ORGANIZATIONAL BEHAVIOR
Integrating Individuals, Groups, and Processes

JOSEPH E. CHAMPOUX
The University of New Mexico

WEST PUBLISHING COMPANY

Minneapolis/St. Paul
New York
Los Angeles
San Francisco

PRODUCTION CREDITS

Artwork Randy Miyake, Miyake Illustration, Incorporated
Composition Carlisle Communications, Ltd.
Copyeditor Patricia Lewis
Indexer Schroeder Indexing Services
Interior Design Diane Beasley
Photo Researcher Eva Tucholka
Cover Image Original work by Christa Giesecke of Pei, Cobb Freed & Partners from the exhibition Mondo Materialis: Materials and Ideas for the Future created by Steelcase Design Partnership. Photography by Elliott Kaufman

Photo Credits to follow Index.

WEST'S COMMITMENT TO THE ENVIRONMENT

In 1906, West Publishing Company began recycling materials left over from the production of books. This began a tradition of efficient and responsible use of resources. Today, up to 95 percent of our legal books and 70 percent of our college and school texts are printed on recycled, acid-free stock. West also recycles nearly 22 million pounds of scrap paper annually—the equivalent of 181,717 trees. Since the 1960s, West has devised ways to capture and recycle waste inks, solvents, oils, and vapors created in the printing process. We also recycle plastics of all kinds, wood, glass, corrugated cardboard, and batteries, and have eliminated the use of Styrofoam book packaging. We at West are proud of the longevity and the scope of our commitment to the environment.

Production, Prepress, Printing and Binding by West Publishing Company.

British Library Cataloguing-in-Publication Data. A catalogue record for this book is available from the British Library.

COPYRIGHT © 1996 BY WEST PUBLISHING COMPANY
610 Opperman Drive
P.O. Box 64526
St. Paul, MN 55164-0526

Printed in the United States of America

03 02 01 00 99 98 97 96   8 7 6 5 4 3 2 1 0

LIBRARY OF CONGRESS CATALOGING-IN-PUBLICATION DATA
Champoux, Joseph Edward.
    Organizational behavior : integrating individuals, groups, and
processes / Joseph Edward Champoux.
        p.   cm.
    Includes Bibliographical references and indexes.
    ISBN 0-314-06242-4 (alk. paper)
    1. Psychology, Industrial.   2. Organizational behavior.
I. Title.
HF5548.8.C353   1996
158.7—dc20
                                                                            95-16979
                                                                                 CIP

To Linda, with love.

Contents in Brief

APPENDICES

Table of Contents

SECTION **I** *Introduction*

Section Overview 0

SECTION II Individual Processes in Organizations

Section Overview   138

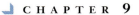

◢ C H A P T E R **12**

Leadership and Management..............322

◢ S E C T I O N   I N T E G R A T I N G   C A S E

III *Group and Interpersonal Processes in
Organizations*.................................354

Preface

Organizational Behavior: Integrating Individuals, Groups, and Processes emerged from more than 20 years of experience in teaching organizational behavior at the undergraduate, graduate, and executive levels. Over that time, I became disenchanted with available organizational behavior textbooks. They did not show the power of organizational behavior theory and concepts for helping people understand their behavior and the behavior of others in an organization. Nor did available books seem "user friendly." They often read like research articles in academic journals and did not consistently show the practical utility of the information presented.

I believe this book addresses my criticisms and will let the reader quickly access and absorb organizational behavior theories and concepts. Although it is firmly grounded in behavioral science theory and research, it is *not* a compendium of research findings. I carefully selected topics and built them into frameworks that are useful for explaining, analyzing, and diagnosing organizational processes.

Organizational Behavior includes topics that apply to one or more issues or problems people face in organizations or are essential background to topics developed later (perception, attitudes, and personality, for example). Each chapter develops its substantive content and shows the student its application through personal assessment exercises or case analysis.

This book is designed for upper-division undergraduate courses and introductory graduate courses in organizational behavior. It describes important behavioral science theory and research that will help a person in both nonmanagement and management situations. For students who do not expect to have management roles, the book offers insights into personal behavior, and the behavior of others, which should help students perform effectively in an organization. For students who are managers or will become managers, *Organizational Behavior* offers insight into managerial situations. For example, the discussion of motivation explains both what motivates the student to behave in certain ways and how managers can affect the behavior of people by using the guidelines of motivation theory.

The book combines macro and micro perspectives. I believe the combined perspectives are essential to understanding organizations and their management. Treating behavioral processes with little or no reference to the design of organizations assumes people's behavior is independent of the organized forms within which they behave. This book describes the relationships between aspects of organizational design and the specific behavioral process under discussion.

Distinctive Pedagogical Features

Organizational Behavior has many distinctive pedagogical features. The following highlights those features.

Chapter sequence roughly parallels a new employee's experience of behavioral processes in organizations. For example, organizational culture (Chapter 5) is followed by organizational socialization (Chapter 6). The chapters then focus on motivation, groups, conflict, and leadership. This sequence is unlike the order of chapters used in many existing texts. I have found it an extremely effective way of communicating the reality of the concepts to introductory students.

Opening Episodes, drawn from press accounts of people, management, and organizations, quickly set a realistic tone for each chapter. The Opening Episodes are real events addressed in the first paragraph of the chapter. Chapter 15, for example, describes a power struggle at the highest level of Amfac, Inc. The result was a deposed executive and conflict among members of the company's board and the remaining managers.

Experiential exercises are integrated into the text to let readers learn something about themselves and how they might behave in the situations discussed in a particular chapter. For example, Chapter 9 uses part of the Job Diagnostic Survey to assess the design of the reader's job. Scoring and interpretation follow each exercise. The implications of the results for the chapter's topics are then developed. Additional experiential exercises appear at the ends of some chapters for use during class.

All experiential exercises are questionnaire-like personal assessment instruments or open-ended response formats. Through these exercises, I am trying to help students develop an understanding of themselves as people and an awareness of how what we are as people affects our reactions in organization situations.

Cases are also directly incorporated into the text. All cases are either press accounts or drawn from them. They are real; none are fictitious although sometimes names are disguised. The goal of the cases is to develop the reader's analytical skills—skills I consider essential to successful management. The cases appear at points that allow the incremental development of the reader's skills. A brief analysis follows each case, applying the chapter's concepts and showing what the reader should have seen in the case. The Instructor's Manual contains more detailed analyses. Additional cases appear at the end of each chapter.

The interwoven experiential exercises and cases are features of the book that let it "work" the conceptual material for the reader. The illustrations of concepts in the experiential exercises help make the ideas come alive, and the cases show how the concepts are applied. The classic "Banana Time" case in Chapter 10, for example, is a rich account of informal group dynamics and the functions of such groups for organizations.

The in-text exercises and cases are key parts of a chapter's development, so they are not set off in distracting boxes that a student can easily ignore. A reader can quickly see concepts in the exercise or case. Adopters should view the exercises and cases as major ways their students will absorb and appreciate important organizational behavior knowledge.

I have built an **integrated perspective** on organizations by linking related theories and concepts, both within chapters and in the sequencing of chapters. Chapters also quickly show how the theories and concepts apply to individuals, groups, and organizational processes. The result is a set of useful insights about organizational behavior and management that will well serve students in their careers.

An **international issues section** in each chapter describes the cross-cultural aspects of the chapter's content and examines the special international issues it raises. For example, this section in Chapter 16 describes the major stressors expatriates and repatriates experience during their international transitions.

An **ethical implications** section in each chapter addresses the ethical issues raised by the chapter's topics. Analyses in these sections build upon the ethical theory background presented in Chapter 3, which is devoted to ethics. They also deal with cross-cultural ethical issues as appropriate. This section in Chapter 6 closely examines the ethical issues surrounding an organization's socialization efforts, especially deliberate efforts to shape a person's behavior.

A **personal and management implications** section in each chapter advises the reader about how the content of the chapter can affect their behavior in an organization. The management implications serve the same function for those who are now managers or expect to be in the future. This section emphasizes the "real world" implications of theories and concepts to show the working utility of the information. In Chapter 8, this section traces several personal effects implied by expectancy theory, equity theory, and behavior modification. It also describes how managers can tailor their view of motivation to the individual qualities of the people they are trying to motivate.

The **Section Integrating Cases** reinforce key ideas for the reader. Each case has enough detail to show a set of related concepts in action. They also offer the chance to do a case analysis with multiple, related concepts. An example is the Section III integrating case which describes how several different leaders transformed their organizations: Lawrence Bossidy at Allied-Signal, Jill Barad at Mattel, and several European executives. This case shows male and female leaders in action and raises several cross-cultural issues in leadership.

Figures clarify chapter content by quickly showing the nature of concepts or relationships among them. I worked closely with an artist to ensure an intuitive rendering of chapter content. The figures are positioned on a page to allow easy reference while reading a chapter. Figure 11-5, which shows conflict management as a thermostat controlling the conflict "temperature" in an organization, is an example.

Photographs are used throughout the book to show major concepts, people, and organizations. Chapter-opening photographs show the chapter's major themes. Opening Episodes typically have a photograph drawn from the press account of the episode. Other photographs illustrate major concepts or issues in a chapter. An exercise in Chapter 6 focuses on the employment expectations created by recruiting materials used by organizations. Photographs of recruiting materials from organizations are a key feature of that exercise.

A list of **key terms** with page number references appears at the end of each chapter. The glossary at the end of the book defines all key terms. Students can use both the key term list and the glossary as study guides.

The **References and Notes** section at the end of each chapter has all citations and some explanatory notes. Students can view this section as a rich resource for library research about a topic, especially for a course paper or term project.

. . . .

↵ *Organization of the Book*

Section I has five chapters that lay critical basic groundwork about organizations. The introductory chapter outlines the goals of the book and how material will be presented. It describes organizations, the roles they play in our lives, and how theories and concepts offer different perspectives on organizations. Functional analysis is developed in the opening chapter because it is used throughout the book as an analytical tool.

Chapter 2 discusses emerging issues affecting modern management: workforce diversity, managing for quality, international issues, and ethics. The first two topics receive detailed treatment to give students a full understanding of the issues. These issues are then woven into many other chapters as appropriate. The international and ethical issues receive brief treatment in Chapter 2 because ethics is fully developed in Chapter 3 and international issues are treated in all other chapters.

Chapter 3 provides detailed treatment of ethics and behavior in organizations. The chapter was separately reviewed by ethicists and assessed by them as accurate in content. This chapter comes early in the book for two reasons: to emphasize the importance of ethics and behavior in organizations and to point the reader squarely at the issue of building an ethical culture in an organization. Each chapter after Chapter 3 has a separate section that discusses the ethical implications of the chapter's topics. Those sections apply many ideas developed in the discussion of ethical theories in Chapter 3.

Chapter 4's description of perception, attitudes, and personality gives some basic background used in later chapters. It includes a discussion of attribution processes, the formation and change of attitudes, and personality development. The discussion of personality development includes the potentially controversial views of the biological bases of personality.

Chapter 5 describes organizational culture. It is included in Section I because of its intimate connection with the emerging issues described in Chapter 2 and the emphasis on ethical values in Chapter 3. The chapter describes the major elements of organizational culture, how the socialization process helps maintain a culture, and the implications for the student in selecting an organization for employment.

Section II focuses on Individual Processes in Organizations. The sequence of chapters from this point on roughly parallels the sequence in which a new employee experiences the behavioral processes of an organization.

Chapter 6 describes organizational socialization and is closely linked to the preceding chapter on organizational culture. This chapter's purpose is to inform the reader of what to expect when first considering an organization as an employee and the dynamics of the socialization process over time. The chapter also describes some limited aspects of careers because different aspects of socialization are experienced as one's career unfolds.

Three chapters follow that develop material dealing with motivation, rewards, and job design. These chapters are designed to let a reader do an analysis and diagnosis of motivation problems. The three topics are brought together in successive chapters because they are inextricably tied together. The chapters describe need theories, cognitive and behavioral theories, and job design theory.

Section III presents material dealing with various aspects of Group and Interpersonal Processes in Organizations. The first chapter of this section describes group and intergroup processes in organizations. The chapter focuses on the role of informal groups in organizations, their functions and dysfunctions, why cohesive groups form, and stages of group development.

Chapter 11 describes conflict in organizations and the management of conflict. Conflict management includes both conflict reduction and conflict stimulation. This chapter includes some discussion of the role of groups in conflict.

Chapter 12 describes various approaches to leadership research and outlines the conclusions that can be drawn from that research. The chapter develops current thinking about trait, behavioral, and contingency approaches to leadership, followed by descriptions of some alternative views of leadership. One view is the Leadership Mystique; another is the distinction between transactional and transformational leadership. Other views include charismatic leadership and Leadership Strategies for Taking Charge. The chapter contrasts leadership and management and shows the difference between the two concepts.

Section IV contains four chapters focusing on several organization processes: communication, decision making, power, political behavior, and stress. Chapter 13 focuses on communication processes in organizations. The chapter first presents a model of the basic communication process. It describes verbal and nonverbal communication, forms of listening, openness in communication (Johari window), ways of improving communication effectiveness, and communication networks. A distinctive feature of this chapter is a discussion of the effects of technology on communication and how it will change the way people interact over long distances.

Chapter 14 begins with a discussion of decision-making processes in organizations. The chapter then moves to a discussion of different models of decision making. Contrasts are drawn between individual and group decision making. The advantages and disadvantages of each are described. The Vroom-Yetton decision process model is fully developed and applied to a set of brief cases.

Chapter 15 discusses both power and organizational politics. The concept of power and its many facets is fully developed. The chapter then moves to ways of building power, and power attributions. The chapter includes a discussion of political strategies, political tactics, and how to do a political diagnosis. It also examines the dark side of organizational politics—deception, lying, and intimidation.

Chapter 16 discusses stress in organizations. This chapter covers types of stressors, incremental and cumulative effects of stress, and ways of managing stress. Descriptions of sources of stress away from work and how these stressors interact with stress experienced at work are unusual features of this chapter. Other sections describe stress diagnosis and stress management strategies.

Section V contains two chapters that develop a macro view of organizations. The first (Chapter 17) describes the contingency view of organizational design (environment, technology, strategy, size). It follows with a discussion of the configuration view of organizational design that includes two typologies based on configurations: (1) mechanistic and organic organizations and (2) the four-part typology of Defender, Prospector, Analyzer, and Reactor.

The second chapter (Chapter 18) describes alternative forms of organization (functional, division, hybrid, and matrix). The chapter also includes descriptions of some evolving forms of organizational design: self-managing teams, a process view of organizational design, the virtual organization, and organization architecture.

Section VI contains two chapters examining organizational change and what the future could be like. Chapter 19 describes organizational change and development. The chapter discusses why organizations must change, how managers cause planned change, and resistance to change. It includes a discussion of organizational development, the role of consultants, and various organizational development interventions.

Chapter 20 closes the book by discussing how organizations and management might look in the future. It draws heavily on current business press discussions about management in the 2000s. Topics include new thinking about making the United States a world-class manufacturing country, increased multinational business and management activities, increased emphasis on using groups and teams in organizations, and major technological changes.

The book has two appendixes. Appendix A develops the foundation ideas for the study of organizations. The material is presented chronologically, beginning with a passage from the Old Testament to illustrate the age of some basic ideas. The remainder of the material develops classical thinking about organizations and their management. The appendix ends in the mid-1930s with what I consider to be the bridge to contemporary thinking about organizations.

Appendix B presents a brief description of how organization research is done. It includes a discussion of research design, sampling, types of measurement scales, reliability, and validity.

. . . .

↵ Ancillary Package

A complete set of ancillary materials accompanies this text. They include an Instructor's Manual, Test Bank, WESTEST™ 3.1 (computer-based test bank), 100 color transparency acetates, and videotapes.

Instructor's Manual

Dr. Edward W. Frederickson of the University of Texas at El Paso worked with me in developing the Instructor's Manual. Special features of the Instructor's Manual are:

- *Detailed lecture outlines.* Three- and four-level outlines of each chapter.
- *Sequels.* Follow-up events that happened after the case description in the text. This material will help with extended class discussion of the in-text cases and Opening Episodes.
- *Additional exercise or case.* One additional exercise or case for each chapter showing concepts not emphasized by the in-text exercise or case.
- *Case analyses.* Detailed analyses of all cases in the text and the additional case noted above.
- *Exercise analyses.* Detailed analyses of all exercises in the text and the additional exercise noted above.

- *Answers to end-of-chapter questions.* Detailed answers to all review and discussion questions, including ways to probe and direct class discussion.
- *Videotapes.* Descriptions covering the key points made in the tapes and discussing their direct connection to the text material (videotape package available to qualified adopters). Included with these descriptions are recommendations of popular movies, available on videotape, which illustrate key parts of chapters. For example, *The Firm* nicely illustrates many parts of the socialization process described in Chapter 6.
- *Instructional television tips.* Observations on ways to make the chapter material effective when teaching by television.
- *Transparency listing.* A complete list of all transparencies, including nontext figures, available to support each chapter.

Test Bank and WESTEST™

A test bank averaging more than 100 multiple choice, true-false, and completion questions per chapter supports this text. Each chapter's questions are arranged topically. The test bank is available in print form to all adopters, and a computer-based version, WESTEST™ 3.1, is available to qualified adopters. WESTEST™ runs on IBM-compatible or Macintosh computers. WESTEST™ is a menu-driven test management system that helps instructors custom design their examinations.

Transparency Acetates

One hundred color transparency acetates are available to qualified adopters. These include transparencies of selected text figures and specially created nontext figures.

Video Program

A set of videotapes drawn from many sources is available to qualified adopters. I chose the tapes to illustrate key points in all chapters. Many tapes support the ethical, international, diversity, and quality issues raised throughout the book. Other tapes show key issues in action such as using rewards at May Kay Cosmetics.

Classroom Testing

I have classroom tested the entire book manuscript with introductory organizational behavior students at the undergraduate, graduate, and executive levels. About 2,000 undergraduate, graduate, and Executive Program students read the manuscript. The feedback from my students has been both positive and helpful for getting a simple and clear presentation. All figures and color transparency acetates were also class-room tested. They have proven to be clear and obvious in their intention.

Avoiding Sexist Language

I am sensitive to the need to avoid sexist language in a modern textbook. I chose to use a single gender throughout a chapter but alternate female and male gender from one chapter to another. My daughter Nicole chose the male gender for Chapter 1 based on the flip of a coin. All even-numbered chapters use the female gender; all odd-numbered chapters use the male gender. Appendix A uses male and Appendix B uses female.

Acknowledgements

My Students

Thousands of my students read the book manuscript during its development while attending my organizational behavior classes at the University of New Mexico. They included undergraduate, Masters of Business Administration (MBA), and Executive MBA students. To involve them in the book's development, my course syllabi included the following comment about the manuscript:

> The copy I have prepared should be error free. If you find any errors—typographical or just plain dumb—please tell me.

They did! I thank them for their feedback, comments, and copyediting efforts. Their continual interaction with this book's development was always a source of encouragement and improvement.

Reviewers

I thank each of the following people for their involvement at various points in the manuscript review process. Your guidance, criticism, and encouragement allowed the continuous improvement of this product.

Maryann Albrecht
University of Illinois at Chicago

Maureen L. Ambrose
University of Colorado at Boulder

Joe Anderson
Northern Arizona University

Kamala Arogyaswamy
University of South Dakota

F. Neil Brady
Brigham Young University

Norman B. Bryan, Jr.
Piedmont College

Rogene A. Buchholz
Loyola University at New Orleans

Thomas Y. Choi
Bowling Green State University

Dennis L. Dossett
University of Missouri at St. Louis

Max E. Douglas
Indiana State University

Bruce H. Drake
University of Portland

John A. Drexler, Jr.
Oregon State University

Ken Eastman
Oklahoma State University

Edward W. Frederickson
University of Texas at El Paso

Daniel Ganster
University of Arkansas

K. Vernard Harrington
Syracuse University

Stanley Harris
Auburn University

Jon P. Howell
New Mexico State University

Y. Paul Huo
Washington State University

I. Edward Jernigan
University of North Carolina at Charlotte

Avis L. Johnson
University of Akron

Bruce H. Johnson
Gustavus Adolphus College

G. Logan Jordan
Purdue University

Ahmad Karim
Indiana University-Purdue University at Fort Wayne

Meryl Louis
Boston University

Jean McEnery
Eastern Michigan University

Karen J. Maher
University of Missouri at St. Louis

Stephen H. Miller
California State University at Hayward

Paula C. Morrow
Iowa State University of Science & Technology

Steven B. Moser
University of North Dakota

Kevin Mossholder
Louisiana State University

Cynthia Pavett
University of San Diego

Lena B. Prewitt
University of Alabama

Jere Ramsey
California Polytechnic State University at San Luis Obispo

Jane Siebler
Oregon State University

Kim A. Stewart
University of Denver

John Tarjan
California State University at Bakersfield

Shari Tarnutzer
Utah State University

John Van Maanen
Massachusetts Institute of Technology

Penny L. Wright
San Diego State University

West Publishing Company Personnel

My special thanks to each of the following people at West Publishing Company. This team brought this book to fruition.

- To Diane Beasley, text designer, for a warm, open, and engaging book design that my University of New Mexico students immediately found appealing.
- To Amy Gabriel, production editor, for keeping me focused on our demanding production schedule and for her skillful management of a complex production process.
- To Robert Horan, acquisitions editor, for his continual support of this book even when he became frustrated with my delays.
- To Patricia Lewis, copyeditor, whose copyediting skills brought polish, sparkle, and smooth flow to the manuscript.
- To Randy Miyake, artist, for the beautiful artwork he developed from my clumsy drawings.
- To Eva Tucholka, photo researcher, for persistence in finding photographs. My best to Max the cat.
- To Janine Wilson, developmental editor, who provided early analyses that helped me control the length of this book and who saved the day when my computer devoured portions of a chapter.
- To Sandi Hiller, editorial assistant, whose quick response to short lead time requests got me critical information.

Other Folks

Some other people made special contributions that I want to acknowledge. My thanks to David Tafoya at the University of New Mexico for help in producing the recruiting material photographs in Chapter 6. And thank you to Wayne Frederickson at the University of Texas at El Paso for his committed efforts in producing the fine Instructor's Manual that accompanies this book.

Feedback and Continuous Improvement

I ask all users of this book to give me feedback about any aspect of its content and design. I want to continuously improve it and need your help to do that. Please send your comments and observations to me at The Robert O. Anderson Schools of Management, The University of New Mexico, Albuquerque, New Mexico 87131. You can also contact me at (505) 856-6253 (voice and FAX) or send E-mail to champoux@unm.edu.

Joseph E. Champoux
Albuquerque, New Mexico

Introduction

. . . .

◢ Section Overview

*F*igure I-1 gives an overview of this book, showing the major sections and the chapters in Section I. This section introduces you to organizations, discusses some major issues that affect organizations and their management, and offers a detailed description of ethics and organizational behavior. The section also describes human perception, attitudes, personality, and the cultures of organizations. Each chapter includes a discussion of the international aspects of the topics and the ethical issues they raise.

Chapter 1 introduces you to the world of organizations. This chapter defines an organization, introduces you to theories and concepts, and shows how you can use them to analyze behavioral issues in organizations. As the chapter explains, you can use theories and concepts in much the same way photographers use camera lenses. Developing an analytical perspective about behavior in organizations is important, so this chapter shows how to analyze a case and then gives you the chance to do a case analysis.

Chapter 2 focuses on four major issues that will affect organizations and their management well into the next century. Those issues are workforce diversity, managing for quality, the global environment of organizations, and ethics. Projected changes in the demographic makeup of the domestic civilian workforce will make the workforce of the future more diverse, and that diversity will present both opportunities and problems for managers. Managing for quality is attracting attention as a way for organizations to be more competitive and meet the needs of increasingly demanding consumers. The global environment of organizations adds still another dimension of diversity, opportunity, and problems. No longer can modern managers assume their markets and competitors are only within the boundaries of their home country.

Much behavior and many decisions in organizations involve ethical issues. Chapter 2 introduces you to ethics, and Chapter 3 examines it in detail. Chapter 3 first considers the social responsibility of modern organizations and then compares ethical and unethical behavior in organizations. In addition to describing the sources of ethics for both societies and individuals, the chapter reviews several theories of ethics and asks you to identify your orientation to ethics. Finally, the chapter addresses the question of how managers can promote ethical behavior and considers the implications that the increasingly global environment of organizations has for ethical behavior.

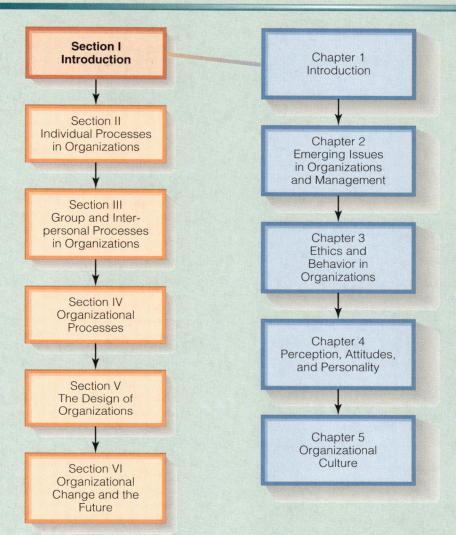

Chapter 4 describes different aspects of perceptual processes, attitudes, and personality. This foundation information underlies organizational processes and many other topics in this book. The chapter starts with a description of human perceptual processes and distinguishes between self-perception (a view of self) and social perception (a view of others); it also describes sources of perceptual error and the processes by which we attribute qualities to people. The chapter next addresses such topics as how attitudes form, how they change, and how attitudes can affect behavior. Finally, personality and its development is discussed from both a social and a biological perspective. The chapter describes several key personality characteristics and types of interest to organizations and management.

Chapter 5 describes many aspects of organizational culture and its effects on organization members. The chapter offers different ways of viewing organizational cultures. It describes the functions and dysfunctions of cultures, explains how to diagnose an organization's culture, and discusses the relationship between an organization's culture and its performance.

1

Introduction

· Organizations in the future will increasingly use groups of people to get work done. Security analysts at Fred Alger Management meet Tuesday nights to discuss clients' portfolios.

After reading this chapter, you should be able to . . .

- Describe the concept of an organization.
- Distinguish between organizational behavior and organizational theory.
- Explain the role of theory and concepts in analyzing organization issues and problems.
- Analyze the intended and unintended consequences of behavior in organizations.
- Do a case analysis using the perspective developed in this chapter.

Chapter Overview

The Bureaucracy Busters

· *T. J. Rodgers, chief executive, Cypress Semiconductor Corporation.*

If you were to ask a CEO in the year 2000 to . . . draw the organization chart of his company, what he'd sketch would bear little resemblance to even the trendiest flattened pyramid around today. Yes, the corporation of the future will still retain some vestiges of the old hierarchy and maybe a few traditional departments to take care of the [routine work] . . . . But spinning around the straight lines will be a . . . [whirling] pattern of constantly changing teams, tasks forces, partnerships, and other informal structures. . . . [I]n tomorrow's corporation teams variously composed of shop-floor workers, managers, technical experts, suppliers, and customers will join together to do a job and then disband, with everyone going off to the next assignment.

Call this new model the adaptive organization. It will bust through bureaucracy to serve customers better and make the company more competitive. Instead of looking to the boss for direction and oversight, tomorrow's employee will be trained to look closely at the work process and to devise ways to improve upon it, even if this means temporarily leaving his regular job to join an ad hoc team attacking a problem. . . .

So far, the adaptive organization exists more as an ideal than as a reality. But you can see aspects of it taking shape . . . at companies such as Apple Computer, Cypress Semiconductor, Levi Strauss, Xerox . . . . Last year, for instance, an informal Xerox team made up of people from accounting, sales, distribution, and administration saved the company $200 million in inventory costs. Cypress, a San Jose, California, maker of specialty computer chips, has developed a computer system that keeps track of all its 1,500 employees as they crisscross between different functions, teams, and projects. Apple is developing a computer network called Spider that . . . instantly tells a manager whether an employee is available to join his project, what the employee's skills are, and where he's located in the corporation.

If you look hard at your own organization you'll probably see something quite similar already going on. In every outfit of more than a few people, there exists an informal organization—social scientists sometimes call it an emergent organization— that operates alongside the formal one. It consists of the alliances between people and the power relationships that actually get work done. It may be as simple as some workers banding together to go outside channels to do a job despite the obstacles set in their way by a pigheaded bureaucrat. This isn't new. What is new is that corporations are finally realizing the need to recognize the informal organization, free it up, and provide it the resources it needs.

The episode opening this chapter suggests that in the future both the way managers design organizations and the types of behavior they encourage may be quite different. Many organizations will keep a hierarchical form to some degree, but they will also use more temporary teams. People can expect to move from one assignment to another, often with dizzying speed, as the opportunities and constraints in the organization's environment change. Individual workers of the future in many organizations also may make decisions that formerly were only within the authority of managers. All forms of behavior in organizations, whether predicted for the future or existing now, are the subject of this book.

This book brings together much of the extensive knowledge about people's behavior in organizations. Such knowledge will help you better understand your own behavior and the behavior of others around you. The understanding you gain from this book will also help you be a better manager now or later in your career.

What Is an Organization?

An **organization** is a system of two or more persons, engaged in cooperative action, trying to reach some purpose.[1] As this simple definition implies, organizations are large or small, have a goal, and require the cooperative interaction of two or more people. Organizations are bounded systems of structured social interaction featuring authority relations, communication systems, and the use of incentives. Examples of organizations include business organizations, hospitals, colleges, retail stores, and prisons.[2]

We are all part of organizations, whether we want to be or not. You are now part of an organization—your college or university. In your daily round of activities, you move from one organization to another. You may shop at a store, deal with a government agency, or go to work. Understanding organizations and their management can give you significant insights into systems that have major effects on you.

Consider for a moment the various classes in which you are now enrolled. Each class has a different professor, often different students, and a different structure. The relationship between professor and students differs from one class to the next. Each class exposes you to a different organization, a different structure, and a different culture.

Reflect on your reactions to your classes. You enjoy some classes more than others. You are pleased or annoyed by some aspects of the way professors manage their classes. The task of this book is to develop an understanding of such phenomena in organizations.

Organizational Behavior and Organizational Theory

Organizational behavior and organizational theory are two disciplines within the social and behavioral sciences that specialize in studying organizations. The term *organizational behavior* is a little misleading because it refers to the behavior of people in organizations—organizations themselves do not behave. **Organizational behavior** tries to understand the behavior, attitudes, and performance of people in organizations. **Organizational theory** focuses on the design and structure of organizations.

As Figure 1-1 shows, several social and behavioral science disciplines contribute to both organizational behavior and organizational theory. The discipline of organizational behavior draws on theory and concepts from various branches of psychology, anthropology, political science, and the sociology of work. From the psychological disciplines comes information about human psychological processes that can affect behavior in an organization. For example, psychology has contributed vast knowledge about human motivation. It tells how a system of rewards can affect a person's behavior and performance in an organization.

Anthropology, political science, and the sociology of work offer other perspectives, theories, and concepts about organizational behavior. Anthropology emphasizes the importance of culture in human systems. It also offers some analytical tools for studying behavior in organizations, one of which is introduced later in this chapter. Political science forms part of the base for studying political behavior in organizations. The sociology of work emphasizes social status and social relationships in the work setting.

The discipline of organizational theory strives to understand the existing design of an organization, ways to redesign an organization, and alternate forms of organiza-

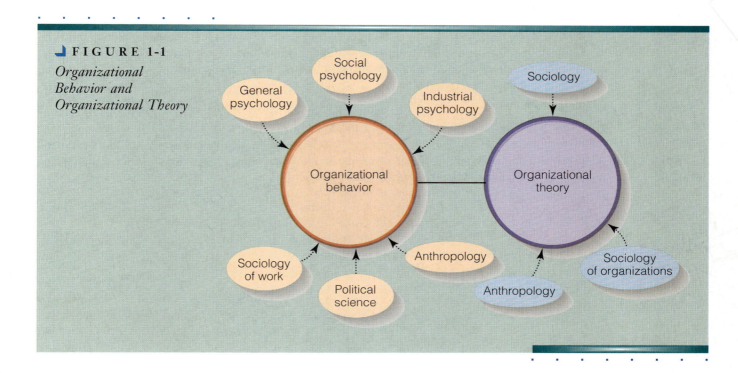

FIGURE 1-1
Organizational Behavior and Organizational Theory

tional design. Sociology offers theories and concepts about social systems and relationships in them. The sociology of organizations, the core of organizational theory, is a specialized part of sociology that focuses on organizations as social systems. Anthropology's theories and concepts about entire societies also contribute to organizational theory.

Figure 1-1 links organizational behavior to organizational theory by a solid line to indicate that neither area of study can ignore the other. Because behavior happens within a specific organizational design, one needs to understand the perspectives of organizational theory. Similarly, human beings design organizations and are embedded in a behavioral system that can strongly affect their behavior.

Both areas of organizational study are important, although this book mainly discusses topics from organizational behavior, such as organizational culture, socialization processes, motivation, and group dynamics. Two chapters (Chapters 17 and 18) focus on organizational design and draw their content from organizational theory. Those chapters also link their observations to organizational behavior.

Theories and Concepts

Each chapter describes both theories and concepts derived from those theories. Each theory uses **concepts** to explain parts of the phenomena to which the theory applies.[3] Think of the concepts as tools, a notion that emphasizes their utility for understanding behavior in organizations. As the book unfolds, you will develop a large collection of theories and concepts. You will learn to use those tools analytically in looking at and solving organizational problems.

WHAT IS THEORY?

Theory has many associations among the general public, and not all of them are positive. On a separate sheet of paper, jot down what the word *theory* means to you. Table 1-1 lists some words and phrases that students often associate with theory.

TABLE 1-1
Words and Phrases Students Often Associate with Theory

Abstract
Boring
Doesn't mean much
Hypothetical
Impractical
Tentative explanation
Unproven
Unrealistic

In reality, though, as Kurt Lewin, a noted social psychologist, said many years ago, "nothing is as practical as a good theory,"[4] a view with which this book agrees. A simple working definition is that "a **theory** is a plausible explanation of some phenomenon."[5] A theory also describes relationships among its concepts. Of course, some theories are stronger and better developed than others. Accordingly, this book describes each theory in detail so you can judge how useful it will be in understanding behavior in organizations. Your task is to assess what you read in the following chapters and decide which theories and concepts will be useful analytical tools.

This book presents two different types of theory. **Descriptive theory** explains behavioral phenomena as they exist. **Normative theory** describes alternatives to existing behavioral phenomena. Writers of normative theory describe the way they think the organizational world should be, not the way it actually is. Most theories discussed in this book are descriptive theories. Normative theories will be clearly identified throughout the book.

 THEORIES AND CONCEPTS AS LENSES

Scientists have long recognized that theories from different scientific disciplines give different views of problems, issues, and questions. Different theoretical perspectives

· *These three views show how different the same scene looks through a wide-angle lens,* top left; *a normal lens,* top right; *and a telephoto lens,* bottom right. *The last view focuses on a way MCI tries to motivate its high performers.*

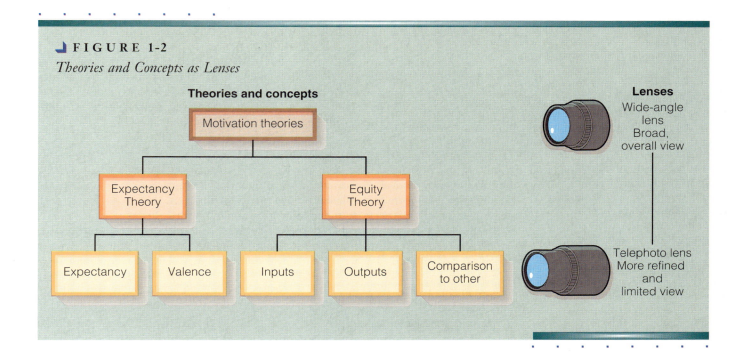

FIGURE 1-2

Theories and Concepts as Lenses

help scientists derive multiple answers to a single question.[6] Similarly, using theories and concepts lets you bring different perspectives to the same organizational issue, problem, or question.

Scientists use theories and concepts in much the same way that photographers use lenses of different focal lengths. A normal lens has an angle of view about the same as human vision. A wide-angle lens gives a broad view of a scene. A telephoto lens lets a photographer isolate the part of a scene on which he* wants to concentrate.

Photographers often start with an overview of a scene. They can then move in and out with lenses of different focal lengths depending on what they want to emphasize. You can do the same with theories and concepts.

Figure 1-2 shows the relationship between theories and concepts and how they can act as camera lenses. Let's assume you are interested in understanding why someone is not doing a job as well as he could do it. As later chapters will explain, motivation is an important element in job performance (the broad view of the scene). Two of the many theories of motivation are called Expectancy Theory and Equity Theory. You may choose these two theories to help you understand the performance problem (narrowing the view of the scene). Each of these theories has concepts that explain part of individual motivation. Expectancy Theory uses the concepts of expectancy and valence. Equity Theory uses the concepts of inputs, outputs, and comparison to other. The individual concepts act as telephoto lenses. Applying each concept to the performance problem focuses your attention on a limited part of the problem, letting you understand that part more fully.

Just as a skilled photographer quickly switches lenses to view a scene from several perspectives, you will learn to use concepts to view behavioral phenomena in organizations from many perspectives. A skilled manager knows the concepts and moves quickly from one to another in analyzing and solving problems in an organization.

---

*Each chapter in this book uses a single gender reference whenever it is necessary to do so. As described in the Preface, a random process decided the gender referent for Chapter 1. Each chapter that follows will alternate male and female referents. Chapter 2 will use female referents, Chapter 3 male referents, and so on. This style was chosen over the more awkward "he or she" method.

Theories and concepts explain behavioral phenomena from the perspective of the intended results of the author of the theory. Unintended consequences often occur with, or instead of, the intended consequences. Consequently, it is useful to examine theoretical concepts both according to what is supposed to happen and what may happen unintentionally.

The consequences of behavior can be examined by using **functional analysis,** an analytical tool borrowed from anthropology.[7] When anthropologists study a society, they divide their behavioral observations into two major groups. First, they decide whether the consequences of behavior are manifest or latent. Then they determine whether the consequences are functional or dysfunctional for the society.

Manifest consequences are the intended results of the actions of an individual. **Latent consequences** are unintended results often of the same behavior. Latent consequences happen but were not intended to happen by the individual. For example, an organization might specify quantity targets for production (manifest consequence), and workers meet the target by accepting poor-quality output (latent consequence).

Functional consequences are results of behavior that are good for the organization and help its adjustment and adaptation. Such results contribute to the organization's progress toward its goals. **Dysfunctional consequences** are results of behavior that are negative for the organization. These results restrict the organization's adjustment and adaptation, impeding it from reaching its goals.

Figure 1-3 shows an analytical device based on functional analysis that you will use at several points in this book. Considering manifest and latent consequences along with functional and dysfunctional consequences produces four classes of behavioral consequences. Although all four are possible, we are interested mainly in two of the four cells in the figure.

Cell I contains manifest functional consequences. These are intended results of behavior that are also good for the organization. People in an organization behave in specific ways expecting something good to happen. They make decisions as managers or employees and want those decisions to have good results. Such actions fall into Cell I.

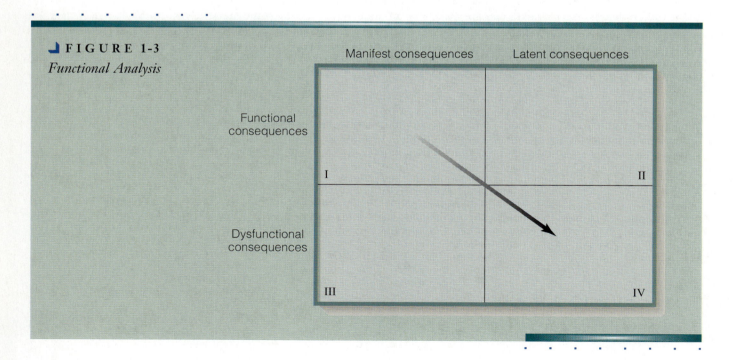

↲ **FIGURE 1-3**
Functional Analysis

Most writers discussed in this book wrote from the perspective of Cell I. When you read about their views, you may think, "This sounds good, but I have seen things that differ from what I am reading." When you have that reaction, you are asking the questions in Cell IV.

While reading this book, deliberately test what it says using the perspective of Cell IV. Theories and concepts will often be presented from the perspective of manifest functional consequences, but those same theories may also have latent dysfunctional consequences. Such an analysis can be a powerful tool because it adds much information to a theory or concept.

C A S E   *Efficiency Controls*

Stop for a moment and apply functional analysis to the following short case. It describes the way a large American corporation assessed the efficiency of a production department. Guide yourself through the case with the following questions:

1. What are the manifest functions of this efficiency control?
2. What are some possible latent dysfunctions of the same control? Did they appear in this situation?
3. What effects could this efficiency control have on production flow and machine maintenance?

CASE DESCRIPTION

"[A] daily efficiency rating was computed, based on the [number of labor hours] of completed units transferred to finished [goods inventory] compared with the number of [labor] hours spent 'on production' during the day of the transfer. [Work in process was not counted when calculating labor hours of completed units, but was counted for 'on production.'] Efficiency was reported daily and accumulated to the end of the month. . . . [E]ach department earned 12 efficiency ratings each year.

"[T]he plant manager accepted the monthly efficiency figures as indicative of every department's accomplishments or progress. He placed a high value on this figure and called his subordinates to task whenever the monthly efficiency figure was low, or whenever it fell significantly under the figure of the preceding month."

Before continuing, note your observations on a separate sheet of paper. Then read the following comments from some foremen in the plant where the efficiency control was used. First, a manufacturing department foreman:

For the last two weeks of the month we're driving hell out of the men. We have to get pieces out, and we're always jammed up at the end of the month. . . . What actually happens is that in the beginning of the month I have to put

all of my men at the beginning of the line to get pieces going for the month's production. This is because we cleaned out the department in the previous month. Then, during the last two weeks I have to put all of the men at the end of the line to finish up the pieces.

A foreman whose department was at the end of the manufacturing process said:

My main trouble is with material flow. I look around the department and either it's empty or I'm overloaded. Most of the rush comes from the 15th to the end of the month. Toward the end of the month the departments send me one or two parts at a time and ask me to rush them through. I guess they want credit for the piece in the month's production report.

Another foreman made the following observations about machine maintenance:

We really can't stop to have our machines repaired. In fact, one of our machines is off right now, but we'll have to gimmick something immediately and keep the machine going because at the end of the month, as it is now, we simply can't have a machine down. We've got to get those pieces out. Many times we run a machine right to the ground at the end of the month trying to get pieces out, and we have to spend extra time at the beginning of the month trying to repair the machine.

CASE ANALYSIS

The efficiency control described here could have been analyzed with functional analysis before it was installed. A skilled analyst could have predicted the latent dysfunctions that eventually happened. With practice, your skills at doing such an analysis will sharpen.

Source: Reprinted by permission of *Harvard Business Review.* An excerpt from "Use and Misuse of Efficiency Controls" by F. J. Jasinski, 34 (July/August 1956). Copyright © 1956 by the president and Fellows of Harvard College; all rights reserved.

Developing an Analytical Perspective

This book will help you develop an **analytical perspective** about organizations. A major goal is increasing your skills for analyzing behavioral problems and issues in organizations. The book uses two methods to develop an analytical perspective: (1) experiential exercises that focus on you as an individual, and (2) cases that present you with situations for analysis and diagnosis.

The experiential exercises are designed to let you learn something about yourself. We are all part of the behavioral processes of organizations. What we are as individuals affects our reaction to events and individuals around us. The possible results for each exercise are interpreted in the context of the concepts discussed. Your results for each exercise emphasize your role in the behavioral phenomena found in organizations.

Case materials are integrated directly into the text allowing you to try some concepts on an actual problem. Some cases describe problems that you analyze and diagnose. You then develop possible solutions to the problems based on your diagnosis. Other cases have no problems. Here you are asked to analyze and explain the behavioral phenomena described in the case. Still other cases present issues being discussed by managers and ask you to predict the probable outcome.

All cases involve real situations, but in some the names of people and organizations have been disguised. Many cases come from the news media and describe current situations happening in real organizations. A brief analysis follows each case. Your instructor can give a more detailed analysis. To get the most benefit from the case, do your analysis first. Then compare it to the analysis in the text and the analysis from your instructor.

Your analytical skills will develop in steps as you do both the experiential exercises and the cases. The first cases in the book are shorter than those toward the end. As you develop your skills at analysis and diagnosis, you will be presented with more complex and rich situations to analyze.

Doing a Case Analysis

You will find the cases most helpful when you follow a structured procedure for the analysis and diagnoses. Table 1-2 and Figure 1-4 show two parts of a procedure you can use to analyze cases.

Use the diagnostic questions in Table 1-2 to be sure you thoroughly understand the facts of the case. Who are the principal characters? They often are employees, managers, and clients of the organization. What aspects of organizational design are

---

TABLE 1-2

Diagnostic Questions for Doing a Case Analysis

- Who are the principal characters?
- What behavior is happening in the case?
- What are the relationships among people and organization units?
- Are there any manifest functional consequences?
- Are there any latent dysfunctional consequences?
- What is the major problem or issue?
- Is organizational design important?
- What concepts would be useful for your analysis?

FIGURE 1-4
The Role of Concepts in a Case Analysis

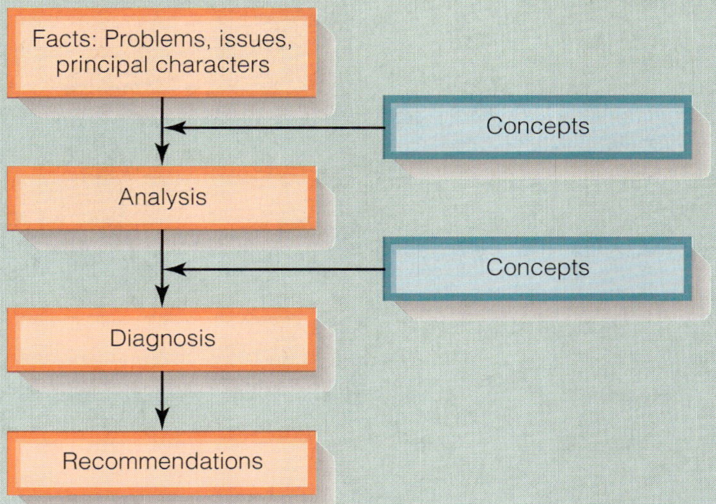

important in the case? What are the relationships between individuals and organization units? What is the behavior of the people in the case? Identify the major problems or issues described in the case. Be sure to identify both manifest functional consequences and, when appropriate, latent dysfunctional consequences.

Next, follow the procedure outlined in Figure 1-4 to apply concepts to your analysis. Reflect on the theories and concepts you have learned up to that point in the book. Identify those you consider applicable to the case. Use the concepts to bring different perspectives to the case, as you would use camera lenses of different focal lengths. The conceptual tools let you see aspects of the case you otherwise would not notice. These tools will also help you detect latent problems and issues not explicitly described in the case.

Your analysis with the conceptual tools also lets you identify symptoms of problems or issues in the case. You proceed in the same way a physician does when he examines a patient. Your patient in this context is the case description. Your diagnosis follows from your understanding of the symptoms, relationships among symptoms, and relationships of the symptoms to the underlying problem.

Your analysis and diagnosis lead to one or more recommendations about what to do. In some circumstances, you may be unable to select a single course of action. Recommend more than one if you believe several possible actions would be right for the facts of the case.

Read the following case and try an analysis and diagnosis. Use any information you have from any source to analyze the case. You already have some limited information from this book to use in an analysis. You also have information from other courses and your experiences. Don't worry about following all the steps of case analysis described earlier.

CASE   *Hovey and Beard Company*

▪ PART I

"The Hovey and Beard Company manufactured wooden toys of various kinds: wooden animals, pull toys, and the like. One part of the manufacturing process involved spraying paint on the partially assembled toys and hanging them on moving hooks which carried them through a

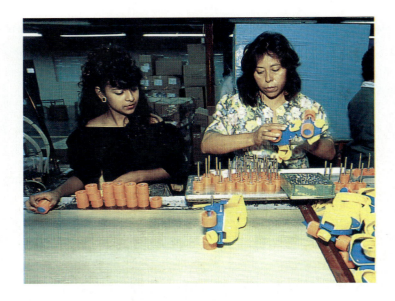

The sequential assembly of these toy roller skates is similar to the sequential painting operation described in the Hovey and Beard case.

drying oven. This operation . . . was plagued by absenteeism, turnover, and low morale. . . .

"The toys were cut, sanded, and partially assembled in the wood room. Then they were dipped into shellac, following which they were painted. The toys were predominantly two colored; a few were made in more than two colors. Each color required an additional trip through the paint room. . . .

"[T]he painting operation had been reengineered so that the eight [workers] who did the painting sat in a line by an endless chain of hooks. These hooks were in continuous motion, past the line of [workers] and into a long horizontal oven. Each [worker] sat at . . . [a] painting booth so designed as to carry away fumes and to backstop excess paint. The [person] would take a toy from the tray [next to the work station], position it in a jig inside the painting cubicle, spray on the color according to a pattern, then release the toy and hang it on the hook passing by. The rate at which the hooks moved had been calculated by the engineers so that each [worker], when fully trained, would be able to hang a painted toy on each hook before it passed beyond reach.

"The [workers] . . . in the paint room were on a group bonus plan. Since the operation was new to them, they were receiving a learning bonus which decreased by regular amounts each month. The learning bonus was scheduled to vanish in six months, by which time it was expected that they would be on their own—that is, able to meet the standard and to earn a group bonus when they exceeded it.

"By the second month of the training period trouble had developed. The [workers] learned more slowly than had been anticipated, and it began to look as though their production would stabilize far below what was planned for. Many of the hooks were going by empty. The [workers] complained that they were going by too fast,

and that the time-study man had set the rates wrong. A few [workers] quit and had to be replaced with new [people], which further aggravated the learning problem. The team spirit that the management had expected to develop automatically through the group bonus was not in evidence except as an expression of what the engineers called 'resistance.' One [worker] whom the group regarded as its leader (and the management regarded as the ringleader) was outspoken in making the various complaints of the group to the foreman. The complaints had all the variety customary in such instances of generalized frustration: the job was a messy one, the hooks moved too fast, the incentive pay was not being correctly calculated, and anyway it was too hot working so close to the drying oven."

What Would You Do if You Were the Foreman?

Make some notes indicating what you would do if you were the foreman. You will see what the foreman did when you return to the case.

PART II

"The consultant who was brought into this picture worked entirely with and through the foreman. After many conversations with him, the foreman felt that the first step should be to get the [workers] together for a general discussion of the working conditions— something, incidentally, which was far from his mind originally and which in his own words would only have been 'begging for trouble.' He took this step with some hesitation, but he took it on his own volition.

"The first meeting, held immediately after the shift was over at four o'clock in the afternoon, was attended by all eight [workers]. They voiced the same complaints again: the hooks went by too fast, the job was too dirty, the room was hot and poorly ventilated. For some reason it was this last item that they complained of most. The foreman promised to discuss the problem of ventilation and temperature with the engineers, and he scheduled a second meeting to report back to the [workers]. In the next few days the foreman had several talks with the engineers, and it seemed that the [workers'] cynical predictions about what the engineers would say were going to be borne out. They and the superintendent felt that this was really a trumped up complaint, and that the expense of any effective corrective measure would be prohibitively high. (They were thinking of some form of air conditioning.)

"The foreman came to the second meeting with some apprehensions. The [workers], however, did not seem to be much put out, perhaps because they had a proposal of their own to make. They felt that if several large fans were set up so as to circulate the air around their feet, they would be much more comfortable. After some discussion the foreman agreed that the idea might be tried out. (Immediately after the meeting, he confided to the consultant that he probably shouldn't have committed himself to this expense on his own initiative; also, he felt that the fans wouldn't help much anyway.) The foreman and the consultant discussed the question of the fans with the superintendent, and three large propeller-type fans were purchased. The decision was reached without much difficulty, since it seemed that the fans could be used elsewhere after their expected failure to provide relief in the paint room.

"The fans were brought in. The [workers] were jubilant. For several days the fans were moved about in various positions until they were placed to the satisfaction of the group. Whatever the actual efficiency of these fans, one thing was clear: the [workers] were completely satisfied with the results, and relations between them and the foreman improved visibly.

"The foreman, after this encouraging episode, decided that further meetings might also be profitable. He asked the [workers] if they would like to meet and discuss other aspects of the work situation. The [workers] were eager to do this. The meeting was held, and the discussion quickly centered on the speed of the hooks. The [workers] maintained that the time-study men had set them at an unreasonably fast speed and that they would never be able to reach the goal of filling enough of them to make a bonus.

"The turning point of the discussion came when the group's leader frankly explained that the point wasn't that they couldn't work fast enough to keep up with the hooks, but that they couldn't work at that pace all day long. The foreman explored the point. The [workers] were unanimous in their opinion that they could keep up with the belt for short periods if they wanted to. But they didn't want to because if they showed that they could do this for short periods they would be expected to do it all

day long. The meeting ended with an unprecedented request; 'Let us adjust the speed of the belt faster or slower depending on how we feel.' The foreman, understandably startled, agreed to discuss this with the superintendent and the engineers.

"The engineers' reaction naturally as that the [workers'] suggestion was heresy. Only after several meetings was it granted grudgingly that there was in reality some latitude within which variations in the speed of the hooks would not affect the finished product. After considerable argument and many dire prophecies by the engineers, it was agreed to try out the [workers'] idea.

"With great misgivings, the foreman had a control with a dial marked 'low, medium, fast' installed at the booth of the group leader; she could now adjust the speed of the belt anywhere between the lower and upper limits that the engineers had set. The [workers] were delighted, and spent many lunch hours deciding how the speed of the belt should be varied from hour to hour throughout the day.

"Within a week the pattern had settled down to one in which the first half hour of the shift was run on what the [workers] called medium speed (a dial setting slightly above the point marked 'medium'). The next two and one-half hours were run at high speed; the half hour before lunch and the half hour after lunch were run at low speed. The rest of the afternoon was run at high speed with the exception of the last forty-five minutes of the shift, which was run at medium.

"In view of the [workers'] reports of satisfaction and ease in their work, it is interesting to note that the constant speed at which the engineers had originally set the belt was slightly below medium on the dial of the control that had been given the [workers]. The average speed at which the [workers] were running the belt was on the high side of the dial. Few if any empty hooks entered the oven, and inspection showed no increase of rejects from the paint room.

"Production increased, and within three weeks (some two months before the scheduled ending of the learning bonus) the [workers] were operating at 30 to 50 per cent above the level that had been expected under the original arrangement. Naturally the [workers'] earnings were correspondingly higher than anticipated. They were collecting their base pay, a considerable piece-rate bonus, and the learning bonus which, it will be remembered, had been set to decrease with time and not as a function of current productivity. (This arrangement, which had been selected by the management in order to prevent being taken advantage of by the [workers] during the learning period, now became a real embarrassment.)"

What Happened Next?

Pause again and note what you think will happen next. The case concludes with a brief description of later events. A detailed analysis follows the case.

"The [workers] were earning more now than many skilled workers in other parts of the plant. Management was besieged by demands that this inequity be taken care of. With growing irritation between superintendent and foreman, engineers and foreman, superintendent and engineers, the situation came to a head when the superintendent without consultation arbitrarily revoked the learning bonus and returned the painting operation to its original status: the hooks moved again at their constant, time-studied designated speed, production dropped again, and within a month all but two of the eight [workers] had quit. The foreman himself stayed on for several months, but, feeling aggrieved, then left for another job."

CASE ANALYSIS

Functional analysis is useful for understanding the events in the Hovey and Beard case. The case also illustrates several concepts you will learn as the book unfolds.

Functional Analysis

Management clearly intended good things to happen by carefully controlling the pace of work in the painting room. The manifest functions of management's actions were increased productivity from the design and control of work pace. The group bonus plan was intended to produce a "team spirit." The workers were expected to pull together for the good of the group and the company.

Some events were not intended by management, but probably could have been predicted. The latent dysfunctions were the repeated complaints about work conditions, decreased output, and harsh feelings directed at both the engineers and management.

Concepts

The case illustrates several concepts and ideas. The goal of the engineers was to increase the efficiency of work processes. The engineers used time-and-motion studies to design standard work activities that are done uniformly by each worker. This approach to work design is expected to increase human productivity.[8] As you saw, though, human beings do not always respond in expected ways when faced with such a standardized system.

The workers had little autonomy when doing their work because the engineers had standardized the pace of work and reduced the workers' ability to make decisions. Letting the workers control their work pace was an effort to increase their autonomy. As you will learn in the chapters on motivation, autonomy plays a key role in the design of jobs that are motivating.

The case illustrates some aspects of human motivation and the use of incentives. Notice that the learning bonus was tied to time and not to the behavior of the workers. Based on what we know about motivation and incentives, we would not expect this incentive method to greatly affect behavior. An alternative method would tie the bonus to improvements in the individual worker's skill and speed.

The company used a group incentive plan, expecting it would bring the workers together and foster team spirit. Such plans work best when the task requires interdependent activity among the workers. This condition did not exist in the Hovey and Beard situation.

The end of the case described a typical problem in using incentives. Because the workers in the paint room were making more money than other workers in the plant, the other workers developed strong feelings of inequity. Management may not have understood why the workers felt as they did. Instead of dealing directly with the inequities by changing the incentive system of the other workers, management chose to "eliminate the problem" by returning the paint room to its original status. This action of management led to the final latent dysfunctions—the workers and the foreman quit.

By drawing on your experience, you may have identified many of these concepts, though you may have expressed them in other terms. Your own experiences also will help you understand many other materials in this book. At the same time, it is important to master the standard words and phrases that are used to describe the concepts and theories in later chapters. Learning those standard terms lets you quickly retrieve applicable concepts and apply them to the cases.

Source: W. F. Whyte, *Money and Motivation* (New York: Harper & Row, 1955), pp. 90–94. Developed by George Strauss and Alex Bavelas. SELECTED EXCERPTS from MONEY AND MOTIVATION by WILLIAM FOOTE WHYTE. Copyright © 1955 by Harper & Row, Publishers, Inc. Copyright renewed 1983 by William Foote Whyte. Reprinted by permission of HarperCollins Publishers, Inc.

Summary

An organization is a system of two or more persons, engaged in cooperative action, trying to reach some purpose.[9] Organizational behavior and organizational theory are both disciplines within the social and behavioral sciences that specialize in studying organizations. Theories and concepts drawn from those disciplines form the foundation of the analytical perspective developed in this book. Theories and concepts let you view organizational issues or problems from different perspectives. They act much like camera lenses in letting you observe a behavioral scene from different angles.

Functional analysis divides the results of a person's behavior into manifest and latent consequences. Manifest consequences are the intended results of the person's action. Latent consequences are the unintended results of the same action. Functional analysis further divides behavior into functional and dysfunctional consequences. Functional consequences are the results of behavior that are good for the organization. Dysfunctional conse- quences are the results of behavior that are bad for the organization.

Developing an analytical perspective on organizations and behavior in them is a central goal of this book. All chapters feature experiential exercises and cases that will help you develop your analytical skills and apply them to real behavioral situations. The last section of this chapter had guidelines for doing case analyses.

. . . .

↵ Key Terms

analytical perspective 10
concepts 5
descriptive theory 6
dysfunctional consequences 8
functional analysis 8

functional consequences 8
latent consequences 8
manifest consequences 8
normative theory 6
organization 4

organizational theory 4
organizational behavior 4
theory 6
theories and concepts as lenses 6

. . . .

↵ Review and Discussion Questions

1. What is theory? Discuss its role in analyzing and diag- nosing organizational issues and problems.
2. Go back and review the concepts you developed when analyzing the Hovey and Beard case. Has anything new occurred to you now that you have finished reading this chapter? Discuss practical experiences with organizations that give you insight into organization phenomena.
3. What are the differences between manifest functions and latent dysfunctions? How are these concepts useful in analyzing and diagnosing organizations?

4. Reflect on five organizations in which you regularly behave. Do you see differences or similarities in your behavior from one organizational setting to another? Why do you think those differences or similarities occur?
5. Discuss how developing an analytical perspective about organizations can be useful to you. How can such a perspective help a person do a better job as a manager?

. . . .

↵ Case

THE BAD BOY OF SILICON VALLEY: MEET T. J. RODGERS, CEO OF CYPRESS SEMICONDUCTOR

The following case describes the behavior of T. J. Rodgers, the chief executive of a semiconductor company. Rodgers sees the world of management differently from his counter- parts in the same industry. Use the following questions to guide you while reading the case:

1. What are the major elements of Rodgers's views of management?
2. Do you believe his ideas will work in this industry?
3. What latent dysfunctions do you see in his way of managing?

Source: Developed from R. Brandt, "The Bad Boy of Silicon Valley: Meet T. J. Rodgers, CEO of Cypress Semiconductor," *Business Week*, December 9, 1991, pp. 64–68, 70.

"When T. J. Rodgers speaks, people bristle. The chief executive of Cypress Semiconductor Corp. calls large chip companies 'dinosaurs.' He accuses their executives of whin- ing for 'political protection' rather than innovating and investing. He complains that current government policies are designed to 'prop up sagging companies.' And he derides Sematech, the government- and industry-funded consortium intended to restore America's edge in semiconductors, as a 'corporate country club' for big business."[10]

Cypress Semiconductor Corp. is a small but successful company that competes in the massive worldwide semicon- ductor industry. With annual sales of $255 million in 1990, it has a small part of the over $25 billion market held by U.S. firms. T. J. Rodgers, the company's chief executive, has a distinctive approach to organizations and management.

Rodgers's management style features frugality, aggres- siveness, and demanding performance standards. He drives himself working 13-hour days with almost nonstop meetings that run until 7 P.M., and he expects his managers to do the same. His evening relaxation includes reading trade magazines and letters. A vacation often features snorkeling in shark-infested waters.

Rodgers's engineering background (Ph.D., Sandford University) may have contributed to his precision approach to management. Software developed by the company tracks manufacturing processes and managers' performance. He regularly reviews performance reports and notes the managers who are five weeks late in reaching their goals. These managers could receive a scathing memo inscribed with "From the Desk of God."

Cypress Semiconductor uses a flexible manufacturing system that enables it to make small lots of specialized chips to customers' specifications. The flexible system lets the company adapt quickly to changes in customer needs. This flexibility is a key part of Rodgers's competitive strategy. The company responds quickly to changing needs, staying ahead of larger, less flexible companies in the industry.

Rodgers believes small companies are better than large ones. He forms new companies to make new products or to manage new manufacturing plants. Each company has its own president and board of directors. Funding comes from Cypress Semiconductor, which keeps an equity interest in the new firm.

Most internal functions operate as profit-and-loss centers, part of Rodgers's effort to encourage entrepreneurial thinking among his managers. Support groups such as testing, for example, charge for their services when requested by an internal department. Rodgers believes managers who request the testing will buy only what they need because they are paying for the tests. " 'Free money is one of the biggest problems of a large company, Rodgers says. 'We've gotten rid of socialism in the organization.' "[11]

. . . .

↳ Case

THE PAYOFF FROM A GOOD REPUTATION

Since the early 1980s, *Fortune* magazine has published a list of the most admired organizations in the United States. This case describes some companies at the top of the list. While reading the case, keep in mind the following questions:

1. What are the key issues raised by the executives in the most admired organizations?
2. Do you perceive those issues as important for managing successfully into the next century?
3. Would any possible latent dysfunctions result from applying the eight criteria *Fortune* uses to assess an organization's reputation?

You won't find it on the balance sheet, and it's not listed in a 10-K or a proxy. If you ask the wizards on Wall Street exactly how it figures into a company's net worth, be prepared for some mighty blank stares. But more and more companies are now coming to realize that when managed correctly, their good name can be their most valuable and enduring asset. Says Laurel Cutler, vice chairman of FCB/Leber Katz Partners, a New York City advertising agency: "The only sustainable competitive advantage any business has is its reputation."

For small companies as well as big ones, the payoff from a good reputation is vast. For starters, it's what puts you first in the minds of consumers and—no small feat—helps keep you there. A solid reputation makes a customer willing to pay more for your product or service. Want the best people working for you? A respected reputation not only helps attract and retain the top minds in your industry, but it also enables you to steal talent away from competitors. It can act as the launching pad for new-product introduction and help open doors more easily for international expansion. And contrary to what you might think, a good reputation, once lost, can be regained.

The outfits that rank high on Fortune's list of the most admired corporations—Merck, Levi Strauss, Rubbermaid, and Harley-Davidson, to mention a few—understand that behind a solid reputation is more than just a well-known name. They earn their esteem by doing what they do well every day in every aspect of their operations, and then by vowing to find a way of doing it better tomorrow. What's more, these companies realize the importance of staying focused on the business that earned them their fame.

At the very least a great reputation is built by offering a superior product or service. "You can't skimp on quality and then pour money into marketing your reputation," explains Alan Towers, president of the consulting firm that bears his name. "To get the most out of your good name, you must continually reinforce the product or service advantage you have over competitors."

The companies that are winning the kudos also understand that consumers are looking beyond quality for something more. If the 1980s are remembered fondly for anything, it will be that they created the sharpest, most-educated customers marketers have ever faced. Sure, these shoppers want the best you have to offer, but they are also interested in what your company stands for: Is your company one they would want to work for? . . .

For example, Herman Miller, the furniture maker in Zeeland, Michigan, no longer uses tropical woods, such as rosewood, from endangered rain forests in its office desks and tables. Instead it uses cherry, which does not come from the tropics. Says CEO Richard Ruch: "We thought first about the environmental aspect and then wondered if the switch would impact sales." In fact, the switch has not hurt sales, which were $869 million in 1990. . . .

When a company is held in high regard, good things happen. On university campuses, the Merck name is golden. Roy Vagelos, 62, the physician, biochemist, and businessman who runs the Rahway, New Jersey, company, tries hard to attract the greatest minds to his research labs. "I still visit about six or eight universities each year, both the medical and business schools, to talk about the discovery of drugs and the wonderful opportunities we have here at Merck," he says. In the past few years the company has been able to lure top scientific talent away from the faculty of such schools as Harvard, Yale, and MIT. . . .

[E]steemed companies often find the road to new-product introductions less bumpy. [Robert] Haas [CEO] of Levi Strauss believes that launching the Dockers brand of casual clothing in 1986 was relatively painless because the San Francisco company made it easy for retailers to do business with it. Says he: "If we hadn't built up that relationship with our retailers over the years, their buyers would not have even looked at the Dockers line, let alone stocked their stores with it." . . .

Rubbermaid—dish drainers, soap dishes, and many of the plastic containers in the average refrigerator come from this Wooster, Ohio, manufacturer—claims that in 1992 it will introduce a new product *every day*. You may think that's just too many dustpans and laundry baskets, but retailers don't. Because Rubbermaid trounces the competition in selection, color, and quality, several retailers, including Wal-Mart, have been testing all-Rubbermaid selling areas in their stores. . . .

When companies turn drummers for their products overseas, they find that a sterling reputation at home translates into an easier time abroad. Demand for Levi's jeans is particularly strong in Europe and Asia. This is one Yankee no one wants to go home, and international operations accounted for 40% of the company's total 1990 sales and about half its pretax operating profits. Rubbermaid's foreign business is only 15% of sales, but CEO Walter Williams is predicting that it will be 25% by the end of the decade. "The beauty about going overseas in a bigger way is that Rubbermaid's reputation has preceded us," he says. "There are not many countries where we would go in and say we're from Rubbermaid and people wouldn't recognize us." . . .

If your good name is worth so much, what happens when you lose it? Says Richard Teerlink, CEO of Harley-Davidson: "We are living proof that you can win your reputation back. But it's not easy." Once the great American motorcycle company—would Peter Fonda and Dennis Hopper have been caught dead easy riding on Kawasakis?—Harley skidded badly in the mid-1970s. "When the competition came in with better bikes, customers left us in hordes," Teerlink recalls. "People said that Harley had a great reputation as being part of Americana. That's nice, but it wasn't enough. No one was going to buy our motorcycles for that reason if they weren't better than the competition's."

By focusing on quality improvements, he revved Harley's engines. Just as important, Teerlink began listening closely to what his remaining customers were telling him. He and his top executives, who often ride their hogs to work, spent weekends participating in cross-country rallies with other bikers and soon developed a keen sense of what the Harley rider wanted. So in the mid-1980s, when Japanese makers were concentrating on sleek aerodynamic styling that concealed the engine, Harley knew enough to stick with its macho bikes.

The Milwaukee company has battled back to the leadership position in the super-heavyweight bike market with a 60% share. . . . Says Teerlink: "It makes me feel good that I can allow my home phone number to be listed in the local directory. When I get calls saying, 'Hey, we like your product,' it's wonderful. That's how you build a relationship with customers, and that's all part of reputation."

- - - - - - - - -

↳ *References and Notes*

[1] C. I. Barnard, *The Functions of the Executive* (Cambridge, Mass.: Harvard University Press, 1938), p. 73.

[2] P. M. Blau and W. R. Scott, *Formal Organizations* (San Francisco: Chandler Publishing Co., 1962); A. Etzioni, *Modern Organizations* (Englewood Cliffs, N.J.: Prentice-Hall, 1964); and W. R. Scott, "Theory of Organizations," in *Handbook of Modern Sociology*, ed. R. E. L. Faris (Chicago: Rand McNally, 1964), 485–529.

[3] R. Dubin, *Theory Building* (New York: Free Press, 1978).

[4] K. Lewin, "The Research Center for Group Dynamics at Massachusetts Institute of Technology," *Sociometry* 8 (1945): 126–36.

[5] Ibid.

[6] T. S. Kuhn, *The Structure of Scientific Revolutions* (Chicago: University of Chicago Press, 1962).

[7] R. K. Merton, *Social Theory and Social Structure* (New York: Free Press, 1968), Ch. 3.

[8] M. E. Mundel, *Motion and Time Study: Improving Productivity* (New York: Prentice-Hall, 1985).

[9] Barnard, *Functions of the Executive*, p. 73.

[10] R. Brandt, "The Bad Boy of Silicon Valley: Meet T. J. Rodgers, CEO of Cypress Semiconductor," *Business Week*, December 9, 1991, p. 64.

[11] Brandt, "The Bad Boy of Silicon Valley," p. 66.

2

Emerging Issues in Organizations and Management (Diversity, Quality, International, Ethics)

· Workforce diversity will bring many types of people together to work in teams.

After reading this chapter, you should be able to . . .

· Understand why the U.S. workforce will increase in diversity well into the next century.
· Describe the direction in which many organizations are headed in managing for quality.
· Discuss some issues and implications of managing organizations in an increasingly global environment.
· Explain some ethical issues that modern managers are asked to consider when they make decisions.

Chapter Overview

OPENING EPISODE *When Will Women Get to the Top?*
Workforce Diversity
EXERCISE *Cultural-Diversity Quiz*
Managing for Quality
CASE *Quality Programs Show Shoddy Results*
The Global Environment of Organizations
Ethics and Behavior in Organizations

When Will Women Get to the Top?

Talk for a while with any woman who has worked her way to the top of a sizable U.S. corporation. You'll get a strong sense that she feels a bit like *Apollo 14* astronaut Alan Shepard when he improvised a six iron out of a piece of lunar equipment and, one-handed in his cumbersome space suit, whacked a golf ball that flickered eerily across the airless surface of the moon. Exhilarated, isolated, keenly aware of the world's attention ("*Houston, can you see me now?*"), female high executives are eager to colonize this unaccustomed terrain with more of their own. But like astronauts, they know too much about the rigors of the journey to believe that it can happen by next Wednesday, or even by next year. Says Carol Bartz, 44, recently named chairman and CEO of Autodesk, a leading maker of software for engineers and architects in Sausalito, California: "I think that women in corporate America are still a generation away from real success."

• *Carol Bartz, CEO and chair of Autodesk, a California software maker.*

Alas, the top men in corporate America appear to agree. A poll of 201 chief executives of the nation's largest companies, conducted exclusively for Fortune by the opinion research firm Clark Martire & Bartolomeo, reveals that only 16% believe it is "very likely" or "somewhat likely" that they could be succeeded by a female CEO within the next decade. And only 18% think it's "very likely" that even after 20 years a woman would be picked to run their companies.

Why? The CEOs in our survey cite a host of reasons, but the biggest barrier, as a few of them admit, is an irrational one—plain and simple discrimination. Notes John H. Bryan, 56, CEO of Sara Lee: "I'm not sure there's a lot that women can do about it. They're already working hard and are very qualified. It shouldn't be this way, but too many senior managers, and particularly CEOs, tend to want to pass their jobs along to someone who's the image and likeness of themselves." John Nelson, 48, who heads Norwest Colorado, a bank holding company, agrees: "The problem with women advancing has more to do with men than with women. Men have dragged their feet."

Thanks for the honesty, guys, but that's pretty discouraging news. And coming during an election year in which, incredibly, some conservative politicians and leaders of the religious right are openly or implicitly condemning the very notion that women *should* work outside the home, it's enough to make even the most optimistic female executive despair. That would be wrong, however, because better days *are* coming. . . .

Toward that end, dozens of corporate colossi, from AT&T to Johnson & Johnson to Xerox, have hired full-time "diversity managers," charged by top management to make the workplace more hospitable to talent of either sex and all colors. In some cases this is pure tinsel and tokenism, but for many companies it's a hard-nosed business strategy. Says Aetna Life & Casualty CEO Ronald Compton, 59, who is largely responsible for the fact that roughly half his company's managers are now women: "I'm not doing this out of the goodness of my heart. I'm selfish. I want the very best people I can get. A lot of them happen to be women." No diversity campaign will succeed without that kind of blessing from the top. . . .

The best reason for believing that more women will be in charge before long is that in a ferociously competitive global economy, no company can afford to waste valuable brainpower simply because it's wearing a skirt. That isn't easy for some folks to accept. "Dealing with change is always painful," notes William Boyle, a Monsanto plant manager who is a big believer in the company's diversity-training programs. "But the days when any U.S. company could stand pat, do things the same old way, and say 'Gosh, look how good we are'—those days are gone."

Source: A. B. Fisher, "When Will Women Get to the Top?" *Fortune*, September 21, 1992, pp. 44, 47, 56. © 1992 Time, Inc. All rights reserved.

his chapter continues the introduction to this book by highlighting four major issues facing modern organizations. Those issues center on the increasing diversity of the U.S. workforce, an emphasis on managing for quality, the increasing global orientation required of managers, and the ethical issues facing organizations. A separate chapter discusses these issues because of their importance to managing successfully in the future.

The case opening this chapter highlights one of these issues—the increasing diversity of the U.S. workforce. Women are coming into the workforce in growing numbers. More and more ethnically diverse people are entering the country and the workforce. Managers will increasingly face a globally competitive environment in which they must use the best talent available, no matter what the person's gender, ethnic background, color, or many other factors.[1] No longer can U.S. executives, mainly white males, accept existing conditions, if they want their organizations to compete effectively. As the case indicated, for some U.S. organizations, these changes will be painful.

- - - - - - - - - -

◢ *Workforce Diversity*

Workforce diversity refers to variations in the composition of the workforce based on personal and background factors of employees or potential employees.[2] Those factors include age, gender, race, ethnicity, and physical ability. Other factors include family status such as a single parent, a dual-career relationship, or a person with responsibilities for aging parents. Figure 2-1 shows the **dimensions of workforce diversity** frequently mentioned by some prominent writers.[3] A quick look at that figure will show you the complexity and scope of the issues surrounding this topic.

Figure 2-2 shows the Bureau of Labor Statistics (BLS) projections of the U.S. civilian labor force growth between 1990 and 2005.[4] The BLS defines the labor force

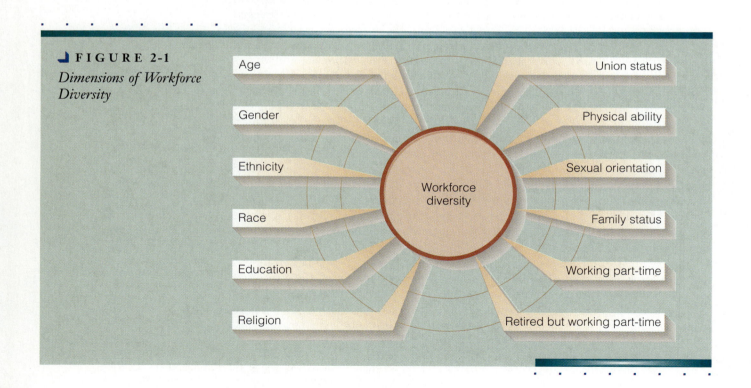

◢ **FIGURE 2-1**

Dimensions of Workforce Diversity

Age

Gender

Ethnicity

Race

Education

Religion

Workforce diversity

Union status

Physical ability

Sexual orientation

Family status

Working part-time

Retired but working part-time

FIGURE 2-2

Projected Growth in the U.S. Civilian Labor Force, 1990–2005

Note: The Bureau of Labor Statistics prepares three projections: low, moderate, and high. Data for this figure came from the bureau's moderate projection, which assumed high net immigration, moderate population growth, and a percentage of the population in the labor force similar to past years. The category Asian/Other includes Native Americans, Alaskan natives, and Pacific Islanders. Hispanic includes both blacks and whites. *Outlook: 1990–2005, Bulletin 2402* (Washington, D.C.: Bureau of Labor Statistics, U.S. Department of Labor, 1992), pp. 93–104.
Source: H. N. Fullerton, Jr., "Labor Force Projections: The Baby Boom Moves on," *Monthly Labor Review* 114 (1991): 33, Table 1.

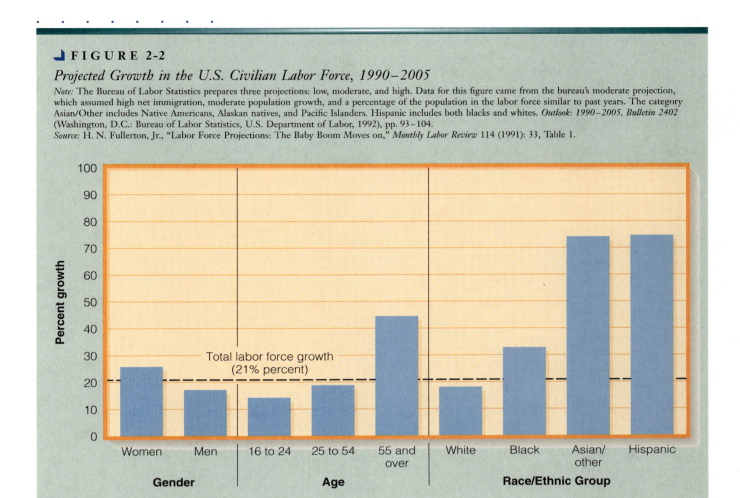

as all people now working or looking for work. BLS projections show the civilian labor force growing by 21 percent during the period 1990–2005.

The number of women in the labor force is projected to grow by 26 percent, a rate above the total projected growth. Projected growth for men is 16 percent, a rate below the total projected growth. Labor force projections by age show a large increase in those age 55 and over and much smaller increases for young workers (16 to 24). The race/ethnic projections show a large increase in minority workers and much smaller increases in white workers. Other data suggest a growth in part-time employment, dual-earner households, and women with young children working outside the home.[5]

If the BLS projections hold true, the workforce of the next century will have more female workers, more minority workers, and more part-time workers. Age diversity will also continue although projections for the year 2005 show less than 15 percent of the labor force at age 55 or over. The expected gender and ethnic profile of the labor force in the year 2005 shows 47 percent women and 28 percent minority workers.[6]

Regional variations will also be significant. The projections discussed so far were for the entire civilian labor force. Local population characteristics will affect the workforce from which a specific organization draws.[7] For example, according to some projections, California's population in 2005 will consist of 50 percent white and 50 percent people of color speaking 80 languages.[8]

People from different social backgrounds, cultures, and language groups bring different worldviews to an organization. They view issues and problems at work through different perceptual lenses. If properly managed, these different views present opportunities to organizations, but they also increase the potential for conflict. The challenge for managers is to focus those diverse views on the mission of the organization while managing the conflict so it remains at a functional level.

People with different needs and expectations also present challenges to an organization's personnel and work policies. Working parents with children often require adaptations in work schedules or on-site day care. Single parents may need time off to take a sick child to a physician. Native Americans may need special work schedules during their culture's periods of celebration. A disabled person can require special access to a building and a specially designed work area. Part-time workers may need to arrange job sharing so the organization can get the value of their talents.

Is workforce diversity a new issue for U.S. managers?[9] The roots of the issue are easily traced to the racial integration of U.S. military forces ordered by President Truman after World War II. That action produced large organizations with racially and ethnically diverse populations. The civil rights movement of the 1960s successfully pressed for legal remedies that removed discriminatory barriers to hiring and promotion in many organizations. Blacks and Hispanics began to appear in growing numbers in organizations. Women began to enter the workforce in increasing numbers; delaying both marriage and childbearing, they chose to pursue careers just like the more prevalent white males. Major changes in immigration to the United States brought increasingly diverse people from many lands, cultures, and language groups. People began retiring from full-time employment between the ages of 55 and 65, but both wanted and needed to work into their later years. Retired people joined the already growing ranks of those who preferred part-time to full-time employment.

In short, workforce diversity has been with U.S. managers since the late 1940s. It has clear roots in the U.S. civil rights movement and the resulting affirmative action programs.[10] The diversity that organizations now experience is a product not only of the increasingly diverse character of U.S. society but also of successful affirmative action and Equal Employment Opportunity programs[11] and government actions such as the Americans with Disabilities Act of 1990. That legislation prohibits discrimination in hiring and promoting people with mental or physical disabilities.[12]

People mean various things by "managing diversity."[13] Some organizations and their managers only react to the increasing diversity they see in their workforce. They seek to manage diversity so people of all backgrounds have equal access to employment, promotion, and personnel policies. Other organizations and their managers "value diversity." They aggressively embrace it and actively try to build a diverse workforce.[14] Such organizations view a diverse workforce as a distinct competitive advantage. In either case, **managing diversity** requires a manager to focus on creating an environment that harnesses the potential of all sources of difference within an organization's workforce.

Managing diversity is not affirmative action in disguise. Instead it is managing to get the greatest contributions from increasingly diverse people. It recognizes that a variety of views from diverse people enrich organization life. Managing diversity does not ask diverse people to give up their individuality and take on the values of the majority. It honors differences among people, but also asks everyone to accept the core values of the organization. Ideally, those core values should be related to the organization's mission such as "An unending pursuit of excellence in customer service." Such a mission statement sets out the organization's goal, not how to reach it. People reach the goal in many different ways because of their diversity.

Why should managers and their organizations care about meeting the expectations and requirements of a diverse workforce? Could they not select people who fit into the organization's existing culture, policies, and procedures? The resounding answer has two parts: (1) Managers will simply have no choice about managing for diversity, and (2) successfully managing for diversity is good business strategy.

The first answer follows from labor force statistics. As Figure 2-2 showed, the U.S. workforce will become increasingly diverse in the future. Organizations that do not have a diverse workforce now are likely to face one in the future, especially as they pursue scarce skilled labor. Other organizations have complied with affirmative action and Equal Employment Opportunity guidelines and directives. Those organizations now have diverse workforces.[15]

The second answer implies a more aggressive management position toward workforce diversity. Good business strategy in the changing world of the 1990s and into the next century requires unleashing all the potential of a diverse workforce.[16] The reasons are twofold: (1) the increasing service character of the U.S. economy, and (2) the need to think and to compete globally to remain competitive.[17]

The growth in service organizations and the need to offer service to customers from all types of organizations are important aspects of the U.S. economy. Almost three-quarters of the employees in the private sector now work in service-based organizations.[18] Managers of other organizations, such as manufacturing, are realizing that they must know their customers' expectations to stay competitive. As society becomes increasingly diverse, customers are becoming more diverse as well. Having a diverse workforce helps managers meet their customers' expectations. For example, the top performing branches at Baltimore-based Maryland National Bank relied on locally recruited tellers. The tellers came from the predominantly African-American neighborhoods they served, letting them better understand their customers.[19]

The global environment of modern organizations adds another layer of complexity to workforce diversity. Many U.S. organizations sell in foreign markets, operate in countries outside the United States, or enter joint ventures with organizations from other countries. Because U.S. organizations operating abroad often employ native-born people at all levels, managers must be able to interact with employees from other countries. To meet the expectations of customers in foreign markets, they need to understand local customs and business practices. Thus, to be successful, U.S. managers must understand cultural differences around the world and not assume customer requirements in foreign markets are the same as at home. A culturally diverse workforce can help U.S. organizations meet these challenges.

Organizations and their managers face many challenges when managing for diversity.[20] The goal of managing for diversity is to unleash the potential of a diverse workforce and channel it toward the organization's goals. The challenge for managers is to provide vision, so everyone understands where the organization is headed. Managers also want to preserve a diversity of viewpoints and enable people to get the satisfaction they uniquely want from their work experiences. The diversity of viewpoints can increase the potential for conflict in the organization, presenting another major challenge to managers.

Managing for diversity forces many organizations to make major changes, such as modifying personnel policies about work schedules, personal leave, language training in English or other languages, and other basic skills. Managers must manage for fairness when meeting the diverse needs of their workforce.[21] For example, a day care policy originally made to meet the needs of working women must apply to all employees despite gender and marital status. Managers will also need to learn new skills such as accepting differences, appreciating language differences, and even learning new languages. The latter can include sign language to communicate with hearing-impaired employees.

Other changes touch the heart of an organization's culture by asking for shifts in its values, rituals, and assumptions.[22] Values suitable to a homogeneous white male culture will need to yield to the heterogeneous values of many diverse groups.[23] Social activities that are rituals in male cultures will need to be changed to allow ready access by female managers, or the activities may be rotated to meet the desires of both groups. For example, if social gatherings of managers usually include only male-oriented sports, other activities should be added. Instead of assuming that all managers like a hard game of flag football, the gathering's organizers could poll people for their preferences.

Cultural-Diversity Quiz

*L*et's pause now so you can reflect on what you know about cultural and workforce diversity. The following exercise asks you several questions about cultural differences among different people. Answer as best you can. Table 2-1 on page 25 has the correct answers and scoring procedure. To get a true assessment, answer the questions before looking at the table.

1. On average, how long do native-born Americans maintain eye contact?
   a. 1 second
   b. 15 seconds
   c. 30 seconds
2. True or false: A universal way to motivate workers, despite cultural background, is through the prospect of a promotion.
3. Learning to speak a few words of the language of immigrant clients, customers, and workers is:
   a. A good idea as the effort communicates respect for the other person.
   b. Not a good idea because they might feel patronized.
   c. Not a good idea because they might be offended if a mistake is made in vocabulary or pronunciation.
4. True or false: American culture has no unique characteristics. It is composed only of individual features brought here from other countries.
5. When communicating across language barriers, using the written word:
   a. Should be avoided. It can insult the immigrant or international visitor's intelligence.
   b. Can be helpful. It usually is easier to read English than to hear it.
   c. Can be confusing. It usually is easier to hear English than to read it.
6. True or false: Behaving formally around immigrant colleagues, clients, and workers—that is, using last names, observing strict rules of etiquette—usually is not a good idea as it gives the impression of coldness and superiority.
7. In times of crisis, the immigrant's ability to speak English:
   a. Diminishes because of stress.
   b. Stays the same.
   c. Improves because of the need to cope with the crisis.
   d. Completely disappears.
8. How many languages are spoken in the United States today?
   a. 0–10
   b. 10–50
   c. 50–100
   d. 100+
9. True or false: Immigrant families in the United States largely make decisions as individuals and have usually abandoned the practice of making decisions as a group.
10. When you have difficulty understanding people with a foreign accent:
    a. It probably means that they cannot understand you either.
    b. It probably means that they recently arrived in this country.
    c. It is helpful if you listen to all that they have to say before interrupting. The meaning might become clear in the context of the conversation.
    d. It is helpful for you to guess at what the speaker is saying and to speak for him or her to reduce the risk of embarrassment.
11. When an Asian client begins to give you vague answers before closing a deal, saying things like "It will take time to decide" or "We'll see," the best thing to do is:
    a. Back off a bit. The client might be trying to say "no" without offending you.
    b. Supply more information and data about your service or product, especially in writing.
    c. Push for a "close." The client's vagueness is probably a manipulative tactic.
    d. State clearly and strongly that you are dissatisfied with the client's reaction to avoid any misunderstanding.
12. Apparent rudeness and abruptness in immigrants often are due to:
    a. Lack of English-language facility.
    b. A difference in cultural style.
    c. Differing tone of voice.
13. True or false: Many immigrant and ethnic cultures place greater importance on how something is said (body language and tone of voice) than on the words themselves.
14. Avoiding public embarrassment (loss of face) is of central concern to which of the following cultures?
    a. Hispanic
    b. Mainstream American
    c. Asian
    d. Middle Eastern
15. True or false: A universal in etiquette is that everyone likes to be complimented in front of others.
16. In a customer-service situation, when communicating to a decision maker through a child who is functioning as interpreter, it is best to:
    a. Look at the child as you speak so he or she will be certain to understand you.
    b. Look at the decision maker.
    c. Look back and forth between the two.
17. Which of the following statements is (are) true?
    a. Most Asian workers like it when the bosses roll up their sleeves to work beside employees.
    b. Taking independent initiative on tasks is valued in most workplaces throughout the world.
    c. Many immigrant workers are reluctant to complain to the boss as they feel it is a sign of disrespect.
    d. Asians are quick to praise superiors to their face as a way of showing respect.

18. True or false: The "V" for victory sign is a universal gesture of good will and triumph.
19. Which of the following statements is (are) true?
    a. It is inappropriate to touch Asians on the hand.
    b. Middle Eastern men stand close as a way of dominating the conversation.
    c. Mexican men will hold another man's lapel during conversation as a sign of good communication.
20. Building relationships slowly when doing business with Hispanics is:
    a. A bad idea. If you don't move things along, they will go elsewhere.
    b. A bad idea. They expect native-born professionals to move quickly and will be disoriented if you do not.
    c. A good idea. It might take longer, but the trust you build will be well worth the effort.

Go to Table 2-1 for the correct answers. Tally the number of correct answers and compare it to the scoring summary in the table.

This quiz assessed your knowledge in many different areas. Note that it included unspoken language such as eye contact and touching other people. It also included ways of working with people for whom English is not a first language. Remember that people of diverse backgrounds have different ideas of the right etiquette or style of social interaction. Working effectively with diverse people, either as coworkers or customers, requires more than knowing a few words of their language. It also requires knowledge of more subtle parts of their cultures. If your score was less than 11 points, you will find much of the information in the citation for this exercise helpful in increasing your cultural-diversity knowledge.

Source: Adapted from S. Thiederman, *Profiting in America's Multicultural Marketplace: How to Do Business across Cultural Lines* (New York: Lexington Books, 1991), pp. xix–xxii. Reprinted with the permission of Lexington Books, an imprint of The Free Press, a Division of Simon & Schuster, from Profiting in America's Multicultural Marketplace: How to do Business Across Cultural Lines by Sondra Thiederman. Copyright © 1991 by Sondra Thiederman.

⌐ TABLE 2-1
Answers and Scoring Summary for the Cultural-Diversity Quiz

ANSWERS

1. a	11. a
2. False	12. a, b, and c
3. a	13. True
4. False	14. a, c, and d
5. b	15. False
6. False	16. b
7. a	17. c
8. d	18. False
9. False	19. c
10. c	20. c

SCORING SUMMARY

Number Correct	Evaluation
16–20	You have a good grasp of cultural diversity. You should do well in the multicultural business world.
11–15	You are culturally aware and probably receptive to learning more about cultural differences.
6–10	You have a way to go but can easily learn more.
0–5	Do not be discouraged. The knowledge reflected in this quiz is new for many people.

Source: Adapted from S. Thiederman, *Profiting in America's Multicultural Marketplace: How to Do Business across Cultural Lines* (New York: Lexington Books, 1991), pp. xxiii–xxiv. Reprinted with the permission of Lexington Books, an imprint of The Free Press, a Division of Simon & Schuster, from PROFITING IN AMERICA'S MULTICULTURAL MARKETPLACE: How to do Business Across Cultural Lines by Sondra Thiederman. Copyright © 1991 by Sondra Thiederman.

A major new thrust of American management is the management for quality of products and services.[24] Although the roots of quality management can be traced to the early 1920s, American organizations did not embrace it until the early 1980s.[25] Quality management has many names including Total Quality Control, Total Quality Management, Total Quality Leadership, Leadership Through Quality, Market Driven Quality,[26] and Continuous Process Improvement.[27] The term *Total Quality Management* embraces all programs of quality management and continuous quality improvement.

Total Quality Management (TQM) is a philosophy and system of management built upon work dating to the 1920s.[28] TQM includes tools and techniques that help organizations manage for quality in services, products, and processes. Although its roots are in manufacturing, it is a management system that can bring major

· *Some founders of the U.S. quality management movement: W. Edwards Deming, top left; Walter A. Shewhart, top right; Armand V. Feigenbaum, bottom left; and Joseph M. Juran, bottom right.*

improvements to any organization. It readily applies to managing all kinds of organizations and the internal processes of any organization or group.

TQM was a distinctly U.S. invention with several important Japanese innovations. The earliest U.S. antecedents to TQM are the works of Walter A. Shewhart, Armand V. Feigenbaum, and Joseph M. Juran at Bell Telephone Laboratories. Shewhart was the first to recognize that variability in manufacturing processes could be attributed to abnormalities or causes common to the process. He developed statistical tools that let managers know when a manufacturing process was out of control and introducing poor quality.[29] In the 1950s, Feigenbaum pressed for Total Quality Control, a method of quality management that required the involvement of people both within and outside a quality control department.[30] Juran did the economic analyses that showed the long-term payoffs of managing for quality.[31] His phrase "gold in the mine" has become a motto of quality management enthusiasts and consultants.

Perhaps the best-known person associated with quality management is W. Edwards Deming, a statistician who started his career with the U.S. Department of Agriculture and the Bureau of the Census.[32] Deming emphasized using statistics to understand and manage process variability. His early teachings had little effect on American managers but strongly influenced the Japanese, who consider Deming the most important American contributor to their methods of managing for quality. He stands as a giant in Japanese quality circles.

The goal of TQM is the management of quality. Although long-term cost reductions and increased profit commonly result, quality management is the goal. TQM focuses an entire organization on continuous improvement in its products, services, or processes.

TQM requires a total systems view of management that reaches beyond the boundary of the organization. It uses an understanding of the interdependence of outside people, outside organizations, and groups within the organization to manage for quality. The list of the stakeholders—groups with an interest in the organization's activities—is long. It includes employees, vendors, suppliers, clients, customers, the community surrounding the organization, coalitions to which the organization belongs, professional or trade associations, and competitors.

TQM asks people to view organizations in a new way. Figure 2-3 shows two contrasting ways of thinking about organizations. Part (a) shows a typical chain-of-command view, which emphasizes reporting relationships and the usual interconnections among people at different levels.[33] Part (b) shows a **TQM view of an organization.** This view expresses the major emphases of TQM: processes, customers, and interdependence with suppliers. It also shows the critical role of feedback in getting continuous quality improvement. Only by directly asking customers and suppliers can an organization discover shifts in expectations and quality requirements.[34]

Many tools and techniques support TQM's philosophy of continuous improvement. These **tools and techniques** were developed to let people watch their work processes to assure a quality product or service. Table 2-2 summarizes some major tools and techniques of TQM. Organizations that move toward TQM must train employees in the use of the tools to get true quality management.

Most tools and techniques shown in Table 2-2 let organizations carefully analyze their processes. Such analyses typically are done by teams of people drawn from all parts of the organization affected by the process. For example, an analysis team examining an organization's hiring process might include members drawn from the Human Resource Department, hiring departments, newly hired employees, and labor union representatives. Such analysis teams often are deliberately diverse in membership to bring many different views to the analysis and improvement of a work process.

Organizations that use TQM enjoy many benefits that do not directly result from other approaches to management. Employee commitment to continuous quality improvement increases. The cost of providing a service or manufacturing a product declines. Service processes function more dependably; products are more reliable.

FIGURE 2-3

Different Views of Organizations

Source: Suggested by W. E. Deming, *Out of the Crisis* (Cambridge, Mass.: MIT Center for Advanced Engineering Study, 1985), p. 4.

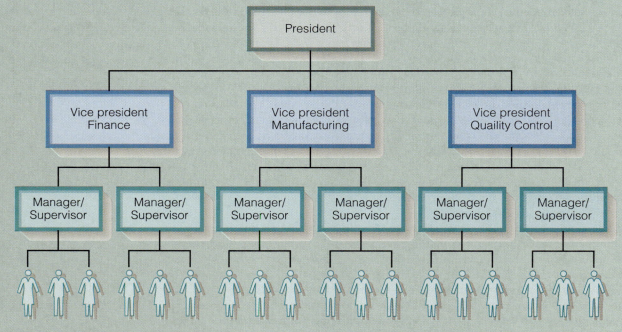

a) A Chain-of-Command Organization

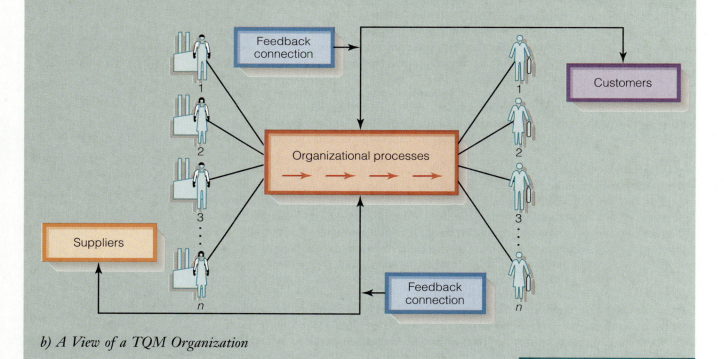

b) A View of a TQM Organization

⌐ T A B L E 2-2

Summary of Total Quality Management Tools and Techniques

CHECKSHEET

A structured method of collecting quantitative data about the results of a process. Lets the user count items such as the number or types of defects in a product.

PARETO CHART

A bar chart displaying the bars in descending order by height. Each bar is a problem measured in the same units. Pareto charts let you isolate the major problems from the minor ones.

FLOWCHART

A diagram that shows the steps, and relationships among steps, in a process. Uses different symbols to show action steps, decision steps, and waiting periods.

CONTROL CHART

A line graph showing the performance of a process over time. The user compares the line showing actual performance to previously computed upper and lower limits of process performance. Quickly shows whether the variability in a process is within or outside the control limits.

CAUSE AND EFFECT DIAGRAM

A drawing that shows the relationship between a problem and its likely causes. The diagram shows relationships among the factors that can affect the variability of a process.

BENCHMARKING

A method of comparing an organization's processes to those of an accepted leader. It shows how the quality of the organization's process compares to one that has already reached high quality.

QUALITY FUNCTION DEPLOYMENT

A concept and a tool for translating customer needs into engineering requirements. Emphasizes the need for cross-functional teams to truly meet customer expectations.*

*J. R. Hauser and D. Clausing, "House of Quality," *Harvard Business Review* (May-June 1988): 63–73.
Source: H. M. Wadsworth, K. S. Stephens, and A. B. Godfrey, *Modern Methods for Quality Control and Improvement* (New York: John Wiley & Sons, Inc. 1986).

TQM is a way of managing that differs from what most managers and organizations have done in the past. It emphasizes a long-term commitment to continuous quality improvement and stresses that quality is everyone's job, not just the job of a quality control or quality assurance department. TQM is intensely customer focused and demands that all members of the organization share that focus. TQM emphasizes high involvement in the work process. It assumes people want high involvement in their work or that managers and supervisors can create that involvement. TQM emphasizes communication in all directions—top-down, bottom-up, and laterally. This feature follows directly from the requirements of cooperation and high involvement. It also is a way TQM generates large amounts of information in the system.

Managers who adopt the TQM philosophy develop a long-term orientation, a commitment to the future. It is not the here-and-now that is important. All the decisions made today in the organization are made with a view of the future. Being good now is not enough. Being great is the goal—a passionate pursuit of continuous improvement.

TQM's emphasis on continuous improvement of all processes in an organization lets people do more with the same resources. Involving everyone in continuous improvement can add challenge to employees' jobs. The long-run result is a committed corps of people with an impassioned focus on mission, customers, and continuous quality improvement.

Not all U.S. organizations that adopted TQM have had successful results.[35] Several prominent failures have occurred, causing some private sector organizations in the United States to reconsider a quality management orientation. The Wallace Co., a winner of the Malcolm Baldrige National Quality Award, filed for Chapter 11 bankruptcy protection.[36] Moving to TQM did not prevent Douglas Aircraft in Long Beach, California, from experiencing massive layoffs. At Florida Power & Light, a leading example of quality management in the United States, major layoffs of the TQM staff followed the appointment of a new chief executive officer. The negative results for many organizations with well-developed TQM programs led some observers to question their long-term effectiveness.[37] Critics felt the costs of such programs often exceeded the benefits of quality.

By the mid-1990s, researchers identified the way improved quality can increase profits. Continuous improvement efforts increase efficiency of processes and reduce their costs. Quality can attract new customers and increase the retention of old customers. According to some estimates, it costs five times as much to get new customers as to keep the present ones.[38] High quality can also make a product or service so attractive that an organization can charge higher prices than its competitors can. Researchers and analysts found that in many cases TQM efforts produced poor results because managers failed to target improvements to areas that had the greatest long-term positive effect on profits.[39] Managers of many quality improvement efforts apparently did not understand how improved quality affected profits.

Total Quality Management supporters remain committed to the quest for managing for quality.[40] The Japanese have had extraordinary success with their quality management efforts, but no other country has achieved such results.[41] U.S. managers may lack the patience and long-term view needed to get the benefits attributed to managing for quality. The following case describes the results of a major study that identifies some difficulties many companies have had.

CASE — *Quality Programs Show Shoddy Results*

*U*se the following questions as guides to your analysis of the case. A brief analysis follows the case. Check with your instructor, and other students, for further observations on this case.

1. What are the main reasons the movement toward managing for quality is floundering?
2. What are key elements of a potentially effective effort to manage for quality?
3. Is Total Quality Management a 1980s fad that will simply fade away?
4. Should U.S. managers let it fade away?

CASE DESCRIPTION

The "total quality" movement, one of the biggest fads in corporate management, is floundering, a broad study suggests.

Despite plenty of talk and much action, many American companies are stumbling in their implementation of quality-improvement efforts, says the study, being released today. A key reason, the study concludes: Many quality-management plans are simply too amorphous to generate better products and services.

Rather than diffusing effort by addressing quality problems across the board, the report proposes that companies should focus on a small number of decisive changes.

"A lot of companies read lots of books, did lots of training, formed teams and tried to implement 9,000 new practices simultaneously," says Terrence R. Ozan, a partner with Ernst & Young, which ran the study with the American Quality Foundation. "But you don't get results that way. It's just too much."

The study represents one of the most comprehensive and critical reviews to date of quality-management programs. In recent years, thousands of organizations have embraced such efforts in a quest for improved performance. Based on a survey of 584 companies in the U.S., Canada, Germany and Japan, the study details failings across a range of quality-improvement activities in the auto, computer, banking and health-care industries. Among its U.S. findings:

- Computer companies involve only 12% of their employees in idea-suggestion programs. Auto makers, which rate highest in this area, involve just 28% of their workers.
- Customer complaints are of "major or primary" importance in identifying new products and services among only 19% of banks and 26% of hospitals.
- Quality-performance measures—such as defect rates and customer-satisfaction levels—play a key role in determining pay for senior managers among fewer than one in five companies across all four industries surveyed. Profitability still matters most.

The results seem even worse when compared with quality programs abroad. Some 73% of surveyed computer makers in Japan and 60% in Germany use customer complaints to help identify new products, compared with 26% in the U.S. Foreign employee-suggestion programs, meanwhile, include larger proportions of workers—34% among Canadian banks, for instance, and 78% among Japanese car makers.

To be sure, there are some bright spots in the U.S.: More than half of all workers in the surveyed companies participate in at least occasional meetings about quality. And the study reports marked increases in quality-related activities during the past three years. But among most U.S. companies, virtually no quality-boosting practices have reached what survey organizers consider lasting and meaningful levels.

"They've got to become habits," says Joshua Hammond, president of the American Quality Foundation, a New York think tank. "If quality is going to have a payoff, it's got to be a routine part of the way you do business."

The findings come at a critical point in the quality movement, which appears to be losing some of its allure after several years of steady growth. The Conference Board, a New York business research group, says attendance at seminars it runs on quality has fallen in the past year. Moreover, the number of companies competing for the Commerce Department's Malcolm Baldrige National Quality Award dropped to 90 this year from 106 last year. . . .

Tom Vanderpool, a quality consultant with Gemini Consulting, Morristown, N.J., says many companies aren't seeing results—and may tire of trying—because they mistakenly isolate quality programs from day-to-day operations. "They tend to put it off as something special, as an objective with 10,000 activities unto itself," he says. "It is not. It is a way to meet business objectives."

Steven Walleck, director of consulting giant McKinsey & Co.'s operations practices, faults the sheer scale of many quality plans. "Most require so much groundwork before results can be expected that you're almost systematically doomed" to waste money on quality-related training and technology, he says. A recent McKinsey study of 30 quality programs found that two-thirds had stalled or fallen short of yielding real improvements, Mr. Walleck adds. . . .

While concluding that companies should target their quality efforts more tightly—what some dub "partial quality management"—the $2 million study doesn't rank which practices work best. But Mr. Hammond suggests that the most successful programs typically include strong personal involvement by senior executives, company-wide awareness of strategic plans and goals, and an emphasis on simplifying processes.

CASE ANALYSIS

Diffused and ill-focused Total Quality Management efforts have likely drained the energy and resources of many companies and kept them from moving forward with decisiveness. Many companies have also had difficulty shifting to a customer focus, when that focus was not a key part of their cultures. Successful quality management efforts have high involvement of senior managers, a clearly defined strategic focus, and accountability of managers to quality and continuous improvement. Concentrating on these features could help U.S. and Canadian managers build a strategic advantage from Total Quality Management and improve its fading image.

Source: G. Fuchsberg, "Quality Programs Show Shoddy Results," *Wall Street Journal,* May 14, 1992, pp. B1, B9. Reprinted by permission of *The Wall Street Journal,* © 1992 Dow Jones & Company, Inc. All Rights Reserved Worldwide.

The Global Environment of Organizations

The **global environment** of organizations demands that modern managers have an international focus that was never required before. Modern managers must begin to think beyond the domestic environment of their organizations. Now the world is their environment and will become increasingly so in the future. For some organizations, thinking internationally means finding new markets outside the home country; for others, becoming a multinational organization operating in many countries; and for others, becoming a transnational organization whose decisions are not limited by country boundaries. Modern managers must think of the entire planet as a source of labor and materials, places of production, and markets.[42]

Modern technology both enables and compels a global view.[43] Thanks to modern aircraft, international travel is common and fast. Telecommunication satellites allow information in all forms to move quickly from country to country. Managers of the

---

TABLE 2-3

Some Dimensions of Country Cultures

Power distance: Degree of inequality among people that a culture considers normal.
- **Low:** People treated as equals despite formal social status (Republic of Ireland, New Zealand, Denmark, Israel, Austria).
- **High:** People accept authority relations and expect those with authority to use it (Malaysia, Guatemala, Panama, the Philippines, Mexico).

Uncertainty avoidance: Value placed on predictability, structure, and stability.
- **Low**: People value flexibility and prefer few formal rules (Hong Kong, Sweden, Denmark, Jamaica, Singapore).
- **High:** People desire written or unwritten rules as a guide for their behavior (Greece, Portugal, Guatemala, Uruguay, Belgium).

Individualism: Value placed on individual behavior, acting alone and not as part of a group.
- **Low:** People prefer to act as members of a group, respect their group, and are loyal to their group (United States, Australia, Great Britain, Canada, the Netherlands).
- **High:** People prefer to act alone and do not expect support from a group (Colombia, Venezuela, Panama, Ecuador, Guatemala).

Masculinity*: Value placed on decisiveness, assertiveness, independence, and individual achievement.
- **Low:** People prefer warm interpersonal relationships and act with tenderness and caring (Costa Rica, Denmark, the Netherlands, Norway, Sweden).
- **High:** People prefer competition and value assertive behavior (Japan, Austria, Venezuela, Italy, Switzerland).

Long-term orientation**: Value placed on persistence, status, and thrift.
- **Low:** Present oriented, respect for tradition, personal stability (United States, Canada, the Philippines, Nigeria, Pakistan).
- **High:** Future oriented, perseverance, valuing status and ordered relationships (South Korea, Japan, Taiwan, Hong Kong, China).

*Although Hofstede named the fourth dimension "masculinity" he felt the values described could apply to women, depending on the dominant gender of the country's culture.
**G. Hofstede and M. H. Bond, "The Confucius Connection: From Cultural Roots to Economic Growth," *Organizational Dynamics* 16 (1988): 4–21.
Sources: G. Hofstede, *Culture's Consequences: International Differences in Work-Related Values* (Beverly Hills, Calif.: Sage Publications, 1984); G. Hofstede, *Cultures and Organizations: Software of the Mind* (New York: McGraw-Hill, 1991); G. Hofstede, "Cultural Constraints in Management Theories," *Academy of Management Executive* 7 (1993): 81–94.

same company working in different countries can easily hold videoconferences. Direct computer transfers of information among countries are as easy as using a computer and a modem to dial the phone number of a computer with a modem in another country.

Advances in technology are not the only reasons modern managers are taking a global view. Regional trade agreements are opening vast new markets,[44] possibly increasing the competition faced by a firm. The North American Free Trade Agreement (NAFTA) that became effective on January 1, 1994, opened the borders of Mexico, Canada, and the United States to easy movement of goods, capital, and services.[45] Europe took similar steps to encourage freer trade among its countries at the end of 1992. Large international market opportunities now exist throughout the world.

Many countries have dropped or plan to drop trade barriers that prevented easy access to their markets. Many Latin American countries are moving toward freer trade.[46] South Korea is letting outside companies operate within its borders. The growing Korean middle class wants quality foreign-made goods, presenting rich new markets to managers with a global view.[47] Several Southeast Asian countries want Western products and are eager to form joint ventures with foreign firms.[48]

The combination of sweeping technological and market changes presents major opportunities to managers with a global orientation. The opportunities are not limited to large organizations. For example, Blue Sky Natural Beverage Co. of Santa Fe, New Mexico, has already been successful in Japan. Although Blue Sky is a small company without the resources of a multinational giant, its managers saw a new market for their products, worked toward it, and successfully entered it.[49]

Thinking globally raises many issues for managers. An obvious difficulty is the language difference among countries. Forming partnerships with local business people or learning the language yourself can help solve the language problem. More difficult are the issues that stem from the vast cultural differences among countries. Understanding these differences can be difficult because outsiders are often not even aware of them. Yet cultural differences affect how a company enters markets, the way it markets goods or services, how it deals with labor laws, and how it builds a loyal customer base.

Cultural differences also define acceptable management behavior and preferences for organizational forms. Table 2-3 shows some dimensions of cultures that have emerged from a cross-cultural research program designed to uncover management and organizational differences in different countries. The table defines five dimensions of culture, describes values and preferences for the low and high ends of each dimension, and lists countries with those characteristics.

Variations along the power distance and uncertainty avoidance dimensions have especially strong implications for management and organizations.[50] Figure 2-4 shows the position of several countries on these dimensions. The countries in each quadrant scored at the low or high ends of the dimensions. Those in the center of the figure had mid-level scores.

People in quadrant I countries prefer well-defined procedures and clear organization structure. Rules and procedures guide daily behavior with managers settling only exceptional matters. Quadrant II countries tend to use formal authority for coordination and simple structures that emphasize senior management's role. People in quadrant III countries rely less on formal rules and organization forms and more on direct interpersonal interactions to coordinate work activities. Quadrant IV countries rely on simple organization forms and the use of direct supervision. The countries in the center of the figure tend to rely on middle management to coordinate activities and to specify the desired results.

Because preferences for management behavior and organization forms clearly differ among cultures, each remaining chapter of this book has a separate section focused on the international issues surrounding the topics of the chapter. The motivation chapters, for example, discuss the international implications of motiva-

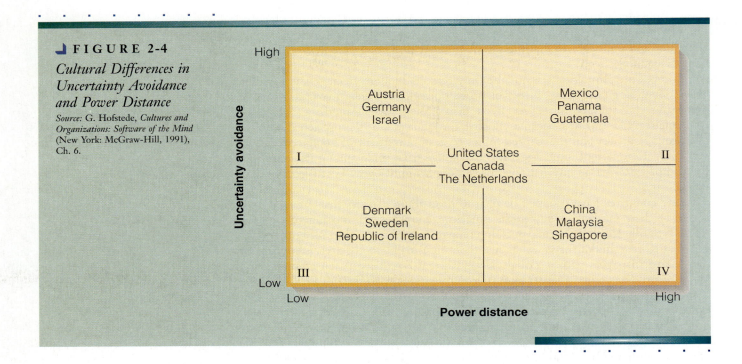

◢ **FIGURE 2-4**

Cultural Differences in Uncertainty Avoidance and Power Distance

Source: G. Hofstede, *Cultures and Organizations: Software of the Mind* (New York: McGraw-Hill, 1991), Ch. 6.

tion. The leadership chapter discusses some leadership issues raised in various countries. Those sections will be important sources of information as you begin to think more globally about managing behavior in an organization.

◢ Ethics and Behavior in Organizations

Modern managers will feel growing pressure from the public and government to behave ethically in all business transactions.[51] This pressure will affect employees of all types of organizations, whether public or private. This section introduces you to ethical issues and behavior in organizations. Chapter 3 describes theories of ethics and addresses ethical issues in more detail.

Ethical behavior is behavior viewed as right and honorable; unethical behavior is behavior viewed as wrong and reprehensible.[52] These seemingly straightforward definitions raise some tough questions for managers and their organizations. First, what standard should be used to judge behavior as ethical or unethical? Different people may have different standards. Second, how should the adjectives used to distinguish ethical from unethical behavior be defined? Right and wrong may mean different things to different people. Furthermore, standards of ethical behavior vary from one country to another. When issues of ethics are combined with the growing opportunities to do business globally, you can see the complexity of ethical questions in organizational behavior.

Questions of ethics abound in organizations and affect many decisions managers must make. Is it ethical for an organization to withhold product safety information from consumers? Is it ethical for a person to use knowledge about human perception to affect the perception of an organization's customers or employees? Is it ethical for an organization to not continuously improve the quality of its products or services when customers do not demand it? Those are only three ethical questions from an almost endless list that managers face today.

Many personal and management implications follow from the four emerging issues discussed in this chapter. A clear implication of increased workforce diversity is the highly varying perceptions of the world held by people with different backgrounds. These varying perceptions can not only affect the quality of social interaction in an organization, but can also provide significant opportunities for creative problem solving.

An organization with a diverse workforce will have both an organization culture and potentially many subcultures defined by the backgrounds of its employees. Employees who share a common language other than English, or a common religion, for example, may form a subculture. Such subcultures can offer support, especially to minority members of the organization who immigrated from another country.

Conflict potential is likely to be high in an organization with a diverse workforce for many reasons. The subcultures just described can develop different values and norms. The naturally different perspectives of people of diverse backgrounds are also potential sources of interpersonal conflict. Managers have the important task of managing that conflict so it is constructively focused. Properly managed conflict, as you will learn later in this book, can help provide creative solutions to complex problems.

A diverse workforce is a major resource for managers with the insight to harness that diversity to pursue the organization's goals. By deliberately diversifying the membership of problem-solving and decision-making groups, managers can ensure that a group brings many different views to problems. This diversity increases the group's potential for finding innovative solutions. Such groups are a central feature of managing for quality.

Total Quality Management's emphasis on continuous improvement through process analysis has several implications for both managers and nonmanagers. Cross-functional teams who do process analysis often include members who typically have not interacted with each other in the past. Such teams go through a series of well-understood stages of development and often experience high levels of conflict while looking at a process from many different views. You will find the later chapters on groups and conflict management to be especially useful in understanding the behavioral processes that often unfold in quality-oriented organizations.

Managers who are trying to shift their organization to a quality and continuous improvement culture must provide strong leadership and help employees adjust to the change. The organizations that have successfully moved toward TQM have had managers who could lead the organization through the necessary but wrenching changes. Such change often meets with resistance from those who do not understand the reason for the change or who think TQM is only a management fad.[53] Later chapters will give you insights about organizational culture, leadership, and organization change.

The global environment of modern organizations is another source of diversity. If you work in a globally based organization, you may be assigned to different countries, serve customers from diverse cultures, or have coworkers from different countries. The effects of global diversity are similar to those of domestic workforce diversity. Interpersonal interactions can become strained by the need to talk in multiple languages or listen to English spoken with many different accents. Conflict potential will also be high because of the diverse backgrounds and viewpoints of people from many cultures. Managers will face the especially strong challenge of managing work groups with high conflict potential.

The implications of the growing emphasis on ethical behavior in organizations touch managers and nonmanagers with equal force. Employees who are not managers can expect pressure either to reveal unethical behavior they observe or to remain silent about it. Employees may also be asked to engage in behavior they consider unethical. Managers will face growing pressure to make ethical decisions and manage their work units to achieve results by ethical means. The next chapter on ethics and behavior in organizations examines these and other issues in detail.

Summary

This chapter introduced you to four emerging topics that will be at the center of managing organizations into the next century. Those topics were workforce diversity, managing for quality, the global environment of organizations, and ethical behavior in organizations.

Bureau of Labor Statistics projections show the workforce becoming increasingly diverse with more female workers, minority workers, and part-time workers. A diverse workforce presents managers with major opportunities to harness diverse talents in the pursuit of organization goals. That same diverse workforce presents managers with the major challenge of managing conflict that can come from diversity in a functional way.

Total Quality Management (TQM) is a system of management built upon work dating to the 1920s. TQM has its roots in manufacturing, but it can help bring major improvements to any organization. It applies to managing all types of organizations and their internal processes. TQM has a strong customer focus and a passion for continuous improvement in meeting customer wants and needs.

Modern technology and increasingly freer trade areas demand an unprecedented international view from modern managers. Organizations that want to expand their markets and profitability require managers with a global view. Managers can now regard the entire world as a source of labor, materials, customers, and places of production. Such a global view clearly implies the need to understand different cultures, different views, and different ways of doing the work of the organization.

The emphasis on ethics in organizations will continue to increase in the future. Ethical behavior is behavior viewed as right; unethical behavior is behavior viewed as wrong. Managers and nonmanagers will face growing demands to behave ethically in all aspects of behavior and decision making associated with their organization. Because standards of ethical conduct vary among countries, the global environment of organizations makes the issue of ethical behavior even more complex.

Key Terms

dimensions of workforce diversity 20
ethical behavior 34
global environment 32
managing diversity 22

tools and techniques of TQM 27
Total Quality Management (TQM) 26

TQM view of an organization 27
workforce diversity 20

Review and Discussion Questions

1. Discuss the predicted changes in the composition of the U.S. workforce into the next century. Compare that profile of the workforce with your work experiences and those of others in your class. What issues have you and others faced if you have worked in an organization high in diversity?

2. The section on workforce diversity traced its roots to affirmative action and Equal Employment Opportunity. Do you think managing for diversity is the same as those two programs or does it require a different view of people with varying characteristics and backgrounds? Discuss this issue openly with students in your class.

3. Discuss the major features of TQM. How does it differ from an inspection-based quality control system? What values does it ask all employees of an organization to accept?

4. As noted earlier in the text, many U.S. managers are rethinking their commitment to TQM. What factors are contributing to this loss of commitment? Does this loss of commitment pose any threat to the competitive position of U.S. organizations throughout the world?

5. Reflect on the types of businesses that are prominent in your area. Would any of them benefit from having a global view of their markets? Is it realistic for managers in

those companies to look beyond domestic borders to find opportunities elsewhere?

6. Discuss the issues that a global orientation raises for managers. Are those issues problems or opportunities for modern managers?

7. Pause and reflect on the section "Ethics and Behavior in Organizations." It was brief because Chapter 3 will give you more detail. With what you now know, are there any ethical issues underlying the decisions made by managers?

. . . .

⤷ Case

GENDER GAP: BUSINESSWOMEN FACE FORMIDABLE BARRIERS WHEN THEY VENTURE OVERSEAS

The increasing diversity of the U.S. workforce and the need to compete globally for markets can collide. This case describes the experiences of some U.S. businesswomen trying to do business overseas. Read and analyze the case. Use the following questions as broad guidelines for your analysis:

1. Must women take any extra steps to be successful in their foreign business efforts?
2. What overall strategy can women use to be successful in international negotiations?
3. Based on the information in this case, and any other information you have, do you believe women in business should not try to compete in the global environment?

The strategy of going global can be tough for any entrepreneur—but it's particularly tough for women.

In many foreign countries, business is still more of a man's world than in the U.S., and women face problems being accepted as professionals. This leads to cultural conflicts that can be hard to handle when an American businesswoman is on unfamiliar turf and doesn't know the rules.

Women find they need to make all kinds of adjustments. Fort Worth business owner Mary Ann Carlile wears her wedding ring overseas—even though she is divorced. She slipped it back on, she says, after a Hong Kong client started asking probing questions about her personal life over a business dinner. Now, she says, the ring serves to discourage such questions. . . .

Of course, women in business still face plenty of problems such as this in the U.S. And traditional barriers to women have eased considerably overseas. But international business experts say that barriers still remain high in many foreign countries. And cultural differences on sex roles often compound the difficulties for American women entrepreneurs.

To cope with the cultural differences, they take extra care to dress conservatively. They take pains to research local cultural mores. And they sometimes take a man along with them for credibility's sake.

Source: B. Marsh, "Gender Gap: Businesswomen Face Formidable Barriers When They Venture Overseas," *The Wall Street Journal,* October 16, 1992, p. R20. Reprinted by permission of *The Wall Street Journal,* © 1992 Dow Jones & Company, Inc. All Rights Reserved Worldwide.

In early correspondence, American women business owners commonly obscure their sexual identity with a foreign prospect by using their initials, rather than a first name. That way, they reason, they won't be rejected out of hand and will get a chance to prove themselves in person. That, however, can lead to awkward surprises on the other side.

Lindsey Johnson, the Small Business Administration's director of women's business ownership, tells of a woman who got eager responses to her initial letters, but "stunned" an international contact when she turned out to be a woman. As a result, she told Ms. Johnson, she will have to take another overseas trips to nail down a deal.

At best, women business owners must work harder to succeed overseas than men, say international experts. "It takes them much longer than their male colleagues to establish the relationships, build the trust, make the entrees," says Robert Moran, director of the cross-cultural communications program at the American Graduate School of International Management in Glendale, Ariz. . . .

Women typically face a "testing period," he says, when they must finesse answers to such questions as, "What are you doing here? Shouldn't you be at home?" Many encounter sexual discrimination or cultural misunderstandings over sexual roles, he adds. He cites one businesswomen who recently called him in frustration over being denied a visa to enter Saudi Arabia simply because she's a woman; her male partner got accepted. . . .

Such cultural roadblocks are one reason that many women shy away from business overseas. The number doing business abroad is so low that the U.S. Small Business Administration started special seminars two years ago to encourage more women-owned businesses to try selling abroad. "There are still people on both sides of the ocean that have a subtle discomfort level in doing business with women because it's so new," says the SBA's Ms. Johnson. . . .

American businesswomen say some other forms of sexism simply leave them spinning their wheels. About 18 months ago, Dorothy Irvine saw a chance to double her firm's annual revenue to $100,000: A small Japanese trading company was looking for a U.S. agent. Ms. Irvine figured that her Evanston, Ill., export-import firm, which trades in Japan, would qualify. She went through proper channels by having a high-level Japanese executive introduce her to the trading company's owner. She met with the owner on four separate trips to Japan, investing thousands of dollars in travel and three weeks of time in preparation.

But the man never took her seriously, Ms. Irvine says. "It was almost as if they were leading me along because I'd been introduced by somebody they respected," she says. She asked an American businessman she knows to sit in on a meeting, she says, and together they concluded that she wasn't getting anywhere because she's a woman. "I would have loved to have had the business," she says. "It was very frustrating."

. . . .

⮑ Case

MAKING SURE DIVERSITY WORKS AT US WEST

The following case offers one senior executive's view of managing diversity. The observations in the case are those of Richard D. McCormick, president and CEO of US WEST, Inc. Assess his observations based on this chapter's discussion of diversity and your personal feelings. Use the following questions as a guide for your evaluation:

1. What is required of managers at all levels to successfully build a diverse organization?
2. What specific actions did Mr. McCormick take to move his managers in the direction he wanted?
3. He makes several assertions about the benefits of work-force diversity. Do you agree with him? Why?

Many CEOs have told me that the key to the entire diversity issue is just to hire people without regard to race or sex or place of national origin, and the cream will rise to the top.

I'm one CEO who thinks they're wrong—that diversity doesn't triumph by just opening the doors on the ground floor. Work force discrimination is alive and well and insidious. Sometimes it's intentional and sometimes unintentional. The Labor Department's study on the "glass ceiling" pointed out three unintentional methods of work force discrimination: word-of-mouth recruiting, lack of access to management development training for women and minorities, and the failure of executives and top management to really promote the advancement of women and minorities. I'm convinced that this last point is the key: concerted, continuous effort by top management. The tone has to be set by the CEO, by words and actions.

When I was CEO of Northwestern Bell, we had many years of good work on affirmative action and equal opportunity. We moved people well in the corporation and saw a lot of progress in our business. . . . Most of the managers said the right things, and had their hearts in the right places, but the old habits lived on in our company. I recall asking one of our officers why I still didn't see any black employees in his department. He told me that they couldn't find any. I then said that I wouldn't find his bonus until he did. Not surprisingly, within about six months he found two qualified blacks.

We had many workshops in both racial awareness and male-female awareness issues, some as long as 15 years ago.

Source: R. D. McCormick, "Making Sure Diversity Works at US WEST," in J. Alster, T. Brothers, and H. Gallo, eds., *In Diversity Is Strength: Capitalizing on the New Work Force* (New York: The Conference Board, 1992), pp. 13–14. Reprinted with permission of The Conference Board.

These were intensive four-day workshops where we really exposed the raw feelings that people have about these issues. The reason is to expose bias, to make people aware of their cultural baggage. This process in our company was voluntary until around 1982. I ran out of volunteers, particularly some officers who never could quite find it in their schedules to get there. In frustration I made it a condition of employment for middle and upper managers: It was amazing how much time suddenly became available.

⮑ WHERE ARE THE WOMEN?

Something else occurred in 1983, when I was president of the company: We have many people in many service clubs that do a lot of good work—Kiwanis, Rotary and others. It just so happened that only men were members of those clubs. We were the largest employer in several states. I was bothered that those organizations were overlooking about half the talent in the community. We urged reform and got nowhere. Finally, I issued a decree in our company saying that we would no longer sponsor memberships in those organizations that discriminated against people on the basis of sex, race—or any other reason. Many of our employees involved in those organizations pressed for reforms. I don't think it was entirely our actions alone that made all the difference, but very quickly we saw those organizations really open their doors and change.

A few years ago when I was starting to feel very good about our company's progress in these areas, a group of black women came to me and told me about some statistics I had been overlooking, namely, that their chances of joining our company and being promoted to what we call the district level or the director level was about 1 in 250, while the chances of that happening for a white male was about 1 in 15. It was an interesting eye-opener for me. Then, black women represented 9 percent of our employee body, about 4 percent of our middle management, and 2 percent of our upper management. Today, black women still constitute 9 percent of our employees, but 6 percent are in middle management and 4 percent are now in upper management.

In all these cases, "waiting for the cream to rise" just wouldn't have worked. The CEO has to set the tone with actions, not words. It's not easy.

⮑ DIVERSITY'S REALITIES

I am frequently criticized for spending so much time on these "soft" issues because financial performance of the company and customer satisfaction are "more important." It's hard to educate managers in this process. About 85 percent of people coming into the work force in this decade will not be white males. In a global competitive environment, we have to tap all the resources—both natural and human—that are available to us. Diversity is one of our six "priority business strategies" as well. There is some self-interest here; it's the right thing to do and it's also good for business. It involves working with the community, with minority youth, with our educational system, and very aggressively working with women- and minority-owned businesses.

Another difficult aspect of this issue is that expectations are rising. Fifty-five percent of our employees are women; 48 percent of our managers are women; 30 percent of our middle managers are women; and 15 percent of our officers are women. I'm pleased with those statistics, compared with those of the past. Moreover, 15 percent of our employees are black; 13 percent of managers are black; 11 percent of middle managers and 8 percent of our officers are black. Again, I feel quite good about those statistics. Yet when I talk to employee groups, they ask why these opportunities are not coming more vigorously and more quickly in our company, and why we have the barriers that we do. . . .

HIGH RISK, HIGH REWARD

Despite the risks, the rewards are great. Through diversity, we're better listeners. If we're better listeners to one another, we'll probably be better listeners to customers. We make better teams because when a diverse work group gets through working out the interpersonal problems, I believe they can tackle anything. Diversity includes a variety of viewpoints, too. Our company used to be made up of a lot of engineers and financial types; but over the last 10 years we've hired many scientists, marketers and others, all to our benefit. Another reward is a better reflection of the marketplace. A diverse group does explore issues better than a group whose members all come from a similar background. . . .

The result of these diversity efforts is a stronger work force. With diverse ideas, we're positioned to attract good people. I'd put our company up against anybody's as an environment that's friendly to women and minorities and all the other people that make up this diverse workplace. We have an environment where people can succeed. The officers and the managerial teams are stronger in our company.

In time, I hope the profile of our company will reflect society in general. We're going to be better team players and better listeners; we will communicate better with employees, customers, vendors and international suppliers. I think I'm going to be stronger in terms of relating to women, blacks and other minority members on my team. I look forward to the day when one of those people holds my job because that is when we will have arrived at US WEST. To me, a company that can unleash that kind of human potential is a company where a young person would want to work and where an investor would want to invest.

References and Notes

[1] J. P. Fernandez, *Managing a Diverse Workforce* (New York: Lexington Books, 1991).

[2] Developed from Fernandez, *Managing a Diverse Workforce;* D. Jamieson and J. O'Mara, *Managing Workforce 2000: Gaining the Diversity Advantage* (San Francisco: Jossey-Bass, 1991); R. R. Thomas, Jr., *Beyond Race and Gender: Unleashing the Power of Your Total Work Force by Managing Diversity* (New York: AMACOM, 1991); and other citations throughout this section.

[3] S. E. Jackson and associates, eds., *Diversity in the Workplace: Human Resources Initiatives* (New York: Guilford Press, 1992); Jamieson and O'Mara, *Managing Workforce 2000*, Chs. 1 and 2.

[4] H. N. Fullerton, Jr., "Labor Force Projections: The Baby Boom Moves on," *Monthly Labor Review* 114 (1991): 31–44.

[5] Fernandez, *Managing a Diverse Workforce*, Ch. 1; C. Tilly, "Reasons for the Continuing Growth of Part-Time Employment," *Monthly Labor Review* 114 (1991) 10–18.

[6] All projections in this section used the moderate projections of the Bureau of Labor Statistics.

[7] Fernandez, *Managing a Diverse Workforce.*

[8] Jamieson and O'Mara, *Managing Workforce 2000*, p. 21.

[9] E. Ginzberg, "Foreword," in Jackson and associates, *Diversity in the Workplace*, pp. xiii–xx.

[10] R. R. Thomas, Jr., "From Affirmative Action to Affirming Diversity," *Harvard Business Review* 90 (1990): 107–17.

[11] S. E. Jackson, "Preview of the Road to Be Traveled," in Jackson and associates, *Diversity in the Workplace*, pp. 3–12; Thomas, "From Affirmative Action."

[12] Jamieson and O'Mara, *Managing Workforce 2000*, pp. 25–27.

[13] R. R. Thomas, Jr., "Managing Diversity: A Conceptual Framework," in Jackson and associates, *Diversity in the Workplace*, pp. 306–17.

[14] M. Loden and J. B. Rosener, *Workforce America! Managing Employee Diversity as a Vital Resource* (Homewood, Ill: Business One Irwin, 1991), Part III.

[15] J. Alster, T. Brothers, and H. Gallo, eds., *In Diversity Is Strength: Capitalizing on the New Work Force* (New York: The Conference Board, 1992); Jackson and associates, *Diversity in the Workplace*; Thomas, "From Affirmative Action."

[16] Thomas, "From Affirmative Action."

[17] S. E. Jackson and E. B. Alvarez, "Working through Diversity as a Strategic Imperative," in Jackson and associates, *Diversity in the Workplace*, pp. 13–29.

[18] M. L. Carey and J. C. Franklin, "Industry Output and Job Growth Continues Slow into Next Century," *Monthly Labor Review* 114 (1991): 45–63.

[19] P. Sellers, "What Customers Really Want," *Fortune*, June 4, 1990, pp. 58–68.

[20] Jackson and Alvarez, "Working through Diversity"; D. Wolf, "Whither the Work Force?" in Alster, Brothers, and Gallo., *In Diversity Is Strength*, pp. 9–10.

[21] Jackson and Alvarez, "Working through Diversity," pp. 26–27.

[22] L. S. Gottfredson, "Dilemmas in Developing Diversity Programs," in Jackson and associates, eds., *Diversity in the Workplace*, pp. 279–305.

[23] J. B. Rosener, "Ways Women Lead," *Harvard Business Review* 68 (1990): 119–25.

[24]Part of this section originally appeared in J. E. Champoux and L. D. Goldman, "Building a Total Quality Culture," in T. D. Connors, ed., *Nonprofit Organizations Policies and Procedures Handbook* (New York: John Wiley & Sons, 1993), pp. 54–55. Copyright © 1993 John Wiley & Sons, Inc. Reprinted by permission of John Wiley & Sons, Inc.

[25]D. A. Garvin, *Managing Quality: The Strategic and Competitive Edge* (New York: Free Press, 1988), Ch. 1; R. R. Gehani, "Quality Value-Chain: A Meta-Synthesis of Frontiers of Quality Movement," *Academy of Management Executive* 7 (1993): 29–42; S. Smith, "Ten Compelling Reasons for TQM," *The TQM Magazine* (1988).

[26]"A Cure for IBM's Blues? Retiring Exec Prescribes a Continuing Focus on Quality," *Information Week*, January 4, 1993, pp. 48–49.

[27]N. E. Rickard, Jr., "The Quest for Quality: A Race without a Finish Line," *Industrial Engineering* 23 (1991): 25–27; J. H. Saylor, *TQM Field Manual* (New York: McGraw-Hill, 1992), p. xix.

[28]G. S. Radford, *The Control of Quality in Manufacturing* (New York: Ronald Press, 1922).

[29]W. A. Shewhart, *Economic Control of Quality of Manufactured Product* (New York: D. Van Nostrand, 1931).

[30]A. V. Feigenbaum, "Total Quality Control," *Harvard Business Review* 34 (1956): 93–101.

[31]J. M. Juran, *Quality Control Handbook* (New York: McGraw-Hill, 1951).

[32]Garvin, *Managing Quality*, Ch. 10.

[33]A. Chandler, *The Visible Hand: The Managerial Revolution in American Business* (Cambridge, Mass.: Belknap Harvard, 1977), pp. 94–109.

[34]W. E. Deming, *Out of the Crisis* (Cambridge, Mass.: MIT Center for Advanced Engineering Study, 1985), p. 4.

[35]J. Mathews, "The Cost of Quality," *Newsweek*, September 7, 1992, pp. 48–49.

[36]N. Ivey, "The Ecstasy and the Agony," *Business Week*, October 21, 1991, p. 40.

[37]R. T. Rust, A. J. Zahorik, and T. L. Keiningham, *Return on Quality: Measuring the Financial Impact of Your Company's Quest for Quality* (Chicago: Probus Publishing Company, 1994).

[38]L. P. Carr, "Applying Cost of Quality to a Service Business," *Sloan Management Review* 20 (1992): 72–77.

[39]Rust, Zahorik, and Keiningham, *Return on Quality*, Ch. 1.

[40]Mathews, "Cost of Quality," p. 49.

[41]J. M. Juran, "Product Quality: A Prescription for the West, Part I: Training and Improvement Programs," *Management Review* 70 (1981): 9–14.

[42]W. B. Johnston, "Global Workforce 2000: The New Labor Market," *Harvard Business Review* 69 (1991): 115–29; R. I. Kirkland, Jr., "Entering a New Age of Boundless Competition," *Fortune*, March 14, 1988, pp. 40–42, 46, 48.

[43]P. Nulty, "How the World Will Change," *Fortune*, January 15, 1990, pp. 44–46, 50–54.

[44]C. M. Aho and S. Ostry, "Regional Trading Blocs: Pragmatic or Problematic Policy?" in W. E. Brock and R. D. Hormats, eds., *The Global Economy: America's Role in the Decade Ahead* (New York: W. W. Norton, 1990), pp. 147–73; S. Ostry, "Governments & Corporations in a Shrinking World: Trade & Innovation Policies in the United States, Europe & Japan," *Columbia Journal of World Business* 25 (1990): 10–16.

[45]B. Davis and J. Calmes, "The House Passes Nafta—Trade Win: House Approves Nafta, Providing President With Crucial Victory," *Wall Street Journal*, November 18, 1993, p. A1.

[46]J. Main, "How Latin America Is Opening Up," *Fortune*, April 8, 1991, pp. 84–87, 89.

[47]L. Nakarmi, "Korea Throws Open Its Doors," *Business Week*, July 29, 1991, p. 46.

[48]L. Kraar, "The Rising Power of the Pacific," *Fortune*, Pacific Rim 1990, pp. 8–9, 12.

[49]S. Robinson, "Exporting Blue Sky to Japan," *Business Outlook, Albuquerque Journal*, October 2, 1989, pp. 1–2.

[50]G. Hofstede, *Cultures and Organizations: Software of the Mind* (New York: McGraw-Hill, 1991).

[51]K. Labich, "The New Crisis in Business Ethics," *Fortune*, April 20, 1992, pp. 167–68.

[52]R. B. Brandt, *Ethical Theory: The Problems of Normative and Critical Ethics* (Englewood Cliffs, N.J.: Prentice-Hall, 1959), Ch. 1; P. E. Davis, ed., *Introduction to Moral Philosophy* (Columbus, Ohio: Charles E. Merrill, 1973), pp. 1–8.

[53]Champoux and Goldman, "Building a Total Quality Culture"; Fuchsberg, G. "Quality Programs Show Shoddy Results," *Wall Street Journal*, May 14, 1992, pp. B1, B9.

3

Ethics and Behavior in Organizations

The United States Government Executive Branch

CODE OF ETHICS

Principles of Ethical Conduct for Government Officers and Employees

1. Public service is a public trust, requiring employees to place loyalty to the Constitution, the laws, and ethical principles above private gain.

2. Employees shall not hold financial interests that conflict with the conscientious performance of duty.

3. Employees shall not engage in financial transactions using nonpublic Government information or allow the improper use of such information to further any private interest.

4. An employee shall not, except pursuant to such reasonable exceptions as are provided by regulation, solicit or accept any gift or other item of monetary value from any person or entity seeking official action from, doing business with, or conducting activities regulated by the employee's agency, or whose interests may be substantially affected by the performance or nonperformance of the employee's duties.

5. Employees shall put forth honest effort in the performance of their duties.

6. Employees shall make no unauthorized commitments or promises of any kind purporting to bind the Government.

7. Employees shall not use public office for private gain.

8. Employees shall act impartially and not give preferential treatment to any private organization or individual.

9. Employees shall protect and conserve Federal property and shall not use it for other than authorized activities.

10. Employees shall not engage in outside employment or activities, including seeking or negotiating for employment, that conflict with official Government duties and responsibilities.

11. Employees shall disclose waste, fraud, abuse, and corruption to appropriate authorities.

12. Employees shall satisfy in good faith their obligations as citizens, including all just financial obligations, especially those—such as Federal, State, or local taxes—that are imposed by law.

13. Employees shall adhere to all laws and regulations that provide equal opportunity for all Americans regardless of race, color, religion, sex, national origin, age, or handicap.

14. Employees shall endeavor to avoid any actions creating the appearance that they are violating the law or the ethical standards promulgated pursuant to this order.

U.S. OFFICE OF GOVERNMENT ETHICS WASHINGTON, D.C. 20005

· *The U.S. government's code of ethics for all government employees.*

After reading this chapter, you should be able to . . .

· Define ethical and unethical behavior.
· Discuss why some scholars believe *It's Good Business* to do business ethically.
· Describe the various theories of ethics and the ethical guidelines each offers.
· Explain how to manage for ethical behavior in an organization.
· Identify some international aspects of ethical behavior in organizations.

Chapter Overview

The New Crisis in Business Ethics, Part I

• *Gary Edwards, president of the Ethics Resource Center, a consulting firm in Washington, D.C.*

As this economic slowdown lingers like some stubborn low-grade infection, managers are putting the heat on subordinates. Many of the old rules no longer seem to apply. Says Gary Edwards, president of the Ethics Resource Center, a consulting firm in Washington: "The message out there is, Reaching objectives is what matters and how you get there isn't that important.

The result has been an eruption of questionable and sometimes plainly criminal behavior throughout corporate America. We are not dealing here so much with the personal greed that propelled Wall Street operators of the Eighties into federal prisons. Today's miscreants are more often motivated by the most basic of instincts—fear of losing their jobs or the necessity to eke out some benefit for their companies. If that means fudging a few sales figures, abusing a competitor, or shortchanging the occasional customer, so be it.

People lower down on the corporate food chain are telling the boss what they think he wants to hear, and outright lying has become a commonplace at many companies. Michael Josephson, a prominent Los Angeles ethicist who consults for some of America's largest public corporations, says his polls reveal that between 20% and 30% of middle managers have written deceptive internal reports.

At least part of this is relatively harmless—managers inflating budget proposals in the hope of ultimately getting what they really need, for example. But a good share of it will almost surely hurt the people and the companies involved, in some cases grievously. The U.S. press, broadcast and print, has become increasingly adept at uncovering corporate misdeeds. Witness the frenzy of reports raising questions about Dow Corning's breast implants. The stock of Corning Inc., one of the two corporate parents of Dow Corning, has declined by about 15% since the scandal erupted, even though the implants represented only around 1% of Dow Corning's revenues and its insurance coverage seems adequate to cover potential litigation.

The Justice Department has become far keener on catching and punishing white-collar criminals since the S&L crisis and the BCCI scandal. Last November tough new sentencing guidelines for corporate crimes went into effect. Warns Josephson: "We are going to see a phenomenal number of business scandals during the 1990s. We are swimming in enough lies to keep the lawyers busy for the next ten years."

The faint sign of good news is that many big U.S. companies have begun to respond to the crisis. According to a survey of Fortune 1,000 companies conducted by Bentley College in Boston, over 40% of the respondents are holding ethics workshops and seminars, and about one-third have set up an ethics committee. Some 200 major U.S. corporations have recently appointed ethics officers, usually senior managers of long experience, to serve as ombudsmen and encourage whistleblowing.

he Opening Episode should give you a clear idea of the agitation in the United States about unethical and illegal behavior in organizations. Such behavior is expected to increase during the 1990s, as are legal actions against it.

A casual review of the press shows that reporters are raising ethical questions about many organizational practices in the United States including the following:

1. Questionable transactions in stock brokerage firms.
2. Firing employees for smoking during nonwork time.
3. Large-scale layoffs at General Motors plants that had harsh effects on people's lives.
4. Questionable loan activities of savings and loan firms that threatened the security of people's savings.
5. Questionable charges to the federal government by contractors.
6. Drug testing and screening for acquired immune deficiency syndrome (AIDS) as a requirement for employment.
7. The shutdown of almost the entire U.S. railroad system by operators in June 1992, following a strike against one railroad.

Unethical or illegal organizational practices are not confined to the United States. The stock markets in Britain, France, Germany, and Australia have all experienced insider trading incidents. The Irish press reported falsification of company records and the questionable purchase of a company in which a chief executive was part owner. In 1987 the Toshiba Corporation sold the Soviet navy advanced milling equipment for building submarine propellers. That transaction violated both Japanese law and an international treaty restricting the sale of military-related technology to then Communist-bloc countries.[1]

The effects of these actions were widespread and reached well beyond the organization. The tough question is whether the actions had ethical implications although some, such as the layoffs, were legal.

Only a few in-depth studies of managers and ethical behavior exist. This type of research requires the cooperation of organizations and their managers, which is often hard to get.[2] Robert Jackall's *Moral Mazes* documents the complex and perplexing world of management decision making where ethics often are not specific decision criteria.[3] Instead, managers find their decisions are bound by context, leading to a situational form of ethics. Veteran managers navigate such moral mazes in ways that let them survive and succeed in their organizations.

Barbara Toffler's study of ethics and management reinforces this view of ethical ambiguity in management decisions.[4] Her extensive interview data showed that ethical dilemmas are common in management decision making and that the choices between right and wrong are not always clear. Although ethical concerns pervaded management decisions and actions, managers rarely used explicit ethical criteria during the decision process.

Gallup polls done between 1981 and 1993 found the public did not view business executives as pillars of ethical behavior.[5] Figure 3-1 shows the results of those polls for executives and other selected occupations. When people were asked which of 25 occupations they believed had "very high" or "high" ethics, pharmacists ranked the highest, car salespeople ranked the lowest, and business executives were about in the middle. People in the United States do not have a particularly positive view of ethics and behavior in organizations.

. . . .

⤷ Social Responsibility of Organizations

Over the years, managers at many organizations have recognized their tarnished ethical image. Those managers and their organizations have increasingly expanded their goals to include social responsibility as well as economic concerns. Many managers now consider the effects of their decisions on the society and external environments in which they operate.[6]

The traditional view of society believed that marketplace transactions should govern it. If each person or organization expressed its desires through marketplace activities, collectively those activities would be in society's interests. Over the years,

FIGURE 3-1

Gallup Opinion Polls on Honesty and Ethics in Various Occupations

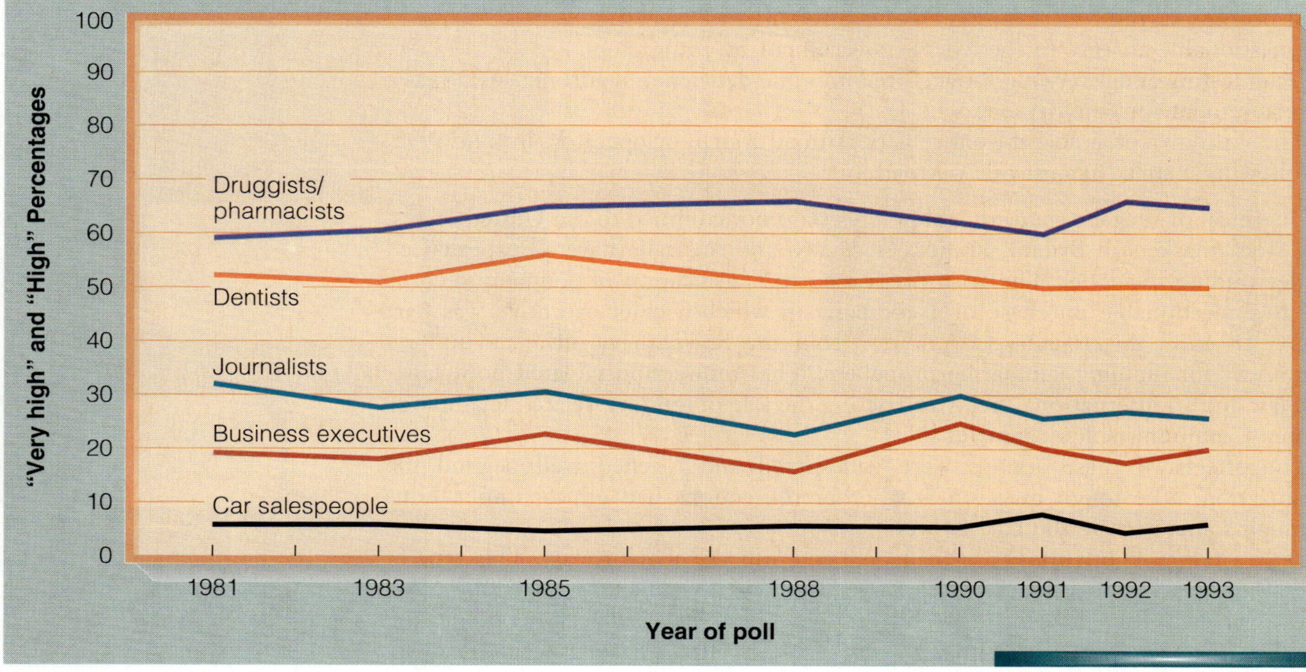

TABLE 3-1

Dimensions of Social Responsibility and Societal Expectations

DIMENSION OF RESPONSIBILITY	SOCIETAL EXPECTATION
Discretionary	Desired
Ethical	Expected
Legal	Required
Economic	Required

the idea that organizations should also be socially responsible gained support until, by the 1950s, it was widely accepted.

Over time, U.S. society placed legal limits on the actions of managers, setting boundaries on its expectations about right and wrong in the business arena. Organizations also began philanthropic activities, such as contributing to local charities and allowing employees to volunteer time, that helped the communities in which they operated.

Table 3-1 lists four **dimensions of social responsibility** of organizations and their managers. Economic and legal responsibilities are required; they form a base for doing business responsibly in our society. Ethical responsibilities add to that base. They involve a largely amorphous and still developing set of social expectations of behavior not covered by the economic and legal responsibilities. The discretionary dimension of social responsibility includes community and philanthropic activities that society desires but does not require or expect.

The three **levels of social responsibility** are institutional, organizational, and individual.[7] The institutional level emphasizes an organization's broad obligations to the society in which it operates. A society holds expectations about what organizations should contribute to it and uses sanctions to enforce those expectations.

The organizational level of social responsibility focuses on a specific organization's function in society and the social issues to which its managers should attend. Different organizations can face different social responsibility issues. For example, society could hold an auto manufacturer accountable for air pollution and safety, whereas providing low-cost housing for the poor could be a peripheral issue for such a firm.

The individual level of social responsibility focuses on the behavior of individual people in an organization, especially managers with decision-making discretion. This level assumes employees are guided by more than their organization's procedures and policies. The individual level of social responsibility asks people to behave ethically when considering the effects of decisions.

The emphasis on ethical behavior in organizations expressed in the individual level of social responsibility is consistent with the growing societal interest in ethics and ethical behavior of all people in an organization. Because ethical behavior has become such an important concern, this chapter discusses ethics at length, and all other chapters of this book include an ethics discussion.

Ethical and Unethical Behavior

Ethical behavior is behavior judged to be good, right, just, honorable, and praise-worthy. Unethical behavior is behavior judged to be wrong, reprehensible, or failing to meet an obligation.[8] The judgment of behavior as ethical or unethical is based on principles, rules, or guides that come from a specific ethical theory, character traits, or social values.[9] A later section of this chapter describes several ethical theories that you can consider for guidelines in behaving ethically.

As Chapter 2 pointed out, the definitions of ethical and unethical behavior pose two nagging issues: the difficulty of finding a standard for judgment on which all reasonable people can agree, and the problem that "good" and "bad" or "right" and "wrong" mean different things to different people and different societies.

More confusion and controversy come from the distinction between what is subjectively and objectively ethical.[10] A person's action is subjectively ethical if the person believes he acted ethically. A person's action is objectively ethical if the person acted according to a rule or law. The same distinction applies to unethical behavior that the person intended (subjectively unethical) and unethical behavior that violates an established rule or law (objectively unethical).

Conflict can arise when a person believes he behaved ethically and other people who observed the behavior believe the person broke a law or rule. For example, doing business efficiently in some countries requires paying bribes. Some firms prohibit such bribes.[11] A manager who pays bribes because he believes it is ethical in a particular country (subjectively ethical) violates his employer's policies (objectively unethical). Conflict can then arise between the employee and the employer over such behavior.

"It's Good Business"

The basic assumption underlying this chapter is that doing business ethically is **good** for **business**. That is the position of Robert C. Solomon, a philosophy professor at the University of Texas, Austin, and Kristine Hanson, a New York businesswoman.

Together, they have written about business ethics and presented ethics workshops around the country.[12]

Solomon and Hanson argue that ethics is the keystone for smooth, effective, and efficient operation of business organizations. If we could not trust another person's word or feel confident that a person would keep contractual agreements, business as we now understand it would agonizingly stop. Although some business people behave unethically and do not get caught, unethical behavior can have long-term negative effects on a business. Customers who feel cheated will not return, or will sue, or will report the cheating business to law enforcement agencies. Ethical businesses develop a reputation of fair business dealings and concern for the effects of their decisions on society. They likely will face fewer punitive or regulatory efforts.

Solomon and Hanson take a long-term view of ethical management. They note that behaving ethically can be more costly in the short term for a business than behaving unethically. For example, when a business adds safety equipment not required by law to a manufacturing operation and another business in the same industry does not, the first company has higher manufacturing costs than the second. Although such ethical concerns can enhance the reputation of the first firm, its higher costs could make it less competitive.

Ethical Issues in Organizational Behavior

As Table 3-2 shows, the organizational behavior topics discussed in this book raise many ethical issues and questions. Each chapter has a separate section that discusses the ethical issues suggested by the behavioral topics of the chapter. The material developed in this chapter plays a central role in those discussions. After reading this chapter, you may wish to read ahead and sample the ethical discussions in later chapters.

People armed with knowledge about behavioral processes in organizations can strongly affect the behavior of other people. Several topics in Table 3-2 raise questions about whether it is ethical to affect the behavior of others without their consent and free will. For example, behavior shaping is a central topic in the motivation chapters. The ethical questions about behavior shaping center on having a person's explicit and free consent to use the shaping process. Discussions about stress in organizations raise ethical issues about the obligation of managers to reduce dysfunctional stress. Those questions, and many others like them, are treated in all the remaining chapters of this book.

Ethics: The Study of Moral Philosophy

Ethics is the branch of philosophy that for centuries has sought answers to the following questions:[13]

1. How can people on this planet live in a just and noble way?
2. Is it right for a person to lie if the lie has positive results for all involved?
3. Do humans have any obligation to nonhuman animals?
4. Should we ignore the environmental effects of decisions, if the decision is otherwise justified by cost or profit?

These questions are all difficult, and different people—and different societies—arrive at different answers.

Ethics is devoted to developing a logical and systematic set of principles that define what is ethical behavior and what is not. Some call ethics moral philosophy. An essential feature of ethics and moral philosophy is its reflective quality—sitting back and looking at the way things usually are done and asking how they *ought* to be done.[14]

TABLE 3-2

Ethical Issues and Questions in Selected Behavioral Areas

CHAPTER	BEHAVIORAL TOPIC	ETHICAL ISSUE OR QUESTION
4	Organizational culture	Knowledge of how an organization's culture affects people's behavior gives managers a chance to control behavior, raising questions of consent and free will.
5	Perception, attitudes, and personality	Knowledge of people's perceptual processes could let managers affect behavior. Again, the question of consent and free will.
6	Organizational socialization	Developing an organization's code of ethics. Socializing new employees to that code of ethics.
7–9	Motivation and rewards	Behavior shaping and the question of free will. Getting people to do something without their explicit and free consent.
10	Groups and intergroup processes	Using knowledge of group dynamics to affect the behavior of people in the organization without their explicit consent.
11	Conflict management	Tolerance for conflict. Stress effects of high levels of conflict.
12	Leadership and management	Inducing others to follow a course of action. Is the action ethical or unethical? What will be the standard of judgment?
13	Communication processes	Using knowledge of communication in organizations to control the flow and accuracy of communication.
14	Decision-making and problem-solving processes	Effects of management decisions on society
15	Political behavior in organizations	Self-promotion. Acting in self-interest, not in the interest of the organization's goals.
16	Stress in organizations	How much stress should people experience at work? Does management have an obligation to reduce dysfunctional stress?
17–18	Organizational design	Using organizational designs to deliberately affect behavior without the free consent of those affected.
19	Organizational change and development	Are the negative effects of change on people ethical? What degree of organizational change induces stress effects in people?

Ethicists also have debated the extent to which an ethical system is absolute or relative.[15] **Ethical absolutism** holds that a system of ethics applies to all people, everywhere, and always. The absolutist refers to an authority such as a religion, custom, or written code for support. **Ethical relativism** says that ethical behavior is whatever a person or society says is ethical. An ethical relativist sees ethics as based on personal feelings or opinion and rejects the view that moral judgments have objective validity.

A position intermediate between the absolutist and relativist extremes sees ethics and moral judgments as changing over the course of human history. What is right (or wrong) at one point in the development of a social system may be wrong (or right) at another point in its development. According to this view, ethical systems evolve with the requirements of a social system so people in that system can behave in ways they judge acceptable.

Only you can decide which position best defines your feelings and beliefs about ethics. You will find that variations in ethical systems around the world present modern managers with extraordinary conflicts about right and wrong in their business decisions.

Ethical Values of Societies and Individuals

Both societies and individuals develop systems of ethical values that serve important functions for them. This section describes how ethical values develop, their functions, and the ways in which they change.

ETHICAL VALUES OF SOCIETIES

All societies have ethical standards that define the behavior they see as right, desirable, and good. The language of all societies distinguishes between good and bad, right and wrong, desirable and undesirable. Ethical standards can be unwritten as in preliterate societies or written as in the more literate.[16]

Ethical systems serve important social functions. They encourage collaborative efforts of organized social forms by providing rules that bring predictability to behavior and help settle clashes of interest. In a world of scarce resources, ethical systems set standards for the allocation of those resources to competing parties. In short, such systems provide "recipes for action"[17] that can reduce internal strife and help a society survive.

Ethical systems are dynamic, not static. Ethical standards must serve the basic needs of the members of a society, or they will be changed. Standards members view as rewarding are kept; other standards may be discarded or revised. Such change is often slow and evolutionary as events unfold within and around a society.

Intercultural contact and the diffusion of ethical standards from one culture to another can also change a society's ethical system. If many people are frustrated by the existing standards, acceptance of the new standards can be quick. Similarly, a society may quickly adopt another country's standards if it perceives them as having high prestige. In a world of extensive personal, audio, and video contacts among societies, diffusion of ethical standards and conflicts among standards are especially likely to occur.

ETHICAL VALUES OF INDIVIDUALS

Individuals develop their ethical values from societal-level values that they learn from their family, religious training, peers, education, and life experiences.[18] The earliest source of ethical values is one's family. The young child learns acceptable behaviors during the early family socialization process, developing an internal ethical standard both by instruction from others and by observation. As a person goes from infancy to adulthood, he develops more complex thinking patterns with which to evaluate life experiences.[19] Those patterns include the person's ethical values. Although people from the same society will have similar systems of ethical values, differences will exist, and those systems can change over time.[20]

People go through three **stages of moral development.** Somes theorists believe that men and women have different experiences at each stage and may end with different views of morality.

The left side of Figure 3-2 shows the stages that have been attributed mainly to men. The stages move from an individually based understanding of morality, to a societal one, and then to a universal moral view. That moral view is labeled an ethic of justice because it applies moral rules to determine what actions are fair. Each stage has different characteristics during its early and later periods.[21]

The first stage of moral development is preconventional. This stage characterizes most children under age nine, some adolescents, and many criminal offenders. In the early period of this stage, the person is self-centered, has no consideration for anyone

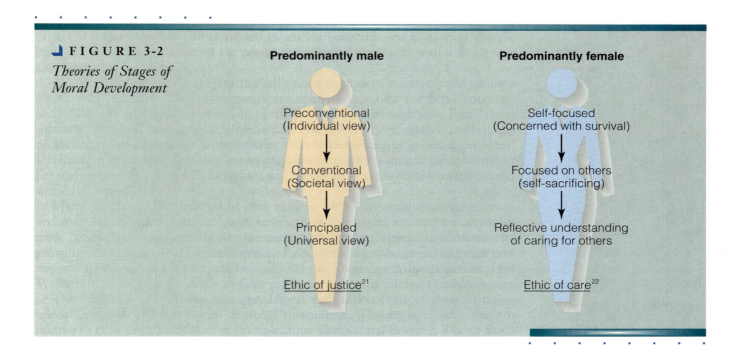

FIGURE 3-2

Theories of Stages of Moral Development

Predominantly male

Preconventional
(Individual view)

↓

Conventional
(Societal view)

↓

Principaled
(Universal view)

Ethic of justice[21]

Predominantly female

Self-focused
(Concerned with survival)

↓

Focused on others
(self-sacrificing)

↓

Reflective understanding
of caring for others

Ethic of care[22]

else's point of view, and obeys rules because they are backed by authority. Moral behavior is almost entirely a function of avoiding punishment. In the later period of this stage, the person becomes aware of the interests of others and the conflicts that arise among multiple interests. Moral behavior, though, stays focused on meeting one's personal interests.

The second stage is conventional. This stage characterizes most adolescents and adults. It features a growing awareness of the expectations important to other people. A person at this stage has learned the importance of trust and loyalty in interpersonal relationships and accepts that mutual agreements take precedence over self-interest. This stage also features the internalization of the moral norms of the person's group or society. The latter part of the conventional stage features an awareness of the surrounding social system. A person fully developed at this stage believes moral behavior strengthens the social system.

The final stage is the principled stage. This stage usually is not reached until after age 20 to 25, and many adults never reach it at all. It is called principled because it features the development of moral principles that guide the behavior of those who reach this stage. These moral principles emerge after the person critically assesses the norms accepted at the conventional stage and concludes that there are universal moral principles, such as the right to liberty. People at this stage have a strong sense of abiding by social contracts. They also are aware that different people have widely varying viewpoints and the difficulty of integrating those viewpoints. People at the latter part of this stage have a fully developed moral point of view centering on two beliefs: (1) a person's actions must always be guided by freely chosen moral principles, and (2) each person must be treated as a free and autonomous individual. Those principles may conflict with existing law, and when they do, the person must follow the moral principle.

The right side of Figure 3-2 shows the three stages of moral development that lead to an ethic of care, so-called because a person with this moral view judges actions based on empathy for others and the person's relationship with them. Some theorists believe an ethic of care and its stages of development are more characteristic of women than men.[22]

The first stage features a strong focus on self with the intent of ensuring survival. This stage is similar to what men usually experience in the preconventional stage, but women often engage in self-criticism for being selfish. The transition to the second stage features a focus on others and a move away from self. People who focus on others and on personal relationships consider actions moral that take account of other people involved in the situation. They focus on feelings, emotions, and the unique qualities of the situation in which the act is happening. The person does not follow abstract rules devoid of reference to people's feelings.

In the third stage, the person enters the most mature stage, characterized by a reflective understanding of caring for others. This stage features not only a strong focus on caring for others as the basis of moral action, but also a balanced view of the self in moral decisions. When choosing an ethical course of action, people in this stage consider the context of behavior, the people in that context, emotions, and feelings.

An ethic of justice refers to abstract rules with little reference to feelings, emotions, and relationships with people. It uses rules to mediate the conflicts that often arise when emotions enter the arena of moral decisions. An ethic of care integrates feelings, emotions, and personal relationships. It is based on the notion that self is interdependent with others, an interdependence that cannot be ignored in moral actions.

The idea that differences in moral development and moral point of view may be gender based has sparked heated debate between moral philosophers and moral psychologists.[23] A conservative interpretation of empirical evidence says people do not have a single moral view that they bring to moral dilemmas. Both men and women use a justice or care view, although they can prefer one to the other. The choice of moral view may vary with the specific moral dilemma. Both men and women may apply a justice view to rights and justice problems and a care view to moral dilemmas involving social relationships.

Ethical values develop throughout a person's life and are affected by the person's social experiences.[24] Ethical values may also change because (1) something directly persuades the person to shift his ethical values, (2) the norms of a social group important to the person affect his values, or (3) conflicts arise between different values.

Sometimes ethical values change because of communications designed to affect our beliefs.[25] Almost daily we are the targets of radio, television, newspaper, and magazine advertising and other forms of communication that try to change our beliefs about something. The arguments about abortion are an example.

People who hold ethical values different from the dominant ethical values of a group important to them will feel social pressures to conform to the norm of the group.[26] Social groups tend to reject individuals who do not conform to their norms. Therefore, if the person with the discrepant ethical value wants membership in the group, he will likely bring his ethical value into alignment with the group norm.

A person's ethical values can conflict with something else the person might desire.[27] Such conflict creates a state of internal tension in the individual, moving the person to reduce the tension.[28] A person can reduce the tension by changing his ethical values. For example, assume an individual who believes it is wrong to lie is asked by a close friend to comment on the friend's attire. The person does not like the friend's attire but does not want to offend the friend. The individual resolves the dilemma by lying and rationalizes the lying as necessary to retain the friendship. Such behavior could lead the person to change his ethical values about lying.

. . . .

⏎ *Theories of Ethics*

This section describes the major theories of ethics that have evolved in the Western world.[29] The following paragraphs describe each theory, its expected results, and objections to each theory.

Utilitarianism asks a person to examine the effects of an action to decide whether the action will be morally correct under utilitarian guidelines. An action is morally right if its total net benefit exceeds the total net benefit of any other action. Utilitarianism assumes a person can know and assess all costs and benefits of his actions. The assessment of all future net benefits includes any significant indirect effects. An action is right if it yields the most benefit for everyone affected by the action including the person doing the action. Utilitarianism forces a single actor to view the effects of an action on many others.

Figure 3-3 shows the two forms of utilitarianism. **Act utilitarianism** asks a person to assess the effects of all actions according to their greatest net benefit to all affected. Under **rule utilitarianism,** a person assesses actions according to a set of rules designed to yield the greatest net benefit to all affected.

Act utilitarians hold that lying is right if it would produce more good than bad. Because they always assess the effects of actions, they reject the view that actions can be classified as right or wrong in themselves. Traditional act utilitarianism has strongly affected economics. You undoubtedly have heard of "marginal utility" and related utility-based ideas in your economics courses.

Rule utilitarianism offers moral rules that should yield the most utility if everyone followed them. A person does not weigh the utility of each action. Instead, he compares the action to rules to see whether it is moral according to those rules. Two principles are central to rule utilitarianism:

1. An action is morally right if it is required by correct moral rules.
2. A rule is correct if the total utility from everyone following the rule is more than the total utility of an alternate rule.

Unlike an act utilitarian, a rule utilitarian does not accept an action as right if it maximizes net benefits only once. Rule utilitarians assess the morality of their actions by referring to a set of absolute rules about what is right or wrong.

Moral philosophers have raised objections to utilitarianism based on the limits they see in its approach to ethics. One objection is that utility can have many different meanings, making it hard to measure for different people. Utilitarianism requires an assessment from the position of the actor because it is not possible to objectively measure costs and benefits for all people affected by an action. A second objection is that some benefits or costs, such as life and health, are hard or impossible to measure. The costs and benefits of uncertain future results of an action are also difficult to assess. Lastly, what should a person count as a cost or a benefit of an action? This

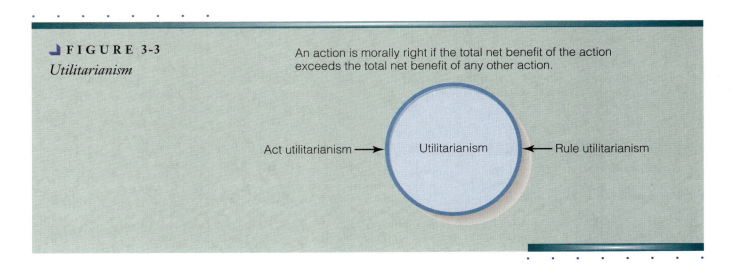

FIGURE 3-3

Utilitarianism

An action is morally right if the total net benefit of the action exceeds the total net benefit of any other action.

Act utilitarianism ⟶ Utilitarianism ⟵ Rule utilitarianism

objection focuses on the difficulty of identifying all the costs or benefits of an action and on the different ways various social groups value the effects of an action.

Utilitarians reply that the costs and benefits of many decisions can be assessed from their monetary equivalents. The benefits of safety equipment in automobiles, for example, can be assessed from the dollars saved in physical damage to people and property. Utilitarians also say precise measurement and full specification of all possible effects of an action are not required by utilitarianism. It asks only for an explicit statement and analysis of effects, recognizing that some measurements will be less accurate than quantitative measures.

Other objections have focused on utilitarianism's approach to moral issues of rights and justice. These objectors say an action that is morally right by utilitarian rules can also violate people's rights or lead to injustice. For example, a company that is deceptive during contract negotiations may win the contract to the benefit of its employees, but in doing so, the company violated the other party's right to full disclosure.

Some moral philosophers have drawn two main conclusions about the limits of utilitarianism: (1) it is difficult to use when an action involves hard-to-quantify values such as life, death, or health, and (2) it does not deal adequately with rights and justice. The following sections describe alternative ethical theories that meet those objections.

RIGHTS

Figure 3-4 shows a rights-based view of ethics. A **right** is a person's just claim or entitlement. The right can focus on what that person does or on the actions of other people toward him. Rights can exist because a legal system defines them (legal right) or because of ethical standards (moral right). Rights let a person do something that is morally or legally correct or entitle a person to have something that is morally or legally correct for that person. The purpose of rights is to let a person freely pursue certain actions without interference from others. Moral rights are universal. They apply to all people everywhere, under any legal system.

Rights have three features. First, other people, groups, and society have a moral duty to respect the rights of others. Second, rights let people pursue their interests as autonomous equals. The areas protected by rights exist despite any presumed social benefits that might come from restricting those rights. Third, rights provide moral justification for one's actions; i.e., people are not justified in interfering with another person's right, but they are justified in helping that person pursue a right. For example, although the right to a fair trial is a basic human right in the United States, employees do not always have a right to due process within their organizations.

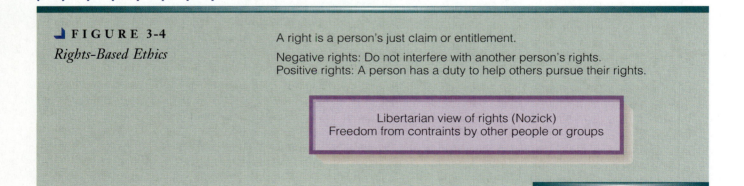

▟ **FIGURE 3-4**

Rights-Based Ethics

A right is a person's just claim or entitlement.

Negative rights: Do not interfere with another person's rights.
Positive rights: A person has a duty to help others pursue their rights.

Libertarian view of rights (Nozick)
Freedom from contraints by other people or groups

A rights-based view of morality says people have certain moral duties toward each other. It rejects the view that the results of actions should be used to assess those actions or to develop rules for guiding behavior. Rights-based ethics express moral rights from the individual's view, not society's. Such ethics do not look to the number of people who benefit from limiting another person's rights. For example, the right to free speech in the United States stands even if a person is expressing a minority or dissenting view. At times, though, utilitarian concerns can override rights. A society can restrict pollution by an organization because of its effects on the health of many other people.

Moral philosophers distinguish between negative and positive rights.[30] Negative rights refer to the duty not to interfere in another's rights. Some writers have proposed such rights for employees. A right to free speech within an organization is an example of a basic employee right.[31] Such a right would let people speak out about actions they feel are wrong. Positive rights refer to the duty to help another person freely pursue an interest to which he has a right. Such rights give a person something he cannot provide for himself, such as a right to proper health care.

Libertarian moral philosophers feel people have only one basic right, the right of freedom from constraints by other people or groups, including the surrounding society.[32] This philosophy views every person as distinct, separate, and equal. All restrictions on people's freedom to do as they wish with their property and labor are immoral according to the libertarian view.

 JUSTICE

Figure 3-5 shows a justice-based view of ethics. Ethical theories based on **justice** use a comparative process that looks at the balance of benefits and burdens that are distributed among members of a group or that result from the application of laws, rules, and policies. Moral philosophers who propose justice-based ethics argue that just results of actions override utilitarian results. Justice-based ethicists usually do not consider an action just if it results in injustice to some members of society although others benefit from the action.

The philosopher John Rawls has proposed a **theory of distributive justice.**[33] He built his theory on the following principles:

The Principle of Equal Liberty:	Each person's basic liberties must equal those of others. Those liberties must also be protected from attack by others.
The Difference Principle:	Societies will have inequalities but must help the disadvantaged (sick, disabled, etc.).
The Principle of Fair Equality of Opportunity:	Everyone must have the same opportunity to gain the best positions offered by society.

The Principle of Equal Liberty includes the basic liberties of many Western societies such as freedom of speech, the right to vote, and the right to hold personal property. The same principle also says organizations cannot invade employee privacy, use bribes to get contracts, or engage in any deceptive practices. Bribery and deception, for example, restrict a person's basic liberty of free choice.

The Difference Principle clearly implies that a society should care for its most needy. It also implies that managers of organizations should use resources efficiently in operating their firms. If they do not, the argument goes, society is less productive than it otherwise can be. If society is less productive, it cannot provide as many benefits to the disadvantaged as it could if it were more productive.

The Principle of Fair Equality of Opportunity says people must be allowed to advance in society based on their effort, contribution, and ability. Organizations must select people for jobs based on their ability to do the job. People who do not have the

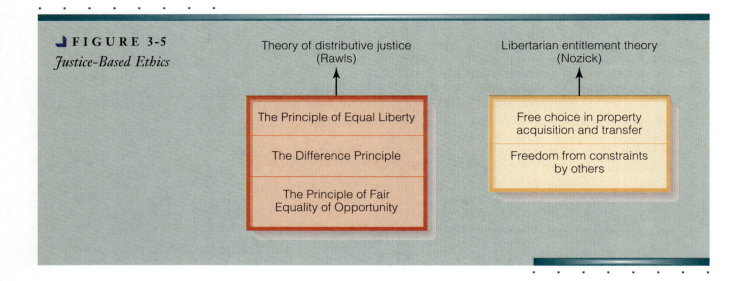

FIGURE 3-5

Justice-Based Ethics

Theory of distributive justice
(Rawls)

The Principle of Equal Liberty

The Difference Principle

The Principle of Fair
Equality of Opportunity

Libertarian entitlement theory
(Nozick)

Free choice in property
acquisition and transfer

Freedom from constraints
by others

needed skills and abilities must have equal access to education and training to let them develop those skills.

Philosopher Robert Nozick proposed a theory of justice based on a libertarian philosophy that contrasts sharply with Rawls's theory.[34] Nozick offered his entitlement theory as a way of understanding justice in acquiring and transferring property. Basically, this ethical theory says the acquisition and transfer of goods and services in a society are just only if done by the free choice of its people. Just transactions include making one's goods, exchanging money or labor for goods, gifts, bequests, gambling winnings, or a lucky find of property with no known owner.

Unjust transactions include stealing, fraud, use of slave labor, swindling, and seizing property. According to the theory, a forced redistribution of property is just only when it is done to correct a previous injustice. The return of stolen property to its proper owner by the police is just. Removing it from the hands of the thief, a constraint on the thief's behavior, does not violate the basic right underlying the theory.

The entitlement theory uses the basic right of freedom from constraint to argue that society cannot force a person to give up any property or services to help others in need. Any redistribution that comes from the free choices of people is just. Any redistribution forced upon a person is unjust, unless it is correcting a past injustice.

 EGOISM

Ethical **egoism** is among the oldest and simplest of Western ethical systems. Moral philosophers distinguish two forms of ethical egoism: individual ethical egoism and universal ethical egoism. An individual ethical egoist judges his actions only by their effects on his interests. Because this form of egoism never considers the interests of other people, moral philosophers usually reject it as a defensible basis of ethics.[35]

Universal ethical egoism, although controversial, can include the interests of others when assessing one's actions. Universal ethical egoism asks a person to weigh the effects of his actions on his interests. The assessment is based on pursuing pleasure and avoiding pain. Although an ethical egoist pursues self-interest, some egoists consider others' interests as a way of reaching their ends. Other egoists consider the interests of others because they want other people to do the same toward them. Some moral philosophers refer to the latter view as "enlightened self-interest."

The objections raised by moral philosophers about ethical egoism focus on its inability to resolve conflicts between one person's self-interest and the interests of another.[36] If each of us pursues his own interests, and those interests conflict with those of another person, that party is prevented from pursuing his interests. Moral philosophers argue that ethical egoism cannot resolve such conflicts independently of the interests of the involved parties.

EXERCISE   *Your Ethical Orientation*

*P*ause now and do the following exercise. It will give you some insights about your ethical orientation.

Read the following statements and the pair of alternatives given for each. Think about each alternative and note the one that you think best represents your feelings on a separate piece of paper.

1. Persons' actions should be described in terms of being
   a. good or bad.
   b. right or wrong.
2. When making an ethical decision, one should pay attention to
   a. one's conscience.
   b. others' needs, wants, and desires.
3. Solutions to ethical problems are usually
   a. some shade of gray.
   b. black and white.
4. It is of more value to societies to
   a. follow stable traditions and maintain a distinctive identity.
   b. be responsive and adapt to new conditions as the world changes.
5. When thinking through ethical problems, I prefer to
   a. develop practical, workable alternatives.
   b. make reasonable distinctions and clarifications.
6. When people disagree over ethical matters, I strive for
   a. some point(s) of agreement.
   b. workable compromises.
7. Uttering a falsehood is wrong because
   a. depending on the results, it can lead to further problems.
   b. it wouldn't be right for anyone to lie.
8. Thinking of occupations, I would rather be a
   a. wise judge, applying the law with fairness and impartiality.
   b. benevolent legislator, seeking an improved life for all.
9. I would rather be known as a person who
   a. has accomplished a lot and achieved much.
   b. has integrity and is a person of principle.
10. The aim of science should be
    a. to discover truth.
    b. to solve existing problems.
11. Whether a person is a liar is
    a. a matter of degree.
    b. a question of kind.
12. A nation should pay more attention to its
    a. heritage, its roots.
    b. future, its potential.
13. It is more important to be
    a. happy.
    b. worthy.
14. Unethical behavior is best described as
    a. a violation of a principle of law.
    b. causing some degree of harm.
15. The purpose of government should be
    a. to promote the best possible life for its citizens.
    b. to secure justice and fair treatment.

Calculate your score using the following formula:

Score = (the number of odd a's + the number of even b's) – 8

Table 3-3 shows an interpretation of different score levels. There are no wrong answers and no unethical scores. About 90 percent of U.S. respondents score in the +5 to –5 range.

This questionnaire was designed to determine whether an individual tends to approach ethical issues from an act utilitarian or a rule utilitarian perspective. Reviewing the earlier section on utilitarianism might also help you interpret your score.

Compare your score to those of others around you. Do the similarities or differences in scores account for any features in yourself or others that you know intuitively?

Source: Adapted from F. N. Brady, *Ethical Managing: Rules and Results* (New York: Macmillan, 1990), pp. 211–12. Reprinted with the permission of Simon & Schuster from the Macmillan College text ETHICAL MANAGING: RULES AND RESULTS by F. Neil Brady. Copyright © 1990 by Macmillan College Publishing Company, Inc.

┘ Society's Efforts to Improve the Ethics of Organizations

Over the past 150 years, the United States and many other countries have taken legal steps to improve the ethics of organizations. Since 1853, consumers have been able to sue corporations for damages resulting from product failure. The Securities Act of 1933 and the Securities Exchange Act of 1934 defined stockholder rights, causing managers to take those rights seriously. As is often observed, regulatory agencies abound in the United States. Each was established by legislation to impose social controls on the behavior of corporations. For example, agencies exist to enforce regulations about the environment, safety, health, equal employment opportunity, and consumer protection. Collectively these regulations have brought major changes in the behavior of employees at all levels in organizations.[37]

A looming question is whether those forms of social control are adequate to produce widespread corporate morality. For several reasons, some business ethicists and attorneys feel they are not. The legal actions allowed by much of the legislation focus on the corporation as an agent and not the decision makers who act illegally. Managers can escape punitive effects and feel justified in taking legal risks for the sake of profits. The laws also assume that managers of corporations have the single goal of maximizing return on investment to shareholders. Although intended to improve morality, the laws do not assume that management decisions should include ethical results. Many managers see the laws and regulations as a burden and offer only minimal compliance. Restrictive interpretations also reduce the effects of the laws. Because a society's laws are designed to protect its citizens, the laws do not extend outside the boundaries of that society. This last issue is especially important for organizations with global operations, a topic addressed later in this chapter.

Enacting tougher laws would not necessarily induce more organization morality. The structure of the laws might prevent them from having the desired effect. Laws must be standardized and apply to general cases, allowing moral slippage in specific instances. Because laws proscribe behavior, they specify minimally acceptable behavior. Because they try to force a person to behave in a specific way, they cannot induce authentic moral behavior, as defined earlier. Societies write laws as reactions to events, not in anticipation of events. Some immoral organizational behavior would always be ahead of any law.

┘ Managing for Ethical Behavior in an Organization

The demand for ethical behavior in organizations is forcing managers to find ways of managing for ethical behavior. **Managing for ethical behavior** involves three steps.

First, managers need to understand the present ethical culture of their organizations. Second, they then need to act to improve that culture. Third, managers must sustain ethical behavior so it becomes well embedded in their organizations.

In following these steps managers encounter a basic dilemma about ethical behavior. Moral philosophers agree that ethical behavior happens because a person freely believes it is the right way to behave. Managers cannot impose ethical behavior by force. Although they can develop a culture that supports ethical behavior, the decision to behave ethically still rests with each person.

UNDERSTANDING THE EXISTING ETHICAL CULTURE

All organizations have a culture, which includes the ethical values and norms guiding the organization's decisions and behavior.[38] Understanding an organization's existing ethical culture is an important first step in managing for ethical behavior.[39]

Typical business values for decision making include maximizing profit, holding a percentage of market share, and getting a target return on investment. Such values become embedded in an organization's culture over time. Other values for decision making can be derived from the ethical theories described earlier. Employee rights, for example, can include a right to privacy and a right to speak freely about organization issues. Utilitarian thinking suggests a decision maker should consider all effects of a decision such as the safety effects of a product and the environmental effects of an organization's manufacturing process. Justice theory implies a value of fair treatment of employees, customers, and clients.

One can discover an organization's values by examining its statements and studying its behavior. Many organizations issue codes of ethics, policies, and other written statements about proper behavior.[40] One can also draw inferences about ethical culture from the decision behavior of managers. If decisions are always guided by profit and investment values, then the types of ethical values described earlier are not present in the organization's culture. If decision makers consider rights and justice effects, then the culture has ethically based values.

An organization's leaders can play a major role in assessing the strengths and weaknesses of the organization's existing ethical character.[41] The assessment tells the organization's leaders the present ethical state of the organization and gives them a base from which to begin improvements.

IMPROVING THE ETHICAL CULTURE

Organizations do not make decisions; they are made by the people in organizations. Those people are guided by personal ethical values and by their perception of the organization's ethical values. Improving the ethical culture of an organization requires changing the ethical values of both the culture and the people in the organization.[42]

Any employee of an organization, with enough courage and stamina, can challenge unethical behavior or lead the organization toward ethical behavior.[43] The challenges include whistle-blowing, sabotaging unethical behavior, or conscientiously objecting to behaving unethically. An employee can also work within the organization, taking a leadership role in getting changes toward ethical behavior.

The fatal launch of the space shuttle *Challenger* in January 1986 provides examples of people acting either as leaders or as individuals in moving toward ethical behavior.[44] Roger Boisjoly, an engineer at Morton Thiokol, which manufactured the booster rockets for the shuttle, argued that the *Challenger* should not be launched after low overnight air temperatures. His research showed the O-ring seals on the rockets could fail, causing an explosion. He was successful in persuading his company's executives to ask for a launch delay, but pressure from NASA caused the executives to reverse that decision. After the *Challenger* explosion, the chief of NASA's astronaut office, John W. Young, circulated a memorandum within NASA showing safety problems in the shuttle program. His internal whistle-blowing efforts led to major changes in the NASA flight safety program. The stress of the experience also led to Boisjoly's permanent departure from Morton Thiokol.

Organizations and their managers have several other methods available for changing their ethical cultures. These methods include codes of ethics, policy guidelines, decision procedures, organizational design, standards of ethical performance, and ethics training.

Codes of ethics are written statements describing behavior prohibited by an organization because it believes the behavior is unethical.[45] Such codes can be based on the theories of ethics described earlier. Codes can come from industry associations, professional associations, or individual organizations. Behaviors most commonly prohibited include kickbacks, illegal political payments, extortion, inappropriate gifts, and conflicts of interest.[46]

Publication of a code of ethics can start the process of changing an organization's ethical values. Such codes let all employees know which behaviors are right and which are wrong. Codes also give managers a basis for sanctioning employees who violate the code. Creating and publishing a code of ethics do not, of course, assure a full change in an organization's cultural values. Much of a code's success depends on the willingness of employees to accept it and make it part of their daily working lives.[47]

Managers can also develop or change policies to improve the ethical culture of their organizations. Policies are written and usually available to all employees. Some typical areas covered by organizational policies are the social responsibility of the organization, employee rights, and the quality of the work environment. Some writers have suggested that such policies amount to "constitutionalizing the corporation."[48] Policies have the same positive and negative features of codes of ethics. They can make an organization's culture more ethical if they are accepted, followed, and enforced.

Decision procedures specify the composition of a decision-making group and the scope of information the group will use to make a decision. Such procedures aim to change an organization's decision processes to include more information about the ethical effects of a decision. A decision-making group for locating a new plant could include members of the affected community and employees affected by the plant's design. Information procedures for new product decisions could require a fresh review of negative test results before final decisions are made.

Changing an organization's design can improve its ethical culture. Separate departments dealing with employee safety and employee rights could be formed; these departments could enforce safety policies and process claims of violations of rights. The organization's board of directors could be expanded to include consumers, persons who are neither shareholders nor employees, employees, and community members.[49] The assumption here is that boards with such diverse members are more likely to have access to more information about critical issues and therefore to make ethical decisions.

Some writers have suggested that organizations develop standards of ethical performance that become part of the organization's performance appraisal process.[50] Such standards prescribe required behavior consistent with existing law and discretionary behavior that accords with the ethical policies of the organization. For example, an ethical standard for sexual harassment might say that all employees shall accept the mandate against sexual harassment in Title VII of the Civil Rights Act.

Since the late 1980s, interest in ethics training for employees has grown.[51] The goal of the training is to help the organization avoid governmental and societal sanctions by preventing unethical and illegal behavior from happening. During training, employees discuss codes of ethics, organization procedures for reporting unethical behavior, ethical frameworks based on ethical theories, and case studies showing ethical and unethical decisions. Another view of ethics training and education assumes it can change a person's basic character.[52] The dimensions of character important for ethical behavior are the person's capacities for ethical sensitivity, ethical reasoning, ethical conduct, and ethical leadership. Such capacities should be the target of development in both university education and organization training programs.

SUSTAINING ETHICAL BEHAVIOR

A sustained pursuit of ethical behavior requires organizations and their managers to engage in activities in three areas.[53] They must (1) teach new employees the ethical values of the organization's culture, (2) use various ways of influencing behavior in an ethical direction, and (3) institutionalize ethical behavior in the culture of the organization.

New employees learn the values of an organization's culture during their early experiences with the organization, including before they join.[54] An important part of an employee's socialization to the culture of the organization involves learning the ethical values of the organization.[55] Making those values explicit before hiring a new employee and reinforcing them during the early employment experience quickly teach the new employee what is right and wrong for that organization.

Managers can also influence the behavior of all employees in an ethical direction. Managers can use ethical performance standards to assess the ethical performance of employees, reinforcing those who behave ethically and punishing those who do not.[56]

A more subtle approach relies on peer reporting of unethical behavior to get employees to comply with an organization's ethical guidelines.[57] Peer reporting refers to coworkers' reports of perceived unethical behavior, a form of whistle-blowing directed at someone with whom a person works. A problem with peer reporting is that it often exposes the reporter to strong social pressure to overlook the unethical behavior. Managers can encourage peer reporting by specifying it as a desired behavior in their code of ethics. Another way to encourage peer reporting is to ensure that unethical behavior by one person will have a negative effect on many others. For example, an organization might punish an entire group of workers for the unethical act of one member of the group.

Ethical behavior has become institutionalized when the desire to behave ethically is part of the cultural fabric of the organization and individuals feel fully supported when they behave ethically. Institutionalized behavior is persistent behavior that is shared by two or more people and woven into the culture of the organization.[58] Three factors can encourage widespread organization learning of ethical behavior. People must see others behave ethically. They must also believe with others that behaving ethically is better than behaving unethically. Management must reward and reinforce ethical behavior as an important step in making it a lasting part of the culture of the organization.[59]

THE TOPICS OF OTHER CHAPTERS AND MANAGING FOR ETHICAL BEHAVIOR

The other chapters of this book have much more information that will help with managing for ethical behavior in organizations. Chapter 5, "Organizational Culture," has a full discussion of culture and how to assess it. That chapter will give you a detailed understanding of organizational culture, what it does for organizations, and how to directly measure its values. Chapter 6, "Organizational Socialization," describes the processes by which people learn the values of their organization's culture. The motivation chapters (Chapters 7–9) describe how managers can use incentives and rewards to affect behavior in their organizations. Group dynamics and the effects of groups on people's behavior are the topics of Chapter 10. Recall from above that peer pressure can strongly affect ethical or unethical behavior in an organization. Leadership and management are topics in Chapter 12, and organizational change is described in detail in Chapter 19. Those two chapters together offer much helpful information about making an organization more ethical.

CASE   *The New Crisis in Business Ethics, Part II*

The following case is the closing portion of the article that was the Opening Episode for this chapter. It describes the responses of several organizations to perceived internal ethical problems. Assess their responses using the information you have learned so far in this chapter. Consider the following questions while reading the case:

1. Do you believe the steps taken by these organizations will reduce unethical behavior? Why?
2. Will some people continue to behave unethically?
3. Is the role of an "ethics officer" important in the success of an ethics program?

CASE DESCRIPTION

Once the scope of the [ethical] problem is clear, the next step is to communicate in no uncertain terms what is expected of managers and other employees. Hewlett-Packard, for example, works hard to ensure that all employees are familiar with its extensive standards for business conduct, which cover everything from conflicts of interest and accounting practices to handling confidential information and accepting gratuities. The standards are high; salespeople are instructed to avoid commenting on a competitor's character or business practices, even to refrain from mentioning the fact that a competitor might be facing a lawsuit or government investigation.

A little innovation helps in getting the message across. Citicorp has developed an ethics board game, which teams of employees use to solve hypothetical quandaries. General Electric employees can tap into specially designed interactive software on their personal computers to get answers to ethical questions. At Texas Instruments, employees are treated to a weekly column on ethics over an international electronic news service. One popular feature: a kind of Dear Abby mailbag, answers provided by the company's ethics officer, Carl Skoogland, that deals with the troublesome issues employees face most often. Managers at Northrop are rated on their ethical behavior by peers and subordinates through anonymous questionnaires.

Source: K. Labich, "The New Crisis in Business Ethics," *Fortune,* April 20, 1992, pp. 172, 176, © 1992 Time Inc. All rights reserved.

More and more companies are appointing full-time ethics officers, generally on the corporate vice-presidential level, who report directly to the chairman or an ethics committee of top officers. One of the most effective tools these ethics specialists employ is a hot line through which workers on all levels can register complaints or ask about questionable behavior. At Raytheon Corp., Paul Pullen receives some 100 calls a month. Around 80% involve minor issues that he can resolve on the spot or refer to the human resources department. Another 10% of callers are simply looking for a bit of advice. But about ten times a month, a caller reports some serious ethical lapse that Pullen must address with senior management. Says he: "Most people have high standards, and they want to work in an atmosphere that is ethical. The complaints come from all levels, and they are typical of what you would find in any business: possible conflicts of interest, cheating on timecards, cheating on expense reports."

Some companies have been motivated to set up an ethics office after a spate of unfavorable publicity. Nynex took the step in 1990 following a series of scandals, including revelations of lewd parties in Florida thrown for suppliers by a Nynex executive. Later 56 middle managers were disciplined or discharged for allegedly receiving kickbacks, and the SEC accused a former unit president of insider trading. The company has since been beating the drum about ethics, but Graydon Wood, Nynex's newly appointed ethics officer, says the job requires a realistic view of human behavior. Says he: "You have to recognize that even with all the best programs, some employees do go wrong. Last year some marketing people didn't report properly, resulting in unjustified commissions. We fired them."

In the current crunch much deception and unethical conduct can be avoided if top managers make sure that the performance goals they set are realistic. Ethicists often cite a classic case that occurred at a GM light-truck plant several years ago. The plant manager got caught with a device in his office that periodically speeded up the line beyond the rate designated in union contracts. Confronted with the evidence, he pointed out that the company's production specifications were based on the line running at maximum allowable speed 100% of the time. He was simply trying to make up for inevitable down time.

Managers must be sure that what they actually do fosters rather than impedes ethical conduct. One sure way to send the word is by rewarding admirable behavior. No code of ethics and no amount of cajolery by the chief executive will have much effect if promotions regularly go to the people who pile up big numbers by cutting corners. Says Kirk Hanson: "Senior management has got to find a way to create heroes, people who serve the company's competitive values—and also its social and ethical values."

These role models could be especially important for younger employees who are trying to survive in what seems to be an increasingly hostile business environment. Michael Josephson reports some dispiriting news about the start that the new generation are off to. He cites surveys of Americans 18 to 30 years old that show between 70% and 80% cheated in high school and between 40% and 50% cheated in college. And—are you ready for this?—between 12% and 24% say they included false information on their résumés.

Commenting on Americans' ethical standards in the 19th century, Alexis de Tocqueville declared that the nation had become great because it was good. He may have overstated a bit, but in pursuit of profits today we may indeed be losing an element vital to our long-term success tomorrow.

CASE ANALYSIS

The organizations and the managers described in the case used many observations made in this section about managing for ethical behavior. The organizations used ethics training and changed their organizational design by forming an ethics office. They also relied on forms of motivation, including both rewards and sanctions. A remaining question is whether those efforts will improve ethical behavior in their organizations.

International Aspects of Ethics

A sharp contrast exists between U.S. attitudes toward business ethics and those of other countries.[60] Of the major capitalist nations, the United States has the highest frequency of reporting ethical violations, the toughest laws, and the greatest prevalence of organization codes of conduct. Europe and Britain have experienced some increase in ethical concerns; Japan shows the least interest in business ethics. Concern for business ethics is more episodic and viewed as faddish in those countries.[61]

Codes of ethics are much less prevalent in Britain, Europe, and Japan than in the United States. U.S. organizations rely heavily on rules applied equally to all people. Organizations in other countries rely more on shared values and a sense of obligation to other people or organizations.[62] The perceived U.S. preoccupation with business ethics prompted the British publication *Economist* to publish an editorial entitled "Hey, America, Lighten Up a Little."[63]

As many organizations become multinational firms, they face additional ethical questions and issues. Multinational firms operate in many countries and are subject to the laws of those countries. The legal and social context of globally oriented organizations can present their managers with ethical dilemmas.[64]

· *Italian citizens protest widespread corruption among politicians by parading an effigy of former Socialist leader Bettino Craxi. The sign says Craxi has received four notices of impending investigations for corrupt activities.*

A LEGAL VIEW

The **Foreign Corrupt Practices Act** of 1977 (FCPA) prohibits a company from using bribes to get business in another country or prevent the restriction of its business.[65] Foreign officials, foreign political parties, and foreign political candidates are the usual targets of bribes. An organization that violates the FCPA faces a maximum fine of $1 million. Individual managers who willfully violate the act face jail terms of up to five years and a maximum fine of $10,000.

The FCPA defines a payment as anything of value, including gifts. Under the act, a practice is corrupt if it tries to induce a person in another country to misuse his official position for the benefit of a company. A practice is also defined as corrupt by its motive. It is not necessary for the practice to be completed, nor must it be illegal in the other country.

The FCPA excludes small payments that are required to complete the ordinary course of business in many countries. Such payments are allowed if they are a usual way of doing business in a country although they would be bribes according to U.S. values. The act also allows entertainment and gifts if they are customary. The need to make small payments to help business along in some countries has presented many organizations with an ethical dilemma. The case describing payoffs in Pacific Rim countries at the end of this chapter discusses some of those dilemmas.

ETHICAL VIEWS

Figure 3-6 shows three ethical views that apply to international affairs and multinational organizations: cultural relativism, ethical realism, and international rights. Each takes a different approach to right and wrong in the international arena. The third view, international rights, describes an ethical theory that applies to the behavior of managers in multinational organizations.

Cultural Relativism

Cultural relativism refers to differences in ethical values among different cultures. It takes a normative ethical view based on the premise that right and wrong should be decided by each society's predominant ethical values.[66]

A cultural relativist bases his argument on three points. First, moral judgments are statements of feelings and opinions and are not wrong or right. Second, moral judgments are based on applicable ethical systems and cannot be judged right or wrong across cultures. Third, because there is no way of proving whether an action is right or wrong, the prudent approach is not to claim that it is either right or wrong. Cultural relativism says managers should behave according to the ethical systems of the countries in which they do business, even if their behavior violates the ethical systems of their home country.

Both classical and contemporary philosophers have rejected cultural relativism's argument that codes of ethics cannot cross national boundaries.[67] They agree, however, that countries vary in what they define as right and wrong.

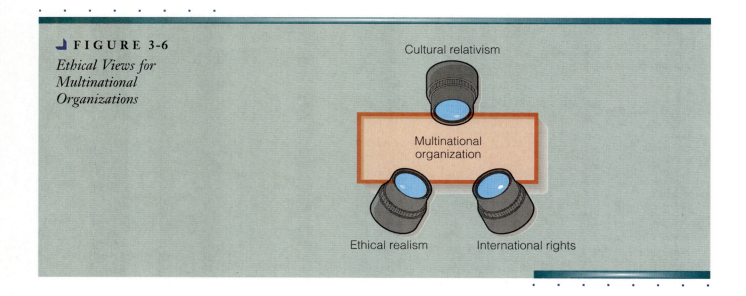

◣ FIGURE 3-6

Ethical Views for Multinational Organizations

Ethical Realism

Ethical realism says that morality does not apply to international activities, behavior, and transactions. The realist arrives at this conclusion by way of some premises about people's moral behavior in the international arena. Because there is no ruling power over international events, people will not behave morally. Because others will not behave morally, one is not morally required to behave according to ethical tenets.[68]

The realist view just described is the traditional view dating to the philosopher Thomas Hobbes. A revised view considers the effects of modern international transactions on people's behavior. The ethicist Manuel Velasquez has offered two revised premises setting out this view:

- When other agents do not adhere to certain tenets of morality, it is not immoral for one to do the same when one would otherwise be putting oneself at a significant competitive disadvantage.[69]
- Without an international sovereign, all rational agents will choose not to comply with the tenets of ordinary morality, when doing so will put one at a serious competitive disadvantage, if interactions are not repeated and that agents are not able to signal their reliability to each other.[70]

Velasquez's second premise marks a major change from the traditional realist view. The revision substitutes interactions among agents in international markets for the third-party enforcer (international sovereign) of ethical rules. Many market interactions are repeated, letting people know whether they can trust each other in those interactions. It is in those repeated interactions that people must behave morally in the international arena.

The global environmental effects of certain decisions illustrate the application of the two principles. The use of chloroflurocarbons adversely affects the global environment. The Montreal Protocol Treaty prohibits its signatories from manufacturing and using those chemicals.[71] Because countries that did not sign the treaty are not bound by it, a multinational firm could decide to move its chloroflurocarbon manufacturing operations from a signatory country to a nonsignatory. Any other decision would put the firm at a serious competitive disadvantage compared to a company that moved and continued manufacturing chloroflurocarbons. The ethical realist concludes that the decision to move the manufacture of chloroflurocarbons is not subject to ethical analysis.

International Rights

At least one business ethicist has proposed an alternative ethical system for international use. Thomas Donaldson, a business ethics professor at Georgetown University, analyzed the cultural relativism and ethical realism arguments against an international system of ethics. He concluded that neither argument excludes the application of a global system of ethics to international affairs. His system is based on human rights and proclaims a set of fundamental **international rights.**[72]

Table 3-4 shows Donaldson's list of fundamental international rights and the correlative duties of multinational organizations. Donaldson argues that such organizations have a minimal duty of honoring each right in the table for all people they employ, everywhere in the world. The multinational organizations are not obliged to those who are deprived of a right, according to Donaldson. This duty exceeds the minimum required for moral functioning and is properly the role of a government. For example, providing food to employees during a famine is the proper role of the host government and not the multinational organization.

Multinational organizations also have a duty to avoid helping to deprive people of these rights.[73] If a multinational organization does business in a country that deprives its citizens of any rights in Table 3-4, the organization is indirectly supporting the deprivation of the right. The morally correct reaction is to cease doing business in such countries. Some U.S. organizations, for example, ceased business operations in South Africa when that country deprived its black citizens of many rights in Table 3-4.

TABLE 3-4

Fundamental International Rights and Correlative Duties of Multinational Organizations

FUNDAMENTAL INTERNATIONAL RIGHT	CORRELATIVE DUTIES			
	Avoid Deprivaton	Avoid Helping to Deprive	Help Protect from Deprivation	Aid Those Who Are Deprived
Freedom of physical movement	X	X		
Ownership of property	X	X		
Freedom from torture	X	X		
Fair trial	X	X		
Nondiscriminatory treatment	X	X	X	
Physical security	X	X	X	
Freedom of speech and association	X	X	X	
Minimal education	X	X	X	
Political participation	X	X	X	
Subsistence	X	X	X	

Source: Suggested by Table 5-1 in T. Donaldson, *The Ethics of International Business* (New York: Oxford University Press, 1989), p. 86. The first, third, and fourth duties were described by H. Shue, *Basic Rights* (Princeton, N.J.: Princeton University Press, 1982). The second duty was described by E. M. Hartman, "Donaldson on Rights and Corporate Obligations," in R. E. Freeman, ed., *Business Ethics: The State of the Art* (New York: Oxford University Press, 1991), Ch. 10.

In some cases, multinational organizations have a duty to protect people from being deprived of their rights, but this duty does not apply to all rights. For example, some business ethicists argue that multinationals not only must honor the right to nondiscriminatory treatment, they must have procedures that protect people from discrimination. Such procedures include informing potential employees of the organization's nondiscriminatory policies and training managers to use those policies. A multinational also has a duty to honor the right of free speech and association by not blocking the formation of a labor union. In addition, the multinational should not press a host government for restrictions that would deprive employees of that right.

The same organization, though, is not morally required to protect its employees from being deprived of the right to own property or to be free from torture. Donaldson argues that actively working to protect those rights falls outside the multinational's ordinary scope of business. As this example shows, ethicists distinguish between the duty to avoid supporting the deprivation of rights and the more active duty of helping to protect from deprivation.

Personal and Management Implications

*A*n overarching implication of this chapter for managers and nonmanagers is the need to understand your system of ethics. The chapter described several views of ethics and let you assess your ethical system. Pause and reflect on what you now know about ethics, your ethical system, and what they imply for your behavior in organizations. For managers, the implications focus on including ethical considerations in decision-making processes. For nonmanagers, the implications focus on potential clashes between your ethics, your managers' ethics, and the ethics of your organization's culture.

Consider how you would respond to a request from your employer for you to behave unethically. If your ethical system differs from that of your supervisor, you will experience high conflict in such matters. Also, if your organization does not have an ethically based culture, you can expect ethical clashes. Such conflicts can expose you to significant stress, especially if your organization does not have procedures for handling ethical disputes.

The introduction to this chapter described the position of two people who teach business ethics. They were unwavering in their position that behaving ethically makes good business sense. Their position is clear: managers *must* include ethical considerations in all decisions, whether they are long-range strategic decisions or day-to-day operating decisions. Whatever the type of decision, Solomon and Hanson insist that managers should behave ethically.

Managing for ethical behavior in organizations carries implications for both managers and nonmanagers. For managers, the implications center on assuring that employees within their areas of responsibility behave ethically. That job is easier if the organization has an ethically based culture, procedures to ensure ethical decisions, and policies that encourage whistle-blowing. If the organization has none of these features, managers must assume personal responsibility for the ethical behavior of their subordinates. Without organization-level help, managers need to develop their own procedures for managing toward ethical behavior.

The personal implications of the discussion about managing for ethical behavior include peer pressure for ethical behavior and reporting unethical behavior. You could feel peer pressure to behave ethically or unethically. In the latter case, you will experience high internal conflict between your ethical values and those held by your peers. Pressure to behave ethically can create conflicts for you if your personal values do not support doing so.

Reporting unethical behavior will be easier for you if your employing organization supports such reporting as described earlier in this chapter. You will feel high social pressure from your peers to avoid reporting if your work group's norms do not support reporting. That pressure will add to any other ethical conflicts you experience but can be especially intense because you are in daily contact with your peers.

These implications become more intense for people working in a multinational organization outside the United States. The ethical conflicts you face in that situation may often be intensified by large differences between your ethical system and that of the host country. To see how sharp such conflicts can be, read the case about payoffs in some countries at the end of this chapter.

. . . .

Summary

Ethical behavior is behavior judged to be good, right, just, honorable, and praiseworthy. Unethical behavior is behavior judged to be wrong, reprehensible, or failing to meet an obligation. The judgment of behavior as ethical or unethical is based on principles, rules, or guides that come from an ethical theory, character traits, or social values. Some ethics scholars have argued that doing business ethically is simply good business.

The four ethical theories that can act as guides to ethical behavior are utilitarianism, rights, justice, and egoism. Utilitarianism asks a person to examine the effects of his actions to decide whether those actions will be morally correct under utilitarian guidelines. An action is morally right if its total net benefit exceeds the total net benefit of any other action. A right is a person's just claim or entitlement. The right can focus on what that person does or on the action of other people toward him. Justice-based ethical theories use a comparative process that looks at the balance of benefits and burdens among members of a group or resulting from the application of

laws, rules, and policies. Egoism focuses on a person's self-interests but can also include the interests of others.

Modern managers are feeling increasing pressure to promote ethical behavior in their organizations, causing them to look for ways of managing for ethical behavior. Managers can follow three steps to manage for ethical behavior in their organizations: (1) understanding the composition of the present ethical culture of their organizations, (2) improving that culture, and (3) sustaining ethical behavior so it becomes well embedded in their organizations.

The section on international aspects of ethics described some legal views, including the Foreign Corrupt Practices Act and its implications for managers of multinational organizations. A case at the end of this chapter about payoffs in some countries also gives more information about the act. Besides the legal views, there are several ethical views such as cultural relativism, ethical realism, and international rights. The last view in particular is attracting increased attention from business ethicists.

▲ Key Terms

act utilitarianism 51	ethical relativism 47	managing for ethical behavior 56
cultural relativism 62	Foreign Corrupt Practices Act 61	rights 52
dimensions of social responsibility 44	international rights 63	rule utilitarianism 51
egoism 54	"It's Good Business" 45	stages of moral development 48
ethical absolutism 47	justice 53	theory of distributive justice 53
ethical behavior 45	levels of social responsibility 45	utilitarianism 51
ethical realism 63		

▲ Review and Discussion Questions

1. Review the discussion of ethical issues in organizational behavior and the summary in Table 3-2. Discuss the areas of organizational behavior where ethical issues have occurred in your experience and the experience of others in your class.
2. The list of contemporary ethical issues in organizations that appeared earlier in this chapter is not complete. What other issues do you see affecting modern organizations and their management?
3. Review the discussion about ethical absolutism and ethical relativism. Discuss those positions in class. Which position do you and other students prefer?
4. Discuss the differences between descriptive ethics and normative ethics.
5. Review the section describing ethical values of individuals and societies. Discuss the ways both societies and individuals form those values.
6. Discuss the three stages of moral development. What are the implications of each stage for a person's behavior? Do you and other students in your class believe you have reached the final stage?
7. Review the four theories of ethics described in the chapter. Also, review the results of the exercise assessing your system of ethics. Compare your results with those of other people in your class. What are the implications for organizational behavior of people having different ethical systems?
8. Discuss the implications of the argument that behaving ethically makes good business sense. How common is that view in contemporary organizations? What do other students in your class think about this argument?
9. In what ways has U.S. society tried to improve the ethics of organizations? Are there any limits to those efforts?
10. The chapter had an extended discussion about managing for ethical behavior in organizations. It also included a case describing what some view as an ethical crisis, including cheating among college students. What are the implications of those discussions for you and others in your class?
11. The chapter discussed three ethical views that apply to international affairs and multinational organizations. Which of those views do you hold? Discuss your view with other students in your class. What are the implications of the different views for behavior in a multinational organization?

▲ Exercise

ETHICAL DILEMMAS IN BUSINESS PRACTICES

Each of the following situations describes some aspect of business practice. Read each scenario and indicate your approval or disapproval using the following scale. List your responses on a separate piece of paper.

Approve   1   2   3   4   5   Disapprove

Source: J. R. Harris, "Ethical Values of Individuals at Different Levels in the Organizational Hierarchy of a Single Firm," *Journal of Business Ethics* 9 (1990): 748–49. Reprinted by permission of Kluwer Academic Publishers.

▲ SCENARIOS

A. Daily, Inc. is a leading manufacturer of breakfast cereals. Conscious of the market shift toward more healthful foods, it recently added a line of all fiber cereals to capitalize on this trend and directed its advertising agency to prepare ad copy which stresses that this cereal helps prevent intestinal cancer among regular users even though there is no scientific evidence to prove or disprove this fact.
B. State Electric, a publicly held electrical generating company, is faced with rapidly escalating costs of its low sulfur coal which it purchases from midwestern suppli-

ers. Reliable estimates show this price trend to continue over the next five years necessitating an across-the-board price increase to customers. Lower cost, high sulfur coal is readily available; however its use will increase State's overall pollution emissions by 25%. Management opts for the high sulfur coal rather than raising the cost per KWH to customers.

C. Doug Watson is a salesman for Delta Drug Company and is responsible for calling on both physicians and pharmacists in a two state area. With commission and bonuses, his annual salary averages about $32,000. Doug has made it a practice of supplementing his salary by at least $1,200 by padding his expense account. He rationalizes this behavior by saying that everyone else in the business is doing it.

D. Frank Pollard, Executive Vice President of United Industries called the personnel director of one of their major suppliers and asks in a non-threatening way that his nephew be interviewed for a job in their organization. The personnel director complies with Pollard's request and arranges for the interview. Pollard's nephew fails miserably on the aptitude test which is required of all applicants; but is hired anyway because United is one of their biggest accounts.

E. One of America's largest automobile manufacturers is the corporate sponsor of the popular TV series ANY-TOWN VICE. The sponsor has been approached by a national coalition of concerned citizens as to the impact of this program on the morals of today's youth. The coalition demands that the sponsor exert its influence on the show's producer to tone down the sex and violence on the program. The sponsor's reply to the coalition is, in essence, that "our job is to sell cars not censor what the public wants to watch on TV."

F. Kiddie Textiles, Inc. a manufacturer of childrens' sleepwear, responded to the appeal by the National Safety Council and treated its entire fall line with the flame retardant agent TRIS. Research found this to be a carcinogenic agent and TRIS treated textiles were subsequently banned from sale in the U.S. Left with more than one million dollars in inventory of the banned products, Kiddie sold the entire lot at cost to an export agent whom it was sure would sell the TRIS-treated sleepwear to markets in underdeveloped countries which had no such ban.

G. The U.S. Patent Office recently issued an exclusive patent to Tiger Automotive for a fuel efficient device which has been proven to increase the average car's mileage by 45%. Given that Tiger is protected from direct competition by its patent, it has decided to price its new product at $45 to auto parts dealers even though it costs less than $1 to produce and distribute.

H. A major supermarket chain, Big Save, has been approached by a group of community leaders requesting that the firm locate a store in the inner city. They desire that low income families, who have little access to the better priced supermarkets in the suburbs, be given an alternative over the higher priced, small grocers who serve the inner-city market. Citing higher costs of facili-

ties and losses due to pilferage and vandalism, Big Save decides not to comply with the group's request.

I. For years the American tobacco industry has been subjected to criticism questioning the legitimacy of its products in the marketplace. More recently, various local action groups have been moderately successful in imposing bans against smoking in public places as well as the workplace. At the Federal level, smoking is prohibited on all regulated airline flights of two hours or less. Feeling that this is a critical issue which may bring about widespread bans against smoking, the tobacco trade association has more than doubled its budget for lobbying efforts to reverse this rule.

J. Johnny Jones is the sales manager for a local automobile dealership. One of his responsibilities is to train new salespersons as they come into the organization. Experience has shown that one of the most difficult tasks in selling automobiles, as in selling other goods, is closing the sale. Jones feels that some customers need to be helped into the decision to buy a particular car, so he teaches his new salespersons several high pressure techniques proven to be successful in closing the sale.

K. First Department Stores, with six suburban locations throughout the metropolitan area, is the largest advertiser in *The Planet Daily News*. The newspaper has been running a series of articles to educate consumers how to better protect their interests in the marketplace. Steve Adams, President of First Department Stores, hears by the grapevine that next Monday an article highly critical of First's credit policies will be featured in the newspaper. The preceding Friday he contacts the editor of the *Planet* and threatens the withdrawal of all advertising if the feature is run.

L. Management of Durable Copy Machines, Inc. has word from reliable sources that its chief competitor is about to unveil a new model which, in all likelihood, will sweep the market and make substantial inroads into Durable's market share and profitability. Sam Samuels, head of engineering for Durable, plays golf regularly with a member of the competitor's design department and is aware of his dissatisfaction with [the] amount of his recent raise. Being made aware of this fact, top management at Durable has instructed personnel to "hire that employee at any cost."

M. The Borden Company is a supplier in the highly competitive building supply industry. In the past, it has experienced difficulty in maintaining customer loyalty among builders and contractors. To address this problem, Borden has developed a plan whereby customers are given points for every $500 worth of merchandise they buy throughout the year. At the end of the year customers are awarded an all-expense vacation for two to various resort areas depending on the number of points accumulated. Prices are, of course, increased to cover this expense.

N. Todd Jackson is the purchasing agent for Wyler Industries and has final say on which of numerous suppliers his firm will buy from. Conscious of the magnitude of purchasing dollars he controls, Jackson has let it be known that in

TABLE 3-5

Scoring Form for Ethics Scenarios

ETHICAL DILEMMA	SCENARIO		SCORE
Fraud	C		____
	N		____
	O		____
		Total	____
Coercion	D		____
	J		____
	K		____
		Total	____
Influence dealing	E		____
	H		____
	I		____
		Total	____
Self-interest	G		____
	L		____
	M		____
		Total	____
Deceit	A		____
	B		____
	F		____
		Total	____

Source: J. R. Harris, "Ethical Values of Individuals at Different Levels in the Organizational Hierarchy of a Single Firm," *Journal of Business Ethics* 9 (1990): 744.

TABLE 3-6

Average Scores of Some Managers, Nonmanagers, and Students

ETHICAL DILEMMA	MANAGERS (N = 72)	NONMANAGERS (N = 40)	UNDERGRADUATE BUSINESS STUDENTS (N = 69)	GRADUATE BUSINESS STUDENTS (N = 17)
Fraud	13.93	12.89	12.86	12.35
Coercion	11.41	11.42	11.58	9.41
Influence dealing	9.07	8.66	8.28	8.94
Self-interest	8.90	8.21	9.09	7.47
Deceit	13.23	13.32	12.43	11.47

Source: J. R. Harris, "Ethical Values of Individuals at Different Levels in the Organizational Hierarchy of a Single Firm," *Journal of Business Ethics* 9 (1990): 744. Reprinted by permission of Kluwer Academic Publishers.

those situations where price and other things are equal, his decision to purchase from a particular vendor can be swayed by the receipt of an "appropriate" gift.

O. John Smith has been recently employed by General Supply, Inc. as a sales rep and has taken over the territory which includes among its potential customers Wyler Industries (mentioned above). General has been unsuc-cessful in selling to Wyler in the past because it has a strict policy against using company funds to provide gifts to any customer or prospective customer. As a novice in the selling profession, Smith is determined to make a sale to Wyler Industries even if he has to pay for a gift for Todd Jackson out of his commission on the sale.

Set up a sheet of paper to look like Table 3-5. Enter the numbers you have recorded for each scenario. Add your scores for the scenarios under each ethical dilemma and enter the total for the dilemma.

Table 3-6 shows the average scores for managers, nonmanagers, and undergraduate and graduate business students at the University of New Mexico. Compare your scores to those shown. Discuss your scores with others in your class to see whether there were any consistent reactions to the scenarios.

↵ Case

WHEN SOMEBODY WANTS A PAYOFF

The following case illustrates some issues raised by the Foreign Corrupt Practices Act and cultural relativism. Consider the following questions while reading the case:

1. How should U.S. managers behave in countries that accept payments (bribes) as a usual way of doing business?
2. Do U.S. managers have any options available that will let them abide by their principles?
3. Note the observation of the Indonesian businessman at the end of the case. Do you accept his viewpoint about corruption?

A European businessman mentioned to a friend earlier this year that he planned to open an office in Thailand. "Are you crazy?" replied the friend, a Malaysian banker. "Don't you know about all the payoffs that'll be required?" "I know," said the European. "They work."

To companies that play it superstraight, East Asia can be disheartening. It's the world's fastest-growing region, but business ethics often seem mired in the past. In booming Thailand, experienced observers say, payoffs have never been so pervasive. In China, corruption among government officials has even fueled popular protests against the regime. In the Philippines, though Marcos is gone, others have inherited his ways. And while the trend in Indonesia is toward less corruption, the country still has a reputation among Western businessmen as the worst in Asia.

So what's a clean-behind-the-ears kind of manager to do? Some companies, convinced that it's impossible to compete in a place like China or Indonesia without getting dirty, don't bother to try. And yet, while it's always better to forsake a deal than sacrifice your principles, old hands in the region argue that there are ways to maneuver around corrupt officials without violating either your own standards or the law. You have to think strategically: Pick a partner whose relationships—rather than payoffs—will open doors; find out what makes the bribe seeker tick; and thoroughly master the local laws.

American companies that succeed in dealing with the problem usually begin by learning what they may and may not do under the Foreign Corrupt Practices Act, the U.S.

law that governs the business conduct of American citizens and companies abroad. Those that take the time to understand the act find that it countenances some surprising things. A few years ago a well-known U.S. consumer products company discovered that local manufacturers in Malaysia and the Philippines were blatantly turning out copies of its most important product, even stamping the company's world-famous logo on the imitation goods. But the American company was loath to turn the matter over to the local police. Why? It seemed the only way to motivate the law enforcers to do their job was to slip them a little cash every now and then. This the American company would not do.

The surprise here: While such grease may be distasteful, there would have been nothing illegal about it in the eyes of American law. The Foreign Corrupt Practices Act, enacted in 1977 following revelations that many large U.S. companies had given bribes to foreign officials, is aimed mainly at stamping out efforts by Americans to win business with such payoffs. The law specifically okays payments to officials to "facilitate" routine government action—everything from processing visas and licenses to providing water, electricity, phone service, police protection, and mail delivery.

Thus, you legally can pay a customs officer $25 in order to make sure he doesn't dally in inspecting your shipment—a task he is supposed to perform anyway. But you can't pay him to process your shipment without inspecting it at all.

Unfortunately, much of the rest of the original act was fuzzy. Last year, in the words of an American lawyer in Thailand, Congress "burned off the fog and mist. Now you have the same mine field, but at least you know where the mines are." Besides clarifying the definition of "foreign official," the amended law substantially eased the obligation that companies once had to keep tabs on the activities of their foreign partners and agents. Under the amended law a company isn't liable for illegal payments made by its representatives unless it actually knows about them, or deliberately looks the other way to avoid knowing. . . .

Corruption is not always easy to recognize. Indeed, an Indonesian businessman argues that it is ultimately a matter of perspective. Is it corrupt, he asks, to hire lobbyists and public relations firms to use their connections to influence legislation and public attitudes? Does taking a public official out to dinner or inviting a client to play golf at your club count as corruption—or as a display of hospitality and appreciation? The point is that in Indonesia and other Asian cultures, the everyday payments that thousands of civil

Source: F. S. Worthy, "When Somebody Wants a Payoff," *Fortune*, Pacific Rim 1987, pp. 117, 118, 122, © 1989 Time Inc. All rights reserved.

Perception, Attitudes, and Personality

· *How do you perceive the person in this photograph? What is her job or occupation? This is Jill Barad, president and chief operating officer of Mattel. She rose from marketing director to her present position in about 10 years, suggesting a strong achievement quality to her personality.*

After reading this chapter, you should be able to ...

· Understand human perceptual processes and how people form impressions of others.
· Describe types of perceptual error and their effects on information people get from their environment.
· Explain attribution processes and their effects on perception and attitudes.
· Discuss the nature of attitudes, how they form, and how they change.
· Explain the different views of human personality development.
· Discuss some dimensions of personality and several personality types.
· Recognize the effects of different cultures on perception, attitudes, and personality.

Chapter Overview

Has Larry Tisch Lost His Touch?

He seems positively enchanted by the glitzy, strobe-lit world he now inhabits, but Laurence A. Tisch must sometimes long for the dull old days. For decades he displayed near-faultless financial wizardry as chief executive of Loews Corp. by buying unpromising enterprises and turning them into gold. . . . Then four years ago Tisch bought a controlling interest in CBS Inc. and began devoting his considerable energies to the faltering media giant. . . .

Long considered a man of humble, almost ascetic tastes, the 66-year-old executive now seems quite comfortable in his elegant, high-ceilinged suite of offices 35 floors up in the CBS building in Manhattan. Surrounded by tasteful bits of art and sculpture, perched behind a great wood slab of a desk, he contends that his brush with glamour has not changed him—"not one iota." He would also have one believe that he presides over a kind of corporate Camelot: "Morale is 1,000% better than it ever was in the past. Everybody is free and easy. There's no politics, no backbiting."

The view is not nearly so pleasant from below. Almost everyone agrees that bloodletting was inevitable when Tisch arrived. . . .

Tisch did what he had to do, eventually slicing off about 1,200 employees, but he failed to anticipate the fishbowl atmosphere of his new job. Echoes reverberated from Central Park to Santa Monica every time the ax fell, and the press portrayed the new guy on top as boorish and bloodthirsty.

The circus really started when Tisch lopped off 150 supersensitive heads in the news division, and Tisch concedes he mishandled the firings: "I should have done more of it by attrition. It was a fiasco, one of those things that just got out of control." But he argues that all concerned have forgotten the sins of the past. "There is no grumbling in the news division," he says. "There is peace. There is harmony."

Morale has in fact picked up from the darkest days, but the mood has settled into a kind of permanent antimanagement siege mentality. Not long ago *CBS This Morning* anchor Kathleen Sullivan got caught growling into an open microphone that CBS now stood for Cheap Broadcasting System. One mordant office wit recently circulated a cost-cutting memo, purportedly from Tisch, that schedules restroom visits in alphabetical order and limits first-aid procedures to normal break periods. "We are no longer allowing surgery leaves of absence," declares the memo. "We hired you as you are and to have anything removed would certainly make you less than we bargained for."

• Laurence A. Tisch, president, CBS Inc. In 1995, Mr. Tisch agreed in principle to sell CBS to Westinghouse Electric Corporation.

Source: K. Labich, "Has Larry Tisch Lost His Touch?" *Fortune,* February 26, 1990, pp. 99–100. © 1990 Time Inc. All rights reserved.

. . . .

The Opening Episode shows how managers often have a different perception of events in their organizations than nonmanagers. Mr. Tisch believed that everything was going smoothly at CBS Inc. Others at lower levels in the organization held a different view. As this chapter unfolds, you will see that people's perceptions of their social world have much to do with their behavior in that world.

This chapter describes three related aspects of human psychology that affect behavior in organizations. The chapter begins with a description of the human perceptual process. It then discusses attitudes, how they develop, and how they change. The chapter closes with a description of human personality, personality development, and personality types. Understanding these basic aspects of human psychology should help you understand behavior in organizations.

Perception is a cognitive process that lets a person make sense of stimuli from the environment. These stimuli affect all senses: sight, touch, taste, smell, and hearing. The stimuli can come from other people, events, physical objects, or ideas.

The perceptual process includes both the inputs to the person and the selection of inputs to which the person attends. The basis of such selective perception is an important part of the perceptual process associated with people's behavior in organizations. A person's perceptual process is a mechanism that helps her adapt to a changing environment.[1]

Figure 4-1 shows the major parts of the perceptual process. The **target** is the object of a person's perceptual process, such as another person, a physical object, an event, a sound, an idea, or a concept. Threshold is the minimum amount of information about the target, or stimulus from the target, for a person to notice its presence. The **detection threshold** is the point at which a person notices that something has changed in her environment. The **recognition threshold** is the point at which a person can identify the target or changes in some attribute of the target.[2]

The target of perception emerges over time from its surrounding context, sometimes slowly and sometimes quickly. People quickly discriminate a high-contrast target from its background, but an ambiguous target takes time to see. The degree of contrast can come from the target's size, color, loudness, or smell. Aspects of the person also affect the speed of emergence. People differ in their degree of motivation to attend to stimuli coming from their environment. They attend more quickly to positively valued stimuli than to negatively valued stimuli. For example, an achievement-oriented employee might notice announcements about promotion opportunities faster than an employee with less achievement motivation.

A person may also use **perceptual defense** to shield herself from negatively valued stimuli. People can block out annoying sounds or disturbing and anxiety-provoking feedback. The latter ability is a particular concern in organizations that do performance appraisals. A person who finds a supervisor's observations unnerving does not hear all the content of the performance review.

Individuals can make two major **perceptual errors:** perceptual set and stereotyping. Perceptual set refers to beliefs about a target based on previous experience with that target. These beliefs act like a set of instructions for processing the information the person gets about the target. The beliefs could have developed from prior association with the target or the person learned them during early family socializa-

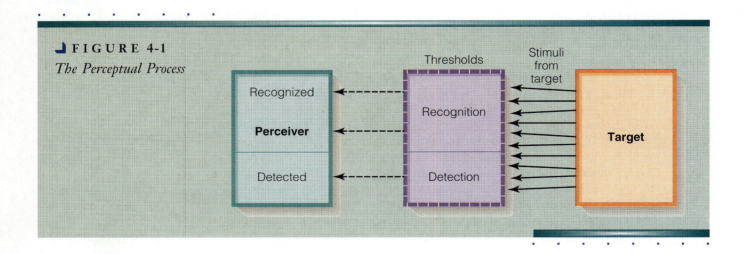

↵ FIGURE 4-1
The Perceptual Process

tion.[3] A person with a perceptual set about a target expects to find certain attributes or qualities associated with the target.

A stereotype is a type of perceptual set that holds beliefs and perceived attributes of a target person based on the group to which the target belongs. For example, a study of samples of Russian and American university students found they held certain images of each other. The Russian students perceived Americans as independent, energetic, and spontaneous. The American students perceived Russians as conservative, orderly, restrained, and obedient.[4]

SELF-PERCEPTION: A VIEW OF SELF

Self-perception is the process by which people develop a view of themselves. Figure 4-2 shows the three parts of self-perception: self-concept, self-esteem, and self-presentation.

Self-Concept

Self-concept is the set of beliefs people have about themselves. It is the view people hold of their personal qualities and attributes. Several factors affect a person's self-concept including the person's observations of her behavior, her recall of past significant events, and the effect of her surrounding social context.

People see their own behavior, and the situation in which their behavior happens, in much the same way they see the behavior of other people.[5] If a person believes that her behavior occurred voluntarily and was not the result of a reward or sanction, she usually concludes the behavior happened because of some personal quality or attribute.

People learn about themselves by comparing themselves to other people with similar qualities.[6] They make such comparisons when they lack clear reasons for their behavior or are otherwise uncertain about themselves. In trying to assess your athletic

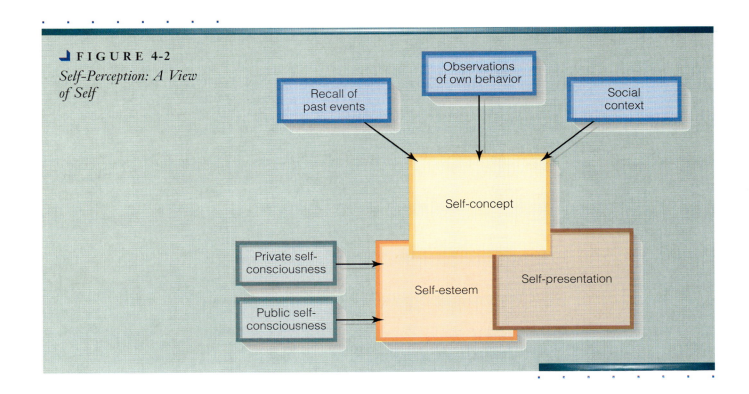

◢ FIGURE 4-2

Self-Perception: A View of Self

Observations of own behavior

Recall of past events

Social context

Self-concept

Private self-consciousness

Public self-consciousness

Self-esteem

Self-presentation

abilities, you may compare yourself to other people of the same gender, size, and weight. In the work setting, you may want to evaluate your abilities to hold a supervisory position. Here you may compare yourself to people with backgrounds similar to yours who have had recent promotions.

We all have had a different series of life experiences, lived in different places, and had different patterns of friendships. People's recall of events that were important in their lives affects their self-concept, but that recall is not without error.[7] People tend to recall events they attribute to themselves and not to a situation or other people. They often overestimate their role in past events.[8] They place more weight on the effects of their own behavior and less on the surrounding situation or other people.

A person's self-concept can have many facets called self-schemas.[9] A **self-schema** is a set of beliefs that help filter and interpret information you get about yourself. The sources of information are the ones described earlier: yourself and other people.

People can entertain views of several possible selves both at work and away from work. Despite this multifaceted quality of self-schemas, people do not present a confusing view of self to others because they can organize their self-schemas into a coherent self-concept.[10] The self-schemas that are prominent in the self-concept vary from person to person. Prominent schemas affect the information a person notices, recalls, and interprets.[11] A person with a prominent independence schema, for example, might overreact to a supervisor who tries to restrict her work-related behavior.

Self-Esteem

Self-esteem is the emotional dimension of self-perception; it refers to the positive and negative judgments people have of themselves. Self-concept is perceptual and cognitive; self-esteem is the feeling a person holds about her self-perception.[12] People's degree of self-esteem plays an important role in behavior. People with low self-esteem tend to be unsuccessful and do not adapt well to stressful events. Those with high self-esteem have the opposite experiences.[13]

People differ in their degree of **self-awareness,** a concept that involves two forms of self-consciousness. People with a private self-consciousness attend to their inner feelings and standards and behave according to a personal standard. Those with a public self-consciousness focus on external standards or norms and behave according to a social standard correct for the situation.[14]

Self-awareness, of course, can cause people to see discrepancies between their ideal self-image and the way they really are, or the way significant others perceive them. People tend to protect their self-esteem from threatening self-discrepancies. We tend to take credit for successes, ascribe failures to other people or the situation, and make excuses for expected failures.[15] We often find it difficult to admit we lack the ability to do some task or feat.[16]

Are such illusions good or bad for people? Some degree of self-deception helps make the social world happier and warmer.[17] Illusions can also lead, though, to self-destructive behavior such as excessive use of drugs, compulsive gambling, and lower achievement than is otherwise possible.[18]

Self-Presentation

The third part of self-perception is **self-presentation,** the behavioral strategies people use to affect how others see them and how they think about themselves.[19] Self-presentations have two goals: to try to affect other people's impressions to win their approval or to increase the person's influence in a situation, or to ensure that others have an accurate impression of the person. Many people feel strongly motivated to have others perceive them accurately, whether positively or negatively.[20]

People tend to pursue one goal more than the other with their self-presenta-tions.[21] Those who are highly conscious of their public image change their behavior from situation to situation. They are conscious of situational norms and readily conform to them. People who want others to perceive them in a particular way behave consistently in different situations. They act in ways they perceive to be true to themselves with little regard for the norms of the situation.

 SOCIAL PERCEPTION: A VIEW OF OTHERS

Social perception is the process by which people come to know and understand each other (see Figure 4-3).[22] When forming an impression of a person, a perceiver first observes the person, the situation surrounding the person, and the person's behavior. The perceiver may form a quick impression by making a snap judgment about that person, or the perceiver may follow the steps in the center of the figure, making attributions and integrating the attributions to form a final impression. No matter how the impression is formed, confirmation biases lead the perceiver to hold tenaciously to it.

Elements of Social Perception

People use three sets of clues when forming their impression of another person. These clues come from the person, the situation surrounding the person, and the observed behavior of the person.

In developing their first impressions, people use different physical aspects of the **person,** such as height, weight, hair color, and eyeglasses. Sometimes those impressions are stereotypes based on physical features. For example, some research suggests people perceive thin men as tense, suspicious, and stubborn; blond women as fun loving; and neatly dressed people as responsible.[23] Such stereotypes result from

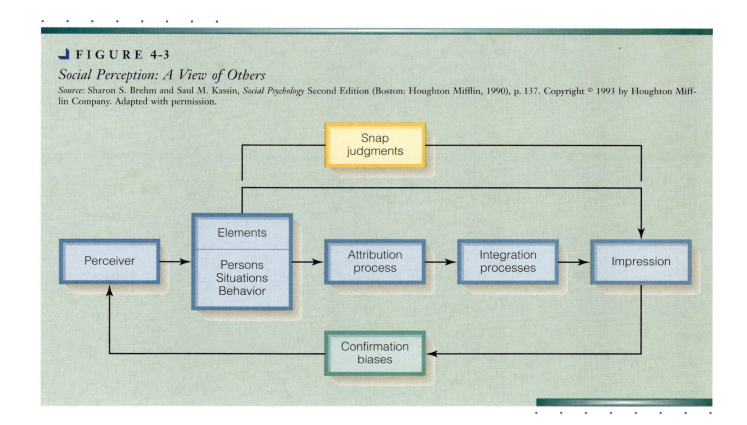

⌐ FIGURE 4-3

Social Perception: A View of Others

Source: Sharon S. Brehm and Saul M. Kassin, *Social Psychology* Second Edition (Boston: Houghton Mifflin, 1990), p. 137. Copyright © 1993 by Houghton Mifflin Company. Adapted with permission.

attributing qualities to people based on previously formed perceptions, despite what is true for the specific person.

We all have preconceptions about the situations in which we see the behavior of other people. Preconceptions develop from our experience with the same or similar situations. Seeing another person in a given situation raises expectations about the behavior that the situation should cause. For example, when two people are introduced, we expect both parties to acknowledge the other and probably to shake hands.

People infer meaning from other people's behavior. They interpret emotions such as fear, happiness, and sadness from facial expressions.[24] They view a person who walks quickly as more powerful and happy than one who walks slowly. In the United States, a person who avoids eye contact during a conversation often is perceived as evasive and shy; one who maintains eye contact is perceived as self-confident.

Attribution Processes

People see, analyze, and explain the behavior of other people. They seek causes of behavior just as scientists search for an explanation of some phenomenon.[25] People use attribution processes to explain the causes of behavior they see in others. The **attribution process** begins with a quick personal attribution followed by some adjustment based on the characteristics of the situation.[26] Figure 4-4 shows an overview of the process.

Through the attribution process people explain observed behavior by characteristics of the person observed or the situation surrounding that person.[27] When people make a personal attribution they say that some characteristic of the person such as her beliefs, disposition, or personality, and not the situation, caused the person's behavior. For example, when you conclude that another student or coworker spends many hours completing a project because she likes to work hard or values hard work, you are making a personal attribution.

Situational attributions turn to the context of the person's behavior to find its causes. You assume that aspects of the situation, not qualities of the person, cause the person's behavior. A situational attribution of a person's hard work would explain the person's behavior by a desire for good grades or other rewards such as a promotion.

Attribution theory says the perceiver uses three types of information when forming a personal or situational attribution: consensus information, distinctiveness information, and consistency information.[28] A perceiver gathers consensus informa-

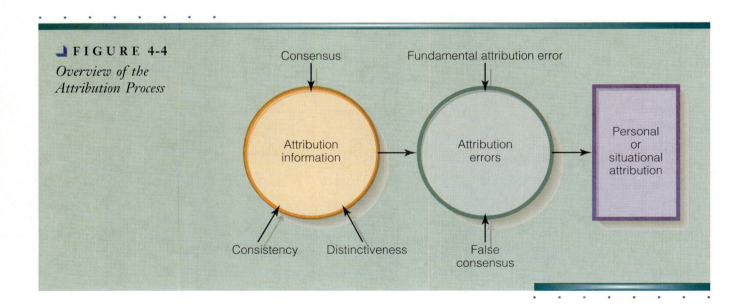

FIGURE 4-4

Overview of the Attribution Process

Consensus

Fundamental attribution error

Attribution information

Attribution errors

Personal or situational attribution

Consistency   Distinctiveness

False consensus

tion by observing other people in the same or a similar situation. If other people show the same behavior as the target person, then the situation, not the person, caused the behavior. If other people behave differently from the target person, then some quality of that person caused her behavior.

Distinctiveness information comes from observing the original person in a different situation. If the person responds differently to the new situation, the perceiver attributes the cause of the original behavior to the situation. If the response is the same, the perceiver attributes the cause to a characteristic of the person.

Consistency information comes from observing the person in a similar situation, but at a different time. Consistency is high if the person's behavior is the same at both times and low if the behavior is different.

Attribution theory says people combine consensus, distinctiveness, and consistency information to decide whether to attribute the causes of observed behavior to the person or to the situation. The perceiver attributes the cause of behavior to the person (personal attribution) when behavior is high in consistency and low in consensus and distinctiveness. The perceiver attributes the cause of behavior to the situation (situational attribution) when consensus and distinctiveness are high, but consistency is low.

Let's see how attribution processes work with an example from a work setting. Assume that you and a coworker are both candidates for a promotion. You believe you are more qualified, but your coworker gets the promotion. Now you try to explain why the promotion went to your coworker.

Attribution theory says you have two choices: the characteristics of the coworker or the characteristics of the situation. You have observed your coworker in different situations and noted wide variations in performance (high distinctiveness; low consistency). You also know your coworker rides a Harley Davidson motorcycle as does your supervisor (high consensus). You are disappointed but do not feel you lost the promotion because of your skills and abilities. The information you have could easily let you conclude that your coworker's promotion resulted from the situation (interest same as supervisor's), not from the coworker's skills and abilities.

The example just given illustrates one of several attribution errors. The **fundamental attribution error** occurs when the situation is underestimated as a cause of another person's behavior and the characteristics of the person are overestimated.[29] When explaining their own behavior, people tend to ascribe its causes to the situation, not to their personal qualities.[30] When explaining the behavior of others, people tend to ascribe its causes to personal qualities, not the situation. Such errors affect the accuracy of the view of the person that emerges from the attribution process. No matter how accurate or inaccurate their perception may be, people tend to overestimate the degree to which others agree with their view. This belief in a **false consensus** reinforces the view the perceiver has of another person.[31]

The person now takes the collection of attributions and begins to integrate them, putting the attributions together to form an impression of the other person. Both the disposition of the perceiver and the way she weighs the individual attributed traits affect the perceiver's final impression. Recent experiences can affect one's interpretation of another person.[32] A positive or negative event just before meeting someone for the first time can affect the resulting impression of the person.[33] One's mood at the time of a first meeting affects that impression. People form positive impressions of others when they are in a good mood and negative impressions when they are in a bad mood.[34]

People can give different weights to traits in the final impression of another person. Different people also arrive at the weights by different routes. First, some people may hold implicit theories about relationships among traits and the relationship of the traits to a person's behavior.[35] Second, some traits may be more central to a person's weighting scheme than others or were the first ones attributed during the early stages of the attribution process.[36] Such traits strongly affect the final impression of another person. Lastly, people often give more weight to negative traits even when positive ones are present.[37]

Confirmation Bias

People sometimes hold so adamantly to their developed impressions of other people that no amount of contradictory evidence will cause them to change their views. Social psychologists call this tendency the **confirmation bias.** It comes in different forms, but always with the same result. People will look for, interpret, and even create information that confirms their prior impressions.[38]

The two major types of confirmation bias are belief perseverance and the self-fulfilling prophecy. Belief perseverance is the tendency of people to stick to their initial impressions of others.[39] These impressions are difficult to change when they make sense to the person, even in the presence of contradictory information.

The self-fulfilling prophecy is the process by which a perceiver's impressions of a person lead that person to behave in ways consistent with the impression.[40] This effect occurs because having formed an impression, the perceiver behaves toward the person in a way consistent with that impression. The person reacts as the perceiver expects, thereby fulfilling the perceiver's prophecy. The problem, of course, is that the perceiver may not have an accurate impression.

Think for a moment about how the self-fulfilling prophecy can operate in a work situation. Assume you are a new employee beginning your first day of work. Your boss quickly develops the impression that you are a high achiever, perhaps because you approach your work with high energy. The boss gives you increasingly more challenging assignments. You rise to the challenge and complete the assignments, fulfilling your boss's prophecy. Of course, just the opposite could happen if your boss's first impression labeled you as a low achiever!

PERCEPTION AND BEHAVIOR

The human perceptual process can play a key role in major areas of behavior in organizations. Table 4-1 lists some behavioral areas and the chapters that discuss them. The table shows them in about the order a new employee would experience them. Let's take a conceptual stroll through these areas and see how your perceptual process could affect your behavior in each area.

Organizational culture involves values and behavioral assumptions that are important to organization members. Before joining an organization, you usually know little about its values and assumptions. After you join, veteran employees may advise you about some key values and correct behaviors during your socialization process. Whatever perceptual sets you carried into the organization can affect your reaction to the new organization. For example, assume you believe people in a business organization should behave formally and dress in business attire. That perceptual set would get a severe shock at Sun Microsystems, which values zany behavior and informal attire.[41]

Perception also underlies people's reactions to motivation systems in organizations. Self-esteem plays an important role in a person's motivation in work organizations. A person's need for esteem can affect her level of motivation. Many organizations use various rewards for different levels of performance. For rewards to work, people must perceive that the rewards are available, that there is a link between performance and getting a reward, and that rewards are distributed fairly.

Accepted theories of job design rest on people's perceptions of the characteristics of their jobs. Each person sees the objective features of jobs in different ways, which will affect their motivational response to those jobs.

Leadership and leadership processes in organizations are a rich area for human perceptual processes to operate. One key factor is the attribution of leadership traits to another person. Charisma, for example, is a leadership trait that can have different meanings to different people. One person might attribute charisma to another person while a second person would not.

⌐ TABLE 4-1

Perception and Organizational Behavior

Organizational culture
   (Chapter 5)
Organizational socialization
   (Chapter 6)
Motivation
   (Chapters 7 and 8)
Job design (Chapter 9)
Leadership (Chapter 12)

↵ *Attitudes*

Attitudes have played a key role in social psychology because of the presumed connection between people's perceptions of their world and their behavior in it. Managers also consider attitudes important. They commonly attribute an employee's poor work performance to a bad attitude about work.

There are almost as many definitions of attitude as there are researchers of attitudes.[42] This book will use the following definition:

> An **attitude** is ". . . a learned predisposition to respond in a consistently favorable or unfavorable manner with respect to a given object."[43]

The object of an attitude can be anything in a person's environment, including physical objects, issues, ideas, events, and people. The evaluative or affective part of the definition is central to the concept of attitude. It is the affective part that conceptually distinguishes an attitude from other psychological concepts such as need, motive, and trait.[44]

As Figure 4-5 shows, an attitude has three separate but related parts:[45]

Cognitive   Perceptions and beliefs about the object of the attitude. The person's perception of the distinguishing features of the object.

Affective   Evaluation and feelings about the object of the attitude. A person's feeling of like or dislike for the object.

Behavioral intentions[46]   How the person wants to behave and what the person says about her behavior toward the object. It is not always the same as the behavior observed following the expression of the attitude.[47]

As an illustration, consider a person's positive attitude about her supervisor. The cognitive part of that attitude is the person's belief that her supervisor has high technical ability. The affective part includes her positive feelings and overall liking of her supervisor. The behavioral intention part includes accepting her supervisor's directions and task assignments.

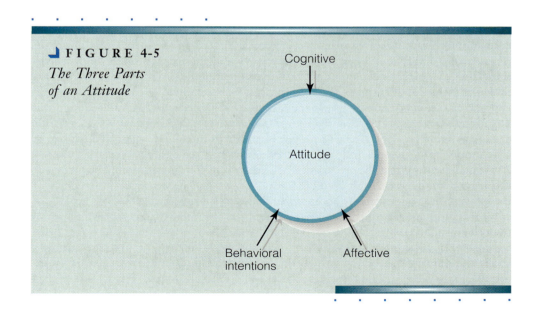

↵ **FIGURE 4-5**

The Three Parts of an Attitude

Cognitive

Attitude

Behavioral intentions

Affective

ATTITUDE FORMATION

A person's beliefs about an object and the amount and type of information the person has about the object both contribute to the **formation of an attitude** about the object.[48] If a person has positive **beliefs** about an object, the person forms a positive attitude about it. If the person believes the object has negative attributes, the emerging attitude will be negative. People form their beliefs by several different routes. The earliest influence on a person's beliefs and resultant attitudes is family upbringing. Each family holds a set of norms and values about what is right and wrong, good and bad. For example, French-Canadian families hold strong beliefs and attitudes about speaking French as their primary language. The children of such families develop positive attitudes about speaking French and negative attitudes about speaking English. As adults, their attitudes about speaking French spill over into attitudes about political candidates' positions on French as the primary language. Similar social influences on attitude formation come from the person's peer groups, work groups, and other social experiences.

Information about an attitude object can come from primary sources such as direct observation and experience or from secondary sources such as radio, television, movies, newspapers, and magazines. If the information associates positive attributes with the object, the person may form a positive attitude. The opposite, of course, could happen if the information associates negative attributes with the object.

ATTITUDE CHANGE

Attitudes are dynamic and change over time. The sources of attitude change are within the person and in the person's social environment. **Attitude change** happens because (1) something persuades the person to shift her attitudes, (2) the norms of a social group important to the person affect her attitudes, or (3) the person becomes uncomfortable with some aspects of her beliefs about certain things.

Persuasive Communication

Common sources of attitude change are the persuasive communications designed to affect our beliefs such as those found in radio, television, newspaper, and magazine advertising. Persuasive communication tries to change the cognitive part of an attitude and assumes the affective part will change in either a positive or negative direction.[49]

Persuasive communication changes attitudes through four separate but related processes. First, the communication must win the target's attention. Television advertising, for example, often plays at a higher volume than the main program to get the attention of the viewer. Second, the target of the attitude change must comprehend the message. A persuasive communication must be presented in a language and format understandable by the target. The third process is acceptance. No matter how logical and persuasive a communication, if the target does not accept it, attitude change will not follow. The last process is retention. If the message is not memorable, attitude change will not last. The latter, of course, is central to the effectiveness of advertising. Our shopping behavior is little affected by advertising we easily forget.

Several factors affect the acceptance of a persuasive communication. The source of the arguments must be both credible to and trusted by the target. The structure of the communication affects its acceptance. Some people respond favorably to logical arguments; others respond favorably to emotional arguments. The characteristics of the target, such as education, knowledge about the content of the message, and prior attitudes, can affect an influence effort. People who hold strongly negative attitudes about the object of the message will not readily change their attitudes to be more positive.

Social Influence

The second major approach to attitude change does not view people as passive receivers of persuasive communications. It sees people as embedded in a social context and affected by the norms or standards held by the social groups a person experiences.[50]

People who hold attitudes different from those of a group important to them will feel social pressures to conform to the norms of the group. Such pressures come from the tendency of social groups to reject people who do not conform to their norms. If the person with the differing attitude values membership in the group, she will likely bring the attitude into alignment with the group norm.

Cognitive Dissonance Theory

People can have multiple beliefs or cognitions about an attitude object. The multiple cognitions can result from persuasive communications or social influence. If discrepancies (**cognitive dissonance**) develop among cognitions, the person feels internal tension and becomes motivated to reduce that tension. The person can reduce the dissonance by changing one or more cognitions. Such change in the cognitive part of an attitude can lead to change in the attitude itself.[51] Here is an example.

Assume you believe in excelling at whatever you do. You are being transferred and want to learn more about your new boss. You check with several people and hear that your new boss is not well liked, leading you to develop a negative attitude about her. After starting your new job, you find that your boss demands high performance and rewards it with praise and pay increases. You should now feel tension from the dissonance between your prior negative attitude and your discovery that the boss's performance demands are consistent with your beliefs about yourself. You likely will dismiss your earlier negative attitude as based on the feelings of people who do not care to excel at their job. By doing so, you bring your cognitions about your new boss into a state of balance or consonance.

SOME ATTITUDES IMPORTANT IN WORK ORGANIZATIONS

Several attitudes that people hold within their work organizations have important implications for behavior and management. The attitudes include general job satisfaction, satisfaction with specific aspects of the organization, and organization commitment.

General job satisfaction is the set of evaluative feelings a person holds about a job and its surrounding context. Satisfaction with specific aspects of an organization focuses on evaluative feelings about pay, fringe benefits, coworkers, and supervision. These feelings play an important role in managing an organization because of their association with employee absenteeism and turnover. People who have low job satisfaction are absent more often or leave the organization, if they have the option of getting another job.[52]

Positive attitudes about supervisors and coworkers can come from comfortable social settings and friendly interactions.

Organizational commitment is another employee attitude associated with absenteeism and turnover. A person with a high commitment attitude accepts the organization's goals, puts in extra effort to reach those goals, and has a strong desire to be a member of the organization. Employees with high commitment attitudes tend to be absent less and stay with an organization longer than those with low commitment attitudes.[53]

Try the following exercise to see where your attitudes about your employing organization fall. It was designed to measure your degree of overall job satisfaction and your degree of satisfaction with specific aspects of your work environment.

Your Work Attitudes

The work attitude survey in Table 4-2 will help you find out how you feel about your current job or a job you have held in the past. The questions in this survey ask you about your job and aspects of your work environment. There are no "trick" questions. This is not a test, and there are no right or wrong answers. Answer each item as honestly and frankly as possible. Part II gives you instructions on how to calculate your attitude scores.

PART I

Using the following scale, indicate how satisfied you are with each aspect of your job and your work environment listed in Table 4-2. Write your answers on a separate sheet of paper.

1	2	3	4	5	6	7
Extremely dissatisfied	Dissatisfied	Slightly dissatisfied	Neutral	Slightly satisfied	Satisfied	Extremely satisfied

PART II: CALCULATE YOUR ATTITUDE SCORES

Calculate your scores for each attitude below by finding the average of your answers to the questions listed to the right of the attitude. Round your answers to one decimal point.

General satisfaction—your overall feelings of satisfaction or happiness with your job:　　Questions 3 and 11

Source: Adapted from J. Richard Hackman and Greg R. Oldham, *Work Redesign* (Reading, Mass.: Addison-Wesley, 1980), (Adapted from pp. 282–84). © 1980 by Addison-Wesley Publishing Company, Inc. Reprinted by permission of the publisher.

Satisfaction with pay and fringe benefits:　　Questions 2 and 10

Satisfaction with job security:　　Questions 1 and 13

Satisfaction with coworkers:　　Questions 5, 8, and 14

Satisfaction with supervision:　　Questions 6, 9, and 16

Satisfaction with personal growth opportunities on the job:　　Questions 4, 7, 12, and 15

Plot your attitude scores on a graph similar to Figure 4-6. The line in the figure plots the averages for the same attitudes for almost 7,000 people from more than 50 organizations throughout the United States.[54] Consider your scores as well above or well below those averages if they differ by 1.0 or more.

ATTITUDES AND BEHAVIOR

There is a connection between attitudes and behavior although it is not a strong one.[55] Many other aspects of organizations, and the people in them, also affect behavior. For example, strong social norms, or rules about a right way of behaving, can affect behavior despite a person's attitude.

A person with strong attitudes about an object, issue, idea, or another person will usually behave in accord with that attitude. You have undoubtedly seen such strong attitudes in action. People who have a strong positive attitude about Macintosh® computers are more likely to buy a Macintosh® than an IBM®-compatible personal computer. People who abhor smoking are not likely to behave in a friendly way toward smokers. Ardent followers of Jesse Jackson are likely to vote for him when he is a candidate for political office.

The strength of the attitude is the key to whether the attitude affects behavior. Three factors associated with attitude strength help determine whether the attitude will directly affect behavior. First, people with strong attitudes often are especially well informed about the object of the attitude.[56] Continuing with the computer example, a Macintosh® lover will know much about what a Macintosh® computer can do. Second, people with strong attitudes usually have gathered information about the object of the attitude directly and personally. They usually do not get the information

TABLE 4-2
Work Attitude Survey Items

1. The amount of job security I have.
2. The amount of pay and fringe benefits I receive.
3. My job in general.
4. The amount of personal growth and development I get in doing my job.
5. The people I talk to and work with on my job.
6. The degree of respect and fair treatment I receive from my boss.
7. The feeling of worthwhile accomplishment I get from doing my job.
8. The chance to get to know other people while on the job.
9. The amount of support and guidance I receive from my supervisor.
10. The degree to which I am fairly paid for what I contribute to this organization.
11. The kind of work I do in this job.
12. The amount of independent thought and action I can exercise in my job.
13. How secure things look for me in the future in this organization.
14. The chance to help other people while at work.
15. The amount of challenge in my job.
16. The overall quality of the supervision I receive in my work.

Source: J. Richard Hackman and Greg. R. Oldham, *Work Redesign* (Reading, Mass.: Addison-Wesley, 1980), (Adapted from pp. 282–84). © 1980 by Addison-Wesley Publishing Company, Inc. Reprinted by permission of the publisher.

FIGURE 4-6
Attitude Survey Averages for Almost 7,000 American Workers

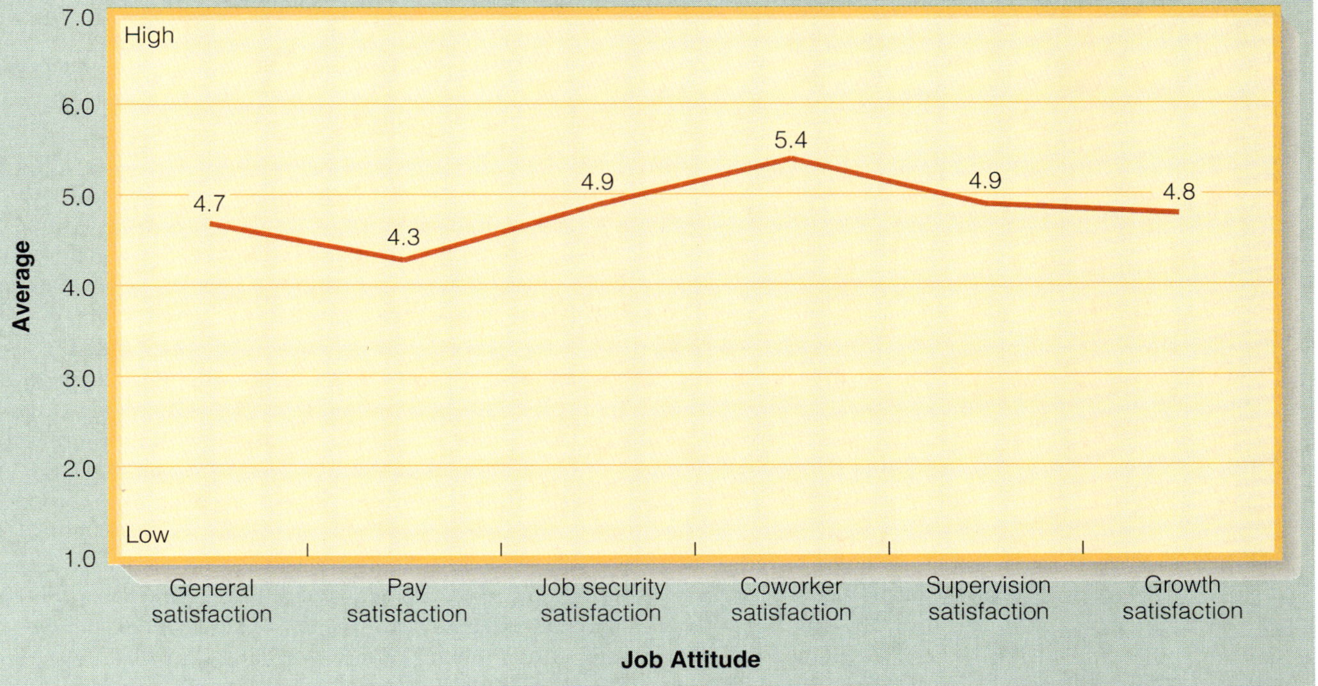

from a secondhand source.[57] Lastly, strongly held attitudes are prominent in the thinking patterns of people who hold them. They are well aware of their attitudes about an object and readily behave in accord with their attitudes.[58]

Social norms are rules of behavior that people learn from groups of people important to them or from their surrounding culture.[59] Such norms are part of the context within which a person behaves. Attitudes affect behavior in the broader context of surrounding social factors. A person forms an intention to behave from her attitude about the behavior and beliefs about the social norms of the behavior. The person's attitude about the behavior is a positive or negative assessment of the behavior. A person will go toward a behavior that is supported by social norms and that she values positively.

The connection between behavioral intentions and behavior is not always as direct as this description implies. For example, suppose you have read a favorable review of a new movie. The review left you with a positive attitude. You also check with some close friends about the same movie. They say it sounds like a good movie and that you ought to see it (social norm). Your behavioral intention is to see the movie, and you make plans to do so. The weather turns bad, though, preventing you from seeing it.

. . . .

Personality

Undoubtedly, you have used or heard phrases such as "That person has an outgoing personality" or "That person has a pleasant personality." The word *personality* carries many meanings for lay people and psychologists.[60] This chapter views personality as a set of traits, characteristics, and predispositions of a person. Personality usually matures and stabilizes by about age 30.[61] The collection of factors that make up an individual's personality affects how that person adjusts to different environments.[62]

PERSONALITY THEORIES

Figure 4-7 shows the three major classes of personality theories developed by psychologists since the early twentieth century. Each class makes different assumptions about human personality and offers a different perspective of how personality develops.

Cognitive Theory

Cognitive theory describes people as developing their thinking patterns as their life unfolds.[63] A person's patterns of thinking affect how the person interprets and internalizes life's events. People move through a series of cognitive development stages.[64] The stages begin shortly after birth with the reflective behavior of the infant and proceed through increasingly more complex modes of perception and interpretation of events in the child's environment. This class of personality theory views a child as neither driven by instincts nor unwittingly shaped by environmental influences. Children are curious and actively explore their social world to understand it. They respond to their environment according to how they understand and interpret its features. Two children in the same environment could interpret and react to it differently.

A child develops cognitive schemata as the child matures and has varied experiences.[65] A schema is a set of models, concepts, and structured patterns of thinking that the child uses to organize and interpret experiences. These schemas change as the child has various experiences and her knowledge base grows. Each person develops different cognitive schemata leading to individualized interpretations and reactions to events. In short, each person develops a unique personality.

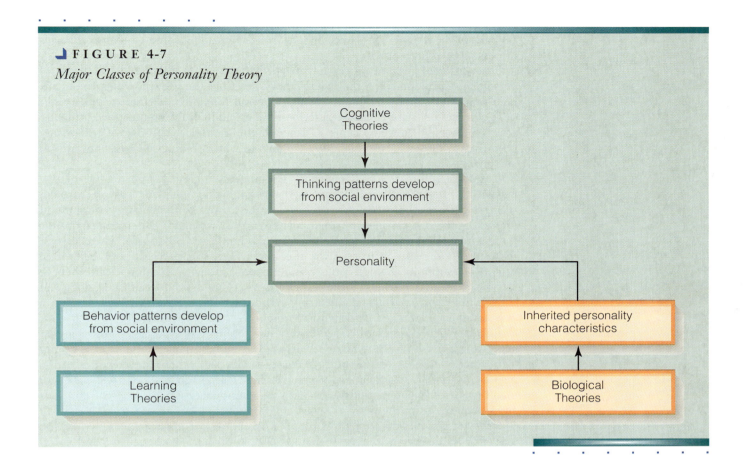

FIGURE 4-7

Major Classes of Personality Theory

```
                        ┌─────────────────┐
                        │   Cognitive     │
                        │    Theories     │
                        └────────┬────────┘
                                 │
                                 ▼
                        ┌─────────────────┐
                        │ Thinking patterns develop │
                        │ from social environment │
                        └────────┬────────┘
                                 │
                                 ▼
                        ┌─────────────────┐
        ┌──────────────►│   Personality   │◄──────────────┐
        │               └─────────────────┘               │
┌───────┴──────────┐                              ┌────────┴─────────┐
│ Behavior patterns develop │                      │ Inherited personality │
│ from social environment │                        │ characteristics │
└───────▲──────────┘                              └────────▲─────────┘
        │                                                  │
┌───────┴──────────┐                              ┌────────┴─────────┐
│    Learning      │                              │   Biological     │
│    Theories      │                              │    Theories      │
└──────────────────┘                              └──────────────────┘
```

Learning Theory

Learning theories of personality have appeared in several forms since the early 1900s.[66] The earliest versions assumed a child was a blank sheet of paper, shaped almost entirely by the social environment. Instincts played no role in these theories.[67] A need to satisfy a set of internal states called *drives* motivated a person's behavior.[68]

A person learns behavior from social interaction with other people. The young child learns acceptable behaviors during early family socialization. Adults continuously interact in different social environments and with different people. As behavior stabilizes, it forms the basic qualities of an individual's personality. Some learning theories view personality development as a continuous process from birth to death. The uniqueness of each personality follows from the variability in each person's social experiences.[69]

Operant-learning theory offered another view of social learning.[70] People learn behavior because external stimuli reinforce the behavior. Reinforcement increases the likelihood of the behavior in the future. The proper application of reinforcers develops complete behavior patterns that form an individual's personality.[71]

The cognitive social-learning theory developed by Bandura accepts the role of reinforcement but sees behavior as largely learned by observation.[72] People learn by observing behavior and its consequences, not by directly responding to reinforcers. They learn by observation and try to imitate the behavior they see.

Biological Theory

Paul Overstreet's popular country song,[73] *Seein' My Father in Me*, described similarities in characteristics of himself and of his father. Overstreet saw himself as talking and walking just like his father, and he described those characteristics as increasing in similarity over time.[74] This song carried strong hints about some **biological theories** of personality development.

Two different sets of research have developed about the biological bases of personality development. Ethological theory describes the ways in which the members of a given species, say, human beings, develop common characteristics as a result of evolution. Behavior genetics describe how an individual's unique gene structure affects personality development.[75] Although the biological theories of personality need more research, results clearly point to some biological basis to human personality.[76]

Ethological theory has deep roots in an evolutionary perspective of human behavior.[77] Behavioral characteristics that have helped humans survive through successive generations become the inborn characteristics of all humans. The simplest example is the distress-like cry of an infant and the response of a person responsible for the infant's care. The infant cries because of hunger or other pain. The caregiver responds to the cry by caring for the infant. Ethologists view both behavioral responses as inborn characteristics common to all humans. Ethologists also believe humans learn from their social experiences. A child who cries, but does not consistently get a warm and nurturing response from a caregiver, may develop a personality characterized by distrust of others.[78]

Behavior genetics describes personality development as a process of behaviorally expressing a person's genotype or set of inherited genes. Behavior geneticists do not view emerging behaviors, abilities, predispositions, and other characteristics of the personality as solely a function of genes. They see personality development as an involved series of interactions between a person's genetically based predispositions and influences from the person's social environment.

Behavior genetics describe three types of heredity-environment interaction.[79] The first type builds from the view that parents contribute both genetic and social influences to the personality development of their children. The parents' genes can predispose them to behave in certain ways. A child's genes can predispose the child to respond in the same ways. For example, parents may be physically active because of their genes. The parents' physical activity is an important part of the child's social environment. The genes the child shares with her parents can predispose the child to respond positively to the presence of physical activity. This example shows how a child's genetic structure and aspects of the child's social environment can reinforce each other in shaping the child's behavior.

In a second type of heredity-environment interaction, the child's genotype affects the character of the social environment the child experiences. A baby predisposed to smiling and activity may receive more social stimulation than one who is moody and passive. Over time, the first baby develops an outgoing, affiliative personality; the second becomes withdrawn and nonsocial.

In the third type of heredity-environment interaction, the child picks certain environmental niches best suited to her genotype. A strong, muscular child might choose contact sports as a leisure activity. A less muscular child might choose golf or fishing. Behaving in such environmental niches can have strong effects on the personality development of the child.

Although some aspects of personality can come from inborn qualities, others are learned. Modern personality researchers largely agree that personality develops from an interaction of internal qualities and the external environment.[80]

 THE *BIG-FIVE* PERSONALITY DIMENSIONS

After almost a century of research, personality psychologists largely agree that five dimensions can describe human personality.[81] Figure 4-8 shows the five dimensions

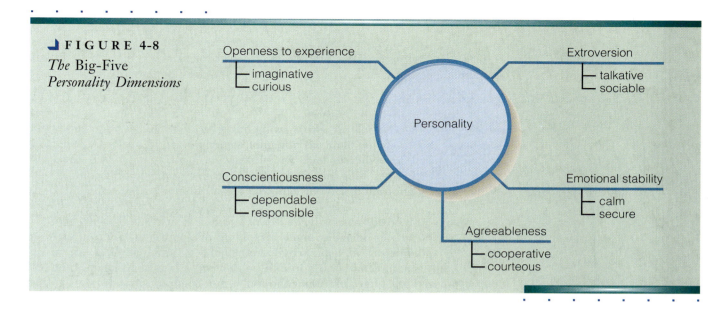

FIGURE 4-8

The Big-Five Personality Dimensions

Openness to experience
— imaginative
— curious

Extroversion
— talkative
— sociable

Personality

Conscientiousness
— dependable
— responsible

Emotional stability
— calm
— secure

Agreeableness
— cooperative
— courteous

and some traits associated with each dimension. These dimensions have appeared in many studies, across many samples, and in studies done in four countries outside the United States (Japan, Israel, the Philippines, and Germany). Although some psychologists feel the dimensions are not precisely specified,[82] they are now widely used in personality psychology.

The following are some typical traits associated with the high and low characteristics of each of the *Big-Five* **personality dimensions.**[83] Reflect on yourself as you read the descriptions and traits. Do any of these dimensions describe your personality?

Extroversion
High: talkative, active, sociable, assertive, gregarious.
Low: reserved, quiet, introverted.

Emotional stability
High: calm, relaxed, secure.
Low: worried, depressed, anxious, insecure, angry, embarrassed.

Agreeableness
High: cooperative, tolerant, good-natured, trusting, courteous, caring.
Low: rude, cold, unkind.

Conscientiousness
High: dependable, thorough, organized, responsible, planful, achievement-oriented, hardworking.
Low: sloppy, careless, inefficient.

Openness to experience
High: curious, intelligent, broad-minded, creative, imaginative, cultured.
Low: simple, unimaginative, conventional

As you will see in a later section, several of these personality dimensions can play a role in people's job performance.

PERSONALITY TYPES

Psychologists also often describe human personality characteristics and dispositions as **personality types.** Many types are useful for understanding and managing behavior in organizations. The following paragraphs describe some personality types that can give you insight into that behavior.

Locus of Control

People differ in whether they feel they control the consequences of their actions or are controlled by external factors. External control personality types believe that luck, fate, or powerful external forces control their destiny. Internal control personality types believe they are largely in control of what happens to them.[84]

Machiavellianism

A Machiavellian personality holds cynical views of other people's motives, places little value on honesty, and approaches the world with manipulative intent. Machiavellians maintain distance between themselves and others and are emotionally detached from other people in their lives. Their suspicious interpersonal orientation can contribute to high interpersonal conflict. Machiavellian personalities focus on personal goals, even if reaching them requires unethical behavior or manipulating other people. Their suspicious orientation also leads them to view their organizational world as a web of political processes.[85]

Type A and B Personalities

During the 1960s and 1970s, much research focused on personality patterns associated with coronary heart disease. The Type A personality emerged as a significant risk factor for that disease. Type A personalities also showed behavior patterns of interest in understanding the behavior of managers and supervisors in organizations.[86]

The Type A personality is aggressive, can quickly become hostile, has a keen sense of time urgency, and focuses excessively on achievement. Such people continuously create new and more difficult goals or engage in more activities than time allows. They do things fast and engage in multiple activities so they can get as much as possible done in a day. They have strong desires to dominate other people and quickly explode in anger over what others consider trivial events. For example, lines at a bank or a stalled vehicle in an intersection can throw a Type A personality into a rage.

Later research showed that some parts of the Type A personality predicted coronary heart disease and other parts were associated with high performance. Hostility was associated with coronary heart disease;[87] striving for achievement was associated with performance.[88]

The contrasting personality type is the Type B personality. Such people have no sense of time urgency and often stop to review their achievements and think about where they are headed in the future. They have high self-esteem, a characteristic that distinguishes them from Type A personalities. Type B personalities are even tempered, are not bothered by common everyday events, and approach the world in a calmer, more considered way than Type A personalities.

Extroversion and Introversion

Extroversion and introversion are two basic and opposite psychological types with deep roots in personality theory. In the early 1920s, psychologist Carl Jung described these types as basic sources of motivation and orientations to the world.[89]

Earlier we saw extroversion as a *Big-Five* personality dimension. This section develops the extroversion-introversion personality types more fully because they are the basis of a widely used personality assessment device described later.

Extroversion features an outward orientation to one's physical world. The extrovert focuses on people and other external objects as a source of ideas, information, stimulation, and meaningful relationships. An extrovert is an outgoing person who enjoys the company of other people and quickly adapts to varying social situations.

Introversion features an inward orientation toward self. The introvert is aware of personal feelings, reflects on personal ideas, and ponders internal images. Outside objects, both people and things, are secondary to the person's own feelings as a source of motivation. The introvert is often overwhelmed by the outside world and does not comfortably adapt to varying social situations.

Jung's extroversion and introversion types are the basis of a widely used personality assessment device called the Myers-Briggs Type Indicator (MBTI). The following case describes the MBTI and its use in many organizations.

. . . .

C A S E　　　　*Personality Tests Are Back*

*T*he following case describes how some companies view the role of personality in managing behavior within their firms. Keep the following questions in mind while reading this case:

1. Do you think such a personality assessment device is useful to managers and nonmanagers?
2. How accurately do you think such devices measure pesonality characteristics?

⌐ CASE DESCRIPTION

"ESFJ SPOKEN HERE," reads the sign on the accountant's desk at Compass Computer Services in Dallas. Her boss, the controller, has a card that says he speaks "ISTJ." The scrambled letters have also been spotted in Transamerica's pyramid in San Francisco, at the Naval Service Weapons Center near Washington, and at Virginia Power Co.'s headquarters in Richmond. They turn up in church-group discussions, on license plates, even in personal ads— "ENFP female desperately seeking INTJ male."

. . . The four-letter combinations are all the hallmarks of a theory of psychological types that is spreading rapidly out of counseling circles into corporate America. According to the tenets, people of different psychological types may have a hard time working together mostly because each has a distinctive way of perceiving the world and making decisions. Make people aware of which types they and their co-workers are, the theory goes, and voilà, communication improves and with it productivity. While some psychologists are not impressed, business people are lapping this stuff up.

The letter combinations stand for personality traits first posited by the Swiss psychologist Carl Jung in 1921 and further amplified after World War II by a mother-daughter team in the U.S., Katherine Briggs and Isabel

Briggs Myers. Just as people are born with a predisposition to be left- or right-handed, says the so-called type theory, they are also predisposed to be either extroverted or introverted (E or I), sensing or intuitive (S or N), thinking or feeling (T or F), and perceiving or judging (P or J). Extroverts are oriented toward the outer world of people and things, introverts toward the inner world of ideas and feelings. Sensing types sniff out detail, while intuitive souls prefer to focus on the big picture. Thinkers want to decide things logically and objectively; feelers base their decisions on more subjective grounds. Perceiving types tend to be flexible and to seek more information, while the judging sort want to get things settled.

. . . In the course of 20 years' work, Briggs and Myers developed a test—or inventory of preferences, as they called it, since there are no right or wrong answers—that indicates an individual's predispositions. It does not measure intelligence, motivation, maturity, or mental health.

The Myers-Briggs Type Indicator, or MBTI as it is commonly known, poses over 100 questions about how the test taker usually feels or acts in particular situations. For instance, in a group, do you often introduce others, or wait to be introduced? (Extroverts tend to introduce, introverts to be introduced.) Do you find it harder to adapt to routine or to more-or-less constant change? (Judging types have a tougher time with change, perceiving types with routine.) Would you rather work under someone who is always kind or always fair? (Feelers go for the kind boss, thinkers prefer a fair boss.) . . .

In 1986 some 1.5 million people took the MBTI, according to its publisher, Consulting Psychologists Press in Palo Alto, California. It is almost certainly the most widely used personality test in the U.S., at least among the allegedly normal population, and the test whose use is growing fastest. Average cost of the test: less than $1. The corporate world is by far the biggest user, and businesses accounted for 40% of test sales last year, double their share of three years ago. Companies that give it include Allied-Signal, Apple, AT&T, Citicorp, Exxon, GE, Honeywell, and 3M. Colleges, hospitals, churches, and the U.S. armed forces also administer the test.

Most companies use the Myers-Briggs Type Indicator primarily in management development programs, to help executives better understand how they come across to others who may see things differently. Converts are going forth to apply type theory to chores ranging from job assignment, performance appraisal, and negotiation to strategic planning and marketing. In defending the new gospel, they stress the damage that botched communications and internecine conflicts can do.

CASE ANALYSIS

The popularity of the MBTI means you may meet it in the future. As with any assessment device, you should view the results as only suggesting a tendency. The dimensions measured by the MBTI are only part of what affects a person's behavior and the quality of social interaction in both work and nonwork situations.

PERSONALITY AND BEHAVIOR

Personality dimensions or types can predispose a person to behave in certain ways.[90] An analysis of results from 162 independent samples found consistent patterns for some *Big-Five* dimensions and job performance.[91] The Conscientious dimension was positively associated with job performance, whatever the person's occupation. Dependable, hardworking, persevering people got higher performance ratings from their supervisors than those who did not have these traits. Extroversion had a stronger positive relationship with job performance for people in sales and management jobs than for people in skilled, semiskilled, and professional jobs. The outgoing, sociable character of the extrovert appeared to fit the interpersonal demands of sales and management jobs.

Some analyses have found relationships between locus of control and behavior in organizations.[92] Internal control personality types tend to perform better than external control personality types. Internals expend more effort, are goal focused, and pursue valued rewards in the work setting. They are also more concerned about their personal success as shown by salary increases and promotions than are externals.

Internals and externals differ in their supervisory or management behavior and the types of supervisory styles they prefer. Internals are action oriented and try to use personal persuasion. They also prefer to work for supervisors with a participative style. Externals are socially oriented, lean toward using coercion, and prefer supervisors with a directive style.

Machiavellian personalities do not develop close ties to other people in the work setting. If they are in a management or supervisory position, they tend to be aloof and cool in their interactions with subordinates. They approach decisions analytically and are little concerned about how their decisions affect other people.[93]

People with Type A and B personalities show distinctly different behaviors in organizational settings.[94] The achievement-striving part of a Type A personality has strong associations with performance.[95] A Type A personality finds it difficult to delegate decision authority. Subordinates who receive such authority must decide in the way the Type A person would and with equal speed. Otherwise the authority is rescinded, and the Type A person does the delegated tasks herself. The Type A person is also highly critical of subordinates' mistakes. The Type B personality readily delegates decision authority and lets people carry out tasks in their own way. Type Bs easily give praise when deserved. They view mistakes as errors from which to learn, not catastrophes deserving reprimand.

International Aspects of Perception, Attitudes, and Personality

*T*his chapter described many aspects of the human perceptual process and gave you some background on sources of perceptual error. Because a person's perceptual process has strong ties to the person's culture, perceptual errors such as stereotyping and attribution errors can be culturally determined.[96]

Some examples of culturally based stereotypes are that the Swiss are punctual, Germans are task-oriented, and Americans are energetic. Individuals who hold these stereotypes, experience many surprises when they meet people from these countries who do not fit the stereotypes. A second form of stereotyping occurs when people project aspects from their own culture onto people and situations in a different culture. People who travel to another country sometimes assume that the new culture mirrors their own.[97] For example, a Korean manager visiting Sweden might assume all women seated behind desks are secretaries. The Korean's behavior, of course, would be partly based on an assumption carried from the home culture. Such behavior would be inappropriate and possibly dysfunctional in Sweden where many women hold management positions.

Cultural differences can also add to attribution error. Applying attributions common in one's home culture to another culture can lead to both surprises and errors in behavior. For example, Canadian and U.S. business people usually use first names and behave informally after they have known each other for a while. Austrian business people continue to use titles and behave formally long after they have formed a business relationship. A North American doing business in Austria would make a serious attribution error by ascribing an Austrian's formality to distrust.

Attitudes and beliefs about organizational design, management, and decision making vary widely across cultures.[98] U.S. managers feel a hierarchical organizational design helps solve problems and guides the division of labor in the organization. French and Italian managers feel a hierarchical design lets people know the authority relationships in the organization. Italian managers, in sharp contrast to those from Sweden, believe that bypassing a manager to reach a subordinate employee is equal to insubordination. Lastly, decision making is less centralized in Swedish and Austrian organizations than it is in organizations in the Philippines and India.[99] As you can see, an organization that crosses national borders and draws its managers from many different countries has a large potential for conflict.

Different cultures emphasize different personality characteristics.[100] People in individualistic cultures, such as the United States, have stronger needs for autonomy than people in more group-oriented cultures, such as Japan. Individuals in cultures that emphasize avoiding uncertainty have a stronger need for security than people in cultures that are less concerned about avoiding uncertainty. Belgium, Peru, Russia, and Spain are examples of cultures that stress uncertainty avoidance. Singapore, Ireland, and India are examples of cultures with lower avoidance tendencies.[101]

· ·

Ethical Issues in Perception, Attitudes, and Personality

Several ethical issues emerge directly from this chapter's discussions of perception, attitudes, and personality. Because almost no empirical research has focused on these issues, much of this section is speculative. The ethical issues that follow from perceptual processes[102] center on errors in perception, attribution processes, and self-presentation.

Perceptual errors can affect how one perceives the behavior of another person. People's perceptual sets include beliefs about what to expect from another person. They could believe that the person is either ethical or unethical and interpret the person's behavior accordingly. That interpretation might not agree with the facts of the situation.

Stereotyping is another form of perceptual error that can filter information about a target person's behavior. This perceptual error should be of special concern as the U.S. workforce becomes more diverse. Many people may carry inaccurate stereotypes about the ethics of people with different social, racial, and ethnic backgrounds. These stereotypes can affect the opinions they develop about the behavior of such people in the workplace.

Self-presentations affect the images other people develop of a person.[103] Some people deliberately manage their presentations so their decisions and behavior appear ethical. Limited experimental evidence suggests some people can favorably manage other people's impressions of their ethical attitudes.[104] The well-understood attribution errors that ascribe causes of behavior to the person or the situation raise questions about accountability for ethical behavior.[105] Individual responsibility is central to ethical behavior. If an observer attributes responsibility for a decision or action to a person, that person could then be judged as behaving ethically or unethically. If an observer attributes the cause of the behavior to the situation, the individual is not held accountable. The latter could happen, for example, if an observer believed the person had behaved unethically because of a directive from the boss. Errors in attribution also could lead a decision maker to conclude that she was not responsible for an unethical act.

There is little reliable and valid information about ethical attitudes.[106] Some evidence points to the absence of a fixed set of ethical attitudes among managers. Instead, attitudes about ethics in organizations and decision making are situational and varying. The morality of behavior and decisions is determined by their social context, not by abstract and absolute rules.[107]

Personal and Management Implications

*T*he types of perceptual errors humans make have several implications. Two common errors come from perceptual sets and stereotyping. If either of these sources of perceptual error gives you an incorrect view of a situation or person, you may behave inappropriately for that situation or person.

The fundamental attribution error is the tendency to underestimate the situation as a cause of another person's behavior. If you suffer from this type of error, you will overestimate the degree to which a person's characteristics explain her behavior. When explaining your own behavior, though, you will tend to ascribe its causes to the situation and not to your personal qualities. Such errors can affect the accuracy of your view about another's characteristics. Whatever the accuracy of your views, you will develop a false consensus, an overestimation of how much others agree with you.

The perceptual errors just described play an important role in an international context because of variations in perception across different cultures. If you have any inaccurate stereotypes of people and situations in other countries, you could blunder interpersonally when placed in these situations.

Recall that when people experience cognitive dissonance, they feel a state of tension and a need to reduce that tension. A common organization situation you could encounter involves a performance appraisal and the rewards you and others get because of that appraisal. Such appraisals are judgments by a manager about people's performance. You may feel your performance was rated lower than it should have been compared to the performance of a coworker. You will feel cognitive dissonance and a need to reduce it. Several ways of reducing the dissonance are available to you such as quitting the organization or seeking a transfer. Chapter 8 examines such dissonance effects more fully in its discussion of Equity Theory.

One of your responsibilities as a manager is assessing the performance of those who report to you. Many job situations will not let you directly measure a person's performance. Instead, you will evaluate or appraise performance based on your knowledge and observations of a person's behavior. Because you are observing the behavior of another person, many perceptual errors described earlier could affect your conclusions about that person's performance.[108] The result could be a performance appraisal that does not accord with what the person believes is just. Such feelings of unfairness can lead the person to engage in behaviors that are dysfunctional for your work unit.

The discussion of attribution processes earlier in this chapter emphasized how people ascribe characteristics and qualities to other people. The attribution processes of those who work for you play an important role in whether they perceive you as a leader. People ascribe leadership qualities to others based on their *implicit leadership theories*.[109] Such theories act as perceptual filters and standards of comparison for the qualities they believe a leader should have. A person perceived as a good leader by one person may not be perceived that way by another.

Organizations will increasingly become multinational in both operation and membership.[110] Many managers in the future will find themselves working directly with managers from other countries. The cultural differences in management orientation described earlier suggest two implications. First, the conflict potential among managers from different countries is high. Second, to reduce that conflict potential, managers from all countries must understand the different orientations they bring to an organization. This chapter touched only briefly on the international aspects of such issues. You will find much more detail in the citations given earlier.

. . . .

↵ *Summary*

Perception is a selective cognitive process that lets a person make sense of stimuli from her environment. Perceptual errors include perceptual set and stereotyping. Self-perception (how you see yourself) has three parts: self-concept, self-esteem, and self-presentation. Social perception is the process of understanding another person using information from the person, from the situation, and from observed behavior. Social perception includes attribution processes, which explain the cause of other people's behavior. People make attribution errors that can lead to inaccurate perceptions and conclusions about another person.

Attitudes are favorable or unfavorable dispositions about an object. The three related parts of an attitude are cognitive, affective, and behavioral intentions. Attitudes can change because something persuades the person to shift her attitudes, the norms of a social group affect her attitudes, or the person becomes cognitively uncomfortable (cognitive dissonance) with some aspects of her beliefs compared to others.

Personality is a set of traits, characteristics, and predispositions of a person. Three views of personality development came from cognitive theory, learning theory, and biological explanations of personality development. The *Big-Five* personality dimensions are extroversion, emotional stability, agreeableness, conscientiousness, and openness to experience. Some personality types of interest are Machiavellian, Type A and B, and extroverted-introverted personalities.

People from different cultures often hold stereotypes about people from other cultures. These stereotypes can be inaccurate, leading to difficulties in interactions in other countries. Cultures also vary in the attitudes held about organizations, their management, and the types of personality characteristics considered important.

. . . .

↵ *Key Terms*

attitude change 82

attitude formation 82

attitudes: cognitive, affective, behavioral intentions 81

attribution process 78

Big-Five personality dimensions 89

biological theory 88

cognitive dissonance 83

cognitive theory 86

confirmation bias 80

detection threshold 74

false consensus 79

fundamental attribution error 79

learning theory 87

perceptual defense 74

perceptual errors 74

personality types 89

recognition threshold 74

self-awareness 76

self-concept 75

self-esteem 76

self-perception 75

self-presentation 76

self-schema 76

social perception 77

target 74

Review and Discussion Questions

1. Review the results of the work attitude exercise you did earlier. Compare your results with those of other students in your class. If there are major differences in attitudes, discuss some possible reasons for these differences.

2. Self-concept, self-esteem, and self-presentation are the three parts of self-perception. How do you see yourself in each of these three areas? Compare your self-view with how some close friends see you. Be prepared for some surprises!

3. Review the description of social perception earlier in this chapter. What do you consider most when forming an impression of a person you have just met? Which types of attribution error are you most likely to make? Discuss these questions with others in your class to see how types of attribution error vary among different people.

4. What do you hold strong attitudes about? Ask some close friends whether you behave in accord with these attitudes.

5. Review the earlier description of the three sources of attitude change. Which of the three causes you to change your attitudes about some object most quickly? Discuss this question with other students in your class to see how the causes of attitude change differ among people.

6. Review the various theories of personality development. Which theory in your opinion is the most realistic explanation of this important process? Why?

7. Review the personality dimensions and types discussed earlier in this chapter. Have you known people who fit some of these personality descriptions? Discuss your interactions with people of the different personality types.

8. Review the brief stereotypes about people from different cultures in the international issues section of the chapter. Are those stereotypes shared by other students in your class? If there are students from other countries in your class, ask them about the stereotypes they hold about U.S. and Canadian people.

9. Review the attribution error discussion in the international issues section. Discuss whether anyone in your class has experienced such attribution errors while traveling in another country.

10. The ethical issues section strongly implied that human perceptual processes can filter the information one gets about other people's actions. Such filtration affects the accuracy of one's judgment about ethical and unethical behavior. Fully discuss the implications of perceptual processes for ethical behavior in organizations.

Case

NEW NOTIONS OF "NORMAL": WORLD'S MOST WIDELY USED PSYCHOLOGICAL TEST GETS FIRST OVERHAUL IN HALF A CENTURY

The following case describes another widely used personality assessment device. Have the following questions in mind while reading this case:

1. Are such paper-and-pencil measures a valid assessment of human personality?

2. Can such devices give people feedback about themselves that they might find damaging?

3. Would you object if an employer asked to assess your personality with such a tool? Would the request be ethical? Why?

Would you consider a woman too masculine if she said she would like to be a soldier? What would you make of a guy who took care not to step on cracks in the sidewalk? Does the statement "I was often sent to the principal's office for

cutting up" suggest the speaker was a class clown or a knife-wielding gang leader?

By turns sexist, confusing and completely out of date, versions of those questions all appeared for decades on the world's most widely used psychological test, the Minnesota Multiphasic Personality Inventory, or MMPI. Millions of people in dozens of countries, being evaluated for character, attitudes and personal behavior, have waded their way through 556 statements, which they must answer true or false.

The test was designed to figure out who is normal and who is not. To do that, the researchers who created it relied on a group of 2,600 middle class, mostly rural, married people from Minnesota. None of them was younger than 16 or older than 65. And they were all white. They were the standard of "normal" psychological fitness against which millions across the world came to be judged by businesses, industries and schools. Now, almost a half century after it was first used, the MMPI has undergone its first major overhaul.

Source: M. Specter, "New Notions of 'Normal': World's Most Widely Used Psychological Test Gets First Overhaul in Half a Century," *Washington Post,* February 5, 1990, p. A3. © 1990 The Washington Post. Reprinted with permission.

⅃ BROADER RANGE REFLECTED

"Society changes, assumptions change and we realized the test needed to reflect a broader range of people," said W.

Grant Dahlstrom, professor of psychology at the University of North Carolina, and a member of a committee that recently introduced a new version of the MMPI. "We took out the sexist references, the religious references and others that have become obscure."

No more can the statement "I like mechanics magazines" be used as a way to gauge a person's "appropriate" sexuality. Also, the blanket use of the word "he" has been supplanted with the more boring and less offensive "person."

The researchers won't reveal specific new questions because they say it might bias the test. But they will say they added questions and some new categories of personality type. In the 1930s, for example, when the test was first introduced, people were either hard chargers or easy-going, big eaters or thin as a rail. Now the test interpretation must account for Type A personalities and anorexics.

"We have included a number of items that reflect the driven, compulsive, schedule-bound, aggressive and competitive style of the Type A," said James N. Butcher, a professor of psychology at the University of Minnesota, and another member of the group that rewrote the test. "We now have certain questions dealing with eating disorders too."

20,000 TEST NEW VERSION

More than 20,000 people randomly selected from phone books and carefully balanced by region, race and sex tested the new version of the MMPI. Different groups of items assess paranoid behavior, hypochondria, anxiety, depression, low self-esteem, anger, cynicism and many other behavioral patterns.

There are a variety of trick questions in the test so that psychologists can evaluate whether people are trying to lie about themselves.

MMPI started out in a medical and psychiatric setting but it quickly spread. Applicants for few high-tension jobs in the United States these days can get by without taking the test. Flight controllers, nuclear power plant operators, airline pilots and officials at such top-secret federal agencies as the National Security Agency all must take it.

"Its [sic] been translated into more than 100 languages," Butcher said. "You could argue that no test has been applied more widely. It needed some improvements. But it has really stood the test of time."

. . . .

 Case

POOR ATTITUDE MAJOR CAUSE OF JOB FRUSTRATION

The following case briefly describes some results of an attitude study done among some midwestern workers. Here are some questions to think about as you go through the case:

1. Do the results of this study seem similar to your present or a past work situation?
2. What role does the difference between expectations and reality play in successful adjustment to a new job?
3. Evaluate Professor Beehr's advice at the end of the case? Do you think people should do as he suggests to avoid unnecessary disappointments?

Poor attitudes, not poor working conditions, are the reasons many frustrated employees consider a job change, a Central Michigan University researcher reports.

The findings stem from a two-year study of workers at five Michigan companies, said Terry Beehr, a psychology professor at the university. [The study was funded by the U.S. Department of Labor.]

Small changes in the workplace probably won't satisfy employees who carry their old restlessness to a new job, Beehr said.

"People who see one job as stressful are prone to seeing all jobs as stressful," he said. "Even when jobs are substantially different, people tend to hold the same kinds of attitudes about them. Some people are more prone to complaining than others and will complain regardless of objective reality." . . .

Most workers experienced an initial satisfaction with their new jobs, but in many cases, the happiness quickly faded, Beehr said.

"By the time we did our follow-up interviews about a year and a half later, the honeymoon was over," he said. "Their encounter with reality drives down those heightened expectations, and the emptiness of unmet expectations takes over. People begin to feel negative about their new jobs."

Those who remained happy with their job changes had taken new positions with tangible benefits such as a higher salary or a better chance for promotion, he said.

The study suggests that disgruntled workers should examine their reasons for leaving before they resign and avoid unrealistic expectations about new jobs, Beehr said.

"I would caution them to make sure the job isn't any worse in any way, including non-work factors such as location," he said.

"If every factor looks at least as good as your current job, go ahead."

Source: Excerpted from "Poor Attitude Major Cause of Job Frustration," Associated Press, 1989. (As the story appeared in *Business Outlook, Albuquerque Journal,* January 9, 1989, p. 7.) Reprinted with the permission of the Associated Press.

[1]W. N. Dember, *Psychology of Perception* (New York: Holt, Rinehart & Winston), 1960.

[2]Ibid., pp. 145–46.

[3]J. B. Davidoff, *Differences in Visual Perception: The Individual Eye* (London: Crosby Lockwood Stapes, 1975), pp. 167–77.

[4]W. G. Stephan, V. Ageyev, C. W. Stephan, M. Abalakina, T. Stefanenko, and L. Coates-Shrider, "Measuring Stereotypes: A Comparison of Methods Using Russian and American Samples," *Social Psychology Quarterly* 56 (1993): 54–64.

[5]D. J. Bem, "Self-Perception: An Alternative Interpretation of Cognitive Dissonance Phenomena," *Psychological Review* 74 (1967): 183–200; D. J. Bem, "Self-Perception Theory," in L. Berkowitz, ed., *Advances in Experimental Social Psychology*, vol. 6 (New York: Academic Press, 1972).

[6]L. Festinger, "A Theory of Social Comparison Processes," *Human Relations* 7 (1954): 117–40.

[7]D. C. Rubin, ed., *Autobiographical Memory* (New York: Cambridge University Press, 1986).

[8]A. G. Greenwald, "The Totalitarian Ego: Fabrication and Revision of Personal History," *American Psychologist* 35 (1980): 603–18.

[9]H. Marcus, "Self-Schemata and Processing Information about the Self," *Journal of Personality and Social Psychology* 35 (1977): 63–78.

[10]Y. M. Epstein, P. Suedfeld, and S. J. Silverstein, "The Experimental Contract: Subjects' Expectations of and Reactions to Some Behaviors of Experimenters," *American Psychologist* 28 (1973): 212–21; K. J. Gergen and M. M. Gergen, "Narrative and the Self as Relationship," in L. Berkowitz, ed., *Advances in Experimental Social Psychology*, vol. 21 (New York: Academic Press, 1988), pp. 17–56; H. Markus and P. Nurius, "Possible Selves," *American Psychologist* 41 (1986): 954–69; G. N. Sande, G. R. Goethals, and C. E. Radloff, "Perceiving One's Own Traits and Others': The Multifaceted Self," *Journal of Personality and Social Psychology* 54 (1988): 13–20.

[11]J. F. Kihlstrom and N. Cantor, "Mental Representations of the Self," in L. Berkowitz, ed., *Advances in Experimental Social Psychology*, vol. 17 (New York: Academic Press, 1984), pp. 1–47.

[12]S. Coopersmith, *The Antecedents of Self-Esteem* (San Francisco: Freeman, 1967).

[13]J. Brockner, "Low Self-Esteem and Behavioral Plasticity: Some Implications," in L. Wheeler and P. Shaver, eds., *Review of Personality and Social Psychology*, vol. 4 (Beverly Hills, Calif.: Sage, 1983), pp. 237–71.

[14]C. S. Carver and M. F. Cheer, "The Blind Men and the Elephant: Selective Examination of the Public-Private Literature Gives Rise to a Faulty Perception," *Journal of Personality* 55 (1987): 525–41; A. Fenigstein, "On the Nature of Public and Private Self-Consciousness," *Journal of Personality* 55 (1987): 543–53.

[15]G. W. Bridle, "Self-Serving Biases in the Attribution Process: A Re-examination of the Fact or Fiction Question," *Journal of Personality and Social Psychology* 35 (1978): 56–71; Greenwald, "Totalitarian Ego."

[16]C. R. Snyder and R. L. Higgins, "Excuses: Their Effective Role in the Negotiation of Reality," *Psychological Bulletin* 104 (1988): 23–35.

[17]S. E. Taylor and J. D. Brown, "Illusion and Well-Being: A Social Psychological Perspective on Mental Health," *Psychological Bulletin* 103 (1988): 193–210.

[18]R. F. Baumeister and S. J. Scher, "Self-Defeating Behavior Patterns among Normal Individuals: Review and Analysis of Common Self-Destructive Tendencies," *Psychological Bulletin* 104 (1988): 3–22.

[19]R. F. Baumeister, "A Self-Presentational View of Social Phenomena," *Psychological Bulletin* 91 (1982): 3–26; J. T. Tedeschi, ed., *Impression Management Theory and Social Psychological Research* (New York: Academic Press, 1981); P. E. Tetlock and S. R. Manstead, "Impression Management versus Intrapsychic Explanations in Social Psychology: A Useful Dichotomy?" *Psychological Review* 92 (1985): 59–77.

[20]W. B. Swan, Jr., "Quest for Accuracy in Person Perception: A Matter of Pragmatics" *Psychological Review* 91 (1984): 457–77; W. B. Swan, Jr., "Identity Negotiation: Where Two Roads Meet," *Journal of Personality and Social Psychology* 53 (1987): 1038–51.

[21]M. Snider, *Public Appearances Private/Realities: The Psychology of Self-Monitoring* (New York: Academic Press, 1987).

[22]Developed from S. S. Brehm, and S. M. Kassin, *Social Psychology* (Boston: Houghton Mifflin, 1990), Ch. 3; S. T. Fiske, "Social Cognition and Social Perception," in L. W. Porter and M. R. Rosenzweig, eds., *Annual Review of Psychology* 44 (1994): 115–94 and other sources cited in this section.

[23]L. Laborite, D. A. Kenya, and T. E. Mallow, "Consensus in Personality Judgments at Zero Acquaintance," *Journal of Personality and Social Psychology* 55 (1988): 387–95; C. P. Herman, M. P. Zanna, and E. T. Higgins, *Physical Appearance, Stigma, and Social Behavior: The Ontario Symposium*, vol. 3 (Hillsdale, N.J.: Erlbaum, 1986).

[24]P. Ekman, W. V. Friesen, and P. Ellsworth, *Emotion in the Human Face* (Elmsford, N.Y.: Pergamon Press, 1972); P. Ekman, W. V. Friesen, M. O'Sullivan, A. Chan, I. Diacoyanni-Tarlatzis, K. Heider, R. Krause, W. A. LeCompte, T. Pitcairn, P. Ricci-Bitti, K. Scherer, M. Tomita, and A. Tzavaras, "Universals and Cultural Differences in the Judgments of Facial Expressions and Emotion," *Journal of Personality and Social Psychology* 53 (1987): 712–17.

[25]F. Heider, *The Psychology of Interpersonal Relations* (New York: Wiley, 1958).

[26]D. T. Gilbert, "Thinking Lightly about Others: Automatic Components of the Social Inference Process," in J. S. Uleman and J. A. Bargh, eds., *Unintended Thought: Limits of Awareness, Intention, and Control* (New York: Guilford, 1989), pp. 189–211.

[27]Heider, *Psychology*; H. H. Kelley, "Attribution Theory in Social Psychology," in D. Levine, ed., *Nebraska Symposium on Motivation* (Lincoln: University of Nebraska Press, 1967).

[28]Kelley, "Attribution Theory"; H. H. Kelley, "The Processes of Causal Attribution," *American Psychologist* 28 (1973): 107–28.

[29]L. Ross, "The Intuitive Psychologist and His Shortcomings: Distortions in the Attribution Process," in L. Berkowitz, ed., *Advances in Experimental Social Psychology*, vol. 10 (New York: Academic Press, 1977).

[30]D. Watson, "The Actor and the Observer: How Are Their Perceptions of Causality Divergent?" *Psychological Bulletin* 92 (1982): 682–700.

[31]B. Mullen, J. L. Atkins, D. S. Champion, C. Edwards, D. Hardy, J. E. Story, and M. Vanderklok, "The False Consensus Effect: A Meta-Analysis of 115 Hypothesis Tests," *Journal of Experimental Social Psychology* 21 (1985): 262–83; L. Ross, D. Greene, and P. House, "The False Consensus Phenomenon: An Attributional Bias in Self-Perception and Social-Perception Processes," *Journal of Experimental Social Psychology* 13 (1977): 279–301.

[32]E. T. Higgins, G. A. King, and G. H. Mavin, "Individual Construct Accessibility and Subjective Impressions and Recall," *Journal of Personality and Social Psychology* 43 (1982): 35–47; D. O. Sears, "The Person-Positivity Bias," *Journal of Personality and Social Psychology* 44 (1983): 233–50.

[33]C. A. Erdley, and P. R. D'Agostino, "Cognitive and Affective Components of Automatic Priming Effects," *Journal of Personality and Social Psychology* 54 (1988): 741–47.

[34]J. P. Forgas and G. H. Bower, "Mood Effects on Person-Perception Judgments," *Journal of Personality and Social Psychology* 53 (1987): 53–60.

[35]D. J. Schneider, "Implicit Personality Theory: A Review," *Psychological Bulletin* 79 (1973): 294–309.

[36]S. Asch, "Forming Impressions of Persons," *Journal of Abnormal and Social Psychology* 40 (1946): 258–90.

[37] J. J. Skowronski and D. E. Carlston, "Negativity and Extremity Biases in Impression Formation: A Review of Explanations," *Psychological Bulletin* 105 (1989): 131–42.

[38] Brehm and Kassin *Social Psychology*, pp. 129–30; M. Snider, "When Beliefs Create Reality," in L. Berkowitz, ed., *Advances in Experimental Social Psychology*, vol. 18 (New York: Academic Press, 1984), pp. 247–305.

[39] Brehm and Kassin, *Social Psychology*, pp. 131–33.

[40] R. Merton, "The Self-Fulfilling Prophecy," *Antioch Review* 8 (1948): 193–210; L. Jussim, "Self-Fulfilling Prophecies: A Theoretical and Integrative View," *Psychological Review* 93 (1986): 429–45; D. T. Miller and W. Turnbull, "Expectancies and Inter-Personal Processes," *Annual Review of Psychology* 37 (1985): 233–56.

[41] W. M. Bulkeley, "Two Computer Firms with Clashing Styles Fight for Market Niche," *Wall Street Journal*, July 6, 1987, pp. 1, 14.

[42] W. J. McGuire, "Attitudes and Attitude Change," in G. Lindzey and E. Aronson, eds., *Handbook of Social Psychology*, vol. 2 (New York: Random House, 1985), pp. 238–40.

[43] M. Fishbein and I. Ajzen, *Belief, Attitude, Intention and Behavior: An Introduction to Theory and Research* (Reading, Mass.: Addison-Wesley, 1975), p. 6. Emphasis added.

[44] Ibid., pp. 6–11.

[45] S. J. Breckler, "Empirical Validation of Affect, Behavior, and Cognition as Distinct Components of Attitude," *Journal of Personality and Social Psychology* 47 (1984): 1191–1205; McGuire, "Attitudes," p. 242; J. J. Rosenberg and C. I. Hovland, "Cognitive, Affective, and Behavioral Components of Attitudes," in C. I. Hovland and M. J. Rosenberg, eds., *Attitude Organization and Change* (New Haven, Conn.: Yale University Press, 1960), pp. 1–14.

[46] Usually described by the more obscure term "conative." McGuire, "Attitudes," p. 242.

[47] McGuire, "Attitudes," p. 242.

[48] Fishbein and Ajzen, "Belief, Attitude, Intention and Behavior, Chs. 5 and 6.

[49] C. I. Hovland, I. L. Janis, and H. H. Kelly, *Communication and Persuasion* (New Haven: Yale University Press, 1953); P. G. Zimbardo, E. B. Ebbesen, and C. Maslach, *Influencing Attitudes and Changing Behavior* (Reading, Mass.: Addison-Wesley, 1977).

[50] K. Lewin, "Group Decision and Social Change," In T. Newcomb and E. Hartley, eds., *Readings in Social Psychology* (New York: Holt, 1947).

[51] L. Festinger, *A Theory of Cognitive Dissonance* (Palo Alto, Calif.: Stanford University Press, 1957).

[52] R. T. Mowday, L. W. Porter, and R. M. Steers, *Employee-Organization Linkages: The Psychology of Commitment, Absenteeism, and Turnover* (New York: Academic Press, 1982).

[53] Ibid., Ch. 2.

[54] J. R. Hackman and G. R. Oldham, *Work Redesign* (Reading, Mass.: Addison-Wesley, 1980), p. 105.

[55] McGuire, "Attitudes," pp. 252–53.

[56] A. R. Davidson, S. Yantis, M. Norwood, and D. E. Montano, "Amount of Information about the Attitude Object and Attitude-Behavior Consistency," *Journal of Personality and Social Psychology* 49 (1985): 1184–98.

[57] Brehm and Kassin, *Social Psychology*, p. 444.

[58] R. H. Fazio, "How Do Attitudes Guide Behavior?" in R. M. Sorrentino and E. T. Higgins, eds., *The Handbook of Motivation and Cognition* (New York: Guilford Press, 1986).

[59] Developed from I. Ajzen and M. Fishbein, *Understanding Attitudes and Predicting Social Behavior* (Englewood Cliffs, N.J.: Prentice-Hall, 1980), Ch. 1; Fishbein and Ajzen, *Belief, Attitude, Intention and Behavior*.

[60] G. W. Allport, *Personality: A Psychological Interpretation* (New York: Henry Holt, 1937), pp. 24–25.

[61] R. R. McCrae and P. T. Costa, Jr., "The Stability of Personality: Observations and Evaluations," *Current Directions in Psychological Science* 3 (1994): 173–75.

[62] M. Snider and W. Ickes, "Personality and Social Behavior," in G. Lindzey and E. Aronson, eds., *Handbook of Social Psychology*, vol. 2 (New York: Random House, 1985), p. 883.

[63] D. T. Kenrick, D. R. Montello, and S. MacFarlane, "Personality: Social Learning, Social Cognition, or Sociobiology?" in R. Hogan and W. H. Jones, eds., *Perspectives in Personality: A Research Annual*, vol. 1 (Greenwich, Conn.: JAI Press, 1985), pp. 215–19; J. Piaget, *The Origins of Intelligence in Children* (New York: International Universities Press, 1952); J. Piaget, *The Construction of Reality in the Child* (New York: Basic Books, 1954); J. Piaget, "The Role of Action in the Development of Thinking," in W. F. Overton and J. M. Gallagher, eds., *Knowledge and Development*, vol. 1 (New York: Plenum Press, 1977).

[64] Detailed description of the stages is beyond the purpose of this chapter. See D. R. Shaffer, *Social and Personality Development* (Pacific Grove, Calif.: Brooks/Cole, 1988), Ch. 4 for a readable description of the stages.

[65] J. Piaget, "Piaget's Theory," in P. H. Mussen, ed., *Carmichael's Manual of Child Psychology*, vol. 1 (New York: Wiley, 1970).

[66] Developed from Kenrick, Montello, and MacFarlane, "Personality: Social Learning, Social Cognition, or Sociobiology?" pp. 211–15; Shaffer, *Social and Personality Development*, Ch. 3 and other sources cited in this section.

[67] J. B. Watson, "Psychology as the Behaviorist Views It," *Psychological Review* 20 (1913): 158–77; J. B. Watson, *Psychological Care of the Infant and Child* (New York: Norton, 1928).

[68] J. Dollard and N. E. Miller, *Personality and Psychotherapy: An Analysis in Terms of Learning, Thinking, and Culture* (New York: McGraw-Hill, 1950).

[69] Ibid.

[70] B. F. Skinner, *Science and Human Behavior* (New York: Free Press, 1953); B. F. Skinner, *Beyond Freedom and Dignity* (New York: Bantam, 1971).

[71] Chapter 8 of this book has a more detailed explanation of Skinner's theory as it applies to motivation.

[72] A. Bandura, *Social Learning Theory* (Englewood Cliffs, N.J.: Prentice-Hall, 1977).

[73] *Billboard*, March 17, 1990.

[74] P. Overstreet and T. Dunn, *Seein' My Father In Me* (Scarlet Moon Music, 1989).

[75] Developed from Kenrick, Montello, and MacFarlane, "Personality: Social Learning, Social Cognition, or Sociobiology?" pp. 211–15; Shaffer, *Social and Personality Development*, 38–51 and other sources cited throughout this section.

[76] T. J. Bouchard, Jr., D. T. Lykken, M. McGue, N. L. Segal, and A. Tellegen, "Sources of Human Psychological Differences: The Minnesota Study of Twins Reared Apart," *Science* 250 (1990): 223–28.

[77] N. B. Jones, "Characteristics of Ethological Studies of Human Behavior," in N. B. Jones, ed., *Ethological Studies of Child Behavior* (London: Cambridge University Press, 1972), pp. 3–33; R. B. Cairns, *Social Development: The Origins of Plasticity of Interchanges* (New York: W. H. Freeman, 1979).

[78] L. A. Sroufe, N. E. Fox, and V. R. Pancake, "Attachment and Dependency in Developmental Perspective," *Child Development* 54 (1983): 1615–27.

[79] S. Scarr and K. McCartney, "How People Make Their Own Environments: A Theory of Genotype/Environment Effects," *Child Development* 54 (1983): 424–35.

[80] Kenrick, Montello, and MacFarlane, "Personality: Social Learning, Social Cognition, or Sociobiology?" pp. 209–11.

[81] J. M. Digman, "Personality Structure: Emergence of the Five-Factor Model." in M. R. Rosenzweig and L. W. Porter, eds., *Annual Review of Psychology* 41 (1990): 417–40; L. R. Goldberg, "The Structure of Phenotypic Personality Traits," *American Psychologist*, 48 (1993): 26–34; R. R. McCrae, "Why I Advocate the Five-Factor Model: Joint Factor Analyses of the NEO-PI with Other Instruments," in D. M. Buss and N. Cantor, eds., *Personality Psychology: Recent Trends and*

Emerging Directions (New York: Springer-Verlag, 1989), pp. 237–45; J. S. Wiggins, and A. L. Pincus, "Personality: Structure and Assessment," in M. R. Rosenzweig and L. W. Porter, eds., *Annual Review of Psychology* 43 (1992): 473–504.

[82]N. G. Waller and Y. S. Ben-Porath, "Is It Time for Clinical Psychology to Embrace the Five-Factor Model of Personality?" *American Psychologist* 42 (1987): 887–89.

[83]M. R. Barrick and M. K. Mount, "The Big Five Personality Dimensions and Job Performance: A Meta-Analysis," *Personnel Psychology* 44 (1991): 1–26; Digman, "Personality Structures"; M. K. Mount, M. R. Barrick, and J. P. Strauss, "Validity of Observer Ratings of the Big Five Personality Factors," *Journal of Applied Psychology* 72 (1994): 272–80.

[84]J. B. Rotter, "Generalized Expectancies for Internal and External Control of Reinforcement," *Psychological Monographs* 80 (1966): 1–28; J. B. Rotter, "External and Internal Control," *Psychology Today* (1971).

[85]R. Christie and F. L. Geis, *Studies in Machiavellianism* (New York: Academic Press, 1970); S. S. Guterman, *The Machiavellians: A Social Psychological Study of Moral Character and Organizational Milieu* (Lincoln: University of Nebraska Press, 1970).

[86]M. Friedman, and R. Rosenman, *Type A Behavior and Your Heart* (New York: Alfred A. Knopf, 1974); M. Friedman and D. Ulmer, *Treating Type A Behavior—and Your Heart* (New York: Alfred A. Knopf, 1984).

[87]S. Booth-Kewley and H. S. Friedman, "Psychological Predictors of Heart Disease: A Quantitative Review," *Psychological Bulletin* 101 (1987): 343–62; H. S. Friedman and S. Booth-Kewley, "Validity of the Type A Construct: A Reprise," *Psychological Bulletin* 104 (1988): 381–84; K. A. Mathews, "Coronary Heart Disease and Type A Behaviors: Update on and Alternative to the Booth-Kewley and Friedman (1987) Quantitative Review," *Psychological Bulletin* 104 (1988): 373–80.

[88]K. A. Mathews, "Psychological Perspectives on the Type A Behavior Pattern," *Psychological Bulletin* 91 (1982): 292–323; K. A. Mathews, R. L. Helmreich, W. E. Beanne, and G. W. Lucker, "Pattern A, Achievement-Striving, and Scientific Merit: Does Pattern A Help or Hinder?" *Journal of Personality & Social Psychology* 39 (1980): 962–67.

[89]C. G. Jung, *Psychological Types* (London: Routledge & Kegan Paul, 1923); C. G. Jung, *Psychological Types or the Psychology of Individuation*, trans. by H. Godwin Baynes. (London: Kegan Paul, Trench, Trubner & Co., 1933).

[90]Digman, "Personality Structure."

[91]Barrick and Mount, "Big Five Personality Dimensions."

[92]P. E. Spector, "Behavior in Organizations as a Function of Employee Locus of Control," *Psychological Bulletin* 91 (1982): 482–97.

[93]Christie and Geis, *Studies in Machiavellianism*, Ch. 17.

[94]Friedman and Rosenman, *Type A Behavior*; Friedman and *Treating Type A Behavior.*

[95]Mathews, "Psychological Perspectives on the Type A Beh tern"; Mathews, Helmreich, Beanne, and Lucker, "P Achievement-Striving, and Scientific Merit."

[96]Developed from N. J. Adler, *International Dimensions of C tional Behavior* (Boston: Kent, 1991), Ch. 3.

[97]P. Burger and B. M. Bass, *Assessment of Managers: An Intern. Comparison* (New York: Free Press, 1979).

[98]A. Laurent, "The Cultural Diversity of Western Conceptions Management," *International Studies of Management and Organizatio* 13 (1983): 75–96.

[99]G. Hofstede, *Culture's Consequences: International Differences in Work-Related Values* (Beverly Hills, Calif.: Sage Publications, 1984), Ch. 3; G. Hofstede, *Cultures and Organizations: Software of the Mind* (New York: McGraw-Hill, 1991).

[100]Adler, *International Dimensions*, Ch. 2.

[101]Hofstede, *Culture's Consequences*, Ch. 4; G. Hofstede, "Cultural Constraints in Management Theories," *Academy of Management Executive* 7 (1993): 81–94.

[102]S. L. Payne, and R. A. Giacolone, "Social Psychological Approaches to the Perception of Ethical Dilemmas," *Human Relations* 43 (1990): 649–65.

[103]Ibid., pp. 655–58.

[104]K. A. Meehan, S. B. Woll, and R. D. Abbott, "The Role of Dissimulation and Social Desirability in the Measurement of Moral Reasoning," *Journal of Research in Personality* 13 (1979): 25–38.

[105]Payne, and Giacolone, "Social Psychological Approaches," pp. 653–54.

[106]D. M. Randall and A. M. Gibson, "Methodology in Business Ethics Research: A Review and Critical Assessment," *Journal of Business Ethics* 9 (1990): 457–71.

[107]R. Jackall, *Moral Mazes: The World of Corporate Managers* (New York: Oxford University Press, 1988), Ch. 5.

[108]J. M. Feldman, "Beyond Attribution Theory: Cognitive Processes in Performance Appraisal," *Journal of Applied Psychology* 66 (1981): 127–48.

[109]B. J. Calder, "An Attribution Theory of Leadership," in B. M. Staw and G. R. Salancik, eds., *New Directions in Organizational Behavior* (Chicago: St. Clair Press, 1977), pp. 179–204.

[110]W. J. Holstein, "The Stateless Corporation: Forget Multinationals—Today's Giants Are Really Leaping Boundaries," *Business Week*, May 14, 1990, pp. 98–105.

5

Organizational Culture

· *A view of The Grand Palace, Bangkok, Thailand. The cultural differences among organizations are similar to the cultural differences among countries.*

After reading this chapter, you should be able to . . .

· Discuss the concept of organizational culture.
· Distinguish among the dimensions of organizational culture.
· Describe the different levels at which we experience an organization's culture.
· Recognize the role of symbols in defining an organization's culture.
· Discuss the functions and dysfunctions of organizational culture.
· Do a diagnosis of an organization's culture.
· Explain the issues involved in creating, maintaining, and changing organizational culture.

Chapter Overview

. . . .

OPENING EPISODE

· *A launch crew prepares a U.S.
Navy fighter jet for launch from an
aircraft carrier. Hand signals and
different-colored uniforms are key
cultural symbols on the deck of an
aircraft carrier.*

Top Gun

When actor Tom Cruise leaped from the cockpit of a Navy jet fighter to the arms of
actress Kelly McGillis in the movie "Top Gun," he made more than a box office hit.
He made a lot of high school students dream of military life, and [in 1987] the
country's three big military academies . . . [cashed in].

Applications . . . [were] up more than 10 percent at the Naval Academy, and at
West Point in New York and the Air Force Academy in Colorado Springs. The Coast
Guard Academy in Connecticut report[ed] no noticeable increase, though it is
smaller than the three other academies, which each admit almost 1,400 new students
a year.

Even at the Army's West Point, admissions officials say cultural phenomena like
"Top Gun" and the popular submarine novel "The Hunt for Red October" combined
with a general patriotic resurgence [at the time] to inspire the nation's college-bound
young to think of the military. . . .

Around the country, members of Congress who nominate 10 candidates per slot
and high school counselors who help students apply say they have seen noticeable
increases in the number of students wanting four years of disciplined schooling
followed by at least five years of military service. . . .

The movie "Top Gun" depicts life in a Navy jet fighter school, and the novel "The
Hunt for Red October" by Tom Clancy describes the adventures of submariners.
Some applicants have cited these in their applications, . . . [said Capt. Harry Seymour,
Jr., the Naval Academy admissions director]. And while it is impossible to measure
their effect, he is convinced they helped increase applications.

"It doesn't hurt to have neat movies like 'Top Gun,' " agreed Capt. Steve LaRue at
West Point. "I think everyone enjoyed the spill-off from that: It's all military. It's not
just the Air Force and the Navy. People forget that the Army has the largest air force
in the world, in terms of helicopters." . . .

"I think a lot of it is a runoff from 'Top Gun,' " said William Dickson, 17, a Fairfax
high school student who has applied to the Air Force Academy. "I'd already applied
to the Air Force Academy about three months before I saw it, but it was kind of
inspirational. First of all, it showed you the rough competition you're going
against—it gave you a goal to try to strive for. And it gave you a picture, more or less,
of what it's going to be like."

Scott Bunney of Castro Valley in California said he applied to the Naval Academy
largely because he wants to fly. "Top Gun" and "The Hunt for Red October" did not
persuade him to apply, he said, but they affected him. "When you think about sitting
behind a desk versus flying a plane or being on a submarine, it's not boring at all. It
makes it exciting."

"The academy is devoid of today's trivia," one applicant wrote to the academy.
"The academy experience leads somewhere. The men and women there are accom-

Source: Excerpted from T. Vesey, "Naval Academy Cruises to Popular Heights. 'Top Gun,' 'Red October'
and Patriotism Boost Military Schools," *Washington Post*, January 19, 1987, pp. B1, B6. ©1987 The
Washington Post. Reprinted with permission.

plishing something—venturing along the edge where the risks are greater, but where the rewards are greater still. Out there, along that edge, I'd like to join them." . . .

"These kids are for real," Seymour said. "Older people can find it hard to understand that this kind of generation is unfolding in front of our eyes."

T he movie *Top Gun* portrays the life of a high-performance naval aviator in training at the Navy's Top Gun flight school. The film showed the culture that developed among those who attend the school. The people who saw the film developed impressions of life as a naval aviator. Those impressions may have affected the career plans of many people.

Organizational culture is a complex and deep aspect of organizations that can strongly affect organization members.[1] Organizational culture includes the values, norms, rites, rituals, ceremonies, heroes, and scoundrels in the history of the organization.[2] It defines the content of what a new employee needs to learn to be accepted as a member of the organization.

Key aspects of organizational culture include a sharing of values and a structuring of experiences in an organization. Different sets of values can coexist among different groups of people throughout an organization. Although values differ from group to group, members of each group can share a set of values. Also, not all people in an organization will fully agree about which values and norms are dominant. Complex organizations usually have enough ambiguity to prevent their members from fully agreeing about which values are salient.[3]

If you have traveled abroad, you have already experienced what it is like to enter a new, different, and "foreign" culture. The architecture you saw was different from that at home. The food was not what you commonly ate. The language may have been different, possibly causing you some difficulty in communication. People in the new culture behaved differently toward each other than you were accustomed to behaving. You probably felt some anxiety about learning your way around the new culture so you would not stand out as a "foreigner." Organizational cultures are similar to cultures of different countries. Your entry into a new organizational culture will have many features of entering the culture of another country.

This chapter uses the following as its definition of organizational culture:

> Any organizational culture consists broadly of long-standing rules of thumb, a somewhat special language, an ideology that helps edit a member's everyday experience, shared standards of relevance as to the critical aspects of the work that is being accomplished, matter-of-fact prejudices, models for social etiquette and demeanor, certain customs and rituals suggestive of how members are to relate to colleagues, subordinates, superiors, and outsiders, and . . . some rather plain "horse sense" regarding what is appropriate and "smart" behavior within the organization and what is not.[4]

All human systems that have endured for some time, and whose members have a shared history, develop a culture. The specific content of an organization's culture develops from the experiences of a group adapting to its external environment and building a system of internal coordination.[5] Each of the different human systems within which you interact has a culture. Your family, your college or university, your employer, and any leisure time organizations such as sororities, fraternities, or cultural organizations all have their own cultures. These cultures can make different—and sometimes conflicting—demands on you.

Each organizational culture divides into multiple **subcultures**. An organization's design creates varying substructures and processes within an organization. Subcultures grow readily within these differentiated parts of the total organization.[6] They also grow readily within departments, divisions, and different operating locations of an organization.

Different occupational groups within an organization often form different subcultures. Specialists in finance, accounting, information systems, and manufacturing often have their own jargon that helps them talk to each other. That jargon becomes an integral part of an occupational subculture and often cannot be understood by those outside the subculture. An information systems specialist easily understands terms like *upload*, *download*, and *token ring networks*, which often are a foreign language to people outside that occupation.

Work force diversity and the global environment of organizations, discussed in Chapter 2, also help build subcultures in organizations. People who come from different social backgrounds and have different values will infuse organizations with a variety of values and points of view.[7] Global operations will require organizations to hire people from the host country. Those employees often will bring values into the organization that differ from those of the organization's home country.

⤶ Dimensions of Organizational Culture

Figure 5-1 shows seven **dimensions of organizational culture.** Each dimension suggests different ways to understand a culture.[8]

The levels dimension describes organizational culture as having different degrees of visibility. The physical qualities of an organizational culture such as logos and other symbols are easy to see. Core values are the least visible.

The pervasiveness dimension views culture as widely dispersed in an organization. Culture affects people, their beliefs, their relationships in and outside the organization, their views of the organization's product or service, their views of competitors, and much more. The list is almost endless and differs from one organizational culture to another.

The implicitness dimension refers to how veteran employees often take the core values of the organization's culture for granted. These employees behave according to certain core values without consciously thinking about them. Those values also are hard for a newcomer to discover because veteran employees assume everyone knows them.

The imprinting dimension suggests organizational cultures often have deep roots in the history of the organization. This dimension applies to well-established cultures with an identifiable history. It also suggests the strong effects organizational cultures can have on their members. Cultures can imprint their values and beliefs on the members of the culture so strongly that people find it hard to shift to new values and beliefs.

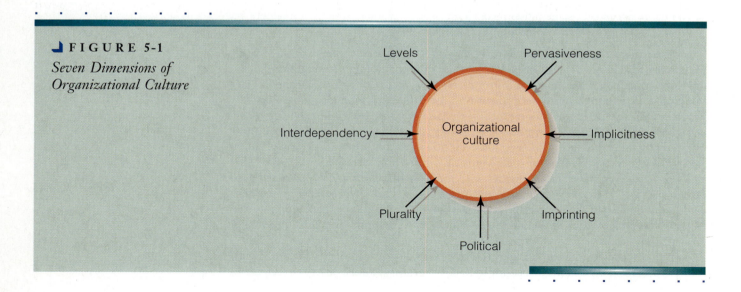

⤶ **FIGURE 5-1**

Seven Dimensions of Organizational Culture

Levels   Pervasiveness

Interdependency → Organizational culture ← Implicitness

Plurality   Political   Imprinting

The political dimension sees culture as connected to systems of power in an organization. Coalitions, cliques, cabals, and alliances can have vested interests in the values that play key roles at different points in the organization's history. Their attachment to those values can make these groups either major sources of resistance to culture change or key resources in bringing culture change.

The plurality dimension emphasizes the existence of subcultures in most organizational cultures. Subcultures can develop vested interests over issues and beliefs. Power struggles in organizations often erupt over such vested interests, especially when managers try to change an organization's culture.

The interdependency dimension suggests the interconnections within an organization's culture and the ways cultures relate to other parts of an organization. Complex connections can exist between subcultures, beliefs, and symbols. The culture may also form connections to other organization systems. For example, the values of an organization's culture often affect the development of the organization's reward system. Some cultures value associating rewards with performance; other cultures do not. Cultures also are interdependent with the external environment of the organization. Employees often behave toward customers and clients according to valued beliefs. Such behavior obviously can affect an important part of an organization's environment.

This chapter discusses most dimensions of culture in detail beginning with levels. The political dimension of culture is so potent in many organizations that an entire chapter is devoted to it (Chapter 15).

Levels of Organizational Culture

Organizational cultures are revealed to us at three different but related levels: artifacts, values, and basic assumptions. These levels vary in their visibility to an outsider, with the first being the easiest to see and the last the most difficult. Figure 5-2 shows the three **levels of organizational culture** and their visibility to an outsider.[9]

Artifacts are the most visible parts of an organization's culture. They are the obvious features of an organization that are immediately visible to a new employee. Artifacts include sounds, architecture, smells, behavior, attire, language, products, and ceremonies.

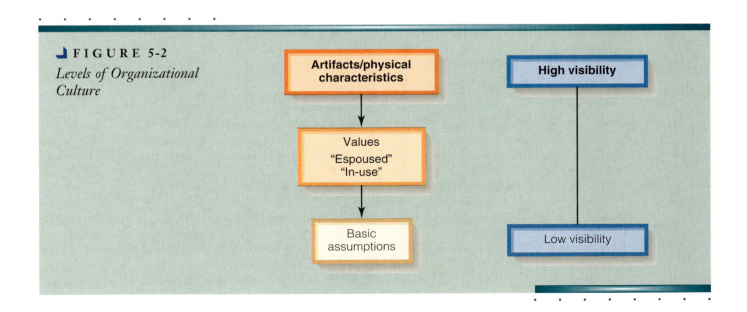

FIGURE 5-2
Levels of Organizational Culture

Artifacts/physical characteristics → Values "Espoused" "In-use" → Basic assumptions

High visibility — Low visibility

Organizations differ in the layout of their interior space and the formality of their working relationships. Do people work in an open office space or behind closed doors? Do people dress formally or informally? Does the interior design give the impression of a cheerful or a somber work environment? Do people refer to each other by first names or do they use formal titles such as Doctor, Mr., Ms., Lieutenant? All these factors are clues to an organization's culture. You can infer some values, norms, and required behavior from such factors. A new employee must first attend to messages from the physical characteristics of the organization and then watch the behavior of veteran organization members.

At the next level of awareness are the values embedded in the culture. **Values** tell organization members what they "ought" to do in various situations. Values are hard for the newcomer to see, but he can discover and learn them. The newcomer must be wary of **"espoused values"** that guide what veteran members say in a given situation. More important are the **"in-use values"** that really guide the behavior of organization members.[10] For example, a new employee learns from talking to superiors that equal opportunity for women and men in promotions is the organization's policy. The person then finds that only men were promoted to management positions in the last five years.

The last level of discovery is almost invisible to a new employee. Even veteran organization members are not consciously aware of the **basic assumptions** of the organization's culture. Like values, these assumptions guide behavior in organizations. As a culture matures, many values become basic assumptions. Basic assumptions deal with many aspects of human behavior, human relationships within the organization, and relationships with elements in the organization's external environment. These assumptions develop over the history of the organization from its ways of dealing with various events.

Veteran members of the organization may not be aware of their basic assumptions until those assumptions are called into question. For example, managers of many American companies may believe that Korean companies cannot produce goods of acceptable quality for American markets. They are rapidly learning that this assumption is not true. The success of Korean companies in electronics and automobiles is causing some American organizations to question their basic assumptions.[11]

Because the assumptions are unconscious, veteran members find it hard to describe them to a new employee. People learn about them from trial-and-error behavior and by watching how veteran employees behave in different situations.

. . . .

⤵ Perspectives on Organizational Culture

The introduction to this chapter suggested there are three perspectives on organizational culture (see page 103). One perspective says organizational cultures consist of shared values and basic assumptions among organization members. A second perspective says subcultures form within an organization's culture. A third perspective implies that ambiguity in organizations prevents pervasive agreement on values and basic assumptions. Figure 5-3 shows all three perspectives. Each perspective lets you see an organization's culture from a different viewpoint, suggesting what you should look for when examining a culture. You will get a fuller understanding of an organization's culture if you use the perspectives together.[12]

The **integration perspective** emphasizes the consensus among people about values and basic assumptions, consistent actions in accord with those values, and the absence of ambiguity. The consensus in values and basic assumptions is the organization's culture. Consistency will appear in the culture's artifacts and the actions of its members. For example, if an organization's values stress the equal status of all employees, then there will be a single employee cafeteria and no designated parking.

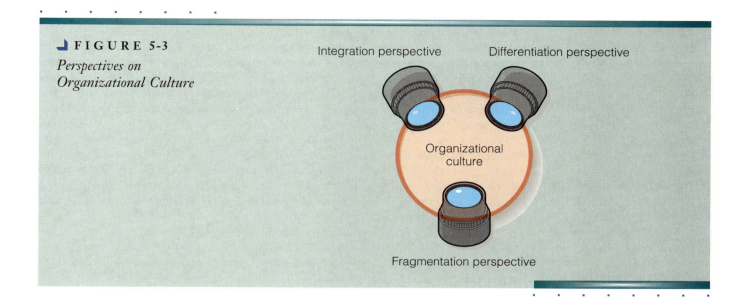

FIGURE 5-3

*Perspectives on
Organizational Culture*

Integration perspective   Differentiation perspective

Organizational
culture

Fragmentation perspective

Culture, for the integration perspective, brings unity, predictability, and clarity to work experiences.

The **differentiation perspective** shows subcultures dispersed throughout an organization's culture. Though these subcultures can have an internal consensus about values and basic assumptions, they differ widely from each other. This perspective lets you uncover inconsistencies between values and artifacts. For example, an organization's management may say all employees are equal in status but have special perquisites for senior executives.

The **fragmentation perspective** focuses on the presence of ambiguity in organizations. It finds that multiple interpretations of values and artifacts are common, making any search for consistency futile. One must note and accept the basic ambiguity of modern organization life.[13]

Ambiguity arises from fast changes both within and outside organizations, the growing diversity of the workforce, and the increasingly global environment organizations must face. Some ambiguity comes from the fleeting quality of many interactions. People may communicate through direct computer interaction, for example, without ever having face-to-face contact. The different viewpoints among members of a diverse or international workforce impose multiple interpretations on the same events. Such differences will not let a consensus about an organization's values and basic assumptions emerge.

Cultural Symbolism

A separate perspective from those just described lets you view an organizational culture as a system of symbols that have meaning only to members of that culture. Some aspects of **cultural symbolism** may have meaning for a wide group of members while other aspects are significant for only a small number of employees. This view of organizational cultures looks at artifacts as described earlier, but also examines anything within the culture that has symbolic meaning to its members.[14]

Cultural symbols have several characteristics. They represent more than the symbol alone by capturing emotional, cognitive, ethical, and aesthetic meanings. Symbols efficiently summarize those meanings for organization members. They serve the important cultural function of bringing order to otherwise complex events and processes, especially those that are repeated.

Symbols can be action symbols, verbal symbols, and material symbols.[15] Action symbols are sets of behaviors that have meaning beyond the obvious aspects of the behavior. Verbal symbols are the stories, slogans, sagas, legends, and jargon that both distinguish people in a culture and carry special meanings for them. Material symbols are found in the physical features of an organization's culture, including architecture, interior decor, and types of clothing.

Symbols vary in complexity. They can be as simple as Xerox Corporation's slogan of "Leadership through Quality," a verbal symbol used in the 1980s to emphasize the company's program of continuous quality improvement and efforts to regain market share in copiers. Symbols can also be more complex such as regularly scheduled meetings where people decide matters but also define the organization's values and priorities in decision making.[16]

The three perspectives of organizational culture described earlier ask you to take differing views of cultural symbols.[17] The integration perspective says symbols and espoused values should be congruent. For example, an organization that says it accepts or values diversity should also provide vegetarian dishes in the company's cafeteria for its vegetarian employees. The differentiation perspective says you will find differences between espoused values and related symbols. An espoused value of equal status among employees may clash with the material symbols of larger offices for higher-status employees. That inconsistency gives you other information about the organization's culture—its lingering conflict between desires for equality and desires for status differences.[18]

The fragmentation perspective offers the most complex view of cultural symbols. It suggests that you examine the meanings of espoused values and cultural perspectives in terms of both what they say and what they do not say. An analysis of a verbal symbol such as a story would look for puns, metaphors, unstated assumptions, and what was not said along with what was said.[19]

As an example of how one gets different information by looking at symbols from different perspectives, consider the following story told publicly by a company president:[20]

> We have a young woman who is extraordinarily important to the launching of a major new (product). We will be talking about it next Tuesday in its first world-wide introduction. She has arranged to have her Caesarean yesterday in order to be prepared for this event, so you—We have insisted that she stay home and this is going to be televised in a closed circuit television, so we're having this done by TV for her, and she is staying home three months and we are finding ways of filling in.[21]

The company president felt he had described deep company feeling and caring for the pregnant woman. He viewed the commitment of the television resources as an important symbol of the company's commitment to its employees.[22] A differentiation analysis suggests other meanings. Perhaps the company was putting the product introduction ahead of the woman's and the baby's needs. The fragmentation perspective adds other meaning to the cultural symbolism of the story. Saying "We have a young woman" could imply strong company control, an implicit assumption of the president.[23]

. . . .

Functions of Organizational Culture

Organizational cultures do many functional things for organizations and management. The two major areas to which they contribute are (1) adaptation to the organization's external environment and (2) coordination of internal systems and processes. Figure 5-4 shows the **functions of organizational culture** and the areas of organization and management activity supported by an organization's culture.[24]

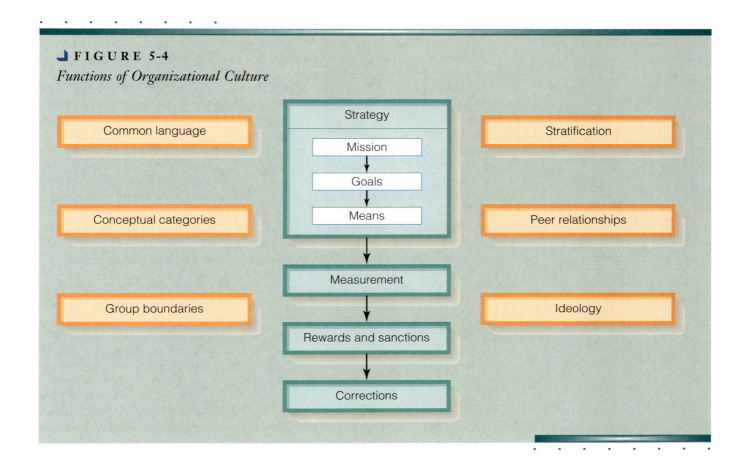

FIGURE 5-4
Functions of Organizational Culture

Common language

Strategy

Mission

Goals

Means

Stratification

Conceptual categories

Peer relationships

Measurement

Group boundaries

Ideology

Rewards and sanctions

Corrections

An organization that has adapted successfully to its external environment can develop a culture with a consensus among members about the organization's mission. Specific goals derived from the mission and the means to reach those goals will be part of the culture. A consensus about a mission among veteran members lets the organization move forward smoothly toward those goals. Members agree about what needs to be done and how it will be done. In short, an organization's culture can help its members develop a sense of identity with the organization and a clear vision of the organization's direction.[25]

An organizational culture that gives its members a clear vision of the organization's mission also presents a consistent image to its markets, customers, and clients.[26] Over time, that image can give an organization a competitive advantage by building commitment to its products or services.

Members of developed organizational cultures agree about how results will be measured and what remedial action will be taken if something goes wrong. Veteran members know almost automatically when things are not going right and how to take corrective action. If there were no consensus about those matters, conflict levels could be dysfunctionally high. With so much conflict among its members, the organization would have difficulty responding rapidly in situations requiring quick action.

Organizational cultures define the rewards and sanctions that managers can use. Rules develop about how good performance will be rewarded and about what sanctions will be levied for poor performance. Some cultures respond to poor performance by saying the individual is not properly matched to the task. Those organizations reassign the person to a new task and let him try again. Other cultures develop specific sanctions that include demotions and terminations.

Organizational cultures differ in the way they use reward systems.[27] Some reward systems emphasize total organization performance, leading to a feeling that members are part of a fraternal group. Other cultures reward individual performance, ignoring the larger system. Members of the latter cultures develop a strong sense of individuality and independence. Later chapters about human motivation discuss the role of reward systems in organizations in more detail.

Culture also helps integrate an organization's subsystems and processes. The integration lets the organization coordinate its various actions effectively. Common language develops within a culture, helping communication. Conceptual categories develop that filter unimportant detail and focus attention on important matters. Perceptual filtration reduces the likelihood that an individual will become overloaded by stimuli defined as unimportant by the culture.

The culture defines boundaries of groups and criteria for inclusion in the group. Well-defined group boundaries enhance member identification with the group and the group's work. Strong groups support and help members get their work done.

Organizational cultures define rules for power, rules for social stratification, and the ways social status is determined. Some accord social status and power to people of high achievement. Others base status and power on seniority.

The nature and quality of peer relationships and interpersonal interactions are defined by the organization's culture. Are interactions characterized by cooperation among peers at any cost or by confrontation and debate? Chapter 11 describes conflict management processes on which this function of culture focuses.

The last function of organizational culture is the development and communication of an ideology of what the organization is all about. An ideology is a set of overarching values that collect all the basic assumptions embedded in the organization's culture. The ideology appears in stories about past successes or descriptions of organization heroes.[28] The heroes may still be with the organization or may have left it long ago or passed on. In either case, what each hero represents stays in the ideology and becomes part of the organization's folklore. The ideology is a strong and sometimes overwhelming guide to action. As such, the ideology is an important element of an organization's culture that must be communicated to and discovered by the newcomer.

All the functions of organizational culture come together to serve an overarching function—reduction of anxiety and uncertainty in human relationships. Rules of conduct and ways of viewing the world outside and inside the organization let members distinguish important stimuli from unimportant. Ignoring some stimuli reduces the chance of overloading the human organism.

▟ Dysfunctions of Organizational Culture

The functional features of an organization's culture can also be dysfunctional. The last paragraph of the preceding section has the clues. Table 5-1 lists the **dysfunctions of organizational culture.**[29]

Changes in an organization's external environment often require changes in an organization's strategy. The existing organizational culture, though, has developed from a particular strategy, and members of the organization who are accustomed to that culture may resist changing the strategy. They may feel that such change will require changes in existing values and basic assumptions. When considering a change in strategy, managers must either dramatically change the existing culture or learn how to manage within its constraints.[30]

The existing organizational culture can lead to dysfunctional results when the organization tries product or market diversification, acquires a new company, or engages in a merger. Analyses of any of these changes ordinarily include financial, physical, and technical aspects of the proposed action, but rarely consider the culture of the target organization. A merger may result in merging incompatible cultures, producing conflicts and inefficiencies.[31] Moving into new markets brings the orga-

▟ TABLE 5-1

Dysfunctions of Organizational Culture

"Culture constrains strategy"
Merging cultures
Creates resistance to change
Conflict from differing views
Communication failures

nization into new subcultures that may not respond in the usual ways to its product or service.

Companies that introduce technologies to gain efficiency in manufacturing or providing service often experience latent dysfunctions. New technology can change familiar ways of acting that have become an accepted part of the existing organizational culture. Power and status may shift to those who know, understand, and can use the new technology. Such shifts undermine the position of those who had power and status in the culture before the new technology arrived. All those factors can lead to conflict, inefficiency, and possible sabotage of the new technology.

Cultures produce different ways of looking at the world and interpreting language and events. People from different subcultures may distrust those from other subcultures because of their different worldviews.[32] Conflict can erupt between people from different subcultures, especially when they passionately hold to different views.

Cultural differences can lead to communication failures between individuals even when they are expressing their thoughts clearly. For example, consider what the following words mean to you:

Tonic   Braces   Bubbler

Tonic is a soft drink in Boston, braces are suspenders in London, and a bubbler is a water fountain in Milwaukee! You might have trouble communicating with people in those cities if you do not know the meaning of those words. Individuals from different subcultures within an organization have similar problems in communication.

Diagnosing Organizational Culture

This section describes the process of **diagnosing organizational culture.** The following observation describes some reasons for doing a diagnosis:

> People at all stages of their careers need to understand culture and how it works because it will likely have a powerful effect on their work lives. People just starting their careers may think a job is just a job. But, when they choose a company, they often choose a way of life. The culture shapes their responses in a strong, but subtle way. Culture can make them fast or slow workers, tough or friendly managers, team players or individuals. By the time they've worked for several years, they may be so well conditioned by the culture they may not even recognize it. But when they change jobs, they may be in for a big surprise.[33]

You can do a diagnosis of an organization's culture from two perspectives: (1) as an outsider considering a job with a certain organization, and (2) as an insider after you have joined an organization.[34]

AS AN OUTSIDER

Diagnosing the culture of an organization as a potential employee will help you decide whether the organization will be a place where you can do well, thrive, and grow or whether the culture will make demands on you that you are unwilling or unable to meet. Although you will not learn all the inner secrets of a culture you have not yet joined, you can find clues about what it would be like to work for that organization.[35]

Study the physical characteristics of the organization.[36] What does the external architecture look like? Does it convey an image of a robust, durable, dependable organization? Does it convey a sense of indifference in the public statement the company makes? Are the buildings the same quality for all employees, or are modern buildings reserved for senior executives? Visits to the headquarters or other work sites

TABLE 5-2
Organizational Culture Diagnosis Worksheet

VISIBLE ARTIFACTS

**I.—PHYSICAL CHARACTERISTICS
(ARCHITECTURE, OFFICE LAYOUT, DECOR, ATTIRE)**

_____

_____

_____

**II.—BEHAVIOR (INTERPERSONAL AND ORAL)
(LANGUAGE, INTERPERSONAL ORIENTATION, USE OF TITLES, RITES,
RITUALS, STORIES, ANECDOTES, HEROINES, HEROES)**

_____

_____

_____

**III.—PUBLIC DOCUMENTS
(ANNUAL REPORTS, PRESS ACCOUNTS,
INTERNAL NEWSPAPERS, NEWSLETTERS)**

_____

_____

_____

INVISIBLE ARTIFACTS*

**IV.—VALUES
(ESPOUSED VALUES, IN-USE VALUES)**

_____

_____

_____

**V.—BASIC ASSUMPTIONS
(ASPECTS OF BEHAVIOR, PERCEPTIONS OF INTERNAL
AND EXTERNAL RELATIONSHIPS, THOUGHTS, FEELINGS)**

_____

_____

_____

*These invisible artifacts are hard for the new employee to see. Although often "second nature" and invisible to organization veterans, they are as important as, and sometimes more important than, the visible artifacts.
Source: Suggested by the analysis in E. H. Schein, *Organizational Culture and Leadership* (San Francisco:Jossey-Bass, 1985, Ch. 1; and T. E. Deal and A. A. Kennedy, *Corporate Cultures* (Reading, Mass.: Addison-Wesley, 1982), Ch. 7.

of an organization can give you valuable insights. Short of a physical visit, photographs in annual reports or press accounts are good approximations.

Read about the company. Examine annual reports and any press accounts about the organization. What do they describe? Do the reports emphasize the people who work for the organization and what they do or the financial performance of the organization? Each emphasis reflects a different culture. The first cares about the people who make up the company. The second may only be looking at the "bottom line." The choice is yours. Which culture do you prefer?

If you visit the organization as part of a recruitment interview, note how you are treated. You are an outsider. Are you treated as one or are you treated as a person about whom the company cares?

Lastly, talk to people who already work for the company. If graduates of your college or university work for the organization, try to contact them. Ask about the history of the company, the criteria of success within the organization, and what it is like to work there every day.

You can develop many clues about an organization's culture by following these suggestions. Only an insider, however, can get to the inner secrets of the culture.

 ## AS AN INSIDER

After you join an organization, you can begin to dig deeper into its culture. Stories and anecdotes are a strong source of evidence about the important qualities of the culture. Watch for similarities among stories told by different people. The subjects emphasized in recurring stories are what is important to the organization's culture. They may include satisfied customers, getting ahead on your merits, or the politics of the organization. Stories often describe organization heroes. What did those heroes do? Pay close attention because a hero's actions likely imply important values in the organization's culture.[37]

Find out the basis of promotions and pay increases. Are promotions based on competence and accomplishment or on tenure and loyalty to the organization? Such differences are clues to different types of organizational culture.

Observations of meetings are also useful sources of information about an organization's culture. Who does the talking? To whom do they talk? Such observations will tell you much about the status structure of the organization. Do participants defer to those with higher status or are all considered equal contributors?

What is the focus of meetings? How much time is spent on various topics? The topics discussed repeatedly and at length are clues about important values of the organization's culture.

Now let's try your skills at diagnosing the culture of two organizations. Use the worksheet in Table 5-2 as a guideline for your diagnosis. Read the case and do your diagnosis first. A short diagnosis follows the case.

CASE   *Sun and Apollo*

*T*his case describes many aspects of two companies that are competing in the same industry. These two companies are trying to sell similar products in the same market. Consider the following questions when reading the case:

1. Do you see differences in the cultures of the two companies?
2. What elements of organizational culture are described in the case?
3. Do you see examples of the physical, value, and basic assumption elements of organizational culture?
4. Can you identify any potential dysfunctions in either company's culture?
5. Would one company be more attractive to you as a potential employer?
6. Which company do you think is more successful?

Source: Excerpted and modified from W. M. Bulkeley, "Two Computer Firms with Clashing Styles Fight for Market Niche," *Wall Street Journal,* July 6, 1987, pp. 1, 9. Reprinted by permission of The Wall Street Journal. © 1987 Dow Jones & Company, Inc. All Rights Reserved Worldwide.

CASE DESCRIPTION

The cover of *High Technology* magazine recently featured two of the world's hottest computer designers posed next to their latest creations. The computers looked similar, but not their makers.

Representing Apollo Computer Inc. of Chelmsford, Massachusetts, was engineer David Nelson, coiffed and immaculately garbed in a gray suit and a silk tie. His rival from Sun Microsystems Inc. of Mountain View, Calif., was William Joy, pictured in a bulky sweater, with a fringe of beard and determinedly unkempt hair.

This is a story of how East Coast meets West Coast—head-on—in the bruising computer marketplace. Five years ago both Sun Microsystems and Apollo Computer were upstart, entrepreneurial firms, striving to make a mark in the horizonless computer business.

"It was like two rowboats in the Pacific Ocean," recalled Robert Smith, Sun's vice president and chief financial officer. "We never saw each other."

• *The Sun Microsystems logo on Sun's headquarters in Mountain View, California,* left; *and the Apollo logo at Apollo's headquarters in Chelmsford, Massachusetts,* right. *Differences in these logos imply differences in the two companies' cultures.*

Today, they are competing chin to chin for sales in their significant niche, the $1.5 billion workstation business, and trying hard to keep at bay such big players as International Business Machines Corp., Digital Equipment Corp., Hewlett-Packard Inc., and Apple Computer Inc. Both companies say the deciding factor in the war—as important as their products and prices—could be their radically different corporate cultures.

To be sure, both companies are go-go computer companies, with fanatical, bearded engineers and executives who glide to work in candy-colored Ferraris.

But Apollo, situated near Massachusetts's famed Route 128, is turning into a buttoned-down, traditional company, eager to overcome a few missteps of its more flamboyant early days. Sun, nestled in the middle of California's Silicon Valley, is ebullient and, at times, downright loony. The company throws monthly beer bashes, and on Halloween employees report to work in gorilla suits.

It is a fight between a company trying to grow up and one that remains intentionally brash and ruthless. The companies' personalities are reflected in their products, their marketing strategies—and the occasional cheap shot fired from the chief executive officer's desk.

"In this country, everything loose rolls to the West Coast," says Apollo's chairman, 53-year-old Thomas A. Vanderslice.

Those are fighting words to Scott McNealy, Sun's extroverted, 32-year-old president. . . . "If I'd set a goal of beating Apollo," says the hyperactive Mr. McNealy, who carries a cellular phone on the golf course, "I'd already be done."

A workstation is a powerful personal computer used by engineers, scientists, printers, and money managers to do such tasks as product design and investment planning. Its graphics are precise—a screen can contain more than one million dots of light—and it can accomplish dozens of tasks at once. Workstations, which retail for $5,000 to $80,000, can also be linked together in a network.

Business is booming. Last year, the workstation market grew 65 percent to $1.5 billion, according to Dataquest Inc., a market-research company. Growth could reach 50 percent again this year. Apollo had a 26 percent share of the market in 1986, compared with Sun's 23 percent.

But Sun is growing considerably faster and is more profitable. In the quarter ended March 31, Sun's sales grew 146 percent to $141 million. That topped Apollo's $123.4 million, a 50 percent increase from the year-earlier period. Sun earned $10.2 million, compared with Apollo's $6.4 million. In addition, Sun sells more units than Apollo, at a lower cost per unit.

[More recently Sun's performance has been described as "breathtaking."[38] Revenues for the fiscal year ending June 1988 were $1.05 billion, almost double the previous year's. Earnings rose by 83 percent.]

[Sun's strategy includes becoming an industry leader in setting computing system standards, using a newly designed high-performance chip, and adopting the UNIX operating system.[39] Sun is perceived by some companies in the industry to be a "presumptuous youngster" who should not presume to set industry standards.][40]

To understand the current state of the battle, it is important to know the brief but turbulent history of the business and the two different paths that the once-similar companies have chosen.

Apollo invented the workstation. The company was founded in 1980 by a prominent electronics engineer, J. William Poduska, who had a track record of successful designs for minicomputers. Thanks to his reputation, the company had no trouble raising capital; his connections in the business gave Apollo an early boost in the marketing of its products. In 1981 it released its first workstation, the DN 100, which sold for $45,000.

In 1984, the rapidly expanding company hired Mr. Vanderslice, a chemistry Ph.D. who rose through the ranks at General Electric Co. and who was once the president of GTE Corp. His job was to guide Apollo's explosive growth. . . .

Meanwhile, on the West Coast, two M.B.A.s from Stanford University joined forces with two local computer whizzes and decided to build and sell workstations. All four men were 27 years old. Their strategy was markedly different from Apollo's. The four men believed the market wouldn't accept a workstation custom-designed by unknown graduate students. So they devised a machine that used a standard operating system called Unix, originally designed by American Telephone & Telegraph Co. It also was designed to communicate with other computers over Ethernet, a widely used local-area network. . . .

Weathering Tough Times

Sun, which never stumbled, continued to chop prices and to move relentlessly into Apollo's customer base. Recently, it dropped prices on its cheapest workstation by 37 percent to $4,995, making it competitive with some personal computers. That workstation is now half the price of Apollo's cheapest machine, and the price cutting elicits a sad shake of the head from Chairman Vanderslice. "I wouldn't have done that," he says. (Nonetheless, Apollo has had to follow the price-cutting trend. . . .)

How the battle proceeds from here is unknown, but many in the industry think the ultimate success of Apollo or Sun will depend on the very different personalities of the companies—crucial factors in determining whether either company can rise to challenges or weather tough times.

Apollo is trying to build an image of solid, long-term reliability, both as a vendor and as an employer. Mr. Vanderslice says that the company's troubles and its recovery have made it more competitive and more mature. Its decisions generally come from the top.

The managers at Sun, in contrast, affect an attitude of sheer, unrestrained invincibility, and its corporate style embodies the open-collar, open-door, protocol-free ambience of California.

Ferrari in the Pond

At Sun, every Friday is a dress-down day. Most workers wear jeans and sport shirts. On April Fool's Day, by tradition, engineers must torment their bosses. This year they placed Mr. Joy's Ferrari on a platform in the middle of the company's decorative pond.

In previous years, the engineers disassembled an executive's car and reassembled it inside his office; they disassembled the man's office and reassembled it in the middle of the pond. The pattern is frighteningly clear, says Mr. Joy: "Car in office, office in pond, car in pond." Next year, he fears, he will find the pond in his office.

[Sun reorganized some of its divisions into groups in 1988. To celebrate the change in status from a division to a group, a "graduation ceremony" was held at Sun's California headquarters. Two thousand employees of the Workstation Division attended the ceremony under a circus big top. Group executives were on stage wearing mortarboards and black gowns. Scott McNealy headed the line. Pat Paulsen, the comedian, was the formal entertainment. He observed, "What's the difference between Sun and the Boy Scouts? The Boy Scouts have adult supervision."[41]]

The office of Mr. McNealy, Sun's president, looks more like a 1960s dorm room than a corporate suite. Pins on a wall map mark the top golf courses in the United States. Also on the wall are a pair of flip-flops—with golf spikes. Robert R. Lux, a Sun vice president who was hired away from Apollo, says, "It was a real eye-opener for me when McNealy came in in a polo shirt and high-fived me in the hallway."

Mr. McNealy favors wide-open discussion among his managers and heated disputes in committees. Mr. McNealy brags that Sun has maintained the hothouse atmosphere of a start-up company. "We're a Fortune 500–size company," he says, "but I have trouble finding a parking space at 5:30."

[Sun is perceived by others in the industry to operate at breakneck speed, a pace they may not be able to sustain. Sun executives are young and hard driving, leading some to conclude they are cocky, if not arrogant.][42]

Empty Parking Lots

In contrast, the parking lots in Chelmsford, at Apollo's low-rise headquarters, are almost empty in the evening and on weekends. Executives urge the staff to work harder. "We're pushing to get people to work the 41st hour every week," says Edward Zander, vice president for marketing.

The atmosphere is decidedly corporate, with closed doors, scheduled meetings and a library hush in the executive suites. Mr. Lux recalls: "It's more a buttoned-jacket style. From 9:15 to 9:20 you discuss an issue and at 9:20 you approve it."

Apollo's managers bristle at comparisons with Sun and the suggestion that they lack an entrepreneurial spirit. "There's a lot to be said for being professional," says Roland Pampel, senior vice president. "We have people doing a lot of fun stuff. That doesn't mean . . . you don't wear suits."

But managers have been instructed to encourage fun on the job. At a recent employee rally, the lordly Mr. Vanderslice startled workers by appearing on stage in a Luke Skywalker costume to do battle with a Darth Vader look-alike. Darth Vader sported a Sun logo on his chest.

Analysts award Mr. Vanderslice high marks for reviving Apollo. "He's doing what everyone thought he was the wrong kind of manager to do—turning around an entrepreneurial company that got in trouble," says Richard Shaffer, the editor of *Technologic Computer Letter*. Mr. Vanderslice's key moves included controlling soaring costs, diversifying markets, and installing quality control to prevent workstations that were too often dead on delivery.

With the market growing rapidly, many analysts predict success for both companies. The big question is whether Apollo can keep up with its flashier competitor. Also important: If the market takes a twist, can the juggernaut Sun recover?

"Sun has the potential to be larger if it pulls off its plans," says Vicki Brown of International Data Corp., a market-research company. If times get tough, she says, "it could end up in a lot of trouble."

Much will depend on the behavior of the major computer makers. IBM is expected to become more competitive in the workstation market, and Digital Equipment recently halved prices on some machines competing directly with Apollo's and Sun's. Hewlett-Packard is already a strong contender. Moreover, new personal computers by IBM and Apple have workstation power.

CASE ANALYSIS

Table 5-3 shows a completed worksheet for the case. As with many organizational cultures, the outsider most readily sees the visible artifacts. The two companies differed sharply in those artifacts. Apollo's managers wore suits and ties and were well groomed. Its East Coast location gave an impression of New England tradition. Parking lots had few cars after 5:30 P.M. Sun's managers and engineers dressed informally and cared little about personal grooming. McNealy's office featured spiked flip-flops and a map showing golf courses around the country. Sun's West Coast location had an air of spontaneity and informality.

The behavior within the two companies also differed. Apollo held meetings behind closed doors. Managers made fast decisions with little heated debate. Decision making at Sun featured much debate. Apollo had few rituals and Sun had many. The latter included "dress-down day" and tormenting the boss on April Fool's Day. Behavior at Sun showed high energy, reflecting much of McNealy's character. The company moved forward at almost breakneck speed.

You can only infer values and basic assumptions from the case because you are an outsider. Apollo valued tradition, professionalism in working relationships, structure, and solidity. Sun valued spontaneity, conflict, and upbeat interpersonal relations. Many values inferred from the case can also be basic assumptions. Managers at Apollo accepted the businesslike approach of the company with little questioning. Sun's managers considered bizarre behavior a basic quality of their company.

Effects on Organizational Culture: Diversity, Quality, Global Environment, and Ethics

The increasing diversity of the workforce will bring different views of the world into organizations. Because employees will have different ways of interpreting experiences, little consensus about core cultural values will develop. Subcultures may form along the dimensions of diversity, increasing the likelihood that the organization's culture will lack homogeneity. Conflict may develop among subcultures, especially in the early stages of moving toward diversity.

Some organizations are not merely reacting to natural changes in their workforce. Managers in those organizations are deliberately building a culture of diversity because they believe it leads to higher performance.[43] The following definition of a culture of diversity comes from two leading writers on workforce diversity:

> By culture of diversity, we mean an institutional environment built on the values of fairness, diversity, mutual respect, understanding, and cooperation; where shared goals, rewards, performance standards, operating norms, and a common vision of the future guide the efforts of every employee and manager.[44]

Managers of organizations moving toward a culture of diversity are seeking a large shift in values, basic assumptions, and ideology.

Managing for quality usually requires a different set of values and basic assumptions from those that often exist in organizations.[45] The values in a quality-oriented and continuous improvement culture include cooperation, trust, caring, a customer focus, and a desire to improve quality. Such cultures view conflict as potentially

Organizational Culture Diagnosis Worksheet: Sun and Apollo

VISIBLE ARTIFACTS

**I.—PHYSICAL CHARACTERISTICS
(ARCHITECTURE, OFFICE LAYOUT, DECOR, ATTIRE)**

- *Apollo:* Gray suit, silk tie, hair style. "Button-down" look. Eastern traditional company. Parking lots empty on evenings and weekends. Closed-door meetings. Corporate-like atmosphere. Age of executives.
- *Sun:* Bulky sweater, unkempt hair, some beard. West Coast location. McNealy's office looks like a 1960s dorm room. Map showing golf courses. Spiked flip-flops. Parking lot full at 5:30 P.M.. McNealy's cellular phone on the golf course. Age of executives. The pond and its role in the pranks.

**II.—BEHAVIOR (INTERPERSONAL AND ORAL)
(LANGUAGE, INTERPERSONAL ORIENTATION, USE OF TITLES, RITES, RITUALS, STORIES, ANECDOTES, HEROINES, HEROES)**

- *Apollo:* Few rituals. Little conflict during decision making. More formality in interpersonal relationships.
- *Sun:* Rituals—gorilla suit, Ferrari in pond, monthly beer busts, dress-down day on Fridays. High level of activity. "High fives." Loony, brash, high conflict.

**III.—PUBLIC DOCUMENTS
(ANNUAL REPORTS, PRESS ACCOUNTS, INTERNAL NEWSPAPERS, NEWSLETTERS)**

Little in the case other than the reporters' accounts.

INVISIBLE ARTIFACTS*

**IV.—VALUES
(ESPOUSED VALUES, IN-USE VALUES)**

- *Appolo:* Solid, businesslike, professional, traditional, reliable.
- *Sun:* Work is fun. Invincible. Be brash and upbeat.

**V.—BASIC ASSUMPTIONS
(ASPECTS OF BEHAVIOR, PERCEPTIONS OF INTERNAL AND EXTERNAL RELATIONSHIPS, THOUGHTS, FEELINGS)**

- *Apollo:* Businesslike behavior and physical appearance. Little conflict during decision making.
- *Sun:* Wide-open discussion. High conflict levels desirable. Spontaneous behavior. Work should be fun.

*These invisible artifacts are hard for the new employee to see. Although often "second nature" and invisible to organization veterans, they are as important as, and sometimes more important than, the visible artifacts.

positive and stress moving decisions to low levels in the organization. Quality-oriented cultures also reject blaming and faultfinding. If there is a big gap between the present values of an organization's culture and those just listed, the organization's management will need to press its culture to change.

As described in Chapter 3, organizations and their managers clearly are under pressure to consider the ethics of decisions and of all behavior in their organizations. That pressure implies the need to consider the ethical dimension of an organization's culture.[46] The ethical dimension includes artifacts, values, and basic assumptions that are directed at ethical behavior. Codes of ethics are artifacts and espoused values.

Over time, they can become basic assumptions and part of the culture's core ideology. An important part of that ideology is the support of ethical dialogues or discussions of the ethical results of actions. Once the value of such dialogues becomes part of a culture's ideology, the dialogues are a required element of behavior in the organization. The discussion of moral issues can then become an integral part of a manager's job.

Each source of effects on an organization's culture has many qualities that often are not part of an organization's present culture. Managers will increasingly face the issue of culture change in their organizations. Culture change usually is not easy and often is strongly resisted by members of the organization. A later section of this chapter describes many issues facing managers who want to change their organization's culture.

. . . .

⌐ *Organizational Culture and Organization Performance*

The popular book *In Search of Excellence*[47] has sparked interest in whether organizational culture is a determinant of an organization's performance. Both that book and many other accounts of culture and performance used anecdotal evidence and nonrandom samples to present positive views of the culture-performance link.[48] Serious reviewers of organizational culture research conclude there is little consistent and systematic empirical knowledge about the culture-performance connection.[49]

A few empirical studies have been designed well enough to allow some observations about the culture-performance link. The following points are summaries of the results of this research. Although not perfect in design, the research had more strong features than weak features.

1. Organizations with cultures featuring well-dispersed participatory decision-making practices had higher returns on investment and sales than those not as well dispersed. The differences in financial performance became even greater over time.[50]
2. Organizations with cultures that had well-organized and adaptable work procedures and presented clear goals to employees outperformed organizations that did not.[51]
3. Such cultural characteristics were stronger predictors of long-term financial performance than short-term performance.[52]
4. Organizations with social responsibility as an espoused value were higher on a composite index of financial performance (return on assets, return on equity, return on sales, and earnings per share) than organizations emphasizing the state of the economy.[53]
5. Within accounting organizations, poorly performing employees quit at a higher rate than higher performing employees in organizations with cultures emphasizing accuracy of work, predictability, and risk taking.[54] There was no difference in the rate of quitting in organizations with cultures valuing collaboration and teamwork. Although the researcher did not directly assess organization performance, those results imply potentially higher performance for the first set of organizations than for the second set.

The problems with empirical research on the culture-performance link led researchers to offer contingency theories of that link. They suggested the performance of an organization is due partly to the congruence between its strategy and its culture or to the congruence between the organization's environment and its culture. The next paragraphs describe the more prominent contingency views.

One view sees organizations gaining competitive advantage when their culture is valuable, rare, and not easily imitated.[55] The value of an organization's culture derives from the guidance it gives to direct people's behavior toward higher performance. Rarity refers to the features of a culture that are not common among competing organizations. Such rarity can come from the unique personalities of the organization's founders and the unique history underlying the culture. Cultures that are not easily imitated make it hard for competitors to change their cultures to get the same advantages. Difficulty of imitation follows partly from the rare features of some cultures and the basic difficulties confronting managers when trying to change a culture.

A second contingency view focuses on environment-culture congruence.[56] Organizations facing high complexity and high ambiguity will require a cohesive culture for effective performance. Such cultures are of the type described earlier under the integration perspective. They feature widely shared values and basic assumptions that guide people's behavior. For organizations facing low uncertainty and low complexity, building a cohesive culture could be costly. Those organizations will reach high performance with more formal control processes such as organization policies, rules, and procedures.

None of these contingency views has been empirically tested. You should ponder them to see whether they are intuitive or logically sound.

. . . .

⌐ *Organizational Culture and Organizational Socialization*

Organizational culture and organizational socialization are intimately connected. Organizational culture defines the content of what an organization wants its members to learn and accept. Organizational socialization is the process an organization uses to teach its members the content of its culture. The socialization process seeks acceptance of the culture's values and basic assumptions from both new and veteran employees.[57]

An organization tries to socialize you to its culture when you first become an employee. The process repeats each time you move within the organization or from one organization to another. Moving to a new physical location, or to a new department or division, exposes you to a new subculture. New socialization efforts follow each move as members of the new culture try to affect your values and behavior.[58]

This discussion has only briefly introduced you to organizational socialization. The next chapter has a detailed description of this important behavioral process and the effects it will have on you throughout your career.

▪ *Basic military training plays a major role in the socialization of recruits to the culture of the U.S. Marine Corps.*

. . . .

⌐ *Creating, Maintaining, and Changing Organizational Culture*

Managers of modern organizations regularly face three decisions about their organization's culture. They can decide to create a completely new culture, usually in a separate work unit or in a new organization. They can work at maintaining their existing organizational culture because they believe it is right for the environments they face. They can decide to change their culture to a new set of values, basic assumptions, and ideologies.[59]

⬛ CREATING ORGANIZATIONAL CULTURE

Creating organizational culture is a deliberate effort to build a specific type of organizational culture. It happens when an entrepreneur forms an organization to pursue a vision or when managers of an existing organization form a new operating unit. The new culture needs an ideology that is understandable, convincing, and widely discussed. The ideology is a key tool for getting commitment from members of the organization to the vision.

Building the culture around that ideology is easier if managers can recruit and select people who already share key parts of the ideology or who can easily develop commitment to it. Formal socialization practices play major roles in building an identity with the ideology. Forging that identity is easier when people's values on entry are close to the values and beliefs of the ideology. Cultural symbols must also be consistent with the ideology. For example, if the ideology has egalitarian values, the organization should have few physical status symbols distinguishing senior managers from other employees.

Subcultures likely will form around demographic patterns, occupations, and technical specializations. Those subcultures also affect the socialization results of new employees. When planning the new culture, managers should try to anticipate both the manifest functions and latent dysfunctions of the likely subcultures.

The environment at the time of founding can shift and present management with new problems and opportunities. Managers will need to be flexible to manage an evolving organizational culture. They also will need to look ahead and plan for leadership succession if they want the culture to continue into the future.

⬛ MAINTAINING ORGANIZATIONAL CULTURE

Maintaining organizational culture does not mean that managers passively and uncritically accept the values and basic assumptions of the present culture. Maintenance of a culture presents managers with a dilemma. They want to hold on to the values that were successful in the past, but they also need to question whether those values are right for the environment the organization now faces.

Culture maintenance requires managers to be aware of what organizational culture is and how it manifests itself in their organization. It requires knowing the existing organizational culture's artifacts, values, and ideologies. A key way managers can become familiar with their culture is by doing a culture diagnosis, as described in an earlier section.

By maintaining their culture, managers want to maintain commitment of the members of the organization to key parts of that culture.[60] They also want to strengthen key values so they are widely held throughout the organization. In short, managers want to hold on to the good part of the organization's culture while helping the organization adapt to its newest challenges.

A key part of culture maintenance is actively looking for and fixing cultural contradictions. Such contradictions can weaken an organization's culture by the ambiguity they present to members of the organization. The differences between espoused values and actual behavior are an example of those contradictions. They also appear as cultural symbols that are inconsistent with expressed values.

Managers need to frequently examine training programs and socialization processes and compare them to the core ideology of the organization's culture. Those programs and processes usually are the first major contact new employees have with the values and basic assumptions of an organization's culture. Inconsistencies between the culture's ideology and what is done in those programs and processes present ambiguities to new employees. Widespread ambiguity will weaken an organization's culture and prevent it from guiding behavior.

Culture maintenance also requires managers to carefully examine any new practices for consistency with their culture's ideology. Introducing drug testing for employment screening in an organization with a culture built around trust might be a contradiction. Such testing might not appear contradictory in an organization that strongly values safety when working in hazardous areas.

CHANGING ORGANIZATIONAL CULTURE

Changing organizational culture requires breaking from some features of the old culture and creating new features. The size and depth of the change will vary depending on the degree of difference between the desired new culture and the old. For example, changing the culture of an organization that has a homogeneous workforce to one that values diversity will require an extended effort. The change will reach deep into the cultural fabric of the organization over a period of many years. Changing an organization's culture is a form of long-term, planned change. This section describes the main features of planned cultural change.[61] Chapter 19 has much more detail.

Successfully managing the change process requires managers to attend to several issues. One is choosing the proper time for change. They are advised to act when the times seem right for culture change or when the situation clearly demands it. An opportune time for culture change might be when the organization wishes to pursue favorable new markets. IBM, for example, changed its culture when it shifted its emphasis away from its historical roots in mainframe computers to small personal computers and workstations.[62] Change also might be required when the organization is performing poorly and faces clear threats to its viability.

Managers should not assume that everyone in the organization will share their view of the need to change. The senior executives of the organization will need to play leadership roles, convincing others in the organization that a culture change is needed and offering a vision of that new culture. Managers will need to move forward with confidence, persistence, and optimism about the new culture. The change effort can focus on many aspects of the organization's culture, such as ideology, values, and symbols, although it is not realistic to expect that all elements of the prior culture will be removed.

Managers should know the roots of their organization's culture and maintain some continuity with the past by keeping elements that are valued widely in the organization.[63] For example, the Federal Bureau of Investigation's efforts to move toward Total Quality Management could be anchored in its perception of itself as the premier law enforcement agency in the world. This approach also lets managers say what will not change as a way of offering familiarity and security to veteran employees. The following describes the major processes of large-scale planned cultural change:

> Large-scale planned cultural change uses four processes to start the change and move the culture to the desired end state.[64] First, the pattern-breaking process destroys old parts of the culture as the organization separates from its past. This process is turbulent and can be disconcerting to many people. The second process is experimenting—with new ideas, innovations, thinking, values, and modes of behavior that support the new culture. Such experimenting focuses on the basic mission and vision of the organization and often builds on the organization's roots.[65]
>
> The third process is visioning. This process gives organization members a clear focus for their activities. It also tells them about the future state of the organization's culture and the important role of its new ideology. The vision can come from a strategic plan, especially if there has been widespread involvement in its development. It also comes from the

Source: Excerpted and adapted from J. E. Champoux and L. D. Goldman, "Building a Total Quality Culture," in T. D. Connors, ed., *Nonprofit Organizations Policies and Procedures Handbook* (New York: John Wiley & Sons, 1993), pp. 61, 64. Copyright © 1993 by John Wiley & Sons, Inc. Reprinted by permission of John Wiley & Sons, Inc.

organization's leaders at all levels. Such leaders play a key role in infusing a vision of the new culture into all members of the organization.

The last process in planned culture change activities focuses on stabilizing or institutionalizing the change. Institutionalization is the process that sustains changes in an organization over time. For organizational culture change, it means moving the culture to its new end state and then holding it in that position. Institutionalization also includes socialization processes needed to teach successive generations of members of the organization about the new culture.[66]

Institutionalized behavior has three characteristics. It is persistent behavior, shared by two or more people in reaction to the same event, that is part of the cultural fabric of the organization. Those are the results wanted by managers trying to move their organizations to a new culture. They want the changes in the organizational culture to last.

Managers can expect to meet resistance to their efforts to change their organization's culture.[67] People often develop deep attachments to valued parts of the old organizational culture and consistent ways of behaving. When culture change affects those valued elements or disturbs established social patterns, strong resistance can develop. Reactions may include lack of cooperation with the change effort, deliberate sabotage of the change effort, or dysfunctionally high levels of conflict. Misunderstandings about the intended goal of the change, or lack of trust between the target of change and the managers pressing the change, can also create resistance reactions.

Resistance to change is a common reaction to any form of organization change. Chapter 19 has an extended discussion of organization change, resistance to change, and ways of reducing that resistance.

EXERCISE   *Diagnosing Your Organization's Culture*

*E*arlier in this chapter you diagnosed the cultures of Sun Microsystems and Apollo Computing. This exercise asks you to diagnose the culture of your employer. If you are not currently working, you can use an employer in your recent past. You also may choose to diagnose your sorority, fraternity, or college or university.

Before starting, you might want to review the guidelines given earlier for diagnosing organizational culture. Use those guidelines and a worksheet similar to the one in Table 5-2 to do your culture diagnosis.

International Aspects of Organizational Culture

*A*n organization operating in a global or international environment will face some special organizational culture issues. The most obvious issues are the effects of varying national cultures on multinational organizations operating in different countries. Local cultures can shape the subcultures of globally dispersed units.[68] National culture, local business norms, and the needs of local customers all can affect the subcultures of such units. For example, the multinational insurance firm AIG follows local practices in collecting monthly premiums. Agents collect monthly premiums at the home of each insured person in Taiwan, but use electronic bank transfers in Hong Kong.[69]

A major issue faced by managers of multinational organizations is the set of values they want globally dispersed operations to have. Do they want the values of the home country to dominate or do they want to adopt those of the local national culture? Managers who want their international units to hold values of the home country place people from the home country in charge of those units. Organizations that hire local people for management positions often first socialize them to the major values of the home country organization. Hewlett-Packard has followed this practice for its worldwide operations so that managers know the "HP Way," whatever their national origins or the country in which they work.[70]

Multinational organizations typically have employees from many countries working side by side. Those employees do not shed their national cultural values when they come to work. The heterogeneity of values in such organizations is extremely high, as is the possibility of subcultures forming along national lines. Some research evidence suggests that instead of masking local differences with organizational culture, multinational cultures may increase ties people have to their native cultures.[71] Managing a multinationally diverse workforce presents all the challenges of managing a domestic diverse workforce described in Chapter 2.

Organizational cultures also differ in the value they place on multinational cultural diversity.[72] Managers may refuse to recognize cultural differences and insist that the home culture way of doing business is the only correct way. Another view suggests recognizing cultural differences among people from different countries and using combinations of those differences for the strategic advantage of the organization. This "cultural synergy" view urges managers to view multinational cultural diversity as a resource.[73] That diversity could lead to better product ideas for culturally diverse markets and better communication with culturally diverse customers.

The cultural synergy view has a set of underlying assumptions that managers could urge upon their organization's culture.[74] Cultural synergy assumes differences among culturally distinct people but also says one can find similarities. It also assumes that people from different cultures will reach the same work goals, but by different routes. Managers should not judge the different routes as good or bad, if they achieve the desired results. The last assumption has clear implications for meeting customer needs. It asks that managers understand "cultural contingency" or reaching desired results with methods that are compatible with the underlying culture. The example earlier in this section about collecting insurance premiums in different countries was a culturally contingent approach.

· ·

Ethical Issues in Organizational Culture

*T*he first ethical issue raised by organizational culture is whether creating, maintaining, and changing organizational cultures are forms of manipulating and exploiting human behavior in organizations.[75] Organizational culture scholars agree that an organization's culture affects the behavior of people in that culture. The ethical issue is what moral action managers should take in managing the cultures of their organizations.

An analysis from the viewpoints of different ethical theories gives different answers. A utilitarian analysis says the moral action is the one that gives the greatest net benefit to the greatest number of people affected by the action. That view concludes that cultural values supporting such action are morally correct. Managers also are morally correct in changing or creating cultures in that direction.

A rights-based analysis suggests people must have the right to make free and informed choices about what affects them. This view argues, for example, for full disclosure to new employees about the values and basic assumptions of the organization's culture. It also argues that employees should be fully informed about any proposed changes to the organization's culture.[76] The libertarian view of rights described in Chapter 3 would reject as immoral an organizational culture that strongly constrains a person's behavior. Managers will have difficulty honoring a rights-based ethic because of the usual lack of conscious awareness of basic assumptions among veteran employees.

Recall that Chapter 3 presented you with two different views of justice ethics. One view emphasized equal liberties, helping the disadvantaged, and equal opportunity to gain rewards. This ethical theory would judge a culture as unethical, for example, if it prevented employees from freely voicing their opinions. It also would judge a culture as unethical if all employee groups did not have an equal chance for advancement. The libertarian view of justice, though, rules as immoral any preferential treatment of one employee at the expense of another. The latter could be a major cultural and ethical issue in an organization with a diverse workforce.

Diagnosing organizational cultures carries two major risks with ethical implications.[77] One risk is that the analysis could be superficial and accept only culture symbols or espoused values as representing the core ideology of the organization's culture. This form of diagnosis could yield observations that are misleading or simply wrong, if in-use values and basic assumptions were different.

The second risk centers on whether the members of the organization are ready to receive feedback about its culture. Organizational cultures often give people protective interpretations about information from the organization's environment. Veteran employees may also hold ideals and basic assumptions that have comfortably guided their behavior in the past. The diagnosis could show those basic assumptions are myths held by veteran employees, not the values expressed in actions. Recall the story earlier in the chapter about the woman who rescheduled her Caesarean operation for the convenience of her company. The prevailing myth in that organization was that the company had an overriding concern for employee welfare, not an overriding concern to introduce products.

Some writers have pressed for the development of a moral dimension of organizational culture.[78] This dimension holds values and basic assumptions about including ethical dialogues in management decision processes. The importance of ethical dialogues must be an explicit part of the organization's ideology and be expressed repeatedly until it becomes a basic assumption. The goal of the moral dimension is to make the discussion of moral issues in decisions a comfortable, desired, and required part of every manager's job.

Personal and Management Implications

The three perspectives on organizational culture suggest that you should not trap yourself into believing that organizational cultures have a uniform set of core values. They often have multiple sets of values among subcultures. Those values can also be contradictory, unclear, and highly ambiguous. Such features of cultures imply that you may encounter difficulties in your socialization to a new culture as a new employee. For managers, those features imply difficulty in doing a clear and unambiguous diagnosis to understand and manage culture.

As a veteran member of an organization, you should be alert to certain pitfalls when doing a culture diagnosis of your employing organization.[79] Objectivity in the diagnosis is important but hard to get when you have been involved in an organization's culture for many years. The emphasis of a culture and its values and basic assumptions are subtle and not easy to see. You will need to exert some effort to reveal the content of the culture and what it does for your organization.

Involving more than one person in the diagnosis can be an important step toward objectivity. Ask someone whose judgment you trust to be a devil's advocate. Avoid making value judgments about the culture. The appointed devil's advocate should let you know when you have wandered. You want a description, not an evaluation, of the culture.

The emerging issues described in Chapter 2 will have effects on organizational culture that will bring both excitement and difficulties to organizations in the future. Employees at all levels will experience increasing conflict potential from both domestic and multinational workforce diversity. Managers will face the challenge of managing that conflict potential so it does not reach dysfunctional levels. Managers of organizations that choose to move toward managing for quality will face the daunting challenge of changing core values in their organization's culture. Nonmanagement employees will also feel pressure to change their behavior to become more customer focused and to seek continuous quality improvement.

Management of an organization's culture is another important implication. It will first be necessary to discover the basic assumptions underlying the culture through a diagnosis as suggested earlier. Identifying the symbols of the culture and communicating them to new employees are important elements of managing a culture. Veteran members of the organization can have some difficulty here because some symbols simply will not be obvious to them.

Managers of modern organizations will feel increasing pressure to include an explicit ethical or moral dimension in their organizational cultures. This will include developing a code of ethics, talking about that code, and prominently displaying it throughout the organization. It will be more difficult for managers to change their existing organizational cultures to make that moral dimension part of the cultural fabric. Nonmanagment employees will also feel this pressure. One key implication for all of us is the growing emphasis on employees' rights to speak out freely in their organizations. That right includes "blowing the whistle" on any unethical behavior we see.[80]

. . . .

Summary

Organizational cultures include the values, norms, rites, rituals, symbols, ceremonies, heroes, and scoundrels in the history of the organization. Organizational cultures define what a new employee needs to learn for acceptance as a member of the organization. Cultures are functional when they help an organization adapt to its external environment and coordinate internal activities. They are dysfunctional when they are the basis of resistance to change or create culture clashes when two different cultures merge.

Organizational cultures are pervasive in organizations, but are often taken for granted by veteran employees. Cultures have strong imprints from their historical roots, become highly interdependent with other organization processes, and can have many subcultures. Organizational cultures also have a political dimension and are often interlocked with the power systems of the organizations.

The levels at which you see organizational cultures vary from visible to almost invisible. Artifacts and other cultural symbols usually are visible to even the newest employee. Basic assumptions, a set of implicit values, are almost invisible to new employees and are only learned after a period of socialization and acceptance. Espoused values and in-use values have mid-level visibility.

Three perspectives view an organizational culture in different ways. The integration perspective sees organizational cultures as widely shared values among organization members. The differentiation perspective says subcultures form within an organization's culture. A fragmentation perspective sees ambiguity in organizations that prevents agreement on values.

Diagnosing an organization's culture is an important way for a potential employee to get information about the organization. It also is an important way for a manager to learn about the culture of his organization. An outsider's diagnosis usually cannot go beyond artifacts and values. The insider not only sees artifacts and values but, with much work, can also uncover basic assumptions.

Managers maintain an existing organizational culture because they believe it is right for the environments they face. They also can try to change their culture to a new set of values, basic assumptions, and ideologies. Those new values can focus on diversity, quality, global competitiveness, or ethical behavior in the organization. Managers can try to create a new culture, usually in a separate work unit or in a new organization. The new culture needs a core ideology that is understandable, convincing, and widely discussed.

. . . .

Key Terms

1. Why do multiple subcultures form in organizations? What implications do subcultures have for a new employee? Give some examples from your employment experience. What effects would you expect the increasingly more global environment of modern organizations to have on subcultures?

2. What are the functions and dysfunctions of organizational culture? What role do basic assumptions play in those functions and dysfunctions?

3. Discuss the procedures for diagnosing an organization's culture. What are the major ethical issues you need to consider when doing such a diagnosis?

4. Review the contingency views of the link between organizational culture and performance. Discuss whether those views are consistent with people's experience and observations. Also discuss the logic of the views to see whether there are any flaws.

5. Review the effects that workforce diversity, managing for quality, a global environment, and an increasing emphasis on ethical behavior are expected to have on organizational culture. Discuss the ways in which those effects could change the cultures of modern organizations.

6. Continue with the preceding question, but explicitly consider the discussion in the section "Creating, Maintaining, and Changing Organizational Culture." Discuss implications for the observations in that section that follow from the effects mentioned in Question 5.

7. Review the section "International Aspects of Organization Culture." Discuss that section with other students in your class, especially if they are from other countries. Also, draw on the experiences of students who have traveled to other countries.

Case

BOB ALLEN RATTLES THE CAGES AT AT&T

Following a traumatic turn of events at AT&T in 1988, Robert Allen, its newly appointed chairman and chief executive, faced hard decisions about the culture of his organization. This case describes what he did. Use the following questions as guides to your analysis of the case:

1. What values did Allen want to inject into the culture of AT&T?

2. Did Allen want his managers to adopt specific behaviors as he tried to change the culture of his organization?

3. Did Allen take any steps as part of the pattern-breaking process of organizational culture change?

4. What should Allen have done to institutionalize AT&T's new culture?

"Mrs. Olson called me early Monday morning just after Jim died—5:29 to be exact. I had seen him at dinner on Friday, and knew there was some deterioration over the weekend, but no one expected his death. Barely before I was awake I was on the telephone with the other top officers. I got them all out of bed. We gathered that morning and began to make plans."

"We were all terribly distraught, but there was so much to do. It was really not until later that we had the time to mourn. Jim was such a vibrant and dynamic person. He really touched the lives of an awful lot of AT&T people, so

it was a shock, and a particularly emotional burden for me because he had also been a good friend. I was aware that I was Jim's choice [to succeed him] and that I would probably be the board's choice. But I really thought I had another year or two to prepare."

On April 19, 1988, the day after James Olson died at 62 of colon cancer and the day before the company's annual meeting, Robert Eugene Allen was elected chairman and chief executive of AT&T. What a way to take over America's largest diversified service company. And what a time. AT&T was losing share in the all-important long-distance market— the major business that the consent decree allocated to it in the 1984 break-up. Within a week of Allen's appointment, the head of the computer operation—one of the company's big bets for long-term growth—quit. At the same time a joint venture with Olivetti of Italy was unraveling, and with it the hope that this quintessentially American company could throw off its fetters and compete globally in the computer market. . . .

[Allen's] major conclusion [after months of thinking about the business was]: AT&T, the most entrenched corporate culture in America, must finally change and change for good. People had been talking about this need ever since divestiture, but too little had happened. The company could no longer operate as the regulated monopoly it once was, satisfied with predictable price increases, complacent about competition, uncritical of costs. To compete in fast-changing markets . . . the phone company of old had to learn to get aggressive, to take chances, and above all, to move quickly.

Allen came to realize that the cultural revolution had to start with him. "Every one of us can fall into the trap of thinking, 'I don't need to change,' " he says. "It's like drug or alcohol addiction. You first have to face up to the fact that you've got a problem." In his first year as chief executive, Allen took strides no predecessor had ever taken. By writing down $6.7 billion in obsolete transmission equipment, he produced $1.67 billion annual loss, the first since AT&T was incorporated 104 years ago. By spending $250 million to acquire Paradyne Corp., a competitor that manufactures data communications equipment, he signaled the end to the not-invented-here syndrome, a self-defeating sense of smugness that permeated [AT&T]. . . .

As for his own style? "I've changed in that I'm not only tolerant of contention, but I encourage it," says Allen. "I am becoming more comfortable with decision-making being much further down in the organization, because that's where the best decisions get made for the customer."

Middle managers are gaining authority. Recently Allen met with several who presented an interim report on a new product proposal. He surprised them by giving the final go-ahead on the idea, even though a feasibility study would not be complete for several months. His decision was meant to make waves beyond that particular project. He says, "It was refreshing to them that I could hear the facts, ask a few questions, make a crisp decision, and turn them loose. Maybe that ought to be normal behavior, but it hasn't been normal behavior around our business." . . .

Though much remains to be done, Allen's first year has produced a string of victories. . . . AT&T has won big government contracts, succeeded in important regulatory battles, and arranged a new venture with Italy's state-owned telephone company that will get it flexing unused muscle overseas. . . . Even William McGowan, head of long-distance archrival MCI, has words of praise for AT&T's managers: "They certainly demonstrated that they realize they have to be more aggressive on costs and on customer responsiveness." . . .

When [Allen] talks about what he is trying to do at AT&T, he gravitates toward the timeless mantras of manager-speak; "quality, quality, quality"; "customer, customer, customer"; "teamwork, teamwork, teamwork." . . .

Settling into his seat on the corporate jet, Allen stretches his legs and sighs. He has spent this day of May in Largo, Florida, at Paradyne Corp., his first visit since AT&T bought the company in February. . . .

The Paradyne purchase is part of Allen's strategy to put AT&T's monopoly-era mentality into permanent amnesia. "We came out of a business that had a single culture," he says. "It was very paternalistic, thorough, slow-moving, and exceptionally proficient in accomplishing its mission, but in a static environment." AT&T didn't have to worry about speed in bringing out new products—it controlled the technology *and* the market. If the company took an extra year to develop a new office telephone system—hey, no problem, it would just sell the old one a little bit longer. Now, says Allen, "if you miss a year, you've missed a whole generation of products." The Paradyne deal demonstrates a quicker way to fill holes in AT&T's product line than internal development.

Paradyne was a good match for AT&T. It is a leading manufacturer of modems that let business computers communicate over nondigital phone systems. Besides, the Florida company had a solid base of business customers in the U.S. and a strong sales force overseas. . . . AT&T Paradyne, as the business unit is called, has already won a million-dollar contract from Deloitte Haskins & Sells, the Big Eight accounting firm.

The latest reorganization—there have been about a half-dozen since divestiture—aims to bring AT&T's businesses closer to the customer. Now 19 business units are organized by product line, such as business communications, switching systems, and network computing systems. Each unit will be responsible for its own profits and losses and will have the authority to make decisions on pricing, marketing, and product development. Says vice chairman Randall Tobias, who is in charge of putting the structure into place: "This is a fundamental change in the way we run the business."

[I]t essentially reverses Jim Olson's old scheme. In his attempt to reorganize the company, Olson consolidated the long-distance organization with the phone and computer groups. His structure had a sensible rationale: The units he inherited, particularly those that sold computer products, behaved like separate fiefdoms and often approached customers with different solutions to the same problem. Says John Malone, president of the consulting firm Eastern Management Group: "You could measure in nanoseconds how long it took the customer to reach the boiling point." To keep customers cool under the new regime, the group presidents will have to make sure that the business units don't go back to getting in one another's way. For large customers, sales reps will work in teams, with members present from each unit that does business with the client.

[Allen] is encouraging new approaches to competition—especially in the superwar over business telephone customers. The long-distance market is booming, thanks to rates that have dropped about 40% since 1984, the proliferation of 800 lines, and those increasingly ubiquitous fax machines. After getting battered by MCI and Sprint in television and print advertisements, AT&T has started getting tougher: Its ads now hit competitors by name.

The head of marketing for the $14-billion-a-year unit that sells long-distance service to businesses is Joe Nacchio, 39, a frank, fast-talking New Yorker with a Type A personality—the antithesis of the old AT&T image of the pasty-faced shut-in who sat at his desk taking customers' orders. In an innovative TV promotion last year, Nacchio offered small-business customers of MCI and Sprint a service guarantee: If they switched to AT&T and were unsatisfied for any reason, the company would pay to switch them back to their former carrier. The campaign attracted 28,952 new clients, and Nacchio says that only five have asked to be moved back. . . .

Then there are the people, the 304,600 survivors of deregulation, reorganization, and top-management changes. Morale, to put it mildly, is shaky. Joel Gross, a telecommunications analyst with Donaldson Lufkin & Jenrette, says, "All the employees are optimistic about the company, but at the same time they are scared out of their minds about their jobs." Allen has not done anything to make them feel more secure: Last year's write-off has a provision for future staff reductions. . . .

Perhaps the most encouraging sign for AT&T is that Allen is finally getting the company's managers to change. Says Gross of Donaldson Lufkin & Jenrette: "A lot of good young bulls below top management will carry the company into the 21st century." Members of this rising generation may bring AT&T all the way into the post-regulatory world.

. . . .

⤷ Case

BRIGHT IDEAS: ANATOMY OF A CORPORATE REVOLUTION

Florida Power & Light Co. is the only U.S. organization to win the Deming Prize, a Japanese award for significant and enduring change to managing for quality. The following case summarizes the process of culture change experienced by the company. Here are some questions to think about while reading the case:

1. What major steps did the company's senior management take to move toward managing for quality?
2. Did the extensive training the company gave its employees do more for the company than merely increasing employee skill levels?
3. What were some reasons for resistance to change?
4. Was management right in persisting in its change effort? Why?

It wasn't always fun being a Florida Power & Light Co. employee. Admitting to someone that you worked there was likely to unleash a scathing harangue about lousy service. Soaring rates and frequent power outages brought the beleaguered utility more customer complaints ten years ago than any other utility in the state.

Fast-forward to 1990. The company hasn't sought a general rate increase in five years. Generators break down so rarely that ratepayers have enjoyed savings of more than $300 million that would have gone for new generating units. Power outages, which used to average 100 minutes per customer each year, are down to 43 minutes per customer. That's well below the national average of 90 minutes—in a state that has more lightning than any other.

Customers are a lot friendlier these days. The company that used to average almost one complaint annually for every 1,000 customers now averages fewer than one per 4,000— the lowest rate in the state. So few complaints are registered in the Miami area, in fact, that the Public Service Commission closed its office there in 1988. . . .

Then this spring came international recognition: Florida Power & Light became the first non-Japanese company to win the prestigious Deming Prize for quality.

The story of how FPL went from a so-so utility to arguably the best in the nation is a story of overhauling a

Source: Excerpted from L. Dusky, "Bright Ideas: Anatomy of a Corporate Revolution," *Working Woman*, July 1990, pp. 58, 59, 63. Reprinted with the permission of Lorraine Dusky.

company culture from top to bottom. It started in 1981 when then FPL chairman Marsh McDonald began a small-scale quality-improvement program. FPL was in deep trouble at the time: Energy prices were skyrocketing; customer dissatisfaction was rising as profits were falling—and Washington was in the mood to deregulate, thereby increasing competition. McDonald's goal was to reorient the company from supplying electricity to meeting customers' needs. He was on the right track, all right, but didn't go nearly far enough in implementing his quality reforms. . . .

Two years later McDonald met the president of Kansai Electric at an international industry meeting in Tokyo. He learned that Kansai was proving that the quality-control concept could be translated to a utility. If Kansai could do it, McDonald mused, why not FPL?

Soon afterward senior executives flew to Osaka to learn firsthand what was going on at Kansai. Some went as skeptics; one who came home a true believer was executive vice president Wayne Brunetti. "If top management isn't convinced that the changes are worth making, don't bother," he says. "Changing a culture is not about sloganeering; it's not something you put in a letter and say 'Go do it.'" "If you're not willing to do it yourself, you won't know what's going on, and employees won't be convinced you care."

Once senior management had the word, they made the mistake of thinking they could simply force-feed it to employees. "I was sent a memo that said, 'Now you belong to a quality-improvement team,'" recalls Katherine Echanique, a procurement clerk. "They didn't ask if I wanted to, and I resented that." She wasn't the only one.

Supervisors and managers weren't exactly gung ho either. Initially they hadn't been invited to join the quality-improvement teams; their workers reported directly to senior executives. From the middle managers' point of view, quality improvement was "something that took their employees away from doing their regular jobs—for which the managers and supervisors were accountable," says Dorothy Norton, general manager of the southern division's 2,000-plus employees. "To make matters worse, the men and women on the quality teams were learning a language that wasn't shared by their own supervisors."

So instead of infusing everything that everybody did, "quality" was something that some employees worked on for an hour a week. A lot of good suggestions came out of those hours, to be sure, but Norton and other senior executives weren't seeing the kind of overall improvement in performance that the Japanese had shown them was possible. . . .

By 1984 three years of tinkering with the culture had produced only lackluster results. Not enough people had become advocates of quality. To inject its fervor into every department—and bring mid-line supervisors into the loop—senior management took several steps: Middle managers became "facilitators," whose job was to coax team members to look for problems to solve and go after them. To be effective, these quality leaders would have to see each employee with new eyes, to assume that every worker was an intelligent individual who genuinely wanted to give his or her best to the company. How to make that shift in thinking? Training.

FPL devised more than a dozen in-house programs, including team-member and facilitator training. Employees were coached to see one another as internal customers and then to try to give these customers what they needed—even if it was something other than what the employee's department usually supplied. . . .

The name W. Edwards Deming, the American guru of quality more revered in Japan than in his native land, also became known throughout the company. One of his basic tenets is that only data-driven solutions count—those based on scientific analysis of numbers and facts, not gut feelings. The slogan around FPL soon became "In God we trust; the rest, bring data." More than 230 employees have taken a five-week course in advanced statistical process control; 8,000 have studied basic statistics; every one of FPL's 15,000 employees has learned how to interpret data.

By this time it was clear that anyone—from installers to group managers—interested in a career at FPL needed to jump aboard the quality bandwagon. Some employees resented the new emphasis at FPL. Line workers, billing clerks and meter readers were being asked to give more to their company. Annoyed by the extra demands, they resisted changing the way they had always done things. . . .

But as more people took up the banner, employees who had waited for 'that quality thing' to fade eventually realized it wasn't going away. Some left the company. About 750 took early retirement. "You are never going to get 100 percent buy-in," says Brunetti. "If you believe that, you are fooling yourself. If you get 75 percent, you are doing marvelous." . . .

[Quality-improvement teams began to discover ideas that worked.] One such idea that caught on was devising umbrellalike protectors to catch bird droppings—a source of corrosion on some lines. This may sound minor, but it's not if it's your line that's been corroded, causing a power outage just as you're warming up the sofa on Super Bowl Sunday. . . .

[A] team in Delray came up with a way to prevent dog bites—no mean feat in Miami, where every other house seems to have a pair of Dobermans on patrol and dog bites were the largest single cause of on-the-job injuries. First, every bill included an insert that asked if the customer had a dog, if it was kept outside and, most important, if it was dangerous. The response was surprisingly high. Second, the data were programmed into the hand-held computers that meter readers carry. Now "BAD DOG" flashes on the screen when a meter reader punches in a location where Fido is on the job. Meter readers then phone the owner before entering. Now dog bites and absenteeism are down; morale and service are up.

Fewer dog bites and bird droppings may sound like small things to hold up as examples of cultural change, but Brunetti insists that "a real breakthrough is the cumulative effect of hundreds—no, make that thousands—of small improvements." . . .

Only when all of these changes had thoroughly imbued the company was FPL transformed. It happened step by step, day by day, an evolution more than a revolution. The old skin had been shed, and in its place a new one was forming.

While the Deming Prize is not well known in the US . . . FPL employees repeated Deming's name so often it seemed like a mantra. And they were well aware of the award's enormous global prestige. To make everyone feel a part of the decision to go for it, then chairman John Hudiburg made the announcement to senior managers and had it broadcast simultaneously to all employees on video monitors. Anne Grealy, a manager in FPL's revenue and regulatory-requirements department, recalls the impact of the announcement: "It was as if you played tennis for a hobby and someone had entered you in Wimbledon." . . .

Before the run for the Deming, an employee survey had revealed some lingering resentment over the way the company had gone about its pursuit of excellence. As a result of the survey, FPL decided that most teams would become strictly voluntary; problem-solving quotas (much like traffic-ticket quotas for cops) would be done away with; annual reviews would not have a separate category for whether or not you served on quality teams—your commitment to quality would be gauged by overall performance. Management was listening. Morale went on the upswing, and FPL fit the last small piece in place. The backwater bureaucracy was no more.

. . . .

↵ *References and Notes*

[1]M. Alvesson and P. O. Berg, *Corporate Culture and Organizational Symbolism* (Hawthorne, N.Y.: Walter de Gruyter, 1992), p. 123; E. H. Schein, *Organizational Culture and Leadership* (San Francisco: Jossey-Bass, 1992); E. H. Schein, "Coming to a New Awareness of Organizational Culture," *Sloan Management Review* 25 (1984): 3–16.

[2]T. E. Deal and A. A. Kennedy, *Corporate Cultures: The Rites and Rituals of Corporate Life* (Reading, Mass.: Addison-Wesley, 1982), pp. 13–15.
[3]J. Martin, *Cultures in Organizations: Three Perspectives* (New York: Oxford University Press, 1992).

[4]J. Van Maanen and E. H. Schein, "Toward a Theory of Organizational Socialization," in L. L. Cummings and B. M. Staw, eds., *Research in Organizational Behavior*, vol. 1 (Greenwich, Conn.: JAI Press, 1979), p. 210.

[5]Schein, *Organizational Culture*, Ch. 1.

[6]Chapters 17 and 18 discuss organizational design.

[7]M. Loden and J. B. Rosener, *Workforce America! Managing Employee Diversity as a Vital Resource* (Homewood, Ill: Business One Irwin, 1991).

[8]A. M. Pettigrew, "Organizational Climate and Culture: Two Constructs in Search of a Role," in B. Schneider, Ed., *Organizational Climate and Culture* (San Francisco: Jossey-Bass, 1990), pp. 413–33.

[9]Schein, *Organizational Culture*, Ch. 2.

[10]C. Argyris and D. A. Schön, *Organizational Learning* (Reading, Mass.: Addison-Wesley, 1978). Argyris and Schön use the concept of "theory in use." This is a slightly modified label for the concept to allow parallel structure in this context.

[11]L. Kraar, "The Tigers behind Korea's Prowess," *Fortune*, Fall 1989, pp. 36–37, 40.

[12]Martin, *Cultures in Organizations*.

[13]Alvesson and Berg, *Corporate Culture*, pp. 194–95, 210–13.

[14]Developed from Alvesson and Berg, *Corporate Culture*; Martin, *Cultures in Organizations*; H. M. Trice and J. M. Beyer, *The Cultures of Work Organizations* (Englewood Cliffs, N.J.: Prentice-Hall, 1993), pp. 86–89 and other citations noted.

[15]T. C. Dandridge, I. I. Mitroff, and W. F. Joyce, "Organizational Symbolism: A Topic to Expand Organizational Analysis," *Academy of Management Review* 5 (1980): 77–82.

[16]Alvesson and Berg, *Corporate Culture*, pp. 86–87.

[17]Martin, *Cultures in Organizations*, pp. 48–50, 87, 145–48.

[18]Ibid., p. 87.

[19]Ibid., p. 148.

[20]J. Martin, "Deconstructing Organizational Taboos: The Suppression of Gender Conflict in Organizations," *Organization Science* 1 (1990): 339–59.

[21]Ibid., p. 339.

[22]Martin, *Cultures in Organizations*, p. 35.

[23]The last two paragraphs taken from Ibid., p. 147.

[24]Schein, *Organizational Culture*, Part II; Trice and Beyer, *Cultures of Work Organizations*, Ch. 1.

[25]Alvesson and Berg, *Corporate Culture*, Ch. 7.

[26]Ibid.

[27]J. Kerr and J. W. Slocum, Jr., "Managing Corporate Culture through Reward Systems," *Academy of Management Executive* 1 (1987): 99–108.

[28]Deal and Kennedy, *Corporate Cultures*, Ch. 3.

[29]Schein, *Organizational Culture*; Trice and Beyer, *Cultures of Work Organizations*, Ch. 1.

[30]Schein, *Organizational Culture*, Part V.

[31]S. Cartwright and C. L. Cooper, "The Role of Culture Compatibility in Successful Organizational Marriage," *Academy of Management Executive* 7 (1993): 57–70; A. Nahavandi and A. R. Malekzadeh, "Acculturation in Mergers and Acquisitions," *Academy of Management Review*, 13 (1988): 79–90; Trice and Beyer, *Cultures of Work Organizations*, pp. 327–30; G. Walter, "Culture Collisions in Mergers and Acquisitions," in P. Frost, L. Moore, M. Louis, C. Lundberg, and J. Martin, eds., *Organizational Culture* (Beverly Hills, Calif.: Sage Publications, 1985), 301–14.

[32]Trice and Beyer, *Cultures of Work Organizations*, pp. 10–11.

[33]Terrence E. Deal and Allen A. Kennedy, *Corporate Culture* (pg. 16), © 1982 by Addison-Wesley Publishing Company, Inc. Reprinted by permission of the publisher.

[34]Developed from Schein, *Organizational Culture*, Ch. 8 and other sources cited in this section.

[35]Deal and Kennedy, *Corporate Cultures*, pp. 129–33.

[36]P. Gagliardi, ed., *Symbols and Artifacts: Views of the Corporate Landscape* (Hawthorne, N.Y.: Walter de Gruyter, 1990).

[37]Deal and Kennedy, *Corporate Cultures*, pp. 133–35.

[38]*Fortune*, August 29, 1988, p. 16.

[39]B. R. Schlender, "Computer Maker Aims to Transform Industry and Become a Giant," *Wall Street Journal*, March 18, 1988, p. 1, M. Rogers, "Silicon Valley's Rising Sun," *Newsweek*, March 21, 1988, p. 62.

[40]Schlender, "Computer Maker," p. 1.

[41]J. B. Levine, "Sun Microsystems Turns on the Afterburners," *Business Week*, July 18, 1988, pp. 114–15, 118. Quotation from p. 114.

[42]Schlender, "Computer Maker."

[43]Loden and Rosener, *Workforce America*.

[44]Ibid., p. 196.

[45]J. E. Champoux and L. D. Goldman, "Building a Total Quality Culture," in T. D. Connors, ed., *Nonprofit Organizations Policies and Procedures Handbook* (New York: John Wiley & Sons, 1993), Ch. 3.

[46]J. A. Waters and F. Bird, "The Moral Dimension of Organizational Culture," *Journal of Business Ethics* 6 (1987): 15–22.

[47]T. J. Peters and R. H. Waterman, *In Search of Excellence: Lessons from America's Best Run Companies* (New York: Harper & Row, 1982).

[48]D. R. Denison, *Corporate Culture and Organizational Effectiveness* (New York: John Wiley & Sons, 1990), p. 2

[49]Alvesson and Berg, *Corporate Culture*, pp. 49–52, 146, 184–86.

[50]Denison, *Corporate Culture*, Ch. 4.

[51]Ibid.

[52]Ibid.

[53]C. Siehl and J. Martin, "Organizational Culture: A Key to Financial Performance?" in B. Schneider, ed., *Organizational Climate and Culture* (San Francisco: Jossey-Bass, 1990), pp. 241–81.

[54]J. E. Sheriden, "Organizational Culture and Employee Retention," *Academy of Management Journal* 35 (1992): 1036–56.

[55]J. B. Barney, "Organizational Culture: Can It Be a Source of Sustained Competitive Advantage?" *Academy of Management Review* 11 (1986): 656–65.

[56]A. L. Wilkins and W. G. Ouchi, "Efficient Cultures: Exploring the Relationship between Culture and Organizational Performance," *Administrative Science Quarterly* 28 (1983): 468–81.

[57]Schein, "Coming to a New Awareness."

[58]Schein, *Organizational Culture*, pp. 12–13; Trice and Beyer, *Cultures of Work Organizations*, Ch. 4.

[59]Trice and Beyer, *Cultures of Work Organizations*, Ch. 9 and 10.

[60]J. Van Maanen and G. Kunda, " 'Real Feelings:' Emotional Expression and Organizational Culture," in B. M. Staw and L. L. Cummings eds., *Research in Organizational Behavior*, vol. 2 (Greenwich, Conn.: JAI Press, 1989), pp. 43–103.

[61]Developed from Champoux and Goldman, "Building a Total Quality Culture," pp. 60–65; Trice and Beyer, *Cultures of Work Organizations*, Ch. 10.

[62]J. W. Verity, "Does IBM Get It Now?" *Business Week*, December 28, 1992, pp. 32–33.

[63]A. L. Wilkins, and N. J. Bristow, "For Successful Organizational Culture, Honor Your Past," *Academy of Management Executive* 1 (1987): 221–29.

[64]G. Barczak, C. Smith, and D. Wilemon, "Managing Large-Scale Organizational Change," *Organizational Dynamics*, 16 (1987): 23–35.

[65]Wilkins and Bristow, "For Successful Organizational Culture."

[66]P. S. Goodman, M. Bazerman, and E. Conlon, "Institutionalization of Planned Organizational Change," in B. M. Staw and L. L. Cummings, eds., *Research in Organizational Behavior*, vol. 2 (Greenwich, Conn.: JAI Press, 1984), pp. 215–46.

[67]Developed from D. Klein, "Some Notes on the Dynamics of Resistance to Change: The Defender Role," in W. G. Bennis, K. D. Benne, R. Chin, and K. E. Corey, eds., *The Planning of Change*, 3d. ed. (New York: Holt, Rinehart and Winston, 1976), pp. 117–24; P. R. Lawrence, "How to Deal with Resistance to Change," *Harvard Business Review* (May-June 1954): 49–57.

[68]Schein, *Organizational Culture*, p. 260.

[69]L. Kraar, "How Americans Win in Asia," *Fortune*, October 7, 1991, pp. 133–34, 136, 140.

[70]Schein, *Organizational Culture*, pp. 259–60

[71]G. Hofstede, B. Neuijen, D. D. Ohayv, and G. Sanders, "Measuring Organizational Cultures: A Qualitative and Quantitative Study across Twenty Cases," *Administrative Science Quarterly* 35 (1990): 286–316; A. Laurent, "The Cultural Diversity of Western Conceptions of Management," *International Studies of Management and Organization* 13 (1983): 75–96.

[72]N. J. Adler, "Cultural Synergy: The Management of Cross-Cultural Organizations," in W. W. Burke and L. D. Goodstein, eds., *Trends and Issues in OD: Current Theory and Practice* (San Diego: University Associates, 1980), pp. 163–84; N. J. Adler, *International Dimensions of Organizational Behavior* (Boston: PWS-Kent, 1991), Ch. 4.

[73]R. T. Moran and P. R. Harris, *Managing Cultural Synergy* (Houston: Gulf Publishing Company, 1981).

[74]Adler, *International Dimensions*, pp. 105–9.

[75]Trice and Beyer, *Cultures of Work Organizations*, pp. 370–72.

[76]Alvesson and Berg, *Corporate Culture*, p. 150.

[77]Schein, *Organizational Culture*, Ch. 10.

[78]Waters and Bird, "Moral Dimension of Organizational Culture," pp. 15–22.

[79]Deal and Kennedy, *Corporate Cultures*, pp. 133–35.

[80]D. W. Ewing, "Civil Liberties in the Corporation," *New York State Bar Journal* 50 (1978): 188–229.

I Introduction

The previous five chapters introduced you to the world of organizations. They also discussed the major emerging issues that will affect managers into the future. Two chapters gave you a close look at ethics and organizational culture. The following case brings together the observations made thoughout Section I and gives you a chance to apply them.

A WEEK ABOARD THE WAL-MART EXPRESS

The following is an extended case focusing on how managers at Wal-Mart manage their culture. Most of the concepts summarized above apply to this case. Do your analysis first and then compare it to the one that follows the case.

Case Description

"I'm really fired up," Andy Wilson is telling the people in the blue smocks, his Alabama accent dripping Dixie. "This is going to be a great store, and I just want you to know how much we 'preciate the job you're doing. Give yourselves a hand." In just a few minutes Wal-Mart store No. 1,784, in Salem, Oregon, will officially open. But not before Wilson, a Wal-Mart regional vice president who has flown 2,000 miles across the country in a De Soto of a prop-engine plane to get here, dusts these newcomers with the cultural pollen that has helped Wal-Mart flower.

"My job isn't important," he continues. "You're the people who make it happen." The session ends with a rousing Wal-Mart cheer—"Give me a W! Give me an A! Give me an L! Give me a squiggly! . . . "—and a solemn pledge by each associate, Wal-Martese for employee, to greet every customer within ten feet, "so help me, Sam."

The speech reminding these hourly workers that they are the very essence of the enterprise, or something like it, will probably be repeated, in all sincerity, by Wal-Mart executives in 100 stores every day. And if each speaker sounds as if he just stepped off a front porch in Tupelo or Arkadelphia, that's because they all did start the week in that metropolis of merchandising, Bentonville, Arkansas.

Wilson is one of 15 regional vice presidents who spend week after grueling week hopscotching their territories. Today it's Salem, which is about as far from Bentonville as any Wal-Mart store that has ever sold a swamp cooler. But Salem is not out of range of Air Wal-Mart, nor of one of the more unique modes of managing ever erected. The inventor was the late Sam Walton, who could never get enough information about what shoppers were buying and who could never talk to enough customers. He figured the best way to find both in quantity was to visit the stores. This he did as he piloted Wal-Mart to spectacular growth. . . .

This process of heading out to the stores begins on Monday . . . when about 50 to 60 corporate officers, buyers, and "regionals" like Wilson hop into the company's fleet of 15 aircraft. The planes, ranging from small puddle jumpers ("*Don't* get in that old Navajo," cautions one veteran) to two small jets, take off from an airfield in nearby Rogers and return on Wednesday or Thursday loaded with information and ideas.

Spending a week with Wal-Mart . . . evokes the notion that the company doesn't have a management organization so much as a whirling cloud of executive particles that coalesces at the end of each workweek. That would be on Saturday, when the company's entire management assembles at 7 A.M., along with some visiting friends and relatives of associates, to review the numbers and hash out problems in brisk parliamentary debates interspersed with inspirational perorations by guest speakers.

At these Saturday fests, the company will make decisions about anything from how to set up displays to where to put new stores, then begin implementing them immediately. Says CEO David D. Glass: "We all get in there and we shout at each other and argue, but the rule is that we resolve issues before we leave." Come Monday it's the big bang again, and the management team explodes across Wal-Mart's universe.

The regional vice presidents like Wilson are a traveling corps of inspectors, scouts, trend spotters, and market researchers. Their specific charge is to execute sales and marketing plans for 15 territories. . . .

In a typical week Wilson, 36, will get to ten to 12 stores across a territory that begins in West Texas, extends across New Mexico and Arizona, and continues up the West Coast into Oregon. Soon he'll add the state of Washington. With a new store opening in his territory every two weeks, he'll be in charge of 125 stores by the end of this year—more than the entire company had when he joined it 16 years ago. Andy's empire racks up more than $2 billion in sales, nearly 5% of Wal-Mart's revenues.

He puts in 200 days a year on the road, typically starting at five in the morning with a three-mile run in a local park or along the roads near the hotel, ending at eight or nine at night with a stroll through a competitor's store. . . .

This week's patrol will cover Northern California and Oregon, Wal-Mart's farthest reaches. The troop moves out at six Monday morning, when Wilson, his regional personnel manager, Lorie Meyer, and Ken Eaton, who is the merchandiser for intimate apparel and hosiery, . . . jam themselves into a twin-prop Aero Commander—basically a van with wings—for the five-hour trip west.

After refueling in Colorado, the plane lands at 9 A.M. local time in Susanville, California, a pleasant perch 4,200 feet up on the northeastern edge of the Sierra Nevada mountain range. With a population of 7,000 and no other retailer of any size within miles, Susanville is a "Wal-Mart town," says the district manager, Rick Crawford, who meets the plane at the tiny airstrip.

Arriving in the store, Wilson does what every regional does: He swims the sales floor like a shark, store subordinates hanging on like retail remoras. Lorie Meyer, trolling for future store managers, heads off to interview some of the assistant managers and observe training programs, while Ken Eaton tours the apparel area with the "depart," or department supervisor.

Susanville, a nine-month-old outlet, proves a disappointing start to the trip. There are gaps on shelves where paint and auto products should be. Some goods are not displayed according to the promotional plans dreamed up in headquarters, and the departs respond to questions with blank stares, as if they had just arrived. That's precisely the problem. Nearly all switched assignments the week before.

There is literally no place to hide bad news. In each location Wilson dips into a terminal that totals up sales by store and department, labor hours, inventory losses, and other information, then compares the data with results for any time period, for any district or region, or for the nation. At Susanville, the visitor is not at all pleased with what he sees. "You have a great opportunity here," he says over and over again to the departs as he points out the store's shortcomings. At Wal-Mart this passes for a chewing out.

The empty shelves demand action. "Whatever you need to do, do it," he tells district manager [Rick] Crawford, who directs associates to head down the road to the nearest Wal-Mart, 120 miles away, and replenish the out-of-stock merchandise immediately via transfer, rather than wait for the next shipment. Crawford arranges to shuttle in a support team from a more established store to retrain the new departs and associates.

As Wilson, Crawford, and two store staffers stand in the garden department, discussing the depleted inventory of growables, a curmudgeonly senior citizen approaches. "Why are you all standing around here with your arms folded? When are you going to get some seeds?" he scolds. Wilson smiles, introduces himself, tells the man that new stock will be here next week. The customer is not impressed with the Man From the Home Office. "I'll get it somewhere else," he growls. "You'll pay too much," Wilson responds. "I don't care what it costs. I want it when I want it," says the man, driving home the point to the regional vice president. The three others try to stifle their amusement at the boss catching hell.

Before Wilson can beat a retreat from Grandpaville, another senior asks him about a weed puller he saw advertised on television. Wilson once again introduces himself, takes down the man's name and number, and promises he'll look into it. This customer *is* impressed: "I like you, Andy. You're interesting." Turns out that Wal-Mart doesn't carry the weed popper—it's one of those cable channel specials—but by the next week the product will arrive, free, at the man's home, and Wal-Mart will have bought itself a steady customer.

By Monday noon Wilson is off to Red Bluff, 100 miles west over the Sierra Nevada. . . . Although the store manager is on vacation, the three assistants seem to have the place humming. But unlike Susanville, there's competition in town—a Kmart—and Wilson leads the assistants on a fast and furious sweep through enemy territory.

The Kmart is ancient but spotless and bristling with signs comparing prices with Wal-Mart's on hundreds of items, favorably of course. Wilson and Crawford, concerned, are flinging items into a shopping cart—shampoo, antifreeze, light bulbs, food—apparently without being spotted as comparison shoppers by the enemy. The bill comes to $153; Crawford pays. The items are lugged back to Wal-Mart and run through the scanner. To everyone's relief, the tab is about $20 lower at Wal-Mart. Wilson and the crew from headquarters head back to the airport for the trip north to Salem, Oregon, where the new store will open the next morning. . . .

Come Tuesday at 9 A.M., the Wal-Mart way is on display at the grand opening in Salem. More than most companies, Wal-Mart is acutely aware of the need to keep the coals of its culture glowing as it rolls into uncharted areas of the country. The company does this by regularly moving experienced managers into new territory. At Salem, the store manager, Mark Blackman, came west after a seven-year hitch in New Orleans. Several assistant managers in Oregon requested a transfer from Colorado, where the high cost of living, particularly in the resort areas, crimps a $20,000 to $30,000 annual salary.

They know better than to get comfortable, because the company's growth demands that assistants move on average every 24 months. Beth Brock, a friendly Oklahoman who now runs a store in Folsom, California, a little farther down the road, is an ultimate Wal-Mart warrior, having moved eight times in ten years with the company. Her reward? Store managers can earn more than $100,000 a year, which goes a long way in most towns.

But now it's time to cut the ribbon in Salem. Mark Blackman introduces himself as the store's new manager, and then presents his wife and wife's sister to the audience of associates and shoppers. The assistant managers introduce themselves and their spouses, adding a few comments about their Wal-Mart careers. Associate Rodney Wright performs a Wal-Mart rap song he composed, and then Blackman presents Wal-Mart checks to the United Way and DARE, a drug education organization. The district manager, Ron Smoot, concludes his stemwinding pep talk with the announcement that the entire staff has purchased Wal-Mart stock. The finish, naturally, is the Wal-Mart cheer, but before the first "Gimme a W!" is heard, the cheer is spelled out in sign language. The company has hired ten associates from a school for the deaf nearby, and all the store supervisors are learning to sign.

With Tuesday off to an energizing start, Wilson heads for the plane and the short, 30-mile trip to Lebanon, Oregon. . . . As he does everywhere, Wilson is constantly making notes on index cards. Country music star Garth Brooks will appear in the area soon, and the store can't get any tour T-shirts, a hot item. Noted. It is also thinly stocked in local styles. Says district manager Smoot: "We asked headquarters for more Western wear and were told it would take 90 days. I need it bad. And I can't get any felt hats." Wilson promises action.

At every store along the tour, Meyer makes a pitch to associates to own stock, which they can buy at a 15% discount to market through a payroll deduction plan. She notes what percentage of each store's employees participate in the plan and tells each group how it compares with the region. The buy-in ranges from 100% in Salem to 30% in Lebanon, below average. The reason, the store manager quietly explains, is that 75% of the store's associates were unemployed when they were hired. It's a timber economy, now as devastated as are the nearby forests from clear-cutting. "We don't want to force our stock on anybody," responds Meyer, who like Wilson is taken aback by the local depression.

Back to the plane. . . . Inside the store [in Klamath Falls, Oregon], Wilson gathers together about 25 hourly workers and department supervisors in the lunchroom. He asks each one his name, the department where he or she works, and what each did before he joined Wal-Mart. And then, "How is your department doing?" After thanking them once again for handling their jobs so well, he asks if there is anything that he or anyone else back at HQ can do for them.

The Q&A with associates, which Wilson will repeat in the next and last stop of the day, Oroville, California, 200 miles away, is part of what the company calls servant-leadership. It's another one of Sam's things, the notion being that the people working in the stores ought to be the ones catered to, not the executives. "You've got to get them to believe that you're listening to them," says Wilson. "Because all the best ideas are going to come from them." He works at it relentlessly, pressing the flesh like a politician and unfailingly praising clerks for their work.

The next morning the plane leaves at six for Folsom, California, the last stop. Manager Beth Brock explains the difference between managing a store in her home state of Oklahoma and one in California. "Here, I do 40% of my business on the weekends, and Friday nights are dead. In Oklahoma, going to Wal-Mart on Friday night was the thing to do." At 10 A.M. Wilson gets the by now familiar high-decibel send-off, and it's back to the airport and a numbing six-hour flight home.

After spending Thursday at the home office planning a meeting—usually he would be on the road—Wilson arrives Friday morning, armed with his stack of index cards for the 7 A.M. operations meeting. It's the first of four assemblies over two days attended by all Wal-Mart officers, including Rob Walton, Sam's eldest son and the company's new chairman.

The congress opens with a report from the battle fronts. And most of the news is good, if not great. Sales are booming. Walton reports from a tour of the company's first stores in New Hampshire. "We're going to blow the doors off this summer," he boasts. . . . But a new emporium in Manassas, Virginia, has problems. . . . The store is messy, and too many products are out of stock. In fact, many of the new Wal-Marts seem to be straining to keep up with the business. Says Glass: "We're leaving hundreds of thousands of dollars on the table. In the aggregate it's millions of dollars. I don't mean to pick on Manassas, but we didn't support that store. We just buried them." Quickly the conversation turns to solutions. Dean L. Sanders, the executive vice president of operations, wants the new-store planning division to devise a supply scheme and test it at a few upcoming openings. Glass approves.

That afternoon many of the same faces get together, over sandwiches and iced tea, for the merchandise meeting. The morning has been devoted to stores; the afternoon is product. Wilson has a couple of things on his index-card agenda: Western wear, the Garth Brooks T-shirts, and shortages in the garden and auto products departments. Brock, the store manager back in Folsom, told him Wal-Mart is missing great business in street-hockey gear, part of the Rollerblade craze. Wilson, who thought so too, announces: "In No. 9 [sporting goods] I don't think we're broad enough in street hockey. We need a 20-foot section. We don't have enough of the pads." The sporting goods buyer says an eight-foot-long section will be ready in two months. "I need it sooner," says Wilson. Sanders, the operations EVP, agrees, and within a week a large display of hockey gear is on its way to Folsom. As for the Garth Brooks T-shirt issue: "I want 1,000 in every store near where he's touring," Wilson says. Done. He then flags the Western wear merchandiser, who promises to get more goods immediately to the Oregon stores.

In Wal-Mart's style, problems pop up like targets in a shooting gallery and are dispatched quickly. For instance, sales and warehouse data show that the store managers aren't ordering fast enough, risking running out of stock. Apparently, they are waiting for directions from Bentonville. "We've got to get rid of this mind-set," says Don Soderquist, the vice chairman and chief operating officer. Sanders immediately offers to create a video that will reemphasize the need for managers to order aggressively. "For $1,200, we can get it to all the district managers overnight," he says. Approved.

The meeting bounces around through a bazaar of products: vitamins (back in the warehouse), fertilizer (there's no spreader setting on the Wal-Mart brand bag; info stickers will be attached), there are no replacement lights for ceiling fans the company sells (ordered). It concludes after two hours, and Wilson heads back to his "office," a desk in the open, tennis-court-size operations room, and dictates a memo via voice mail to all his district managers, telling them about the actions taken and what to expect next week.

Next morning it's show time: the now famous Wal-Mart Saturday get-together that somehow combines entertainment with no-nonsense business, sort of "Family Feud Meets Ernst & Young." About 500 folks show up in the auditorium; the dress code is church picnic. Kin are welcome, and today brothers, cousins, and in-laws of associates are all introduced to the crowd, which greets each name with a round of applause. When an associate group from Sam's Club, Wal-Mart's warehouse club, is introduced, the group stands up and whoops and hollers.

Soderquist, a big Midwesterner with a booming voice, emcees the show. There is plenty to yell about today. "We had an excellent week!" Soderquist intones, announcing sales figures that are about 25% ahead of last year and up 13% for same-store sales.... Each regional vice president then reports on new stores. Glass once again praises the effort in Illinois, and applause greets Wilson's announcement that 100% of the Salem store's staff have bought stock. Finally Soderquist reads the week's honor roll, the stores that showed the greatest year-to-year improvement for the week.

Now it's time for the guest speaker, Dr. Frederick Humphries, president of Florida A&M University, a leading black college. Humphries is what might be called a supply-side educator: "Tell us what you want," he exhorts the audience, "and we'll make them for you. You want computer scientists? We'll make them for you." He concludes his speech, about producing the next generation of African American businessmen, to a standing ovation.

Case Analysis

The case had many examples of verbal, material, and action symbols. It opened with the Wal-Mart cheer, a verbal symbol that appeared throughout the case. The words people used were also symbols: "associate" instead of employees, "depart" as a short way of saying department supervisor, "You have a great opportunity here" as a form of Wal-Mart sanction of behavior, and "Whatever you need to do, do it" as an expression of required responsive behavior. The whoops and hollers following the introduction of the Sam's Club associates at the Saturday gathering expressed support and identity with all parts of the corporation.

Another verbal symbol, but distinct from the spoken words mentioned above, was the sign language used at the opening of the store in Salem, Oregon. Not only was the cheer spelled in sign language, but store supervisors were learning to sign. Both the hiring of deaf associates and the use of sign language are important symbols of valuing diversity.

Material symbols appeared often in the case. The presentation of the Wal-Mart checks to the United Way and DARE at the opening of the Salem store symbolically reached out to the store's community. Several references to buying Wal-Mart stock suggest the importance of employee ownership in the culture of this organization. Buying the weed popper for a customer, even when Wal-Mart did not sell the item, was a material symbol of its commitment to its customers. The corporate headquarters offices were functional and showed almost no status distinctions. One observer likened the offices to a regional truck depot.[1]

The Friday and Saturday meetings had ritualistic meaning. Those meetings were the reason for the frenzied week of traveling. Friday morning focused on stores; Friday afternoon focused on products. Those events happened repeatedly on each Friday. They featured important action symbols, or behavior, that expressed some basic assumptions of the Wal-Mart culture.

Action-oriented events filled the Friday meetings. Managers attacked any problems raised by anyone in the meetings. The discussions in the meetings appeared heated yet well focused on solving a problem. The fast pace of the meetings implied a strong action orientation of the Wal-Mart culture.

The Saturday meeting also featured guest speakers, such as Dr. Frederick Humphries, president of a leading black college in Florida. He emphasized what his college was doing to help build the next generation of black business people. The standing ovation, another action symbol, implied the value Wal-Mart places on diversity.

The case implies values of an intense customer focus, care for associates, decisiveness, no delays in solving problems, and all executives supporting the store managers. The company had a strong profit orientation, but saw the other values as a way to get to that goal. Values of decisiveness and problem solving showed in Andy Wilson's hectic weekly travel and the fast-paced Friday meetings. You can see the caring for associates in the family involvement in the Saturday meetings, the lack of pressure to buy stock by the associates in the Lebanon, Oregon store, the seeking of ideas from associates in all stores visited, and training of newly transferred store managers and department supervisors.

Although the case does not mention Total Quality Management (TQM), the behavior in the case and the associated values are all consistent with TQM's intense customer focus. The desire for decentralized decision making at the store level for stock reorders also is consistent with a TQM philosophy. Decentralization to this level helps meet customer needs and can build responsive stores.

Evidence for some values appears so often that likely they are basic assumptions in the Wal-Mart culture. The heated meetings at Wal-Mart headquarters featured such continued conflict they implied a basic assumption that conflict is good if it leads to resolution. Concern for employees, as shown in the repeated symbols mentioned earlier, points to a basic assumption of caring. Other evidence appears in the lack of status distinction and the servant-leadership emphasis, instilled in this culture by its founder and hero, the late Sam Walton.

Focusing on the customer also looks like a basic assumption. It has its roots in Sam Walton's passion for learning about customer wants, needs, and expectations. It shows in the repeated symbols of customer focus: greet any customer within ten feet ("so help me, Sam") and buying the weed popper.

The strong customer focus is most likely part of the core ideology of the Wal-Mart culture. The stores described in the case all faced different markets. Some emphasized Western wear; others stressed Rollerblade equipment; still others needed Garth Brooks T-shirts. In each instance, the Friday meetings led to fast action to respond to those market needs.

Other information not in the case suggests Sam Walton held those basic assumptions as his tenets of doing business.[2] He believed in the following:

1. Treat employees as partners. Share both bad news and good news.
2. Encourage employees to challenge the obvious.
3. Employees must get involved.

The entire case is an example of how the managers of one organization maintain its present culture and create new cultures. Traveling managers used all types of cultural symbols to reinforce Wal-Mart values in existing stores. Examples include responding to customer needs in the Folsom, California store and seeking employee ideas in Klamath Falls, Oregon.

Wal-Mart executives focused on creating culture in new stores. They managed cultural symbols in their desire to infuse those stores with the Wal-Mart way. The Salem, Oregon store was not just new, it was in new territory for the company. Experienced managers from other stores were moved into the new store. Other symbols focused on the new store included the rap song composed by an associate, doing the Wal-Mart cheer—but only after spelling it in sign language—and the proud announcement by Wilson of 100% participation in the stock plan.

The Wal-Mart culture must work for them. The company has grown at a compound rate of 30 to 40 percent for almost 20 years.[3] Growth rates in sales, net income, and earnings per share between 1987 and 1991 also point to success. Sales grew 29 percent, net income grew 27 percent, and earnings per share grew 26 percent.[4]

References and Notes

[1] J. Huey, "Wal-Mart: Will It Take Over the World?" *Fortune*, January 30, 1989, pp. 52–64.

[2] J. H. Boyett and H. P. Conn, *Workplace 2000: The Revolution Reshaping American Business* (New York: Penguin Books USA, 1991), pp. 339–40.

[3] Huey, "Wal-Mart," p. 53.

[4] Financial information reported by Wal-Mart Stores Inc. Taken from *Compact Disclosure,*® Disclosure Incorporated, Bethesda, Maryland, October 1992.

Individual Processes in Organizations

Section Overview

*F*igure II-1 shows an overview of the major sections of this book and the chapters in Section II. This section introduces you to some major individual processes in organizations. The main topics are organizational socialization, motivation, rewards, and the job design effects on motivation. Each chapter discusses international aspects of the topics and the ethical issues they raise.

Chapter 6 describes a powerful organization process called organizational socialization. It is often the first process you experience after joining a new organization. The chapter opens with a description of roles, role behavior, and the types of transitions people make as they move through roles in an organization. It then focuses on the three stages of organizational socialization. The first stage, called anticipatory socialization, happens before a person joins an organization. The entry/encounter stage follows the anticipatory stage. In this stage, you compare expectations formed in the anticipatory stage to the reality you see after entry. The last stage (metamorphosis) features the emergence of the self-image an organization wants a person to have. Chapter 6 includes a discussion of the effects of individual differences on socialization and describes the characteristics of an effective socialization process.

Chapters 7 and 8 focus on major theories of human motivation. Chapter 7 describes the major need theories; Chapter 8 describes cognitive and behavioral theories. The need theories include the Hierarchy of Needs Theory, Existence-Relatedness-Growth Theory, and McClelland's Achievement Motivation Theory. Chapter 7 also describes Herzberg's Motivator-Hygiene Theory, which is not a need theory, but is closely related to them and acts as a bridge to Chapter 8.

Chapter 8 describes some cognitive and behavioral theories of motivation. The two cognitive theories are Expectancy Theory and Equity Theory. Expectancy Theory shows how people's beliefs about effort, performance, and resulting outcomes can affect their motivational state. Equity Theory addresses the question of fairness in the distribution of rewards by managers. The two theories combine to form an analytical tool for understanding motivational issues in organizations.

Chapter 8 then describes two motivational techniques: Behavioral Modification and Goal Setting Theory. Behavior Modification shows how to shape behavior by associating consequences with behavior. The discussion includes the side effects of

```
┌──────────────────┐
│    Section I      │
│   Introduction    │
└──────────────────┘
         │
         ▼
┌──────────────────┐
│   Section II      │            ┌──────────────────┐
│ Individual        │────────────│    Chapter 6      │
│ Processes         │            │  Organizational   │
│ in Organizations  │            │  Socialization    │
└──────────────────┘            └──────────────────┘
         │                                │
         ▼                                ▼
┌──────────────────┐            ┌──────────────────┐
│   Section III     │            │    Chapter 7      │
│ Group and Inter-  │            │   Motivation:     │
│ personal Processes│            │  Need Theories    │
│ in Organizations  │            └──────────────────┘
└──────────────────┘                     │
         │                                ▼
         ▼                      ┌──────────────────┐
┌──────────────────┐            │    Chapter 8      │
│   Section IV      │            │ Motivation: Cognitive│
│  Organizational   │            │ and Behavioral    │
│  Processes        │            │Theories and Techniques│
└──────────────────┘            └──────────────────┘
         │                                │
         ▼                                ▼
┌──────────────────┐            ┌──────────────────┐
│   Section V       │            │    Chapter 9      │
│ The Design of     │            │ Intrinsic Rewards │
│  Organizations    │            │ and Job Design    │
└──────────────────┘            └──────────────────┘
         │
         ▼
┌──────────────────┐
│   Section VI      │
│  Organizational   │
│  Change and the   │
│     Future        │
└──────────────────┘
```

punishment and the criticisms made of this approach to human motivation. Goal Setting Theory describes how specific, challenging, reachable goals that are accepted by a person lead to higher performance than goals that are "fuzzy," unchallenging, not reachable, or not accepted. The chapter also discusses the steps in the technique of goal setting.

Chapter 9 explains how job design affects people's experience of internal rewards. The chapter develops the Job Characteristics Theory of Work Motivation, a well-researched theory that can guide the design of motivating jobs. The chapter also discusses how the context of a job can affect its motivational qualities and gives you guidelines for diagnosing and redesigning jobs. A separate section discusses group-based job design and compares it to jobs designed for individuals.

6

Organizational Socialization

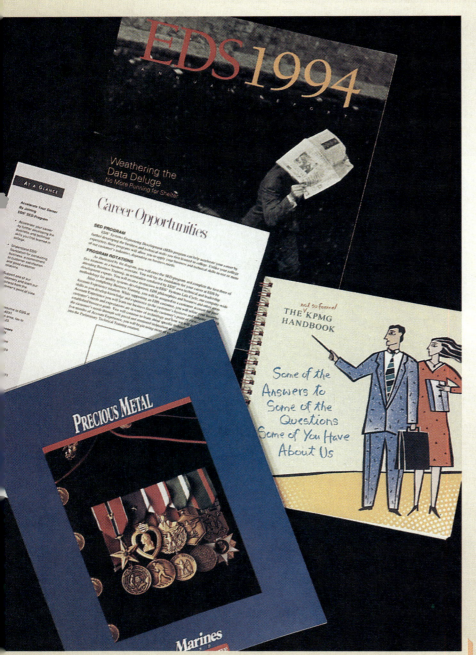

- Many organizations use recruiting brochures to attract potential new employees. For many college students, these brochures are their first glimpses of organizations that might employ them.

After reading this chapter, you should be able to . . .

- Explain organizational socialization as a process that develops and communicates an organization's culture.
- Distinguish between roles, role behaviors, and boundary transitions.
- Describe the stages of organizational socialization and how they repeat during a work career.
- Distinguish the socialization issues in expatriate and repatriate adjustment.
- Discuss the ethical issues in organizational socialization.

Chapter Overview

OPENING EPISODE

Women Challenging "Old Boy" Network

Tired of running up against the "old boy" networks of corporate America, the women of Susquehanna University's business school here have created a network of their own.

The school began assigning mentors to each woman majoring in business last year. This year's mentors, Susquehanna graduates already in the business world, met their charges earlier this month.

The "old girl" network doesn't include poker games, golf outings or hunting trips. It does include discussions on getting ahead and juggling home and career.

"I wish I had had someone to talk to about business while I was in school," said Mary Mack, a 1983 graduate assigned to freshman Colleen Supinkski of Easton, Pa.

Mack, who runs a Washington computer programing business, said she entered the business world thinking it would be just like her textbooks said. Instead, she said, promotions at the company she previously worked for were based on who one knew, and its "family atmosphere" chilled when she wanted a transfer.

The Susquehanna students are assigned mentors in the second semester of their freshman year. Twenty-one are starting the program this year; 18 started last year.

"I'm concerned about having a husband, kids, two dogs and being a career woman," said Kim Dunkle, a sophomore from West Chester who began the program last year. "I'm nervous that I'm not going to be able to do it."

Mentors are required to meet with the students at least twice a year for the student's four years of college. Students are encouraged to call or write at least four times a year.

Source: K. P. Kissel, "Women Challenging 'Old Boy' Network," Associated Press, 1993. (As the story appeared in *Business Outlook*, *Albuquerque Journal*, March 1, 1993, p. 3.) Reprinted with the permission of the Associated Press.

· *The business school at Susquehanna University, Selinsgrove, Pennsylvania.*

The Opening Episode shows how some women business students are trying to get accurate information about their future careers in business. The mentoring program should help them understand the adjustments required by multiple work and nonwork roles. Although they have not left their university, the students' socialization to roles in their career has already begun. This chapter describes organization socialization and shows you where in that process the Susquehanna University mentor program falls.

Organizational socialization is the process by which people learn the content of an organization's culture.[1] It is a powerful process that not only affects the individual's behavior but also helps shape and maintain the organization's culture. One scholar has defined organizational socialization as the " . . . process by which a new member learns the value system, the norms, and the required behavior patterns of the . . . organization or group . . . [the person] is entering."[2] Organizations almost inevitably leave their imprint on individual members through the socialization process.[3]

Two ideas are embedded in the above definition. First, the definition tells us what an individual must do to participate as a successful member of an organization. The socialization process is one way an organization tries to affect its members' motivation to participate. Second, the " . . . values, norms, and required behaviors . . ." are the contributions the organization expects from its successful members. Those contributions must about equal the inducements from the organization if the person is to join and stay in the organization.

Values, norms, and required behaviors are all part of the culture of an organization.[4] As described in Chapter 5, organizational culture includes the values, norms, rites, rituals, ceremonies, heroes, and scoundrels in the history of the organization.[5] It defines the content of what a new employee needs to learn to be accepted as a member of the organization.

Organizational socialization is usually the first behavioral process a person experiences after joining an organization. Accordingly, this chapter starts by describing how the process affects a new employee trying to learn a new culture. It then describes how the socialization process unfolds through different stages in one's relationship with the organization. You will eventually see that people are socialized to multiple cultures throughout their careers.

This chapter examines organizational socialization from your perspective both as an individual affected by the process and as a manager using the process. The information you gain here will increase your understanding of the socialization process as it affects you. Such understanding will let you make choices about the organizations you may wish to join after graduation. You also will gain insights into what will happen to you shortly after you join the organization and throughout your career.

Managers use the organization's socialization process to affect the behavior of people they hire or who move into their work unit. Understanding the dynamics and content of the process lets a manager use it more effectively than she might otherwise.

Organizational socialization in the broadest sense is a process by which people adjust to new organizations, new jobs, and new groups of people. It focuses on getting employees to acquire the values, attitudes, and role behaviors defined as important by the culture.[6] It also is concerned with the development of work skills and adjustment to the norms and values of the immediate work group.[7] In short, organizational socialization deals with the basic question of individual-organization fit.

. . . .

◢ Roles and Role Behavior

Organizations ask us to take on roles that have certain behavioral requirements. The roles develop from the division of labor of the organization and its organizational design. Other aspects of roles are defined by the organization's culture.

A role is a set of activities, duties, responsibilities, and required behaviors that the organization wants an individual to acquire. The behaviors that are part of a role are the contributions the organization wants in exchange for the inducements it is willing to give (pay, fringe benefits, and the like). The two must roughly balance for the individual to agree to the role.

ROLE BEHAVIOR

Each role has role behaviors that vary according to what the organization requires of a person.[8] There are three types of role behaviors: pivotal, relevant, and peripheral. **Pivotal role behaviors** are behaviors an individual must accept to join and remain a member of the organization. These behaviors are "the price of membership," the basic contributions the organization expects in exchange for its inducements. Examples of pivotal role behaviors include valuing a job well done, attire, belief in a hierarchy of authority, viewing conflict as constructive, and accepting the profit motive.

Relevant role behaviors are behaviors considered desirable and good by the organization, but not essential to membership. These behaviors can include appearance, extra work efforts such as committee work, and lifestyle.

Peripheral role behaviors are behaviors that are neither necessary nor desirable. An example of a peripheral role behavior is occasional chatting and visiting with coworkers during the work day. Management tolerates such behavior if it is not excessive and does not interfere with work performance. If management eventually decides the behavior as unacceptable, it can then become either pivotal or relevant.

Role behavior that is pivotal in one organization may only be relevant in another and vice versa. Variations in what is pivotal and relevant can also be found within the same organization.

ROLE EPISODES

A series of **role episodes** communicates pivotal and relevant role behaviors. These episodes start when an organization recruits an individual for employment and continue during the early months of employment. Figure 6-1 shows the content and dynamics of a role episode.[9]

One or more persons are role senders. Before a person joins the organization, the role sender is often the company's recruiter. After the person joins the organization, the role sender is the individual who hired or will supervise the new employee. Other role senders are coworkers throughout the organization.

The role sender defines a sent role's pivotal and relevant role behaviors by communicating information about the role either orally or in writing. Job descriptions, company policies, and the employee handbook often communicate pivotal role behaviors. Relevant role behaviors are communicated orally and less formally than pivotal role behaviors.

The focal person receives the role behavior sent by the role sender. The person then enacts the role behavior according to the way she perceives it. The focal person's perception forms the received role. She either complies with the role sender's request or resists it.

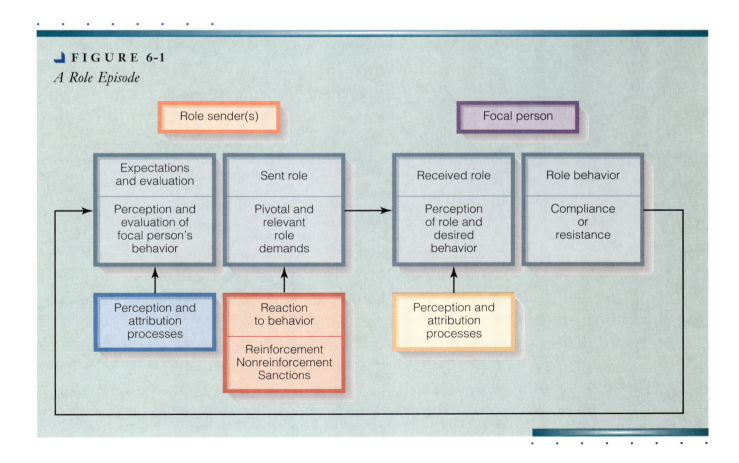

FIGURE 6-1

A Role Episode

The role sender perceives the focal person's behavior and assesses how closely it matches the sender's perception of the content of the role. The role sender can react to the behavior of the focal person in one of three ways: reinforcement, sanctions, or nonreinforcement (ignoring). If the behavior is acceptable, the focal person may receive some reinforcement, such as a compliment for doing a good job. If the focal person has not complied with the requested role behavior, the role sender may apply sanctions such as a reprimand. Reinforcement and sanctions are most likely to be used for pivotal and relevant role behaviors. Role senders often ignore (nonreinforcement) peripheral role behavior, at least until they decide whether the behavior is pivotal or relevant.

The role episode repeats with the same role sender. The episode ends when compliance is obtained, noncompliance is accepted, or the focal person is terminated by the organization. Alternatively, a new employee can leave the organization. She might quit if the behavior is unacceptable to her or if the inducements from the organization no longer equal her contributions.

The role episode can repeat with other managers or coworkers as the role senders. Often managers and coworkers send conflicting role behaviors to a new employee. She likely will comply with the role sender she believes has the most control over her destiny in the organization.

Managers find themselves behaving as role senders and focal persons simultaneously. As role senders, they try to affect the behavior of those who report to them, especially new employees. At the same time, the managers to whom they report view them as focal persons and try to shape their behavior, especially if they are considered good candidates for promotion.

Perception plays an important role in role episodes. Many aspects of perception described in Chapter 4 operate during role episodes. Both the role sender and the focal person may experience selective perception which can lead to disagreements about the content of the person's role. Attribution processes may also operate. If a new employee does not do well, she might attribute her failure to lack of guidance from the role sender and not to her misunderstanding of the role content.

. . . .

↵ Boundary Transitions

The socialization process is continuous throughout a person's association with an organization, but is most intense before and after boundary transitions.[10] **Boundary transitions** occur when a new employee crosses the organization's boundary upon joining the organization. They also occur as the person's career unfolds and she crosses other boundaries within the organization. The employee is most susceptible to organizational influences just before and just after those transitions.[11]

Boundary transitions have three dimensions: functional, hierarchical, and inclusionary.[12] Each dimension presents different features of an organization's socialization process to a person. Figure 6-2 shows the boundary transitions within a three-dimensional cone. The figure emphasizes the different direction of movement of each dimension of a boundary transition.

When you first join an organization, you cross its functional boundary. Most likely, you will take a job in a single department such as accounting, finance, marketing, or human resources. These departments do many major work functions of the organization. You may cross other functional boundaries in the same organization if it has a program of employee development emphasizing experience in several functional areas.

The socialization process of the functional dimension emphasizes the development and use of skills and abilities in doing a particular task. The process also emphasizes "how we do things around here," which may or may not be what you

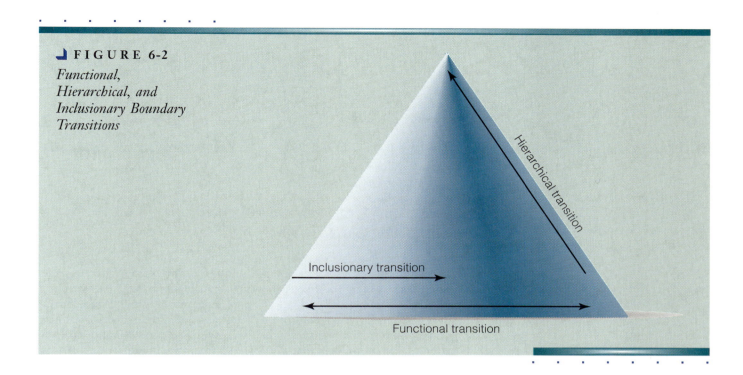

Functional, Hierarchical, and Inclusionary Boundary Transitions

Hierarchical transition

Inclusionary transition

Functional transition

learned in college. Basic values of an organization's culture are communicated following a functional boundary transition.

If you successfully master the requirements following a functional boundary transition, you may be promoted to a higher position. At this point, you experience the hierarchical dimension of a boundary transition. Now you are moving upward in the organization into a position with more authority. It may be a supervisory or management position or a more senior staff position within a functional area. The socialization process following the hierarchical boundary transition may emphasize being rewarded for good performance, taking on more responsibilities, and becoming more involved in organization affairs. If you were promoted into a different functional area, you also would experience the socialization processes for the functional dimension of the boundary transition.

The hierarchical dimension has an additional characteristic as well. Take another look at Figure 6-2. Notice that hierarchical transitions also feature inward movement. Such transitions bring you closer to the center of the organization. The socialization process at a hierarchical transition includes many things about the heart of the organization's culture.

The last dimension of boundary transitions is the inclusionary dimension, which usually operates in concert with the first two dimensions. The inward movement of this boundary transition emphasizes that you are a newcomer to an existing system. You will be expected to prove yourself before you will be accepted by veteran members of the organization.

The socialization process of the inclusionary dimension heavily emphasizes values, norms, and required behaviors. Acceptance of those values and norms will be critical to your acceptance by others already in the system. Over time it could mean acceptance into the heart of the organization and admission to its "inner circle."

The early period following a boundary transition is highly important from both the individual's and the organization's perspective. During this time, you learn the performance expectations of the organization. Your success in the organization depends partly on getting a job assignment that fits your skills, needs, and values.

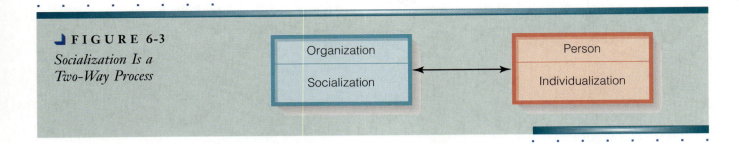

FIGURE 6-3

Socialization Is a Two-Way Process

Organization		Person
Socialization	←→	Individualization

Individual and Organization Perspective on Organizational Socialization

The socialization process is a two-way process, not a one-way process. At the same time the organization is trying to affect your values and behavior, you are trying to keep certain aspects of your individuality.[13] The organization wants to put its mark on you, and you want to put your mark on the organization. You presumably value who you are, and you want the organization to recognize and use what you value in yourself. Figure 6-3 shows this constant interplay between the organization's efforts at **socialization** and your bid for **individualization.**

As an individual, you have a unique set of skills and talents and want to satisfy a unique set of needs. You feel a desire to preserve your individual identity. Simultaneously, you feel a need for acceptance by your employing organization and its members so they will use your talents and abilities.

Members of an existing organizational culture feel they must require some degree of conformity to the values and behaviors the culture considers necessary for its survival. Uniform values and behavior among organization members can decrease the potential for conflict. The organization also needs innovative behavior if it is to remain viable and survive in a changing environment. Organizations face the following problem: getting what they need for effective role performance without overspecifying behavior for the role.[14]

Now you can see the basic dilemma of organizational socialization for both the individual and the organization. The process is a "tug-of-war" between the individual's need to be who she is and the organization's need to mold her to its image of her.

Let's now see how this drama unfolds as a person begins the process of choosing a new job and entering a new organization.

Stages of Organizational Socialization

Organizational socialization happens in three stages: Choice: Anticipatory Socialization, Entry/Encounter, and Change: Metamorphosis. The product of one stage becomes the input to the next stage. Understanding the stages of socialization is important from your perspective as an individual because of the experiences you are likely to have at each stage. It also is important from a management perspective because each stage helps the socialization process achieve what the organization wants it to achieve.[15]

Figure 6-4 shows the three stages of socialization. You will experience the stages of socialization not only in your first job, but in successive positions within the same organization, as well as in a new position in a different organization. The first two stages include several processes of socialization. These **socialization processes** are methods organizations use to shape the values and behavior they would like you to have.

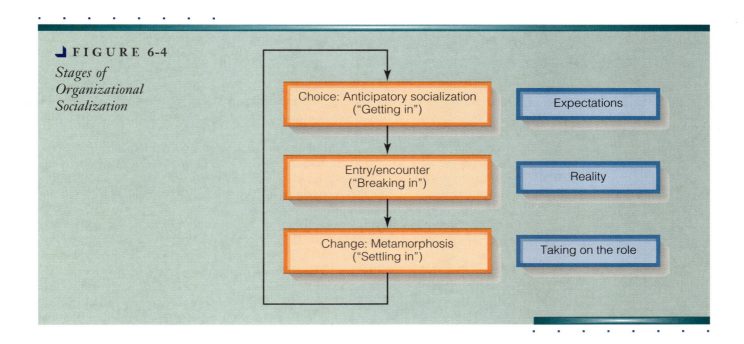

FIGURE 6-4

Stages of Organizational Socialization

Choice: Anticipatory socialization ("Getting in") → Expectations

Entry/encounter ("Breaking in") → Reality

Change: Metamorphosis ("Settling in") → Taking on the role

CHOICE: ANTICIPATORY SOCIALIZATION ("GETTING IN")

Choice: anticipatory socialization is the first stage of socialization a person experiences.[16] This stage happens before a person joins an organization or takes a new job in the same organization. It prepares the individual for entry into an organization as a new employee. The mentoring program described in the Opening Episode occurs during this stage.

Although the person is outside the organization, the events during the anticipatory stage are a first glimpse of the organization's culture. Her expectations or beliefs about what it will be like to be a member of the organization develop during this stage. In short, when we consider a new position or a new organization, we predict what life will be like in the new situation.

The individual and the organization both face two important issues at the anticipatory stage.[17] One issue involves the question of realism. Does the potential new employee have a realistic idea of the organization's culture? Does the individual understand the specific job requirements? Organizations present an image of themselves and the jobs that need to be done. Individuals develop expectations about working in the organization from that image. The basic question is whether that image is a true and accurate portrayal of life in the organization.

Realism is the responsibility of both the organization and the individual. The organization should present both the positive and negative side of what it is like to work for the company. The potential employee should also present an accurate picture of herself.[18] She must know what she can do and not oversell or undersell herself to the organization.

An image of life in the organization is the basic product of the anticipatory stage of socialization. A new employee develops an image of the organization, and the organization develops an image of her. The degree of congruence in those images will prove critical to the mutual adaptation of the two parties.

The second issue focuses on congruence between the individual and the organization. You have a set of skills and abilities. Are those skills and abilities congruent with the needs of the organization? You also have a set of needs and values. Can the organization satisfy those needs and offer you a congruent set of values?

These two sets of issues are important for both parties because lack of realism and congruence are associated with high turnover, low satisfaction, low organizational commitment, and poor job performance. Errors at the anticipatory stage have negative effects for both the individual and the organization.[19]

Socialization Processes

Organizations use several socialization processes in the anticipatory stage. Although all the processes are available to any organization, different organizations use them in varying degrees.

Recruitment activities are important processes within the anticipatory socialization stage. As you approach graduation, you will begin seeking a job by reading recruitment advertising or brochures. Company recruiters will come to your campus to interview students. You also may talk to former students who are now working for a company in which you are interested.

The recruiting activities create a set of expectations about working for the organization. Although you have not yet joined the company, you develop a set of beliefs about working in the firm. The recruitment process—and choosing a company—socializes you to a set of beliefs or expectations about that organization before you even join it.

Some companies also use screening and selection devices to make hiring decisions. Such devices include written tests, oral interviews, and simulation of a job unfamiliar to you. Written tests can assess skills, interests, and psychological characteristics. Oral interviews augment an employment application and any written tests. Job simulations test a person's strengths and weaknesses in new and unfamiliar situations.[20]

Screening and selection devices can be used with potential new employees and existing employees who may be seeking promotion. NCR Corp.'s "early identification program"[21] used all three methods to identify existing employees with executive potential. Employees with psychological and interest profiles similar to those of existing senior executives were considered to have the most future potential. The selection and screening procedures yield the same results by identifying a nearly homogeneous group of people from which the organization can draw.

During these recruitment activities, the organization and the potential new employee should both consider the realism of images they project. Lack of realism in the anticipatory stages creates problems for both parties after the person enters the organization.

Realistic Job Previews

Many organizations have recognized the importance of creating **realistic expectations** during the anticipatory stage of socialization. These organizations use many ways to give potential new employees a Realistic Job Preview. This approach to recruiting sharply contrasts with approaches that describe only the positive qualities of the organization.

Realistic Job Previews are balanced descriptions of important characteristics of the job and the organization. The descriptions include important sources of both satisfaction and dissatisfaction.[22] The preview is given to a potential employee before the applicant has accepted a job offer. Research evidence shows that Realistic Job Previews can help build realistic expectations about the organization, increase satisfaction after joining the organization, and reduce turnover.[23]

Organizations use several approaches to Realistic Job Previews. Some organizations use recruiting brochures that give an accurate description of what it is like to work for the organization. Others use videotapes and films lasting 25 to 80 minutes. The films show many aspects of the work situation that the recruit could face. They include descriptions by present employees of what they like and do not like about their jobs. Some organizations are starting to use work site visits for applicants for nonmanagerial, entry-level jobs.[24] Site visits have not been commonly used in the past for applicants to such positions.

Similar previews are also being used to a limited degree in company mergers. Realistic Merger Previews keep employees informed about the progress of a merger and its likely effects on their jobs.[25] The previews have reduced employee uncertainty and increased their sense that the company cared, was honest, and could be trusted.

Realistic Job Previews are a deliberate effort by an organization to set expectations. The intention is to create expectations that are neither unrealistically high nor unrealistically low.[26] By creating realistic expectations, the organization avoids the negative results that could occur if a new employee's image of the organization is sharply out of line with reality.

◢ E X E R C I S E   *Organizational Recruiting and Expectations*

*F*igure 6-5 shows some recruiting materials used by three organizations—the U.S. Marine Corps; Electronic Data Systems Corp. (EDS), a major firm in the computer and information technology industry; and KPMG Peat Marwick, a professional accounting firm. The materials present the recruit with a large amount of information about these organizations.

The Marine Corps', brochures emphasize pride, teamwork, and challenge, Photographs show Marine recruits in physically demanding training and portray the diversity of the Marine Corps. The brochures also illustrate the various jobs available to recruits, foreign travel, and career movement.

EDS's recruiting materials have two features. The upper brochure in Figure 6-5b describes the widespread effect of the company in many aspects of people's lives, such as credit card transactions and travel reservations. EDS portrays itself as a powerful provider of information services worldwide. The bottom sheet invites the recruit to be part of EDS's world. The back of the sheet offers facts about the company and career opportunities.

KPMG's recruiting materials include the handbook, computer diskettes, and postcards for following up contacts with recruits. The handbook describes the diversity of the company, expected career development, performance-based compensation plan, and available personal time. The computer diskettes for both PC and Macintosh® have more detailed information about careers, KPMG's worldwide locations, and the extensive fringe benefit program. For example, a person who passes the CPA examination in the first year receives $1,500—$750 if she passes it in the second year.

Write your impressions, images, and feelings about these materials on a separate piece of paper. What are your expectations about working in each organization?

◢ INTERPRETATION

You might have noted sharp differences in these recruiting materials. The Marine Corps materials have strong colors and stand out boldly. EDS features a description of the company's varied activities and an invitation for the recruit to be part of their world. KPMG Peat Marwick used pastels that present a warm image of the company.

The Marine Corps materials in Figure 6-5a can convey an image of pride and strong transition.[27] Parts of the dress uniform could give you an impression of formal relationships within the Corps. The sword, although no longer used in battle, symbolizes the Marine Corps' deep ties to its past. The medals imply bravery and honor. The Bronze Star on the left of the several medals is the fifth highest honor awarded by the United States. Wearing the uniform might put you above the crowd.

The EDS materials in Figure 6-5b can impart a sense of excitement about the information and computer technologies that are the heart of the company's business. The broad range of activities suggests variety in work experiences as the person grows with the company. EDS has an industry reputation of providing its new hires with high-quality training, which suggests they get a good start on a technology-based career.

The KPMG Peat Marwick recruiting materials in Figure 6-5c present a less formal image of the company than the stereotypes many people may have of accounting firms. Warm pastel colors portray a desired informality. Describing the performace-based pay plan and the bonus for passing the CPA examination emphasizes the importance of individual performance.

Of course, there is much more to the internal reality of each organization than the recruiting materials show. Marine Corps training is grueling, and some jobs are routine (supply clerk) while others are glamorous and exciting (aviator). EDS remains a conservative company although it is trying to break from a past that included a strict dress code.[28] Accounting firms hire accounting students who work toward their CPA. They begin as junior accountants and work long hours in their early years.

Recruiting materials are an important source of information about any organization you might consider as a potential employer. Remember, though, what the materials exclude can be as important as what they include!

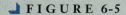

FIGURE 6-5
Recruiting Materials from Three Organizations

a.

b.

• *(a.) U.S. Marine Corps (b.) Electronic Data Systems Corp. (c.) KPMG Peat Marwick*

c.

ENTRY/ENCOUNTER ("BREAKING IN")

Assume a person has accepted a job with an organization. She crosses the boundary of the organization on the first day of employment and begins to experience the second stage of socialization—**entry/encounter.** The anticipatory stage of socialization built expectations about what it is like to work for the organization. Now the new employee will learn whether those expectations are consistent with the reality of organization life.[29]

FIGURE 6-6

The Sense-Making Process during the Entry/Encounter Stage

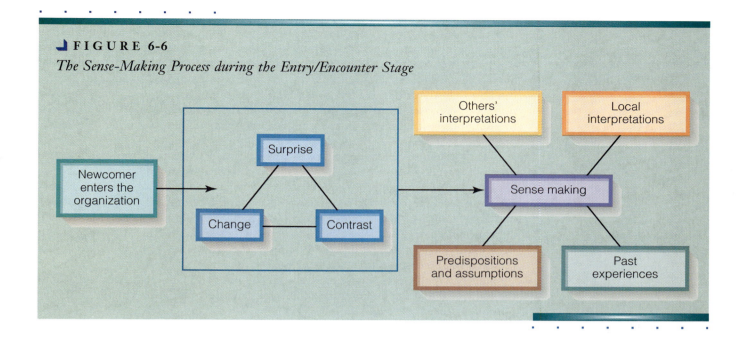

If the new employee was highly motivated to join the organization, she will be eager to be socialized by the organization.[30] Because she is new to the organization, she will want to "learn the ropes" from knowledgeable insiders. She also will seek information from many sources to reduce her natural feelings of uncertainty.[31] In the entry/encounter stage, she will learn the role she is to play and the culture of the organization, among other things.

Early experiences during the entry/encounter stage feature change, contrast, and surprise, the three major parts of the **sense-making process.**[32] Figure 6-6 shows the sense-making process and the relationships among its parts.

Change refers to differences in the major features of the employee's old and new roles. For example, she should feel a sharp change between her role as a college or university student and her first job after graduation. She will go from being a senior (at the top of the undergraduate status order) to being a "human resource analyst trainee" (at the bottom of the Human Resource Department). The bigger the differences between the new and old roles, the more change with which the new employee must cope.

Contrast refers to aspects of the new setting that jump out at her and get her attention. These features will likely include the physical qualities of the new setting and the obvious values and behaviors of the new culture. The degree of contrast she experiences depends on the differences between the new setting and the old. For example, as a college student, she may not have had a personal computer. She used machines in a computer laboratory along with other students. She takes a new job and is given her own personal computer along with extensive word processing and spreadsheet software. This single feature of the new situation will stand out in bold relief from other aspects of the setting.

The feature of **surprise** in entry/encounter experiences is partly grounded in the comparison of expectations from the anticipatory stage to the reality of the entry/encounter stage. The company recruiter assured her that her job would have high autonomy. She starts the new job and discovers it has low autonomy. Surprise!

Surprise events move a person to attribute meaning to those events as described in the discussion of attribution processes in Chapter 4. The new employee initially bases the meaning of an event on her predispositions, assumptions, and experiences with similar events in a previous role. Others around her in the new work setting know what to expect from various situations. She is new to the setting and does not yet share that information. Local interpretations in Figure 6-6 refer to understandings among coworkers about what to expect from the boss and the shared meaning given to events. Individuals also have their own impressions of meaning for such events that have developed from their longer association with the organization. Other employees can be a rich source of explanation of the meaning of "surprises." As a newcomer, she may not be conscious of how little she knows about the meaning of events. That meaning may not be shared with her until she is accepted by veteran members of the organization.

During the entry/encounter stage, the organization wants to give the employee a new self-image. The pivotal and relevant role behaviors are the basis of the new self-image. Some organizations require many pivotal role behaviors. Such organizations ask for a large change in self-image as do military organizations during basic military training. Others require only a few pivotal role behaviors and ask for a small change in self-image. Various parts of the same organization will also ask for different degrees of change in self-image. Whatever the degree of change in self-image required by the organization, the basic process of change is the same.

The entry/encounter stage serves several purposes and raises some issues for both the individual and the organization. The issues and purposes are intertwined and are not independent of each other.[33]

Clarification of the new employee's role in the organization is a major purpose of the entry/encounter stage. Role clarification includes the definition of the person's role by both the organization and her immediate work group. An issue for the individual at this point is whether the two role definitions are the same!

A second purpose of the entry/encounter stage is to teach the new employee about tasks, duties, and responsibilities, including the priorities of conflicting work assignments. The supervisor's evaluation of the new persons' performance plays a key role in the new employee's socialization. From these evaluative interactions with her immediate supervisor, the new employee learns the nuances of the organization's culture.

A third purpose of the entry/encounter stage is to teach the new employee about the norms of the immediate work group. Norms are rules of behavior that govern social interactions within the group. They include rules about social status and the bases of power and influence in the group. New employees learn who the informal leaders are and where power rests within the group. Performance norms often exist, and they are not always congruent with what either the organization or the new employee values!

The various purposes of the entry/encounter stage can make different and conflicting demands on a person. The new employee may get conflicting messages about job performance within the immediate work group. The norm of the work group may be either higher or lower than the performance desired by the organization and the employee's immediate supervisor. A new employee must resolve the conflicting behavioral demands to adjust successfully to the new role in the organization.

The new employee's job may require a high degree of interaction with other groups in the organization. These groups may place different and conflicting behavioral demands on her. Successful adjustment to her new organization role requires managing such intergroup role conflicts. New employees can experience much pressure and stress when adapting to these various sources of role conflict.

There is another major set of roles involved in the entry/encounter stage. These are the individual's nonwork roles—the roles played by the person outside the employing organization. Roles such as mother, father, spouse, or student all place demands on the person. Adaptation to new organization roles, with their multiple sources of conflict, can put stress on roles outside work. Successful adaptation to the organization's demands involves successful management of all the individual's roles, both at work and away from work.

Sources of Socialization during the Entry/Encounter Stage

Source: Suggested by E. H. Schein, "Organizational Socialization and the Profession of Management," *Industrial Management Review* 9 (1968): 6.

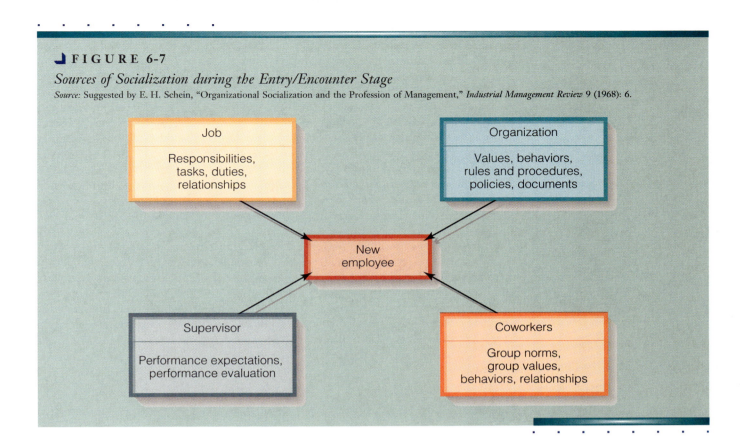

As you can see, there are multiple **sources of organizational socialization.** Figure 6-7 shows the sources of socialization you will experience when you enter a new organization. As a new employee, you will be bombarded from all sides with socialization efforts by the organization, immediate supervisor, coworkers, and the job itself.

Socialization Processes

Organizations use many different socialization processes to give new employees a new self-image. Three steps are involved in creating that **new self-image.**[34]

The first step is unfreezing the old self-image. The organization wants the new employee to discard some or all aspects of her old self-image. The second step is **changing** to the new self-image. The organization uses a series of role episodes to communicate pivotal and relevant role behaviors to new employees. These behaviors and associated values will become part of the new self-image. The last step is **refreezing,** which puts the new self-image solidly in place. The new employee now has acquired the norms, values, and required behaviors the organization considers important.

The processes organizations use in the entry/encounter stage produce different degrees of change in self-image. Not only do the processes communicate different types of role behavior, but they communicate it with different intensity.

Indoctrination programs teach the formal rules and procedures of the organization. Such programs are used when an organization considers the rules and procedures to be pivotal role behavior. Organizations dealing with classified or sensitive materials often use an indoctrination program to show how to handle such materials. The programs are presented in classroom-like settings or on videotape. As a result, the rules and procedures are presented uniformly to many different new employees.

A new employee may be assigned to a veteran employee as an apprentice. The veteran shows the new employee how to do the technical parts of the job. She also can tell the new employee about the formal rules and procedures of the organization. Socialization by apprenticeship can produce highly varied results because the organization has less control over the content of the socialization process than it does in an indoctrination program.[35]

Many organizations use formal training programs to develop skills they consider important to a given job. The major accounting firms have extensive training programs for new accounting graduates. Although the new graduate has received academic training in accounting, the firm now wants to show how it does an audit. Such training programs usually communicate much more than just skills and formal job duties. They also often convey the values and norms of the firm. The new accounting graduate will quickly learn what it means to be a "KPMG Peat Marwick auditor."

Organizations can quickly unfreeze a new member from her old self-image with debasement or upending experiences.[36] Some organizations give a new employee an extremely easy or extremely hard task to do in the early employment period. An easy task assignment for a recent college graduate may be humiliating, causing the new employee to question who she is and what she is doing. A hard task may humiliate for different reasons—it is beyond what the graduate can do now. Both task assignments have the same effect. The college graduate questions her self-image, making her ready for change by the organization.

CHANGE: METAMORPHOSIS ("SETTLING IN")

> When Gregor Samsa woke up one morning from unsettling dreams, he found himself changed in his bed into a monstrous vermin. He was lying on his back as hard as armor plate, and when he lifted his head a little, he saw his vaulted brown belly, sectioned by arch-shaped ribs. . . . His many legs, pitifully thin compared with the size of the rest of him, were waving helplessly before his eyes.
>
> Franz Kafka, *The Metamorphosis*[37]

The change new employees undergo in most organizations is usually not as dramatic as the transformation of Gregor Samsa into a beetlelike insect! Change takes place during the encounter stage, as it slowly and surely flows and blends into the **metamorphosis stage.** The word *metamorphosis* emphasizes the extraordinary changes that can happen to people from organizational socialization processes.[38]

If a new employee has successfully resolved the demands from the multiple sources of socialization, she now begins to feel comfortable in her new role. She has some degree of mastery of job requirements and responsibilities. She has accepted the more obvious values of the organization's culture. She has adjusted to the norms of her immediate work group and now feels accepted by her peers. Her self-confidence is increasing, and the anxiety of the early employment period is decreasing.

Some socialization processes clearly separate this stage from the entry/encounter stage with rites and rituals. Examples of rites and rituals include graduation ceremonies at universities and some management training programs and the ceremonies that mark the end of basic military training or graduation from a military academy. Other organizations do not have such ceremonies so this stage is not clearly separated from the encounter stage.

The metamorphosis stage can have three possible results: a rebellious response, a custodial response, and an innovative response. Figure 6-8 shows each response.[39] A **rebellious response** is a possible outcome if a new employee does not accept the socialization demands of different sources. Failure to accept the demands may cause her to leave the organization or to be terminated. Rebellion, from the organization's perspective, is a clear case of a socialization failure.[40]

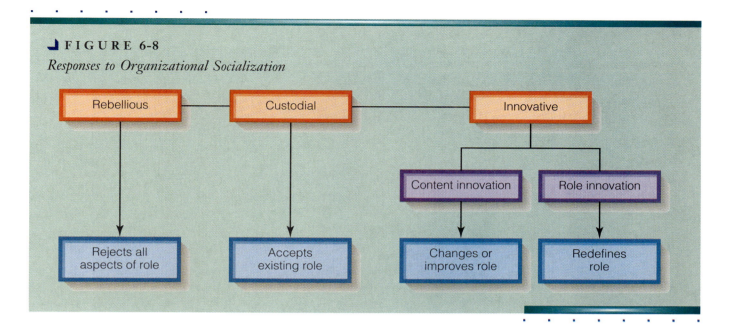

FIGURE 6-8

Responses to Organizational Socialization

A **custodial response** occurs when the employee conforms to the requirements of the role, accepting all aspects of its content and process. Such a response may happen because it makes sense to a new employee. She may decide that if the organization has been successful in the past doing things this way, she should not try to change it now.

A new employee may decide not to accept things the way they are and may choose an innovative response instead. Such a response comes in two different forms: content innovation and role innovation. **Content innovation** changes and improves the knowledge base and process characteristics of the role. The employee may decide that the way decisions were made in the past or the data upon which certain reports were based are not good enough for the job that needs to be done now. **Role innovation** is a more startling form of innovation. This response rejects most aspects of the role and the norms associated with it. Role innovation is clearly a form of rebellion. Unlike the rebellious response described earlier, if the organization and groups within it accept this response, the organization keeps the innovations.

 **C A S E**   *Life at IBM*

The following case describes part of the socialization process at IBM. Use the following questions as a guide to your analysis. A brief analysis follows the case.

1. What are the pivotal and relevant role behaviors? How do employees learn those role behaviors?
2. What are the key values of IBM's core ideology?
3. What are sources of socialization for IBM employees?
4. Does the case raise any ethical issues for you?

Source: S. Chace, "Life at IBM: Rules and Discipline, Goals and Praise Shape IBMers' Taut World," *Wall Street Journal*, April 8, 1982, 1, 14. Reprinted by permission of the *Wall Street Journal*, © 1982 Dow Jones & Company, Inc. All Rights Reserved Worldwide.

CASE DESCRIPTION

When Thomas J. Watson Sr. died in 1956, some might have thought the IBM spirit of the stiff white collar was destined to die with him. But indications are that the founder's legacy of decorum to International Business Machines Corp. still burns bright. Consider the way an IBM man on a witness stand in San Francisco the other day replied when questioned about an after-hours encounter with a competitor:

Q. "All of you were in the hot tub with the Qyx district manager?"
A. "The party adjourned to a hot tub, yes. Fully clothed, I might add."

That an IBMer invited to a California hot tub should fear that propriety demanded a swimsuit wouldn't surprise many people who have ever worked for the giant company. . . . IBM has a reputation in the corporate world for . . . [a] standout trait: an almost proprietary concern with its employees' behavior, appearance and attitudes.

What this means to employees is a lot of rules. And these rules, from broad, unwritten ones calling for "tasteful" dress to specific ones setting [sales] quotas, draw their force at IBM from another legacy of the founder: the value placed on loyalty. Mr. Watson believed that joining IBM was an act calling for absolute fidelity to the company in matters big and small. . . .

And just in case an IBM employee isn't a self-starter in the loyalty department, the company has a training regimen geared to instilling it. In brief, this consists of supervising new trainees closely, grading them, repeatedly setting new goals for them, and rewarding them amply for achievement. Suffused in work and pressure to perform, employees often develop a camaraderie, an esprit de corps.

What it all amounts to is a kind of IBM culture, a set of attitudes and approaches shared to a greater or lesser degree by IBMers everywhere. This culture, as gleaned from talks with former as well as current employees, is so pervasive that, as one nine-year (former) employee puts it, leaving the company "was like emigrating."

To George McQuilken, who left IBM to found his own company, Spartacus Computers, Inc., "the hardest part about being gone was the first few times I tried to make a decision on my own about anything, like what hotel to stay in, or who I wanted to hire."

For those who don't leave, IBM returns the loyalty. . . . The most valued of these employees are sometimes known within the world of IBM as "sorries"—people the computer company would be especially sorry to lose. . . .

Virginia Rulon-Miller was once an IBM sorry. A self-described "lifer" at IBM, she got into trouble when her interpretation of IBM's largely unwritten rules clashed with that of her superiors. Unlike most separations from IBM—quiet resignations to pursue other interests—hers was a messy divorce that ended up in court. . . .

On a June day in 1979, . . . [Ms.] Rulon-Miller abruptly turned in her keys and her plastic identification card and fled IBM, after her boss confronted her with her relationship with Matt Blum, once an IBM super-salesman and at that time a manager at a competing office-products company. In an emotionally charged interview, her boss said she was being given a nonmanagement post at the same salary. To her, steeped in IBM's get-ahead culture, this was tantamount to being released, and she said so. She sued, charging wrongful dismissal. . . .

At the trial, IBM conceded that [Ms.] Rulon-Miller was a loyal employee with an outstanding record and that there was no indication she had ever passed company secrets to her boyfriend. But, it argued, the mere existence of a relationship between business rivals was a conflict. "She clearly cared very much for Matt Blum," IBM said. "And she clearly cared for his success. And if that is the case, she had a conflict of interest."

[Ms.] Rulon-Miller's lawyers argued that what really worried IBM was the possibility she would defect to Matt's company, Exxon Corp., Qyx, encouraging other IBM [salespeople] to defect as well. The jury sided with her, saying in effect that the company couldn't dictate an employee's off-the-job behavior. It awarded her $300,000 in compensatory and punitive damages. IBM has said it would appeal, but it won't discuss the case with a reporter. . . .

How does IBM inspire positive feelings even in former employees who take it to court? Largely by following Mr. Watson's basic formula: systematic goading toward excellence, combined with constant supervision and frequent rewards. Its more flamboyant aspects are gone; probably no IBMer will ever again be feted as Otto E. Braimayer, an early 40-year employee, once was, with a formal dinner featuring 40 waiters carrying in 40 cakes. But management-by-merit-badge techniques continue to keep employes arriving at 7:30 A.M. to attend meetings before their regular duties begin. . . .

Tight discipline is also enforced by near-constant observation and grading. At sales training schools, trainees know what can happen if they fail to leave their rooms "broom clean": They may be called back to try again, or their manager may be charged for the cleanup. Vigilance even extends to the evening hours. Instructors take notice of who is burning the midnight oil preparing for the next day's product-demonstration tests and who seems to have a crush on whom. "Report cards" grade trainees on matters ranging from product knowledge and presentations to attitude—enthusiasm, confidence, sincerity, cooperation, work with others, desire to learn. . . .

Once out in the field, [salespeople] get a quota of IBM machines to be placed in their territories. Each year the quota is raised or the territory cut or both, partly to test employees' ingenuity in selling more products to the same people. Customers need to be sold hard; IBM takes back the commission if a customer decides to return rented equipment after a year or so. . . .

Achievement is followed by immediate rewards. Insiders say the most cherished of these isn't money. It's having your name and quota on the bulletin board with a notation saying '100%.' It's having a party thrown for you at your branch because you have satisfied a prickly customer. It's a steady flow of letters of commendation.

Says one ex-IBMer: "If you burp the right way, they send you a certificate." . . .

Gina Rulon-Miller . . . burped the right way. Her file overflowed with notes. "Dear Gina, thank you . . . for the excellent job you did in setting up our case studies at your branch last month" or "for helping to make this business show a success." Or, "Your performance in purchase and new equipment placements has been tremendous." Congratulations "for qualifying for your third 100% club. . . . May the force be with you."

The notes and the quotes, the training and the praise are very effective. "People work their brains out," says [Ms.] Rulon-Miller's brother Todd, an IBM veteran who now works for an American Express Co. unit. The results please IBM, too. Asked whether company officials ever wonder if IBM has too many rules, a spokesman replies: "IBM has an adequate number of rules. We think they are proper and necessary. But we always try to challenge bureaucracy, so that any time we felt a rule was extraneous or unnecessary, we would seek to eliminate it."

The hard work that the IBM atmosphere inspires has another effect, Todd Rulon-Miller believes. "A close clique forms from the pressure everyone feels," he says. "The first thing they want to do at night is go out and have drinks with each other. Then they start blending business and social life. They rent cabins in Tahoe together, buy a sailboat, join a softball team, play golf."

When a member of the clique leaves the office, he may want to keep up his IBM-based social life. So it was that Matt Blum, the IBM salesman, even after his defection to Exxon was playing third base for a softball team of IBMers the night an IBM man showed up dressed as a big typing ball from an IBM Selectric typewriter to cheer the team on. Mr. Blum shared beer and golf with his IBM buddies. He braved San Francisco Bay in a communal sailboat. And he invited the (clothed) IBMers into his hot tub. . . .

In California State Supreme Court in San Francisco last December, it became clear that IBM didn't have written rules about the propriety either of golf games with competitors' employees or of close personal relationships with them—to say nothing of hot-tub parties. The company officials who testified couldn't agree about whether moving [Ms.] Rulon-Miller out of management was a disciplinary act, or about how it squared with IBM's code of "respect for the individual." One IBM loyalist said the switch was merely a way to accommodate her personal relationship by removing her from a potential source of conflicts.

The jurors didn't buy that, concluding that IBM had acted with "oppression or actual malice" in its dealing with [Ms.] Rulon-Miller. But their verdict didn't do much to clarify the company's encompassing but unwritten code of behavior, a code that pervades the life of every IBM professional. One former IBMer, reflecting on his years at corporate headquarters in Armonk, N.Y., describes the way that atmosphere affected him: "In my 15 years there," he says, "I never lost the feeling that I was breaking a rule. But I never knew what the rule was."

CASE ANALYSIS

IBM, at the time of this case, expected several pivotal and relevant role behaviors of its employees. Some of those role behaviors were not explicit, creating ambiguity in interpretation by some employees, especially Ms. Rulon-Miller. Pivotal role behaviors include loyalty, dressing tastefully, and the performance plan. Relevant role behaviors include helping other trainees, being sincere, and cooperating with everyone. The central value of IBM's core ideology was complete loyalty to the company in all parts of one's life.

Sources of socialization and socialization processes included the company's training programs, supervisors or managers, other trainees, and peers at work. Socialization efforts were continuous and intense, leaving strong imprints on many employees. Although Ms. Rulon-Miller had been with the company for many years, she was perceived as behaving in ways that did not accord with the core value of complete loyalty. The ethical issue should be clear. Did IBM violate Ms. Rulon-Miller's rights by reacting as it did to knowledge about her nonwork activities?

Individual Differences and Socialization

People do not react uniformly to socialization experiences. Their reactions vary depending on the person. An individual's skills and abilities play a role in the speed with which a person learns job duties during the socialization process.[41] People with high levels of job-related skills and abilities learn job duties more quickly than people with few such skills and abilities. Success in learning job duties may be perceived positively by those watching the newcomer's reactions to the organization.

Skills and abilities are not the only **individual differences** that affect people's reactions to **socialization** experiences. People also vary in their beliefs about how successful they will be in dealing with this new, ambiguous, and possibly threatening experience. Such self-efficacy beliefs are associated with different responses to the socialization process. People with low self-efficacy adopt a custodial response. People high in self-efficacy adopt innovative responses.[42]

Recall the discussion about perception and attribution processes in Chapter 4. It argued that people have strong perceptual filters that alter or impart meaning to the information they get from their environment. Selective perception affects how accurately they perceive information from socialization agents. A newcomer may not perceive the information in the way the socialization agent intended. Conflict can develop between the newcomer and the agent because of those differences in perception.

Attribution processes work in much the same way.[43] The newcomer imparts meaning to information sent by a socialization agent based on the newcomer's experience with situations perceived to be similar. The socialization agent and the newcomer usually do not have a common set of experiences and therefore do not give the same meaning to a set of information. The different meanings may lead to conflict. Such inappropriate attributions can make it difficult for the newcomer to adapt. Adaptation is more successful, of course, when the newcomer and the socialization agent impart the same meaning to information.

The last individual difference comes from the different needs people may try to satisfy from their work experiences.[44] If a newcomer has a strong need to associate with other people, she may be highly influenced by members of her work group. If a newcomer has a strong need to achieve, she may aggressively pursue new job duties while trying to show her socialization agent(s) that she can quickly master a demanding job. You will learn much more about needs and motivation in upcoming chapters.

↳ *Characteristics of an Effective Socialization Process*

The characteristics of an **effective socialization process** described in this section came from a careful consideration of the research evidence about the effects of organizational socialization. This section is included so you as a potential new employee of an organization can judge the socialization processes to which you will be exposed. Don't forget! Part of the socialization process happens to you before you join an organization. The rest happens after you join.[45]

The characteristics of effective socialization processes described here are useful guidelines for managers to follow in designing a socialization process for new people coming to work for them. Managers must recognize that the selection mechanisms used by an organization are an intimate part of the socialization process. First, managers can thoroughly analyze the skill and ability requirements of various jobs. Second, they should base the selection of new employees on those skill requirements. Lastly, managers can reward and reinforce the skills and abilities of recruits during their socialization experiences.

Organizations should provide realistic descriptions of the jobs that need to be done, the available training, the reward system, and promotion opportunities. Realistic descriptions will attract people who feel the organization offers what they want and will discourage other individuals who realize the fit between themselves and the organization would be poor. Those who choose the organization based on a realistic description should find the socialization process easier than it would have been without the description.

The socialization process should focus on the day-to-day activities a new employee needs to know. Skills required by the job should be emphasized. Other things such as "What are we as an organization?" and "What do we highly value?" should also be communicated. In short, the socialization process must tell the new employee what she needs to know to be successful, assuming she has the necessary skills and abilities.

Feedback about performance is highly important during the early stages of socialization. Unfortunately, many organizations do performance appraisals at fixed intervals, often within the first 6 to 12 months of employment. Giving feedback more often than specified by organization policy can be effective during the early period of socialization. The feedback also should be ongoing during this period of potential high anxiety for the new employee.

Several of the preceding issues highlight the importance of the immediate supervisor in the socialization process. Supervisors should focus on assigning tasks that challenge the newcomer and satisfy her needs. Feedback on performance is critical and should not be restricted to the formal feedback required by organization policy. The supervisor can also act as a "buffer," protecting the new employee from conflicting demands outside the work group.

The new employee experiences some anxiety during the early employment period. The socialization process may overpower the new person, impairing her job performance. The new employee will want to know her chances of success in the new role. Here again, the supervisor is important in giving valuable feedback about how the person is doing and what her future is likely to be.

The informal socialization processes within work groups need to be fully understood. Do the groups communicate positive or negative feelings about the organization? If employees feel good about the organization, socialization at this level can be both effective and efficient. In short, the informal group can help in the socialization process. If employees hold negative feelings, the new employee will be exposed to conflicting socialization cues and demands. How the person adjusts depends on which source of socialization the person considers most important to her success.

International Aspects of Organizational Socialization

*T*he increasingly global environment of many organizations will present opportunities to work in different countries to more people than ever before. Each time a person moves to and from an international assignment, she experiences an international role transition.[46] Just as in domestic job changes, she also experiences the stages of socialization, boundary transitions, and the sense-making process. At the same time, the international context creates some special issues for each part of the socialization process.

A person going to an assignment outside her home country is an expatriate, and a person returning from an assignment is a repatriate. Both movements have elements of culture shock.[47] The potential culture shock for the expatriate is easy to understand because she is moving from her home country to another country. The repatriate also can experience culture shock upon returning to her home country. During a typical international assignment of three to four years, the home country could have changed in ways unknown to the expatriate. On return, she enters a culture with many new features.

Expatriates and repatriates both go through a period of cross-cultural adjustment that occurs along three related dimensions: adjustment to a new job and work environment, adjustment to interacting with local nationals, and adjustment to the general culture of the country.[48] An organization's socialization process can help adjustments along those dimensions. Making cross-cultural training part of the socialization process can give people information that can smooth international role transitions.[49]

 ISSUES IN EXPATRIATE ADJUSTMENT

Expatriate adjustment has aroused much interest because of the high incidence of failures and the costs associated with those failures. Between 16 and 40 percent of U.S. employees sent to other countries return before the end of their assignment. One estimate puts the direct cost of expatriate failures for U.S. multinational organizations at over $2 billion a year. That figure does not include unmeasured costs such as lost business, damage to the organization's reputation, and loss of employee self-esteem.[50]

Expatriates face some special difficulties during the early part of socialization to their new assignment.[51] Their lack of knowledge about the local norms and rules of behavior important to insiders can lead to difficulty crossing the inclusionary boundary in international assignments. Expatriates can also experience dramatic changes, contrasts, and surprises during the sense-making process. The size of the differences depends on the degree of difference between the expatriate's home culture and the other country's culture. Both difficulties argue for more preparation for international job transitions than for domestic job changes.

Multinational organizations typically select people for international assignments based almost solely on successful performance in domestic roles. The underlying assumption is that success in domestic operations will automatically translate into success abroad. Several researchers recommend selection criteria other than successful domestic performance. Those criteria include experience from an earlier international assignment, openness to differences among people, and willingness to learn about another culture. Researchers also recommend using the same criteria in assessing the adjustment potential of a spouse and other family members.[52]

The socialization of expatriates should include cross-cultural training. Although research evidence shows that cross-cultural training is effective in smoothing expatriate adjustment, only about 30 percent of expatriates get such training before leaving their home country.[53] The training usually offered is not comprehensive;

typically, it includes an orientation to the other country's culture and its physical environment. Spouses are not included in such training,[54] although it is becoming clear that their adaptation plays a key role in successful expatriate adjustment.

Some countries are simply harder to adjust to than others. The greater the difference between the other country's culture and the home culture, the harder the adjustment. Some research indicates that India, Liberia, and some Southeast Asian countries, for example, are especially difficult for U.S. employees. Women face a special issue in cultures with male-dominated norms and values. Female expatriates—and wives of male expatriates—find adjustment to such cultures especially difficult.[55]

Career development programs and policies of multinational organizations have been suggested as ways of smoothing expatriate transitions.[56] Such programs and policies can show the career connections between the expatriate assignment, a repatriate assignment, and long-term career progress with the company. Multinational organizations can also assign at-home mentors to help guide the expatriate while abroad.

ISSUES IN REPATRIATE ADJUSTMENT

When returning to her home country, a repatriate who has been gone for several years may not have an accurate image of her home culture. During the anticipatory stage before leaving the international assignment, she can develop inaccurate expectations of life back home.[57]

Home leave or required visits to the home office can help maintain accurate expectations. Required interactions with people in the home office because of task interdependence can also increase the flow of information. Such interactions can happen by any communication medium, including telephone, facsimile, international teleconference, and direct computer connection.

A repatriate's adjustment will also be easier if she had the mentor in the home office mentioned earlier. The mentor could keep her informed of major policy and strategic changes back home. In short, maintaining a flow of accurate information about changes in the home organization and culture gives the repatriate accurate expectations about her return.

The degree of adaptation to the other country's culture can affect adaptation to the home culture. Although such adaptation is functional for working in the international assignment, it is dysfunctional for adaptation on return. To have a successful repatriation adaptation, the repatriate will need to unlearn much of what made her successful abroad.

Many perquisites that go with an international assignment can be dysfunctional to repatriation adjustment. Such assignments often have salary differentials and housing allowances that have high social status in the host country. Repatriation removes those differentials, possibly leading to a downward shift in perceived status and poorer housing conditions.

Almost no multinational organizations offer predeparture training to employees preparing to return to the home organization. Such training could parallel that of expatriates by including information on culture shifts in the home culture and major changes in the home organization. Training on return could also help repatriation adjustment. Such training could become part of the organization's formal socialization program for its repatriates.

. . . .

Ethical Issues in Organizational Socialization

*O*rganizational socialization processes pose ethical questions to potential employees, present employees, and the organization's managers. Because socialization processes can shape a person's values and behavior to those wanted by the organization, several ethical issues center on informed consent. Should the organization tell the potential new employee that it will deliberately try to change some of her values and behavior? Should present employees be told that each time they change positions in the organization, their values and behavior will also change to some degree? A related issue centers on an organization's training programs. Such programs often have both socialization and training goals. Should an organization reveal those goals to employees before they enter the programs?

Debasement experiences are an especially effective way of forcing a person to shed an old self-image. Most organizations use mild forms of debasement of the type described earlier. Sororities, fraternities, basic military training, and the military academies all use stronger forms of debasement that can create feelings of fear and intimidation. Debasement experiences pose a clear ethical dilemma for organizations and their managers. The U.S. Air Force Academy settled that dilemma in 1993 by changing its policies about the treatment of first-year cadets by upper-class cadets. Read the case at the end of the chapter and decide for yourself whether that policy change ends the ethical dilemma for the academy.

The discussions of anticipatory socialization emphasized the importance of having accurate expectations about working for a particular organization. An ethical issue is raised when an organization knowingly withholds negative information from potential employees. Some organizations use Realistic Job Previews to give potential employees a balanced view of the organization. At what point does an organization move into the unethical arena by not giving a balanced view of itself? The same issues are raised when a potential employee knowingly withholds information about herself that could affect her performance or retention by an organization. At what point does she move into the unethical arena by not giving a balanced view of herself?

 ·

Personal and Management Implications

*T*he anticipatory stage of socialization has an especially important implication for everyone. Get as much information as you can about the organizations that interest you. Examine existing documents for clues about the organization's culture. Materials such as annual reports and press accounts about what the organization does can be useful sources. If possible, contact existing employees of the organization to get some idea about the organization's culture from an informed insider. The accuracy of your image of the organization and its culture will make your adaptation to the organization much easier. Getting accurate information at this stage is highly important for taking an assignment in another country. The latter will feature much that is new about the external culture surrounding the organization.

Depending on the information you have about an organization, you may have a hard time making sense of your early experiences. Many surprises await you, and your task is to make sense out of those surprises. Try to get information from knowledgeable insiders about the type of early experiences you may have, a task that can be difficult in an international assignment. Find out about them before joining the organization so you can understand the meaning of those experiences. The less you know before you join, the greater the number of surprises after entry.

Be accurate and candid in the way you present yourself. Know your values, skills, abilities, and limits. You play a key role in the other side of a Realistic Job Preview. There is a strong need for a "Realistic Employee Preview" as well. You may need to temper the accuracy of your presentation with your knowledge of the culture of the target organization. Some organization recruiters would react adversely to a candid self-presentation, especially if their organization's culture supports and values some degree of deception.

The importance of a Realistic Job Preview to the retention and performance of new employees cannot be overemphasized. Managers should let potential new employees know both the good and bad points about working for the organization. Such accurate information becomes highly important for new employees taking an assignment in another country. Include information about the local culture in the Realistic Job Preview. You will find the socialization process much easier if newcomers have had a Realistic Job Preview.

Managers play a potent role in the socialization process. Your behavior as a manager sends signals and cues about important values in the culture. For example, if the organizational culture values punctuality highly, your behavior should reflect your acceptance of this value. If it values ethical behavior in all organization actions, you must behave in ways that show you accept that value.

Recall the sense-making process, which is an important part of a new employee's adaptation to experiences in the entry/encounter stage. This process has several implications for you as a manager.[58] The newcomer needs information about the meaning of events experienced as "surprises." Support getting interpretive information to the newcomer from peers. Encourage the newcomer's peers to "tell it like it is," without any fear of reprisal. Informal associations of newcomers and veterans are helpful ways of making local interpretations and other's impressions quickly available to the newcomer. Building bridges between newcomers and veterans also helps boundary transitions to assignments in other countries.

The performance appraisals you do with a newcomer are also an important mechanism for giving feedback about how the person sees and interprets the organization. Tell her the meaning you see in events that have happened to her and show her the events are part of the routine life of the organization. The latter is especially true for events newcomers might interpret as "goofy" but are highly valued by you and the organization.

. . . .

◤ *Summary*

Organizational socialization is a powerful process that affects an individual's behavior and helps shape and maintain an organization's culture. It usually is the first behavioral process a person experiences after joining an organization. Part of the socialization process happens before you join an organization. Other parts happen after joining.

Organizations ask us to take on specific roles that have behavioral requirements. The three types of role behavior are pivotal (required), relevant (desired), and peripheral (tolerated). You learn those role behaviors in a series of role episodes that unfold during your socialization experience. The socialization process is continuous throughout a person's association with an organization, but it is most intense before and after boundary transitions. Boundary transitions have three dimensions: functional (job), hierarchical (promotion), and inclusionary (inward movement).

The anticipatory stage of socialization builds expectations about life in the organization before you enter the organization. You compare those expectations to the reality you experience in the entry/encounter stage. The entry/encounter stage happens to you after you cross the boundary of the organization and begin your first day of employment. Change, contrast, and surprise are the three parts of the sense-making process that all new employees experience. That process pummels the person with information and experiences that she must correctly interpret for successful adaptation to the organization's behavioral requirements. After successful adaptation to socialization demands, you pass through the metamorphosis stage. In this stage, you experience your final adaptation to the organization's demands.

Organizations operating in an international context face special socialization issues. People moving to other countries (expatriates) experience boundary transitions and stages of socialization as they do in domestic job changes. On return to their home country, repatriates can experience culture shock while readapting to their home culture.

Several ethical issues center on whether there is a need for informed consent about an organization's goal of shaping a person's values and behavior by its socialization processes. The broad ethical question is: "Should the organization tell potential and existing employees about the goals of its socialization process?"

Key Terms

boundary transitions 144
change: metamorphosis stage 154
choice: anticipatory socialization 147
content innovation 155
custodial response 155
effective socialization process 159
entry/encounter stage 150
individual differences and
   socialization 158

new self-image 153
organizational socialization 141
pivotal, relevant, and peripheral role
   behavior 142
realistic expectations 148
Realistic Job Previews 148
rebellious response 154
role episode 143

role innovation 155
sense-making process 151
socialization processes 146
socialization versus
   individualization 146
sources of organizational
   socialization 153

Review and Discussion Questions

1. Discuss the relationships between organizational culture and organizational socialization.
2. Which of the three types of role behavior is the most important for an organization? Why?
3. Describe the three stages of organizational socialization. What are the relationships among the stages?
4. What is the role of individual differences in organizational socialization? What reactions do you expect to have to the socialization processes of a new employer? Why?
5. What types of socialization processes are available to organizations? What functions does each serve for both the individual and the organization?
6. What dysfunctions are likely to happen in the anticipatory stage of socialization? How can an organization reduce those dysfunctions?
7. Discuss the responsibilities of both the individual and the organization to present an accurate image of themselves. Why is accuracy important to both parties? What ethical issues surround the presentation of an accurate image?
8. Discuss the dynamics of a role episode. What effects do the perceptual processes described in Chapter 4 have on a role episode?
9. Review the three dimensions of a boundary transition. What levels of an organization's culture does each dimension reveal?
10. Discuss the responses individuals can have to organizational socialization. Which of those responses is most likely to be yours?
11. What are the major sources of socialization in the entry/encounter stage? Which of those is likely to receive the most attention from a newcomer?
12. Discuss the special issues that surround socialization during international job changes. If students in your class have experienced any international transitions, ask about their views of the observations in the international section of this chapter.
13. What are the ethical issues raised by organizational socialization? Discuss those issues. Are they real issues that managers should address, or are organizations justified in proceeding as they have in the past?

Case

KNOW THY POTENTIAL EMPLOYER

This case describes some databases available on CompuServe®, an on-line computer service available to subscribers. CompuServe says these databases are a source of information about potential employers. Assess them using the following questions as guides:

1. Will the information available help you develop more accurate expectations about an employer during the anticipatory stage of socialization?

Source: Excerpted from M. Naver, "Know Thy Potential Employer," *CompuServe Magazine*, March 1991, p. 15. Reprinted with the permission of Michael Naver.

2. These databases contain much information. Is there so much information that a person searching the databases would be overwhelmed?

Any job counselor will tell you that learning all you can about your target industry and company is an important part of your job search. With its wide variety of company information databases, CompuServe can make the learning easier.

Online databases range from those that provide summary information about a company and its products to those that offer detailed financial and product reports. Some provide such valuable information that they are used by professional recruiters, according to Scott Gerber, CompuServe financial products manager.

"These databases are a strong job-search tool," says Gerber. "The information is timely and convenient to get, and you can search from home or from your office. It's your chance to use the same research tools as professional recruiters."

Here's a summary of CompuServe company information databases:

- Disclosure II Reports . . . offers detailed financial information on 10,500 companies. The information is culled from the reports corporations file with the Securities and Exchange Commission—the same information that Wall Street analysts use in evaluating a company's performance.

  With Disclosure II, you can learn who the company owners are, what businesses the company is in, which of them have the greatest impact on earnings, and quarterly income statements and balance sheets. . . .

- Company Screening . . . takes information on the 10,500 companies and reduces it to subsets that meet your criteria, such as a particular industry, size of a company, geographic area or performance. After you've narrowed your search to a few companies that meet your criteria, use Disclosure II to get detailed information on each of them. . . .

- Standard & Poor's Online . . . offers recent summary information on 4,700 companies, including business summaries and recent stock market information.

  The information here is less detailed than in Disclosure II but also less expensive—$1 per company, as opposed to $5–$10 per company. . . .

In addition to researching a company's financial standing, you'll want to learn about the company's products. Several CompuServe research databases suit this purpose.

- IQuest . . . is one of the most comprehensive information and reference services available anywhere. IQuest gives you access to 850 publications, databases and indexes spanning the worlds of business and government. . . .

- D&B–Dun's Market Identifiers® . . . offers directory information on more than 6.7 million US establishments, both public and private. The information available about a company can include the name and address, as well as company characteristics such as sales figures, number of employees, net worth, corporate family relationships and executive names. Similar information is also available on international companies via the D&B–International Dun's Market Identifiers® database . . . or the D&B–Canadian Dun's Market Identifiers® database. . . .

- Business Dateline . . . is a searchable database providing full-text articles from more than 115 regional business publications in the United States and Canada. Use Business Dateline to look for background information on smaller companies or subsidiary companies. . . .

- Newspaper Library . . . contains full-text articles from 48 US newspapers. . . . This database is another good source for background information on smaller or privately held companies. . . .

- Corporate Affiliations . . . is a searchable database containing company profiles and information on corporate linkages for parent companies and their affiliates. Included are most large public and private companies and their subsidiaries throughout the world. Information available on a company can include the name, address, stock exchanges, business description, executive names, total sales, assets, and net worth and liabilities, if available.

. . . .

 Case

AIR FORCE ACADEMY GUNS DOWN HAZING

This case describes changes in the hazing policy at the U.S. Air Force Academy. Consider the following questions while reading the case:

1. What positive and negative effects do you see for such debasement experiences?
2. Does hazing raise any ethical issues?
3. Has the Air Force Academy settled those ethical issues with its policy changes?

The Stairway to Heaven used to be real hell for freshmen at the Air Force Academy.

The rite of passage called for freshmen to run up a set of stairs while upperclass cadets would scream in their faces, call them names and order them to do push-ups while reciting the mission of the Air Force.

Source: G. Anton, "Air Force Academy Guns Down Hazing," *Colorado Springs Gazette Telegraph.* (As the story appeared in the *Albuquerque Journal,* February 16, 1993, pp. A1, A10.) Reprinted with the permission of the *Colorado Springs Gazette Telegraph.*

But not any more.

A cadet squadron sending its freshmen up a stairway got in trouble last week simply for yelling too loudly and getting too close. Their actions violated a new training policy that forbids upperclassmen to use "negative motivation" to discipline first-year cadets.

"Freshmen might as well be our friends now," commented junior Kay Aquino.

So what's wrong with that? Well, upperclass cadets are responsible for training and disciplining freshmen. That's been done through a rigorous and regimented system that included verbal abuse and meaningless tasks. Although the academy has long discouraged fear or punishment as a tool, some time-honored practices were allowed to continue—until now.

The new policy, which took effect Jan. 22, [1993] limits the time freshmen can be ordered around by upperclass cadets to five hours a week. It is allowed only between 6 A.M. and 8 P.M., and cannot interfere with meals, athletic training, studying, chaplain's time or military events.

7

Motivation: Need Theories

· *This Federal Express team found and fixed a billing problem that cost their company $2.1 million a year. Many companies use teams as problem-solving tools. People with strong social needs will likely feel motivated to work on such teams.*

After reading this chapter, you should be able to . . .

· Discuss the role of needs in behavior in organizations.
· Describe the major need hierarchy theories of motivation.
· Appreciate that the important needs vary from person to person.
· Understand how some needs may be learned.
· Distinguish between motivator and hygiene factors in a person's environment.
· Discuss the international and ethical issues in motivation.

Chapter Overview

Leaving the Fast Track for the Convent

Mary Anne Reese was well on her way to having it all.

As a successful corporate lawyer, she owned a three bedroom house with a view of the Great Smoky Mountains, vacationed in the Caribbean and still could blow an occasional paycheck on a spontaneous shopping spree.

But a year ago this fall, she gave it all up and entered a convent. She joined the Sisters of Mercy of the Union, one of the largest orders of Catholic nuns in the world.

"There was something missing from my life as a yuppie," says Reese, 30, who has the natural good looks of an Ivory soap commercial star.

"I had a big house all to myself and was eating out in expensive restaurants every other night. But I needed a lifestyle that was more community-oriented. I wanted my life to make a difference, and that was more valuable to me than money or the things I had."

Reese is one of a dwindling number of USA women answering the call to religious life. She is the only Sisters of Mercy candidate in her province, an area that includes, Kentucky, Ohio, Tennessee and Jamaica.

The national statistics are just as grim. Every year since 1980, an average of 1.4 candidates entered 251 religious communities surveyed by the National Conference of Religious Vocation Directors. Twenty years ago, an average of 7.79 women joined individual religious communities.

In 1963, there were about 177,000 nuns; today there are approximately 114,000.

One reason for the drop: Women have more options today than they did 20 years ago. And more Catholics are choosing to serve the church as lay ministers rather than as sisters, priests and brothers, says Sister Sarah Marie Sherman, executive director of the National Sisters Vocation Conference.

Religious orders also are becoming more selective about whom they'll accept, she says. Most young women today, like Reese, have college educations and some "life experience" before they enter religious life.

Reese's convent is a comfortable brick house on a quiet residential street shared with four other sisters. On a tour of their home, Reese points out the "chapel"—a stark room with a crucifix on a small, draped pedestal. The sisters sit in here every morning in beanbag chairs and sip coffee while they say prayers. "There are no kneelers at this house," Reese says, smiling.

Her bedroom is decorated with religious pictures and bright Tennessee quilts. In the corner is a personal computer she uses for writing poetry, short stories and letters.

Though some sisters still wear long robes, rosaries and habits, Reese and her housemates dress in everyday clothes. Reese's typical garb: sweatshirt and jeans.

Reese knows the vows she'll take—poverty, chastity, obedience and service to the poor, sick and uneducated—seem strange to most people. "The theories of it stand against values that society and Madison Avenue exalt: Who can I use, what can I use, what can I grab here, and total individualism at all costs."

"Our society builds everything around sex and exalts sex as something you can't live without. I think religious (orders) are saying, 'No, that's not true. You can have deep relationships and intimacy without necessarily physically expressing that.'"

Reese has been serious about three men since college. But she had no qualms about giving up dating: "I don't feel a call to put all my energy into one relationship or one small family unit. I need more broadness than that."

· *Mary Anne Reese*

Her mother, Mary Reese, agrees. "She could probably have gotten married had she wanted to. But marriage wasn't programmed into her life."

She wasn't surprised that her only child entered a convent. The family's Irish Catholic roots are deep: Mary Anne attended Catholic grade schools, high school and college; an uncle is a priest.

Reese worked closely with Sisters of Mercy in her last job as an in-house lawyer for St. Mary's Medical Center in Knoxville, Tenn. As a lawyer, Reese made enough "to be statistically called a yuppie."

"My idea of a good time was to go to the mall and spend everything I just made on clothes or camping equipment. This friend and I created what we called Buyers Anonymous. Anytime one of us got the urge to go spend money we'd call the other one. But it was counterproductive because the other one would go along and spend money, too. My friend's now a Dominican nun."

"I was never a good manager of money. That's another advantage of this," she jokes.

During the summer of '84, she realized there was an emptiness in her life. She contacted the Sisters of Mercy and met with a vocation director once a month for a year before entering the convent last October.

Now Reese works as a youth minister for the Jesuit Renewal Center in a nearby suburb. She helps high school kids get to know themselves and each other better on overnight retreats.

Her voice quivers when she talks about teen suicide and drug abuse—problems that have touched many of the kids' lives. "I can't say enough about my job. It's the most important work I've ever done."

Reese has just begun the arduous process of becoming a nun. Ahead of her:

- Another year as a "candidate" or postulant.
- Two years as a novice. That's when she receives the title of "sister."
- First vows: She relinquishes her right to all money and property.
- Final vows: Three to six years after first vows.

Her salary goes to the community, and she is given a small allowance for personal expenses. "I haven't really wanted for anything," she says. "Now and then I'll get interested in a luxury cruise to France and I can't do that."

In her first year as a novice, she can't hold a job and must spend most of her time in prayer and reflection. That'll be tough, Reese says. "I'm one of those people who defines my identity so much in terms of my job. What am I going to say, 'Hi, I'm a novice'?"

She also must give up her car: "That will kill me. My car has a personality. It's my significant other."

Reese isn't sure what her future in the convent holds, but hopes to combine her legal background with her interest in teens—possibly working with runaways.

Would she want to be a priest if the church changed its rules? "Yes . . . but I'd want to see the priesthood change so the priesthood of *all* people is affirmed. I wouldn't want to be a priest who holds sole power in a church, but more an enabler of all people."

She understands other women's reluctance to enter religious life. "Not everybody wants to get into something when he or she can't see the end result. I'm entering the Sisters of Mercy today but I don't know what that means five, 10, 20 years from now.

"I think religious life as we know it is dying in a lot of ways. But I think there will be rebirth into something else. I think what I see happening is God is calling people into religious life for specified periods of time and not necessarily the rest of their lives."

Reese gives herself a 60 percent chance of remaining in the convent.

"There are some days when I want to pack my bags and get out. There are some days when I absolutely love it and want to spend the rest of my life here. Overall, I have a general happiness and contentment."

Was Mary Anne Reese motivated by something to stop being a corporate lawyer and enter a convent, or was her behavior the result of random events? This chapter and the next two describe aspects of human motivation in work organizations that will give you insights into Ms. Reese's behavior. You will see that her behavior is understandable. It shows she made choices among different courses of action.

The amount of space devoted to motivation in this book is deliberate. It is based on the conviction that enhancing and sustaining employee motivation is a manager's major function. Psychologists have developed many theories of motivation to explain why people behave in one way and not in another.

The theories share several assumptions.[1] First, they assume that behavior has a starting point, a direction, and a stopping point. Second, the behavior is voluntary and under the control of the individual. These theories try to explain why we choose to read one book over another or shop at Safeway instead of Krogers. They do not deal with involuntary or automatic responses such as breathing or eye blinking. Third, the theories assume that behavior is not random, but has a specific purpose and direction. Based on those assumptions, this chapter will use the following definition of motivation:

> Motivation . . . [refers to] those psychological processes that cause the arousal, direction, and persistence of voluntary actions that are goal directed.[2]

Managers usually want a certain level of job performance from an individual. Motivation is one stage in a sequence of stages leading to that level of performance.[3] Figure 7-1 shows the sequence of stages, with motivation as the first stage. Note the distinction between "behavior" and "performance." The behaviors individuals choose may or may not lead to the desired level of job performance.

Knowing the different theories helps you understand some elements of your behavior and the behavior of others. These theories also suggest ways in which managers can affect and direct your behavior. From a management perspective, understanding these theories helps a manager build and manage a system of motivation. They also give you the conceptual base for analyzing and diagnosing motivation problems in organizations.[4]

Organizations intentionally or unintentionally build "motivation systems." These systems hold assumptions about which behaviors are important for job performance and what affects those behaviors.[5] The three motivation chapters give you information that will help you understand how such a motivation system should be built. Motivation theories also give you the tools you need to analyze an organization's existing motivation system. They also help you understand why an employee is or is not performing as needed. Chapter 8 will give you the opportunity to analyze the motivation system you are now working in as an employee.

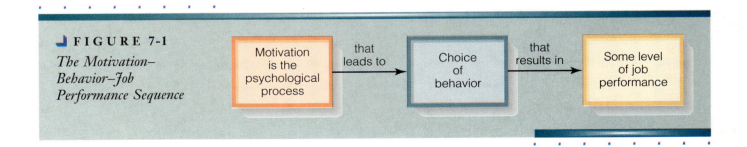

⬛ **FIGURE 7-1**

The Motivation–Behavior–Job Performance Sequence

Motivation is the psychological process → *that leads to* → Choice of behavior → *that results in* → Some level of job performance

Overview of Where We Are Headed

Figure 7-2 is an overview of the first two motivation chapters. The figure will help you navigate these chapters and understand the different emphases of the various theories. The theories of motivation fall into two groups: need theories, which this chapter describes, and cognitive and behavioral theories, which Chapter 8 discusses. Each motivation theory uses different mechanisms to explain why people behave as they do.

Need theories of motivation use characteristics or attributes of the person to explain motivation. These theories apply to healthy personalities and do not try to explain disorders such as psychoses. This chapter describes four need theories in the order shown in Figure 7-2. Murray's Theory of Human Personality gives a basic understanding of the role of needs in deciding human behavior. Maslow's Hierarchy of Needs Theory and Alderfer's E.R.G. Theory add to our understanding about the role of needs. McClelland's Achievement Motivation Theory describes the way needs develop and the role of three needs in shaping and directing behavior.

Herzberg's Motivator-Hygiene Theory does not fit cleanly into either of the theory groups. It gives useful observations about motivation and is a transition between the need theories of this chapter and the cognitive and behavioral theories in Chapter 8.

The two cognitive theories are Expectancy Theory and Equity Theory. Expectancy Theory describes the decision process people use to choose among courses of action. This theory introduces the role of various types of rewards or outcomes people get for their behavior. Equity Theory complements Expectancy Theory by

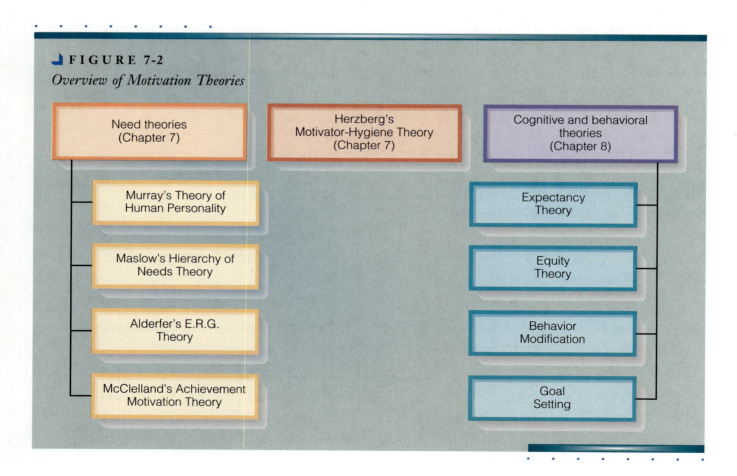

FIGURE 7-2

Overview of Motivation Theories

Need theories (Chapter 7)	Herzberg's Motivator-Hygiene Theory (Chapter 7)	Cognitive and behavioral theories (Chapter 8)
Murray's Theory of Human Personality		Expectancy Theory
Maslow's Hierarchy of Needs Theory		Equity Theory
Alderfer's E.R.G. Theory		Behavior Modification
McClelland's Achievement Motivation Theory		Goal Setting

explaining comparisons people make with others and why people may or may not feel fairly treated. A feeling of unfairness motivates the person to behave in ways that reduce the unfairness.

The two behavior theories are Behavior Modification and Goal Setting. Behavior Modification is a technique built on concepts that emphasize the role of external consequences in shaping and directing human behavior. Goal Setting is also a motivation technique. It emphasizes how to set goals that people will want to reach.

. . . .

❑ Murray's Theory of Human Personality: The Concept of Needs

Henry Murray and his colleagues at Harvard University spent many years studying human personality. Their research program used interviews, questionnaires, and in-depth clinical studies of selected people to develop a pioneering theory of human needs and behavior.[6]

Murray's Theory of Human Personality makes some assumptions about human beings and their behavior. This theory views people as adaptive when facing a dynamic and changing environment. Human behavior is goal directed and purposeful. Both factors internal to the person (needs) and factors in the person's external environment govern behavior.[7] Human beings learn from their interactions with their external environment and from their earlier experiences. They also hold preconceptions about what the future will be like. In Murray's view, a college student would have some notion of what college life would be like, based on earlier experiences in the educational system. As you experience college life, you develop new preconceptions about future college experiences.

The concept of need is basic to Murray's explanations of human behavior. **Need** is a hypothetical concept used to explain observable differences in behavior among different individuals or of the same person over time. In Murray's words:

> Between what we can directly observe—the stimulus and the resulting action—a need is an invisible link, which may be imagined to have the properties that an understanding of the observed phenomena demand.[8] . . . [It is a] hypothetical process within . . . [the person which over time] "points" activity and co-ordinates it.[9]

The theory puts needs into two classes. Physical needs are concerned with the satisfaction of the basic physical processes of the human body, such as the needs for food, air, water, and sex. Psychological needs focus on emotional and mental satisfaction.[10] Some examples include a need to be around other people and a need to achieve difficult goals. Table 7-1 is a partial list of the psychological needs that Murray and his colleagues identified.

Mary Anne Reese in the Opening Episode made choices about her new career that give us hints about her basic need structure. The order of nuns she joined emphasizes helping others. She also had to live in a close, communal setting in a convent. Both behaviors suggest Ms. Reese is strong in the Need for Nurturance and Need for Affiliation (see Table 7-1). The order's requirement to give up personal ownership of physical possessions and deferring to the authority of her order suggests a low Need for Acquisition and a strong Need for Deference.

❑ CHARACTERISTICS OF NEEDS

Needs are latent internal characteristics activated by stimuli or objects a person experiences. The person tries to behave in a way that satisfies an activated need. Some needs cause us to go toward objects we like. Other needs cause us to go toward

TABLE 7-1

Some Needs in Murray's Theory of Human Personality

NEED	DESIRE TO:
n Acquisition*	gather property, belongings, and objects.
n Order	organize and systematically arrange objects; be clean, neat, and tidy.
n Achievement	attain difficult goals; perform as well as possible.
n Recognition	receive credit for actions; to seek honors and recognition.
n Exhibition	draw attention to oneself.
n Dominance	command, control, and influence others; affect the direction of a group.
n Deference	respect authority; admire a person with authority.
n Autonomy	be independent and not be influenced by others.
n Affiliation	associate with others, have friends, and join groups.
n Nurturance	help others, give aid, improve the condition of other people.
n Blamavoidance	behave conventionally; obey rules; avoid punishment.
n Aggression	attack another person; deride, blame, and try to harm others.

*The small *"n"* in front of the name of each need is the psychologist's abbreviation for the word "need."
Source: H. A. Murray, *Explorations in Personality* (New York: John Wiley & Sons, 1938), pp. 80–83.

objects we dislike. If you have a high Need for Affiliation and meet someone you know and like while walking around the campus, you will probably strike up a conversation with that person. If you have a strong Need for Aggression, you may deliberately seek someone you dislike and try to hurt that person.

Some needs in Table 7-1 involve things people want to avoid. People strong in the Need for Blamavoidance avoid social situations where there may be pressure to engage in behavior they consider unacceptable. Such situations would cause them excessive stress. For example, a person may avoid groups of people who do not share his values and might ask the person to do something unacceptable.

Needs, especially those that are opposites, may show rhythmic patterns over time. Managers are good examples of people whose behavior can be directed at satisfying needs that are opposites. A manager could satisfy a Need for Dominance in his relationships with subordinates. Yet the same manager is subordinate to someone else in the organization and might engage in behavior directed at the Need for Deference. Though these needs are distinct opposites, a healthy person has little difficulty displaying the different behaviors required.

Needs that are opposites can also be useful for understanding contradictory or puzzling behavior. A person may satisfy a Need for Dominance in work activities, especially if he has a management or supervisory position. The same person may abandon a leadership role in his nonwork life by choosing to follow others (Need for Deference).

Multiple needs often decide a person's behavior. One need may be the primary basis of behavior, and other needs simply serve the primary need. If you choose to join a sorority or fraternity on your campus, you may be seeking to satisfy a Need for Affiliation. You also may believe that a record of extracurricular activities in college is important for getting a desirable job after graduation. Your primary need here may be the Need for Achievement. Your Need for Affiliation is serving it by moving you to join a student organization.

People's needs can lead to conflicts. Although mild conflicts often are not harmful, unresolved strong inner conflicts can be the root of some psychological or emotional disorders.

IMPLICATIONS OF MURRAY'S THEORY FOR BEHAVIOR IN ORGANIZATIONS

Murray's theory offers a general explanation of human behavior. In this book, we are, of course, mainly interested in understanding our own behavior, and the behavior of others, in organizations. How can this theory be of use in that context?

The first thing to note is that many needs have the potential to shape and direct behavior. Not all people have equal amounts of the needs in Murray's list. As will become clear, an important aspect of needs is that they vary in importance among different people.

Needs can direct behavior toward some things and away from others. Managers in organizations often control the objects toward which behavior is directed. Understanding how an individual's need structure affects his reactions to such objects lets managers more effectively influence the behavior of people in their organizations. A person with a strong need for recognition, for example, should respond favorably to praise from a supervisor.

We often are puzzled by another's behavior because of what we believe about that person. You may be working with someone you consider to be a "loner," a person who does not associate much with a wide range of people. The same person, however, regularly associates with people who can give him technical help at work. The person probably has a high Need for Achievement and some Need for Affiliation. The latter need acts in the service of the achievement need. Murray's theory helps us understand behavior that otherwise is puzzling.

Conflicts among needs can be useful in understanding some behavior you will see in organizations. A person with a strong Need for Acquisition and a weak Need for Achievement could simultaneously aspire to and want to avoid a promotion. Murray's ideas should help you understand that behavior. Such insights into behavior can help you be more effective in either a management or a nonmanagement role.

Let's now look at your need profile. The following exercise lets you quickly assess the needs that are most important to you.

EXERCISE   *Your Profile of Needs*

*T*urn back to Table 7-1, which lists several needs from Murray's Theory of Human Personality. Using the following scale, rate the importance of each need to you:

Unimportant 1 2 3 4 5 6 7 Important

On a separate piece of paper, write the number from the scale that represents how important each need is to you.[11]

This exercise should have given you some insight into the needs that are important to you. It did not list all needs, so others may also be important. The needs you rated as most important will have the strongest effect on your behavior. Keep those needs in mind as other need theories are discussed in this chapter.

⤷ Maslow's Hierarchy of Needs Theory

Murray's theory showed us that needs are an essential and powerful force directing human behavior. In contrast to Murray's long list of needs, Abraham H. Maslow felt that needs could be condensed into five groups of basic needs whose satisfaction is sought by all healthy adults. Maslow felt those needs were so basic that they motivate the behavior of people in many different cultures. Chronic frustration of those needs could produce psychopathological results.[12]

The following are the five basic need categories in **Maslow's Hierarchy of Needs Theory:**

- **Physiological needs** are the basic requirements of the human body: food, water, sleep, and sex.
- **Safety needs** are the desires of a person to be protected from physical or economic harm. Healthy adults normally do not want to be hurt so people avoid harm and seek safety.
- **Belongingness and Love needs** include the desire to give and receive affection and to be in the company of others. Also referred to as a social or affiliation need.
- **Esteem needs** deal with a person's self-confidence, sense of worth, and evaluation of self. Esteem needs are of two types. Esteem from others is the valuation of our worth that we get from others. Self-esteem is the feeling a person has about himself or herself, a feeling of self-confidence and self-respect.
- **Self-actualization needs** describe the desire for self-fulfillment. According to Maslow, self-actualization is ". . . the desire to become more and more what one is, to become everything that one is capable of becoming."[13]

· *Steve Young, quarterback for the San Francisco Forty-Niners, prepares to throw a pass during the 1995 Superbowl. Strong esteem needs likely play a role in success as a professional football player.*

Maslow felt the five needs formed a **need hierarchy** according to their prepotency (Figure 7-3). By **"prepotency"** Maslow meant that the needs at the bottom of the hierarchy dominate human behavior if all needs are unsatisfied. A person living in poverty concentrates on satisfying physiological needs and does not try to satisfy the needs at the top of the hierarchy.

According to the theory, people must satisfy the needs at the bottom of the hierarchy before higher-level needs emerge as important. An unsatisfied need is a potential motivator of behavior. Once a person satisfies a need at one level, the need at the next level in the hierarchy becomes the focus of behavior. Physiological needs are satisfied first, followed by safety, belongingness and love, esteem, and self-actualization needs. A satisfied need is no longer a motivator.

Maslow did not feel a need has to be completely satisfied before the next higher need becomes important. Most people who are working have almost completely satisfied their physiological and safety needs, but they usually still have some unsatisfied belongingness and love, esteem, and self-actualization needs. Although we may eat periodically during the day when we are hungry, balanced regular meals satisfy this part of our physiological needs. Our behavior, then, focuses more continually on the satisfaction of the higher-order needs, which happens throughout our total set of life activities.

As with Murray's theory, behavior can focus on more than one need. For example, a person actively seeks a promotion at work because he sees the promotion leading to more money (physiological and safety needs). The person may also feel the promotion will be an important satisfier of his esteem and self-actualization needs.

Maslow felt most people seek satisfaction of the basic needs in roughly the order shown by the hierarchy, although the hierarchy is not rigid. A strongly creative person may pursue the expression of creativity (self-actualization) at the expense of more basic needs such as maintaining an adequate diet (physiological needs). A chronically unemployed person is so concerned with staying alive (physiological) that esteem and self-actualization needs simply are not important. Lastly, people obsessed

FIGURE 7-3

Maslow's Hierarchy of Needs

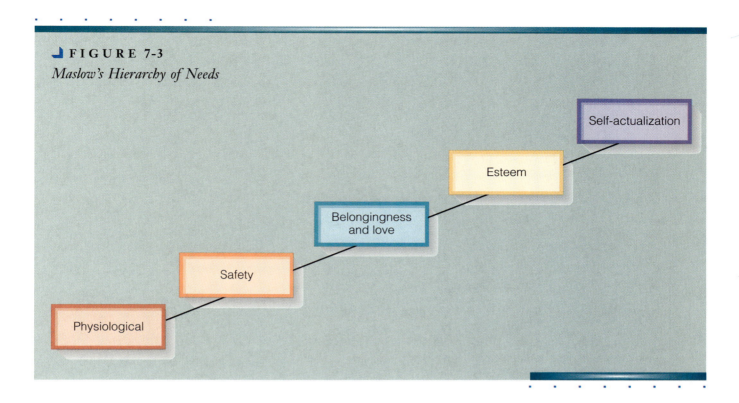

with seeking affection (love needs) or receiving feedback from others (esteem needs) will not see other needs in the hierarchy as important.[14]

Maslow did not think that needs were the only basis of human behavior. The context or environment within which the person behaves also is important. Needs are useful explanatory concepts of people's behavior, but we must also consider the person's situation and how it affects behavior.

"Maslow's need hierarchy theory . . . presents the student of work motivation with an interesting paradox: The theory is widely accepted, but there is little research evidence to support it."[15] That gloomy quotation is the first sentence in a comprehensive review of research directed at the theory. Although research has occasionally given some support to Maslow's theory,[16] most parts of the theory have not been consistently supported when empirically tested.

Maslow derived the theory clinically as a dynamic explanation for changes and development in human personality, especially its role in neurotic behavior. The theory was not always specific enough to let investigators develop testable hypotheses and design studies that used the proper tests.[17] Two studies that used good tests of progression through the hierarchy did not empirically support that part of the theory.[18] Although Maslow found the theory of use in his clinical work, he was well aware of the tentative nature of his conclusions.[19]

E.R.G. Theory

Clayton P. Alderfer, a psychologist at Yale University, has proposed a variation to Maslow's theory called **E.R.G. Theory.** Many aspects of Alderfer's theory are similar to Maslow's theory, but other aspects are unique and give us additional insights into the effects of needs on human behavior.[20]

Alderfer described three groups of basic human needs: Existence, Relatedness, and Growth. **Existence needs** are a person's physical and material wants. **Relatedness**

FIGURE 7-4

The Existence, Relatedness, and Growth Need Hierarchy (E.R.G. Theory)
Source: Suggested by David Lee Robbins.

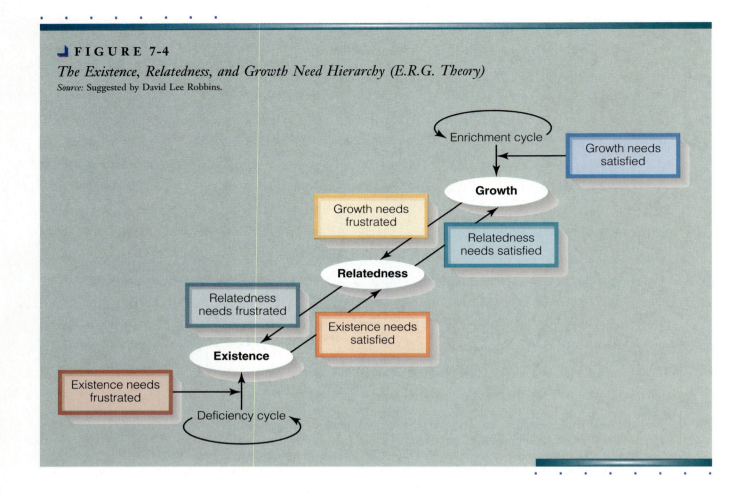

needs are the desires to have interpersonal relationships with other people and to develop intimate relationships with people important in our lives. **Growth needs** are the desires to be creative and productive, to use one's skills, and to develop additional capabilities. These three groups of needs form a hierarchy: existence, relatedness, growth. All people have those needs, although in varying degrees. Figure 7-4 shows the structure of E.R.G. Theory.

Note the similarities between Alderfer's E.R.G. Theory and Maslow's Hierarchy of Needs Theory. Alderfer's existence needs are the same as Maslow's physiological and safety needs. Relatedness needs are the same as belongingness and love needs. Growth needs include both esteem and self-actualization needs.

In Alderfer's theory, needs affect an individual's behavior in much the same way as described by Maslow. A need that is not satisfied is a motivator. Once the need is satisfied, it is no longer a motivator. If both lower-order and higher-order needs are unsatisfied, the lower-order needs will be the most important motivators of behavior.

Movement through the need hierarchy is both similar to and different from that described by Maslow. Satisfaction of a need leads to movement upward in the hierarchy. A need does not require full satisfaction for upward movement to occur. Frustration of a need that a person is trying to satisfy leads to movement down the hierarchy.

The first form of movement is **satisfaction-progression,** which is the same as described for Maslow's Hierarchy of Needs Theory. The second form of movement is **frustration-regression,** a concept introduced by E.R.G. Theory that gives additional insight about motivation and human behavior. The two forms of movement are best seen through an illustration.

Assume you are seeking a promotion at work and apply for a new position. Many others have applied but only one person will be selected. The people who work with you strongly support you for the promotion. Working hard for the promotion implies you have strong growth needs that you are trying to satisfy by getting the promotion. After a prolonged wait, you learn you have not been selected. Your growth needs are now frustrated. E.R.G. Theory predicts you will move down the hierarchy and focus on relatedness needs. In this situation, you will turn to your coworkers for further support while adjusting to the disappointment of not being promoted. If your growth needs are strong, however, sometime in the future you will try to satisfy them again.

Two other concepts in E.R.G. Theory extend it beyond Maslow's Hierarchy of Needs Theory. A person can become locked into a **deficiency cycle** at the bottom of the hierarchy. If an individual cannot satisfy his existence needs, he will more strongly desire those needs. Under conditions of scarcity, a person could become obsessed with satisfying existence needs.

A different cycle operates at the top of the hierarchy. A person who successfully satisfies growth needs desires them even more. This **enrichment cycle** leads a person to want to grow and develop continually. The individual will also seek multiple environments to satisfy his needs for growth. For example, an individual who is successful in a challenging and demanding job should experience the enrichment cycle. He will continue to seek challenges in activities away from work such as leading a community group or playing competitive sports.[21]

Alderfer's original research supported many parts of the E.R.G. Theory, but not all. The elements of the theory that have the most important implications for management received the most support.[22] Progression and regression were supported, but movement through the hierarchy was not as simple and clear-cut as Alderfer originally thought. The research showed some thresholds in need satisfaction levels that are related to movements in either direction. The enrichment cycle had empirical support, especially in settings that offered challenge and discretion. A person with an intensified desire for growth could also seek growth satisfaction in more than one setting. Some research other than Alderfer's has given additional support to the theory.[23]

EXERCISE   *Your Need Hierarchy*

Go back to your need profile from the earlier exercise and rank each need from most important to least important using the ratings you assigned them. If you rated two needs equally, leave them in their original order. Consider these questions while reviewing your list:

Which of your needs are the most important?
Your most important needs are the ones you seek to satisfy in the choices you make among different behaviors.

Were all needs close together in importance?
If the needs are close in importance, several needs may be the focus of your behavior simultaneously. Go back to the example about the effect of multiple needs and consider whether your behavior closely fits that description.

Was there a break in rated importance?
A sharp break in importance between adjacent needs implies that the needs up to the break are your dominant needs. The needs after the break play subsidiary roles in your behavior.

This exercise did not show you the dynamic features of the need hierarchy theories such as movement through the needs. It only showed your need hierarchy right now and not how it could be at any other time.

David McClelland and his colleagues studied the role of the Need for Achievement, the Need for Power, and the Need for Affiliation in deciding human behavior. McClelland and some of his colleagues most thoroughly studied the Need for Achievement, although they investigated all three needs.[24] **McClelland's Achievement Motivation Theory,** and other directly related theories of personality such as Murray's, are the product of an impressive research program spanning almost 40 years.[25] The research was done by different investigators and with many samples, although some controversy has surrounded their measurement methods.[26] Atkinson and his colleagues have successfully rebutted the criticism, allowing some confidence in the research results.[27]

The three needs are each associated with different behavior. As you read the following descriptions of the behavior of a person with high need strengths in each need, think about your own behavior. Possibly one of McClelland's needs is most characteristic of you.

People with a strong **Need for Achievement** take responsibility for the results of their behavior and want to solve problems.[28] Such people like to find the means for overcoming obstacles. They want to succeed, but they are willing to take calculated risks. High Need for Achievement people analyze situations, try to understand the chances of success, and set moderate achievement goals for themselves. Such goals are neither too easy nor too difficult to reach. These people prefer to set performance standards for themselves and do not respond well to externally applied incentives. They seek situations that allow achievement satisfaction and prefer nonroutine tasks to routine assignments. They look for and welcome feedback about how well they are doing. Skills, abilities, training, and experience all add to the performance of an achievement-motivated person.[29] A highly motivated person who also has high ability will outperform an equally motivated person with lower ability.

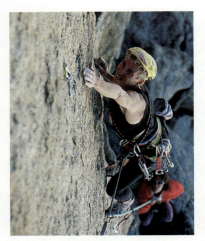

· *Strong achievement needs can drive people to reach tough goals such as scaling a sheer cliff face. High achievers like to solve problems and take calculated risks.*

How does the Need for Achievement develop? McClelland felt people acquired the Need for Achievement through socialization to the values of their culture. Because the need was acquired, it could also be learned. He based this conclusion on the results of his extensive studies of the presence of Need for Achievement concepts and themes in the folklore, mythology, and art of various societies. His research showed that societies emphasizing the Need for Achievement from generation to generation had higher levels of economic development than societies that did not.[30]

A person with a strong **Need for Power** focuses on ". . . controlling the means of influencing the behavior of another person"[31] and having a strong effect on other people. Note the emphasis in the definition on influence and controlling the means of influence. The means of influence can be anything available to the person to control the behavior of another. A high Need for Power person actively searches for the means of influence. He could use a superior-subordinate relationship or external rewards, for example, to control the behavior of another.[32]

McClelland distinguished between two different ways of expressing the Need for Power.[33] One form of expression uses personal dominance, physical aggression, and exploitation. People who have learned to express the need for power in this way view situations from a win-lose perspective. They must win and the other party must lose. McClelland did not feel such power behavior resulted in the type of leadership required by organizations.

The second form of expression focuses on persuasion and interpersonal influence. The person tries to arouse confidence in those he wants to influence. If, for example, a person who expresses a Need for Power in this way is the head of a group, he will clarify the goals of the group and persuade members to achieve those goals. His influence efforts will emphasize the ability of group members to reach goals, and he will try to develop in those members a belief in their competence. Of the two types of power, McClelland felt the second one characterized effective leaders in organizations.[34]

A person with a strong **Need for Affiliation** focuses on "establishing, maintaining, and restoring positive affective relations with others."[35] He wants close and warm relationships with other people. Such people seek the approval of others, especially those about whom they care. Strong Need for Affiliation people like other people, want other people to like them, and want to be in the company of others.[36] Separation from a loved one is undesirable, whether it is physical separation or psychological separation caused by an argument or a fight.[37]

What does McClelland's theory tell us about behavior in organizations, both your behavior and the behavior of others? The answer to this question requires us to consider all three needs that McClelland and his colleagues studied.

Money plays an important role for both high and low achievers, but for different reasons.[38] The high Need for Achievement person wants concrete feedback about performance. Such people want to know when they have been successful. Making a profit, or receiving a bonus, is a concrete statement about success or failure. The high achiever will not value the money as an end in itself. The monetary reward is a symbol of success and feedback about job performance.[39] The low achiever, on the other hand, views the monetary reward as an end in itself. An organization could get increased performance from a low Need for Achievement person by rewarding improved performance with more money.

More money alone does not get high performance from high Need for Achievement people. The job must be challenging, and the person must be responsible for what is done. Such people want to feel successful at doing something over which they have control. As you will see in Chapter 9, the design of a person's job can be an important element in job performance for the reasons just given.

McClelland's research found that managers and executives usually had higher Need for Achievement scores than people in other occupations.[40] This does not mean that people in many other achievement-oriented occupations such as scientists, professors, and artists are low achievers. It simply means that the nature of Need for Achievement behavior as described above fits well with the role demands of managers and executives. McClelland summarized his view as follows:

> The achievement motive should lead individuals to seek out situations which provide moderate challenge to their skills, to perform better in such situations, and to have greater confidence in the likelihood of their success. It should make them conservative where things are completely beyond their control, as in games of chance, and happier where they have some opportunity of influencing the outcome of a series of events by their own actions and of knowing concretely what those actions have accomplished. [41]

The Need for Achievement and the Need for Power are related in important ways that have implications for behavior in organizations.[42] Both needs lead to assertive behaviors in trying to get something done. The high Need for Achievement person is task centered and future oriented and performs to an internal standard of excellence. The high Need for Power person engages in behavior that draws attention to the person for the effect he is having. Such people are more risk taking and present oriented and assess situations for their change potential. Both types of people are important for successful organizations. High Need for Achievement managers are important to keep an organization going, but high Need for Power people can bring dramatic changes and innovations.[43] McClelland's research also found high Need for Power and low Need for Affiliation in more totalitarian-oriented countries.[44] We can speculate that this pattern of needs is associated with an authoritarian management style that relies on close supervision.[45]

Look back at your profile of needs. The profile assessed both Need for Achievement and Need for Affiliation. Need for Dominance in Murray's theory is close in meaning to McClelland's Need for Power.

Frederick **Herzberg's Motivator-Hygiene Theory** is not based directly on needs. It also does not fit neatly with the cognitive and behavioral theories described in the next chapter. It is useful as a transition between purely need-based theories and those based on cognitive and behavioral processes.

In developing his theory, Herzberg did his early research with samples of accountants and engineers. Each person was interviewed and asked to recall a past work event he found especially positive or especially negative. The interview responses were content analyzed to decide whether any systematic relationship existed between positive and negative events and aspects of the job or work organization.[46]

Herzberg found that reports of negative events had items that mostly involved a person's job context. Negative reports described company policy, its administration, working conditions, and supervision more often than reports of positive events. The positive reports described aspects of the job itself, a feeling of achievement, and a feeling of responsibility. The person's salary was mentioned about the same proportion of time in both negative and positive reports.

Herzberg called the items predominantly found in descriptions of negative events **dissatisfiers.** He called those found in descriptions of positive events **satisfiers.** Dissatisfiers could lead to high levels of employee dissatisfaction. If management improved the dissatisfiers, employees would feel a reduction in dissatisfaction, but not higher satisfaction. The satisfiers could lead to high levels of employee satisfaction, but their absence or a person's failure to experience them would not produce dissatisfaction.

Herzberg's observations on satisfaction and dissatisfaction differed from commonly held views. The traditional view saw a single continuum with satisfaction at one end and dissatisfaction at the other. Herzberg's research suggested two distinct continua, one for satisfaction and one for dissatisfaction. Figure 7-5 compares the traditional view of satisfaction with the one suggested by Herzberg. In short, different aspects of an employee's experiences contributed separately to satisfaction and dissatisfaction.

Herzberg eventually called the satisfiers **motivators** and the dissatisfiers **hygiene factors.**[47] Table 7-2 lists Herzberg's motivators and hygiene factors. Notice that

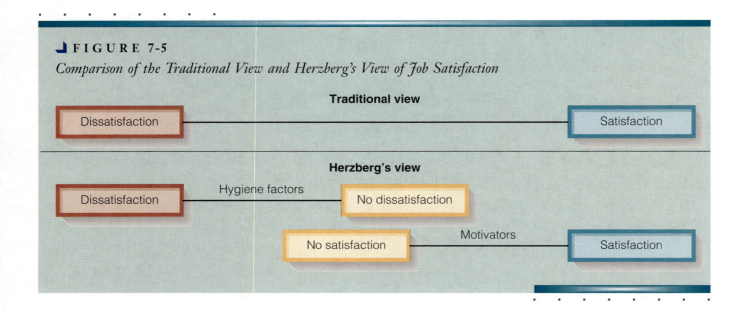

↵ FIGURE 7-5

Comparison of the Traditional View and Herzberg's View of Job Satisfaction

Traditional view

Dissatisfaction ———————————————— Satisfaction

Herzberg's view

Dissatisfaction —— Hygiene factors —— No dissatisfaction

No satisfaction —— Motivators —— Satisfaction

TABLE 7-2

Herzberg's Motivators and Hygiene Factors

MOTIVATORS	HYGIENE FACTORS
Achievement	Company policy and administration
Recognition	Supervision
Work itself	Interpersonal relations
Responsibility	Working conditions
Advancement	Salary

motivators are either in the job itself or are an individual's personal response to job and work experiences. The hygiene factors are in the context surrounding the job, external to both the individual and the job.

The Motivator-Hygiene Theory offers specific recommendations about how to improve employee motivation.[48] Managers first must improve the hygienic conditions of work (e.g., company policies, their administration, quality of supervision, and working conditions) before trying to increase motivation. Negative hygienic conditions distract employees from experiencing the motivators. Once the work context is improved, the manager can try to provide the motivators by redesigning jobs using a process Herzberg called job enrichment. By adding more responsibility and autonomy to the job, the manager creates the opportunity for an employee to experience the motivators. Chapter 9 discusses job redesign and its effect on human motivation in detail.

Empirical research designed to test the Motivator-Hygiene Theory has had mixed results. The work of Herzberg and his colleagues, using the retrospective interview technique, has supported the distinction between motivators and hygiene factors. Work by other researchers, using other research methods, has not produced confirming evidence.[49] Some also have questioned the basic validity of retrospective interviews.[50] As Chapter 4 explained, people can attribute positive work experiences to themselves and negative experiences to external factors.

There are, of course, two sides to this critique. Herzberg responded to the question of attribution by arguing that more conventional methods of measurement also produce bias. His use of retrospective interviews was a deliberate effort to avoid such bias.[51]

· ·

International Aspects of the Need Theories of Motivation

*T*he need theories described in this chapter were the work of U.S. scholars. Early empirical research also often used U.S. samples. A major issue centers on whether those theories are culture bound.[52] Although the concept of needs holds across cultures, people with different cultural backgrounds may express and satisfy those needs differently.[53]

The accumulated research evidence shows Maslow's Hierarchy of Needs Theory does not hold in many countries in the form proposed. Different needs appear as driving forces in different countries.[54] Many U.S. workers respond to self-actualization. Security and affiliation needs are the strongest needs among Latin American workers. French and German workers have a strong need for security. The strong cooperative and affiliation orientation of New Zealanders suggests the belongingness and love needs are central in that country.

The results of one large study of the central values of different countries imply differences in saliency of needs among different countries. Different needs apparently are at the top of the hierarchy for workers in different cultures.[55] Self-actualization

Presumably, you are pursuing a college education because you have chosen some career that "feels good" to you right now. Reflect on your need structure and your future career to be sure they are congruent. It is better to think carefully now about career choices given your needs than to experience some painful frustrations in the future.

E.R.G. Theory described an "enrichment cycle" as possible for those who can satisfy growth needs and then come to desire them even more strongly. This is a form of self-motivation that will be useful to you as a manager. A key issue here is how to induce an enrichment cycle in another person.

The design of jobs and the nature of task assignments induce high levels of self-motivation, a motivation similar to the enrichment cycle. Chapter 9 gives a complete description of intrinsic rewards and job design. That discussion should help you in thinking about what you can do as a manager to redesign jobs to make them more motivating.

Summary

The motivation theories described in this chapter offer major insights into human behavior. Figure 7-6 summarizes the major concepts of each theory and indicates their common points.

Murray's Theory of Human Personality is a broad and complex picture of needs and behavior. His theory allowed for a complex collection of needs that often served as multiple bases of behavior.

Maslow's Hierarchy of Needs Theory and the changes made to it by E.R.G. Theory suggest that some needs that can be a source of motivation are stronger than others. Those needs can dominate the attention of the person for some time. Murray had made the same suggestion, but the two hierarchical theories put it into bold relief.

McClelland's Achievement Motivation Theory gave much detail about the behavior associated with three needs, especially the Need for Achievement. The behaviors associated with the Needs for Achievement and Power were both important for success in organizations, although for different reasons.

Herzberg's Motivator-Hygiene Theory distinguished factors in the job itself from those in the work context. Factors in the job were the motivators; those in the work context were the hygiene factors. The motivators directly added to motivation. Hygiene factors could lead to dissatisfaction, but improving them would not lead to motivation.

International aspects of the need theories in this chapter raised questions about whether these theories are culture bound. Although the concept of needs holds across cultures, people with different cultural backgrounds can have different patterns of needs, motivators, and hygiene factors.

The discussion of ethical issues surrounding the need theories of motivation focused on broad ethical issues created by a manager's knowledge of human motivation. Those issues will crystallize in the next two motivation chapters as we build more detailed theories of human motivation.

Key Terms

belongingness and love needs 176
deficiency cycle 179
enrichment cycle 179
E.R.G. Theory 177
esteem needs 176
existence needs 177
frustration-regression 179
growth needs 178
Herzberg's Motivator-Hygiene
    Theory 182

hygiene factors (dissatisfiers) 182
Maslow's Hierarchy of Needs
    Theory 176
McClelland's Achievement Motivation
    Theory 180
motivators (satisfiers) 182
Murray's Theory of Human
    Personality 182
need 173
Need for Achievement 180

Need for Affiliation 181
Need for Power 180
need hierarchy 176
physiological needs 176
prepotency 176
relatedness needs 177
safety needs 176
satisfaction-progression 178
self-actualization needs 176

FIGURE 7-6

Summary of Need Theories

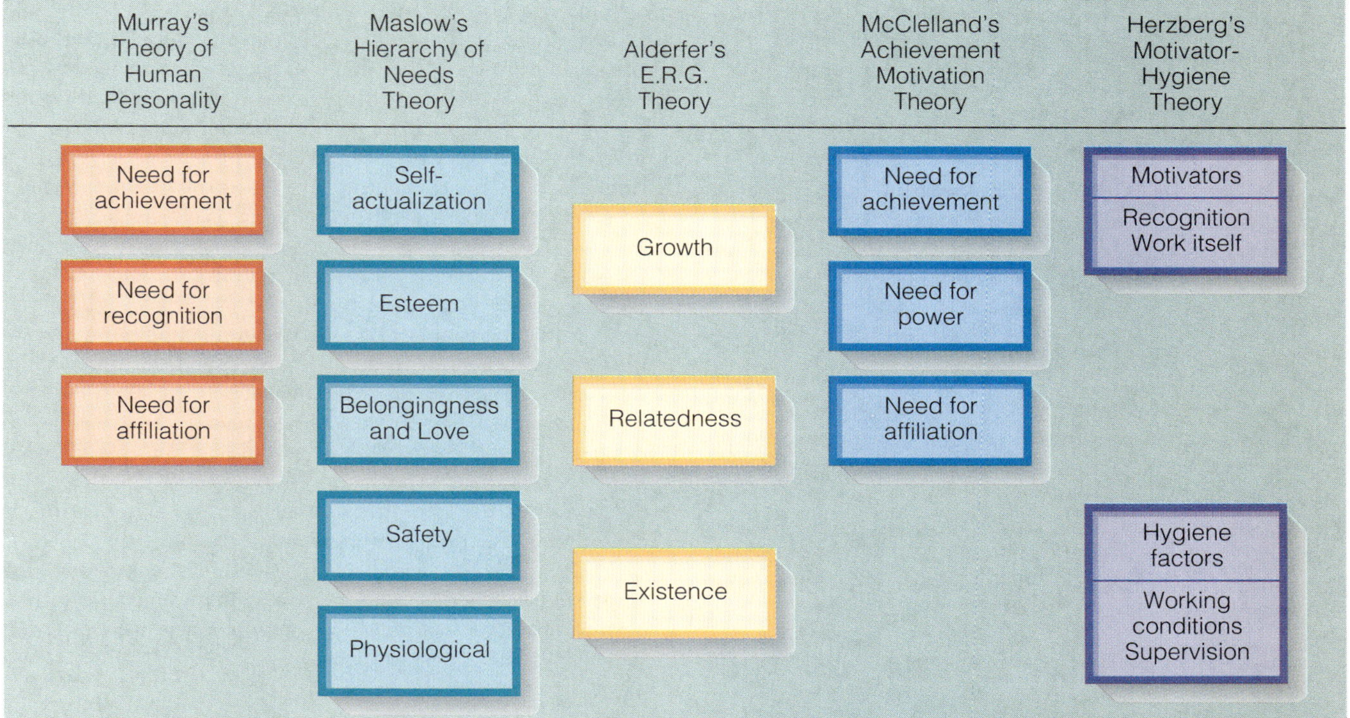

Murray's Theory of Human Personality	Maslow's Hierarchy of Needs Theory	Alderfer's E.R.G. Theory	McClelland's Achievement Motivation Theory	Herzberg's Motivator-Hygiene Theory
Need for achievement	Self-actualization	Growth	Need for achievement	Motivators — Recognition, Work itself
Need for recognition	Esteem		Need for power	
Need for affiliation	Belongingness and Love	Relatedness	Need for affiliation	
	Safety			Hygiene factors — Working conditions, Supervision
		Existence		
	Physiological			

Review and Discussion Questions

1. What are the similarities and differences between Maslow's Hierarchy of Needs Theory and Alderfer's E.R.G. Theory?

2. Based on your experiences, which of the two need theories mentioned in Question 1 fits your sense of reality? Use examples of situations and behavior to make your points.

3. Discuss the satisfaction-progression and frustration-regression principles from E.R.G. Theory. Give examples of the functioning of each principle.

4. Which parts of Herzberg's Motivation-Hygiene Theory made useful contributions to our understanding of motivation in organizations?

5. Discuss the major common points of all the theories described in this chapter.

6. What is the relationship between monetary rewards and different needs? How should managers view money as a motivator for people with different needs?

7. Discuss the two "Faces of Power" described by McClelland. Which have you or other students in the class experienced? Which of the two types of power do you respond to best? Why?

8. What implications for the practice of management do you see in the theories of motivation discussed in this chapter? How does a manager's knowledge of people's needs help him do a better job of managing?

9. Review the discussion of ethical issues and the need theories of motivation. Discuss those issues with the goal of taking a strong position on them.

10. Discuss the international aspects of the need theories described in this chapter. If any students in your classes are from other countries, ask them whether the statements hold true for people raised in a traditional way in their culture or whether people show the same profiles as many Americans.

Case

LIFE IN JAPAN AFTER NEW JERSEY

The international issues section of this chapter discussed some research results and observations that suggest needs and need structures are culturally based. This case describes some experiences of a young Japanese woman returning to Japan from a four-year stay in the United States.

1. What does the case imply about the stability of a person's needs after exposure to another culture for a long time?
2. Will patience alone let repatriated Japanese families re-accept all parts of their home culture?

You've got to, you know, really, like, feel bad for Mayu Omura, 12. There she was in suburban Richwood, New Jersey, living the totally awesome life of an affluent American preteen—gossiping about boys, cruising the malls, staying hip to the new fashions. A big Schwarzenegger fan, she saw *Terminator 2* four times.

Then her father, Haruki, an executive at KDD, Japan's largest international telecommunications company, was transferred back to Tokyo this summer after nearly four years in the U.S. Suddenly Mayu had to cope with a far less

expansive life. Sighs she: "I miss my friends very much, and also our big house. Everything was so much bigger there.

Hundreds of these Japanese youngsters are undergoing similar culture shock nowadays as they return to Japan from their fathers' global postings. Since the numbers posted overseas are going up, the problem is likely to increase in the future. While executives might have little trouble plugging back into the work routine after a stretch abroad, their families often yearn for lost freedom. Wives refuse to fade into the background once again, and many children bristle at the strict discipline of their local schools.

In a survey conducted by Friends, a Tokyo group that helps returning families cope, kids complained about everything from the uniforms and haircut regulations imposed by Japanese schools to authoritarian teachers and docile peers.

Some parents living overseas seek to ease reentry ahead of time. They send their children to the handful of traditional Japanese schools in the U.S. and other foreign countries. But for those like the Omuras, who let their kids attend American schools, the only answer seems to be patience.

Mayu intends to get back to the U.S. someday. Meanwhile she seeks a dose of Americana whenever she can. She even went to see *Terminator 2* in Tokyo, but it just wasn't the same. Says she: "I was the only one laughing at the funny parts—maybe they didn't get the jokes."

Source: C. Mikami, "Life in Japan after New Jersey," *Fortune,* December 2, 1991, pp. 13–14. © 1991 Time Inc. All rights reserved.

Case

PURSUIT OF SELF-ESTEEM IS A BIG BUSINESS

This case describes efforts to build self-esteem in children so they will feel good about themselves throughout their lives. Discuss the reactions of the critics at the end of the case. Try to answer the following questions:

1. Are these misguided efforts?
2. Is self-esteem an important need in shaping successful adult behavior?
3. Can people learn how to change their self-esteem?

The message on the star-shaped mirror at a new Museum of Science and Industry exhibit poses a true or false question to children: "A total person can say, 'I like myself!'"

Press the False button, and stormy music rumbles. Punch True, and the child is rewarded with magical tinkly sounds.

For decades, children have been sent to the loud and lively Museum of Science and Industry to learn about scientific and technical matters that many parents couldn't explain.

Now the fancy gadgets are helping to teach children something else they may not be learning at home: self-esteem.

For years, teaching self-esteem has been dismissed as a feel-good crusade, taken seriously only in California, where a government-funded task force was set up several years ago to study the topic. But now the self-esteem fervor is catching on, even in the skeptical Midwest. Poor self-esteem has become, some experts say, the root of many social evils, from teen-age pregnancy to drug use to murder.

Childhood is viewed now as rocky terrain to be negotiated carefully at the risk of destroying a fragile self-image.

Today one-third of all elementary schools in the country use curriculums designed to boost pupils' self-image, according to the National Council for Self-Esteem....

"The self-esteem you develop early in life tends to persist," said Dr. Jerome Schulman, a Children's Memorial Hospital psychiatrist who developed the Museum of Science and Industry's Starway exhibit. "And people with poor self-esteem go through life feeling lousy about themselves."

...People who don't like themselves tend to have a similarly low opinion of other people and go through life taking their frustrations out on themselves and others, he said.

The pursuit of self-esteem has become a big business.

Source: Excerpted from T. Wiltz, "Pursuit of Self-Esteem Is a Big Business," *Chicago Tribune,* July 7, 1992, Section 2, pp. 1–2. (As the story appeared in the *Albuquerque Journal,* August 12, 1992, p. B1.) Reprinted by permission: Tribune Media Services.

It's grist for talk shows and a favorite topic of dozens of self-help books and psychological studies.

Even citizens of Eastern Bloc countries are trying to jump on the bandwagon, reports Robert Reasoner, president of the 10-year-old International Council for Self-Esteem.

"The bottom line is, self-esteem is in a sense a social vaccine we can use to reduce deviant behavior," said Reasoner, who pioneered self-image curriculums about a decade ago as superintendent of the California-based Moreland School District.

"I see it as the one hope for making a better society," Reasoner said.

"Self-esteem is the cheapest, most effective way of getting at social issues."

But what is self-esteem?

"It's keeping your cool when you're scared," said Matt Johnson, a 9-year-old from Denver, as he played in the Kids' Starway exhibit at the Museum of Science and Industry. . . .

"It's when you like yourself," said Maria Hurst, a 3rd-grader at Brentano Elementary School, a Chicago public school which includes self-esteem lessons in its curriculum. "I heard it in reading. I like myself. I like the way I act."

Critics argue that there are hazards in the self-esteem craze. Blindly praising children for every little thing creates spoiled children who think the world revolves around them, experts say.

"Kids are becoming praise junkies," said Nancy Curry, a University of Pittsburgh psychoanalyst who serves as a consultant to the children's television show, "Mr. Rogers Neighborhood.". . .

As a result, "The concept of self-esteem has become trivialized," said Curry. . . .

"We're seeing more narcissism among children, a lot of selfishness," Curry said. "We see children who have a very strong sense of entitlement."

Healthy self-respect can't be taught in school, according to Curry and other self-esteem detractors. Children learn to feel good about themselves by loving parents who are willing to set limits for their kids while teaching them to respect others, they say.

. . . .

↵ *References and Notes*

[1]T. R. Mitchell, "Motivation: New Directions for Theory, Research, and Practice," *Academy of Management Review* 7 (1982): 80–88.

[2]Ibid., p. 81.

[3]Ibid., pp. 82–83.

[4]M. G. Evans, "Organizational Behavior: The Central Role of Motivation," in J. C. Hunt and J. D. Blair, eds., "1986," *Yearly Review of Management of the Journal of Management* 12 (1986): 203–22.

[5]Mitchell, "Motivation," p. 82.

[6]H. A. Murray, *Explorations in Personality* (New York: John Wiley & Sons, 1938); H. A. Murray, *Assessment of Men* (New York: Holt, Rinehart, & Winston, 1948).

[7]Murray dealt with other factors internal to the person, the details of which do not change the essence of what is presented here. Factors external to the person were stimuli to which the person reacted. Murray's word for such stimuli was *press*.

[8]Murray, *Explorations*, p. 60.

[9]Ibid., p. 73.

[10]Murray's original terms were *viscerogenic* and *psychogenic*, respectively.

[11]Developed from Murray, *Explorations*, pp. 80–83.

[12]A. H. Maslow, "Preface to Motivation Theory," *Psychosomatic Medicine* 5 (1943): 85–92; A. H. Maslow, "A Theory of Human Motivation," *Psychological Review* 50 (1943): 370–96.

[13]Maslow, "Theory of Human Motivation," p. 382.

[14]Ibid., p. 386.

[15]M. A. Wahba and L. Bridwell, "Maslow Reconsidered: A Review of Research on the Need Hierarchy Theory," *Organizational Behavior and Human Performance* 15 (1976): 212–40.

[16]V. F. Mitchell and P. M. Mougdil, "Measurement of Maslow's Need Hierarchy," *Organizational Behavior and Human Performance* 16 (1976): 334–49.

[17]Wahba and Bridwell, "Maslow Reconsidered"; D. T. Hall and K. E. Nougaim, "An Examination of Maslow's Need Hierarchy in an Organizational Setting," *Organizational Behavior and Human Performance* 3 (1967): 12–35.

[18]Hall and Nougaim, "Examination of Maslow's Need hierarchy"; E. E. Lawler III and J. L. Suttle, "A Causal Correlation Test of the Need Hierarchy Concept," *Organizational Behavior and Human Performance* 7 (1972): 265–87.

[19]A. H. Maslow, *Eupsychian Management* (Homewood, Ill.: Dorsey, 1965), pp. 55–56.

[20]C. P. Alderfer, *Existence, Relatedness, and Growth: Human Needs in Organizational Settings* (New York: Free Press, 1972).

[21]J. E. Champoux, "A Sociological Perspective on Work Involvement," *International Review of Applied Psychology* 30 (1981): 65–86.

[22]Alderfer, *Existence*.

[23]R. E. Kaplan and K. A. Smith, "The Effect of Variations in Relatedness Need Satisfaction on Relatedness Desire," *Administrative Science Quarterly* 19 (1974): 507–32; J. P. Wanous and A. A. Zwany, "A Cross-Sectional Test of Need Hierarchy Theory," *Organizational Behavior and Human Performance* 18 (1977): 78–97.

[24]D. C. McClelland, *The Achieving Society* (Princeton, N.J.: D. Van Nostrand, 1961); D. C. McClelland, "Business Drive and National Achievement," *Harvard Business Review* (July-August 1962): 99–112; D. C. McClelland, "Toward a Theory of Motive Acquisition," *American Psychologist* 20 (1965): 321–33.

[25]Two excellent volumes capture much of the important work of both McClelland and his colleague Atkinson. A. J. Stewart, ed., *Motivation and Society* (San Francisco: Jossey-Bass, 1982); J. W. Atkinson, ed., *Personality, Motivation, and Action: Selected Papers* (New York: Praeger, 1983).

[26]D. R. Entwisle, "To Dispel Fantasies about Fantasy-Based Measures of Achievement Motivation," *Psychological Bulletin* 77 (1972): 377–91.

[27]J. W. Atkinson, K. Bongort, and L. H. Price, "Explorations Using Computer Simulation to Comprehend Thematic Apperceptive Measurement and Motivation," *Motivation and Emotion* 1 (1977): 1–26; J. W. Atkinson, "Studying Personality in the Context of an Advanced Motivational Psychology," *American Psychologist* 36 (1981): 117–28.

[28]McClelland, *The Achieving Society*.

[29]J. W. Atkinson, "Motivational Determinants of Intellective Performance and Cumulative Achievement," in J. W. Atkinson and J. O. Raynor, eds., *Motivation and Achievement* (Washington, D.C.: Winston, 1974).

[30]McClelland, *The Achieving Society*.

[31]J. W. Atkinson and D. Birch, *An Introduction to Motivation*, 2d. ed. (New York: Van Nostrand, 1978), p. 82.

[32]J. Veroff, "Development and Validation of a Projective Measure of Power Motivation," *Journal of Abnormal and Social Psychology* 54

(1957): 1–8; D. C. McClelland, "The Two Faces of Power," *Journal of International Affairs* 24 (1970): 29–47.

[33]D. C. McClelland, *Power: The Inner Experience* (New York: Irvington, 1975); D. C. McClelland and D. H. Burnham, "Power Is the Great Motivator," *Harvard Business Review* 55 (1976); 100–10.

[34]McClelland and Burnham, "Power Is the Great Motivator."

[35]Atkinson and Birch, *Introduction to Motivation*, p. 82.

[36]J. W. Atkinson, R. W. Heyns, and J. Veroff, "The Effect of Experimental Arousal of the Affiliation Motive on Thematic Apperception," *Journal of Abnormal and Social Psychology* 49 (1954): 405–10.

[37]T. E. Shipley, Jr. and J. Veroff, "A Projective Measure of Need for Affiliation," *Journal of Experimental Psychology* 43 (1952): 349–56.

[38]McClelland, "Business Drive and National Achievement."

[39]McClelland, *The Achieving Society*, pp. 233–37.

[40]McClelland, "Business Drive and National Achievement."

[41]McClelland, *The Achieving Society*, pp. 238–39.

[42]J. Veroff, "Assertive Motivations: Achievement versus Power," in A. J. Stewart, ed., *Motivation and Society* (San Francisco: Jossey-Bass, 1982), Ch. 4.

[43]D. C. McClelland and D. G. Winter, *Motivating Economic Achievement* (New York: Free Press, 1969).

[44]McClelland, *The Achieving Society*, pp. 168–69.

[45]McClelland had much the same speculation, although at a societal level. See McClelland, *The Achieving Society*, p. 394.

[46]F. Herzberg, B. Mausner, and B. Snyderman, *The Motivation to Work* (New York: Wiley, 1959); F. Herzberg, *Work and the Nature of Man* (Cleveland: World Publishing Company, 1966).

[47]Herzberg, *Work and the Nature of Man*.

[48]F. Herzberg, "One More Time: How Do You Motivate Employees?" *Harvard Business Review* 46 (1968): 54–62.

[49]R. J. House and L. A. Wigdor, "Herzberg's Dual-Factor Theory of Job Satisfaction and Motivation: A Review of the Evidence and a Criticism," *Personnel Psychology* 20 (1967): 369–89; N. King, "Clarifi-

cation and Evaluation of the Two-Factor Theory of Job Satisfaction," *Psychological Bulletin* 74 (1970): 18–31.

[50]V. H. Vroom, *Work and Motivation* (New York: John Wiley & Sons, 1964), p. 129.

[51]Herzberg, *Work and the Nature of Man*, Ch. 8.

[52]G. Hofstede, "Motivation, Leadership, and Organization: Do American Theories Apply Abroad?" *Organizational Dynamics* 9 (1980): 42–63; G. Hofstede, *Culture's Consequences: International Differences in Work-Related Values* (Beverly Hills, Calif.: Sage Publications, 1984).

[53]N. J. Adler, *International Dimensions of Organizational Behavior* (Boston: PWS-KENT, 1991), pp. 152–60.

[54]L. J. Bourgeois III and M. Boltvinik, "OD in Cross-Cultural Settings: Latin America," *California Management Review* 23 (1981): 75–81; G. H. Hines, "Cultural Influences on Work Motivation," in P. Warr, ed., *Personal Goals and Work Design* (London: John Wiley & Sons, 1976), Ch. 2; D. Sirota and J. M. Greenwood, "Understand Your Overseas Work Force," *Harvard Business Review* 49 (1971): 53–60.

[55]Hofstede, "Motivation"; Hofstede, *Culture's Consequences*, pp. 255–56.

[56]Adler, *International Dimensions*, pp. 154–55.

[57]Hofstede, "Motivation"; Hofstede, *Culture's Consequences*, pp. 126–28, 255–57.

[58]Adler, *International Dimensions*, 156–57.

[59]C. Argyris, *Personality and Organization: The Conflict between System and the Individual* (New York: Harper & Brothers, 1957); R. Likert, *New Patterns of Management* (New York: McGraw-Hill, 1961); D. McGregor, *The Human Side of Enterprise* (New York: McGraw-Hill, 1960).

[60]L. E. Davis and A. B. Cherns, eds., *The Quality of Working Life*, vol. 1 *Problems, Prospects, and the State of the Art* (New York: Free Press, 1975).

[61]Adler, *International Dimensions*.

[62]Champoux, "Sociological Perspective."

[63]Ibid.

Motivation: Cognitive and Behavioral Theories and Techniques

· *Albin Wolowiec Jr. shows off his profit-sharing check. In 1994, Chrysler Corporation's workers received an average of $8,000 each from the company's profit-sharing program. Such payments are motivators for many people.*

After reading this chapter, you should be able to . . .

· Describe how people develop expectations about what will happen to them.
· Appreciate differences in the values people place on the results of their behavior.
· Understand the differences between extrinsic and intrinsic outcomes.
· Discuss the role of equity in human motivation and behavior.
· Describe the powerful technique of Behavior Modification.
· Use the technique of Goal Setting.
· Discuss some international aspects of motivation.

Chapter Overview

Tony Dorsett and the Dallas Cowboys

• *Tony Dorsett making a play for the Dallas Cowboys in the late 1980s.*

Dallas Cowboys President Tex Schramm said Thursday he will not trade Tony Dorsett even though the 10-year veteran running back fumed over Herschel Walker's five-year, $5 million contract.

"I told him I didn't even intend to talk about trading him," Schramm said after meeting with Dorsett. "We'd never trade Tony. He is too much a part of our organization."

Dorsett said he wanted to be traded or given a raise in view of the deal made with Walker, a refugee with the hibernating USFL who came to terms Wednesday. Dorsett warned that if his demands were not met, he could be a "disruptive force" on the Cowboys.

Schramm said Thursday: "Tony would like to pull back what he said. He feels sorry he let it flow out. He didn't mean it. He was just mad and being egged on by the media.

Dorsett, who receives an annual salary of about $450,000 plus fringe benefits, agreed he got out of control.

However, Dorsett did not apologize.

"My feelings haven't changed a great deal," Dorsett said. "I had a nice conversation with Tex so they would know where my head is at and I know where they are at. I think the contract surprised everybody and I showed some immaturity. It was a fit of rage." . . .

Dorsett did not repeat he wanted to be traded but did not take it back.

Asked about the reaction of the fans, he said, "I'm not worried about the boo birds. They don't put bread and butter on the table. They have a tendency to forgive and forget."

Schramm said he and Dorsett "shook hands before he left. Sure, he was still a little hurt but he'll be OK. He's a good kid, a good man." . . .

Walker, who is expected to practice in a Cowboys uniform for the first time today, agreed to a guaranteed contract on Wednesday.

Asked if he would renegotiate Dorsett's contract, Schramm replied, "I feel comfortable with his contract."

Dorsett, who had fallen into financial trouble over several sour business ventures, missed training camp last year until the Cowboys renegotiated his contract.

Dorsett had originally welcomed the thought of playing in the same backfield with another Heisman Trophy winner, but was steamed when details of Walker's contract came out.

"If this team does not pay me like they are paying their other back, I would suggest strongly that the team try to trade me or pay me because I'll be very unhappy and . . . I can be a very disruptive force," said Dorsett.

"I don't want to be here. When you pay a guy more than me, you've told me he's your back. I'm not second fiddle to anyone."

Walker was to return from personal business in New Jersey and attend but not play in Saturday night's exhibition game in Los Angeles against the Raiders.

Schramm said he can remember grumbling among the Cowboys' players when Dorsett was signed in 1977.

Source: Excerpted from "Cowboys: We'd Never Trade Tony," Associated Press, 1986. (As the story appeared in the *Albuquerque Journal,* August 15, 1986, pp. D1, D5.) Reprinted with the permission of the Associated Press.

"It's just a historic thing," Schramm said. "Tony came in as the Heisman Trophy winner out of Pittsburgh and got a big salary and some of the veterans started grumbling. It happens every year with No. 1 draft choices. It's a fact of the game."

Walker, 24, the 1982 Heisman Trophy winner, set a professional football rushing record for one season with 2,411 yards for the USFL New Jersey Generals in 1985....

Walker has yet to comment on Dorsett's remarks but said earlier he had a lot of respect for Dorsett.

"It would be an honor to play with him because Tony has a lot of class," Walker said. "Just look at what he has accomplished. I've always admired Tony. We're not going to have any problems. We both want to win."

T his chapter describes two groups of motivation theories that differ from those in Chapter 7. One group uses cognitive processes to explain human behavior. The other group focuses on observable behavior, not cognitive processes.

The two cognitive process theories are Expectancy Theory and Equity Theory. Expectancy Theory describes internal processes of choice among different behaviors. Equity Theory describes how people react when they feel unfairly treated by organizations. Later this chapter uses Equity Theory to examine Tony Dorsett's reaction to Herschel Walker's contract. As we will see, Dorsett's behavior is a fully understandable reaction to his feelings of being treated unfairly.

The second group of theories, called Behavioral Theories, focuses on observable behavior. These theories do not use internal psychological processes to explain human behavior. This characteristic is a central and sometimes controversial feature of Behavior Modification. The technique of Goal Setting is also included in this group because of its emphasis on setting external goals that a person tries to reach. It uses cognitive processes to explain behavior but mostly focuses on how to set goals for people to reach.

⌐ Expectancy Theory

The **Expectancy Theory** of motivation is a useful tool for analyzing motivation issues and problems.[1] Because it can help you understand human behavior, it can serve as an analytical tool. A review of the research literature shows mixed support for Expectancy Theory as described here.[2] Despite the mixed support, the theory has intuitive appeal and works well as an analytical tool.

Expectancy Theory makes certain assumptions about what people do when deciding how to behave. Some will be familiar to you because they are similar to the assumptions described for need theories in Chapter 7. The following are the four assumptions underlying Expectancy Theory:

- Forces in the environment and the individual interact to affect behavior.
- People choose among different courses of action.
- People make those choices based on preferences for the outcomes of those actions.
- The choices among alternatives are rational and are based on a person's perceptions of the value of the results of various actions. An individual goes toward outcomes valued positively and avoids outcomes valued negatively.

The first assumption is similar to Murray's Theory of Human Personality, which was described in Chapter 7. People have certain characteristics (needs) they are trying to satisfy. The immediate environment may present opportunities for the satisfaction of those needs. People choose behavior directed at satisfying those needs in that particular environment.

People have different preferences for different outcomes. You have specific preferences for various course grades, and your preferences may differ from those of other students. Some students will be satisfied with an "A" or a "B." Others are determined to get an "A." Still others simply want to avoid receiving a "C," "D," or "F."

The assumptions of Expectancy Theory suggest that if you value receiving an "A" more than receiving any other grade, you will behave in a way that lets you get that grade. Of course, you also will need to believe that getting an "A" is possible. If you believe an "A" is possible, you will take notes in class, record class lectures, and spend considerable time studying. You also will avoid behavior that will not lead to getting the "A" such as socializing instead of studying.

THE BASIC CONCEPTS OF EXPECTANCY THEORY

Three concepts form the basic structure of expectancy theory. The first two concepts deal with a person's expectancy that actions will lead to certain outcomes. The third concept deals with a person's preference among these outcomes.

Expectancy is a person's belief that ". . . a particular act will be followed by a particular outcome."[3] It is a subjective probability that a person's action will be followed by a particular outcome. If the person believes the outcome is certain to happen, the expectancy is 1. If the person believes the action will not lead to that outcome, the expectancy is 0. Expectancy can take on any value between 0 and 1. An expectancy of .50 means a person believes there is a 50–50 chance that an act will be followed by a given outcome.

The first expectancy concept is a person's belief that effort leads to a desired or required level of performance.[4] Effort is the extent to which a person tries to perform as desired. Because many factors affect whether a person can perform as desired, Expectancy Theory formulates this uncertainty as the **Effort-Performance Expectancy** ($E{\rightarrow}P$). For example, a person works hard and meets an important deadline.

A second expectancy concept describes a person's belief that performance will be followed by some outcome. The **Performance-Outcome Expectancy** ($P{\rightarrow}O$) describes the perceived connection between a person's performance and any outcomes she may get for that performance. Those outcomes can include a pay increase, promotion, quality award, or praise from the boss.[5] Continuing the deadline example, the person receives a bonus for meeting the deadline.

The third concept in Expectancy Theory is valence. **Valence (V)** is the preference people have among outcomes. Outcomes an individual wants to receive have positive valence. Outcomes a person wants to avoid have negative valence. If the person is indifferent to an outcome, the valence is 0. Valences have a range of values expressing the degree of attraction or avoidance a person associates with the outcome.

The basic concepts of Expectancy Theory are not new. They have their roots in the principle of hedonism.[6] People pursue pleasant experiences and avoid unpleasant experiences. Adam Smith noted over three hundred years ago that human beings cognitively calculate the likely losses and payoffs of various courses of action.[7]

THE RELATIONSHIPS BETWEEN EXPECTANCIES AND VALENCES

Expectancy Theory describes specific relationships between expectancies and valences in explaining how and why people choose among behaviors. Figure 8-1 shows a simplified version of Expectancy Theory and the relationships among the three concepts.

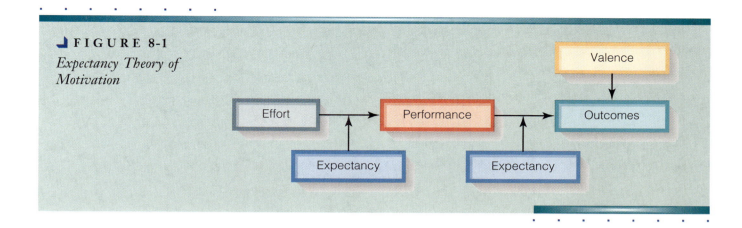

FIGURE 8-1

Expectancy Theory of Motivation

Expectancy Theory says people perceive a connection between effort and a desired or required level of performance. People also perceive a link between that level of performance and an outcome. Lastly, people have different preferences for different outcomes.

The following formula shows the relationships among the three concepts more directly:

$$\text{Motivation} = f \sum_{i=1}^{n} (E{\rightarrow}P)_i \times (P{\rightarrow}O)_i \times V_i$$

The formula shows two important features of Expectancy Theory. First, multiple outcomes are possible for behavior. Those outcomes may be something positively valued (a raise) or negatively valued (being fired). A person's perception of the valence of all possible outcomes for a behavior decides the choice of behavior. People go toward positively valent outcomes and avoid negatively valent outcomes. They also may need to consider several possible outcomes at once in their evaluation.

Second, the expectancies and valences are expected to combine multiplicatively when a person assesses different courses of action. Here you can see the importance of a value of 0 for an expectancy or a valence. If an outcome is positively valent, but you know you cannot get it (expectancy = 0), the theory predicts you will not be highly motivated. Similarly, if you are indifferent to an outcome (valence = 0), you also will not be highly motivated even though you believe you can get the outcome.

TYPES OF OUTCOMES

The outcomes people get for performance divide into two types: extrinsic and intrinsic. **Extrinsic outcomes** are outcomes people receive from someone else for their performance. **Intrinsic outcomes** are rewards a person gives to herself. Figure 8-2 is an expanded version of the theory showing both extrinsic and intrinsic outcomes.

Extrinsic outcomes include pay increases, promotions, supervisor's praise, quality awards, larger office space, and other rewards that are external to the person. Managers can give or withhold extrinsic outcomes for an employee's performance. The employee has control over the performance she is willing to give, but does not directly control the outcome she gets. There is also a time delay between the employee's performance and the extrinsic outcome. For example, organizations usually give pay increases annually or semiannually. The time lag of many extrinsic outcomes can reduce their effect on motivation.

Employees have much more control over the intrinsic outcomes they experience. Because the individual controls intrinsic outcomes, there is also little time delay

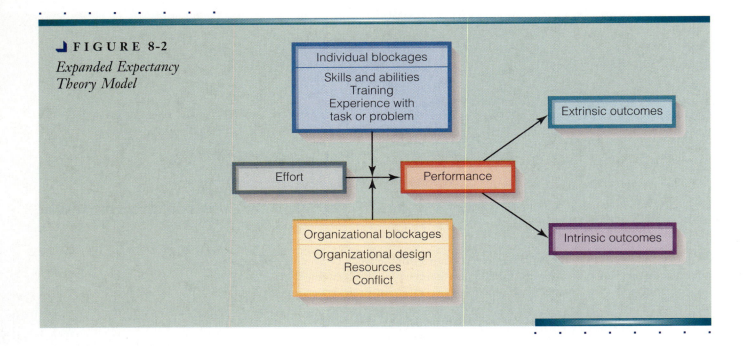

between the performance and the outcome. The absence of a time lag increases the effect intrinsic outcomes can have on motivation.

Managers and organizations do not directly deliver intrinsic outcomes, nor can they require a person to experience such outcomes. People experience intrinsic outcomes from doing work that they consider challenging and that uses many different skills and abilities.[8] Managers can affect the design of jobs and assign tasks people will find challenging. In this way, managers can provide the opportunity for people to experience intrinsic outcomes.

Intrinsic outcomes are believed to be associated mainly with higher-order needs such as self-actualization.[9] Extrinsic outcomes can be related to many different needs, including physiological, esteem, and self-actualization. The amount of money a person makes clearly helps satisfy physiological needs by providing food and shelter. An individual's salary and merit pay increases also are signs of her accomplishment. They give the individual feedback about how the organization feels about her performance.

■ INDIVIDUAL AND ORGANIZATIONAL BLOCKAGES

The linkage between effort and performance is not always direct or free of obstacles. Individual or organizational blockages can cause a person to perceive a low effort-performance expectancy.

Individual blockages derive from a person's perceived skills and abilities, real skills and abilities, and experience with the task to be done, as well as from the difficulty of the task itself.[10] If the person believes she has the skills to do the job and has had experience with a similar task, she should perceive a high effort-performance expectancy. Her motivation to do the job will then be high. If the task assignment is beyond the person's present skills and abilities, or the person has had no experience with the task, she will perceive a low effort-performance expectancy. Her motivation will also be low.

Organizational blockages include lack of resources to do a task, inadequate training to do a job, high levels of conflict within the organization, and the design of the organization. If the organization does not give an individual adequate resources, such as the tools and equipment needed to do the job, the person will perceive a low expectancy between effort and performance. If the organization has not adequately trained the person to do the job, expectancy will also be low. When the job requires a level of cooperation among individuals that is impossible to get due to conflict in the organization, the effort-performance expectancy will again be low. The conflict may be high because the organization is complex and not well coordinated. Organizations may also be designed so a manager has little direct authority over the person she is trying to motivate.[11] In each case, Expectancy Theory predicts low motivation.

Let's see how Expectancy Theory applies to you. By doing the following exercise, you will develop a better understanding of the motivation system within which you now work.

E X E R C I S E   *Expectancy Theory and You*

*A*nswer the following questions about the job you have now or one you recently held. Different things can happen to people who do their jobs *especially well* or *especially poorly.*

PART I

Using the following scale, indicate on a separate sheet of paper the likelihood that each of the things listed below would happen if you did your job *especially well.*

```
0 — 1 — 2 — 3 — 4 — 5 — 6 — 7 — 8 — 9 — 10
0%-10%-20%-30%-40%-50%-60%-70%-80%-90%-100%
No chance              50/50              Would
   of                 Chance of          happen
happening             happening          for sure
```

1. You will get a larger pay increase or make more money.
2. You will be promoted.
3. You will be transferred to a better job.
4. Your supervisor will praise you.
5. You will have more job security.
6. You will be given an opportunity to do the things you do best.
7. You will be given an opportunity to develop your skills and abilities.
8. You will feel better about yourself as a person.
9. You will get a feeling that you've accomplished something worthwhile.

PART II

Using the following scale, indicate on a separate piece of paper the likelihood that each of the things listed below would happen if you did your job *especially poorly.*

Source: Adapted from D. A. Nadler and E. E. Lawler III, "Motivation: A Diagnostic Approach," J. R. Hackman, E. E. Lawler III, and L. W. Porter, eds., *Perspectives on Behavior in Organizations* (New York: McGraw-Hill Book Company, 1977), Tables 3-1 and 3-2, p. 37. Reprinted with the permission of David A. Nadler and Edward E. Lawler III.

```
0 — 1 — 2 — 3 — 4 — 5 — 6 — 7 — 8 — 9 — 10
0%-10%-20%-30%-40%-50%-60%-70%-80%-90%-100%
No chance              50/50              Would
   of                 Chance of          happen
happening             happening          for sure
```

1. You won't get a larger pay increase or make more money.
2. You won't be promoted.
3. You won't be transferred to a better job.
4. Your supervisor will not praise you.
5. You will be among the first to be fired or laid off.
6. You will not be given an opportunity to do the things you do best.
7. You will not be given an opportunity to develop your skills and abilities.
8. You will not feel better about yourself as a person.
9. You will not get a feeling that you've accomplished something worthwhile.

PART III

Different people want different things from their work. Here is a list of things a person could get from a job. Using the following scale, indicate on a separate piece of paper how *desirable* each item in the list is *to you.*

```
-3 —— -2 —— -1 —— 0 —— +1 —— +2 —— +3
Extremely          Neither           Extremely
undesirable       desirable          desirable
                     nor
                 undesirable
```

1. The size of the pay increase you get or the amount of money you can make.
2. Getting a promotion.
3. Being transferred to a better job.
4. The praise you get from your supervisor.
5. The amount of job security you have.
6. The opportunity to do the things you do best.
7. The opportunity to develop your skills and abilities.

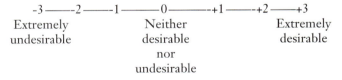

8. The opportunity to do something that makes you feel good about yourself as a person.
9. Accomplishing something worthwhile.

PART IV: INTERPRETATION OF YOUR RESULTS

Prepare some figures similar to those shown in Figure 8-3. Plot your answers to the above questions on the figures. The numbers in parentheses below the labels for each outcome correspond to the question numbers.

Plot your answers from Parts I, II, and III as follows:

- Parts I and II on Figure 8-3a.
- Parts I and III on Figure 8-3b. The scale for expectancy (Part I) is on the left side of the figure. The scale for valence (Part III) is on the right.
- Parts II and III on Figure 8-3c. The scale for expectancy (Part II) is on the left side of the figure. The scale for valence (Part III) is on the right.

Connect the points with a line according to the legend at the bottom of each figure.

Your answers to the three parts of the questionnaire indicate your perceptions of the motivation system in which you work. Each figure gives you a different view of the motivation system. The three figures considered together will give you insights into the level of motivation you feel when working.

Figure 8-3a compares your expectancies for outcomes you *will get* for doing a good job to your expectancies for outcomes you *will not get* for doing a poor job. Both lines should be high and close together if the motivation system worked according to Expectancy Theory. "Close together" means less than 10 percentage points difference between the two lines. Most of the time such an ideal state will not happen. Wherever the two lines come close together, both the positive and the negative use of a particular outcome were occurring. The convergence of the two lines suggests a balanced approach to motivation by your manager or supervisor.

If the line for doing a good job is below the line for doing a poor job, the outcome was withheld for poor performance more than it was given for good performance. If the line for doing a good job is above the line

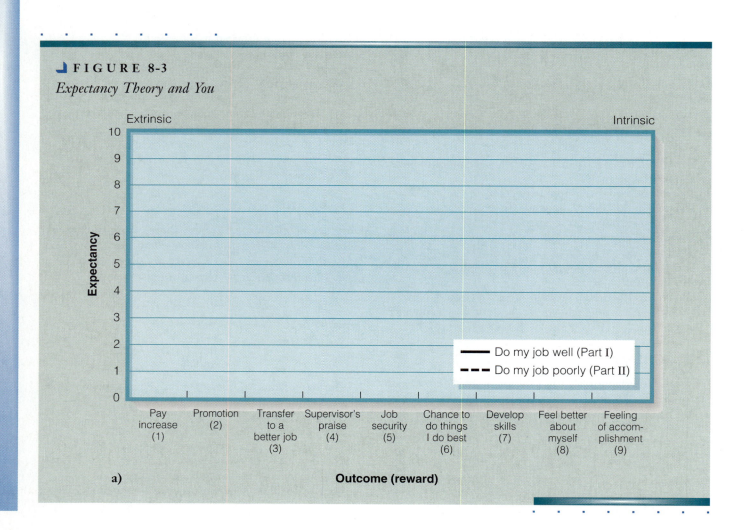

FIGURE 8-3
Expectancy Theory and You

a)

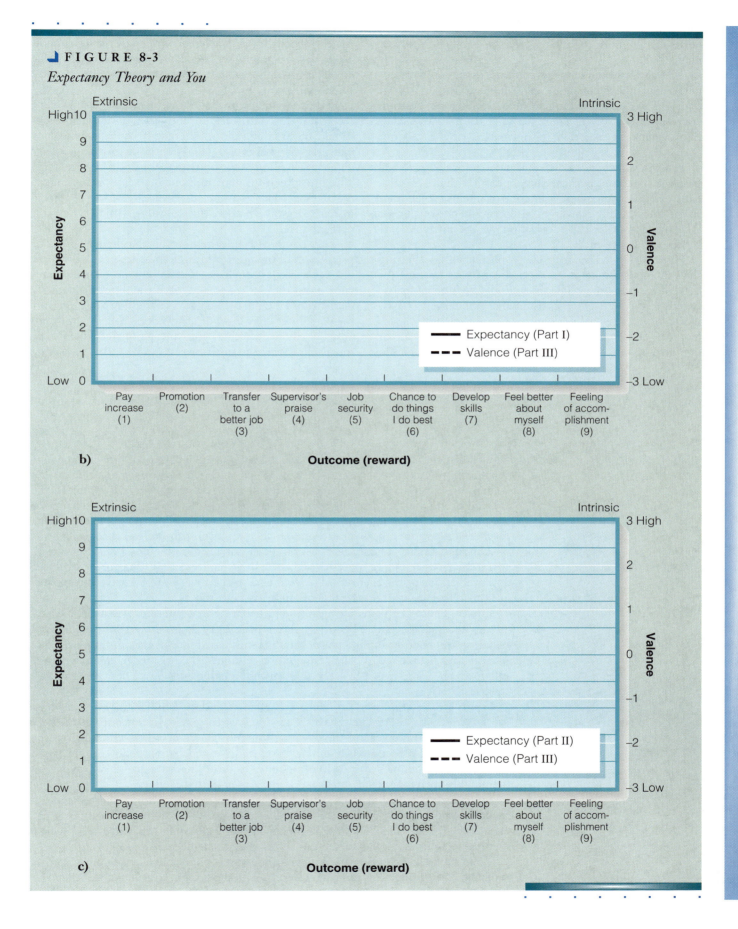

for doing a poor job, the outcome was given for good performance more than it was withheld for poor performance.

This result has two interpretations. First, you have not performed poorly on your job, and your supervisor or manager has no reason to withhold an outcome. Second, your supervisor or manager may not want to use sanctions when she sees poor performance, or she did not correctly assess your performance.

You will usually get a different pattern for extrinsic and intrinsic outcomes because someone other than you controls extrinsic outcomes. You control intrinsic outcomes so the lines usually converge. In short, you personally use a balanced approach to motivation for the intrinsic outcomes you experience.

Figure 8-3b compares your expectancies for getting the outcomes for good performance to your valence for each of the outcomes. The lines should be high and close together if your supervisor or manager behaved consistently with Expectancy Theory. "Close together" means less than 10 percentage points on the expectancy scale or one scale point difference on the valence scale. Figure 8-3b answers two major questions. First, are you getting what you value if you do well? If you are, your motivation level should be high. Second, are you getting what you *do not value* if you do well? If you are, your motivation level should be low.

Figure 8-3c compares your expectancies of not receiving the outcomes if you do poorly. The lines should be high and close together if your supervisor or manager is behaving consistently with Expectancy Theory in withholding outcomes for poor performance. The interpretation here is about the same as for Figure 8-3b. Was what you valued withheld for poor performance? Or, was what you did not value withheld for poor performance?

The combined information in the figures is your perception of the motivation system where you now work or have worked in the past. Reflect on your feelings about your motivation at work, and see if the figures accurately depict those feelings. The figures should provide answers for you about your level of motivation. You also will find answers about whether you are motivated mainly by intrinsic or extrinsic outcomes.

Equity Theory

Equity Theory is a useful way to explain the behavioral dynamics of human exchange relationships. Any social relationship in which one person gives something to get something in return is an exchange relationship. Because one party is giving to the exchange, and another party is receiving, either party may perceive the exchange as inequitable. Many exchange relationships exist, such as marriage, parent-child, teacher-student, members of a team, and the employer-employee exchange.[12]

Although Equity Theory research has been criticized on methodological grounds, research evidence points more toward accepting than rejecting the general structure and predictions of the theory.[13] The elements of the theory most useful to managers are those that have stood the test of empirical research.

Equity Theory explains motivation and behavior in a different way than Expectancy Theory. Expectancy Theory suggests people try to maximize the outcomes of behavior and choose among behavioral outcomes based on this maximization. Equity Theory says people try to balance the ratios of inputs to outcomes from an exchange relationship.[14] You will see later that strong relationships exist between the two theories.[15]

Equity in the employer-employee exchange should be familiar to you from your job experiences. There likely have been times when you have felt unfairly treated. Possibly, you did not receive the pay raise you felt you deserved, or you received the same pay raise as a coworker, but felt you had worked harder than she did. Both instances are examples of possible inequity. Equity Theory explains why you felt inequitably treated and suggests several responses to that feeling.

Inputs are personal characteristics and behaviors a person brings to the employment exchange. These characteristics include the person's training, education, skills, experience, gender, age, and ethnic background among other attributes. People also contribute some level of effort and individual performance.

The person contributing the inputs decides their importance or relevance to that exchange. If the contributor perceives the inputs to be relevant, then they are relevant, even though the other party to the exchange may not see them that way. For example, you may feel your pay increases each year should be based on your performance. Your employer, however, bases pay increases on the length of time an employee has been with the company. You feel your performance is a relevant input to the employment exchange. The company does not treat it as relevant for pay increases and ignores individual performance when making pay decisions. You may feel inequitably treated in this exchange, if other things happen as described below.

An individual can receive many positive and negative outcomes from the employment exchange. Positive outcomes include pay, fringe benefits, pleasant working conditions, friendly coworkers, competent supervision, and intrinsic outcomes from the job itself. Negative outcomes include unpleasant or hazardous working conditions, a monotonous job, quarrelsome coworkers, and close, controlling supervision. The individual alone decides whether an outcome is positive or negative.

People assess the ratio between their relevant outcomes and their relevant inputs. Each person compares this ratio to the ratio she perceives for another person or group of people. The ratio can also be compared to similar ratios in the past or to some absolute standard of fairness. Let's call the person making the comparison *person* (you) and the object of comparison *other* (say, a coworker).

A feeling of **equity** happens when an individual perceives the ratios as roughly balanced:

$$\text{Person} \quad : \quad \text{Other}$$

$$\frac{\text{Outcomes}_p}{\text{Inputs}_p} = \frac{\text{Outcomes}_o}{\text{Inputs}_o}$$

The ratios are approximately equal when the outcomes and inputs of both person and other are perceived by person to be about the same. This happens in a work situation when an individual believes she and a coworker are paid the same amount and that their relevant inputs are about the same.

A feeling of equity can also occur when other's outcomes are higher (or lower) than person's and other's inputs also are higher (or lower). This form of equity is common in organizations. You should not feel inequitably treated if your supervisor gets a higher salary than you. More responsibility, seniority, and experience often accompany the higher salary. Of course, if you do not perceive those inputs as present, you will feel a state of inequity!

Inequity exists for person if either of the following conditions results from the comparison:

$$\text{Person} \quad : \quad \text{Other}$$

$$\frac{\text{Outcomes}_p}{\text{Inputs}_p} < \frac{\text{Outcomes}_o}{\text{Inputs}_o} \qquad \textbf{Negative inequity} \\ \text{(“underpayment”)}$$

$$\frac{\text{Outcomes}_p}{\text{Inputs}_p} > \frac{\text{Outcomes}_o}{\text{Inputs}_o} \qquad \textbf{Positive inequity} \\ \text{(“overpayment”)}$$

As these formulas show, people can experience two types of inequity. People may feel underpaid for what they give the organization (negative inequity). They also can feel they are paid more than their work is worth (positive inequity). The amount of inequity experienced is proportional to the size of the perceived discrepancy in the two ratios. The point at which a person experiences inequity is higher for positive inequity than negative inequity. People may attribute some amount of overpayment to "good fortune" or see it as their just reward for high levels of effort in the past.

Equity Theory can be changed by adding a time dimension. It suggests strong feelings of inequity develop over time.[16] Past inequities may have a cumulative effect. A new inequity experience can push people over a threshold so that they act explosively after the new inequity experience. Thus, people's present behavior can only be understood from their history of inequity experiences.

EQUITY THEORY AND EXPECTANCY THEORY COMBINED

Equity Theory gives some strong warnings about what can happen when managers use extrinsic outcomes to reward performance. By combining Equity Theory with Expectancy Theory, the need to consider equity whenever extrinsic outcomes are used becomes explicit.

Figure 8-5 shows the two theories combined. The figure emphasizes the role of perceived equity in producing a feeling of satisfaction from the distribution of extrinsic outcomes. Low levels of satisfaction can result if the person perceives an inequitable distribution of extrinsic outcomes.

EQUITY SENSITIVITY

People's response to a state of inequity can differ. Some writers have proposed three types of **equity sensitivity:** equity sensitives, benevolents, and entitleds.[19] Figure 8-6 shows the three types and the state of the equity comparison for each. So far no empirical studies of these types have been done.

Equity sensitives are people who react to felt inequity in the way equity theory describes. Benevolents accept fewer outcomes for their inputs than other people would accept. They accept negative inequity and do not try to reduce the feeling as described by the theory. They may have altruistic tendencies and freely give more than they get. Entitleds have high thresholds of inequity and accept positive inequity with no feelings of guilt. They may feel the world owes them their due and think whatever outcomes they get are their just reward.

FIGURE 8-5

Expectancy Theory and Equity Theory Combined

Source: L. W. Porter and E. E. Lawler, III, *Managerial Attitudes and Performance* (Homewood, Ill.: Richard D. Irwin, 1968), adaption of Figure B, p. 165. © Richard D. Irwin, Inc., 1968.

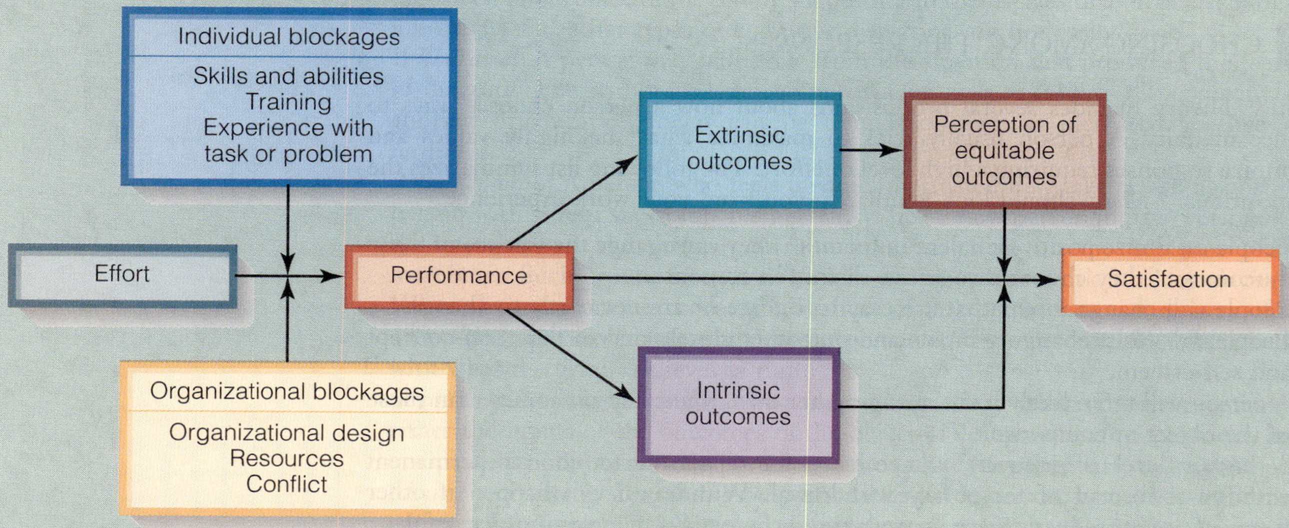

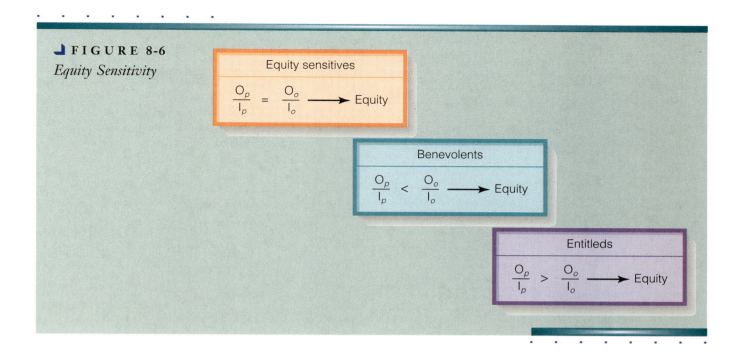

FIGURE 8-6
Equity Sensitivity

Equity sensitives

$$\frac{O_p}{I_p} = \frac{O_o}{I_o} \longrightarrow \text{Equity}$$

Benevolents

$$\frac{O_p}{I_p} < \frac{O_o}{I_o} \longrightarrow \text{Equity}$$

Entitleds

$$\frac{O_p}{I_p} > \frac{O_o}{I_o} \longrightarrow \text{Equity}$$

EXERCISE *Equity Theory Analysis of Tony Dorsett's Reaction*

Go back and reread the Opening Episode about Tony Dorsett, keeping in mind what you now know about Equity Theory. Identify the inputs and outcomes for both Tony Dorsett and Herschel Walker. List them on a separate sheet of paper using a format similar to Table 8-1. Also identify what Dorsett intended to do about his feelings of inequity.

INTERPRETATION

The inputs for Dorsett were his age, experience, and contributions to the Dallas Cowboys for 10 years. He also was a Heisman Trophy winner. His outcomes were his $450,000 salary and fringe benefits.

Walker's inputs were his age, experience, and professional football rushing record. Walker also was a Heisman Trophy winner. Walker's outcomes were his five-year $5 million contract.

We can only speculate about Dorsett's perception of how his ratio of inputs to outcomes compared to the same ratio for Walker. Dorsett clearly felt his salary was inequitable compared to Walker's. He reacted with anger and rage.

What did Dorsett do about his feelings of inequity? He first spoke out to the press. He wanted the Cowboys to trade him (withdrawal) or increase his salary (change outcomes). If that did not happen, he suggested he could be a "disruptive force."

Behavior Modification

Behavior Modification is an approach to human motivation and behavior that differs in many ways from Expectancy Theory and Equity Theory.[20] The theory underlying **Behavior Modification** does not use cognitive processes to explain what a person does.[21] Instead, it relies on observed behavior both to explain existing behavior and to change its direction. The theory assumes people engage in behavior that has positive outcomes,[22] avoid behavior that has unpleasant outcomes, and avoid behavior that fails to produce positive outcomes.

⏌ T A B L E 8-1

Equity Theory Analysis of Tony Dorsett's Reaction

DORSETT		WALKER	
Inputs	Outcomes	Inputs	Outcomes

DORSETT'S RESPONSE TO INEQUITY

The following four principles guide the application of the theory to the management of behavior in organizations:

- *Principle of Contingent Reinforcement.* A consequence has its strongest effect on behavior only if delivered when the desired behavior happens.
- *Principle of Immediate Reinforcement.* A consequence has its biggest effect on behavior if it occurs immediately after the behavior happens.
- *Principle of Reinforcement Size.* Large consequences have stronger effects on behavior than small consequences.
- *Principle of Reinforcement Deprivation.* The longer a person is deprived of a reinforcer, the stronger its effect on behavior in the future.

⏌ A METHOD OF BEHAVIOR MODIFICATION

Behavior Modification in organizations combines four approaches to affecting behavior with different schedules of controlling the consequences of behavior. It also uses the technique of shaping to change behavior gradually when a single big change is not possible.

Approaches to Affecting Behavior

Managers try to shape behavior by applying or withdrawing consequences of the behavior. Those consequences are either positive or negative for the target person. Managers use four approaches to affect the nature and direction of behavior: positive reinforcement, punishment, extinction, and negative reinforcement. Figure 8-7 shows each approach and the expected effect on the target person.

Positive reinforcement applies a positive event to increase the frequency or strength of desirable behavior. For example, a manager who receives a quality improvement suggestion from an employee could give that employee praise and recognition. Positive reinforcement of that behavior increases the likelihood the person will repeat the behavior in the future.

Punishment applies a negative event to decrease the frequency of behavior considered undesirable by the manager. When the undesirable behavior appears, the

206   S E C T I O N I I · *Individual Processes in Organizations*

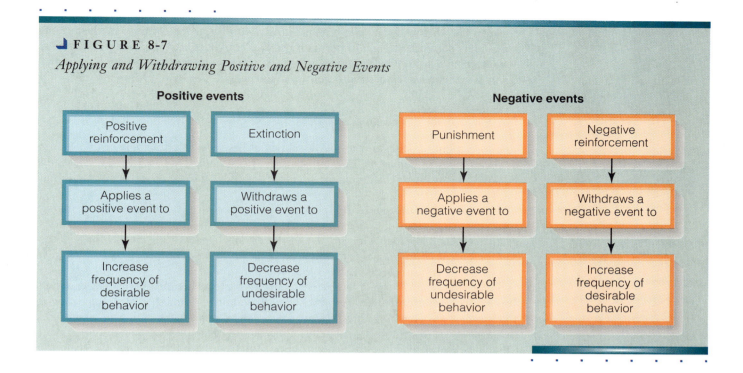

FIGURE 8-7

Applying and Withdrawing Positive and Negative Events

manager applies some sanction to the employee's behavior. The sanction might be a reprimand or time off without pay. Punishment stops behavior but does not change its direction. Because it does not prescribe desired behavior, punishment cannot produce new behavior. Punishment also has side effects that may be undesirable. A separate section later in the chapter describes those side effects.

Extinction withdraws something the employee considers positive to decrease the frequency of an undesirable behavior. Note that punishment and extinction have the same target—undesirable behavior—but differ sharply in other respects. Punishment applies a negative event to a behavior; extinction withdraws a positive event from a behavior. An example should make the difference clear.

Assume you are a manager who holds regular staff meetings each Monday morning. One member of your staff often disrupts meetings by telling jokes. Other staff members usually laugh at the person's behavior, giving positive reinforcement. The behavior continues because of this reinforcement. You decide that you have had enough and want to stop the behavior.

You could use punishment and orally reprimand the disruptive employee during the staff meeting. The behavior will stop, but the negative side effects could be strong, as you will see later. Extinction is an indirect approach to get the same result as punishment. You first get the others in the meeting to cooperate by not laughing at, or otherwise reinforcing, the employee's behavior at the next meeting. You are asking them to withhold something the disruptive employee values. If the other employees consistently withhold laughter from meeting to meeting, the disruptive employee's behavior will eventually stop. The frequency of the disruptions will gradually decline until they are completely gone or extinguished.

Negative reinforcement increases the frequency of desirable behavior by withdrawing or withholding a negative event. Although both negative reinforcement and punishment use a negative event, they do it in distinctly different ways. Punishment applies a negative event; negative reinforcement withdraws or withholds a negative event.

Negative reinforcement causes the person to whom it is applied to try to escape from or avoid a negative event. An example of this effect can be seen when a supervisor scolds a person for being late for work. The person being scolded "escapes" from the negative event by showing up for work on time in the future. Coworkers see the interaction between the late employee and the supervisor. Those coworkers avoid any future scolding by coming to work on time. In both cases the result is an increase in desired behavior following the negative reinforcement.[23]

Schedules of Reinforcement

Reinforcement of behavior can follow schedules based on the time between behaviors or the number of behaviors. Because spacing of consequences has different effects on behavior, choosing a reinforcement schedule depends on the goal of the person doing the reinforcement.[24]

Continuous reinforcement applies a consequence after each behavior. Thanking someone each time she does something for you is an example of continuous reinforcement. The behavior will be exhibited at a steady high rate as long as the reinforcement continues. If the consequence is withheld deliberately or accidentally, the behavior will quickly vanish.

Figure 8-8 shows the intermittent reinforcement schedules managers can use. **Intermittent reinforcement** uses a schedule based on the time between behaviors or the number of behaviors. Intermittent schedules produce more enduring changes in behavior than continuous schedules. There are four intermittent reinforcement schedules. Ratio schedules use the number of behaviors; interval schedules use time between behaviors.

With a fixed ratio schedule, a consequence is applied after a fixed number of behaviors. A sales commission system is an example of a fixed ratio schedule. The salesperson usually earns a commission for each sale. The behavioral response under a fixed ratio schedule is high and steady, but stops quickly when the consequence is withheld.

With a variable ratio schedule, the consequence follows a varying number of behaviors. An example is complimenting employees for good performance, but not praising each occurrence of good performance. The behavioral response is high, steady, and enduring. The uncertainty of a variable ratio schedule may contribute to the lasting quality of the behavior.

With a fixed interval schedule, a consequence is applied a constant time after the behavior. The most common example is receiving a paycheck at the end of a pay period. The time between paychecks may be one week, two weeks, or one month.

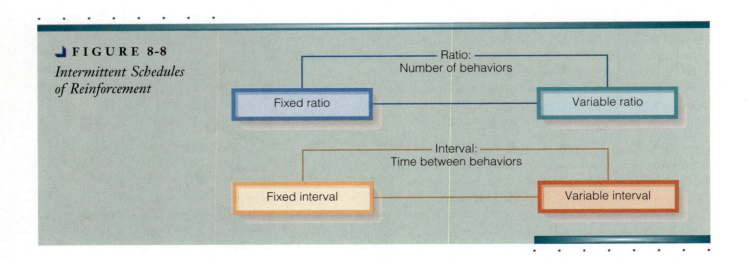

◢ FIGURE 8-8

Intermittent Schedules of Reinforcement

Ratio:
Number of behaviors

Fixed ratio — Variable ratio

Interval:
Time between behaviors

Fixed interval — Variable interval

Whatever the pay period, it is a predictable and fixed length of time. The behavioral response is strongest just before the consequence. A fixed interval paycheck will not have much effect on job performance but will strongly reinforce membership in the organization.

With a variable interval schedule, a consequence is applied after different periods between behavior. The effect on behavioral response is strong and steady. Behavior endures and is not extinguished easily. A manager who walks around the organization at random times and praises employee performance when warranted is using a variable interval schedule. Note again that the uncertainty of the reinforcement may contribute to the enduring quality of the behavior.

Shaping

Shaping is a technique designed to make gradual changes in a person's behavior while aiming for a target behavior. Managers often face situations where the desired change in a person's behavior cannot happen in one step. Shaping provides a way of moving a person's behavior toward the target a step at a time. Figure 8-9 shows the process used in shaping. An example should clarify the use of this technique.

An employee may need to learn a new job or a new procedure. The change is big given what the person is doing now. A manager who uses shaping gives positive reinforcement on a continuous schedule as the employee gradually learns the new job or procedure. Behavior that does not move toward the target is treated with extinction. Once the target is reached, the manager changes the reinforcement schedule to an intermittent one. When the behavior is well in place, the manager can give reinforcement less frequently.

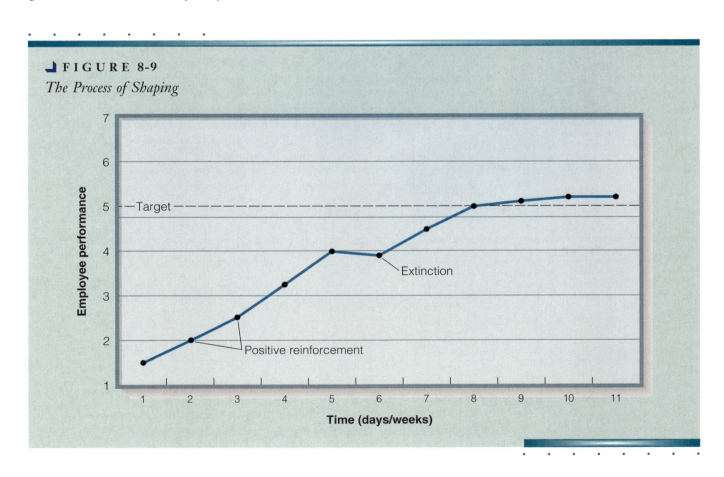

FIGURE 8-9

The Process of Shaping

SIDE EFFECTS OF PUNISHMENT

The continual use of punishment can lead to the undesirable **side effects of punishment** shown in Figure 8-10.[25] People may also perceive extinction as punishment, possibly resulting in side effects as well.[26] The side effects of extinction should be less strong than those of punishment.

Punishment stops behavior temporarily but does not cause the person to adopt more desirable behavior. In addition, the undesirable behavior often returns when the source of punishment is not present. Because punishment does not lead to learning new behavior, it is far less potent as a shaping tool than positive reinforcement.

A person who is punished continually may react emotionally. Anger, hostile behavior toward the source of punishment, and sabotage of equipment and the work process, are all possible reactions. Punishment can also lead to inflexible behavior, particularly when it is applied during the early employment period when a new employee is especially attentive to cues about the right type of behavior.[27] A new employee who is reprimanded after challenging one of the boss's decisions is unlikely to engage in that behavior later.

Some research evidence also indicates that the person receiving punishment develops negative feelings toward the source of punishment.[28] A climate of distrust, and even hate, can develop between a manager and subordinates, undermining the manager's ability to effectively shape behavior.

BEHAVIOR MODIFICATION AND EXPECTANCY THEORY CAN COMPLEMENT EACH OTHER

Many scholars treat Behavior Modification and Expectancy Theory as two different methods of explaining human motivation and behavior. A closer look at the two theories suggests they may complement each other in important ways.[29]

Both theories include probabilities. Behavior Modification affects the probability that a behavior will happen by using consequences to increase the occurrence of a behavior. Expectancy Theory uses probabilities (expectancies) to describe cognitions that people have about the connections between effort and performance and performance and outcomes. Positive reinforcement increases those probabilities. The two theories do not seem to be in conflict, although their focus is different.

Behavior Modification uses external consequences to change behavior or develop new behavior. Expectancy Theory says behavior has two types of outcomes, intrinsic and extrinsic. The intrinsic outcomes cannot be controlled directly by a manager and

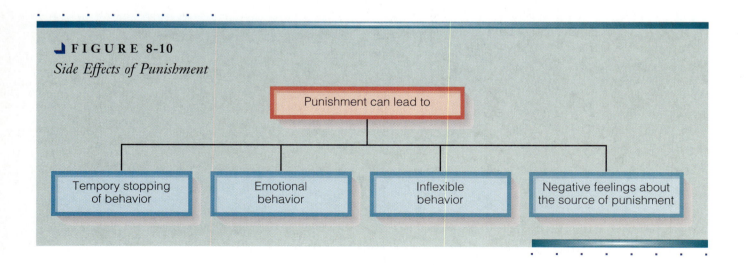

FIGURE 8-10
Side Effects of Punishment

Punishment can lead to

Tempory stopping of behavior

Emotional behavior

Inflexible behavior

Negative feelings about the source of punishment

do not fit into a Behavior Modification framework. You will find from the three motivation chapters that managing both extrinsic and intrinsic outcomes is important in changing and developing human behavior in organizations.

CRITICISMS OF BEHAVIOR MODIFICATION

Most of the basic research behind Behavior Modification was done with pigeons and rats. Some critics do not feel the research results can be extended to humans.[30] One critic describes the extension to human beings as "applied ratomorphism."[31] Adherents of Behavior Modification agree that humans are different from rats and pigeons, but they believe animal and human behavior can be controlled by the same mechanisms. Those mechanisms are the basis of Behavior Modification.

Another criticism based on the differences between animals and humans points out that the organized systems within which humans behave are more complex than the laboratory settings of much early research. People in organizations are subject to conflicting consequences and social pressures. Such conflicts make their behavior more difficult to control than that of an animal in an experiment.[32] Empirical research results soften this criticism. Field research done in controlled institutional settings such as schools and mental hospitals,[33] along with basic experimental research,[34] supports the program of Behavior Modification outlined in this chapter. Other empirical research done in business organizations usually was well designed and showed positive improvements in the target behavior.[35]

Behavior Modification does not use cognitive concepts to explain human behavior as do Expectancy and Equity Theory. It focuses on external forces working on the person. Because of this orientation, some critics believe Behavior Modification takes an excessively mechanistic view of human behavior. People remember experiences and develop expectations about the future. In short, people have consciousness and can reason.[36]

Responses to this criticism have two parts. Although Behavior Modification does not use cognitions to explain behavior, B. F. Skinner the theory's principal researcher, felt such cognitions existed. He did not consider them necessary to explain the causes of behavior, though, and they are not themselves the causes. Instead, one looks outside the person for those causes.[37] In addition, a later modification of the original work by Skinner and his colleagues specifically allows for cognitions in explaining behavior. This approach is consistent with the techniques of Behavior Modification described above.[38]

. . . .

Goal Setting Theory

Edwin A. Locke and his colleagues spent many years studying the effects of goals on human behavior and performance. Their research led to the development of a motivational technique called **Goal Setting**. Empirical research done by several independent researchers supports the theory.[39]

Goals that are specific, challenging, reachable, and accepted by a person lead to higher performance than goals that are "fuzzy," unchallenging, not reachable, or not accepted. Goal specificity includes what needs to be done, how much needs to be done, and the performance period.[40] High performance is partly the result of clear expectations about what to do and when to do it. People told to "do their best" do not perform as well as those who have specific task goals to reach. Goal Setting affects behavior through the psychological processes of directing attention, stimulating effort, persisting in the effort, and finding ways to do the task well.[41]

Acceptance of the goal is important, but how one gets acceptance is not. People do about the same whether goals are set unilaterally by supervisors or set jointly by themselves and their supervisors. Although research has not found participation in goal setting to be important for commitment to the goal, participation can be useful for reaching the goal. Participation increases information about the way a goal can be reached. The information can let employees discover better ways of doing the job.

People also need feedback about their performance while they are performing. Rewards for behavior leading toward the goal result in higher performance, even when the goal is not reached. Goal Setting without feedback is not effective in improving performance.[42] Note the similarity between this aspect of Goal Setting and shaping in Behavior Modification.

The Goal Setting technique uses the following steps to set goals:[43]

- Specify the employees tasks, duties, and responsibilities.
- Specify how the employee's performance will be assessed. Be specific about the way job performance will be assessed and the behaviors that will be part of the assessment.
- Specify the goal or target to be reached. If employee performance can be quantified, then a specific amount of output can be stated. If performance cannot be quantified, then the goal or target should be specified clearly. The goal must be clear and high enough to be challenging but not so high as to be unreachable.
- Specify the time span of employee performance. Here the employee learns about deadlines, the time within which she must reach the goal. That time may be short or long—one week, one month, or two years, for example.
- Set priorities among goals. When several goals are set, distinguish the more important goals from the less important. A simple ranking of goals tells the employee which are the most important.
- Specify both the difficulty and the priority of goals. If goals vary in difficulty of achievement, then reaching all or part of a difficult goal is a better performance than reaching a simple goal. Achieving goals of low priority is not as high a level of performance as achieving goals of high priority. Making distinctions at this step lets both the employee and the supervisor understand variations in the difficulty and importance of goals.
- Review the goals for needed coordination and cooperation with others. If an employee's goals cannot be accomplished without the cooperation of others, then the goals of many employees may have to be coordinated. This step is necessary to reduce conflict among goals in situations where employees are interdependent.

The Goal Setting steps are designed to produce goals that are specific about both the task to be done and the time within which it must be done. Specificity is further enhanced by stating how performance will be measured and the priorities among multiple goals. The challenge of the goal follows from its degree of difficulty.

The Goal Setting technique does not view goals as static. Goals often are based on the past and some predictions about the future. As circumstances change, goals may need to change. An important element is the ability to change goals after they have been set because the circumstances surrounding employee performance have changed. For example, a sales quota may be set for a salesperson based on a prediction about the economy over a one-year period. If economic conditions change sharply, the sales quota should also be changed. If the goal is not adjusted downward when the economy turns down, the goal becomes unreachable, and employee performance will drop. If the economy turns up and the goal is not revised upward, the goal becomes too easy, and the employee will not perform up to her capabilities.

Goals are not set and the employee turned loose to reach the goal. The supervisor and the organization play important roles in goal accomplishment. The organization should train employees to increase their skills and let them reach increasingly more difficult goals. Management must also provide resources such as money, equipment, and time to get the job done. Lastly, it is especially critical that an employee know how well she is doing while trying to reach some goal.

There are many connections between Goal Setting and the theories discussed earlier. The Effort-Performance Expectancy increases because of employee training and resources. Feedback and rewards for performance enhance the Performance-Outcome Expectancy. If goals are sufficiently challenging, intrinsic outcomes also should result. The elements of Goal Setting Theory and the steps in setting goals should all contribute directly to improved employee motivation.

. . . .

International Aspects of the Cognitive and Behavioral Theories of Motivation

The theories described in this chapter have two underlying assumptions that could restrict their application in countries outside the United States. The first says that the individual controls decisions about future actions.[44] The second says a manager can deliberately shape the behavior of people who work for her. Both assumptions reflect U.S. values of free will and individualism. All the theories described in this chapter were developed by U.S. scholars. Are they so culture-bound that they have limited application elsewhere in the world?

Some observers believe Expectancy Theory has such strong roots in U.S. values it likely does not apply to other cultures. The U.S. value of strong individualism leads to a need to explain our actions as a way of getting something for them or satisfying some need.[45] Expectancy Theory also emphasizes individual control of one's destiny, another strong U.S. value that is not characteristic of all cultures.[46] For example, Muslim managers believe something happens mainly because God wills it to happen. The Chinese of Hong Kong believe luck plays a role in all events. Both are examples of attributing control to external not internal factors.[47]

Only two studies offer evidence of Expectancy Theory's validity in other cultures. One study focused on female life insurance sales representatives in Japan who worked under a complex commission system tied to their performance. Its results accorded well with U.S. findings of the same period.[48] A second study, done among textile workers in Russia, linked valued extrinsic rewards, praise, and recognition directly to worker performance.[49] Workers received those outcomes when they increased output. Productivity increased as predicted by Expectancy Theory.

Japan is more collectivistic than Russia. It is not yet clear from research whether managers will find Expectancy Theory a good guide in countries that do not have individualistic values or attribute control to external factors.

The discussion of the international aspects of Need Theories in Chapter 7 highlighted the large cultural differences in what people viewed as their most important needs and values. Such differences will have strong effects on the types of outcomes people from different cultures will see as positively valent.[50] U.S. managers usually view a pay increase as a positively valent outcome. A group of workers in Mexico who had received a pay increase later reduced their work hours. The higher pay let them live the way they wanted and reduce their work hours so they could enjoy other parts of their life. They placed a higher value on their life outside work than on the pay increase.[51]

The cross-cultural effects on Equity Theory and its predictions about behavior are not clear. Different cultures could define fairness in different ways. Because it is an individualistic theory, it could have limited application in collectivistic societies.[52]

Research on Locke's Goal Setting Theory has been done in Israel, former West Germany, Japan, several Caribbean islands, and some English-speaking countries outside the United States.[53] Results of those studies were consistent with the U.S. work that formulated the theory and technique as described earlier. One study of U.S. and Israeli students found the U.S. students were not affected by how goals were

Summary

This chapter focused on motivation from two distinctly different perspectives: one was internal to the individual and the other was external. Expectancy Theory explains different internal states of the process of motivation. The Effort-Performance Expectancy is the perceived connection between an individual's effort and her performance. Both individual and organizational blockages reduce the belief that a person's effort will lead to a given level of performance. A second expectancy describes the perceived connection between performance and the outcomes for performance. The Performance-Outcome Expectancy is a person's belief that performance will be followed by one or more extrinsic or intrinsic outcomes. Of great importance is the value, or valence, people put on those outcomes. Managers need to attend to what subordinates value for their performance and then reward good performance with valued outcomes.

Equity Theory showed us that a manager must be careful when using extrinsic outcomes for job performance. If a person feels inequitably treated in comparison to someone else, the individual may decrease her performance or leave the organization.

Behavior Modification does not use cognitive processes to describe human motivation and behavior. It looks outside the individual at the consequences of a person's behavior. The techniques of Behavior Modification center on controlling those consequences to direct and shape behavior.

Goal Setting Theory describes other ways of directing and shaping a person's behavior. Goals that are specific, challenging, reachable, and accepted by a person lead to higher performance than goals that do not have those characteristics. Managers can follow the Goal Setting steps to improve the performance of a subordinate.

The motivation theories described in this chapter were all developed by U.S. scholars. Those theories have two underlying assumptions that reflect U.S. values of free will and individualism. The International Aspects section discussed whether the assumptions limit the application of these theories in countries outside the United States.

Key Terms

Behavior Modification 205

continuous reinforcement schedules 208

Effort-Performance Expectancy (E→P) 194

equity 201

equity sensitivity 204

Equity Theory 200

Expectancy Theory 193

extinction 207

extrinsic outcomes 195

Goal Setting Theory 211

individual blockages 196

inputs 200

intermittent reinforcement schedules 208

intrinsic outcomes 195

negative inequity 201

negative reinforcement 207

organizational blockages 196

Performance-Outcome Expectancy (P→O) 194

positive inequity 201

positive reinforcement 206

punishment 206

responses to inequity 202

shaping 209

side effects of punishment 210

valence 194

Review and Discussion Questions

1. What has been your experience with the connection between job performance and outcomes? Were positive outcomes used more often than negative outcomes?

2. In the past have you experienced blockages between your effort and performance? Were they individual blockages or organizational blockages? What form did the blockages take? What did you or your manager or supervisor do about the blockages?

3. Discuss the different types of equity sensitivity. Where do people in your class put themselves? Who are the equity sensitives, benevolents, and entitleds?

4. Review the various reactions to inequity described earlier. How have you reacted to inequity in the past?

5. To whom have you compared yourself in the past when making equity comparisons? Have an open discussion in class about other students' bases of comparison.

6. Review the criticisms raised earlier about Behavior Modification. Discuss those criticisms. Do those criticisms limit the use of Behavior Modification in organizations?

7. Review the ethical issues about managers affecting the motivation of people in work organizations. What are your feelings about those issues? What do other students in your class think about those issues?

8. Review the discussion of the international aspects of the motivational theories described in this chapter. Ask students from outside your country to comment on the observations made in that section.

↵ TABLE 8-2

Checklist of Rewards

Coffee break treats	Desk accessories
Office with a window	Profit sharing
Friendly greetings	Special job assignment
Company car	Stock options
Invitations to coffee/lunch	Paid-up insurance policies
Redecoration of work environment	Solicitation of suggestions
Company picnics	Private office
Larger office	Equipment
Extended breaks	Smile
Compliment on work progress	Permission to work on personal
Beer parties	project on company time
Feedback about performance	Commendations
Vacation trips	Job with more responsibility
Promotion	Professional travel
Wall plaques	Formal awards
Newspaper articles	Incentive plan
Permission to leave early	Employee of the month

. . . .

↵ *Exercise*

BRAINSTORMING ABOUT REWARDS

Managers often feel constrained about the rewards they can give their subordinates for high performance. Many more rewards are available than we ordinarily believe.

Table 8-2 shows rewards that managers can give for high performance in many organizations. First, write on a separate sheet of paper the rewards you could get where you now work, *if your supervisor or manager chose to use them.* Add to the list if you feel a reward is missing.

Second, meet in groups of no more than seven students each. Compare and discuss your lists. Look for commonali-

ties and differences among the lists. Create a new list representing all the rewards listed by at least one person in the group. Then spend about 20 minutes brainstorming. Come up with anything as a reward that at least one person in the group values (positive valence) for high performance. Don't hesitate to be bizarre!

Rank order each reward from most important to least important to members of the group. Each group should then describe their top five rewards. Discuss the reasons for commonalities and differences among each group's top five rewards.

. . . .

↵ *Case*

REWARDS AND SELF-MANAGING TEAMS

This case describes the approaches some companies use to reward their self-managing teams. Companies often use such teams when managing for quality and seeking continuous process improvement. Consider the following questions and issues while reading the case:

1. What are the equity issues raised in the case? Give examples.
2. Are there any potential dysfunctions from the reward approaches described?

Source: B. Dumaine, "Who Needs a Boss?" *Fortune,* May 7, 1990, pp. 58–60. © 1990 Time Inc. All rights reserved.

3. Evaluate both the recommendations of the consultant Thomas Kuczmarski and Japan's national competition among teams.

There remains considerable debate among employees, managers, and consultants over the best way to compensate team members. Most companies pay a flat salary. And instead of handing out automatic annual raises, they often use a pay-for-skills system that bases any increase not on seniority but on what an employee has learned. If, say, a steelworker learns how to run a new piece of equipment, he might get a 5% raise.

While the young and eager tend to do well with pay-for-skills, some old-school blue-collar workers like Chaparral Steel's Neil Parker criticize aspects of the system. Says he:

"New guys come in who are aggressive, take all the courses, and get promoted ahead of guys who have been here years longer and who showed up for overtime when the company really needed us. It's not fair." As Parker suggests, pay-for-skills does set up a somewhat Darwinian environment at the mill, but that's just the way Chaparral's management likes it.

When teams develop a hot new product, like Rubbermaid's auto office, or save money, like the Federal Express team that caught $2.1 million in billing errors, you would think they would clamor for rewards. Not necessarily. In many cases, surprisingly, a little recognition is reward enough. The Fedex team members seem perfectly content with a gold quality award pin and their picture in the company newsletter. Says one: "We learn more in teams, and it's more fun to work in teams. It's a good feeling to know someone is using your ideas."

In his book *Managing New Products* Thomas Kuczmarski, a consultant to many of the Fortune 500 industrials, argues that recognition isn't enough. "In most companies multidisciplinary teams are just lip service because companies don't provide the right motivation and incentive. Most top managers think people should just find 20% more time to work on a new team project. It's a very naive and narrow-minded approach." His modest proposals: If a new product generates $1 million in profits, give each of the five team members $100,000 in the first year. Or have each member write a check for $10,000 in return for 2% of the equity in the new product. If it flies they're rich; if it flops they lose their money.

Kuczmarski admits that no major corporation has adopted his provocative system, although he says a few are on the verge of doing so. One objection: Jack Okey, a Honeywell team manager, flatly states that it would be bad for morale to have, say, a junior engineer making more than a division vice president. "If you want to be an entrepreneur, there are plenty of entrepreneurial opportunities outside the company. You can have entrepreneurial spirit without entrepreneurial pay."

Perhaps. Awards dinners and plaques for jobs well done are common in the world of teams, but Texas Instruments vice president James Watson thinks more can be done. He cites the example from Japan, where there is a nationwide competition among manufacturers' teams. Sponsored by the Union of Japanese Scientists and Engineers, the competition pits teams selected by their companies against one another. Once a year the teams travel to Tokyo to make presentations before judges, who decide which performs best at everything from solving quality problems to continuously improving a manufacturing process. The winners get showered with prizes and media coverage.

. . . .

⬤▶ *References and Notes*

[1] Developed from V. H. Vroom, *Work and Motivation* (New York: John Wiley & Sons, 1964); L. W. Porter and E. E. Lawler III, *Managerial Attitudes and Performance* (Homewood, Ill.: Richard D. Irwin, 1968); E. E. Lawler III, "Job Attitudes and Employee Motivation: Theory, Research, and Practice," *Personnel Psychology* 23 (1970): 223–37.

[2] H. Garland, "Relation of Effort-Performance Expectancy to Performance in Goal-Setting Experiments," *Journal of Applied Psychology* 69 (1984): 79–84; H. Garland, "A Cognitive Mediation Theory of Task Goals and Human Performance," *Motivation and Emotion* 9 (1985): 345–67; H. G. Heneman III and D. P. Schwab, "Evaluation of Research on Expectancy Theory Predictions of Employee Performance," *Psychological Bulletin* 78 (1972): 1–9; R. J. House, H. J. Shapiro, and M. A. Wahba, "Expectancy Theory as a Predictor of Work Behavior and Attitudes: A Reevaluation of Empirical Evidence," *Decision Sciences* 5 (1974): 481–506; C. W. Kennedy, J. A. Fossum, and B. J. White, "An Empirical Comparison of Within-subjects and Between-subjects Expectancy Theory Models," *Organizational Behavior and Human Performance* 32 (1983): 124–43; T. R. Mitchell, "Expectancy Models of Job Satisfaction, Occupational Preference, and Effort: A Theoretical, Methodological, and Empirical Appraisal," *Psychological Bulletin* 81 (1974): 1053–77; D. P. Schwab, J. D. Olian-Gottlieb, and H. G. Heneman III, "Between-subjects Expectancy Theory Research: A Statistical Review of Studies Predicting Effort and Performance," *Psychological Bulletin* 86 (1979): 139–47.

[3] Vroom, *Work and Motivation*, p. 17.

[4] The word *performance* appears throughout the explanation of Expectancy Theory. You can substitute the word *behavior* if you like. The description of the theory focuses on a single class of behavior for this explanation, but this does not restrict the application of the theory.

[5] Some descriptions of Expectancy Theory add the concept of "instrumentality" and use a different numerical notation than used here (Vroom, *Work and Motivation*). This chapter uses the modification to Expectancy Theory given by Porter and Lawler (*Managerial Attitudes*). No harm is done to this chapter's explanation of the theory by omitting "instrumentality."

[6] Vroom, *Work and Motivation*, pp. 9–10.

[7] A. Smith, *The Theory of Moral Sentiments* (London: A. Millar, 1759; facsimile edition, New York: Garland Publishing, 1971). Suggested by J. H. Turner, "Toward a Sociological Theory of Motivation," *American Sociological Review* 52 (1987): 15–27.

[8] J. R. Hackman and G. R. Oldham, *Work Redesign* (Reading, Mass.: Addison-Wesley, 1980); J. R. Hackman and G. R. Oldham, "Motivation through the Design of Work: Test of a Theory," *Organizational Behavior and Human Performance* 16 (1976): 250–79.

[9] Porter and Lawler, *Managerial Attitudes*, Ch. 8.

[10] Ibid., Ch. 8 and 9; D. A. Nadler and E. E. Lawler III, "Motivation: A Diagnostic Approach," in J. R. Hackman, E. E. Lawler III, and L. W. Porter, eds., *Perspectives on Behavior in Organizations* (New York: McGraw-Hill, 1977), pp. 28–36.

[11] Chapters 17 and 18 discuss the organizational design concepts just mentioned.

[12] J. S. Adams, "Inequity in Social Exchange," in L. Berkowitz, ed., *Advances in Experimental Social Psychology* (1965) pp. 276–99; J. S. Adams, "Toward an Understanding of Inequity," *Journal of Abnormal Social Psychology* 67 (1963): 422–36; P. Kollack, P. Blumstein, and P. Schwartz, "The Judgment of Equity in Intimate Relationships," *Social Psychology Quarterly*, 57 (1994): 340–51.

[13] J. Brockner, J. Davy, and C. Carter, "Layoffs, Self-esteem, and Survivor Guilt: Motivational, Affective, and Attitudinal Consequences," *Organizational Behavior and Human Decision Processes* 36 (1985): 229–44; J. Brockner, J. Greenberg, A. Brockner, J. Bortz, J. Davy, and C. Carter, "Layoffs, Equity Theory, and Work Performance: Further Evidence of the Impact of Survivor Guilt," *Academy of Management Journal* 29 (1986): 373–84; J. P. Campbell and R. D.

Pritchard, "Motivation Theory in Industrial and Organizational Psychology," in M. D. Dunnette, ed., *Handbook of Industrial and Organizational Psychology* (Chicago: Rand McNally, 1976), pp. 63–130; R. J. Harris, "Pinning Down the Equity Formula," in D. M. Messick and K. S. Cook, eds., *Equity Theory: Psychological and Sociological Perspectives* (New York: Praeger, 1983), pp. 207–41; P. S. Goodman and A. Friedman, "An Examination of Adam's Theory of Inequity," *Administrative Science Quarterly* 16 (1971): 271–88; E. E. Lawler III, "Equity Theory as a Predictor of Productivity and Work Quality," *Psychological Bulletin* 70 (1968): 596–610; R. T. Mowday, "Equity Theory Predictions of Behavior in Organizations," in R. M. Steers and L. W. Porter, eds., *Motivation and Work Behavior* (New York: McGraw-Hill, 1979), pp. 124–46.

[14]C. I. Barnard, *The Functions of the Executive* (Cambridge, Mass.: Harvard University Press, 1938). There is strong similarity between some elements of Equity Theory and Chester Barnard's concept of the inducement-contributions balance discussed in Appendix A. In both cases, some balance (equity) must exist for the individual to accept the inducements offered for the person's contributions.

[15]Lawler, "Equity Theory as a Predictor."

[16]R. A. Cosier and D. R. Dalton, "Equity Theory and Time: A Reformulation," *Academy of Management Review* 8 (1983): 311–19.

[17]Suggested by ibid.

[18]Adams "Inequity in Social Exchange"; J. S. Adams and S. Freedman, "Equity Theory Revisited: Comments and Annotated Bibliography," in L. Berkowitz and E. Walster, eds., *Advances in Experimental Social Psychology*, vol. 9 (New York: Academic Press, 1976), pp. 43–90.

[19]R. C. Huseman, J. D. Hatfield, and E. W. Miles, "A New Perspective on Equity Theory: The Equity Sensitivity Construct," *Academy of Management Review* 12 (1987): 222–34.

[20]Other names for the concepts in this section include operant conditioning and positive reinforcement. The phrase "Behavior Modification" says more completely what is being tried, especially in a management context. Developed from F. Luthans and R. Kreitner, *Organizational Behavior Modification and Beyond: An Operant and Social Learning Approach* (Glenview, Ill: Scott, Foresman, 1985); W. C. Hamner, "Reinforcement Theory," in H. L. Tosi and W. C. Hamner, eds., *Organizational Behavior and Management* (Chicago: St. Clair Press, 1974), pp. 93–112; and other references cited in this section.

[21]B. F. Skinner, *Science and Human Behavior* (New York: Free Press, 1953); B. F. Skinner, *Beyond Freedom and Dignity* (New York: Bantam, 1971); B. F. Skinner, *About Behaviorism* (New York: Knopf, 1974).

[22]E. L. Thorndike, *Educational Psychology: The Psychology of Learning*, vol. 2 (New York: Columbia University, Teachers College, 1913).

[23]Hamner, "Reinforcement Theory," pp. 100–101.

[24]W. F. Dowling, "Conversation with B. F. Skinner," *Organizational Dynamics* 1 (Winter 1973): 31–40; C. B. Ferster, and B. F. Skinner, *Schedules of Reinforcement* (New York: Appleton-Century-Crofts, 1957).

[25]For more details about the side effects of punishment see Skinner, *Science and Human Behavior*; A. Bandura, *Principles of Behavior Modification* (New York: Holt, Rinehart, & Winston, 1969).

[26]W. R. Nord, "Beyond the Teaching Machine: The Neglected Area of Operant Conditioning in the Theory and Practice of Management," *Organizational Behavior and Human Performance* 4 (1969): 375–401.

[27]R. Katz, "Time and Work: Toward an Integrative Perspective," in B. Staw and L. L. Cummings, eds., *Research in Organizational Behavior*, vol. 2 (Greenwich, Conn.: JAI Press, 1980), pp. 81–127. Also see Chapter 6 and the discussion of the early part of the socialization process in organizations.

[28]R. D. Arvey and A. P. Jones, "The Use of Discipline in Organizational Settings: A Framework for Future Research," in L. L. Cummings and B. M. Staw, eds., *Research in Organizational Behavior*, vol. 7 (Greenwich, Conn.: JAI Press 1985), pp. 367–408.

[29]F. Petrock and V. Gamboa, "Expectancy Theory and Operant Conditioning: A Conceptual Comparison," in W. R. Nord, ed., *Concepts and Controversy in Organizational Behavior*, 2d. ed. (Santa Monica, Calif.: Goodyear Publishing Company, 1976), pp. 175–87.

[30]Developed from Luthans and Kreitner, *Organizational Behavior Modification and Beyond*, Ch. 9 and other sources as noted.

[31]M. Hammer, "The Application of Behavioral Conditioning Procedures to the Problems of Quality Control: Comment," *Academy of Management Journal* 14 (1971): 529–32.

[32]F. L. Fry, "Operant Conditioning in Organizational Settings: Of Mice or Men?" *Personnel* 51 (1974): 17–24; W. F. Whyte, "Pigeons, Persons and Piece Rates: Skinnerian Theory in Organizations," *Psychology Today* 5 (April 1972): 67–68, 96, 98, 100.

[33]Nord, "Beyond the Teaching Machine"; C. E. Schneier, "Behavior Modification in Management: A Review and Critique," *Academy of Management Journal* 17 (1974): 528–48.

[34]B. F. Skinner, *About Behaviorism* (New York: Vintage 1976); B. F. Skinner, *Contingencies of Reinforcement* (New York: Appleton-Century-Crofts, 1969).

[35]K. O'Hara, C. M. Johnson, and T. A. Beehr, "Organizational Behavior Management in the Private Sector: A Review of Empirical Research and Recommendations for Further Investigation," *Academy of Management Review* 10 (1985): 848–64.

[36]E. A. Locke, "The Myths of Behavior Mod in Organizations," *Academy of Management Review* 2 (1977): 543–53; E. A. Locke, "Myths in 'The Myths in the Myths about Behavior Mod in Organizations,'" *Academy of Management Review* 4 (1979): 131–36.

[37]Skinner, *Science and Human Behavior*; Skinner, *About Behaviorism* (1974).

[38]A. Bandura, *Social Learning Theory* (Englewood Cliffs, N.J.: Prentice-Hall, 1977).

[39]E. A. Locke, D. B. Feren, V. M. McCaleb, K. N. Shaw, and A. T. Denny, "The Relative Effectiveness of Four Methods of Motivating Employee Performance," in K. D. Duncan, M. M. Gruneberg, and D. Wallis, eds., *Changes in Working Life* (London: John Wiley & Sons, 1980), pp. 363–83; E. A. Locke and G. P. Latham, *Goal Setting: A Motivational Technique That Works!* (Englewood Cliffs, N.J.: Prentice-Hall, 1984); E. A. Locke and G. P. Latham, *A Theory of Goal Setting & Task Performance* (Englewood Cliffs, N.J.: Prentice-Hall, 1990); E. A. Locke, K. N. Shaw, L. M. Saari, and G. P. Latham, "Goal Setting and Task Performance: 1969–1980," *Psychological Bulletin* 90 (1981): 125–52; K. I. Miller and P. R. Monge, "Participation, Satisfaction, and Productivity: A Meta-Analytic Review," *Academy of Management Journal* 29 (1986): 727–53; J. C. Naylor and D. R. Ilgen, "Goal Setting: A Theoretical Analysis of a Motivational Technology," in B. M. Staw and L. L. Cummings, eds., *Research in Organizational Behavior*, vol. 6 (Greenwich, Conn.: JAI Press, 1984), pp. 95–140.

[40]Naylor and Ilgen, "Goal Setting," p. 97.

[41]Locke, et al., "Goal Setting."

[42]Locke, et al., "Relative Effectiveness," pp. 363–88.

[43]Locke and Latham, *Goal Setting*.

[44]B. M. Staw, "Organizational Behavior: A Review and Reformulation of the Field's Outcome Variables," *Annual Review of Psychology* 35 (1984): 627–66.

[45]G. Hofstede, "Motivation, Leadership, and Organization: Do American Theories Apply Abroad?" *Organizational Dynamics* 9 (1980): 42–63; G. Hofstede, *Culture's Consequences: International Differences in Work-Related Values* (Beverly Hills, Calif.: Sage Publications, 1984), p. 255; G. Hofstede, *Cultures and Organizations: Software of the Mind* (New York: McGraw-Hill, 1991).

[46]N. J. Adler, *International Dimensions of Organizational Behavior* (Boston: PWS-KENT, 1991), pp. 157–60.

[47]Ibid., p. 158.

[48]T. Matsui and I. Terai, "A Cross-Cultural Study of the Validity of the Expectancy Theory of Motivation," *Journal of Applied Psychology* 60 (1979): 263–65.

[49]D. H. B. Welsh, F. Luthans, and S. M. Sommer, "Managing Russian Factor Workers: The Impact of U.S.-Based Behavioral and Participative Techniques," *Academy of Management Journal* 36 (1993): 58–79.

[50]Adler, *International Dimensions*, pp. 157–60.

[51]Ibid., p. 159.

[52]E. E. Sampson, "Psychology and the American Ideal," *Journal of Personality and Social Psychology* 35 (1977): 767–82.

[53]Locke and Latham, *Theory of Goal Setting*, p. 43.

[54]M. Erez and P. C. Earley, "Comparative Analysis of Goal-Setting Strategies across Cultures," *Journal of Applied Psychology* 72 (1987): 658–65.

[55]Hofstede, "Motivation, Leadership, and Organization," pp. 56–59.

[56]Locke and Latham, *Theory of Goal Setting*, pp. 211–13.

[57]L. K. Trevino, "The Social Effects of Punishment in Organizations: A Justice Perspective," *Academy of Management Review* 17 (1992): 647–

76; L. K. Trevino and G. A. Ball, "The Social Implications of Punishing Unethical Behavior: Observers, Cognitive and Affective Reactions," *Journal of Management* 18 (1992): 751–68.

[58]Locke, "Myths of Behavior"; Locke, "Myths in 'The Myths.'"

[59]C. R. Rogers and B. F. Skinner, "Some Issues Concerning the Control of Human Behavior: A Symposium," 124 *Science* (1956): 1057–66.

[60]R. Kreitner, "Controversy in OBM: History, Misconceptions, and Ethics," in L. Frederiksen, ed., *Handbook of Organizational Behavior Management* (New York: Wiley, 1982), pp. 71–91.

[61]Ibid., p. 89.

[62]Ibid., p. 88.

9

Intrinsic Rewards and Job Design

· *Many jobs in the future will feature extensive use of computer technology. Here, Boeing engineers work with a virtual reality simulation of the interior of the Boeing 777.*

After reading this chapter, you should be able to . . .

· Discuss the role of job design in giving people opportunities to experience intrinsic rewards.
· Describe the major theories of job design.
· Appreciate how the work context affects people's reaction to the design of their jobs.
· Explain the process of diagnosing and re-designing jobs.
· Distinguish between the design of jobs for individuals and the design of jobs for groups.
· Explain the role of job design in stress.

Chapter Overview

· *Routine, repetitive work such as processing chickens can be a stressor for workers.*

Stressful, Low-Clout Jobs Bad for Heart

The prime candidates for heart attacks aren't hard-driving Type A executives, but workers who face high demands but have little job control, say five new studies of more than 1 million people.

The research is the first to show a direct cause-and-effect link between control on the job and heart-attack risk.

"The workers at greatest risk are people who have very little or no decision-making power," says Robert Karasek, industrial engineer at the University of Southern California at Los Angeles, and an expert on the role of work in health.

Of all those studied, the 10 percent at highest risk are four times as likely to get heart attacks as the 10 percent at lowest risk, says Karasek.

"The health risk of low job control in developing heart disease is roughly the same as the risk from smoking or high serum cholesterol," he says.

Among the latest findings [he cited] in a 1987 book on the subject are four Swedish studies of more than 1 million people and a USA study of 1,000 men and women. Karasek was a collaborator on all five projects. The findings:

At lowest risk of heart attacks are those with low demand/high control work—"a declining breed," says Karasek. Among them: foresters, blacksmiths, bookbinders, and maintenance workers whose jobs demand little technical skill or hustling.

In between are employees with high demand/high control tasks (managers and many top professionals), along with low demand/low control workers. These include people like janitors, watchmen, billing clerks.

At highest risk are high demand/low control workers who have many tasks and time pressures but little say over how the job is done. They include assembly-line workers, cooks, and representatives at large public utilities who answer complaints but exert little authority.

Source: M. Elias, "Stressful, Low-Clout Jobs Bad for Heart," *USA Today,* September 24, 1986, p. D1. Copyright 1986, *USA Today.* Reprinted with permission.

I t is not hard to understand the stressful effects of demanding jobs such as those of a senior executive or a heart surgeon. Karasek's research points to how the design of jobs that do not require such skills may also produce stress. His research suggests that people doing jobs with high workload demands and low discretion in decision making will experience stress.[1] The jobs of telephone operators, assembly workers, and materials handlers often have those characteristics.

This chapter describes how the design of jobs affects motivation, satisfaction, and stress. The previous chapters on motivation spent much time discussing the role of extrinsic rewards in developing and guiding human behavior in organizations. According to those theories of motivation, both extrinsic and intrinsic rewards are important in human motivation. The conditions under which people experience the two types of rewards differ sharply from each other, however.

This chapter also focuses on what organizations and managers can do to create a context within which employees can experience intrinsic rewards. Although managers can use extrinsic rewards directly, they have only indirect control over intrinsic rewards. A manager cannot tell an employee to experience intrinsic rewards such as self-esteem or self-actualization. The manager can only create a context or set of job experiences that lets the employee experience intrinsic rewards.

. . . .

⤵ *Intrinsic Rewards and Job Design*

During the eighteenth century, the Scottish philosopher Adam Smith made some early observations on job design and its effects on workers.[2] Appendix A describes his observations on making an ordinary straight pin. Making a pin required many small tasks with each worker performing a specialized function. Smith noted that such work designs had both manifest functions and latent dysfunctions for workers and organizations. The manifest functions included higher productivity and skill development. The latent dysfunctions included little physical or social activity outside work.

The job design approach just described is a mechanistic one based on research flowing from industrial engineering. Three other approaches have also emerged: motivational, biological, and perceptual/motor.[3] Table 9-1 summarizes some features of each approach and describes their manifest functions and latent dysfunctions.

The **mechanistic approach** to job design used task simplification and specialization to get higher output, less mental overload, and decreased training time. Its latent dysfunctions of low motivation and low job satisfaction stimulated psychologists to search for a job design approach that remedied those dysfunctions.

The **motivational approach** developed theories of job design centered on task variety, worker autonomy, and performance feedback. These theories predicted improved job satisfaction, motivation, and performance. Jobs designed using the motivational approach however, often increased training time and associated costs.[4]

⤵ TABLE 9-1

Selected Features and Results of Different Job Design Approaches

APPROACH	SELECTED FEATURES	MANIFEST FUNCTIONS	LATENT DYSFUNCTIONS
Mechanistic	Task specialization Task simplification Repetition	Decreased training time Fewer errors Higher output Less mental overload	Low job satisfaction Low motivation High absenteeism
Motivational	Variety of tasks Autonomy Performance feedback	High job satisfaction High motivation High job involvement High performance Low absenteeism	Higher training time Higher training costs Greater chance of mental overload and stress
Biological	Physical demands Endurance Movements Workplace climate	Decreased physical effort and fatigue Low absenteeism High job satisfaction	High costs for changes and improvements in equipment and work environment
Perceptual/motor	Mental demands Attention Concentration Information processing	Fewer errors and accidents Less mental overload Less stress	Low job satisfaction Low motivation

Source: M. A. Campion and P. W. Thayer, "Job Design: Approaches, Outcomes, and Trade-offs," *Organizational Dynamics* 15 (1987): 66–79.

For the most part, the biological and perceptual/motor approaches focus on different aspects of job design. The **biological approach** focuses on the physical demands of a job. It tries to design jobs that do not exceed the physical abilities of workers. For example, tools are designed to fit comfortably in a person's hand, decreasing effort and fatigue. Workstations also are designed for comfortable seating and body movement. Such changes and improvements, though, have associated costs.

The **perceptual/motor approach** focuses on the mental demands of a job. This approach aims to reduce mental overload from the amount of information a worker processes. For example, dials and gauges used to monitor a work process are designed for easy reading and grouped in a way that does not confuse workers. Efforts to reduce the mental demands of jobs often have the latent dysfunction of low job satisfaction from too little mental stimulation.

This chapter focuses mainly on motivational approaches to job design. It fully develops some job design theory that can guide an organization's efforts in redesigning jobs to raise levels of intrinsic rewards. Although the chapter's focus is on motivation, it does not ignore the contributions of other approaches to job design.

The Job Characteristics Theory of Work Motivation

The **Job Characteristics Theory** of Work Motivation is a well-developed and well-understood theory of job design.[5] It is a cognitive theory with many similarities to the cognitive theories of motivation described in Chapter 8. Figure 9-1 presents an overview of the theory. Much empirical research supports many parts of the theory as described in this section.[6]

The theory says the design of a person's job produces two major classes of outcomes. **Behavioral outcomes** are observed employee behavior such as individual productivity and quality of work. **Affective outcomes** are the individual's internal reactions to a job's design such as job satisfaction and motivation. The theory expects high levels of behavioral outcomes to follow high levels of affective outcomes (especially motivation).

People experience a set of **critical psychological states** that produce positive affective and behavioral outcomes. The characteristics of a person's job induce the critical psychological states. A person has perceptions about the objective qualities of his job, such as tasks, duties, responsibilities, activities, and the like. The theory uses those perceptions to explain the presence and level of the critical psychological states.

The center of Figure 9-1 isolates perceived job characteristics, critical psychological states, and affective outcomes as factors internal to the person. Both the objective

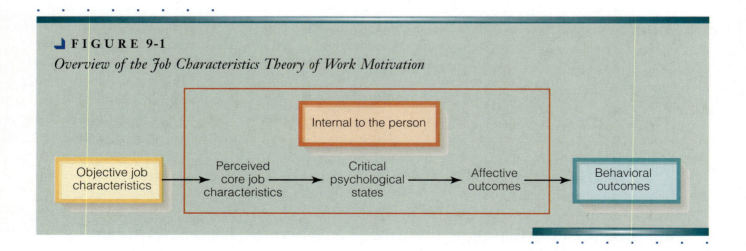

◢ FIGURE 9-1

Overview of the Job Characteristics Theory of Work Motivation

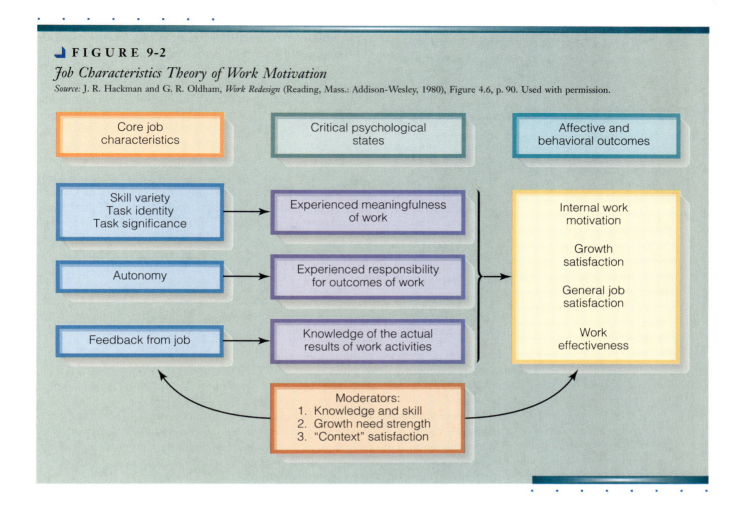

FIGURE 9-2

Job Characteristics Theory of Work Motivation

Source: J. R. Hackman and G. R. Oldham, *Work Redesign* (Reading, Mass.: Addison-Wesley, 1980), Figure 4.6, p. 90. Used with permission.

job characteristics and the behavioral outcomes are external to the person. The theory is strongly cognitive in its explanation of people's reactions to their jobs. It includes direct connections, however, to aspects external to the person. Those external factors are important to fully understanding people's responses to work design.

Figure 9-2 shows the detailed structure of the Job Characteristics Theory of Work Motivation. The following sections describe each group of variables in that figure.

AFFECTIVE AND BEHAVIORAL OUTCOMES

The theory predicts that the design of a person's job will produce several affective and behavioral outcomes.[7] The affective outcomes are internal work motivation, growth satisfaction, and general job satisfaction. The figure shows the behavioral outcomes as "work effectiveness," which refers to the quality of a person's work performance and the quantity of work produced. The design of a person's job can add to or detract from work effectiveness.

The affective outcome internal work motivation is most closely associated with work effectiveness. **Internal work motivation** is a feeling of self-reward from doing the job itself. Think of it as intrinsic motivation,[8] an idea closely tied to the intrinsic rewards you saw in the Chapter 8 discussion of Expectancy Theory. That chapter described how a person's job performance could lead to intrinsic rewards. Those intrinsic rewards are central to internal work motivation. A person who does a job well experiences intrinsic rewards, which then reinforce his work behavior. They act as a form of self-propulsion causing the person to want to continue to do the job well. A person who experiences high internal work motivation should show high work effectiveness. The opposite also is true.

Growth satisfaction is associated with the opportunities a person has to experience personal growth and development from the work itself. If the job design allows such opportunities, we expect a high degree of growth satisfaction. Jobs that produce feelings of high internal work motivation and result in high work effectiveness should also provide opportunities for personal growth and development and the resulting growth satisfaction.

The last affective outcome is general job satisfaction. Job design can affect general feelings about work and the work organization. Although many other factors affect those feelings, the job is a basic connection between a person and the employing organization. Consequently, a person's job has some influence on feelings of overall job satisfaction.

CRITICAL PSYCHOLOGICAL STATES

For a job to produce high levels of the affective and behavioral outcomes, the individual must experience three critical psychological states:

- *Knowledge of the actual results of work activities.* The person must know how well or how poorly he is doing while doing the work itself. The individual would have neither positive nor negative feelings if he did not know the results of work activities.
- *Experienced responsibility for outcomes of the work.* A person must also control the outcomes of his work activities. If the employee believes external factors such as coworkers, equipment, or the supervisor were responsible for the outcomes of the job, he likely will not feel particularly good about having done a good job or particularly bad about having done a poor job.
- *Experienced meaningfulness of the work.* The person doing the job must experience the work as important. Work perceived as unimportant by the person doing the job is not likely to produce high levels of affective and behavioral response.

All three critical psychological states must be present to produce the highest level of positive affective and behavioral outcome. A job where the employee controls the results of meaningful work and learns about how he is doing while doing the job itself should produce a positive response.

PERCEIVED AND OBJECTIVE JOB CHARACTERISTICS

The following description divides job characteristics into two groups: perceived and objective. The Job Characteristics Theory itself does not carefully distinguish perceived from objective job characteristics. There are good practical and theoretical reasons, however, to make the distinction.[9]

Five **core job characteristics** must be present to produce the critical psychological states. People have perceptions of the objective characteristics of their jobs that form their impressions of the core job characteristics. The following are the five core job characteristics used by the theory:[10]

- *Skill variety.* The degree to which the job has many different activities using several skills, abilities, and talents of the person.
- *Task identity.* The degree to which the job lets a person do a whole piece of work from start to finish.
- *Task significance.* The degree to which the person doing the job perceives it as important to others in the organization or clients of the organization.

- *Autonomy.* The degree to which the person has discretion in deciding how the job will be done and when it will be done.
- *Feedback from the job itself.* The degree to which the person learns about the quality of his job performance while doing the task. Feedback from the job includes feedback from clients directly served by the job, but not feedback from a supervisor or coworkers.

The objective characteristics of a person's job are associated with perceived job characteristics, although the association is not direct. A job that may appear simple and routine to an outsider may not appear that way to the person doing the job. A later section of this chapter discusses the factors affecting the connection between the objective and perceived job characteristics.

The five core job characteristics are not equally related to the critical psychological states. Figure 9-2 shows skill variety, task identity, and task significance as associated with experienced meaningfulness of the work. If these job characteristics are present, the person could experience the work as meaningful. All three characteristics do not need to be present to induce a state of meaningfulness. The three job characteristics associated with experienced meaningfulness can have offsetting effects among themselves. For example, a job that is not perceived as significant may be a whole job, using many skills and abilities. Such a job should be meaningful to the person doing the job.

The remaining two core job characteristics are related to different psychological states. Jobs high in autonomy should produce a feeling of personal responsibility for the outcomes of the work. Jobs that give feedback while doing the job should let the person know the actual results of work activities.

The concept of **motivating potential** summarizes the effect of the five core job characteristics on the critical psychological states. The following formula shows how the theory expects the job characteristics to combine to result in some level of motivating potential for a job:[11]

$$\text{Motivating Potential Score (MPS)} = \left[\frac{\text{skill variety} + \text{task identity} + \text{task significance}}{3} \right] \times \text{autonomy} \times \text{feedback from the job itself}$$

The formula emphasizes the strong effect autonomy and feedback from the job itself can have on motivating potential. The theory does not expect a job low in autonomy or in job-related feedback to produce high levels of affective or behavioral response. Figure 9-2 shows the reasons for this effect. Autonomy and job feedback are related to two of the three psychological states, experienced responsibility and knowledge of results. Low levels of those psychological states are associated with low affective and behavioral response.

RELATIONSHIPS PREDICTED BY THE THEORY

Figure 9-3 shows the basic relationships predicted by the theory. On the left side of the figure is the positive relationship expected between motivating potential and internal work motivation. Jobs high in motivating potential should produce higher internal work motivation than jobs low in motivating potential.

Note the use of the word "potential" in the preceding paragraph. Jobs high in motivating potential offer an *opportunity* for an individual to experience high levels of motivation and satisfaction. Incumbents of such jobs should also perceive the jobs as meaningful and important. There is always a chance that other factors within the person or within the work context will block the job's potential.

The theory includes the **moderator variables** shown at the bottom of Figure 9-2 to accommodate the chance that blockages will inhibit the motivating potential of a job.

• *Charlie Chaplin, as he appeared in his film* Modern Times. *Chaplin's film satirically portrayed early twentieth-century factory jobs. Such jobs had low motivating potential.*

Relationships Predicted by the Job Characteristics Theory of Work Motivation

Basic relationship — High / Low — Internal work motivation — Motivating potential — Low (<50) Middle (50–150) High (>150)

Effect of moderators — High / Low — Motivating potential — Low (<50) Middle (50–150) High (>150)
Moderator is positive or high
Moderator is negative or low

· *Modern commercial jet aircraft present a complex environment to pilots. This job likely has high motivating potential.*

Those variables are called moderators because they change or affect the relationships among parts of the theory. Some are factors in the person (individual moderators); others surround the person while he is doing the job (work context moderators). Each variable allows for differences in the way people respond to the motivating potential of their jobs. The theory, therefore, does not assume a universal, positive response to jobs high in motivating potential.

Figure 9-2 shows three moderator variables: knowledge and skill, growth need strength, and satisfaction with the context of the job. The right side of Figure 9-3 shows the change in the basic relationship expected from these variables.

Assume a person is trying to do a job high in motivating potential. Because of its high motivating potential, the person could perceive the job as meaningful and important. A person with the necessary skills and abilities should do that job successfully. High motivating potential combines with the person's knowledge and skill to produce high internal work motivation. A person without the necessary skills and abilities should not do the job as successfully as a person with the necessary skills and abilities. In this case, the person is failing at a job perceived to be meaningful and important. This combination of events produces a low level of internal work motivation.

People's needs can also affect their reaction to job design. Some people have strong needs for personal growth, development, and learning from the job itself.[12] Others have weak needs for such growth. Such desires for growth and development from the job itself are characteristic of people with strong needs for achievement or self-actualization as discussed in Chapter 7.

The concept of **growth need strength (GNS)** captures the variability in growth needs among different people. People with strong growth needs should respond more positively to jobs high in motivating potential than people with weak growth needs. Individuals with strong growth needs are more ready to respond to the motivating potential of a job than people with weak growth needs. Individuals with weak growth needs may be "stretched" by the demands of a job high in motivating potential. They would find such work experiences stressful and not do as well as someone with strong growth needs.

The last set of moderators focuses on the work context (**context satisfaction** in Figure 9-2), which includes quality of supervision, the compensation system, job security, and immediate coworkers. A negative work context distracts a person from experiencing the qualities of a job high in motivating potential. A person working in a positive work context would perceive it as supportive, letting the person experience the motivating qualities of the job itself.

The right side of Figure 9-3 summarizes the expected moderating effect of the three sets of variables. The relationship between motivating potential and internal work motivation (or performance and satisfaction) is still positive. If a moderator variable is positive, the theory predicts a more positive response to a level of motivating potential than when a moderator variable is negative. The line with the steeper slope shows the form of this moderating effect. When the moderator variable is negative, the theory predicts a less positive response to the motivating potential of the job. The line with the shallower slope shows the latter relationship.

The expected moderating effects have not had consistent empirical support. The moderating effect of skill has not been studied. One study found that knowledge, as assessed by education level, had an opposite moderating effect. Managers with less education had more favorable affective responses than those with more education.[13] Various studies did not always find the moderating effects of GNS or failed to find them in the form the theory predicts.

Moderating effects of the context satisfactions also have not always appeared as predicted.[14] The theory expects a negative work context to distract a person from experiencing the intrinsic motivating qualities of a job with a high Motivating Potential Score (MPS). Empirical research about this part of the theory has had mixed results. Some research has supported the predictions of the theory.[15] Other research has suggested an opposite effect.[16] The research evidence suggests two different reactions to a negative work context: the distraction effect suggested by the theory, and an escape effect where people turn to the job to escape a negative work context.[17]

Let's pause now to see what the Job Characteristics Theory of Work Motivation says about your job and your reaction to it. Do the following exercise. It focuses on your present job or one you held in the past.

EXERCISE   *The Design of Your Job*

PART I

Answer the following questions about your present job or one you held in the recent past.[18] If you have not held a job, refer to your present role as a student. Each question describes a job characteristic from the Job Characteristics Theory of Work Motivation. Each question has its own scale. Read all parts of the scale before deciding which number best expresses the amount of the job characteristic in your job. Record the number you pick for each question on a separate piece of paper.

1. How much *variety* is there in your job? That is, to what extent does the job require you to do many different things at work, using a variety of your skills and talents?

1	2	3	4	5	6	7
Very little; the job requires me to do the same routine things over and over again.			Moderate variety			Very much; the job requires me to do many different things, using a number of different skills and talents.

Source: J. Richard Hackman and Greg R. Oldham, WORK REDESIGN (pp. 278–280), © 1980 by Addison-Wesley Publishing Co., Inc. Reprinted by permission of the publisher.

2. To what extent does your job involve doing a *"whole" and identifiable piece of work*? That is, is the job a complete piece of work that has an obvious beginning and end? Or is it only a small *part* of the overall piece of work, which is finished by other people or by automatic machines?

1 —————— 2 —————— 3 —————— 4 —————— 5 —————— 6 —————— 7

| My job is only a tiny part of the overall piece of work; results of my activities cannot be seen in the final product or service. | My job is a moderate-sized "chunk" of the overall piece of work; my own contribution can be seen in the final outcome. | My job involves doing the whole piece of work from start to finish; the results of my activities are easily seen in the final product or service. |

3. In general, how *significant or important* is your job? That is, are the results of your work likely to significantly affect the lives or well-being of other people?

1 —————— 2 —————— 3 —————— 4 —————— 5 —————— 6 —————— 7

| Not very significant; the outcomes of my work are *not* likely to have important effects on other people. | Moderately significant. | Highly significant; the outcomes of my work can affect other people in very important ways. |

4. How much *autonomy* is there in your job? That is, to what extent does your job permit you to decide *on your own* how to go about doing the work?

1 —————— 2 —————— 3 —————— 4 —————— 5 —————— 6 —————— 7

| Very little; the job gives me almost no personal "say" about how and when the work is done. | Moderate autonomy; many things are standardized and not under my control, but I can make some decisions about the work. | Very much; the job gives me almost complete responsibility for deciding how and when the work is done. |

5. To what extent does *doing the job itself* provide you with information about your work performance? That is, does the actual work *itself* provide clues about how well you are doing—aside from any "feedback" co-workers or supervisors may provide?

1 —————— 2 —————— 3 —————— 4 —————— 5 —————— 6 —————— 7

| Very little; the job itself is set up so I could work forever, without finding out how well I am doing. | Moderately; sometimes doing the job provides "feedback" to me; sometimes it does not. | Very much; the job is set up so that I get almost constant "feedback" as I work about how well I am doing. |

PART II

Each question in Part I assessed your perception of one of the five core job characteristics. The following table shows the job characteristics measured by each question:

JOB CHARACTERISTIC	QUESTION
Skill variety	1
Task identity	2
Task significance	3

JOB CHARACTERISTIC	QUESTION
Autonomy	4
Feedback from the job itself	5

Using your answers in Part I and the following formula, calculate the Motivating Potential Score (MPS) for your job. The MPS is a summary index showing your job's potential to provide intrinsic motivation. The numbers in parentheses are the question numbers.

$$MPS = \left[\frac{\begin{smallmatrix}(1)\\ \text{skill}\\ \text{variety}\end{smallmatrix} + \begin{smallmatrix}(2)\\ \text{task}\\ \text{identity}\end{smallmatrix} + \begin{smallmatrix}(3)\\ \text{task}\\ \text{significance}\end{smallmatrix}}{3} \right] \times \begin{smallmatrix}(4)\\ \text{autonomy}\end{smallmatrix} \times \begin{smallmatrix}(5)\\ \text{feedback from}\\ \text{the job}\end{smallmatrix}$$

Plot your scores for the core job characteristics on a graph similar to Figure 9-4. The question numbers are in parentheses under the name of each job characteristic.

PART III: INTERPRETATION

The following interpretation describes your reaction to your job using predictions from the Job Characteristics Theory of Work Motivation. Deviations from the following description will occur if you do not react as the theory predicts, or if the theory is incomplete.

Compare your MPS to the national norm in Figure 9-4. The norm is the average MPS for 6,930 people working in 876 different jobs in 56 organizations around the country.[18] If your MPS is about 50 points lower than the norm, your job should not be an important source of

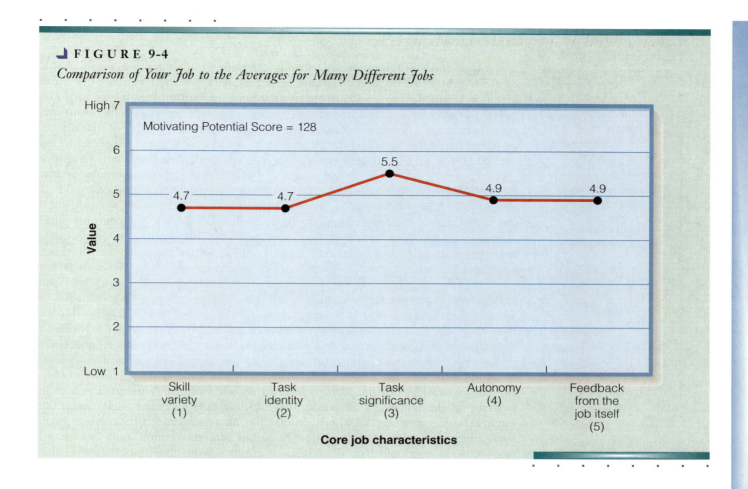

FIGURE 9-4

Comparison of Your Job to the Averages for Many Different Jobs

Motivating Potential Score = 128

(Value axis: High 7, 6, 5, 4, 3, 2, Low 1)

4.7 — Skill variety (1)
4.7 — Task identity (2)
5.5 — Task significance (3)
4.9 — Autonomy (4)
4.9 — Feedback from the job itself (5)

Core job characteristics

intrinsic motivation or growth satisfaction. Because the job itself gives you few intrinsic outcomes, you may view the job as instrumental for getting extrinsic outcomes, especially money.

If your MPS is about 50 points higher than the norm, your job should be a source of motivation. It can give you considerable opportunity for growth satisfaction. You likely enjoy your work and look forward to going to work each day. The previous statements would be even more positive if you are also high in growth need strength.

Now examine the profile of the five core job characteristics in Figure 9-4. That profile shows the specific job characteristics that contributed to your low or high MPS. Compare your profile to the line for the national norms. If your job's characteristics differ from the norm by about 1 point, you can consider those characteristics to be

significantly higher or lower than the norm. Remember that autonomy and feedback from the job itself heavily influence your MPS. Your score may be high or low because of those two job characteristics alone.

Why are the job characteristics high or low? Without knowing the specific job and its context, we can only speculate about what is affecting your MPS. Consider the following questions and think through their implications:

- How does the technical process affect each job characteristic?
- How does your supervisor's or manager's behavior affect each job characteristic?

This chapter addresses those questions in more detail later. You may find it useful to come back after reading that material and rethink the questions.

Contextual Factors in Job Design

Contextual factors such as the design of an organization, technologies in the work process, and management behavior can affect the designs of people's jobs and their

FIGURE 9-5

Context Factors and the Job Characteristics Theory of Work Motivation

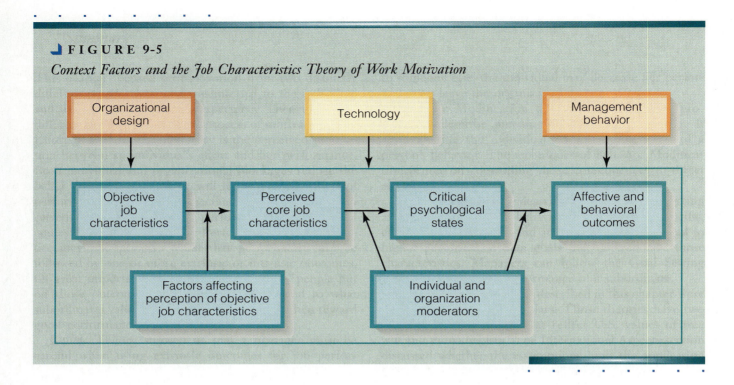

reaction to them.[19] Figure 9-5 shows the major context factors discussed in the following sections. Note carefully the implications of those contextual factors for the design of the job you could be doing after graduation.

ORGANIZATIONAL DESIGN AND JOB DESIGN

A major feature of organizational design that affects the design of jobs is the degree of specialization the organization has chosen for its division of labor. Highly specialized tasks tend to be low in most of the core job characteristics, resulting in low motivating potential. Less specialized tasks will be higher in the job characteristics and higher in motivating potential. You can easily see the differences between assembly line work and the job of a manager.

Organizations with centralized decision-making processes restrict the scope of decision making and responsibility of individuals lower in the organization. Centralized decision making yield jobs low in skill variety and autonomy. The person may also do only a small part of a larger task, reducing task identity. Lastly, if the individual does not make important decisions because they are made at a higher level, task significance may also be reduced. You probably can see the effect those actions can have on motivating potential and the resultant levels of motivation, performance, and satisfaction.

Organizations with decentralized decision-making processes have the opposite effect on job characteristics and motivating potential. Employees may perceive their jobs as being more significant, having more wholeness to them (task identity), and allowing more autonomy. Motivating potential could be higher than it is in a centralized organization.

Span of control is the number of people directly reporting to a supervisor or manager. Because of the direct relationship between a manager and his subordinates, variations in span of control affect the design of both the manager's job and the subordinates' jobs. A manager with a narrow span of control can pay closer attention to the work of subordinates than a manager with a wide span of control. Such behavior potentially can reduce the autonomy of the subordinates. A wide span of control has the reverse effect. Here we expect increased autonomy and skill variety from more job duties. Recall that the theory expects autonomy to greatly affect motivating potential. The span of control, therefore, could have a strong effect on the motivational quality of jobs.

Span of control also affects the duties and design of the manager's job. A narrow span of control lets the manager have more control over subordinates' work. A wide span of control reduces the opportunity for day-to-day control. It also increases the time available for a manager to do other types of managerial work, such as long-range planning and budgeting. A manager's task identity could be higher when he has a wide span of control because he is more involved in the "big picture." Skill variety also could be increased because the manager is using a wider range of skills than is required by a narrow span of control.

TECHNICAL PROCESS AND JOB DESIGN

The technical process of an organization is the major way the work of the organization gets done. The nature of the process affects the characteristics of a person's job[20] by either impeding or helping job design. Large capital investment in an existing technical process can limit the redesign of jobs. The cost of changing a physical facility or replacing an existing manufacturing process often prevents managers from considering new ways of designing jobs. On the other hand, adopting a particular technical process can help the redesign of work. A company that adopts a group-based technical process can redesign jobs to take advantage of that technology.[21]

Mass-production technical processes usually have highly standardized jobs. Such jobs are routine, not highly skilled, and individually are a small piece of a larger set of activities. Skill variety, task identity, task significance, autonomy, and feedback from the job itself could be low. In contrast, technologies that do custom-designed work have jobs that are nonstandard, not narrowly defined, and not repetitive. All core job characteristics and motivating potential could be high.

Computer-based automated processes can control the pace of a complex, expensive, and often dangerous manufacturing process. Workers follow standardized procedures when monitoring the process. A person doing a monitoring job should not perceive much skill variety, task identity, and autonomy because of the routine character of the job and the standardized control procedures. Task significance could be high because of the cost and danger of the process. The dials and gauges the person monitors also build feedback into the job.

Many manufacturing companies have changed their manufacturing approach by adopting flexible manufacturing techniques, robotics, group-based manufacturing, "just-in-time" inventory management, and Total Quality Management.[22] Each approach could require or induce changes in the design of jobs of those working in such manufacturing systems.[23]

Flexible manufacturing techniques let companies respond quickly to changing customer requirements. Such technologies require workers to be flexible. This requirement increases the skill variety and autonomy of their jobs.

Group-based manufacturing technologies need jobs designed around groups of people, not individuals. You will read about many aspects of group-based job design later in this chapter.

"Just-in-time" inventory management removes buffers from within the technical process.[24] The tighter links among parts of the technical process require workers to respond quickly to any disruptions in the manufacturing process. Such responses call for jobs designed with more skill variety, autonomy, and feedback from the job itself.

Jobs in organizations are related, sometimes in ways that are not immediately clear. A change in one job can often affect other jobs in the organization.[25] Managerial and subordinate jobs are a clear case of the interdependence of jobs in an organization. The relationship of management behavior to job design must be considered from two perspectives. The first is the effect of a manager's behavior on the design of the job of a subordinate. The second is the effect of a change in the job of a subordinate on a manager's job.

Managers using close control over subordinates (close supervision) will narrow the scope of a subordinate's work. The subordinate's job becomes narrowly defined with little decision-making discretion. Under those circumstances we expect low skill variety, task identity, and autonomy. Managers using general control and delegation of decision-making authority have the opposite effect on a subordinate's job. Skill variety, task identity, and autonomy should all increase under such circumstances.

Managers who involve their subordinates in the decision-making process will affect many job characteristics.[26] Involvement in decision making requires the subordinate to use previously unused skills and abilities. Such involvement can show a person the importance of his role in the larger scheme of things for the organization. Because involvement can increase the employee's commitment to the decision, the manager can allow the employee more discretion in carrying out the decision. When a manager increases employee participation in decisions, skill variety, task significance, and autonomy of the subordinate's job could increase.

Managers with an achievement orientation emphasize high performance goals and stress subordinate achievement.[27] Such managers will assign subordinates more complex tasks and give subordinates more responsibility for getting the job done. This type of management behavior should increase skill variety, autonomy, and task significance.

. . . .

⌐ *Diagnosing and Redesigning Jobs*

Jobs in organizations can be diagnosed to decide whether they should be redesigned. The safest approach to job redesign uses a theoretical orientation to guide the questions that need to be asked about jobs in any organization.[28] This chapter has developed a conceptual framework that should prove useful in that task.

The first step in any redesign program is getting information about the existing state of jobs in the organization. The information should be collected by multiple methods of measurement. Questionnaires can be used and supplemented with personal interviews and direct observations.

One questionnaire that can be used is the **Job Diagnostic Survey (JDS).**[29] Norms are available for many types of jobs allowing results from one organization to be compared to the results for similar jobs in other organizations. You used part of the JDS when you assessed the characteristics of your present job earlier in this chapter.

Data collected with the JDS will show the overall MPS of individual jobs, the job characteristics, and affective responses. The MPS can be compared to norms to decide whether a job has an excessively low score. Then the job characteristics that are responsible for that low MPS can be identified.

The JDS also provides information about employee GNS and levels of satisfaction with the work context. If a job is a target for a redesign activity, the GNS should be examined to decide whether employees in that job are ready to respond to a redesigned job (high GNS). The context satisfactions give important information about whether employees perceive the work context as positive. Although the JDS does not measure employee knowledge and skills, any job redesign activity must consider whether employees have the necessary knowledge and skills to do the

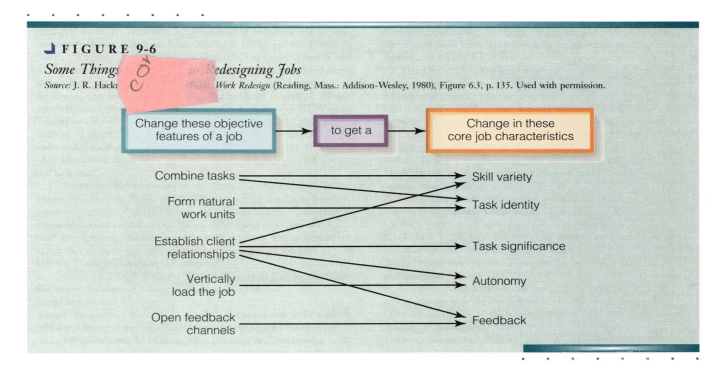

FIGURE 9-6

Some Things ~~____~~ ____ Redesigning Jobs
Source: J. R. Hackr____ ____ ____ *Work Redesign* (Reading, Mass.: Addison-Wesley, 1980), Figure 6.3, p. 135. Used with permission.

redesigned work. If they do not, it may be necessary to include a training program along with the program to redesign jobs.

The employees who provide the data should see the results to verify their accuracy. Asking the employees to suggest ways their jobs can be redesigned can also elicit useful information.

Assume an organization has identified one or more jobs as candidates for redesign. What can managers change to affect each core job characteristic? Figure 9-6 shows the objective features of a job that can be changed and the expected effect the changes will have on the core job characteristics.[30]

Combining existing tasks from several jobs into the new job increases skill variety because additional skills are needed to do the job. Task identity also increases because the new job will have increased "wholeness." By establishing client relationships, people doing a job that serves others inside or outside the organization can directly contact their clients. The job incumbent will use new interpersonal skills (skill variety). The interaction can let the individual know the importance of the task to the client (task significance). Because the job incumbent can directly contact the client, autonomy also is increased. Lastly, the person doing the task can get direct feedback from the client about how well or poorly he is doing (feedback from the job itself).

Group-Based Job Design

Up to this point, the discussion has focused on job design for individual employees of an organization. Some tasks, however, are better done by groups of people than by individuals. Here is what Hallmark Cards did some years ago:

> Under the old system, an artist worked on a single item—a classical daughter-to-dad Father's Day card, for instance—then passed the card on to an editorial worker for a dose of dewy prose, and thence onward to marketing, which would decide whether the card would sell or not. Under the new approach, artist, writer, and marketing expert work as a team on a broad category of cards—say, the entire Father's Day line. Rejects are lower, and it takes fewer people to produce a new line of cards.[31]

The team used at Hallmark is a **self-managing work group.**[32] Such groups have three characteristics. First, they are intact groups, whether permanent or temporary, whose members are interdependent while doing the tasks of the group. Both members and nonmembers perceive the groups as real. Second, the group produces a defined product, service, or decision. Third, the members of the group control the task and interpersonal processes of the group. They have the authority to make task assignments within the group and decide how and when the work will be done. This third characteristic of the group is the major source of its self-managing quality.

The design of the task that the group will do partly derives from our knowledge about how to design work for individuals. The organization must also consider the composition of the group and the rules the group develops about its job performance. The problem for the organization is to design both the task the group will do and some aspects of the group itself. Chapter 10 gives you other information about groups important for **group-based job design.**

 ## DESIGN OF THE GROUP TASK

Designing jobs for a group is done in much the same way as for individuals. Each core job characteristic is still necessary, but it is now defined for a group task, not an individual task. Skill variety requires the group to use many different skills in doing the task. The task must still be a whole task (task identity) that the members of the group perceive to be important to others (task significance). The group task must give group members discretion in getting the work done (autonomy). This discretion includes task assignments within the group, the work processes the group will use, and the setting of priorities for the tasks of the group. The work should give feedback to members of the group while the task is being done (feedback from the job itself). As you can see, the elements used in designing a group task are much the same as the job characteristics of an individual task.

 ## DESIGN OF THE GROUP

One important element to consider in designing the group is its composition. Obviously, members of the group must have the skills and abilities needed to perform the tasks. The size of the group is important. If the group is too large, the group process becomes inefficient, and productivity will be lower than desired.[33] There is no formula for finding the optimal size of the group. Careful analysis of the task requirements usually will show how many people the group needs. If more people than needed are included, they may get in each other's way.

The self-managing characteristic of the group and the degree of autonomy designed into the group's task require group members to have the interpersonal skills necessary to manage the interpersonal processes in such activities. A balance also must be struck between the heterogeneity and homogeneity of group members. If the people in the group are different from each other, managing the interpersonal processes may be more difficult than if the members were similar to each other. A group whose members are similar in background and perspective, however, may be less likely to find creative solutions to work problems. Highly homogeneous, enduring groups often suffer from "groupthink," a phenomenon that blocks the discovery of creative solutions by the group.[34]

People who work together in a group develop norms about how its work should be done and how much work should be done. Those norms are rules of conduct that can control the behavior of members of the group. The problem for management is to encourage norms consistent with the task to be done and the desired level of productivity.

When the work group is designed, those responsible for its design (either management or an outside consultant) can help group members talk through various approaches to the work of the group. The goal is to help build a climate that encourages open discussion of existing and developing group norms. From this process, members of the group can learn that it is all right to discuss and change the performance norms of the group.

 ## WHAT CAN WE EXPECT TO HAPPEN?

Properly designed groups and group-based jobs can produce several desirable results. The presence of the core job characteristics, adjusted for a group work process, could lead to high levels of effort, motivation, and performance. The composition of the group, its size, individual skills and abilities, and balance between heterogeneity and homogeneity could lead to a high level of knowledge and skill to do the work of the group. Individual members of the group also could feel good about their membership in the group and feel satisfied with their experiences in the group.

Self-managing work groups can develop such strong norms that group members try to exert control over each other's behavior.[35] Positive performance norms help focus members on successfully completing the group's tasks. Strong behavioral norms also focus group members on quickly discovering ways of successfully dealing with work problems the group might face.

 ## INDIVIDUAL AND CONTEXTUAL CONSIDERATIONS

As with individual job design, the organization must consider several individual and contextual characteristics before trying group-based job design. If the individual and contextual characteristics do not support a group approach, success with group-based job design is unlikely.

Group-based job design makes more interpersonal demands on individuals than does individual job design. Chapter 7 described how the importance of people's social needs can vary. The most likely candidates for a group-based approach are people with strong needs for affiliation. Such people should enjoy the interpersonal processes found in a self-managing work group. The individuals in a group should also have strong growth needs. Such needs show a readiness to respond to the design of the task of the group. Strongly affiliative people with weak growth needs might find the group attractive more because of the social interaction than because of the intrinsic qualities of the tasks of the group. For this reason, individuals who have both strong growth needs and strong social needs are highly desirable.

CASE

Who Needs a Boss?

*T*he following case describes the efforts of several companies to expand their use of self-managing work teams. Consider these questions while reading the case:

1. Which job characteristics are most likely to be affected by the changes described?
2. Are the approaches of these companies consistent with the guidelines and discussion of group-based job design?

◢ CASE DESCRIPTION

Many American companies are discovering what may be *the* productivity breakthrough of the 1990s. Call the still-controversial innovation a self-managed team, a cross-functional team, a high-performance team, or, to coin a phrase, a superteam. Says Texas Instruments CEO Jerry Junkins: "No matter what your business, these teams are the wave of the future." Corning CEO Jamie Houghton, whose company has 3,000 teams, echoes the sentiment: "If you really believe in quality, when you cut through everything, it's empowering your people, and it's empowering your people that leads to teams."

We're not talking here about the teamwork that's been praised at Rotary Club luncheons since time immemorial, or the quality circles so popular in the 1980s, where workers gathered once a week to save paper clips or bitch about the fluorescent lights. What makes superteams so controversial is that they ultimately force managers to do what they had only imagined in their most Boschian nightmares: give up control. Because if superteams are working right . . . they manage themselves. No boss required. A superteam arranges schedules, sets profit targets, and—gulp—may even know everyone's salary. It has a say in hiring and firing team members as well as managers. It orders material and equipment. It strokes customers, improves quality, and, in some cases, devises strategy.

Superteams typically consist of between three and 30 workers—sometimes blue collar, sometimes white collar, sometimes both. In a few cases, they have become a permanent part of the work force. In others, management assembles the team for a few months or years to develop a new product or solve a particular problem. Companies that use them—and they work as well in service or finance businesses as they do in manufacturing—usually see productivity rise dramatically. That's because teams composed of people with different skills, from different parts of the company, can swoop around bureaucratic obstacles and break through walls separating different functions to get a job done. . . .

Source: B. Dumaine, "Who Needs a Boss?" *Fortune*, May 7, 1990, pp. 52, 55, 58.

Some large organizations still feel a need to exercise oversight of superteams' activities. What to do with a team that louses up quality or orders the wrong machinery? James Watson, a vice president of Texas Instruments' semiconductor group, may have the answer. At one of TI's chip factories in Texas, Watson helped create a hierarchy of teams that, like a shadow government, works within the existing hierarchy.

On top is a steering team consisting of the plant manager and his heads of manufacturing, finance, engineering, and human resources. They set strategy and approve large projects. Beneath the steering team, TI has three other teams: corrective-action teams, quality-improvement teams, and effectiveness teams. The first two are cross-functional and consist mainly of middle managers and professionals like engineers and accountants. Corrective-action teams form to tackle short-lived problems and then disband. They're great for those times when, as the technophantasmic novelist Thomas Pynchon writes, there's fecoventilatory collision: the s— hits the fan.

By contrast, TI's quality-improvement teams work on long-term projects, such as streamlining the manufacturing process. The corrective-action and quality-improvement teams guide and check effectiveness teams, which consist of blue-collar employees who do day-to-day production work, and professional workers.

What's to keep this arrangement from becoming just another hierarchy? "You have to keep changing and be flexible as business conditions dictate," says Watson. He contends that one of the steering team's most important responsibilities is to show a keen interest in the teams beneath it. "The worst thing you can do to a team is to leave it alone in the dark. I guarantee that if you come across someone who says teams didn't work at his company, it's because management didn't take interest in them." Watson suggests that the steering team periodically review everyone's work, and adds, "It doesn't have to be a big dog-and-pony show. Just walk around and ask, 'How are you doing?' "

Last spring a group of executives from a Fortune 500 manufacturer traveled to Midlothian, Texas, to learn how Chaparral Steel managed its teams. Efficient superteams have helped make Chaparral one of the world's most productive steel companies. During the tour, one executive asked a Chaparral manager, "How do you schedule coffee breaks in the plant?"

"The workers decide when they want a cup of coffee," came the reply.

"Yes, but who tells them when it's okay to leave the machines?" the executive persisted.

Looking back on the exchange, the Chaparral manager reflects, "The guy left and still didn't get it."

The case described both temporary and permanent groups with clearly defined tasks. Members of many teams worked on interdependent tasks. They also had unusually large decision-making authority leading to almost complete self-management of the team's activities.

Most of the core job characteristics discussed earlier should be positively affected although no direct data appeared in the case. Skill variety and autonomy should increase because of the increased decision-making authority within the teams. Task identity should rise because these teams tend to do larger and more complete tasks. Task significance could increase if the team members perceive the results of their work as important to the organization and its customers. Feedback could come from the job itself, depending on its design. Feedback also can come from members of the team and not the boss.

◢ Factors Affecting Perceptions of Objective Job Characteristics

The Job Characteristics Theory has not always been clear on whether the core job characteristics are the "objective" characteristics of the job or those perceived by the job incumbent.[36] The social context of a person doing a job affects his perception of the job's objective features. Therefore, a person's perceptions of job characteristics are not necessarily an accurate picture of the job's objective features. As Chapter 4 described, though, perceptions can strongly affect people's behavior.[37]

The **Social Information Processing Theory** is an alternative to the Job Characteristics Theory.[38] This view holds that interactions with other people affect a person's perceptions of job characteristics. For example, social interactions with coworkers and supervisors can lead a person to cognitively develop a view of the characteristics of the job. Informational cues about the task can come from either present or previous coworkers. They may describe the job in positive or negative terms, affecting the current incumbent's perception of the job.[39] This socially constructed view may not be the same as the "objective" features of the job.

The Social Information Processing view of task design has the following implications for those considering job redesign:[40]

- Participation in the job design process may produce feelings of high satisfaction independent of any job design changes.
- Using the Job Diagnostic Survey, or any other questionnaire, before changing the design of jobs may sensitize people to certain job characteristics they had not noticed before.
- Perceptions of the job characteristics can be manipulated by the social information made available to employees by managers and coworkers in the organization.

Research focused on the Social Information Processing Theory has produced mixed results. Some studies support the theory's predictions while others do not.[41] A conservative conclusion points to the Social Information Processing Theory as a complement to the Job Characteristics Theory.[42] The largest change in perceptions of job characteristics and satisfaction can occur in the presence of *both* changes in the objective job characteristics (job redesign) and oral cues by supervisors.[43] Information given to employees about the design of their jobs, and the favorable effects of that information on their perceptions of the task, may be important elements in a job redesign activity.[44]

◢ Time and Job Reactions

People's perceptions of the characteristics of their jobs—and their reactions to their jobs—are also related to **time**.[45] As you learned earlier in the chapter about organizational socialization (Chapter 6), people experience organizations in identifiable stages. During each stage people attend to different aspects of their job and work context, causing the job characteristics to take on varying importance over time.

During the early part of the employment period (about the first six months), people have little interest in the characteristics of their job that can give them intrinsic rewards (skill variety and autonomy). Nor are they ready to respond to the qualities of the job believed to produce high motivation and satisfaction. Their attention during this early period focuses more on their place in the new task environment and on learning the social and technical aspects of the job and the organization.

Because his attention is on learning a new social milieu, the individual puts more emphasis on feedback from the job itself and on task significance. The person also will emphasize other sources of feedback such as that received from coworkers and supervisors. The person's attention is on the context of the job and not on the intrinsic qualities of the job itself.

The reactions just described apply to both newcomers to an organization and to veteran employees who move to new jobs within the same organization. And as Chapter 6 described for socialization experiences in general, when people move from one job to another or from one organization to another, they have the same reactions to the characteristics of the job in the early employment period.

During the period from six months to three years on the job, people attend to all the job characteristics described as important for motivation and performance. The intrinsic qualities of the job itself will be important to them, and they are ready to respond to those qualities. But as time goes on, and the employee masters more complex work, the individual becomes increasingly unresponsive to the intrinsic qualities of the job. The individual will perceive the job as less challenging even though the objective job has not changed. According to one writer:

> . . . in time even the most challenging job assignments and responsibilities can appear less exciting and more habitual to job holders who have successfully mastered and become increasingly accustomed to their everyday task requirements.[46]

With mastery of the job, and felt acceptance in the social environment, the person again turns his attention to contextual features like the quality of supervision, the reward system, and his coworkers. In short, the person puts more emphasis on extrinsic factors during the early and late stages of adaptation to a job. Intrinsic factors receive more emphasis during the middle stage while the person is mastering the task.

. . . .

↵ *Job Design and Stress*

The Opening Episode described how jobs at both the upper and lower reaches of an organization can be stressful for incumbents. Jobs can be stressful if they are too complex, but jobs at lower levels of an organization that have low decision discretion (autonomy) can also be stressful.[47] This type of job may be moderately high in some core job characteristics but low in autonomy, producing a low MPS.

Figure 9-7 shows the basic relationship between the design of a job and stress. Part of what is said here is speculative, because research has confirmed only some relationships shown in the figure. For example, only the upward-sloping segment of the curve on the right side of Figure 9-7 was found in samples of employees from many different organizations.[48] Everything in this section, however, was derived logically from several theoretical and empirical considerations.

Much of what this chapter has said about job characteristics and people's reactions to their jobs deals with the state of activation of an individual induced by the job itself. People have an optimal level of stimulation for effective task performance.[49] Going above this level (extremely high MPS) overtaxes the individual and can

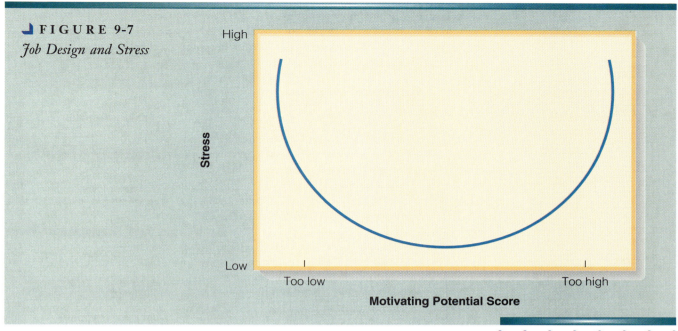

FIGURE 9-7
Job Design and Stress

[Figure axes: Vertical axis labeled "Stress" ranging from Low to High; Horizontal axis labeled "Motivating Potential Score" ranging from "Too low" to "Too high"]

produce high stress and decreased motivation and performance. Jobs with low MPS do not give a person enough stimulation. The individual may then engage in non-task-related behaviors such as talking to coworkers or visiting the water fountain to introduce "enough" stimulation.

Jobs with extremely high MPS are associated with decrements in affective response or behavior. This suggests that job redesign activities should include identifying jobs with extremely high MPS. These jobs should then be "de-enriched," reducing them to a lower, more optimal level of MPS (the center of Figure 9-7).[50] Autonomy, or discretion in decision making, may emerge as an important job characteristic that is associated with stress at all levels of an organization.[51]

International Aspects of Job Design

*T*he International Aspects section of Chapter 7 emphasized differences in the motivational needs that are driving forces in different countries. For example, people in the United States emphasize self-actualization, people in France stress a need for security, and people in the Scandinavian countries emphasize belongingness and love (social) needs.[52] Two implications follow from those cultural differences. Because all cultures do not view self-actualization from work experiences as important, striving for intrinsic rewards from job redesign does not apply to all cultures. Another implication is that cultural differences should guide the choice of individual-based or group-based approaches.

U.S. managers have mostly used individual-based approaches to job design although that emphasis has shifted in the quest to manage for quality. You saw an example of that shift in the earlier case about self-managing work teams. On many occasions in Total Quality Management, group-based job design (self-managing work teams) makes sense. Managers in other countries have mainly emphasized group-based job design. Sweden and Norway in particular have restructured their work systems around self-managing work teams,[53] an approach consistent with their more socially oriented values, desire for quality interpersonal relationships, and little emphasis on competition among individuals.[54]

Changing specific job characteristics also is likely to lead to different reactions in different cultures. For example, efforts to increase autonomy and task identity are not likely to be accepted in countries such as Belgium, Mexico, Greece, Thailand, Turkey, and France. French managers in particular abhor recommendations to decentralize their decision authority, and their subordinates do not expect them to do so.[55]

Ethical Issues in Job Design

Several areas in job design and redesign raise ethical issues for organizations and their managers. The clearest set of issues derives from the discussion about job design and stress. Although research evidence is still accumulating, it suggests that jobs that are excessively low or excessively high in MPS are especially stressful. The ethical issues pivot on whether managers should knowingly assign people to such jobs, redesign such jobs, or arrange for robots and other forms of automation to do the work of low MPS jobs.

Knowingly assigning people to jobs that can induce a dysfunctional stress response poses a clear ethical dilemma to managers. They could argue on utilitarian grounds that such jobs let people earn a living, benefiting people and society. Another utilitarian argument could say that such benefits do not exceed the stress-related costs. Still another argument, based on rights or justice, says it is unethical to expose people to such working conditions. As with any ethical dilemma, the answers do not come quickly or easily.

Jobs with excessively high MPS, which are known to induce dysfunctional stress responses, are candidates for redesign into two or more new jobs. Managers could argue from a utilitarian view that increasing the number of jobs increases labor costs, reduces profit, and reduces the benefits to many people such as customers and stockholders. The counterargument, of course, is the harm to some people from dysfunctionally high stress. The answer to this ethical dilemma is neither simple nor clear. In any event, it is a clear example of a situation in job design where an ethical dialogue should occur.

The work of jobs with low MPS could be done in many cases with automated equipment, sparing people from exposure to potentially dysfunctional stress. If the people are not reassigned to other jobs, the adverse effects on employment that result raise additional ethical questions. A case at the end of the chapter describes robots in an IBM factory. Review that case to get a sense of the ethical questions that automated manufacturing raises for modern organizations.

Self-managing work teams, as described in the earlier case, raise some ethical questions for at least two reasons: (1) people with a low need for affiliation may have little desire for team-based work, and (2) some people may not want high involvement in their work roles, preferring high involvement in nonwork roles instead.[56] Those reasons imply at least two ethical questions. Should involvement in such teams be voluntary for those already employed by a company? Should job applicants be fully informed about the company's use of teams and the likelihood of a team assignment if they are hired?

Multinational and transnational organizations face ethical issues that derive from the cultures in which they operate. As Chapter 7 described, people around the world differ in the needs they consider central to their personalities and lives. People in many countries do not readily accept moving decision authority below the managerial level. They perceive decision making as the proper role of managers, not nonmanagers. This orientation is especially true of Mexico, many South American countries, India, Hong Kong, and Singapore. Employees in Sweden and Austria, however, expect high involvement in decision making.[57] Should managers honor the host national culture, or should they adhere to their home organization's emphasis on self-managing work teams?

The ethical issues raised in this section have no easy answers. The answers can come only from an ethical dialogue guided by explicit ethical values.

Several important implications emerge from this chapter for you and for the design of jobs. The first is related to you as a person and the nature of the needs you are trying to satisfy at work. Recall from Chapter 7 that people (including yourself) vary in the needs they are trying to satisfy in their jobs and careers. The issue for you is the degree of congruency that exists between your need structure and the type of career you are now pursuing. A job congruent with your various needs should be highly satisfying and motivating to you.

Second, reflect upon the outcomes for your work performance that you highly value (Chapter 8). If you place more emphasis on intrinsic outcomes, jobs designed according to the Job Characteristics Theory should be a source of satisfaction and motivation for you. If you place more emphasis on extrinsic outcomes, the opposite conclusion is true. The intrinsic motivational qualities are less important to you than the extrinsic outcomes you get for good performance.

The last implication deals with your relative preferences for jobs designed for groups versus individuals. If you have strong affiliation needs, you should be comfortable with jobs designed for groups or teams of people. If your affiliation needs are weak, you should prefer jobs designed for individuals.

Managers should actively search for ways to tap the growth needs of their employees. You would like to have maximum discretion in designing jobs to fit the needs people are trying to satisfy at work. Remember, though, the importance of growth needs varies from country to country. Unfortunately, getting congruence between individual needs and job design is not always possible. The design of the organization and the underlying technical process may constrain you from being as flexible as you might prefer.

Another important issue is whether the design of jobs you manage is congruent with the organization's technical process. A highly interdependent technical process suggests using individual job design. A technical process built upon teams requires a group-based approach to job design. Incongruity between the technical process and the type of job design can lead to unnecessary frustration for your subordinates.

Changing your behavior as a manager can produce significant changes in the job design of your subordinates. Delegating decision authority increases the autonomy and task significance of your subordinates' jobs. Involving subordinates in decisions can increase skill variety and task significance. If people working for you have strong achievement needs and are unhappy with the jobs they are doing, consider changing some aspects of your management behavior. The change in your behavior will lead to important changes in the design of the jobs of your subordinates. These issues will be raised again in Chapter 12, which returns to the question of leadership and management.

Summary

The Job Characteristics Theory of Work Motivation describes how the design of jobs affects motivation, performance, and satisfaction. The theory specifies several core job characteristics that can affect three internal psychological states and induce high levels of motivation and performance.

The theory includes both individual and work context factors that can affect (moderate) the expected positive relationships between job characteristics and levels of motivation and performance. The strength of a person's need for growth on the job must be strong for a high positive response to the characteristics of the job. Many other factors in a job's context can help or hinder job design such as the design of the organization, technical process, and management behavior.

The diagnosis and redesign of jobs start by getting information about the present state of jobs using a questionnaire similar to the Job Diagnostic Survey. Data collected with the JDS show the job's MPS, the core job characteristics, and affective responses. The MPS can be compared to norms to decide whether a job has an excessively low score. Then the job characteristics that are responsible for that low MPS can be identified.

Jobs can be designed either for groups or for individuals. The basic approach is the same for each. Other factors considered in group-based job design include the internal dynamics of the group and group norms. Countries differ in whether they emphasize individual-based or group-based job design. Scandinavian organizations have emphasized self-managing work teams more than individual-based approaches to work design.

An alternative to the Job Characteristics Theory describes how perceptions of job characteristics develop and the factors that can affect those perceptions. Supervisors, coworkers, and the job redesign process all can positively or negatively affect perceptions, even when the job is not changed.

Jobs can be stressful if they have an extremely high MPS, a point that should not be surprising to you. Jobs that make high performance demands, but are low in autonomy, also can stress incumbents. The potential stress effect of job design is a major ethical issue facing managers.

↳ Key Terms

affective outcomes 224
behavioral outcomes 224
biological approach 224
context satisfaction 229
core job characteristics 226
critical psychological states 224
group-based job design 236

growth need strength (GNS) 228
internal work motivation 225
Job Characteristics Theory 224
Job Diagnostic Survey (JDS) 234
knowledge and skill 228
mechanistic approach 223
moderator variables 227

motivational approach 223
motivating potential 227
perceptual/motor approach 224
self-managing work group 236
Social Information Processing Theory 239
time and job reactions 239

↳ Review and Discussion Questions

1. Discuss examples of work contexts within which you and your fellow students have held jobs. Did the design of the job take advantage of the work context or did it conflict with the work context?

2. Discuss the factors that affect a person's perception of the objective characteristics of a job. What implications do you see for a job redesign strategy?

3. Jobs can be designed for groups or individuals. What individual needs should be strong in people who will work in a group or team setting? Which countries tend to emphasize one approach instead of the other?

4. Discuss the role of individual differences in job design. Which needs discussed in earlier chapters are closely related to the concept of growth need strength? Will you find differences in important needs in different cultures around the world?

5. Discuss the role of time in your reactions to the characteristics of your job. If the students in your class differ in age, discuss the different experiences people of different ages have had with time and job reactions.

6. The argument was presented that jobs with high performance demands and little individual control (autonomy) are stressful. Discuss this argument using examples from your own experience or the experience of others in the class.

7. Review the discussion of ethics and job design. Are those real issues facing managers in modern organizations?

↳ Case

THE TREADFREE DATA ENTRY OPERATORS

The following case will let you diagnose the job of some data entry operators. It includes data collected with the Job Diagnostic Survey. Here are some questions to have in mind while reading the case:

Source: Developed from J. Richard Hackman, and Greg R. Oldham, WORK REDESIGN (pp. 131, 133), © 1980 by Addison-Wesley Publishing Co., Inc. Reprinted by permission of the publisher.

1. Given the results of the diagnosis, how would you change this job?

2. What steps would you take to improve this job's core characteristics?

All data entry for the Treadfree Manufacturing Corporation was done in one organization unit, headed by a Manager of Data Entry Services. This manager is responsible for two supervisors, two clerks, and about twenty data entry and data verification machine operators. Most of the operators are young, on their first or second full-time job, and have high school diplomas.

As seen in Figure 9-8, most work came from five departments: accounting (30 percent), engineering (10 percent), sales (20 percent), personnel (20 percent), and production staff (10 percent). Another 10 percent of the work comes from miscellaneous departments throughout Treadfree.

Representatives of client departments bring work to be done to a receiving clerk seated at a desk at a corridor window in the data entry room. The clerk accepts the work, completes a work order form that indicates job specifications (such as special formats or codes), and the due date for the job. The data and work order form are then given to Supervisor I, who checks the materials to make sure that they are clear and legible, and that the due date is realistic given other work in progress. If there is a problem with the work as submitted, Supervisor I returns it to the receiving clerk, who calls the client and resolves the difficulties. Problems having to do with due dates are negotiated directly between Supervisor I and the client.

Supervisor I keeps a queue of jobs to be done on the shelves by her desk, and when a data entry operator becomes free, gives the next job to be done to that individual. For especially large or especially urgent jobs, the supervisor may break the work into several parts and give the parts to several operators. Occasionally it is necessary to have an operator set aside work in progress to do part of a rush job.

When a job (or portion of a job, if the work was broken up when assigned) is completed, it is given by the data entry operator to Supervisor II. This supervisor makes a quick check for accuracy of codes and formats, and notes the due date for the work to be completed. He then places the work in a queue on his shelves and gives the next highest priority job to the next available verifier. All jobs are verified using a machine which confirms that data were entered correctly. Verifiers correct any errors they find.

After a job (or portion of a job) has been verified, it goes to the assembly clerk. The assembly clerk compiles the original work submitted with a printout of the entered data. The assembly clerk then calls the client to say that the job may be picked up at the assembly clerk's corridor window.

Supervisor I is responsible for the receiving clerk, the ten data entry operators, and any problems having to do with scheduling or due dates. When work is especially heavy, she may obtain permission from the manager to bring on some part-time help. Supervisor II is responsible for the assembly clerk, the ten verifiers, and any problems having to do with quality and accuracy. If clients discover problems in the work

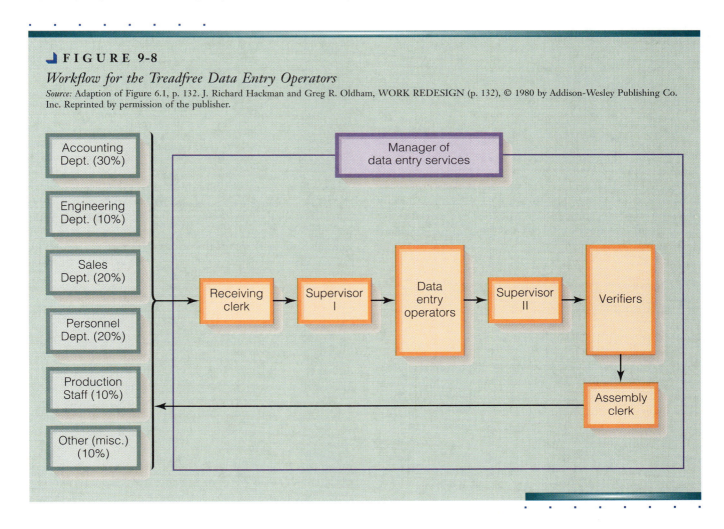

FIGURE 9-8

Workflow for the Treadfree Data Entry Operators

Source: Adaption of Figure 6.1, p. 132. J. Richard Hackman and Greg R. Oldham, WORK REDESIGN (p. 132), © 1980 by Addison-Wesley Publishing Co. Inc. Reprinted by permission of the publisher.

Diagnostic Profile for the Treadfree Data Entry Operators

Source: J. Richard Hackman and Greg R. Oldham, WORK REDESIGN (p. 134), © 1980 by Addison-Wesley Publishing Co., Inc. Reprinted by permission of the publisher.

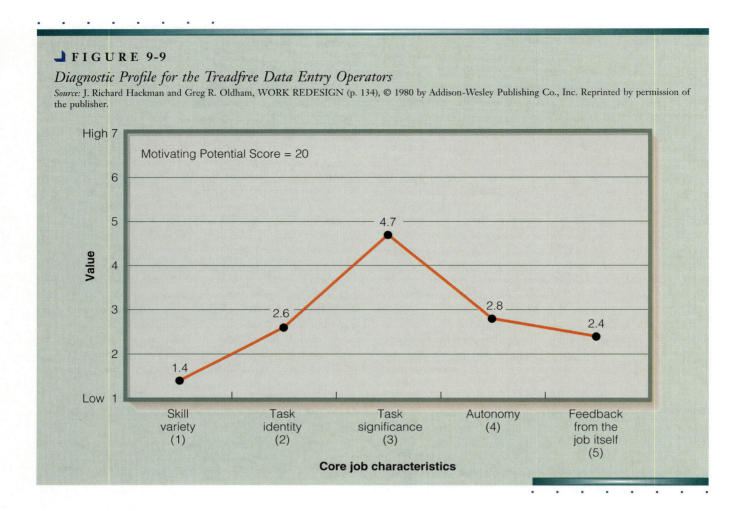

after picking it up, they contact Supervisor II, who will have someone who is free (or can be made so) among the verifying staff do the corrections. Since it takes somewhat longer to initially enter data than it does to verify it, having the verifiers do any corrections "balances" the workloads of the data entry operators and verifiers. On occasion, however, it is necessary for Supervisors I and II to move someone from data entry to verifying or vice versa to deal with a "lump" in the workflow.

An evaluation of the job using the Job Diagnostic Survey (JDS) yielded the diagnostic profile shown in Figure 9-9. The job characteristic scores have been confirmed using multiple observers (supervisors and outside researchers) and multiple methods (interviews and the JDS).

▗ Case

ROBOTICS AT IBM

The following case describes the introduction of manufacturing robots at one of IBM's manufacturing facilities. Many workers were displaced by the robots; others remained to work in an automated manufacturing environment. Address the following questions in your analysis:

Source: J. Marcom, Jr., "Slimming Down: IBM Is Automating, Simplifying Products to Beat Asian Rivals," *Wall Street Journal*, April 14, 1986, pp. 1, 20. Reprinted by permission of the *Wall Street Journal*, © 1986 Dow Jones & Company, Inc. All Rights Reserved Worldwide.

1. What effects did the introduction of robotics have on the jobs of these workers who continued to work in the plant?
2. Which job characteristics of those people were the most likely to be affected by the move to robotic manufacturing?
3. What are the ethical implications of moving to such manufacturing methods? Consider this question from utilitarian, rights, and justice perspectives.

Americans bought four million low-priced computer printers last year, and 80% of them came from Japan. Following a familiar pattern, the Japanese printer makers took technology developed by International Business Machines Corp., drove costs down, pushed reliability up and quickly dominated the $2 billion-plus retail market.

But here, tucked among the trees of IBM's 1,250-acre complex, a new building symbolizes the U.S. computer giant's determination to strike back. About the size of a Kmart—and about as plain-looking—the factory produces the Proprinter, among the first payoffs from a far-reaching IBM drive to best the Japanese.

Spurred by growing competition from Japan and other Asian countries, IBM in the late 1970s set a new goal: to become the world's lowest-cost producer of computers and related equipment. It began a radical rethinking of its manufacturing processes. Turning the tables, IBM sometimes borrowed Japanese techniques. . . .

The Charlotte plant, designed to build one million printers a year, is crucial to IBM's bid to compete in a market that the Japanese conquered years ago. In it, a battery of machines molds plastic into Proprinter parts. Conveyors take bins filled with covers, frames and circuitry to robots that methodically snap together the finished product. People are scarce; one person mans a station on each assembly line, and a few others stand by if the computers running the factory call for help. . . .

IBM, however, says the Proprinter is just the first of several products to be made by the new Charlotte plant. Similar automated plants making other products are opening around the U.S. A $350 million overhaul of IBM's Lexington, Ky., typewriter plant is nearly complete. Robots at a new facility in Austin, Texas, assemble the IBM Personal Computer Convertible, a $1,995 portable computer announced early this month. In Raleigh, N.C., a new robotized assembly line is building color monitors for IBM computer terminals; IBM has been buying the assembled monitors in Japan. . . .

The push for automation entails a winnowing of IBM's product line to fewer, more versatile products—offering greater economies in manufacturing and, IBM says, greater reliability. It also results in a shift in IBM's labor needs [requiring the retraining of] assembly workers . . . as technicians, programmers or secretaries. IBM did 3,000 retraining courses for its 6,000 workers at Lexington, some of whom were retrained more than once.

Few American companies, and no other electronics concern, can match IBM's resources. Many of the robots, much of the design and factory-management software and all the computers used in its factories are IBM's own. Despite a sales slowdown last year, IBM increased spending on new plants and property 33% to $6.1 billion. The pace continues strong, and much of the effect won't be seen for years.

"The amount of money we're spending in 1986 for 1990 through 1995 is extraordinary," says John F. Akers, the president and chief executive.

The changes brought by IBM's push are dramatic in older plants. The Selectric typewriters that IBM has built in Lexington since 1962 are among IBM's highest-volume products, but the plant fell short in crucial measures of efficiency. IBM made a bewildering variety of models and options—the Selectric used 2,700 parts and came in 55,000 combinations—which required huge inventories of parts and finished goods. And there were 36 color choices.

As cheap microelectronics began to replace complex mechanical innards, dozens of new competitors emerged. IBM decided 36 colors were a luxury that it couldn't afford, and it shifted to a Model T approach. IBM tore out the rows of workbenches where skilled workers carefully put together the Selectric. In went a winding 7 1/2-mile-long computer-controlled railroad along which robots snap keys on keyboards, flexible machining systems place chips on circuit boards, and video cameras automatically check the print quality of finished products. IBM cut the human labor time in each machine by 75%. . . .

The machine was "designed for automation," another oft-heard buzzword at IBM nowadays, with 60 parts, against 150 for comparable printers when IBM began designing the product two years ago. One molded-plastic side frame took the place of 20 other parts. Motors twist and lock in place, eliminating four screws, four nuts and four washers. The design is "the real key," says Frank A. Metz Jr., an IBM senior vice president and group executive.

The parts are designed to snap together easily but tightly, regardless of whether robots or humans do the snapping. Instead of making a blanket decision to automate, IBM decided separately the most efficient way to do each task, comparing robots, special-purpose machine tools, manual assembly and outside contracting. In Charlotte, robots do must of the work. But a human is needed to make one adjustment that affects the distance of print head to platen, the plate against which the head strikes a piece of paper.

"We wanted it to be a gnat's eyelash—with the robot it ends up being that plus a bit," says J. Charley Rogers Jr., product manager.

The fewer parts there are, the more reliable the product and the smaller the inventory-management job. IBM is gearing up to make many of the parts in the Charlotte factory. It requires outside suppliers to make frequent deliveries—with zero defects—following the Japanese "just-in-time" practice to minimize inventories. The plant doesn't even have a warehouse. . . .

The factory has eight separate assembly lines, allowing IBM to phase in production gradually and switch production to yet-to-be-announced models. The plant's robots could conceivably be reprogrammed to make, say, toasters, if they fit the standard "platform" of the printer case. Personal computers seem one obvious possibility; IBM says the Austin plant making the PC Convertible uses a process similar to Charlotte's.

Trays filled with parts are carried to an automated storage system, which holds a few hours' supplies and serves trays as needed to the robot assembly stations. Throughout, computers control the process and flash error messages to operators when, for instance, a robot is unable to insert a part. An overhead conveyor carries finished goods from assembly areas to test areas and on to a highly automated packing line.

IBM figures packing machines—which include machines to mold the Styrofoam pads that cushion the printer in the box—cut packaging costs by more than half to $2 a printer. The next human hands to touch the product, once it leaves the test station, are the buyer's, when the box is opened.

[1]R. A. Karasek, "Job Demands, Job Decision Latitude, and Mental Strain: Implications for Job Redesign," *Administrative Science Quarterly* 24 (1979): 285–308; R. A. Karasek, "Job Socialization and Job Strain: The Implications of Two Related Psychosocial Mechanisms for Job Design," in R. Gardell and G. Johansson, eds., *Working Life: A Social Science Contribution to Work Reform* (New York: John Wiley & Sons, 1981), pp. 75–94.

[2]A. Smith, *An Inquiry Into the Nature and Causes of the Wealth of Nations* (London: George Routledge & Sons, Limited, 1893, originally published in 1776), Ch. 1.

[3]M. A. Campion and P. W. Thayer, "Job Design: Approaches, Outcomes, and Trade-offs," *Organizational Dynamics* 15 (1987): 66–79.

[4]M. A. Campion and C. L. McClelland, "Interdisciplinary Examination of the Costs and Benefits of Enlarged Jobs: A Job Design Quasi-Experiment," *Journal of Applied Psychology* 76 (1991): 186–98.

[5]J. R. Hackman and G. Oldham, "Motivation through the Design of Work: Test of a Theory," *Organizational Behavior and Human Performance* 16 (1976): 250–79; J. R. Hackman and G. Oldham, *Work Redesign* (Reading, Mass.: Addison-Wesley, 1980), and other citations throughout this section.

[6]L. R. Berlinger, W. H. Glick, and R. C. Rodgers, "Job Enrichment and Performance Improvement," in J. P. Campbell and R. J. Campbell, eds., *Productivity in Organizations: New Perspectives from Industrial and Organizational Psychology* (1988), pp. 219–54; M. A. Campion, "Interdisciplinary Approaches to Job Design: A Constructive Replication with Extensions," *Journal of Applied Psychology* 73 (1988): 467–81; Campion and McClelland, *Interdisciplinary Examination"*; J. E. Champoux, *"A Multivariate Test of the Job Characteristics Theory of Work Motivation,"* *Journal of Organizational Behavior* 12 (1991): 431–46; Y. Fried and G. R. Ferris, "The Validity of the Job Characteristics Model: A Review and Meta-Analysis," *Personnel Psychology* 40 (1987): 287–322; R. W. Griffin, "Effects of Work Redesign on Employee Perceptions, Attitudes, and Behaviors: A Long-Term Investigation," *Academy of Management Journal* 34 (1991): 425–35; Hackman and Oldham, *Work Redesign*, p. 97; G. Johns, J. L. Xie, and Y. Fang, "Mediating and Moderating Effects in Job Design," *Journal of Management* 18 (1992): 657–76; K. H. Roberts and W. Glick, "The Job Characteristics Approach to Task Design: A Critical Review," *Journal of Applied Psychology* 66 (1981): 193–217.

[7]The original presentations of the theory did not describe the connections between affective and behavioral outcomes as is done here. The connections appear logical and allow easier and clearer description of the theory.

[8]E. L. Deci, *Intrinsic Motivation* (New York: Plenum Press, 1975).

[9]R. W. Griffin, *Task Design: An Integrative Approach* (Glenview, Ill.: Scott, Foresman, 1982).

[10]Hackman and Oldham, *Work Redesign*, pp. 78–80.

[11]Ibid., p. 81.

[12]Growth need strength is not always discussed as specific to the job itself. It is clear from the way it is measured that this was the authors' intent. See Hackman and Oldham, *Work Redesign*, pp. 287–93.

[13]Johns, Xie, and Fang, "Mediating and Moderating Effects."

[14]Fried and Ferris, "Validity of the Job Characteristics Model"; Hackman and Oldham, *Work Redesign*; E. A Hogan and D. A. Martell, "A Confirmatory Structural Equations Analysis of the Job Characteristics Model," *Organizational Behavior and Human Decision Processes* 39 (1987): 242–63; Griffin, *Task Redesign*; Roberts and Glick, "Job Characteristics Approach"; B. T. Loher, R. A. Noe, N. L. Moeller, and M. P. Fitzgerald, "A Meta-Analysis of the Relation of Job Characteristics to Job Satisfaction," *Journal of Applied Psychology* 70 (1985): 280–89; P. E. Spector, "Higher-Order Need Strength as a Moderator of the Job Scope–Employee Outcome Relationship: A Meta-Analysis," *Journal of Occupational Psychology* 58 (1985): 119–27; R. B. Tiegs, L. E. Tetrick, and Y. Fried, "Growth Need Strength and

Context Satisfactions as Moderators of the Relations of the Job Characteristics Model," *Journal of Management* 18 (1992): 575–93.

[15]G. R. Oldham, "Job Characteristics and Internal Motivation: The Moderating Effect of Interpersonal and Individual Variables," *Human Relations* 29 (1976): 559–69.

[16]A. A. Abdil-Halim, "Individual and Interpersonal Moderators of Employee Reactions to Job Characteristics: A Re-Examination," *Personnel Psychology* 32 (1979): 121–37; J. E. Champoux, "The Moderating Effect of Work Context Satisfactions on the Curvilinear Relationship between Job Scope and Affective Response," *Human Relations* 34 (1981): 503–15; J. E. Champoux, "A Multivariate Test of the Moderating Effect of Work Context Satisfactions on the Curvilinear Relationship between Job Scope and Affective Outcomes," *Human Relations* 45 (1992): 87–111; G. R. Ferris and D. C. Gilmore, "The Moderating Role of Work Context in Job Design Research: A Test of Competing Models," *Academy of Management Journal* 27 (1984): 885–92.

[17]Champoux, "A Multivariate Test" (1992).

[18]Hackman and Oldham, *Work Redesign*, p. 105.

[19]The material in this section depends heavily on Griffin, *Task Design*. Other sources are noted in the appropriate places. Some material also is speculative because little research has been done in many of the areas discussed.

[20]D. J. Brass, "Technology and the Structuring of Jobs: Employee Satisfaction, Performance, and Influence," *Organizational Behavior and Human Decision Processes* 35 (1985): 216–40; D. A. Buchanan and D. Boddy, "Advanced Technology and the Quality of Working Life: The Effects of Word Processing on Video Typists," *Journal of Occupational Psychology* 55 (1982): 1–11.

[21]M. H. Safizadeh, "The Case of Workgroups in Manufacturing Operations," *California Management Review* 33 (1991): 61–82.

[22]M. R. Kelley, "New Process Technology, Job Design, and Work Organization," *American Sociological Review* 55 (1990): 191–208; P. L. Nemetz and L. W. Fry, "Flexible Manufacturing Organizations: Implications for Strategy Formulation and Organization Design," *Academy of Management Review* 13 (1988): 627–38; R. J. Schonberger, *Japanese Manufacturing Techniques: Nine Hidden Lessons in Simplicity* (New York: Free Press, 1982); R. J. Schonberger, *World Class Manufacturing: The Lessons of Simplicity Applied* (New York: Free Press, 1982).

[23]J. W. Dean, Jr., and S. A. Snell, "Integrated Manufacturing and Job Design: Moderation Effects of Organizational Inertia," *Academy of Management Journal* 34 (1991): 776–804.

[24]R. J. Schonberger, "The Transfer of Japanese Manufacturing Management Approaches to U.S. Industry," *Academy of Management Review* 7 (1982): 479–87.

[25]J. A. Davy, R. E. White, N. J. Merrit, and K. Gritzmacher, "A Derivation of the Underlying Constructs of Just-in-Time Management Systems," *Academy of Management Journal* 35 (1992): 653–70.

[26]V. Vroom and P. Yetton *Leadership and Decision Making* (Pittsburgh: University of Pittsburgh Press, 1973).

[27]R. J. House, "A Path-Goal Theory of Leader Effectiveness," *Administrative Science Quarterly* 16 (1971): 321–38.

[28]Hackman and Oldham, *Work Redesign*, Chs. 5 and 6; Griffin, *Task Design*.

[29]Hackman and Oldham, *Work Redesign*; Griffin, *Task Design*.

[30]Hackman and Oldham, *Work Redesign*, pp. 135–42.

[31]B. Saparito, "Cutting Costs without Cutting People," *Fortune*, May 25, 1987, p. 27.

[32]J. R. Hackman, "The Design of Self-Managing Work Groups," in B. King, S. Streufert, and F. E. Fiedler, eds., *Managerial Control and Organizational Democracy* (Washington, D.C.: Winston & Sons, 1978); Hackman and Oldham, *Work Redesign*, Ch. 7; E. Sundstrom, K. P. De

Meuse, and D. Futrell, "Work Teams: Applications and Effectiveness," *American Psychologist* 45 (1990): 120–33.

[33]I. D. Steiner, *Group Process and Productivity* (New York: Academic Press, 1972).

[34]I. L. Janis, *Groupthink*, 2d. ed. (Boston: Houghton Mifflin, 1982); G. Moorhead, "Groupthink: Hypothesis in Need of Testing," *Group and Organization Studies* (December 1982). Chapter 14, "Decision-Making and Problem-Solving Processes," examines the groupthink phenomenon in more detail.

[35]J. Barker, "Tightening the Iron Cage: Concertive Control in Self-Managing Teams," *Administrative Science Quarterly* 38 (1993): 408–37.

[36]Roberts and Glick, "Job Characteristics Approach," p. 196.

[37]G. Salancik and J. Pfeffer, "An Examination of Need-Satisfaction Models of Job Attitudes," *Administrative Science Quarterly* 22 (1977): 427–56; G. Salancik and J. Pfeffer, "A Social Information Processing Approach to Job Attitudes and Task Design," *Administrative Science Quarterly* 23 (1978): 224–53; R. W. Griffin, M. A. Welsh, and G. Moorhead, "Perceived Task Characteristics and Employee Performance: A Literature Review," *Academy of Management Review* 6 (1981): 655–64; J. Thomas and R. W. Griffin, "The Social Information Processing Model of Task Design: A Review of the Literature," *Academy of Management Review* 8 (1983): 672–82.

[38]Salancik and Pfeffer, "Examination of Need-Satisfaction Models"; Salancik and Pfeffer, "A Social Information Processing Approach."

[39]C. A. O'Reilly and D. F. Caldwell "Informational Influence as a Determinant of Perceived Task Characteristics and Job Satisfaction," *Journal of Applied Psychology* 64 (1979): 157–65; S. E. White and T. R. Mitchell, "Job Enrichment versus Social Cues: A Comparison and Competitive Test," *Journal of Applied Psychology* 64 (1979): 1–9.

[40]Salancik and Pfeffer, "A Social Information Processing Approach."

[41]Berlinger, Glick, and Rodgers, "Job Enrichment"; D. F. Caldwell and C. A. O'Reilly, "Task Perception and Job Satisfaction: A Question of Causality," *Journal of Applied Psychology* 67 (1982): 361–69; R. W. Griffin, "Objective and Social Sources of Information in Task Redesign: A Field Experiment," *Administrative Science Quarterly* 28 (1983): 184–200; Thomas and Griffin, "The Social Information Processing Model"; M. Kilduff and D. T. Regan, "What People Say and What They Do: The Differential Effects of Informational Cues and Task Design," *Organizational Behavior and Human Decision Processes* 41 (1988): 83–97.

[42]Griffin, *Task Design*, pp. 169–71.

[43]Griffin, "Objective and Social Sources of Information."

[44]Griffin, *Task Design*, p. 171.

[45]R. Katz, "Job Longevity as a Situational Factor in Job Satisfaction," *Administrative Science Quarterly* 23 (1978): 204–23; R. Katz, "The Influence of Job Longevity on Employee Reactions to Task Characteristics," *Human Relations* 31 (1978): 703–25; R. Katz, "Time and Work: Toward an Integrative Perspective," in B. Staw and L. L. Cummings, eds., *Research in Organizational Behavior*, vol. 2 (Greenwich, Conn.: JAI Press, 1980), pp. 81–127; R. Katz, "Managing Careers: The Influence of Job and Group Longevities," in R. Katz, ed., *Career Issues in Human Resource Management* (New York: Prentice-Hall, 1982), pp. 154–81.

[46]Katz, "Managing Careers," p. 160.

[47]Karasek, "Job Demands."

[48]J. E. Champoux, "A Three Sample Test of Some Extensions to the Job Characteristics Model of Work Motivation," *Academy of Management Journal* 23 (1980): 466–78; Champoux, "Moderating Effect"; Champoux, "A Serendipitous Field Experiment"; Champoux, "A Multivariate Test" (1992). Some of Karasek's findings also suggest the downturn. See Karasek, "Job Demands," p. 304.

[49]W. E. Scott, Jr., "Activation Theory and Task Design," *Organizational Behavior and Human Performance* 1 (1966); 3–30.

[50]Champoux, "A Three Sample Test."

[51]Karasek, "Job Socialization"; M. L. Fox, D. J. Dwyer, and D. C. Ganster, "Effects of Stressful Job Demands and Control on Physiological and Attitudinal Outcomes in a Hospital Setting," *Academy of Management Journal* 36 (1993): 289–318.

[52]G. Hofstede, *Culture's Consequences: International Differences in Work-Related Values* (Beverly Hills, Calif.: Sage Publications, 1984).

[53]C. Berggren, *Alternatives to Lean Production: Work Organization in the Swedish Auto Industry* (Cornell International Industrial and Labor Relations Report No. 22, December 1992).

[54]G. Hofstede, "Motivation, Leadership, and Organization: Do American Theories Apply Abroad?" *Organizational Dynamics* 9 (1980): 42–63; Hofstede, *Culture's Consequences*, Ch. 6.

[55]Hofstede, "Motivation," pp. 56–59.

[56]Champoux, "A Three-Sample Test."

[57]Hofstede, *Culture's Consequences*.

II   *Individual Processes in Organizations*

◢ BALANCING ACT

*T*he executive described in this case has used many ideas developed in this section, probably without realizing it. He has done much to motivate his subordinates to high performance levels. Read the case. Use the concepts and ideas developed so far in the book for your analysis. What is this executive doing right and why does it work?

Case Description

As Vice President of research at Genentech Inc., a biotechnology company, David W. Martin Jr. is the bridge between two different worlds: business and academia.

His boss, a former venture capitalist, is interested in products and profits; his subordinates, 200 high-powered scientists, are dedicated to ideas and research. Dr. Martin's job is to ensure that the twain somehow meet.

The trickiest part of this delicate balancing act, says the thin, energetic executive, is to keep his scientists focused on product-oriented research without destroying their motivation.

"You want them to feel they have the freedom to follow their instincts," he says, sitting in his small, book-lined office in South San Francisco. "But you don't want them to go off on tangents that are unlikely to be productive for the company in the long run."

To keep the focus, he uses very few sticks, but just about every carrot available to the "progressive" manager, from granting increased autonomy to cheerleading in the hallways to handing out checks and stock options. And he tolerates the odd behavior of his unbuttoned-down subordinates, who have been known to tamper with a colleague's report for fun and to post phony corporate memos asking for contributions for executive pay raises.

Managing high-technology researchers is one of the most daunting management tasks around, Robert Burgelman, an associate professor of management at Stanford Business School, observes. "You can't plan a breakthrough," he says. "Scientists are oriented toward methods and managers are oriented toward results."

Source: Developed from K. A. Hughes, "Balancing Act: How One Manager Walks the Narrow Line between Corporate Goals and Basic Research," *Wall Street Journal*, November 10, 1986, p. 14D. Reprinted by permission of the *Wall Street Journal*, © 1986 Dow Jones & Company, Inc. All Rights Reserved Worldwide.

Dr. Martin, 45 years old, came from the scientists' camp. Four years ago he was a professor in medicine and biochemistry at the University of California in San Francisco. He had spent four years in medical school, 20 years doing medical and scientific research—and no time ever in business.

Recruited to be Genentech's first-ever vice president, research, he tried to prepare by taking a course at the California Institute of Technology on managing research and development. It was "expensive and worthless," he says. "It didn't teach you how to motivate, how to say no, how to prioritize, how to focus or how to organize highly trained scientists." Gaylord Nichols, director of programs for the Industrial Relations Center at Cal Tech, responds, "He completely misunderstood the course. The course was geared toward planning research and development rather than the management of scientists."

In the end, Dr. Martin learned his management skills simply by doing them, in what he now describes as an "initiation by fire."

He says he was lured to Genentech, where he has an annual research budget of more than $10 million, by the chance to prove that basic research could be profitable. His annual salary of $220,000 and a hefty package of stock options weren't a consideration, he says, because he already was well-paid.

Genentech, founded a decade ago, was the first biotechnology company to go public. . . . It was the first biotech concern to take a drug from discovery to market—a cloned human growth hormone. Dr. Martin's responsibility is to continue that success by bringing along new products. He meets every week with Genentech's chief executive officer, Robert A. Swanson, who, he says, conveys one steady message: "More products, more products."

But the ideas for those products must be coaxed from Dr. Martin's squadron of scientists. That requires much special care, including, for example, an offbeat management system that features awards of autonomy.

Dr. Martin allows his best scientists to "follow their noses" full time with little supervision, in the hope that such research eventually will yield a product. About half the scientists are allowed to devote about 20% of their time to their own projects. The rest are kept on a tight rein.

"If you tell scientists to give 100% to a project, and they aren't interested, you won't get a product," he explains. "But if you say, put 75% into this and 25% on your own work, they work much harder."

Most of Genentech's current research uses gene splicing to produce or "clone" human proteins for use as treatments against diseases. Over the past three years, company scientists have cloned "factor VIII," a blood-clotting agent needed by hemophiliacs. They have also cloned tumor necrosis factor, which appear to break apart tumor cells, and inhibin, a substance that may lead to the production of a male contraceptive.

In overseeing that research, Dr. Martin isn't simply a businessman trying to bend the lofty interests of researchers to his own capitalist ends. As a veteran biochemist with a reputation for research in inherited immune deficiencies, he also uses his technical knowledge to lead his workers. He says he spends about one-third of his 75-hour to 85-hour workweek poring over medical and scientific journals.

"He knows the scientific literature better than anyone else I've ever seen," says David Goeddel, Genentech's director of research in molecular biology. "That forces everyone else to keep up."

Beyond that, Dr. Martin uses an array of incentives. One way to persuade scientists to pursue profitable projects is to give them a piece of the company. All his researchers own some Genentech stock, whose price has shot up some 700% since its first public offering in 1980, making some of them millionaires.

Yet they remain scientists, albeit unusually wealthy ones. Despite their stakes in the company, some of the scientists given free range have wandered into projects that aren't likely to yield commercially useful results. Dr. Martin has allowed one group of his stars to work on a vaccine for acquired immune deficiency syndrome, or AIDS, though he thinks liability problems would make questionable the commercial value of any such product.

One staff scientist, Arthur Levinson, spends about half his time on cancer research that isn't expected to produce commercial results for years. In return, however, Mr. Levinson pitched in to help develop a vaccine for hepatitis B, and came up with a more efficient way to produce it.

To keep scientists on track, Dr. Martin most frequently applies what he calls "subtle pressure." Projects that he considers useful are given his enthusiasm and support. And when those projects succeed, he reaches into his desk to write a "Genencheck"—a quick reward of up to $1,000. For special break-throughs, he doles out stock options.

Sometimes he also engaged in cheerleading—literally. To foster peer recognition for a scientist bringing in a successful project, Dr. Martin has been known to lead his researchers in a chant of "Ahooo! DNA! DNA! DNA!" (DNA is the genetic code responsible for the growth and development of living organisms, and so is the starting point of most of the scientists' work.)

Dr. Martin rarely will flatly refuse to allow a scientist to embark on a project. But he will set short deadlines for work he considers unpromising. He once turned down a project on leuroregulin, a possible anti-cancer agent. But, he recalls, the scientist pushing the project "begged." He was given six weeks to reach a particular milestone. When he failed to do so, Dr. Martin pulled the plug. By that time, he says, the scientist agreed it was time to quit.

But some scientists will disregard even a flat "no," he says. Earlier this year he tried to halt work on developing interleukin-1 and interleukin-2, proteins that help regulate the immune system, on the ground that there were better projects with clearer product applications. He later discovered that a scientist, working on his own time, had managed to clone interleukin-1. That was interesting science—but not particularly good for the company. Dr. Martin says he simply told the wayward scientist that his time would be better spent on more useful projects.

Dr. Martin says he's tried to make it understood that, after four of his refusals, work on a given project really must stop. If a scientist perseveres after that, Dr. Martin gradually strips away his technicians and equipment, making continued disobedience all but impossible.

For all that, Dr. Martin says his single biggest error as a high-tech manager came not with unruly scientists but with subservient ones. Some scientists, he says, came to take his suggestions as commands. One hapless crew pursued for six weeks an approach he mentioned. "The researchers just didn't know what a suggestion from a vice president meant," he says.

Mistakes like that are rare. Homegrown though it is, Dr. Martin's management system to work. Possibly the highest praise comes from Mr. Goeddel, the molecular biologist, who says, "No one good has left since he's been here."

Case Analysis

Scientists are difficult people to manage. They want autonomy and like to pursue their own research interests. They have a strong Need for Achievement and highly value recognition of their work by their peers. Scientists identify more with their profession than with the company employing them, making the job of managing scientists almost impossible.[1] Dr. Martin's background as a scientist helped him understand those characteristics of scientists. He showed his understanding by the way he used increased autonomy as an extrinsic reward for good performance.

Although the case described Martin's actions as mainly focused on motivation, he also was affecting the socialization of his scientists. Genentech's culture included some clearly defined pivotal role behaviors. The scientists' research had to focus on product development. They could not pursue only what interested them as scientists. Mr. Swanson, the chief executive officer, was clear in his desire for "more products, more products."

Martin directed several of his motivational efforts toward ensuring the pivotal role behavior. For example, if a scientist did not redirect his behavior after four tries, Martin pulled the scientist's equipment and technicians to get the pivotal role behavior. Martin steadfastly focused on ensuring the pivotal role behavior and reinforcing the cultural value of innovative and profitable product development.

You also saw an example of peripheral role behavior. Dr. Martin clearly tolerated his scientists' unusual behavior such as tampering with reports and asking for contributions for executive pay raises.

Dr. Martin's motivational efforts served important socialization goals. The cultural values of the veteran scientists got continual reinforcement. New scientists would both see those efforts and experience them directly, giving the newcomers clear direction in the Entry/Encounter stage of socialization. This culture had strong values of continued high performance and innovation. Mr. Goeddel's comment at the end of the case is evidence of such values.

Dr. Martin was consistent in using valued extrinsic rewards. He correctly identified both monetary incentives and increased autonomy as highly valued by his scientists. By giving a "Genencheck" when a scientist completed a project successfully, Dr. Martin reinforced the expectancy of performance leading to extrinsic outcomes. His actions increased his scientists' perception that high performance leads to high rewards. He reinforced pivotal role behavior by the same actions.

Dr. Martin used several different approaches to manage motivation. He used positive reinforcement and punishment most frequently. Dr. Martin used Goal Setting when he wanted to redirect a scientist's behavior. Note how specific he was in setting the time deadline in the leuroregulin project.

Dr. Martin focused more on the Performance-Outcome Expectancy than on the Effort-Performance Expectancy. Of the two expectancies, he needed to worry less about the latter because of the training and experience of his scientists. Although not all scientific projects will produce desired results, judgment based on experience and knowledge plays a key role in identifying projects with a high chance of success.

References and Notes

[1] A. Gouldner, "Cosmopolitans and Locals," *Administrative Science Quarterly* 2 (1957): 282–92; W. Kornhauser, *Scientists in Industry* (Berkeley: University of California Press, 1963).

Group and Interpersonal Processes in Organizations

. . . .

Section Overview

*F*igure III-1 is an overview of the major sections of this book and the chapters in Section III. This section introduces you to group dynamics and interpersonal processes in organizations. The main topics include behavior in and between groups, conflict in organizations, and leadership and management. Each chapter discusses international aspects of the topics and the ethical issues they raise.

The first chapter in this section (Chapter 10) describes group and intergroup processes in organizations. It begins by distinguishing between formal and informal groups in organizations and then lays a basic conceptual foundation. The chapter offers various perspectives on groups in organizations. It then asks you to do a short exercise that assesses some of your needs that can be related to your behavior in a group. The chapter builds a model of group formation that should help you understand how and why cohesive groups form in organizations. Chapter 10 features a section on the group dynamics effects of workforce diversity. It includes discussions on group effectiveness and how you can become an effective member of a group. The chapter also examines how managers can use groups in their organizations in ways that avoid typical group dysfunctions.

Chapter 11 focuses on conflict management in organizations. It begins by defining conflict and distinguishing it from competition and cooperation. The chapter describes three philosophies of conflict—traditional, behavioral, and interactionist. It builds a perspective from those philosophies that provides a background for the rest of the chapter. Conflict episodes are then discussed along with the dynamics of conflict behavior. The episodic feature of conflict in organizations is a key point. The chapter develops a model of conflict management that can guide you in choosing when to reduce conflict and when to increase conflict. That model can also help you diagnose conflict in an organization.

The third chapter in this section (Chapter 12) describes leadership processes in organizations. It views leadership as an influence process that uses several bases of power to affect the behavior of other people. Several approaches to the study of

FIGURE III-1
Section III Overview

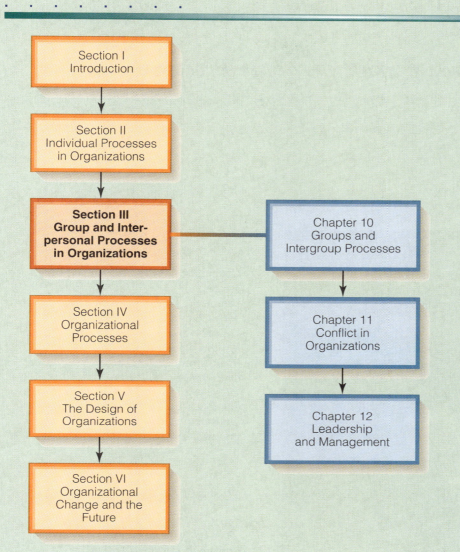

Section I
Introduction

Section II
Individual Processes
in Organizations

**Section III
Group and Inter-
personal Processes
in Organizations**

Chapter 10
Groups and
Intergroup Processes

Chapter 11
Conflict in
Organizations

Section IV
Organizational
Processes

Chapter 12
Leadership
and Management

Section V
The Design of
Organizations

Section VI
Organizational
Change and the
Future

leadership have evolved over the years. The trait approaches looked for personal qualities that distinguished effective from ineffective leaders or leaders from followers. Behavioral approaches focused on leader behavior and leader effectiveness. Contingency approaches studied the effects of different behaviors in different situations. The chapter also describes some alternative views to the major approaches. It builds a summary perspective of leadership, distilled from the various approaches and views of leadership in organizations.

10

Groups and Intergroup Processes

• *Groups form a major part of modern organizational life. Understanding groups and their dynamics will help you adapt to the groups you will find in organizations.*

After reading this chapter, you should be able to . . .

- Distinguish between formal and informal groups.
- Define the basic conceptual tools for understanding groups.
- Describe how and why cohesive groups form in organizations.
- Identify and explain the stages of group development.
- Discuss the factors that affect group effectiveness.
- Understand the ways managers can use groups in organizations.

Chapter Overview

. . . .

▶ OPENING EPISODE

Diverse Work Groups Marked by Innovation, Cultural Barriers

Khanh Vu's department at Sun Microsystems in San Jose, Calif., could be a tower of Babel: Thirty-one of the 35 engineers Khanh supervises come from 11 different nations in the Americas, Africa, the Middle East and Asia.

They bring to their work the passions, assumptions and prejudices unique to their cultures. While each engineer is an expert technician, few are fluent in the culture that surrounds them at Sun, the culture of American business.

They are the first generation of a remarkable new international work force, whose growth is inevitable as business goes global. Nowhere in the United States is the mix more diverse and the range of cross-cultural issues more complicated than in Silicon Valley.

With few models to imitate, work groups like Khanh's often must invent the future as they go. In some ways, says Khanh, the very lack of shared cultural assumptions seems to set the group free, giving them a creative edge.

"This is a very diverse environment—we are willing to try anything," he said.

Although diverse work groups such as Khanh's can be a source of innovation and creativity—benefits of great importance in Silicon Valley—such groups are complex and not without problems. In the workplace, language equals power, and employees at any level who are not fluent in both the language and the culture of their bosses are in a weak position.

In Silicon Valley, the integration of foreign-born workers is a central concern. According to the 1990 census, 26 percent of Santa Clara County's labor force is foreign-born. In some firms, a 50–50 work force is not uncommon, and there are companies employing up to 80 percent foreign-born workers, says consultant Marian Stetson-Rodriguez of the Sunnyvale, Calif., firm of LinguaTec. . . .

Supervising such a complex work force requires caution. Khanh, who was born in Vietnam, recalls the time when a small crisis erupted in his department. An engineer—a man—planned to be away on business. Khanh assigned one of the man's colleagues—a woman—to check in with him by phone, at home. It seemed like a good plan—both were Iranian, and they shared a native tongue.

However, the male engineer was appalled. How, he demanded, could he explain to his family these calls from a strange woman?

Warned off, Khanh found someone in another department—a man—to do the task. He had picked up another lesson in the largely uncharted business school of intercultural hard knocks—discuss everything first.

"Those are the kinds of things you just have to learn," he said. "You just have to ask a lot. If it's not going to be good, I will be corrected."

▸ *The diversity of these engineers can disturb the smooth functioning of a group in getting work done. Workforce diversity will affect group dynamics in many organizations.*

Source: Excerpted from M. Lewis, "Diverse Work Groups Marked by Innovation, Cultural Barriers," Knight-Ridder Newspapers. (As the story appeared in the *Albuquerque Journal Business Outlook*, February 22, 1993, p. 22.) Reprinted by permission. Knight-Ridder Tribune News Service.

Even when everyone in a workplace speaks English and wears some version of the gray flannel uniform of American business, huge cultural differences may lie just beneath the surface, according to Farid Elashmawi, whose consulting firm is called Tech Trans.

For example, he said, Americans revere independence, risk-taking, egalitarianism and decisive action—even occasional brashness—in their employees.

"In Japan, however, group harmony, group consensus and group achievement might be valued. In an Arab country, family identification, religious affiliation and seniority are important," he said.

Some of the greatest strains can arise when traditional Asian values clash with the American business culture.

Take the experience of James Hsieh, an immigrant from Taiwan, who says he spends his days slipping back and forth between his Asian self and his Americanized self.

In his department—marketing—at Hewlett-Packard Co., Hsieh feels he must be gregarious, forthright, even aggressive—more "American" than most Americans.

Yet, walking down the hall to consult with a group of Taiwanese engineers, he feels pressure to put on his Asian persona—humble and deferential, less blunt and aggressive. It's not behavior that his Taiwanese colleagues expect from an "American" colleague, yet they hold him to the old-country standard, he said.

W orkforce diversity brings special opportunities and problems to work groups in organizations. Culturally based differences in values and interpersonal orientation can shape group dynamics in unexpected ways. This chapter offers basic information about group and intergroup processes in organizations. Some of its observations, though, will vary depending on the diversity of a group.

This chapter describes several aspects of groups, group dynamics, and intergroup processes in organizations. The chapter builds upon premises that emphasize the inevitability of groups in organizations. Those premises also view groups as having both good and bad effects for individuals, managers, and organizations.[1]

Groups can powerfully influence people's behavior. Knowledge of how and why groups form, and an understanding of their dynamics, can help you function better within a group or manage group activities. This chapter's orientation toward groups in organizations is captured by the now classic statement:

[G]roups exist; they are inevitable and ubiquitous; they mobilize powerful forces having profound effects upon individuals; these effects may be good or bad; and through a knowledge of group dynamics there lies the possibility of maximizing their good value.[2]

Formal and Informal Groups

"A group is a collection of people who interact with each other regularly over . . . time and perceive themselves to be mutually dependent . . . [in] the attainment of one or more common goals."[3] This definition has some important elements. A group is a collection of people trying to do a task or reach a goal. The people regularly interact with each other and depend on each other to do their tasks. The degree of mutual dependence is a function of the design of the jobs the people are doing and the design of the organization.

Formal groups are either functional groups within an organization or task groups.[4] Functional groups are clusters of people formed by the design of the organization such as divisions, departments, sections, and work units. They are a product of the organization's division of labor, the way the organization has divided its total work to reach its goals. Such groups are often permanent, but may change when the organization decides to redesign its structure.

Organizations form task groups as temporary groups to carry out specific duties, usually special projects. Committees, project teams, and task forces are examples of task groups. Other examples from Total Quality Management are process action teams and continuous improvement teams. Because they usually disband when their assignment is completed, temporary task groups do not have the enduring qualities of permanent groups.

The formal groups in an organization are visible and easily identified from an organization chart or a listing of departments. Whenever you go into an organization and consult a directory to find the department you want, you are looking at a list of the formal groups for that organization. The people in an organization's formal groups usually are not asked whether they want to associate or interact with the other members of the group. They are assigned to their groups and may interact with people in the same group or with people in other formal groups.

Interaction patterns within organizations can affect the formation of **informal groups** within and across formal groups. Informal groups may form along interest lines, such as the task specialization of individuals, hobbies, or other concerns. They may be friendship groups whose members associate with each other both at work and away from work. Outsiders and newcomers cannot readily see informal groups, which are part of the background of the organization. The informal groups form a "shadow organization" exerting powerful forces, both good and bad, on the formal organization.[5]

Basic Concepts for Understanding Groups in Organizations

Several basic concepts will help you understand the dynamics of groups in organizations.[6] **Cohesiveness** and norms are two such concepts. A group is cohesive when its members are attracted to the group's task, to its prestige, and to other members of the group.[7] Members of cohesive groups like to be together, care about each other, and typically know each other well. Cohesive groups also tend to perform better than noncohesive groups, especially if they are small.[8]

Group **norms** are unwritten rules of behavior for members of a cohesive group. The norms define acceptable behavior and roles of group members. Norms include levels of performance valued by the group, teamwork within the group, and relationships with managers and other aspects of the formal organization.[9] New members learn a group's norms through its socialization process. A cohesive group will put great pressure on a new member to conform to those norms.

There are two types of **conformity** to group norms, compliance and personal acceptance.[10] **Compliance** means a person goes along with the group's norms, but does not accept the norms. A person may comply to help the group appear united to outsiders or to prevent conflict within the group. **Personal acceptance** means an individual's beliefs and attitudes are congruent with the norms of the group. Personal acceptance is the more powerful of the two types of conformity. Because the person has internalized the group's norms, she may strongly defend those norms and try to socialize new members to them. Conformity to group norms is not necessarily bad; it can bring order to a group's activities.[11] Because members know what to expect from each other and share performance expectations, conformity often leads to more effective group performance. A section later in the chapter discusses the dysfunctions of excessive conformity.

Behavior in groups falls into two major classes: required and emergent. **Required behavior** is what a person must do because of membership in the organization and as part of the person's role in the formal group. Required behaviors include being at work at a specific time, performing job duties in a certain way, and interacting with specific people in another department to complete a task.[12] **Emergent behavior** grows from interactions among group members. Such behavior can focus on work tasks or be purely social.[13] The norms of a group can define emergent behavior. Organizations do not prescribe emergent behaviors and often do not formally acknowledge that such behavior happens. The newcomer to an existing cohesive group will not immediately understand the function and meaning of many emergent behaviors. The following example illustrates the difference between required and emergent behavior.

At 3 P.M. every day a particular pattern of behavior occurred in a law firm. Members of the firm called the behavior "M&M™ Time." The firm's offices were in a large rectangular area on a single floor of a downtown office building. The offices of the attorneys were on the outside perimeter while the secretarial staff occupied the center of the rectangle. At 3 P.M. one secretary would take a large brandy snifter of M&M™ candies from a drawer of her desk. She would place the snifter on her desk, making enough noise for the attorneys in the surrounding offices to hear. The attorneys would fly out of their offices and line up to take a handful of candy. They would linger by the secretary's desk talking among themselves about their leisure time activities or about technical aspects of their cases. After about 20 minutes, the attorneys would return to their offices.

This law office had developed a pattern of social interaction that regularly occurred between 3:00 and 3:20 P.M. The informal social interaction during M&M™ Time was emergent behavior. The managing partners of the firm did not require the behavior. Nevertheless, that behavior served important functions for the participants. It broke up their work day and gave them a chance to relax or to discuss cases informally with their colleagues.

. . . .

⤴ *Perspectives on Groups in Organizations*

This chapter's perspective on groups in organizations has three parts. The first focuses on what groups can do in organizations; the second, on how groups affect people in organizations; and the third, on the role groups can play for managers of organizations. You will see that cohesive groups can have both positive and negative effects on the management of an organization.

⤴ FUNCTIONS OF GROUPS IN ORGANIZATIONS

Figure 10-1 shows the different functions of groups in organizations. As you learned in Chapter 6, groups can be an important source of socialization of organization members. Whether the result of the socialization will be functional for the organization depends on the group's orientation to management.

Groups can be a source of rewards for members, serving as an important motivational system. Praise and other rewards offered by the group can reinforce member behavior. That behavior can be desirable or undesirable from the perspective of managers in the organization.

Groups also provide support for their members while they work. This function of groups is especially important to those doing hazardous work, where the intimate cooperation of all members of the group is necessary to do a job safely.

Groups also serve a social function, especially if they are informal groups. The social function can appear as well-defined games and themes that occur at predictable times. The law firm's M&M™ Time was an example of a group's social function.

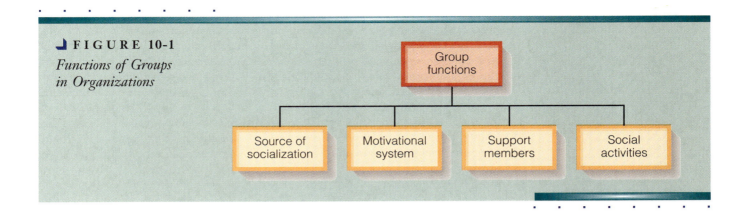

◢ FIGURE 10-1

Functions of Groups in Organizations

Group functions

- Source of socialization
- Motivational system
- Support members
- Social activities

 INDIVIDUAL PERSPECTIVE

Groups are unavoidable, exist everywhere in organizations, and can strongly affect your behavior.[14] When you first enter an organization or transfer to another part of the same organization, you are assigned to a formal group that may be called a department, section, or work unit, depending on the organization.

An informal group can exist within a formal group. One or more persons within that informal group will interact with you. The interactions will be frequent at first. Members of the group will give you information about what the group believes about the organization and its management. The group will try to affect your behavior by communicating its norms to you. If you persist in rejecting the group's norms, you will eventually become an "outsider." If you show that you accept the informal group's norms, other members of the group may accept you as a new member.

If you have a low need for affiliation and little desire to interact with other people, you likely will reject the influence of the group and will move away from its members. As you move away, members of the group will try even harder to attract you to them. If you reject their efforts, you will become an "outsider." Your needs profile from an exercise later in this chapter will give you some information about the strength of your need for affiliation.

If you have a strong need for affiliation, you will value interaction with members of the group and move toward them. Interactions with the group will be frequent. If you accept the norms of the group, and the group accepts you, you become a new member.

As mentioned earlier, groups serve important functions for people. Their informal social activities may help you satisfy social needs. If the job is hazardous, a cohesive group can provide essential support. Because organizations do not always fully define jobs and tasks, members of a group are an important source of information about how to do the work.[15]

 MANAGEMENT PERSPECTIVE

Groups can have both good and bad effects on an organization.[16] The powerful effects that cohesive groups have on individual behavior does not guarantee that the behavior will be functional for the organization or management. The pattern of behavior depends on the norms of the group. If the norms are supportive of the organization and management, the behavior of group members should be functional for the organization. The opposite happens when the norms of the group are antagonistic. In that case, dysfunctional behavior can be expected.

Cohesive groups with norms supportive of management can have several other functional consequences for an organization and management.[17] If tasks are interdependent, the cooperative behavior of cohesive group members helps task accomplishment. A cohesive group can produce innovative work behavior that has obvious uses for the organization. Cohesive groups are self-policing and may stamp out deviant behavior. Control over individual behavior in cohesive groups is more immediate than controls used by managers.[18]

For these reasons, managers need to understand the ways groups develop, the direction groups take, and their effect on individual behavior. If managers understand the processes of group formation, they can deliberately promote the formation of cohesive groups.

EXERCISE   *Your Manifest Needs*

*B*efore going on, it will be useful for you to learn some things about yourself that are important for understanding groups in organizations. Do the following exercise before reading further in this chapter.

◢ INSTRUCTIONS

Table 10-1 lists 20 statements that describe various things people do or try to do on their jobs.[19] How accurately does each statement describe your behavior at work? If you are not now working, refer to a past job you have had. If you have not held a job, refer to your present role as a student.

Use the following scale to record your responses on a separate sheet of paper. Answer all questions frankly. There are no right or wrong answers.

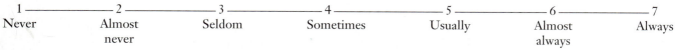

1	2	3	4	5	6	7
Never	Almost never	Seldom	Sometimes	Usually	Almost always	Always

Table 10-2 shows the scoring instructions. Follow the instructions carefully. You will get an average score for each of four needs.

◢ INTERPRETATION OF YOUR RESULTS

The Manifest Needs Questionnaire (MNQ) you just completed measures the strength of four needs with important implications for your interpersonal behavior at work.[20] The score tells you the strength of each of the four needs. Scores range from a low of 1 to a high of 7. Assess your scores by comparing them to the averages for some management students shown in Table 10-3. If you scored at least 0.5 higher than the average for a need, you have a high score. If you scored 0.5 or more lower than the average, you have a low score.

The next paragraphs describe probable behavior for people who scored high or low for each need. If you scored close to the average for a need, you may display a mixture of characteristics of persons with low and high scores.

The Need for Affiliation (nAff) is a person's desire to be in the company of other people at work. If you had a low score, you are not inclined to be outgoing toward others. If you had a high score, you likely start social interactions and enjoy the company of others. You also may be willing to go along with the wishes of people whose friendship you value.

The Need for Dominance (nDom) is a person's desire to control a situation or other people. If your score for this need is high, you try to exert control in work situations. If you had a low score, you tend to give up control of your work situation to others.

The Need for Autonomy (nAut) is the extent to which a person wants to control her work activities and not have them controlled by others. If your score was high, you likely do not want your work directed by others. If you had a low score, you likely will accept supervisory control.

The Need for Achievement (nAch) is the desire to grow and develop from the job itself. If you had a high score, you try to grow, develop, or self-actualize from your work experiences. You may also take calculated risks and want success from your efforts. If your score was low, you do not wish to grow and develop from your work experiences. You avoid risky situations and prefer to share responsibility for task accomplishment with others.

The lower part of Table 10-3 shows selected profiles or combinations of need scores. If you have a high need for affiliation, high need for dominance, and low needs

TABLE 10-1

Manifest Needs Questionnaire

1. I do my best work when my job assignments are fairly difficult.
2. When I have a choice, I try to work in a group instead of by myself.
3. In my work assignments, I try to be my own boss.
4. I seek an active role in the leadership of a group.
5. I try very hard to improve on my past performance at work.
6. I pay a good deal of attention to the feelings of others at work.
7. I go my own way at work, regardless of the opinions of others.
8. I avoid trying to influence those around me to see things my way.
9. I take moderate risks and stick my neck out to get ahead at work.
10. I prefer to do my own work and let others do theirs.
11. I disregard rules and regulations that hamper my personal freedom.
12. I find myself organizing and directing the activities of others.
13. I try to avoid any added responsibilities on my job.
14. I express my disagreements with others openly.
15. I consider myself a "team player" at work.
16. I strive to gain more control over the events around me at work.
17. I try to perform better than my coworkers.
18. I find myself talking to those around me about nonbusiness related matters.
19. I try my best to work alone on a job.
20. I strive to be "in command" when I am working in a group.

Source: R. M. Steers and D. M. Braunstein, "A Behaviorally-based Measure of Manifest Needs in Work Settings," *Journal of Vocational Behavior* 9 (1976): 254, Table 1. Reprinted with the permission of Academic Press, Inc.

for autonomy and achievement (Profile 1), you enjoy the company of others and will start interactions with members of an existing group. Your high need for dominance suggests you may try to take control of the group from an existing group leader, leading to interpersonal conflict between yourself and that leader.

If you have a high need for affiliation and a high need for achievement, but are low on the other two needs (Profile 2), you might try to interact with members of an existing group. If you believe the group will be important to your success in the organization, you could feel a strong desire to become an accepted member of the group. If you also have a high need for dominance (Profile 3), you may try to affect the group's direction to enhance your own success in the organization. The latter tendency, of course, could result in interpersonal conflict between you and an existing group leader.

If you are low in the needs for affiliation, dominance and autonomy, but have a high need for achievement (Profile 4), you will likely not interact with members of an existing group. You will prefer to achieve success in the organization from your efforts alone. The members of an existing group may try to attract you to the group, but you will resist becoming a member of the group.

The same pattern of behavior would be exhibited if you have a high need for autonomy instead of a high need

TABLE 10-2

Manifest Needs Questionnaire Scoring Procedure

Calculate your average need scores using the following formulas. Note that you subtract 8 from some scores.

- **Need for Affiliation:** The sum of Item 2 + Item 6 + (Item 10 − 8) + (Item 14 − 8) + Item 18. Divide the total by 5.
- **Need for Dominance:** The sum of Item 4 + (Item 8 − 8) + Item 12 + Item 16 + Item 20. Divide the total by 5.
- **Need for Autonomy:** The sum of Item 3 + Item 7 + Item 11 + (Item 15 − 8) + Item 19. Divide the total by 5.
- **Need for Achievement:** The sum of Item 1 + Item 5 + Item 9 + (Item 13 − 8) + Item 17. Divide the total by 5.

Some Possible Score Profiles from the Manifest Needs Questionnaire

PATTERN	NEED FOR AFFILIATION	NEED FOR DOMINANCE	NEED FOR AUTONOMY	NEED FOR ACHIEVEMENT	BEHAVIOR PATTERN
Comparison means:					
Ninety-six management students in the mid-1970s*	4.1	4.2	3.7	4.3	
Twenty-two University of New Mexico under-graduate management students, Spring 1992	3.9	4.6	4.1	5.2	
1	High	High	Low	Low	High social interaction and possible opposition to an existing group leader.
2	High	Low	Low	High	High social interaction and strong desire to be a member of an existing group, if you believe it will be important for your success in the organization.
3	High	High	Low	High	High social interaction and possible opposition to an existing group leader. You might try to affect the group's direction toward your success in the organization.
4	Low	Low	Low	High	Prefer to achieve success in the organization by yourself.
5	Low	Low	High	Low	Prefer to control your work and not be controlled by others in the organization.
6	Low	Low	High	High	Prefer to achieve success in the organization by yourself and control your work.

*R. M. Steers and D. N. Braunstein, "A Behaviorally-based Measure of Manifest Needs in Work Settings," *Journal of Vocational Behavior* 9 (1976): 256, Table 2. Mean scores of the ninety-six management students reprinted with the permission of Academic Press, Inc.

for achievement (Profile 5). Because you prefer to control your work, and not have others control your behavior, you will strongly resist efforts to draw you toward an existing group. That behavioral tendency will be especially strong if you are high in the needs for both autonomy and achievement (Profile 6). You want to achieve success in the organization by yourself and keep control of your work.

Keep your need pattern from the MNQ in mind as you read this chapter. Your pattern has implications for the types of social interactions you will experience and whether you will become involved in group activities. ↵

Why Do People Join Informal Groups?

Although people have little choice about the formal groups to which an organization assigns them, they voluntarily join informal groups.[21] Like other people, you may join informal groups for any of several reasons or for a combination of reasons.

Sometimes people are attracted to an informal group because of similar attitudes, beliefs, and opinions. Membership in an informal group can satisfy needs that are not satisfied by other aspects of a person's work experiences. A person with a strong need for affiliation can satisfy that need through membership in an informal group. A person with a strong need for dominance can join an informal group in the hope of emerging as a group leader.

Some individuals may value the activities or goals of the group. Others may view membership in the group as useful for other ends. A person could feel, for example, that membership in a specific informal group will help her get a promotion in the organization.

A Model of Cohesive Group Formation

This section builds a conceptual model that you can use to analyze how and why cohesive groups form in an organization. The model applies to both formal and informal groups. Central to the model are the concepts of activities, interactions, and sentiments.[22]

ACTIVITIES, INTERACTIONS, AND SENTIMENTS

Activities are the formal requirements of the organization such as job duties and responsibilities. Activities follow from formal group membership and the division of labor of the organization. The physical layout of the work area and the technical process of the organization can also demand certain activities. Activities are the same as required behaviors; they are behaviors a person must do because of membership in the organization.

Interaction refers to social interaction between two or more people. The interaction can be face-to-face with two people talking to each other or through memoranda and reports. Interactions can also occur by means of telecommunications devices, televideo devices, personal computers, or electronic mail. The cases at the end of this chapter describe these forms of interaction.

Sentiments are attitudes, beliefs, and feelings about the person or persons with whom you interact. Sentiments develop from social interactions and are feelings of like or dislike for one another.

Figure 10-2 shows arrows linking activities to interactions and interactions to sentiments. Required behavior can lead to social interaction. People are required to

· *Required work activities bring people together. They will develop feelings (sentiments) about each other from their social interaction.*

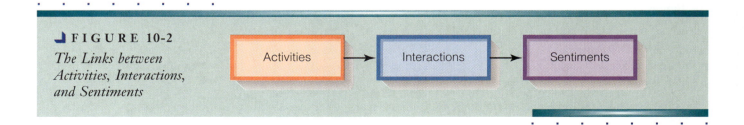

◢ FIGURE 10-2

The Links between Activities, Interactions, and Sentiments

Activities → Interactions → Sentiments

do certain things as employees of the organization (activities). Those required activities bring a person into contact with one or more other people (interaction).

For example, a payroll clerk must take payroll forms to the data processing department by 1 P.M. each Thursday. The clerk delivers the forms to a specific person in the data processing department. The interaction between the two clerks occurs because of a required work behavior. During the interaction, they learn about each other's background and interests and discover they have common interests, or the reverse. From this information, they can develop positive or negative feelings (sentiments) about each other.

Work activities lead to patterns of social interaction that let people sort out their sentiments. If they find they share similar interests, likes, and dislikes, they can be attracted to each other. A cohesive group can form if the interactions involve several people.

FACTORS AFFECTING COHESIVE GROUP FORMATION

Several **factors** in the physical layout of work areas, work processes, organizational design, and job design affect the **formation of cohesive groups.**[23] Those factors will either allow social interaction or restrict it. If the factors allow social interaction, and positive sentiments emerge among those who interact, a cohesive group should form. A manager who understands those factors can use them to encourage the formation of a cohesive group or to build barriers against its formation.

Table 10-4 lists the factors that allow or restrict social interaction. If people are physically close together, the potential for social interaction is high. If they are widely separated, the potential is low. The physical separation of formal groups forms clear boundaries between the groups. A clearly defined boundary increases the potential for social interaction within the formal group but not between the groups. A less well-defined boundary decreases that potential. The ambient noise level affects whether people can talk easily to each other while working. A high noise level decreases the chance of oral communication (interaction). A low noise level increases that chance.

Job activities requiring interaction among workers, as in the payroll clerk example, increase the prospect of the formation of a cohesive group. Similarly, incomplete job descriptions can require an individual to go to a coworker for help (interaction). The opposite characteristics decrease the likelihood of social interaction.

Free time at work during rest periods and the ability to move around while working increase the potential for social interaction. A job that does not require close

TABLE 10-4

Factors Affecting the Formation of Cohesive Groups

FACTORS ALLOWING SOCIAL INTERACTION	FACTORS RESTRICTING SOCIAL INTERACTION
Proximity of people	Distance between people except when telecommunications are used
People not physically isolated from other groups	Physical barriers (walls, machines, etc.) separating formal groups
Low noise level	High noise level
High required interaction	Low required interaction
Incomplete job descriptions	Job descriptions that thoroughly describe job duties
Free time at work: liberal rest periods and breaks	Little free time at work: restrictions on rest periods and breaks
Not physically tied to workstation	Physically tied to workstation
Low degree of attention required by work	High degree of attention required by work
Low absenteeism and turnover	High absenteeism and turnover

attention lets the worker interact with other nearby workers. The opposite characteristics decrease the potential for social interaction.

Absenteeism and turnover within a formal group also affect social interaction. High absenteeism decreases the chance of the same group of people interacting with each other from one day to the next. Low absenteeism has the opposite effect. High turnover increases the instability of group membership. The continual presence of new people causes the group to focus on socializing the new people, decreasing the likelihood of a stable pattern of social interaction.

BASES OF ATTRACTION

Physical factors alone do not fully explain the formation of a cohesive group. **Bases of attraction** explain why people who can potentially interact are sufficiently attracted to each other to form a cohesive group.[24]

Similarities in attitudes, beliefs, gender, ethnic background, age, social status, and education can be the basis of people's attraction to each other. Individuals are attracted to each other because they share common experiences. Membership in a group can also satisfy a person's desire for social interaction, causing the person to be attracted to group members. Individuals may perceive a group as instrumental to reaching some goal. For example, you may join a college sorority or fraternity because you believe that companies like to hire college graduates who have been involved in such organizations.

SUMMARY

Figures 10-3 and 10-4 summarize the Model of Cohesive Group Formation. Required work activities lead to social interaction when the factors allowing interac-

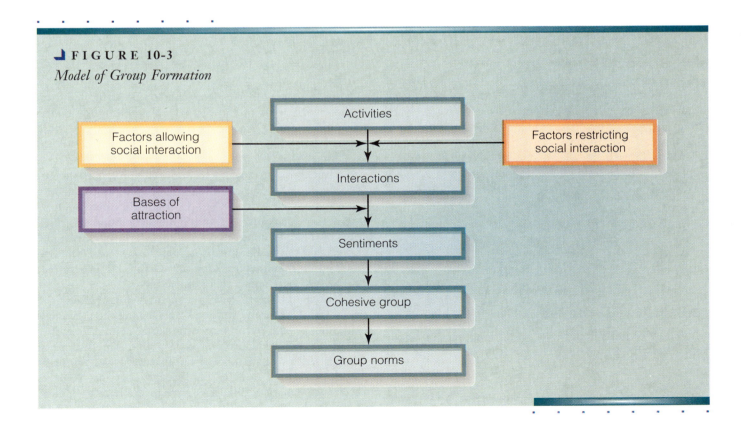

◢ FIGURE 10-3
Model of Group Formation

Activities

Factors allowing social interaction

Factors restricting social interaction

Bases of attraction

Interactions

Sentiments

Cohesive group

Group norms

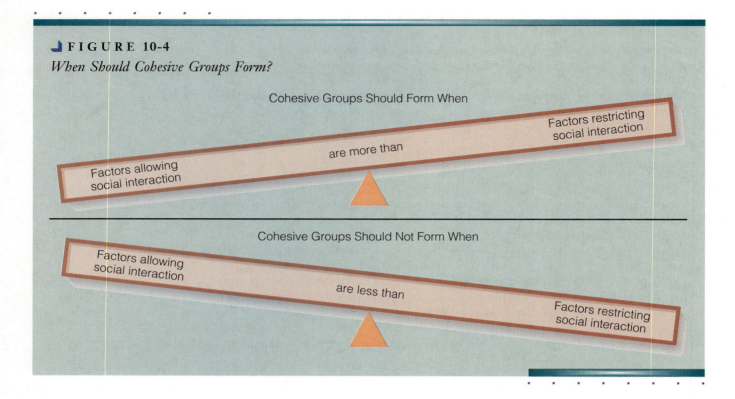

FIGURE 10-4

When Should Cohesive Groups Form?

Cohesive Groups Should Form When

Factors allowing social interaction — are more than — Factors restricting social interaction

Cohesive Groups Should Not Form When

Factors allowing social interaction — are less than — Factors restricting social interaction

tion exceed those restricting it. The bases of attraction affect the formation of sentiments during the interactions. If individuals are attracted to each other, mutually positive sentiments can develop. A cohesive group then forms with norms governing the behavior of group members.

CASE   *Donald Roy and "Banana Time"*

*T*he following case is from Donald Roy's account of his experiences while entering an existing cohesive informal group. Roy was a graduate student in the Department of Sociology of the University of Chicago at the time. Roy refers to himself in the first person. All names are fictitious. Use the following questions as a guide for your analysis:

1. Which factors in the situation allowed social interaction? Which factors restricted it?
2. What were some bases of attraction?
3. Did a cohesive group form? What was the evidence for cohesiveness?

CASE DESCRIPTION

My fellow operatives and I spent our long days of simple repetitive work in relative isolation from other employees of the factory. Our line of machines was sealed off from other work areas of the plant by the four walls of the clicking room. The one door of this room was usually closed. Even when it was kept open, during periods of hot weather, the consequences were not social; it opened on an uninhabited storage room of the shipping department. Not even the sound of work activity going on elsewhere in the factory carried to this isolated work place. There were occasional contacts with "outside" employees, usually on matters connected with the work; but, with the exception of the daily calls of one fellow who came to pick up finished materials for the next step in processing, such visits were sporadic and infrequent.

Moreover, face-to-face contact with members of the managerial hierarchy were few and far between. No one bearing the title of foreman ever came around. The only company official who showed himself more than once during the two month observation period was the plant superintendent.... [H]e managed to pay his respects every week or two. His visits were in the nature of short businesslike, but friendly exchanges....

Source: Excerpted. Reproduced by permission of the Society for Applied Anthropology from D. F. Roy, " 'Banana Time'—Satisfaction and Informal Interaction," *Human Organization* 18 (1960): 158–61.

The clicking machines were housed in a room approximately thirty by twenty-four feet. They were four in number, set in a row.... To the rear of one of the end machines sat a long cutting table; here the operators cut up rolls of plastic materials into small sheets manageable for further processing at the clickers.... [See Figure 10-5 for the layout of the Clicker Room.]

The clickers were ... punching machines, ... similar to ... punch presses, their leading features were hammer and block. The hammer, or punching head, was approximately eight inches by twelve inches at its flat striking surface. The descent upon the block was initially forced by the operator, who exerted pressure on a handle attached to the side of the hammer head. A few inches of travel downward established electrical connection for a sharp, power-driven blow....

Introduction to the new job with its relatively simple machine skills and work routines, was accomplished with what proved to be, in my experience, an all-time minimum of job training. The clicking machine assigned to me was situated at one end of the row. Here the superintendent and one of the operators gave a few brief demonstrations, accompanied by bits of advice which included a warning to keep hands clear of the descending hammer. After a short practice period, at the end of which the superintendent expressed satisfaction with progress and potentialities, I was left to develop my learning curve with no other supervision than that afforded by members of the work group. Further advice and assistance did come, from time to time, from my fellow operatives, sometimes upon request, sometimes unsolicited....

Absorbed at first in three related goals of improving my clicking skill, increasing my rate of output, and keeping my left hand unclicked, I paid little attention to my fellow operatives.... Their names, according to the way they addressed each other, were George, Ike, and Sammy. George, a stocky fellow in his late fifties, operated the machine at the opposite end of the line; he ... had emigrated in early youth from a country in southeastern Europe. Ike, stationed at George's left, was tall, slender, in his early fifties, and Jewish; he had come from Eastern Europe in his youth. Sammy, number three man in the line, and my neighbor, was heavy set, in his late fifties, and Jewish; he had escaped from a country in Eastern Europe just before Hitler's legions had moved in. All three men had been downwardly mobile as to occupation in recent years. George and Sammy had been proprietors of small businesses; the former had been "wiped out" when his uninsured establishment burned down; the latter had been entrepreneuring on a small scale before he left all behind him to flee the Germans. According to his account, Ike had left a highly skilled trade which he had practiced for years in Chicago.

I discovered also that the clicker line represented a ranking system in descending order from George to

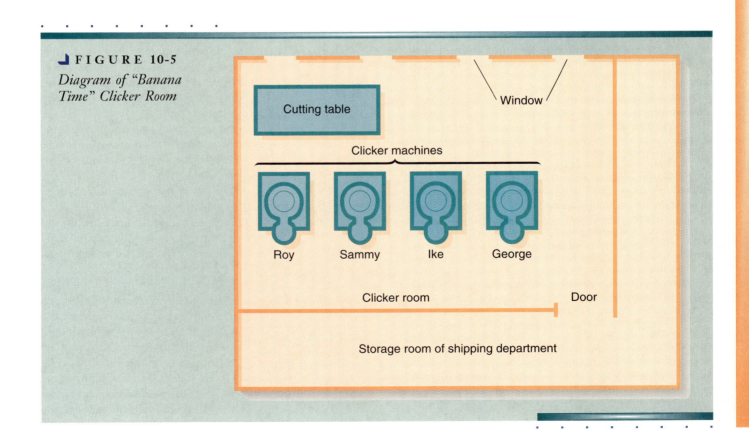

◢ FIGURE 10-5

Diagram of "Banana Time" Clicker Room

Cutting table

Window

Clicker machines

Roy   Sammy   Ike   George

Clicker room   Door

Storage room of shipping department

myself. George not only had top seniority for the group, but functioned as a sort of leadman. His superior status was marked in the fact that he received five cents more per hour than the other clickermen, put in the longest workday, made daily contact, outside the workroom, with the superintendent on work matters which concerned the entire line, and communicated to the rest of us the directives which he received. . . . Ike was next to George in seniority, then Sammy. I was, of course, low man on the totem pole. . . .

It was evident to me, before my first workday drew to a weary close, that my clicking career was going to be a grim process of fighting the clock. . . . I had struggled through many dreary rounds with the minutes and hours during the various phases of my industrial experience, but never had I been confronted with such a dismal combination of working conditions as the extra-long workday, the infinitesimal cerebral excitation, and the extreme limitation of physical movement. . . . [S]tanding all day in one spot beside three old codgers in a dingy room looking out through barred windows at the bare walls of a brick warehouse, leg movements largely restricted to the shifting of body weight from one foot to the other, hand and arm movements confined, for the most part, to a simple repetitive sequence of place the die,—punch the clicker,—place the die,—punch the clicker, and intellectual activity reduced to computing the hours to quitting time. It is true that from time to time a fresh stack of sheets would have to be substituted for the clicked-out old one. . . . Now and then a box of finished work would have to be moved back out of the way, and an empty box brought up. . . . And there was the half hour for lunch, and occasional trips to the lavatory or the drinking fountain to break up the day into digestible parts. But after each momentary respite, hammer and die were moving again. . . . Before the end of the first day, Monotony was joined by his twin brother, Fatigue. I got tired. My legs ached, and my feet hurt. . . .

I began to take serious note of the social activity going on around me; my attentiveness to this activity came with growing involvement in it. What I heard at first, before I started to listen, was a stream of disconnected bits of communication which did not make much sense. Foreign accents were strong and referents were not joined to coherent contexts of meaning. It was just "jabbering." What I saw at first, before I began to observe, was occasional flurries of horseplay so simple and unvarying in pattern and so childish in quality that they made no strong bid for attention. . . .

But, as I began to pay closer attention, as I began to develop familiarity with the communication system, the disconnected became connected, the nonsense made sense, the obscure became clear, and the silly actually funny. And, as the content of the interaction took on more and more meaning, the interaction began to reveal structure. . . .

This emerging awareness of structure and meaning included recognition that the long day's grind was broken by interruptions. . . . [The] interruptions appeared in daily repetition in an ordered series of informal interactions. . . . As phases of the daily series, they occurred almost hourly, and so short were they in duration that they disrupted work activity only slightly. . . .

Most of the breaks in the daily series were designated as "times" in the parlance of the clicker operators, and they featured the consumption of food or drink of one sort or another. There was coffee time, peach time, banana time, fish time, coke time, and, of course, lunch time. Other interruptions, which formed part of the series but were not verbally recognized as times, were window time, pickup time, and the staggered quitting times of Sammy and Ike. . . .

My attention was first drawn to this times business during my first week of employment when I was encouraged to join in the sharing of two peaches. It was Sammy who provided the peaches; he drew them from his lunch box after making the announcement, "Peach time!" On this first occasion I refused the proffered fruit, but thereafter regularly consumed my half peach. Sammy continued to provide the peaches and to make the "Peach time!" announcement, although there were days when Ike would remind him that it was peach time, urging him to hurry up with the mid-morning snack. Ike invariably complained about the quality of the fruit, and his complaints fed the fires of continued banter between peach donor and critical recipient. . . .

Banana time followed peach time by approximately an hour. Sammy again provided the refreshments, namely, one banana. There was, however, no four-way sharing of Sammy's banana. Ike would gulp it down by himself after surreptitiously extracting it from Sammy's lunch box, kept on a shelf behind Sammy's work station. Each morning, after making the snatch, Ike would call out, "Banana time!" and proceed to down his prize while Sammy made futile protests and denunciations. George would join in with mild remonstrances, sometimes scolding Sammy for making so much fuss. The banana was one which Sammy brought for his own consumption at lunch time; he never did get to eat his banana, but kept bringing one for his lunch. At first this daily theft startled and amazed me. Then I grew to look forward to the daily seizure and the verbal interaction which followed.

Window time came next. It followed banana time as a regular consequence of Ike's castigation by the indignant Sammy. After "taking" repeated references to himself as a person badly lacking in morality and character, Ike would "finally" retaliate by opening the window which faced Sammy's machine, to let the "cold air" blow in on Sammy. . . . Opening the window would take a little time to accomplish and would involve a great deal of verbal interplay between Ike and Sammy, both before and after the event. Ike would threaten, make feints toward the window, then finally open it. Sammy would protest, argue, and make claims that the air blowing in on him would give him a cold; he would eventually have to leave his machine to close the window. Sometimes the weather was slightly chilly, and the draft from the window unpleasant; but cool or hot, windy or still, window time arrived each day. . . . George's part in this interplay . . . was to encourage Ike in his window work. He would stress the tonic values of fresh air and chide Sammy for his unappreciativeness.

Following window time came lunch time, a formally designated half-hour for the midday repast and rest break. At this time, informal interaction would feature exchanges between Ike and George. The former would start eating his lunch a few minutes before noon, and the latter, in his role as straw boss, would censure him for malobservance of the rules. Ike's off-beat luncheon usually involved a previous tampering with George's alarm clock. Ike would set the clock ahead a few minutes in order to maintain his eating schedule without detection, and George would discover these small daylight saving changes. . . .

About mid-afternoon came fish time. George and Ike would stop work for a few minutes to consume some sort of pickled fish which Ike provided. Neither Sammy nor I partook of this nourishment, nor were we invited. For this omission I was grateful; the fish, brought in a newspaper and with head and tail intact, produced a reverse effect on my appetite. George and Ike seemed to share a great liking for fish. Each Friday night, as a regular ritual, they would enjoy a fish dinner together at a nearby restaurant. On these nights Ike would work until 8:30 and leave the plant with George.

Coke time came late in the afternoon, and was an occasion for total participation. The four of us took turns in buying the drinks and in making the trip for them to a fourth floor vending machine. Through George's manipulation of the situation, it eventually became my daily chore to go after the cokes; the straw boss had noted that I made a much faster trip to the fourth floor and back than Sammy or Ike.

Sammy left the plant at 5:30, and Ike ordinarily retired from the scene an hour and a half later. These quitting times were not marked by any distinctive interaction save the one regular exchange between Sammy and George over the former's "early washup." Sammy's tendency was to crowd his washing up toward five o'clock, and it was George's concern to keep it from further creeping advance.

CASE ANALYSIS

Table 10-5 summarizes the concepts used in this analysis and gives an example of each from the case. The required work behavior of Donald Roy and the other men in the clicker room was operating the clicker machines and cutting or moving materials. The jobs they did were simple and routine. The required work activities did not

TABLE 10-5

Concepts Used to Analyze the Banana Time Case

CONCEPTS	EXAMPLE FROM CASE
Required behavior activities	Operating clicker machines; cutting and moving materials.
Factors affecting group formation:	
Physical isolation	Clicker room separated from rest of factory by walls. Almost no interaction with people outside the room.
Proximity	Machines close enough to allow interaction.
Free time	Rest periods, breaks. Little interaction with management.
Lack of noise	Low noise level allowed conversations.
Attention required by work	Simple, routine tasks. Little attention required other than to prevent injury.
Interaction	Could talk freely. The three men interacted with Roy to give him advice on how to do the work.
Bases of Attraction:	
Gender	All men.
Age	All except Roy in their 50s.
Ethnicity	Eastern European; Jewish.
Common experiences	George, Ike, and Sammy previously had hard times in business.
Emergent behavior	Well-developed roles in the times and themes. The times and themes were an expected part of the workday.
Cohesiveness	
Norms	

bring the four men directly into interaction, although several factors in the work setting allowed the high social interaction described in the case.

Walls separated the clicker room from the rest of the factory resulting in almost no interaction with people outside the room. The machines were close enough (proximity) to allow interaction. The noise level was low enough, even with the machines operating, to let the men talk (interaction). The jobs were simple and did not require much attention except to prevent injury by the clicker machine.

The bases of attraction were gender, age, ethnicity, and common experiences. All clicker operators except Roy were men in their 50s. George, Ike, and Sammy were from Eastern Europe; Ike and Sammy were Jewish. The three men also shared the common experience of having done badly in business in the past. Note that Donald Roy shared few of the characteristics that were the bases of attraction for the other three men. The times and themes were emergent behaviors that occured throughout the day. They had well-developed, clearly defined roles for the three men, implying that they formed a cohesive group.

Processes of Group Development

Three models of group development processes describe different ways groups develop from their beginning to their maturity. Each model offers a different and complementary view of group development.

STAGES OF GROUP DEVELOPMENT MODEL

Groups can develop in a series of stages with each stage emphasizing something different.[25] Early aspects of development focus on the social structure of the group: norms, roles, social status, and relationships among roles.[26] Each stage has different implications for member behavior and group performance. The stages are not discrete and clearly identifiable states. They are plateaus in the group's evolution from beginning to end. Groups of strangers who have not done the task of the group before are most likely to experience all stages of development.[27]

The **stages of group development** are a controversial area of group and group dynamics research. Little research has examined the stages in organizational settings.[28] Although some prominent group scholars have accepted the stages of development,[29] a conservative conclusion says the stages only apply to newly formed groups.[30] That conclusion suggests that knowledge about group development could be especially important in an organization that deliberately uses groups to do its work.

Table 10-6 lists the stages of group development and the characteristics typical of the group at each stage.[31] The stages affect both the social structure of the group (norms, roles, status relationships) and the group's orientation to its tasks.

Group Formation

During the group formation stage, members of the group first meet each other and learn about the task or tasks to be done. The group defines its boundaries both socially and for the tasks of the group. People who have never been together before introduce themselves to each other. They reveal their characteristics and abilities to other group members, sometimes slowly. The members also discuss preliminary ideas about how to do the group's task.

Intragroup Conflict

The intragroup conflict stage then begins to evolve. Discussions focus on social roles within the group appropriate to getting the task of the group done. Informal leaders begin to emerge, even though a formal leader was appointed, as is often the case for

TABLE 10-6

Stages of Group Development

STAGE	EMPHASIS WITHIN THE GROUP
Group formation	Learn about each other and the task.
	Define social and task boundaries.
Intragroup conflict	Discuss social roles.
	Emergence of leadership.
Group cohesion	Define roles and relationships among roles.
	Has an identifiable culture.
	Conflict focuses on different ways of doing the task.
Task orientation	Members accept the group's norms.
	Energy focuses on getting things done.
Termination	Disband or redefine the group's goals.

a formal task group. Power struggles may erupt between competing informal leaders. Conflict arises about how the group should do the tasks of the group. People often struggle to keep their identity and autonomy as the group tries to give an identity to the individual. New members entering an existing cohesive group experience the power and force of the socialization process of the group at this stage.[32]

Group Cohesion

By the group cohesion stage, the group has defined its roles and the relationships among roles. Appropriate behavior of various members has been worked out. Members accept each other, and an identifiable group culture emerges.

Conflict is less intense at this stage than during the previous stage. If conflict is accepted as part of the group's norms, the group defines acceptable conflict behavior. The conflict at this stage focuses less on the social structure of the group than on different ways of doing the group's task.[33] Conflict can arise if an individual sharply deviates from the group's norm about task behavior.

Task Orientation

Members of the group are comfortable with each other at the task orientation stage and have accepted the group's norms. The members of the group have settled upon their goals and worked out their division of labor. The task or tasks are now defined, and energy focuses on getting things done.

Termination

Some groups eventually reach their goals, disband, and end their existence as an identifiable group. Other groups redefine their task and membership. If either event happens, the group returns to the first stage of development and restarts the evolutionary process.

Repetition of the Stages

Functional groups and cohesive informal groups reach the task orientation stage of development and plateau there. Under certain conditions, however, such groups repeat the stages and experience redevelopment.[34] When newcomers join an established group, the group's social structure and ways of doing its task often are altered. Established members of the group, especially formal or informal leaders, have the task of socializing the new member to the norms of the group. All the forces and dynamics of socialization processes described in Chapter 6 come into play for the newcomer.

Organizations that undergo a major redesign often redistribute existing members of the organization into new formal groups. The people are not new to the organization, but they are new to the groups in which they find themselves. The stages of group development repeat as groups affected by the reorganization try to redevelop. Such redevelopment of groups is especially characteristic of organizations using a matrix design[35] and those rebuilt after mergers, acquisitions, or takeovers.[36]

 ## MULTIPLE SEQUENCE MODEL

According to the stage view of group development, groups begin at a starting point and progress steadily toward their ending stage. Some research has shown that many groups do not develop in such an orderly way. According to the **multiple sequence model,** different groups develop in widely differing patterns.[37]

The multiple sequence model uses four phases to describe the development process. An orientation phase is a period where group members share information about the group's task, feel uneasy with each other, and have little focus to their activities. A conflict phase features disagreements about task approaches, the growth of factions, and antagonistic interactions. The development phase has a strong task focus and consensus about the group's direction. An integration phase has low task orientation but a strong focus on support of each member.

Table 10-7 shows some sequences identified in the research that led to the development of the model. Groups can vary in both the number of phases that unfold during development and the sequence of the phases. Levels of task difficulty, conflict, and the need for information likely disturb a group's orderly progress through the phases. For example, group I was a group of college students trying to choose a topic for a term project. During the early phases, the group experienced high conflict and confrontation among members. Repeated conflict phases happened until the group found a topic that all members accepted.

PUNCTUATED EQUILIBRIUM MODEL

The **punctuated equilibrium model** describes the group development process as interrupted by major change events, conflict, and upheaval. It does not see group development as proceeding in an orderly way through a series of stages. This model

TABLE 10-7
Multiple Sequences of Group Development

GROUP	SEQUENCE OF PHASES
I	Orientation, conflict, development, conflict, development, conflict, orientation, development
II	Orientation, development, conflict, integration, development
III	Orientation, conflict, orientation, conflict, orientation, conflict
IV	Orientation, conflict, development, integration, development, conflict

Source: M. S. Poole, "Decision Development in Small Groups II: A Study of Multiple Sequences in Decision Making," *Communication Monographs* 50 (1983): 228, 229, 231.

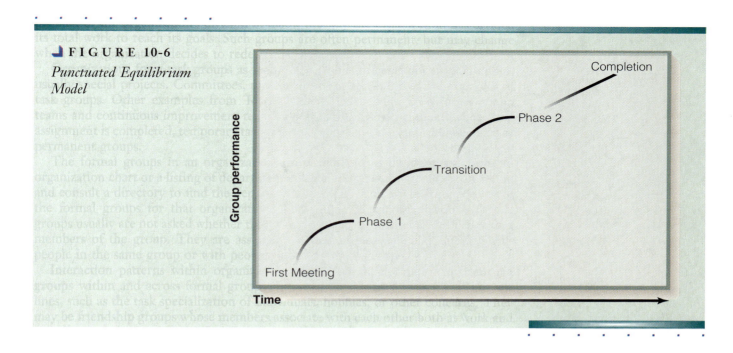

FIGURE 10-6

Punctuated Equilibrium Model

Completion

Phase 2

Transition

Phase 1

First Meeting

Group performance

Time

of group development applies especially to temporary problem-solving groups with a deadline.[38]

Groups can move through the five phases and events shown in Figure 10-6. The First Meeting is a critical starting point that sets behavior patterns that last well into the group's development. Members of the group build a framework that strongly defines their orientation to tasks, relationships with the group's external environment such as supervisors, and interpersonal relationships. Phase 1 features continued work on the group's task as defined by the First Meeting. A critical Transition occurs at the midpoint of a group's schedule. Some groups become unhappy with their progress and redefine the framework guiding their behavior. Other groups reconfirm the framework and accelerate toward Completion. Phase 2 focuses on task completion and the desire to finish the group's assignment. At the Completion phase, the group delivers its final product and disbands.

The research that developed the punctuated equilibrium model found recurring patterns in the groups studied. The First Meeting established a framework that affected the group throughout Phase 1. Different groups showed different behavior patterns during that period. They usually experienced the Transition phase halfway to their deadline, despite varying periods of time for task completion. The Transition also was the point at which group members were most likely to accept redirection of the group's efforts. Although the phases usually happened at the same periods in a group's development, the behaviors within each phase varied widely among groups. The latter is a major difference between the punctuated equilibrium model and the stage model of group development.

Sources of Factors Affecting Cohesive Group Formation

Earlier we saw how several factors can affect the formation of cohesive groups. This section looks more closely at the specific sources of those factors. Table 10-8 summarizes the factors and their sources.

Many companies use an "open space" concept in office design. Using dividers about four feet high, large open office areas can give people a sense of belonging to

TABLE 10-8

Sources of Factors Affecting the Formation of Cohesive Groups

	SOURCE OF FACTOR			
FACTOR	Physical Layout	Technical Process	Organizational Design	Job Design
Proximity	X	X		X
Physical isolation	X	X		
Noise	X	X		
Required interaction		X	X	X
Incomplete job descriptions		X	X	
Free time at work		X	X	
Physically tied to workstation		X		
Attention required by work		X		
Absenteeism, turnover	X			X

a group. The absence of solid high walls can encourage interaction. The openness also reduces a sense of physical isolation. Individuals can see and possibly talk to people from other formal groups. Open areas tend to have a high ambient noise level, though, which can make interaction difficult. The noise reduces the ability to talk, either face-to-face or by telephone.[39]

The technical process of the organization affects all factors. The next paragraphs briefly describe two technologies discussed in Chapter 17. The goal of the analysis is to discover the ways in which the technical process allows or restricts social interaction. You can similarly analyze any other technical process to discover its effect on social interaction.

A mass-production technical process, as found in a factory assembly line, can have a high noise level. Workers must often stay at their workstations and devote a high level of attention to their work to complete tasks successfully and safely. These factors reduce the potential for social interaction. Workers usually are not free to take breaks at their discretion, but must wait until a relief person is available to take their place on the line.[40]

The continuous process technologies found in oil refineries, chemical plants, and nuclear power plants also have many effects on the factors. The control rooms of such facilities usually are bounded by walls and frequently have restricted access. Several people often work together in the same room, so proximity and physical isolation could increase social interaction and identification among people within the formal group. Workers usually must stay at their workstations, attending to the status of the system or process by monitoring gauges and dials.

Organizational design can affect required interaction, completeness of job descriptions, and free time at work. Some organizations have well-defined job descriptions and restrict employee rest periods and breaks; both factors can reduce interaction. At the same time, specialization of functions within departments and work units can require employees to interact with each other to complete the total package of work. The final effect on group formation depends on which characteristics of a bureaucracy are strongest.

Some organizations have high levels of ambiguity and incompletely specified job descriptions. The fewer restrictions on employee behavior increase opportunities for social interaction. The ambiguity in such organizations can cause employees to interact to get information about their roles. Because of more chances for interaction, cohesive groups are likely to form in such ambiguous work environments.

The design of jobs affects proximity, required interaction, completeness of job descriptions, absenteeism, and turnover. Because job design frequently follows from

collectivistic or individualistic values can be important. Countries with collectivistic values emphasize the goals of the group over those of the individual, insist on loyalty to the group, and stress cooperation among group members. Countries with individualistic values focus on the person, not the group. Examples of collectivistic countries are Hong Kong, Colombia, and the Philippines. Individualistic countries include Canada, Great Britain, and the United States.[51]

Some limited research evidence indicates that individualists perform poorest when working in a group.[52] People with collectivistic values perform their best in a homogeneous group and worst in a hetereogeneous group. Such evidence implies local cultural values should be considered when designing an effective group in an international environment.

A group's cohesiveness affects its effectiveness in many ways. There is more communication within a cohesive group. Members of cohesive groups help each other and are more satisfied with the group and its task. Cohesive groups more strongly affect member behavior than groups that are not cohesive.

 GROUP SIZE

Productivity typically is lower in large groups than in small ones.[53] Group size has several effects including the following:

- Satisfaction with the group's activities decreases as size increases.
- Participation of members drops as size increases.
- The strength of bonds among group members decreases as group size increases.
- Large groups have more resources for doing the group's task.
- Reaching agreement about a group's activities or making decisions is more difficult in large groups than in small ones.
- A leader more likely emerges as group size increases.
- Large groups make communication and coordination of group members difficult.
- People in large groups find it difficult to learn about each other. For example, in a three-person group, the number of possible relationships is 6; in a four-person group, 25; and in a six-person group, 301!

 TASK

Two characteristics of a group's task affect how well a group performs. Tasks with high cooperation requirements are better done in small groups.[54] People working on difficult tasks do better when the group allows feedback while doing the task. A group norm of letting people know how they are doing will help such feedback. Feedback can also be encouraged by keeping the group size small enough to let people know the performance of other group members.

The complexity of a group's task guides the degree of centralization or decentralization the group should have. Groups do complex tasks more effectively when they use decentralized communication and decision-making structures (see Chapter 13). Groups doing simple tasks can use a centralized structure effectively.

 IMPLICATIONS FOR DESIGNING GROUPS

This discussion of factors affecting group effectiveness has several implications for designing groups to do different tasks. You can consider these implications from the perspective of a manager designing a group, a chair of a committee, or a member of a group.

Assume you would like to get high interaction among diverse people in a group. You want that interaction both because you would like the group to become cohesive and because you want the group to produce many ideas about an issue or problem.

You should first consider the physical environment in which the group will work. A group clearly bounded from other groups will have high interaction within the group. A round table or circular work area usually allows more interaction than a rectangular table.

A rectangular table emphasizes the leadership roles of the head positions. If you are the formal leader such as a committee chair, you could choose to sit at the head of a rectangular table. If no formal leader is appointed, but you believe certain group members have leadership qualities, you can put one of those people at the head of a table.

You can then consider the degree of cohesiveness you would like the group to have. High cohesiveness follows when members have compatible characteristics. You will find cohesive groups useful for tasks requiring high levels of interdependence and cooperation. High diversity among members of the group, though, is a useful way of increasing conflict within the group. That conflict can be an important source of new ideas. Generating ideas is especially important for problem-solving and decision-making groups that are looking for creative solutions to problems. Chapter 11, incidentally, discusses conflict management. You may wish to look at that chapter if you want to learn more about managing conflict within groups.

Although small groups have many advantages over large groups, large groups can bring more resources to the group's task. Large groups present coordination and communication problems. If you are considering a large group, you should weigh the costs and benefits carefully.

Groups with an even number of members can break into opposing subgroups of the same size. Think carefully about whether you want opposing subgroups to form. Using an even-numbered group size is another way of increasing the conflict potential within the group. Such conflict can bring different viewpoints to the group's task or problem.

· · · · · · · · ·

◢ Using Groups in Organizations

Managers and organizations are increasingly using groups to get work done. Many groups become the highly autonomous self-managing work teams described in Chapter 9. If properly designed, such groups adopt the good features of face-to-face work groups and use knowledge about groups and their dynamics.[55]

There are several natural places where organizations can deliberately use groups. Managers can use groups to make decisions. Ambiguous problems, about which a manager has little information, lend themselves to group decision making.[56] A manager can build a decision-making group by using observations made in this chapter. The manager should be careful, though, for cohesive decision-making groups can suffer from groupthink as noted later. It then becomes necessary for the manager to promote conflict within the group to avoid this dysfunction.

Many manufacturing organizations have shifted the focus of their manufacturing technologies from individuals to groups. These companies form "production cells" centered on making a specific product or major subassembly.[57] Racks of parts and equipment form the boundaries of each group. The groups are small enough for people to know each other well. Such groups should eventually display the qualities of cohesive groups described in this chapter.

Some service organizations also have used group-based job design. One insurance firm has used self-managing work teams with success. The company reduced the processing time of claims to 5 days with the group-based approach. The earlier individual-based approach took 20 days.[58]

Quality circles are another example of how organizations use groups. Japan pioneered the use of such groups based on quality management ideas introduced by U.S. consultants in the 1950s.[59] The Japanese call them "quality control circles," showing their emphasis on solving quality control problems. The members of each quality control circle are the regular members of a work group. They meet periodically to find and fix quality control problems.

U.S. managers want quality circles to focus on more than quality control problems. Membership may reach beyond the immediate work group, causing social interaction of individuals across formal work groups. In the United States, the circles typically are temporary. They can also be part of a larger organization change program.

These examples are only a few of the more prominent ways organizations deliberately use groups. Other examples include committees, task forces, and project teams. Look around in an organization in which you participate. You cannot fail to find both formal and informal groups in abundance. The task for you is to understand your behavior within the groups to which you belong. The task for you as a manager is to manage effectively the dynamics of groups for which you are responsible.

. . . .

Dysfunctional Consequences of Groups

Groups sometimes have **dysfunctional consequences** for either the member or the organization.[60] Groups can take more time to do some tasks than individuals. The group structure takes time to develop. Conflict in the early stages of group development takes time to settle.

People who are members of cohesive groups often experience some loss of their individual identity. Groups give individuals a degree of anonymity, causing some people to behave in atypical ways. Responsibility for negative results of the group's actions can become diffused among group members. Because no single person takes responsibility for a bad decision, people in groups can escape accountability for their behavior.

Social loafing, free-rider effects, and sucker effects can occur within groups.[61] Social loafing (or the free-rider effect) can develop when a person perceives her effort in the group as unimportant or as not easily observed by others. Sucker effects happen when other group members perceive the free rider and reduce their effort to remedy their feelings of inequity. In both cases, group members reduce their effort toward the group's goals, possibly lowering overall group performance.

A cohesive group can put strong pressure on its members to conform to its norms. Such conformity can lead to high levels of uniformity of behavior within the group. It also can lead to close monitoring of member behavior to ensure compliance with the group's norms. The amount of control a group exerts over its members can exceed the control of individual managers or supervisors.[62] The almost continual interaction among group members keeps them under the watchful "eye of the norm."[63]

Uniformity in decision-making groups can also lead to groupthink.[64] Groupthink is a major dysfunction of cohesive decision-making groups. Groups suffering from groupthink strive for consensus, typically consider only a few alternatives before a decision, and do not periodically reexamine the assumptions underlying their decisions. The obvious results for an organization are a less effective decision-making process and poor-quality decisions. Chapter 14 fully describes groupthink.

. . . .

Intergroup Processes in Organizations

Intergroup processes happen at the point where members of two or more groups must interact to complete a task. Such processes feature interactions among members of different groups in an organization, such as manufacturing, quality assurance, finance, marketing, and design engineering. Although behavior at group interfaces is called intergroup behavior, groups do not interact directly. Members of groups interact with each other, representing the interests of their group. The basic management issue is the effective coordination of activities that require contributions of people from different groups.

Interdependence among tasks in organizations is a major reason for intergroup behavior.[65] The interdependence comes from connections among people that result from the design of the organization and its work processes. A major contemporary source of interdependence is the growing use of cross-functional teams in managing for quality.

People from different groups can have different orientations to tasks, time, and goals.[66] Marketing people may have a strong customer focus; manufacturing people usually are cost and schedule conscious; research and development people often take a long-term view. These different orientations can affect the quality of social interaction among members of different groups.

Several social psychological forces affect intergroup interactions.[67] People typically view their group as composed of members with differing characteristics and other groups as having homogeneous members. People also tend to favor people from their own group and to place positive value on its purpose. Such social psychological responses can lead to categorization, stereotyping, and perceptual distortion of members from other groups.

Intergroup behavior often leads to conflict between groups, partly as a result of these social psychological forces. That conflict must be managed to keep it at a functional level so people can reach their work goals.[68] Conflict management is an almost inevitable and key part of managing intergroup processes.

The intergroup processes described above apply to both formal and informal groups. As organizations become increasingly affected by workforce diversity, formal groups likely will have more diverse members. Not only will diversity have positive and negative effects on intragroup processes, it can have similar effects on intergroup processes.

Workforce diversity could have important effects on behavior between members of informal groups. Because informal groups form around bases of attraction, cohesive informal groups could form based on workforce demography. Characteristics such as gender, race, country of origin, and age could be the basis of such groups. Stereotyping and perceptual distortion of people from such informal groups can affect the quality of intergroup behavior among group members.

· ·

International Aspects of Groups in Organizations

Cross-cultural factors affect groups, group dynamics, and intergroup processes in several ways. The tendency to accept group pressure for conformity to the group's norms, for example, varies among cultures. The Japanese encourage high conformity to the norms of a group that has the person's primary loyalty. Experimental research with German students showed a low tendency to conform. Conformity was moderate among people in Hong Kong, Brazil, Lebanon, and the United States. Such evidence suggests caution in carrying your home country view of conformity into other cultures.[69]

All societies pressure deviates to conform to norms,[70] but the strength of the pressure and the intensity with which deviates are rejected vary from culture to culture. Some limited experimental evidence showed that French, Swedish, and Norwegian groups were highest in pressure to conform and in the intensity with which they rejected deviates. German and British groups were much lower in those pressures. Such results imply that understanding cultural differences in conformity is important for managers in organizations operating in different countries.

Cross-cultural research on intergroup processes is limited, but nevertheless some implications can be inferred.[71] Collectivistic cultures expect little expression of conflict during intergroup interactions.[72] They favor suppressing conflict with little discussion about the feelings of different group members. Such cultures prefer to personalize the interaction—to focus on the people, despite what group they represent. Group membership is a more important part of the interaction in collectivistic cultures than in individualistic cultures.

The cross-cultural differences in group and intergroup behavior emphasize major areas of cultural diversity for organizations operating in a global environment. The following are several observations about managing such culturally diverse groups.[73]

Managers should select group members of about equal ability and not choose members on cultural factors alone. The manager can also tell each member about the achievements of other members. Try to develop mutual respect between group members and avoid judgments based on cultural or ethnic stereotypes.

Recognize differences; do not hide or ignore them. Managers can encourage group members to discuss the cultural differences in the group. Help the group discover and use different, and potentially positive, ways of viewing the group's task. View the differences as potential cultural synergy that can lead to high group performance.

Do not let one cultural group dominate another within a group. Such dominance can come from the culture viewed as most advanced, the culture of the host country, or the culture of the home country of the employing organization. The goal is to get the best of different cultural views focused on the group's task. Actively manage group processes by giving each member feedback about her contribution. Use this feedback to help all members understand how the group's cultural diversity is contributing to its success.

· ·

Ethical Issues about Groups in Organizations

*T*he major ethical issues about groups in organizations center on conformity to group norms and the question of informed free choice. Cohesive groups develop powerful forces of socialization to their norms. If their socialization efforts are unsuccessful, such groups reject deviant members. A person can expect assignment to a formal group as a regular part of an employment contract but may have little knowledge of the presence of informal groups and their norms before joining the organization. The ethical question becomes: Are managers required to inform recruits about all cohesive groups in the organization?

A second ethical issue centers on deliberately using groups to get work done and the selection of their members. People with weak affiliation needs usually do not enjoy high levels of interpersonal interaction. Self-managing work teams and process action teams in managing for quality, for example, require extensive interaction among members for success. Do managers have an ethical duty to screen people for membership based on the strength of their social needs? Should managers make membership on such teams voluntary, so people can choose whether or not to join a team?

Conflict levels within groups, especially heterogeneous groups, can be high and continuous. Such heterogeneity can come from deliberate selection of members or mirror the diversity of an organization's workforce. Some people find high conflict stressful. Do managers have an ethical duty to screen people for group membership based on the amount of conflict they can tolerate?

· ·

Personal and Management Implications

*T*he implications of groups for you as an individual derive from the ways a cohesive group can affect your behavior. You need to consider both your results from the Manifest Needs Questionnaire and the tendency of cohesive groups to strongly affect behavior. If you like to interact with people, you likely will become a member of an existing informal group. If the group is cohesive, its norms will affect your behavior. Of course, if you do not care to interact with others, you will probably not become a member, and the group will have little effect on you.

The norms of a cohesive group do not always accord with the wishes of management and the organization. During your early socialization in an organization, a group may present you with performance norms that contradict the organization's norms. You can experience much internal conflict when trying to decide which performance norms to accept. If you value group membership highly, you will likely accept the group's norms. If those norms also contradict the performance norms of management, you may find yourself at odds with the organization.

The positive side of a cohesive group for you is the support it can give its members. If the tasks of the group are interdependent, group support should help you get your job done. The group can also be an important source of information about how to do the tasks. A cohesive group can help you "learn the ropes" quickly.

Recall from Chapter 6 that the early stages of socialization are both important and potentially stressful. The stages of group development you experience when entering groups of varying maturity put pressures upon you along with their socialization efforts.[74] Organizations that use temporary teams expose their employees to repeated pressures from both the stages of group development and the socialization process.

The management implications derive from two major properties of cohesive groups: (1) their powerful effect on individual behavior and (2) group norms. Managers should consider how they can use the positive qualities of cohesive groups. Such groups can support individual performance and help develop innovative solutions to problems. As you saw in Chapter 9, some organizations have designed entire work systems around groups.

Deliberately constructing the factors that help group formation—or reducing the factors that impede group formation—is a major implication for management. Managers can affect whether a cohesive group will form. More difficult is getting group norms that accord with your goals and those of your organization. The leadership information in Chapter 12 and the organizational development information in Chapter 19 should help you create a climate for the development of groups with the norms you want.

When you deliberately use groups in an organization, you need to understand the stages of group development and the effects of those stages on group members. You can help the stages of group development in many ways. Give newcomers an accurate picture of what it is like to work in a group before they join. Anticipatory socialization and Realistic Job Previews, described in Chapter 6, can inform newcomers about the group before they arrive. The more accurate the information, the more it will help the individuals adjust to the group. Well-informed newcomers will also minimally disturb the existing group social and task structure.

People who choose to work outside their home country will be affected by cultural differences in groups and group dynamics. One simply cannot carry home country assumptions about the right way to behave in groups into another culture. Although our knowledge is still limited, the available evidence suggests you should inquire about cultural differences in such behavior.

↵ Summary

A group is a collection of people doing a task or trying to reach a goal. Formal groups are either task groups or functional groups such as departments and work units. Informal groups form within and across formal groups.

The basic concepts for understanding groups in organizations are norms, cohesiveness, required behavior, and emergent behavior. People join informal groups for many reasons such as satisfying social needs. People with strong dominance or power needs can satisfy those needs through leadership roles in groups.

The stages of group development each emphasize something different for members of the group. Conflict levels typically are high during the early stages of group development. Later stages focus on the tasks the group is doing.

Several factors in the physical layout of work areas, work processes, organizational design, and job design affect the formation of a cohesive group. If such factors allow social interaction, and positive feelings emerge among those who interact, a cohesive group should form.

Several factors influence a group's effectiveness. The physical environment, social environment, size, and type of task all influence group effectiveness in different ways. Each factor has implications for designing groups in organizations to get work done.

Managers can use groups deliberately in ways described earlier. Organizations use groups for decision making. Many manufacturing organizations arrange their manufacturing process around groups, not individuals.

Cultural differences in group dynamics suggest one should learn about those differences before taking an assignment in another country. The pressure to conform to group norms and the value placed in conformity to those norms vary from culture to culture. Cultures also differ in how much conflict between groups they will accept.

The major ethical issues about groups in organizations center on conformity to group norms and the question of informed free choice. Cohesive groups develop powerful forces of socialization to their norms. Such groups reject deviant members after unsuccessful efforts to get conformity to norms. Are managers ethically required to tell recruits about all cohesive informal groups in the organization?

◢ Key Terms

activities 265
bases of attraction 267
cohesiveness 259
compliance conformity 259
dysfunctional consequences of groups 283
emergent behavior 260
factors affecting cohesive group formation 266

factors affecting group effectiveness 279
formal groups 258
informal groups 259
interaction 265
multiple sequence model 274
norms 259

personal acceptance conformity 259
punctuated equilibrium model 274
required behavior 259
sentiments 265
social structure of groups 277
stages of group development 272

◢ Review and Discussion Questions

1. Discuss different score profiles from the Manifest Needs Questionnaire. What are the implications of different profiles for social interaction?
2. What is likely to happen to a new employee in the presence of a cohesive group? Use examples from your own experience.
3. Why are cohesive groups important to us as individuals?
4. What are some reasons why managers should be concerned about the presence of groups and group cohesiveness?
5. What factors help or impede cohesive group formation? Reflect on your experiences to find examples of the factors.
6. Discuss the "Model of Cohesive Group Formation." Does it apply to your experiences and the experiences of others in your class?
7. Discuss the stages of group development. What behavior or events does each stage emphasize?

8. Discuss the major aspects of the social structure of groups. What are the sources of the social structure of groups?
9. What factors affect group effectiveness? Discuss the implications of those factors for using groups effectively in organizations.
10. Discuss the functions and dysfunctions of groups. What can managers do to reduce the dysfunctions and increase the functional effects of groups?
11. How should managers reward group performance? You might want to review the earlier motivation chapters (Chapters 7 and 8) for some hints.
12. Review the ethical issues raised by groups and group dynamics. Should managers be concerned with these issues? Why?

GROUP COMPUTING CHANGES THE RULES

The following case describes how people will interact electronically in the future. Consider the following questions while reading this case:

1. Will this form of interaction increase?
2. Will electronic interaction be limited to computer and video links?
3. Do you expect people who interact electronically to form cohesive groups? Why or why not?
4. Is it possible for cohesive informal groups to form across such physical distances? Why?

[The] time-independent nature of electronic-mail [E-mail] communication allows a completely new kind of group to exist—one that does not depend on geographical proximity to be tightly knit. . . .

In published studies of work-group computing systems, three classes of computer support for group activity are commonly described. The first category, face-to-face meetings, is largely restricted to research and development laboratories in universities and corporate institutions. A few individual consultants have combined their own mental skills with software and hardware to achieve a degree of computer support for face-to-face meetings. . . .

A second category of computer support for group activity comprises remote meetings, a concept more popularly

Source: Excerpted from P. Karon, "Group Computing Changes the Rules," *PC Week*, June 7, 1988, pp. 55, 59. Reprinted from *PC Week*, June 7, 1988. Copyright © 1988 Ziff-Davis Publishing Company.

known as teleconferencing. Like the face-to-face meetings, the key to this kind of group activity is that the people involved are all meeting at the same time, even if they are in different locations. This requires a fairly complicated blend of technologies, ideally consisting of video links and computer screen–sharing systems.

The last category of group-computing applications are the most realized in the PC-user community . . . . [They] provide links among colleagues who are not necessarily working in either the same place or at the same time. . . .

Electronic mail is, of course, the most common of these asynchronous group-computing systems. For the most part, however, E-mail applies to only those aspects of work that involve communication, rather than other productive aspects of worker activities.

A few other kinds of commercial products such as group decision-support software and group-authoring packages have begun to address the workplace from a group-computing perspective. But most group-computing schemes in use are informal systems put together in offices where employees are used to and dependent upon microcomputers, and are familiar with linked environments.

For now, most work-group systems are simple variations on the themes of [Local Area Networks] and E-mail. More complex systems have also begun to widen in use, such as desktop-publishing schemes with different people contributing text, graphics or other forms of data for inclusion under a single cover. For most jobs, group computing is still emerging, observers say. The challenge is to make sure that the changes it stirs truly enhance productivity in the office.

BOEING KNOCKS DOWN THE WALL BETWEEN THE DREAMERS AND THE DOERS

This case describes the concurrent engineering effort at the Boeing Co. Consider the following questions and observations while reading the case:

1. What factors contribute to and restrict the development of cohesive groups in this situation?
2. What advantages and disadvantages do you see for concurrent engineering?
3. Note the examples of interaction that is not face-to-face.

"Have you hugged an engineer today?" That's the question on Garnet W. Hizzey's door at Boeing Co.'s 777 airplane

Source: D. J. Yang, "Boeing Knocks Down the Wall between the Dreamers and the Doers," *Business Week*, October 28, 1991, pp. 120–21. Reprinted from October 28, 1991 issue of *Business Week* by special permission. copyright © 1995 by the McGraw-Hill Companies.

operation in Renton, Wash. Since Hizzey is the plane's production-engineering manager, that might sound like a forlorn plaint. Actually, it's more a vivid reminder that sweeping changes are afoot.

In big companies, at least, design engineers and manufacturing types hardly ever mix. And until now, Boeing was like most other companies, sorting the dreamers into one fiefdom and the doers into another, with an invisible barrier between. Relations between the two focused on griping about "the other side of the wall"—usually when designers cooked up something that manufacturing considered too expensive or hard to make. With the 777, though, "we won't have the luxury of whining," says Hizzey. His job is to make the widebody transport, which is scheduled to take its maiden flight in mid-1994, easier and cheaper to manufacture than its predecessors. To do that, his 400 engineers are working side by side with designers, an approach called concurrent engineering (CE).

Costly Changes. Hizzey and his crew are at the core of a massive makeover of the way companies develop products.

Until recently, designers had a pretty free hand. They would toss the design over the wall to production, then keep on making improvements. Each change, no matter how trivial, typically cost upwards of $10,000. Yet it hasn't been unusual for a complex product to be modified hundreds of times, sometimes even early in production. With the 777, Boeing wants to get the details right before production starts—and weed out all those avoidable costs.

That requires juggling just a few pieces, such as the 132,500 engineered parts in every plane, plus three million rivets, screws, and other fasteners. Boeing can do this because of a huge computer system that runs a European-developed solids-modeling program called Catia. It lets engineers iron out bugs on video screens, where fixes are cheap, instead of on expensive life-size models called mock-ups. The new process brings together representatives from design, production, and Boeing's outside suppliers, with regular input from airline customers, maintenance, and finance. "The magic is, you can simulate [assembly] before you actually do it," says Alan R. Mulally, vice-president in charge of 777 design. Boeing hopes this will save as much as 20% of the 777's estimated $4 billion to $5 billion development cost.

Paperless Plane. It should also help the world's No. 1 planemaker keep up with the competition. Paperless design was pioneered by such companies as Motorola, Xerox, Digital Equipment, and Ford Motor. In the 1980s, Northrop Corp.'s B-2 stealth bomber was made from scratch without blueprints, a process in which Boeing participated as a subcontractor. McDonnell Douglas Corp. subsequently developed a similar program for jet fighters, which it is now using to develop a commercial helicopter, too. Then in early October, Airbus Industrie, the government-backed European passenger-jet consortium, rolled out two new products of a four-year paperless-design project: One is Airbus' new long-range jet, the A340; the other is a short-range counterpart, the A330.

The first customer for the 777, United Airlines Inc., ordered 34 planes a year ago, and today, Boeing has more than 7,000 people working on the job. About half are in 238 so-called design-build teams. The engineers are linked through 2,033 computer workstations in Seattle, 484 in Wichita, where Boeing will build the nose, and 70 in Philadelphia—plus 220 in Japan, where local suppliers are helping design the main body sections.

Integrating the overall aircraft design plus the digital blueprints for the various production processes is a huge number-crunching chore: Boeing had to patch together eight of IBM's biggest mainframes. But this cuts out much of the handwork that slows a project and inflates its cost. For instance, craftspeople used to fashion master models, or plaster duplicates, of every part to help guide suppliers that make molds for them. Now, precise computer data will be zipped electronically to the mold-makers. Only for highly complex assemblies, such as flap mechanisms, will Boeing do mock-ups.

Such advances don't come cheap. Boeing's research-and-development expenses will nearly double this year, to about 1.5 billion, and they could hit $2 billion in 1992. Then,

there's the $2.5 billion to build two new plants for the 777, including a major expansion of the Everett (Wash.) factory, already the largest in the world. Boeing figures these front-end investments will be balanced by back-end savings. But the outlays, combined with tepid orders—only 72 so far for the $120 million plane—unnerve Wall Street, where Boeing shares have been treading water for a year in the 45-to-50 range. Even top Boeing Execs are circumspect. "You have to be concerned when you make that much of a technology leap," says Chairman Frank Shrontz.

Actually, even aside from Boeing's role on the B-2, CE and paperless design aren't entirely new to the company: It used them three years ago for an engine strut on the 767. Errors fell dramatically, and the job was finished ahead of time. So far, that's true for the 777, though some suppliers grumble about computer incompatibilities that force them to start with a paper blueprint and then reenter data into their computers. Despite these glitches the project is on schedule. Some 25% of the design will be done by March, 1991, and it should be 90% finished by February 1993—just after assembly begins.

Easy Fix. Manufacturing engineers, who wouldn't normally be involved for another year, have already made their mark. For three decades, the skin on Boeing jets has had a bend in it where the top of the wing meets the side of the fuselage. This covers the inside rib of the wing, the structure that attaches the wing to the body. In the assembly process, putting just the right bend in several aluminum body panels that fit side by side has been "like an art form," says Hizzey—difficult, time-consuming, and costly. On the 777, his production engineers suggested redoing the wing-body joint to eliminate the bend. The designers agreed—and solved 30 years of manufacturing headaches by altering one line on a computer screen.

Each design-build team is assigned a part of the plane, such as tail-fin panels or passenger-entry doors. Major suppliers sit on these teams, too, and the biggest contractors—Mitsubishi, Fuji, and Kawasaki Heavy Industries—have real-time tie-ins with Boeing's computers. The teams meet at least every two weeks to review their work with other interested parties, who might range from purchasing officials to airline customers. "I try to think of these teams as little companies," says Stephen R. Johnson, who heads a group of 10 teams designing the wing's trailing edge. "They each have cost targets and weight targets—and board meetings."

Once the design and manufacturing engineers no longer felt obliged to posture, adds Johnson, they were able to empathize with each other. They even share offices. This has been somewhat traumatic for designers, who now get instant reactions from production engineers. Yet most have bought into the concept. "There were a few agnostics, but they are among the keenest advocates now," says Hizzey.

Designers used to resent it even more when customers put in their two bits. Gordon A. McKinzie, United's 777 program manager, says he spotted rolling eyes when Boeing engineers learned that United and the No. 2 customer, All Nippon Airways Co., would be snooping around. But later, the designers agreed with a United suggestion that the longest wing flap be divided in half to make repairs easier. And they're considering a United request to use more-durable stainless steel bolts and to make door latches so they won't catch fingers as they close. McKinzie says he's amazed at Boeing's candidness: "We feel very privileged to be part of their agony."

Boeing concedes that togetherness has its problems. Some teams lack needed resources or skills, some people were adamantly opposed at the start to sharing data, and some team leaders were inexperienced at running interdepartmental meetings. "Working together is not an esoteric warm and fuzzy thing," says Mulally. "It takes a lot of management and care and nurturing."

Because the process is being refined as it goes on, producing the first 777 will likely take six months more than the usual 48. But if CE brings the project in on schedule and on budget, Boeing will adopt it companywide. So next time, paperless development should be not only cheaper, but smoother and faster, too.

. . . .

➤ References and Notes

[1] D. Cartwright and R. Lippitt, "Group Dynamics and the Individual," *International Journal of Group Psychotherapy* 7 (1957): 86–102.

[2] Cartwright and Lippitt, "Group Dynamics," p. 90.

[3] K. Wexley and G. A. Yukl, *Organizational Behavior and Personnel Psychology* (Homewood, Ill.: Richard D. Irwin, 1977), p. 123.

[4] D. Cartwright and A. Zander, *Group Dynamics: Research and Theory* (New York: Harper & Row, 1960), pp. 36–38.

[5] R. F. Allen and S. Pilnick, "Confronting the Shadow Organization: How to Detect and Defeat Negative Norms," *Organizational Dynamics* 1 (Spring 1973): 6–10.

[6] Developed from G. C. Homans, *The Human Group* (New York: Harcourt, Brace & World, 1950); G. C. Homans, *Social Behavior: Its Elementary Forms* (New York: Harcourt, Brace & World, 1961).

[7] L. Festinger, "Informal Social Communication," *Psychological Review* 57 (1950): 271–82.

[8] B. Mullen and C. Copper, "The Relation between Group Cohesiveness and Performance: An Integration," *Psychological Bulletin* 115 (1994): 220–27.

[9] Allen and Pilnick, "Confronting the Shadow Organization."

[10] C. A. Kiesler and S. B. Kiesler, *Conformity* (Reading, Mass.: Addison-Wesley, 1969).

[11] M. E. Shaw, *Group Dynamics: The Psychology of Small Group Behavior*, 2d ed. (New York: McGraw-Hill, 1976), pp. 259–60.

[12] R. Dubin, *The World of Work* (New York: Prentice-Hall, 1958), Ch. 4.

[13] Ibid., pp. 61–76.

[14] H. J. Leavitt, "Suppose We Took Groups Seriously," in E. L. Cass and F. G. Zimmer, eds., *Man and Work in Society* (New York: Van Nostrand Reinhold, 1975); P. Selznick, "Foundations of the Theory of Organization," *American Sociological Review* 13 (1948): 25–35; Shaw, *Group Dynamics*.

[15] Dubin, *World of Work*, Ch. 16; Wexley and Yukl, *Organizational Behavior*, Ch. 7.

[16] C. I. Barnard, *The Functions of the Executive* (Cambridge, Mass.: Harvard University Press, 1938); Selznick, "Foundations"; Wexley and Yukl, *Organizational Behavior*, Ch. 7.

[17] Dubin, *World of Work*, Ch. 6.

[18] J. Barker, "Tightening the Iron Cage: Concertive Control in Self-Managing Teams," *Administrative Science Quarterly* 38 (1993): 408–37.

[19] R. M. Steers and D. M. Braunstein, "A Behaviorally-based Measure of Manifest Needs in Work Settings," *Journal of Vocational Behavior* 9 (1976): 251–66.

[20] Developed from D. C. McClelland, J. W. Atkinson, R. A. Clark, and E. L. Lowell. *The Achievement Motive* (New York: Appleton-Century-Crofts, 1953); H. A. Murray, *Explorations in Personality* (New York: Oxford University Press, 1938).

[21] Shaw, *Group Dynamics*, pp. 83–97.

[22] Homans, *Human Group*; Homans, *Social Behavior*.

[23] Developed from A. P. Hare, *Handbook of Small Group Research* (New York: Free Press, 1976); Shaw, *Group Dynamics*, Ch. 4; C. R. Walker, R. H. Guest, and A. N. Turner, *The Foreman on the Assembly Line* (Cambridge, Mass.: Harvard University Press, 1956).

[24] E. Berscheid and E. H. Walster, *Interpersonal Attraction* (Reading, Mass.: Addison-Wesley, 1969); Shaw, *Group Dynamics*, pp. 84–91.

[25] Hare, *Handbook*, Ch. 4; Shaw, *Group Dynamics*, Ch. 4.

[26] Shaw, *Group Dynamics*, p. 97.

[27] J. A. Seeger, "No Innate Phases in Group Problem Solving," *Academy of Management Review* 8 (1983): 683–89.

[28] B. W. Tuckman and M. A. C. Jensen, "Stages of Small Group Development Revisited," *Group and Organization Studies* 2 (1977): 419–27.

[29] For example, Shaw, *Group Dynamics*, pp. 101–5.

[30] Seeger, "No Innate Phases."

[31] The names of the stages used here are not identical to those found in other textbooks. Those names came from a careful review of the group dynamics literature. The labels used best convey what is happening within the group at each stage. Developed from Hare, *Handbook*; B. W. Tuckman, "Developmental Sequence in Small Groups," *Psychological Bulletin* 64 (1965): 384–99; Tuckman and Jensen, "Stages of Small Group Development"; S. L. Obert, "Developmental Patterns of Organizational Task Groups: A Preliminary Study," *Human Relations* 8 (1983): 37–52; Shaw, *Group Dynamics*, Ch. 4.

[32] J. P. Wanous, A. E. Reichers, and S. D. Malik, "Organizational Socialization and Group Development: Toward an Integrative Perspective," *Academy of Management Review* 9 (1984): 670–83.

[33] Chapter 11 has much more about the role of conflict in groups and organizations.

[34] Wanous, Reichers, and Malik, "Organizational Socialization," p. 671.

[35] See Chapter 18.

[36] Wanous, Reichers, and Malik, "Organizational Socialization," p. 671.

[37] M. S. Poole, "Decision Development in Small Groups I: A Comparison of Two Models," *Communication Monographs* 48 (1981): 1–24; M. S. Poole, "Decision Development in Small Groups II: A Study of Multiple Sequences in Decision Making," *Communication Monographs* 50 (1983): 206–32.

[38] C. J. G. Gersick, "Time and Transition in Work Teams: Toward a New Model of Group Development," *Academy of Management Journal* 31 (1988): 9–41; C. J. G. Gersick, "Marking Time: Predictable Transitions in Task Groups," *Academy of Management Journal* 32 (1989): 274–309.

[39] T. R. V. Davis, "The Influence of Physical Environment in Offices," *Academy of Management Review* 9 (1984): 271–83; G. R. Oldham and N. L. Rotchford, "Relationships between Office Characteristics and Employee Reactions: A Study of the Physical Environment," *Administrative Science Quarterly* 28 (1983): 542–56.

[40] Walker, Guest, and Turner, *Foreman*.

[41] L. W. Porter and R. M. Steers, "Organizational, Work, and Personal Factors in Employee Turnover and Absenteeism," *Psychological Bulletin* 80 (1973): 151–76; V. H. Vroom, *Work and Motivation* (New York: Wiley, 1964).

[42]N. J. Adler, *International Dimensions of Organizational Behavior* (Boston, Mass.: Kent, 1991), Ch. 5; S. E. Jackson, "Team Composition in Organizational Settings: Issues in Managing an Increasingly Diverse Work Force," in S. Worchel, W. Wood, and J. A. Simpson, eds., *Group Process and Productivity* (Newbury Park, Calif.: Sage Publications, 1992), pp. 138–73; R. T. Mowday and R. I. Sutton, "Organizational Behavior: Linking Individuals and Groups to Organizational Contexts," in L. W. Porter and M. R. Rosenzweig, eds., *Annual Review of Psychology* (1993): 195–229; R. C. Ziller, "Homogeneity and Heterogeneity of Group Membership," in C. G. McClintock, ed., *Experimental Social Psychology* (New York: Holt, Rinehart & Winston, 1972), pp. 385–411.

[43]Mowday and Sutton, "Organizational Behavior," pp. 205–7.

[44]M. E. Gist, E. A. Locke, and M. S. Taylor, "Organizational Behavior: Group Structure, Process, and Effectiveness," *Journal of Management* 13 (1987): 237–57.

[45]T. H. Cox, S. A. Logel, and P. L. McLeod, "Effects of Ethnic Group Cultural Differences on Cooperative and Competitive Behavior on a Group Task," *Academy of Management Journal* 34 (1991): 827–47.

[46]W. E. Watson, K. Kumar, and L. K. Michaelsen, "Cultural Diversity's Impact on Interaction Process and Performance: Comparing Homogeneous and Diverse Task Groups," *Academy of Management Journal* 36 (1993): 590–602.

[47]Developed from Cartwright and Zander, *Group Dynamics*, Ch. 34; Shaw, *Group Dynamics*, Ch. 8.

[48]K. Benne and P. Sheats, "Functional Roles of Group Members," *Journal of Social Issues*, 2 (1948): 41–49.

[49]Cartwright and Zander, *Group Dynamics*, pp. 655–64.

[50]Developed from Hare, *Handbook*, Gist, Locke, and Taylor, "Organizational Behavior."

[51]G. Hofstede, *Culture's Consequences: International Differences in Work-Related Values* (Beverly Hills, Calif.: Sage Publications, 1984), Ch. 5.

[52]P. C. Earley, "East Meets West Meets Mideast: Further Explorations of Collectivistic and Individualistic Work Groups," *Academy of Management Journal* 36 (1993): 319–48.

[53]R. Z. Gooding and J. A. Wagner III, "A Meta-Analytic Review of the Relationship between Size and Performance: The Productivity and Efficiency of Organizations and Their Subunits," *Administrative Science Quarterly* 30 (1985): 462–81; Hare, *Handbook*; Mullen and Copper, "Relation between Group Cohesiveness and Performance," p. 213.

[54]Shaw, *Group Dynamics*, pp. 322–23.

[55]L. D. Ketchum and E. Trist, *All Teams Are Not Created Equal* (Newbury Park, Calif.: Sage Publications, 1992), Ch. 8; E. Sundstrom, K. P. De Meuse, and D. Futrell, "Work Teams: Applications and Effectiveness," *American Psychologist* 45 (1990): 120–33.

[56]V. H. Vroom and P. W. Yetton, *Leadership and Decision-Making* (Pittsburgh: University of Pittsburgh Press, 1973).

[57]R. J. Schonberger, *Japanese Manufacturing Techniques: Nine Hidden Lessons in Simplicity* (New York: Free Press, 1982); R. J. Schonberger, *World Class Manufacturing: The Lessons of Simplicity Applied* (New York: Free Press, 1982).

[58]J. Hoerr, "Worker Teams Can Rev Up Paper-Pushers, Too," *Business Week*, November 28, 1988, pp. 64, 68, 72.

[59]D. A. Garvin, *Managing Quality: The Strategic and Competitive Edge* (New York: Free Press, 1988).

[60]Shaw, *Group Dynamics*, pp. 398–402.

[61]S. J. Karau, and K. D. Williams, "Social Loafing: A Meta-Analytic Review and Theoretical Integration," *Journal of Personality and Social Psychology* 65 (1993): 681–706; J. A. Shepperd, "Productivity Loss in Performance Groups: A Motivation Analysis," *Psychological Bulletin* 113 (1993): 67–81.

[62]Barker, "Tightening the Iron Cage."

[63]Ibid., p. 432.

[64]I. L. Janis, *Victims of Group Think* (Boston: Houghton Mifflin, 1973).

[65]J. D. Thompson, *Organizations in Action* (New York: McGraw-Hill, 1967).

[66]P. R. Lawrence and J. W. Lorsch, *Organization and Environment* (Homewood, Ill.: Irwin, 1967).

[67]R. J. Fisher, *The Social Psychology of Intergroup and International Conflict Resolution* (New York: Springer-Verlag, 1990); D. M. Messick and D. M. Mackie, "Intergroup Relations," in M. R. Rosenzweig and L. W. Porter, eds., *Annual Review of Psychology*, vol. 40 (1989), pp. 45–81.

[68]E. H. Neilsen, "Understanding and Managing Intergroup Conflict," in J. W. Lorsch and P. R. Lawrence, eds., *Managing Group and Intergroup Relations* (Homewood, Ill.: Irwin, 1972).

[69]C. S. Coon, "The Universality of Natural Groupings in Human Societies," *Journal of Educational Sociology* 20 (1946): 163–68; L. Mann, "Cross-Cultural Studies of Small Groups," in H. C. Triandis and R. W. Brislin, eds., *Handbook of Cross-Cultural Psychology, Social Psychology*, vol. 5 (Boston: Allyn & Bacon, 1980), pp. 155–209; L. Mann, "Cultural Influences on Group Processes," in M. H. Bond, ed., *The Cross-Cultural Challenge to Social Psychology* (Newbury Park, Calif.: Sage Publications, 1988), pp. 182–95.

[70]Coon, "Universality of Natural Groupings."

[71]W. B. Gudykunst, "Culture and Intergroup Processes," in M. H. Bond, ed., *The Cross-Cultural Challenge to Social Psychology* (Newbury Park, Calif.: Sage Publications, 1988), pp. 165–81.

[72]See pages 32–34 for a description of collectivistic and individualistic values.

[73]The rest of this section was developed from Adler, *International Dimensions of Organizational Behavior*, Ch. 5.

[74]Wanous, Reichers, and Malik, "Organizational Socialization," pp. 670–76.

11

Conflict in Organizations

After reading this chapter, you should be able to . . .

- Define conflict and conflict behavior in organizations.
- Describe the different philosophies of conflict management.
- Distinguish between functional and dysfunctional conflict.
- Understand different levels and types of conflict in organizations.
- Analyze conflict episodes and the linkages among them.
- Understand the role of latent conflict in an episode and its sources in an organization.
- Describe a model of conflict management.
- Use various techniques to reduce and increase conflict.
- Appreciate some international and ethical issues in conflict management.

· *Discussion and debate are a form of conflict in organizations. A major challenge for many people is to manage the conflict for its positive effects and to avoid its dysfunctions.*

Chapter Overview

. . . .

OPENING EPISODE

Conflict at Gallaudet University

Chanting slogans they could not themselves hear, they marched on the Capitol 1,800 strong, celebrating a victory for a cause that until last week the world at large—and even they themselves—barely knew existed. To call it by its proper name, do as they did: touch a forefinger to one's mouth, then one's cheek, thrust a fist defiantly to the sky. This translates to "deaf power." Less than a week after the trustees of Gallaudet University, the prestigious school for the deaf in Washington, D. C., had chosen a new president, a student-faculty strike had forced her resignation and virtually certain replacement by a deaf educator. For the first time in memory, deaf people as a group had spoken up and found, to their astonishment, that the world would listen.

Protests began Sunday night, minutes after the trustees chose as Gallaudet's seventh president (in 124 years) Elisabeth Ann Zinser, an experienced college administrator whose only handicap was that—like all her predecessors—she could hear. Gates to the campus were blockaded, and the air was filled with the flying fingers of outrage as students rallied, passionately but peacefully; anyone who was brought to his feet by a rousing speech had to sit back down again so the people behind him could see the rhetoric. Zinser was reviled, hung in effigy and—in an elaborate digito-lingual pun—dubbed with the sign-language gesture for "sinner." Four days into the strike, after meeting with students and administrators, she resigned, in deference "to this extraordinary social movement of deaf people." This echoed a sentiment of Gary Olsen, a 1965 graduate of Gallaudet and executive director of the National Association of the Deaf. "It's a national issue. Deaf people have been oppressed too long." . . .

· *Students opposing the appointment of Dr. Elisabeth Ann Zinser as president of Gaullaudet University in Washington, D.C.*

The injustice of having a nondeaf president at Gallaudet, a federally chartered and funded institution, had certainly been pointed out in the months since former president Jerry C. Lee stepped down in August. All but a handful of the school's 2,100 students are hearing-impaired, and an estimated 95 percent of the nation's deaf professionals—in fields such as education, law and engineering—are Gallaudet graduates. The matter even attracted the notice of Vice President George Bush, not otherwise known as a fan of affirmative action, who wrote the university search committee that Gallaudet "has a responsibility to set an example and . . . appoint a president who is not only highly qualified but who is also deaf." The question gained force when the field was narrowed to Zinser and two deaf candidates, including a popular Gallaudet dean, I. King Jordan. But, led by the patrician and, some say,

Source: J. Adler, "Deaf Students Speak Out, and the World Listens," *Newsweek*, March 21, 1988, p. 79. From NEWSWEEK, March 21, 1988. © 1988, Newsweek, Inc. All rights reserved. Reprinted by permission. Sequel: M. Sinclair, "Gallaudet Realizes Its Dream. 1st Deaf President Officially Welcomed," *Washington Post*, October 22, 1988, pp. B1, B2. © 1988 The Washington Post. Reprinted with permission. Concluding observation: L.A. Walker, "I Know How to Ask for What I Want," *Parade Magazine*, April 23, 1989, p. 4. Observation of Roslyn Rosen to Lou Ann Walker.

autocratic chairwoman Jane Bassett Spilman, the trustees chose Zinser in a 10–4 vote, with all the voting deaf trustees opposed.

Zinser's selection gave rise to additional student demands, including the appointment of a majority of deaf trustees and the resignation of Spilman. Those issues are sure to be discussed at a special board meeting this week. In seven years on the board, Spilman has never learned to sign, and her choice of Zinser seemed to express a preference for a president whom *she* could talk to. Since a major part of a university president's job is to raise money, one could argue for choosing someone who could go to a cocktail party and talk with his hands full. But that is precisely the argument the deaf students reject, because by implication it closes off whole fields of human endeavor. "The time has come for the plantation mentality which has for so long controlled this institution and others serving the deaf to end," said psychology professor Allen Sussman. Perhaps, someday, the president of, say, Princeton will be deaf, in which case it might not matter so much that the president of Gallaudet is.

. . . .

↲ SEQUEL

[T]he deaf community at Gallaudet University rose up and gave voice to a dream. [S]tomping their feet and roaring to the rafters, they watched that dream come true.

Dwarfed by a giant television screen that conveyed his hand signs to the campus' jammed field house, I. King Jordan was inaugurated [October 21, 1988] as the first deaf president of Gallaudet, the school founded 124 years ago to serve the needs of hearing-impaired people.

Speaking to 3,500 people gathered in the field house and to thousands of others watching around the country by satellite, Jordan called for a new commitment to excellence. . . .

The 20-minute address was repeatedly interrupted as the audience clapped, yelled and stomped their feet in approval—particularly when Jordan recalled the events that began . . . with a demonstration by the "Deaf President Now" committee and led to his own selection as president.

[E]vents . . . were organized and serious, and they took place under cloudy gray skies. All of this was in sharp contrast to the sunny days of uncertainty and spontaneity [in the] spring [of 1988] when student demonstrators shut down the university to protest the board's initial decision to name Elisabeth Ann Zinser. . . . Zinser resigned shortly after she was appointed to make it possible for Jordan to be named president.

"It didn't happen by accident," [said U.S. Sen. Tom Harkin, the chairman of the Senate subcommittee on the handicapped], . . . "it didn't happen because some benevolent person granted your wish, it happened because you made it happen." . . .

. . . Jordan has sought to capitalize on the publicity of the spring protests, to establish good relations with congressional leaders who provide most of the university's budget and to bring peace and unity to the campus, which was torn by conflicts during the demonstrations.

[One observer noted] "that one of the best repercussions of the Gallaudet protest is visibility—for an invisible disability."

. . . .

The turmoil at Gallaudet University pitted students and faculty against the trustees and a newly appointed president. The conflict erupted explosively, as if it had been brewing in the background for some time. It is not difficult to understand what happened. Gallaudet University had never had a hearing-impaired president. The desire for a deaf president most likely built slowly over the school's 124-year history. The appointment of yet another president who could hear was the spark that ignited the conflict. The resignation of Zinser and the appointment of Jordan followed the protests and student-faculty strike. The enthusiastic welcome of the new president suggests the community's impatience with a series of presidents who were not hearing impaired. Now Jordan must manage the conflict to bring the opposing groups back to a more collaborative and cooperative relationship.

The way the conflict at Gallaudet University rose and then fell is also characteristic of conflict in organizations. Factors surrounding people in organizations create a potential for conflict behavior. The behavior results and then managers must address the conflict. The conflict behavior subsides if managers remove the true cause of the conflict. This chapter gives you the information you need to understand and manage the dynamics of conflict behavior in organizations.

. . . .

❏ Conflict: What Does the Word Mean to You?

Before going any farther, let's find out what the word *conflict* means to you. Jot down the words you associate with conflict. Are the words on your list mainly positive or negative? Does your list have *any* positive words?

A check of an electronic thesaurus for words associated with conflict produced a list of 110 synonyms for both the noun and verb forms of the word. Most words were negative! Table 11-1 shows a sample of these synonyms. Clearly, the word *conflict* has a negative connotation in English.

Behavioral scientists widely recognize that conflict in organizations is a basic process that needs managing.[1] In the early 1990s, some conflict scholars argued that conflict should be viewed as vital to continuous improvement in organizations and that conflict management was crucial to its successful use.[2] Many managers, though, believe they should eliminate conflict from their organizations.[3] Social scientists who have studied conflict also have usually focused on its negative results.[4] Although this chapter's observations are supported by the results of much conflict research,[5] you will find parts of this chapter unsettling if you have a negative view of conflict. Conflict in organizations is a fascinating subject in its own right and something that any manager needs to understand thoroughly.

. . . .

❏ Definition of Conflict in Organizations

Broadly defined **conflict** behavior ranges from doubt or questioning to annihilation of an opponent.[6] A narrower definition says conflict in organizations is opposition, incompatible behaviors,[7] or antagonistic interaction. Conflict in organizations includes interactions in which (1) one party opposes another party, or (2) one party tries to prevent or block another party from reaching his goals. Critical elements of conflict are interdependence with another party and the perception of incompatible goals.[8] The parties in conflict can be individuals or entire groups within the organization.[9]

The range of events considered conflict is deliberately broad. It includes disagreements, debates, disputes, and active efforts to prevent someone from getting what he wants. Annihilation of an opponent is more characteristic of international conflicts (war) than modern organizations.

. . . .

❏ Conflict and Cooperation

Conflict and cooperation are different concepts.[10] Cooperation refers to people working together to reach mutually desired goals. Cooperation often is necessary when people are dependent on each other to reach a goal. Yet conflict and cooperation are not opposites. The absence of cooperation does not necessarily mean the presence of conflict, nor does the absence of conflict mean the presence of cooperation.

❏ **TABLE 11-1**

Some Synonyms for the Word "Conflict"

Battle	Marathon
Duel	Regatta
Struggle	Altercate
Contention	Clash
Dissension	Fight
Division	Quibble
Disharmony	Wrangle
Brush	Jar
Encounter	Interfere
Run-in	Engage
Bout	

Source: Taken from the electronic thesaurus of Microsoft® Word, Version 4.0. The sample took every fifth synonym from the thesaurus.

Later this chapter describes conflict as happening in episodes. As the conflict episodes ebb and flow, periods of cooperation may occur. Task groups where members must work together to reach their goals often display a common pattern. At some point, especially in the group's early stages of development,[11] the members can fiercely disagree about how to reach the group's goals. Conflict develops at this point in the form of discussions and disagreements. If the members of the group eventually agree about how to reach the goals, the conflict recedes and cooperation returns.

Conflict in organizations can serve useful functions when properly managed. Cooperation is not the only desirable state within an organization. Having cooperation without any conflict could result in a stagnant organization and complacent management.[12]

Philosophies of Conflict Management

There are three different **philosophies of conflict management.**[13] According to the traditional philosophy, all conflict is bad and potentially destructive for the organization. This philosophy sees conflict as an annoyance that managers must end.

The behavioral philosophy sees conflict as inevitable in organizations. The nature of organizations creates a potential for conflict, and members of the organization should accept it as part of organization life. Although the behavioral philosophy recognizes the positive role of conflict in organizations, it does not endorse deliberately increasing conflict.

The first two philosophies of conflict are mainly descriptive. The third, the interactionist philosophy, has a strongly normative perspective about conflict management. The interactionist philosophy has four parts:

- Conflict is essential to the survival of an organization.
- If necessary, managers should encourage conflict in organizations.
- Conflict management includes both increasing and reducing conflict.
- Conflict management is a major responsibility of a manager.

Reflect on these philosophies. Which philosophy best represents your approach to conflict?

Perspective on Conflict

The perspective of this chapter is based on the last two philosophies just described. It does not view conflict as bad for an organization or suggest that managers should remove all conflict, as the traditional philosophy recommends. Like the behavioral philosophy, this perspective views conflict as an inevitable part of organization life, and like the interactionist philosophy, it sees conflict as necessary for organization growth and survival. The latter is especially true if the organization is in an environment requiring innovation and change.[14]

Conflict management, including both increasing and decreasing conflict, is a basic responsibility of a manager. The goals of this chapter are to (1) help you develop an understanding of conflict processes in organizations and (2) show you how to diagnose conflict situations. That knowledge can help you do a better job of managing conflict.

Functional and Dysfunctional Conflict

Functional conflict works toward the goals of an organization or a group. **Dysfunctional conflict** blocks an organization or a group from reaching its goals.[15] Conflict is dysfunctional when it is either higher than needed by a group to reach its goals or so low that a group is less effective than it could be in reaching its goals. Because the boundary between functional and dysfunctional conflict is often fuzzy, deciding what level of conflict is functional requires a manager to understand both the positive and negative results of conflict. A knowledgeable manager then tries to manage conflict to keep it within functional bounds.

Conflict that is functional in one group can be dysfunctional in another group. A process analysis team that is trying to solve a difficult quality problem, for example, might need more conflict than a group doing routine tasks. The conflict requirements of a group or an entire organization can also change with time. Conflict that is functional at one point can be dysfunctional at another point. Organizations or groups that have enjoyed an unchanging environment may need more conflict to help adapt to a turbulent environment.

The assessment of whether conflict is functional or dysfunctional is made from the perspective of the organization, not the perspective of individual participants.[16] We all differ in how much conflict we can tolerate. The conflict requirements of the group in which you work may be higher than what you are comfortable experiencing. The level of conflict can still be functional for the group although one or more members feel uncomfortable.

Dysfunctionally high conflict can produce excessive levels of tension, anxiety, and stress. It can drive out people who could be valuable to the group but cannot tolerate such a high level of conflict. Dysfunctionally high conflict can also reduce trust, leading to continual antagonistic interactions. As a result, one or more parties to the conflict may withhold or distort information. Poor-quality decision making can result when conflict reaches a dysfunctional level. The conflict can also become the focus of management's attention, diverting valuable resources from other tasks.

Dysfunctionally low conflict is the opposite of functional conflict. The organization or group does not encourage new ideas or tolerate different points of view. Decisions are made with poor information. The organization encourages traditional approaches, although the external environment requires innovation and change. This description of dysfunctional conflict may strike you as strange because of the widespread idea that conflict is bad for organizations.[17]

Mary Parker Follett, an early writer about organizational conflict, used the phrase "constructive conflict" in her writings. She felt conflict unshackles people from a mind-set that considers only existing alternatives and problem solutions.[18] Follett believed conflict can lead to innovation and change by generating new information and new ideas.[19] Conflict can reduce stagnation by forcing participants to examine new ideas and solutions to old problems.[20]

The Opening Episode described conflict between the students and administration at Gallaudet University. The conflict levels were high with extremely antagonistic interactions among the groups involved. Only time will tell whether this conflict was functional for Gallaudet University.

Conflict management involves maintaining conflict at a level that is functional for the group. If the conflict level is dysfunctionally high, managers should reduce the conflict. If the conflict level is dysfunctionally low, managers should increase the conflict. Much of the rest of this chapter will show you how to manage conflict to get its functional results.

. . . .

Levels and Types of Conflict in Organizations

Organization conflict occurs at several levels and appears in different forms. Figure 11-1 shows a classification of organization conflict by level and type. The various levels and types of conflict often have different sources and roots. Understanding the levels and types of conflict can help a person diagnose a conflict episode and do an effective job of conflict management.

FIGURE 11-1

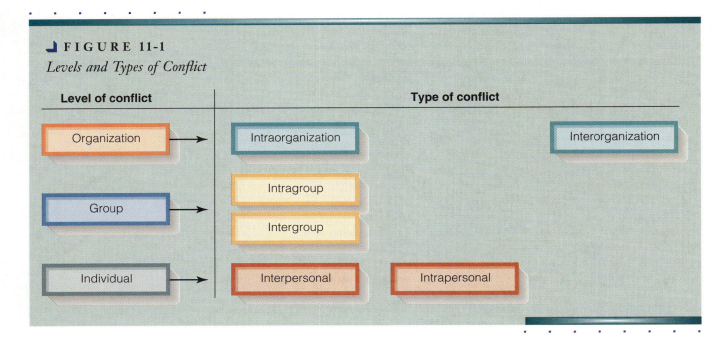

Levels and Types of Conflict

INTRAORGANIZATION CONFLICT

Intraorganization conflict includes all types of conflict occurring within an organization. This type of conflict happens at the interfaces of organization functions created by the design of the organization.[21] Such conflict can occur along the vertical and horizontal dimensions of the organization. Vertical conflict develops between managers and subordinates.[22] Horizontal conflict occurs between departments and work groups. Two department managers, for example, may be in conflict because the organization has not clearly defined their areas of authority. Their decision-making areas overlap, and each wants the other to give up some authority.

Other types of intraorganization conflict are intragroup conflict and intergroup conflict. **Intragroup conflict** is conflict among members of a group. Conflict within a group is likely to be highest during the early stages of group development when there are strong differences among members. The conflict can be about ways of doing tasks or reaching the group's goals. Note that conflict within a group is also interpersonal conflict.

Intergroup conflict is conflict between two or more groups in an organization.[23] This type of conflict often has its roots in the design of the organization.[24] For example, the Opening Episode described an intergroup conflict involving three groups: the students and faculty together, at least one administrator, and the trustees. The organizational design of Gallaudet University formed the groups that became involved in the conflict.

Interpersonal conflict is conflict between two or more people,[25] such as between a customer and a sales clerk or between two people within an organization. Interpersonal conflict is the most basic form of conflict behavior in organizations. Although the discussions above focused on the interfaces at which intraorganization conflict can happen, the conflict behavior actually occurs at the interpersonal level.[26]

Interpersonal conflict happens for many reasons, including basic differences in views about what should be done, efforts to get more resources to do a job, or differences in orientation to work and time in different parts of an organization. Interpersonal conflict can also arise because of intrapersonal conflict. A person may release the internal tension of intrapersonal conflict by lashing out at someone during an interpersonal interaction.

INTRAPERSONAL CONFLICT

Intrapersonal conflict is conflict that occurs within an individual. The conflict arises because of a threat to the person's basic values, a feeling of unfair treatment by the organization, or from multiple and contradictory sources of socialization. The Theory of Cognitive Dissonance, discussed in Chapter 4, described how people react to intrapersonal conflict. People will feel internally uncomfortable and try to reduce the discomfort. Another form of intrapersonal conflict is negative inequity, described in Chapter 8. Individuals who perceive themselves as getting less for their contributions to the organization than they believe they deserve experience intrapersonal conflict.

Intrapersonal conflict can also arise when an employee sees actions within an organization that he considers illegal or unethical. Individuals base such judgments on their personal values and ethics. The tension created by the intrapersonal conflict can lead the individual to act directly against the organization. This act of "whistle-blowing" pits the individual against other members of the organization in what can become extremely heated conflict behavior.[27]

INTERORGANIZATION CONFLICT

Interorganization conflict is conflict between two or more organizations that results from relationships between them. For example, an organization may become highly dependent on its suppliers or distributors, increasing the potential for conflict over delivery times or other agreements. The hostile takeover of one organization by another is also a form of interorganization conflict.[28]

Interorganization conflict is not the same as competition between organizations. Two organizations can compete in the same market without engaging in conflict behavior. Burger King and McDonald's are competitors in the fast-food business, but neither organization tries to prevent the other from doing business.

· · · · · · · · ·

Conflict Episodes

Conflict researchers view conflict processes in organizations as a series of episodes that ebb, flow, and vary in duration.[29] The episode model used in this chapter is one of several such models in the research literature. Although the models vary in specific features, they share many common elements. Each sees antecedents to conflict (latent conflict) that lead to conflict behavior. An episode ends with an aftermath that links it to a later episode.[30] Figure 11-2 shows the stages of a **conflict episode.**

LATENT CONFLICT

Latent conflict refers to factors in the person, group, or organization that might lead to conflict behavior. These conditions are the antecedents to conflict and are a potential for conflict in an organization.

Think of latent conflict as lurking in the background waiting for the right conditions to emerge as conflict behavior. Just as a latent image on a piece of exposed film becomes visible in the presence of certain chemicals, latent conflict rises to the level of awareness under certain conditions. Some basic forms of latent conflict are scarce resources such as limited budgets or equipment and incompatible goals of both individuals and groups. More than one form of latent conflict can be present concurrently. A later section describes possible latent conflicts found in organizations.

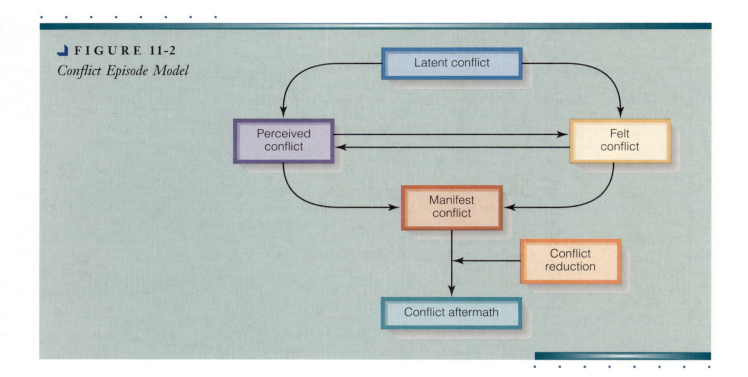

FIGURE 11-2
Conflict Episode Model

Latent conflict

Perceived conflict

Felt conflict

Manifest conflict

Conflict reduction

Conflict aftermath

PERCEIVED CONFLICT

Even when latent conflict factors are present, conflict may not be **perceived** by those potentially in conflict. Two mechanisms limit the perception of conflict. People can block out mild conflict by suppressing their awareness of it. If many conditions exist for conflict in an organization, individuals may focus on them selectively, letting them successfully manage the conflict. All the perceptual mechanisms discussed in Chapter 4 operate for perceived conflict.

Latent conflict does not always precede the perception of conflict. People can perceive themselves in conflict when no latent conditions exist. A common example is misunderstanding another person's position on an issue. The misperception substitutes for the antecedent. Increased communication can reduce the perception of conflict in such a case.

FELT CONFLICT

Felt conflict is the emotional part of a conflict episode. At least one individual personalizes the conflict and focuses on the parties involved, losing sight of the underlying issues. Some conflict episodes never enter the felt conflict stage. Two individuals disagree but neither feels any hostility toward the other. They treat the disagreement as an issue to settle that has nothing to do with them personally.

Other conflict episodes have a strong felt conflict element. Feelings between the two parties can become intense. They express hostility orally and in extreme cases physically. This type of conflict episode is what you likely recall if you have strong negative feelings about conflict. The arrow from perceived conflict to felt conflict in Figure 11-2 indicates the possibility of personalizing conflict once the parties perceive that the conditions for conflict are present. Conflict episodes with strong felt conflict are among the more difficult to manage well.

Felt conflict also includes the values and attitudes the parties to a conflict episode hold about each other. High levels of trust and a value orientation of interpersonal cooperation can lead to lower perceived conflict. The opposite attitudes and values can lead to high perceived conflict. The arrow from felt conflict to perceived conflict in Figure 11-2 indicates that felt conflict can lead to perceived conflict.

 ## MANIFEST CONFLICT

Manifest conflict is the actual conflict behavior between the parties to the conflict episode. It can be oral, written, or physical aggression. Oral manifestations are the arguments we often see either between ourselves and another person or between other people. Written manifest conflict is the exchange of memoranda or other documents designed to make a point or win an argument. Physical aggression is strongly negative conflict behavior intended to injure an opponent.

 ## CONFLICT AFTERMATH

Conflict episodes end with a **conflict aftermath.** If the conflict episode is settled to the satisfaction of the parties involved, the conflict aftermath will be clear of any potential latent conflicts for a new episode. When the conflict ends but the basis of the conflict is still present, the aftermath holds the latent conflicts for a new conflict episode. For example, disputes over the allocation of scarce resources often are settled by compromise. No one gets exactly what he wants so the aftermath contains the latent desires for more resources. A new episode may start later because of the latent conflict left in the aftermath of a previous episode. As you will see later, each method of reducing conflict leaves a different conflict aftermath.

Go back and reread the Opening Episode. Now that you understand more about the episodic quality of conflict in organizations, you should now see how and why the conflict at Gallaudet University unfolded in this way.

 ## RELATIONSHIPS AMONG CONFLICT EPISODES

Figure 11-3 shows the relationships among conflict episodes. Each conflict episode links to the next by the connection between the conflict aftermath and the latent conflict. Breaking that connection is the challenge of effective conflict management. Effective long-term reduction of dysfunctionally high conflict, requires discovering the latent conflicts and removing them from the conflict aftermath. You will discover that one cannot always completely clear the aftermath of a conflict episode. In this sense, conflict is a fact of organization life.

 ## PRESSURES ON CONFLICT EPISODES

Conflict episodes occur in a social context that can put **pressure** on the parties to the conflict.[31] Managers of departments and work units often find themselves in conflict with another manager. Each manager represents a constituency with a stake in the outcome. "Winning" the conflict episode can become important to one manager or the other because of pressure to win from his constituency. Because of this pressure, the conflict may not end with the most satisfactory resolution, increasing the chances that latent conflict will remain in the conflict aftermath of the episode.

Organizational cultures take different approaches to conflict behavior. Cultures that believe certain levels of conflict are functional may support using problem-solving conflict behavior designed to get at the true underlying issues. This type of organizational culture supports ending a conflict episode without the latencies for another episode.

FIGURE 11-3

Relationships among Conflict Episodes

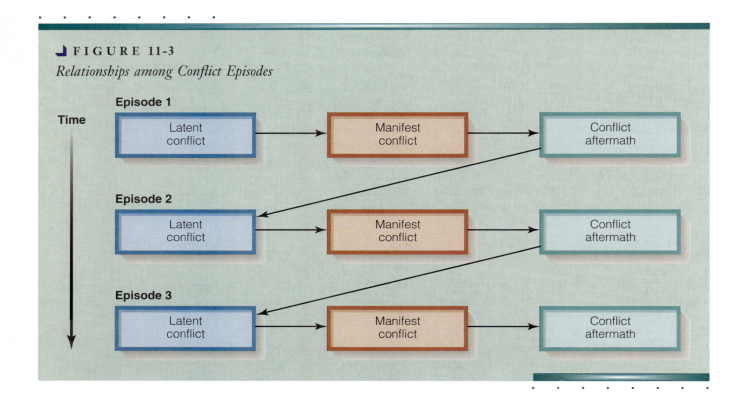

Other cultures encourage the repression of conflict behavior in the belief that it is unacceptable to the system. In this case, people may internalize the conflict and develop strong, but repressed, negative feelings about another party. A later conflict episode can erupt with almost explosive levels of felt conflict. Conflict in such systems can reach dysfunctionally high levels.

EXERCISE Orientations to Conflict

*T*he **orientation to conflict** that people bring to an episode can affect their behavior during the episode.[32] Understanding your orientation and the possible orientations of others can help you understand behavior in a conflict episode. If you must manage conflict, understanding these orientations can help your diagnosis of the conflict. The following exercise assesses your conflict orientation.

DESCRIPTION

Using the following scale, indicate the degree to which the statements in Table 11-2 describe your behavior in potential conflict situations.[33] Record your answers on a separate piece of paper.

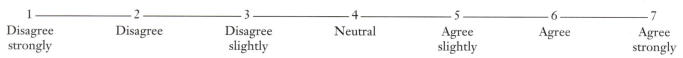

1	2	3	4	5	6	7
Disagree strongly	Disagree	Disagree slightly	Neutral	Agree slightly	Agree	Agree strongly

Tally your scores according to the following key:

Dominance = Item 1 + Item 2 + Item 7 + Item 16
Collaborative = Item 8 + Item 10 + Item 13 + Item 17
Compromise = Item 3 + Item 5 + Item 9 + Item 18
Avoidance = Item 4 + Item 11 + Item 14 + Item 19
Accommodative = Item 6 + Item 12 + Item 15 + Item 20

1. I am usually firm in pursuing my goals.
2. I try to win my position.
3. I give up some points in exchange for others.
4. I feel that differences are not always worth worrying about.
5. I try to find a position that is intermediate between the other person's and mine.
6. In approaching negotiations, I try to be considerate of the other person's wishes.
7. I try to show the logic and benefits of my position.
8. I always lean toward a direct discussion of the problem.
9. I try to find a fair combination of gains and losses for both of us.
10. I try to immediately work through our differences.
11. I try to avoid creating unpleasantness for myself
12. I might try to soothe the other's feelings and preserve our relationship.
13. I try to get all concerns and issues immediately out in the open.
14. I sometimes avoid taking positions that would create controversy.
15. Rather than negotiate the things on which we disagree, I try to stress those things upon which we both agree.
16. I press to get my points made.
17. I consistently seek the other's help in working out a solution.
18. I propose a middle ground.
19. There are times when I let others take responsibility for solving the problem.
20. I sometimes sacrifice my own wishes for the wishes of the other person.

Source: Thomas-Kilmann Conflict Mode Instrument, pp 2–5. © Copyright 1974, Thomas-Kilmann Conflict Mode Instrument. Xicom, Inc. Woods Road, Tuxedo, New York. Adapted with permission by: Joseph E. Champoux, Ph.D.

⌐ INTERPRETATION

This section describes the typical behavior of a person who scored high for an orientation. The behavior is less characteristic of a person with a low score. A high score is 18 points or more; a low score is 6 points or less. Do not be surprised if you had a high score for more than one orientation. People can use more than one orientation because they have different predispositions. They also can use more than one orientation because different conflict situations call for different orientations.

A person with a dominance orientation to conflict wants to win the conflict episode and overwhelm the other party. A person with this orientation cares more about his position than about the position of the other person. Conflict episodes in which at least one party has a dominance orientation can escalate and become highly emotional and unpleasant. Dominance-oriented people are unlikely to accept a solution to the conflict that does not give them a feeling of winning a battle. A dominance orientation is useful, though, in situations requiring quick action, in conflicts where a choice must be made among unpopular alternatives, or in situations when survival of a unit or an organization is at stake.

A person with a collaborative orientation wants to satisfy the desires of all parties to the conflict. This orientation gets commitment to the final conflict result and blends the insights of everyone involved. A person with a collaborative orientation enters the conflict episode with a sincere desire to find a solution that satisfies each party to the conflict. This orientation is difficult and time-consuming. There is no assurance that the desires of each party can be satisfied, especially in conflicts over scarce resources. The conflict episode can drag on as the collaborative-oriented person searches for a satisfactory solution. Such behavior can be frustrating to the other party who may not share the same orientation, adding to hostile behavior during the episode.

A person with a compromise orientation splits the difference, so each party gets only part of what he wants. The episode features "horse-trading," giving something to get something. Because each party gets something from whatever "deal" is made, the episode can close without harsh feelings between the parties. The compromise orientation works in situations with deadlines for resolution or where a temporary solution to a complex problem is all that is practical. It also is useful when neither party's goals are particularly important and more time-consuming orientations are difficult to justify.

An avoidance orientation can reflect a low tolerance for conflict. The person avoids conflict by backing away

TABLE 11-3
Main Features of Each Conflict Orientation

- **Dominance:** Person wants to win the conflict episode and overwhelm the other party. Views conflict episodes as battles to fight and win.
- **Collaborative:** Person wants to satisfy the wishes of all parties to the conflict and sincerely desires to find a solution that satisfies everyone.
- **Compromise:** Person splits the difference so each party gets only part of what he wants. Conflict episodes feature "horse-trading," giving something to get something.
- **Avoidance:** Person backs way from a conflict episode, possibly because of low tolerance for conflict.
- **Accommodative:** Person focuses on needs and desires of the other party to the conflict, ignoring his own needs and desires.

from a conflict episode. The orientation may also reflect apathy about the issues or that the person perceives the issues as trivial. An avoidance orientation is useful for letting people cool off from a conflict episode. It also is useful where possible damage from facing the conflict exceeds the benefits of fixing the conflict. Individuals with an avoidance orientation find it hard to talk through the basis of conflict. They want to walk away from the episode, but doing so prevents them from getting to the real basis of the conflict. The conflict episode is likely to be short-lived, and its results will probably not be fruitful.

A person with an accommodative orientation focuses on the other party to the conflict. He ignores his needs and desires in deference to what the other party wants. The conflict episode can be brief when a party has an accommodative orientation. The behavior during the episode will not be highly emotional, at least on the part of the person who is trying to pacify the other. As a result, the needs of the other party are likely to be satisfied, but not those of the person with the accommodative orientation. People use an accommodative orientation when they see they are losing the conflict episode. They also use it when continued conflict could damage their long-term goals.

Table 11-3 lists the main features of each conflict orientation. Refer to the table while reflecting on your pattern of scores and the following questions:

- Which orientations have you used most frequently and least frequently?
- Which orientations have you found most effective and least effective?

- What were the situations where the different orientations were most and least effective?
- Which patterns emerged among other students in your class?

A person's orientation toward conflict can change as the conflict episode unfolds. Whether a change in orientation occurs depends on how firmly the person holds to the orientation, the importance of the issues to the person, and his perception of an opponent's power. A dominance-oriented person presses to win important issues but can shift to a compromise orientation. The shift can happen if the person perceives that the other party's power and potential to win the conflict episode is stronger than his.

Each orientation has a different effect on the aftermath of a conflict episode. Avoidance, accommodative, and dominance orientations leave well-defined aftermaths that can result in later conflict. A collaborative orientation can leave the cleanest aftermath when it successfully identifies and satisfies the desires of all parties to the conflict. A clean aftermath reduces the chance of future conflict over the same issues. Compromise is a middle ground, leaving some aftermath, but not as much as the first three orientations.

Research evidence strongly indicates that a collaborative orientation to conflict yields more positive long-term benefits for organizations than the other four orientations. Benefits include better-quality decisions, increased trust, and increased satisfaction with the results of a conflict episode.[34]

Latent Conflict: The Sources of Conflict in Organizations

Recall that latent conflicts are antecedents to a conflict episode. Many natural conditions of organizations act as latent conflicts. Such latencies lurk in the background

Scarce resources

Organization differentiation

Rules, procedures, policies

Cohesive groups

Interdependence

Communication barriers

Ambiguous jurisdictions

Reward system

→ Latent conflict

and trigger conflict when the right set of conditions occurs. The presence of latent conflict does not always lead to manifest conflict although the latencies create a high potential for conflict. Latent conflict also is important to understand because the latencies give us clues about how to reduce dysfunctionally high conflict.

The latent conflicts described in this section are major sources of conflict in organizations.[35] Some latent conflicts are especially characteristic of large organizations. The latencies discussed here are representative but not exhaustive of sources of conflict. Creative diagnosis of organization conflict requires identifying conflict latencies. Any specific conflict episode can have variations on the latent conflicts described here. Figure 11-4 shows the latent conflicts discussed below.

Dependence on scarce resources is a common latent conflict in organization. The scarce resources can be tangible, such as money, equipment, and facilities, or intangible, such as knowledge and expertise.[36] Individuals or groups often find themselves dependent on the same facility to do their work. The resource is finite and cannot be expanded quickly. The dependence on the single facility can bring individuals into conflict. A common example is a single copying machine within a department. Several people could want to use the machine simultaneously, and an argument could erupt between two potential users. The single machine as a scarce resource was the latency for the conflict episode.

Organization differentiation,[37] which is discussed later in Chapter 17, can be a major source of conflict in organizations. The differentiation produces groups and work units with different goals, time horizons, views of the world, and languages. For example, research and development people typically think in the long term and have their own scientific jargon. Production people want to get tasks done now according to a specific schedule. The various orientations produced by this differentiation form a latency that can lead to a conflict episode when members of the different units must interact.

Organizations have many rules, procedures, and policies to guide decision making about recurring events. The same procedures and policies intended to get smooth organization functioning are a latent conflict.[38] This type of latent conflict could be lurking in your college or university. Each school usually has policies governing when a new section of a class can be opened. For example, your school may say 100 students must be enrolled in a section of a course before a new section can be opened. A professor, however, may prefer that his classes not exceed 60 students. The

· *University computer centers are often a scarce resource and a latent conflict in the closing weeks of a semester or a quarter. "Computer Cathedral" at the University of Michigan has enough resources to avoid this latent conflict.*

professor closes the class at 60. Students complain to an administrator. The administrator and the professor begin a conflict episode, the latency for which was a previously existing policy.

Cohesive groups develop a culture of their own. The members of such groups strongly identify with the group and care about what it represents. Groups also can differ in what they value. Conflict can erupt when members of such groups interact with each other.[39]

High interdependence among people at work is another source of conflict in organizations. This latent conflict can be caused by the type of technical process used by the organization. It also can be found where work is designed around groups and not individuals.[40] Whatever its source, interdependence in organizations forces people to interact with each other. The required interaction increases the potential for conflict within the organization.

Communication barriers are another source of latent conflict in organizations. If individuals or groups do not interact frequently with each other, misunderstandings can develop between the groups. This type of latent conflict is common in organizations with shift work. The day shift does not interact with the evening shift except briefly at the change of shifts. Members of each shift develop opinions about the quality of the other shift's work. As those opinions become diverse, the potential for conflict during the change in shifts increases.

Ambiguous jurisdictions are another common latent conflict. This latency occurs when the organization has not clearly defined individuals' areas of decision authority. "Turf battles" erupt when two people or groups believe they have the responsibility for the same activity. This type of latent conflict is common in a matrix organization, if the organization has not clearly defined the areas of jurisdiction.[41] Many people in such organizations work for more than one person. Conflict can arise when those people receive conflicting orders from their multiple bosses.

The reward system of the organization is another area of latent conflict. Reward systems that encourage different and incompatible behavior are a significant source of latent conflict. A common example is the design of reward systems for sales and manufacturing people. Sales people receive a commission for selling. Manufacturing managers get rewards for keeping costs down. Sales people can make more sales by offering early delivery dates, but those dates may not fit into manufacturing's production schedule. The conflict potential is high and can lead to a conflict episode when sales and manufacturing interact.

. . . .

Conflict Management

Conflict management focuses on maintaining conflict at functional levels for a department, work unit, or an entire organization. Conflict management does not mean the complete elimination of conflict, nor does it refer only to conflict reduction. It means maintaining conflict at the right level to help the department, work unit, or organization reach its goals.[42]

Basic to the process of conflict management is the selection of a desired level of conflict. The desired level of conflict varies according to the **perceived conflict requirements** of the unit. Several factors affect the choice of the desired level of conflict. Organizational cultures place differing values on debate, disagreement, and conflict itself. Managers in organizational cultures that support debate, doubt, and questioning may perceive a higher desired level of conflict than those who do not. The nature of the organization's product or service also affects the desired level of conflict. Creative and innovative products or services require a higher level of conflict than more routine and predictable products and services. Organizations facing fast-changing external environments require higher conflict levels for successful adaptation than organizations facing stable external environments.

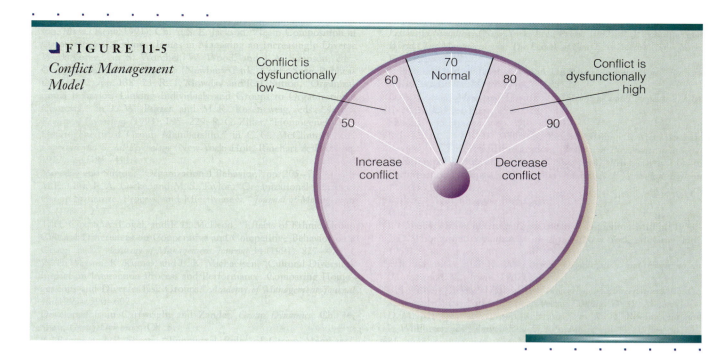

FIGURE 11-5

Conflict Management Model

Conflict is dysfunctionally low — 50 60 70 Normal 80 — Conflict is dysfunctionally high — 90

Increase conflict

Decrease conflict

Desired conflict levels for an organization, department, or work unit can vary from one group to another and for the same group over time.[43] If an organization's environment shifts from stable to turbulent, then the right level of conflict becomes higher. A shift in the opposite direction causes the right level of conflict to become lower.

The preceding paragraphs emphasized a manager's perception of the desired level of conflict. The manager's **tolerance for conflict** affects his perception of a unit's conflict requirements. A manager who avoids conflict likely has a lower tolerance for conflict than a manager who actively engages in functional conflict behavior. Even when a work unit requires a specific conflict level, the manager's tolerance for conflict affects his perception of the desired level.

Figure 11-5 shows a model of conflict management. The figure shows the process of conflict management as a thermostat, emphasizing a manager's monitoring of conflict levels. If conflict levels are at about the desired level, the manager (thermostat) does nothing. If the conflict level is dysfunctionally high, the manager tries to

· *This concurrent engineering team at NCR Atlanta brought a new check-out counter terminal to market in half the normal time. The new terminal had 85 percent fewer parts than earlier versions and an assembly time of two minutes. Maintaining conflict at a functional level within such teams is a key aspect of their success.*

reduce the conflict. If the conflict level is dysfunctionally low, the manager tries to increase the conflict. In the same way a thermostat maintains a desired room temperature, conflict management maintains a desired conflict level.

What are the symptoms that a manager can read to decide whether the conflict level is dysfunctionally high or low.[44] Low trust in a work unit, deliberate distortion of information, high levels of tension during interpersonal interactions, and antagonism between parties are all signs of dysfunctionally high conflict. In extreme cases, dysfunctional conflict can take the form of sabotage of the organization's products or services or violence against other parties.

Suppression and withdrawal are two symptoms of dysfunctionally low conflict.[45] Suppression includes denial of differences and a desire to perceive similarities between parties that do not exist. Repressing controversial information and prohibiting disagreements about legitimate issues also are signs of suppression. Withdrawal includes reduced communication to avoid interactions that could lead to controversy, the belief in "peace at any price," and walking away from a disagreeable interaction.

. . . .

❏ *Reducing Conflict*

Several approaches exist for **reducing conflict** in organizations. The approaches divide into three groups: lose-lose, win-lose, and win-win. Although these approaches usually are called methods of conflict resolution, this chapter refers to them as methods of conflict reduction because many do not eliminate conflict.[46] Table 11-4 lists the methods of conflict reduction described in this section. Managers must use caution when reducing conflict to make sure it does not fall to a dysfunctionally low level.

❏ TABLE 11-4
Methods of Conflict Reduction

LOSE-LOSE METHODS	WIN-LOSE METHODS	WIN-WIN METHODS
Avoidance	Dominance	Problem solving
Compromise	Authoritative command	Integration
Smoothing	Majority rule	Superordinate goal
Separation		Exchange members
Buffering		Expansion of resources
Third-party intervention		
Reference to rules		

❏ LOSE-LOSE METHODS

Lose-lose methods of conflict reduction do not try to deal directly with the conflict. None of the parties to the conflict episode get what they want. Sometimes the lose-lose approaches ignore the conflict altogether and do not try to reduce it.

Avoidance is an obvious way to reduce conflict in the short run, but it does not permanently reduce the conflict. A conflict episode can recur when the parties meet again. Withdrawal may happen because one party to the conflict has a low tolerance for conflict or because one party has an avoidance orientation to conflict. The conflict episode is stressful, and the party simply wants to avoid the confrontation.

Anyone trying to manage conflict must be aware of the prospect of avoidance. Although manifest conflict levels will not be high, the latent conflict is still there. Later conflict episodes can arise and surprise those managing conflict.

Compromise uses bargaining and negotiation to reduce conflict. Each party to the conflict gives up something to get something he values. Although manifest conflict drops, the conflict aftermath is not cleared. The parties to the conflict have not completely resolved the underlying issues.

When the latent conflict is scarce resources, compromise is a common reduction method because resources often cannot be expanded quickly. The conflict over the copying machine described earlier offers an opportunity for compromise: let each party copy part of what he needs and return later to copy the rest. The manifest conflict behavior subsides, but the latent conflict is not removed.

Smoothing emphasizes the similarities between the parties to the conflict. Discussion centers on similar points of view, not differences. Because the differences are not discussed, they remain in the conflict aftermath and become a latent conflict that may spark a later conflict episode.

Separation of the parties in conflict reduces manifest conflict. This method is useful when a quick response to conflict is necessary to prevent immediate damage. Separation has the disadvantage of not addressing the issues underlying the conflict. The conflict episode ends with a predictable conflict aftermath. A later conflict episode can happen if the parties do not stay separated.

Buffering is a way of reducing conflict caused by interdependence of people's tasks and duties.[47] Interdependent production tasks often have buffer stocks of parts or materials between individual workers. Such buffers decouple the workers, reducing the chance of conflict from interdependence of the tasks. This approach to conflict reduction can be effective but depends on the management of the buffer stocks.

Managers who use third-party intervention submit conflicts to a neutral person for solution. Arbitration of labor disputes is a common example of third-party intervention. The third party may try to reduce the conflict by giving something to each party in the conflict episode. In this respect, it is much like compromise with the third party suggesting the compromise. Also like compromise, a conflict aftermath is left behind. The issues often are not satisfactorily resolved for all concerned.

You have probably settled a dispute with another person by flipping a coin. You were using a reference to rules method to reduce the conflict. In this method, managers use an existing rule to settle the conflict or arrange one such as flipping a coin. When an employee asks for time off, a manager may refer to some existing policy about days off. Referring to the policy avoids facing the conflict. A conflict aftermath remains for those who lose from reference to rules.

WIN-LOSE METHODS

Win-lose conflict reduction methods make one party to the conflict a clear winner and the other party a clear loser. Such techniques leave a conflict aftermath that can result in a new conflict episode.

Dominance happens when one party to a conflict simply overwhelms the other. Dominance can occur because one party has higher organization status or is physically overpowering. It can also happen when one party to the conflict has a low tolerance for conflict. You can think of dominance as the "flip side" of avoidance. If one party has an appeasement or avoidance conflict orientation, the other party can easily dominate the episode. Dominance leaves a conflict aftermath because it does not try to discover why the conflict occurred.

Organizations widely use authoritative command for conflict reduction, partly because of the formal authority relationships found there. Two people in conflict refer their conflict to a common superior who decides the solution to the conflict. Manifest conflict stops, but the conflict episode ends with a conflict aftermath.

Decision-making groups faced with conflict over issues can use majority rule to reduce the conflict. Each issue is put to a vote letting some members of the group win and others lose. If the alternatives are acceptable to all concerned, this method can work effectively. If the same people lose repeatedly and personalize the loss, majority rule leaves a potentially destructive aftermath.

With win-win conflict reduction methods, each party to the conflict episode gets what he wants. Win-win approaches do not leave a conflict aftermath because they directly address the causes of the conflict and try to remove them. Although these techniques do not strongly differ, they have some useful distinctions.

Problem solving tries to find the true basis of a conflict episode.[48] This method tries to make sure all differences among the parties are fully exposed. All parties to the conflict encourage and support minority views to be sure they get full expression. The parties view differences as important sources of information leading to creative solutions to the conflict.

Organizations and managers who use problem solving do not have a negative view of conflict. They see conflict episodes as constructive opportunities for creative solutions to problems. Properly done, problem solving leaves little or no conflict aftermath.

Integration seeks solutions that are in the best interests of all parties.[49] It assumes that people's deeply held interests and desires are the basis of conflict. This approach tries to find a solution that fully meets the goals of each party.

A superordinate goal is a goal desired by all parties to the conflict but unattainable by any party alone.[50] Superordinate goals compel cooperation even if the parties otherwise do not wish to cooperate. Organizations using group-based incentive programs are using a form of superordinate goal. Everyone in the group wants to get the reward, but no one can do it alone.

Superordinate goals should work well where the latent conflict is high interdependence. The superordinate goal operates in the background, forcing the members of the group to cooperate. Later conflict episodes are less likely in the presence of a continually operating superordinate goal.

When conflict is based on misunderstandings because of different group membership, a manager can exchange members between the groups to reduce the conflict. A goal of the exchange is to increase interaction among those in conflict. The exchange and interaction let each person see how the other group functions. The individuals come to learn the point of view of the opposing group. This process is time-consuming but effective in clearing up misperceptions. Little conflict aftermath will remain if the exchange continues for a long enough period to change people's perceptions and attitudes.

Expansion of resources is the desired approach in episodes that have resource constraints as the latent conflict. This approach has obvious limitations, with cost being a major one. In the copying machine example earlier, the desired solution would be more copying machines, but this may not be possible if the organization has a limited budget. Low-cost personal copiers may be a solution available to managers in the future.

Increasing Conflict

The interactionist philosophy of conflict management says a manager should **increase conflict** when it becomes dysfunctionally low. The goal of increasing conflict is to get the functional qualities of conflict described earlier, such as more information for decisions and creative solutions to problems. Table 11-5 summarizes the main features of methods to increase conflict.

Increasing conflict must be done skillfully and cautiously so conflict levels do not become dysfunctionally high. The manager's role is to structure situations as described below and not express opinions or take positions on issues. This role is especially important because it can encourage subordinates to express their views.[51]

Groups with members of different social backgrounds, education, expertise, organization positions, and opinions have high conflict potential. By deliberately forming heterogeneous groups to find creative solutions to problems, a manager tries to use the functional qualities of conflict. Organizations with a diverse workforce have an especially rich resource for forming groups with high conflict potential.

A manager of a decision-making group can ask one member of the group to play the role of devil's advocate. This person deliberately criticizes a position that has emerged as dominant within the group. Alternatively, the manager can ask each person in the group to critique the alternatives under consideration. Each of these approaches recognizes the information-generating function of conflict.

Dialectical inquiry is a structured debate of opposing views about solutions to a decision problem. Two people or groups prepare arguments and debate the question in the presence of the person who makes the final decision. One argument presents the prevailing opinion about a decision. The other argument presents a believable and plausible alternative. The decision maker forms a final decision by drawing upon information presented by both sides.[52]

Managers can also try to develop an organizational culture with a set of values and norms that support openness about debate and opinions. They must devote time to building this type of culture. Searching for quick solutions to problems can lead to pressure to reduce differences and emphasize similarities.

Increasing interdependence among individuals increases conflict potential. The use of "just-in-time" inventory management makes the production process more dependent on incoming raw materials and parts. The parts of the organization connecting inventory with production are more interdependent under "just-in-time" management than under more traditional warehousing methods.[53]

The design of the organization's reward system can also increase conflict. Extrinsic rewards can powerfully affect behavior. Using rewards to get different behavior from individuals and groups can increase conflict levels in the organization.

CASE — *How Ford and Mazda Shared the Driver's Seat*

*T*his case describes a collaborative automobile design effort between Ford Motor Co. and Mazda Motor Corp. Read the case with the following questions in mind:

Source: J. B. Treece, "How Ford and Mazda Shared the Driver's Seat," *Business Week*, March 26, 1990, pp. 94–95. Reprinted from March 26, 1990 issue of *Business Week* by special permission, copyright © 1990 by the McGraw-Hill Companies.

1. Could the people described in the case have anticipated the latent conflicts that were present? Why? What were those latent conflicts?
2. Did the key managers do an effective job of managing the conflict episodes?

In March, 1985, Gordon B. Riggs flew to Hiroshima on an urgent mission from Ford Motor Co. Two years earlier, Ford had commissioned Mazda Motor Corp. to engineer a new version of Ford's best-selling Escort, which the No. 2 U.S. auto maker planned to build in North America using mostly Japanese parts. But a hitch had developed. Ford decided its new-car fleet wouldn't average the 27.5 miles per gallon that Washington required by 1991 unless the high-mileage Escort was included in the calculation. And under the fuel-economy rules, the Escort could be counted only if at least 75% of it was made at home. Riggs, who headed Ford's small-car programs, had to break the news to Mazda—and find a way to add more U.S. parts to the Escort than the two partners had planned.

From that crisis sprang a product-development effort that Michinori Yamanouchi, a Mazda senior managing director, calls "innovative in automotive history." Over the next five years, Ford styled the outside of the car while Mazda engineered the inside. Mazda taught Ford how to keep a strict development schedule, and Ford proved to Mazda that U.S. suppliers can turn out high-quality parts. In fact, the two worked together so well that when the 1991 Escort hits the showrooms on Apr. 26, it will arrive on time, within its $2 billion budget, and performing better than planned. As a result, the Escort project could help encourage more joint product development in many industries—and in autos, for sure. "We have done a global program now," says Dee T. Kapur, who ended up managing Ford's end of the project. "Maybe in six or seven years, it will be a normal way of doing business."

The CT20, as the new Escort was code-named, culminates a decade of work toward what former Ford Chairman Donald E. Petersen calls the "global car." His idea, which failed with the original Escort, was to engineer on one continent a car that could be built and sold on several, thus making the best use of costly engineering resources. The Chevrolet Prizm, which Toyota Motor Corp. and General Motors Corp., make in Fremont, Calif. was a start in this direction. But the CT20 goes much further. It is to be assembled in 12 locations for annual global sales of 900,000 units in 90 markets, either as the Escort or one of various Mazdas—the 323, Protege, or Familia. And Mazda has handed off its design to Ford, which will build the car with virtually no further Japanese input in Ford plants in Hermosillo, Mexico, and Wayne, Mich. "The Escort exemplifies all we have been striving for," says Petersen, who drove the first one off the Wayne assembly line on Feb. 26.

Small Squabbles. Striving is putting it mildly, says Riggs, recalling his return to Hiroshima. He had been Ford's envoy there from 1979 to 1984, looking after the 24% stake it owns in Mazda, Japan's No. 5 carmaker. Job 1, the first production model of the CT20 wasn't due until 1990. But Riggs knew that Mazda would lock in the design much earlier than Ford, and that it wouldn't put up with the late styling tweaks so common in Detroit. So he quickly assembled a Ford team that knew Mazda's methods, choosing Toshiaki Saito to head it. A Japanese who had joined Ford out of design school, Saito had just supervised the exterior styling of the Ford Probe, which was based on Mazda's sporty MX-6 and built by Mazda for Ford. In six months he had Ford approvals for the CT20's styling, and his team moved to Hiroshima to get Mazda's reaction.

Almost immediately, the debate began. Mazda's designers questioned whether Ford's license-plate recess was big enough for every market. Sure enough, Malaysian plates wouldn't fit. Ford wanted a certain design for roof rails, the gutter above the doors that drains off rain. Mazda resisted, and negotiations dragged on for two weeks, until Saito finally pulled his designers aside. "You can't delay Job 1," he insisted, and Ford dropped the request.

The disputes crossed over into more than styling. Which rust-resistant alloy to use for door flanges? What length should the wheelbase be? Mazda chose two lengths for different models, the shorter one to achieve better handling on cramped Asian roads, while Ford opted for just one. But Ford agreed to give buyers a choice of two suspensions, a stiff one for handling or a soft one for comfort. To reduce noise, Mazda wanted the engine improved, while Ford wanted other adjustments. The compromise was to retune the engine, add more insulation, and install the motor on softer rubber mounts. "There was a lot of frustration," says Kei Kado, general manager of Mazda's office of international business development. "We often needed to call the U.S. But it was midnight, so we had to wait half a day at least." The engine delays added up to scarcely a week, not much by Ford standards. But to Mazda that was a week to make up.

Precise Parts. Then suddenly, in mid-1986, it seemed the headaches might all be for naught. Riggs had cleared his first hurdle easily, sticking a Ford engine in the CT20 to push up its U.S. content. But now the problem was cost. Ford hoped the 1991 Escort would be its first subcompact to make money, not just help meet mileage standards and attract first-time buyers. But the CT20 was way over budget as the yen's sharp rise pushed up Japanese component prices. "The whole program was thrown up in the air," recalls Arthur S. Hyde, the head of Ford's engineering team in Hiroshima. Briefly, Ford considered importing the car from Taiwan, where it makes an Escort look-alike called the Mercury Tracer. But then, the partners realized that the cheap dollar would cut costs for them if they used more American parts in the U.S. model. With that decided, Riggs left the program, replaced by Kenneth R. Dabrowski, who knew the parts business better.

[51]Brown, *Managing Conflict*; Robbins, *Managing Organizational Conflict*; D. Tjosvold, "Implications of Controversy Research for Management," *Journal of Management* 11 (1985): 21–37.

[52]R. A. Cosier and C. R. Schwenk, "Agreement and Thinking Alike: Ingredients for Poor Decisions," *Academy of Management Executive 4* (1990): 69–74; R. O. Mason, "A Dialectical Approach to Strategic Planning," *Management Science* 15 (1969): B–403 to B-414.

[53]R. J. Schonberger, "The Transfer of Japanese Manufacturing Management Approaches to U.S. Industry," *Academy of Management Review* 7 (1982): 479–87.

[54]G. Hofstede, *Culture's Consequences: International Differences in Work-Related Values* (Beverly Hills, CA: Sage Publications, 1984), Ch. 4 and 5.

[55]W. B. Gudykunst, "Culture and Intergroup Processes," in M. H. Bond, ed., *The Cross-Cultural Challenge to Social Psychology* (Newbury Park, Calif.: Sage Publications, 1988), pp. 165–81.

12

Leadership and Management

• *Joan E. Spero, undersecretary for Economic, Business and Agricultural Affairs, is the driving force behind the effort to focus the State Department on economic diplomacy.*

After reading this chapter, you should be able to . . .

- Understand leadership as an influence process in organizations.
- Describe the bases of power and their relationship to leadership and management.
- Distinguish the trait, behavioral, and contingency theories of leadership.
- Discuss some alternative views of leadership.
- Explain the role of neutralizers, substitutes, and enhancers of leader behavior in organizations.
- Distinguish between leadership and management.
- Analyze the effects of self-managing teams on leadership.
- Appreciate some international and ethical issues that surround leadership and management.

Chapter Overview

· · · · · · · · · · · · · · · ·

▷ OPENING EPISODE

Stafford at Pillsbury Co.

As 51-year-old John M. Stafford walked into a hotel meeting room in Naples, Fla., ... to resign as chairman and chief executive of Pillsbury Co., a piano player in the lobby a few feet away was crooning, "Oh, What a Beautiful Mornin.' "

It was a fitting end. During a turbulent three years as head of the giant Minneapolis-based food and restaurant concern, Mr. Stafford time and again seemed out of step with those around him and with his businesses. During his tenure, sales and earnings fell, leadership positions in such moneymakers as baking mixes and pizza eroded, few new products were introduced and Pillsbury's Burger King chain lost market share to McDonald's. In recent months, the company has widely been rumored to be a takeover candidate. . . .

Mr. Stafford from the start struck people as weak. In 1985, for example, there was a meeting of Pillsbury's restaurant-group executives to discuss the future of the troubled JJ. Muggs chain. Some of those present had been assured beforehand that Mr. Stafford supported the chain. But in the meeting, Mr. Spoor [the former chairman] attacked the chain, insiders say, and indicated he wanted to close it. One source who was there says that Mr. Stafford went over to the other side during the meeting and that within 15 minutes after it ended, everyone in the Pillsbury restaurants group knew about it. The source asserts that nobody trusted Stafford after that.

Mr. Stafford was cautious and reluctant to spend for expansion. When executives at Distron, the $1 billion Pillsbury unit that supplies food to Burger King and some other restaurants, asked for $2 million last year to buy about 20 refrigerated tractor-trailers, Mr. Stafford said he would get back to them. He never did. . . .

Former Pillsbury executives say that Mr. Stafford was so preoccupied with numbers and procedure that the businesses suffered. He always had subsidiaries working on projections, they say. Each unit files a five-year plan every year and spends most of the summer and fall preparing it. "We were always planning—never executing," says one former executive.

Mr. Stafford's first big move after becoming chairman was to establish a committee to write a lengthy explanation of the company's "Mission and Values." It was his most visible effort to change Pillsbury's corporate culture, but rivals within Pillsbury quickly began sniping that he lacked a clear vision of his own. . . .

· *The Pillsbury Center, Minneapolis, Minnesota.*

Mr. Stafford's reliance on numbers permeated the company. Last year he named a financial man—Charles Olcott, previously head of investor relations—to run Burger King, amazing other restaurant executives, who believed that Burger King needed a marketing wizard to turn things around after the disastrous "Herb the Nerd" ad campaign. . . .

At headquarters in Minneapolis, executives barely hid their lack of respect for Mr. Stafford. He was sometimes called "the wooden soldier" because of his stiffness and inflexibility. Mr. Campbell, the head of Pillsbury's restaurant businesses, is well-known by insiders for an unflattering imitation of Mr. Stafford sitting stiffly at his desk and making a point by waving his glasses in a predictable pattern.

. . . .

T he reporters who described John M. Stafford at Pillsbury focused both on Stafford's traits and his behavior in different situations. Stafford's traits included cautiousness, reluctance, and inflexibility. His behavior included a tendency to focus on procedure and rely heavily on numbers for decisions. Note also the drop in trust among his subordinates and the absence of a clear vision for the direction of the company. You will find as this chapter unfolds that traits, behavior, trust, and vision play key roles in leadership and management in organizations.

Leaders can hold formal organization positions or emerge spontaneously within an organization.[1] The formal positions carry titles such as Manager, Supervisor, Foreman, or Vice-President. Both the formal qualities of the position and the characteristics of the person holding it contribute to leadership. Other people play leadership roles although they do not hold formally appointed positions. Such leaders are emergent leaders and often are found within formal and informal groups in organizations.[2]

Leadership is a process of social influence involving two or more people: the leader and a follower or a potential follower.[3] The influence process has two dimensions. The first is the intention of the formal or emergent leader to affect the behavior of at least one other person. The second is the extent the target of the influence effort perceives it as acceptable. Perception and attribution, which were discussed in Chapter 4, are important elements of the leadership process in organizations. The person who is the target of the influence effort must attribute it to a specific person and consider it acceptable.

. . . .

↳ *Influence Processes in Leadership and Management*

Much of the success of leaders in organizations depends on the influence they have over others. A manager's power decides the amount of influence she has over a subordinate. A manager can draw on several sources or **bases of power** that come from both her formal management position and her personal characteristics.[4]

◪ ORGANIZATIONAL BASES OF POWER

The organizational bases of power are legitimate power, reward power, coercive power, and information power. Legitimate power derives from the manager's position. The organization gives the manager decision authority that she can use to affect the behavior of subordinates. Assigning tasks and setting goals for completing them are examples of legitimate power.

Reward power derives from the manager's ability to tie positive outcomes to a subordinate's behavior. A manager has high reward power if she can give positive outcomes for desirable behavior. Positive outcomes can include praise, pay increases, or time off. The use of reward power to provide positive outcomes makes the manager more attractive to the subordinate. You will see later in this chapter that understanding subordinates' desires for various outcomes is an important part of leadership.

Coercive power refers to efforts to affect the behavior of another person through fear of punishment. A manager has high coercive power if she has the authority to penalize subordinates. A manager has low coercive power if she has no such authority. The spoken or unspoken threat of a poor evaluation of a subordinate's performance is an example of coercive power.

Information power derives from the control and distribution of information in an organization.[5] Deliberately controlling the receipt and distribution of information increases a manager's information power. When information is scarce, others become more dependent on the manager for information.[6]

Each management position in an organization has certain amounts of organization-based power. The amount of power in a position varies, depending on the organization's policies about rewards and punishments. The person who assumes the position has some organization-based power available to affect the behavior of subordinates. When the person leaves the position, the power stays behind and does not travel with the person to a new position.

 ## PERSONAL BASES OF POWER

The personal bases of power are referent power and expert power. Referent power is based on the personal liking an individual subordinate has for a manager. The more the subordinate identifies with the manager, the stronger the referent power. A manager who is disliked by a subordinate has low referent power.

Expert power derives from the manager's technical knowledge and expertise. A manager with the knowledge and skills needed for group success has high expert power. A manager with little knowledge has low expert power. The source of the manager's influence is the subordinates' dependence on the manager for the information they need to do their job successfully.

The personal bases of power flow from qualities or attributes of the manager. Those bases also depend on the attribution of those qualities to the manager by subordinates. The personal bases of power available to a manager with one group of subordinates will not be available to the same manager with a different group of subordinates.

 ## RELATIONSHIPS AMONG THE BASES OF POWER

Figure 12-1 shows the cumulative effects of the organizational and personal bases of power. The amount of power a leader or manager has depends on the number of bases she has available.

Some leaders and managers will have only the organizational bases of power to influence people. Other leaders and managers will have both organizational and personal bases. Those people will be in the enviable position of having many organizational sources of power at their disposal. They are liked by their subordinates and perceived to be an important source of help in doing their job. The importance of the latter situation will become clearer as the description of leadership processes in organizations unfolds in this chapter.

The organizational bases of power are related in several ways. The organization either authorizes (legitimate power) a manager to reward or penalize subordinates, or it gives the manager no such authority, leading to low levels of reward and coercive power. The organization can also give a manager the authority to access and distribute certain types of information (information power). Think of legitimate,

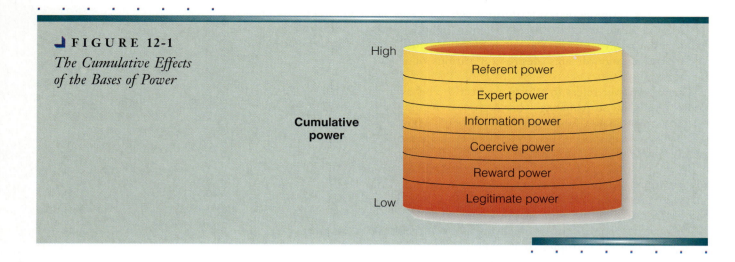

FIGURE 12-1

The Cumulative Effects of the Bases of Power

reward, coercive, and information power as stacked upon each other to form the cumulative power in a formal organization position (Figure 12-1).

Referent power derives from the degree of attractiveness of the manager to the subordinate. Reward power increases the manager's attractiveness; coercive power decreases it. The judicious and fair use of both rewards and sanctions increases the manager's referent power over subordinates. The chapters on motivation have more complete descriptions of how rewards and sanctions can affect behavior.

Trait Approaches to Leadership

The Opening Episode illustrated how people in leadership and management positions are often described by their traits. Personality psychology also relies on traits to explain consistencies in people's behavior across situations.[7] It is not surprising that the earliest studies of leadership in organizations focused on the psychological and personal characteristics that distinguished leaders from nonleaders or leaders from followers.[8] Some scholars have defined a trait as follows:

> A **trait** is defined as any distinctive physical or psychological characteristic of the individual to which the individual's behavior can be attributed. Traits are thus inferred from observation of an individual's behavior.[9]

Much leadership research has focused on finding a set of **leadership traits** that were the qualities of a successful leader or distinguished leaders from followers.[10] The traits investigated were physical factors such as height and weight, social characteristics such as interpersonal skills and status, and personality characteristics. Leaders were intelligent, aware of their situations, and able public speakers. Leaders had higher IQs than their followers but were not successful if they were much more intelligent than their followers. Leaders with knowledge that applied to their situation and who knew how to get things done could move people to high levels of achievement. Leaders carried out their responsibilities. They were self-confident, took the initiative, and persisted when the going got rough. Leaders had high energy and showed a high level of physical and social activity. They were cooperative and able to persuade group members to cooperate. Leaders were adaptable and able to change with changing situations.[11]

Does this trait profile sound logical to you? Common sense tells us that such qualities should be the characteristics of leaders. As described in the Opening Episode, Stafford at Pillsbury lacked many of these qualities.

Some reviews of past research have found the traits of intelligence, dominance, self-confidence, energy, and task-relevant knowledge to be consistently associated with leadership.[12] Leaders are bright, self-confident, high-energy people who know something about the situation they are trying to affect and take control when they must. A later review of leadership research identified these six traits as consistently associated with leadership: "... **drive, the desire to lead, honesty/integrity, self-confidence, cognitive ability, and knowledge of the business.**"[13] Three traits were found in both reviews: self-confidence; cognitive ability, which includes intelligence; and knowledge of the business, which is similar to task-relevant knowledge. Desire to lead and honesty/integrity expand the list of traits. Leaders want to affect the behavior of others. Effective leaders also have honesty and integrity, which help them gain the trust of their followers.

The leadership research community is becoming increasingly aware that traits play an important role in leadership. Personality psychologists have argued that traits are associated with consistent behavior across situations. They also have shown that the relationship between traits and behavior is not as small as many had argued in the past.[14] Some studies have reported stable leadership in groups with varied tasks and membership. Leaders varied their behavior according to the needs and task requirements of the group.[15]

EXERCISE   *Your Traits*

*T*he following are among the many traits people can have. On a separate piece of paper, list the traits you believe best describe you.

Active
Energetic
Intelligent
Knowledgeable
Verbal fluency
Adaptable
Alert to situations
Dependable
Emotionally adjusted
Cooperative
Interpersonally skilled
Sensitive

Persistent
Sociable
Extrovert
Take the initiative
Insightful
Drive
Dominant
Self-confident
Honest
Original
Desire to lead

Review the traits you listed and see how many of them were discussed earlier in the chapter. The more leader-related traits you listed, the more likely you have some qualities of a leader.

Behavioral Theories of Leadership

Leadership researchers eventually realized that traits alone did not fully explain leadership effectiveness. As a result, they turned to studying leader behavior in the late 1950s. Two complementary behavioral theories of leadership were designed to describe the behavior that distinguished leaders of effective and ineffective work groups. One set of researchers was at the University of Michigan; the other set was at Ohio State University.

THE UNIVERSITY OF MICHIGAN STUDIES: PRODUCTION-CENTERED AND EMPLOYEE-CENTERED BEHAVIOR

The University of Michigan Studies of leadership behavior sought to understand the leadership behavior of the best and poorest performing units in an organization. The criteria of unit effectiveness included meeting the organization's productivity goals, employee attitudes, turnover, absenteeism, and costs.

The Michigan researchers conceptualized two dimensions of leadership behavior: Production-centered behavior and Employee-centered behavior.[16] **Production-centered** leader behavior focused on the tasks that had to be done, pressured subordinates to perform, and had little concern for people. Such leaders did not trust people to work on their own and therefore supervised them closely. Production-centered leaders had little understanding or appreciation for the social system within their work units. They did not set high performance goals. Interaction with subordinates was brief and choppy, focusing on specific instructions for doing the job.

Employee-centered leader behavior focused on the people themselves, their personal success, and the quality of the social system that formed within the work unit. Such leaders had high performance goals for their work units and communicated their performance expectations to their subordinates.

The Michigan researchers felt their research showed Employee-centered leadership was more likely to lead to higher work unit performance than Production-centered leadership. They also felt that Production-centered leadership could lead to high productivity but had several latent dysfunctions. The dysfunctions were poor employee attitudes with resulting higher turnover or absenteeism, little group loyalty, and high levels of distrust between subordinates and their leaders.[17]

Employee-centered leadership combined a strong concern for the social aspects of the work unit with high performance expectations. High performance expectations can be a key element in getting high levels of work performance.[18] Here you can begin to see how motivation can be an important tool for effective leaders.

THE OHIO STATE LEADERSHIP STUDIES: INITIATING STRUCTURE AND CONSIDERATION

The Ohio State Leadership Studies also consistently found two dimensions of leadership behavior: Initiating Structure and Consideration. **Initiating Structure** is the task-oriented dimension of leader behavior. Leaders high in Initiating Structure make individual task assignments, set deadlines, and clearly lay out what needs to be done. They act decisively without asking for the suggestions and ideas of subordinates. Leaders low in Initiating Structure tend not to take the initiative. These leaders practice "hands off" management, leaving people alone and letting them define the tasks and deadlines for themselves. Excessively high Initiating Structure, especially when combined with strong elements of coercion, is associated with high turnover, high grievance rates, and low satisfaction. A moderate amount of Initiating Structure can help get good task performance in situations where people are not trained or face high task ambiguity.[19]

Consideration is the people-oriented dimension of leadership behavior. Leaders high in Consideration show concern for members of their group. They are empathic, interpersonally warm, and interested in developing relationships with their subordinates based on mutual trust. They actively seek the suggestions and opinions of their subordinates and accept and carry out those suggestions. Leaders low in Consideration often publicly criticize a subordinate's work. They lack concern for the feelings of others and have little interest in the quality of their interpersonal interactions. High Consideration is associated with high job satisfaction, low turnover, and group cohesion. The last two factors can help maintain a group's level of performance.[20]

Contingency Theories of Leadership

Neither the trait nor behavioral approaches offered completely satisfactory explanations of leadership in organizations causing researchers to develop contingency theories of leadership. Such theories viewed successful leadership as dependent upon the situation faced by a leader. The two contingency theories described in this section strongly differ. The first views the leader as unable to change behavior readily; the second sees the leader as able to choose from a repertoire of behaviors. Each theory offers different ways of thinking about how a leader fits the requirements of a situation.

FIEDLER'S CONTINGENCY THEORY OF LEADERSHIP

Fred E. Fiedler studied leadership in widely varying groups such as manufacturing groups, boards of directors, managers, and military combat teams. His work built a contingency theory of leadership that considered the characteristics of the leader and the characteristics of the situation.[21]

Fiedler's theory assumes leaders are predisposed to a particular set of leader behaviors. Leaders are either task-oriented or relationship-oriented. **Task-oriented leaders** are directive, structure situations, set deadlines, and make task assignments. **Relationship-oriented leaders** focus on people, are considerate, and are not strongly directive. Leaders had either one of the two predispositions, but not both.

Although the two types of leaders are similar to the behavioral dimensions discussed earlier, there is an important distinction between Fiedler's contingency theory and the behavioral theories. Fiedler's theory assumes the predisposition to a particular style of leadership is difficult to change. It is a basic disposition of the leader with almost personality-like qualities.

Fiedler's theory focuses on the extent to which situations let the leader influence subordinates. Situations differ in how favorable they are for a leader to exert influence because of variations in three dimensions: leader-member relations, task structure, and position power. Fiedler felt leader-member relations was the most important dimension and position power was the least important.

Leader-member relations describe the quality of the relationship between subordinates and leader. This dimension includes the amount of trust between leader and subordinates and whether the leader is liked and respected by the subordinates. The leader-member relations dimension has strong connections to the referent and expert bases of power.

Task structure describes the extent to which the work is well defined and standardized or ambiguous and vague. When task structure is high, the work is predictable and can be planned. Low task structure describes an ambiguous situation with changing circumstances and unpredictable events.

Position power refers to the formal organization authority of the leader. This power is separate from any personal power the leader might have. A situation with high position power lets the leader hire people and directly reward or punish behavior. A leader with low position power cannot do such things. In the latter situation, policies may constrain the leader from using any rewards or punishments.

The position power dimension is related to the organizational bases of power. A high position power situation has a high degree of legitimate, coercive, and reward power. The opposite is true of a low position power situation.

The three dimensions allow classification of situations according to how favorable the situation is for the leader's influence.[22] Figure 12-2 shows a classification based on a dichotomy of each dimension. Situations described as favorable allow high leader influence; situations described as unfavorable allow little leader influence. Fiedler's

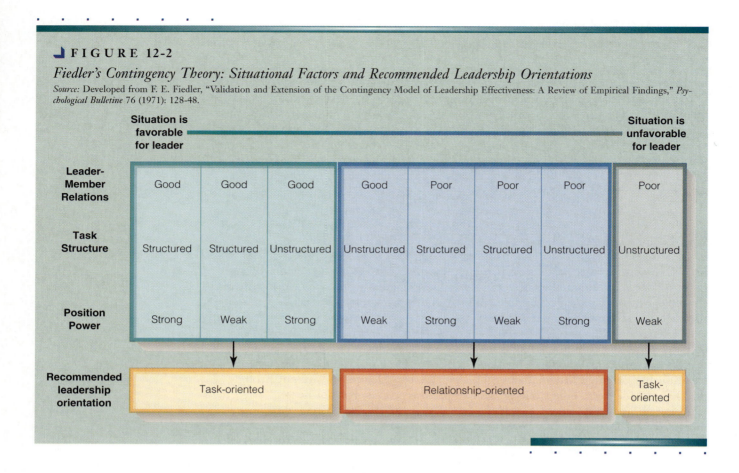

Fiedler's Contingency Theory: Situational Factors and Recommended Leadership Orientations

Source: Developed from F. E. Fiedler, "Validation and Extension of the Contingency Model of Leadership Effectiveness: A Review of Empirical Findings," *Psychological Bulletin* 76 (1971): 128-48.

	Situation is favorable for leader							Situation is unfavorable for leader
Leader-Member Relations	Good	Good	Good	Good	Poor	Poor	Poor	Poor
Task Structure	Structured	Structured	Unstructured	Unstructured	Structured	Structured	Unstructured	Unstructured
Position Power	Strong	Weak	Strong	Weak	Strong	Weak	Strong	Weak
Recommended leadership orientation	Task-oriented			Relationship-oriented				Task-oriented

contingency theory makes two broad recommendations about leadership: task-oriented leaders are more effective in highly favorable or highly unfavorable situations; relationship-oriented leaders are more effective in situations between those two extremes.

Fiedler did not think organizations could easily and reliably select leaders to match the situations in the organization. He also was not optimistic about the effectiveness of leadership training designed to change leaders. He argued strongly that the situation had to be changed to fit a leader's predispositions—" 'engineer' the job to fit the [leader]."[23] Alternately, the leader can be trained to understand her approach to leadership. The leader learns ways to change the situation so she can be successful.[24]

The relationship between a successful leader type and the characteristics of the situation is logical and easy to understand in some situations, but less clear in others. For example, in the first situation on the far left of the figure, the leader is well liked and the task is clear. Focusing on the task in this situation may seem right. The situation on the far right also makes sense. The leader has nothing to lose by being task-oriented if everything in the situation already is unfavorable! It is less clear why a relationship-oriented leader is right for some situations shown for that orientation. It would seem hard for a relationship-oriented leader to be effective in a group where she is disliked. This type of leader also is nondirective and possibly lets the structure of the task affect subordinate behavior.

 HOUSE'S PATH-GOAL THEORY OF LEADERSHIP

Robert J. House developed the path-goal theory of leadership to resolve inconsistencies in much previous leadership research. A contingency theory says characteristics of the situation govern the choice of leader behavior. Although path-goal theory and Fiedler's theory are both contingency theories, they view the contingency relationship differently.[25] An extensive analysis of empirical studies of the theory showed partial support for the theory.[26]

Path-goal theory sees the leader's role as one of affecting a subordinate's motivation to reach desired goals. The leader affects a subordinate's motivation by using rewards when desired goals are reached, being supportive while the subordinate is trying to reach the goals, making task assignments that are inherently motivating, and clearing barriers en route to goal accomplishment. The name of the theory summarizes what a leader does—clearing subordinates' paths to the accomplishment of desired goals. The leader's behavior can enhance a subordinate's motivation and increase a subordinate's job satisfaction. Acceptance of the leader by the subordinate should also increase. The developers of path-goal theory nicely captured the desired outcomes of leader behavior in the following statement:

> [T]he motivational functions of the leader consist of increasing the number and kinds of personal payoffs to subordinates for work-goal attainment, and making paths to these payoffs easier to travel by clarifying the paths, reducing road blocks and pitfalls, and increasing the opportunities for personal satisfaction en route.[27]

Path-goal theory proposed four leader behaviors instead of the two widely used until that time. The following are the four behaviors described by the theory:

Directive	Directive leader behavior focuses on what must be done, when it must be done, and how it must be done. This behavior clarifies performance expectations and the role of each subordinate in the work group.
Supportive	Supportive leader behavior includes concern for subordinates as people and the needs they are trying to satisfy. Supportive leaders are open, warm, friendly, and approachable. They care about the people who work for them and treat their subordinates as equals.
Participative	Participative leader behavior includes consultation with subordinates and serious consideration of subordinates' ideas before making decisions. Participative leader behavior also means the leader actively seeks the suggestions and ideas of subordinates as part of her approach to decision making.
Achievement-oriented	Achievement-oriented leader behavior emphasizes excellence in subordinate performance and improvements in performance. An achievement-oriented leader sets high performance goals and shows confidence in the abilities of subordinates to reach those goals.

The four behaviors of path-goal theory have several important qualities. Directive and supportive behavior are the same as Initiating Structure and Consideration. These two behaviors have been consistently a part of leadership research and are basic to the functioning of leaders in organizations. Participative leader behavior emphasizes the decision-making function of leaders. Note that subordinate participation emerges as an important part of decision making.

Achievement-oriented leader behavior gets to the heart of subordinate motivation. Chapter 8 showed how high and achievable performance goals are a key part of high work performance. The expressed confidence of the leader also emerges as an important contributor to motivation.

The path-goal theory described two sets of contingency factors that play an important role in the choice of leader behavior. The sets of factors were (1) personal factors of subordinates and (2) work environment factors.

Personal factors are subordinates' perception of their ability, their perceptions of the source of control (locus of control) over what happens to them, and their views about people in authority positions (authoritarianism). **Work environment factors** include tasks, the nature of the system of authority in the organization, and the primary work group.

Figure 12-3 shows the structure of path-goal theory. The four leader behaviors are described as a "repertoire" to emphasize that the leader chooses among the behaviors. The theory does not suggest leaders should use all the behaviors at the same time. The choice of behavior changes as circumstances facing the leader change. Those circumstances include contingency factors from the person and from the work environment.

Subordinates whose ability is less than that required by the task are likely to respond positively to directive leader behavior. They welcome clarification of their duties and tasks because their level of ability makes it difficult to complete the task. High-ability subordinates may feel such leader behavior is redundant because they already know what to do and do not need the boss telling them how!

People can perceive the locus of control of their behavior as either internal or external to them. Subordinates who feel their behavior is responsible for the results they achieve (internal control) are likely to respond positively to participative behavior and less positively to directive behavior. Because they feel in control, they do not want the leader to direct them to task completion. Instead, they would like to affect decisions that lead to task accomplishment. Low participative and directive leader behavior work better for subordinates who feel externally controlled.

People high in authoritarianism are strongly status-oriented; they readily accept the direction of people in an authority position and want to please them. People low in authoritarianism are flexible and tend not to defer to authority. People high in authoritarianism will accept directive leader behavior; people low in authoritarianism will prefer participative behavior.

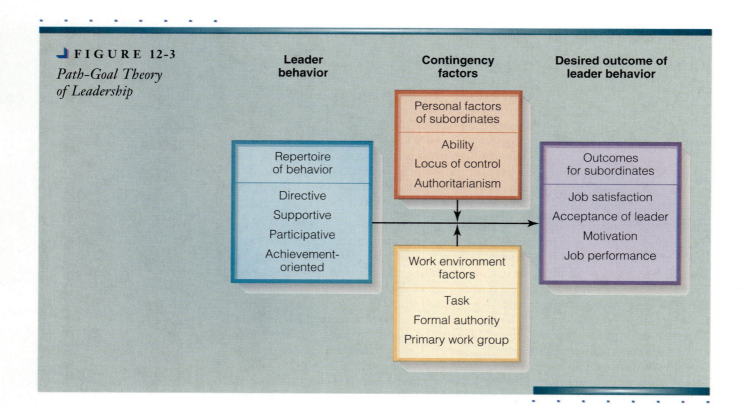

FIGURE 12-3
Path-Goal Theory of Leadership

The three work environment factors contribute to a work environment that varies in its degree of ambiguity. Routine tasks done in a setting with clearly defined relationships among roles and standard operating procedures are less ambiguous than tasks done in a more fluid setting. Formal authority also contributes to the degree of ambiguity. Well-defined authority in a leader's role lets a leader clearly define work roles and set clear goals.

Primary work groups consisting of people strongly identified with each other often develop well-defined procedures for doing the group's work. The opposite is true of work groups where people do not strongly identify with each other. The first type of group presents an unambiguous environment to the subordinate; the second presents an ambiguous environment.

Path-goal theory suggests different leader behaviors for work environments with different degrees of ambiguity. Subordinates working in a low-ambiguity situation can clearly see what must be done and how to do it. Directive leader behavior will be perceived as redundant and could reduce subordinate satisfaction and motivation. A better behavioral choice is supportive because it can offset possible negative effects of routine tasks. Directive leader behavior, though, is a useful way to bring structure to an ambiguous situation. Such behavior could clarify what needs to be done and reduce subordinate frustration with the uncertainty of the situation.

EXERCISE *Your Behavior Repertoire*

*T*able 12-1 describes several leader behaviors. To what extent do you behave in the ways described? Using the following scale, record on a separate piece of paper the number from the scale that best describes your belief about how you behave.

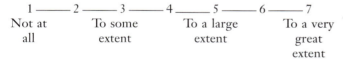

1	2	3	4	5	6	7
Not at all		To some extent		To a large extent		To a very great extent

Several leadership theories in this chapter described the behaviors listed in Table 12-1. Those theories have implications for how a leader behaves in various situations. The number of different behaviors available to you contributes to the flexibility you have to behave differently in different situations. Few behaviors suggest inflexibility; many behaviors suggest flexibility. Reflect on the pattern of behaviors revealed by this exercise while you read the section "Perspectives Offered by Each Leadership Theory" later in the chapter.

Alternative Views of Leadership

The next sections describe several alternative views of leadership that differ from those described so far in this chapter. Look for similarities and dissimilarities to what has already been said about leadership in organizations.

THE LEADERSHIP MYSTIQUE

Expressing frustration with the direction in which academic research in leadership had gone, E. E. Jennings made the following observations about leadership theory:

> Leadership theory suffers from a defect—it does not represent leadership—not as historians define it and as leaders themselves practice it. . . . [T]he theorists have not rediscovered the essential difference between leadership and management and blindly perpetuate the myth

TABLE 12-1
Leader Behaviors

- *Directive.* — Directive leader behavior focuses on what must be done, when it must be done, and how it must be done. This behavior clarifies performance expectations and the role of each person in the work group.

- *Supportive.* — Supportive leader behavior includes concern for subordinates as people and the needs they are trying to satisfy. Supportive leaders are open, warm, friendly, and approachable.

- *Participative.* — Participative leader behavior includes consultation with subordinates and serious consideration of subordinates' ideas before making decisions. Participative leader behavior also means the leader actively seeks the suggestions and ideas of subordinates.

- *Achievement-oriented.* — Achievement-oriented leader behavior emphasizes excellence in subordinate performance and is always trying to get improvements in performance. An achievement-oriented leader sets high performance goals for subordinates. She shows confidence in the abilities of subordinates to reach those goals.

- *Reconciliation.* — Reconciliation resolves conflicting demands placed on the work unit, thereby reducing disorder within the work group.

- *Tolerance of uncertainty.* — A person with this type of leader behavior does not worry about uncertainty, feels little anxiety in the face of uncertainty, and deals with uncertainty without much stress.

- *Influence with supervisors.* — A person with this type of leader behavior can influence her superiors. She builds amiable relationships with superiors.

Source: The first four behaviors came from R. J. House, "A Path–Goal Theory of Leadership Effectiveness," *Administrative Science Quarterly* 16 (1971): 321-338 and R. J. House and T. R. Mitchell, "Path–Goal Theory of Leadership," *Journal of Contemporary Business* 8 (1974): 81-97. The last three behaviors came from R. M. Stogdill, *Individual Behavior and Group Achievement* (New York: Oxford University Press, 1959).

that the two concepts are interchangeable. For centuries man has endowed leadership with special meaning. The manager arrived relatively lately on the scene of human debate and enterprise. The two ideas were never intended to be fused. Great leaders were seldom effective managers.[28]

If Jennings is right, this chapter has described management, not leadership. Leaders are powerful agents of change in their organizations. Managers want to build and administer effective, smoothly functioning organizations. Leaders change organizations; managers maintain them.[29]

Jennings's **leadership mystique** captures his view of leadership.[30] His leadership mystique is a set of ideas, values, and beliefs that Jennings feels is the essence of leadership. The leadership mystique has three dimensions:

- A sense of mission.
- A capacity for power.
- A will to survive and persevere.

A leader has a sense of mission, a vision of some future state for her organization. The vision is more than a strategic plan. It is a dream about something that the leader wants to create. It does not now exist but it *will* exist. The mission becomes part of the heart, soul, and ego of the leader. It is the leader's heroic vision of the possible. She pursues that mission at great personal sacrifice. The leader describes the mission with intense passion, trying to enlist others to pursue it with her.

A capacity for power refers to getting and using power to pursue the mission. The leader uses both organizational and personal bases of power to achieve the mission. Leaders have no fear of power, nor do they believe having power is undesirable. Power—and the capacity to get it—is basic to achieving the mission.

Leaders are often frustrated in their pursuit of their mission. They must have a will to survive and persevere in reaching their mission. The third quality of the leadership mystique deals with impediments to achieving the mission—financial backers, competitors, government restrictions, and so on. A leader has ". . . a will to persevere against a discourteous, unbelieving world of sometimes total opposition."[31]

Think about it. Are managers and leaders different? A later section describes some views about that question.

TRANSACTIONAL AND TRANSFORMATIONAL LEADERSHIP

After many years of studying leadership processes, Bernard M. Bass developed a conceptualization describing transactional and transformational leadership. He feels the distinction is both real and necessary for understanding differences in results of leadership processes.[32]

Transactional Leadership

Transactional leadership focuses on exchange relationships between leader and follower. The two parties exchange agreements about what needs to be done. The leader clarifies role and task requirements and builds enough confidence in the subordinate to get the job done. The leader may help the follower reach the agreed-upon goals. Transactional leaders show subordinates how their needs will be satisfied if they do what is required. If the follower reaches the goals, the leader gives positive feedback and other rewards for job accomplishment. If the goals are not reached, the leader uses sanctions. Transactional leaders focus on the care, maintenance, administration, and management of an organization.

The two major parts of transactional leadership are contingent reinforcement and management by exception. Contingent reinforcement refers to a leader's use of positive or negative consequences. The selection of consequences depends on whether the follower is successful or unsuccessful in doing what is desired. Management by exception means the leader reacts to what a follower does only when performance does not meet expectations.

Transactional leaders relate to their subordinates in several ways:

- They know what subordinates want to get from their work.
- They try to give subordinates what they want, if it is justified by their performance.
- They promise and use rewards for effort and performance.
- They focus on the self-interests of subordinates to get the work done.

Subordinates who work for a transactional leader do what is required and not much more. If successful, subordinates not only receive the promised rewards, but also feel good about themselves for a job well done.

Most of the leadership theories discussed so far in this chapter, especially the path-goal theory, described transactional leadership processes. Transactional leaders also rely heavily on the motivation theories and techniques described in Chapters 7 and 8.

Transformational Leadership

Transformational leadership differs sharply from transactional leadership. It emphasizes charisma, individualized consideration, and intellectual stimulation.

Charisma is the most important part of transformational leadership because of the power it gives a leader.[33] Followers of charismatic leaders trust them, identify with them, and have high confidence in them. Charisma is an attribution by the follower. A leader perceived as charismatic by one person may not be perceived as charismatic by another. Personal traits play a strong role in charisma. Charismatic leaders often have a high degree of self-confidence, self-esteem, and self-determination.

Individualized consideration includes a developmental orientation, individualized orientation, and mentoring. The transformational leader wants subordinates to experience continual growth and development. She delegates challenging tasks to subordinates to encourage growth and development.

An individualized orientation means the transformational leader recognizes variations in skills, abilities, and desires for growth opportunities among subordinates. The transformational leader knows her subordinates well. The transformational leader also gives individual counseling, guidance, and support and constructively critiques a subordinate's performance. A key part of individualized consideration is the degree to which the leader shows genuine interest in the subordinate.

Mentoring is the process by which transformational leaders help develop subordinates by using the leader's knowledge and experience. Transformational leaders act as role models and show their followers the job performance they want by the example of their own behavior. The leader may do the role modeling either consciously or unconsciously.

Intellectual stimulation refers to the transformational leader's ability to build high awareness of problems and solutions to problems. Such leaders induce changes in the values and beliefs of subordinates. They stimulate subordinates to image new and different future states for the group. Intellectual stimulation is more than a change in present direction. It demands a large leap in the values, beliefs, and problem focus of subordinates.

Transformational leaders get their intellectual stimulation from superior technical ability and personal brilliance. They also create and manage symbols and images that represent their vision for the group or the organization. Emotional stimulation can be part of intellectual stimulation. The transformational leader imbues followers with a consciousness about some future state and the role each follower will play in attaining that future state.

Transformational leaders can have the following effects on their subordinates:

- They raise the subordinates' level of awareness and consciousness about the value of work results.
- They develop more awareness of ways subordinates can reach work outcomes.
- They get subordinates to transcend their immediate self-interest.
- They develop commitment to the work group, team, or organization.
- They extend subordinates to reach for higher-level needs.

Transformational leaders strive for major increases in performance beyond that needed to reach immediate organization goals. They bring excitement to the workplace and build strong emotional bonds between themselves and their subordinates. Transformational leaders work toward what they believe is right and good for the organization, not its present direction. They often bring dramatic changes to an organization's culture and are remembered long after they are gone.

Organizations need transformational leaders in times of crisis and distress.[34] Turbulent external environments require the inspiration and creative problem solving of a transformational leader. In short, transformational leaders can be the key to an organization's survival during times of rapid change and uncertainty.

CHARISMATIC LEADERSHIP

Charismatic leaders attract devoted followers who energetically pursue the leader's vision. Charismatic leaders move their followers to extraordinary heights of performance, profoundly affect their aspirations, build emotional attachment to the leader, and win commitment to the leader's vision. Followers focus on the interest of the organization mission more than on their self-interest. Charismatic leaders win the loyalty of their followers and inspire them to self-sacrifice in the pursuit of a vision.[35]

Research focused on charismatic leadership has described a constellation of behaviors that distinguish charismatic leaders from other types of leaders and managers.[36] Charismatic leaders see well beyond their organization's current situation and develop a view of the future that is different from the present. They develop and widely communicate an inspirational vision—a vision they describe as better in specific ways from the present. Such leaders form bonds of trust between themselves and their followers. Charismatic leaders empower others in their organizations to carry out the vision.

Looking beyond the present situation includes scanning the environment for new market opportunities, predicting changes in markets and technologies, and looking for ways to keep their organization aligned with its outside environment. Charismatic leaders are impatient with present conditions and press their organizations to continuously improve. They push their organizations toward a new state by creating dissatisfaction with the present.

Creating and communicating an inspirational vision is a key behavior of charismatic leaders. To communicate, they use all suitable media with which they feel comfortable. Such media include written documents, speeches, conversations with individual employees, television, and direct electronic communication. Charismatic leaders are especially skilled at framing messages that clearly express and support their vision.

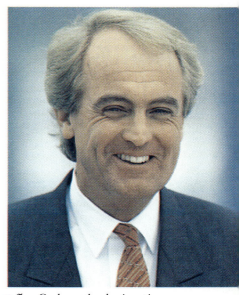

Building trust between the manager and her followers is a key part of getting commitment to the leader's vision. Charismatic leaders behave in ways that are consistent with statements about the vision. The leader also tries to forge values supporting the vision into the cultural fabric of the organization. For example, Jan Carlzon, the charismatic former chief executive of Scandinavian Airlines System (SAS), reinforced customer-oriented values when he refused to accept a magazine or newspaper while traveling on SAS before all other passengers were offered one.[37]

Charismatic leaders are especially skilled at tapping unused motivational energy in their followers. They rely on empowerment, an approach that helps followers develop self-confidence in their ability to fulfill the leader's vision. Such leaders often design experiences to stretch their followers to new levels of performance. By giving them feedback, charismatic leaders help steer followers in the desired direction and inspire them to higher levels of performance.

Jan Carlzon, the charismatic former chief executive of SAS, helped transform that organization's cultural values.

 SUMMARY

Table 12-2 summarizes the main features of the alternative views of leadership. The leadership mystique and charismatic leadership emphasize the role of vision or mission in the leadership process. Both suggest a leader should play a forward-looking role. Each view also has distinctive features such as the intellectual stimulation of transformational leadership and the use of power in the leadership mystique. Transactional leadership has the distinctive features of management by exception and using rewards and sanctions (contingent reinforcement) to affect behavior.

TABLE 12-2

Alternative Views of Leadership in Organizations

LEADERSHIP MYSTIQUE

Sense of mission
Capacity for power
Will to survive and persevere

TRANSACTIONAL LEADERSHIP

Contingent reinforcement
Management by exception

TRANSFORMATIONAL LEADERSHIP

Charisma
Individualized consideration
Intellectual stimulation

CHARISMATIC LEADERSHIP

Looks beyond the present
Creates and communicates an inspirational vision
Builds trust
Empowers others

Substitutes, Neutralizers, and Enhancers of Leadership Behavior

Substitutes, neutralizers, and enhancers each operate differently in the relationship between a leader and a subordinate. Figure 12-4 shows the different relationships for substitutes, neutralizers, and enhancers.[38]

Substitutes for leadership act in place of the leader, making leader behavior unnecessary. The substitute, not the leader, affects subordinate attitudes and behavior. Some leadership theories described in this chapter have suggested that characteristics of the task, subordinate, organization, and work group can substitute for the leader. For example, path-goal theory suggested that people doing routine and predictable tasks would find directive leader behavior redundant. The nature of the task, not the leader, guides the person's behavior. Tasks allowing high levels of intrinsic motivation also substitute for motivational influences from the leader.

Neutralizers prevent leader behavior from affecting the attitudes and behavior of subordinates. A neutralizer breaks the connection between leader behavior and subordinate response. A neutralizer has no direct effect on the subordinate. Instead, it is a block between the leader and the subordinate. For example, work groups often develop norms or rules that control the behavior of group members. If those norms are not consistent with what the group leader wants, the norm neutralizes the leader's efforts to influence the group. Employees with a professional orientation, such as scientists and university professors, often turn to their professional peers for recognition and rewards. That orientation can neutralize supportive leader behavior and any efforts at recognition by the leader.

Enhancers strengthen the connection between leader behavior and subordinate satisfaction and performance. If a leader controls rewards for a subordinate's performance, and the subordinate perceives a direct connection between performance and getting the reward, the reward system enhances the leader's influence over

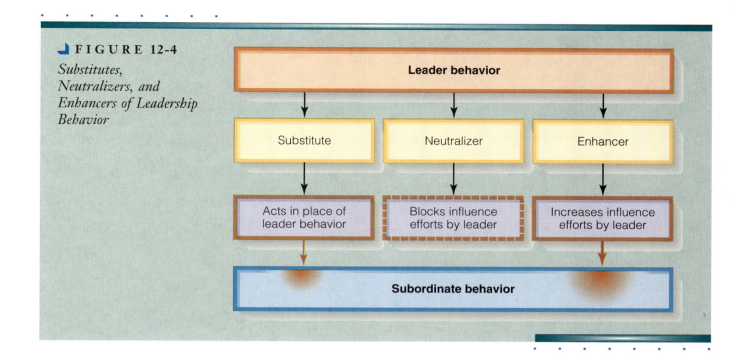

Leader behavior

Substitute Neutralizer Enhancer

Acts in place of leader behavior   Blocks influence efforts by leader   Increases influence efforts by leader

Subordinate behavior

the subordinate. Similarly, organization policies that let the leader hire and fire enhance the leader's influence over subordinates by increasing her coercive power. The bases of power described earlier can cumulatively act as enhancers of leadership behavior.

Table 12-3 summarizes possible substitutes, neutralizers, and enhancers of leadership behavior. A leader, or potential leader, is well advised to discover which of them are present in her leadership situation.

Leadership Perceptions: "We Know a Leader When We See One"

The discussions of leadership in this chapter have focused on the traits and behavior of leaders. Human perceptual processes underlie people's observations of leader traits and behaviors. Researchers have developed two different but related views of leadership perceptions. The first view builds on perceptual categories; the second view describes the process of leadership attribution. Figure 12-5 shows both views for easy comparison.

LEADERSHIP CATEGORIZATION

According to the **Leadership Categorization** view of leadership perception, people observe the behavior of another person and then quickly compare those observations to a cognitive category describing a leader. Figure 12-5a shows a simplified version of the Leadership Categorization Process.[39]

A person's perceptual process, as described in Chapter 4, helps filter observations from the person's environment. The person compares her perceived observations to a cognitive category that is either a leadership prototype or a leadership exemplar. A leadership prototype is a person's cognitive image of the characteristics, qualities, behaviors, and traits that make up a leader. For example, some people might view

TABLE 12–3

Substitutes, Neutralizers, and Enhancers of Leader Behavior

CHARACTERISTICS	SUBSTITUTE FOR LEADERSHIP	NEUTRALIZER	ENHANCER
TASKS			
Unambiguous, routine	Initiating Structure		
Task gives feedback	Initiating Structure		
Intrinsically motivating	Relationship-oriented behavior		
INDIVIDUALS			
Ability	Initiating Structure		
Professional orientation	Initiating Structure	Supportive leader behavior	
ORGANIZATION			
Reward system, control by leader			Leader influence (reward power)
Reward system, no control by leader	Leader influence		
Rules, procedures, policies	Initiating Structure		Leader influence (coercive power)
WORK GROUP			
Cohesive, organizationally congruent norms			Leader influence
Cohesive, organizationally incongruent norms		Leader influence	

Source: Suggested by Table 1 in S. Kerr and J. M. Jermier, "Substitutes for Leadership: Their Meaning and Measurement," *Organizational Behavior and Human Performance* 22 (1978): 375–403. Developed from Kerr and Jermier "Substitutes for Leadership" and J. P. Howell, P. W. Dorfman, and S. Kerr, "Moderator Variables in Leadership Research," *Academy of Management Review* 11 (1986): 86–102.

leaders as intelligent and industrious while others think of leaders as honest and outgoing.[40] A leadership exemplar is a specific person people regard as a leader such as Margaret Thatcher, or Martin Luther King, Jr.

A key step in the Leadership Categorization Process is deciding whether the perceived observations match the leadership prototype or exemplar. If they do not match, the observer decides the observed person is not a leader. If they match, she decides the observed person is a leader.

LEADERSHIP ATTRIBUTIONS

Attribution of leadership follows the attribution processes described in Chapter 4.[41] Figure 12-5b shows the steps in a simplified version of the process.

Individuals observe the behavior of other people and the effects associated with the behavior. An observer can also infer other behaviors from the observed behavior. For example, an observer might conclude that a talkative person who interacts with many people in a group has much job-related information. The observer made the inference from the talkative and interactive behavior she saw.

In the next step in the process, the observer assesses the observed and inferred information for evidence of leadership. A key factor in this step is whether the

Leadership Perceptions

Source: (a) A simplified version of the process drawn from R. G. Lord, "An Information Processing Approach to Social Perceptions, Leadership and Behavioral Measurement in Organizations," in B. Staw and L. L. Cummings, eds., *Research in Organizational Behavior*, vol. 7 (Greenwich, Conn.: JAI Press, 1985), pp. 87–128; R. G. Lord, R. J. Foti, and C. DeVader, "A Test of Leadership Categorization Theory: Internal Structure, Information Processing and Leadership Perceptions," *Organizational Behavior and Human Performance* 34 (1984): 343–78; R. G. Lord and K. J. Maher, *Leadership and Information Processing: Linking Perceptions and Performance* (New York: Unwin Hyman Academic, 1991).
(b) A simplified version of the process drawn from B. J. Calder, "An Attribution Theory of Leadership," in B. M. Staw and G. R. Salancik, eds., *New Directions in Organizational Behavior* (Chicago: St. Clair Press, 1977), pp. 179–204.

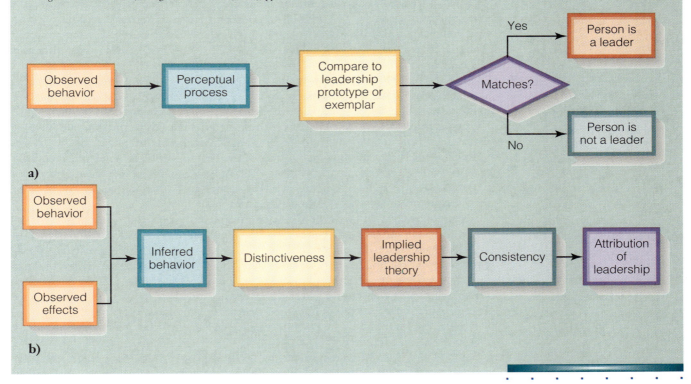

behavior is specific to one person or is widely shared by other people in a group. An observer accepts only distinctive behavior as evidence of leadership. The observer then compares the distinctive behavior to an implicit leadership theory. Such theories act as perceptual filters and standards of comparison for the leadership qualities a person believes are important for a leader to have. Some people think decisiveness is an important leadership quality. If a leader shows decisiveness, then the person is a leader. The observer now decides whether the behavior is consistent across situations and over time. If she sees similar behavior from the same person in different situations and at different times, she will build a strong attribution of leadership.

The attribution of leadership traits may explain what happened to Stafford at Pillsbury in the Opening Episode. Stafford's predecessor was decisive, a quality that the people at Pillsbury valued. Stafford was not decisive and was judged to be a poor leader.

⌐ Perspectives Offered by Each Leadership Theory

The various theories of leadership described in this chapter make useful contributions to the analysis of leadership requirements in organizations. Each theory gives a different perspective on leadership. Remember that people's perceptual processes can affect whom they regard as a leader.

The trait approach to leadership concluded that certain qualities distinguish successful from unsuccessful leaders. Selecting leaders according to their traits must be done cautiously and with a watchful eye on the requirements of the situation. Popular descriptions of leaders also use traits. Recall the description of Stafford in the Opening Episode of this chapter. He had traits just the opposite of those of the successful leaders found in the trait research.

The behavioral approaches emphasized the role of leader behavior, not traits. They also focused on two enduring behaviors, people and task. The analysis of leadership requirements and problems in organizations should not lose sight of those two dimensions of leader behavior. The contingency approaches said the situation makes a difference. Fiedler's theory and House's path-goal theory offer different perspectives on contingency aspects of leadership.

Fiedler's theory implies that one should accept the leadership style of those who are unable or unwilling to change their leadership behavior. If the organization judges a leader to be valuable, then the situation of the leader should be changed to let the person be successful. Fiedler's theory also sensitizes us to the difficulties a new leader may face in following a popular leader. As the Opening Episode described, Stafford took a different approach to leadership than his predecessor at Pillsbury, but he inherited a situation partly built by his predecessor. Despite difficulties with several aspects of Fiedler's theory, it sends clear signals that the leader-situation fit may be important for successful performance.

Path-goal theory implied the need for careful analysis of the contingency factors present in a situation. Many concepts in this book about motivation, job design, and group dynamics are important tools for the analysis of leadership situations. Path-goal theory also implied more flexibility in leader behavior than the other theories did. The choice of behavior follows an analysis of the situation. This perspective suggests a new leader should assess the situation and then choose the behavior that fits the situation. Unfortunately, some people do not have the needed behavioral flexibility. In that case, it may be necessary to turn to the perspective given by Fiedler's contingency theory.

Leadership mystique, transformational leadership, and charismatic leadership offer related perspectives on leadership. Each theory considers vision, charisma, and knowledge of both tasks and people to be qualities of effective leaders. Although closely related to traits, these qualities imply a high level of interaction between a leader and her subordinates. An effective leader has a vision of a future state, communicates that vision, excites others to follow, and knows much about both the tasks to be done and the people who will do the tasks. Read the case at the end of the chapter describing a reporter's observations on business leaders; then come back to this section and reflect upon the total notion of leadership.

Substitutes, neutralizers, and enhancers of leadership suggest thoroughly analyzing a leadership situation. Substitutes suggest leaders should avoid behavior subordinates will perceive as redundant. If a substitute is producing desirable subordinate behavior, a leader is well advised to leave a good situation alone. Neutralizers advise leaders to avoid behavior that will not affect subordinates. Because neutralizers act as blocks between a leader and a subordinate, the leader should find ways to remove or reduce the neutralizer. Enhancers work for the leader, who should capitalize on them to get the highest possible influence in a situation. Leaders can also create other enhancers to increase their level of influence.

. . . .

Women, Men, and Leadership

Do women and men exhibit different leadership behavior? That question has been the center of a continuing debate since the 1980s. Those who feel there is a

· *Hazel O'Leary, secretary of the Department of Energy*, left; *and Jack Welch, chief executive, General Electric Corporation*, right. *Both executives have led their organizations through turbulent times.*

difference base their argument on presumed differences in the socialization of women and men. Supposedly, the socialization of men leads to a competitive, aggressive leadership style while the socialization of women results in a nurturant, caring leadership style.[42]

One study showed some differences in the leadership behavior of women and men. Women's leadership behavior was similar to transformational leadership. Men's leadership behavior was similar to transactional leadership. Women described themselves as sharing power, sharing information, and encouraging their subordinates' self-worth. Men described themselves as using authority that came from their position and relying on rewards and punishments to shape subordinates' behavior.[43] The design of this study, however, restricts the generalization of its results. The sample was drawn from members of the International Women's Forum and male leaders the respondents nominated. The 31 percent response rate also limits interpretation of these results.

Empirical evidence from other sources says there is no documented difference in the leadership behavior of women and men in equivalent organization positions.[44] This area needs more research to find whether differences exist. Such research will let us better understand leadership behavior as more women move into leadership positions. The case at the end of this section of the book describes the leadership activities of a woman and a man. You might want to read that case now to see how those two leaders chose to behave.

· · · · · · · · · ·

Leadership and Self-Managing Teams

Managers in organizations are increasingly using self-managing teams to get work done. Chapter 10 described the characteristics of such teams. This section addresses the leadership issues raised by self-managing teams.

The use of self-managing teams changes the traditional distribution of decision authority in an organization. Teams take on much decision authority formerly exercised by managers and supervisors. In addition to doing their regular work of producing a product or providing a service, such teams often establish work schedules, set performance goals, assess team member performance, purchase supplies, assess quality, interact with vendors, and interact with internal or external customers.[45] Managers and supervisors typically decided such matters before the teams were formed. The redistribution of decision authority changes the roles of managers and supervisors outside the team and defines new roles for team members.

Each team typically has a team leader who is either selected by team members or appointed by a manager or supervisor outside the team.[46] Some team leaders hold the job permanently. Other teams rotate members through the position. The growing popularity of self-managing teams increases the likelihood that you could become a member of such a team and rotate through the team leader position.

The leadership issues raised by self-managing teams center on the bases of power of the team leader, the person's traits, and the types of leadership behavior exhibited. The authority given to the team by management outside the team affects the amount of legitimate, reward, coercive, and information power available to the team leader. Whether the leader will also have expert power or referent power depends on the person. All the observations made earlier in this chapter on the bases of power apply to the leaders of self-managing teams.

The role of traits in the leadership process and the different leader behaviors described earlier in this chapter also apply to team leaders. For example, a team member who rotates into the team leader role might not have leadership traits, or other team members might not attribute them to the person. Leaders of self-managing teams could benefit from viewing the team leader role from the different perspectives offered by the various theories.

Managers and supervisors outside the team do not cease to be leaders or managers. The nature of their work shifts from close day-to-day supervision to long-range planning, team guidance, team development, resource support, and political support from more senior management. Much of the behavior of external leaders and managers focuses on developing the self-managing part of self-managing teams.[47]

. . . .

Management and Leadership

Historians, scholars, and other observers have often distinguished management and leadership. Managers and leaders play different roles in an organization. Managers sustain and control organizations; leaders try to change them. Organizations also have different needs for those roles at different levels and at different times in their history.[48]

Leaders have a vision of how the organization could be better and can inspire followers to pursue that vision. They are willing to take risks, especially if they perceive high payoffs from a course of action. They readily use power for influence, pulling people along instead of using punishment to coerce people into compliance. Leaders actively seek opposing views to identify options to a course of action. Because of their relentless pursuit of a vision, risk-taking behavior, and desire to use conflict, they often plunge an organization into chaos while pursuing that vision.

Managers follow the present vision for the organization; they do not create a new one. They solve problems and try to bring order to the workplace, while ensuring the commitment of people to the organization's goals. Managers take fewer risks than leaders. They use available rewards and sanctions coupled with their knowledge of human motivation to get predictable behavior.

People are appointed to supervisory, management, and executive positions. The names of the positions vary, but each denotes an appointed management position in an organization. Each position can have different requirements for management and leadership. Some positions require only management. Other positions require large amounts of leadership and have little need for management. Still others need a mixture of leadership and management.

An organization's requirements for management and leadership will change as the factors affecting the organization change. Because leaders are important change agents, they play key roles when the external environment is changing fast. Managers play key roles in stable external environments. An organization has little need for a strong change agent if little is changing around it.

Different organization levels may have different needs for managers and leaders. Management may be required at the top with leadership needed at lower levels. Decentralized organizations are especially likely to exhibit this pattern.

Reflect on this section after reading the two cases at the end of the chapter describing observations on leadership and management. See whether the cases give examples of different leadership and management requirements in organizations.

International Aspects of Leadership and Management

The core values that define the relationships between leaders and followers or managers and subordinates vary from country to country. People in countries with values that specify strongly hierarchical relationships in organizations react more positively to directive approaches than to participative approaches. A directive approach is congruent with the values of many Latin American countries, India, Hong Kong, and France. More participative approaches fit the values of countries like Austria, Sweden, Great Britain, Canada, the United States, and Germany.[49] Variations in cultures suggest trying to match a leader or manager's behavior to what that culture expects.

Leader and manager behavior may not always vary for multinational organizations operating in different countries. Uniformity could occur because the company selects managers with behaviors and orientations valued by the firm. Socialization practices could also give people a consistent set of core values that will not vary from country to country.[50]

A long line of research shows cultural differences in response to directive leadership and management. Such leadership and management behavior includes Initiating Structure, Production-centered, Task-oriented, and directive behaviors discussed earlier in the chapter. Workers in countries with authoritarian values expect their leaders and managers to behave in an autocratic way.[51] Other cross-cultural leadership research is finding evidence that the positive effects of a supportive leadership and management style may not vary from culture to culture. It also appears that managers who tie positive rewards to people's performance will get positive results in whatever country they manage.[52]

Japanese managers from senior executives to managers several levels lower are more transformational than transactional in their leadership style. The individualized consideration part of transformational leadership was a major feature of Japanese managers' behavior. They press for high performance and sacrifice from their subordinates but also show a real interest in their welfare. The contingent reinforcement part of transactional leadership also does not fit well with Japanese customs. Employees are not expected to seek individual rewards for high performance, nor are they expected to show interest in such rewards.[53]

Ethical Issues in Leadership and Management

Leadership uses social influence to deliberately affect another person's behavior. Such changes in a person's behavior can happen without a person consciously deciding to change. Leaders can also use much of the behavioral knowledge in this book to shape and direct others' behavior. A major ethical issue focuses on whether such efforts are an unethical manipulation of other people's behavior.[54]

Behavior changes induced by leadership may also change a person's attitudes, values, and beliefs. For example, a leader's efforts to move her organization toward Total Quality Management may try to transform an organization's values to include an emphasis on customers, processes, and continuous improvement not just on profit or cost. Individual employees may undergo similar changes. That possibility has led some observers to suggest that leadership may have a brainwashing-like effect on people.[55]

These possible results of leadership have led some observers to try to discover the qualities of ethical and unethical leaders. An ethical leader confronts moral dilemmas, rewards ethical behavior, and builds an ethical organizational culture.[56] Such qualities are especially important to consider when leaders have strong effects on their followers. Transformational leaders, with strong charismatic features, can get strong commitment to their vision from followers who accept the vision. This type of leadership can clearly have ethical or unethical results.

At least one study found that ethical and unethical charismatic leaders behaved differently in many ways.[57] That study suggested that ethical leaders did the following:

- Encouraged and developed critical thinking among followers. Actively sought different views so critical issues were examined from many perspectives.
- Helped followers develop in ways consistent with their needs, aspirations, and abilities.
- Invited negative and positive feedback without reprisal. Did not fear criticism.
- Pursued the goals of the organization, not their self-interest.
- Developed a shared vision.
- Recognized the contributions of everyone to successfully achieving that vision.
- Shared information widely with followers. Actively sought other people's views about critical issues.
- Had high moral standards that caused the leader to resolve ethical dilemmas.

As a result of these actions, ethical leaders succeed in continuously growing and developing people who are major assets to the leader in jointly solving problems. Unethical leaders create followers who have disciple-like attachment to the leader but are unable to strike out alone.

Personal and Management Implications

Do you feel you have some traits associated with leadership? If you do, the chances are good you will find yourself in a leadership role in the future. If you are now involved in clubs or campus organizations, do you try to exercise leadership? Both your traits and your present behavior give you some clues about possible leadership roles you will play in the future.

What type of leadership behavior do you prefer? Do you prefer more people-centered behavior or more task-centered behavior? Do you want to work for someone who emphasizes achievement? Would you like to participate in decisions that are likely to have a strong effect on you? Knowing the type of leader behavior you like will help you assess new job situations in the future. The cross-cultural differences in preferences described in the international section imply that desirable leader behavior varies from culture to culture. If you work outside your home country, you can expect variations in leader behavior preferences.

Transformational leaders often get higher performance from subordinates than the subordinates ever expected to achieve. Don't be surprised by your behavior if you find yourself working for a transformational leader. Such leaders create genuine excitement in subordinates and persuade them to act in extraordinary ways.

The distinction drawn earlier between management and leadership is important for managers to consider. A supervisory or management position may need more management behavior than leadership behavior, although the position may require some leadership behavior. Analyze your situation. If it requires change, then leadership behavior in the different forms described in this chapter is required. If the situation is stable, then it needs management behavior that maintains and cares for your part of the organization.

Managers responsible for hiring other managers or supervisors often unknowingly use personal traits in their selection decision. If you use traits in your hiring decisions, you should examine the situation to be sure the individual you are considering will be successful. Note also that two behaviors, people and task, persist throughout the leadership research. All leaders and managers use these basic behaviors.

The contingency theories of leadership advise you to analyze the situation you are managing. If you do not have the behavioral flexibility suggested by path-goal theory, Fiedler's theory guides you toward the situations suited to your predispositions. If your behavior is flexible, path-goal theory guides you in a joint analysis of your situation and the behavior required for success. Consider both contingency approaches when reviewing your situation and your behavioral predispositions. The contingency view can be important to you if the people reporting to you come from different cultures.

Both leadership mystique and transformational leadership emphasize the role that charisma and a vision of the future play in leadership success. Do you have those qualities? Can you infuse your subordinates with excitement about the future? Think about it! Those two qualities may be the keys for successful leadership performance.

The discussion of substitutes, neutralizers, and enhancers of leadership gave you guides to aspects of your situation that change your influence over subordinates. Many factors in your situation can affect your influence over those who work for you.

Summary

Leadership is an influence process involving two or more people. One person's influence over another follows from six bases of power: legitimate, reward, coercive, information, referent, and expert.

Trait theories describe traits that are consistently associated with leadership such as intelligence, dominance, self-confidence, energy, the desire to lead, honesty, and task-relevant knowledge. Behavioral theories to leadership describe task- and people-oriented behavior as stable dimensions of leader behavior. Two contingency theories give different views of how situations affect leader behavior. Fiedler's contingency theory of leadership says leaders have a predisposition to focus on people or task. House's path-goal theory of leadership says leaders can choose from four behaviors and combine them according to the needs of the situation. Those behaviors are directive, supportive, participative, and achievement-oriented.

Alternative leadership theories include the leadership mystique, transactional versus transformational leadership, and charismatic leadership. Each theory emphasizes the role of charisma and vision in effective leadership.

Situations surrounding leaders have many factors that substitute for leader behavior, neutralize the behavior, or enhance the behavior. Understanding the characteristics of the situation is an important step in being an effective leader in an organization.

Leaders and managers play different roles in organizations. Leaders try to change organizations; managers sustain and control them. Organizations also have different needs for those roles at different levels and at different times in their history.

The growing use of self-managing work teams in U.S. and Canadian organizations is changing the role of leaders inside and outside the teams. Many observations in this chapter apply to such teams and can guide team leaders and those who coordinate activities of several teams.

The core values that define the relationships between leaders and followers or managers and subordinates vary across cultures. People in countries with values that specify hierarchical relationships in organizations react more positively to directive approaches than to participative approaches.

An ethical leader confronts moral dilemmas, rewards ethical behavior, and builds an ethical organizational culture. Such qualities are especially important to consider for leaders who have strong effects on their followers.

achievement-oriented leader
  behavior 331
attribution of leadership 340
bases of power 324
Consideration 328
directive leader behavior 331
Employee-centered behavior 328
enhancers 338
Initiating Structure 328

leader-member relations 329
Leadership Categorization 339
leadership mystique 334
leadership traits 326
neutralizers 338
participative leader behavior 331
personal factors 332
position power 329
Production-centered behavior 328

relationship-oriented leaders 329
substitutes 338
supportive leader behavior 331
task-oriented leaders 329
task structure 329
transactional leadership 335
transformational leadership 336
work environment factors 332

◗ Review and Discussion Questions

1. Review the leadership traits described earlier. Discuss the traits that you and others in your class believe you have.
2. People differ in what they view as traits and qualities of an effective leader. What traits do you and others in your class attribute to effective leaders? Discuss the similarities and differences among the traits ascribed to leaders. Why were there similarities and differences?
3. Review the two behavioral approaches to leadership. What are the similarities and differences in the two approaches?
4. Review the three dimensions in Fiedler's contingency theory that affect a leader's influence in a situation. Try to identify an example of one of the eight situations shown in Figure 12-2. Did the leader in that situation behave as predicted by the theory? If not, did you perceive the leader to be effective or ineffective? Discuss how Fiedler's theory explains why the leader was effective or ineffective.
5. The path-goal theory of leadership described how two sets of contingency factors, personal factors of subordi-

nates and work environment factors, affect the choice of leader behavior. Discuss how these factors affect the choice of leader behavior. Give examples from your experience and the experience of others in your class.
6. Review the alternative views of leadership. Do those views differ from the other theories of leadership? Why?
7. Have you ever been in a situation where substitutes, neutralizers, and enhancers of leadership existed? What did the leader do in that situation? What effect did the substitutes, neutralizers, and enhancers have?
8. Is there a difference between leadership and management? What roles do leaders and managers play in organizations?
9. Discuss the observations on leadership and self-managing teams. In what specific ways will the growing use of such teams change leadership processes in organizations?
10. Review the observations in the international and ethics sections of the chapter. Discuss the ethical implications of different preferences for leader behavior in different cultures.

◗ Case

THE NEW NON-MANAGER MANAGERS

The following case describes some dramatic changes in the roles of middle managers and the effects of those changes on non-managers. Here are some questions to think about while reading this case:

1. Do you think you could behave the way the non-managers behave in the case? Why?
2. Are these non-managers behaving in ways you prefer?

3. What areas of organizational behavior already covered in your course apply to what these non-managers are trying to do?

It's still open season on the American middle manager, and big guns continue to bag their daily limit without difficulty. Hardly a day passes without some formerly blue-chip outfit like GM, IBM, or Sears dispatching another couple of thousand or so to the corporate afterlife. The American Management Association reports that while middle managers are only about 5% of the work force at the 836 companies it surveyed, they account for a plump 22% of the past year's layoffs.

Source: B. Dumaine, "The New Non-Manager Managers," *Fortune,* February 22, 1993, pp. 80–81. © 1993 Time Inc. All rights reserved.

The reasons are no mystery. Middle managers have always handled two main jobs: supervising people, and gathering, processing, and transmitting information. But in growing numbers of companies, self-managed teams are taking over such standard supervisory duties as scheduling work, maintaining quality, even administering pay and vacations. Meanwhile, the ever-expanding power and dwindling cost of computers have transformed information handling from a difficult, time-consuming job to a far easier and quicker one. Zap! In an instant, historically speaking, the middle manager's traditional functions have vaporized.

That's bad enough. At the same time, competition is forcing many companies to squeeze costs without mercy. Guess who looks like a big, fat target? Says Cynthia Kellams, a management consultant at Towers Perrin: "If you can't say why you actually make your company a better place, you're out."

Knowing precisely what middle managers won't be doing much of anymore is only so useful. What *will* they, or their late Nineties equivalents, be doing? For an answer, look at those who are prospering. Call them the new managers, or—better yet—the new, non-manager managers. Many, perhaps most, are baby-boomers who bring a radically new set of values to the workplace. The 78 million Americans born between 1946 and 1964 tend to be an irreverent bunch. Many don't see the CEO as much of a hero. In fact, they often think the big guy gets in the way. They like to call themselves leaders, facilitators, sponsors—anything but managers.

More significantly, boomer managers want something other than the reassuring routine of the organization man. They want challenging and meaningful work. Says Lou Lenzi, a general manager at RCA who helped create Pro-Scan, a successful new line of televisions: "For me there is a certain amount of professional pride, the satisfaction of making something happen."

For a closer glimpse of tomorrow's manager, consider Cindy Ransom, 37, a middle manager—er, sponsor—passionate about her job at Clorox. Three years ago Ransom asked her workers at a 100-person plant in Fairfield, California, to redesign the plant's operations. As she watched, intervening only to answer the occasional question, a team of hourly workers established training programs, set work rules for absenteeism, and reorganized the once traditional factory into five customer-focused business units. As the workers took over managerial work, Ransom used her increasing free time to attend to the needs of customers and suppliers.

Last year Clorox named Ransom's plant the most improved in the company's household products division, its largest. Did money spur her to help work the change? That certainly doesn't hurt, but she cites a more compelling reason: to see the people who work with her succeed. Says she: "When I read about America losing its competitive edge, it really pisses me off. It gets me motivated to make a difference in my little corner, to make my factory competitive enough so my people can be employed here until they retire." For her reward, Ransom won't move up in the hierarchy, but will get to apply her skills at a Clorox plant overseas, which suits her just fine.

Managers like Ransom, committed to coaching, sponsoring—heck, why not use the term—empowering their people, are still rare. Says James Champy, CEO of CSC Index, a consulting firm in Cambridge, Massachusetts, that specializes in reengineering organizations: "We won't see them in great numbers for another five to ten years. But corporate America is definitely going in that direction."

Another reason the new manager is coming into vogue: Middle managers who master skills such as team building and intrapreneurship and who acquire broad functional expertise will likely be in the best position to get tomorrow's top corporate jobs. That's because the role of the top executive is becoming more like that of a team player and broker of others' efforts, not that of an autocrat.

Look at Drypers, a small but fast-growing maker of disposable diapers. This profitable Houston company, whose sales last fiscal year grew 24% to $140 million, operates with an office of the chief executive that consists of five managing directors, all with equal power. The five, each of whom has functional responsibility like finance, marketing, and manufacturing, work much like a middle management team, sharing information and kicking around ideas. No major decision is made until the five managing directors arrive at consensus. A lone CEO might be able to make a decision faster, but at Drypers, once a decision is made, all functions feel they own it, which helps wonderfully their inclination to put it into effect swiftly.

For example, the company last year developed and launched technologically advanced, disposable training pants called Big Boy and Big Girl in six months, fast by industry standards. After only a half year on the market, the new line has an impressive 20% market share in southeastern Texas. Says managing director David Pitassi: "When you have a shared vision, it's a very powerful thing."

. . . .

↳ Case

OBSERVATIONS ON LEADERSHIP

This case describes a business reporter's observations about the qualities that make good leaders at the top of American

Source: K. Labich, "The Seven Keys to Business Leadership," *Fortune,* October 24, 1988, pp. 58–64. All emphases in original. © 1988 Time Inc. All rights reserved.

corporations. Use the following questions to guide your analysis of this case:

1. What is your reaction to these observations? Do you feel they are valid?
2. How do they relate to the various leadership theories discussed in this chapter?
3. Do you now work for someone who has the qualities described or have you worked for such a person in the past?

TRUST SUBORDINATES

Managers have been hearing it for years, yet many of them still don't believe: The corporate command-and-control structure, with virtually all authority and responsibility residing in a chief executive at the top of a management pyramid, is fast giving way. The model that management consultants and B-school professors advocate instead is one they call the high-commitment organization. It requires pushing responsibility down the ladder and relying far more on the energy and talent of the entire work force. Your workers haven't been evincing much energy and talent? Maybe that's because they don't trust the company to reward those qualities, and perhaps *that's* because the company doesn't trust the workers to exhibit them.

Management experts say the key to making a high-commitment organization work is mutual trust between top executives and employees. The ability to engender that trusting relationship has become the No. 1 leadership test. Says Steven F. Dichter, a partner at management consulting firm McKinsey & Co.: "You can no longer afford to manage for average performance, and if you want to get that extra margin from employees you have to loosen all the boundaries." ...

An important initial step toward giving more authority to lower-level employees is letting them have a voice in decisions. ... "Employee involvement requires participative management," says [Donald E.] Petersen, [Ford Motor Company CEO]. "Anyone who has a legitimate reason, who will be affected by a decision, ought to have the feeling that people want to know how he or she feels." Such worker involvement was a major factor in the improved quality of Ford's cars in the Eighties, which played a large role in its financial turnaround. Industry veterans who remember the company a decade ago say the change in attitude among employees is almost palpable. ...

Another benefit of giving subordinates lots of authority: The policy helps them become leaders who may one day take charge of the company. Is it any wonder that such detail-obsessed CEOs as Harold Geneen of ITT and Harry Gray of United Technologies left messy succession problems in their wake? By contrast, look at Johnson & Johnson's James E. Burke, who is passionate about decentralized management. ... He says, "We spend time with our managers, but we tell them it is their responsibility to run their company." One reason: "Leaders are developed by challenges."

DEVELOP A VISION

... [E]mployees keep an eye on the long term. Like anyone being led, they like to know where they're going and why, and they hate to be whipsawed by changing goals. Steve S. Chen, 44, left Cray Research ... because he had a vision of a supercomputer that Cray decided not to build. "This machine *will* be built, it *has* to be built," says Chen. "The future of technology in this country is at stake." Evidence of a vision's potency to inspire: About 40 colleagues followed Chen out the door.

Don't underestimate the power of a vision. McDonald's founder, Ray Kroc, pictured his empire long before it existed, and he saw how to get there. He invented the company motto—"Quality, service, cleanliness, and value"—and kept repeating it to employees for the rest of his life. ...

Of course a leader must be able to sell his vision, and that can be difficult. The instantly classic example: Richard Ferris's attempt to assemble a vast travel conglomerate of United Airlines, Hertz rental cars, and Westin and Hilton International hotels under the Allegis name. The projected synergies would have taken a long time to develop, and investors were not persuaded to follow Ferris to the payoff. Last year, rather than give Allegis allegiance, they decided the company was more valuable in pieces.

KEEP YOUR COOL

While crisis isn't the only test of leadership, it's the acid test. By demonstrating grace under pressure, the best leaders inspire those around them to stay calm and act intelligently. Example: John J. Phelan Jr., 57, chairman of the New York Stock Exchange, who was particularly graceful even as stock prices plunged around him ... [in October 1987]. Under powerful urging to shut the exchange and halt the bloodletting, Phelan stood fast and kept his doors open. He held a series of crucial press conferences, helping to prevent more panic selling by displaying dispassionate decisiveness. He maintains that genuine leadership necessarily involves stepping forward in a crisis. "You have to take a position, whether you like it or not," he says. "The natural inclination is to hide in a hole for a while. But if you don't talk about some of the problems, you create a credibility gap." ...

ENCOURAGE RISKS

Effective corporate leaders encourage employees not only to take chances but also to readily accept error. They make clear to one and all that the future of the enterprise rests on willingness to experiment, to push in new and untested directions.

The best way for a leader to convey that message—or any message—is by leading the charge personally. Frederick W. Smith, 44, set an entrepreneurial tone for Federal Express when he founded the company 15 years ago. A former Marine Corps officer back from Vietnam, Smith risked several million dollars he had inherited from his father on a longtime dream of starting up an overnight air delivery service. At the time no obvious nationwide market for such a service existed and few industry experts thought one would develop quickly. Smith persisted and assembled an international delivery empire that earned $188 million on revenues of $3.9 billion in fiscal 1988. Even with all his success, Smith continues to resist the safe route; sometimes he stumbles. He introduced an electronic message transmission service call ZapMail in 1984 and lost $233 million on it. His philosophy of risk is succinctly stated in the Federal Express Manager's Guide, a folksy compendium of leadership tips that functions as a sort of company bible. "Fear of failure must never be a reason not to try something different," it says. Employees know that Smith lives by it.

BE AN EXPERT

Another hallmark of successful corporate leaders is that they do their homework. The troops will follow a lot more willingly if they are confident that the man or woman in front knows at least as much as they do. What August Busch of Anheuser-Bush doesn't know about beer probably isn't worth knowing; ditto with Corning's Jamie Houghton on the subject of glass. Both run companies that dominate the competition.

Both CEOs also run family-dominated companies and were educated in their respective industries virtually from birth. . . . Apple Computer Chairman John Scully . . . [did not have that advantage. He] has achieved much-noted success as a corporate leader, even though he knew almost nothing about personal computers when he came to Apple in 1983 after years as a marketer at PepsiCo. Aware of his problem, he immediately set about solving it. "I'm essentially an intuitive leader, and you can only be intuitive about something you understand," [says] Scully. . . .

Armed with the proper mindset, Scully quickly filled in the gaps, and his mastery of the personal computer business became obvious during his famous showdown with company founder Steve Jobs in 1985. Given a choice between the two, top executives and board members who had once harbored suspicions about Scully because of his lack of technical background rallied round him. . . .

INVITE DISSENT

A company run by an effective leader is a place where dissent is desirable. . . . James Burke of Johnson & Johnson is a boss who actively courts fractious types. "My style is to encourage controversy and encourage people to say what they think," he says.

That practice paid off during J&J's extended crisis over Tylenol poisoning. Relying on his staff's sometimes noisy advice, Burke seized the initiative when seven people died from cyanide-laced Tylenol capsules in 1982. He recalled some 30 million Tylenol packages and sent out new ones with elaborate safety seals. . . . [H]e stayed cool in numerous media appearances in which he explained his efforts and soothed anxious consumers. All the while he was entertaining often sharply differing opinions about what he should do, and he believes he made better decisions as a result. . . .

As president of Xerox's 33,000-person U.S. marketing group, Addison Barry Rand, 43, has amassed an impressive reputation for inspiring his staff. An important element of his success has been an unqualified willingness to accept a variety of opinions and integrate them into his management strategy. Says Rand, . . . "The higher you get in an organization, the more important it is to have people who will tell you when you are right or wrong. If you have 'yes' people, then either you or they are redundant."

SIMPLIFY

Effective leaders possess an extraordinary ability to focus on what is important and reach elegant, simple answers to complex questions. It is not a matter of settling for an easy answer or quick fix, but of zeroing in on essentials. Drew Lewis, 56, now chairman of Union Pacific, has built his career on an exceptional knack for locking onto the most vital parts of a problem and executing deceptively simple solutions. In the 1970s he helped rescue a gaggle of faltering eastern railroads by forming Conrail. As chairman of Warner Amex, he renegotiated major cable contracts and thereby greatly reduced the company's huge losses. He's at it again with Union Pacific, restructuring and streamlining a company with a big railroad and other diverse holdings. He has already sold assets, entered the waste management business, and reduced the 52,000-person work force by 6,000. Characteristically, he has attacked bureaucracy with special vigor, directing a reduction of management layers in the railroad from nine to four. . . .

EPILOGUE

Leaders shake things up, which may be one reason we don't have more of them. "A lot of top executives simply don't want to cope with change, and it becomes harder to move them the more successful their company has been," says Eric R. Zausner, a managing director at the consulting firm Booz Allen & Hamilton. The problem can be especially severe at a large corporation, which may have an entrenched bureaucracy with no recognition of its stake in making change work. Some leadership experts say that is one of the many woes facing top management at General Motors. Chief Executive Roger Smith has fought the problem, trying to inject some spirit into middle managers. But the bureaucracy has fought back.

. . . .

References and Notes

[1] R. J. House and M. L. Baetz, "Leadership: Some Empirical Generalizations and New Research Directions," in B. M. Staw, ed., *Research in Organizational Behavior* (Greenwich, Conn.: JAI Press, 1979), pp. 341–423.

[2] Ibid., p. 344.

[3] Ibid., p. 342–46.

[4] J. French and B. Raven, "The Bases of Social Power," in D. Cartwright, ed., *Studies in Social Power* (Ann Arbor, Mich.: Institute for Social Research, 1959), pp. 150–67.

[5] B. H. Raven and A. W. Kruglanski, "Conflict and Power," in P. Swingle, ed., *The Structure of Conflict* (New York: Academic Press, 1970).

[6] J. P. Kotter, *Power in Management* (New York: AMACOM, 1979); A. Pettigrew, "Information Control as a Power Resource," *Sociology* 6 (1972): 187–204.

[7] D. T. Kenrick and D. C. Funder, "Profiting from Controversy: Lessons from the Person-Situation Debate," *American Psychologist* 43 (1988): 23–34.

[8]Developed from B. M. Bass, *Bass & Stogdill's Handbook of Leadership: Theory, Research, and Managerial Applications* (New York: Free Press, 1990), Ch. 4 and 5; W. O. Jenkins, "A Review of Leadership Studies with Particular Reference to Military Problems," *Journal of Educational Psychology* 44 (1947): 54–79; R. D. Mann, "A Review of the Relationships between Personality and Performance in Small Groups," *Psychological Bulletin* 56 (1959): 241–70; H. L. Smith and L. M. Krueger, "A Brief Summary of Literature on Leadership," *Bulletin of the School of Education, Indiana University* 9 (1933): 1–80; R. M. Stogdill, "Personal Factors Associated with Leadership: A Survey of the Literature," *Journal of Psychology* 25 (1948): 35–71.

[9]House and Baetz, "Leadership," p. 348.

[10]A. G. Jago, "Leadership: Perspectives in Theory and Research," *Management Science* 28 (March 1982): 315–36.

[11]R. G. Lord, C. L. De Vader, and G. M. Alliger, "A Meta-Analysis of the Relation between Personality Traits and Leadership Perceptions: An Application of Validity Generalization Procedures," *Journal of Applied Psychology* 71 (1986): 402–10; Stogdill, "Personal Factors," pp. 44–45.

[12]Bass, *Handbook*, Chs. 4 and 5; Mann, "A Review of the Relationships"; House and Baetz, "Leadership," p. 349.

[13]S. A. Kirkpatrick and E. A. Locke, "Leadership: Do Traits Matter?" *Academy of Management Executive* 5 (1991): 48–60. Quotation taken from p. 49; emphasis added.

[14]Kenrick and Funder, "Profiting from Controversy."

[15]D. A. Kenny and S. J. Zaccaro, "An Estimate of Variance Due to Traits in Leadership," *Journal of Applied Psychology* 68 (1983): 678–85; S. J. Zaccaro, R. J. Fotie, and D. A. Kenny, "Self-Monitoring and Trait-Based Variance in Leadership: An Investigation of Leader Flexibility across Multiple Group Situations," *Journal of Applied Psychology* 76 (1991): 308–15.

[16]R. Likert, *New Patterns of Management* (New York: McGraw-Hill, 1961); R. Likert, *The Human Organization: Its Management and Value* (New York: McGraw-Hill, 1967).

[17]Likert, *New Patterns of Management*, pp. 58–60.

[18]E. A. Locke and G. P. Latham, *A Theory of Goal Setting & Task Performance* (Englewood Cliffs, N.J.: Prentice-Hall, 1990).

[19]Bass, *Handbook*, Ch. 24; J. M. Howell and P. J. Frost, "A Laboratory Study of Charismatic Leadership," *Organizational Behavior and Human Decision Processes* 43 (1989): 243–69; R. M. Stogdill, *Individual Behavior and Group Achievement* (New York: Oxford University Press, 1959).

[20]Bass, *Handbook*, Ch. 24.

[21]F. E. Fiedler, "Engineer the Job to Fit the Manager," *Harvard Business Review* 43 (1965): 115–22; F. E. Fiedler, *A Theory of Leadership Effectiveness* (New York: McGraw-Hill, 1967); F. E. Fiedler, "Validation and Extension of the Contingency Model of Leadership Effectiveness: A Review of Empirical Findings," *Psychological Bulletin* 76 (1971): 128–48.

[22]Developed from Fiedler, "Validation and Extension."

[23]Fiedler, "Engineer the Job," p. 115.

[24]F. E. Fiedler, "The Leadership Game: Matching the Man to the Situation," *Organizational Dynamics* (Winter 1976): 6–16.

[25]R. J. House, "A Path-Goal Theory of Leadership Effectiveness," *Administrative Science Quarterly* 16 (1971): 321–38; R. J. House and G. Dessler, "The Path-Goal Theory of Leadership: Some Post Hoc and a Priori Tests," in J. G. Hunt, ed., *Contingency Approaches to Leadership* (Carbondale: Southern Illinois University Press, 1974); R. J. House and T. R. Mitchell, "Path-Goal Theory of Leadership," *Journal of Contemporary Business* 3 (1974): 81–97.

[26]J. C. Wofford and L. Z. Liska, "Path-Goal Theories of Leadership: A Meta-Analysis," *Journal of Management* 19 (1993): 857–76.

[27]House and Mitchell, "Path-Goal Theory," p. 85.

[28]E. E. Jennings, "On Rediscovering the Leader," in J. W. McGuire, ed., *Contemporary Management: Issues and Viewpoints* (Englewood Cliffs, N.J.: Prentice-Hall, 1974), p. 390.

[29]Jennings, "On Rediscovering the Leader," pp. 390-96.

[30]E. E. Jennings, *An Anatomy of Leadership* (New York: Harper & Row, 1960); Jennings, "On Rediscovering the Leader."

[31]Jennings, "On Rediscovering the Leader," p. 391.

[32]B. M. Bass, *Leadership and Performance beyond Expectations* (New York: Free Press, 1985); B. M. Bass, "From Transactional to Transformational Leadership: Learning to Share the Vision," *Organizational Dynamics* 18 (1990): 19–31.

[33]Bass, *Leadership and Performance*, pp. 42–43.

[34]Ibid., Chs. 9–10.

[35]R. J. House, "A 1976 Theory of Charismatic Leadership," in J. G. Hunt and L. L. Larson, eds., *Leadership: The Cutting Edge* (Carbondale: Southern Illinois University Press, 1977), pp. 189–207; R. J. House, W. D. Spangler, and J. Woycke, "Personality and Charisma in the U.S. Presidency: A Psychological Theory of Leader Effectiveness," *Administrative Science Quarterly* 36 (1991): 364–96; Howell and Frost, "A Laboratory Study"; B. Shamir, R. J. House, and M. B. Arthur, "The Motivational Effects of Charismatic Leadership: A Self-Concept Based Theory," *Organization Science* 4 (1993): 577–94.

[36]J. A. Conger, *The Charismatic Leader: Behind the Mystique of Exceptional Leadership* (San Francisco: Jossey-Bass, 1989), pp. 9–10.

[37]J. Carlzon, *Moments of Truth* (Cambridge, Mass.: Ballinger, 1987), pp. 94–95.

[38]J. P. Howell, D. E. Bowen, P. W. Dorfman, S. Kerr, and P. M. Podsakoff, "Substitutes for Leadership: Effective Alternatives to Ineffective Leadership," *Organizational Dynamics* (1990): 21–38; J. P. Howell, P. W. Dorfman, and S. Kerr, "Moderator Variables in Leadership Research," *Academy of Management Review* 11 (1986): 86–102; S. Kerr, "Substitutes for Leadership: Some Implications for Organizational Design," *Organization and Administrative Sciences* 8 (1977): 135–46; S. Kerr and J. M. Jermier, "Substitutes for Leadership: Their Meaning and Measurement," *Organizational Behavior and Human Performance* 22 (1978): 375–403; P. M. Podsakoff, B. P. Niehoff, S. B. MacKenzie, and M. L. Williams, "Do Substitutes for Leadership Really Substitute for Leadership? An Empirical Examination of Kerr and Jermier's Situational Leadership Model," *Organizational Behavior and Human Decision Processes* 54 (1993): 1–44; P. M. Podsakoff, S. B. MacKenzie, and R. Fetter, "Substitutes for Leadership and the Management of Professionals," *Leadership Quarterly* 4 (1993): 1–44.

[39]R. G. Lord, "An Information Processing Approach to Social Perceptions, Leadership and Behavioral Measurement in Organizations," in B. Staw and L. L. Cummings, eds., *Research in Organizational Behavior*, vol. 7 (Greenwich, Conn.: JAI Press, 1985), pp. 87–128; R. G. Lord, R. J. Foti, and C. DeVader, "A Test of Leadership Categorization Theory: Internal Structure, Information Processing and Leadership Perceptions," *Organizational Behavior and Human Performance* 34 (1984): 343–78; R. Lord, R. Foti, and J. S. Phillips, "A Theory of Leadership Categorization," in J. G. Hunt, U. Sekaran, and C. A. Schriesheim, eds., *Leadership: Beyond Establishment Views* (Carbondale: Southern Illinois University Press, 1982), pp. 122–41.; R. G. Lord and K. J. Maher, *Leadership and Information Processing: Linking Perceptions and Performance* (New York: Routledge, 1993).

[40]Lord, Foti, and DeVader, "A Test of Leadership Categorization Theory."

[41]Developed from B. J. Calder, "An Attribution Theory of Leadership," in B. M. Staw and G. R. Salancik, eds., *New Directions in Organizational Behavior* (Chicago: St. Clair Press, 1977), pp. 179–204.

[42]M. Loden, *Feminine Leadership or How to Succeed in Business without Being One of the Boys* (New York: Times Books, 1985).

[43]J. B. Rosener, "Ways Women Lead," *Harvard Business Review* 68 (1990): 119–25.

[44]Bass, *Handbook*, Ch. 32; G. H. Dobbins and S. J. Platz, "Sex Differences in Leadership: How Real Are They?" *Academy of Management Review* 11 (1986): 118–27.

[45]R. S. Wellins, W. C. Byham, and J. M. Wilson, *Empowered Teams: Creating Self-Directed Work Groups That Improve Quality, Productivity, and Participation* (San Francisco: Jossey-Bass, 1991).

[46]Ibid., Ch. 7.

[47]C. Manz and H. P. Sims, Jr., "Leading Workers to Lead Themselves: The External Leadership of Self-Managing Work Teams," *Administrative Science Quarterly* 12 (1987): 106–28; C. Manz and H. P. Sims, Jr., *Superleadership: Leading Workers to Lead Themselves* (Englewood Cliffs, N.J.: Prentice-Hall, 1989).

[48]W. Bennis and B. Nanus, *Leaders: The Strategies for Taking Charge* (New York: Harper & Row, 1985) pp. 21, 23, 40–41, 92–93, 218–26; J. P. Kotter, "What Leaders Really Do," *Harvard Business Review* (1990): 103–11; G. A. Yukl, *Leadership in Organizations* (Englewood Cliffs, N.J.: Prentice-Hall, 1994), pp. 4–5; A. Zaleznik, "Managers and Leaders: Are They Different?" *Harvard Business Review* 55 (1977): 67–80; A. Zaleznik, "The Leadership Gap," *Academy of Management Executive* 4 (1990): 7–22.

[49]G. Hofstede, "Motivation, Leadership, and Organizations: Do American Theories Apply Abroad?" *Organizational Dynamics* (1980): 42–63; G. Hofstede, *Culture's Consequences: International Differences in Work-Related Values* (Beverly Hills, Calif.: Sage Publications, 1984), Ch. 9; G. Hofstede, "Cultural Constraints in Management Theories," *Academy of Management Executive* 7 (1993): 81–94; I. Vertinsky, D. K. Tse, D. A. Wehrung, and K. Lee, "Organizational Design and Management Norms: A Comparative Study of Managers' Perceptions in the People's Republic of China, Hong Kong, and Canada," *Journal of Management* 16 (1990): 853–67.

[50]Bass, *Handbook*, p. 761.

[51]Bass, *Handbook*, Ch. 34; L. Mann, "Cross-Cultural Studies of Small Groups," in H. C. Triandis and R. W. Brislin, eds., *Handbook of Cross-Cultural Psychology. Social Psychology*, vol. 5 (Boston: Allyn & Bacon, 1980), pp. 155–209.

[52]P. W. Dorfman and J. P. Howell, "Dimensions of National Culture and Effective Leadership Patterns," in E. G. McGoun, ed., *Advances in International Comparative Management* (Greenwich, Conn.: JAI Press, 1987), pp. 127–50.

[53]Bass, *Handbook*, pp. 799–800.

[54]H. P. Sims, Jr. and P. Lorenzi, *The New Leadership Paradigm: Social Learning and Cognition in Organizations* (Newbury Park, Calif: Sage Publications, 1992), Ch. 13.

[55]Ibid., pp. 272–73.

[56]F. Bird and J. Gandz, *Good Management: Business Ethics in Action* (Toronto: Prentice-Hall, 1991).

[57]J. M. Howell and B. J. Avolio, "The Ethics of Charismatic Leadership: Submission or Liberation," *The Executive* 6 (1992): 43–54.

III *Group and Interpersonal Processes in Organizations*

⊿ LEADERS AND MANAGERS

*T*his case describes the approaches to leadership and management of two senior U.S. executives and some European executives. What differences do you see in their approaches? Are there any similarities? An analysis follows the descriptions.

Lawrence Bossidy

Lawrence A. Bossidy, chief executive of Allied-Signal since July 1991, grew up in Pittsfield, Massachusetts, in the shadow of General Electric's big transformer works. In high school he was a star pitcher, a fastballing south-paw who hero-worshiped New York Giant screwball ace Carl Hubbell. . . .

Bossidy has a paunch now, and his 57-year-old left arm isn't what it was, but he's still throwing heat. In his first 15 months on the mound for the Morristown, New Jersey, company, operating profits increased 28.5%. Return on shareholders' equity leaped from 8.9% to 17%. And the stock, 29⅜ when Bossidy's appointment was announced, was recently 55½. The Tigers, by contrast, finished sixth, 21 games out.

Bossidy's performance at Allied-Signal is an object lesson in corporate transformation. Says he: "Change can be done faster than most people think." And he's out to prove it—not just by cutting (though he has done that) but also by preparing the company to grow and add jobs. Shamelessly picking off tools and talent from GE, Xerox, and other companies, Bossidy has set himself the ultimate test of cycle-time reduction: increasing the speed of corporate revolution. "Personally, I couldn't do it any other way," he says. "I'm not mature enough. I had to get it all out on the table."

In this case, "all" meant housecleaning and culture change—urgently and simultaneously. The key features: ambitious goals like 8% annual revenue growth, a total-immersion total quality program, an aggressive plan to

recast the company's supply chain, and a top-to-bottom change in human resources management. Informal as well as impatient, Bossidy is determined to accomplish the kind of transformation that took GE more than a decade in less than half the time. "We couldn't have done it this fast 15 years ago," he admits, crediting pioneers like GE, Motorola, and Xerox for showing him how. Says Ralph Reigns, who became head of Allied-Signal Automotive in November 1991 after stretches at United Technologies, Mack Trucks, and ITT: "I've never seen anything move as fast."

The company Bossidy joined was the creation of Edward L. Hennessy Jr., one of the grand acquisitors of the Eighties, who turned sleepy Allied Chemical into a multibillion-dollar power in automotive components, aerospace, and engineered materials. But by 1991 the house that Ed built was ramshackle. Debt was 42% of capital, and cash was pouring out like heat through an uninsulated roof.

Hennessy was already looking for an heir. Bossidy . . . was an obvious candidate. But he said no when Allied-Signal's board proposed to sit him at Hennessy's feet, not crowning him CEO till Hennessy retired on an unspeci-fied date. Bossidy had been No. 2 long enough. His counteroffer: Hennessy could remain chairman till the end of 1992, with Bossidy CEO from the get-go.

The new chief has been telling people to move faster ever since. His first day, a new company forecast predicted a negative cash flow of $435 million in 1991 and $336 million in 1992. A survey taken a month before showed that executive morale was, he says, "the worst I'd ever seen." Within ten weeks, Bossidy started dropping shoes. First came a restructuring plan. It chopped $225 million from capital spending, reduced the annual dividend to $1 a share from $1.80, put eight small divisions up for sale, cut 6,200 salaried jobs, and combined ten data-processing centers into two. Those steps were supposed to cut the cash drain to $250 million in 1991 and to zero this year. What actually happened was stunning: Negative cash flow of $195 million last year and a positive $255 million in the bag for 1992. In all, an $831 million turnaround from the July 1991 forecast.

Credit some of it to Bossidy's other shoe. With the restructuring, he outlined lofty goals for folks to "see the promised land and know when they got there." Targets

Sources: T. A. Stewart, "Allied-Signal's Turnaround Blitz," *Fortune,* November 30, 1992, pp. 72–74. © Time Inc. All rights reserved.

Barad: J. A. Oliver, "Mattel Chief Followed Her Instincts and Found Success," *Marketing News,* March 16, 1992, p. 15. Reprinted with permission from *Marketing News,* published by the American Marketing Association, Joyce Anne Oliver, 1992.

Euromanagers: P. Hofheinz, "Europe's Tough New Managers," *Fortune,* September 6, 1993, pp. 114, 116. © Time Inc. All rights reserved.

included 6% annual gains in productivity and big jumps in operating profit margin from 4.7% in 1991 to 9% in 1994, return on equity from 10.5% to 18% over the same period, and working capital turnover from 4.2 times a year to 5.2. . . .

A statement of corporate vision and values came out with the goals. It was the handiwork of Allied's top 12 executives, who compose the leadership committee, and it accomplished the dual job of raising the senior executives' sights and bringing them together with Bossidy to see what they could agree on. Much of the statement is standard, bracing stuff: the vision of being "one of the world's premier companies, distinctive and successful," and the values of satisfying customers, integrity, and teamwork. But it galvanized people. And one aspect caught everyone's attention. Asks Frederic Poses, who runs the engineered materials division: "Did you notice the most interesting value on the list? Speed."

Bossidy chose total quality management to turn the vision and values into reality. Hennessy had already hired James Sierk to be vice president of quality and productivity. Sierk came from Xerox's Baldrige Award team, where he prepared the famous "Wart Report," which became Xerox's agenda for continuing improvement after it won the prestigious quality prize. Bossidy strongly buttressed Sierk's efforts at Allied-Signal. Says Noel Tichy, a University of Michigan business professor who led GE's renowned Management Development Institute in the mid-Eighties and follows Bossidy's work at Allied-Signal: "TQ is a joke in a lot of places. Larry put a hardness into the process with a clear set of goals, values, and methods."

He changed the timetable first. "I'd laid out a five-year plan," Sierk recalls. "Larry told me to do it in two." By the end of 1993, the CEO wanted all 90,000 employees to complete a four-day course in the use of tools like process maps to hunt for unnecessary work and benchmarking to study other companies' successes. (They're ahead of schedule.)

Bossidy was determined that total quality become a part of normal operations rather than a separate bureaucracy. To that end, Sierk told Coopers & Lybrand, the firm he hired to set up the course, that within three months the consultants were to finish training a generation of trainers and then scoot, leaving employees to carry on the work. The students were people like Doreen Mannix, 34, a production manager at Allied-Signal's sprawling chemical plant in Hopewell, Virginia, who became a "master facilitator" as well as doing her regular work, and spent three months on the road—even traveling to Singapore—to teach quality methods to employees in all three divisions of the company. Bossidy also set a deadline for Sierk. After three years he was to close his office and be prepared to take an operations job.

The training itself is unique. Employees come to the course in natural work groups—colleagues who build part of a brake system, for example—and bring a real-life problem, like reducing idle machine time. Trainers and supervisors must approve the choice in advance. This ensures that the problem is neither trivial nor too big for the team to fix, and it almost forces managers to okay team proposals later. During their four-day training, teams work on their problem. Then they return to their jobs to complete it with help from trainers on-site.

In Tempe, Arizona, aerospace worker Barbara Peters had a very personal project—to save her job. Peters and her teammates, who hand-finish machine hardware, saw the company send $25,000 a month in work to outside vendors and smelled the unemployment office. The team found that in-house work was expensive because antiquated tumblers did a poor job of prepping the hardware for finishing. Cashing their management-approval chit, they got the company to buy new tumblers, a $60,000 expenditure that should save $240,000 a year.

Using real problems, not classroom training, hardwires the quality effort to performance. Evidence? Allied-Signal achieved its increased productivity and working capital goals over the past 12 months despite flat sales.

Jill Barad

Taking time to tell people how good they are is one of the best ways management can reward people for their efforts, said Jill Barad, president of Mattel USA.

"We in management tend to focus on what's not being done, how people aren't performing instead of recognizing that our people have delivered in the past and are quite capable of delivering again," she pointed out. "We must constantly remind people of their strengths so they can make the most of those behaviors."

During the last decade, Barad worked her way up from product manager to Mattel's senior ranks largely by launching a series of innovative and highly successful new products, mainly dolls, for young girls.

Most important to marketing success, she believes, is following your own instincts, what you really believe to be true. She is known for working with people to help them see that vision of where she wants the company to go so they can breathe new life into older product lines and create new ones.

In late 1990, her vision caused 31-year-old Barbie to exceed $700 million in revenue, breaking a record and bringing total Mattel sales to $1.4 billion. Last year, Barbie sales rose above $800 million while overall revenue approached $1.6 billion.

"No one is a one-man band, and if they are they don't last very long," Barad noted. "You have to bring a lot of people along with you. For people to feel the momentum, the energy and enthusiasm you feel, they have to see what you see and believe that it can be real."

"They must believe that your combined efforts in some way can benefit them, the company, and the greater us."

The biggest strategic change for Mattel in recent years was to focus on core brands. For years, she recalled, Mattel wanted to be good at everything it touched.

"The answer and opportunity was to capitalize on what we had already established a base of business in, rather than spending dollars on many diverse toy lines that may or may not be what young people wanted," she said.

"Barbie was the best example of that. We increased the Barbie business by 70% in the past three years since we went back to building our basic brands."

The company's large doll business was less than $40 million before Barad and her managers employed this focused strategy. In the old days, the company was coming up with a new doll every year and had to replace that volume again and again.

Today, three major brands of large dolls represent $220 million in revenue.

"We've really stuck with this strategy and capitalized on what we think are very long-lasting niches in the marketplace that won't go away, because they are based on fundamental play patterns that children have," she said.

"I like to do things that are based on fundamental needs because they are predictable, constant, and ever-lasting."

One lesson she draws on frequently is: What is obvious is usually true.

"You don't have to dig for deep, dark secrets," she noted. "You just have to look at what is and what is not, and put it together in a fresh and contemporary way."

She learned this lesson early in her career when she worked as a beauty consultant for Love Cosmetics while she was a student at Queens College in New York.

Barad thinks she may always have been drawn to the flair and intensity of fashion and cosmetics, even as a child. She remembers being fascinated by "all the colors, textures, and scents" found within the cosmetics section, as well as the soda fountain, of the New York–based pharmacies owned by her grandparents.

After college and before joining Mattel, Barad held several positions in the cosmetics industry. She was a brand manager for Coty Cosmetics in New York and later worked as an account executive handling the Max Factor account for Wells, Rich Greene Advertising in Los Angeles.

Today she shares the position of president of Mattel USA with David Mauer. Barad is responsible for fashion dolls, large and small dolls, plush and activity toys, and other marketing and packaging services.

Mauer is responsible for boys, infant, and preschool toys and a newly launched game division. She and Mauer, with chairman John Amerman, are leaders of customer service teams, a new concept in the toy industry.

"Our role is to work with a particular distribution customer to learn everything we can about what their organization is striving to achieve," she said. "We share that information with all the people at Mattel who need to know and get everyone moving to change and implement the right processes and systems to better meet those customers' needs.

"We've increased our business far more in accounts where we've initiated this customer service strategy and plan to implement it for every account."

Euromanagers

The new European management style contains elements of reengineering, total quality management, and other trends popular in the U.S., but it also has its own flavor. It could be called the supply-side revolution, because a big part of it is aimed at pressuring suppliers to raise productivity and reduce their own costs.

ABB's Percy Barnevik has been a master of the technique, but its real father may be the contentious José Ignacio "Inaki" López de Arriortúa, 52. López became a managerial legend when, as purchasing chief at General Motors, he cut $2 billion out of the U.S. automaker's expenses, mainly by badgering parts makers to cut prices or risk losing GM's business. But the accusation by GM that López pilfered secret documents before defecting to Volkswagen last winter—which López denies—has badly tarnished his reputation. López's usefulness to VW—he has already achieved big productivity gains—may be in jeopardy.

And López has detractors outside of GM. Because their own costs are so high, many German suppliers claim VW is asking too much of them. Martin Herzog, secretary of the powerful Association of the German Motor Industry, blasts López for "ruining [the parts industry] with his rude supply policy," while Günter Mordhorst, CEO of Varta, a $1.4-billion-a-year battery maker, accuses López of "mass murder."

France's Valeo (1992 sales: $3.8 billion) is one European parts maker that can compete. CEO Noël Goutard, 61, has changed almost everything. A new budget is now made up every six months instead of once a year so the company can shift or readjust its strategy more quickly. Goutard put workers into teams responsible for organizing their own activities. Each team meets for five minutes or so every morning and for an hour once a week to talk about problems and ways to improve. Every worker is expected to make ten suggestions for improvements a year, and Goutard insists that all suggestions be considered within ten days. Says he: "We couldn't just copy the Japanese. We had to develop our own management system."

Goutard says workers have accepted the changes enthusiastically: "People like to work for a company that is prepared to confront market conditions." Last year, despite major layoffs, Valeo hired 800 graduate engineers. As Goutard notes, "We're moving out of unskilled labor and into skills." By the end of next year, he wants half the staff of the purchasing department to be trained engineers.

Now the results are apparent. Set foot inside Valeo's headquarters on Paris's quiet Rue Bayen and ask anybody how the company managed to increase profits by 26% last year in the ferociously competitive parts market. "Quality, service, price," comes the answer. Goutard has so effectively conveyed these buzzwords from the top to the bottom of his organization that even the farthest-flung outer-office secretary sounds like Peter Drucker.

Valeo has also laid off nearly 9,000 workers and moved some production overseas, but Goutard says that Europe still has strengths as a manufacturing base. He insists that he has acquired factories in Korea, Brazil, Mexico, and Turkey not just to cut costs but also to get a better foothold in those fast-growing markets. Still, he wants to keep some production at home to stay close to the European market. Speaking of Europe, he notes, "I've never seen changes take place without strong incentive. The incentives are here now: erratic markets, Japanese competition, intense job pressure. They are forcing change."

Where did Goutard learn so much about management? "Listening to customers," he says. "They can teach you everything you need to know." Just how good is Valeo? Last year, when he was still at GM, Inaki López gave Valeo an award for delivering the best value and service.

Barnevik, 52, the rangy Swede with a Stanford MBA, has forged a competitive powerhouse out of ABB by taking the concept of leanness to extremes. He turned ABB into 5,000 profit centers, each with its own balance sheet, then shrank headquarters drastically. His now famous cut-then-cut-again style reduced his Zurich corporate staff from 4,000 to 200. "We dislike headquarters," he says. "They cost a lot of money, and they disturb the people who are doing the real business." His formula? Cut the staff to 10% of its original size, let it run for a couple of years, then go back and cut it again by farming out every administrative chore that you can get done for less money outside.

As a result, Barnevik has turned two sleepy European engineering companies into a highly competitive machine (1992 sales: $29.6 billion). In a recession year, profits slipped just 4%, to $1.1 billion. He has made few friends along the way, though, except among shareholders. Europeans marvel at his achievement but grumble that the man is a slave driver who has terrified his staff.

Barnevik has also embraced supply-side management. Many supplies for ABB's 5,000 business units world-wide are purchased by a single center in Mannheim, Germany, run by two Swedes, Sune Karlsson and Roland Andersson. At every other board meeting one of them reports on the latest savings from working more closely with suppliers. Karlsson and Andersson visit suppliers not only to insist on lower costs but also to show managers how to attain them. "It's a win-win situation," says Karlsson. "We're helping them lower ABB's costs, and we're also helping them improve their competitiveness."

ABB has also begun urging suppliers to help with R&D. Instead of giving a supplier a new design, the company asks it to create its own design within certain parameters—at lower cost. Andersson says that one Japanese supplier, which he won't name, was asked to take on such a project. The result was a new part 30% cheaper than the earlier version. Says he: "Our first reaction was to get angry and say, 'Why didn't you do this before?' They said, 'Because you didn't ask.'"

Not everyone does things so radically. In fact, Nestlé CEO Helmut Maucher, 65, suggests that friendliness is as effective a management technique as Barnevik's neutron bomb tactics. His philosophy: "If you do things quietly, step by step, you avoid causing friction. But you can look back over five years and see that radical change was accomplished."

In his nearly 12 years as CEO, Maucher has quietly expanded his company, based in Vevey, Switzerland, through a series of shrewd and well-managed acquisitions. Nestlé's sales have doubled, from $17 billion to $38 billion, and Maucher vows that they will double again by the end of the century through forceful expansion in Third World markets. Says he: "Only 25% of our products are sold in the developing world, where 80% of the population lives. I see growth possibilities everywhere."

While Maucher plans expansion, he has handed over daily management of the world's third-largest food company (according to the 1993 Fortune Global 500) to Ramón Masip, 52, a suave, urbane Spaniard who embodies the new type of hard-driving Euromanager. Over lunch on the sixth floor of Nestlé's stylish offices overlooking Lake Geneva, Masip is a picture of Iberian courtesy and charm. He chats amiably about his rise from a Nestlé market researcher to chief operating officer. But when talk turns to the difficulty of running one of the most truly global corporations, his eyes narrow slightly and this gregarious manager briefly flashes the sharp teeth behind that warm smile. Lest his visitor underestimate him, Masip calmly ticks off a list of factories he has closed—including several back home in Spain, where the unemployment rate exceeds 21%. Says he: "Sometimes you have to cut off a finger to save an arm."

Europe still has a long way to go in overcoming the competitive drag of its too generous social welfare system and its laid-back approach to management. But if the trend toward a new management style continues, and even picks up, Europe could become a paradigm of how to manage in the new global economy.

The Old World is capable of producing the archetypal manager for the 21st century. More than many Americans or Japanese, Europeans are often very comfortable in international situations. The better-run companies—like Nestlé—have corporate boards that closely resemble the

U.N. Security Council. Says Paul Strebel, a professor at the International Institute for Management Development in Switzerland: "Our cultural diversity is a huge asset." Adds Roland Berger, head of Germany's Roland Berger & Partner consulting firm: "Europeans are better equipped for globalization."

The question is how far European society will let managers take their tough new approach. With workers and managers long accustomed to virtual lifetime employment guarantees, Europe has watched its structural unemployment rise to 10.5%—and it won't go down soon. Barnevik estimates that as few as one-third of the major companies in Europe are prepared to survive under increasing global competitive pressure. Says he: "We face productivity challenges that were undreamed of in the 1970s."

The risk over the long term is that rising unemployment may bring back overregulation and protectionism rather than force the loosening of these stifling restrictions. As Maucher puts it, "The question is whether Europe is politically able to be competitive."

The time when European management methods are taught at Harvard is still a way off. But make no mistake: At this moment, European managers are gearing for the competitive challenges of the 21st century. And they are doing it fast.

Case Analysis

The managers described in this case all had to bring about large-scale organizational change. They needed to transform their organizations and change strategic direction. Each manager, though, had a different approach and emphasized different factors.

Lawrence Bossidy did not accept the common belief that large-scale change cannot happen fast. His approach to transforming Allied-Signal reflected his impatience. He also used specific goals so his managers could "see the promised land and know when they got there."[1] The research on Goal Setting described in Chapter 8 clearly pointed to the motivational quality of specific, challenging goals.

The company's vision statement began to focus people on customers, teamwork, and speed. Bossidy chose Total Quality Management, a philosophy and system of management that focuses on customers. It also uses teams to focus on specific problems and find solutions. Bossidy saw Total Quality Management as the way to transform his company.

Jill Barad's approach at Mattell USA was distinctly different from Bossidy's at Allied-Signal. Her goal, however, was the same as Bossidy's: refocus Mattell on its core businesses. Managers had earlier tried unsuccessfully to expand into new business areas.

Barad developed a strategy based on toys that fit the basic play patterns of children. She believed that strategy would bring the company long-term continuing revenue because play patterns do not change fast. Her results with the Barbie doll testify to the success of her strategy.

Barad's style of management and leadership features positive rewards, recognition of people's achievements, and a strong team focus. Although she had the vision for the needed strategic change, she felt she needed the commitment of many other people. They had to share her vision and believe it was achievable. Her repeated successes suggest she has taken the right approach.

The European managers not only approached their tasks differently from earlier generations of European managers, but also differed among themselves. Except for Maucher at Nestlé, they had a demanding and well-focused approach to changing their organizations. Increasing global competition and shifts in markets created the need for change.

All the managers shared several underlying themes including setting tough goals, increasing those goals, focusing on customers, giving service, and emphasizing quality. All the companies had a strong commitment to Total Quality Management. Building supplier relationships, and demanding more from suppliers are not European traditions. Some suppliers had trouble adjusting to the new system, but the successes indicate it is working.

Europe's cultural diversity may give new European managers a competitive edge in global competition. Such managers have experience in working across national boundaries. As Professor Strebel noted, "Our cultural diversity is a huge asset."[2]

References and Notes

[1] Stewart, "Allied-Signal's Turnaround Blitz," p. 73.
[2] Hofheinz, "Europe's Tough New Managers," p. 116.

Organizational Processes

. . . .

Section Overview

*F*igure IV-1 is an overview of the major sections of this book and the chapters in Section IV. The four chapters of this section describe some major organizational processes, including communication, power, politics, decision making, and stress. Each chapter discusses international aspects of the topics and the ethical issues they raise.

Chapter 13 describes communication processes in organizations. The basic communication process has a sender, a receiver, and a message going over a communication channel. Noise surrounding the process can distort messages. Communication in organizations occurs in networks of various forms. Verbal communication includes oral, written, electronic, and video communication. Nonverbal communication includes gestures, facial expressions, and the sender's voice. The meaning of nonverbal communication varies across cultures.

Chapter 14 describes decision processes in organizations. It presents several decision-making models that have different assumptions and limitations. The various models likely apply to different decision types and decision situations. Individuals do well with some types of decisions while groups are better for other types of decisions. The chapter presents a model that can guide your choice of approach, depending on the characteristics of the decision problem. Cohesive decision-making groups often suffer from a major dysfunction called groupthink. The chapter also discusses methods of improving decision making, some of which can help avoid groupthink.

Power and political behavior (Chapter 15) are major processes that can affect the behavior of all employees in organizations. People's sources of power include charisma, important work activities, and their political network. Attribution processes can affect a person's perception of someone else's power, even when the other party has little power. Political maneuvering in organizations includes political strategy and political tactics. Strategy is a person's political plan, which often focuses on career development or resource allocation decisions. Tactics are individual steps in carrying out the plan such as controlling a meeting agenda or building coalitions with important people or groups. Doing a political diagnosis of an

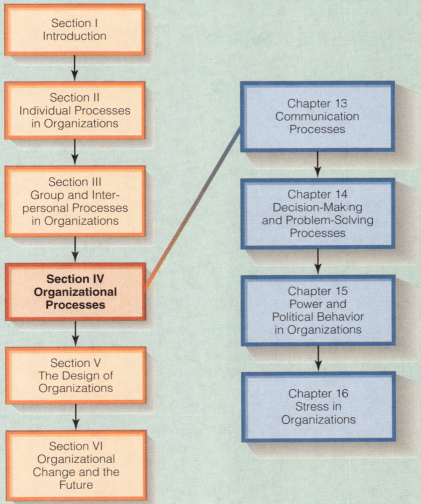

Section I
Introduction

Section II
Individual Processes
in Organizations

Section III
Group and Inter-
personal Processes
in Organizations

**Section IV
Organizational
Processes**

Section V
The Design of
Organizations

Section VI
Organizational
Change and the
Future

Chapter 13
Communication
Processes

Chapter 14
Decision-Making
and Problem-Solving
Processes

Chapter 15
Power and
Political Behavior
in Organizations

Chapter 16
Stress in
Organizations

organization lets a person see her political position compared to others in the system. Sadly, political behavior has a dark side—deception, lying, and intimidation.

The section closes with a chapter (Chapter 16) describing stress in organizations. It begins with several models of stress and brings them together into an integrated model. That model should help guide your understanding of how factors in a person's environment can lead to either positive or negative stress. A section of the chapter shows you how to diagnose stress for yourself and for an organization. The latter should help managers understand how their organizations induce stress responses in employees. Individuals and organizations can manage stress in several ways including stress reduction, stress resiliance, and stress recuperation.

13

Communication Processes

· MILLSTAR, one of the largest communication satellites, lets U.S. military forces communicate worldwide.

After reading this chapter, you should be able to . . .

· Explain the basic communication processes of organizations.
· Understand the effects of verbal and non-verbal communication.
· Distinguish between the functions and dysfunctions of organizational communication.
· Discuss the features of active listening and the different forms of listening.
· Describe ways of making communication processes more effective.
· Understand the effects of new technology on communication.
· Describe communication networks and the roles that can emerge within a network.

Chapter Overview

. . . .

OPENING EPISODE

Putting More Oomph in Your Oratory

· Business Week *reporter Dick Janssen,* left, *gets feedback from communications trainer Bert Decker after viewing a videotape of Janssen's presentation.*

Robert Burns once wrote of the yearning to see ourselves as others see us. Today, thanks to the camcorder, the poet could see himself—and then be critiqued. How would he like that? I think I know.

I found out, as many managers do, by taking a crash course in communicating. Much of the time, I felt like a butterfly under a magnifying glass. By the time I was released, though, I had confronted some dismaying habits and had a headful of pointers on how to handle any audience.

A number of image gurus run such programs for corporate clients. Among the largest firms are New York's Communispond (212 687-8040), Atlanta's Speakeasy (404 261-4029), and Chicago's Executive Technique (312 266-0001). Decker Communications, based in San Francisco (415 546-6100), taught my one-day senior-executive course, which costs $2,500. Pricey—but the limit is six students; a two-day session for 15 costs less.

Our instructor, Bert Decker, displays all the empathy of a drill sergeant: "I've trained over 32,000 people, and there isn't anyone who comes here who really wants to be here," says Decker, a former documentary filmmaker. Yet the motivation to tough it out is strong: Managers spend 94% of their time communicating, "giving off cues about ourselves dozens of times a day."

I soon find out what sort of cues. After taking my turn standing up and telling the class about my job and family, I am whisked off to watch a video replay. There I am, in living color, looking at the floor and occasionally heavenward. Staring longingly at the (off-limits) shelter of the lectern. Clutching my prop, a ballpoint pen, and using it to make feeble gestures. Rocking backward, with my voice a guarded monotone. And, sin of sins, I often stall with a meaningless "uh."

The tape ends. I am shaken and don't believe that I will be redeemed as a speaker in just one day. But my coach finds glimmers of hope. After the first minute, I had let a smile break through, and I even said something mildly amusing. (Personal and audience-tailored anecdotes are in; jokes are out.) And, while I didn't use my hands expansively enough, I never put them in my pockets. It is time for one of Decker's upbeat generalizations: "We are all better than we think we are."

My peers, meanwhile, display flaws of their own. An advertising exec fails to leave room in her speech for commas or periods that would let listeners keep up with her rapid-fire thoughts. A manufacturing honcho's delivery is so wooden that he might have been reading aloud from a physics text.

Soon, Decker tosses us some surprise ad-lib topics. Mine is "feet," and what counts here is not accuracy but free association and enthusiasm. ("They're vital to the shoe

Source: D. Janssen, "Putting More Oomph in Your Oratory," *Business Week*, June 4, 1990, p. 165. Reprinted from June 4, 1990 issue of *Business Week* by special permission, copyright © 1990 by The McGraw-Hill Companies.

industry," I offer.) Later, in pursuit of persuasion, we have to outline and deliver a speech on a real-life situation, such as urging a skeptical sales force to push low-end merchandise.

In between, we absorb Decker's minilectures on principles. A speech, he proclaims, should convey an overall impression rather than just facts and figures: "You have to reach people emotionally, not mechanically, if you want to cause change." Our words are only a small part of a message we convey and are easily undercut by visual cues such as poor posture or darting eyes.

To avoid such a problem, he reminds us of things our mothers probably taught us, plus some finishing touches. Like not slouching. We learn to stand with our knees flexed, tilting slightly forward, a nuance of body language meant to serve us as well at a cocktail party as on the speaker's platform. Instead of averting our eyes from one amorphous glob of an audience, we learn to seek eye contact with an individual—for three to six seconds, max, that is. We find we do gain encouragement from this fleeting but intimate human contact. Then we move on to nurture rapport with another listener.

More vidotapes show we are improving. And we are made privy to some of the subtler secrets of well-coached CEOs and pols. Never say: "That's a good question." (It reflects poorly on other questions.) Look away fast from a hostile questioner, so you don't get locked into a counterproductive debate. When you avoid making a direct reply, use the question as a bridge to a point you wish to make.

To make the most of a crash course, follow up on your own later. All it takes is a videocamera or just a mirror and simple cassette tape recorder. When will I start finding the time for this? Well, uh. . . .

. . . .

The Opening Episode showed the importance many managers place on effective communication in their organizations. Video replays of an oral presentation showed presenters the nonverbal cues people use when communicating. The replay was important feedback to those in the workshop, allowing them to begin improving their communication skills. This chapter discusses many aspects of both verbal and nonverbal communication and the important roles they play in an organization.

The following quotation expresses the chapter's orientation to communication processes in organizations:

> The word *communication* will be used here in a very broad sense to include all of the procedures by which one mind may affect another. This, of course, involves not only written and oral speech, but also music, the pictorial arts, the theatre, the ballet, and in fact all human behavior."[1]

This quotation came from the opening of a now classic work describing an early theory of communication. The heart of the definition is in the first sentence. All communication in organizations tries to affect the behavior of at least one other person. Communication can change the way a person perceives his environment and thereby lead to changes in behavior.[2]

Organizational communication includes the purpose, flow, and direction of messages and the media used for those messages.[3] Such communication happens within the complex, interdependent social systems of organizations.[4] Think of organizational communication as another view of behavior in organizations. This chapter calls such behavior "message behavior," behavior that includes sending, receiving, and giving meaning to messages.

Communication processes in organizations are continuous and constantly changing; they do not have a beginning or an end, nor do they follow a strict sequence.[5] During communication, the sender creates messages from one or more symbols to which he attaches meaning. Messages can be oral, written, or nonverbal; they can also be intentional or unintentional. Messages deal with tasks to be done, maintenance of organizational policies, or information about some state of the organization. They can go to people inside the organization or outside.

Communication processes exhibit major differences across cultures. Organizations may encounter these differences when they operate internationally or as a result of diversity in the domestic workforce. A later section discusses the cross-cultural differences that can affect communication processes.

Organizational communication happens over a pathway called a network. The network can be formal as defined by formal organizational positions and relationships among those positions. It can also be informal as defined by informal patterns of social interaction and the informal groups described in Chapter 10. Communication over the network goes in any direction: downward, upward, or horizontal. Communication networks in organizations are interdependent, interlocking, and overlapping systems of human interaction. They involve relationships among individuals, within and among groups, or dispersed almost randomly throughout an organization.

◢ The Basic Communication Process

Figure 13-1[6] shows the sequence of the **basic communication process.** The sender decides what message to send and encodes it using symbols he assumes the receiver will understand. The sender converts the message to a signal and sends the message over a communication channel to the receiver. The channel can be a person's voice, an electronic device, a written medium, or a video medium. The receiver decodes the message received over the channel and interprets its meaning. The receiver responds to the communication by acting in a manner consistent with that interpretation.

The feedback loop at the bottom of the figure implies interdependence between the sender and receiver during the communication process.[7] The sender interprets the response of the receiver and can send an additional message for clarification.

Various distortions, errors, and foreign material often affect the quality of the signal. The noise in the model represents these distortions; they are additions to the

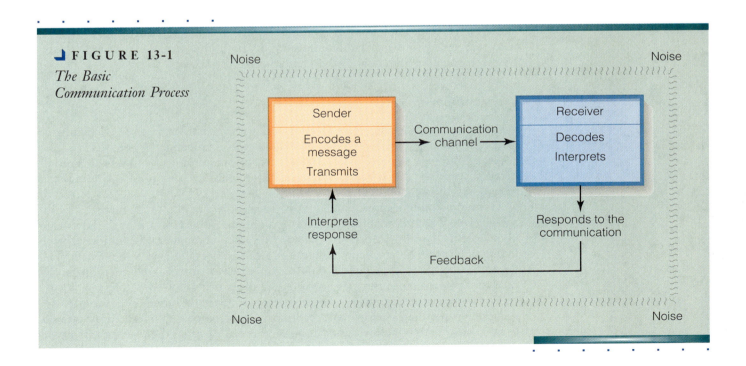

◢ FIGURE 13-1

The Basic Communication Process

signal not intended by the sender. Noise surrounds the entire communication process in organizations and can make communication less effective. A later section discusses communication dysfunctions that result from the presence of noise.

Types of Communication

Verbal and nonverbal communication are the two major types of communication found in organizational communication processes. **Verbal communication** includes oral, written, and electronic forms of communication. **Nonverbal communication** includes eye movements, gestures, facial expressions, tone of voice, and the like.[8]

Both types of communication can appear together in a communication process and interact to create meaning for a receiver. Nonverbal communication adds much of the feeling and emotion that a sender wants to give to a message.[9] Nonverbal communication often has more effect than verbal communication on the meaning receivers give a message.[10]

VERBAL COMMUNICATION

Oral and written messages are the two major forms of verbal communication found in most organizations. The following paragraphs discuss many characteristics of the different forms of verbal communication you will likely find in today's organizations.

Oral Communication

All forms of speech between a sender and receiver are **oral communication.**[11] It can occur during face-to-face interaction or by telephone, radio, or television. Although oral communication usually has the immediate attention of the receiver, the message can be recorded and played later; cassette recordings, telephone answering devices, and computer-recorded voice mail are examples.

Oral communication leaves no permanent, retrievable record of the message and response unless the interaction is transcribed or recorded. When the sender wants to affect the receiver's opinion on some matter, oral communication is more effective than written. Nonverbal communication by both the sender and the receiver, however, can affect the final interpretation of the message.

Written Communication

Written communication is any form of handwriting, printed memo and report, or message sent over an electronic medium such as a computer network.[12] The receiver's response is more delayed in written communication than in oral communication because the receiver must read the message before interpreting and responding to it.

Written communications compete with each other for the time and attention of the receiver. They also compete with oral communication, a form with the advantage of at least the vocal presence of the sender. Written communication can have some interaction with nonverbal communication, although it is not always immediate. The way a sender gives a memo or report to a receiver, for example, can affect the receiver's perception of the message when he reads it.

Written communication has several advantages over oral communication. It is a retrievable and almost permanent recording of a message. Comprehension often is greater with written than with oral communication[13] because the receiver can reread a written communication to be sure he understands the sender's intended meaning. For this reason, managers commonly use memoranda to document agreements.

Electronic and Video Communication

As modern technology develops, **electronic and video communication** are becoming increasingly important. Such communication includes electronic mail, computer networks, fax machines, computer conferencing, and videoconferencing. These methods of communication offer several advantages:

- High-speed transmission and reception.
- Accurate transmission of a message.
- Easy dispersal of the same message to people in scattered locations.
- Direct interaction and quick feedback.

Videoconferencing also allows people in different places to see each other while they talk. A later section of this chapter discusses emerging technologies and their effects on communication in detail. A case at the end of the chapter provides examples of videoconferencing.[14]

NONVERBAL COMMUNICATION

Nonverbal communication is behavior that communicates but does not use written or spoken words. Examples include gestures, posture, seating position, pitch of voice, speed of speech, and the physical environment of the communication interaction. People use all of these to communicate explicitly or implicitly with each other. Table 13-1 lists behaviors that are forms of nonverbal communication. Individuals combine verbal and nonverbal communications to create unique communication styles.[15]

TABLE 13–1
Forms of Nonverbal Communication

TYPE OF NONVERBAL BEHAVIOR	EXAMPLES
Gestures	Finger pointing, moving hands, winking, nodding head.
Paralanguage	Voice quality, voice tone, yawning, grunting
Idiosyncratic acts	Licking lips, scratching, touching parts of body, handling nearby objects.
Postures	Standing or sitting with legs outstretched and arms spread or legs and arms close to body. Slouching, leaning forward bowing.
Spatial behavior	Choosing a near or far chair to sit on. Arrangement of furniture.
Clothing	Formal versus informal, choice of colors, appropriateness for occasion.
Physical signs	Visible: furrowed brow, changes in skin color, sweat on brow. Olfactory: Body odor Audible: breathing sounds, intestinal sounds, smacking lips. Tactile: wet handshake, weak or strong hand shake.

Source: S. Duncan, "Nonverbal Communication," *Psychological Bulletin* 72 (1969): 118-37; G. F. Mahl, *Explorations in Nonverbal Behavior* (Hillsdale, N. J.: Lawrence Erlbaum Associates, 1987), pp. 3-4.

Nonverbal communication can contradict, amplify, or complement verbal communication. A supervisor who does not maintain eye contact during a conversation may not be perceived as sincere by a subordinate. A professor who says you should ask questions when you do not understand and then leaves time for questions reinforces your perception that he wants you to understand.

The rest of this section describes four aspects of nonverbal communication: (1) physical aspects of the person, (2) the physical environment of communication, (3) time, and (4) communication with signs and signals. The interpretations given here are North American. A later section of this chapter gives interpretations from other cultures. See the citations for a description of the almost endless forms of nonverbal communication available to us.

Physical Aspects of the Person

Physical aspects of the person such as voice, facial expressions, gestures, body movements, and posture are all forms of nonverbal communication. Each can regulate, add to, or detract from the intended meaning of the sender.[16]

Receivers infer meaning from how a sender vocalizes a verbal message. Receivers often can sense a sender has positive feelings about the receiver when the sender speaks rapidly, fluently, and with few references to self. A sender who increases the volume and rate of his speech can also persuade a receiver to accept a message. A receiver may perceive deceit when the sender makes many speech errors and talks slowly.

Facial expressions tell much about feelings, especially when the person is unwilling or unable to express his feelings. A smile while speaking can connote liking for the receiver. A frown can indicate disgust or despair, feelings the sender may not want to mention.

Senders can use gestures, such as punctuated hand and arm movements, to emphasize parts of their message. Senders who look away from the receiver imply uncertainty about their message. A shift in posture, such as leaning forward, implies the sender will make a new and possibly important point. Moving closer to the receiver can also imply a positive attitude toward that person.

Physical Environment of Communication

The physical setting of a communication interaction is the second major type of nonverbal communication. It includes all aspects of using space, including the distance between the sender and the receiver.

A person who remains seated behind a desk puts a barrier between himself and a visitor.[17] Such an arrangement may unintentionally tell the visitor that the seated person is cold, distant, and even uninterested in the visitor. Increasingly, U.S. managers are arranging tables and comfortable chairs in an open area of the office. Coming out from behind the desk makes a guest feel more comfortable, and the arrangement gives a feeling of openness.

North Americans normally hold business conversations with a distance of 5½ to 8 feet between speakers.[18] Any closer distance can make the receiver uncomfortable and cause the person to move away. As a later section will explain, this North American custom does not hold in many other countries. The difference in distance between speakers is an especially difficult cross-cultural issue in communication.

Time

The third type of nonverbal communication is one's orientation to and use of time.[19] North American business people consider it rude to arrive late for an appointment or a meeting. They interpret lateness as disrespect for themselves and for the organization they represent.

North Americans are also distinctly future oriented. They consider the long term to be about 5 to 10 years. You will find later that time orientations and the meaning of time vary among cultures.

Communication with Signs and Signals

Communication with signs and signals is a pervasive part of our lives.[20] Turn signals on motor vehicles, traffic control signals, and caution flags of highway workers are all common examples. A handshake is an important and almost everyday physical sign. Some people in North America believe a firm handshake indicates confidence and a weak handshake indicates uncertainty.

⌐ Functions of Organizational Communication

Organizational communication processes serve several important functions for an organization and its management. The **functions of organizational communication** include information sharing, feedback, integration, persuasion, emotion, and innovation. Figure 13-2 summarizes those functions.[21]

Communication processes help share information with people both inside and outside the organization. The information includes descriptions of the organizer's mission, strategy, policies, and tasks. Descriptions of the organization's mission go to organization members, to stockholders, and, through advertising and other media, to people outside the organization. Information about task direction and feedback on task performance mainly go to members of the organization. Information sharing also affects decision processes in an organization. As you will see in Chapter 14, information plays a basic role in helping managers make accurate decisions. An organization's communication processes either serve the decision process in a functional way or add to the dysfunctions described in the next section.

The feedback function of organizational communication lets people know about the quality of their job performance.[22] Feedback can reduce uncertainty, give people important cues about levels of performance, and act as a motivational resource. Reducing uncertainty is especially important during the early stages of learning a task. Giving the right behavioral cues early lets people know which behaviors will lead to valued rewards and which will not. Feedback can be given orally face-to-face or provided more formally through the organization's performance appraisal system.

An organization's communication process helps integrate and coordinate the diverse functions of the organization. Communication among design engineering, manufacturing, and marketing helps coordinate the successful development of new products. Organizations operating across national boundaries have the more complex

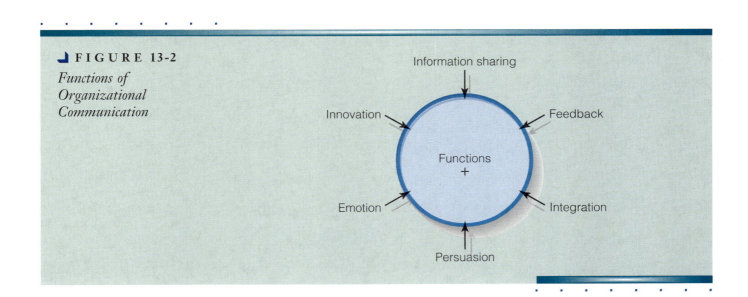

⌐ FIGURE 13-2

Functions of Organizational Communication

requirement of integration across cultures. The later discussion of the international aspects of communication highlights cross-cultural issues.

A key part of the definition of communication is its role in affecting the behavior of someone else. People in organizations use communication processes to persuade other people to behave in a way the communicator desires. The persuasion function of communication often plays a key role in large-scale organizational change. For example, Craig Weatherup, the head of a Pepsi-Cola division, used extensive meetings to convey his vision to the company's 30,000 employees.[23] Also, recall the Opening Episode's description of training managers to be more effective communicators. The managers wanted to increase their communication skills so they could affect the behavior of other people.

The emotional function of communication focuses on the human side of the organization. People often need to express their feelings of satisfaction or dissatisfaction with their tasks, supervision, and the context within which they work. An organization's communication process can play a useful function for its members by letting them express their feelings. A case at the end of this chapter describes how one organization found an innovative computer-aided way of encouraging employees to express their emotions.

Modern organizations feel they must turn out a continuous stream of innovative services and products to meet competition in both domestic and world markets. The communication process lets an organization gather information from its external environment and move it to key decision points within the organization. As managers make innovative decisions, they can move information about those decisions to people both inside and outside the organization. By supporting innovation, the communication process plays a major role in the adaptation of the organization to its ever-changing external environment.

. . . .

Dysfunctions of Organizational Communication

Figure 13-1 showed the basic model of communication surrounded by noise.[24] Noise subsumes all forms of error that can happen during communication. The source of errors can be the sender, the receiver, the message, and the medium of communication. Such noise or errors lead to **dysfunctions of organizational communication.** Figure 13-3 summarizes these dysfunctions. A later section describes ways of decreasing these dysfunctions to improve communication effectiveness.

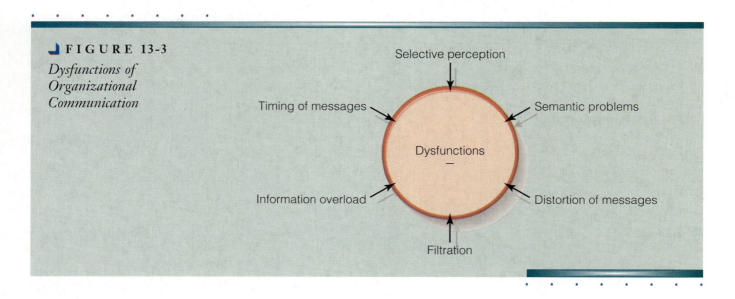

FIGURE 13-3

Dysfunctions of Organizational Communication

Selective perception

Timing of messages

Semantic problems

Dysfunctions
—

Information overload

Distortion of messages

Filtration

Selective perception lets receivers block out information they do not want to hear in a message.[25] Receivers might want to block out threatening information or information that disagrees with their existing beliefs. They might also want to block some information to reduce the amount they need to process. Despite the intended meaning of the sender, the receiver "selectively listens" to the communication. The receiver then uses the perceived information in the message to develop his meaning of it. Selective perception can also affect the information the sender gets from the receiver about the receiver's interpretation of the sender's message. The sender's assessment of the accuracy of the receiver's interpretation can affect the sender's reaction to the receiver. For example, the sender might repeat the message several times if he believed the receiver did not understand it correctly.

Semantic problems are communication dysfunctions that happen when receivers interpret a communication differently than the sender intended.[26] Some words have different meanings for different people. For example, general words or phrases such as "good," "average," and "do your best" can have widely varying interpretations. Such words often are at the center of semantic problems in oral and written performance appraisals commonly done in organizations. Try it yourself. Ask some of your friends what they mean by the words or phrases in quotation marks in this paragraph.

Other semantic problems stem from the jargon used by professional or technical groups and the ingroup language of different functional groups in an organization.[27] Accountants talk about "burden," manufacturing engineers discuss "metrology," and computer specialists "upload and download."[28] Such language helps communication within the group because its members know the language.[29] It can cause serious communication dysfunctions, however, among members of different groups and among the different functions of an organization.

Distortion of messages can happen when the sender and receiver do not have the same frame of reference. We all have had different experiences that give different meanings to our present experiences. The attributes, background, organizational position, and culture of the sender and receiver may differ, causing them to interpret messages differently. A later section of this chapter discusses other aspects of culture that affect communication within and among organizations operating in different countries.

Receivers distort messages by making assumptions about the sender and what his message means. Such assumptions can cause the receiver to begin decoding and take action before hearing the entire message. Both the meaning and the action may not be what the sender intended.

Senders can filter the content of their messages either intentionally or unintentionally. Filtration reduces the information content of the message, possibly leading to misinterpretation by the receiver. The sender may intentionally filter a message because of fear of the receiver's reaction. The filtration might be unintentional if the sender does not understand the entire problem or issue he wants to communicate. Both types of message filtration produce messages without enough information to let the receiver interpret them accurately.

Information overload is a communication dysfunction that happens when a person gets more information than he can process effectively.[30] It typically occurs when people have too little time to process the information. Hurried and harried receivers often do not have enough time to accurately decode, absorb, and respond to a message. People also have limits on the amount of information they can process.

Receivers can react to information overload in several ways. They may ignore or screen out some messages to prevent overwhelming themselves with incoming information. Sometimes they delay their response to incoming messages to a later, less busy time. Another reaction is especially insidious because it increases information overload throughout a communication system. An overloaded sender or receiver may not pass on the information needed to understand a message. Alternatively, he may duplicate a message already sent. In either case, the receiver will ask questions to help him understand the intended meaning. The questioning itself increases information overload in the system.[31]

The timing of messages affects whether communication dysfunctions will happen.[32] Messages with short deadlines do not leave enough time for accurate interpretation. The action taken by the receiver may not be the action intended by the sender. Dysfunctions can also happen when a sender transmits a message well ahead of the time for action. Receivers do not always remember such messages so no action takes place.

Senders get the action they intend from a message only if the receiver accepts it.[33] The credibility and power of the sender play a central role in the acceptance. Such factors are important in organizational communication because the position held by a sender often gives him power over the receiver. This relationship is a central feature of superior-subordinate communication. If the subordinate does not consider the sender to be a credible source of a message, he is unlikely to accept the message.

E X E R C I S E *Complex Words and Jargon*

*T*ry the following exercise. It should show you how complex words and jargon can introduce major dysfunctions into an organization's communication process.

Read the following correct but complex words and jargon and note on a separate piece of paper the meaning you give to each word. The dictionary or professional meaning of each word appears at the end of the exercise. Don't look ahead. First see whether you understand these words.

COMPLEX WORDS

Obsequious	Diffident
Obfuscate	Ubiquitous
Obeisance	Obdurate

JARGON

BRB	CUL
Plasma	SPC
Emoticons	Newbie
PAT	TAP

CORRECT MEANINGS

BRB   "Be right back." A common electronic mail acronym.

BTW   "By the way." Another common electronic mail acronym.

Diffident   Lacking confidence in oneself.

Emoticons   Symbols embedded in text on the Internet to show feelings and emotions. For example, :-) viewed sideways is a happy face.

Newbie   A new user of the Internet.

Obdurate   Not easily moved to pity or sympathy.

Obeisance   A gesture of respect or reverence. Deference.

Obfuscate   To darken. To confuse.

Obsequious   Excessively willing to serve or obey.

PAT   An acronym from Total Quality Management that means Process Action Team.

Plasma   As used in nuclear physics: a high-temperature ionized gas that is electrically neutral.

SPC   An acronym from Quality Assurance meaning Statistical Process Control.

TAP   A U.S. Air Force acronym meaning Technology Area Plan.

Ubiquitous   Present, or seeming to be present, everywhere at the same time.

Do not feel embarrassed if you did not know the meaning of some of these words. The complex words listed here are not widely used. Jargon is the special language of professions and in-groups. To understand it, you need to either be part of the profession or in-group or interact regularly with them. Unfortunately, a person using those words in written or oral communication would leave many receivers bewildered. You should now see how important appropriate language is for effective communication.

Sources: Except as noted below, meanings are from *Webster's New Universal Unabridged Dictionary*, 2d ed. (New York: Simon & Schuster, 1979).

BRB and BTW: D. Angell and B. Heslop, *The Elements of E-Mail Style: Communicate Effectively via Electronic Mail* (Reading, Mass.: Addison-Wesley, 1994), p. 94.

Emoticons: Angell and Heslop, *Elements of E-Mail Style*, pp. 111–12; E. Baig, "Ready to Cruise the Internet?" *Business Week*, March 28, 1993, pp. 180–81.

Newbie: Baig, "Ready to Cruise the Internet?"

Listening

Many people in the communication profession consider listening a primary skill for success in almost any activity. It is the first skill a person learns as a child, followed by speaking, reading, and writing. Listening is also a big part of human communication activities. Estimates vary, but they suggest people spend about 50 percent of their time listening.[34]

Listening is different from hearing. Hearing is a physiological process of detecting and processing sounds. **Listening** is the mental process of assigning meaning to the sounds. It is also an active process with the listener choosing from among listening behaviors depending on the form and purpose of the listening.

The **listening process** includes both intrapersonal and interpersonal activities.[35] A person receives a message from another person (interpersonal), tries to interpret it (intrapersonal), and responds to the other person to show the meaning imputed to the message (interpersonal). The process repeats during a communication interaction as both parties try to reach mutual understanding.

ACTIVE LISTENING

With **active listening,**[36] the listener is responsible for the completeness of a speaker's message. A listener's role in the communication process is not one of passively absorbing a spoken message and deriving meaning from it. With active listening, the listener is responsible for hearing a speaker's message correctly. It involves accurately hearing the facts in a message and understanding the speaker's feelings about the message. Active listening features a deliberate effort to understand a message from the speaker's viewpoint.

The meaning of a message includes both its content and the sender's feelings. In active listening, a listener attends to all verbal and nonverbal cues to get the total meaning. Verbal cues include message content, speed of speech, body movements, and the like. A listener may ask questions to get the speaker to clarify a point. A listener may also rephrase the message until the speaker is satisfied the listener understands its meaning. A manager can use active listening to help positively manage conflict. Active listening helps the manager understand the true wants of the parties to the conflict (see Chapter 11).

· *Active listening shows respect for a speaker and increases the accuracy of the communication process.*

Active listening can have positive effects on a speaker. It lets the speaker know that a listener cares about the message, respects the speaker's opinion, and wants to understand the speaker. Active listening gives speakers the sense that their message is important and that the listener is sincerely interested.

TYPES OF LISTENING

Organizational communication involves four **types of listening.** Each has a different function and set of behavioral requirements for a listener.[37] As Figure 13-4 shows, two types of listening are basic and act as a foundation for the other types. The others are alternate forms of listening that serve different functions for the listener and the speaker.

Discriminative listening distinguishes among various audio and visual stimuli. It is the most basic form of listening that must happen before any other types. Discriminative listening requires concentrating on stimuli and being sensitive to differences among them. It also includes attending to both verbal and nonverbal stimuli to begin getting the message.

FIGURE 13-4

Types of Listening

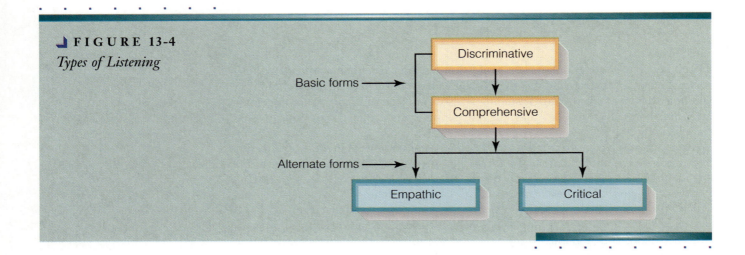

Comprehensive listening moves beyond distinguishing among stimuli to understanding the message. Listening for comprehension plays a big role in organizations because people often need to listen to business presentations, participate in group discussions, attend videoconferences, and so on. Comprehensive listening is also an important part of the educational process when students listen to discussion and lectures. During comprehensive listening, the listener does not judge the speaker or the message. Effective comprehensive listening also requires a large vocabulary to understand a broad range of speakers. The listener asks questions to assure accurate understanding. Intense concentration also is needed because the human brain can simultaneously listen and think, causing the listener's mind to wander and miss part of the message.

Empathic listening lets a speaker talk through a problem without the listener reacting critically. The goal is to have the speaker find the solution with the listener offering supportive responses. Effective empathic listening requires effective discriminative and comprehensive listening. It also requires the listener to see the speaker's message from that person's point of view—the essence of empathy. A manager can use empathic listening when counseling an employee about performance problems. It lets the manager hear the employee's point of view, not just the manager's.

Critical listening requires the listener to assess the messages received, the listener, and the medium. People listen this way to judge persuasive messages. A listener can develop skills to decide whether the speaker is making a logical argument based on evidence or using an emotional appeal to sway the listener. Critical listening is used in organizational communication when listening to opposing views and recommendations during a decision process.

Openness in Communication: The Johari Window

The **Johari window** is a graphical model that suggests aspects of human communication that can affect openness, accuracy, and trust among people during the process.[38] It focuses on awareness during communication, giving insights into many aspects of communication dynamics. The model applies to all communication media discussed in this chapter. Figure 13-5 shows the basic Johari window.

The model was named by and for its creators: Dr. Joseph Luft and Dr. Harrington V. Ingham. The name of the model is pronounced as though you were saying a combined form of their first names, Joe and Harry.

FIGURE 13-5

The Johari Window

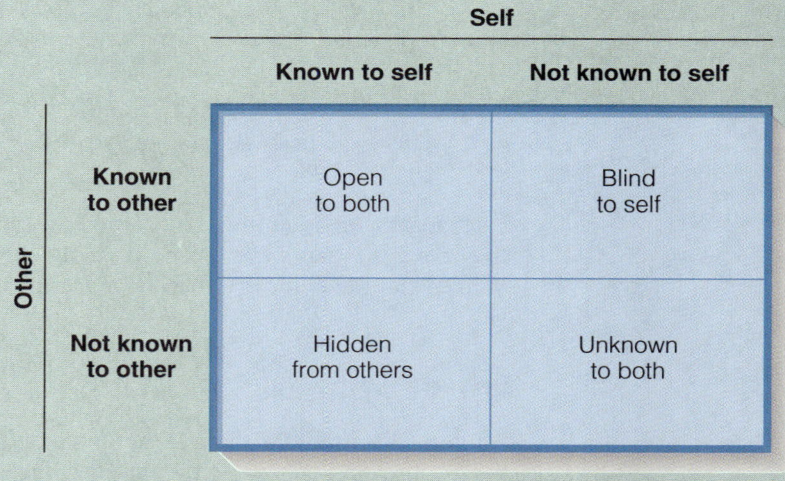

	Self	
	Known to self	**Not known to self**
Known to other	Open to both	Blind to self
Not known to other	Hidden from others	Unknown to both

The window forms from jointly considering two dimensions: (1) information during communication that is known or unknown to a person (self) and (2) information during communication that is known or unknown to another person during communication (other). The result is a window with four quadrants that offer different observations and insights about communication processes in organizations. For simplicity, the following descriptions focus on two people during a communication interaction. These observations also apply to any number of people or groups who are trying to communicate.

Quadrant 1 (Open to Both) describes the area where both parties share information about themselves. Each party is aware of the feelings, motives, and actions of the other party. Quadrant 1 describes the amount of openness during communication, a quality expected to improve communication accuracy, increase trust, and reduce defensiveness during interaction. According to the model, people have a characteristic amount of openness from one interaction to another. People can also vary their degree of openness from person to person and at different times with the same person. For example, people in newly formed work groups or teams often are less open with each other in the early stages of group formation than in later stages (see Chapter 10).

Quadrant 2 (Blind to Self) is the area where self is unaware of his feelings, motives, and actions, although they are known to the other party. The other person has information about self that self is not aware of or is not ready to recognize. Communication interactions with peers are affected by information that is known to others but not to self. For example, self usually accords superiors unusual courtesy but treats peers in a cool manner that they find offensive.

Quadrant 3 (Hidden from Others) is the area where self holds information about himself and others but uses discretion in revealing that information. Self controls the amount of information that he wants to reveal about his feelings, motives, and actions. For example, a manager who has treated a clerk rudely might internally feel guilt, but not reveal it. He also could express his feelings about the incident, which would increase openness during communication.

Quadrant 4 (Unknown to Both) describes the area during communication where neither party is aware of the feelings, motives, and actions of the other party. One discovers the content of this quadrant only by looking back at behavior and inferring from it. The unknown area can also bring surprises to a communication interaction because either party might unknowingly insert information into a communication that neither party expects. For example, a quiet competent person is promoted to a supervisory position and becomes a domineering tyrant. A person who has worked well on individual tasks suddenly becomes withdrawn after assignment to a cross-functional team.

. . . .

↰ *Improving Communication Effectiveness*

Participants in organizational communication can **improve communication effectiveness** in several ways.[39] The previous discussion of communication dysfunctions implied the following approaches to improvement.

↰ SENDER

Senders can improve their communication effectiveness by (1) understanding the background and culture of the receiver, (2) asking for feedback about a message, and (3) getting training in oral and written communication.

Senders who understand the background and culture of the receiver will be more effective than senders who do not have that understanding. A receiver's background includes his education, social status, and professional or technical training. The last is important because of the special meaning such training can give to many words. Because jargon can lead to communication dysfunctions, a sender avoids dysfunctions by not using it. A sender's knowledge of the receiver will let him send messages with enough content to communicate as intended.

Knowledge of the receiver's culture plays an important role in communication across national boundaries. Senders need to take special care when communicating with people from other cultures. This suggestion applies to oral communication, written communication, and nonverbal communication. A later section on the international aspects of communication gives more information on those points.

Asking for oral or written feedback to a message helps a sender improve his communication effectiveness. The feedback gives the sender some observations on the receiver's perception and interpretation of the message. The sender can then adjust the message as needed for clearer understanding.

Formal training in improved written and oral communication can improve a sender's effectiveness. The Opening Episode of this chapter described training to improve oral communication effectiveness. Training in written communication skills can focus on basic writing skills such as sentence structure and the right level of complexity for various audiences. Senders can also use personal computer software tools such as Grammatik® and RightWriter® to analyze their written communication.[40] Although neither of these tools automatically makes a person a more effective writer, they offer observations on a person's writing that can improve effectiveness.

↰ RECEIVER

Receivers can improve their communication effectiveness in the following ways: (1) know the sender, (2) know themselves, (3) practice active listening, and (4) use the feedback loop of the communication process.

A receiver can improve communication effectiveness by knowing and understanding the sender. If the sender is in an organization subunit that uses its own language, then the receiver needs to learn that language or ask the sender to clarify the message. The same suggestion applies to jargon used by senders with a professional or technical background. In both situations, the receiver is at a disadvantage in the communication process because he does not readily understand the language used by the sender.

The receiver's knowledge of self can also improve communication effectiveness. If the receiver uses jargon or in-group language, he will interpret messages with that jargon in the background. The jargon introduces noise into the communication process and can distort the messages received. The receiver's perceptual process can also make the communication process less effective. Awareness of how both jargon and the receiver's perceptual process can alter the meaning of messages helps a receiver improve communication effectiveness.

Practicing active listening can improve a receiver's listening effectiveness. The earlier section on listening described how a receiver can improve his listening behavior.

Receivers can use the feedback loop of the communication process to improve their role in that process. A receiver can ask a sender to clarify a message, especially if the sender typically uses jargon or in-group language. The receiver can also state his understanding of the message, so the sender can react to that interpretation. Both feedback activities require close interdependence between sender and receiver to improve communication.

MESSAGE

The construction of the message can play a key role in communication effectiveness. Many people do not easily understand long messages with complex language. Messages using language highly different from the receiver's language can also be misinterpreted. Differences in language include jargon, in-group language, and languages of different cultures. Simple concise messages, in language shared by the sender and the receiver, are more effective than long complex messages riddled with jargon. The exercise earlier in this chapter illustrated the difficulty you can have in understanding complex words and jargon.

MEDIUM

The medium of message transmission should have little noise if the communication process is to be effective. You can easily illustrate this for yourself by tuning a radio to a distant station. The static you hear is noise in the communication channel. The static makes it difficult for you to understand the radio message.

A sender can overcome or reduce noise in communication by using multiple channels. A manager can follow an oral message, such as instructions to a subordinate, with a written memo summarizing the conversation. The manager can also meet with a subordinate to discuss a memo sent earlier. In both cases, the manager is using multiple channels to improve communication effectiveness.[41]

The discussion of perception in Chapter 4 emphasized that people perceive high-contrast objects faster than low-contrast objects. A sender can introduce high contrast into messages by using paper or ink of a different color than is normal for written communications. A sender can also change the setting in which he sends oral messages. For example, when announcing major shifts in the direction of Sandia National Laboratories, the organization's president, Dr. Al Narath, met with 4,000 employees on a parade field.[42]

ORGANIZATION

Organizations have several ways of improving the effectiveness of their communication systems. A major first step is an organization-communication audit.[43] Such audits assess and diagnose the current state of the organization's communication system.

An organization-communication audit yields information that helps managers answer questions like the following:

1. How much information are organization members now getting about job duties, job performance, pay, benefits, and the like? How much information do they think they get about each of these and related items?
2. Do organization members perceive the organization's communication practices as effective?
3. Do people know the mission and goals of the organization?
4. How much trust do organization members place in the organization's communication system?
5. What is the structure of the organization's formal and informal communication networks? Are these the right networks to support the mission and goals of the organization?

From the results of an organization-communication audit, managers can determine the need for major organizational changes to improve communication effectiveness. Those changes can include building an organizational culture that supports trust, openness, upward communication, and active debate. Much of the information on organizational change and development in Chapter 19 applies to the changes suggested by an organization-communication audit.

Organizations can provide training in oral communication, written communication, and listening. This chapter's Opening Episode showed one approach to improving oral communication effectiveness. Workshops for improving written communication and developing listening skills[44] also are available.

Modern computer technology lets organizations enhance their communication systems. Electronic message systems such as written electronic mail, voice electronic mail,[45] local area networks, and computer conferencing let a sender transmit the same message quickly to many people. Quick feedback responses also are possible with such systems. Although speed is a major functional consequence, computer-based communication lacks the feelings and emotional information that can come from nonverbal communication. Users developed Emoticons on the Internet, for example, to add feelings and emotions to text messages.[46] Because the expected effects of technology on organizational communication are so great, the next section discusses them in detail.

· · · · · · · · ·

⌐ *Technology and Communication*

Some forecasters predict emerging **technology** will lead to major changes in organizational communication processes. Table 13-2 summarizes some of those technologies.[47] The technologies are available to almost any organization although if they are to improve an organization's communication processes, they must be used in various combinations. Existing and expected combinations of these technologies will bring about nearly revolutionary changes in the way people will communicate in the future. The changes will also have major effects on the design of organizations and behavior in them.

TECHNOLOGY

The ordinary telephone will remain a major communication device among people in developed nations. Major changes will come from fiber optics and new satellites. Digital cellular phones will allow communication among cellular users in most parts of the world. Digital cellular systems also allow wireless fax and modem transmissions. Laptop or notepad computers will include digital cellular fax devices and

▸ TABLE 13–2

Emerging Technologies That Can Affect Organizational Communication

TECHNOLOGY	EXAMPLES AND EFFECTS
Computers	New computer technology includes parallel processor mainframe computes, pen-based notepads, and multi media personal computers. The latter will feature a scanner, sound board, CD-ROM, and fast, high-resolution video that is able to do animated presentations. Personal computers will come in all sizes, from desk top versions to hand-held portable versions.
Satellites	The Low Earth Orbit satellite system planned for launch in the late 1990s will open cellular phone connections to almost all parts of the world. Direct broadcast satellites will feature stronger television broadcast signals with higher-quality video and audio than now available.
Video displays	Thin, flat-panel displays will allow smaller computer monitors and smaller television sets. They will give high-quality video in either color or monochrome.
Digital electronics	Digital electronic devices represent all forms of information as 0s and 1s. computers can create, process, record, and send such information. Digitized information includes text, sound, images, and numeric data.
Distributed computing	Distributed computing includes networks of computers within organizations and networks among organizations. Modern technology will allow connections among computers by telephone lines, cable, and satellite.
Fiber optics	Fiber optic cables use thin strands of glass to move digital information with light particles called photons. This technology can carry 100 times the information of conventional copper wires. Any digital device can use a fiber optic connection.
Lasers	Laser devices emit a high-intensity, well-controlled beam of light. Lasers will pay a key role in optical data storage.
Optical data storage	Optical data storage devices read digitally recorded information with a laser. The recorded information includes any combination of sound, text, data, still images, and video images. A key advance of this technology is the ability to store large amounts of information in a small space. Modern devices will allow fast retrieval of the information.

Source: D. Burrus, *Technotrends: How to Use Technology to Go Beyond Your Competition* (New York: HarperBusiness, 1993), pp. 325-47.

modems. Combine the latter with the proposed Low Earth Orbit satellite systems, and you can quickly see the flexibility and mobility of future communication.

Distributed computing technology will grow in use. People within an organization will continue to communicate directly on a computer network with electronic mail. Digital technology will let all forms of text, images, audio, video, and numeric data move across a network. Satellites and fiber optics will allow high-speed connections among networks at any of an organization's locations. An organization with global operations, for example, could move all forms of information quickly to distant places.

Distributed computing will also affect communication among organizations. Commercial networks such as CompuServe and Prodigy can connect any subscribers to each other. In 1994 the Internet linked 15 million people with 1.5 million computers running 13,000 networks in about 100 countries.[48] Interconnections among such networks form the emerging information highway, a technology that can connect people in almost any organization.[49]

Personal computers will see increasing use for communication. When personal computers have modems and fax devices, people in an organization can quickly communicate with each other. Satellite and fiber optic links will let them transmit any media such as text, numeric data, graphic images, and video images. By communicating with their personal computers, people in different countries can lessen the effects of time zone differences. For example, someone in Calgary, Canada, could send an electronic mail or fax message to someone in Bucharest, Romania, before the latter person arrives for work.

Videoconferencing allows face-to-face communication over almost any distance.[50] The systems available in the early 1990s used fiber optic telephone links and high-speed data compression to send video images. People in a videoconference can see each other, speak to each other, show graphic images, and send documents by fax. Such systems are a substitute for traveling to distant sites for meetings.

New technology will allow desktop videoconferencing.[51] A small camera mounted on a computer monitor sends the video image to the receiving computer. The other party has the same configuration, making two-way video and audio interaction possible. A small window opens on each person's computer screen letting them see each other. Other parts of the screen can show the text of a report the two parties are revising or graphics for an upcoming joint business presentation. Fiber optics and new satellite technology let desktop videoconferencing happen between locations almost anywhere in the world.

Multimedia personal computers can help a person manage information media of any form. Such computers feature scanners, sound boards, business presentation software, CD-ROMs, and, for advanced users, animation software. Business presentations of the future can include full-color three-dimensional graphics, photographs, video images, background sound, and text. Properly designed, such presentations can have dramatic effects on an audience. The overhead projector with black and white slides will give way to a multimedia business presentation controlled by a personal computer and the presenter. Such presentation will make large audience communication not only possible but dramatic as well.

ORGANIZATIONAL EFFECTS

Communication researchers have noted some organizational effects that new communication technologies can have on organizations.[52] Direct communication by computer or fax can reduce social status cues allowing more free and open communication. Senior managers, for example, can send messages to almost anyone connected on a computer network and ask for responses. People at all levels in the organization can respond, something they probably would not have done before the network.

Such direct communication reduces face-to-face communication and alters usual communication relationships. Direct electronic messages typically do not include nonverbal communication such as tone of voice and facial expressions, although they are important to meaning. Videoconferencing, of course, can offset the absence of nonverbal information.

Different technologies lead to different changes in customary relationships. When senior managers send messages directly to people at different levels in the organization, they bypass middle managers. The middle managers in turn may feel disconnected from the communication process and become concerned about their role in the organization. Maintaining a single integrated database using Electronic Data Interchange technology has both positive and negative effects. Information is updated almost immediately as transactions take place with suppliers and customers. Authorized users can get that information from their computer terminals. Customary relationships are changed, however, because people usually do not need to go through their supervisor to get the information.

With telecommuting, people can work at home using a computer connected by telephone lines to their office network. As technology develops, the number of telecommuters is expected to increase from 7 million in 1994 to an estimated 45 million by 2000. Positive effects include increased productivity, reduced commuting and related automobile emission pollution, and easier management of work and family time. Negative effects include the absence of face-to-face contact and interference with family life.

These observations plus some research and anecdotal evidence suggest that modern communication technology will lead to fewer management levels in organizations.[53] Flatter organizations can result with more people sharing critical information. With more eyes and minds looking at the same information, people will more likely discover creative solutions to an issue or problem. For example, MTV Network's sales force met unexpected resistance from cable operators to the introduction of MTV's Comedy Central. Sales people at different locations entered their daily experiences into the computer network. A pattern emerged: Turner Broadcasting System was offering its Cartoon Channel at unheard of low prices. MTV responded by changing its prices, saving many cable deals that were still pending.

CASE *Computer-Aided Conferencing*

*T*his case illustrates how computer technology can change the way people meet. Consider the following questions while reading the case:

1. Did people's behavior change in these meetings as a result of the technology?
2. Which changes benefited these organizations? What were the benefits?
3. Were there any latent dysfunctions from using the technology? What were they? What could be done to avoid them?

CASE DESCRIPTION

There's a bloody meeting going on. "This company has no leader—and no vision," says one frustrated participant. "Why are you being so defensive?" asks another. Someone snaps: "I've had enough—I'm looking for an-

other job." Rough stuff—if these people were talking face-to-face. But they're not. They're sitting side-by-side in silence in front of personal computers, typing anonymous messages that flash on a projection screen at the head of the room.

Electronic encounter groups like this could soon be the meeting place of Corporate America, if some key high-tech companies and researchers have their way. Most enticing is what happens during so-called electronic meetings: People become brutally honest. The anonymity of talking through computers "turns even shy people powerful," says Alethea O. Caldwell, president of Ancilla Systems Inc., an Elk Grove (Ill.) health care company that used an electronic meeting to hammer out its five-year plan.

Timesaver

The delivery may be bruising, but the honest answers offer valuable, unfiltered information. Samuel L. Eichenfield, president of Greyhound Financial, a division of Greyhound Dial Corp, asked 20 staffers at a recent electronic meeting to rate their bosses. The results? "One

Source: J. Bartimo, "At These Shouting Matches, No One Says a Word," *Business Week*, June 11, 1990, p. 78. Reprinted from June 11, 1990 issue of *Business Week* by special permission, copyright © 1990 by McGraw-Hill, Inc.

manager enrolled in a management-improvement session, and another took a strategic-planning course," says Eichenfield.

Outwardly, electronic meetings are simple: Up to 50 people sit around a horseshoe-shaped table, empty except for a series of PCs. A complex local-area network tracks and sorts by topic and order of response every sentence typed in by participants. It then displays them on the projection screen. When attendees want to vote on an issue, the computers tally the results and display them. At the end of the meeting, everybody gets a printed synopsis.

IBM is one of the biggest boosters of electronic meetings. In 1986, it gave the University of Arizona $2 million to perfect the concept and since then has built 18 electronic-meeting rooms at IBM sites and plans 22 more. Eighty employees at IBM's Federal Sector Div. are pitching the concept to such customers as Procter & Gamble Co. and General Motors Corp. and to other IBM units. So far, 7,000 IBMers, including Chairman John F. Akers, have taken part. These sessions, says IBM project manager Christopher J. McGoff, have "brought people together" who have traditionally skirmished, such as employees from product development and marketing.

Even managers who wince when electronic meetings make peers out of subordinates give the format high marks for efficiency. Chitchat is eliminated, and discussions don't digress. A study by IBM and the University of Arizona claims that electronic meetings are as much as 55% faster than traditional one. Phelps Dodge Mining Co. in Phoenix has proof. Last year, it had its planning meeting electronically. Usually, says Robert E. Johnson, Phelps Dodge's director of research and business development, this session takes days. This time, it lasted 12 hours. A big plus: "A lot of people were able to talk at once" without stepping on toes, he says.

IBM won't have the electronic-meeting market to itself for long, Andersen consulting is building two electronic-meeting rooms that will accommodate long-distance sessions as well. And the University of Arizona has spawned a startup, Ventana Corp. Ventana plans to run electronic meetings for customers and sell a software package for those who want to lead their own sessions.

'It's Sad'

Electronic meetings attract diverse groups. Last year, Arizona's Democratic state legislators and Southwest Gas

Corp. were among dozens of companies using them. But they do have some key drawbacks. While anonymity prevents bloody noses, it makes it impossible for people to get credit for a good idea, says Ventana CEO J. F. Nunamaker. Also, computer-shy participants may have trouble keeping up with those who can pound out messages rapidly. And even though a crude computer shorthand can mimic human touches such as some facial expressions . . . many participants find the process unnatural.

Critics say these problems prove there's no substitute for oral communication. Notes one participant in a recent electronic meeting: "It's sad that we can't talk without sitting at terminals." Maybe. But some similar sentiments have been heard before. In the 1890s, people said the bane of human communications would be a new invention, the telephone.

CASE ANALYSIS

Electronic meetings of the type just described will become more common as companies learn about the available technology. Other technologies such as satellites will let meetings include people from almost anywhere. Such meetings let people safely say how they feel about important issues. Developments in computer technology will continue to bring large-scale change to organization communication systems of the future.

Communication Roles in Organizations

Individuals in organizations play different **roles** and serve different functions in the communication process. The five roles are initiator, relayer, liaison, terminator, and isolate. The following descriptions emphasize the relative frequency of the communication behaviors of each role.[54]

Initiators start communications and send more messages than they receive or pass on to someone else. Relayers receive and pass on more messages than they start or end. The liaison role is more complicated than either the initiator or relayer. A liaison connects two parts of an organization but is not a member of either part.[55] A liaison person helps coordinate organizational functions by getting messages from one part of an organization to another.[56] Liaisons can hinder the flow of messages, however, if they become bottlenecks in a communication network.

The last two roles involve more passive communication behavior. Terminators are at the end of a communication network and mainly get messages. They infrequently send messages or relay information to others in the organization. Isolates are usually outside the normal communication process. They send, receive, or relay only a few messages.

Communication Networks

Communication in organizations takes place within a structured system called a network. Networks take different forms, as described later in this section. The formal design of the organization defines some networks. Others emerge from informal social interaction within organizations, such as the behavior described in Chapter 10.[57]

Figure 13-6 shows several possible communication networks using lines to show communication channels between nodes. Communication between nodes of a network can be bidirectional. The following discussion of communication networks applies to all forms of communication whether face-to-face, by electronic media, or by video media.[58]

PAIR-WISE COMMUNICATION

Pair-wise communication is any form of oral or written communication between two people.[59] It is widespread in any organization and forms the basis of its communication process. Pair-wise communication occurs between superiors and subordinates, between individuals of different status with no direct reporting relationship, between peers, and between friends. Whenever you chat with a friend, for example, you are involved in pair-wise communication. Each person in a pair focuses attention on the other party. This feature distinguishes pair-wise communication from the other forms of communication described in this section. The direction of pair-wise communication can be top-down, bottom-up, or lateral.

Figure 13-6a shows the simplest form of pair-wise communication, the dyad. The figure also shows the serial chain, a series of connected dyads.[60] The serial chain network forms when three or more dyads become connected. Every person in a serial chain except the originator acts as a receiver, interpreter, and sender when relaying messages from one node to the next. Each person in the serial chain can communicate only with adjacent positions, a characteristic of messages that must follow an organization's formal reporting channels. Serial chains are common in organizations, with much of both formal and informal communication flowing along such chains.

FIGURE 13-6

Communication Networks

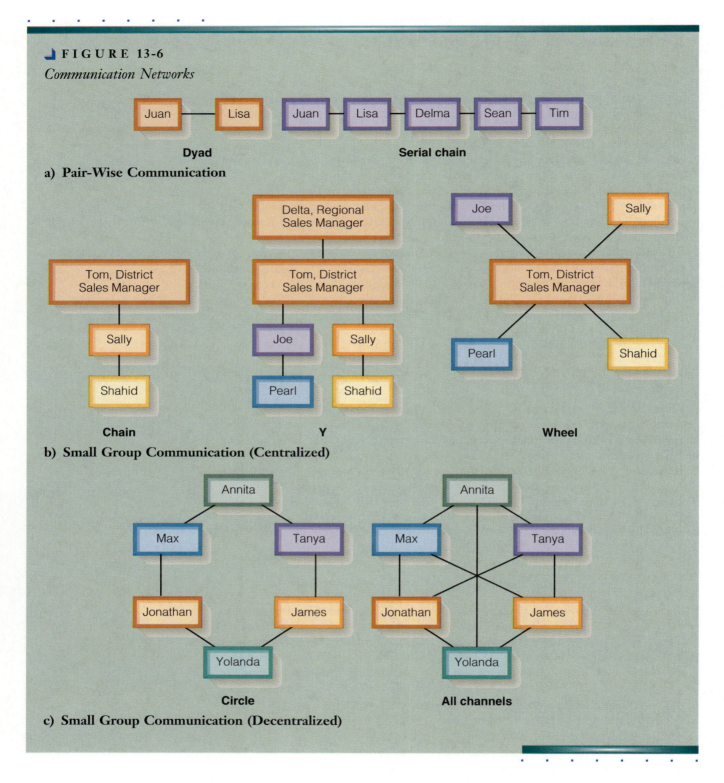

a) **Pair-Wise Communication**

b) **Small Group Communication (Centralized)**

c) **Small Group Communication (Decentralized)**

SMALL GROUP COMMUNICATION

Small group communication involves three or more people directly interacting during the communication. The groups can be face-to-face or widely dispersed if the communication process uses an audio, video, or computer-based medium.[61]

Small group communication occurs within an organization's departments, work units, and cross-functional teams. It also happens within informal groups that form in an organization. Communication interaction within small groups rotates among group members in either a structured or a random pattern. Whether the group is in one location or dispersed, communication takes place within either a centralized or a decentralized communication network.

Centralized Communication Networks

Figure 13-6b shows **centralized communication networks.** In these networks, a single person is a key figure in sending and receiving messages, no matter where they go in the network.[62] In centralized networks, only one or a few parts of the network have the potential to get information.[63]

The chain and Y are forms of the serial chain. A person at the apex of the chain or Y sends messages and receives responses to them. People below the apex relay those messages to the next person in the chain. The flow reverses as responses return through the nodes of the chain to the person at the apex. The different levels of nodes in the chain and the Y resemble the different reporting levels in organizations.

The wheel restricts communication to the person at the center of the wheel. The person in the hub position also has high communication independence. Messages can flow bidirectionally to and from the hub. People in the nodes at the ends of the spokes usually cannot communicate with each other. An example of a wheel network in an organization is a dispatcher who sends vehicles to various destinations.

Decentralized Communication Networks

Figure 13-6c shows **decentralized communication networks.** In these networks, communication flows freely, with no one person playing a central or controlling role.[64] Decentralized networks spread the potential to get information throughout the network, so that all parts have about equal information status in the network.[65] No person in the network depends exclusively on anyone else.[66]

The circle network lets people communicate with those on each side, but does not let them communicate across the circle. The all-channels network decentralizes communication even further. Communication flows freely among members of the network without restriction. Managers use all-channels networks in the freewheeling decision groups described in Chapter 14.

Advantages and Disadvantages of Each Network

Centralized and decentralized communication networks have different advantages and disadvantages.[67] Centralized networks are faster and have fewer errors when solving simple problems or tasks, but are less effective with complex problems or tasks. Decentralized networks are faster and more accurate with complex problems than with simple problems. They also process more messages and yield higher satisfaction among network members, whatever the type of problem or task.

LARGE AUDIENCE COMMUNICATION

Large audience communication involves getting a message from one person or a few people to many people. The sender designs a message before sending it to the audience. Such messages usually are sent continuously with no interruption from the audience. The audience can include twenty, hundreds, thousands, or, with the help of radio and television, millions of people. Some typical organization examples are department meetings, briefing sessions, training programs, orientation meetings, and new product or service introductions.[68]

The following features of large audience communication distinguish it from small group communication:

1. The sender (speaker) is the dominant figure. He is the source of the information for the audience. The audience has the passive role of listening while the sender gives his message.
2. Audience size prevents each person in the audience from interacting with all the others.
3. There is little face-to-face interaction between the sender and individual receivers in the audience. The absence of interaction is a direct result of audience size. Some spontaneous interaction can happen such as booing or cheering the speaker. Also, a speaker may encourage questions from the audience to stimulate interaction.
4. Large audience communication in organizations usually occurs in a formal setting such as a conference room, auditorium, or video center.

Relationships between Communication Roles and Networks

Figure 13-7 shows where each role can appear in a communication network. The likelihood that a given role will appear in an organization's communication processes depends in part on the design of the organization and the structure of its communi-

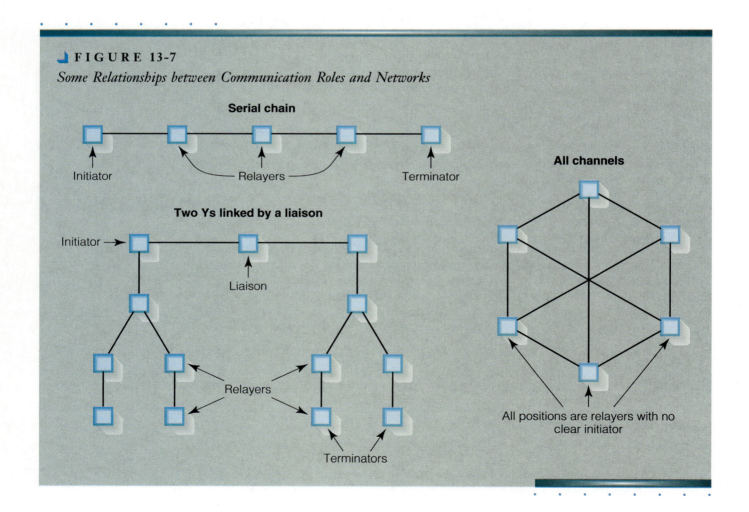

FIGURE 13-7

Some Relationships between Communication Roles and Networks

Serial chain

Initiator — Relayers — Terminator

Two Ys linked by a liaison

Initiator
Liaison
Relayers
Terminators

All channels

All positions are relayers with no clear initiator

cation networks. Centralized organizational designs and centralized communication networks will have initiators at upper levels and terminators at lower levels. A serial chain will also feature an initiator at the beginning of the chain and a terminator at the end.

Decentralized organizations and decentralized communication networks, such as the all-channels network shown in Figure 13-7, are likely to have more relayers than more centralized structures. More people will have access to information in such a network than in the more centralized ones. Decentralized networks also do not have clearly defined initiators because that role moves freely among the positions in the network. Terminators are hard to find in an all-channels network until a single communication interaction ends.

Figure 13-7 also shows a liaison role performing its typical function of linking communication networks in which it is not a member. By linking networks, the liaison serves as a coordination mechanism in organizations.

The figure deliberately does not show the isolates. Isolate roles emerge in physically separated work groups—groups of people outside the mainstream work activities of the organization or at geographically dispersed locations.[69] Isolates also arise in work situations that require little interaction or where the work itself requires the constant attention of the person.

International Aspects of Organizational Communication

This chapter alluded to cross-cultural issues in communication at several points. Those issues go beyond the spoken and written language of another country. Although English is widely spoken when doing business in non-English-speaking countries, nonnative speakers will not always understand your message correctly due to nonverbal communication differences.[70]

Different meanings of nonverbal communication can be a special problem for those who travel to or work in different countries. The next paragraphs describe some cultural differences in some major nonverbal behaviors: using space and orientation to time.[71]

In the United States, office space is divided about equally among those who work in an area. When someone new is assigned to the work area, the workers freely rearrange the space to make room for the newcomer. In French offices, in contrast, workers grudgingly give up space to a new person and typically assign him undesirable space such as a desk facing a blank wall.

North Americans ordinarily stand 5½ to 8 feet apart while speaking. In Latin American cultures, people stand much closer. When a North American speaks to a Latin American in that person's home country, the Latin American moves close to the North American, who then feels uncomfortable and backs away. The Latin American then perceives the North American as cold and distant, an unintended communication of the nonverbal behavior.

Orientations to time and the meaning of time differ widely among cultures. Latin Americans view time more casually than North Americans. The latter value promptness in keeping appointments, a nonverbal behavior that is even more strongly emphasized by the Swiss. A North American or a Swiss might feel insulted if people were late for an appointment, even though no insult was intended.

Egyptians usually do not look to the future, a state they define as anything more than a week away. South Asians think of the long term as centuries, not the typical five- or ten-year view of North Americans. The Sioux Indians of the United States do not have words for "time," "wait," or "waiting" in their native language. You can readily see that misunderstandings about time could arise in a face-to-face business meeting of people from different countries or among people in a culturally diverse workforce.

*A*n organization's communication processes play an important role in presenting an ethical image to people inside and outside the organization. Internal processes include newsletters, satellite television broadcasts, direct mailings, and postings on bulletin boards. External processes include annual reports, press releases, and public statements by senior executives. What does the organization say and not say about ethical behavior and ethical decisions? Those statements—or their absence—form the ethical image of the organization.

Organizations can manage external impressions of their behavior by offering their own accounts of behavior that protesters say was unethical. The protest may come from a special interest group that believes the organization has behaved unethically. An organization's response is a communication in any form designed to affect the perception of others inside or outside the organization. A response is designed to make the organization, or individual members, look more ethical than charged.[72]

Research on impression management identified the following major types of response:

1. Denials say the organization was not responsible for the event or that the organization did not cause the event.
2. Excuses say the organization cannot be held responsible because some factors limited its control over the event.
3. Justifications say the organization is responsible for the event, but the accuser is using inappropriate ethical standards to assess the event.
4. Concessions say the organization caused the event and could have prevented it from happening.

Some limited research evidence suggests that managers use justifications more often than the other three types when responding to an ethics charge.[73] Managers use justifications because they provide a chance to describe the organization's standard of behavior and show that the protester's standard is wrong for that organization. Justifications also let an organization appeal to other stakeholders it considers more important than the protesters.

Communication processes play a key role in sustaining ethical values in an organization's culture. Part of the communication happens during the socialization of new employees. Communication can help sustain ethical values in an organization's culture through repeated references to how the organization includes ethical considerations in its decision processes.

An ethical issue centers on how much an organization should disclose to employees, customers, suppliers, and the community in which it operates. The groups may raise several ethical questions including the following:

1. Does the organization have an ethical obligation to fully reveal negative information about its plans to employees? Such information includes planned layoffs, transfers, and other large changes that could disrupt people's lives.
2. How much should an organization tell its customers or clients about the safety of its products, the level of error in its services, and the results of its testing programs? Would it matter whether the organization made cars or footballs or provided health care services? In other words, do organizations whose products are more likely to lead to injury if defective have a greater responsibility to disclose information to customers and clients about the reliability of their products or services?
3. The disclosure issue extends to suppliers also. Should an organization tell its suppliers how it chooses among them, its contracting process, and the basis of its commitment to a supplier?

A growing ethical issue surrounds communication privacy in organizations. Do employees have the right to private communications in the work setting that cannot be revealed to anyone without their consent? That ethical issue will grow in the future as more employees using personal computers become part of computer networks in organizations. Existing software lets both network managers and senior managers read employees' voice mail, E-mail, and other computer files. The underlying ethical issue is whether people's rights to privacy extend to such computer surveillance.[74]

. . . .

Personal and Management Implications

*C*ommunication processes in organizations have several implications. One personal implication follows from your participation in various communication processes in your family, work setting, and college or university. By participating, you directly affect the quality of those processes. The earlier discussions about how to improve communication effectiveness as a sender or a receiver are particularly important to your personal effectiveness in a communication process.

Communication in the future, whether in work organizations or our homes, will take different forms as new technology develops. You will be able to communicate with many different people at distant locations and engage in widespread interaction via electronic and video media. In short, you likely will not limit your communication activities in the future to face-to-face or written forms.

The discussion of communication roles implied that you play some of those roles in the communication processes in which you are involved. The isolate role could be a problem for you because it implies you are outside the mainstream communication process. If you want to reduce your isolation, you will need to actively increase the information flow to you from other parts of the process.

You undoubtedly display many forms of the nonverbal behavior described earlier in the chapter. Inappropriate nonverbal behavior can reduce your communication effectiveness. Take advantage of opportunities to have yourself videotaped while making a formal presentation. Such feedback can be especially revealing about aspects of your presentation you cannot easily see. Many elements of nonverbal behavior can negatively affect your communication effectiveness.

If you will be traveling to different countries or working for a multinational organization, the discussion of cultural differences in meanings of nonverbal behavior should be useful to you. Sensitivity to those differences will improve your effectiveness in different locations. You may want to review some citations in the international section as preparation for international travel.

The communication processes a manager uses do not stand by themselves. They strongly affect several management roles. For example, the persuasion function of communication affects the leadership role that many managers play in organizations. Chapter 12 described that role in detail. A leader's ability to persuade stems in part from communication effectiveness, as described earlier in this chapter.

The information sharing function of communication is directly related to the decision processes of organizations. Chapter 14 looks at such processes. The quality of your organization's communication processes affects the quality of the decisions you and other managers make. Many earlier observations on improving communication effectiveness apply here as well.

Managers can easily experience information overload as demands for their time increase. You will see increasing use of the electronic and video forms of communication described earlier. Although these methods of communication will make communication easier, they can also make the flow of communication so fast that managers can be overwhelmed.

Communication networks vary in their effectiveness for dealing with routine versus nonroutine problems. The choice of a network to support your decision processes is another important factor in the quality of your decisions. You may wish to review the earlier section on communication networks before reading Chapter 14's treatment of decision making.

Managers usually do performance appraisals of those who report directly to them. Such appraisals typically include an interview between the manager and the subordinate. If you do such appraisals, reflect on the physical setting of the interview. Do you meet with the subordinate in your office, seated behind your desk, or do you choose a neutral location with more informal seating? Go back to the section describing nonverbal communication. Some observations made there directly relate to your communication effectiveness during a performance appraisal interview.

Summary

Communication processes in organizations involve a sender, a receiver, and a message flowing over a communication channel. The process includes feedback the sender gets from the receiver in the receiver's response to the message. Noise surrounds the entire process, helping to distort messages.

Communication has both verbal and nonverbal forms. Verbal communication includes oral communication, written communication, electronic communication, and video communication. Nonverbal communication includes gestures, facial expressions, and the voice of the sender. Nonverbal communication can contradict, amplify, or complement verbal communication.

Organizational communication has several functions and dysfunctions. It is a process that lets people share information and helps managers integrate or coordinate different parts of the organization. Dysfunctions include selective perception, semantic problems, and information overload. There are several ways to improve communication effectiveness such as training, asking for feedback from a receiver, and understanding cultural differences in communication.

Listening is an active process with the listener choosing from among listening behaviors. Active listening involves accurately hearing the facts in a message and understanding the speaker's feelings about the message. It features a deliberate effort to understand a message from the speaker's viewpoint.

Technology forecasters predict major changes in organizational communication processes because of emerging technologies. The technologies include digital cellular phones, satellites, and videoconferencing.

Individuals in organizations can play different communication roles: initiator, relayer, terminator, and isolate. Communication in organizations occurs within different communication networks. Some communication is pair-wise, involving only two people. Small group communication uses either centralized or decentralized networks. Large audience communication features a single sender and multiple receivers.

Key Terms

active listening 373
basic communication process 365
centralized communication
 networks 385
communication roles 383
decentralized communication
 networks 385
dysfunctions of organizational
 communication 370

electronic and video
 communication 367
functions of organizational
 communication 369
improving communication
 effectiveness 376
Johari window 374
listening 373
listening process 373

nonverbal communication 366
oral communication 366
pair-wise communication 383
small group communication 384
technology and communication 378
types of listening 373
verbal communication 366
written communication 366

Review and Discussion Questions

1. Quickly review the description of the basic communication process presented earlier in this chapter. Discuss the effect of "noise" on the process. What forms of "noise" have you and other students in your class experienced?

2. What is the role of the feedback loop in the basic communication process? How can both the sender and the receiver use it to improve communication effectiveness?

3. Review the ways senders can improve communication effectiveness. Have you used any of those methods to improve your communication?

4. Review the ways receivers can improve communication effectiveness. Try some of those methods with other students in your class to see if they help make communication more accurate. Discuss active listening and its role in improving communication effectiveness.

5. The section, "International Aspects of Communication," offered several observations on the different meanings nonverbal communication behaviors may have in different cultures. Discuss those behaviors with students from other countries or with those who have traveled to other countries. What was their experience with such nonverbal behavior?

6. Discuss the layout of your classroom for this course. What is the reason for this design rather than a different design? Does the layout help or restrict social interaction? Does it create spatial and social distance between the students and the professor?

7. Review the section, "Dysfunctions of Organizational Communication." Have you experienced any of those dysfunctions during your college education? Discuss and compare your experiences with those of other students in your class.

8. What types of nonverbal behavior do the professor and students of your class display? How does this behavior affect your interpretation of the messages they send?

9. Ask some close friends to describe the nonverbal behavior they see from you when you talk. Ask them whether such behavior adds to or detracts from the meaning of what you say.

10. Review the technologies that forecasters expect will change communication processes in the future. Which technologies are used at your college or university? Discuss the experiences of students in your class with those or similar technologies.

11. Discuss the role of an organization's communication process in managing for ethical behavior in the organization. How can the communication process help sustain ethical values in the organization's culture?

. . . .

↵ Case

COMPUTER-AIDED VIDEOCONFERENCING

This case describes new technology that could change communication patterns in organizations. Read the case with the following questions in mind:

1. What likely effects will videoconferencing have on interaction in organizations?
2. Do you expect that people will object to meetings held electronically? Why?
3. Would widespread use of this technology affect the formation of cohesive groups? How?
4. What do you see as positive and negative aspects of videoconferencing?

Datapoint's Minx, a desktop workstation-based videoconferencing system, may be one of those endangered species that's being restored to health.

When Datapoint introduced the systems a few years ago, few people snapped them up, despite the product's ability to let workers stay at their workstations and still hold conferences with colleagues. . . .

In a few years it just may be possible to have cost-effective desktop videoconferencing. PictureTel Corp., for example, recently demonstrated a link between its codec and a workstation equipped with a small camera and a video-signal converter connected to the codec. . . .

[W]ith the advent of small camcorders in the home-video market, there's a raft of small cameras that can be placed inconspicuously on top of a computer monitor. High-speed dial-up telecommunications lines are widely available, and some international standards now exist that define how videoconferencing systems from different vendors can work together.

PC technology has advanced, too. There are several cards on the market that translate television signals into VGA input for display on a PC monitor, and vice versa. . . .

Several manufacturers are working on methods for delivering voice, video and data to the multimedia stations of the future. . . .

What we need now is a reason to do all this. Some cynics believe that, apart from training, there is little need for multimedia workstations.

Will people who are accustomed to meeting as a group in a conference work well sitting at their desks? It may take getting used to at first, but putting video over the network has a number of benefits. . . .

For design engineers and architects having a conference with a client in another city, instead of carting cumbersome architectural drawings on a plane they can use desktop videoconferencing to talk to a client remotely, transmit the drawings and discuss changes to the design, make the actual changes during the meeting and show the client the results.

The wide area network links will be especially handy in emergencies where time is of the essence. Should an oil spill or other calamity call into question a corporation's reputation, remote links between the corporation and its public relations and advertising firms would enable the company to come up with a presentation to express its point of view much faster.

Source: M. Kramer, "Cost-effective Videoconferencing Will Be Worth the Wait," *PC Week,* June 18, 1990, p. 61. Reprinted from *PC Week,* June 18, 1990. Copyright © 1990 Ziff-Davis Publishing Company.

Exercise

ANALYZE YOUR WRITING

This exercise gives you a chance to analyze a sample of your writing to see how effectively it communicates. Effective written communication requires a direct, positive writing style that omits unnecessary words. A direct, positive style uses the active voice and avoids noncommittal language. See the references in the source lines for this exercise for more information on writing effectively.

USE THE ACTIVE VOICE

Using the active voice instead of the passive voice brings more vigor, energy, and sparkle to one's writing. Many people needlessly use the passive voice without even being aware they are using it. The following sentences show the difference in structure between active and passive voice:

- Active: We enjoyed our afternoon classes.
- Passive: Our afternoon classes were enjoyed by us.

Note that the passive voice sentence is longer, more awkward, and less clear than the active voice sentence. Unnecessarily using the passive voice makes your writing wordy and hazy.

Passive voice uses some form of the verb "to be" (is, was, were, etc.) with the past participle of another verb. The verb phrase "were enjoyed" in the above example was formed in just that way.

AVOID WRITING ROADBLOCKS

The path to clear and concise writing can be filled with many roadblocks, including awkward phrases, clichés, folksy phrases, muddy phrases, pompous phrases, redundant phrases, and wordy phrases. The following paragraphs briefly describe each roadblock and give a few examples.

Awkward Phrases

Awkward phrases are technically correct, but they are stilted and hard to understand. Awkward phrases slow readers down because they cannot quickly grasp the writer's intended meaning. Here are two examples of awkward phrases with their less awkward substitutes:

"as a consequence of" → "because"
"only a difference being" → "except"

Sources: For general information on effective writing, see W. Strunk, Jr. and E. B. White, *The Elements of Style* (New York: Macmillan, 1959), Ch. 2. For help in avoiding passive voice, see P. G. Perrin, K. W. Dykema, and W. R. Ebbitt, *Writer's Guide and Index to English* (Chicago: Scott, Foresman, 1965), p. 732 and Strunk and White, *Elements of Style*, pp. 13–14.

Clichés

Clichés are overused, commonplace, and stale expressions. Writers often use clichés when they write hastily or try to fill up space. Here are two examples of clichés with their recommended substitutes:

"a large number of" → "many"
"due to the fact that" → "because"

Folksy Phrases

Folksy phrases are either too informal for business writing or sound like a regional dialect. Such phrases often appear in casual conversation, but you usually should avoid them in formal academic or business writing. Here are two examples with their recommended substitutes:

"along the same line" → "like"
"meet up with" → "meet"

Muddy Phrases

Muddy phrases are just that—cloudy and hazy phrases that prevent the reader from quickly understanding what a writer is trying to say. Here are two examples with their recommended substitutes:

"at your earliest convenience" → "soon"
"have been shown to be" → "are"

Pompous Phrases

Pompous phrases are excessively formal. A writer may use them, thinking they will positively impress a reader, but pompous phrases usually just make the writing wordy and harder to understand. Here are two pompous phrases with their recommended substitutes:

"accentuate" → "stress"
"elucidate" → "explain"

Redundant Phrases

Redundant phrases use words that repeat each other's meaning. The extra words clutter the sentence while adding almost nothing to the writer's intended meaning. Here are two examples with their recommended substitutes:

"attach together" → "attach"
"final outcome" → "outcome"

Wordy Phrases

Using more words than necessary is a common problem. Notice how many of the preceding roadblocks were described as wordy. Many other commonly used phrases can be expressed in fewer words with no loss of meaning. The following are two examples with their recommended substitutes:

"except in a small number of cases" → "usually"
"for the simple reason that" → "because"

DO AN ANALYSIS OF SOME OF YOUR WRITING

Now you can analyze some of your writing to see if you can make it clearer. Take about five pages from a term paper you

Source: W. Holder, *Punctuation + Style User's Guide* (San Diego, Calif.: Oasis Systems, 1982). This manual describes some early computer-based writing analysis programs. The examples of phrases came from pp. 27–71. Reprinted with the permission of Wayne Holder.

wrote for a class. Go through the pages with a highlighter and mark the places where you used the passive voice. Look for verb phrases beginning with some form of the verb "to be." Then rewrite those sentences in the active voice.

Next, scan the same five pages for the phrases listed in Table 13-3. Revise your writing with the recommended substitutes. After you make these revisions, your paper should be more vigorous and energetic than it was originally. If you did not make many revisions, you already have a strong, direct writing style.

◢ TABLE 13–3

Some Writing Roadblock Phrases and Recommended Substitutes

ROADBLOCK PHRASES	RECOMMENDED SUBSTITUTES
a case in point	(an overused phrase – avoid)
along this line	similarly
alternative choice	choice
an example of this is	thus
at which time	when
conjecture	guess
consensus of opinion	consensus
consequently	so
considerable number of	many
depreciate in value	depreciate
during the course of	during or while
early beginnings	beginnings
except for	except
facilitate	ease or simplify or help
facts and figures	facts
fewer in number	fewer
finalize	complete or finish or end
for the reason that	because or since
from the standpoint of	according to
had a need for	needed
has proved itself to be	has proved or is
in a number of cases	some
in conjunction with	with
in light of	because
in terms of	about
involve the necessity of	require
it is apparent	apparently
it is of interest to note that	note that
lots of	many
make mention of	mention
on a few occasions	occasionally
only difference being	except
owing to the fact that	because or due to or since
with the result that	so

Source: Excerpted from W. Holder, *Punctuation + Style User's Guide* (San Diego, Calif.: Oasis Systems, 1982) pp. 27–71. The table shows a small sample of possible roadblock phrases. Reprinted with the permission of Wayne Holder.

♪ References and Notes

[1] C. E. Shannon and W. Weaver, *The Mathematical Theory of Communication* (Urbana, Ill.: University of Illinois Press, 1949), p. 3. Emphasis in original.

[2] D. F. Roberts, "The Nature of Human Communication Effects," in W. Schramm and D. F. Roberts, eds., *Process and Effects of Mass Communication* (Urbana, Ill.: University of Illinois Press, 1971), p. 361.

[3] G. M. Goldhaber, *Organizational Communication* (Madison, Wisc.: Brown & Benchmark, 1993).

[4] L. W. Porter and K. H. Roberts, "Communication in Organizations," in M. D. Dunnette, ed., *Handbook of Industrial and Organizational Psychology* (Chicago: Rand McNally, 1976), p. 1567.

[5] D. K. Berlo, *The Process of Communication* (New York: Holt, Rinehart & Winston, 1960).

[6] Developed from Shannon and Weaver, *Mathematical Theory*; Berlo, *Process of Communication*, pp. 102–3, 109–16.

[7] E. M. Rogers and R. Agarwala-Rogers, *Communication in Organizations* (New York: Free Press, 1976), Ch. 1.

[8] R. W. Pace and R. Boren, *The Human Transaction* Glenview, Ill.: Scott, Foresman, 1973), pp. 24–26.

[9] G. W. Porter, "Nonverbal Communication," *Training and Development Journal* 23 (1969): 3–8.

[10] Porter and Roberts, *Communication in Organization*," p. 1564.

[11] H. Guetzkow, "Communications in Organizations," in J. G. March, ed., *Handbook of Organizations* (Chicago: Rand McNally, 1965), pp. 538–39.

[12] Ibid.

[13] Porter and Roberts, "Communication in Organizations," p. 1563.

[14] G. P. Huber, "A Theory of the Effects of Advanced Information Technologies on Organizational Design, Intelligence, and Decision Making," *Academy of Management Review* 15 (1990): 47–71.

[15] Developed from S. Duncan, "Nonverbal Communication," *Psychological Bulletin* 72 (1969): 118–37; G. M. Goldhaber, *Communication* (Dubuque, Iowa: Wm. C. Brown, 1986), Ch. 5; M. L. Knapp, *Essentials of Nonverbal Communication* (New York: Holt, Rinehart & Winston, 1980); M. L. Knapp, M. J. Cody, and K. K. Reardon, "Nonverbal Signals," in C. R. Berger and S. H. Chaffee, eds., *Handbook of Communication Science* (Newbury Park, Calif.: Sage Publications, 1987), pp. 385–418; G. F. Mahl, *Explorations in Nonverbal Behavior* (Hillsdale, N.J.: Lawrence Erlbaum Associates, 1987); A. Mehrabian, *Nonverbal Communication* (Chicago: Aldine-Atherton, 1972).

[16] Mehrabian, *Nonverbal Communication*, Chs. 1, 2, and 6.

[17] R. Harrison, "Nonverbal Communication: Explorations into Time, Space, Action, and Object," in J. H. Campbell and H. W. Hepler, eds., *Dimensions in Communication* (Belmont, Calif.: Wadsworth, 1970), pp. 158–74.

[18] E. T. Hall, *The Silent Language* (Garden City, N.Y.: Doubleday, 1959).

[19] Ibid., Ch. 1.

[20] Porter, "Nonverbal Communication."

[21] Goldhaber, *Organizational Communication*; D. R. Ilgen, C. D. Fisher, and M. S. Taylor, "Consequences of Individual Feedback on Behavior in Organizations," *Journal of Applied Psychology* 64 (1979): 349–71.

[22] Ilgen, Fisher, and Taylor, "Consequences of Individual Feedback."

[23] B. Dumaine, "Times Are Good? Create a Crisis," *Fortune*, June 28, 1993, pp. 123–26.

[24] Developed partly from Guetzkow, "Communications," pp. 550–58 and other sources cited throughout this section.

[25] Porter and Roberts, "Communication in Organizations," p. 1564.

[26] Shannon and Weaver, *Mathematical Theory*, pp. 115–16.

[27] Guetzkow, "Communications," p. 551.

[28] Burden refers to overhead costs of organizations such as the cost of operating a Human Resource Management Department, metrology is a system of weights and measures, upload means send data to another computer, and download means receive data from another computer.

[29] Guetzkow, "Communications," pp. 551, 553.

[30] Guetzkow, "Communications," pp. 551–53; C. A. O'Reilly, "Individual and Information Overload in Organizations: Is More Necessarily Better?" *Academy of Management Journal* 23 (1980): 684–96.

[31] O'Reilly, "Individual and Information Overlaod," p. 692.

[32] R. L. Dilenschneider and R. C. Hyde, "Crises Communications: Planning for the Unplanned," *Business Horizons* 28 (1985): 35–41.

[33] C. I. Hovland, I. L. Janis, and H. H. Kelly, *Communication and Persuasion* (New Haven: Yale University Press, 1953); P. G. Zimbardo, E. B. Ebbesen, and C. Maslach, *Influencing Attitudes and Changing Behavior* (Reading, Mass.: Addison-Wesley, 1977).

[34] J. H. Seibert, "Listening in the Organizational Context," in R. N. Bostrom, *Listening Behavior: Measurement and Application* (New York: Guilford Press, 1990), Ch. 8; M. Purdy, "What Is Listening?" in D. Borisoff and M. Purdy, *Listening in Everyday Life: A Personal and Professional Approach* (Lanham, Md.: University Press of America, 1991), Ch. 1.

[35] S. C. Rhodes, "Listening: A Relational Process," in A. D. Wolvin and C. G. Coakley, *Perspectives on Listening* (Norwood, N.J.: Ablex Publishing, 1993), Ch. 11.

[36] C. R. Rogers and R. E. Farson, *Active Listening* (Chicago: Industrial Relations Center of the University of Chicago, 1976).

[37] A. D. Wolvin and C. G. Coakley, "A Listening Taxonomy," in A. D. Wolvin and C. G. Coakley, *Perspectives on Listening* (Norwood, N.J.: Ablex Publishing, 1993), Ch. 2.

[38] J. Luft, *Of Human Interaction* (Palo Alto, Calif.: National Press Books, 1969); J. Luft, *Group Process: An Introduction to Group Dynamics* (Palo Alto, Calif.: Mayfield Publishing, 1984).

[39] Pace and Boren, *Human Transaction*.

[40] Reference Software; San Francisco, California publishes Grammatik and holds its trademark. RightSoft, Incorporated, Sarasota, Florida, publishes RightWriter and holds its trademark.

[41] H. J. Hsia, "On Channel Effectiveness," *Audio-Visual Communication Review* 16 (1968): 245–61.

[42] Based on local news reports, Albuquerque, New Mexico.

[43] Goldhaber, *Communication*, Ch. 10.

[44] L. K. Steil, "Listening Training: The Key to Success in Today's Organizations," in D. Borisoff and M. Purdy, *Listening in Everyday Life: A Personal and Professional Approach* (Lanham, Md.: University Press of America, 1991), Ch. 7.

[45] F. J. Derfler, Jr., "Building Workgroup Solutions: Voice E-Mail," *PC Magazine*, July, 1990, pp. 311–29.

[46] D. Angell and B. Heslop, *The Elements of E-Mail Style: Communicate Effectively via Electronic Mail* (Reading, Mass.: Addison-Wesley, 1994), pp. 111–12.

[47] Developed from D. Burrus, *Technotrends: How to Use Technology to Go Beyond Your Competition* (New York: HarperBusiness, 1993); A. Gunn, "Connecting Over the Airwaves," *PC Magazine*, August 1993, pp. 359–62, 365, 360, 376, 378, 384; and other sources cited throughout this section.

[48] A. Kantor, "Internet: The Undiscovered Country," *PC Magazine*, March 15, 1994, pp. 116–17; W. Schatz, "Internet: Open for Business?" *Informationweek*, February 14, 1994, pp. 34, 36, 39, 40.

[49] C. Lazzareschi, "Wired: Businesses Create Cyberspace Land Rush on the Internet," *Los Angeles Times*, August 22, 1993, D1, D2, D4.

[50] M. Kramer, "Cost-Effective Videoconferencing Will be Worth the Wait," *PC Week*, June 19, 1990, p. 61.

[51] B. Machrone, "Seeing Is Almost Believing," *PC Magazine*, June 16, 1994, pp. 233–36, 238, 241, 245, 246, 251.

[52]S. E. O'Connell, "Human Communication in the High Tech Office," in G. M. Goldhaber and G. A. Barnett, eds., *Handbook of Organizational Communication* (Norwood, N.J.: Ablex Publishing, 1988), pp. 473–82.

[53]A. D. Shulman, R. Penman, and D. Sless, "Putting Information Technology in Its Place: Organizational Communication and the Human Infrastructure," in J. S. Carrol, ed., *Applied Social Psychology and Organizational Settings* (Hillsdale, N.J.: Lawrence Erlbaum Associates, 1990), pp. 155–91; J. R. Wilke, "Computer Links Erode Hierarchical Nature of Workplace Culture," *Wall Street Journal*, December 9, 1993, pp. A1, A9.

[54]Developed from P. R. Monge, and E. M. Eisenberg, "Emergent Communication Networks," in F. M. Jablin, L. L. Putnam, K. H. Roberts, and L. W. Porter, eds., *Handbook of Organizational Communication: An Interdisciplinary Perspective* (Newbury Park, Calif.: Sage Publications, 1987), pp. 304–42; Porter and Roberts, "Communication in Organizations," p. 1569; Rogers and Agarwala-Rogers, *Communication*, pp. 132–40; H. Sutton and L. W. Porter, "A Study of the Grapevine in a Governmental Organization," *Personnel Psychology* 21 (1968): 223–30.

[55]Rogers and Agarwala-Rogers, *Communication*, pp. 135–38.

[56]E. Jacobson and S. Seashore, "Communication Practices in Complex Organizations," *Journal of Social Issues* 7 (1951): 28–40; Rogers and Agarwala-Rogers, *Communication*, pp. 135–38.

[57]Monge and Eisenberg, "Emergent Communications Networks."

[58]Pace and Boren, *Human Transaction*, pp. 29–33.

[59]Goldhaber, *Communication*, Ch. 6; Pace and Boren, *Human Transaction*, Ch. 10.

[60]Pace and Boren, *Human Transaction*, pp. 29–33.

[61]Ibid., pp. 31, 318–329.

[62]Goldhaber, *Communication*, p. 288.

[63]Porter and Roberts, "Communication in Organizations," p. 1568; M. E. Shaw, "Communication Networks," in L. Berkowitz, ed., *Advances in Experimental Social Psychology* (New York: Academic Press, 1964), pp. 111–47.

[64]Goldhaber, *Communication*, p. 288.

[65]Porter and Roberts, "Communication in Organizations," p. 1568.

[66]Shaw, "Communication Networks," p. 125.

[67]Ibid.

[68]R. F. Bales, *Interaction Process Analysis: A Method for the Study of Small Groups* (Cambridge, Mass.: Addison-Wesley, 1950); Goldhaber, *Communication*, Ch. 8; Pace and Boren, *Human Transaction*, pp. 31–32, Ch. 11; A. P. Hare, *Handbook of Small Group Research*, 2d ed. (New York: Free Press, 1976).

[69]K. A. Davis, "Management Communication and the Grapevine," *Harvard Business Review* 31 (September-October, 1953): 43–49.

[70]N. J. Adler, *International Dimensions of Organizational Behavior* (Boston: PWS-Kent, 1991), Ch. 3.

[71]Hall, *Silent Language*; E. T. Hall, *The Hidden Dimension* (Garden City, N.Y.: Doubleday, 1966).

[72]D. E. Garrett, J. L. Bradford, R. A. Meyers, and J. Becker, "Issues Management and Organizational Accounts: An Analysis of Corporate Responses to Accusations of Unethical Business Practices," *Journal of Business Ethics*, 8 (1989): 507–20.

[73]Ibid.

[74]J. Coates, "Computer Privacy? It's Not a Given," *Chicago Tribune*, May 23, 1993, pp. 7–1, 7–6.

14

Decision-Making and Problem-Solving Processes

· *Decision making in organizations includes decisions by individuals and by groups. Here, a manager is absorbed in late-night thought before picking a course of action.*

After reading this chapter, you should be able to . . .

· Understand the nature of decision making in organizations.
· Describe several models of decision making and the perspectives they bring to the decision process.
· Distinguish between individual and group decision making and identify the situations for which they are best suited.
· Discuss the sources of bias and error in decision making.
· Understand the process of escalation of commitment to a losing course of action.
· Recognize groupthink and how to avoid it during group decision making.
· Explain several methods of improving decision processes in organizations.

Chapter Overview

. . . .

◢ O P E N I N G   E P I S O D E

Decision Making aboard a Damaged DC-10

A determined crew struggled to control a crippled DC-10 and disagreed over what steps to take before the July 19 crash in which 112 of the 296 people on board were killed, a transcript released Monday shows.

The transcript of the cockpit voice recorder chronicles the final 33 minutes, 34 seconds of United Airlines Flight 232 after the airliner's tail engine exploded, apparently hurling debris that destroyed the plane's hydraulic control system.

The crew, alternating between hope and despair, discussed possible options for keeping control of the aircraft. At one point, the crew members discussed whether to try to lower the plane's flaps.

"Hell, let's do it," said Capt. Alfred C. Haynes. "We can't get any worse than we are. . . ."

Haynes and three others in the cockpit—all of whom survived—managed to steer and to control the plane's altitude by applying power selectively to the two working jet engines. But, as they attempted to land in Sioux City, Iowa, the plane cartwheeled and burst into flames.

The transcript, released by the National Transportation Safety Board, showed the crew disagreeing seconds before impact about whether to shut off power to the plane's two functioning engines. As they neared the runway, Haynes ordered the power eased in an attempt to slow the plane for its inevitable crash.

"Ease the power back . . . ease the power back," Haynes said 22 seconds before impact.

"Maybe you can pull 'em all the way off," the first officer, William Records, suggested. Haynes then told pilot Dennis Fitch to "close the throttles."

"Close 'em off," Records repeated.

Fitch declared: "Nah. I can't pull 'em off or we'll lose it. That's what's turning ya."

At one point, the captain asked: "Anybody got any idea about puttin' the gear down right now?" After a back-and-forth conversation, Haynes decided, on the advice of Fitch, to lower the gear.

About five minutes later, trying to stabilize the plane after a steep bank, a crew member tentatively identified as Fitch said, "Damn it, I wish we hadn't put that gear down."

Crew members said also that company engineers, with whom they were in radio contact, were no help because the DC-10 manual covers what to do if two of the three hydraulic systems are lost, but not if all are knocked out.

· *The end of United Airlines Flight 232 in Sioux City, Iowa. Critical decisions during the final moments saved the lives of 184 of the 296 people aboard the DC-10.*

Source: K. Davis, "Cockpit Transcript Details Last Minutes of DC-10," *Los Angeles Times*, September 19, 1989, p. I-15. Copyright, 1989, Los Angeles Times. Reprinted by permission. Article by Kevin Davis.

Twenty minutes before the crash, Haynes discussed evacuation procedures with a flight attendant and hinted that he thought the crew would be killed.

"You'll get the command signal to evacuate," he said. "But I really have my doubts you'll see us [pause] standing up, honey. [pause] Good luck, sweetheart."

"Thanks. You, too," the attendant replied.

Finally, there's a single word one second before impact. "God."

The decision situation in the Opening Episode involved a crisis in landing a badly damaged DC-10. Although most decision situations in organizations allow time for more thoughtful reflection on alternatives, the basic issue facing decision makers is the same. Decision makers try to pick the right decision from a set of alternatives.

The decision-making process has three steps: defining a decision problem, creating alternative courses of action, and choosing among them using specified or unspecified criteria. The criteria for choosing among alternatives can include the cost, profit, danger, or pleasure of each alternative. Although decision making focuses on choice, it also intends to reach a goal.[1]

Decision making fits within the larger context of problem-solving activities in organizations. Individuals in organizations, especially managers, face problems, opportunities, and events requiring action. To find the root causes of those problems, opportunities, and events, individuals use a problem-solving process. Decision making is the part of the problem-solving process that identifies a problem and chooses a course of action.[2]

Although decision making is a basic function of the role of managers, nonmanagers also make decisions.[3] Organizations that embrace Total Quality Management or use the self-managing teams described in Chapter 10 involve many nonmanagers in decision processes. Throughout this chapter, the term *decision maker* refers to a person at any level in an organization who picks a course of action when faced with a decision situation.

Types of Decision Strategies

The two major types of decision strategies are programmed decisions and unprogrammed decisions.[4] Three dimensions define the characteristics of each strategy. Figure 14-1 shows the two decision strategies and their related dimensions.

The routine-nonroutine dimension describes whether the decision is common or unusual. The recurring-nonrecurring dimension describes whether the decision happens repeatedly or infrequently. The certainty-uncertainty dimension describes the degree of predictability of the decision. Risk embraces a large part of the certainty-uncertainty dimension. Situations of complete certainty or uncertainty are not as common as risky situations. When making decisions under risk, the decision maker assesses the probability of the alternatives during the decision process.[5]

Decision makers use a programmed decision strategy for routine, recurring, and predictable decisions. This strategy relies on existing rules and standard procedures, uses well-known decision criteria, and applies uniform processing to a decision problem. Examples include the handling of exchanges and returns after Christmas and the recording and processing of accrued vacation and sick leave time. Such decisions are considered highly programmed because they are structured and treated with existing procedures.[6]

Decision makers use an unprogrammed decision strategy for nonroutine, nonrecurring, and unpredictable decisions. This decision strategy is usually used when

FIGURE 14-1

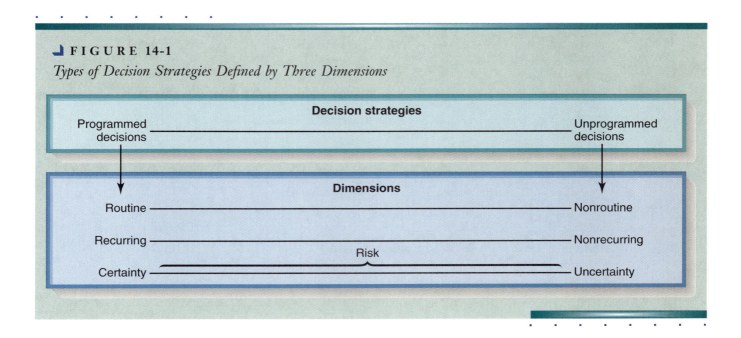

FIGURE 14-1

Types of Decision Strategies Defined by Three Dimensions

decision makers face novel or unusual events that they have not encountered in the past. Such unstructured events require creative problem solving for effective decision making.

These two decision-making strategies are end points of a continuum. As this chapter will explain, organizational decision making features many variations of the two strategies.

The Process of Decision Making

The process of decision making in organizations is much more than choosing from alternate courses of action. It involves several interrelated phases only one of which is choice. Figure 14-2 shows these phases. The next section describes several specific decision-making models that modify this general process.[7]

The decision process can be dynamic. It can unfold linearly or be restarted at any earlier phase. A decision maker can also repeat or restart the entire process, depending on the conditions that unfold during the process. Decision makers can move in both directions in the sequence and even stop for an extended time at one phase.[8]

The first phase is problem identification and diagnosis. The organization faces an issue or problem that needs a solution. The issue or problem could be as simple as a request by a customer or an employee to do something not covered by existing policies or as major as widespread unethical behavior in the organization. Whether the problem is simple or difficult, its presence invokes the decision process.

The first phase also includes identification of criteria that will show that the issue is resolved or the problem is solved. This element is important because it is tied directly to the last phase, assessing the effects of the decision. The criteria should be as explicit and as measurable as possible so managers can determine the success or failure of the decision.

The second phase focuses on developing alternatives for dealing with the issue or solving the problem. The decision maker searches for alternatives and information about the alternatives. The search can be informal, such as a telephone call for advice

FIGURE 14-2

The Decision-Making Process

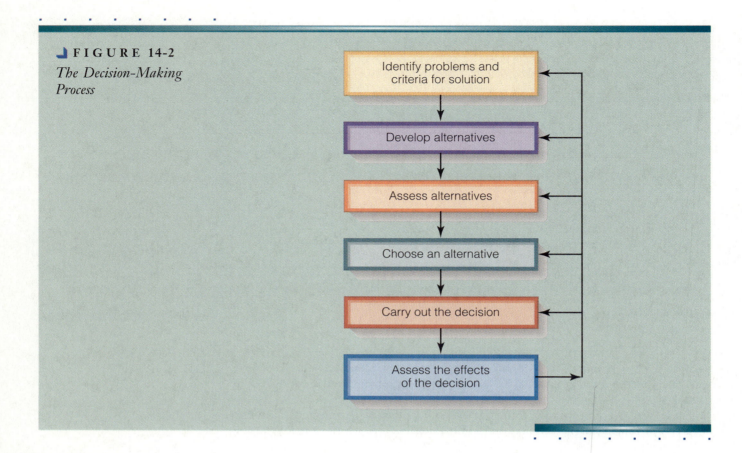

on a simple but unusual issue, or formal, such as a market survey to find out why the company's product is losing market share.

When faced with a complex problem, the decision maker may look at many different alternatives and consider them simultaneously. During the search, the decision maker often faces time and cost constraints, which can lead to imperfect or incomplete information about each alternative.

Decision makers discard alternatives they view as unacceptable solutions to the problem or issue, based on the criteria developed in the first phase. Acceptability, of course, is a judgment based on the decision maker's perception of the alternatives. Acceptable alternatives then become part of the decision maker's set of possible alternatives that move to the assessment phase of the decision process.

The decision maker now compares and assesses the alternatives in the feasible set. She examines each alternative to see what desirable and undesirable results it is likely to have. An important consideration is whether those affected by an alternative are likely to accept it. The degree of acceptance can affect the success of the decision. The decision maker also considers the amount of risk each alternative involves and the certainty of its results.

Once the assessment is completed, the decision maker must choose from the alternatives. Although people commonly associate decision making only with this phase, decisions are actually made by means of the entire dynamic and interdependent process just described.

The process of choosing the best alternative is not always neat and tidy. Decision makers may face several dilemmas at this phase including the following:

1. Two or more alternatives appear equally good. If the decision maker is truly indifferent, a random process such as a coin toss can make the choice.

2. No one alternative can solve the issue or problem. Here the decision maker can use a set of alternatives to solve the problem or restart the decision process to search for better alternatives.
3. No alternatives offer enough positive results to offset expected negative effects. The decision maker can restart the process to see if better alternatives exist. Note that in both this and the previous dilemma a decision has been made—it was the decision not to decide.[9]
4. The decision maker perceives many alternatives as acceptable. The decision maker can go back to the previous phase to get more information about the alternatives and then try to make a choice.

Once a choice is made, the decision maker is ready to carry out the decision. Moving the decision to action is often as complicated as making the decision. Those asked to carry out the decision may accept decisions about simple issues, but resist tough decisions about complex problems. The major issues in this phase go beyond the quality of the decision. They focus squarely on managing a successful implementation.

The last phase in the decision process is assessing the effects of the decision. The criteria for evaluating the decision come from the first phase. The people asked to carry out the decision measure the results and compare them to the criteria. If the results are not those desired, corrective action may be required. If it becomes clear that the criteria need revision, the entire process restarts.

. . . .

 Models of Decision Making

Problem-solving and decision-making processes can follow several models. Each model describes variations in the decision process and includes different assumptions. These assumptions imply that the models apply to different types of decisions in modern organizations.

THE RATIONAL MODEL

The **Rational Model** of decision making has its roots in the classical economic theory of the firm and statistical decision making. According to this model, a decision maker approaches a decision problem in the following way:[10]

1. The decision maker has a goal she wants to maximize or minimize. That goal can be profit, revenue, market share, cost, and so on.
2. The decision maker knows all alternatives and their results. She has complete information about each alternative. The decision maker is also fully knowledgeable about the degree of risk and uncertainty associated with each alternative.
3. The decision maker uses some function to give a preference ordering to the alternatives under consideration. The decision maker knows that function at the beginning of the decision process.
4. The decision maker applies the preference ordering function to the set of alternatives and chooses the alternative that maximizes the goal.

The Rational Model sees decision making proceeding sequentially from beginning to end. It does not have dynamic properties such as revising the goal or extending the search for new alternatives.

THE BOUNDED RATIONALITY MODEL

The **Bounded Rationality Model** assumes decision makers have limitations that constrain rationality in the decision process. Those limits include the absence of complete information about alternatives and their results, cost constraints, time constraints, and limitations in dealing with complex problems.[11]

Because of these limitations, decision makers may not consider all possible alternatives and therefore may not choose the alternative that maximizes a goal. Instead, the decision maker selects an alternative that is good enough to reach the goal. Selecting a satisfactory but not optimal alternative is known as **satisficing behavior,** a term that emphasizes the decision maker's search for satisfactory, not optimal, solutions. The following classical analogy shows the distinction between optimizing and satisficing.

> An example is the difference between searching a haystack to find the sharpest needle in it and searching the haystack to find a needle sharp enough to sew with.[12]

The Bounded Rationality Model is both open and dynamic. Decision makers attend to forces and constraints imposed by the environment of the decision. As new information comes into the decision process, they can change both the goal of the decision problem and the set of alternatives. If the decision maker does not find a satisficing alternative in the set under consideration, she broadens the search for more alternatives.

UNSTRUCTURED DECISION-MAKING MODELS

Unlike the two models just described, many decisions do not have a structure that allows orderly progression from identification of the decision problem to selection of an alternative. **Unstructured decisions** often are unprecedented, significant, and complex events that defy program-like decision processes.[13] To put it more dramatically, unstructured decision making is a

> process characterized by novelty, complexity, and openendedness, by the fact that the organization usually begins with little understanding of the decision situation it faces or the route to its solution, and only a vague idea of what the solution might be and how it will be evaluated when it is developed. Only by groping through a recursive, discontinuous process involving many difficult steps and a host of dynamic factors over a considerable period of time is a final choice made. This is not ... decision making under *uncertainty* ... where alternatives are given even if their consequences are not, but decision making under *ambiguity* where almost nothing is given or easily determined.[14]

Decision makers solve such complex, unstructured, and ambiguous problems by breaking them into manageable parts to which they apply more structured approaches to decision making. The novelty of such problems usually does not allow an optimizing approach to selecting an alternative. Decision makers rely on satisficing approaches for finding solutions to unstructured problems.[15]

Unstructured decisions are especially vulnerable to factors that can disturb orderly movement through the decision process. The process can be affected by political forces trying to stop a decision, make false starts because of inadequate information about the problem, or run into blank walls when an alternative does not solve the unstructured problem.[16] The decision maker assesses many alternatives simultaneously using a series of cycles for finding and assessing them.[17] During the process of finding and evaluating alternatives, one alternative can emerge as the preferred choice. Such an "implicitly favored" alternative emerges during the decision process, not just at the end of the process. During the search for alternatives, the decision maker rejects those that are unacceptable and adds those that are acceptable to the set, even though she has already identified a preference.

The decision maker then moves to a stage of confirming the implicitly chosen alternative. During this stage, she tries to arrive at the belief that her implicit preference was the right choice. Many aspects of selective perception, distortion, and attribution discussed in Chapter 4 operate during this phase. The task for the decision maker is to believe that her implicit favorite is better than at least one alternative to which it is compared.

 THE GARBAGE CAN MODEL OF DECISION MAKING

The **Garbage Can Model** of decision making was developed to explain decision making under conditions of high ambiguity. Conditions of ambiguity arise in organizations when goals are not clear, organizational participants change fast, and the technologies of the organization are either poorly understood or rapidly changing. The fast-changing global environments of many organizations also add ambiguity.[18]

Decision making under ambiguity does not lend itself to the more rational, structured approaches described earlier. In ambiguous situations, a decision maker may not know all the alternatives available and the results of each alternative. She also may not have a clear set of rules to guide choices from the alternatives.

The Garbage Can Model sees decision making under ambiguity as a time-sensitive process of four almost independent streams or flows (Figure 14-3). The four streams are problem streams, solutions streams, participant streams, and choice opportunity streams. These streams are constantly moving through an organization. The confluence of the streams at some point results in a decision.

Problem streams are the issues or problems facing the organization or part of it at a particular time. Solutions streams are the solutions available to a decision maker. Those solutions may have no direct connection to the problems needing solution. Participant streams are the decision makers and others who are available to decide. The choice opportunity streams are the chances to decide.

The garbage can metaphor was chosen deliberately and is not an attempt at humor. The contents of a real garbage can consist of whatever people have tossed

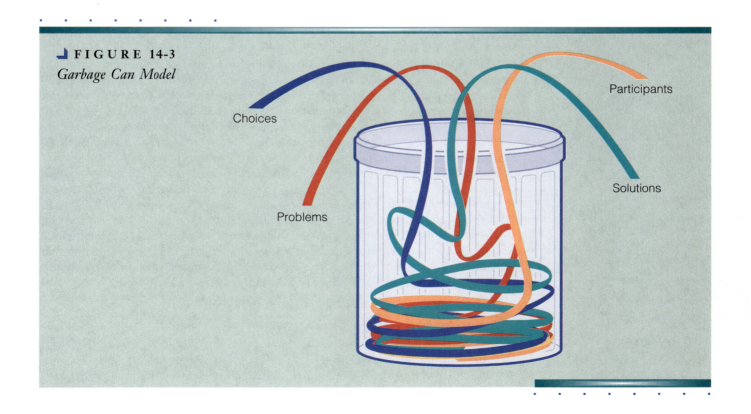

FIGURE 14-3
Garbage Can Model

Choices

Participants

Problems

Solutions

into the can. A decision-making garbage can is much the same. The four streams flow toward the garbage can. Whatever is in the can when a decision is needed contributes to that decision. The Garbage Can Model sees decision making in organizations as chaotic: solutions look for problems to solve, and decision makers make choices based on the arbitrary mix of the four streams in the garbage can.

 ## POLITICAL MODELS OF DECISION MAKING

Political models of decision making assume that individuals and groups in organizations pursue their self-interest and try to reach decisions that serve their interests. These models see decision making as a power- and conflict-based process featuring bargaining and compromise as ways of reducing conflict. The decisions that emerge from this process usually do not satisfy everyone involved.[19]

Political models of decision making view power as a central feature of the decision process. Such models define power as the ability or capacity of an individual or group to overcome an opponent. According to the models, individuals or groups try to gain power and affect decisions by developing strategies such as controlling information critical to a decision and building coalitions within the organization to gain support for a position. Political forces within an organization are most likely to affect resource allocation decisions such as budget allocations.

 ## HUMBLE DECISION MAKING

Modern decision makers face complex decisions because of the extensive information available to them and the increasingly global aspects of their decisions. Computer technology and advanced communications equipment let decision makers get more information than they can realistically process. For example, many people in business use electronic information services such as the Dow Jones News/Retrieval®.[20] It allows easy access to many databases with information about companies and economic activities around the world. The quantity and complexity of the information can easily exceed a decision maker's ability to use it effectively.

The complexity of modern decisions and the possibility of information overload prompted a prominent scholar to suggest that we adopt more **humble decision-making processes.**[21] Such processes recognize the inability of humans to absorb and process the large amounts of information available to them.

A humble decision process is adaptive and dynamic. The decision maker recognizes that she cannot have all information needed for an optimal decision, so she makes trial-and-error decisions, checking the results along the way. Trial-and-error is a distinguishing feature of humble decision making and sets it apart from the other models. With humble decision making, the decision maker revises a decision whenever new information says it needs revision. Since decision makers may have to wait for new information, the humble decision-making process includes delays, which are viewed as part of the process, and not as a negative development. In short, humble decision making is not a rigid approach to decision making and problem solving. It explicitly recognizes that the environment of modern decision making is so complex that it can easily exceed the abilities of decision makers.

 ## PERSPECTIVES OF EACH MODEL

Each decision-making model applies to different decision problems. The Rational and Bounded Rationality Models are suited to well-structured problems. Ill-structured problems are better approached by the models developed for unstructured,

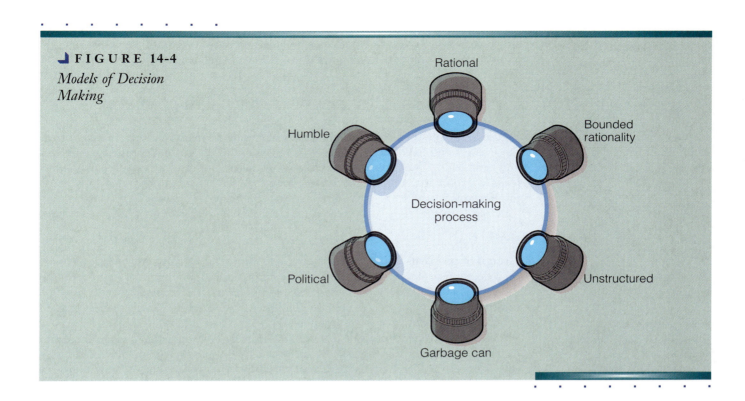

FIGURE 14-4

Models of Decision Making

Rational

Bounded rationality

Humble

Decision-making process

Political

Unstructured

Garbage can

ambiguous situations.[22] The unstructured decision models and the Garbage Can Model likely describe such decision processes more accurately than the rationality models.[23]

Each model also offers a different perspective on decision-making processes in organizations (see Figure 14-4). The Rational Model sees the process as having known alternatives and views the decision maker as able to decide among them. The Bounded Rationality Model softens that view and advises you about human limitations and using satisficing behavior.

Unstructured decision-making models see problems as ambiguous and unstructured. Decision makers should be prepared to hit blank walls, make false starts, and be affected by political forces. The Garbage Can Model carries lack of structure and ambiguity to an extreme. Rather than seeing the decision process as orderly and rational, this model sees it occurring at the confluence of four streams that just happen to land in the garbage can at a certain time.

The political models emphasize the role of power and self-interest in decision processes. They also include political behavior that happens outside the decision process; for example, a decision maker can organize a coalition to win support for a decision before the decision is made.

Humble decision making cautions decision makers to approach decision processes with a sense of humility about how much information they can process. It also suggests decision processes are rarely rational and feature many trial-and-error moves.

Individual and Group Decision Making

Individual and group approaches to decision making apply to different types of decision problems. Individuals do a good job with well-structured problems that have several tightly coupled parts. Groups do a better job with ill-defined problems consisting of loosely coupled parts. They work well with problems too complex for a single person to solve. Such decisions include those affecting multiple constituencies and decisions needing the commitment of those affected to get effective execution.[24]

ASSETS AND LIABILITIES OF GROUP DECISION MAKING

Figure 14-5 lists the **assets and liabilities of group decision making.**[25] Recognizing these assets and liabilities can help you understand what group decision making can and cannot do. The assets and liabilities also raise implications for the person who leads a group through the decision process. A later section fully develops these implications.

Assets

Groups of people can bring more knowledge, information, skills, and abilities to bear on a decision problem. The heterogeneity of a decision-making group can stimulate discussion and debate about how to solve the problem. Each person gives a piece of information or knowledge to the decision process. The debate can also let people see solutions they would not have thought of alone.

When groups make decisions, everyone in the group understands more about the decision. Participants in the process know which alternatives were reviewed and why one was selected and others rejected. Such involvement reduces communication failures and the perception of decision makers as arbitrary. Communication is continuous throughout the decision process and is not limited to the announcement of a decision.

Participation in a decision-making group can lead to increased acceptance of the decision. If they perceive their participation as legitimate, participants can develop a sense of ownership of decisions, reducing resistance while carrying out the decision. Workers in many countries outside the United States, however, feel that management should make certain decisions without any involvement of the workers.[26]

Group decision making can increase the job satisfaction of those involved in the decision process for several reasons. Participants often can use skills and abilities they value to help solve meaningful problems. The resulting decisions may reflect important interests of the participants. Those who participate in a group decision process may also find the involvement satisfying, especially if they have a strong need for affiliation.

Group decision making also helps the personal development of participants, enabling them to work on more complex problems in the future. Group decision making can improve collaborative problem-solving skills, develop trust among those who participate, and enhance interpersonal skills. Such developments can have long-term payoffs for an organization, especially if it wants to continuously improve the skills and abilities of its members.

FIGURE 14-5

Assets and Liabilities of Group Decision Making

Assets	Liabilities
Increased information and knowledge	Pressure for conformity
Acceptance of the decision	Dominant individual
Understanding the decision	Favored alternative
Job satisfaction	Winning the argument
Personal development	More time to reach decision

Liabilities

Although group decision making clearly has assets, unfortunately it also has liabilities. Individuals who participate in group decision making can feel strong social pressures to conform to some emerging norm. That norm may be associated with certain alternatives that begin to look right to many members of the group. Pressure is placed on those who disagree to get them to accept the favored alternatives. Conforming to such social pressure will come easily to those members with a strong desire to be accepted by the group. The section on groupthink later in the chapter discusses this problem further.

Often one person emerges as the dominant figure in the group, especially if the group had no appointed leader from the outset. Such people become dominant by increasing their participation, being particularly persuasive, or persisting in their position. Unfortunately, the dominant people may not have the best ideas or the best solution to the decision problem.

As the group uncovers alternatives, individuals can develop strong preferences for a particular alternative. Although that alternative may not be the best solution to the problem, attention begins to focus on converting those who do not agree with the favored alternative. The goals of some participants, and possibly of the group, can be deflected from finding the best solution to winning the argument.

Group decision making takes time. It is ill-suited for decisions about problems needing a fast response. Crises usually do not allow group decision making. The time liability of group decision making includes not only the time of the principal decision maker, but the time of everyone involved in the process. The major liabilities of group decision making, including the time required, all point to the key role the group leader plays in reaching an effective decision.

THE ROLE OF THE GROUP LEADER

If group decision making has so many assets, then why do we hear the popular saying "A camel is a horse designed by a committee?"[27] Whether group decision making will succeed depends on many factors, but an important one is how the person who is the nominal group leader manages the group process.

Formal decision-making groups usually have an appointed leader; informal decision-making groups usually do not. One or more leaders emerge within informal decision groups as the group moves through the stages of group development. Whatever the source of the leader, she plays a key role in managing the processes so the group makes effective decisions.

The actions described below try to increase the assets of group decision making while reducing the liabilities. An informal leader may have little control over many of the following factors especially in the early stages of the process. A formal group leader has a better chance of systematically using the following suggestions than does an informal group leader.

The physical setting[28] of a decision-making group can affect the quality of the decision process. Rectangular tables encourage those at the heads of the table to have more influence than the people along the edges. Round tables encourage more open interaction patterns, possibly increasing information in the decision process. The meeting room should be large enough to let group members work comfortably. Clear boundaries, such as walls around the group, will help develop a cohesive group.

Membership of the group can affect the quality of decisions.[29] Two criteria guide decisions about group composition: (1) the need to win acceptance of the decision, and (2) the need for information to solve the problem the group faces. The group should include people affected by the decision or those who will carry out the decision. Their inclusion can increase their acceptance and commitment to the

• *The physical setting of a decision-making group can affect the quality of the decision process. Rectangular tables can encourage a person at the head of the table to have more influence than the people along the edges.*

decision and allow easier implementation. People included in the group should also have the knowledge and skills needed to make a good decision.

The group leader should not view the composition of the group as static. The membership might need changing as the decision process unfolds. It may be necessary to add new members if it becomes clear that the group needs other information or if a new constituency will be affected by the group's decision.

Choosing the right **size** for a decision-making group presents the group leader with clear alternatives. A small group (about five to seven members) can have too few people to generate enough information about the decision problem. Larger groups increase the information potential but pose coordination problems. As group size increases, participation of individual members decreases, and the information they might have contributed is lost.[30]

Once the group's size and composition are settled and the decision process begins, the group leader needs to attend to several important dynamics within the group. A major task for the group leader is conflict management.[31] The group leader should focus the conflict on the decision problem, not on group members. Managing conflict during a group decision process includes identifying dominant members who may be pressing their favored positions at the expense of a quality group decision. The group leader also needs to watch for members who have good information about the problem but withdraw from the conflict. The leader should encourage those people to contribute to the discussion.

The group leader's orientation to conflict plays a key part in effective conflict management. A leader who prefers to avoid conflict and quickly tries to stop it if it starts risks losing important information. If the leader enjoys conflict, she may allow it to become dysfunctionally high.

The group leader must decide about the degree of structure of the group's discussion. A systematic, well-synchronized discussion can lead to high-quality decisions.[32] In a structured approach to problem solving, the leader affects the structure of the discussion, but not the identification and choice of solutions. It is a delicate balancing act and one that takes a skilled leader. Inexperienced leaders can quickly yield to the temptation to affect the result of the decision process. A less-structured approach to decision making is the freewheeling brainstorming approach described later in this chapter. That method turns members of the group loose to generate any idea they think applies to the problem.

. . . .

 ## Choosing Between Individual and Group Approaches to Decision Making

Managers can choose from several alternative social processes for making decisions. The available approaches differ for decision problems affecting individuals and those affecting groups.[33]

ALTERNATIVE SOCIAL PROCESSES FOR DECISION MAKING

Tables 14-1 and 14-2 show several approaches to decision making. Table 14-1 describes approaches for decisions affecting individuals. Table 14-2 describes approaches for decisions affecting groups.

The tables identify the decision-making approaches with a combination of letters and Roman numerals. The letters represent the major characteristics of a process; the Roman numerals are variants of a process. The approaches labeled with an "A" tend to be authoritative in character where the decision maker makes the decision. The "C" approaches are consultative with the decision maker getting information and

TABLE 14-1

Different Approaches to Decisions Affecting Individuals

SYMBOL	DEFINITION
AI	You solve the problem or make the decision yourself using information available to you at the present time.
AII	You obtain any necessary information from the subordinate, then decide on a solution to the problem yourself. You may or may not tell the subordinate the purpose of your questions or give information about the problem or decision on which you are working. The person's input is clearly in response to your request for specific information. He or she does not play a role in the definition of the problem or in generating or evaluating alternative solutions.
CI	You share the problem with the relevant subordinate, getting the person's ideas and suggestions. Then *you* make the decision. The decision may or may not reflect your subordinate's influence.
GI	You share the problem with one of your subordinates, and together you analyze the problem and arrive at a mutually satisfactory solution in an atmosphere of free and open exchange of information and ideas. You both contribute to the resolution of the problem with the relative contribution of each being dependent on knowledge rather than on formal authority.
DI	You delegate the problem to one of your subordinates, providing the person with any relevant information that you possess, but giving the person full responsibility for solving the problem alone. Any solution that the person reaches will receive your support.

Source: V. H. Vroom and P. Yetton, *Leadership and Decision-Making* (Pittsburgh: University of Pittsburgh Press, 1973), p. 13, Table 2.1. Reprinted from LEADERSHIP AND DECISION-MAKING, by Victor H. Vroom and Philip W. Yetton, by permission of the University of Pittsburgh Press. ©1973 by University of Pittsburgh Press.

advice from others before deciding. The "G" approaches use group processes to make decisions. The "D" approaches feature delegation of decision making.

If you view the approaches in Tables 14-1 and 14-2 as social processes for making decisions, these approaches have several characteristics as you move from the "A" approaches to the "G" and "D" approaches:

1. Social interaction increases between the decision maker and others involved in making the decision.
2. Those taking part in the decision process have increased involvement that can lead to more influence on the decision and increased commitment to the decision. They can also have a better understanding of the problem because of their involvement in making the decision.
3. The social processes for making a decision become increasingly more complex and feature increased potential for conflict.
4. The time to make a decision increases.

With these features of the approaches to decision making in mind, let us now see which approach you would select for some decisions. Try the following exercise. It was designed to show you how the alternative approaches to decision making can operate.

┛ **T A B L E   14-2**

Different Approaches to Decisions Affecting Groups

SYMBOL	DEFINITION
AI	You solve the problem or make the decision yourself using the information available to you at the present time.
AII	You obtain any necessary information from subordinates, then decide on a solution to the problem yourself. You may or may not tell subordinates the purpose of your questions or give information about the problem or decision on which you are working. The input provided by them is clearly in response to your request for specific information. They do not play a role in the definition of the problem or in generating or evaluating alternative solutions.
CI	You share the problem with relevant subordinates individually, getting their ideas and suggestions without bringing them together as a group. Then *you* make the decision. This decision may or may not reflect your subordinates' influence.
CII	You share the problem with your subordinates in a group meeting. In this meeting you obtain their ideas and suggestions. Then *you* make the decision, which may or may not reflect your subordinates' influence.
GII	You share the problem with your subordinates as a group. Together you generate and evaluate alternatives and attempt to reach agreement (consensus) on a solution. Your role is much like that of chairperson, coordinating the discussion, keeping it focused on the problem, and making sure that the critical issues are discussed. You can provide the group with information or ideas that you have, but you do not try to "press" them to adopt "your" solution, and you are willing to accept and implement any solution that has the support of the entire group.

Source: V. H. Vroom and P. Yetton, *Leadership and Decision-Making* (Pittsburgh: University of Pittsburgh Press, 1973), p. 13, Table 2.1. Reprinted from LEADERSHIP AND DECISION-MAKING, by Victor H. Vroom and Philip W. Yetton, by permission of the University of Pittsburgh Press. © 1973 by University of Pittsburgh Press.

┛ **E X E R C I S E**   *Types of Management Decision Processes*

*T*he following cases describe two decision situations. Read each case. Then review the decision processes described in Tables 14-1 and 14-2. Select the approach you would use to make the decision described in each case. Note the reasons for your choice on a separate piece of paper.

┛ **CASE I: OIL PIPELINE**

You are a general foreman in charge of a large gang laying an oil pipeline. It is now necessary to estimate your expected rate of progress in order to schedule material deliveries to the next field site.

You know the nature of the terrain you will be traveling and have the historical data needed to compute the mean and variance in the rate of speed over that type of terrain. Given these two variables it is a simple matter

Source: V. H. Vroom and P. W. Yetton, *Leadership and Decision-making* (Pittsburgh: University of Pittsburgh Press, 1973), p. 41. Reprinted from LEADERSHIP AND DECISION-MAKING, by Victor H. Vroom and Philip W. Yetton, by permission of the University of Pittsburgh Press. © 1973 by University of Pittsburgh Press.

to calculate the earliest and latest times at which materials and support facilities will be needed at the next site. It is important that your estimate be reasonably accurate. Underestimates result in idle foremen and workers, and an overestimate results in tying up materials for a period of time before they are to be used.

Progress has been good and your five foremen and other members of the gang stand to receive large bonuses if the project is completed ahead of schedule.

CASE II: DATA COLLECTION

You are on the division manager's staff and work on a wide variety of problems of both an administrative and technical nature. You have been given the assignment of developing a universal method to be used in each of the five plants in the division for manually reading equipment registers, recording the readings, and transmitting the scoring to a centralized information system. All plants are located in a relatively small geographical region.

Until now there has been a high error rate in the reading and/or transmittal of the data. Some locations have considerably higher error rates than others, and the methods used to record and transmit the data vary between plants. It is probable, therefore, that part of the error variance is a function of specific local conditions rather than anything else, and this will complicate the establishment of any system common to all plants. You have the information on error rates but no information on the local practices which generate these errors or on the local conditions which require the different practices.

Everyone would benefit from an improvement in the quality of the data, as it is used in a number of important decisions. Your contacts with the plants are through the quality-control supervisors who are responsible for col-

lecting the data. They are a conscientious group committed to doing their jobs well, but they are highly sensitive to interference on the part of higher management in their own operations. Any solution that does not receive the active support of the various plant supervisors is unlikely to reduce the error rate significantly.

SOME POSSIBLE RESULTS OF THIS EXERCISE

Because both cases asked for decisions affecting groups of people, you should have selected a decision process from Table 14-2. The following describes the reactions of groups of students to these two cases. How do their reactions compare to yours?

Students typically selected all the decision processes shown in Table 14-2 for Case I. Those who picked the "A" processes argued they had enough information to make the decision. Those who picked the "C" or "G" processes said they wanted to get more information for two reasons. First, they wanted the information so they could increase the accuracy of their decision. Second, they wanted to involve the workers affected by the decision because their bonuses were at stake.

The reaction to Case II was usually more uniform. More than 90 percent of the students in a group selected the GII process. They typically cited the lack of information available to the decision maker. That information was in the five plants, requiring the involvement of the quality-control supervisors in the decision-making process. The students also argued that involvement of those supervisors should help offset feelings of management interference.

When considering social processes for decision making, two questions need answers. The descriptive question asks which of the social processes decision makers use and why. The results of the exercise illustrated your answer to this question. The second question is normative. This question asks which of the social processes a decision maker should select to decide about specific problems and issues in organizations.

Source: V. H. Vroom and P. W. Yetton, *Leadership and Decision-Making* (Pittsburgh: University of Pittsburgh Press, 1973), pp. 43-4. Reprinted from LEADERSHIP AND DECISION-MAKING, by Victor H. Vroom and Philip W. Yetton, by permission of the University of Pittsburgh Press. © 1973 by University of Pittsburgh Press.

THE VROOM-YETTON DECISION-MAKING MODEL

A normative model of decision making has been proposed that guides a person's choices among the alternative approaches to decision making described above. The **Vroom-Yetton Model** uses a set of rules that protect the acceptance and quality of the decision. The model selects the approach indicated by those rules as best for the decision problem under consideration.

The Vroom-Yetton Model considers decision problems to have certain qualities, characteristics, or attributes. The decision maker assesses the characteristics of the decision problem by asking some diagnostic questions. The answers to those questions guide the decision maker to the model's recommended approach for that decision problem.

The following summarizes the problem attributes used by the Vroom-Yetton Model.[34]

1. The importance of the quality of the decision.
2. The amount of information the decision maker has about the problem.
3. The degree to which the decision problem is structured or unstructured. Structured problems have clear alternative solutions and ways of choosing among them.
4. The importance of subordinates' acceptance of the decision to effectively carry out the decision.
5. The likelihood that subordinates will accept the manager's decision.
6. The extent to which subordinates accept the goals of the organization and the goals to be reached by the solution.
7. The amount of conflict among subordinates that could arise as they discuss alternative solutions. This conflict happens in the decision process, not after a decision.

The authors of the normative model developed a decision tree that you can use to diagnose a decision problem. Figure 14-6 shows the decision tree for both individual and group problems.

The decision tree has boxes or nodes linked by lines. Above the nodes are letters, which are keyed to the diagnostic questions shown in the figure. These questions let you analyze the attributes of a decision problem.

To use the decision tree for a decision problem, first decide whether you are working with an individual or group problem. If the problem affects only one person other than yourself, it is an individual problem. If the problem affects more than one person, it is a group problem.

Start on the left side of the decision tree. State the problem and begin answering the diagnostic questions. Answer yes or no to Question A, "Is there a quality requirement such that one solution is likely to be more rational than another?" Follow the line associated with your answer to the next node. Answer the question above the node with a yes or a no. Continue until you reach an end point showing a set of alternative decision-making approaches. The figure identifies the alternatives with the letters used earlier in Tables 14-1 and 14-2.

The list of alternatives at an end point is the feasible set of alternatives. The Vroom-Yetton Model offers two different solutions to picking an alternative from the feasible set. The first solution, called the Time-Efficient solution, picks the alternative on the left side of the set. This alternative takes less time to reach a decision than the alternatives farther to the right. The second solution, called the Time-Investment solution, picks the alternative on the right side of the feasible set. This solution picks more group-oriented decision approaches with the goal of developing the decision skills of the participants.

Now go back to the exercise and use the decision tree to select an alternative. Compare what the model chooses to what you chose earlier. Your instructor can tell you which alternative the authors of the model considered correct.

The Vroom-Yetton Model has received broad general support from several research efforts.[35] No one suggests the model guarantees perfect decisions. Research evidence says that decisions made by processes in a model-selected feasible set have consistently been of higher quality than decisions made by processes outside the feasible set. The effectiveness, quality, and acceptance of decisions decline as the number of rule violations increase.[36] Because the decision tree applies the rules underlying the model, a manager using the model can expect those benefits. One study focused on the model's prescription of group processes (CII and GI) when conflict is likely among subordinates and acceptance of the decision is important. That study showed subordinates were more likely to accept a decision from a group decision process than an individual one.[37]

A new model has been proposed that considers five new attributes of decision problems.[38] Those attributes address such issues as the time available to make a

◢ **FIGURE 14-6**

Decision Tree for Individual and Group Problems

Source: V.H. Vroom and P. Yetton, *Leadership and Decision-Making* (Pittsburgh: University of Pittsburgh Press, 1973), p. 194, Figure 9.3. Reprinted from LEADERSHIP AND DECISION-MAKING, by Victor H. Vroom and Philip W. Yetton, by permission of the University of Pittsburgh Press. © 1973 by University of Pittsburgh Press.

A. Is there a quality requirement such that one solution is likely to be more rational than another?
B. Do I have sufficient information to make a high-quality decision?
C. Is the problem structured?
D. Is acceptance of decision by subordinates critical to effective implementation?
E. If I were to make the decision by myself, is it reasonably certain that it would be accepted by my subordinates?
F. Do subordinates share the organizational goals to be attained in solving this problem?
G. Is conflict among subordinates likely in preferred solutions? (This question is irrelevant to individual problems.)
H. Do subordinates have sufficient information to make a high-quality decision?

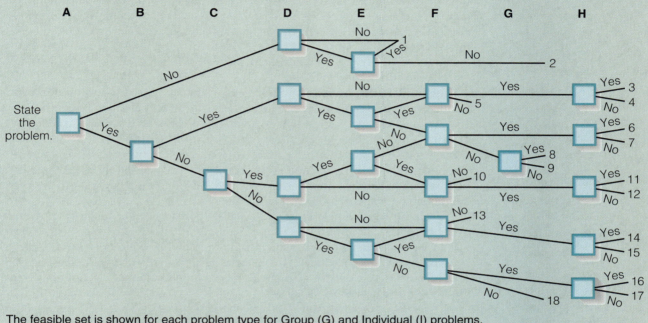

The feasible set is shown for each problem type for Group (G) and Individual (I) problems.

1 { G: AI, AII, CI, CII, GII / I: AI, DI, AII, CI, GI
2 { G: GII / I: DI, GI
3 { G: AI, AII, CI, CII, GII / I: AI, DI, AII, CI, GI
4 { G: AI, AII, CI, CII, GII / I: AI, AII, CI, GI

5 { G: AI, AII, CI, CII / I: AI, AII, CI
6 { G: GII / I: DI, GI
7 { G: GII / I: GI
8 { G: CII / I: CI, GI

9 { G: CI, CII / I: CI, GI
10 { G: AII, CI, CII / I: AII, CI
11 { G: AII, CI, CII, GII / I: DI, AII, CI, GI
12 { G: AII, CI, CII, GII / I: AII, CI, GI

13 { G: CII / I: CI
14 { G: CII, GII / I: DI, CI, GI
15 { G: CII, GII / I: CI, GI
16 { G: GII / I: DI, GI

17 { G: GII / I: GI
18 { G: CII / I: CI, GI

decision, the geographical location of subordinates, the information subordinates have to help with the decision, and subordinate development. The new model also expanded the allowable answers for most of the attributes from two to five. The resulting model is so complex that a computer program is needed to get the most benefit from applying the model. Some limited research evidence has shown that following the model's recommendations can increase the effectiveness of a decision process.[39]

Judgment Biases

The description of decision-making models started with models that see the process as rational and ended with models that take a less rational view and see decision makers using less than optimal judgment. Many factors affect human judgment during the decision-making process. This section outlines those factors and presents some exercises to assess your personal **judgment biases.**

HEURISTICS

Decision makers use several **heuristics** or guidelines to simplify the task of processing the often bewildering array of information they amass during decision making. These strategies let them move quickly through the process but also limit the information to which they attend. Although heuristics can lead to accurate decisions, they often introduce biases in human judgment. People are not always aware that they use heuristics. The next paragraphs describe three heuristics. Which do you tend to use when faced with a decision?

The **availability heuristic**[40] refers to the tendency to recall and use information that is easily retrievable from memory. Such information usually is vivid, emotional, specific, and recent. Information without those characteristics might apply to the decision problem but will be less available to the decision maker. For example, managers who do performance appraisals often recall events in the recent past better than events that happened earlier; as a result, they do not have a continuous stream of information for the entire performance period. The result could be an unbalanced and possibly unfair performance appraisal.

The **representativeness heuristic**[41] leads a decision maker to compare a current event to past events about which the person has knowledge or beliefs. If the current and past events are not comparable or if the decision maker's beliefs are incorrect, the decision may not be accurate. This heuristic includes stereotypes. Using stereotypes with an increasingly diverse workforce can lead to inaccurate or discriminatory hiring and promotion decisions.

Anchoring and adjustment[42] is a heuristic decision makers use to get a starting point for a decision and then adjust beyond that point. It can play a big role in setting a person's hiring salary or developing a budget. For example, a manager might establish a new employee's salary by increasing the person's present salary by some percentage. The salary offer will not necessarily reflect the new employee's true value to the organization. The anchoring and adjustment heuristic is tenacious, tying the decision maker to the original anchor even when other information indicates it is irrational.

THIRTEEN POSSIBLE BIASES

When heuristics are right for the decision problem, they can help managers make good decisions. They help the person process information and simplify complex decisions. When the heuristic is not right for the decision, it can introduce systematic judgment biases that lead to wrong or irrational decisions. Heuristics can work alone or in combination to bias a person's judgment.[43]

Table 14-3 summarizes 13 possible biases and gives an example of each. The biases are grouped under the heuristic that is their most likely source. The last two biases stem from more than one heuristic.

The availability heuristic leads to judgment biases that adversely affect the accuracy of information used in a decision process. Inaccuracies come from the

---

AVAILABILITY HEURISTIC BIASES

EASE OF RECALL

People tend to recall vivid, recent events more easily than others. A person perceives easily recalled events as happening more often than less easily recalled events.

Example: Recent, dramatic events have more effect on a performance appraisal than older, less remarkable events.

RETRIEVABILITY

People tend to assess the frequency of events inaccurately because human memory can retrieve common information more rapidly than unusual information.*

Example: A manager underestimates the number of Hispanics employed by the organization because she sees the name Sanchez more often than the less common name Sena.

PRESUMED ASSOCIATIONS

People usually overestimate the likelihood of two events happening simultaneously because they can easily recall similar associations. They tend not to consider less easily recalled, but logically possible, associations.

Example: A manager may assume the English-speaking ability of some members of a diverse workforce is associated with lack of intelligence.

REPRESENTATIVENESS HEURISTIC BIASES

INSENSITIVITY TO BASE RATES

People usually ignore logically derived rates of occurrence of events (base rates) when they have other descriptive information about the event.

Example: More students in an MBA program will likely have undergraduate degrees in psychology than in Russian studies.†

INSENSITIVITY TO SAMPLE SIZE

Statistical logic says large samples yield more reliable estimates than small samples. People often fail to recall the role of sample size when judging the reliability of sample estimates.

Example: A manufacturing manager examines the first 10 items produced and concludes that product quality is poor.

MISCONCEPTIONS OF CHANCE

People often judge the randomness of a sequence of events from its appearance, although the number of events is statistically too small for that conclusion.

Example: The manufacturing manager in the previous example then questioned the randomness of a sampling process that had the following result: good, good, good, good, bad, good, bad, bad, bad, good. Statistical theory says that sequence is equally as likely as any other sequence when drawn randomly.‡

REGRESSION TO THE MEAN

Extreme events tend to regress to the mean or average of the events on later occurrences. Because the event is extreme (either high or low), a later event will likely occur away from that extreme.

Example: A supervisor believes a salesperson's extremely high performance in one quarter will be followed by similar performance in the next quarter.

TABLE 14-3 (cont.)

CONJUNCTION FALLACY

People tend to judge the simultaneous occurrence of two events as being more likely than one event alone. Statistical logic says that the probability of one event occurring is equal to or greater than the probability of both happening together.
Example: A manager who decides to simultaneously introduce two products could overestimate initial sales because the two products were introduced together.

ANCHORING AND ADJUSTMENT BIASES

INSUFFICIENT ANCHOR ADJUSTMENT

People start with an initial value for an estimate and tend not to adjust far from that anchor. The result often is a bad estimate because of strong cognitive ties to the anchor.
Example: Managers often prepare annual budgets by using the previous year's budget as a starting point. The tendency to not adjust far from that anchor could create a budget with sizable error.

CONJUNCTIVE AND DISJUNCTIVE EVENTS BIAS

People often overestimate the likelihood of conjunctive events or events that must occur together. They also underestimate the likelihood of separate or disjunctive events.
Example: A manager forms multiple cross-functional teams to recommend improvements in a large process. All the teams must come together to fit their improvements into the process.

OVERCONFIDENCE

People tend to be overconfident about the accuracy of their judgment when answering difficult questions about which they have little knowledge.
Example: A manager estimates the annual sales of Gillie's Hatch Valley Chile Company in Hatch, New Mexico. Gillie's is a real but little known company which does not publish its sales figures.

MULTIPLE HEURISTIC BIASES

CONFIRMATION TRAP

People tend to search for information that supports what they believe is true. They tend not to seek information that can challenge their views.
Example: A manager tentatively decides to introduce a product and seeks only confirming evidence to reach a decision.

HINDSIGHT

After learning of the negative result of a decision, people usually overestimate the degree to which they would have decided correctly.
Example: The product above does poorly, and the manager's boss says "I knew it was a bad idea."

Source: M. H. Bazerman, *Judgment in Managerial Decision Making*, (New York: John Wiley & Sons, 1994), pp. 45–46, Table 2.2.
*A. Tversky and D. Kahneman, "Extensional versus Intuitive Reasoning: The Conjunction Fallacy in Probability Judgment," *Psychological Review* 90 (1983): 293–315.
†Adapted from D. Kahneman and A. Tversky, "On the Psychology of Prediction," *Psychological Review* 80 (1973): 237–51.
‡Bazerman, *Judgment in Managerial Decision Making*, p. 24.

content of recalled information, estimates of the frequencies of events, and errors in association. The representativeness heuristic yields judgment biases that affect estimates of the occurrence of events and misperceptions about whether a series of events is random or not. Anchoring and adjustment biases affect a decision maker's ability to make accurate estimates that can affect project completions or budgets. The last two biases are both broad and common. Hindsight can create a false sense of one's predictive ability while the confirmation trap can lead to behavior that avoids disconfirming and uncomfortable information.

FRAMING EFFECTS

The presentation of decision problems can lead to **framing effects,** another form of bias that affects decision makers. Differences in presentation or framing of the problem affect their choices.[44] As an illustration, read Decision Problems 1 and 2 in Table 14-4 and choose an alternative for each.

Psychological research on decision making has consistently shown that people prefer Program A for Decision Problem 1 and Program D for Decision Problem 2. Perhaps you did the same. Now look closely at the problems. The only difference between them is the wording: the programs in Problem 1 are phrased as gains and those in Problem 2 as losses. People prefer to avoid risks (risk-averse behavior) when

---

TABLE 14-4

Framing Effects and Decision Problems

PROBLEM 1

Assume you are a plant manager faced with the prospect of laying off 600 workers. You are considering two alternative programs to reduce the number of people laid off.
- If you choose Program A, you will save 200 jobs.
- If you choose Program B, there is a 33% chance that the 600 workers will be saved and a 67% chance that no workers will be saved.

PROBLEM 2

Assume you are a plant manager faced with the prospect of laying off 600 workers. You are considering two alternative programs to reduce the number of people laid off.
- If you choose Program C, you will lay off 400 workers.
- If you choose Program D, there is a 33% chance of no layoffs and a 67% chance that you will lay off all 600 workers.

PROBLEM 3

Examine the following decisions and note the alternative you prefer for each:
- Decision I. Choose between:
  - A. A sure gain of $240
  - B. A 25% chance to gain $1,000 and a 75% chance to gain nothing
- Decision II. Choose between:
  - C. A sure loss of $750
  - D. A 75% chance to lose $1,000 and a 25% chance to lose nothing

Source: A. Tversky and D. Kahneman, "The Framing of Decisions and the Psychology of Choice," *Science* 211 (1981): 453–58. Problems 1 and 2 based on the example on p. 453. Problem 3 was taken from p. 454.

facing decisions involving gains. They prefer to take risks (risk-seeking behavior) in decisions involving losses.

Go back to Table 14-4 and read Problem 3, which asks you to make two concurrent decisions. Most people choose alternative A for Decision I and alternative D for Decision II. Rational decision theory says a decision maker should choose the alternative with the greatest expected value.[45] You calculate expected value by weighing the result with its probability of happening. Alternative B is better than A for Decision I [Expected value: $(\$1,000 \times .25) + (\$0 \times .75) = \$250$]. Neither option is better in Decision II.

Framing decisions as losses may contribute to excessively risky decision behavior. Decision makers tend to avoid sure losses of the type shown in Decision Problem 3, Decision II (Table 14-4). Hoping to regain losses through the risky alternative, they may engage in excessive and possibly inappropriate risky decision behavior. Such decision behavior may be associated with high levels of decision failures.[46]

The overwhelming judgment biases[47] caused by framing decision problems suggest decision makers need to understand how framing can affect their decisions. They also should view a decision problem from different frames to see whether they get contradictory results.[48] Some research points to success from reframing decision problems. Although such efforts add time to the decision process, better decisions might result.[49]

EXERCISE *Your Judgment Biases*

*L*et's pause a moment to let you try the following exercise. It will help you assess your judgment bias.

This exercise presents you with three decision problems. Note your decision for each problem on a separate piece of paper. A later discussion tells you the correct decision for each problem.

THE PROBLEMS

Problem 1

Fortune magazine ranked the following 10 corporations among the 500 largest United States–based firms according to 1991 sales volume.

Group A: Apple Computer, Levi Strauss, Maytag, Quaker Oats, Zenith Electronics

Group B: Conagra, Allied-Signal, Textron, Amerada Hess, United Technologies

Which group of five organizations (A or B) had the larger total sales volume?

Problem 2

Susan is finishing her MBA at a prestigious university. She is interested in the arts and once considered a career as a musician. Is Susan more likely to take a job?

a. in the management of the arts?
b. with a management consulting firm?

Problem 3

A newly hired engineer for a computer firm in the Boston metropolitan area has four years of experience and good all-around qualifications. When asked to estimate the starting salary for this employee, my secretary (knowing little about the profession or the industry) guessed an annual salary of $23,000. What is your estimate?

THE CORRECT ANSWERS

Problem 1

Most people pick Group A although the correct answer is Group B. The corporations in that group had sales large enough to rank in the Fortune 100. No company in Group A had sales that large. Likely you were more familiar with the consumer firms in Group A than the industrial firms in Group B. That familiarity led you to believe you knew more about those companies, illustrating the availability heuristic and the ease of recall bias.

Source: Adapted from M. H. Bazerman, *Judgment in Managerial Decision Making* (New York: John Wiley & Sons, 1994), pp. 12–16. Copyright © 1994 by John Wiley & Sons, Inc. Reprinted by permission of John Wiley & Sons, Inc.

Problem 2

Most people analyze this decision problem by thinking about the types of people who would take the jobs described in alternatives A and B. That approach usually leads to choosing A and not B. A different analysis would ask about the number of MBAs who take jobs in art management versus consulting jobs. Knowledge of base rate data should lead you to choose B and not A. This problem illustrates people's insensitivity to base rates that follows from the representativeness heuristic.

Problem 3

Did my secretary's estimate affect your estimate of the engineer's starting salary? Most people say no. Research on the anchoring and adjustment heuristic points to a strong effect from the anchor, whatever its relevance and source.[50] People can become so tied to the anchor that they do not adjust upward to the actual average starting salary of $55,000!

Escalation of Commitment

Assume you face the following decision problem. What would you do?

> You take a position with a well-known firm with an excellent reputation. You believe that it offers an excellent career opportunity in a firm that you can grow with. After two years you are not progressing as [fast] as you had expected. You decide to invest large amounts of unpaid overtime [to prove] your contribution to the company. You still do not get the recognition that you expect. By now, you have been with the organization for several years and would lose [many] benefits, including a vested interest in the company's pension plan, if you decide to leave. You are in your late 30s and feel that you have invested your best years with this company. Do you quit?[51]

This decision problem illustrates a common dilemma faced by decision makers. Should they abandon a losing course of action or increase their commitment to it in the hope of getting future positive results and recovering past losses? Research evidence suggests they are likely to commit more resources, a process called **escalation of commitment** to a losing course of action.[52]

Commitment escalation typically happens in sequential decision processes involving decisions that can have strong effects on an organization. Such decisions include capital investment decisions, major research and development investments, plant expansions, and the like. Decision makers watch the effects of their decisions to see whether intended results occur. Some decisions succeed and others fail. It is when they fail that irrational decision behavior happens.

Rational decision theory emphasizes using future costs and benefits, not past or sunk costs, in assessing alternatives.[53] Economists argue that sunk costs should play no role in a present decision, but decision makers often do not see them as psychologically sunk. As a result, past decisions can have negative effects on present ones.

Figure 14-7 shows some factors that contribute to escalation of commitment to a losing course of action.[54] The decision maker might feel a need to justify past actions to herself for ego protection or to others who assess her performance. She may feel a personal responsibility for the decision's success. Pressures for consistency in decision behavior and the desire to appear as a rational decision maker can result in irrational escalation. Framing of the decision problem could also affect commitment escalation.[55]

Recall from the discussion on framing effects that decision makers tend to avoid risk for positively framed problems and seek risk for negatively framed problems. The latter tendency could contribute to commitment escalation that leads to failure. A failing project appears to the decision maker as a choice among losses. The first choice is to stop the project and accept the sunk costs. That option has a 100 percent chance of happening if the action is taken. The second choice is to consider an option with some probability of loss and some probability of success. That is the risky choice and the one a decision maker will likely take when the problem is framed as a loss.

· *The Shoreham Nuclear Power Plant on Long Island, New York. Escalation of commitment to a losing course of action resulted in an investment of $5 billion and a plant that never started operation.*

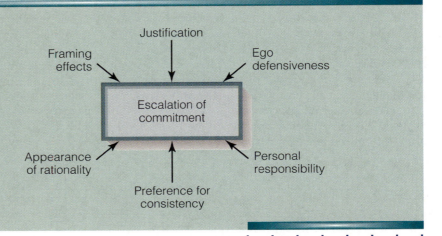

FIGURE 14-7

Contributors to Escalation of Commitment to a Losing Course of Action

Source: J. Ross and B. M. Staw, "Organizational Escalation and Exit: Lessons from the Shoreham Nuclear Power Plant," *Academy of Management Journal* 36 (1993): 701–32; G. Whyte, "Escalating Commitment to a Course of Action: A Reinterpretation, *Academy of Management Review*" 11 (1986): 311–21.

Groupthink

Groups can make bad, even disastrous decisions. A major example is the space shuttle *Challenger* tragedy. Despite evidence of safety hazards, senior managers at the National Aeronautics and Space Administration (NASA) pressed for the launch.[56] Why do group decision processes go awry?

One explanation is the phenomenon of groupthink, an ugly disease that can infect a cohesive decision-making group. Such groups have members who have worked closely together for some time and share a common set of values. These groups also often operate during times of crisis, putting stress on their members to reach a commonly agreed-upon decision.[57]

Groupthink is another explanation for excessively risky decisions. An earlier section discussed framing effects and how decision makers react to problems framed as losses. The groupthink view adds another perspective to understanding such behavior.[58]

Groupthink involves excessive conformity to a group norm that supports agreement among group members. Decision-making groups with groupthink have lost their ability to critically assess alternative solutions to a problem. They also have lost the ability to examine the effects of past decisions critically, especially decisions that have become dysfunctional for the organization. Another major feature of groupthink is the absence of ethical concerns for the effects of the group's decisions.

Groupthink does not affect decision-making groups simply because they are cohesive. The nature of the norms of such groups is the key to groupthink. If those norms have the qualities just described, then the decision process becomes seriously dysfunctional. If those norms feature support for continuously and critically examining alternatives, the decision-making group will not suffer from groupthink.

Here are the symptoms of groupthink. Watch for them whenever you work in a decision-making group.

- *Invulnerability.* Members of the group have an illusion of security and protection from harm. This feeling assures group members there is little danger in what they are doing. It also leads the group to accept excessive risks in the decision alternatives considered.
- *Rationalization.* Members of the group develop and use rationalizations that help them fend off signs of danger. The rationalizations act as perceptual filters, letting the group discount negative feedback about past decisions or alternatives under consideration.

A Boardroom Drama as Time Ran Out for Amfac's CEO: Sloan's Talk of Spinning Off Hawaiian Land Proved His Undoing

A surly storm pelted San Francisco outside Amfac Inc.'s boardroom on the morning of Nov. 20. The tempest was a perfect backdrop to what was going on inside, where emotions between Chief Executive Ronald R. Sloan and Chairman Henry A. Walker Jr. were coming to a head. Now, Amfac's board would decide the fate of the once-proud trading company and its richest asset: 56,700 acres of Hawaiian land.

For most of his 18 months as CEO, Sloan had promised investors a restructuring plan. The aim: to boost Amfac's stock—even if it meant disposing of its undervalued property and, with it, ties to Hawaii stretching back 139 years. Investors eagerly bid up the shares to a record 40¾ before the market crash in October.

But minutes after the meeting started, it was clear that Sloan had run out of time. According to one witness, Walker ally Kenneth F. Brown quickly brought the conflict to a climax: He moved to ask Sloan to resign. The board agreed. When Sloan refused, directors voted to fire him. Walker, 65, then reclaimed the post of CEO, at least until he can appoint a successor. Also removed: Amfac's general counsel and its chief spokesman.

· · · · · · · · ·

▸ **SUSPENDED DIVIDEND**

The shakeup was just the start of what may yet be a messy dismantling of Amfac. Until the recent runup, Amfac shares had traded in a narrow range below 35 despite tantalizing estimates that the shares represent $50 to $70 in hidden value.

But it hasn't been the undeveloped Hawaiian land alone that's weighed on the stock. Amfac in 1984 suspended the dividend on common shares after taking fat write-offs for ill-planned diversifications such as seafood processing and off-price retailing. And Amfac last year lost $66.6 million on about $2 billion in revenues, the third massive loss in four years. Through nine months this year, Amfac has posted profits of $15.9 million but only after a $16 million pretax boost from the sale of property.

Frustrated investors had thus backed Sloan. They believed the 26-year Amfac veteran had resolved to boost the shares. With advice from Morgan Stanley & Co., Sloan had even contemplated selling or spinning off any or all of Amfac's five units: wholesale distribution, food processing, Hawaiian agriculture and development, retailing, and resort management. Sloan declined to comment but some of his partisans say he figured the sooner Amfac moved, the better to take advantage of the past year's astounding runup in Hawaiian land prices. And since his compensation formula had been changed in September to reflect shareholder values, he had every reason to push his strategy.

But Sloan ran into trouble. One friendly director resigned in October. Sources close to Sloan say he tried filling the vacancy. But before Sloan could get his own candidate's commitment, Walker's supporters rescheduled a nominating committee meeting and picked instead a Honolulu attorney who runs Amfac's Hawaiian operations. Just before the Nov. 20 meeting, another Sloan ally quit.

· *Ronald R. Sloan, former chief executive of Amfac Inc.*

Source: J. B. Levine, "A Boardroom Drama As Time Ran Out for Amfac's CEO," *Business Week*, December 7, 1987, p. 59. Reprinted from December 7, 1987 issue of Business Week by special permission, copyright © 1987 by The McGraw-Hill Companies.

The resignations were problems enough. But there was also Hawaii Governor John D. Waihee III, who on Nov. 17 heard financial columnist Dan Dorfman speculate about Amfac's potential breakup on a television newscast. Waihee directed the state employee pension fund to start buying the stock. He also telexed other large shareholders with a warning: He would fight any plan that might parcel off acreage to uncaring owners and threaten the 8,500 Amfac jobs in the state. He also asked a state panel to rescind commercial zoning on a 577-acre Amfac development near Honolulu set for construction next year.

Walker says the board had to move against Sloan because it was caught between stockholders and the governor. As for himself: "I'm simply in the middle." Moreover, some Amfac directors had suspected that Sloan was inciting investors to remove recalcitrant directors. That fear intensified in October when New York–based Odyssey Partners asked regulators for permission to boost its stake to 15% from 4%.

. . . .

SIDESTEPPING THE LAW

"Nothing could be further from the truth," insists E. Thomas Unterman, Amfac's outside counsel, who was dismissed along with Sloan. In fact, some investors siding with Sloan suspect that certain directors urged Hawaiian officials to oppose Sloan's plan. But Walker and Waihee deny that. Directors "didn't contact me," says the governor. "The news was bad enough that I contacted them."

Walker had expressed philosophic support for spinning off the Hawaiian land. But, sources close to Sloan say, Walker recently seemed to favor more modest changes, perhaps divesting only Amfac's mainland pharmaceutical distributor. That may be one way to sidestep Hawaiian law, which requires a three-fourths vote of shareholders to sell "substantial" assets in the state. The board is set to review the issue again on Dec. 13. "We'll still consider total breakup," Walker says, "but in light of the violent opposition by the state of Hawaii."

That's unlikely to satisfy institutional investors, who own more than half of Amfac. "Walker is going to do the absolute minimum restructuring to get shareholders off his back," predicts Robert M. Sussman of New York's Quantum Fund. "But we're not going to sit by and watch Henry Walker screw us." Which should make it obvious that Amfac's in for more stormy weather.

. . . .

The Opening Episode described a major target of political behavior in organizations, executive selection. Executive selection, including dismissal and hiring, is only one of several such targets. Others include the allocation of resources, such as budgets, people, and equipment, and deciding the mission of the organization. The episode also showed the importance of having a power base and allies in the organization. Sloan's power base was the board of directors and some frustrated stockholders, but time worked against him. He could not move fast enough to fill the board vacancy. Other political players were faster and filled the vacancy with a supporter of his opponent, Henry Walker.

You may believe that political behavior is something that happens only during local, state, and national elections. Political behavior actually pervades organizational life, affecting everyone, not just senior executives.

Discussions of political behavior in organizations use a special language. Table 15-1 lists some words and phrases used in this chapter and their definitions. These words and phrases indicate the key roles power and influence play in organizational politics. This chapter focuses squarely on the development and use of power in organizations and the role political behavior processes play in using that power. As you will also see, political behavior often gives power to people who do not have it from their formal organizational position.[1]

TABLE 15-1

Some Words and Phrases Used to Describe Political Behavior in Organizations

WORD OR PHRASE	BRIEF DEFINITION
Alliance	An association of individuals, groups, or organizations trying to reach a common goal.
Cabal	A group of people trying to reach their political goals. Often involves secretive behavior and political intrigue.
Clique	An exclusive group of people; often snobbish.
Coalition	A temporary alliance of political factions to reach a specific goal.
Co-optation	The process of bringing an estranged faction into a decision process, but the opposition does not let the faction have much effect on decisions.
Opponent	An adversary. Can be a person, group, or organization.
Opposition	A person, group, or organization that blocks the efforts of another person, group, or organization from reaching their goals.
Political behavior	Exercising influence and using power during interactions within and between organizations.
Political strategy	A long-range plan of political action.
Political tactics	Specific short-range behaviors selected to achieve a political strategy.
Power	The ability to affect the behavior of other people. Also, the ability to affect the direction of a department or an entire organization.

Power

Before presenting this chapter's view of power, let's find out what power means to you. Take a sheet of paper and list the words or phrases that come to you when you think about power.

Table 15-2 lists some synonyms of the word *power*. Perhaps your list included some of these synonyms. The synonyms imply that power is a force that can give direction. It is also a force that can be a source of control and dominance. Although power has negative associations for many people[2] it can have positive effects in organizations.

Power is a person's ability to get something done the way he wants it done.[3] It is the ability to affect other people's behavior and overcome resistance to changing direction. Power often is used to overcome opposition and get people to do what they otherwise might not do.[4] It includes the ability to gather physical and human resources and put them to work to reach whatever goals the person wants to reach.[5] As you can see, little in this definition is negative.

Figure 15-1 shows actual power, potential power, and the potential for power as distinct facets of power in organizations.[6] **Potential power** exists when one party perceives another party as having power and the ability to use it. **Actual power** is the presence and use of power. The use of power may or may not successfully reach desired results. Use of power, whether successful or unsuccessful, is actual power.[7] **Potential for power** is the chance that individuals or groups have to build a power base with resources they control. The facets of power imply a perceptual basis of power. Power exists when one party perceives another party to have potential power, actual power, or the ability to build a power base.

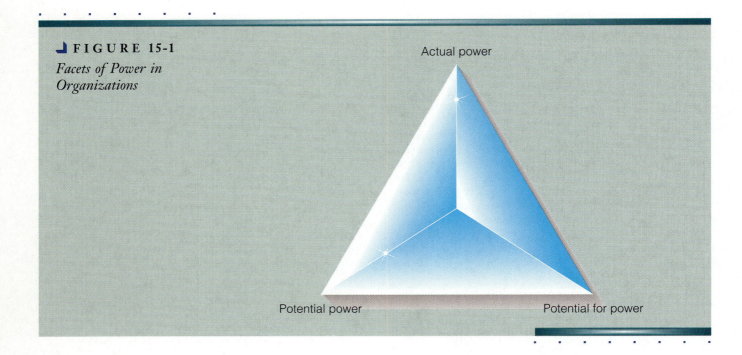

FIGURE 15-1

Facets of Power in Organizations

Actual power

Potential power

Potential for power

Power relationships in organizations have the three dimensions shown in Figure 15-2.[8] The relational dimension is the social interaction part of power. Power in organizations happens during social interactions between people and groups. The dependence dimension views power as owing to the reliance of one party on the actions of another. Dependence is high when valued results are unavailable from another source. High power follows from high dependence. The sanctioning dimension refers to the ability of one party to affect the results for the other party by using rewards, penalties, or both. This dimension of power has both actual and

TABLE 15-2

Some Synonyms of the Word Power

current, electricity, juice;
administration, administrators, authorities, bureaucracy, civil service, commission, department, direction, forces, government;
management, ministry, officials, powers, rule, rulers;
authority, clout, control, influence, leverage, prestige, pull, weight;
intensity, severity, tumult, turbulence, violence;
authority, command, commission, control, direction, domination;
jurisdiction, management, mastery, might, rule;
agent, catalyst, factor, force;
ardor, beef, brawn, drive, energy, force, intensity, lustiness, might, muscle, pep, potency, punch, steam, strength, verve, vigor, vim, virility, vitality;
capacity, potential;
charisma, dominance, influence, leadership, magnetism, personality, strength.

Source: Electronic thesaurus of Microsoft Word, Version 5.0A.

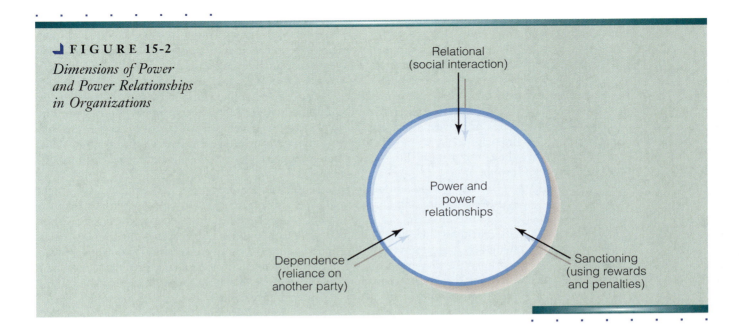

FIGURE 15-2

Dimensions of Power and Power Relationships in Organizations

Relational
(social interaction)

Power and power relationships

Dependence
(reliance on another party)

Sanctioning
(using rewards and penalties)

potential aspects. Actual sanctioning arises because of observations of sanctioning behavior. Potential sanctioning arises from expected sanctions or from the person's reputation for using sanctions.[9]

Power and authority are different concepts, although a person can have both power and authority.[10] Authority is the right to make decisions and to give direction to other people in an organization. Such authority comes to a person because of his position in the organization. It often is formally recognized in writing so people know their authority relationships. Look back at the definition of power given earlier. That definition associated power with a person's ability to get things done, not with the person's position in an organization. A person with power can be at any level in an organization, not just at the senior levels.

Power flows and is exercised in all directions in organizations.[11] It flows downward along the vertical dimension of organizations within superior-subordinate relationships. Power can also flow upward within superior-subordinate relationships. Here the subordinate exercises influence over the superior, a process some have called "managing the boss."[12] The third direction of power is lateral. Managers usually are highly dependent on others at the same level for cooperation and resources. A manager needs to influence people and groups outside his direct reporting relationships. Such influence extends to people and groups in other departments, in other work units, and outside the organization.[13]

Power is dynamic, not static.[14] As the organization's external environment changes, different subsystems of the organization, different individuals, and different coalitions may emerge as seats of power. Individuals, departments, and work units that are powerful at one point in the organization's history may not be powerful at another point. For example, individuals and units responsible for marketing a successful new product are likely to develop power, but if the product's market share drops, their power will likely subside.

This chapter sees power as essential to the functions of leadership and management.[15] Power is more than simply dominance. Instead, power is the capacity to get things done in an organization. Powerful managers and leaders can achieve more, get more resources for their subordinates, and give their subordinates more chances to develop and grow. Power is also a necessary part of controlling one's fate and building self-esteem.[16]

Who is the more powerful person? Does the person standing have higher social status? Does the person operating the terminal have the only knowledge of the language on the screen?

POWER, LEADERSHIP, AND MANAGEMENT

Powerful leaders and managers delegate decision authority to subordinates and view their subordinates' talents as a resource. Such leaders and managers can more easily change their subordinates' working conditions than powerless leaders and managers can. The powerful can get the resources and information subordinates need to be effective. They take risks and press for innovations in their organizations. Subordinates of powerful leaders and managers can develop from the new experiences and increase their promotion opportunities. Powerful leaders and managers often share their power with their subordinates, creating more total power for the entire work group.[17]

Because having and using power are key characteristics of a leader, powerlessness is more a feature of managers and supervisors than of leaders. Those with little or no power use close supervision and do not delegate authority to subordinates. They often distrust their subordinates and view talented subordinates as threatening. Such managers and supervisors stick to the rules and do not take risks. Subordinates who work for the powerless do not have the chance to develop from involvement in new activities. Powerless managers and supervisors strongly focus on the work of their group, protecting it from outside interference. Their work group becomes "their" territory, a symbol they use to try to increase their significance in the organization.

BUILDING POWER

Figure 15-3 shows six major **sources of power** in organizations. Leaders and managers can identify and use these sources to build their power base. An important step in **building power** is a political diagnosis. A later section of this chapter describes how to do a diagnosis.[18]

A person can derive power from his knowledge, skill, reputation, and professional credibility. People with specialized knowledge have power if other people depend on that knowledge to do their jobs. A person's reputation builds from a series of successes. Power grows as a manager or leader develops a positive reputation. Giving

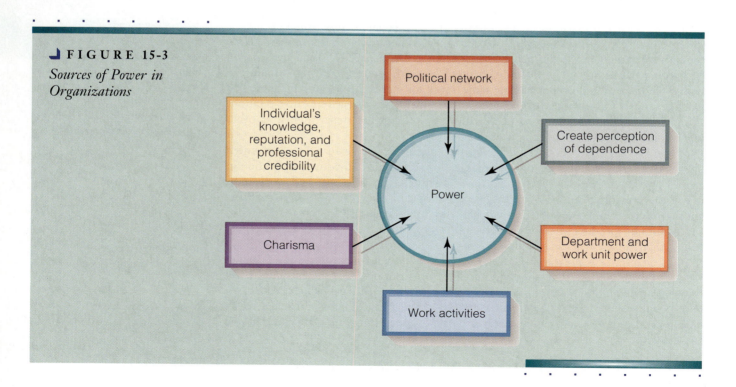

FIGURE 15-3

Sources of Power in Organizations

- Political network
- Individual's knowledge, reputation, and professional credibility
- Create perception of dependence
- Charisma
- Power
- Department and work unit power
- Work activities

talks at professional meetings and serving on committees of professional associations, for example, can increase one's professional credibility, which can lead to influence both outside and inside the organization.

Chapter 12 discussed charisma as an important quality of leadership. Its importance comes from the power a charismatic person has over others. Those who attribute charisma to a manager or leader feel inspired by his ideas and become committed to carrying them out. Although charisma is mainly a personality-like quality, managers and leaders can learn to make effective and influential appeals to others. Charisma is especially important as a source of power in lateral relationships where the manager or leader has no direct authority.

A person's work activities can also be a source of power. Work activities that are extraordinary, visible, and appropriate to the goals of the organization are important sources of power. Extraordinary work activities usually are risky activities successfully done. Other people in the organization notice the results and develop positive feelings about the successful person. A person who is continuously successful at high-risk work activities may come to be regarded as charismatic.

A person can create a strong power base by building a **political network** within an organization. A political network depends on the person's communication channels in the organization. The communication can follow the formal organizational design or be informal in character. Chapter 13 discussed this aspect of power and political behavior more fully.

A leader or manager builds a political network by getting the support of others, including subordinates and those outside his direct authority. Doing favors for others can help build support by developing a sense of indebtedness to the manager or leader. Favors are especially important in developing support in lateral relationships. Forming alliances with other peer leaders and managers adds to a person's power base in an organization.

Creating a perception of dependence is still another way to build power in an organization. The perception comes from the belief that the leader or manager controls scarce resources, including people, equipment, money, information, and rewards, and can use these resources to help or impede other people. Note that the leader or manager does not actually need to control the resources. The perception of control is the key to this method of building power.

The last source of power in an organization is the power base of the work unit headed by the manager or leader. This source of power depends on the department's ability to cope with uncertainty, the uniqueness of its functions, changes in the external environment, and its centrality to the work flow of the organization. The movement of power among departments is part of the dynamic character of power.

Departments that reduce uncertainty for an organization can have high power. For example, human resource management departments that become expert in affirmative action, equal employment opportunity, and workforce diversity can increase their power in their organizations.[19] Departments offering a service available from few other sources in the organization have high power. Departments at key points in the work flow of an organization also enjoy considerable power. Managers or leaders whose departments hold a central position or perform a unique function in an organization can build a strong power base for themselves.

ATTRIBUTION OF POWER

Chapter 4 described attribution processes of social perception. Attribution processes also operate when power is ascribed to people at all levels in an organization. The power a person ascribes to another person may not be the same as the actual power of the other party.

Both personal characteristics and the context in which a person works can lead to the **attribution of power**. Personal characteristics include formal position in the organization, technical knowledge, and position within a communication network. A person whose formal position has high status and authority will have high formal authority. Others who interact with that person will ascribe to him high power and potential influence. A person with high technical knowledge can be perceived in the same way, especially in a technical organization. Holding a central position in a communication network may lead others to perceive the person as having high power because of his access to information.[20]

The formal and informal contexts of the person also affect attributions of power. The formal context includes membership in a powerful group or project. A member of such a group can mirror the power of the group and have high power attributed to him. A similar attribution process works for members of informal coalitions and social networks, if an observer believes the coalition or network is powerful.

◢ **TABLE 15–3**

Descriptions of Power Use Styles

STYLE 1

Work gets accomplished by working effectively behind the scenes. Sometimes it is best to take action without others' being aware of what is happening, so that quietly, and without fanfare, work can get done. Other times, it is best to get work accomplished by creating a favorable impression on others, either by complimenting them on their efforts and ideas, or presenting one's own work efforts, or giving praise and recognition to others for their efforts, which can be effective ways to get work accomplished.

STYLE 2

Work gets accomplished by building contacts and a network of support for one's efforts. Work is rarely accomplished without the assistance of others. Sometimes appeals to reason, logic, or emotion convince others to lend their support. Other times, exchanging one's resources (time, rewards, expertise) for others' resources (information, privileges, promotion) creates this base of support. Ultimately, work gets done through a bargaining and negotiation process, whereby people exchange valued resources to aid one another in task accomplishment.

STYLE 3

Work gets accomplished by exerting pressure on others to get it done. Whether one issues directives, orders, or makes demands, it is necessary to be forceful to get things accomplished. Sometimes it is important to remind people of the potential loss of their pay, privileges, or jobs to ensure that work is carried out. In other cases, just telling someone to do something is all that is required. Essentially, task accomplishment calls for a clear statement of expectations and careful follow-up. Work gets done by monitoring and reviewing others to ensure that work is completed.

STYLE 4

Work gets accomplished by utilizing certain problem-solving and decision-making techniques. Listening skills, the acknowledgment of individual differences, the utilization of each person's resources and contributions, the management of conflict, and the development of trust among people are all essential components of this decision-making process. Ultimately, work gets accomplished by attempting to create win-win situations for everyone. When people take part in decision making, assume responsibility, recognize the legitimacy of others' concerns, and search together for common goals and means to solve their problems, work gets done.

STYLE 5

Work gets accomplished by generating enthusiasm and commitment in others for task accomplishment. One develops this commitment by creating a vision of future possibilities and by giving others a sense of mission and purpose in their work. Sometimes one can generate this commitment in others by creatively using language and symbols. Other times, forging strong bonds of identification between individuals will strengthen this commitment and, by sheer weight of one's presence, energy, personality, and enthusiasm, one can energize others to action.

Source: Adapted from N. C. Roberts, "Organizational Power Styles: Collective and Competitive Power under Varying Organizational Conditions," *Journal of Applied Behavioral Science* 22 (1986): 448, Table 2. Italics omitted. Reprinted with permission from NTL Institute, "Organizational Power Styles," by Nancy C. Roberts, pp. 448-49, *Journal of Applied Behavioral Science*, Vol. 22, No. 4, copyright December 1986.

TABLE 15-4

TABLE 15-4

Average Percentage of Use of Each Power Style by 347 Practicing Managers

| | STYLE NUMBER IN TABLE 15-3 AND STYLE NAME | | | | |
| | 1 | 2 | 3 | 4 | 5 |
	Impression Management	Transactional	Directive	Consensus	Charismatic
Used with peers	17%	22%	7%	31%	18%
Used with supervisors	21%	21%	4%	32%	16%
Used with subordinates	15%	13%	13%	30%	23%

Source: N. C. Roberts, "Organizational Power Styles: Collective and Competitive Power under Varying Organizational Conditions," *Journal of Applied Behavioral Science* 22 (1986): 449, Table 3. Reprinted with permission from NTL Institute, "Organizational Power Styles," by Nancy C. Roberts, pp. 448-49, *Journal of Applied Behavioral Science*, Vol. 22, No. 4, copyright December 1986.

EXERCISE *Using Different Power Styles*

*P*eople have different approaches to using power in organizations. The following exercise will help you understand your **power styles.**

Table 15-3 describes five styles of using power to get work done in an organization. Read each style and note on a separate sheet of paper the percentage of time you use each style when interacting with peers, your supervisor, or subordinates, if you are a manager or supervisor. Record a separate percentage for the time you use a style with each group.

INTERPRETATION

Table 15-4 shows the percentage of time 347 managers used each style in their organizations. The table shows the usage separately for interactions with peers, supervisors, and subordinates. The five labels in the heading of the table are the names of the power styles described in Table 15-3.

The five styles fall into three groups. Impression Management and Directive are each forms of competitive power styles that people can use to overcome the opposition of another party. Competitive power styles use either force or coercion (Directive) or deceit and manipulation (Impression Management).

The Consensus and Charismatic power styles are each forms of a collective use of power. These styles feature a more cooperative use of power with all parties pooling their resources to reach a common goal. People move toward common ends because of individual choice, not coercion. The Consensus power style features joint problem solving. The Charismatic power style excites members of an organization to move toward mutually desired goals.

The Transactional power style can be either competitive or collective, depending on a person's intention in using this style. Some amount of cooperation is needed to have a transaction. If the power interaction focuses on the allocation of scarce resources, the style can become distinctly competitive.

The percentages in Table 15-4 show that the managers used a mixture of power styles. Managers used the Directive power style more in their interactions with subordinates than with their peers and supervisors. Those managers also used the Consensus style more than any other style in all three situations. They used Impression Management and Transactional styles between 28 percent and 42 percent of the time. Those two styles use political behavior more than the other three power styles.

Your percentages should also show a mixture, although they may not be the same as those in the table. You can reflect on whether you use each style more or less than the practicing managers in the various situations. Differences between your pattern and those of the practicing managers may be due to differences in your experience in using power in organizations.

Political Behavior

Political behavior in organizations focuses on getting, developing, and using power to achieve a desired result in situations of uncertainty or conflict over choices. Such behavior often happens outside accepted channels of authority in an organization. You can view political behavior as unofficial, unsanctioned behavior to reach some goal.[21]

A person can use political behavior to build the bases of power described earlier. People also use political behavior to affect decisions, get scarce resources, and earn the cooperation of people outside their direct authority. Political behavior ebbs and flows with the dynamics of power described earlier. A person's need for power can also affect his willingness to become involved in an organization's inevitable political processes.

The political processes of organizations have two characteristics that distinguish them from other organizational processes: power and influence.[22] Behavior that uses power, builds power, or tries to influence others is political. Such behavior tries to control a result and can feature high levels of conflict. Political behavior can be directed at reaching organizational goals or individual goals that do not benefit the organization. An example of the latter is a manager who drives his work unit to high levels of performance just to enhance his reputation. His demands could increase the stress on people in the work unit and have long-term dysfunctional effects such as damaged equipment.

When a manager stimulates conflict to increase his power base or to affect a decision process, he has moved into the political arena. A manager, for example, may know that his opponent in a decision-making group has a low tolerance for conflict. By taking strong positions on an issue, the manager can introduce conflict and possibly unnerve his opponent.

Political behavior is especially important in managing lateral relationships. Three lateral relationships in particular feature political behavior.[23] Line-staff relationships put a staff person in a position of influencing someone else in the organization to approve an important project. Managers of human resource management and finance departments usually do not have line authority over those who approve a project and carry it out. They often use their bases of power, and the political tactics described in a later section, to influence others to adopt the project.

The second type of lateral relationship is competition for resources. Managers use political behavior when competing for resources such as money, people, equipment, and office space. They compete with other managers at the same organizational level for those resources, but none of the managers can decide the resource allocations directly. Because resource allocation decisions are a common battleground of political behavior, a later section looks at those decisions in more detail.

The third type of lateral relationship is interdependence in the work flow. Managers of some work units are often dependent on other work units. Successful completion of earlier stages in the work flow is necessary for the success of the dependent work unit. Managers must negotiate with the managers of earlier work units to assure an efficient work flow. Such interdependence is common in serially interdependent manufacturing (assembly lines) and service processes. Processing of insurance claims is an example of the latter.

Political behavior and the political processes of organizations can also lead to the institutionalization of the current power holders.[24] Institutionalization is the product of a mature political process. Those in power build an organizational structure, develop policies, and create information systems that support their power bases. Once in place, these structures prevent people with little power from gaining power against the established coalition.

 POLITICAL MANEUVERING IN ORGANIZATIONS

Political maneuvering in organizations consists of political strategies and political tactics. The latter are specific political activities used to reach the goal of a strategy.

Political Strategies

A **political strategy** is a plan to reach a goal using specific political tactics. It may or may not be written. The strategy specifies the goal to reach and the political means to reach that goal. A well-designed political strategy includes a plan for dealing with changes in the political context within which the person pursues the goal. The plan explicitly recognizes that political events in organizations do not always happen as expected. A political strategy specifies various combinations and sequences of political tactics to deal with different political events as the strategy unfolds.

The use of political strategies is not restricted to executives, managers, and supervisors. Strategies are available to people at all levels of an organization. This aspect of political strategies is one reason political behavior is so pervasive in organizations. It also helps to explain the intrigue organizational politics brings to organizational life.

Researchers have documented political strategies in the following areas:

1. Decisions about resource allocations such as budgets, choice of senior executives, and the design of the organization.[25]
2. Development and enhancement of a person's career.[26]
3. Performance appraisals prepared by a person's supervisor or manager.[27]
4. Decisions about pay increases.[28]

Political Tactics

Political tactics involve either building power or using power unobtrusively. A political strategy can use a mix of tactics, moving from one to another as the political landscape changes. Table 15-5 summarizes five major political tactics.[29]

Decision-making processes can have a distinctly political dimension. Politically oriented decision makers can affect the choice of alternatives that favor themselves or their organizational units. A decision maker can exert his power to deftly affect the process by selectively emphasizing his favored alternative. The alternative emphasized is one that will favorably affect the power of the decision maker or his unit.

A politically oriented decision maker can also call upon an outside expert or consultant. Because the consultant is an outsider, he can bring an aura of objectivity and legitimacy to the decision alternatives under consideration. Decision makers call in consultants when power within the decision-making process is about equally dispersed and the issue is critical to either the organization or the individual. When power is well balanced, the decision maker needs another lever to increase his power within the process.

An unobtrusive way of using power in an organization is to control the decision-making agenda. People who want matters to stay as they are often use this tactic. By

---

⌐ TABLE 15–5

Political Tactics

Selectively emphasizing decision criteria	A decision maker can affect a decision process by selectively emphasizing the importance of a favored alternative.
Using outside experts	A politically oriented decision maker can call upon an outside expert or consultant to swing the power balance in a decision process toward his favored alternative.
Controlling the agenda	Controlling the agenda includes deciding whether an issue or problem is considered at all and, if it is considered, its position on the agenda.
Building coalitions	People build coalitions when they want to create a power base and amass power resources to reach the goals of their political strategy.
Co-optation	A person uses co-optation to persuade others to favor his position.

controlling the agenda, they can decide both whether an issue or problem is considered at all and, if it is considered, where it will appear on the agenda. Items toward the end of an agenda may get less attention than those presented earlier. Decisions made about earlier issues on the agenda can affect later decisions.[30]

People build coalitions when they want to create a power base to reach the goals of their political strategy. The coalition can be internal, formed around individuals and groups within the organization. It can also be external, formed around people and groups outside the organization. In both cases, the individuals or groups are believed important to the political actor's position.

A person uses co-optation as a political tactic to persuade outsiders or insiders to favor his position. Through co-optation, he tries to lure people to his side. The targets of co-optation are either potential opponents or people whose help can smooth the way to the goals of a political strategy. Placing outsiders on boards of directors, advisory councils, or task forces can give them information that persuades them that a particular issue or position is important. A politically savvy person can use committees to co-opt insiders. Particularly nasty issues or problems requiring information from many sources and the commitment of those sources to a decision can benefit from a committee approach.

Several other political tactics do not fit neatly with those already described. These tactics often are manipulative approaches aimed at persuading a target of the merits of one's position. The target may or may not be aware of the goal of the influence effort or that an influence effort is happening. Some examples of these miscellaneous tactics include blaming others, selectively using information, and impression management. Blaming others is a political tactic used when a person wants to avoid association with a negative event. A person can try to influence another individual by selectively presenting, distorting, or withholding information. A third miscellaneous tactic is impression management. Dressing according to perceived organizational norms, taking credit for successes even when unjustified, and presenting an image of being associated with important events and information are examples of impression management.

POLITICAL DIAGNOSIS

A **political diagnosis** helps one understand the location of power in an organization and the type of political behavior that is likely to happen. It identifies politically active individuals and coalitions in the organization, the amount of power they have, and the likely ways they will use their power. The diagnosis also examines political networks in the organization.[31]

Individuals

A political diagnosis focused on individuals has the following purposes:

1. Identify the powerful and politically active people in the organization.
2. Learn the power base of each of those people.
3. Assess each person's skill in using his power base.
4. Decide how each person is likely to use power.
5. Identify the goals each person is trying to reach through power and political behavior.

The political diagnosis collects information in each of these areas. Information is gathered from organizational records and key informants inside and outside the organization.

An individual-level diagnosis begins by identifying presumably powerful people in the organization from an organizational chart and a description of titles and duties. This part of the diagnosis also includes identifying individuals external to the organization who play important roles in its political processes. Some examples of external individuals are union officials, people from regulatory agencies, and key financial backers of the organization. One needs to use caution in ascribing power to a person because of position and title. Some people with powerful sounding titles may not actually have power. Other parts of the diagnosis supplement this first step.

A sample of people in the organization can then be interviewed about the reputation of the initially identified power holders. One can also identify major decisions and the people involved in those decisions. These steps test the conclusions from the first step.

Once the power holders have been identified, their power base must be assessed. The power base depends on both the resources available to the person and his political skill in using those resources. Resources include budget discretion, rewards, sanctions, and information. A power base is strong if the person has discretion in using resources that are important for major issues facing the organization. The power base becomes stronger when there is little substitute for the person's resources and the resources apply to a wide range of situations.

The political skill of a power holder is determined by how effectively he uses his resources. A diagnosis assesses a person's ability to develop a general political strategy and use the political tactics described earlier. It also is necessary to assess the person's flexibility in using the resources available. This step in the diagnosis relies on both archival information such as minutes of key decision-making groups and reports and people in the organization familiar with the power holder's background. These sources can also give information about how the power holder is likely to use his power and the goals he wants to reach.

Coalitions

The political diagnosis then moves to identifying and assessing coalitions in the organization. A **coalition** is an alliance of individuals who share a common goal. Coalitions are also interest groups that try to affect decisions in the organization. Coalitions can have members from widely scattered parts of the organization. The goals of a political diagnosis of coalitions are the same as those listed earlier for individuals.

Information from veteran informants inside and outside the organization can help identify coalitions. Reports of past major decisions are also a useful source of information. Any stable group of people who regularly affect major decisions is a coalition.

The power of a coalition depends on the power bases of its individual members. One can use the methods of assessing an individual's power base described earlier to do an initial assessment of a coalition's power. The coalition's power also depends on the stability of its membership and its effectiveness in managing its group processes. An unstable, mismanaged coalition will lose the advantages of the power of its individual members. Assessing the power of a coalition can require direct observation of the coalition in action, using the conceptual tools described in Chapter 10. One can infer how a coalition is likely to use its power from the political styles of its high-status members. Often such members strongly affect the norms of the coalition. The political goals of a coalition are most easily assessed from its public statements.

Political Networks

The diagnosis of political networks gets at the heart of an organization's political processes. Political networks form from affiliations and alliances of individuals and coalitions. Political networks can control the flow of information and other resources through the organization. They also can give support to those in the network and provide a common ideological view.

The diagnosis of networks depends upon knowledge from informants and direct experience in the organization. The diagnosis should identify the people and coalitions that have major influence within the network. Information from the diagnosis of individuals and coalitions helps identify those strategic positions. The diagnosis should also identify the individuals with informal access to the organization's decision-making processes. Such people play key political roles in affecting the results of major decisions.

 ## THE DARK SIDE OF ORGANIZATIONAL POLITICS: DECEPTION, LYING, AND INTIMIDATION

Unfortunately, organizational politics also has a dark side: deception, lying, and intimidation. The gloomy aspects of political behavior help explain why it has a negative image in the eyes of many people.

Deception

> A prince being thus obliged to know well how to act as a beast must imitate the fox and the lion, for the lion cannot protect himself from traps, and the fox cannot defend himself from wolves. One must therefore be a fox to recognize traps, and a lion to frighten wolves. Those that wish to be only lions do not understand this. Therefore, a prudent ruler ought not to keep faith when by so doing it would be against his interest, and when the reasons which made him bind himself no longer exist. If men were all good, this precept would not be a good one; but as they are bad, and would not observe their faith with you, so you are not bound to keep faith with them. . . . But it is necessary to be able to disguise this character well, and to be a great feigner and dissembler; and men are so simple and so ready to obey present necessities, that one who deceives will always find those who allow themselves to be deceived.[32]

This advice from Niccolò Machiavelli promotes the use of **deception** to build and hold power. Today, hundreds of years after Machiavelli's observations, deceptive behavior is still a part of organizational life. Such behavior tricks another party into arriving at incorrect conclusions or selecting the wrong alternative in a decision process. Deceptive behavior happens in organizations when an individual's personal goals become more important than the goals of the organization. Here are some examples of deceptive behavior:[33]

1. A manager does not want change but never actually says he does not want change. Instead, he authorizes an endless series of studies that result in everyone forgetting the proposed change.
2. An executive appears to select successors based on ability but really selects them based on loyalty to his ideas.
3. An Equal Employment Opportunity (EEO) manager proposes expanding his staff to develop a training program to improve job opportunities for underrepresented groups. Many judge the overt goal as the worthy pursuit of diversity. The EEO manager's covert goal is to increase his chances of a promotion to a higher level, something never discussed in the proposal.

The costs of such behavior to organizations are clear: high economic costs of endless studies, selection of less-capable successors, and the higher cost of an otherwise worthy diversity enhancement program.

Despite its costs, some argue that deceptive behavior is functional for organizations. Deceptive behavior brings political intrigue and a sense of uneasiness to an organization. The maneuvering of the deceptive behavior lends an air of excitement to otherwise routine daily activities. No one knows upon arriving at work which "hidden agenda" will play out on a given day.

Lying

Lying is the intentional misstatement of the truth where the liar is trying to mislead another party and knows what he is saying is untrue. Note that lying differs from deception; they are not synonyms. Lying helps the liar build power by distorting information in favor of the liar. A person lies to gain a political advantage. Although lying can help a person reach his political goals, the long-term effects include a loss of power, especially if others discover the lie.[34]

Intimidation

The third gloomy side to political behavior is the indirect and direct **intimidation** of someone who wants to reform organizational practices but does not have the authority to cause such changes. Such people typically are in lower-level positions in an organization. They may perceive middle and upper management as incompetent or acting in ways they regard as illegal or immoral.[35]

Managers perceive the reformer as threatening their authority. They first react by trying to intimidate the reformer indirectly. If indirect intimidation does not silence the reformer, the intimidation escalates to a more direct form. Here are some management actions that can intimidate a reform-minded subordinate:

1. The manager assures the subordinate that he misperceives the situation and his suggestions are not valid. If the reformer persists, the manager suggests an investigation to find the truth. The results of the investigation will show the reformer that the charges have no basis.
2. The next level of intimidation isolates the reformer from others in the organization. A manager first reduces or ends communication with the reformer and restricts his interactions with others in the organization. If the reformer persists, a manager can physically isolate the person by transferring him to a position that has low visibility or is physically distant from the part of the organization to which the reformer objects.
3. The third level of intimidation focuses on the character and motives of the reformer. A manager defames the reformer by suggesting to others that he is incompetent or even psychopathological.

These methods of intimidation try to prevent the reformer from building support among others in the organization. The intimidation also tries to drive the reformer out of the organization. If none of the methods work, managers can escalate to the last level—firing the person.

. . . .

C A S E   *Road Rough for Women at Big Three*

*T*his case describes some political maneuvering of women executives and engineers at the three U.S. automobile makers. Use the following questions as a guide for your analysis:

1. Did these women use a political strategy to advance in their organizations? If they did, which political tactics did they use?

Source: D. J. Morrow, "Road Rough for Women at Big Three," *Albuquerque Journal*, January 31, 1993, pp. H3, H4. Reprinted by permission: Tribune Media Services.

2. Did they do a political diagnosis to develop their strategy and tactics?

◢ CASE DESCRIPTION

Stephanie Bergeron knew it was a risky move. After a promising 11-year career at General Motors, she accepted a position four years ago as Chrysler's assistant general auditor, a job traditionally held by a man.

Bergeron has climbed the corporate Everest rapidly and now serves as Chrysler's manufacturing group con-

troller. In her current post, she supervises a staff of 550 and oversees the finances of Chrysler's manufacturing operations. [She became Assistant Treasurer—Corporate Finance for Chrysler Corporation in November 1994.]

Bergeron is representative of the paradox facing female executives at the Big Three automakers. The good news: Women now hold a bigger slice of the managerial pie than they did five years ago and appear to have escaped the downsizing ax better than their male counterparts.

The bad news: Women in senior level management positions, such as Bergeron, are the rare exception. Three years ago, five women served as vice presidents at General Motors, Ford and Chrysler. Today, the number has dwindled to two—Shirley Young at General Motors and Helen Petrauskas at Ford—and won't likely increase anytime soon.

"If Detroit had more women in management, it wouldn't have to be downsizing as furiously as it is now," said Laurel Cutler, a former Chrysler vice president who is now vice chairman of Foote Cone & Belding, a New York advertising agency. "You can't remain isolated from half the car market and expect to come out ahead."

To find out how female professionals at the Big Three were navigating the corporate maze, the Detroit Free Press and the University of Michigan sent questionnaires to some 650 professional women, querying them on everything from salary to sexual harassment.

Most of the 103 replies told a similar story. Frustrated by a visible old-boys network, female professionals have a tough time finding mentors.

"You need a sponsor to be accepted, or you'll be overlooked time after time for promotions," said one of Chrysler's female managers. "To fill new positions, these men are going back to their familiars, meaning their friends and associates."

The mentor search is particularly tough for women, because most of them look for men. According to several of the women surveyed, men make better mentors because they tend to have more contacts and have a better knowledge of the company's political currents.

"Men are generally not comfortable mentoring women," said Mary Mattis, vice president of Catalyst, a New York research firm. "The woman can't initiate this relationship because of the innuendo. The man doesn't want to initiate it because he's afraid people will talk about him." . . .

"Women are moving up, but their progress has been very, very slow," said Dee Soder, president of Endymion, a New York–based executive advisory firm. "It's even worse when you consider how many years women have been in the pipeline. There's a vast pool out there of untapped talent." . . .

"Is manufacturing a good career for women?" asks Shirley Young, GM's vice president of consumer market development. "There's no question that it will be. There are certain barriers that come when there are not large numbers of women. Anytime you're in that stage, you have the plus of being the first and the loneliness of being the first."

To overcome the isolation, women are starting to lean on each other. Two GM engineers—Nancy Simioni and Jeanne Polan—formed PMS, the Professional Mother's Society, when they became pregnant with their first children in 1986.

"At first Nancy and I got together to talk about where to get professional maternity clothes," said Polan, who is expecting her fourth child. "Since then the group has expanded to about 20 women and has become an open forum." . . .

Even though the survey revealed common threads in several areas, there were striking differences of opinion among women at the three companies. Chrysler's crew was older and better paid than Ford's or GM's, and had vocal complaints about discrimination and an active old-boys network.

Ford's female executives were happier in their jobs than their crosstown colleagues, but still saw significant room for improvement. For example, several criticized Ford's family leave policy because it didn't allow men to spend enough time with their newborns.

"It's interesting that women didn't mention their own leaves," said Sally Staebler, one of Ford's corporate lawyers. "Women are treated very fairly here. When I first came to Ford 14 years ago, I couldn't believe some of the good assignments they gave women. There is nothing closed to a woman lawyer in this company." . . .

How can more women make it to the top? Most of the women polled believe the key is in broadening one's career path. Fast-trackers should go into engineering and manufacturing and avoid the three traditionally "pink," or female, professions: public relations, personnel and purchasing. . . .

"A lot of people don't know what an engineer is," said Susan Cischke, the chief engineer at Chrysler's proving grounds in Chelsea. "I liked math and science when I was in school, but a lot of girls stayed away from these classes. To really make it in corporations as engineers, women need to get an early foundation when they're in school."

The hours are long for both male and female executives, but the rewards can be sweet. A growing number of women are moving through the ranks in non-traditional areas. For example, GM has a group of female engineers working on their new Camaro/Firebird project, while Cischke supervises much of Chrysler's product testing.

Women are already responsible for several showroom changes. "We really consider the human factors of the car," said Elizabeth Pilibosian, lead development engineer on GM's Camaro/Firebird project. "One of the things women worry about is their fingernails, so we made the buttons larger. Men liked the changes as well, because the old buttons weren't large enough for their hands."

CASE ANALYSIS

The case showed how women in male-dominated parts of three large organizations had to do some political maneuvering to advance their careers. Their diagnosis of the political systems of their organizations showed a need to build a political system for themselves. For the most part, they built a political network and formed coalitions with other aspiring women. Men controlled the long-established political systems in the organizations. Women built their own network to get around the male-dominated systems.

International Aspects of Political Behavior in Organizations

*T*his section presents some observations on the international aspects of political behavior in organizations. Some observations are speculative because there has been little direct assessment of political behavior in organizations across cultures. Several observations came from known cultural differences that can affect the attribution of power to a person and that person's political behavior.[36]

People from different cultures hold different beliefs about the proper relationship between individuals who have power and those who do not. Some cultures see a directive and autocratic use of power as correct. Other cultures define a consultative or democratic approach as correct. Such cultural differences affect reactions to the use of power and related political behavior. Different individuals within those cultures, of course, can have different beliefs about power relationships.

People in the Philippines, Mexico, many South American countries, India, Singapore, and Hong Kong value a directive use of power. A consultative-oriented manager[37] is not as respected in those countries as a manager who gives clear directions and instructions to subordinates. Workers in those countries ascribe power to a directive manager and weakness to a consultative one. Status symbols also play important roles in defining who has power and who does not. The political processes within the organizations of those countries should also mirror the power orientation of the underlying culture. Consultative-oriented managers have a distinct disadvantage when trying to maneuver through the political systems of power-directive cultures.

People in the Scandinavian countries, Israel, Switzerland, Austria, and New Zealand have an opposite orientation. Workers in those countries expect their managers to involve them in the decision-making process. A directive manager from India or Singapore, for example, would not be well accepted by workers in Scandinavian organizations. Though such a manager enjoys high power in his home culture, the same manager would have little power in Scandinavian cultures.

Cultures vary widely in their orientation to uncertainty. Some cultures value the reduction of uncertainty. Other cultures see uncertainty as a manageable aspect of organizational life. Workers in Greece and France expect managers to maintain low levels of uncertainty. A manager who cannot keep uncertainty low has little power and influence over his workers. Workers in Denmark and the United States, however, have a higher tolerance for uncertainty. Nonmanagers in those countries expect managers to make risky decisions. Such workers could ascribe high power to risk-taking managers and low power to those who avoid risk. The degree of power ascribed to various managers affects their ability to influence others with political tactics.

Workers in the United States, Australia, Great Britain, Canada, and the Netherlands are more individualistic than workers from many South American countries. The latter value family ties and conformity to social norms. South American workers expect managers to look after them. Managers who show genuine interest in their subordinates' private lives enjoy higher power in South American organizations than they do in North American organizations.

The preceding observations all examined culturally based differences in sources of power and the attribution of power by one party to another. Although we know little about political processes in organizations in different cultures, some limited observations can be made.

Scandinavian managers typically depend on informal social contacts and consensus building as their major political strategies.[38] Such strategies involve many people throughout the organization. The strategies unfold more slowly than those of faster-moving, less consensus-oriented U.S. managers.

Managers from different countries also have different views of organizations as political systems. French and Italian managers are motivated to get and use power in their organizations. They have a distinctly political orientation to their organizations, focusing their work days on building and using power. Danish and British managers have the opposite orientation. They focus more on reaching organizational goals than on building individual power bases.

Knowledge of cultural differences will help managers understand the reactions of people in different cultures when they try to exercise power. Experience in the political systems of organizations in one's home culture do not always carry over to organizations in other cultures.

Ethical Issues about Political Behavior in Organizations

Political behavior in organizations raises many questions about what is ethical behavior and what is not. You may have sensed some ethical issues as you read this chapter. If any of the discussions of power or political behavior caused you to ponder the "rightness" of the observations, you were raising implicit ethical questions.[39]

Using power and political behavior in an organization to serve only one's self-interest is unethical, if you reject an egoistic view of ethics and accept a utilitarian view. Similarly, political behavior that uses excessive organizational resources to reach a personal goal is also unethical. These observations suggest any political strategy and its associated tactics are unethical if they do not serve the goals of the organization or at least of a larger group of people than the single political actor. For example, an individual who ignores equipment maintenance to push products through a manufacturing process for personal gain is behaving unethically.

Using power and political behavior to violate another person's rights is also unethical. Political tactics such as blaming others, ingratiation, and co-optation violate others' rights. A co-opted individual, unless he understands the goal of the political actor, has not consented to be influenced. Making accusations against someone violates that individual's right to an impartial hearing of the charges.

A sense of justice strongly argues for fair treatment, fair pay, and the fair administration of rules and procedures. Giving preferential treatment to someone to build a sense of obligation is unethical.

Does this discussion of ethics and political behavior mean political behavior is inherently unethical? No! If you accept the discussions of ethics in Chapter 3, political behavior, the use of power, and influence efforts that have the following characteristics are all ethical:

1. Such behavior should serve people outside the organization and beyond the single political actor.
2. Individuals should clearly know the intent of the actor and give their free consent, implicitly or explicitly, to be influenced.
3. The right of due process should not be violated while the political behavior unfolds.
4. The administration of the organization's resources, procedures, and policies should allow fair treatment of all affected people.

These guidelines should help you distinguish an organizational statesman from a person playing "dirty politics."[40]

. . . .

Personal and Management Implications

*P*ower and organizational politics have some implications for you as an individual or as a manager. Several implications follow from the three facets of power. You should easily see actual power because this is power in use. Potential power and potential for power are less obvious, but no less important. Think of potential power as latent power ready to spring into use when conditions call for actual power. Knowing who has potential power, including yourself, lets you navigate the political system of your organization.

Potential power and potential for power strongly suggest doing a political diagnosis of your organization. That diagnosis will help you find power potentials. For example, potential for power exists when a person has scarce resources needed by others in the organization. You may have knowledge or information not commonly available. Recognizing that you have such a scarce resource is a first step in building a power base. Potential for power suggests you should examine what you do in the organization to see whether any latent conditions exist to build power. You can then develop appropriate political strategies from the results of the diagnosis.

Potential for power suggests caution when using your power in an interaction with someone in the organization. The other party may react to you by discovering his power potential and begin building a power base. He could then oppose you in ways you did not expect.

Political maneuvering is a pervasive part of organizational life. Such maneuvering is not restricted to those in management or supervisory positions. The sections describing political strategies and political tactics apply to both nonmanagers and managers. You can use those strategies and tactics to pursue desired goals in your organization.

Power attribution, unfortunately, is a two-edged sword. You may attribute power to others in the organization and act accordingly, but your attribution may not be correct. Also, you may believe you have power over someone else, but the other party may not attribute power to you. Part of the political intrigue of organizations has its roots in the attribution process. You may want to review that section of Chapter 4 to get more details about this important psychological process.

The process of power attribution implies caution when you perceive another person has high power over you. You might unknowingly attribute high power to a peer because of his association with a powerful project. Yet the peer and others in the organization may not share your perception of his power. Your attribution of power can lead you to unnecessarily defer to the peer and be influenced more than is justified by the situation.

Managing lateral relationships in an organization can test any manager's political skills. Because you have no direct authority over others in such relationships, you must use a political approach to these interactions. The political tactics need not be any of the villainous ones described in the section on the dark side of organizational politics. Managing these relationships, however, can require a careful political diagnosis.

Using political strategies and tactics raises ethical questions about your behavior. You might want to review the "Ethical Issues about Political Behavior" section before embarking on a political road in your organization. You will need to decide for yourself what ethical guidelines you will follow. Your personal ethics will guide you in the choice of political strategies and tactics.

The section describing some international aspects of organizational politics clearly implied caution for you if you work as a manager in different countries. Orientations to power and organizational politics vary from country to country. Cross-cultural differences point to developing an understanding of those differences before using any political tactics.

↵ Summary

Power is a person's ability to get something done the way the person wants it done. It includes the ability to gather physical and human resources and put them to work to reach whatever goals the person wants to reach. Power has three facets: potential power, actual power, and potential for power.

Political behavior in organizations focuses on getting, developing, and using power to reach a desired result. Lateral relationships in organizations are the major places where power and political behavior play key roles.

Political strategies are broad plans for reaching some goal using political tactics. Political strategies usually focus on resource allocation decisions, career development, management succession, and the redesign of organizations.

Political tactics are political behaviors that become part of a political strategy. There are five major political tactics: (1) selectively emphasize decision criteria, (2) use outside experts, (3) control the agenda, (4) build coalitions, and (5) co-optation. Miscellaneous tactics include impression management, sanctions, and ingratiation.

A political diagnosis helps one understand where power is located in an organization and the type of political behavior that is likely to happen. A political diagnosis focuses on individuals, coalitions, and political networks.

People from different cultures hold different beliefs about the proper relationship between those who have power and those who do not. Some cultures see a directive and autocratic use of power as correct. Other cultures view a consultative or democratic approach as correct.

The ethical issues section took a distinctly normative position about political behavior in organizations. Using power and political behavior in an organization to serve only one's self-interest is unethical. Using political behavior and power in a manner that violates a person's rights is also unethical.

Key Terms

actual power 435
attribution of power 439
building power 438
coalition 445
deception 446
intimidation 447

lying 447
political diagnosis 444
political network 439
political strategy 443
political tactics 443

potential for power 435
potential power 435
power relationships 436
power styles 441
sources of power 438

Review and Discussion Questions

1. Review the discussion of power at the beginning of this chapter. Discuss with other students in your class their reactions to power. Be sure to examine whether they think power serves positive or negative functions for an organization.
2. Power has the three facets of actual power, potential power, and potential for power. Discuss the implications of the three facets for all employees of an organization.
3. Review the ways managers can build power in organizations. Discuss the experiences people in your class have had with managers trying to build a power base.
4. What were your reactions to the earlier descriptions of political strategy and tactics? Discuss your reactions with other students in your class.
5. Review the description of the ethical issues surrounding political behavior in organizations. Do you accept or reject the normative positions taken from the various ethical theories? How do other students in your class feel about those ethical issues?
6. Review the discussion of international differences in power and political behavior. Check with students from different countries about whether they see political behavior in their country's organizations in the ways described earlier.
7. Review the discussion of the difference between leadership and management in Chapter 12. Discuss the role power plays in being an effective leader or manager.
8. Discuss the role of power attribution on the effects of power within an organization. How does the attribution process affect an individual's power potential?
9. This chapter argued that organizational politics has its dark side. Discuss your experiences and those of others in your class with the dark side of organizational politics.

Case

A GAME OF CHICKEN BETWEEN THE TEAMSTERS AND UPS: A LEADERSHIP RACE AND THIN PROFITS HAVE BOTH SIDES DRIVING

This case is an example of how the internal political processes of one organization can affect the internal political processes of another. Consider the following questions in your analysis of this case:

1. What are the political pressures on Teamsters President William J. McCarthy? What do you predict McCarthy will do? Will he accept a United Parcel Service (UPS) offer or will he call a strike?
2. What are the political pressures on UPS? Do you think the company is willing to sit out a strike as a political tactic to get a settlement it can accept?

Source: A. Bernstein, "A Game of Chicken between the Teamsters and UPS," *Business Week*, August 6, 1990, p. 32. Reprinted from August 6, 1990 issue of Business Week by special permission, copyright © 1990 by The McGraw-Hill Companies.

United Parcel Service long has enjoyed tranquil relations with its unionized workers. Many of the 140,000 Teamsters at the company complain about its rigorous, minutely timed work schedules. But top Teamsters officials usually have settled contracts amicably by winning hefty wages—up to 30% more than those paid at nonunion competitor Federal Express Corp. The union has never called a national strike, not even in 1987, when members rejected the company's terms by 53%.

But there are signs of trouble. UPS officials fear a walkout when the Teamsters' contract expires on July 31. The reason: Teamsters President William J. McCarthy is under pressure to drive a harder bargain. A militant dissident named Ron Carey is running against him for the union's top office, and since Carey hails from the largest UPS local, this contract has become a political battleground.

DISCONTENT

What's more, the 71-year-old McCarthy has personally taken charge of the UPS bargaining—an unusual step. And while even dissidents from the Teamsters for a Democratic Union doubt that most UPS workers really want to strike, McCarthy has set the stage for a walkout. He capriciously has recommended turning down UPS's final offer, fanning rank-and-file discontent. Says one top Teamsters official who has participated in the bargaining: "If the contract is turned down by one vote, Billy is capable of calling a strike."

The two sides actually agreed long before the deadline to try for an early settlement. But profit margins at the $12.4 billion company slumped to 5.6% last year from 8% in 1987, largely because of a big push overseas and increased competition from Federal Express overnight deliveries. As a result, UPS tried to hold the line. Management said that its final offer would be a mere 11% increase over three years: a $1.50-an-hour wage hike plus a benefit increase of 75¢ an hour. On June 26, McCarthy called together several hundred local leaders and told them he would recommend against the deal.

Almost immediately, UPS changed its tune. Fearing customers would flee if they smelled a strike, UPS returned to the table and upped its offer by more than 25%. It added a cost-of-living adjustment worth about 18¢ an hour over three years, a further 30¢ an hour in benefits, and onetime bonus payments in the first year. . . .

➤ MONEY SQUEEZE

The proposal is weighted toward part-timers, who make up about 45% of the work force and earn much less than full-timers. Including the bonuses, part-time workers probably would come out well ahead of inflation, while full-

timers would wind up even. But, says a top Teamsters official, "that's not really a bad offer, given what other unionized workers are getting these days." Nevertheless, McCarthy still didn't buy it. Even though his final wage demand was only 15¢ an hour higher, he called a membership vote and recommended rejecting the United Parcel Service offer. McCarthy didn't respond to requests for an interview.

With ballots due by the end of July, both sides say the vote is a toss-up. UPS officials have launched a hard-sell campaign, sending letters to warn that a "No" vote will produce a strike. But many drivers feel UPS is trying to squeeze money out of the union to fund its expansion overseas. Says a 10-year veteran driver from Kansas City, Kan.: "Their spending across the water is going to come back to haunt them."

Indeed, the standoff already is making UPS customers nervous. UPS would shut down if its 62,000 Teamsters drivers walked out. The U.S. Postal Service says its volume jumped in mid-July as UPS customers began to book business elsewhere in anticipation of a walkout. Michael S. Coughlin, the Deputy Postmaster General, says the service plans to ration parcels it would receive in a UPS walkout. "We can't handle 10 million additional parcels overnight," he says.

With so much at stake, UPS may return to the table before the Teamsters walk out. Jim Kelly, the company's chief negotiator, insists that what's on the table is "our best and final offer." But he also says he will sit down again if the offer is rejected. The real wild card seems to be McCarthy. Given the politics at stake, there's no telling which way he'll go.

. . . .

➤ *Case*

THE SECRET WAR INSIDE GRACE & CO.: A SCHEME TO TOPPLE THE CEO HAS BROUGHT GRACE TO GRIEF

The following case shows the political intrigue that occurred at senior levels in an organization. Similar political intrigue though can happen at any other level as well. Here are some questions to have in mind as you read the case and consider your analysis:

1. Who are the key figures in this political drama? Were they inside or outside the organization?
2. Did any alliances or coalitions form? If they did, what purpose did they serve?
3. Do you believe the political behavior will be functional or dysfunctional for the company?

Source: E. Lesly, "The Secret War Inside Grace & Co.," *Business Week,* April 17, 1995, pp. 40–41. Reprinted from April 17, 1995 issue of Business Week by special permission, copyright © 1995 by The McGraw-Hill Companies.

4. J. Peter Grace died on April 19, 1995.[1] What effect do you expect his death to have on the future of W. R. Grace & Co.?

The roots of the current management crisis at W. R. Grace & Co. go back to late 1992. J. Peter Grace had fallen ill with cancer, and his longtime lieutenant J. P. Bolduc, former executives say, began pressing the board to name him chief executive. The board—loyal to Grace but knowing the octogenarian executive needed to be eased out—agreed. In 1993, Bolduc became the first person outside the Grace family to head the chemical and health services company. Peter Grace, who had been CEO for 47 years, remained chairman.

And Peter Grace remained bitter. For the next 2½ years, as former executives and other sources close to the company tell it, Grace simmered while Bolduc stripped him of the rich perquisites he and his family may have regarded as their birthright. Bolduc took away Grace's private Gulfstream IV jet, and he trimmed Grace's personal corporate staff from

[1]E. Lesly, "Fall from Grace," *Business Week,* May 29, 1995, p. 63.

about 10 to 4. Last November, he insisted that the company disclose in the proxy millions of dollars of perks and loans made to the Grace family. But Bolduc pushed too hard, and the backlash was severe. On Mar. 2, he resigned, citing differences with the board.

What really lay behind Bolduc's fall from grace? First came reports that Bolduc had been forced out after insisting on disclosure of the Graces' perks. Outraged institutional shareholders applied such pressure that Peter Grace and nine other board members agreed not to stand for reelection at the annual meeting on May 10. But many insiders remained disturbed by the way events unfolded at Grace. In a Mar. 23 memo to other board members obtained by BUSINESS WEEK, director Robert C. Macauley complained that "we are living a lie." And, finally, on Mar. 30, the company said publicly that Bolduc had been asked to resign after several employees accused him of sexual harassment—charges Bolduc denies.

The real story, as pieced together by BUSINESS WEEK, however, may be far more complicated. Former executives and others close to the company contend that Bolduc's downfall came after a small group of Grace executives and outside board members became convinced that Bolduc had to go.

A key figure in Bolduc's departure is Constantine L. Hampers, a Grace executive who runs its National Medical Care Inc. unit. It has been dogged by the Food & Drug Administration, which has cited it for selling nonsterile medical equipment several times since 1993—but it is also Grace's biggest profit generator. The company says the problems have been resolved.

As Bolduc moved to centralize Grace's operations and lower overhead, Hampers grew increasingly angry. Hampers says that last December he told the board he would resign when his employment contract expired in 1996. Hampers acknowledges that he wanted Bolduc gone, though he says his threat to leave was not a ploy to oust Bolduc.

Hampers is a complex character. A physician who started NMC in 1968, he sold it to W. R. Grace for approximately $238 million in 1984. Hampers in 1988 was charged in a 14-count indictment with smuggling the skins of endangered Mexican jaguars and ocelots into the U.S. He pleaded guilty to a reduced charge in 1990, according to the company's proxy. He remained very much in charge of NMC, and he didn't think much of Bolduc. Says Hampers: Bolduc "was terrible to work for. He never understood operating. I just did not want to work for him."

Hampers became allied with other Bolduc critics inside the company. A former executive says they include Peter Grace, his son Patrick Grace, and three outside board members—former New Hampshire Senator Gordon J. Humphrey, consultant Virginia A. Kamsky, and Macauley, founder of a Catholic charity. Humphrey and Kamsky did not respond to requests for interviews. Some directors on the 22-member board "felt [Bolduc] was pushing Grace too

far," says a former executive whose account was confirmed by several others. "Then Gus Hampers came out of the woodwork. They got together to support Gus Hampers as CEO and get rid of Bolduc."

At some point, a private investigator came into the picture. Hampers says he hired Kroll Associates Inc.—and is personally paying for its services. Hampers says he is convinced that there is a campaign afoot to prevent him from getting the top job at the company, and that is why he hired investigator Jules Kroll. "The purpose was to look into who was conducting a campaign of innuendo and rumors" against Hampers, Kroll says.

The former executive contends, however, that Hampers actually hired Kroll to investigate Bolduc. Hampers denies that. "I'm not looking for dirty laundry [on Bolduc]. I'm looking for a conspiracy against me," he says.

Meanwhile, Grace's board in February launched its own investigation of Bolduc, hiring retired federal Judge Harold Tyler. His original assignment was to give an opinion on the necessity of disclosing the Grace family perks in the proxy. Then, allegations that Bolduc had sexually harassed female employees came up, and Tyler was directed to investigate that issue as well, Macauley says.

◢ LATE-NIGHT DEAL

Damaging information on Bolduc was easily found, according to several former executives who paint Bolduc as a rough-hewn taskmaster, though smart and effective. "J. P. went around and harassed all the people all the time," says the former executive. According to a company statement, Tyler told the board on Feb. 28 that "grounds existed to find that Mr. Bolduc had sexually harassed certain employees." Tyler did not respond to BUSINESS WEEK'S request for an interview. Through an attorney, Bolduc denies ever acting inappropriately.

But the Tyler report sealed his fate, and Bolduc negotiated a $20 million severance package in a late-night meeting with director Roger Milliken. In his Mar. 23 letter to board members, Macauley questioned the propriety of the payment. "Neither I nor many of the other board members have the faintest idea as to the reasoning," it says.

After the upheaval, Hampers publicly offered himself as the best candidate to be the next CEO, and Macauley says the majority of Grace directors support him. But investors are violently opposed to the idea, since Hampers is regarded as too closely tied to the Grace family. The company "sanctioned a witch-hunt against their chief executive," says one institutional shareholder who has been agitating for corporate-governance reforms. "Our primary objective is that Gus Hampers not get the job." His hope: that the litigation-wary board will hire an outsider as CEO.

After all the *Sturm und Drang* at Grace, though, it may be tough to lure a good manager to take the job.

[1]D. Mechanic, "Sources of Power of Lower Participants in Complex Organizations," *Administrative Science Quarterly* 7 (1962): 349–64.

[2]R. M. Kanter, "Power Failures in Management Circuits," *Harvard Business Review* 57 (July-August 1979): 65–75; J. P. Kotter, "Power, Dependence, and Effective Management," *Harvard Business Review* 55 (Winter 1977): 125–36; N. H. Martin and J. H. Sims, "Thinking Ahead: Power Tactics," *Harvard Business Review* 34 (November–December 1956): 25, 26, 28, 30, 32, 34, 36, 40.

[3]G. R. Salancik and J. Pfeffer, "Who Gets Power and How They Hold Onto It: A Strategic Contingency Model of Power," *Organizational Dynamics* 5 (Winter 1977): 3–21.

[4]J. Pfeffer, *Managing with Power: Politics and Influence in Organizations* (Boston: Harvard Business School Press, 1992).

[5]R. M. Kanter, *Men and Women of the Corporation* (New York: Basic Books, 1977).

[6]D. H. Wrong, "Some Problems in Defining Social Power," *American Journal of Sociology* 73 (1968): 673–71.

[7]S. B. Bacharach and E. J. Lawler, *Power and Politics in Organizations* (San Francisco: Jossey-Bass, 1980), p. 25.

[8]Ibid., pp. 15–26.

[9]Wrong, "Some Problems in Defining Social Power."

[10]Bacharach and Lawler, *Power and Politics*, pp. 27–32; Kotter, "Power, Dependence, and Effective Management," pp. 217–18; J. Pfeffer, *Power in Organizations* (Marshfield, Mass.: Pitman, 1981), pp. 4–6. Appendix A has a more extended discussion of different types of authority in organizations.

[11]L. E. Griener and V. E. Schein, *Power and Organization Development* (Reading, Mass.: Addison-Wesley, 1988).

[12]J. J. Gabarro and J. P. Kotter, "Managing Your Boss," *Harvard Business Review* 58 (1980): 92–100.

[13]R. E. Kaplan, "Trade Routes: The Manager's Network of Relationships," *Organizational Dynamics* 2 (Spring 1984): 37-52.

[14]Griener and Schein, *Power and Organization Development*, pp. 35–37; Salancik and Pfeffer, "Who Gets Power," pp. 14–15.

[15]Kanter, *Men and Women*; Kanter, "Power Failures."

[16]R. May, *Power and Innocence* (New York: W. W. Norton, 1972).

[17]Developed from Kanter, *Men and Women*; Salancik and Pfeffer "Who Gets Power."

[18]Developed from Griener and Schein, *Power and Organization Development*; Kanter, *Men and Women*; Kotter, "Power, Dependence, and Effective Management"; Salancik and Pfeffer, "Who Gets Power."

[19]Griener and Schein, *Power and Organization Development*, p. 34.

[20]C. J. Fombrun, "Attributions of Power across a Social Network," *Human Relations* 36 (1983): 493–508.

[21]Griener and Schein, *Power and Organization Development*; D. L. Madison, R. W. Allen, L. W. Porter, P. A. Renwick, and B. T. Mayes, "Organizational Politics: An Exploration of Managers' Perceptions," *Human Relations* 33 (1980): 79–100; H. Mintzberg, *Power in and around Organizations* (Englewood Cliffs, N.J.: Prentice-Hall, 1983), p. 172; Pfeffer, *Power in Organizations*, p. 7; Salancik and Pfeffer, "Who Gets Power."

[22]B. T. Mayes and R. W. Allen, "Toward a Definition of Organizational Politics," *Academy of Management Journal* 2 (1977): 635–44.

[23]Griener and Schein, *Power and Organization Development*, pp. 20–22.

[24]Salancik and Pfeffer, "Who Gets Power."

[25]Pfeffer, *Power in Organizations*, p. 2.

[26]T. A. Judge and R. D. Bretz Jr., "Political Influence Behavior and Career Success," *Journal of Management* 20 (1994): 43–65.

[27]G. R. Ferris, T. A. Judge, K. M. Rowland, and D. E. Fitzgibbons, "Subordinate Influence and the Performance Evaluation Process: Test of a Model," *Organizational Behavior and Human Decision Processes* 58 (1994): 101–35.

[28]K. M. Bartol and D. C. Martin, "When Politics Pays: Factors Influencing Managerial Compensation Decisions," *Personnel Psychology* 43 (1990): 599–614.

[29]Developed from R. W. Allen, D. L. Madison, L. W. Porter, P. A. Renwick, and B. T. Mayes, "Organizational Politics: Tactics and Characteristics of Its Actors," *California Management Review* 22 (1979): 77–83; Bacharach and Lawler, *Power and Politics*, pp. 120–29; D. Kipnis, S. M. Schmidt, C. Swaffin-Smith, and I. Wilkinson, "Patterns of Managerial Influence: Shotgun Managers, Tacticians, and Bystanders," *Organizational Dynamics* 12 (Winter 1984): 58–67; Pfeffer, *Power in Organizations*, Ch. 5; L. W. Porter, R. W. Allen, and H. L. Angle, "The Politics of Upward Influence in Organizations," in L. L. Cummings and B. M. Staw, eds., *Research in Organizational Behavior,* vol. 3, (Greenwich, Conn.: JAI Press, 1981) pp. 181–216.

[30]Pfeffer, *Power in Organizations*, pp. 150–54.

[31]Developed from A. T. Cobb, "Political Diagnosis: Applications in Organizational Development," *Academy of Management Review* 11 (1986): 482–96; Griener and Schein, *Power and Organization Development*, Ch. 7.

[32]N. Machiavelli, *The Prince and the Discourses* (New York: Modern Library, 1940), pp. 64–65.

[33]Developed from Griener and Schein, *Power and Organization Development*, Ch. 5.

[34]R. J. Lewicki, "Lying and Deception: A Behavioral Model," in M. H. Bazerman and R. J. Lewicki, eds., *Negotiating in Organizations* (Beverly Hills, Calif.: Sage Publications, 1983), pp. 68–90.

[35]Developed from R. O'Day, "Intimidation Rituals: Reactions to Reform," *Journal of Applied Behavioral Science* 10 (1974): 373–86. O'Day summarizes the research observations of many people since the 1950s.

[36]Developed from G. Hofstede, *Culture's Consequences* (Beverly Hills, Calif.: Sage Publications, 1984).

[37]See Chapter 14 for descriptions of various decision-making approaches such as consultative.

[38]Hofstede, *Culture's Consequences*, p. 261.

[39]Developed from G. F. Cavanagh, D. J. Moberg, and M. Velasquez, "The Ethics of Organizational Politics," *Academy of Management Review* 6 (1981): 363–74; M. Velasquez, D. J. Moberg, and G. F. Cavanagh, "Organizational Statesmanship and Dirty Politics: Ethical Guidelines for the Organizational Politician," *Organizational Dynamics* 12 (Autumn 1983): 65–80.

[40]Velasquez, Moberg, and Cavanagh, "Organizational Statesmanship," p. 80.

16

Stress in Organizations

· *Floor traders at the Mexico City Stock Exchange the day after Mexico devalued the peso. The frenzied activity is a stressor for these traders.*

After reading this chapter, you should be able to . . .

- Understand the body's natural responses to stressful events.
- Discuss various models of the stress response.
- See that stress is not always bad for people.
- Describe the sources of stress in modern living.
- Understand burnout as a special case of stress.
- Distinguish between individual and organizational strategies of stress management.
- Recognize how working in another country presents its own sources of stress.
- Appreciate the ethical issues raised by stress in organizations.

Chapter Overview

Job Stress Crushing Workers Worldwide

If it's getting harder to go to work, there may be good reason. The U.N.'s International Labor Organization says job stress is increasing to the point of a worldwide epidemic affecting some of the most ordinary jobs.

Waitresses in Sweden, teachers in Japan, postal workers in America, bus drivers in Europe and assembly-line workers everywhere are all showing increasing signs of job stress, an ILO report said Monday.

Pressure to keep up with machines, no say about the job and low pay for long hours have left millions of workers burned out, accident-prone or sick, the report says. And frequently now workers must cope with the growing practice of supervisors electronically monitoring performance by computer.

"We now know that stress is a global phenomenon," said ILO job-stress expert Vittorio G. Di Martino in an interview. "We thought in the past that it his mostly white-collar workers in the industrialized countries. It's time to put that myth to rest."

The report, "Job Stress: The 20th Century Disease," points to growing evidence of problems around the world, including developing countries, where, it says, companies are doing little to help employees cope with the strain of modern industrialization.

The international organization estimates the cost of job stress in the United States alone at $200 billion annually from compensation claims, reduced productivity, absenteeism, added health-insurance costs and direct medical expenses for related diseases such as ulcers, high blood pressure and heart attacks.

Stress-related injury claims on the job have climbed from 5 percent of all occupational disease claims in 1980 to 15 percent a decade later, the report says.

Work pressure is so intense in Japan that Japanese have coined a phrase for death by overwork: Karoshi. A survey cited in the report says 40 percent of all Japanese workers fear they literally will work themselves to death.

Major factors in the stressful nature of a job are not only the demands of the work itself but the lack of control many workers have over their jobs, said Di Martino.

"Blue-collar workers face high demand but very little control and little autonomy in the way they can cope with the pressure," he said.

As the use of computers spreads throughout the world, workers in many countries are being subjected to new pressures.

In airline offices, government agencies, insurance companies, mail-order houses and telephone companies, workers find themselves constantly checked by employers who can monitor everything from how quickly they perform a task to the frequency and length of breaks.

"This may be reassuring for the employer but not for the worker," the report says.

· Japanese businessmen typically fall asleep in their hotel lobby following a stressful business day.

Source: D. Briscoe, "Job Stress Crushing Workers Worldwide," Associated Press, 1993. (As the story appeared in the Albuquerque Journal, March 23, 1993, pp. A1, A5). Reprinted with the permission of the Associated Press.

Stress is an unavoidable feature of modern living. As the Opening Episode shows, it is also a worldwide phenomenon that appears in many cultures. Stress in organizations has high personal, organizational, and social costs.

Table 16-1 shows some observations on stress taken from the preface of a book describing some early research on the human stress response. These observations suggest stress is an unavoidable part of living. Simple everyday events such as crossing a street or an annoying draft can be sources of stress. Exciting events such as college graduation or marriage can also cause stress. Stress is not always bad for us, especially if we prepare our physical and psychological systems to cope with it.

A person experiences stress when an event in her environment presents a constraint, an opportunity, or an excessive physical or psychological demand. The first condition for stress occurs when a constraint blocks a person's efforts to reach a desired goal. The individual can experience stress while trying to overcome the constraint. The second condition for stress is more positive. An opportunity from the person's environment may present her with a chance to get something she values.

The third condition for stress returns to the negative. Some event in the person's environment presents excessive physical or psychological demands. The individual experiences stress while trying to satisfy those demands.

The words *stressor* and *stressors* refer to objects or events in a person's physical and social environment that can induce a stress response. Stressors can be present in any of the environments through which a person passes during a daily round of activities. Those environments include the work environment, the nonwork environment, and the surrounding social, economic, and cultural environments.

Stressors must be present for a person to experience stress. The presence of a stressor does not mean all people will react with a stress response. A person's perceptual process decides whether the presence of a stressor leads to a stress response.[1] One person may perceive a stressor as a challenge to overcome, while another person perceives the same stressor as a threat.

Stress is not always bad for a person. Some amount of stress can energize and motivate the individual to behave in desired ways. Selye's observations on stress in Table 16-1 express this view of stress. As noted earlier, stress can also be a response to an opportunity. It can help move a person toward valued results offered by the opportunity. Stress is also useful in times of threat or danger. Upon perceiving a threat, a person's adrenaline flows and her heart rate increases, preparing her to face the threat.

People have different stress responses to events in their environment. Some people quickly feel high amounts of stress. Others feel less stress or no stress at all. Variations

---

◢ **TABLE 16-1**

Some Observations on Stress by Dr. Hans Selye

No one can live without experiencing some degree of stress all the time. You may think that only serious disease or intensive physical or mental injury can cause stress. This is false. Crossing a busy intersection, exposure to a draft, or even sheer joy are enough to activate the body's stress-mechanism to some extent. Stress is not even necessarily bad for you; it is also the spice of life, for any emotion, any activity causes stress. But, of course, your system must be prepared to take it. The same stress which makes one person sick can be an invigorating experience for another.

Source: H. Selye, *The Stress of Life* (New York: McGraw-Hill, 1976), p. vii.

in stress responses are related to a person's skills, abilities, and experiences with those events.[2]

Because it can have both positive and negative effects, it is important to understand stress, especially stress in organizations. For individuals, dysfunctional stress is associated with increased cardiac risk and the abuse of alcohol or other drugs. For organizations, dysfunctional stress is associated with high absenteeism rates, high turnover, reduced productivity, and poor decisions.[3] As described in the Opening Episode, job stress costs U.S. organizations an estimated $200 billion a year.[4]

Some stress is also necessary to energize people to work at the levels needed by many organizations. The optimal level of stress varies from person to person. All of us can benefit from understanding our stress responses and learning how to manage stress to reduce its negative effects. If you are a manager now, expect to be one in the future, or would like to better understand your manager, you need to know how people respond to stressors and how that response can vary.

Models of the Stress Response

This section describes several models of the stress response that give you background for the more complex stress analysis models described later. It first describes a general model of the stress response that shows how people respond to stressors in their environment. It then describes more complex models and closes with a description of an integrated model of the stress response.

THE GENERAL ADJUSTMENT SYNDROME: "FIGHT OR FLIGHT"

· *An encounter with this hissing cougar should induce the "fight or flight" response in almost anyone.*

An early model of stress response was the **General Adjustment Syndrome.** That model viewed the stress response as a natural human adaptation to a stressor in the individual's physical or psychological environment. Adaptation to the stressor happens when the person chooses behavior that lets her change the stressor (a fight response) or leave the presence of the stressor (a flight response). This general model of stress is well documented in medical research.[5]

The stress response unfolds in the three closely related stages shown in Figure 16-1. The first stage is **Alarm.** The body prepares to fight or adjust to the stressor by increasing heart rate, respiration, muscle tension, and blood sugar.

The second stage is **Resistance.** The body tries to return to a normal state by adapting to the stressor. The adaptation can be closing a window to prevent an irritating draft or quickly stepping back on the sidewalk to avoid an oncoming car. When a person repeatedly experiences a specific stressor or constantly resists a stressor, the body moves to the third stage of stress, **Exhaustion.**

During the Exhaustion stage, the body begins to wear down from exposure to the stressor. If a person experiences the stressor long enough and does not effectively manage the source of stress, then stress-related illnesses can appear (high blood

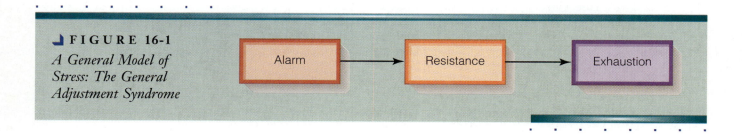

◢ FIGURE 16-1

A General Model of Stress: The General Adjustment Syndrome

Alarm → Resistance → Exhaustion

pressure, headaches, ulcers, insomnia, and the like). This stage of the stress response is when the damaging effects of stress occur, both for the individual and for the organization. Later sections of this chapter describe ways of building your body's resilience to stress, so the Exhaustion stage does not occur.

The stress response leads to either distress or eustress. **Distress** is the dysfunctional result of stress. A person suffers distress when she does not successfully adapt to the stressor or does not remove the stressor from her environment. **Eustress** is a positive result of stress; it occurs when the person has successfully adapted to the stressor or the degree of stress has not exceeded the person's ability to adapt to it. A later section focuses on managing stress to avoid distress and get eustress.

We all have experienced the General Adjustment Syndrome. Recall some event in the past that alarmed you—turning into a dark alley, perhaps, or riding a horse that suddenly reared, or hitting the brakes on a car because of an oncoming truck, or suddenly discovering a major error in a report due to your boss in one hour. In such circumstances, you should have experienced the reactions described by the syndrome: your heart rate increased; the palms of your hands became sweaty; and you started to breathe fast. These were all natural responses invoked by your central nervous system's reactions to a threat. Stress is a natural human response to a condition that is overwhelming, either for a moment or for a long time.

 ## THE TRANSACTIONAL MODEL OF STRESS

The General Adjustment Syndrome emphasizes physiological responses to stressors. A later model introduced important psychological processes and responses. The **Transactional Model of Stress** emphasizes perceptual processes, learned responses to stressors, and individual personality variations.[6] It has been widely researched since the early 1950s using methods ranging from field research to laboratory experiments. The model's basic functioning has held under such extensive scrutiny.[7]

This model views people's relationships to stressors in their environment as dynamic transactions between people and their situations. Stress happens when environmental conditions prevent a person from satisfying some need or reaching a valued goal. The response to a stressor partly depends on the person's earlier experiences with the same stressor or a similar situation. Differences among people also affect their perception of environmental demands and constraints. For some people, a specific stressor induces a stress response; for other people, it does not.

 ## THE PERSON-ENVIRONMENT FIT MODEL

The **Person-Environment Fit Model** says the goodness of fit between a person and her work environment affects the amount of stress the person experiences.[8] This model of stress is a widely accepted and heavily researched explanation of the stress response.[9] The model has strong intuitive appeal because it views the stress response as jointly determined by the characteristics of the person and of the person's environment. Although some evidence points to the ability of the model to explain variation in stress response,[10] some analysts have found serious methodological problems with past research.[11]

The degree of fit happens along two dimensions. The first is the extent to which a person's job satisfies the needs the person brings to the work setting. A job that does not let a person satisfy her needs is more stressful than one that satisfies those needs. The second dimension focuses on a person's skills and abilities and the skill and physical demands of a job. Congruence, or good fit, between the skill and physical demands of a job and the person's abilities and skill is less stressful than the opposite. You probably have felt stress from such incongruence when you started a class in college that took you beyond your level of skill and ability.

The model views people as interacting with their work environments. That interaction requires continual adjustments of self and work environment as elements of each change over time. A person develops more skills, abilities, and needs as her career unfolds. Organizations also change with time, especially when they introduce new work technologies or change their design.

Because a better fit decreases stress, a person can try to change some elements of both self and the work environment to improve that person-environment fit. A person can improve her skills and abilities through training. She can also negotiate with her supervisor to change the job content to include more decision authority. Such changes can alter job content to align it better with the person's present skills, abilities, and needs.

The changes just described alter qualities of the person or work environment. The person can also distort her perception of self, environment, or both. Such distortions can overstate or understate a person's abilities or the demands coming from the work environment. Perceptual distortion acts as a defense mechanism against the felt stress coming from a poor person-environment fit.

THE JOB DEMANDS–JOB DECISION LATITUDE MODEL

Another model also focuses on the stress effects of people's jobs. The **Job Demands–Job Decision Latitude Model** uses two constructs to explain the stress effects of jobs.[12] The first is job demands, which include the pace of work, amount of work, and conflicting work requirements. The job demands in the model are psychological demands, not physical demands. Although a job may have high physical demands that lead to fatigue, the psychological demands can lead to a stress response. A person may tire because of the pace of work but also can feel anxiety about keeping up the pace and getting work done on time.

The second construct in the model is job decision latitude. This construct describes a worker's decision authority and the different skills used on the job. Stress results when a job is high in demands and low in decision latitude. Here, the worker does not have the authority to behave in ways that let her successfully manage high job demands. An example is the job of a customer service representative of a public utility who handles customer complaints but has almost no authority to fix the target of the complaint. The least stress comes from jobs high in latitude and low in demand, such as the jobs of maintenance workers and foresters.

AN INTEGRATED MODEL OF STRESS

Figure 16-2 shows an **Integrated Model of Stress** that describes sources of stress and the conditions under which those sources evoke a stress response. It combines many pieces from the preceding models to form a detailed model of responses to stress.[13]

The Integrated Model of Stress has not received much direct research attention. This model was developed from different contributions in the stress research literature. Because it was not empirically tested as a whole model, it is useful mainly as a tool for analyzing and managing stress in your life. It also is a management tool for managing stress in organizations.

Some parts of the model have solid footing such as the role of perception in filtering stressors[14] and the role of some moderators. The evidence is strong for the moderating effects of Type A personalities, social support, diet, and exercise.[15] There is also research evidence of gender differences in distress reactions. In one study, women reported higher levels of distress than men, partly because of multiple work and nonwork roles. Men reported lower distress but incurred more severe physical illnesses than women.[16]

An Integrated Model of Stress

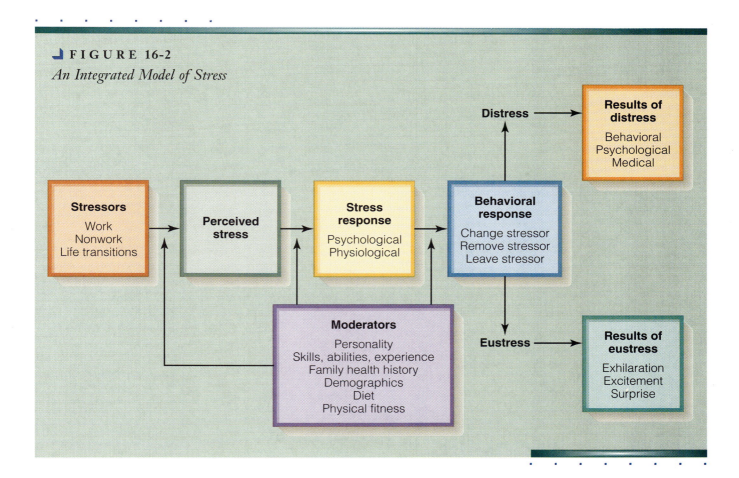

Overview

The antecedents of stress are shown as stressors. They occur in work experiences, nonwork experiences, and various life transitions. As people's perceptual processes filter the stressors, a stress response results. That response involves physiological and psychological changes that result in the person choosing behavior in response to the stressor. The behavioral choice affects whether the person feels distress or eustress. If the person perceives a stressor as excessively demanding or as a harmful constraint, distress will result. If the person perceives a stressor as a source of challenge or as an exciting opportunity, she will feel eustress. Both distress and eustress have the different results shown in the figure.

Stressors

Stressors occur within work organizations, in the nonwork part of people's lives, and during major life transitions. Table 16-2 lists possible stressors in each of these areas. Stress researchers have mentioned everything shown in the table. Many stressors have also been the objects of systematic research.[17]

Other chapters of this book describe several aspects of organizations listed as work-based stressors in Table 16-2. Those chapters should help you develop a deeper understanding of the attributes and processes of organizations that can induce a stress response. Where appropriate, the following discussion refers you to specific chapters for more information about a topic.

Stressors: The Sources of Stress in People's Lives

WORK STRESSORS

Job-Based	Role-Based	Career-Based	Physical Environment	Social Environment	Organizational Factors
Work overload	Role ambiguity	Job security	Lighting	Relationship with superior	Organizational culture
Work underload	Role overload	Obsolescence	Glare	Relationship with subordinates	Degree of responsibility
Heavy work	Role conflict	Underpromotion	Flicker	Relationship with coworkers	Organizational change
Time pressures	Responsibility	Overpromotion	Noise	Group pressures	Technological change
Deadlines		Career ceiling	Vibration	Conflict	Participation in decision making
Number of decisions		Retirement	Motion	Crowding	Political behavior
Hours of work			Heat		Communication quality
Work pace			Cold		Performance feedback
Travel requirements			Wind		Physical moves
			Dust		
			Fumes and vapors		
			Radiation		
			Increased atmospheric pressure		
			Decreased atmospheric pressure		
			Danger		
			Night shifts and loss of sleep		

NONWORK STRESSORS	LIFE TRANSITION STRESSORS
Economic uncertainty	Children moving out
Political uncertainty	Death of loved one
Family	Divorce
Financial	Having a child
Legal	Marriage
Dual career	Premarital breakup
Relocation	Unemployment
Nonwork organizations	

The list of stressors in Table 16-2 is formidable, possibly leaving you with the feeling that stressors are inescapable in modern life. Although stressors are a real part of living, not all people experience distress from them.

Work Stressors. The six classes of work-based stressors come from the job a person does and the environment within which the person does that job. Job-based stressors include work overload and work underload. The first is easy to see as a potential stressor. If a person has too much to do or is asked to do tasks beyond her skills and abilities, stress can result. Although work underload is less obvious as a stressor, the results of stress research say a person can experience stress when she has too little to do.[18]

A fast work pace, doing heavy work, tight deadlines, and making many decisions are also work stressors. A person's hours of work are a separate stressor. Both the number of hours and the timing of work hours can be stressors. The timing of work hours can interact with nonwork factors, such as the need for child care while the person works at night.

The travel requirements of a job can also add to perceived stress. Managers who are responsible for operations in several locations, for example, may frequently travel to those locations. Having to deal with busy airports, adjust to time changes, and cope with temporary living arrangements in hotels and motels can create stress. Stress from international traveling adds the dimensions of time changes, new languages, and different cultures.

Role-based stressors come from the roles people have in organizations.[19] A role includes a person's work duties, the performance expectations of other people, and the person's relationships with others in the organization. Role ambiguity becomes a stressor when a person does not have enough information about a work role. Such ambiguity happens when an individual does not know the goals of the work role, the expectations of those who interact with the work role, and the scope of her responsibilities. Role overload is similar to work overload. It refers to the total requirements of all roles a person must play in the organization, not just the immediate work role. For example, a manager reports to someone higher in the organization, is responsible for the work done in her group, and must carry out her immediate task assignments. All those requirements can add up to a set of demands that exceed the person's abilities, resulting in role overload. Role conflict emerges when a person gets conflicting task demands or is asked to do tasks beyond what she perceives as justified for the role.

The table lists responsibility as a separate role-based stressor because some research shows different stress effects from responsibility for people versus responsibility for objects, such as budgets, equipment, and physical plant. Distress—and its negative physical effects—is more likely among people with significant human responsibilities.[20]

The career-based stressor group includes potential stressors such as worries about job security, disappointment about how far one has gone in a career (career ceiling), promotions to jobs that do not use one's talents (underpromotion), and promotions that go beyond what a person can do (overpromotion). Obsolescence can become a potential stressor when an organization quickly changes its technologies. Skills a person used with one technology are no longer needed with the new technology. A pending retirement can be a major stressor for many people who have not prepared for the transition. People who have worked for many years suddenly find they must fill the hours that were once occupied by work.

The physical environment within which people work also presents potential stressors.[21] Most items listed are obvious and need little explanation. Stressors from atmospheric pressure refer to working at high altitudes or underwater. The former leads to decreased oxygen and potentially decreased work performance. The latter can be stressful because pressurized environments create unusual physiological demands from pressurized oxygen and nitrogen. The effects of glare, light flicker, and radiation are getting increasing attention because of the widespread use of video display terminals.

The social environment of work also has potential stressors. Social environment includes the immediate work group, relationships with people in other work groups, and participation in teams of people from different parts of an organization. The social environment extends beyond groups and includes the quality of a person's relationships with others in the organization.

Stressors can also come from group pressures to meet a certain performance standard or pressures to do your individual work in a group-defined way. Conflict among the members of a group and between groups in an organization can also be potential stressors. Crowding too many people into a physical area is a potential stressor because of its effects on privacy, noise level, or heat. Chapters 10 and 11 can help you understand the effects of groups and conflict and help you manage them as stressors.

Many natural aspects of work organizations can be potential stressors. An organizational culture that has high performance requirements or defines high levels of conflict as desirable can be a potential stressor for many people. Fast change in an organization's design or work processes can create high uncertainty. People who do not participate in decision making may feel little control over their work destiny. The quality of communication in the organization may be poor, leaving people wondering what is happening. High levels of political behavior can be significant stressors for many, especially those who do not understand how and why such behavior occurs in organizations.

Nonwork Stressors. The nonwork side of people's lives also has many potential sources of stress. Nonwork refers to all activities of a person happening outside the work organization that are not part of the person's work role or work responsibilities. Such activities include involvement in one's family, religious activities, leisure activities, and community organizations.

Potential stressors exist at a societal level, at a family level, and in nonwork organizations. At a societal level, potential stressors come from political and economic uncertainty. Nonwork stressors include political and economic uncertainty, though such uncertainties also affect work organizations. Political uncertainty includes major changes in the political climate or orientation of your society, internal or civil strife, and international disputes (wars). Economic uncertainty includes recessions and the accompanying employment uncertainty for many people.

Many aspects of family life can present multiple stressors to a person. Potential stressors are family instability, marital instability, financial uncertainty, and legal problems. When relocation is necessary because of a job transfer or regular rotation during military duty, the entire family is uprooted and moves to a new place. Children must adjust to new schools. Each spouse must adjust to life in a new and often strange place.

Involvement in nonwork organizations such as religious societies, community organizations, and political office carries its own set of stressors. For example, if you are active in the administration of several community organizations, the time demands of your activities can be a significant stressor.

The increasing number of dual-earner and dual-career couples adds still another dimension to nonwork stressors. Stressors from dual careers are especially complex because each partner faces potential stressors in the work setting. They then face potential stressors in their nonwork setting. Depending upon the couple's success in managing a dual-career relationship, those stressors can combine. The combinations of stressors can overwhelm the dual-career couple and explode into the negative results of distress.[22]

Life Transition Stressors.[23] The last section of Table 16-2 lists some common life transition stressors. Life transitions occur when a person leaves one role and begins another or experiences major changes in the definition of a role. The table lists the life transitions in alphabetical order because of wide variation in the way people experience them. As people go through the life cycle, they may marry, have children, and then watch the children leave the family home. They may marry late in life, or not at all, or remarry after divorce or the death of a spouse. The changes experienced in these transitions can induce distress for many people.

Life transitions do not always produce distress. Ending a bad marriage is different from ending a good marriage. A person might perceive the death of a chronic alcoholic as relief from a burden. Leaving a job and work organization that a person hated can also remove a significant stressor.

Both retirement and promotion are work stressors with transition qualities. At retirement, for example, a person moves from an active role in a work organization to one or more roles in another part of her life.[24] Promotion moves a person out of one role to another at a higher level in an organization.

Perceived Stress

Human perception plays an important role in whether a stressor will lead to a distress or eustress response. Although perception is not always recognized as part of the stress response, both Selye's observations on stress shown in Table 16-1 and the Transactional Model of Stress implied a role for **perceived stress** in the model.

A stressor can be an exciting opportunity to one person and a threat to another. Some people see the Iditarod Trail Race from Anchorage to Nome, Alaska, with a sled and dog team as a challenge to eagerly pursue while others view it as an unthinkable source of harm. The music of Metallica is distressful noise to many parents, but a source of exhilaration to their teenagers. An upcoming trip to Venice excites some and causes others to tremble. The perceptual process is at work when people encounter stressors. Selective perception and attribution processes both affect how people perceive stressors.

Stress Response

The **stress response** has both physiological and psychological aspects. These psychophysiological responses lead to behavior focused on the stressor.[25]

The physiological response to perceived stress is an integrated set of bodily functions all directed at preparing the body to respond to the stressor. The bodily changes ready a person to either fight the stressor or run from it. Although the response involves a complex network of neurophysiological reactions, the immediate reaction to perceived stress happens fast.

The sympathetic nervous system and the endocrine system of the body play an integrated role in the stress response. Seconds after perceiving a stressor, messages stream from the cortex to the hypothalamus to the pituitary gland. The endocrine system increases the levels of several hormones in the bloodstream, including ACTH (adrenocorticotrophic hormone), adrenaline, and noradrenaline. These hormones increase the levels of fatty acids and glucose in the bloodstream. Heart rate and blood pressure rise, as the heart pumps more blood to the brain and muscles. Breathing rate increases as the sympathetic nervous system and the endocrine system ready the body to face the stressor.

The general psychological response includes apprehension and increased alertness. An individual's specific psychological response can be either positive or negative. A positive response includes feelings of exhilaration, excitement, challenge, and opportunity. A negative response includes feelings of anxiety, fear, and threat. Although the physiological part of the stress response is about the same for all of us, people vary in their psychological response to perceived stress. It is here that you can begin to see how stress can have negative effects.

Behavioral Response

Now that the person is ready to act, she must choose the right **behaviorial response** for the stressor. Stressful situations often do not leave much time for decision. For example, a pilot faced with an in-flight emergency often has little time to decide what to do. The stress response readies the pilot to respond fast; training and experience let the pilot make the right choices. Even in less dramatic situations, an individual must still act. We all face the dilemma of choosing the right behavior for a specific stressor. The wrong choice can lead to distress; the right choice can lead to eustress.

Figure 16-3 shows the groups of stressors described earlier. They are arranged to show the likely relationships among stressors with arrows indicating the probable direction of effects or interactions among the groups.[26] As the figure implies, it is unwise to treat one group of stressors as isolated from the others. The following discussion uses Figure 16-3 to give you some broad clues about how to accurately identify the stressor causing your stress response and help you choose an appropriate behavioral response.

The work stressors show organization factors surrounding the others because such basic, and often major, aspects of organizations can profoundly affect other parts of organizational life. Changes in organizational design, the introduction of new technologies, or the relocation of entire operations can affect people's jobs, roles, social environment, and careers.

FIGURE 16-3
Relationships among Stressors

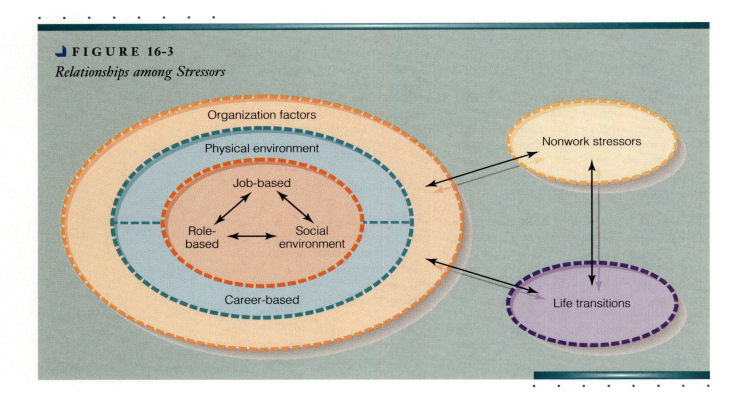

The figure shows the physical environment and career factors as sources of stress surrounding the job, role, and social factors. The main effects of the environment and career factors fall on roles, jobs, and the social environment. For example, no heat in a building in Fargo, North Dakota, during January will negatively affect job performance, meeting role expectations, and social interaction at work! An important promotion that enhances a person's career can positively affect the same factors.

As the two-headed arrows imply, job, role, and social environment stressors all interact and usually do not operate separately from each other. Excessive role demands can easily lead to feelings of work overload, as demands from many people elsewhere in the organization pummel an employee. Group-based social pressures for specific performance levels interact with job and role. Group norms of low performance press an individual to reduce performance to remain an accepted member of the group. Compliance with the norm, however, does not let the person meet the role expectations held by her supervisor. The individual is torn by having to decide which of these conflicting demands she should satisfy.

Nonwork stressors and life transitions each affect the other. Life stages, such as becoming a parent or having the children leave the family home, insert sources of stress into the family. A single person with long ties to a certain place can feel stress from an unexpected job transfer. How the person responds to such stressors decides whether the stressor is adequately removed so that the stress effects away from work do not affect behavior and performance at work. The two-headed arrows connecting the work stressors to the nonwork and life transition stressors indicates the often-noted spillover effects of work experiences on experiences away from work.[27] In short, stress experienced at work can carry over to one's nonwork life and add to the stressors one experiences in that sphere.

Results of Distress

The **results of a distress response** happen when a person does not choose the right behavior to manage the stress response, is predisposed to distress, or has not built a resilience to common stressors. The results of distress are the effects usually associated with the word *stress*.

Table 16-3 shows the behavioral, psychological, and medical results of distress. The behavioral results include high levels of smoking, drug use, appetite disorders, proneness to accidents, and violence. Behavioral distress effects can reach into one's nonwork life affecting family and marital relations, spouse and child abuse, sleep patterns, and sexual functioning. The psychological results of stress include severe anxiety, alienation, depression, and psychosomatic effects such as speech difficulties. You may have experienced the latter when starting a class presentation and discovering you had no voice. After a while, the anxiety passed and your voice returned. You temporarily experienced an unfortunate psychological result of distress.

Stress researchers have linked heart disease, stroke, back aches, ulcers, and headaches to distress. Some of these medical results are tied to the behavioral reactions described earlier. For example, increases in smoking and drug use can induce heart problems or a stroke. The natural stress response includes a rise in serum cholesterol and blood pressure. Each of these natural effects, if sustained over a long time, can lead to either a stroke or a heart attack.

Stressful life events probably do not lead directly to physical disorders such as stroke and heart disease. Stressors likely intertwine in complex and not yet well-understood ways with other parts of a person's lifestyle.[28] More varied research designs using multiple measurement methods will help clarify our understanding of stress in organizations and other parts of people's lives.[29]

Results of Eustress

Eustress is the exhilaration of winning a competition, the excitement of an unexpected high grade in a course, the birth of a child, a windfall of money, the surprise of receiving an unexpected gift. The list of eustress events could go on and on. Because perceived stress plays an important role in the behavioral response to a stressor, one person's source of eustress can be another person's source of distress. Consider the different reactions of people to a promotion at work. Some people grow and develop from the promotion (eustress). Others incur severe medical and psychological disorders such as hypertension and chronic depression (distress).[30]

Among the many things people can do to help reduce the effects of distress or increase the chance of **eustress results** is to develop an understanding of personal characteristics that increase the likelihood of distress effects. The next section

◢ **TABLE 16-3**

The Behavioral, Psychological, and Medical Results of Distress

BEHAVIORAL RESULTS	PSYCHOLOGICAL RESULTS	MEDICAL RESULTS
Increased smoking	Anxiety	Heart disease
Increased drug and alcohol use	Alienation	Stroke
Appetite disorders	Depression	Backaches
Proneness to accidents	Psychosomatic effects such as speech difficulties	Ulcers
Proneness to violence		Headaches
Disturbed family and marital relations		
Spouse and child abuse		
Disturbed sleep patterns		
Sexual dysfunctioning		

describes those characteristics. Another possibility is to increase one's resilience to stress, which is discussed in a later section.

Moderators of Stress

Stress researchers have emphasized the role of several personal characteristics as **moderators** of perceptions and behavioral responses to stressors. Such moderators can change the relationships shown in Figure 16-2. For example, a physically fit person may have a less severe response to perceived stress than a person who is not physically fit. The moderators include personality characteristics; skills, abilities, and experience; family health history; demographics such as gender, ethnicity, and age; diet; and physical fitness.[31]

Personality. Stress researchers have associated two personality types with differences in perceptions of stressors and responses to them. Hardy personalities can adapt positively to stressors; Type A personalities tend to adapt negatively to stressors.

Personality hardiness is a personality type described by three dimensions: commitment versus alienation, control versus powerlessness, and challenge versus threat.[32] People with hardy personalities approach life's events with a strong commitment to reaching their goals, believe they have at least some control over their life's direction, and see life's events as a source of challenge and personal growth. Research evidence points to commitment and control as consistently related to positive stress responses.[33]

People with low and high personality hardiness respond to stressors in distinctly different ways. Figure 16-4a shows the response of a low hardiness personality. Part (b) of the figure shows the response of a high hardiness personality.

Low hardiness personalities assess stressors pessimistically. They view stressful life events as unchangeable disruptions to the normal course of their behavior. Their reaction follows from their alienation from life's events, a feeling of having little control over events, and a view of stressors as a threat. Low hardiness personalities try to escape from stressors, not change them.

High hardiness personalities assess stressors optimistically. They view stressful life events as challenges to overcome. The reaction of high hardiness personality stems from a commitment to life goals, a feeling of having control over events, and a view of stressors as a source of challenge. High hardiness personalities take decisive action to change the stressors, not escape from them.

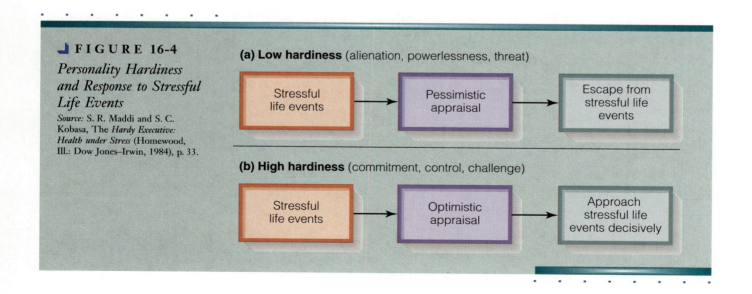

FIGURE 16-4

Personality Hardiness and Response to Stressful Life Events

Source: S. R. Maddi and S. C. Kobasa, The *Hardy Executive: Health under Stress* (Homewood, Ill.: Dow Jones–Irwin, 1984), p. 33.

(a) Low hardiness (alienation, powerlessness, threat)

Stressful life events → Pessimistic appraisal → Escape from stressful life events

(b) High hardiness (commitment, control, challenge)

Stressful life events → Optimistic appraisal → Approach stressful life events decisively

Here is an example from your role as a college student. Students typically face many stressors toward the end of a semester or quarter. Library research papers are due as finals' week approaches. Low hardiness personalities will likely see these events as threatening and try to avoid them for as long as possible. These students' procrastination makes the stressors worse because they meet their deadlines by working long, weary hours. High hardiness personalities will likely see the same events as a challenge and try to organize their schedules to meet deadlines in a timely way. The response of the high hardiness personality can help reduce the amount of distress she experiences.

The second personality type studied by stress researchers is the Type A described earlier in Chapter 4. A Type A personality is aggressive, can quickly become hostile, focuses excessively on achievement, and has a keen sense of time urgency. Type A personalities like to move fast and often do more than one activity concurrently. Some aspects of the Type A personality predict coronary heart disease, and other aspects predict high performance. Hostility is strongly associated with coronary heart disease.[34] Striving for achievement has strong associations with performance.[35]

The opposite personality type is the Type B personality. Such people feel less time urgency, often stop to ponder their achievements, and reflect on where they are headed. They have high self-esteem, a characteristic that distinguishes them from Type A personalities. They are even tempered and are not bothered by everyday events.

The descriptions of Type A and B personalities contain clues to their effects on perceptions and responses to stress. A Type A's hurried approach to life can lead to a perception of stressors as constraints and not opportunities. Type A personalities want accomplishments and can readily perceive blockages even when no constraints are present. A Type B's more even-tempered approach lets the person see more opportunities than constraints. Type A personalities can also increase the demands made on them.[36] In short, the Type A personality is more likely to feel distress than a Type B personality. Some research results also suggest that Type A personalities with low hardiness have the greatest risk of suffering the illness effects of distress.[37]

Skills, abilities, and experience. A person experienced with similar stressors will have less distress than a person for whom a stressor is new. Experience reduces uncertainty and ambiguity, letting the person accurately perceive the stressor and choose the right response. Training to develop one's skills and abilities has a similar effect.

Family health history. Your family's health history often can tell you whether you are predisposed to the negative health effects of distress. Medical histories of hypertension, high serum cholesterol levels, and ulcers point to a chance of experiencing the ill effects of stress. Such histories only suggest a predisposition. Proper stress management, as described in a later section, can offset the negative results of distress.

Demographics. Some demographic characteristics point to a greater likelihood of experiencing certain stressors or experiencing distress. Working people with family responsibilities often feel many work and nonwork stressors simultaneously. They often feel pressures to get ahead in a career while also managing child rearing, social relationships, and a home.

One's ethnic background also suggests unique stressors. Racial prejudice at work and away from work is an obvious stressor. Ethnic minorities also feel pressures for career advancement so they can be role models for others with a similar ethnic background.

Biological age also changes a person's perception of stress and response to a stressor. With age comes experience, which can reduce the experience of distress as described earlier. The aging process also changes the body's physical response to a stressor. An older person, for example, is more likely to have increased blood pressure from a stressor than a younger person.

Diet. The saturated fat and sodium content of one's diet can affect the long-term results of stress. Excessive sodium intake contributes to high blood pressure. Excessive saturated fat adds to serum cholesterol levels. Recall from an earlier section that increases in blood pressure and serum cholesterol are both natural stress responses. Excesses in one's diet worsen these conditions, however, possibly leading to long-term negative results for the person.

Physical fitness. One way of managing stress is through physical fitness. An aerobic exercise program helps reduce serum cholesterol and increases one's resilience to stressors. A physically fit person is less likely to feel the harmful effects of distress than a person who is less fit.[38]

TABLE 16-4
Sources of Stress

LIFE EVENT	POINTS
Death of a spouse	99
Divorce	91
Marriage	85
Death of close family member	84
Fired at work	83
Pregnancy	78
Marital separation	78
Jail term	72
Personal injury or illness	68
Death of close friend	68
Retirement	68
Change of financial state	61
Spouse begins or stops work	58
Marital reconciliation	57
Christmas	56
Change in health of family member	56
Foreclosure of mortgage or loan	55
Sex difficulties	53
Addition of new family member	51
Change to different line of work	51
Business readjustment	50
Mortgage over $10,000 [Present day amount of $50,000]	48
Change in residence	47
Change in number of arguments with spouse	46
Change in responsibilities at work	46
Begin or end school	45
Trouble with boss	45
Revision of personal habits	44
Trouble with in-laws	43
Vacation	43
Change in living conditions	42
Son or daughter leaving home	41
Outstanding personal achievement	38
Change in work hours or conditions	36
Change in school	36
Minor violations of law	30
Change in eating habits	29
Mortgage or loan less than $10,000 [Present day amount of $50,000]	27
Change in sleeping habits	27
Change in recreation	26
Change in church activities	26
Change in number of family get-togethers	15

Source: Adapted from "The 1990's Stress Scale," *Albuquerque Journal,* December 16, 1991, p. B1. Reprinted by permission: Knight-Ridder Tribune Media Services.

*T*his exercise will help you identify some sources of stress you have experienced or may encounter in the future. Table 16-4 lists many events that could happen to you. Record the points for each event you experienced in the past year on a separate piece of paper. Add the events to get a total. Above 300 points is the danger level.

Burnout

Burnout is a chronic state of emotional exhaustion stemming from an unrelenting series of on-the-job pressures with few moments of positive experience. It is a special case of distress and an often-used popular term to refer to stress. Burnout is work-related distress usually experienced by people in jobs with high levels of interpersonal interaction or in jobs that require helping other people.[39] Individuals who experience burnout usually have high emotional investment in their work, derive a major part of their self-esteem from their work, and have few interests away from work. They also have high performance standards for themselves, especially for what they can do to help someone who needs aid.[40]

Burnout follows the process shown in Figure 16-5. Repeated exposure to work stressors results in emotional exhaustion. For example, nurses who repeatedly tend the same terminally ill patients can become emotionally exhausted. Depersonalization of relationships follows emotional exhaustion as a coping response. This response views the people served as objects instead of humans, a way of building an impersonal barrier to the stressor. The final stage of the burnout process is reduced personal accomplishment. People at this stage lose interest in their work, experience decreased efficiency, and have little desire to take the initiative.

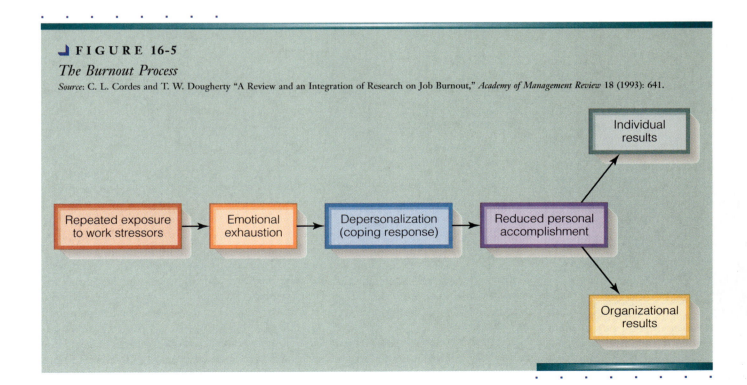

◢ FIGURE 16-5

The Burnout Process

Source: C. L. Cordes and T. W. Dougherty "A Review and an Integration of Research on Job Burnout," *Academy of Management Review* 18 (1993): 641.

The burnout process produces many individual and organizational results. Individual results include headaches, mood swings, cynicism, increased use of drugs and alcohol, questioning of self, and family conflicts. Organizational results include inflexibility in dealing with organizational clients, negative work attitudes, increased absenteeism, and decreased work efficiency.

Occupations that experience high levels of burnout include nurses, customer service representatives, and social workers. Research physicists, forest rangers, and laboratory technicians experience low burnout. Intermediate levels of burnout result from jobs such as librarian, receptionist, and sales representative.[41]

The research evidence about the effects of burnout is especially compelling. Chronic exposure to stressors in the workplace is associated with serious ill effects.[42] One researcher summarized burnout as follows: "Burnout seems more widespread, of longer duration, and has more somber consequences than many observers believe."[43]

⅃ Stress Management

Stress management has a goal of maintaining stress at an optimal level for both the individual and the organization. Because some stressors are unavoidable and some amount of stress is not bad for many people, this section does not say that all stress should be reduced.[44]

Individual and organizational strategies of stress management fall into three groups. Stress reduction strategies aim to decrease the number of stressors affecting a person. Stress resilience strategies try to increase a person's ability to endure stressors and not feel dysfunctional results. Stress recuperation strategies aim to help the person bounce back from stress with methods that are not physically harmful.

The stress management strategies described in this section have been widely discussed in the popular press and by medical practitioners and stress researchers. Little directly evaluative research has rigorously measured the effects of these strategies.[45] A 1991 report of an exhaustive review of published work also concluded that little can be said about the effectiveness of many training strategies.[46] The effectiveness of diet, aerobic exercise, and physical fitness, though, are better understood. Existing empirical research points to their recuperative and resilience effects.[47]

⅃ INDIVIDUAL STRATEGIES

The strategies for **individual stress management** show how to gain control over stress in a person's life. This section presents the strategies but does not give a step-by-step description of each strategy. The associated citations have those details.

Stress Reduction

Stress reduction strategies decrease the amount of stress a person experiences. Some strategies are obvious, old, and deceptively simple. The most obvious is to avoid events and circumstances that cause distress. If you do not enjoy crowds, then do your holiday shopping when crowds are few. If you do not enjoy driving in heavy traffic and congestion, avoid such traffic.

A key element in stress avoidance is planning. Knowing what to expect, and knowing potential stressors, lets a person prepare for them. If the stressors are unavoidable, planning helps the person prepare for them. You often cannot avoid traffic congestion, but you can plan and choose routes that give you the least amount of stress.

Entering a new organization and new job often is a stressful experience. Learning about the organization and job before accepting a position prepares a person for new

· *Making telephone calls early in a workday is a recommended method of managing stress.*

stressors. A company's annual reports and business press accounts of a company's activities can give you some clues.

A less obvious source of stress that people can avoid are chemicals and food. Some chemicals are in people's environments and hard to avoid. Others come from the chemicals and foods people eat. Caffeine, nicotine, alcohol, and other drugs are stressors, especially in excess.[48] Omitting such substances from one's diet or using them in moderation can significantly reduce those stressors.

This chapter earlier emphasized the role of perception in deciding whether stressors were present. A person can use perceptual processes to reduce stress. Isolating oneself affectively (psychological withdrawal) from potential stressors can reduce their harmful effects. People in naturally stressful occupations, such as emergency room personnel, develop the ability to block perceptually the plethora of stressors in their work. An alternative is to selectively ignore some stressors by looking for positive elements in the situation. For example, if you find traffic congestion stressful, you can think of it as an opportunity to watch humanity in action.[49] Lastly, some stressors simply are an inevitable part of certain experiences. Certified public accountants (CPAs) know the closing days before income tax deadlines are long, hard, and tiring. The experienced CPA recognizes the inevitable and does not try to resist those stressors.

Time management skills help many people manage the multiple demands that are often placed upon them in both work and nonwork settings.[50] Such skills include setting priorities between multiple tasks and developing a schedule for doing important tasks. Time management skills include reducing interruptions while working, limiting the length of telephone calls, and reducing the number and length of meetings.

Role overload avoidance is still another strategy for individual stress reduction. This strategy features dropping tasks, avoiding excessive obligations, and simply knowing when to say no. Many managers can delegate less important but time-consuming tasks to their subordinates. Decentralizing decision making not only reduces the role load of the manager, it can improve the design of the subordinate's job. Saying no and negotiating reasonable deadlines let you avoid excessive obligations and their associated stressors.

Social support while doing stressful tasks and building social support networks can help many people reduce stress.[51] Such social support can develop in both work and nonwork situations. Sources of social support include supervisors, coworkers, family members, and professional organizations. These sources can give people any of the four forms of social support: emotional, appraisal, informational, and instrumental.

Emotional support includes caring and empathic listening to a person who feels troubled. Appraisal support gives information to a person about her performance. This form of social support is especially useful to a new employee who is trying to manage the stressors of a new job. Informational support involves giving a person information that lets her more easily handle task demands. Instrumental support includes pitching in to help a coworker having trouble completing a task. This form of support often appears in cohesive groups faced with demanding work.

All of these are ways of reducing stressors and their negative effects. The stressors of a situation may so overwhelm a person that the only way out is leaving the situation. Leaving can take a variety of forms ranging from a job transfer to complete withdrawal from the organization.

Stress Resilience

Stress resilience strategies help a person develop physical and psychological stamina against potentially harmful stressors. The most widely recommended stress resilience strategies feature physical exercise, diet, and weight control.

The two major types of exercise are aerobic and anaerobic. Aerobic exercise features physical activity lasting 20 to 30 minutes that raises the heart rate, respiration, and the metabolic rate. Walking, swimming, cycling, jogging, and mountain climbing are aerobic activities. Vigorous racket games, cross-country skiing, and aerobic dancing are other forms of aerobic exercise. Such exercising can be done both inside and outside. For example, a skiing machine or a stationary bicycle can be used indoors. Stress resilience comes from heart and lung conditioning, decreased blood pressure, and decreased serum cholesterol.[52]

Anaerobic exercise includes recreational sports such as bowling and nonstrenuous activities such as gardening and light weight lifting. All such activities offer diversions from earlier stressful events. Weight lifting also helps muscle tone and general conditioning. It can add to one's self-image, possibly helping a person face potential stressors with confidence.

A proper diet, combined with a regular exercise program, helps a person's stress resilience by increasing her physical and psychological stamina.[53] A balanced diet low in sodium and saturated fats helps keep blood pressure and serum cholesterol within acceptable bounds. The combination of diet and exercise lets a person manage her weight. Diet, exercise, and weight control help a person face stressors from any source more easily. A physician should be consulted before making a major change in one's present diet or exercise program.

Stress Recuperation

Several strategies help people recover from their exposure to stressors. These methods of **stress recuperation** help people rejuvenate physically and psychologically, especially after severe distress. The methods all feature some type of activity ranging from vigorous exercise to positive thinking.

The previous section described aerobic exercise as a way to build resilience to stress. It is also a good way to recuperate from distress. Some evidence shows vigorous exercise causes hormonal secretions that lead to relaxed feelings.[54] The recuperative effects of exercise are a form of natural biochemical relaxation.

Relaxation training is a major element of recuperative strategies. As the name implies, relaxation training teaches people how to relax. The methods include ancient forms of meditation found in Eastern religions and modern secular methods of relaxation such as Clinically Standardized Meditation. Some techniques emphasize physical relaxation; others emphasize mental relaxation. Likewise, some techniques can be self-taught while others require a trained instructor. All relaxation techniques induce the same physiological mechanism called the relaxation response.[55] The relaxation response is a natural physical process that includes decreased respiratory, heart, and metabolic rates.

All relaxation methods have several elements in common. A person must be in a comfortable position in a quiet environment to elicit the response. The lack of distractions lets the person focus on something other than an external object. The object of focus can be a sound (the *mantra* of classical mediation) or a mental object. Through training, the person learns to develop a passive attitude during relaxation by excluding external stimuli and worrisome thoughts. When regularly practiced, the result is the relaxation response described earlier.

Table 16-5 lists the major forms of relaxation training. The table briefly describes each method and indicates whether it can be self-taught or requires an instructor. The citations in the table have more detailed descriptions of the methods.

Meditation is another way to reach a relaxed state.[56] It is treated separately from relaxation training because of its mystical connotations. Most people have experienced meditation; it is simply focused awareness. That focus can be anything, including objects, sounds, and images. Meditation techniques teach people how to focus their awareness in healthy ways. Such focused awareness leads to profound relaxation and recuperation from distress.

Classical meditation techniques derive from Eastern religions with roots in the sixth century. A well-known method in the West is Transcendental Meditation, introduced by Maharishi Mahesh Yogi in the 1950s. Other religious-based methods

TABLE 16-5

Major Forms of Relaxation Training

RELAXATION METHOD	BRIEF DESCRIPTION	SELF-TAUGHT OR REQUIRES INSTRUCTOR	SOURCE FOR DETAILED DESCRIPTION
Relaxation response	An adaptive antistress bodily response that decreases heart rate, muscle tension, breathing rate, and metabolic rate. Has the elements common to relaxation methods described in the body of the text.	Self-taught	H. Benson and M. Z. Klipper, *The Relaxation Response* (New York: William Morrow, 1976).
Progressive relaxation	A method of physical relaxation focused on the major muscle groups. People learn to systematically tense and relax muscle groups sequentially. Requires a quiet place, low lighting, and comfortable position.	Requires instructor	E. A. Charlesworth and R. G. Nathan, *Stress Management: A Comprehensive Guide to Wellness* (New York: Ballantine Books, 1985), Chapter 5.
Biofeedback	Gives visual or auditory feedback about muscle tension, heart rate, or blood pressure. People learn to use that information to relax muscles, reduce heart rate, etc.	Requires instructor	J. C. Quick and J. D. Quick, *Organizational Stress and Preventive Management* (New York: McGraw-Hill, 1984), pp. 245–47.
Momentary relaxation	Builds upon training in the other relaxation methods. Features brief relaxation from quiet, closed eyes, and deep breathing. Can be done almost anywhere. Requires only a few minutes of time.	Self-taught	K. Albecht, *Stress and the Manager: Making It Work for You* (New York: Touchstone Books, 1986).

of meditation derive from Zen Buddhism, Chinese Taoism, and Japanese Shintoism. All these meditation techniques require training and usually are not self-taught.

Clinically Standardized Meditation is a relaxation and distress recuperation method that is more intense than the relaxation methods.[57] It was developed as an alternative to the Eastern Meditation methods and designed to be more acceptable to Westerners. It requires time to learn, but can be self-taught with the help of videotapes and manuals. Training is also available from qualified instructors.

Releasing one's emotions in any of several safe ways can help a person rebound from distress. Some of these emotional releases do not always receive social approval. Many are almost ancient ways of releasing one's feelings from distress.

Many people release their feelings by talking to others, writing out their feelings, or acting out their feelings. Talking to others includes people at work and away from work. The people one talks to at work may be those who are stressors. The discussions can focus on a person's feelings about the stressor and its effects on the person.

Writing about one's feelings in letters and memoranda can help reduce tension from the stressors and focus on remedies. Writing while the emotion is fresh vents the emotion. Returning to the writing a few days later lets the person assess her views while in a calmer state. The writing may simply function as an emotional release, or it can go forward with recommendations for reducing the distress.

Acting out one's emotions and feelings can also release the tension of distress. A person can act out her feelings privately, including shouting loudly, crying, aggressively throwing rocks in a lake, or vigorously punching a speed bag. There are two simple guidelines for acting out emotion: (1) it should do no harm to anyone and (2) it must work for the person.

Other forms of stress recuperation feature rest, diversion, and a balanced work-nonwork lifestyle. Getting adequate rest prepares a person for inevitable stressors. Three-day weekends and extended vacations give a person a chance to rest, recover, and immerse in other activities. Balancing one's work and nonwork life lets a person recover through involvement in outside work interests. It is also possible for a person to find eustress in nonwork activities that can compensate for the distress of work activities. For example, the quiet of stamp collecting may compensate for the distress of demanding work. Competition in a marathon may compensate for the distress from excessively routine work.[58]

Psychotherapy, medical therapy, and counseling are forms of stress recuperation that are often needed when a person has advanced distress effects. Some therapy and counseling programs focus on behavior change such as altering Type A behaviors, drug abuse, and cigarette smoking. Medical therapy includes prescription drugs and surgery. A physician can prescribe drugs to fight anxiety, depression, and hypertension. Surgery can repair severe cardiovascular damage that was distress induced.

CASE   *Managing Stress to Fight Burnout*

*T*he following is a press account of some observations on individual stress management. Consider the following questions while reading the case:

1. What are some elements of the stress management program recommended by the consultant?
2. What obstacles do you see for yourself or other people in following the recommended program?

CASE DESCRIPTION

You feel too tired to get out of bed. Even if you could muster the motivation, you're so cynical about your work that you wonder what it's all for.

When you do get out of bed, facial tics get worse. You find yourself getting angry and judgmental. You walk and talk faster, but forget what you say and take twice as long

to get your work done. Stomach aches and fatigue become part of your daily experience.

Behaviors and attitudes such as these may signal the approach of "burnout"—a battering form of depression that can cost you your job and ruin your health.

But pretending to cope will only get you so far.

"You always have to play like you're in perfect command of the situation, even if you're going nuts," Wolfgang Hultner, general manager of Mandarin Oriental San Francisco, said at a recent San Francisco Chamber of Commerce seminar on avoiding burnout. "The hotel business is like show business—you're always on stage. You have to keep on smiling."

The secret to handling the crunching pressures of daily life is not reducing stress, but learning how to manage it.

"Stress is the sense of enthusiasm that gets us going," said Janelle Barlow, a licensed clinical therapist and chief trainer for TMI of North America, an internal management training company. "Most people do better with a

Source: J. Morian, "Managing Stress Key to Combating Job Burnout," *Palo Alto Peninsula Times Tribune*. (As the story appeared in the *Albuquerque Journal*, November 11, 1990, p. D2.) Reprinted by permission: Knight-Ridder Tribune News Service.

little bit of pressure, but if that pressure is increased, performance drops off."

Getting rid of that despondent, hopeless feeling and regaining physical vitality all comes down to changing the way you think and act, Barlow said.

Instead of elevating your blood pressure, change your behavior. Use your head, social skills and business experience to cope with irritating scenarios, she said.

Examine your behavior to see if you're making your day harder for yourself. Get enough sleep and tackle uncomfortable tasks early in your day. Set priorities for your daily activities and avoid dwelling on the list of things left to do. Perpetual worrying will make you physically tired, Barlow said.

Take a short trip to the "stress management cubicle"— what Barlow calls the bathroom—for a break from the pressure. And make sure you take time out before making major decisions.

Another way to break the pressure is to use things in your environment to bring on relaxation. Pick out cues, like a ringing telephone or a stop light, and every time you come into contact with the cue, say out loud, "I am," breathe in, and then say "relaxed," and breathe out.

Exercise is crucial to releasing stress. Barlow suggests writing exercise into your daily plan as an appointment and to honor it regardless of work demands.

Also, listen to your "self talk," or what you tell yourself.

Gary Pike, who started as a one-man public relations firm and built his business in San Francisco into Pike Communications, said he used self-assessment to discover what was causing the most stress and unhappiness. After realizing that he had to let go of some of the responsibilities in his company, he was happier and had more time to focus on doing what he does best—sales calls.

CASE ANALYSIS

Many of Janelle Barlow's observations were discussed in more detail earlier in this chapter. Getting enough sleep, doing hard tasks early in the day, and setting task priorities are all methods that can help people manage stress. Individuals can create their own programs of stress management from the methods available to them. Obstacles you might face in following a stress management program are disciplined time management and the behavioral change required by a regular exercise program. Organizations and their managers can also help with stress reduction, stress resilience, and stress recuperation. The organizational strategies for stress management in the next section follow from these observations for individuals.

ORGANIZATIONAL STRATEGIES

The goal of **organizational stress management** is to achieve the optimal level of stress required by the goals of the organization. That level of stress varies according to individual differences and organization needs.[59]

Stress Reduction

Stress reduction strategies include training programs, personnel policies, job design, and organizational design. Training programs can focus on job-related training that improves a person's ability to do a job. Such training can improve the fit between a person's abilities and the demands of the job. It also is a way of reducing stress from role overload. Other training programs can show people how to do time and stress management. Time management includes a set of techniques and procedures that help people manage time effectively. Stress management training can include any of the individual stress reduction and stress recuperation techniques that lend themselves to formal training. The latter include the relaxation training techniques described in Table 16-5, Clinically Standardized Meditation, and Transcendental Meditation. By offering such training at little cost or no cost, organizations give their employees a major employment benefit.

Organizations can also design their selection, placement, and career development policies and procedures to help people with stress reduction. These procedures should be designed to improve person-job fit by identifying skill requirements and skill availability among employees. Selection, placement, and career development policies also include removing people from dysfunctionally stressful situations. Such people can be placed in situations better suited to their skills, abilities, and interests. Organizations can also enhance their policies and procedures by sponsoring self-assessment and career development workshops, which can help people learn about their skills, abilities, and interests.

The job design discussions in Chapter 9 presented an approach to job redesign that can help managers create a better fit between people and their jobs. Improved fit reduces stressors that come from the work itself. Role analysis is another approach to the person-job fit. Its procedures let individuals learn the expectations others in the organization have for their work role.[60] Both approaches can reduce role ambiguity and role overload.

Managers can use several organizational design options to reduce stress. Many people perceive centralized organizations as distressful because of the degree to which they are controlled and the lack of discretion they have while working. Decentralized organizations and self-managing work teams let people have more autonomy, reducing stressors from feelings of little self-control.[61]

The values emphasized by an organization's culture can help reduce stress. An organization can explicitly recognize the stressors produced by its work activities. It can also say that it does not want its employees to experience the dysfunctions of distress. The values can then emphasize the importance of social support—the helping and caring that offset the effects of stressors. Other values that can reduce stress include taking stress breaks and exercising on company time.

Physical work conditions and the physical layout of the workplace can reduce stressors. Some obvious improvements are noise control, proper ambient temperature, and removal of noxious odors. The physical layout of the workplace can help or hinder social interaction. By changing the layout, managers can help build cohesive groups and social support networks.

Managers can also help reduce nonwork stressors for their employees. Flexible work schedules can make it easier for employees with school-age children to manage their responsibilities. Flexible work schedules also help reduce stressors from daily commuting in cities with high traffic congestion. Day care benefits or day care centers at work are helpful for employees with preschool children.

Stress Resilience

Organizations can use the individual stress resilience strategies of physical exercise, diet, and weight control to help their employees resist the effects of distress. On-site space for aerobic and anaerobic exercise lets employees exercise without traveling far from their workplace. Such exercise centers can also have trained instructors who design exercise programs for stress resilience.

Company cafeterias can offer diet options that let employees maintain a stress-resilient diet. Providing foods that are low in sodium and saturated fat enables employees to choose something other than the usual high-sodium, high-fat dishes. Organizations can offer complete programs of diet and exercise, giving their employees guidance on the right balance of each.

Stress Recuperation

The exercise centers that help develop stress resilience also promote stress recuperation. Strong aerobic exercise following a stressful day lets people recuperate from stress before going home. Working off the effects of stress before leaving the workplace helps prevent stress from work from spilling over to nonwork. Organizations can also support stress breaks during the work day to help their employees rebound from unavoidable distress.

Some training programs used for stress reduction also apply to stress resilience. Organizations can offer on-site or off-site relaxation training and workshops on meditation. In either case, offering such training during regular work hours enhances its availability and makes it a significant employee benefit.

Employee assistance programs can offer stress-oriented therapy or counseling programs that focus on behavior change such as altering Type A behaviors, drug and alcohol abuse, and cigarette smoking. Counseling programs within organizations supplement stress management training. They usually are available to help people who cannot manage stress effectively by themselves.

C A S E   *Your Boss as a Stressor*

*T*he following case presents one person's view of how managers and supervisors can induce stress in their subordinates. It also describes how those same managers and supervisors can reduce stress in their organizations. Read the case and assess it using information in this chapter and any other chapters in this book. Guide your assessment with the following questions:

1. Are these realistic behaviors that happen often in organizations?
2. Can managers and supervisors easily change their behavior to make it less stressful for their subordinates?
3. How perceptive must people be to see that they are behaving as described in the case?

CASE DESCRIPTION

Does your secretary wince when you hand her a new project?

Is your assistant disorganized? Do others on your staff complain of constant headaches or seem jittery or nervous?

Many managers have never considered the possibility that they may be contributing to the stress disorders afflicting their employees. But according to Dr. F. J. McGuigan, director of the Institute for Stress Management at U.S. International University in San Diego, some bosses may be "stress inducers." . . .

What are the management techniques that can cause employees to feel stressed?

Each individual will react differently to direction from a manager. But McGuigan suggests these as examples of behaviors that could add to employee tension:

- Piling excessive amounts of work on employees and giving them little direction as to priorities. . . .
- Calling frequent, lengthy meetings, and then criticizing employees for not spending enough time at their desks getting work out.
- Setting impossibly high goals in the mistaken belief that it will make employees try harder.

Source: "Boss, Are You Stressing Out Your Employees?" Business Wire, 1986. (As the story appeared in *Business Outlook, Albuquerque Journal*, February 3, 1986, p. 28.) Reprinted with the permission of Business Wire.

- Putting employees on the spot, especially in front of others, rather than giving them time to research answers to your questions.
- Repeatedly taking employees off one project to work on others, requiring them to juggle many projects at the same time. . . .
- Involving the entire staff in every problem or crisis even though some of the individuals can do nothing to help alleviate the difficulty. . . .
- Bringing up employees' past mistakes when you are correcting them for current errors.
- Managers also need to realize that if they themselves are overly tense, their short tempers, frantic activities and disorganization can be picked up on by their employees who will follow the example, McGuigan says.

What can you do to help your employees be less stressed and more productive?

- Spend more time thinking about how you would feel if you were in your employees' shoes. Try to imagine what it would be like having yourself for a boss.
- You can tactfully question employees directly, or preferably have someone from outside the company or from another department, such as employee relations, quiz your employees anonymously. . . .
- Help your employees give priorities to assignments. . . .
- Try to keep emergency projects presented to you to a minimum by helping your employees anticipate future needs. . . .
- Work on sharpening your communication skills so employees really understand your directives. Ask employees for feedback and listen to what they tell you.
- Be quick to praise and reinforce good work.
- If reprimands are necessary, try to give them in a calm manner rather than shouting at the employee.
- Encourage your employees to learn the stress reducing techniques of Progress[ive] Relaxation, to stop stress-increasing habits such as smoking and to get adequate rest and exercise.
- Learn to work "differentially" relaxed yourself. McGuigan explains that differential relaxation means using only the necessary energy for the work you are doing, not wasting energy needlessly.

The behavior of managers can often be a significant stressor. The methods for reducing such stress suggested by McGuigan include many things suggested by this chapter and others in this book. Praise, reinforcement, and reprimand are all part of the motivation system in an organization. Communication skills of individual managers are part of the communication system of an organization. Chapter 13 discussed communication in detail. Reducing stress in an organization includes both stress management and improvements in other systems that affect people's behavior.

International Aspects of Stress in Organizations

*T*his section describes some contributors to stress that arise from an organization's international activities. It examines stress issues in four areas: (1) business trips to other countries, (2) relocation to another country for an extended time, (3) working in an organization within another country, and (4) returning home. Each area commonly adds to stress.[62]

Traveling to another country on a business trip exposes a person to several potential stressors. Crossing time zones, adjusting sleep patterns, entering a different culture, and learning how to move about in that culture can all add to stress. People will vary, of course, in their stress response. If they perceive travel as a source of stress, they are likely to have a distress reaction and feel apprehensive. Other people may have a eustress reaction and view the experience as a challenge. Both people will have a stress response, but with different results.

A stronger and more lasting source of stress is relocation to another country for an extended time.[63] Unlike business travel to another country, a move can last for several years and involve an entire family. Consequently, a person experiences many more stressors than during a business trip.

The expatriate enters the new culture and experiences the culture shock common to travel to any new country. The culture shock is intensified by the longer stay, often the presence of an entire family, living quarters other than a hotel, and possibly servants who do household chores. The ways and mores of a new culture cascade upon the expatriate and her family. Different rules of behavior, new relationships, and a different language all must be mastered quickly, if the expatriate is to function effectively in the new environment. The crush of information acts as a form of role overload and exposes the expatriate to many stressors.

An especially strong stressor for expatriates is discovering early in their tour that they are ineffective in getting tasks done in the local culture. They quickly discover that effective task behavior in their home culture does not work in the host culture. If expatriates do not quickly adapt to the ways and mores of that culture, their continual frustration could lead to questions about their self-efficacy.

Because the expatriate's family often joins in the move, the family unit meets new nonwork stressors early. Family members have had to sever ties with friends and relatives back home. Spouses are left alone for extended periods as the expatriates immerse themselves in mastering new task environments. Children not only must adapt to new schools, they must adapt to schools in a new environment. School-age children are gone during the day, leaving a spouse to master relationships with servants and shop in unfamiliar stores. The entire family often sees big differences in its quality of life and in its social and physical environment. All these together are nonwork stressors surrounding the expatriate and her family.

The culture shock stressors can be particularly grueling for spouses of expatriates, especially wives.[64] Women foreigners often cannot work for pay in the host country. They may have many free daytime hours, during which they try to build relationships with servants, learn how to shop, interact with members of the local population who may be unaccustomed to foreigners, and face long periods of loneliness and boredom. If a wife left a job or career behind to join her husband, she has lost something that gave meaning to her life. Altogether, these factors are significant stressors for an expatriate's wife and can add to stress in their marriage.

The effects of culture shock usually pass after six months, if the expatriate and family successfully adapt to unavoidable stressors. The expatriate, though, has already faced a diverse set of work-based stressors, uniquely defined by the local culture.

Each chapter of this book has included a section describing the international aspects of the chapter's major topics. Those sections showed you the behavioral differences you can expect in organizations of various countries and cultures. The behavioral differences are the fabric of the organizational cultures one encounters in different countries. Depending on the country you are coming from and the country you are going to, you will experience congruence or incongruence between the behaviors you are accustomed to and those you will see. Understanding and adapting to behavioral differences can be stressful for many people.

A way of reducing this stress is to understand the behaviors you will see in the new country. Many companies give their employees predeparture cultural training. The international sections of other chapters in this book are also a source of information for you. You may wish to review them to get a picture of differences in organizational behavior from country to country.

After expatriates have adapted to differences in behavior in a new country, they may face a new challenge when they return to their home country to continue their career in a domestic operation of the same company. Returning to one's homeland presents the repatriate with its own set of stressors.[65]

Repatriates often assume that nothing will have changed while they were gone. Yet, during the repatriate's time overseas, the repatriate has changed, as have family members, relatives, friends, and coworkers in the home country. While living abroad, expatriates often recall only positive features of their home culture. Returning to their home country can cause as much culture shock as entering a foreign country. Many stressors are the same. The ways and mores of the home country are different from those of the country just left. Any negative features forgotten while gone will have a particularly shocking effect.

Repatriates also experience a form of organizational culture shock when returning to an organization in their home country. Earlier chapters described differences in typical organizational behavior among countries. If the repatriate is returning to a home country whose organizational cultures differ from the one left behind, she can experience the stress of culture shock.

· ·

Ethical Issues in Stress in Organizations

Stress in organizations raises many ethical issues. Both the business and the more general press report regularly on work-related stress. Many states allow work-based stress claims under worker compensation laws, raising the specter of high social and economic costs of work-based stress.[66] The following are some ethical issues that could be raised about stress in work organizations:

1. Managers often decide to change a work environment. The change may involve technology, organizational design, or the physical aspects of the organization, including relocating the company. Such changes can adversely affect the person-environment fit for some, but not all employees. Do managers have an ethical duty to reduce potential stress by preparing their employees for changes? Do managers have an ethical duty to refrain from making changes that might be good for the company but would cause high stress for employees?

2. A person's physical work environment can present many stressors. The Occupational Safety and Health Administration has set standards for many stressors, including noxious fumes, radiation, and unsafe working conditions. Is it unethical for managers to knowingly expose workers to such hazards in an effort to reduce operating costs?

3. An organization's selection and placement policies can affect the quality of the person-environment fit.[67] The likelihood of a good fit can be improved if both the potential recruit and the organization have accurate information about each other. Is it unethical for an organization to knowingly distort information about the job, the organization, or the likely career path for the recruit? Is it unethical for a recruit to knowingly distort information about herself to improve her prospects of receiving an offer of employment? Chapter 6 also addressed this issue when discussing Realistic Job Previews.

4. When harmful stress appears to result from a present poor person-environment fit, is the organization required to provide career counseling or help the person find a better-fitting job within or outside the organization?[68]

5. Because work and nonwork stressors may combine to have harmful effects, knowledge about such stressors can help a manager understand the total stress effects on an employee. How much should an individual reveal about her nonwork world to an organization? Should managers concern themselves with nonwork stressors when judging the total stressor exposure of an employee? To what extent is it unethical to ask about an employee's nonwork life?

Personal and Management Implications

*T*he earlier discussion of models of the stress response gave you different views of the human stress response. The models describe the natural character of the response, its unavoidable quality, and how it varies from person to person. The Integrated Model of Stress includes several moderators that emphasizes the importance of interactions between the person and the environment.

One main implication is the need to learn and understand your individual stress response. What experiences do you consider stressful? How do you react to those experiences? What characteristics of yourself as a person either amplify or weaken your response to unavoidable stressors? For example, Type A personalities approach experiences with impatience, often adding to the natural stressors they meet daily.

The discussion of stress management offered many observations on individual ways of reducing stress, increasing stress resilience, and recovering from stress. Pay special attention to your diet and physical condition as ways of increasing your stress resilience. Examine the role of exercise in your lifestyle. As the section explained, exercise not only increases one's resilience to stress, but plays a role in recovering from stress. If you do not regularly exercise now, you might want to add physical activity to your lifestyle.

The section on stress recuperation described the many methods available to help people recover from stress. If you feel you do not know how to recover from stress in healthy ways, you might want to learn more about methods of relaxation, for example. Table 16-5 lists many readable sources about these methods of stress recuperation. You should also find out whether your employing organization sponsors workshops on stress management or offers counseling. If you feel you are not coping with stressors effectively, follow these suggestions to find out more about effective and healthy stress recuperation for you.

All these personal implications also apply to you as a manager. Other implications follow from that role as well. The earlier case describing managers as stressors had several implications for you in that role.

Reflect on your behavior toward those who work for you. Do you demand more than they can deliver? Do you set deadlines that are almost impossible to meet? In short, as a manager, are you a stressor in the environment of your subordinates? You will find it revealing, informative, and possibly frightening to learn that your subordinates perceive you as a stressor. Ask them and be sure to listen carefully to their observations. Then compare their comments to observations about stress throughout this chapter. Of course, it is always possible you are not behaving as a stressor.

Reflect upon your organization. Does it have any organizational strategies that reduce stress, increase stress resilience, or help people recover from stressors? If it does not, are you able to encourage their development? You can easily learn what is now being done by consulting with your Human Resources Department.

The jobs of managers have their own set of stressors not always found in other types of jobs. Many management jobs require repeated travel away from home. Managers with such jobs are exposed to the natural stressors of traveling. Those stressors have a different quality if the travel is international. The implications for managers in jobs requiring travel center on ways of avoiding stress, having high resilience to those stressors, and recuperating quickly in healthy ways from unavoidable stressors.

Management jobs often also carry more responsibility than nonmanagement jobs. Those responsibilities can be significant stressors for many people. One implication asks whether you have been trained for your management position. If you have not had the right training, you may not be ready to handle the responsibilities of the position. The second implication asks whether you are in a job suited to your personal characteristics. The latter implies reducing stress by leaving the position.

. . . .

↵ Summary

Stress is an unavoidable aspect of modern living. People experience stress when an event in their environment presents a constraint, an opportunity, or an excessive physical or psychological demand. Not all stress is bad. Some stress can energize a person to behave in desired ways.

Several models of the stress response have evolved since the early 1900s with each giving a different view of stress. The Integrated Model of Stress combines many elements of the earlier models to form a detailed model of responses to stress.

The Integrated Model describes stressors as occurring in work experiences, in nonwork experiences, and during major life transitions. The model includes the role of perception in filtering stressors. A stressor can be exciting to one person and a source of harm to another. The model describes moderators of the stress response such as personality, skills, family health history, demographics, diet, and physical fitness. The Integrated Model also describes the results of both distress and eustress.

Burnout is a chronic state of emotional exhaustion stemming from an unrelenting series of on-the-job pressures with few moments of positive experience. It is a special case of distress and an often-used popular term to refer to stress. Burnout is work-related distress usually experienced by people in jobs that require helping other people.

Stress management includes strategies individuals can use to manage stress in their lives and organizations can use to help employees manage stress. Different strategies aim to reduce stress, increase stress resilience, and help people recuperate from stress.

Stressors can arise from the international activities of organizations. Four areas in particular contribute to stress: (1) business trips to other countries, (2) relocation to another country for an extended time, (3) working in an organization within another country, and (4) returning home.

Many ethical issues surround stress in organizations. This section emphasized the roles of managers, nonmanagers, and organizational policies in dealing with sources of stress. The ethical issues often pivot on the amount of knowledge people have about sources of stress in their work environments.

. . . .

↵ Key Terms

Alarm, Resistance, Exhaustion 460
behavioral response 467
burnout 473
distress 461
eustress 461
General Adjustment Syndrome 460
individual stress management 474
Integrated Model of Stress 462

Job Demands–Job Decision Latitude Model 462
moderators of stress 470
organizational stress management 479
perceived stress 467
Person-Environment Fit Model 461
results of distress 468

results of eustress 469
stress recuperation 476
stress reduction 474
stress resilience 475
stress response 467
stressors 463
Transactional Model of Stress 461

↵ Review and Discussion Questions

1. Review each model of stress described in this chapter. What are the major differences among the models? What unique and common perspectives does each model give to you? How can you use this information at work?

2. Review the sources of stressors described in the chapter. Which of those sources are playing the biggest role in your life now? Which sources do you expect to play big roles in the future?

3. What is the role of perception in the stress response? You may find it useful to review the perception portion of Chapter 4 and discuss its implications for understanding the stress response.

4. Not all stress is bad for people. Eustress is possible and can be exhilarating for many. Discuss the conditions under which you believe you experience eustress. Com-

pare those conditions to the conditions of eustress of some of your friends.

5. Review the section on ways of managing stress. Which methods are easiest for you to follow now? Which methods should you consider in the future? As a manager, which of these methods can you affect for others?

6. The section on ethical issues raised several ethical issues or questions about stress. Review those issues and discuss them in class. Identify the positions different people take on each issue.

7. Both travel and transfer to foreign locations can be a source of stress for many people. Discuss with others in your class experiences you have had with foreign travel or foreign assignments. Which parts of those experiences were the most recurring stressors?

↵ Case

OVERSTRESSED BY SUCCESS: FOR SCORES OF CEOs, IT'S TERRIFYING AT THE TOP

The following case describes the stress and terror felt by many executives at the top of their organizations. Although you may not now be at that level of management, many stressors identified in the case are common to management at any level. Have the following questions in mind while reading the case:

1. Which stressors described in the case likely appear in most management roles?

2. Do you have any of the personal qualities described in the case that suggest you could be stress-prone in a senior management role?

3. What role does one's nonwork life play in relieving the stressors that cannot be escaped in many management jobs?

Saying that Rick Chollet had it all doesn't quite say it all. Chollet, the son of struggling French immigrants, built a small mail-order tool business called Brookstone into a hugely successful national purveyor of adult toys and gadgets. He was handsome, happily married, loved by employees and colleagues—and as it turned out, deeply despondent. Last March 18, out of the blue it seemed, Chollet took his life. "Please forgive me, but the thought of going through the torture of living is just too much to bear," he wrote to his family before locking the garage door of his New Hamp-

Source: D. Gelman, "Overstressed by Success: For Scores of CEOs, It's Terrifying at the Top." From NEWSWEEK, June 3, 1991, p. 56. © 1991 Newsweek, Inc. All rights reserved. Reprinted by permission.

shire house, climbing into his BMW and turning on the engine. His wife, Susan, later revealed that Chollet had been depressed for half of his adult life. People put him on such a pedestal, she said, that he constantly feared letting them down. "He swung from feeling totally powerful to totally helpless." . . .

[P]sychiatrists say it can be terrifying at the top. Many high-powered company chiefs like Chollet harbor suicidal feelings along with their stock options and chamber of commerce trophies. Often, they are so bent on maintaining a veneer of authority that they have trouble acknowledging they need help. Psychiatrists nevertheless treat scores of stressed-out execs. "I think half the successful work force is depressed," says Douglas LaBier, a Washington, D.C., psychoanalyst who heads the Project on Adult Lives, one of a growing number of programs focused on treating professionals.

Executives at the top are often propelled there by strong drives that are accompanied by rigid personal standards. Some suffer stress because they are perfectionists about their own work, some because they feel overly responsible for setting a shining example for others. When host Eileen Prose recounted the story of Chollet's suicide on Channel 5, on Boston's morning "Good Day" show, a woman viewer called in to say she, too, had attempted suicide recently because of the pressures of running a prosperous business, and feared she might try it again. "It's just so overwhelming," the caller said. "Everyone looks at me as a leader and all I want to do is run."

Women chiefs may feel especially conflicted about success because often they are brought up to put the needs of others first. They don't necessarily resort to suicide. Instead, says Tanya Korkosz, a psychiatrist at Leadership Consulting Group in Belmont, Mass., they may unwittingly sabotage themselves by gaining weight or developing chronic medical problems. Psychotherapist Steven Berglas, author of "The Success Syndrome: Hitting Bottom When You Reach the Top," adds that execs may adopt such "self-handicapping" behavior so they can blame any subsequent failure on something other than their own incompetence. This gives them a way of "quitting without appearing to quit."

There are, in fact, any number of reasons for executive blues. One major cause is what Berglas calls "encore anxiety," fear that they won't be able to repeat or sustain earlier achievements. Some executives may be secretly convinced they got to the top by an undeserved stroke of luck, unlikely to recur. They live in dread of exposure. Gerald Kraines, a psychiatrist who treated Chollet for depression, estimates that 20 to 30 percent of CEOs he encounters through his work as a consultant on organizational stress fall in the category of fearing their inadequacy will be found out. The trouble is, he says, they compensate by driving themselves more and more. "They're on a treadmill where they can never savor their success, because they have to keep working harder." . . .

Dealing with executives in distress can be more complicated than treating ordinary patients, say the handful of experts beginning to specialize in that area. For one thing, in the process of keeping anxieties hidden from others executives manage to conceal them from themselves. The first, perhaps hardest, step is getting the executive to recognize he's depressed, says Jeffrey Lynn Speller, director of Harvard Medical School's Leadership Research Project and author of "Executives in Crisis." Once that is done, Speller concentrates on helping patients reconstruct their self-esteem around their personal lives instead of their jobs. Specialists say many troubled execs have molded their lives according to a distorted sense of what their parents or others expect from them. The therapist tries to broaden the patient's definition of achievement.

One unique treatment approach is ACCEL, a four-week program for "high-functioning individuals" at Timberlawn Psychiatric Hospital in Dallas, Texas. Psychiatrist Mark Unterberg says he founded the VIP program four years ago after a CEO who had been admitted for a nervous breakdown grew even shakier in the hospital's restrictive environment. Unterberg realized executives had to be kept busy and allowed to use phones to pursue the healthy aspects of their lives. Patients are put on a regimen of five and six group-therapy sessions per day. Each is assigned to at least two psychiatrists, sometimes a third if substance abuse is involved.

VIPs' resistance to treatment can be strong. One CEO had not taken a vacation in 14 years, believing that if he did, his employees would think he was shirking his duty. Psychiatrists recognize, of course, that there are hundreds of healthy executives who thrive on such unrelenting work and challenge. But hundreds of others may feel like they're on a treadmill to oblivion, unable to get off until they fall off. Or, like Rick Chollet, until they jump.

. . . .

➧ *Exercise*

NEW STRESS SOURCES

Psychologist Georgia Witken surveyed almost three thousand women about stress in their lives. Her survey suggested women today face new sources of stress. The following lists the life events the women found stressful and the points they gave each event.

Review the life events that follow. Note on a separate piece of paper the points for the events that happened to you in the past year. Find the total of the points and add it to the total points you got for the exercise on p. 473. Remember, you are at increased risk of illness or serious depression if your total is over 300 points.

Life Event	Points
Disabled child	97
Single parenting	96
Remarriage	89
Depression	89
Abortion	89
Child's illness	87
Infertility	87
Spouse illness	85
Crime victimization	84
Husband's retirement	82
Parenting parents	81
Raising teens	80
Chemical dependency	80
Parent's illness	78
Singlehood	77
Moving	76
Adoption	74
Son or daughter returning home	61
Own retirement	58
Commuting	57

Source: "New Stress Sources," *Albuquerque Journal,* December 16, 1991, p. B1. List of stressors: Reprinted by permission: Knight-Ridder Tribune Media Service.

[1]M. T. Matteson and J. M. Ivancevich, "Organizational Stressors and Heart Disease: A Research Model," *Academy of Management Review* 4 (1979): 347–57.

[2]R. S. Lazarus, *Psychological Stress and the Copying Process* (New York: McGraw-Hill, 1966), Ch. 1.

[3]J. C. Quick and J. D. Quick, *Organizational Stress and Preventive Management* (New York: McGraw-Hill, 1984), Ch. 1.

[4]D. Briscoe, "Job Stress Crushing Workers Worldwide," Associated Press. (As the story appeared in the *Albuquerque Journal*, March 23, 1993, pp. A1, A5.

[5]Developed from H. Selye, *The Stress of Life* (New York: McGraw-Hill, 1956); H. Selye, "The Stress Concept: Past, Present, and Future," in C. L. Cooper, ed., *Stress Research* (New York: John Wiley & Sons, 1983), pp. 1–20. Dr. Hans Selye did the basic psychophysiological research about human stress responses, to which he gave the name General Adaptation Syndrome. The phrase "fight or flight" came from the earliest stress research done by Cannon. See W. B. Cannon, "The Influence of Emotional States on the Functions of the Alimentary Canal," *American Journal of Science* 137 (1909): 480–87; W. B. Cannon, "Organization for Physiological Homeostasis," *Physiological Review* 9 (1929): 339–430.

[6]Lazarus, *Psychological Stress*, Ch. 1; R. S. Lazarus, J. Deese, and J. F. Osler, "The Effects of Psychological Stress upon Performance," *Psychological Bulletin* 49 (1952): 293–316.

[7]Lazarus, *Psychological Stress*; R. S. Lazarus and S. Folkman, *Stress, Appraisal, and Coping* (New York: Springer Publishing, 1984).

[8]J. R. P. French, W. Rogers, and S. Cobb, "A Model of Person-Environment Fit," in G. V. Coelho, D. A. Hamburgh, and J. E. Adams, eds., *Coping and Adaptation* (New York: Basic Books, 1974), 316–33; R. V. Harrison, "Person-Environment Fit and Job Stress," In C. L. Cooper and R. Payne, eds., *Stress at Work* (Chichester, England: John Wiley & Sons, 1978), pp. 175–205.

[9]J. R. Eulberg, J. A. Weekley, and R. S. Bhagat, "Models of Stress in Organizational Research: A Metatheoretical Perspective," *Human Relations* 41 (1988): 331–50.

[10]R. D. Caplan, "Person Environment Fit: Past, Present, and Future," in C. L. Cooper, ed., *Stress Research: Issues for the Eighties* (New York: John Wiley & Sons, 1983), pp. 35–78.

[11]J. R. Edwards and C. L. Cooper, "The Person-Environment Fit Approach to Stress: Recurring Problems and Some Suggested Solutions," *Journal of Organizational Behavior* 11 (1990): 293–307.

[12]R. A. Karasek Jr., "Job Demands, Job Decision Latitude, and Mental Strain: Implications for Job Redesign," *Administrative Science Quarterly* 24 (1979): 285–308; R. A. Karasek, "Job Socialization and Job Strain: The Implications of Two Related Psychosocial Mechanisms for Job Design," in R. Gardell and G. Johansson, eds., *Working Life: A Social Science Contribution to Work Reform* (New York: John Wiley & Sons, 1981), pp. 75–94; R. A. Karasek Jr., "Control in the Workplace and Its Health-Related Aspects," in S. L. Sauter, J. J. Harrell, and C. L. Cooper, eds., *Job Control and Worker Health* (Chichester, England: Wiley, 1989), pp. 129–59.

[13]Developed from Quick and Quick, *Organizational Stress*; Matteson and Ivancevich, "Organizational Stressors and Heart Disease"; M. T. Matteson and J. M. Ivancevich, *Controlling Work Stress: Effective Human Resource and Management Strategies* (San Francisco: Jossey-Bass, 1987), Ch. 2, and other sources cited throughout.

[14]S. V. Kasl and C. L. Cooper, *Stress and Health: Issues in Research Methodology* (New York: Wiley, 1987).

[15]Quick and Quick, *Organizational Stress*; A. J. McMichael, "Personality, Behavioural, and Situational Modifiers of Work Stressors," in C. L. Cooper and R. Payne, ed., *Stress at Work* (Chichester, England: John Wiley & Sons, 1978), pp. 127–47.

[16]T. D. Jick and L. F. Mitz, "Sex Differences in Work Stress," *Academy of Management Review* 10 (1985): 408–20.

[17]Developed from C. L. Cooper and J. Marshall, "Sources of Managerial and White Collar Stress," in C. L. Cooper and R. Payne, ed., *Stress at Work* (Chichester, England: John Wiley & Sons, 1978), pp. 81–105; C. L. Cooper and J. Marshall, "Occupational Sources of Stress: A Review of the Literature Relating to Coronary Heart Disease and Mental Ill Health," *Journal of Occupational Psychology* 49 (1976): 11–28.

[18]Cooper and Marshall, *Stress at Work*.

[19]R. L. Kahn, D. M. Wolfe, R. P. Quinn, J. D. Snoek, and R. A. Rosenthal, *Organizational Stress: Studies in Role Conflict and Ambiguity* (New York: John Wiley & Sons, 1964), p. 94.

[20]Cooper and Marshall, *Stress at Work*, pp. 87–88.

[21]See E. C. Poulton, "Blue Collar Stressors," in C. L. Cooper and R. Payne, ed., *Stress at Work* (Chichester, England: John Wiley & Sons, 1978), pp. 51–79 for more detail about how physical stressors work.

[22]N. Gupta and G. D. Jenkins Jr., "Dual Career Couples: Stress, Stressors, Strains, and Strategies," in T. A. Beehr, and R. S. Bhagat, eds., *Human Stress and Cognition in Organizations: An Integrated Perspective* (New York: John Wiley & Sons, 1985), pp. 141–75.

[23]B. Wheaton, "Life Transition, Role Histories, and Mental Health," *American Sociological Review* 55 (1990): 209–23.

[24]A. E. McGoldrick and C. L. Cooper, "Stress at the Decline of One's Career: The Act of Retirement," in T. A. Beehr and R. S. Bhagat, eds., *Human Stress and Cognition in Organizations: An Integrated Perspective* (New York: John Wiley & Sons, 1985), pp. 177–201.

[25]Quick and Quick, *Organizational Stress*, Ch. 3; R. S. Schuler, "Definition and Conceptualization of Stress in Organizations," *Organizational Behavior and Human Performance* 25 (1980): 184–215.

[26]Suggested by J. E. McGrath, "Stress and Behavior in Organizations," in M. D. Dunnette, ed., *Handbook of Industrial and Organizational Psychology* (Chicago: Rand McNally, 1976), pp. 1351–96. See pp. 1391–92.

[27]J. E. Champoux, "A Sociological Perspective on Work Involvement," *International Review of Applied Psychology* 30 (1981): 65–86.

[28]D. C. Ganster and J. Schaubroeck, "Work Stress and Employee Health," *Journal of Management* 17 (1991): 235–71; S. V. Kasl, "Pursuing the Link between Stressful Life Experiences and Disease: A Time for Reappraisal," in C. L. Cooper, ed., *Stress Research: Issues for the Eighties* (New York: John Wiley & Sons, 1983), pp. 79–102; S. V. Kasl, "Stress and Disease in the Workplace: A Methodological Commentary on the Accumulated Evidence," in M. F. Cataldo and T. J. Coates, eds., *Health and Industry: A Behavioral Medicine Perspective* (New York: Wiley, 1986), pp. 52–85.

[29]S. E. Sullivan and R. S. Bhagat, "Organizational Stress, Job Satisfaction and Job Performance: Where Do We Go from Here?" *Journal of Management* 18 (1992): 352–74.

[30]Quick and Quick, *Organizational Stress*, Ch. 3.

[31]Developed from Cooper and Marshall, *Stress at Work*, pp. 97–101; Ganster and Schaubroeck, "Work Stress"; McGrath, "Stress and Behavior in Organizations," pp. 1391–92; Quick and Quick *Organizational Stress*, pp. 63–73; Schuler, "Definition of Stress," pp. 192–95.

[32]R. J. Ganellen and P. H. Blaney, "Hardiness and Social Support as Moderators of the Effects of Life Stress," *Journal of Personality and Social Psychology* 47 (1984): 156–63; S. C. Kobasa, "The Hardy Personality: Toward a Social Psychology of Stress and Health," in G. S. Sander and J. Suls, eds., *Social Psychology of Health and Illness* (Hillsdale, N.J.: Lawrence Erlbaum Associates, 1982), pp. 3–32; S. R. Maddi and S. C. Kobasa, *The Hardy Executive: Health Under Stress* (Homewood, Ill.: Dow Jones–Irwin, 1984).

[33]J. G. Hull, R. R. Van Treuren, and S. Virnelli, "Hardiness and Health: A Critique and Alternative Approach," *Journal of Personality and Social Psychology* 53 (1987): 518–30.

[34]S. Booth-Kewley and H. S. Friedman, "Psychological Predictors of Heart Disease: A Quantitative Review," *Psychological Bulletin* 101 (1987): 343–62; D. C. Ganster, J. Schaubroeck, W. E. Sime, and B. T. Mayes, "The Nomological Validity of the Type A Personality among Employed Adults," *Journal of Applied Psychology* 76 (1991): 143–68; K. A. Mathews, "Coronary Heart Disease and Type A Behaviors: Update on and Alternative to the Booth-Kewley and Friedman (1987) Quantitative Review," *Psychological Bulletin* 104 (1988): 373–80.

[35]K. A. Mathews, "Psychological Perspectives on the Type A Behavior Pattern," *Psychological Bulletin* 91 (1982): 292–323; K. A. Mathews, R. L. Helmreich, W. E. Beanne, and G. W. Lucker, "Pattern A, Achievement-Striving, and Scientific Merit: Does Pattern A Help or Hinder?" *Journal of Personality & Social Psychology* 39 (1980): 962–67.

[36]K. L. Froggatt and J. L. Cotton, "The Impact of Type A Behavior Pattern on Role Overload–Induced Stress and Performance Attributions," *Journal of Management* 13 (1987): 87–90.

[37]F. Rhodewalt and S. Agustsdottir, "On the Relationship of Hardiness to the Type A Behavior Pattern: Perception of Life Events versus Coping with Life Events," *Journal of Research in Personality* 18 (1984): 212–23.

[38]Quick and Quick, *Organizational Stress*, pp. 249–52.

[39]C. L. Cordes and T. W. Doughterty, "A Review and an Integration of Research on Job Burnout," *Academy of Management Review* 18 (1993): 621–56; S. E. Jackson, R. L. Schwab, and R. S. Schuler, "Toward an Understanding of the Burnout Phenomenon," *Journal of Applied Psychology* 71 (1986): 630–40; C. Maslach, *Burnout: The Cost of Caring* (Englewood Cliffs, N.J.: Prentice-Hall, 1982); A. Shirom, "Burnout in Work Organizations," in C. L. Cooper and I. Robertson, eds., *International Review of Industrial and Organizational Psychology* (Chichester, England: Wiley, 1989), pp. 25–48.

[40]L. Moss, *Management Stress* (Reading, Mass.: Addison-Wesley, 1981).

[41]Cordes and Dougherty, "A Review," pp. 643–44.

[42]R. T. Golembiewski, "Burnout as a Problem at Work: Mapping Its Degree, Duration, and Consequences," *Journal of Managerial Issues* 1 (1989): 86–97; Maslach, *Burnout*; B. Perlman and E. A. Hartman, "Burnout: Summary and Future Research," *Human Relations* 35 (1982): 283–305.

[43]Golembiewski, "Burnout," p. 86.

[44]Developed from E. A. Charlesworth and R. G. Nathan, *Stress Management: A Comprehensive Guide to Wellness* (New York: Ballantine Books, 1984); A. Ellis, "What People Can Do for Themselves to Cope with Stress," in C. L. Cooper and R. Payne, eds., *Stress at Work* (Chichester, England: John Wiley & Sons, 1978), pp. 209–22; A. A. McLean, *Work Stress* (Reading, Mass.: Addison-Wesley, 1979); D. Ornish, *Stress, Diet, and Your Heart* (New York: Penguin Books, 1982), Ch. 2; Quick and Quick, *Organizational Stress*.

[45]J. E. Newman and T. A. Beehr, "Personal and Organizational Strategies for Handling Job Stress: A Review of Research and Opinion," *Personnel Psychology* 32 (1979): 1–41.

[46]D. Druckman and R. Bjork, *In the Mind's Eye: Enhancing Human Performance* (Washington: National Academy Press, 1991).

[47]Druckman and Bjork, *In the Mind's Eye*; Quick and Quick, *Organizational Stress*, Chs. 3 and 11.

[48]Charlesworth and Nathan, *Stress Management*.

[49]L. I. Pearlin and C. Schooler, "The Structure of Coping," *Journal of Health and Social Behavior* 19 (1978): 2–21.

[50]A. Lakein, *How to Get Control of Your Time and Your Life* (New York: Peter H. Wyden, 1973).

[51]S. Cohen and T. A. Wills, "Stress, Social Support, and the Buffering Hypothesis," *Psychological Bulletin* 98 (1985): 310–57; J. S. House, *Work Stress and Social Support* (Reading, Mass.: Addison-Wesley, 1981); J. Suls, "Social Support, Interpersonal Relations, and Health: Benefits and Liabilities," in G. S. Sander and J. Suls, eds., *Social Psychology of Health and Illness* (Hillsdale, N.J.: Lawrence Erlbaum Associates, 1982), pp. 255–77.

[52]Quick and Quick, *Organizational Stress*, pp. 249–52.

[53]Ornish, *Stress, Diet, and Your Heart*.

[54]S. R. Gambert, et al., "Exercise and the Endogenous Opioids," *New England Journal of Medicine* 305 (1981): 1590–91.

[55]H. Benson, *The Relaxation Response* (New York: William Morrow, 1975).

[56]Ornish, *Stress, Diet, and Your Health*, Ch. 10; Quick and Quick, *Organizational Stress*, 236–38, 241–43.

[57]P. Carrington, *Freedom in Meditation* (New York: Anchor Press, 1978).

[58]Champoux, "A Sociological Perspective."

[59]Developed from Quick and Quick, *Organizational Stress*, Chs. 8 and 9 and other sources cited in this section.

[60]W. L. French and C. H. Bell, *Organization Development: Behavioral Science Interventions for Organization Improvement* (Englewood Cliffs, N.J.: Prentice-Hall, 1984).

[61]Karasek, "Job Demands"; Karasek, "Control in the Workplace."

[62]Developed from N. J. Adler, *International Dimensions of Organizational Behavior* (Boston: PWS-Kent, 1991).

[63]See Adler, *International Dimensions*, Chs. 8 and 9 for more detail.

[64]Ibid., Ch. 9.

[65]N. J. Adler, "Reentry: Managing Cross-Cultural Transitions. *Group and Organization Studies* 6 (1981): 341–56; Adler, *International Dimensions*; C. Howard, "The Returning Overseas Executive: Culture Shock in Reverse," *Human Resources Management* 13 (1974): 22–26.

[66]R. Grover, "Say, Does Workers' Comp Cover Wretched Excess?" *Business Week*, July 22, 1991, p. 23.

[67]Suggested by Harrison, "Person-Environment Fit," pp. 197–200.

[68]Ibid.

IV   *Organizational Processes*

↲ IT'S HOW YOU PLAY THE GAME

*T*he following case continues the description of Jill Barad's activities at Mattel, Inc. The close of Section III introduced you to her leadership style. Apply what you have learned in the chapters of this section to the case. An analysis follows the case description.

Case Description

Maybe it's too obvious to compare Jill Elikann Barad to her star product, Barbie. But it's tempting. After all, Barad has a pretty face, a knockout wardrobe—and a great career. Since joining Mattel, Inc., in 1981, she has risen through the ranks so quickly that in 1988 *USA Today* dubbed her "the toy industry's Princess of Power." And that was before Barad became president of the company's Girls and Activity Toys Division late last year.

At 38, Barad has managed to escape the fate of so many executive women who butt up against the legendary glass ceiling on their climb to corporate America's uppermost rungs. And she's done it in the toy industry—a business notoriously cutthroat and fickle. Barad even survived, and thrived, after a major Mattel shake-up that cost many others their jobs.

Not bad for a onetime aspiring actress whose sole movie credit is a nonspeaking part as Miss Italian-America in a Dino De Laurentiis turkey, *Crazy Joe.* But Barad's rise hasn't been without controversy—whether because of others' jealousy, lingering sexism or her personal style. Her admirers say she has prevailed through a combination of charm, talent and underlying toughness; detractors say Barad worked her way up the ladder with a false smile, cutting out anyone who got in her way. Barad herself says, "I think of myself as very goal-oriented. I'm an achiever." That much is certain. Barad can point to a string of successes that include updating Barbie and introducing the Heart Family (a cute quartet of Mom, Dad, baby girl and boy) and many of Mattel's popular dolls. Says competitor Larry Bernstein, president of Hasbro Toys, a division of Hasbro, Inc., "Jill seems to have

what we call 'the feel' for the product. She understands what little girls want and how to execute that."

Barad clearly understands the feminine impulse to dress well and look good. She started out as a beauty consultant with Love Cosmetics while still a student at Queens College in New York. After a brief stint as a gofer to producer De Laurentiis, Barad joined Coty Cosmetics as a traveling representative, training department-store cosmeticians in the art of applying makeup. She parlayed a knack for new-product ideas into an entry-level management position with the company and became brand manager for Coty's entire line in less than three years.

She quit the company in 1978 to marry Thomas Barad, then a producer/personal manager (now an executive with Paramount Pictures), and relocated to Los Angeles, where she was hired by the Wells, Rich, Greene ad agency to handle the Max Factor account. After taking a few years off to have her first child, she reentered the job market by pitching to Mattel the idea (though it didn't take off) of selling cosmetics to little girls. (More recently she came up with the L'il Miss Makeup doll.)

For anyone critical of her promotion of cosmetics to such an impressionable group, Barad offers this rebuttal: "Cosmetics, although we talk about them as exterior covering, also are helpful and protective and make women—and now men—feel good about themselves," she says. And it's what's below the surface that matters, of course, says Barad, who sometimes finds that the focus is on her beauty rather than her brains. ("From casual observation, she is very adroit at using her looks," says one rival toy-company executive.) Barad is quick to point out that she couldn't have acquired her track record simply because of her looks—"not for nine years and four different management groups."

That Barad has come so far is a testament to both her tenacity and the willingness of Mattel to ignore gender as a factor in its promotions. (Women account for about 45 percent of the company's work force, with nine holding high-ranking officer positions.) Within a few weeks of telling Mattel management that she was pregnant with her second child, Barad was promoted to director of marketing.

But it wasn't always so wonderful at Mattel. The mercurial nature of the toy business aside, the going got especially tough at the company in the mid-'80s, when its Masters of the Universe empire crumbled. (Barad's con-

Source: K. Masters, "It's How You Play the Game," *Working Woman,* May 1990, pp. 88–91. First appeared in WORKING WOMAN in *May 1990.* Written by *Kim Masters.* Reprinted with the permission of WORKING WOMAN Magazine. Copyright © *1990* by WORKING WOMAN, Inc.

tribution to the line, the sinewy She-Ra, Princess of Power, stayed on the market only briefly.) Having expanded on the strength of that franchise, Mattel was saddled with too much inventory and too many employees. As the crisis deepened, the company became increasingly political. Recalls one ex-employee, "It would have made one of the best soap operas you've ever seen."

While some might have fled, Barad stuck it out. She accepted a transfer out of the marketing division to product development—a move many thought curious. "[Mattel] was always considered a marketing-driven company," explains Barad, "so moving over to product development meant, to some people, that you were leaving the mainstream." But she says she was willing to be flexible. "I think a lesson for everybody is that you don't have to have this clear path that you've planned out for five or ten years and think that's the only way to succeed. I took the chance that there was something to be gained."

John W. Amerman, who assumed the helm at Mattel in 1987, soon after Barad made her lateral move, says she was wise to take the chance that her talent would be recognized. "A lot of people talked to Jill and said, 'This is good for your long-term career,' " he says. "And it's all paid off for her."

But at the time, not everyone approved of how Barad played the game. When, for example, Barad's boss (reputed to have been a close friend as well) fell out of favor with the higher-ups, Barad "abandoned her other alliances in a hurry," says an executive who worked with her then. "The company was going to hell, and she not only survived it, she rose up out of the ashes."

Tom Wszalek, a former member of Barad's team who now is with the Disney Channel, has a softer appraisal of Barad's actions. "Whether or not Jill supported [her boss], I don't think she did things to consciously undermine her." And Barad denies any allegations of betrayal on her part. "I never switched alliances," she states emphatically.

Barad soon regained her upward mobility, and new management has turned Mattel around. The company has built up its most successful product lines—Barbie and Hot Wheels—and added a line of preschool toys licensed by Disney. In 1987 the company lost $113 million on revenue of $1 billion. But the following year, Mattel made $36 million on revenue of $990 million. Performance continued to improve in 1989, with an $80 million gain on revenue of $1.2 billion.

Barad has overseen a significantly improved performance by Barbie—revenues grew 30 percent in 1988 and another 20 percent in 1989. In addition to revamping Barbie, Barad has launched such successful doll lines as the Heart Family, P. J. Sparkles and L'il Miss Makeup (a concept that allowed Barad to achieve her long-standing ambition to bring little girls and makeup together.)

In the year she debuted, 1988, L'il Miss Makeup gave Mattel $40 million worth of business. Barad got the

brainstorm for the doll from an innovative color-change process introduced with Hot Wheels Color Racers. Since, as Barad explains, the biggest problem for a makeup doll was that "little girls are so heavy-handed that you always wind up with a mess," the solution involved not actually having to apply any makeup. When a wand filled with cold water touches the doll's face, it activates the color-change process; likewise, warm water makes the color disappear.

Barad came up with the concept only weeks before the annual industry fair at which manufacturers present their new products. "Within two weeks we had L'il Miss Makeup, and I think it was five months later that we were shipping her into the marketplace," Barad recalls. The following year, L'il Miss Dress Up was added to the line; this year, L'il Miss Magic Hair.

Mattel chairman and CEO Amerman cites Barad's success with the L'il Miss line as an example of her ability to come up with a new idea and execute it. He says that he was impressed with Barad even before he took over, having been president of Mattel's international division for several years prior: "You look around the company, you decide who's good, who can be counted on, who's got the ideas. Jill has always been that type of person in my mind."

A key part of Barad's modus operandi is her ability to convert a potential negative into a positive. She admits that she was bored and felt stripped of her identity when she quit work to have her first child, but Barad quickly characterizes the experience as "a real learning time for me." Her darkest hours during the Mattel shake-up gave her "a much more well-rounded perspective on the business." How does she describe her professional philosophy? "There's no such thing as 'can't.' "

Somehow it's not so surprising, then, to learn that Barad bases much of her management style on a strategy she picked up from a sports coach on how to inspire a slumping player. Instead of berating an athlete for screwing up, Barad says, the coach told her "he would take [the player] in a room and show him a tape of all his brilliance and say, 'You're the only one who did that. All of that came from you.' " Explains Barad, "It's a way to give [someone] confidence that there's nobody better." So when it comes to motivating her staff of 500, Barad says that she tries to "continually inspire my people to believe that we can do it."

As far as confidence goes, Barad appears always to have had enough faith in herself to push ahead—going back to those early days of her career when she escaped from the makeup artist's smock at Coty by sending unsolicited product-marketing proposals to management. That confidence has allowed her to make decisions and act on them fast. Tom Wszalek remembers when they were launching a new Barbie ad campaign, based on the slogan We Girls Can Do Anything. Barad wanted a dramatic 60-second commercial, but Wszalek recalls saying that the commercial hadn't been budgeted for. "She said, 'Let's just go for it. We'll worry about how to budget it later.' And it turned out to be a real centerpiece commercial," he says.

Sometimes, however, that push for quick action had the potential for problems. Wszalek recalls a major public-relations event for Barbie that was held in February 1986 at one of the Hudson River–pier exhibition halls in New York: "It was very complicated. We commissioned Andy Warhol to do a painting of Barbie and worked with the designer Billy Boy in Paris, who had a collection of haute couture for Barbie on exhibit there. Jill was saying, 'We really ought to cut this deal and get him to bring the collection over here for a traveling exhibit around the country.' I was wrestling with whether we could make it work financially or otherwise, but I certainly felt a lot of pressure and heat to make it happen.

"We got a lot of publicity," he continues, "but I ended up cutting a deal that was not very good. I spent a lot more money than I should have." But again the show's traveling success outweighed the high price tag. And as for the little matter of going well over budget—something that, for most executives, would constitute a Big Mistake—Barad was able to escape unscathed.

As is still (unfortunately) the case for most high-powered women executives, Barad's career has forced her to make some painful choices and personal sacrifices. Once, when she walked into her son's third-grade classroom for a parent-teacher meeting, the teacher exclaimed, "Oh, so Alexander really does have a mother." Barad admits that she felt awful and says she tries very hard to make time for Alexander, 10, and his brother, Justin, 7. When either of the boys calls her at work, she says, he's never put on hold. But, she adds, "There are realities to the fact that I cannot be everywhere. I've accepted that. I try to put my priorities in order—and it works out better some times than others."

In the end, says Barad, she's satisfied that she's doing her best. "This is me," she says. " I work hard. And I'm never going to please everyone and be what they all want me to be."

Case Analysis

The case describes Jill Barad's behavior within Mattel's political system and some aspects of her approach to major decisions. It also suggests that senior executives, especially women, have many stressors in their lives.

Jill Barad's political strategy focused on managing her career with Mattel. She was ambitious and clearly wanted to move to senior positions within the company. Barad formed alliances within the company that were political tactics to advance her career. Her transfer from marketing to product development was likely done to broaden her experience, although several observers felt it was a bad move.

Barad had both supporters and detractors inside and outside the company. Different perceptions of her behavior led to different conclusions about her motives. She is also an attractive woman, which led some to conclude that her physical attractiveness helped her advance.

Barad's decision approach featured large amounts of intuition and risk taking. She had strong personal feelings and beliefs that helped her guide Barbie to renewed success. Her acceptance of risk clearly showed in her decision about the 60-second commercial. She also showed acceptance of risk by moving from marketing to product development. Barad's approach to decisions also featured speed and decisiveness.

Stressors in Barad's life came from both the work and the nonwork sectors. On the work side, she felt pressures to make successful decisions. Barad was also trying to advance within the company during a difficult period. On the nonwork side, she experienced the common stressors of career women with school-age children. She wanted to balance her work and nonwork priorities, but admitted that it did not always work well.

SECTION V

The Design of Organizations

. . . .

◢ *Section Overview*

*F*igure V-1 shows an overview of the major sections of this book and the chapters in Section V. This section has two chapters. The first outlines two major views of organizational design: (1) the contingency view and (2) the configuration view. The second chapter describes alternative forms of organizational design. Each chapter discusses international aspects of the topics and the ethical issues they raise.

Chapter 17 describes the contingency and configuration views of organizational design. According to the contingency view, an organization's strategy, external environment, technical process, and size affect its design. Two perspectives can guide manager's thinking about the external environment and organizational design. The information perspective views managers as designing organizations to help manage uncertainty in the external environment. The resource perspective sees organizational design as focused on the degree of interdependence between the organization and other organizations in the external environment.

The configuration view of organizational design builds upon the contingency view but does not limit the factors affecting design to four. It sees many factors affecting organizational design—industries, organizational and national cultures, existing organizational members and groups, and the ideology that drives the organization's culture. Configuration theories predict that clusters of factors occur naturally. The variations in the clusters or configurations affect how well an organization does in marketing, meeting customer needs, and reaching cost and profit goals.

Chapter 18 describes alternative forms of organizational design. They include the common and widely used functional, divisional, and hybrid designs; a complex form called matrix; and several evolving forms. Organizational design by function collects major activities of an organization into almost homogeneous groups. For example, all accounting, manufacturing, and engineering activities are assigned to separate departments and work units. Organizational design by division divides the organization's activities according to customers served, operating locations, and the like. Each division has all the functions it needs to operate properly. Some organizational designs feature a combination of the functional and divisional forms.

Organizational design by matrix is a complex form that aligns an organization along two dimensions. One dimension focuses on the functional activities of the organization. The other dimension focuses on projects that serve the organization's

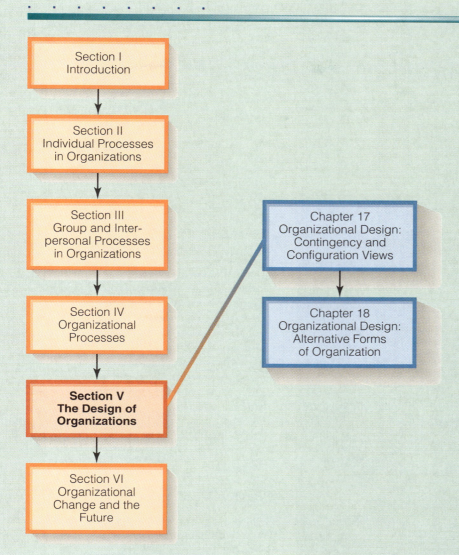

Section I
Introduction

Section II
Individual Processes
in Organizations

Section III
Group and Inter-
personal Processes
in Organizations

Chapter 17
Organizational Design:
Contingency and
Configuration Views

Section IV
Organizational
Processes

Chapter 18
Organizational Design:
Alternative Forms
of Organization

**Section V
The Design of
Organizations**

Section VI
Organizational
Change and the
Future

customers. Many people in a matrix organization report to two bosses, one boss from the functional side and the other from the project side.

Several evolving forms of organizational design are growing in use. Self-managing work teams let managers build an organization around decentralized teams that focus on a complete part of a service or product of the organization. The process view of organizational design moves away from a hierarchical view and says organizations are a series of interconnected processes. Those processes do the main work of the organization. Virtual organizations use networks to build connections between the host organization and many other organizations at scattered locations. Organization architecture is a view of organizational design that uses an architectural metaphor. It asks managers to view organizational design as having form, purpose, and balance among its parts. An organization's architecture includes the informal organization, political processes, reward system, and culture.

17

Organizational Design: Contingency and Configuration Views

· *Developing an organization's strategy often is a first step in deciding the organization's design.*

After reading this chapter, you should be able to . . .

- Describe how organizational design can get information to decision makers and help coordinate activities in an organization.
- Discuss the contingency view of organizational design.
- Distinguish between the organizational design effects of strategy, external environment, technical process, and size.
- Discuss the configuration views of organizational design.
- Distinguish between Defender, Prospector, Analyzer, and Reactor organizational forms.

Chapter Overview

Cummins Engine Company

In articles about innovative management, Cummins Engine Co. of Columbus, Ind. frequently gets a mention. And its Clovis [New Mexico] subsidiary, Cummins Natural Gas Engines Inc., reflects the parent's philosophy.

The 14-year-old Cummins plant here is the only engine maker in the state. Mechanics build natural gas engines the size of a small car. But don't look for an assembly line. They assemble them one at a time to customer specifications according to Jim McDade, former plant supervisor and now materials manager.

"We sell horsepower per dollar," said McDade. "That's what we're out in the marketplace competing against.". . .

Cummins Engine, ranked 160th on the Fortune 500 list, was "most admired" in January among industrial and farm equipment companies. Senior executives surveyed by Fortune weighed such measures as quality of management and products, innovativeness, long-term investment value, financial health, ability to attract and keep talented people and community and environmental responsibility. . . .

The Clovis plant makes eight engines ranging from the four cylinder, 495-cubic-inch to the 1,710-cubic-inch, V-12.

They are naturally aspirated (breathe on their own with the intake stroke) or turbo-charged. The engines will run on natural gas, propane, methane, or—used in cogeneration—digester gas.

· *Thomas Pitts assembles a custom engine at the Cummins Engine plant in Clovis, New Mexico.*

Prices range from about $8,000 to $120,000 with all features.

Beginning with a long block built to Cummins specifications at its plant in [Puña,] India, one mechanic will assemble an entire engine because "each engine is so individual," McDade said.

"The customer decides exactly what he wants on an engine, and we build it. It didn't used to be that way. We used to build one engine, and put everything on it," he said.

Each engine is tested and then cleaned and painted "Cummins beige" before leaving the plant by common carrier. The plant makes about 20 engines of various sizes each month. . . .

Management, he said, is not above turning a wrench. "We all do exactly what it takes to get it out the door. We get along."

The parent company is one of a handful to pursue new kinds of labor-management relations, according to Business Week. The traditional division of work "into narrow tasks requiring little training or commitment" has succumbed to "production teams with broader jobs, rotating assignments and considerable management."

The new systems also drop union work rules and minimize managerial supervision while giving employees a voice in decision making.

Source: Excerpted from S. Robinson, "Firm Sells 'Horsepower Per Dollar,' New Mexico Engine Plant to Step Up Production," *Albuquerque Journal*, May 10, 1987, p. D1. Reprinted by permission of Albuquerque Publishing Company.

. . . .

T he Opening Episode described the manufacturing process used at Cummins Engine Company's manufacturing plant in Clovis, New Mexico. The engines are not assembled in sequential steps as on a traditional assembly line. Mechanics build each engine entirely and can rotate among jobs within the plant. The manufacturing or technical process used in this plant affects the way both workers and managers behave.

This chapter develops two major views of organizational design. The contingency view argues that a manager's choice of organizational design is driven and constrained by several factors inside and outside the organization. The configuration view says certain clusters of context, technical, and design factors let an organization be more effective than other clusters. The chapter develops both views as analytical tools for assessing an existing organizational design or choosing a new one.

❏ What Is Organizational Design?

Organizational design refers to the way managers structure their organization to reach the organization's goals. The allocation of duties, tasks, and responsibilities between departments and individuals is an element of organizational design. Reporting relationships and the number of levels in the organization's hierarchy are other structural elements.[1]

Organizational charts usually show the formal design of an organization. They show the configuration of the organization as it is or as the managers of the organization would like it to be. Such charts typically use boxes to show positions in the organization and lines connecting the boxes to show reporting relationships.[2] Figure 17-1 shows an organizational chart for a hypothetical manufacturing company. It quickly gives you an image of how managers have divided the major tasks of the organization and the major reporting relationships. For example, all manufacturing, engineering, and marketing are grouped under one person, the Operations Vice-President. Such grouping emphasizes the close ties that are usually needed in modern manufacturing between those who design, build, and market products.

Organizational charts are incomplete pictures of the division of labor in an organization. They usually do not show all communication links, integrating mecha-

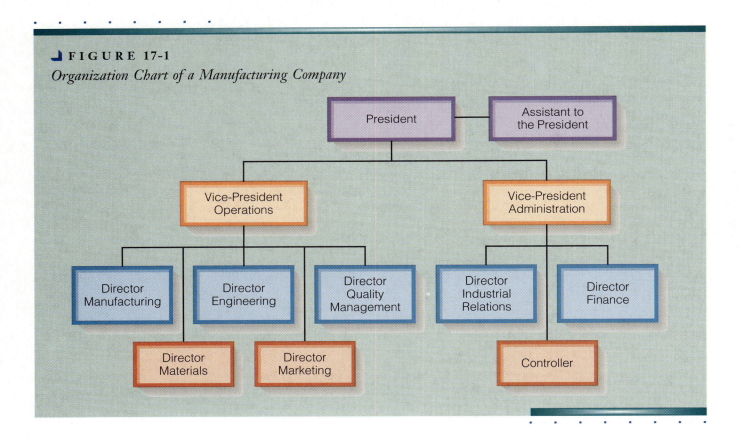

❏ **FIGURE 17-1**

Organization Chart of a Manufacturing Company

nisms, behavioral processes, and informal arrangements within the organization. Nevertheless, organizational charts are useful for showing the basic intended design of an organization.

The design of an organization is much more than the lines and boxes on an organizational chart. "[I]t is a pattern of interactions and coordination that links the technology, tasks, and human components of the organization to ensure that the organization accomplishes its purpose."[3] Organizational design includes the different ways organizations divide their work between people and work units.

An **organization's design has two basic goals.** It must get information to the right places for effective decision making, and it must help coordinate the interdependent parts of the organization. When the organization's design is not right for what it is doing, managers may not get the information they need to predict problems and make effective decisions.[4] They also may not react quickly enough to problems because the existing organizational design blocks needed information. Conflict levels in the organization could be excessively high, implying misalignments in the organization's design.[5] The existing structure may not do an effective job of monitoring changes in the external environment. It may fail to signal managers that a decision is needed now because of such environmental changes.

This chapter gives you some conceptual frameworks for analyzing and understanding the design of organizations. These frameworks let you answer the following questions:

- If you are designing a new organization from the beginning, what should its design be?
- If you are examining an existing organization, is the current organizational design correct for what the organization is doing and for the environment in which it exists?
- Has the external environment changed, requiring changes in the present design of the organization?

This chapter is closely related to the one that follows. The present chapter develops two analytical frameworks that you can use to examine existing and potential organizational designs. Chapter 18 shows you specific approaches to organizational design.

. . . .

 ## Some Background Concepts

Some basic background concepts are helpful in describing the design of organizations. This chapter and the following one use these concepts to discuss organizational design. This section briefly describes each concept. Appendix A has more detail on each concept and some related ideas.

Division of labor	The partitioning among members of the total tasks, duties, and responsibilities of the organization.
Span of control	The number of people reporting directly to a supervisor or manager. The Vice-President of Operations in Figure 17-1 has a span of control of five.
Delegation of authority	Moving decision authority to positions below a manager in an organization.
Centralization/ decentralization	A centralized organization has decision authority at the upper levels of the organization. A decentralized organization has decision authority at the lower levels of the organization. These concepts form a continuum describing degrees of centralization or decentralization.

The **line and staff** parts of an organization differ from each other.[6] The line organization does the work that is tied directly to the organization's goals. This is the part of the organization involved in day-to-day ongoing work activities. For example, in the manufacturing firm shown in Figure 17-1, the operations part of the organization is the line organization. The administrative part is the staff organization.

The staff organization is the group of specialists who give advice and support to the line. Staff includes people in personnel, finance, accounting, management information systems, and strategic planning. They serve in various roles such as advisory, record keeping, data gathering, planning, and the like. Such roles do not have direct authority over the line organization.

The distinction just made between line and staff is clean and clear-cut. In practice, however, that distinction is not always clear, leading to dysfunctional conflict between the line and staff parts of the organization.[7]

. . . .

The Contingency View of Organizational Design

The contingency view of organizational design asks managers to assess four factors before deciding on the design of an organization. The factors are the external environment, the organization's strategy, its technical process, and its size. Each factor alone can affect design decisions, or they can act as a collection of forces that both constrain design choices and drive them.[8]

OVERVIEW

Figure 17-2 shows the major contingency factors of organizational design. The **external environment** includes the organization's competitors, customers, suppliers, distributors, government regulators, legislation affecting it, countries of operation, labor unions, culture, and the like. An organization's **strategy** describes the organization's goals and the ways its managers expect to reach those goals. The **technical process** is the system the organization uses to produce its products or services. The **size** of the organization both directly affects organizational design and changes the effects of the other factors.

Figure 17-2 shows the boundary between the organization and its external environment as a broken line. The line is broken to stress that organizations are open systems with permeable boundaries. A system is a set of interdependent parts forming an organic whole. **Open systems** can act on their external environment and are affected by activities in that environment. Open systems have transactions and exchanges with various parts of their external environment. Closed systems have no such transactions. They are self-contained and operate independently of their external environment. This chapter assumes modern organizations are open systems that interact with their environments.

Figure 17-3 shows some relationships among the contingency factors. The external environment of an organization is dynamic and can change, forcing managers to form a new strategy for dealing with the change. Carrying out that strategy can require a change in some aspect of the organization's design, technical process, or both. The figure shows organizational size affecting several factors. A later section describes some effects of the size of organizations.

Figure 17-3 shows organizational culture surrounding the relationships among the contingency factors. Organizational culture forms the context within which managers decide about organizational design and redesign. For example, an organization's culture can be a source of resistance to change (see Chapter 5). Managers will need to understand their organization's existing culture before beginning an organizational redesign effort.

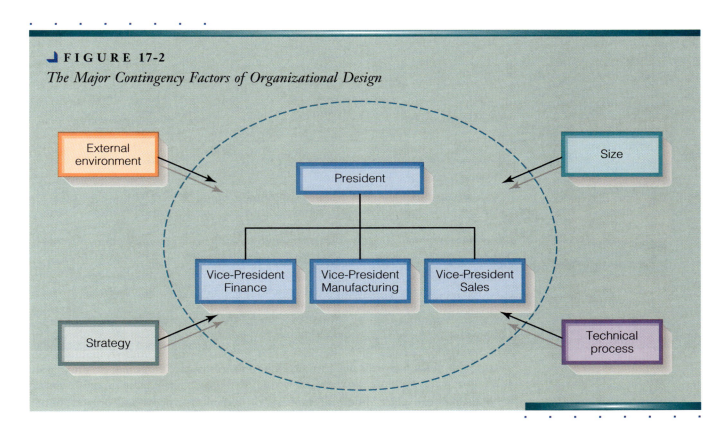

FIGURE 17-2

The Major Contingency Factors of Organizational Design

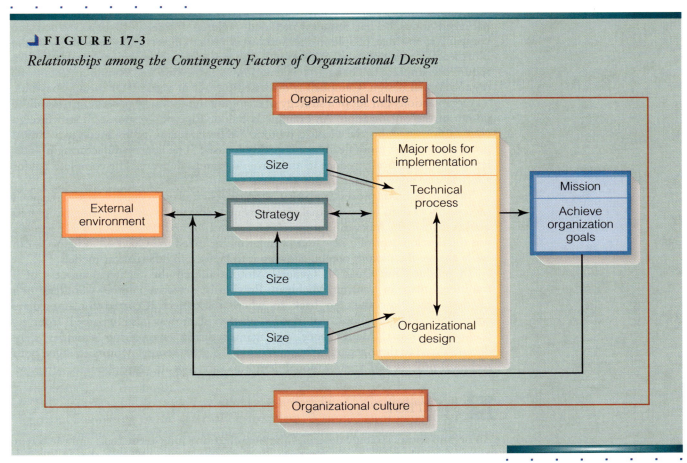

FIGURE 17-3

Relationships among the Contingency Factors of Organizational Design

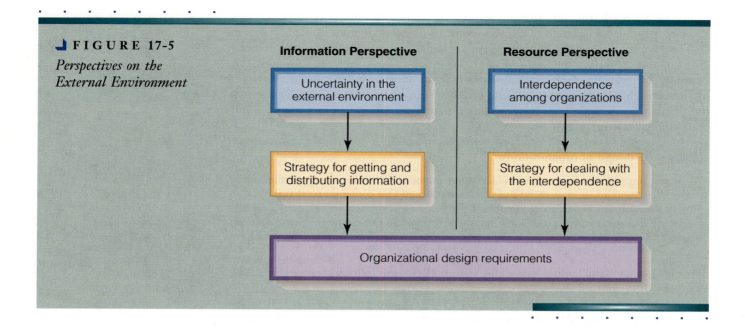

FIGURE 17-5

*Perspectives on the
External Environment*

Information Perspective

Uncertainty in the
external environment

Strategy for getting and
distributing information

Resource Perspective

Interdependence
among organizations

Strategy for dealing with
the interdependence

Organizational design requirements

The second element adding uncertainty to an organization's environment falls on a continuum ranging from static to dynamic. A static external environment is unchanging or slowly changing. A dynamic external environment is filled with quickly moving events that could conflict with each other. The degree of change creates uncertainty in predicting future states of the environment.

Figure 17-6 depicts both environmental dimensions. The figure shows four possible states of the external environment with varying degrees of uncertainty. A simple-static environment has the lowest uncertainty; a complex-dynamic environment has the highest uncertainty. Both simple-dynamic and complex-static environments are about midway between the other two.

Different aspects of the external environment may vary along the dimensions just described. Each element of the environment may be different from the others, so that the various elements make different and contradictory demands on the organization. Reconciling these demands is the complex task management faces in designing the organization.

The Information Perspective uses the concepts of differentiation and integration to describe variations in internal structure and processes found in organizations.[21] **Differentiation** refers to variations in the formal structure and behavior of members within different units of an organization. Each unit's design can have a different degree of centralization and decentralization, span of control, or number of managers.[22] Differentiation is a response to environmental uncertainty. Various parts of an organization such as divisions or departments specialize in handling the uncertainty in their sector of the external environment. That specialization leads to differences in the behavioral processes within those divisions and departments.

The required behavioral processes of a work unit can produce different attitudes and different goal and time orientations among its members. For example, manufacturing usually requires an emphasis on meeting near-term targets and goals. The members of a manufacturing work unit are also likely to have a short-term time perspective. A planning department, because it is doing long-range planning, may require a much longer time focus from its members.

The same characteristics of the external environment that require differentiation of an organization also call for a certain degree of **integration**.[23] The different goals and orientations of the various units create high conflict potential among the units' managers. The environmental demands, however, may require the managers to

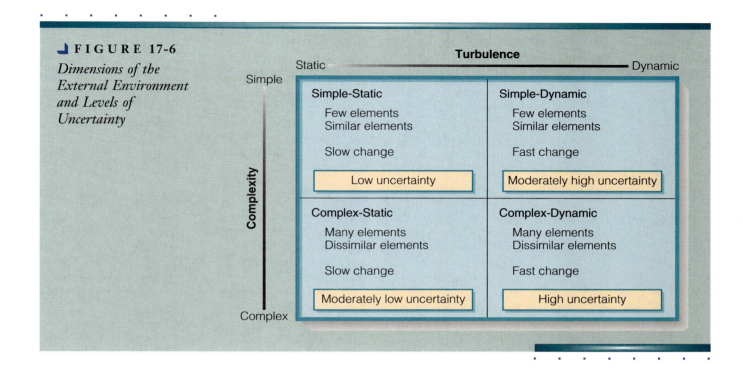

FIGURE 17-6

Dimensions of the External Environment and Levels of Uncertainty

collaborate and cooperate. For example, a sales manager may try to increase sales volume by promising delivery dates that are difficult for manufacturing to meet. If the manufacturing manager tries to meet the delivery dates, production costs may increase. Cooperation between the two units would better serve the interests of the customer and meet the goals of the organization. The different goal orientations of the units, however, can bring the two managers into conflict. Integration is "the quality of the state of collaboration that exists among departments that are required to achieve unity of effort by the demands of the environment."[24]

When an organization is highly differentiated, its design, processes, and members' orientations vary significantly. The resulting differences in the organization demand integration. Highly differentiated organizations that are successful have a higher degree of integration than less-successful organizations with an equal amount of differentiation. Successful organizations use more, and more complex, integrative mechanisms than less-successful organizations.[25]

Integrating mechanisms can include reporting systems, individuals, temporary teams, computer networks, video conferences, or even an entire department of the organization. They also include organizations and groups outside the organization such as suppliers and customer alliances.[26] Those forms of integration are consistent with the quest for process improvement and customer focus of Total Quality Management. Such devices also help managers deal successfully with the conflicts that can develop in highly differentiated organizations.

A final issue facing managers is the right amount of differentiation for the organization. Organizations that are either overdifferentiated or underdifferentiated might be less successful than organizations with more balanced differentiation.[27] For example, a plastics organization had combined its Basic and Applied Research activities into one department. Basic Research was concerned with the state of science and making major scientific discoveries. Applied Research used existing scientific knowledge to make marketable products. These different orientations led to high internal conflict in the department. As a result, the department was less successful in meeting its goals than were separate departments carrying out the same activities in other organizations. These separate departments were internally more homogeneous.

Resource Perspective

The **Resource Perspective** focuses on an organization's dependence on its external environment for economic and material resources. Managers often respond to dependence by trying to control parts of the environment or by changing the environment to a more favorable state. Such managerial responses can lead to changes in the design of the organization.[28]

The Resource Perspective starts with the observation that organizations depend to varying degrees on their external environment for financial and material resources. Managers ask such questions as (1) How much dependence now exists? and (2) How much dependence should we accept? They can respond to perceived high dependence in several ways.

Managers can increase **linkages with other organizations** by contracts, board of directors' membership, and joint ventures. Long-term buying contracts ensure a supply of critical parts or materials. Managers from key vendors may be invited to join the organization's board of directors. Joining the board can give the vendor a sense of having a stake in the organization to which he sells. Organizations use joint ventures when they feel they do not have the necessary financial or technical resources to compete in a specific market. Joint ventures let an organization develop the resources while maintaining autonomy.[29]

Increasing interorganization linkages makes an organization more dependent on its external environment. Managers may then feel a need to decrease that dependence and increase the organization's autonomy. An organization can use two methods to increase its control over the external environment and decrease the power other organizations have over it.

Acquisition of and merger with another company give an organization control over a key element in its external environment. The acquisition may be a company in the same line of business (**horizontal integration**) or a company that is a supplier or distributor (**vertical integration**).[30] The latter type of acquisition can help the organization forge closer ties with key suppliers and distributors.

Organizations can also affect the external environment by trying to make it more favorable. Advertising is a common and widespread effort to affect buyer behavior. Lobbying directly or through a trade association can get desired legislation that is favorable to the organization. Litigation is still another strategy organizations use to affect events in their external environment.

Integration of the Two Perspectives

Managers can respond to the external environment by using either the Information Perspective or the Resource Perspective or a combination of the two. If environmental uncertainty is a key factor, managers could emphasize the Information Perspective. They can change the organization's strategic plan to deal with the changed environment. They may then find they must also change the organization's design to be sure enough information about the environment gets into the organization.

Faced with a highly uncertain external environment, an organization's strategic response could be an effort to tame that environment. If sources of supply are important but potentially volatile, the organization might enter into a long-term buying contract with a supplier. The contract increases the organization's dependence on that vendor and puts the organization under the vendor's control. Management may then respond by acquiring the supplier. Now the organization's external environment is redefined and enlarged to contain elements that apply to the supplier. Management's job is complicated by the need to attend to the new environmental elements along with the elements that were present originally.

The perspectives can be used in combination, if shifts in the environment require it. The two perspectives can lead to different strategic responses that may then require changes in organizational design to carry out the strategy.

The technical process converts an organization's inputs (material, human, monetary) into its outputs. The process may be mechanical as in manufacturing organizations, or it can be a service to clients as in banks, hospitals, or insurance companies. The process can also be largely mental as in organizations that solve problems or create new ideas, products, and services. Research and development organizations, advertising agencies, and software development companies are examples of the latter.

The design of the technical process can predetermine much of the behavior of the people who work in the process. Technical processes vary in work pace, worker control, complexity, degree of routine, predictability, and degree of interdependence within the process. The behavior can be associated with mechanical and manual processes, or it can involve thinking and analytical activities. The technical process decides both what is done and the pace at which it is done.[31]

Types of Technical Processes

Figure 17-7 shows some common technical processes described in this section and the organizations that typically use them. Later sections describe the relationship between the technical processes and the external environment, the characteristics of each type, the behavioral demands the processes make on people, and the effects the processes have on organizational design.

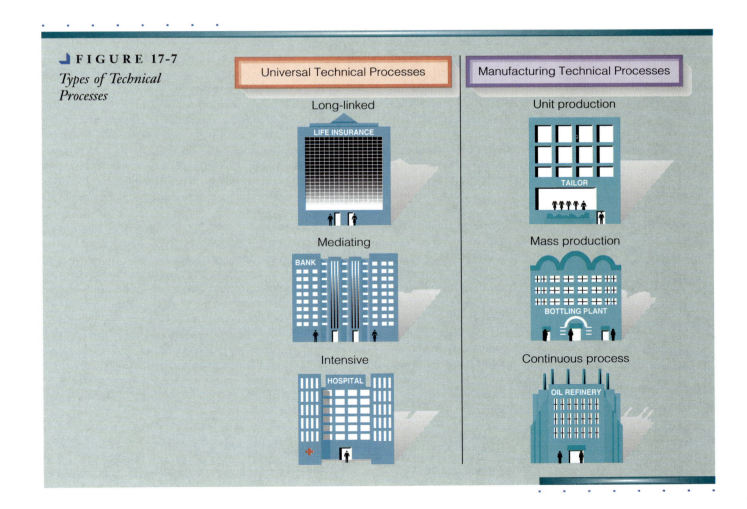

⬛ **FIGURE 17-7**

Types of Technical Processes

Universal Technical Processes

Long-linked — LIFE INSURANCE

Mediating — BANK

Intensive — HOSPITAL

Manufacturing Technical Processes

Unit production — TAILOR

Mass production — BOTTLING PLANT

Continuous process — OIL REFINERY

Unit production is a technical process in which an entire product is made to an individual customer's specifications.[32] This technical process typically uses skilled workers who from their training and experience know how to do their job. Tasks are not narrowly defined or repetitive, so workers have some control over the pace and content of their work. A custom tailor, for example, uses a unit production process to make clothing for a customer. The description of Cummins Engine Co.'s production of pump engines in the Opening Episode was another example of a unit production process.

Mass-production technology uses a series of interconnected steps to produce a product. Researchers also call this technology long-linked because each step in the process depends on steps preceding and following it.[33] The success of the total process depends on each step being done as planned. Such technologies are common in mass-production manufacturing and many service organizations. The technical process controls the production rate, giving workers little control over the pace of their work. Mass-production workers use fewer skills than workers in a unit production process to do narrowly defined, repetitive tasks. Long production runs of a single item are common. Individual customers are not involved because the output of the process often is placed in inventory for sale. Soft drink companies such as PepsiCo use mass-production technology.

Modern manufacturing technologies are changing the nature of the long-linked, mass-production technology. Although the process still involves a series of interconnected steps, flexible manufacturing systems make it possible to turn out small numbers of different products.[34] Such systems use robots, computer-controlled machines, and a central computer system to control machine setups, materials transfer, and the product produced. The step-wise process remains, but the speed and flexibility of the process greatly increase. A case later in the chapter shows how one company uses a flexible manufacturing system to make electric motors.

Continuous process technology is characterized by high capital investment in plant and equipment. The process is fast moving and can be costly or dangerous should it go awry. Automated equipment often controls the process. Workers are more involved in monitoring the production process than in producing products. The level of productivity is largely built into and controlled by the process itself. Worker intervention usually occurs only when a problem arises. Chemical and oil refineries use a continuous process technology.

A **mediating** technology links interdependent individuals or organizations to complete a transaction. Banks link borrowers and depositors. Telephone companies link a caller with someone who will receive the call. Such organizations are the links among parties, mediating their transactions.

Mediating technologies apply standard procedures to different clients. The clients may be physically dispersed and can interact with the organization at different times. The organization brings the different people and organizations together and then processes their transactions according to standard rules and procedures. A bank, for example, would create risks for itself if it did not analyze each loan application in the same way.

An **intensive** technology draws different elements from its available technology and applies them to a single object. As the object responds, the technical process reacts, varying both the selection and application of elements based on the state of the object. A hospital is a good example of an intensive technology. The hospital applies various elements of its technology to a single object, the patient. Depending on the patient's condition, technical elements may be drawn from radiology, cardiology, laboratory, or pharmacy. As the patient responds, the hospital changes the number and type of technical elements applied.

Technical Process and the External Environment

Technical processes vary in their degree of connection to the external environment. Managers can take many actions to uncouple the technical process from or couple it to the external environment. **Uncoupling the technical process** protects it from environmental disturbances. **Coupling the technical process** exposes it to environmental disturbances. Such coupling efforts are done in full recognition that the technical process may be disturbed. Uncoupled technical processes usually make smooth and predictable behavioral demands; coupled technical processes can have unpredictable effects on worker behavior.

Uncoupling the Technical Process. Managers of organizations that have large capital investments in their technical processes want to use the technical process constantly and protect it from environmental disturbances. Four methods can be used to uncouple the technical process from the environment: (1) buffering, (2) smoothing and leveling, (3) anticipation, and (4) rationing.[35]

Buffering protects the technical process on either the input side or the output side by stockpiling raw materials or warehousing finished product. Electrical utilities, for example, protect the generation of electricity from variations in shipments of coal or oil by stockpiling those materials at the generation site. Toy manufacturers warehouse toys to meet high seasonal demand.

Managers use smoothing and leveling processes to shift demand for products or services from peak demand periods to times of less demand. An example that you probably have experienced is the variation in long-distance telephone rates at different times of the day. Long-distance calls are most expensive on weekdays between 8 A.M. and 5 P.M., a period of high business demand. Rates are lowest between 11 P.M. and 8 A.M. on the same days—periods of low use of long-distance equipment and lines. The different rates encourage leveling of demand for long-distance service.

Managers use anticipation to have the organization's product or service ready when there are fluctuations in demand. Restaurants, for example, plan for variations in demand by using different staffing levels at different times of the day. Managers also use strategic planning to predict future directions and decide what the organization should do in the future.

The last response occurs when the first three responses do not work or are not available to managers. Rationing is frequently used under emergency conditions. Hospitals, for example, cannot afford to invest the funds necessary to maintain themselves at the level required to meet the demands of infrequent catastrophic events. Bed space is rationed during a disaster by assigning beds only to those most seriously hurt.

Coupling the Technical Process. Many organizations are experimenting with ways of coupling their technical processes to the external environment. Some organizations are adopting just-in-time production practices that closely tie the technical process to the environment.[36] Raw materials, parts, subassemblies, and so on arrive as needed. There is no stockpiling of materials or other inventory maintenance to buffer the technical process. Just-in-time production requires both managers and nonmanagers to be fully aware of the status of the production process. Suppliers must also be concerned with the quality of what they supply because poor-quality materials, parts, or subassemblies can cripple the technical process. Organizations adopting this new approach to production management create strong interdependencies between manufacturing and suppliers in the external environment.

Characteristics of Each Technical Process

Technical processes can be characterized by (1) the extent to which they create routine or nonroutine work environments, (2) the types of skills required of workers, and (3) the degree of interdependence between people and work units. Interdependence can exist both within the technical process and between the process and other parts of the organization to which it is linked.[37]

Unit production technologies require frequent decisions because different objects will have different requirements. Unexpected elements in jobs that have not been done before often require decisions from workers or supervisors. Communication levels are high and have a strong problem-solving orientation. Worker interdependence is high because each person contributes to the object.[38]

Mass-production technologies create routine, predictable work settings for both managers and workers. Workers have little discretion about how to do their work. Disruptions caused by material shortages or equipment failures require quick action from management. Such technologies are routine and predictable when everything works right. If the process is dangerous, management and workers must constantly be aware of the state of the process so problems can be predicted and crises avoided. When something goes wrong, decisions must be made quickly and with knowledge of the total system.[39]

Mass-production technologies create interdependence within the technical process and between the process and other work units.[40] The technical process is interdependent with the purchasing department at the beginning of the process and the shipping department at the end. Planning the content and length of production runs aids coordination among these interdependent work units. Communication and frequent decisions are necessary during the planning process. Once production is underway, standard procedures substitute for individual decisions and communication. Interdependence increases with modern manufacturing technologies. Computer technology forges strong, real-time links between the technical process and other parts of the organization.[41]

Mediating technologies create some degree of uncertainty for management because of the physical and temporal separation of clients. Managers cannot predict with certainty the time and place of client transactions. Different parts of an organization with a mediating technology operate independently of each other when processing client transactions. They are linked together, however, when trying to reach the organization's goals and must coordinate their activities by using standard procedures for processing transactions.

Intensive technologies require a high degree of cooperation among the technical elements and much face-to-face communication. Coordination requirements also are high because many different parts of the technology must be brought together to transform the object successfully. Intensive technologies feature complex interdependence among work units.[42] The object in process can enter and reenter work units as its condition changes and the technical process responds to its condition. Many decisions must be made when the object is processed. Mutual adjustment and a high level of face-to-face communication coordinate the different parts of the system.

Technical Process and Organizational Design

The research examining relationships between the technical process and organizational design has aroused considerable controversy.[43] Questions about how to measure and classify technical processes muddy the conclusions we can draw from published reports. There has also been strong disagreement about the importance of technology as a contingency factor of organizational design.[44] Some studies support it as a factor; other studies do not. With these cautions in mind, some conclusions emerge from systematic reviews of the research literature.[45]

Routine technologies feature centralized decision making that uses formal written rules and procedures to guide decisions. Such centralization is more characteristic of small organizations than large organizations. Organizations that use routine technologies and have many professional employees use fewer formal procedures than organizations with fewer professionals. Organizations that use complex, nonroutine technologies tend to have more departments, fewer levels of authority, and more participation in decision making than organizations that use more routine technologies.

Different types of technical processes have different forms of organizational design.[46] The span of control of first-line supervisors is greater in mass-production technologies than in continuous process technologies. Organizations using continuous process technologies have taller hierarchical designs than organizations using mass-production or unit production technologies. Duties and responsibilities are less well-defined in the decentralized unit production and continuous process technologies than in the more centralized mass-production technology. Modern manufacturing technologies, however, let managers decentralize decision authority within mass-production technology more than in the past.[47] Decentralization and loosely defined duties give managers needed flexibility to manage the production of different products.[48]

Continuous process technologies also use a decentralized organizational design.[49] The more costly and potentially more dangerous continuous process technology requires a closer supervisor-worker relationship than the more routine mass-production technology. Fast response to a process gone awry is necessary in a continuous process technology.

Mass-production technologies often have formal procedures to guide decisions about the state of the process. The routine, predictable character of this technology allows a centralized organizational design with high standardization.[50] Organizations with the less routine, less predictable unit production or continuous process technologies need a more flexible and responsive organizational design.

 ORGANIZATION SIZE

Organizations usually develop more formal written rules and procedures as they increase in size. Large organizations have more management levels and more structured work activities than small organizations and often use a decentralized form.[51]

Large organizations are more differentiated and need more integrating mechanisms than small organizations.[52] Managers in large organizations make decisions guided by written rules and procedures. Small organizations can have an organic form with a simpler design than large organizations use.[53] Small organizations also have less differentiation and integration, fewer formal written procedures, and narrower spans of control.

Organization size influences the effects of the technical process on organizational design. Technical process is more strongly associated with organizational design in small organizations than in large organizations. People in the technical process have less control over work procedures in large organizations than in small ones.[54]

· ·

 C A S E   *Campbell Soup Co.*

Read the following case and analyze it using the concepts described up to this point in the chapter. Consider the following questions while reading the case:

Source: Developed from "Campbell to Sell More Businesses," Associated Press, 1990 (As the story appeared in the *Albuquerque Journal*, June 30, 1990, p. C4); C. Dugas and M. N. Vamos, "Marketing's New Look: Campbell Leads a Revolution in the Way Consumer Products Are Sold," *Business Week*, January 26, 1987, pp. 64–69; B. Saporito, "Campbell Soup Gets Piping Hot," *Fortune*, September 9, 1991, pp. 142–44, 146, 148.

1. What were the changes in the external environment that required a management response?
2. Did the company change its strategy? If so, in what specific ways?
3. Did management redesign part of the organization to align it with the new strategy? If they did, what were the changes?

⌐ CASE DESCRIPTION

The Campbell Soup Co. was in trouble. Its market share had dropped to 62 percent in the late 1980s from 83

The Campbell Soup Co. corporate headquarters in Camden, New Jersey.

percent in the mid-1950s. New product development had slowed to a walk. The heirs of the company's founder John T. Dorrance feuded about selling the company and griped about its poor performance. What had happened to a company known as a leading marketer of consumer products and with a brand name that was over 100 years old?

The external environment of Campbell had shifted in several significant ways. During the 1980s, more women and ethnic minorities entered the workforce, single-parent households increased, and the population became older. Traditional meal preparation changed with each family member preparing his or her own meal. Such demographic and behavioral shifts increased the demand for greater variety in easily prepared foods. Convenience in food preparation overrode any commitment to Campbell's tomato or chicken noodle soup.

Campbell had grown into a slow-moving centralized organization with strong manufacturing ability. Marketing decisions were centralized in its Camden, New Jersey headquarters. Uniform advertising campaigns reached across the United States through the mass media. These characteristics did not fit the needs of a diverse and fast-changing environment.

R. Gordon McGovern became chief executive in the mid-1980s and quickly tried to shift Campbell to a marketing focus by moving decision making closer to customers. He formed 50 divisions whose managers had profit and loss responsibility. Marketing activities were spread across the United States in 22 regions. Each region had a marketing and sales force with its own advertising and sales promotion budget.

The result was a sharp shift from a uniform mass advertising approach to one that was tailored to a regional market. Skiers in Nevada's Sierra Mountains receive hot soup samples at a ski resort. New York City football fans were the targets of a radio promotion for Swanson Frozen dinners. A Sacramento, California Span-

ish radio station featured an advertising campaign for V8 juice, a popular drink among Hispanics.

The new marketing strategy did not produce immediate dramatic improvements. McGovern resigned in 1989 and was replaced by David Johnson, an executive with a reputation for turning around lackluster organizations. Johnson refined the company's strategy by focusing only on frozen and heat-processed foods. He formed 40 business units that had responsibility for all aspects of marketing, manufacturing, and logistics. Johnson also slashed costs by closing inefficient or excess manufacturing plants. The result: operating profits increased by 30 percent in the fiscal year ending July 1991.

CASE ANALYSIS

The Campbell Soup Co. case shows how managers can react to shifts in the external environment. The company developed a new strategy and began to change the organization's design so it could achieve that strategy.

The external environment shifted from a uniform mass market to several different market sectors. The demography of American consumers had changed. The number of single parents and working women had increased. Consumers wanted more variety and breadth in food offerings. There was a shift from family meal preparation to individual food preparation. Convenience in preparing foods was now a major consideration of many consumers.

The environment of Campbell Soup became more complex because of the changes in demography. Marketing of Campbell's products faced a more uncertain environment than before. Management's lag in response resulted in a loss of market share.

The design of Campbell Soup's organization had to change to help meet the goals of the new strategy. A centralized marketing organization worked for a uniform mass market. The shift to regional marketing and sales required a decentralized organization. McGovern began moving marketing decisions away from headquarters in Camden, New Jersey. The decisions now are made at a local level closer to consumer tastes.

The new chief executive, Johnson, continued decentralizing Campbell and cut costs by closing plants. Johnson focused the company's strategy more sharply and prepared the company for an even more diverse future by improving its fiscal performance.

The Configuration View of Organizational Design

The configuration view of organizational design builds upon the contingency view but does not limit the factors affecting design to the external environment, strategy, technical process, and size. Instead, the configuration view sees many factors affecting organizational design—industries, organizational and national cultures, existing organization members and groups, and the ideology that drives the organization's culture.[55] Configuration theories predict that clusters of factors occur naturally. These clusters or configurations have various effects on how well an organization does in serving its markets, meeting customer needs, and reaching cost and profit goals.

Configuration theories feature typologies describing generic organization forms that vary in effectiveness. The typologies include the factors needed to describe an organization's design, its context, and aspects of its processes that will let it perform effectively. The theories and their typologies view relationships among factors as bidirectional. They also expect different configurations to be equally effective. For example, to succeed in a dynamic environment, managers could develop successions of innovative products or find specific market niches. Such strategies will work well only when they are configured with the right organizational design, technical process, and behavioral processes in the organization.

TWO CONFIGURATION TYPOLOGIES

Researchers have proposed two configuration typologies that have empirical support in the organizational design literature. The first typology features two generic organization forms—mechanistic and organic. The second typology features four generic forms—Defender, Prospector, Analyzer, and Reactor. The next two sections describe the typologies and give examples of each.

Mechanistic and Organic Organizations

Recall that external environments of organizations can fall on a continuum ranging from certainty to uncertainty. Two different types of organizational design are right for the two different environments.[56] Figure 17-8 shows the alignment of the two types of organizations with the external environment.

A **mechanistic organization** fits a highly certain external environment. Mechanistic organizations have the following characteristics:

- Clearly specified tasks.
- Precise definition of rights and obligations of organization members.
- A hierarchical structure of control, authority, and communication.
- A tendency toward vertical interaction and communication.

Mechanistic organizations have predictable and formal internal relationships and rely on written rules and procedures. This organizational design suits recurring, predictable events where the organization's response can be standardized.

Mechanistic
organizations

Organic
organizations

Certainty ————————————— Uncertainty

External environment

An **organic organization** fits an uncertain external environment. Organic organizations have the following characteristics:

- Roles that are not highly defined.
- Tasks that are continually redefined through interaction with other members of the organization.
- Little reliance on authority and control to direct the activities of organization members. Organic organizations rely on individuals' commitment to organization goals.
- Decentralized control and decision making.
- Fast decision-making processes.[57]
- Communication that is both lateral and vertical.

Less-defined roles and continual redefinition of tasks give organization members the flexibility they need to respond to changing events. Decentralization of decision making lets people deal with the different situations presented by the changing external environment. A speedy decision process lets managers keep up with fast environmental shifts.

Defender, Prospector, Analyzer, and Reactor Organizations

The second configuration typology describes the four types of organizations shown in Figure 17-9: Defender, Prospector, Analyzer, and Reactor.[58] The Defender and Prospector anchor the end points of a continuum with the Analyzer midway between them. The Reactor is not on the continuum because this typology views it as a maladapted organization form.

Defender organizations succeed in stable environments with well-defined market segments for their products and services. They develop a committed customer base that lets them provide a predictable flow of products or services to the marketplace. Because their environment is stable, Defenders achieve a competitive cost advantage from specialization, repeated use of well-understood technical processes, and low costs of product manufacturing or service delivery. The Defenders' organizational design features well-defined functions, centralization, and formal procedures. They can also use a long-range planning process because their external environments change slowly. Many companies producing products with strong brand recognition such as Jaguar automobiles are Defender organizations.

Prospector organizations succeed in dynamic environments that are unpredictable and fast changing. They prosper by continually watching their external environment to find new markets. Prospectors focus on developing new products or services that fit fast-changing customer needs, desires, and expectations. Because they focus on developing new products and services, Prospectors often change their external

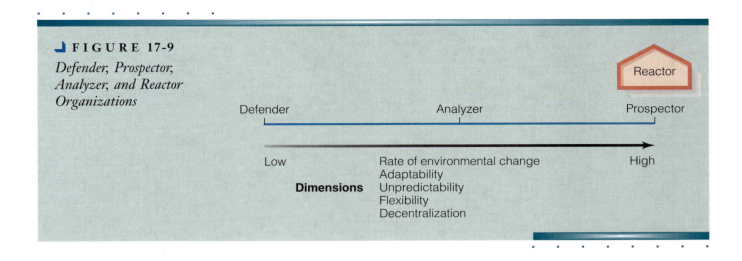

Reactor

Defender   Analyzer   Prospector

Low   Rate of environmental change   High
                    Adaptability
Dimensions   Unpredictability
                    Flexibility
                    Decentralization

environment as well as respond to it. Prospector organizations have high decentralization, little task specialization, few levels of management, and high interdependence between people and work units. Their technical processes emphasize flexibility so they can quickly introduce new products. Changes in the external environment have few negative effects on Prospectors because of their constant monitoring, adaptation, and the change they often bring to that environment. Their constant quest for newness brings internal change that prevents them from enjoying the advantages of stable organizational design and stable technical processes. Successful personal computer companies such as Acer in Taiwan are examples of Prospector organizations.

Analyzer organizations have some features of both Prospector and Defender organizations (see Figure 17-9). To keep costs low, they strive for efficiency in their technical processes for producing stable products and services. They also develop new products and services to maintain a competitive edge in changing markets. Analyzer organizations constantly scan their external environment for successful new products and services from Prospectors. Then the Analyzers quickly introduce their own versions to capture a piece of the market. Because these organizations feature both stability and change, one part of their organizational design is routine, formal, and centralized. Another part features temporary task groups, decentralization, and few formal procedures. Major drug manufacturers such as Whitehall Laboratories invest in research and development for new products while successfully marketing established products such as Advill®.

Reactor organizations have an unbalanced configuration of external environment, organizational design, strategy, and technical process. Managers of Reactor organizations have poorly adapted to environmental changes over time. Poor adaptation can occur for three reasons: (1) lack of a strategy that is both clear and widely known throughout the organization, (2) a technical process and organizational design that are not well linked to a strategy, or (3) management's insistence on keeping a strategy, technical process, or organizational design that is no longer right for a changed environment.

The first three organization types have a balanced configuration of external environment, strategy, technical process, and organizational design (see Figure 17-10). Some research points to greater success for organizations with balanced configurations.[59] The last organization type, the Reactor, is less effective than the others. Figure 17-11 shows four possible unbalanced configurations for Reactor organizations.

Balanced Configuration:
Defender, Analyzer, and
Prospector

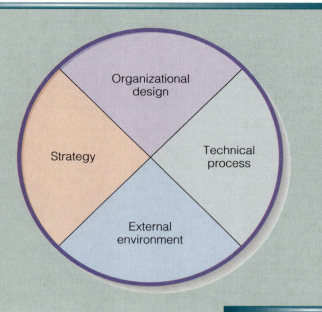

■ FIGURE 17-11

Unbalanced Configurations: Reactor Organizations

Unbalanced configuration 1

Unbalanced configuration 2

Unbalanced configuration 3

Unbalanced configuration 4

Baldor Electric

The following case describes Baldor Electric's responses to its changing environment. Here are some questions to consider while reading the case:

1. Is Baldor a mechanistic or an organic organization?
2. Which of the four types of organizations does it most closely resemble: Defender, Prospector, Analyzer, or Reactor?

CASE DESCRIPTION

Chastity is nice. And temperance gets applause. But constancy, among the virtues, pays off in cash when properly employed—as Baldor Electric, an electric motor maker in Fort Smith, Arkansas, is finding. Along with much bigger brethren like General Electric, Reliance Electric, and Emerson Electric, Baldor slogged through a decade of lousy sales for the U.S. motor industry. But unlike some of those others, it emerged with bigger market share, record sales and profits, and a reputation for quality second to none. . . .

The danger to Baldor came from overseas. In the late 1970s foreign manufacturers began pumping out low-cost commodity-type motors from automated factories in Japan, South Korea, and Taiwan. "And they weren't even breathing hard," says Jim Raba, spokesman for the National Electrical Manufacturers Association. The dollar's rise increased their advantage. Some American manufacturers, including Westinghouse, originator of the alternating-current motor, got out of the business altogether. Others—including GE and Emerson—moved some production offshore to capture lower costs. . . .

Source: Excerpted from A. Farnham, "Baldor's Success: Made in the U.S.A.," *Fortune*, July 17, 1989, pp. 101, 102, 104, 105. © Time Inc. All rights reserved.

Baldor did not. It stayed the course—which sounds great if you're on the right course. Staying the wrong course has little merit, as the crew of the *Exxon Valdez* can attest. More than a few security analysts thought Baldor's compass had been magnetized. They kept asking when management would wise up. Remembers Roland Boreham Jr., 64, Baldor's chairman: "We caught hell because we looked like an oddball."

If not actually odd, Baldor is at least a niche player. The company makes only industrial electric motors, not the kind found in consumer appliances, the business that Emerson dominates. Baldor's motors turn up in factories and worksites. There are explosion-proof motors (for mining, oil, and gas applications) and lint-proof motors (for the textile industry). Small Baldor motors run heart pumps in hospitals. Larger ones flip battleship windshield wipers back and forth. The largest, at 500 horsepower, roll steel. Being specialized, such motors command premium prices. While none is a big seller by McDonald's standards, collectively they give Baldor more than 10% of the $1-billion-a-year U.S. industrial motor market.

Half the company's 1988 sales came from selling standard motors (over 2,500 different models). The rest came from custom work—building motors for a variety of manufacturers, most of which require short lead times. Baldor can design, produce, and deliver a motor in six weeks.

Boreham, the man most people credit with keeping Baldor home, worried about going offshore. Trained at UCLA as a meteorologist (and electrical engineer), he forecast that when updrafts buoying the dollar subsided, Baldor would lose any price advantage gained by moving. And as a quality maven, he feared production abroad might damage Baldor's reputation. Engineers consistently give the company's motors high marks for reliability and workmanship.

• *Part of Baldor Electric's manufacturing system in Fort Smith, Arkansas. The company's flexible manufacturing system lets it build electric motors to each customer's specifications.*

Tolerant of nothing less than total quality where copper wire and insulation are concerned, Boreham is somewhat less scrupulous about personal possessions. He speaks admiringly of a friend's Yamaha graphite golf clubs but plays with a set Andrew Carnegie would have recognized. His daughters, he says, needle him to buy better clothes. A contemplative man who likes to help write the company's annual report, he smokes Prince Albert tobacco ($8.50 the pound) in pipes he suspects "may not be very good." (They aren't.) So absorbed is he in motors that his wife—whose sense of humor is perhaps obscure—once hung a picture of one over their bed.

Since Baldor adjusts so much of its production to suit special demands—the company's average lot produced is only 50 motors—it was insulated, to a degree, from commodity competition. It felt the squeeze another way. "A flood of motors coming over wasn't our big worry," Boreham says. "Our fear was foreign machinery coming in." When the dollar rose, foreign-made industrial machinery began entering the U.S., all of it powered by foreign motors. By 1987, the National Electrical Manufacturers Association estimates, $1 billion a year in offshore motors was arriving via this channel. As these wore out, U.S. owners began ordering overseas replacements. Making matters worse, two markets Baldor relied on—energy and agriculture—coincidentally went into slumps. By 1982 the combined effects on sales were hard to ignore. Recalls Boreham: "After 21 straight years of sales increases, we learned humility." From 1981 to 1983 profits tumbled by a third. . . .

The victory cost plenty. Between 1977 and 1982—around the same time other motor companies were bowing out—Baldor tripled its rate of capital investment, upgrading milling equipment, cutters, lathes, and winders. President and chief operating officer Quentin Ponder designed a home-grown version of just-in-time manufacturing, which Baldor calls flexible flow. Under Baldor's batch system, making an order had taken up to four weeks. Ponder cut that time to five days.

Flex-flow eliminates progressive assembly. Each worker puts together a complete motor from a tray of parts in front of him. The tray is tagged with a computer printout telling him what kind of motor he's building, how to assemble the parts, and how to test the completed product. Successive trays may hold parts for different kinds of motors, and a worker may assemble as many as 20 different models in a shift. . . .

To bolster its reputation for quality, Baldor in 1987 sent all 96 of its middle-level managers through quality expert Philip Crosby's training program in Orlando, Florida. It sent nearly 2,000 of its 2,500 employees through in-house classroom instruction. Baldor's investment in training confirms the company's commitment to—and high opinion of—its non-union work force. The company hasn't laid off a worker in Fort Smith since 1962. It offers profit sharing (a local rarity) and pays close to union wages. Its workers by and large return the compliment. Turnover is low, and workers tend to regard jobs at Baldor as careers. Workers voted 10 to 1 to reject an attempt to unionize a Baldor plant in Oklahoma. "It's hard to get a 10-to-1 vote on whether it's a nice day or not," says Boreham. Tom Netherton, business manager for the International Brotherhood of Electrical Workers, says he plans to make his own effort next year. Isn't he fighting an uphill battle? "Well," he allows, "you have to do something for entertainment in Fort Smith."

Randy Goldsmith, a 32-year-old lathe operator, says he has seen big changes since he arrived at Baldor in 1975. "Nobody had the pride then they do now," he says. "Not the workers, not the company. It used to be we had these clips to check the tolerances of the shafts we made. If the clip didn't fit—well, you could push on it harder and say it was OK. Now we check with these electronic snap gauges." The digital gauges are accurate to one ten-thousandth of an inch. Goldsmith, who signs off on every shaft he makes, says, "If anything's wrong with it, they know my address.

Chastened by its onetime dependency on agriculture and oil, Baldor has been broadening its product line, adding 300 new models to its last catalogue alone, as it explores less cyclical markets such as food handling and fitness. The fitness motor turns joggers' treadmills, while the food industry product, called a Wash Down motor, is designed to take dousings with hot, soapy water. It sells at a 40% to 50% premium over competing alternatives, yet Dick James, engineering manager of Mushroom Cooperative Canning, a mushroom growers' association in Kennett Square, Pennsylvania, uses at least 140 of them to drive his canning and freezing lines. He says, "Downtime is costly. We had several motors prior to Baldor, but they didn't last. They're bombarded all day long with hot water, and at night, when they cool, ordinary motors suck in water, ruining the bearings." Since Baldor introduced its first Wash Down four years ago, the model's unit sales have grown nearly 50% annually.

Perhaps the most impressive evidence of Baldor's renewed staying power is its sales abroad, which began expanding even when the dollar was high. These now account for 11% of total sales, with exports growing at twice the rate of domestic sales. The company's strategy overseas is to sell to neglected niches. In Japan it found one: dental lathes. "It took us three years to get an order," says John McFarland, Baldor's director of international sales. "We had to make quite a few modifications to suit the buyers." This small bite into the Japanese motor business has led to orders from Toyota, among others. In selling to foreign markets, whose design standards often differ from those of U.S. customers, Baldor has an important edge in its ability to fine-tune small orders, even from across an ocean.

Contemplating Baldor's past, especially its decision not to move production abroad, Boreham puffs his pipe and muses, "Pride takes you one direction, short-term profit another. Pride usually wins out if you're a confident person." In Baldor's case, pride—a stubborn, costly, and almost atavistic commitment to home, work force, and product—has served the company well. Contemplating the future, what could go wrong? For the near term, at least, not much. Unless scientists at the University of Utah discover perpetual motion.

CASE ANALYSIS

Baldor Electric's management forged it into an organic organization with all the features of a Prospector. To see how close Baldor is to a Prospector, reread the earlier description of Prospectors now while the case is clearly in your mind.

The company's external environment featured complex, rapid change both domestically and internationally. Baldor's management formed a strategy focused on high-quality electric motors for different market niches. Successfully carrying out that strategy required a decentralized organizational design and a flexible technical process. The company's nimble organization, skilled workforce, and flexible technical process let it quickly adapt to its customers' changing needs. Baldor Electric has a fully balanced configuration of factors that have helped it become a success.

International Aspects of Organizational Design

*T*he international context of organizations can increase the complexity of their external environments. The elements of the external environment described earlier multiply when an organization moves into the global arena. Countries vary in cultural orientation, labor laws, consumer preferences, buying and selling traditions, and economics. Multiple country operations can further increase the environmental complexity of multinational organizations.[60]

An organization facing an external environment high in international dimensions of complexity may require more differentiation. Such organizations may need separate functions to manage currency transactions and to follow local labor laws. The increased differentiation requires more integrating mechanisms to coordinate those activities.

Countries vary in their acceptance of ambiguous or uncertain situations. They also vary in their acceptance of differences in power and authority based on organization position.[61] The choice of mechanistic or organic organizational designs is more complex in an international context than a domestic one. The ambiguous and uncertain roles and relationships that often go with an organic design may not fit cultural expectations about such relationships. Although managers from a home country might favor an organic organization, the local culture might favor a mechanistic one.[62] The opposite is also possible. For example, an organic organization fits the cultural expectations of many Nordic countries. A mechanistic form fits the expectations of many Mediterranean countries, China, and Hong Kong.[63]

Ethical Issues and Organizational Design

*M*anagers can face several ethical issues when considering the external environment of their organizations or assessing strategic options. They can affect their external environments by lobbying activities. Such efforts are common in the United States, where they are considered both legal and ethical. Bribing government officials, however, is illegal under U.S. law.

Managers face constant choices about using new technologies in their organization's technical processes. Such changes can affect an organization's employment levels and create stress for those who need to learn new ways of working. The ethical issues center on the stress effects of such changes and the effects on displaced workers.

Strategic responses to environmental shifts also raise ethical questions. Many organizations have been pressed to become smaller, leaner, and more efficient to stay competitive. Procter and Gamble, for example, cut 13,000 jobs and closed 30 plants in 1993.[64] Among the first decisions made by Apple Computer's new chief executive officer in July 1993 was the layoff of 2,500 workers.[65]

A utilitarian analysis would focus on the net benefits of both sets of management actions. Many people would gain from those actions, including shareholders, customers, and the remaining employees. The employees who lost their jobs were a clear cost. Management's actions were ethical if the total benefits exceeded the costs.

The international section noted that different cultures often expect different organizational designs. Managers operating in an international environment can face a complex ethical dilemma. Should they choose an organizational design according to their home culture or according to the local culture?

Personal and Management Implications

Several implications derive from this chapter's discussion of organizational design. Differentiation of organizations can be a basis of interpersonal conflict. If you are in conflict with someone from another part of the organization, try to recall the effects of differentiation on people's perception of and orientation to time. Such factors may be the basis of your conflict, not "personality differences."

The type of technical process used by an organization affects the design of jobs. The pace of work and degree of autonomy in a job are due partly to the technical process. Unit production allows more autonomy than mass production. The latter more directly controls work pace than the former. You may wish to reflect on the technical process used in organizations you consider for future employment.

The contingency factors of organizational design can change over time, requiring management to respond with a new design. A new organizational design can introduce many changes for you. Established relationships with others in the organization may be disrupted. Old, and possibly comfortable, ways of behaving will be altered. Only you know how well you cope with change. A significant source of change for you in the future will be the redesign of your employing organization. Chapter 19 discusses how managers can change organizations and what you can do to cope with change.

Managers must continually watch the external environment for changes that require a change in strategy. If strategy is changed, both the organizational design and the technical process should be reexamined. If the environment becomes turbulent, managers should consider moving to an organic form of organization. Any changes required are not always easy to make. Resistance to change by people in the organization is common.

Organizations can become more complex and more differentiated in design as they grow larger. A highly differentiated organization can produce conflict. Mergers of organizations with different cultures and designs can also lead to conflict.

Remaining competitive in a fast-changing external environment often requires managers to change the technical process of their organization. The existing technical process or organizational design can constrain such change.[66] Managers must be aware of when a new technical process is needed. As organizations change their technical processes, managers must also be aware of needed changes in organizational design. Some research evidence described earlier points to specific changes in organizational design required by different characteristics of the technical process.

Changing an organization is not easy. Chapter 19 describes the methods of change available to a manager and the types of resistance to change that can be expected. It also describes many aspects of organizational design that can contribute to conflict. Knowing how to manage conflict effectively will be important to you as a manager.

Summary

Organizational design refers to the way managers structure organizations by assigning tasks and responsibilities to departments and individuals and defining reporting relationships among them. The design of an organization helps get information to the right places for effective decision making and helps coordinate the interdependent parts of the organization.

The contingency view of organizational design focuses on strategy, external environment, technical process, and size. An organization's external environment can change, requiring managers to form a new strategy. That strategy is then carried out by changing the technical process, organizational design, or both. Routine technologies centralize decision making and use written rules and procedures to guide decisions. Complex, nonroutine technologies can have more complex organization forms with more departments or divisions than nonroutine technologies. Managers can use buffering, smoothing, anticipation, and rationing to protect the technical process from environmental disturbances.

The configuration view of organizational design sees many factors affecting the design such as industries, organizational and national cultures, existing organization members and groups, and the ideology that drives the organization's culture. Configuration theories predict that naturally occurring clusters of factors will have various effects on how well an organization does in serving its markets, meeting customer needs, and reaching cost and profit goals.

Two configuration typologies have empirical support in the organizational design literature. One typology features two generic organization forms—mechanistic and organic. The first is successful in a static environment; the second is successful in a dynamic environment.

The second typology features four generic forms—Defender, Prospector, Analyzer, and Reactor. Defender organizations use well-defined functions, centralization, and formal procedures to succeed in stable environments with clearly defined market segments. Prospector organizations use decentralization, little task specialization, few levels of management, and high interdependence between people and work units. Prospectors succeed in dynamic environments that feature unpredictable and fast change. Analyzer organizations have some features of both Prospector and Defender organizations. Reactor organizations have an unbalanced configuration of external environment, organizational design, strategy, and technical process.

Key Terms

Analyzer 515

buffering 509

continuous process 508

coupling the technical process 509

Defender 514

differentiation 504

external environment 500

goals of organizational design 499

horizontal integration 506

Information Perspective 503

integration 504

intensive technology 508

interorganizational linkages 506

mass production 508

mechanistic organization 513

mediating technology 508

open systems 500

organic organization 514

Prospector 514

Reactor 515

Resource Perspective 506

size 500

strategy 500

technical process 500

uncoupling the technical process 509

unit production 508

vertical integration 506

Review and Discussion Questions

1. What are the major contingency factors of organizational design? How are they related to each other?
2. Review the examples in the chapter and discuss how companies reacted to changes in the contingency factors.
3. Review the two typologies offered by the configuration view of organizational design. Discuss the similarities and differences you see between them.
4. Why are mechanistic organizations appropriate for a static environment and organic organizations appropriate for a dynamic environment?
5. What are the different types of technical processes? Describe the typical organizations that use each technical process.
6. Do different technical processes have any organizational design implications? If so, what are they?

7. How can managers protect an organization's technical process from environmental disturbances?

8. How is organization size related to organizational design? Does organization size affect the relationship of technical process to organizational design?

9. Review the international and ethics sections in the chapter. Discuss the ethical issues that surround organizational design questions in different countries. Should managers choose a design according to the local culture or according to their home culture?

. . . .

↵ *Case*

GOING GLOBAL

This case reviews what some small businesses are doing to compete globally. Consider the following questions while reading the case:

1. Which of the two perspectives on organization environment apply to the case?
2. Do the issues described apply to companies of any size?
3. Are there special dangers for small companies that enter international markets?

Broad Street Books never intended to be a global player.

After only three years in business, the small Philadelphia publisher is marketing one book in London and is seeking to distribute another throughout Europe. It is considering producing the company's latest release in Spanish.

"We never thought about being an international company," says Edward Moran, a partner in the firm. "We just saw market opportunities in other countries for our books and went after them."

These days, many small businesses are deciding that going global is a promising way to expand. Cognetics Inc., a Cambridge, Mass., consulting firm, says the number of small companies now tapping the global market is rising fast. And of 51,000 exporters it tracked recently, 87% employed fewer than 500.

"Going global is the theme now, even for small companies," says Byron Battle, a senior consultant with Arthur D. Little Co. "They're realizing there are lots of markets out there that aren't in a constant [slowdown]."

Going global, of course, is filled with pitfalls for even the biggest, most sophisticated companies. Deep pockets and huge support staffs can only do so much to combat the inevitable culture clash that comes from going abroad; knowing what works in the U.S. isn't a guarantee of success anywhere else.

But for a small business with limited resources, an overseas venture can be even more daunting. Cumbersome labor laws in foreign countries make it difficult to set up shop. Customs and language differences create thorny obstacles. Keeping tabs on products and services can be complex. And the capital required to launch an international business can be formidable.

But entering the global market isn't necessarily overwhelming for companies that choose the right method. Here are [some] ways that small businesses are expanding into the global marketplace.

Source: J. A. Lopez, "Going Global," *Wall Street Journal,* October 16, 1992, p. R20. Reprinted by permission of *The Wall Street Journal,* © 1992 Dow Jones & Company, Inc. All Rights Reserved Worldwide.

↵ FINDING A FOREIGN DISTRIBUTOR

Like Mr. Moran of Broad Street Books, many entrepreneurs find foreign distributors offer a low-cost and low-risk way to position products overseas. The distributors purchase the product, provide the sales team and find the buyers. What's more, they already have established relationships with foreign stores and customers, something that would take American companies years to develop.

But distributors sometimes have only marginal commitment to selling an individual manufacturer's products. And companies can go woefully wrong if they pick the wrong distributor, warns Bryan Robertson, president of Subsidiary Services Intl., a Providence, R.I., company that provides small- and medium-sized companies with international marketing services.

Often, he says, small-business owners check only credit records and neglect other important details, such as how and where the distributor sells the products. "All of this is important if you're going to build a brand," Mr. Robertson explains.

Consider B. D. Baggies, a New York men's-shirt maker owned by Apparel Group. The company accepted the first foreign distributor that offered to sell the shirts in stores across Europe.

"Later, we found that the distributor wasn't right. They were selling our shirts to women's stores as a unisex product," explains Charles W. McConnell, B. D. Baggies' president. "We were small and didn't check it out. We weren't optimizing our business."

Since then, the company has carefully screened distributors and now does business in about 40 countries with their help.

↵ JOINT VENTURES

Some companies prefer to have a greater presence abroad than a distributor offers, but fret that establishing their own operation or office abroad may be too complicated or too expensive. That's when a joint venture can be beneficial, says James C. Collins, a Stanford Business School professor.

Kija Kim, president of Harvard Design & Mapping Co., Cambridge, Mass., used a partnership to enter the Japanese market. Ms. Kim, who provides a technology that helps map toxic-waste-disposal sites, last summer joined forces with a Japanese waste-management firm.

In just one year, she has been involved in two multi-million-dollar projects. Today, she is forging ahead on other bids. She uses her partner's offices for her staff. The partner has also helped her build a long list of contacts.

Of course, satisfying partnerships and joint ventures are difficult to arrange. If not structured properly or monitored, a company can lose control of its product. Just finding a suitable partner can be a monumental task. And too many times, overeager U.S. businesses jump at the first foreign partner they meet.

"Small businesses have ants in the pants," says Hans B. Koehler, director of the Wharton School's Wharton Export Network, which helps small- and medium-sized businesses expand into global markets. "This is something that can't be rushed. It's like a marriage. You have to look around and make certain there's no one you're going to like better."

However, before scouting for a partner, a company should first sit down and examine what characteristics its foreign partner should possess. For instance, a software business may want to match up with a computer company, or a pants maker may want to join forces with a shirt manufacturer. But Mr. Koehler advises companies to look for partners that have similar ideals and goals. What's more, he cautions against joining forces with a corporate conglomerate, which can "gulp you up. They have so many more resources to bring to bear."

But how does a company find a satisfying partner? One good resource is foreign chambers of commerce. Once a company has a profile of an ideal mate, a foreign chamber can provide lists of potential partners. Other sources are international accounting firms, trade associations and small-business consultants.

Ms. Kim found her partner with help from the state of Massachusetts, which was conducting a trade mission. On the tours, she met with various Japanese companies and officials. She quickly established a strong rapport with N.S. Environmental Science Consultants of Japan, and soon the two companies were planning a partnership. "It was like a marriage," Ms. Kim says.

However, there was more than just chemistry involved. Ms. Kim thoroughly investigated her new partner beforehand and then sat down to discuss how the joint partnership should be structured. Lawyers later drew up a binding contract. Many companies neglect to investigate their new partners, Mr. Koehler says, and that's why many joint ventures go sour.

There are other precautions a company should take. One is to set performance standards, says Stanford's Mr. Collins.

That will help ensure that the foreign company will properly promote the products. Another is to audit results as a means of guarding profits. And finally, Mr. Collins says, the company should keep a strong presence. Too often small companies get too wrapped up in their domestic business and neglect their international partnership, says Subsidiary Services' Mr. Robertson.

In some countries, partnerships provide a way to hurdle barriers. In Brazil, for instance, foreign companies must manufacture their products there if they want to sell them in that country. For many small businesses, setting up a manufacturing arm abroad is too expensive. However, a partnership provides a back-door entrance, Mr. Koehler says.

LICENSING AGREEMENTS

Licensing agreements often seem alluring: What could be nicer than extra income with so little extra work?

Many agreements work well. The licensee takes the American product or concept and commercializes it in a foreign country, sending the licenser regular checks.

Nonetheless, experts frequently warn against licensing deals. Subsidiary Services' Mr. Robertson says the agreements usually result in a total loss of product control and profits.

"They seem like a quick hit," says Mr. Robertson. "But they're really a big risk."

If the agreement isn't negotiated properly, the licensee can do just about anything with the product. Mr. Robertson says there have been instances in which a company purchased the licensing rights and then shelved the product so it wouldn't compete against its own. Others gain the purchasing rights to produce a competing product in the United States.

"You have to be very clear about what can and cannot be done with the product," Mr. Robertson warns. For instance, a New York apparel maker licensed its name in Europe and has been facing skidding international profits because of quality problems, Mr. Robertson says. Clothing that the licensees produce in Europe falls below American standards, he adds. Because of clauses in the contracts with licensees, the apparel company can't regain the rights to its own brand.

. . . .

 Case

MANUFACTURING BICYCLES AT HUFFY CORPORATION

Here is another case that will let you further apply the concepts developed in this chapter. Try to answer the following questions after you have read the case:

Source: Excerpted from R. E. Winter, "Upgrading of Factories Replaces the Concept of Total Automation," Wall Street Journal, November 30, 1987, pp. 1, 8. Reprinted by permission of The Wall Street Journal, © 1987 Dow Jones & Company, Inc. All Rights Reserved Worldwide.

1. What type of technical process does the case describe?
2. Was the company's organizational design consistent with that type of technical process?
3. Did Huffy's management couple or uncouple the technical process from the external environment?

At Huffy's 32-year-old Celina, Ohio, bicycle factory, 1,700 employees turn out more than 15,000 bicycles a day. Five years ago, it required 2,200 employees to make 10,000 bikes daily.

. . . [F]resh attention is being paid to blemish-free products and to ensuring a smooth and rapid flow of parts through the plant. [Huffy] . . . uses the popular just-in-time inventory management system, in which suppliers furnish parts and materials precisely when they are needed. Employees get involved in the decisions, making them more willing to continue to change. Officials talk constantly of new goals, in contrast to the old factory maxim "If it ain't broke, don't fix it."

As a result, Huffy says, the Celina plant has become the most productive bike factory in the world, requiring only 0.7 hour of work to make a bike. That is a quarter to a third of the time needed in [Asia], says Barry J. Ryan, Huffy's vice president for finance. . . .

Huffy in 1983 closed a brand-new plant in Oklahoma, as imported bikes kept taking a larger share of the market and the automated equipment at the plant didn't live up to expectations, among other things. So Huffy concentrated on improving the Ohio plant.

Huffy says the program has helped it meet the foreign competition. "Our two big advantages over Taiwan bike producers are quality and the ability to respond to the market," says John L. Mariotti, the president and general manager of Huffy's bicycle unit.

. . . [Q]uality improvement begins with [Huffy's] . . . suppliers, who now must certify that parts and materials meet specifications. Those who can't or won't are dropped. Besides ensuring better . . . bicycles, this emphasis on certification eliminates inspectors who formerly culled out bad parts.

[Huffy] . . . workers . . . inspect their own work and . . . act as a quality control on the person or machine just ahead of them in the production process. Problems are corrected before dozens of defective bikes . . . are produced.

Shorter production cycles also help cut costs by reducing inventories, the third major goal of plant upgrades. Many manufacturers formerly tried to lower costs and guard against shortages by buying in large quantities. Now, however, computerized production planning and electronic communications between customer and supplier eliminate the need for big stockpiles of materials.

. . . Huffy requires suppliers to ship frequently to meet production schedules. Huffy receives steel daily from Armco Inc.'s Middletown, Ohio, plant. About a week after steel comes into the Huffy plant, it goes out as a bicycle. Five years ago, the process took three times that long. "We're relentless in seeking improvement," Mr. Mariotti says. "Our goal is to have things [arrive] . . . in the morning and go out that evening."

He measures the inventory cut by the drop in the number of big tubs that are used to store and move parts. Only 700 are needed now, down from about 3,000 five years ago. Back then, he recalls, "you could hardly walk through the aisles because of stacks of parts."

Enlisting employees' support also is important in upgrading production. Says Mr. Mariotti: "They must understand their jobs are best protected by their own productivity and product quality."

Huffy drives home that message by issuing monthly checks separate from the paychecks, with each employee receiving his or her share of a 50-50 split of cost savings. Savings are measured by improvements in the ratio between bikes completed and hours recorded at the plant's time clocks. Usually this check is about 5% to 8% of the basic wage.

Mr. Mariotti says he prefers this so-called gain sharing to profit sharing because it isn't affected by bike prices, "which employees can't do anything about."

. . . [A] team approach is used for some jobs. For instance, Huffy's Connie Stolenburg, Carolyn Phillips and Craig Myers operate a production cell making the forks that hold the front wheels. Machines shape the parts, weld them together, grind the welds smooth, drill holes and cut threads. The three workers feed the machines, inspect the parts and determine when something is amiss.

They are paid a base rate of $7.65 an hour and can earn more if they exceed a quota. But only perfect forks count, and they must fix any that are defective.

At another cell, eight people assemble bicycle wheels. They switch jobs periodically so they don't get bored. One afternoon, Joann Wilkins is lacing the 36 spokes into each wheel hub. Before the afternoon is over, the 11-year veteran will lace 264 hubs, a task that keeps her moving steadily, but not frantically. "I like working in a group a lot better than doing one job by myself," she says.

. . . .

◢ References and Notes

[1] J. Child, *Organization* (New York: Harper & Row, 1977). See Appendix A for more description of such concepts.

[2] K. K. White, *Understanding the Company Organization Chart* (New York: American Management Association, 1963).

[3] R. Duncan, "What Is the Right Organization Structure? Decision Tree Analysis Provides the Answer," *Organizational Dynamics* (Winter 1979): 59.

[4] Ibid., pp. 77–79.

[5] Chapter 11 has a detailed discussion of aspects of organizational design and conflict.

[6] M. Jelinek, "Organization Structure: The Basic Conformations," In M. Jelinek, J. A. Litterer, and R. E. Miles, eds., *Organizations by Design: Theory and Practice* (Plano, Texas: Business Publications, Inc., 1986), pp. 125–39; White, *Understanding the Company Organization Chart*, pp. 32–44.

[7] M. Dalton, "Conflicts between Staff and Line Managerial Officers," *American Sociological Review* 15 (1950): 342–51.

[8] A. C. Bluedorn, "Pilgrim's Progress: Trends and Convergence in Research on Organizational Size and Environments," *Journal of Management* 19 (1993): 163–91; W. A. Randolph and G. G. Dess, "The Congruence Perspective of Organizational Design: A Conceptual Model and Multivariate Research Approach," *Academy of Management Review* 9 (1984): 114–27.

[9] C. Dugas and M. N. Vamos, "Marketing's New Look: Campbell Leads a Revolution in the Way Consumer Products Are Sold," *Business Week*, January 26, 1987, pp. 64–69.

[10]A. Farnham, "Baldor's Success: Made in the U.S.A.," *Fortune*, July 17, 1989, pp. 101–6.

[11]J. B. Treece, "It's Time for a Tune-up at GM: Quality and Cutting Costs Are Tops on the New President's Agenda," *Business Week*, September 7, 1987, pp. 22–23.

[12]W. J. Hampton, "General Motor's Little Engine That Could," *Business Week*, August 3, 1987, pp. 88–89.

[13]A. D. Chandler, Jr., *Strategy and Structure: Chapters in the History of the Industrial Enterprise* (Cambridge, Mass.: M.I.T. Press, 1962), p. 13; J. R. Galbraith and R. K. Kazanjian, *Strategy Implementation: Structure, Systems, and Process* (St. Paul: West Publishing Company, 1986), p. 1; H. Mintzberg, "The Strategy Concept I: Five Ps for Strategy," *California Management Review* 30(1) (1987): 11–24; H. Mintzberg, "The Strategy Concept II: Another Look at Why Organizations Need Strategies," *California Management Review* 30(1) (1987): 25–32.

[14]D. Miller, C. Dröge, and J. Toulouse, "Strategic Process and Content as Mediators between Organizational Context and Structure," *Academy of Management Journal* 31 (1988): 544–69.

[15]Galbraith and Kazanjian, *Strategy Implementation*, p. 1.

[16]Chandler, *Strategy and Structure*, p. 14.

[17]T. L. Amburgey and T. Dacin, "As the Left Foot Follows the Right? The Dynamics of Strategic and Structural Change," *Academy of Management Journal* 37 (1994): 1427–52.

[18]B. W. Keats and M. A. Hitt, "A Causal Model of Linkages among Environmental Dimensions, Macro Organizational Characteristics and Performance," *Academy of Management Journal* 31 (1988): 570–98; Miller, Dröge, and Toulouse, "Strategic Process"; R. D. Russell and C. J. Russell, "An Examination of the Effects of Organizational Norms, Organizational Structure, and Environmental Uncertainty on Entrepreneurial Strategy," *Journal of Management* 18 (1992): 639–56.

[19]J. R. Galbraith, *Organizational Design* (Reading, Mass.: Addison-Wesley, 1977).

[20]Duncan, "What Is the Right Organization Structure?"

[21]P. R. Lawrence and J. W. Lorsch, *Organization and Environment* (Homewood, Ill.: Richard D. Irwin, 1967).

[22]P. M. Blau, "A Formal Theory of Differentiation in Organizations," *American Sociological Review* 35 (1970): 201–18.

[23]Blau, "A Formal Theory"; Lawrence and Lorsch, *Organization and Environment*.

[24]Lawrence and Lorsch, *Organization and Environment*, p. 11.

[25]Ibid.

[26]J. E. Ettlie and E. M. Reza, "Organizational Integration and Process Innovation," *Academy of Management Journal* 35 (1992): 795–827.

[27]Lawrence and Lorsch, *Organization and Environment*.

[28]Developed from J. Pfeffer and G. R. Salancik, *The External Control of Organizations: A Resource Dependence Perspective* (New York: Harper & Row, 1978).

[29]M. Aiken and J. Hage, "Organizational Interdependence and Intraorganizational Structure," *American Sociological Review* 33 (1968): 912–30.

[30]J. Pfeffer, "Merger as a Response to Organizational Interdependence," *Administrative Science Quarterly* 17 (1972): 382–94.

[31]R. Dubin, *The World of Work* (Englewood Cliffs, N.J.: Prentice-Hall, 1958), pp. 62–65.

[32]Developed from J. Woodward, *Management and Technology* (London: Her Majesty's Stationary Office, 1958); J. Woodward, *Industrial Organization: Theory and Practice* (Oxford: Oxford University Press, 1965).

[33]J. D. Thompson, *Organizations in Action* (New York: McGraw-Hill, 1967).

[34]J. Heizer and B. Render, *Production and Operations Management: Strategies and Tactics* (Boston: Allyn & Bacon, 1991), Ch. 7; R.J. Schonberger, *World Class Manufacturing: The Lessons of Simplicity Applied* (New York: Free Press, 1986), pp. 97–99.

[35]Thompson, *Organizations in Action*.

[36]R. J. Schonberger, "The Transfer of Japanese Manufacturing Management Approaches to U.S. Industry," *Academy of Management Review* 7 (1982): 479–87; Schonberger, *World Class Manufacturing*.

[37]C. Perrow, "A Framework for Comparative Organizational Analysis," *American Sociological Review* 32(1967): 194–208.

[38]Thompson, *Organizations in Action*.

[39]C. Perrow, *Complex Organizations: A Critical Essay*, 3d ed. (New York: Random House, 1986), pp. 146–54.

[40]Thompson, *Organizations in Action*.

[41]Heizer and Render, *Production*, Ch. 7.

[42]Thompson, *Organizations in Action*.

[43]L. W. Fry, "Technology-Structure Research: Three Critical Issues," *Academy of Management Journal*, 25 (1982): 532–52.

[44]H. E. Aldrich, "Technology and Organizational Structure: A Reexamination of the Findings of the Aston Group," *Administrative Science Quarterly* 17 (1972): 26–43; C. L. Hulin, and M. Roznowski, "Organizational Technologies: Effects on Organizations' Characteristics and Individuals' Responses," in L. L. Cummings and B. M. Staw, eds., *Research in Organizational Behavior* (Greenwich, Conn.: JAI Press, 1985), pp. 39–85.

[45]Fry, "Technology-Structure Research"; C. C. Miller, W. H. Glick, Y. Wang, and G. P. Huber, "Understanding Technology-Structure Relationships: Theory Development and Meta-Analytic Theory Testing," *Academy of Management Journal* 34 (1991): 370–99.

[46]Woodward, *Management and Technology* and *Industrial Organization*; W. L. Zwerman, *New Perspectives on Organization Theory* (Westport, Conn.: Greenwood Publishing Corporation, 1970).

[47]J. W. Dean, Jr., S. J. Yoon, and G. I. Susman, "Advanced Manufacturing Technology and Organization Structure: Empowerment or Subordination?" *Organization Science* 3 (1992); 203–29.

[48]T. K. Reeves, B. A. Turner, and B. C. Smith, "A Theory of Organization and Behavior in Batch Production Factories," *Administrative Science Quarterly* 17 (1972): 81–98.

[49]P. N. Khandwalla, "Mass Output Orientation of Operations Technology and Organizational Structure," *Administrative Science Quarterly* 19 (1974): 74–97.

[50]Reeves, Turner, and Smith, "A Theory of Organization"; Zwerman, *New Perspectives on Organization Theory*.

[51]Bluedorn, "Pilgrim's Progress"; Child, *Organization*; P. H. Grinyer and M. Yasai-Ardekani, "Strategy, Structure, Size, and Bureaucracy," *Academy of Management Journal*, 24 (1981): 471–86; Miller, Dröge, and Toulouse, "Strategic Process"; Khandwalla, "Mass Output Orientation."

[52]P. M. Blau, C. M. Falbe, W. McKinley, and P. K. Tracy, "Technology and Organization in Manufacturing," *Administrative Science Quarterly* 21 (1976): 20–40.

[53]Zwerman, W. L., 1970.

[54]Aldrich, "Technology and Organizational Structure"; D. J. Hickson, D. S. Pugh, and D. C. Pheysey, "Operations Technology and Organization Structure: An Empirical Reappraisal," *Administrative Science Quarterly* 14 (1969): 378–97; J. H. K. Inkson, D. S. Pugh, and D. J. Hickson, "Organization Context and Structure: An Abbreviated Replication," *Administrative Science Quarterly* 15 (1970): 318–29; D. S. Pugh, D. J. Hickson, C. R. Hinings, and C. Turner, "Dimensions of Organization Structure," *Administrative Science Quarterly* 13 (1968): 65–105.

[55]A. D. Meyer, A. S. Tsui, and C. R. Hinings, "Configurational Approaches to Organizational Analysis," *Academy of Management Journal* 36 (1993): 1175–95.

[56]Developed from T. Burns and G. M. Stalker, *The Management of Innovation* (London: Tavistock, 1961).

[57]K. M. Eisenhardt, "Making Fast Strategic Decisions in High-Velocity Environments," *Academy of Management Journal* 32 (1989): 543–76; W. Q. Judge and A. Miller, "Antecedents and Outcomes of Decision Speed in Different Environmental Contexts," *Academy of Management Journal* 34 (1991): 449–63.

[58]R. E. Miles and C. C. Snow, *Organization Strategy, Structure, and Process* (New York: McGraw-Hill, 1978).

[59]D. H. Doty, W. H. Glick, and G. P. Huber, "Fit, Equifinality, and Organizational Effectiveness: A Test of Two Configurational Theo-

ries," *Academy of Management Journal* 36 (1993): 1196–1250; Miles and Snow, *Organization Strategy*, Ch. 13.

[60]A. K. Sundaram and J. S. Black, "The Environment and Internal Organization of Multinational Enterprises," *Academy of Management Review* 17 (1992): 728–57.

[61]G. Hofstede, *Culture's Consequences: International Differences in Work-Related Values* (Beverly Hills, Calif.: Sage Publications, 1984); G. Hofstede, *Cultures and Organizations: Software of the Mind* (New York: McGraw-Hill, 1991); G. Hofstede, "Cultural Constraints in Management Theories," *Academy of Management Executive* 7 (1993): 81–94.

[62]G. Hofstede, B. Neuijen, D. D. Ohayv, and G. Sanders, "Measuring Organizational Cultures: A Qualitative and Quantitative Study across Twenty Cases," *Administrative Science Quarterly* 35 (1990): 286–316.

[63]I. Vertinsky, D. K. Tse, D. A. Wehrung, and K. Lee, "Organizational Design and Management Norms: A Comparative Study of Managers' Perceptions in the People's Republic of China, Hong Kong, and Canada," *Journal of Management* 16 (1990): 853–67.

[64]G. Stern, "P&G Will Cut 13,000 Jobs, Shut 30 Plants," *Wall Street Journal*, July 16, 1993, pp. A3, A4.

[65]R. Kelly, "Spindler Rocks the Apple Cart," *Information Week*, July 12, 1993, p. 12.

[66]P. D. Collins, J. Hage, and F. M. Hull, "Organizational and Technological Predictors of Change in Automaticity," *Academy of Management Journal* 31 (1988): 512–43.

18

Organizational Design: Alternative Forms of Organization

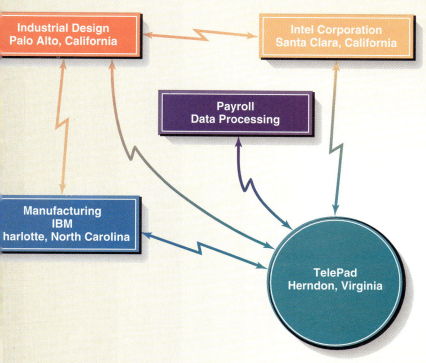

Industrial Design
Palo Alto, California

Intel Corporation
Santa Clara, California

Payroll
Data Processing

Manufacturing
IBM
harlotte, North Carolina

TelePad
Herndon, Virginia

· *Telepad in Herndon, Virginia, is an example of a virtual organization. This evolving organization form relies heavily on telecommunications technology to link its distant parts.*

After reading this chapter, you should be able to . . .

· See the relationships between the concepts of Chapter 17 and the choice of a specific form of organization.
· Describe the design features of functional, divisional, hybrid, and matrix organization forms.
· Discuss the strengths and weaknesses of each form.
· Describe the conditions under which managers choose one form of organization over another.
· Explain the characteristics of several forms of organizations that are likely to evolve in the future.

Chapter Overview

IBM's Reorganization

International Business Machines Corp. announced a reorganization Thursday that it calls the biggest decentralization since the 1956 death of its legendary leader, Thomas Watson Sr.

The delegation of authority away from the Armonk, N.Y., headquarters is intended to make the world's biggest computer company "more open, more flexible and more agile," chairman-chief executive John F. Akers told reporters.

"In some respects we (will) have several IBM companies instead of one, integrated computer and communications company," Akers said.

Financial analysts said the reorganization—which includes the naming of two vice chairmen—would not do much for the sluggish revenues of the $50 billion giant in the short term. . . .

IBM is establishing five independent businesses with worldwide development responsibilities for particular product lines, ranging from mainframes to personal computers. The five businesses will also be in charge of U.S. manufacturing.

Also being created is IBM United States, which will oversee those five lines of business and be in charge of all U.S. operations.

The five new lines of business are: Enterprise Systems, for the company's big System 370 mainframe computers and related products; Application Business Systems, for the System 36 and 38 mid-size computers and related products; Personal Systems, for personal computers and other products; Communication Systems, for communications products; and Technology Products, for semiconductors and packaging.

"They've been struggling for years now trying to figure out how to manage product development," says John McCarthy, an industry analyst with Forrester Research, a Cambridge, Mass., research company.

IBM's sluggish product development cycle has been due, analysts say, to infighting between marketing people who knew what customers needed and wanted, and product development engineers who knew what new technology was possible to deliver. The resultant bickering left the company's management committee to resolve product decisions. As a consequence, IBM's development cycle slowed down, missing opportunities during a period when the industry began turning out new products faster than ever for a rapidly evolving market.

"By delegating more . . . [authority] from IBM's management committee to the new, highly independent lines of business, we will be able to speed technological innovation and move products to the marketplace more quickly," said . . . Akers.

Perhaps the most serious omission from the current restructuring was that little was done to focus the company's structure toward its announced future direction—software development. Software is expected to be the key "value" ingredient as computer hardware, over time, becomes more generic and less profitable.

"For years now they've been talking about how software is going to be the future of their revenue streams," McCarthy says. "But software is going to be buried deep within these new business units. The product side is all hardware based.

"I question whether the reorganization really fits with what they've been telling us about their long-term strategy," he says.

Source: Excerpted and developed from "IBM Announces Plan for Decentralization," Associated Press, 1988. (As it appeared in the *Albuquerque Journal,* January 29, 1988, p. C20.) Reprinted with the permission of Associated Press; M. Clayton, "IBM Restructuring Aims to Introduce the Right Hand to the Left Hand," *Christian Science Monitor,* February 2, 1988, p. 10. Reprinted with permission of *Christian Science Monitor.*

· *John F. Akers, former chairman and chief executive of International Business Machines Corporation.*

I BM's management redesigned the organization around major product lines, domestic operations, and international locations to help them more effectively manage new product development. The company's product line includes personal computers, mainframe systems, communications systems, and supporting software. IBM had to make sense out of its diverse product line to effectively and efficiently manage the company. Industry analyst McCarthy raised questions, though, about whether IBM's new reorganization is right for its strategy. Only time will tell whether the company has made the right choice. Although IBM chose a specific form of organization that emphasized its major product lines, many other forms with different emphases are also available to managers.

This chapter describes many alternative forms of organizational design available to managers. It discusses different organization forms used for differentiation and integration or to carry out a resource dependence perspective. The design chosen depends on the organization's strategy, its external environment, its technical process, and its size, as well as on the need for a balanced configuration of these factors.

The three major forms of organizational design are functional, divisional, and matrix. Managers also combine functional and divisional designs into a hybrid design to get the better features of each. The divisional structure has several variations, creating an extensive list of design choices.

Several newer forms of organizational design are evolving and beginning to see widespread use. Those forms focus on teams or processes or link widely dispersed organizations and individuals to form an extended organization.

There are no formulas to guide choices among the designs.[1] Each design has advantages and disadvantages, and managers try to choose the design that offers the most benefits and the fewest limitations.[2] Understanding the advantages and disadvantages of each design lets the manager use informed judgment in picking the basic configuration for an organization and variants within it.

Each organizational design makes different behavioral demands. The implications of each form of organization for you, personally and as a manager, are described at the end of this chapter.

. . . .

◢ Organizational Design by Function

Organizational design by **function** groups the tasks of the organization according to the activities they perform. A functional configuration divides the organization into major units or departments such as accounting, finance, manufacturing, engineering, management information systems, and the like. Functional configurations can vary from one organization to another. The functional units found in an organization depend on its goals and tasks.[3]

Table 18-1 shows the design factors of a functional organization. The strategy of a functional organization focuses on a few products or services in well-defined markets with few competitors. The external environment is stable, has little uncertainty, and is simple in form. The technical process is routine and has little interdependence with other parts of the organization. The product or services are standardized, letting the organization apply the technical process repeatedly, according to well-defined procedures.

Figure 18-1 is the organization chart for the hypothetical manufacturing company introduced in Chapter 17. This company has a clear functional design with each function shown below the two vice-presidents. The functions include manufacturing, engineering, marketing, finance, and industrial relations. Each box in the figure is a major element that the company feels is important for its effective functioning.

The chart has little detail but gives you some idea of the environmental sectors the company considers important. Each major function differentiates the company and

TABLE 18-1
Characteristics of Organizational Design: Functional Organization

DESIGN FACTORS

Strategy: Specialized organization producing a few products or services for a well-defined market.

External environment: Stable, little uncertainty, little competition, simple.

Technical process: Routine, low interdependence, applied repeatedly to a limited product or service line.

Size: Small to medium.

STRENGTHS

Specialization.

Specialists are together and can develop collegial relationships.

Career paths for specialists.

Supports in-depth skill development.

Brings focus to goals of each function.

Simple and efficient system for communication, decision making, and administration within functions.

Economies of scale within functions.

WEAKNESSES

Slow response to environmental changes.

As the environment changes, has difficulty coordinating the functions.

Referral of decisions can overload senior management.

Adds to a shortsighted view of the mission of the organization.

Innovations not broadly based because of specialization.

Difficult to coordinate multiple products or services.

Source: R. L. Daft, *Organization Theory and Design* (St. Paul, Minn.: West Publishing Co., 1995), Ch. 6; R. Duncan, "What Is the Right Organization Structure? Decision Tree Analysis Provides the Answer," *Organizational Dynamics* 7 (Winter 1979): 64.

aligns it with each sector. For example, Marketing focuses on the customer, a key element in the success of many firms. Marketing does not manufacture products. It tries to sell the products using promotions in different media such as print advertising and television advertising.

The organization chart also illustrates the combined use of staff and line within a functional design. The line organization shown in Figure 18-1 is Operations. The functions within Operations do the major operating tasks of designing the product and manufacturing it with high quality. The rest of the functions are staff, serving in support and advisory roles to the line organization. Finance supports Operations by focusing on sources of money for plant expansion. Industrial Relations supports the entire company by trying to maintain a committed workforce.

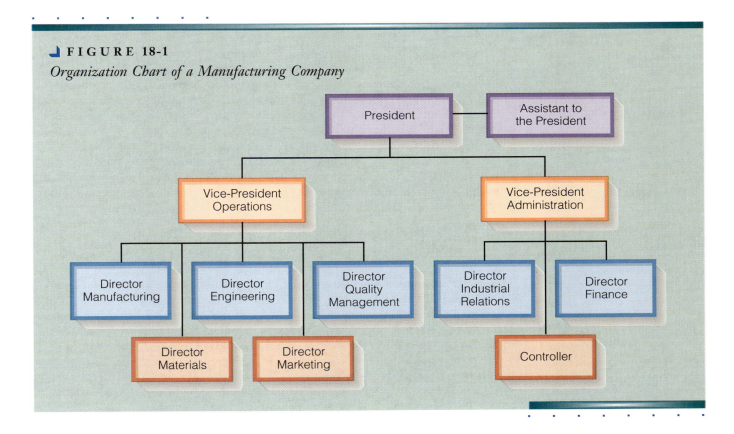

FIGURE 18-1

Organization Chart of a Manufacturing Company

STRENGTHS AND WEAKNESSES

Table 18-1 also shows the strengths and weaknesses of organizational design by function. A functional design emphasizes specialization within the organization by grouping similar activities into single units or departments. The design brings specialists together in one place. Most accountants are in the accounting function, most financial analysts are in the finance function, and most engineers are in the engineering function. Such groups let collegial relationships develop among specialists. The groups encourage the development of specialized skills and sharing of information. Career paths for the specialists are clear. A person who begins as a junior accountant can follow a career path within the accounting function to as high as she aspires.

Each function can experience economies of scale. If engineers need specialized equipment, the equipment is put in a centralized place where any engineer can use it. The organization saves money by not duplicating the equipment at several locations.

Organizational design by function is a simple and efficient system for communication, decision making, and administration. Reporting relationships and responsibilities are clearly defined. If a manager in engineering has questions about accounting policies, she gets an answer from someone in the accounting function. Decisions about manufacturing processes are made within the manufacturing function. If a design change to a product is needed, the decisions may be made together with engineering.

The weaknesses of functional designs partly derive from the strengths of this configuration. Its weaknesses start to show when the external environment of the organization shifts to a state ill-suited to a functional design. A functional design usually does not help managers respond quickly to external changes. The emphasis on specialization promotes a tunnel-vision view of the goal of each function. Engineers usually do engineering, financial analysts usually do financial analysis, and so forth. The environment can shift, however, requiring a broader view and review of the organization's strategy. Getting a broader view can be difficult within a functional design, especially if it has existed for some time. Note that the structure itself produces a set of widely accepted behaviors and perceptions within the organization. Those perceptions restrict managers from quickly responding to external changes.

The slowness in response is accompanied by confusion among lower-level managers about the direction they should take. They often face new situations with which they have had little experience. They feel unsure about decisions and refer many decisions upward in the organization. As changing demands are made on the organization, the referrals can become excessive and overload senior management. The focus on individual specialization makes innovations based on interdisciplinary approaches unlikely. Innovations will be restricted to individual specializations and not broadly based on interactions among the specializations.

BEHAVIORAL DEMANDS OF A FUNCTIONAL ORGANIZATION

Functional organizations emphasize the technical skills of those within each function. The organization rewards behavior associated with the technical contribution of the function. Individuals work in an environment populated with others who share common backgrounds and views. Such homogeneity can lead to narrow views of the function's contribution to the total organization. Carried to its extreme, the emphasis on a functional contribution can produce dysfunctional behavior for the organization[4] and limited career opportunities.

Organizational Design by Division

Organizational design by **division** uses decentralization as its basic approach. The basis of the decentralized divisions can be the organization's products, services, locations, customers, programs, or technical processes. A divisional design is especially useful for a strategy focused on different products or services. It also is useful when the organization's strategy calls for high customer or client satisfaction with its products or services. Some organizations have such a complex relationship with their external environment that they simultaneously use several different bases for a divisional structure.

Organizations often evolve from a functional design to a divisional form. As the external environment changes, managers may find that the organization must diversify its activities to stay competitive. As the organization adds new activities, managers may find that the functional design does not let them manage as efficiently as they must. They often try to solve the problem by moving or evolving the present functional form of organization to a divisional design.[5]

Table 18-2 shows the design factors of a divisional organization. An organization needs a divisional structure when the external environment is complex, is changing rapidly, and has moderate to high uncertainty. Technical processes in divisional organizations often are nonroutine and interdependent with other parts of the organization. Organizations with continuous process technologies, such as oil and chemical refineries, often use a divisional form. The divisional form focuses attention on costly and potentially dangerous processes. A divisional structure is also a common management reaction to large organization size.

Figure 18-2 shows part of the divisional organizational design of Colgate-Palmolive Co. The company based its divisional structure on major operating areas around the world.

Think for a moment about the logic behind Colgate-Palmolive's organizational design as shown in Figure 18-2. The company's products face distinctly different

TABLE 18-2

Characteristics of Organizational Design: Divisional Organization

DESIGN FACTORS
_____

Strategy: Focused on specific products, services, locations, customers, or processes. Has many different products or services. Wants customer or client satisfaction.

External environment: Changing, moderate to high uncertainty, many competitors, complex.

Technical process: Nonroutine, high interdependence. Organizations with continuous process technologies may have fast-changing, costly, or dangerous processes.

Size: Large.

STRENGTHS
_____

Adaptable to differences in products, services, clients, location, or processes and changes in the external environment.

Gives high visibility to products, services, customers, etc.

High satisfaction to customers or clients because of clear responsibilities within the organization for the product or service.

WEAKNESSES
_____

Can lose well-focused technical specialization and in-depth technical development.

Loses the economies of scale of the functional organization.

Redundancies in functions.

Difficult to get uniform application of organization policies with decentralized and duplicated functions.

Becomes focused on the specialized goals of a division.

Integration across decentralized units often is difficult.

Source: R. L. Daft, *Organization Theory and Design* (St. Paul, Minn.: West Publishing Company, 1995), Ch. 6; R. Duncan, "What Is the Right Organization Structure? Decision Tree Analysis Provides the Answer," *Organizational Dynamics* 7 (Winter 1979): 66.

markets in different world regions. Marketing of Colgate-Palmolive products in the United States likely is different from marketing products in Latin America or the Asia Pacific region.

Colgate-Palmolive's international divisions face sharply different legal and cultural environments in Europe, Latin America, and Asia Pacific countries. Grouping international operations into divisions separate from domestic operations lets the international divisions develop specialized skills and abilities for dealing with international questions that do not arise in domestic operations. In this example, you can see that the organizational division of labor is similar to an individual division of labor. The divisional organization chosen by Colgate-Palmolive is well suited to responding and adapting to differences in product type, product marketing, and cultural differences of the various international locations.

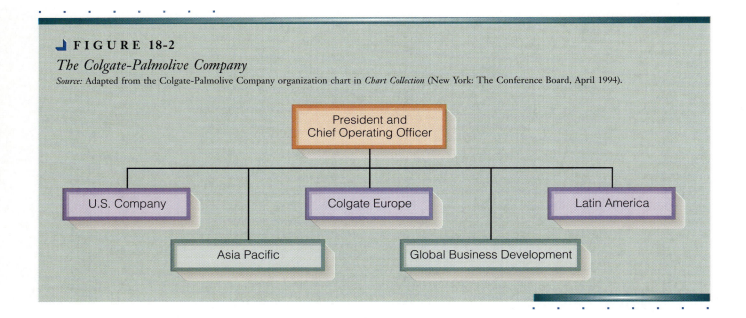

 STRENGTHS AND WEAKNESSES

Table 18-2 lists the strengths and weaknesses of organizational design by division. This design easily adapts to differences in products, services, clients, location, and the like. Products can differ not only in how they are manufactured, but also in how they are marketed.

Products, services, and customers are highly visible in a divisional structure. The names of the products or a broad class of products often appear in the company's organization chart. A customer can quickly find the locus of responsibility for a product or service from the chart.

The weaknesses of a divisional structure come partly from its decentralized qualities. Economies of scale are lost, because many functions of the organization such as accounting, personnel, and purchasing are duplicated within each division. Technical specialization is not as focused as it is in a functional design. Specialists in one division cannot talk readily with similar specialists in another division. Uniform application of personnel and purchasing policies is also difficult with functions decentralized and dispersed among the divisions.

Managers within divisions become focused on the goals of the division. As in a functional organization, managers can lose sight of the general organization strategy. Integration of the divisions toward achieving the organization strategy and integration of the functions within each division are more difficult than in a functional organization. The integrating mechanisms in Figure 18-2 are the company presidents and the division managers. Other integrating mechanisms are necessary to successfully integrate an organization differentiated by divisions.

BEHAVIORAL DEMANDS OF A DIVISIONAL ORGANIZATION

Divisional organizational design emphasizes autonomy in decision making of people in many parts of the organization. Individuals at various levels can become more involved in the basic activities of the organization. Decentralized organizations also put individuals in contact with people from many parts of the organization. Such organizations put more interpersonal skill demands on people than functional organizations.

Decentralized organizations reward behavior that goes toward the goals of the decentralization. Such behavior focuses on a product, customer, service, or location. Emphasizing that behavior increases its importance to the individual, often making the behavior an end in itself. The latter is a dysfunction of bureaucracy discussed in Appendix A under the topic of bureaupathology.

. . . .

⌐ *Hybrid Organizational Design*

Managers often combine functional and divisional designs. They use this **hybrid** form to get the benefits and reduce the weaknesses of the two configurations used separately. Divisions are used in the same way described earlier. The divisions decentralize some functions, and the headquarters location centralizes others. The centralized functions often are the costly ones for the organization.[6]

The combination of both function and division in an organization shows the complexity of the problem managers face in deciding how an organization should be differentiated. The complexity of the differentiation also leads to difficulty in getting the needed integration.

Table 18-3 shows the design factors of a hybrid design combining functions and divisions. Many factors are the same as those listed for a divisional organization. Many products or services are involved. Often the organization needs to use resources efficiently and to adapt to changes in the external environment. Organization size is a design factor because the cost of maintaining a corporate headquarters and related staff often cannot be borne by a small organization.

Figure 18-3 shows part of the organization chart of Unilever de Argentina S.A. The first row of the chart shows the functional areas of the company. The second row shows the divisions.

The functional areas provide specialized support activities, such as human resources and finance, to each division and the entire company. Human resources include safety, hygiene, and management development. The financial function includes company-wide finance, accounting, and auditing. The divisions focus activities according to specific market areas such as personal care products and foods. Each division includes marketing and sales activities focused on the product assigned to the division.

⌐ STRENGTHS AND WEAKNESSES

Table 18-3 also lists the strengths and weaknesses of a hybrid design. The first three strengths are the same as those for a divisional organization. Economies of scale are possible in some functional areas. Expensive shared resources do not need to be decentralized and duplicated at high cost to the organization. Managers use the hybrid form to get the best effects of both a functional and a divisional organization.

Weaknesses of the hybrid design follow directly from trying to get the best features of both the functional and the divisional forms. The first three weaknesses in Table 18-3 were also listed in Table 18-2 for a divisional organization. An added weakness is the potential for high administrative overhead if the staff at corporate headquarters expands without control. There is high potential conflict between decentralized divisions and centralized corporate headquarters units. Division managers want autonomy to do what they believe they do well. Centralized headquarters units may want to exert control over divisions even when doing so may not be effective.

⌐ **TABLE 18-3**

Characteristics of Organizational Design: Hybrid Design

DESIGN FACTORS

Strategy: Focused on specific products, services, locations, customers, or processes. Has many different products or services. Wants customer or client satisfaction and efficient use of organization resources.

External environment: Changing, moderate to high uncertainty, many competitors, complex.

Technical process: Both routine and nonroutine. High interdependence with both functions and divisions. Organizations with continuous process technologies may have fast-changing, costly, or dangerous processes.

Size: Large.

STRENGTHS

Adaptable to differences in products, services, clients, location, or processes and changes in the external environment.

Gives high visibility to products, services, customers, etc.

High satisfaction to customers or clients because of clear responsibilities within the organization for the product or service.

Efficient use of expensive shared resources. Some areas realize economies of scale.

Gains some of a functional organization's strengths from specialization of some functions.

WEAKNESSES

Difficult to get uniform application of organization policies with decentralized and duplicated functions.

Becomes focused on the specialized goals of a division.

Integration across decentralized units often is difficult.

Potential for high administrative overhead.

Potential conflict between decentralized divisions and centralized corporate headquarters units.

Source: R. L. Daft, *Organization Theory and Design* (St. Paul, Minn.: West Publishing Company, 1995), Ch. 6.

⌐ BEHAVIORAL DEMANDS OF A HYBRID DESIGN

Organizations that combine functional and divisional forms make behavioral demands similar to both types of organizations. Individuals in different parts of the organization feel different sets of demands. Those in the functional areas are rewarded for behavior associated with their technical expertise. The functional specialists supporting division operations are rewarded for achieving division goals. The two sources of pressure for different types of behavior are not always consistent. Such inconsistency can lead to conflict about the right role of a functional specialist.

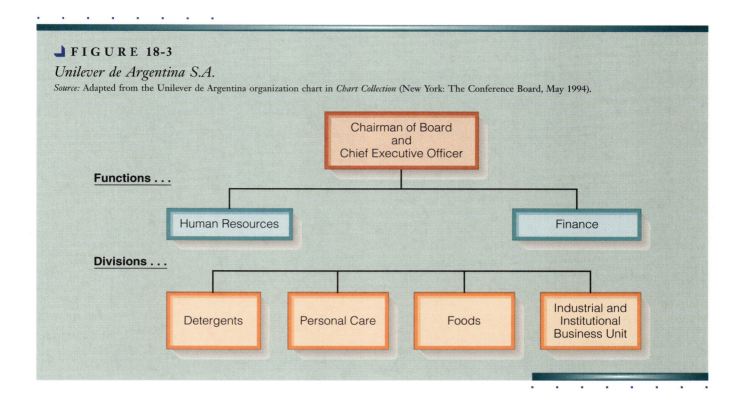

FIGURE 18-3

Unilever de Argentina S.A.

Source: Adapted from the Unilever de Argentina organization chart in *Chart Collection* (New York: The Conference Board, May 1994).

Functions . . .

Divisions . . .

- Chairman of Board and Chief Executive Officer
- Human Resources
- Finance
- Detergents
- Personal Care
- Foods
- Industrial and Institutional Business Unit

EXERCISE   *Organizational Design and You*

*P*ause now to do the following exercise. It can help you understand some alternative forms of organizational design.

If you are currently working, try to get an organization chart from your employer. If none is available, draw one from your understanding of the functions of various work units. Show reporting relationships among units with solid lines as in the organization charts earlier in this chapter. If you are not currently working, use a chart for an organization to which you belong, a company where a friend or relative works, or your college or university.

After getting or developing the chart, examine it with the following questions in mind:

- Are any major elements of the organization's strategy visible in the chart?
- Is it a functional, divisional, or hybrid organization?
- If it is a divisional form, on what basis did the company organize the divisions—product, customer, location, or process?
- Based on what you know up to now, does the organizational design make sense? Is it effective in reaching the goals of the organization? Why or why not?

Matrix Organizational Design

Organizations often use a **matrix** design when two separate sectors of the external environment demand management attention. For example, if the organization produces products using advanced technology and its customers have highly specialized needs, both changes in technology and changes in customer needs require management's attention.[7] Organizations also move to a matrix form after other organizations in their region or industry have adopted it.[8]

The word *matrix* evolved during the 1950s within the aerospace industry to describe the gridlike organizational design used in project management. This design

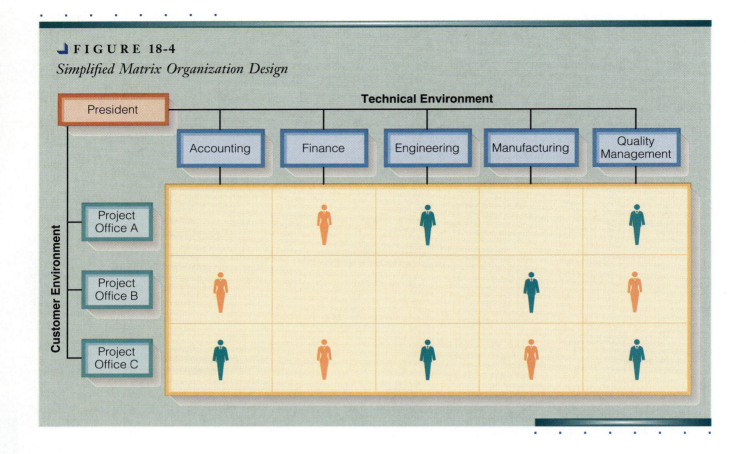

FIGURE 18-4
Simplified Matrix Organization Design

specifically rejected the long-standing recommendation of unity of command with each employee getting direction from only one boss.[9] It uses multiple authority structures, so that many people report to two managers.

Figure 18-4 shows a simple matrix organizational design. People from different functional areas of the company (the top row) are assigned to various projects (the left column). Each person assigned to a project reports to at least two supervisors or managers; one supervisor is in the functional area, and the other is in a project.

The mixture of people from the functional areas varies according to the needs of the projects. Some projects, such as Project Office C in Figure 18-4, need people from all functional areas. Other projects, such as Project Office A and B, need people only from some functional areas. After a person finishes a project, she returns to the functional area.

Multiple reporting relationships are a basic feature of matrix organizations, distinguishing them from the forms discussed earlier. Although reporting to two or more managers may appear odd, many people have experienced this relationship as children when both their mother and father have authority. Children often skillfully navigate these multiple authority relations.

Table 18-4 shows the design factors of a matrix form of organizational design. The following are the conditions under which an organization may choose a matrix design:

Pressures from the external environment for a dual focus.

The example from the aerospace industry described fast changes in technology and customer needs. Those pressures moved managers to adopt the multiple focus of the matrix form.

Characteristics of Organizational Design: Matrix Organizations

DESIGN FACTORS

Strategy: Focused on specific products or projects to meet customer requirements. Also requires development and enhancement of technical skills in the organization. Recognizes the need to focus on both market and technology.

External environment: Changing, high uncertainty, many competitors, complex. Both product and technology environments are changing.

Technical process: Nonroutine. High interdependence in the technical process to meet the requirements of a product or project.

Size: Moderate to large.

STRENGTHS

Responsive and flexible in the face of changing demands.

Pools expensive resources and uses them on several projects.

Potentially high human involvement and motivation.

People have more information about the total project.

WEAKNESSES

Dual-authority relationships contribute to ambiguity, confusion, power struggles, and stress.

The absence of high interpersonal skills leads to low communication and conflict.

Decision making can be slow.

Lack of highly skilled management amplifies all weaknesses.

Source: R. L. Daft, *Organization Theory and Design* (St. Paul, Minn.: West Publishing Company, 1995), Ch. 6.

High uncertainty within the multiple sectors of the external environment creates high management information needs.

Multiple elements in the external environment are changing fast, creating high uncertainty about future states of the environment. As described in Chapter 17, high uncertainty creates a strong need for more information.

Constraints on human and physical resources.

Most organizations have constraints on expanding their human or physical resources. This is especially true when the resources are expensive human specialists or costly technical equipment. The matrix form of organization encourages sharing those resources and allows flexibility in meeting competing requests.

Managers can design a matrix organization in different ways.[10] Some organizations use a matrix form within specific functional areas only. Such an arrangement is common in a marketing department. Managers responsible for a brand or group of

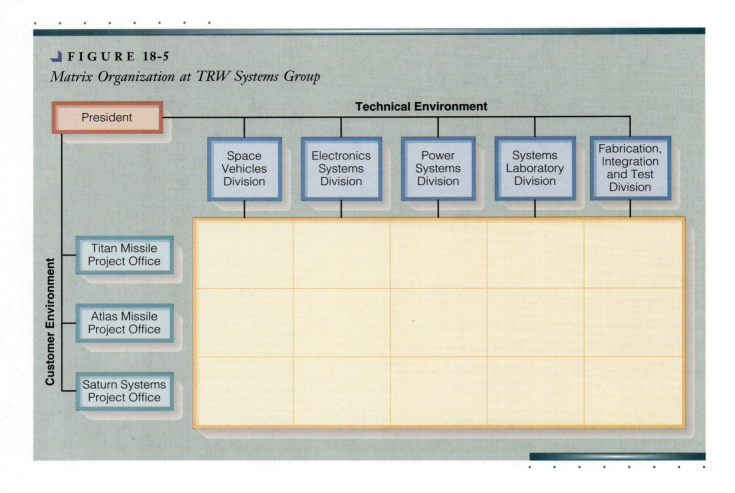

Matrix Organization at TRW Systems Group

brands bring all the marketing skills together to focus on the products. Other organizations use temporary matrix forms to complete specific projects. The matrix organization disbands after the project is completed. Still other organizations have the matrix form as a permanent feature of their organizational design.

Technical specialists within a matrix organization may work for one project or be shared among many projects. The sharing of technical specialists is a particular strength of matrix organizations.

Figure 18-5 shows the organizational design of an early user of the matrix form, TRW Systems Group (TRW).[11] The divisions across the top of the chart group the technical specialties of the company. Each is a major technical area and a major technical strength of TRW. The technical areas get high visibility from their placement in major divisions.

Major projects are grouped into the Project Offices shown on the left side of the figure. Each is a large project for two different customers. The United States Air Force funded the missile projects. The National Aeronautics and Space Administration funded the Saturn Systems Project. Each customer has different requirements.

The boxes at the intersection of the project offices and the divisions are the point at which the two sides of the matrix come together. Each intersection is the application of a specific technical area to a project's requirements. When a technical specialist from a division finishes work on a project, she is reassigned to another project.

■ STRENGTHS AND WEAKNESSES

Table 18-4 lists the strengths and weaknesses of a matrix organization. The strengths of matrix organizations include responsiveness, flexibility, efficient use of expensive resources, and potentially high levels of human motivation and involvement.[12] The dual focus of matrix organizations lets management respond quickly to changes in market or product demand. Matrix organizations share scarce and often expensive human and physical resources among different projects. Individuals in a matrix organization can get information about a total project, not just about their particular specialty.

The weaknesses of matrix organizations include high levels of ambiguity because of dual or multiple authority relationships for many people. Ambiguity in authority relationships can encourage power struggles among managers who compete for dominance. People reporting to both a functional and a project manager can experience opposing demands from the two managers. Matrix organizations are complex systems with high conflict potential. Such conflict can reach dysfunctionally high levels in these organizations. All the weaknesses of a matrix design can act as significant stressors for people in such organizations.

Managers in matrix organizations may decide more slowly than in the other forms of organization. Decision making is slow because of the need to consider total project goals, not only those of a functional specialty. Also, many people are involved in the decisions, increasing the amount of time required to decide a course of action.

 ## BEHAVIORAL DEMANDS OF A MATRIX ORGANIZATION

Matrix organizations place high demands on the skills of their managers. Because of the high conflict potential in matrix organizations, managers need well-developed conflict management skills. Chapter 11 examined conflict management in detail. When the manager's conflict management skills are not sufficient, matrix organizations become seriously dysfunctional.

Matrix organizations demand high levels of coordination, cooperation, and communication. The communication often is face-to-face and in groups or teams. Communication must be descriptive and not evaluative to be effective. A high level of interpersonal skill is needed to successfully function in matrix organizations. Both managers and nonmanagers must have such skills. Individuals who do not like high levels of human contact will be uncomfortable in matrix organizations.

CASE · *The TRW Systems Group*

*T*his case describes one company's experience with a matrix form of organization. Have the following questions in mind while reading and analyzing the case:

1. Why did TRW use a matrix organization?
2. How did TRW carry out the matrix form?
3. What are the behavioral demands of the matrix organization in this company?

CASE DESCRIPTION

The origins of the TRW Systems Group go back to 1953 when Ramo-Wooldridge (RW) established a privileged

Source: Excerpted from S. M. Davis and P. R. Lawrence *Matrix* (Reading, Mass.: Addison-Wesley, 1977), pp. 91–99. Stanley M. Davis and Paul R. Lawrence, MATRIX (excerpted from text on pp. 91–99). ©1977 by Addison-Wesley Publishing Company, Inc. Reprinted by permission of the publisher.

relationship with the United States Air Force to perform systems engineering and forward planning on the USAF's intercontinental ballistic missile (ICBM) program. RW grew quickly by linking itself with the accelerating ICBM program, but its close relationship with the USAF prohibited it from bidding on hardware contracts. In 1958 RW joined with Thompson Products to form TRW, Inc. The part of the composite organization that was engaged in the USAF's ICBM work was retitled the TRW Systems Group. One year later, the TRW Systems Group exchanged its privileged relationship for one that allowed it to compete for hardware contracts in addition to the systems engineering activities to which it had until then been restricted.

Between 1960 and 1963, TRW Systems completed the transition from a "sheltered captive" of the Air Force to a fully independent, competitive aerospace company. Dur-

ing this period the number of employees increased from less than 4000 to 6000. Sales volume grew from $60 million to $125 million. Whereas in 1960, 16 contracts distributed among eight customers accounted for the sales volume, by 1963 these numbers had become 108 contracts and 42 different customers.

Although TRW Systems dropped its privileged systems engineering role, it maintained the systems management for three major ICBM programs for which it had held responsibility: the Titan missile, the Atlas missile and the Saturn system. Figure 18-5 . . . [shows] the organization [design] TRW Systems used in 1963 to manage these three programs. . . . Each [project] office reported at the same level as each functional division. . . .

Most of TRW Systems' programs were at the state of the art of their particular technology. The Titan, Atlas, and Saturn programs and the many smaller projects they assumed called on the best technology available in rocket propulsion systems, guidance and control systems, electric power systems, telecommunications, digital systems, mechanical design, metals technology, etc. TRW Systems acquired some of that technological knowledge from government and university research and development laboratories and through a varied set of subcontractors. But they developed most of it themselves through original research and by keeping their engineers and scientists in close proximity with their respective professional bodies and sources of outside technological development. They viewed this functional capability as their primary strength.

TRW Systems' customers, however, didn't buy functional competence. They purchased a specific output that applied that knowledge via the . . . project offices. TRW Systems' contracts were for projects and programs that were highly uncertain and frequently subject to changes from other components of the aerospace systems with which they interfaced. The [program] offices worked closely with their customers, interpreting their requirements, modifying them where necessary, and converting

them to specifications they could relate to the functional resource groups. . . .

The typical project office which coordinated the contract activities numbered from 30 to 40 people and was concerned with the planning, coordinating, and systems engineering of the project. . . . Customer contact and responsibility for cost, schedule, and performance lay with them. The actual design and technical work was carried out by the different functional departments. A large hardware contract for a space vehicle required the integration of all of TRW Systems' capabilities to produce the systems of the subprojects. For example, the assistant [project] manager (APM) for planning and control was responsible for cost and schedule control. . . . The APM for systems engineering was responsible for formulating the project's systems requirements and making sure that everything was designed to fit together in the end. And the APM for product integrity was responsible for developing and implementing a reliability program for the entire project including all of its subprojects. . . .

Each . . . subproject was assigned to a specific functional organization. The manager of that functional organization appointed a subprogram manager (SPM) with the concurrence of the project manager. The SPM was responsible for the total subproject and was delegated management authority by both the functional management and the APM to whom the SPM reported operationally for the project. Normally the SPM reported administratively to a laboratory or department manager in the functional organization.

The SPM worked full time directing his subproject, but was not a member of the project office; he remained a member of his functional organization. He represented both the [project] office and functional management in his authority over the divisional people working on his subproject. He spoke for the project in such matters as scheduling personnel and facility assignments, expenditure of funds, customer requirements and design interfaces. He also, however, represented the laboratory or division in such issues as technical approach, cost-effective scheduling, and the impact of design changes. The project manager provided his evaluation of the SPM's performance to the SPM's functional manager for the SPM's salary review. . . .

TRW Systems was organized into five operating divisions; specifically, the Space Vehicles, Electronic Systems, Systems Laboratory, Power Systems and . . . [Fabrication, Integration, and Test (FIT)] Divisions. Each of the divisions served as a technology center which focused on the disciplines and resources necessary to practice its technology. Although each division was organized differently, they shared a similar pattern of organization. . . .

Reporting to the division general manager were several operations managers. The operations managers were each in charge of a group of laboratories which were engaged in similar technologies. Each laboratory included a number of functional departments which were organized around technical specialties. Most divisions had a fabrication or manufacturing operations group headed by an operations manager. . . .

Each of the divisions at TRW Systems was a mixture of projects and functional departments and was generally organized around a fairly logical grouping of technical disciplines. Nevertheless, there was considerable cross-divisional coordination. TRW Systems approached the structural problem of which [projects] and which functions should go together with an "order-disorder" notion. They wanted the freedom to be able to organize in whatever way seemed best at the time—"the flexibility to be responsive"—rather than be forced into a bureaucratic logic that dictated that specific functions belonged with specific [projects], etc. It was a deliberate structuring to make . . . projects go to other divisions to get support; part of a philosophy of encouraging the interdependent relationships they needed if they were to function with little or no duplication of specialties. . . .

The manager of the functional organization appointed a subproject manager with the concurrence of the project manager. The subproject manager was assigned responsibility for the total subproject activity and was delegated management authority by the functional division management and by the assistant project manager to whom he reported operationally for the project. He was accountable for performance in his functional specialty to the manager of his functional area, usually a laboratory manager. The functional manager was responsible for the performance evaluation of the subproject manager. The subproject manager thus represented both the [project] office and his functional area and was responsible for coordinating the work of his subproject with the engineers within the functional area. Normally each functional area was involved in work on several projects simultaneously. . . .

Both sides of the matrix had different forms of organizational power and thus different pressures converged on the SPM. The [project] office had power in the form of money which the functional managers needed to fund their activities. The technical managers had the competence to make state-of-the-art projects succeed and were strong enough to ensure that technical performance was not sacrificed for the cost and schedule expediencies that underlaid the drive of the [project] people. To support this balance, TRW Systems insisted that the SPM remain under direct functional jurisdiction.

CASE ANALYSIS

TRW Systems Group needed to emphasize both its technical capabilities and its customer requirements. The company felt it had a high level of technical competence in its scientists and engineers. Those people stayed at the cutting edge of their disciplines by being in close contact with professional organizations and academic research activities.

TRW's customers bought a product, not technical knowledge. They often had special requirements. Projects varied in emphases and mixes of technical requirements. Customers differed not only in what they wanted but also in when they needed delivery.

Technical knowledge and customer requirements gave TRW a dual focus. Figure 18-5 shows how the technical resources of the company were placed in functional divisions. The major projects formed the other axis of the matrix. Individuals at the intersection of project and function effectively worked for two different managers.

TRW Systems Group experienced high ambiguity in its roles and the relationships among them. Individuals needed to respond flexibly to changing customer requirements. People in the matrix had high levels of interdependence with each other. The functional managers, for example, depended on the projects for their source of funding. Such dependence for funding is a common feature of a matrix design.

Evolving Forms of Organizational Design

Managers are trying several new ways of designing their organizations. Some forms focus on teams and work processes. Others try to balance the formal and informal parts of an organization. The most unusual form, the virtual organization, links widely scattered organizations to form a network focused on a specific goal.

 SELF-MANAGING TEAMS

Many changes unfolding in the external environment of organizations emphasize the need to focus on customers and flexibly respond to changing needs. Managers are finding it necessary to move decisions to lower levels in their organizations to meet both requirements. The need to meet diverse local requirements becomes even more important as organizations increasingly become more global in outlook.[13]

An organization that relies on **self-managing teams** uses decentralization to move decisions to the teams and authorizes those teams to decide about product design, process design, and customer service. Such teams have the authority to act so they can give the organization needed flexibility and tailor responses to specific customers. Many such teams also feature people from different functions in the organization. In this way, the teams deliberately use functional differences in ways of thinking to get more creative solutions to problems.

Decentralization and self-managing work teams let managers flatten their organizations by removing one or more layers of management. The result is often a nimble organization poised to meet the changing opportunities and constraints in the external environment. A case at the end of this chapter gives you some examples of this new and evolving form of organization.

 A PROCESS VIEW OF ORGANIZATIONAL DESIGN

The **process view** of organizational design discards the packaging of duties and tasks offered by a functional or divisional approach. It asks managers to view their organization as a series of interconnected processes that weave across multiple functions. The packaging of tasks focuses on the results of a process, not on people's skills or functions. People are assigned responsibility for all or part of a process where they will use multiple skills. They also have the decision authority to act within their process.[14]

Insurance companies usually process insurance applications with a stepwise process that went from function to function. Individual clerks did repetitive tasks focused on a small part of the process. The steps included checking the application, rating it, and offering the customer a quotation. One company changed its view of itself from function to process.[15] Individual case managers were assigned to each application. They processed the entire application with the help of individual computers and expert systems that guided the manager through the process. The case manager went to someone for help only when an application raised major issues that required advice from a physician or an underwriter. The company reduced its processing time from an average of 5 to 25 days to 2 to 5 days. It also increased its responsiveness to customers because a case manager had all the information she needed to answer a customer's questions.

THE VIRTUAL ORGANIZATION

A **virtual organization** is a temporary network of companies or individuals that focus on reaching a specific target or responding to new opportunities. Information technology links all members of the network wherever they may be in the world.[16]

The term *virtual organization* borrows its metaphor from computer technology. Virtual memory is a computer programming technique that lets a programmer have more memory than is available on the computer. Software simulates memory by using space on a disk drive. When the program runs, it is unaware that the software gives it virtual memory instead of real memory.

The metaphor carries to the virtual organization. Any company that lacks a particular skill or resource enters an agreement with a company or person (consultant or contract employee) with that skill or resource. Information technology links the companies and individuals so they can operate as if they were a single organization. The number of elements in a virtual organization network is defined by the skills, talents, and resources needed to reach the goal.

Unlike the other designs discussed in this chapter, companies in a virtual organization network have little direct control over the functions done by other members of the network. This approach to organizational design requires new behaviors of managers. High trust in network members is a central feature of a virtual organization. Conflict management and negotiation behaviors play a key role because of the need to maintain functional relationships among parts of the network. Interdependencies among organizations in a virtual organization require them to work together to reach a mutually desired goal.

TelePad in Herndon, Virginia designs, builds, and markets a handheld pen-based computer with a workforce of 24 employees. The company has no manufacturing plants, limited internal design talent, and only a few engineers. The company linked to IBM's plant in Charlotte, North Carolina to build the computer, to an industrial design company in Palo Alto, California for its external design, to Intel Corp. for engineering help, and to a data processing firm to process its payroll. The company links to over two dozen other companies to get its product to consumers. Ron Oklewiczs, Telepad's president, puts his marketing talent to work selling the computer to government agencies and private industry. A virtual organization lets TelePad do what it does best—market the computer. Meanwhile others in the network do what they do best—design, build, package, and ship the computer.

ORGANIZATIONAL ARCHITECTURE

Organizational architecture is a way of thinking about organizational design, not a specific form of it. This section examines the architectural view because it is evolving as a new method for managers to use in designing and redesigning organizations.[17]

Organizational architecture deliberately uses an architectural metaphor to focus managers on viewing organizational design as having form, purpose, and balance among its parts. It views organizational design as more than functions, divisions, or reporting relationships. An organization's architecture includes those elements along with the informal organization, political processes, reward system, and culture. Design issues center on getting balance among the parts to help the organization carry out its strategy.

The architectural view of organizational design asks the organization architect to take a systems view of the organization. That view considers the external environment as described in Chapter 17. It also includes knowledge of the organization's history, its present culture, and the nature of individuals and groups in the organization. The architect believes the design of the organization depends on the organization's strategy, its external environment, and its nature. The latter includes people, tasks, and technical process.

All forms of organizational design described in this chapter are available to the organization architect. Her dilemma is to find the mix of those forms that is right for a particular organization. The right mix could mean large change for the organization. For example, a process view of organizations is vastly different from a functional view. An organization designed around functions must undergo major changes if it is to take a process view.

International Aspects of Alternative Forms of Organization

*T*he previous chapter noted that some organizational forms are more congruent with the values of certain cultures. That concern continues with this chapter and becomes clearer when looking at the alternative forms described earlier. Functional and divisional designs may be more congruent with the values of countries that want to avoid uncertainty and accept hierarchical differences in power. Such countries include many Latin countries and Japan.[18]

Countries that avoid ambiguity are not likely to accept a design with little predictability of human behavior. Matrix organizations typically have multiple authority relations and high ambiguity, making them unacceptable in countries such as Belgium, France, and Italy.

Cultures vary in how successfully they use self-managing teams. U.S. managers have begun to emphasize these teams as they have shifted to managing for quality. Managers in many Scandinavian countries also use self-managing teams with considerable success. Sweden and Norway have restructured their work systems around self-managing work teams,[19] an approach consistent with their more socially oriented values, need for quality interpersonal relationships, and little emphasis on competition.[20]

The virtual corporation can use communications and computer technology to link organizations around the world. Members of such alliances can use an organizational design that is consistent with local culture values. As global relationships of this type increase, they will add to the complexity of managing in the international environment.

Ethical Issues about Alternative Forms of Organization

*S*everal organization forms described in this chapter can produce high levels of interpersonal and intergroup conflict. They also can feature ambiguity in both roles and relationships among roles. Some alternative forms also imply extensive change for most organizations.

Matrix organizations often produce conflict and ambiguity. Moving to a process view of organizations usually requires large-scale organizational change. The virtual organization asks people to enter new and unusual relationships. Both conflict and change can lead to stress responses in some people.

Organizational change of the extent required by these forms of organizational design can induce high stress levels in some employees. The ethical issue for managers is whether that stress becomes dysfunctionally high, leading to long-term psychological and physiological disorders.

For international organizations, the issue continues the ethical dilemma raised in Chapter 17. Should managers consider local cultural values when assessing alternative forms of organization outside their home country? Both the changes required by some alternative forms and the nature of authority relationships in them can induce high stress in people who find such alternatives culturally unacceptable. The ethical dilemma centers on the values that should guide the manager's decision. Should she use home country values or those of the local culture?

Personal and Management Implications

*E*ach organization form discussed in this chapter has implications for you as a member of such organizations. These implications follow from both the design of each form and the behavioral demands the different forms make on people.

AAL assigned the activities of different functional areas to about 20 teams of 20 to 30 people each. It formed five groups of these teams with each group serving agents from different regions. Members of the teams receive training that develops their skills across the original functional areas. All teams can process any transaction no matter how complex it is.

Field agents interact regularly with only one team, not many different people as happened with the functional design. AAL calls it "one-team processing." The regular interaction with a few people has helped the agents and teams develop close, supportive relationships.

AAL's change to self-managing teams was followed by a 75 percent decrease in processing time. The company cut three layers of supervision and 55 jobs as the teams increased their self-managing responsibilities. The company helped these displaced workers find other positions in the organization. AAL also introduced a pay plan that lets employees earn more money when they increase their skills.

The company also heard some complaints about the new design. Employees reported increases in felt stress and the loss of old friendship patterns they had formed under the functional design. Some employees also felt uncomfortable taking on managerial roles within the teams that they believed were not right for them.

. . . .

⌐ Case

A PROCESS VIEW AT FORD MOTOR COMPANY

This case describes part of Ford Motor Company's process approach to organizational design. Consider the following questions while reading the case:

1. Is this approach as radical a change for an organization as the author implies?
2. In what specific ways does this approach ask managers to shift their view of an organization?
3. Are any negative results associated with the process approach?

Japanese competitors and young entrepreneurial ventures prove every day that drastically better levels of process performance are possible. They develop products twice as fast, utilize assets eight times more productively, respond to customers ten times faster. Some large, established companies also show what can be done. . . . [Ford Motor Company has reengineered its accounts payable processes and gained a competitive edge as a result.]

In the early 1980s, when the American automotive industry was in a depression, Ford's top management put accounts payable—along with many other departments—under the microscope in search of ways to cut costs. Accounts payable in North America alone employed more than 500 people. Management thought that by rationalizing processes and installing new computer systems, it could reduce the head count by some 20%.

Ford was enthusiastic about its plan to tighten accounts payable—until it looked at Mazda. While Ford was aspiring to a 400-person department, Mazda's accounts payable organization consisted of a total of 5 people. The difference in absolute numbers was astounding, and even after adjusting for Mazda's smaller size, Ford figured that its accounts payable organization was five times the size it should be. The Ford team knew better than to attribute the discrepancy to calisthenics, company songs, or low interest rates.

Ford managers ratcheted up their goal: accounts payable would perform with not just a hundred but with many hundred fewer clerks. It then set out to achieve it. First, managers analyzed the existing system. When Ford's purchasing department wrote a purchase order, it sent a copy to accounts payable. Later, when material control received the goods, it sent a copy of the receiving document to accounts payable. Meanwhile, the vendor sent an invoice to accounts payable. It was up to accounts payable, then, to match the purchase order against the receiving document and the invoice. If they matched, the department issued payment.

The department spent most of its time on mismatches, instances where the purchase order, receiving document, and invoice disagreed. In these cases, an accounts payable clerk would investigate the discrepancy, hold up payment, generate documents, and all in all gum up the works.

One way to improve things might have been to help the accounts payable clerk investigate more efficiently, but a better choice was to prevent the mismatches in the first place. To this end, Ford instituted "invoiceless processing." Now when the purchasing department initiates an order, it enters the information into an on-line database. It doesn't send a copy of the purchase order to anyone. When the goods arrive at the receiving dock, the receiving clerk checks the database to see if they correspond to an outstanding purchase order. If so, he or she accepts them and enters the transaction into the computer system. (If receiving can't find a database entry for the received goods, it simply returns the order.)

Under the old procedures, the accounting department had to match 14 data items between the receipt record, the purchase order, and the invoice before it could issue payment to the vendor. The new approach requires matching only three items—part number, unit of measure, and supplier code—between the purchase order and the receipt record. The matching is done automatically, and the computer prepares the check, which accounts payable sends to

Source: M. Hammer, "Reengineering Work: Don't Automate, Obliterate," *Harvard Business Review* 68 (July–August 1990): 105–6. Reprinted by permission of *Harvard Business Review*. An excerpt from "Reengineering Work: Don't Automate, Obliterate" by Michael Hammer, 68 (July–August 1990). Copyright © 1990 by the President and Fellows of Harvard College; all rights reserved.

the vendor. There are no invoices to worry about since Ford has asked its vendors not to send them. . . .

Ford didn't settle for the modest increases it first envisioned. It opted for radical change—and achieved dramatic improvement. Where it has instituted this new process, Ford has achieved a 75% reduction in head count, not the 20% it would have gotten with a conventional program. And since there are no discrepancies between the financial record and the physical record, material control is simpler and financial information is more accurate.

. . . .

References and Notes

[1] J. R. Galbraith, "Matrix Organization Designs," *Business Horizons* 14 (1971): 29–40.

[2] M. Jelinek, "Organization Structure: The Basic Conformations," in M. Jelinek, J. A. Litterer, and R. E. Miles, eds., *Organizations by Design* (Plano, Tex.: Business Publications, 1981).

[3] Developed from E. Dale, *Planning and Developing the Company Organization Structure* (New York: American Management Association, 1952); R. Duncan, "What Is the Right Organization Structure? Decision Tree Analysis Provides the Answer," *Organizational Dynamics* 7 (Winter 1979): 59–80; Jelinek, "Organization Structure."

[4] See Appendix A for a discussion of such dysfunctional behavior called bureaupathology.

[5] Developed from Dale, *Planning and Developing*; Duncan, "What Is the Right Organization Structure"; R. E. Hoskisson, C. W. L. Hill, and H. Kim, "The Multidivisional Structure: Organizational Fossil or Source of Value?" *Journal of Management* 19 (1993): 269–98; Jelinek, "Organization Structure."

[6] Developed from R. L. Daft, *Organization Theory and Design* (St. Paul, Minn.: West Publishing Company, 1995), Ch. 6.

[7] Developed from L. R. Burns, "Matrix Management in Hospitals: Testing Theories of Matrix Structure and Development," *Administrative Science Quarterly* 34 (1989): 349–68; S. M. Davis and P. R. Lawrence, *Matrix* (Reading, Mass.: Addison-Wesley, 1977); S. M. Davis and P. R. Lawrence, "Problems of Matrix Organizations," *Harvard Business Review* 56 (1978): 131–42; Duncan, "What Is the Right Organization Structure?"; R. C. Ford and W. A. Randolph, "Cross-Functional Structures: A Review and Integration of Matrix Organization and Project Management," *Journal of Management* 18 (1992): 267–94.

[8] L. R. Burns and D. R. Wholey, "Adoption and Abandonment of Matrix Management Programs: Effects of Organizational Characteristics and Interorganizational Networks," *Academy of Management Journal* 36 (1993): 106–38.

[9] See Appendix A for a discussion of unity of command.

[10] E. W. Larson and D. H. Gobeli, "Matrix Management: Contradictions and Insights," *California Management Review* 29 (Summer 1987): 126–38.

[11] Developed from Davis and Lawrence, *Matrix*, pp. 91–101.

[12] Developed from Davis and Lawrence, *Matrix*; Duncan, "What Is the Right Organization Structure?" pp. 59–80; Larson and Gobeli, "Matrix Management."

[13] Developed from E. E. Lawler III, "The New Plant Revolution Revisited," *Organizational Dynamics* (Autumn 1990): 5–14; E. E. Lawler III, "The New Plant Approach: A Second Generation Approach," *Organizational Dynamics* (Summer 1991): 5–14; M. H. Safizadeh, "The Case of Workgroups in Manufacturing Operations," *California Management Review* 33 (Summer 1991): 61–82; M. S. Scott Morton, ed., *The Corporation of the 1990s: Information Technology and Organizational Transformation* (New York: Oxford University Press, 1991).

[14] M. Hammer, "Reengineering Work: Don't Automate, Obliterate," *Harvard Business Review* 68 (1990): 104–11; M. Hammer and J. Champy, *Reeingineering the Corporation: A Manifesto for Business Revolution* (New York: HarperCollins, 1993); T. A. Steward, "Reengineering: The Hot New Managing Tool," *Fortune*, August 23, 1993, pp. 40–43, 46, 48.

[15] Hammer, "Reengineering Work," pp. 106–7.

[16] J. A. Byrne, "The Virtual Corporation: The Company of the Future Will Be the Ultimate in Adaptability," *Business Week*, February 8, 1993, pp. 98–102; J. A. Byrne, "The Futurists Who Fathered the Ideas," *Business Week*, February 8, 1993, p. 103.

[17] Developed from D. A. Nadler and M. L. Tushman, "Designing Organizations That Have Good Fit: A Framework for Understanding Architectures," in D. A. Nadler, M. S. Gerstein, R. B. Shaw, and associates, *Organizational Architecture: Designs for Changing Organizations* (San Francisco: Jossey-Bass, 1992), Ch. 2; M. S. Gerstein, "From Machine Bureaucracies to Networked Organizations: An Architectural Journey," in D. A. Nadler, M. S. Gerstein, R. B. Shaw, and associates, *Organizational Architecture*, Ch. 1.

[18] G. Hofstede, *Culture's Consequences: International Differences in Work-Related Values* (Beverly Hills, Calif.: Sage Publications, 1984), pp. 264–66; G. Hofstede, *Cultures and Organizations: Software of the Mind* (New York: McGraw-Hill, 1991); A. Laurent, "The Cultural Diversity of Western Conceptions of Management," *International Studies of Management and Organization* 13 (1983): 75–96.

[19] C. Berggren, *Alternatives to Lean Production: Work Organization in the Swedish Auto Industry* (Cornell International Industrial and Labor Relations Report No. 22, December 1992).

[20] G. Hofstede, "Motivation, Leadership, and Organization: Do American Theories Apply Abroad?" *Organizational Dynamics* 9 (1980): 42–63; Hofstede, *Culture's Consequences*, Ch. 6.

V The Design of Organizations

GENERAL FOODS

*T*his case describes how a major food packaging company changed its strategy when shifts occurred in its external environment. Consider these questions while reading the case:

1. What parts of the company's external environment changed?
2. Was the company's original organizational design correct before the environment shifted?
3. Is the new organizational design correct for the company's new environment and strategy? Why?

Case Description

General Foods is a large food packaging company with headquarters in White Plains, New York. Over the years, the company had developed a significant presence in the packaged foods industry. From the 1940s through the 1960s, General Foods built strong brand recognition for its products. The company was the third largest national advertiser with an advertising budget of $160 million in 1971. Its 30 brand names covered 430 food items.

Brands such as Maxwell House, Jell-O, Kool-Aid, Birds Eye, and Sanka were household names. By 1966, General Foods was ahead of its competition in all major food types other than cereals. It also was the uncontested leader in instant coffee, desserts, and dog food. The company's profit of 6 percent of sales was the highest in the food industry.

The company built its growth strategy on acquisitions and expansion of its broad product groups and market segments identified along brand-name lines. The goal of the strategy was continual year-to-year growth in earn-

Sources: Developed from "Jockeying Begins as Ferguson Rises at GF," *Advertising Age*, December 11, 1972, p. 8; N. Giges, "GF Stress New Product Area in Major Reorganization Move," *Advertising Age*, February 12, 1973, pp. 1, 57; "The Rebuilding Job at General Foods," *Business Week*, August 25, 1973, pp. 48–51, 53–55; "GF Revamp Strategy: Growth through Efficiency," *Advertising Age*, June 3, 1974, pp. 1, 63; "James L. Ferguson: General Foods' Super-marketer," *MBA Executive*, March/April 1980, pp. 1, 6–7, 9, 11; "GF Splits Marketing and Sales," *Sales and Marketing Management*, May 19, 1980, p. 10; "Changing the Culture at General Foods," *Business Week*, March 30, 1981, pp. 136, 140; J. L. Ferguson, "General Foods' Formula for Facing Changing Times," *Progressive Grocer*," September 1982, pp. 34–35.

ings. The company experienced such growth in earnings and market share from the 1940s through the 1960s.

In 1968 the Federal Trade Commission (FTC) forced the company to divest itself of S.O.S. Soap Pads because of fears the company was dominating products sold through supermarkets. The commission also ruled that General Foods could not acquire any company that sold its products nationally through supermarkets or heavily used consumer advertising.

The company changed its strategy and began a series of acquisitions hoping that success in the new areas would fuel continual growth in earnings. It acquired Vivian Woodward Corporation, W Atlee Burpee Co., Kohner Bros. (toys), and the Burger Chef and Rix fast-food chains. The acquisitions did not prove strongly profitable. General Foods took a one-time write-off of $39 million in 1972 following the liquidation of Rix and the closing of unprofitable Burger Chef outlets. Sales of grocery products other than coffee increased by only 2.7 percent in fiscal year 1972. The total effect was a drop of 2.3 percent in net earnings for fiscal 1972. This was the first time in almost 20 years the company had experienced no earnings growth.

General Foods began to face competition in areas where it had traditionally been strong. As the pioneer developer of decaffeinated coffees, its Maxim, Brim, and Max Pax brands had helped General Foods to continue expanding its market share in coffee. Nestlé had introduced its Taster's Choice brand of decaffeinated coffee, which had significant effects on General Foods' market share. By 1973, Maxim's market share had dropped to 7.5 percent and Taster's Choice had risen to 12.6 percent.

The company was also experiencing competition from a new area. Grocery chains faced with profit margins of only 0.6 percent began to step up the introduction of their own higher-margin private label items. Store private labels could undercut national brands by 3¢ or 4¢ an item.

General Foods also began to have difficulties in merchandising products. There was little coordination among product families. As one food broker said: "Maxwell House didn't give a damn what Jell-O was doing, and both of them cared less about Post cereals."[1]

Other environmental changes were occurring around the company. The characteristics of American consumers began to change. Two-earner couples were increasing.

The traditional role of the woman as the shopper was changing. Both men and women were increasingly involved in grocery purchases. Two-earner couples, with or without children, began to demand more convenience in food preparation. American consumers also were showing an increasing concern for weight control, nutrition, and health. They now sought foods low in sugar and sodium and substitutes for animal protein.

Not only had General Foods failed to introduce any major new product lines in recent years, but the new products it introduced had failed, including Pick-Up Stix Pizza snacks, Cool'n Creamy Puddings, Toast-'ems, Snackwiches, and Thick 'n Frosty shakes. In the past, the company spent as much as 43 weeks test marketing a potential new product as it had done with Maxim. Now it was bringing products to market after only six months of testing. The life cycle of new products also started to decline. Whereas the life cycle had been two to three years in the mid-1960s, by the early 1970s, it had dropped to six months or less.

Economic conditions and government policies put additional pressures on the company. Inflation was running high. The federal government had introduced price controls in an effort to control inflation. Because General Foods bought items such as coffee and rice in the commodities market, it felt major cost pressure in manufacturing its products. At the same time, the government's price controls prevented the company from passing all or most cost increases through to the consumer.

In 1972, several management and organization changes were made. Arthur Larkin, Jr., chairman and chief executive officer (CEO), retired early in April. C. W. Cook assumed his post. In December 1972, James L. Ferguson was named president and chief operating officer. He was made responsible for all General Foods' domestic and international grocery activities and its technical research activities.

Figure V-2 shows General Foods' organization chart at the end of 1972.[2] General Foods had organized the divisions of its Grocery Group by major brand names and the technology used to produce its products. The Maxwell House Division had always been separate from the other grocery divisions and produced only ground and instant coffees. The Birds Eye Division produced and marketed frozen products including entrees, vegetables, juices, puddings, and pies. Breakfast cereals came from the Post Division along with the Tang and Start breakfast drinks. The Kool-Aid Division developed and marketed packaged beverage mixes, seasoned coatings mixes, and salad dressing mixes. Canned puddings, gelatin dessert products, and pudding mixes came from the Jell-O Division. Each division was responsible for the development and marketing of new products and the continued marketing of existing products.

General Foods began a major reorganization in February 1973 and progressed with it gradually throughout 1973. Figure V-3 shows a portion of the new organization chart. James L. Ferguson became chief executive officer in August 1973, assuming duties formally held by C. W. Cook.

The Maxwell House Coffee Division was unchanged. Products and activities in the traditional brand-name divisions were reallocated to three new divisions. Pet Foods was merged into a separate division.

All new product development activities were removed from the product divisions and placed in a New Product Development Division. This new division was responsible for all noncoffee product development activities. Market research activities, formerly done within each product division, were assigned to corporate staff. Other support activities such as Sales, Personnel, and Production were combined at the corporate level. The new division would do some new product development work and product research internally, but were to focus most of their attention on marketing.

J FIGURE V-2

General Foods Grocery Group Organization before 1973

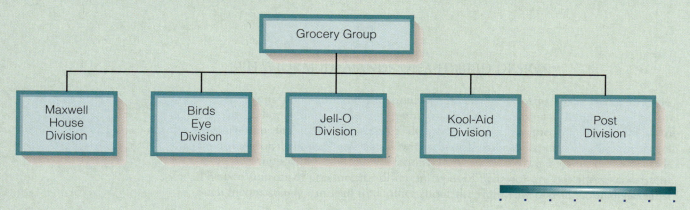

General Foods Grocery Group Organization after 1973 Reorganization

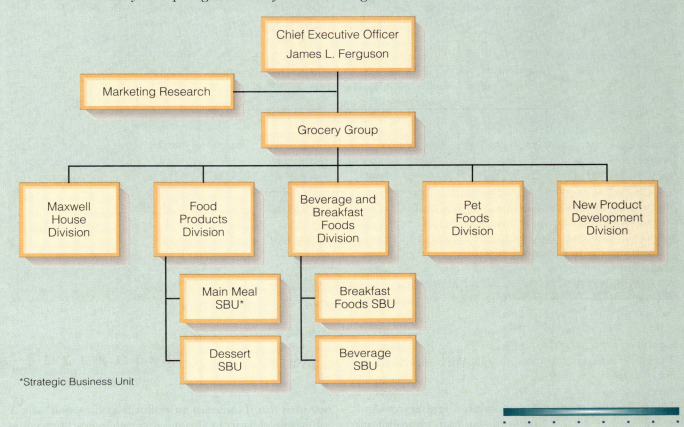

*Strategic Business Unit

The new Food Products Division had two Strategic Business Units (SBU). The Main Meal SBU had all Birds Eye vegetables products, seasoned coating mixes, salad dressings, and oven cooking bags. The Dessert SBU became responsible for Birds Eye fruits, all dessert products from the Jell-O division, frozen toppings from the Birds Eye division, and other products such as Calumet baking powder and Baker's chocolate.

The Beverage and Breakfast Foods Division also had two SBUs. The Breakfast Foods SBU got all cereal products from the Post Division, plus Log Cabin syrups. The Beverage SBU was responsible for all Kool-Aid drink mixes, Birds Eye frozen orange juice, Instant Postum, and Start and Tang breakfast drinks.

Management duties were reassigned. Senior management was to make strategic decisions and be responsible for the implementation of strategy. Operating managers in the divisions were to focus on their operational responsibilities. As described by Ferguson: "From now on, the working level will not only be permitted to take full operating responsibility, it will be required to."[3]

The new strategy at General Foods would strongly emphasize new product development. Instead of introducing many new products and hoping for some successes, the company would carefully test new products and only those with potential would make it to market. The company's research activities would also refocus from a short-term view to a long-term one of finding major breakthroughs.

Mr. Ferguson commented on the old and new strategies at General Foods:

> Over a period of time ... we became aware that our growth depended more on individual new products than from an effectively coordinated strategy against a given market segment. This worked fine as long as market growth was healthy and the winners continued in a steady stream at reasonable cost. But when things tightened up, it became clear that the nature of the game was changing, and we were losing out on benefits that could come from a more coordinated approach.[4]

Case Analysis

The General Foods case shows you how an organization's strategy can affect its design. General Foods' original strategy emphasized increases in market share through acquisitions that matched existing product areas. The company wanted steady year-to-year growth in earnings. The strong brand recognition helped the company for many years.

The company's external environment shifted sharply in the late 1960s. The FTC restricted the company's acquisition strategy. General Foods responded to the FTC's decision by moving into areas where it had little knowledge and experience. At the same time, consumers changed both their buying patterns and types of products bought. Product life cycles shortened. Competition increased from both traditional areas such as other packaged food companies and nontraditional areas such as grocery store private labels. Economic shifts also occurred making the external environment complex and dynamic. The external environment now presented company management with high uncertainty.

Ferguson saw a need to both develop a new strategy and change the design of the organization to carry out that strategy. The company now needed to focus on new product development and more effective marketing of its existing products. The lack of internal coordination needed to be replaced by increased coordination among related product types. The earlier emphasis on brands only was replaced by more integration of the various brands.

Before the changes by Ferguson, General Foods was highly differentiated but had a low degree of integration. The differentiation resulted both from its size and its many brands—430 food items. The old organization structure did not let management do a proper job of integration. The company's performance dropped because of its inadequate integration.

Although not described by the case in this way, the new organizational design directly addressed the dual issues of differentiation and integration. Related products were grouped together in divisions regardless of brand. The SBUs refined each group so managers could build a marketing strategy around menu lines. Putting marketing research at the top of the organization raised its status and visibility in the company. Ferguson sent a clear message—new products are important to General Foods.

Ferguson changed the organizational design to fit his new strategy, making the design of General Foods a major tool for carrying out that strategy. The company also needed to address the nature of its internal processes. Where should it fall on the mechanistic-organic continuum? Recall from Chapter 17 that organic organizations work well in dynamic environments. The high uncertainty of the complex-dynamic environment of General Foods called for the internal processes of an organic organization.

References and Notes

[1] "The Rebuilding Job at General Foods," *Business Week*, August 25, 1973, p. 53.

[2] The organization chart in Figure V-2 shows only the elements important to this case.

[3] "GF Revamp Strategy: Growth through Efficiency," *Advertising Age*, June 3, 1974, p. 1.

[4] "The Rebuilding Job at General Foods," p. 51.

Organizational Change and the Future

. . . .

Section Overview

*F*igure VI-1 is an overview of the major sections of this book and the chapters in Section VI. This section has two chapters that bring the book to a close. One describes organizational change; the other looks into the future. Each chapter discusses international aspects of the topics and the ethical issues they raise.

Chapter 19 describes organizational change and development. The chapter describes the forces for and against change and the difference between planned and unplanned change. Planned change can have as its targets the organization's culture, decision processes, or design. There are two models of planned organizational change. The evolutionary model sees change happening incrementally over-time. The revolutionary model views change as unfolding over periods of stability followed by bursts of change activity.

People in organizations often resist change because they feel they will lose something valued or have familiar relationships disrupted. Managers can view resistance to change as a problem to overcome or a source of new information about their organization. The chapter describes several ways managers can reduce resistance.

Organizational development is a systematic approach to planned change that uses much of our knowledge from the social and behavioral sciences. Organizational development happens in a series of phases and typically uses an internal or external consultant. The consultant helps the organization learn how to change and continue its development after the consultant leaves. Action research is a data-based approach to change that uses data to diagnose the current state of the organization.

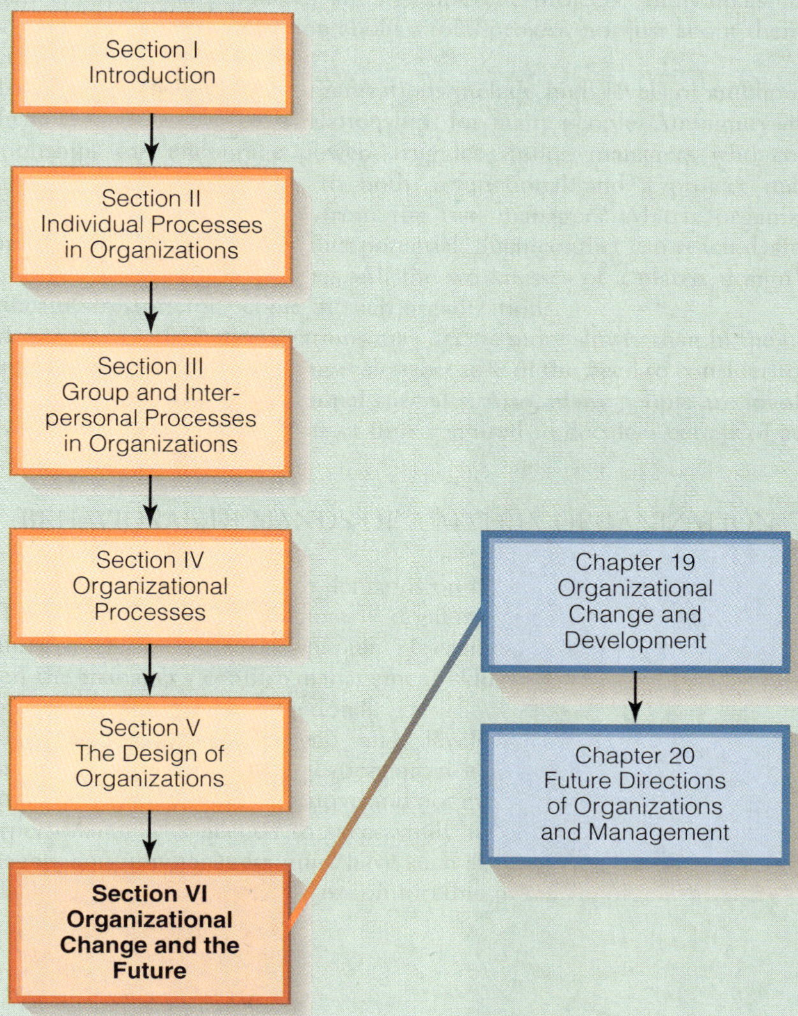

FIGURE VI-1

Section VI Overview

```
┌─────────────────┐
│    Section I    │
│  Introduction   │
└─────────────────┘
         │
         ▼
┌─────────────────┐
│   Section II    │
│   Individual    │
│   Processes     │
│ in Organizations│
└─────────────────┘
         │
         ▼
┌─────────────────┐
│   Section III   │
│ Group and Inter-│
│ personal        │
│ Processes       │
│ in Organizations│
└─────────────────┘
         │
         ▼
┌─────────────────┐                    ┌─────────────────┐
│   Section IV    │                    │   Chapter 19    │
│  Organizational │                    │  Organizational │
│    Processes    │                    │     Change and  │
└─────────────────┘                    │   Development   │
         │                             └─────────────────┘
         ▼                                      │
┌─────────────────┐                             ▼
│   Section V     │                    ┌─────────────────┐
│  The Design of  │                    │   Chapter 20    │
│  Organizations  │                    │ Future Directions│
└─────────────────┘                    │ of Organizations │
         │                             │ and Management  │
         ▼                             └─────────────────┘
┌─────────────────┐
│   Section VI    │
│  Organizational │
│  Change and the │
│     Future      │
└─────────────────┘
```

Chapter 20 examines the future of organizations and management. It examines the future for domestic changes, international changes, and technological changes. All those changes will press organizations and their managers to change in several ways. Organization and management changes will require new strategies, new organizational designs, and changes in management behavior.

19

Organizational Change and Development

· *Hewlett Packard engineers in Singapore are proud of their new printers that print in several Asian languages. The company has responded to fast-changing Asian markets by offering printers capable of handling local languages.*

After reading this chapter, you should be able to . . .

· Discuss the pressures on managers to change their organizations.
· Describe the types of organizational change.
· Explain the phases and targets of planned organizational change.
· List some reasons for resistance to change in organizations.
· Describe the organizational development techniques managers can use to change their organizations.
· Understand some international aspects of organizational change and development.

Chapter Overview

. . . .

OPENING EPISODE

Bob Allen Is Turning AT&T into a Live Wire

Almost a year after the breakup of American Telephone & Telegraph Co., the company's board of directors fumed at the eight-figure losses of the Consumer Products Division. The board ordered the division's operations chief to turn a profit or get out of that business. They had said the unthinkable: abandon the business that was the basis of the company—making telephones.

The Consumer Products Division was a stunning example of the organizational characteristics that plagued AT&T. It was a highly centralized organization that was not nimble enough to keep up with its faster moving rivals. The company's culture valued aversion of competition and conflict. It had lost touch with its customers and was slower than its competitors to bring products to market.

Robert E. Allen became AT&T's chair in April 1988 following the sudden death of former chair James E. Olson. Allen quickly assessed the state of the company by traveling extensively to research facilities, service centers, and manufacturing plants. Allen identified the core problem as a stodgy, plodding organization with a culture formed by more than 70 years of regulated monopoly status. The breakup of AT&T in 1984 did not change the company's culture to one that supported a competitive orientation.

Allen set out to change the company's culture to one with a strong customer focus, flexibility, and the ability to adapt to a fast-changing external environment. He wrote a statement of his desired new direction at home on a Saturday. His vision statement for the company stressed winning in its markets, technological leadership, passionate commitment to customers, and increasing shareholder value. The vision statement went to all employees the following week. Allen then set out to change AT&T.

The new organizational design moved much decision authority from senior executives to presidents of business units. Each business unit would focus on specific products or services and operate as a separate business within the company. For example, the Transmission Systems business unit was a $2.5 billion business in 1989. It had five subordinate units that focused on specific aspects of transmission such as cellular radio and fiber optics. The subordinate units were separate profit-and-loss centers whose managers were responsible for their success.

The new organizational design reversed the earlier centralized form. Managers of the business units had marketing, pricing, and product development authority within their units. They did not need any higher approval to launch new products or services—a major feature of the earlier AT&T. Once he had formed the business units and named their presidents, Allen presented his final plan to 131 top executives in March 1988. Here is a reported account of the close of that presentation:

> Allen looked on impassively as his team vigorously debated the merits and pitfalls of the
> new structure. "There were some very candid views expressed," he recalls. Then a hush

· *Robert E. Allen, chairman of AT&T, has brought revolutionary change to that company. His efforts have made AT&T a formidable competitor in the telecommunications industry.*

Source: Developed from J. J. Keller and M. Maremont, "Bob Allen Is Turning AT&T into a Live Wire," *Business Week*, November 6, 1989, pp. 140–52. The quotation that concludes the episode is from p. 144.

A T&T's Robert Allen was trying to transform a stodgy, ponderous organization. He had a clear vision of what his company could be and was trying to achieve that vision. Allen faced the increasingly common problem of creating an organization that could respond to fast changes in its external environment. AT&T could no longer rely on monopoly status for success in its markets. It would have to compete in what had become a turbulent, complex, fast-changing environment. Three years after Allen started his change efforts, AT&T had not finished its transformation.[1]

An early section of this chapter describes the sources of pressure on managers to change their organizations. Such pressures for change will continue in the future, making it necessary to understand how organizational change takes place and what it does to people in organizations. It also will be useful for you to know the probable effects on you as a member of a changing system. You will be better prepared to adapt to such change, or cope with it, if you understand the change processes of organizations.

As a manager or nonmanager, you may also need to change all or part of an organization in the future. Successfully changing an organization requires knowing how to manage change and cause change deliberately. Managers also need to understand the forces in people and organizations that resist organizational change and how to reduce such resistance.

Several earlier chapters gave you information that will help you understand intentional organizational change. The earlier discussions of organizational culture in Chapter 5, motivation in Chapters 7 and 8, job design in Chapter 9, leadership in Chapter 12, and power and political behavior in Chapter 15 are all useful for understanding and managing change processes.

Forces for and against Change

The forces for change that press managers to change the organization can come from outside or inside the organization.[2] Competition for market share can force managers to change the organization's strategy and then its structure to carry out that strategy. The Campbell Soup case in Chapter 17 is an example of this sequence of changes.

Threats of acquisition can induce management to change the organization's structure and internal processes to inhibit the takeover effort. If managers are to respond to the increased interest in global markets and the need to compete across many borders, they will have to consider major changes in their organizations.[3] Increasing workforce diversity and growing interest in managing for quality are also forces for change.

Internal forces for change appear as dissatisfaction, discontent, felt stress, loss of control over internal processes, and dysfunctionally high conflict. Decision processes may have become dysfunctionally slow; turnover and absenteeism may be high; and communication among different parts of the organization may have almost stopped. Such problems, or combinations of them, can press managers to try to change their organizations.

FIGURE 19-1

Forces for and against Change

A Force Field

| Present state of the organization | | Desired state of the organization |

Forces for change | **Forces against change**

Workforce diversity → ← Homogeneous workforce

Total Quality Management → ← Quality inspectors

International emphasis → ← Previous domestic emphasis

A — Time — A'

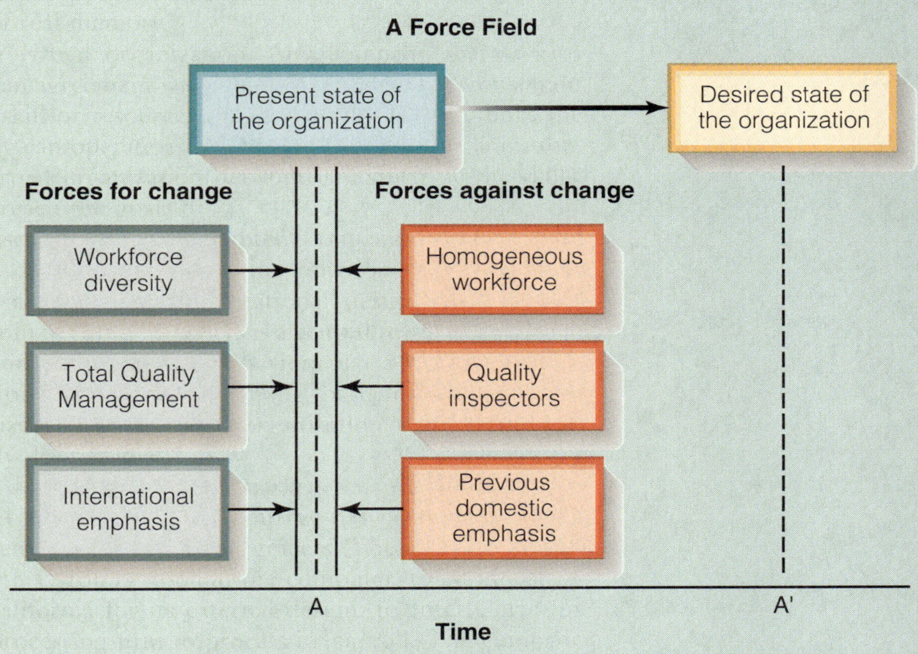

Forces for change often face forces opposing change. The opposing forces can also lie inside or outside the organization. Resistance to change inside the organization can come from individuals and groups who do not want the change to happen. Outside the organization, special interest groups, such as consumer groups and unions, may oppose the organizational change. A later section of this chapter describes many reasons people resist change in organizations.

Managers can respond to pressures for change in two ways. They can deny the importance of the pressures for change and continue to manage as they have in the past. Such a reaction can have strong negative effects on an organization, if it truly needs to change.

The second reaction is to accept the need for change and move forward with a deliberate, planned change effort. For example, Pratt & Whitney's management had developed an arrogant, unresponsive attitude toward its customers for jet engines. As a result, the company's profits dropped to a 13-year low in 1986.[4] The marked decline in profits convinced Robert F. Daniell, the company's CEO, to begin a program of planned change.

Figure 19-1 shows the forces for and against change acting as a force field[5] around the present state of the organization. This chapter describes how managers and other agents of change can affect that force field and move the organization to a desired new state.

Unplanned and Planned Organizational Change

Organizational change involves movement from the present state of the organization to some future or target state.[6] The future state may be a new strategy for the organization, changes in the organization's culture, introduction of a new technology, and so on. These are just a few examples; many other possible future states exist.

Organizational change is either unplanned or planned. Unplanned organizational change occurs when pressures for change overwhelm any efforts to resist the change. Such change may be unexpected by management and can result in uncontrolled, if not chaotic, change effects on the organization. In other cases, management may anticipate the change, but be unable to avoid it.

Planned organizational change involves deliberate and systematic efforts by managers to move an organization, or a subsystem, to a new state. Planned change includes deliberately changing the organization's design, technology, tasks, people, information systems, and the like. For example, the Opening Episode described how Allen at AT&T induced planned change by forming a new vision of the future and moving decision authority to lower levels. Although managers try to follow a plan for change, it does not always move forward smoothly. The plan often hits blockages, causing managers to rethink their goal and plan.[7]

Planned organizational change defines a desired future state for the organization, analyzes and diagnoses the present state of the organization, and manages the process that moves the organization from its present state to the desired future state.[8] Often a consultant serves as a change agent to help managers bring about planned organizational change. The consultant may be external to the organization or part of a staff function that specializes in helping managers carry out planned organizational change.

Targets of Planned Organizational Change

The targets of a planned organizational change effort are as varied as organizations. The early phases of planned change establish the need for change and identify the target that needs changing to reach the desired future state. The target can be an organization's culture, decision processes, or communication processes. Managers may need to change the design of tasks or the design of the organization. They may want to introduce technologies or adopt a new strategy for the organization. The choice of the target must be made only after careful assessment of the current state of the organization and the need for change.[9]

Planned Organizational Change

The reasons for organizational change, the scope of change, and the intensity of change vary. Change can happen because managers react to environmental shifts or because they anticipate the future state of the organization's environment. Sometimes change happens incrementally, letting the organization evolve from its present state to a future state. Such incremental change does not affect all organization systems. For example, an organization might change its pay scale to stay market competitive. Change can also have more dramatic effects on an organization. A strategic shift, for example, can have almost revolutionary effects on an entire organization by affecting the design of the organization, job design, the informal organization, and support processes. Researchers have proposed two contrasting models of planned organizational change to explain these two types of change: the evolutionary model and the revolutionary model. The models describe different change processes for evolutionary and revolutionary change.[10]

EVOLUTIONARY MODEL OF ORGANIZATIONAL CHANGE

Evolutionary change happens incrementally over time as managers adapt an organization's design and processes to changes in its external environment. This view of planned organizational change dominated academic and practitioner thinking until the early 1980s. The **evolutionary model** of organizational change sees change happening in small bits that add to a total amount of change. Figure 19-2 depicts the evolutionary change process.

The evolutionary model of organizational change views change as happening in a series of phases.[11] A manager or other change agent develops a need for change among those affected. The change agent then tries to move the organization or a part of it toward the changed state. During the last phase, the change agent **stabilizes the change** and makes it an ongoing part of the organization. The phases do not have distinct boundaries; each phase blends into the next phase in the sequence. Although the three phases often occur during a planned change effort, organizational change does not always happen in a linear fashion. Unexpected events can occur along the way, forcing a return to an earlier phase.

One example of evolutionary change was Microsoft Corporation's recognition that it was not ready for the sweeping effects of the Internet on people's ways of communicating with personal computers.[12] The company announced in 1994 that it would offer software to allow easy access to the Internet. For this industry giant, producing such software and adding new support systems for it were small changes in the company's total products and systems.

REVOLUTIONARY MODEL OF ORGANIZATIONAL CHANGE

Rather than seeing organizational change happening in smooth phases, the **revolutionary model** sees organizational change as unfolding over long periods of stability followed by bursts of major change activities.[13] After the big changes occur, the organization settles into another stable period.

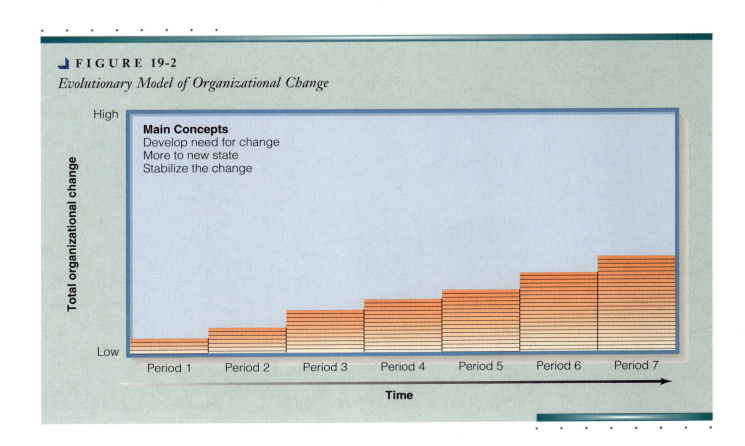

◢ FIGURE 19-2

Evolutionary Model of Organizational Change

Main Concepts
Develop need for change
More to new state
Stabilize the change

y-axis: Total organizational change (High / Low)

x-axis: Period 1   Period 2   Period 3   Period 4   Period 5   Period 6   Period 7

Time

Figure 19-3 depicts the revolutionary change process and lists the main parts of this type of organizational change. The three concepts anchoring this view are equilibrium periods, revolutionary periods, and deep structure. During **equilibrium periods,** an organization moves steadily toward its mission and goals. **Revolutionary periods** feature feverish change activities aimed at changing the strategic direction of the organization. **Deep structures** are enduring features of an organization's design, processes, and relationships with its external environment that let the organization succeed. For example, until personal computers and minicomputers overtook mainframe computers in many markets, IBM viewed its mission as designing and selling mainframes. Its deep structure supported that mission and strongly focused its members on the mainframe market.[14]

Research focused on revolutionary organizational change suggests two events can trigger a revolutionary period: (1) dissatisfaction with the organization's performance and (2) strong feelings among organization members that it is time for change.[15]

The first event is a response to a felt misfit between the organization's deep structure and its current environment, technical process, and mix of organizational members. Dissatisfaction develops following clear organizational failure or when many believe failure is imminent. For example, IBM's Chief Executive Officer (CEO) John Akers resigned in January 1993 following a period of dismal financial performance.[16] The company's board of directors appointed Louis V. Gerstner Jr., an outsider, as the new CEO. Gerstner forged a new direction for the company, creating a turbulent period. In less than two years, he reduced its workforce by 55 percent, cut costs, reduced prices, and increased product development. By the end of 1994, analysts had estimated profits at $2.8 billion, and cash on hand had climbed to almost $11 billion. A turbulent period indeed, but the results were positive.[17]

The second event can happen when organization members feel uneasy with the current equilibrium period and develop feelings of little forward movement. Al-

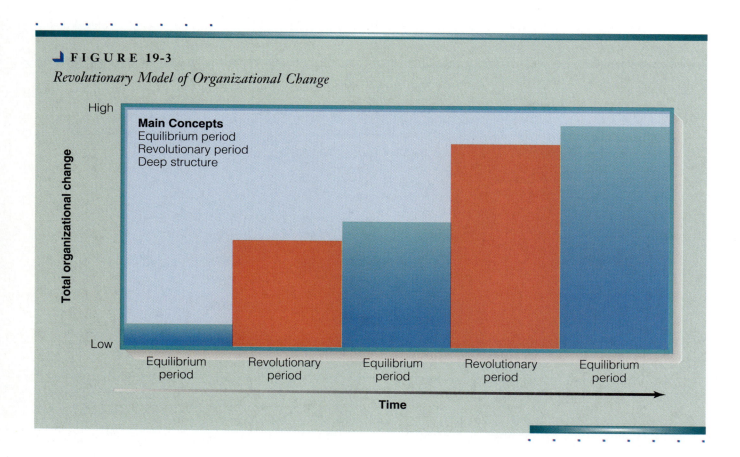

FIGURE 19-3
Revolutionary Model of Organizational Change

Main Concepts
Equilibrium period
Revolutionary period
Deep structure

(y-axis: Total organizational change — Low to High)

Equilibrium period · Revolutionary period · Equilibrium period · Revolutionary period · Equilibrium period

Time

though little research has focused on this event, some results suggest it can happen in new venture organizations.[18] Managers seem to reach a milestone in the development of the new organization, sense a need for major change, and embrace it—starting a new turbulent period.

Resistance to Change

People in organizations often resist both planned and unplanned organizational change. Although the target of the change may be the design of the organization, people's jobs, or the underlying technology, the change also affects social systems in the organization. People develop long-standing and familiar patterns of social interaction. When an organizational change affects these networks of social interaction, strong resistance can develop. It may take the form of lack of cooperation with the change effort, deliberate sabotage of the change effort, or dysfunctionally high levels of conflict.[19] This section will describe types of resistance in general. A particular change effort will lead to specific types of resistance.[20]

REASONS FOR RESISTANCE TO CHANGE

Figure 19-4 shows several reasons people resist organizational change.[21] Some people may perceive the change as causing them to lose something valued. For example, a change could reduce the social status of an individual or a group. If the individual or group valued their status, they are likely to resist the change.

Misunderstandings about the intended goal of the change or lack of trust between the target of change and the change agent can create resistance reactions. Misunderstandings can arise because the change agent did not fully explain the goal of the change. Lack of trust may develop because the change agent is an outsider or comes from a part of the organization that the target has long distrusted.

Resistance to change can also occur when all parties involved in the change do not share a common perception about the value of the change. The change agent and

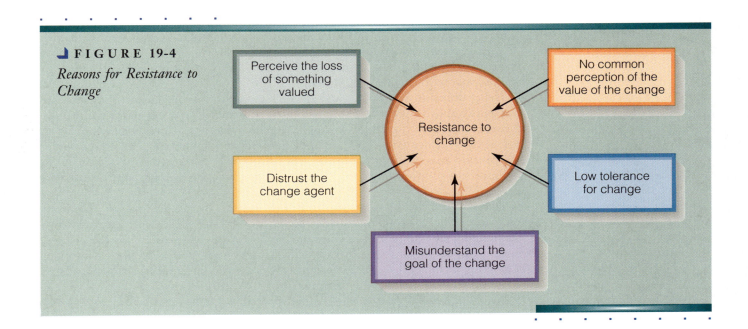

FIGURE 19-4

Reasons for Resistance to Change

Perceive the loss of something valued

No common perception of the value of the change

Resistance to change

Distrust the change agent

Low tolerance for change

Misunderstand the goal of the change

those who are the target of the change often have different expectations about the effects of the change. Later, this section discusses how such differences make resistance to change a valuable tool for managing change.

Lastly, the people who are the target of the change may have low tolerance for change and the uncertainty associated with it. People vary in their ability to change their behavior quickly. Those who resist change because of low tolerance may believe the change would be good for them and the organization. They simply cannot alter their behavior as fast as the change requires.

MANAGERS' ORIENTATION TO RESISTANCE TO CHANGE

Managers can have two different reactions to resistance to change. They can treat the resistance as a problem to overcome or view it as a signal to get more information about the reasons for the resistance.[22] Managers who view resistance as a problem to overcome may try to forcefully reduce it. Such coercive approaches often increase the resistance.[23]

Alternatively, managers may see resistance as a signal that the change agent needs more information about the intended change.[24] The targets who will be affected by the change may have valuable insights about its effects. An alert change agent will involve the targets in diagnosing the reasons for the resistance. In this way, managers can use resistance to change as a tool to get needed information.

Should managers and change agents see the absence of resistance to change as a stroke of good fortune? There are many reasons to think they should not. The absence of resistance is also a signal to managers and change agents.[25] A change that is automatically accepted can be less effective than one that has been resisted and actively debated. The resisters play an important role by focusing the change agent's attention on potentially dysfunctional aspects of the proposed change.[26]

MANAGING THE CHANGE PROCESS TO REDUCE RESISTANCE

Resistance reactions may focus on the change, the method of change, or the change agent. Figure 19-5 offers several methods of reducing resistance once it starts. The method or methods used depends in part on the target of the resistance to change.[27]

Resistance often develops when the change agent and the target of change differ strongly in such characteristics as level of education, physical appearance, values, and language. Using change agents with characteristics congruent with those of the target reduces resistance reactions.[28] For example, if the target of the change effort is a group of people who dress informally at work, a change agent would be ill-advised to wear formal business clothes.

Using dramatic ceremonies and symbols to signal disengagement from the past can quickly move a system forward with little resistance.[29] The ceremony can include recognition of a job well done on some program coming to an end. This approach to managing a change effort can be especially effective in industries such as aerospace, where shifts in technology make old programs obsolete. Ceremoniously burying the old program and launching the new one can go a long way to reducing resistance to change.

Communicating information about the change is another way to head off resistance. The communications can be written or oral, presented to groups or to single individuals. The communication should explain the reasons for the change, how it will happen, and the effects it will have on various groups in the organization. Especially with highly technical change, an explanation in simple and understandable terms helps reduce resistance reactions.

Involving the key people who will be affected by the proposed change also helps reduce resistance. They should be involved early in the change effort, especially in diagnosing the system to see whether change is needed. This suggestion does not

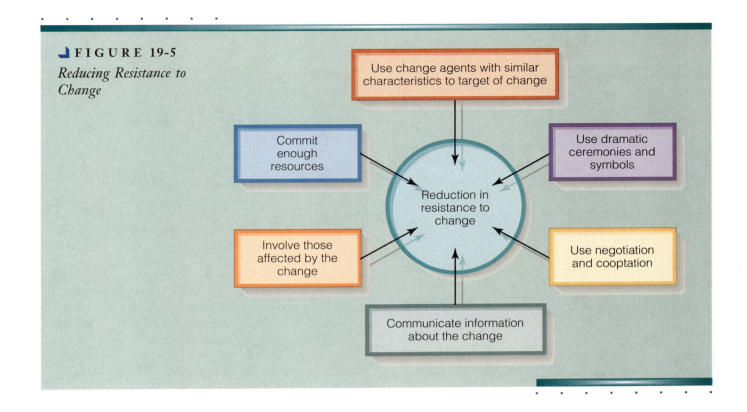

FIGURE 19-5

Reducing Resistance to Change

Use change agents with similar characteristics to target of change

Commit enough resources

Use dramatic ceremonies and symbols

Reduction in resistance to change

Involve those affected by the change

Use negotiation and cooptation

Communicate information about the change

mean inviting members of the target system to participate just to give them a superficial sense of contributing to the change. Their involvement is necessary to get crucial information from those most intimately involved in the target system. Such information lets managers and change agents design an effective change effort.

Managers can support a major change effort by committing enough resources to make the change easier on those affected. Ample resources are particularly important if the change involves moving to a new and complex technology. Managers can expect resistance reactions when people must learn new, more complex ways of doing their work. Management can head off such resistance by committing enough resources to train people to use the new technology.

When a powerful person or group is a potential source of resistance, negotiation may be necessary. These people may not be powerful enough to prevent the change, but they can create a significant source of resistance. Negotiations are common when unionized employees are asked to change their work behavior. A union contract may need revision to get major changes in the way work is done.

A more indirect and politically based approach involves various forms of manipulating those who are the target of change. Cooptation is a political strategy that aims to persuade important individuals or groups to endorse the change by inviting them to play a role in designing the change effort. Cooptation is different from the involvement described earlier. Here, the change agent is not seeking information to build an effective change program. The change agent or manager simply wants the important person or group to accept the change program. Of course, cooptation can backfire. The coopted individual or group may affect the design of the change effort to benefit themselves at the expense of the larger organization's goals.

Managers and change agents sometimes have no choice other than to force change onto the target system. Coercion is often necessary when the change must come quickly or is undesirable to the target system. Pressing or forcing a system to change can also increase resistance to change, making the manager or change agent's job even more difficult.

Progressive

The following case describes the change strategy used by a CEO to improve his organization. Assess his approach.

1. Which type of planned change approach did he use?
2. Is there evidence that the change is working? If so, what is this evidence?

CASE DESCRIPTION

Peter Lewis, the CEO of Progressive, a highly successful Cleveland auto insurer that sells policies mostly to high-risk drivers, knew his people took pride in their relationship with customers. They believed they provided the best service of any auto insurer in America. To make employees feel they *had* to change, Lewis communicated a message guaranteed to get their attention. Says he: "I told them that our customers actually hate us."

The idea wasn't off the wall. California voters had recently passed Proposition 103, a law that mandated cuts in auto insurance rates. The new regulation convinced Lewis that drivers, fed up with sky-high insurance premiums, simply hated insurance companies. He also saw that Allstate, a new competitor, was starting to steal market share by offering lower prices. So Lewis told the employees of his highly profitable company that all was not well. "I said our customers felt like the people in the movie *Network* who were all hanging out of apartment windows screaming, 'I'm mad as hell, and I'm not going to take it anymore!'"

Source: B. Dumaine, "Times Are Good? Create a Crisis," *Fortune,* June 28, 1993, p. 126. © 1993 Time Inc. All rights reserved.

Lewis cajoled, argued, and reasoned for months until his top executives began to agree to his ideas for change. His plan had two goals. To stay competitive, Lewis felt the company had to revamp its claims process and cut prices. He could do the latter only by firing some 1,300 employees, 19% of the work force. All this at a time when the company was enjoying healthy growth.

Resistance was formidable. Progressive's claim system was the best in the industry—why change it? Lewis persisted, and today the system is faster and more efficient. For example, Progressive gives customers an 800 number they can call 24 hours a day, seven days a week. Within a few hours of an accident, a Progressive claims agent can visit the customer, often cutting a check on the spot. The company found that settling claims faster—in 11 days on average, vs. 18 before—meant less paperwork, fewer hours spent by claims adjusters on each case, and fewer lawyers getting involved. All these changes added up to big savings for Progressive. And customers were happy to get their money faster.

When it came to the layoffs, Lewis recalls, "the shock was enormous. It destroyed morale." To try to reverse some of the damage, he explained that the motive was to reduce costs and make pricing more competitive, and thus the company more profitable—an honest message but unlikely to lift spirits. To convince his people that higher profits were worth the pain, Lewis in 1992 launched a profit-sharing program for all supervisors and hourly workers.

Would he do it again? Lewis thinks so: "A few years ago we had momentum; we had a lot of stuff going for us. But we could see that our competitors were going to kill us if we didn't do something fast." So far Progressive is

• *Peter Lewis, chief executive of Progressive, a Cleveland auto insurer that specializes in high-risk policies. Lewis brought wrenching change to his company to get a strong customer focus.*

very much alive. The company's stock appreciated 70% over the past 12 months.

CASE ANALYSIS

Peter Lewis wanted to change his company's customary way of doing business. He believed he would meet strong resistance and used a method that shook people loose from their cultural roots. The method Lewis used is an example of revolutionary change described earlier. By including the profit-sharing program, Lewis was able to reward desirable behavior. The improved claims service and 70 percent increase in stock value suggest that his radical approach to changing Progressive is working.

Organizational Development

Organizational development is a long-term, systematic, and prescriptive approach to planned organizational change. Although it uses a systemwide view, it can focus on a single subsystem of an organization. Organizational development applies the theories and concepts of the social and behavioral sciences to the problem of changing an organization. It also uses the knowledge of the behavioral sciences as the source of techniques to cause change.[30]

The following statement by one of the key proponents of organizational development describes its goals:

> (1) enhancing congruence between organizational structure, processes, strategy, people, and culture; (2) developing new and creative organizational solutions; and (3) developing the organization's self-renewing capacity.[31]

The self-renewing emphasis distinguishes organizational development from other approaches to planned organizational change.[32] Organizational development views organizations as complex social and technical systems. An organizational development effort can focus on human processes in the organization, the organizational design, job design, technology, and many other aspects of the organization.

A careful examination of the goals of organizational development reveals its prescriptive feature.[33] Organizational development tries to create an organization with enough flexibility to change its design according to the nature of its tasks and external environment. It builds mechanisms within the organization that let members get feedback about the state of the organization. The feedback then lets all members engage in activities directed at continuous improvement.

Organizational development views conflict as an inevitable part of organization life. It tries to build a culture that says conflict can be positively managed to reach the organization's goals. The culture also needs a norm that says people with knowledge, not just those in appointed decision-making roles, should have authority and influence in decision making. Organizational development asks organization members to take charge of their destiny and to be involved in the change process.

PHASES OF ORGANIZATIONAL DEVELOPMENT

The practice of organizational development unfolds in the series of phases shown in Figure 19-6. Each phase flows into the next phase. These are phases—not steps—because in practice, there are no clear demarcations between them.[34]

The figure suggests organizational development unfolds in a forward-moving fashion. Information developed during the effort, however, may suggest needed changes. For example, during the evaluation phase, managers may discover they need more data from the diagnosis phase. The arrows linking later to earlier phases in the figure indicate that phases can repeat.

The following description of the phases assumes an internal or external organizational development consultant is involved in the effort. Such consultants typically

■ **FIGURE 19-6**

Phases of Organizational Development

Source: T. G. Cummings and C. G. Worley, *Organizational Development and Change* (Minneapolis/St. Paul: West Publishing Company, 1993), Adapted from Figure 3-1, p. 54 with the permission of West Publishing Company.

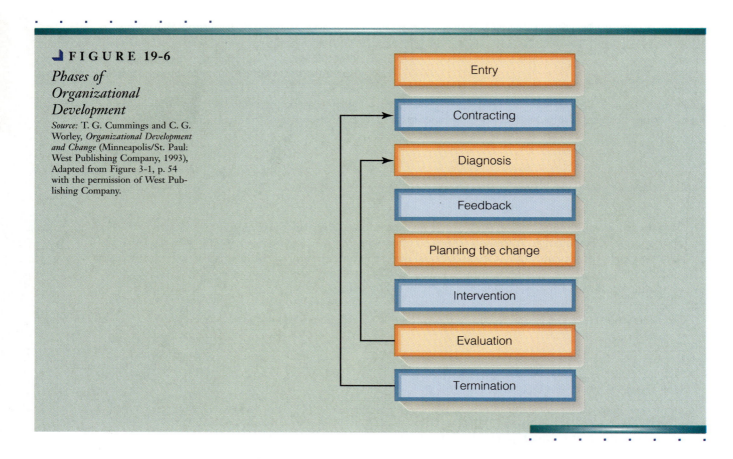

have the training and experience that let them serve as key resources to the managers trying to use organizational development. Not all organizational development efforts use consultants; small organizations and those with limited resources, for example, tend not to use them.

Entry

The first phase (**Entry**) is the point at which the consultant has direct contact with the client. The client usually begins the contact, especially if the consultant is an external one. Internal consultants may also make the first contact because helping managers in their organization is often part of their job description.

This phase includes all the dynamics of establishing a client-consultant relationship. Key elements are the mutual evaluation of each other and the conclusion that the client and consultant can develop a compatible working relationship.

Contracting

If both parties consider the entry phase successful, they move to the **contracting** phase. An organizational development contract can range from an oral agreement to a document that legally binds both parties. The contract describes both party's expectations and outlines what they will do during the organizational development program.[35] Neither party should look upon the organizational development contract as a static agreement. As the organizational development program unfolds, the parties should reexamine or renegotiate the contract.

Diagnosis

During the **diagnosis** phase, the consultant gets information about the client system and diagnoses its state. An alert consultant begins the diagnosis phase as early as the first contact with the client. Initially, the diagnosis may involve observing the behavior and reactions of the client and the physical characteristics of the client system. Later the diagnosis can include systematic data collection using interviews, surveys, and company records. The consultant summarizes the results of the analysis and diagnosis in preparation for feedback to the client system.

Feedback

The consultant then has a series of **feedback** meetings with members of the client system. The number of meetings depends on the scope of the organizational development program. If the program focuses only on one work group, the consultant would meet first with the manager or supervisor of the group and then with the other members of the group. If more groups are targeted, more meetings will be needed.

Feedback meetings typically include several steps. First, the consultant presents his analysis of the data collected in the diagnosis phase. A discussion follows in which the consultant answers questions and clarifies the presentation as needed. The consultant then gives a preliminary diagnosis of the client system. This step has the distinctive organizational development feature of collaboration of the client. The consultant and the members of the client system work together to arrive at a diagnosis of the current state of the client system. The active involvement of the client can lead to changes in the consultant's original diagnosis.

Planning the Change

The diagnosis and feedback phases, when done well, lead to **planning the change** required in the client system. The planning phase can occur during the feedback meeting if the change is simple or if the client system is small. Often this phase happens at some later time.

The client and consultant also work collaboratively during the planning phase. They identify alternative courses of action and the effects of each alternative. After selecting the change alternatives, they lay out the steps needed to bring about that change. A distinctive feature of the planning phase in organizational development is that the client decides the nature of the change program—not the consultant.

Intervention

Once the change program is underway, the consultant and client collaboratively intervene in the client system to move it to the desired future state. The **intervention** can include activities such as changes in job and organizational design, a conflict reduction program, or management training. A later section describes many available organizational development interventions.

The consultant's role during this phase is one of helping the intervention and forecasting dysfunctional results. Members of the client system may resist the intervention. Involving these people in the diagnosis and feedback phases should reduce resistance at the intervention phase. The able consultant helps the client interpret the resistance and develop methods of reducing it, if they jointly decide they should.

Evaluation

Activities in the **evaluation** phase focus on whether the organizational development effort had the effect the client wanted. The evaluation can range from simply asking whether the client feels pleased to conducting a well-designed research effort to show empirically the effects of the intervention. Any evaluation, whatever its depth, should be done independently of the consultant who helps the organizational development program. The evaluation should also give the client system information about the next steps to take.

Termination

The consultant's involvement with a specific intervention terminates at some point. If the intervention did not move the client system to the desired end state, the consultant's relationship may end completely. If the intervention was successful and the client system has the ability to change and develop, an external consultant's direct involvement with the client comes to an end although some contact usually remains.

In contrast, internal consultants usually stay with their part of the organization and continue some involvement with the client system. Their involvement, though, is usually not as strong as in earlier phases of the organizational development effort.

Both external and internal organizational development consultants want the client system to become independent of the consultant. The goal of independence is consistent with the consultant's role of helping the client system become self-reliant in its change and development. Independence does not mean the consultant has no further contact with the client. Effective organizational development consultants often develop long-term relationships with clients, moving from one organizational development project to another within the same organization.

EXERCISE — *Your Assumptions and Values about Organizational Development*

*P*ause for a moment and examine your assumptions and values about organizational development. The following statements express the assumptions and values of many organizational development consultants. Quickly read each statement and note your response on a separate piece of paper using the following scale:

Disagree   Neither agree   Agree
            nor disagree

1. Emotions are best handled in work organizations by repressing them—feelings are taboo on the job.
2. Most managerial and administrative groups, teams, and committees lack problem-solving skills.
3. In order for a group or team to optimize its effectiveness, the formal leader can not perform all its leadership functions.
4. What happens in one section, unit, part, or sub-system of an organization will affect and be influenced by other parts of the organization.
5. When provided with a working environment which supports and challenges them, most people will strive to grow and acquire new knowledge, skills, and abilities.
6. Most organizations will become more effective if they become more responsive to the needs of their members.

7. Understanding people's feelings, and skill in working with feelings, opens up avenues for improved organizational performance.
8. A major avenue towards increasing organizational effectiveness is through creating conditions under which members can make greater contributions to organization goals.
9. Most people desire to make, and are capable of making, a higher level of contribution to the attainment of organization goals than most organizational environments will permit.
10. The ordinary organization member inherently prefers to avoid responsibility, has little ambition, and wants security above all.

If you disagreed with statements 1, 2, and 10 and agreed with most of the other statements, your assumptions and values are *similar* to those of many organizational development consultants. If you agreed with statements 1, 2, and 10 and disagreed with most of the other statements, your assumptions and values are *dissimilar*.

Incongruence between your assumptions and values and those of many organizational development consultants could lead to conflict between you and such consultants if you should meet them later in your career. Such conflict might develop because your assumptions and values would prevent you from understanding the orientation of the consultant. Of course, conflict is less likely if your assumptions and values are congruent with those of the consultant because you will readily understand the consultant's orientation.

Source: R. McLennan, *Managing Organizational Change* (Englewood Cliffs, N.J.: Prentice-Hall, 1989), pp. 104–7, questions 3, 5, 7, 9, 11, 19, 20, 21, 29, and 32. McLennan, Roy, MANAGING ORGANIZATIONAL CHANGE, ©1989, pp. 104–107. Adapted by permission of Prentice Hall, Upper Saddle River, New Jersey.

THE ORGANIZATIONAL DEVELOPMENT CONSULTANT

Organizational development consultants play a different role for a client than other types of consultants. Their role is based on three beliefs. First, they believe the client system is better able than the consultant to solve its problems. The client knows more about its system than the organizational development consultant does and can use that knowledge to find solutions. Second, the client system can discover the solutions, if the consultant helps the client build processes that allow their discovery. Third, the client, not the organizational development consultant, is always responsible for changing its system.[36]

The role of the organizational development consultant is one of collaborative facilitation. Both the organizational development consultant and the client system have equal status in discovering problem solutions. An organizational development consultant asks questions of the client system and encourages the client to find answers. All these role characteristics strongly argue for a marginal relationship with the client system and neutrality or impartiality about problem solutions.[37] The organizational development consultant sits at the edge and is not deeply involved in solving the client system's problems.[38]

Types of Consulting Activities

There are three broad types of consulting activities. First, a client can buy expert knowledge. The client may face a difficult problem and turn to a consultant for a solution. In this situation, the client identifies the problem before hiring the consultant. The client temporarily hands the problem to the consultant and waits for the consultant to return a solution. A common example is turning to a lawyer for legal analysis of alternative courses of action.[39]

The second type of consultant activities resembles the relationship of a doctor to a patient. The client (patient) thinks something is wrong, but has not diagnosed the problem or identified a potential solution. In this situation, the client relies on the consultant for both the diagnosis and the solution of the problem. The client is highly dependent on the consultant until the consultant provides a workable solution.

The third type of consultant activities is the kind used in organizational development. Consultants who practice organizational development offer their skills to develop processes that the client system uses to diagnose and solve its problems. The expert knowledge offered by such a "process consultant"[40] focuses on the process of finding a solution, not on finding a specific solution to a problem. The consultant actively involves the client in assessing and diagnosing the problem and identifying alternative solutions. This type of consultant activity is an aggressively collaborative effort with the client. A major assumption of the process consultant is that the client will develop problem-solving skills for dealing with future problems.

Internal and External Organizational Development Consultants

Consultants can come from either inside or outside the organization targeted for the development effort.[41] Internal consultants are employees of the target organization; often they are found in a Human Resource Management Department or in a department dedicated to organizational development. External consultants are employees of an organization outside the client system; they are either self-employed or employed by a consulting firm. Many have academic appointments and do part-time organizational development consulting as part of their professional activities. Internal and external organizational development consultants both have advantages and disadvantages.[42]

An internal organizational development consultant usually knows the business of the organization and the role played by the client system. An internal organizational development consultant also knows the culture and political structure of the organization. The external organizational development consultant must learn these matters to understand observed behavior—a learning that costs the client system. Internal organizational development consultants often cannot assess and diagnose as effectively as external consultants because of their close relationship to the client system. The internal consultant's position in the organization can also restrict his effectiveness in recommending interventions to individuals in higher positions.

The advantages of an external organizational development consultant are the opposite of the disadvantages of the internal organizational development consultant. The external consultant brings a fresh eye to the client system. He probably can help the client system quickly discover the problem and the solutions. Unfortunately, the external organizational development consultant must also be accepted by the client system. Such acceptance often takes longer for the external consultant than for the internal consultant.

Combinations of internal and external organizational development consultants can bring important advantages to an organizational development effort.[43] The inside knowledge of the internal consultant can give the outside consultant insights about the organization. The internal consultant can also provide continuing help to the client system, when the external consultant is absent. Lastly, the external consultant can often recommend interventions to those higher in the organization in ways not available to the internal consultant.

Skills and Abilities of an Organizational Development Consultant

Organizational development consultants need specific skills and abilities to play effective roles in organizations. These skills and abilities fall into four areas: (1) intrapersonal skills, (2) interpersonal skills, (3) general consultation skills, and (4) organizational development theory.[44]

Intrapersonal skills such as analytical ability, active learning skills, flexibility, and innovation are necessary for effective consultation. These skills play key roles in collecting, analyzing, and diagnosing data from an organization. Interpersonal skills are important because of the need to develop an effective relationship with people in the client system. Such skills include listening, developing a trust-based relationship with members of the client system, and talking the client system's language.

General consultation skills include asking the right diagnostic questions and knowing how to collect and analyze data. Other skills focus on selecting an intervention and moving it into the client system to cause the desired change. An organizational development consultant needs thorough knowledge about the interventions available and how to apply them to a specific client system. A later section of this chapter describes many possible interventions.

The last set of skills is knowledge about organizational development theory. Much of the information presented throughout this textbook is the basic knowledge needed by an organizational development consultant. In short, the consultant should have a thorough understanding of the behavioral and social sciences as they apply to organizations. Without that knowledge, the consultant and the client system stumble through the organization trying to bring about change.

Assumptions and Values of Organizational Development Consultants

Table 19-1 lists the assumptions and values held by organizational development consultants. Not all organizational development consultants have the same mix of assumptions and values. Understanding the assumptions and values that consultants likely hold can help managers smooth the early stages of an organizational development effort.[45]

It also helps for managers to understand their own assumptions and values about organizational change and development. The exercise you did earlier let you assess

T A B L E 19-2 (cont)

Structural and Technological Intervention:

Organizational design

Focuses on finding changes in the design of the organization to improve the organization's effectiveness. Possible design changes include the functional, divisional, and matrix organizational designs described in Chapter 18.

Collateral organization

Creates a separate but parallel organization to the formal organization. The collateral organization draws its members from anywhere in the organization. It is useful for solving problems that require information from many parts of the formal organization.

Job design

Examines ways of redesigning jobs in the organization to improve motivation and performance. The jobs may be redesigned around individuals or around self-managing work teams.

Technology

Can change the core technology of the organization to improve the functioning of the organization. It can examine the introduction of a vast array of new technologies anywhere in the organization.

Human Resource Management Interventions:

Goal setting

Focuses on collaborative goal setting by managers and subordinates. Goal setting can improve communication and increase commitment to work goals.

Reward systems

Examines an organization's reward system to find ways to make it more effective in improving employee performance. This intervention looks at many aspects of rewards and motivation including individual needs and fairness. Chapters 7 and 8 described the effects of those factors on human motivation.

Career planning and development

Helps people design and manage their careers. It gives people the knowledge and information they need to make informed career choices. Those choices include the type of job they are now in and the way their career can unfold in the organization. The major target of this intervention is the congruence of people's needs and the jobs and careers they have. Such congruence is expected to lead to higher performance and satisfaction.

Stress management

Tries to identify people who are experiencing dysfunctionally high stress, identify the work factors adding to the stress, and teach people how to manage stress. The goal is to reduce the negative effects of stress on absenteeism, turnover, health, and performance.

Strategy Interventions:

Open-systems planning

Views the organization as an open system in the way described in Chapter 17. It systematically analyzes and diagnoses the external environment of the organization and develops a strategic plan for the organization's response to that environment.

Organizational culture

Diagnoses an organization's culture to see whether it is consistent with the culture needed to carry out the organization's strategic plan. The organizational culture intervention is closely tied to the immediately preceding intervention. See Chapter 5 for a discussion of how to analyze and diagnose an organization's culture.

involvement in goal setting can have positive effects. Survey feedback used alone can have little effect.[57] Research results show the effects as clearly positive for quantity and quality of work but less positive for turnover and absenteeism. The strongest interventions were of the structural/technological and human resource management types. Effects were also stronger in small organizations than in large organizations.[58] Multiple interventions can also positively affect employee attitudes, although team building, goal setting, and T-groups used alone can do the same. Effects usually are stronger for supervisory than for nonsupervisory employees.[59]

· ·

CASE   *Process Consultation at Apex Manufacturing Corporation*

*T*he following case describes the way an external consultant helped the management of an organization learn how to improve its meeting processes. While reading the case, pay close attention to the relationship of the consultant to the client system.

CASE DESCRIPTION

The company was a large manufacturer organized into several divisions. The top management team, consisting of the president and division managers, was experiencing communication problems resulting from a recent reorganization. The company was expected to grow rapidly in the next few years, and team members felt they should work on group problems now. They sought help from an external consultant who was an expert in process consultation.

An initial meeting was set up between one of the key managers in the group and the consultant. The meeting was intended to acquaint the two parties and to explore the possibility of establishing a consulting relationship. The manager recounted the group's desire to work on group problems and their need for external help. He also voiced his concerns that the president needed help in handling key people and the president and his subordinates communicated poorly. The consultant agreed to attend one of the team's weekly meetings. At this time, he would meet the president and the other executives and discuss further what could and should be done.

At the initial team meeting, the consultant found a lively interest in having an outsider help the group. Members were willing to enter into an open-ended relationship in which each step of process consultation would be jointly agreed upon by all parties. The consultant explained his approach to process consultation and suggested that he sit in on the weekly meetings. He also

proposed to interview each member over the next several weeks as a way of getting further acquainted with team members. During the initial meeting, the consultant observed that the president was informal yet powerful and confident. He seemed to tolerate process consultation so long as he saw some value in it. The consultant concluded (and subsequently confirmed) that the group's problems resulted mainly from interactions between the president and his subordinates; relationships among the subordinates were less important.

In interviewing team members over the next several weeks, the consultant focused on the president-subordinate relationship. This focus included questions about what went well or poorly with the relationship; how the relationship affected job performance; and how members would like to see the relationship changed. This information provided the consultant with a better understanding of the causes underlying the ineffective team meetings. It told him how members viewed the key relationship with the president.

During the weekly team meetings, the consultant noticed that group process was fairly healthy. Members spoke when they felt like it, issues were fully explored, conflict was openly confronted, and members felt free to contribute. Although this climate was constructive, it created a major difficulty for the group. No matter how few items were discussed, the team was never able to finish its work. As the backlog of items became longer, members' frustrations grew. Meetings became longer and more of them were scheduled, yet there was little success in completing the work.

The consultant suggested that the team was overloaded; the agenda was too large and consisted of a mixture of operational and policy issues without recognition that each type of issue required a different allocation of time. He asked members to discuss how they might develop a more effective agenda for the meetings. After a half-hour of sharing feelings, members decided to sort the agenda into several categories and to devote some meetings exclusively to operating issues and others to

Source: E. F. Huse and T. G. Cummings, *Organization Development and Change* (St. Paul, Minn.: West, 1985), pp. 106–7. Reprinted with the permission of West Publishing Company.

policy matters. The operating meetings would be short and tightly run; the policy meetings would last one full day each month at an off-site location and explore one or two large questions in depth. It was also decided that the consultant would attend only the full-day policy meetings. Time would be set aside for any theory inputs from the consultant as well as for process analysis of the meetings.

The full-day meetings changed the climate of the group dramatically. It was easier to establish close informal relationships during breaks and meals. Because there was sufficient time, members felt they could work through their conflicts instead of leaving them dangling. The level of trust in the group increased, and members began to share more personal reactions with each other. In fact, one whole meeting was devoted to giving and receiving feedback from team members, including the president. The consultant suggested that only one person be discussed at a time; that person only listened and did not respond until all the members had a chance to give feedback. Members were encouraged to discuss the strengths and weaknesses of each member's managerial and interpersonal style. The consultant added his own feedback on points he had observed about that member's

behavior. The exercise was successful in deepening relationships and in exposing areas for future work.

CASE ANALYSIS

The case illustrates how external consultants typically begin their work with an organization. The beginning of the case described how the consultant and client established their relationship. The consultant and the client assessed each other. Once they reached an agreement, the consultant could move to the early stages of assessing and diagnosing the top management team's meetings.

As an outsider, the consultant could see the dysfunctions of the team's meetings more readily than the team members. The members had experienced the dysfunctional behavior for so long they likely thought it was normal. Note that the consultant asked the team members to look at their processes and begin developing their own solutions. The team eventually discovered and put into place the solutions to their dysfunctional meetings. The client system fixed its problems, not the consultant. The approach this consultant used is a hallmark of organizational development consultants—the approach of "collaborative facilitation" mentioned earlier in this chapter.

International Aspects of Organizational Change and Development

*T*he intellectual roots of organizational development are mainly in the United States although some branches stem from England, northern Europe, and Scandinavia.[60] The assumptions and values of organizational development consultants, and the nature of the various interventions, reflect the values of those cultures. These assumptions and values are highly different from the assumptions and values found in other nations.

People in different countries have different values and different orientations to organizations as human systems. Latin American countries often have less egalitarian social values than those found in the United States. Workers have strong loyalty to their superior and see a directive management style as both correct and appropriate. Social class distinctions are also strong in Latin American countries as is the belief that superiors are more competent than subordinates.[61]

French and Italian managers tend to see organizations as hierarchically oriented systems of authority relations. Swedish and U.S. managers usually do not see organizations as strongly hierarchical. French and Italian managers often view organizations as political systems in which they try to gain power for themselves. The French also tend to have a manipulative perspective about organizational change.[62]

Countries vary in the degree of uncertainty they find tolerable and in their approaches to conflict. People in southern European and Latin American countries prefer to avoid uncertainty, whereas those in the Scandinavian countries can tolerate more uncertainty. People in Latin American countries also use nonconfrontational approaches to managing conflict.[63]

The differences in values and orientations to uncertainty and conflict have clear implications for the selection of an organizational development intervention.[64] In countries that emphasize uncertainty avoidance, interventions should be predictable

· *Rio de Janeiro, Brazil. Predictable and management directed organizational development interventions will likely work well in Latin American organizations.*

and logical in structure and should avoid conflict. The hierarchical and power orientation of managers in many countries suggests using structured and controlled interventions that avoid confrontation across different levels in the organization. In many countries, the intervention needs to be perceived as coming from the top of the organization.

Cultural differences imply some changes in the usual approaches to organizational development described in this chapter. Early data-gathering stages of organizational development should include an assessment of the assumptions and values held by members of the organization.[65] Culture-specific organizational development interventions could be developed with the help of local social and behavioral scientists.[66]

Multinational organizations, or "stateless corporations," operate across national boundaries.[67] The members of such organizations come from many different countries. They have few if any shared values, making the job of selecting an intervention almost impossible.[68]

The last implication that follows from the cultural differences described above is another value dilemma for the organizational development consultant. As described earlier, such consultants typically have humanistic, feeling-based values. Yet, they may need to select an intervention that fits a target culture, but does not agree with those values![69]

Ethical Issues in Organizational Change and Development

*O*rganizational change and development activities present both the client system and the consultant with several possible ethical dilemmas. In all instances, the ethical dilemmas lead to less effective and possibly harmful organizational development programs.[70]

One dilemma follows from misrepresentation and collusion. An organizational development consultant may misrepresent his capabilities, skills, or experience for helping the client system identify and solve its problems. The misrepresentation may occur to ensure that the consultant gets a fee from the potential client. Managers in the client system may misrepresent themselves and the true nature of their problems because they are reluctant to reveal their shortcomings to the consultant, other managers in the organization, or competitors.

Collusion occurs when either party tries to exclude other parties or parts of the client system from involvement in the organizational development effort. The consultant may collude to exclude others to protect his activities from scrutiny. The client system may collude with the consultant or others to avoid issues the client system finds too difficult or distasteful to resolve.

Ethical issues surround the use of data in an organizational development effort. Usually the data are collected under conditions of confidentiality and voluntarism. Any violation of either of these conditions is a breach of ethics. Such data should not be used punitively against those who provided the data. Because consultants and client systems can easily distort or alter data, ethical issues surround the handling and feedback of data.

Another type of ethical dilemma involves the manipulation or coercion of people in the client system. The issue here is whether individuals are asked to change their values and behavior without full awareness and consent. Several organizational development interventions described earlier are powerful techniques for changing people. Ethical considerations require that participants in an organizational development intervention be informed of the potential effects on them. Both forced participation and failure to inform participants about potential effects of an intervention are breaches of ethics.

A fourth class of ethical dilemmas involves conflicts in the values and goals that are the focus of the organizational development program. Should they be the values and goals of the organizational development consultant or of the client system? Because a major goal of organizational development is developing a client system's abilities to solve its problems, the values and goals of the client system should be the focus of activities. Satisfying the goals and values of the organizational development consultant instead could be a breach of ethics.

The last class of ethical dilemmas overlaps with the first. It focuses on the technical abilities of both the organizational development consultant and the client system. Consultants clearly should not recommend interventions that they are incapable of helping to put into place. They also may be inept during the assessment and diagnosis of the client system, resulting in the choice of an inappropriate intervention. Client systems should not accept interventions that push them beyond their ability to execute the intervention.

Personal and Management Implications

*T*he discussions about organizational change and development throughout this chapter suggest three major personal implications. The first deals with change, the second focuses on your values, and the third follows from whether you will be fully informed of the effects of an intervention.

Because many organizations are finding they must change to adapt to their changing environment, you are likely to feel the effects of organizational change in the future. Reflect on what you have learned in this chapter. Are you likely to resist change or accept it? Don't forget, resistance can be helpful to an organization. Resistance reactions can also mean dysfunctional adaptation of yourself to much needed change in an organization.

Recall that organizational development consultants have a set of assumptions and values about people in organizations. A major implication for you is whether your personal values are congruent with those of such consultants. They believe most people want to grow and develop in a challenging and supportive environment. They feel managers should use conflict constructively in changing or managing the organization. They also see human feelings as basic data to use in assessing and diagnosing the organization.

Reflect on these assumptions and values and on the results of the exercise you did earlier. Do you share the consultants' values? If you do not, you may find organizational change and development interventions stressful and threatening.

All data collected during the early phases of a planned change or organizational development effort must be treated confidentially. Further, organizational development interventions often will have direct effects on your behavior within the organization. Will you be informed about the effects of interventions? Will the data you give to an organizational development consultant be handled confidentially? You should think about these issues because you are likely to meet them in the future.

Recall the discussion earlier about the different orientations managers can have to resistance to change. If you now view resistance as a problem to overcome, you will find it useful to reflect on the discussion about using resistance reactions diagnostically. They can be an important source of information to managers about the state of the system. Such information can help effect organizational change in a more functional way.

Your assessment of an organizational development consultant, whether internal or external, is an important first step in developing a relationship with that consultant. Be sure you fully know the consultant's skills and abilities. Also, a complete discussion of values and assumptions will tell you whether you can work effectively with the consultant. Modern organizational development efforts are based on full collaboration between the client and consultant. Such collaboration will not go smoothly if there is conflict between the basic values and assumptions of the parties.

Managers are increasingly carrying out organizational development directly, often with the help of an internal or external organizational development consultant.[71] As you develop your skills, and those of others in your organization, you might begin organizational development without a consultant. You may then face the value and ethical dilemmas described earlier. Managing the organizational change and development effort can become a key part of your role as manager. Many topics discussed in this chapter, and more fully developed in the sources cited, should serve you well in that activity.

Before beginning organizational change and development efforts at locations outside your home country, you will need to understand the orientation to change of people from the local culture. As discussed earlier, cultures vary in their orientation to authority and to uncertainty. Such cultural differences imply the need for different intervention and change strategies for the parts of the organization that are in different cultures.

Summary

Organizational change includes both unplanned and planned change. Unplanned change happens when forces for change overwhelm the organization. Planned organizational change is deliberate and unfolds in a series of phases that are not always distinct from each other. Planned change efforts can have different targets including the organization's culture, decision processes, task design, and organizational design.

People in organizations resist change for many reasons. Managers may view resistance to change as a problem to overcome or as a new source of information about the organization. The chapter described some ways to manage the change process to reduce resistance.

Organizational development is a systematic approach to planned change using the theories and concepts from the social and behavioral sciences. It happens in a series of phases and often uses an action research approach. Action research uses data to assess the current state of the organization and to diagnose the organization to identify needed changes.

Organizational development in its earliest stages usually uses a consultant. Such consultants come from inside or outside the organization. Organizational development consultants hold certain assumptions and values about people in organizations that can lead to dilemmas for the consultant. These values also have strong implications for the relationship of the consultant to the client system.

Managers and consultants can choose from four classes of organizational development interventions: (1) human process interventions, (2) structural and technological interventions, (3) human resource management interventions, and (4) strategy interventions.

Organizational development has its intellectual roots mainly in the United States with some branches in England, northern Europe, and Scandinavia. The assumptions and values of consultants, and the nature of many interventions, reflect the values of those cultures. Those assumptions and values are different from the assumptions and values found in many other nations.

Key Terms

action research 576
contracting 570
deep structures 564
diagnosis 570
entry 570
equilibrium periods 564
evaluation 571
evolutionary model 563
feedback 571

human process interventions 577
human resource management
   interventions 577
intervention 571
move toward the change state 563
need for change 563
organizational development 569
organizational development
   consultants 573

planning the change 571
resistance to change 565
revolutionary model 563
revolutionary periods 564
stabilize the change 563
strategy interventions 577
structural and technological
   interventions 577
terminates 572

1. Discuss your values about organizational change and development and ask other students in your class about their values. Freely exchange thoughts and positions about values. An open discussion of value differences will illustrate for you and others in your class a goal of organizational development.

2. Discuss the ethical issues faced by both the client system and the organizational development consultant. Which issues should be most troubling to practicing managers? How should managers handle those ethical dilemmas?

3. Review the phases of organizational development. What are the major issues faced by both the client system and the organizational development consultant in each phase? Which of the ethical dilemmas discussed earlier are most likely to appear in each phase?

4. Review the section describing the international aspects of organizational change and development. Discuss the constraints different cultures put on an organizational development consultant. What opportunities also might exist because of cultural differences?

5. Review the description of action research. What are the features of action research that distinguish it from other approaches to planned organizational change?

6. The chapter described the different orientations managers can have to resistance to change. Which orientation do you personally hold? Discuss with other students in your class the orientations they have to resistance to change. Was there agreement about an orientation or were there big differences in orientation?

7. Describe the major classes of organizational development interventions. What are the goals of each? Which specific interventions are likely to have the quickest effects on the client system? Which are likely to have the most lasting effects?

8. Discuss the advantages and disadvantages of internal and external organizational development consultants. When is an organization most likely to use one or the other? Discuss the usefulness of a team of internal and external organizational development consultants.

Case

JUST HOW TOUGH IS TONY TERRACCIANO? WITH REAL ESTATE FLAGGING, FIRST FIDELITY'S CEO HAS HIS HANDS FULL

This case describes a bank executive's direct approach to organizational change. Consider the following questions while reading the case:

1. What is your reaction to Mr. Terracciano's tough-minded direct approach? Discuss your feelings about this case with other students in your class.

2. Based on the information you have in the case, do you feel that Mr. Terracciano's approach was justified by the situation at First Fidelity Bancorporation of Newark? Compare his approach to organizational change with the approaches of the executives in the case that follows.

When Tony Terracciano was president of Pittsburgh's Mellon Bank Corp., bank officials once called in a manager whose department was generating solid growth. Instead of a pat on the back, one person at the meeting says the executive was told to cut costs by 10%. When he objected Terracciano asked sharply: "I wonder if the No. 2 guy in your department can get costs down?" The manager didn't have to be asked again.

Source: J. Weber, "Just How Tough is Tony Terracciano?" *Business Week,* July 9, 1990, p. 62. Reprinted from July 9, 1990 issue of *Business Week* by special permission, copyright © 1990 by The McGraw-Hill Companies.

Anthony P. Terracciano, 52, doesn't pull any punches. He says he doesn't remember the Mellon incident. But as he reshapes New Jersey's troubled super-regional bank, First Fidelity Bancorporation of Newark, it has become part of his reputation. On Feb. 1, his first day as chief executive of the $30 billion bank, he named three outside executives to key jobs, shoving aside bank veterans. Five weeks later, he cut 1,400 out of 13,500 employees. By mid-May, he uncovered so many bad loans that he now plans to add up to $300 million to loan-loss reserves, spawning a second-quarter loss that could top $100 million. Says Terracciano: "I'm not a believer in the idea that time is an unlimited resource."

STREET ADMIRERS

So far, Terracciano's hard-knuckled style is winning fans. First Fidelity insiders praise him for creating a consistent loan policy for the bank's eight remaining subsidiary banks and for setting out to coordinate the banks' computers. Such efficiencies eluded prior management, which masterminded a disappointing merger with Fidelcor Inc. of Philadelphia in 1988. Productivity rankings by investment firm Keefe, Bruyette & Woods Inc. put First Fidelity near the bottom on a 1989 list of 50 banks. "We'll make the top 10 by the time we're finished," vows Terracciano.

He has even found believers on Wall Street, where his loud, combative style is appreciated. Several analysts have restored buy recommendations on the stock, which is below

[29]Burke, *Organizational Development*, p.p. 118–19.

[30]Developed from French, Bell, and Zawacki, *Organizational Development*, pp. 5–14; R. Beckhard, *Organizational Development: Strategies and Models* (Reading, Mass.: Addison-Wesley, 1969).

[31]M. Beer, *Organizational Change and Development* (Santa Monica, Calif.: Goodyear Publishing, 1980), p. 27.

[32]French, Bell, and Zawacki, *Organizational Development*, p. 14.

[33]Beckhard, *Organizational Development*.

[34]Developed from Burke, *Organizational Development*, pp. 68–79; D. A. Kolb and A. L. Frohman, "An Organizational Development Approach to Consulting," *Sloan Management Review* 12 (1970): 51–65.

[35]M. R. Weisbord, "The Organizational Development Contract," *OD Practitioner* 5 (1973): 1–4.

[36]Developed from Beer, *Organizational Change*; Beer and Walton, "Organizational Change," 1987; French, Bell, and Zawacki, *Organizational Development*, pp. 10–11.

[37]N. Margulies and A. P. Raia, *Conceptual Foundations of Organization Development* (New York McGraw-Hill, 1978), Ch. 4.

[38]Beer, *Organizational Change*.

[39]Developed from E. H. Schein, *Process Consultation* (Reading, Mass.: Addison-Wesley, 1969); E. H. Schein, "The Role of the Consultant: Content Expert or Process Facilitator?" *Personnel and Guidance Journal* 56 (1978): 339–43.

[40]Schein, *Process Consultation*.

[41]Developed from Burke, *Organizational Development*, Ch. 8.

[42]R. R. Blake and J. S. Mouton, *Consultation: A Handbook for Industrial and Organizational Development* (Reading, Mass.: Addison-Wesley, 1983), pp. 564–65.

[43]Ibid.

[44]Cummings and Worley, *Organizational Development*, Ch. 2.

[45]Developed from P. E. Connor, "A Critical Inquiry into Some Assumptions and Values Characterizing OD," *Academy of Management Review* 2 (1977): 635–44; W. L. French, "Organizational Development Objectives, Assumptions, and Strategies," *California Management Review* 12 (1969): 23–34; W. L. French and C. H. Bell, *Organizational Development: Behavioral Science Interventions for Organization Improvement* (Englewood Cliffs, N.J.: Prentice-Hall, 1984), Ch. 4; M. Sashkin and W. W. Burke, "Organizational Development in the 1980s," *Journal of Management* 13 (1987): 393–417.

[46]Connor, "A Critical Inquiry."

[47]N. M. Tichy, "Agents of Planned Social Change: Congruence of Values, Cognitions, and Actions," *Administrative Science Quarterly* 19 (1974): 164–82.

[48]N. M. Tichy, "An Interview with Roger Harrison," *Journal of Applied Behavioral Science* 9 (1973): 701–29; N. M. Tichy, "An Interview with Max Pages," *Journal of Applied Behavioral Science* 10 (1974): 8–26; Tichy, "Agents of Planned Social Change"; Connor, "A Critical Inquiry."

[49]Connor, "A Critical Inquiry," p. 639.

[50]Developed from M. A. Frohman, M. A. Sashkin, and J. J. Kavanagh, "Action-Research as Applied to Organizational Development," *Organization and Administrative Sciences* 13 (1976): 129–61.

[51]Developed from French and Bell, *Organizational Development*; Cummings and Worley, *Organizational Development*.

[52]F. Friedlander and L. D. Brown, "Organizational Development," in M. R. Rosenzweig and L. W. Porter, eds., *Annual Review of Psychology*, vol. 25 (Palo Alto, Calif.: Annual Reviews, 1974), pp. 313–41.

[53]Ibid.

[54]J. M. Nicholas and M. Katz, "Research Methods and Reporting Practices in Organizational Development: A Review and Some Guidelines," *Academy of Management Review* 10 (1985): 737–49; J. I. Porras and R. C. Silvers, "Organizational Development and Transformation," in M. R. Rosenzweig and L. W. Porter, eds., *Annual Review of Psychology*, vol. 42 (Palo Alto, Calif.: Annual Reviews, 1991), pp. 51–78.

[55]D. A. Garvin, "*Managing Quality: The Strategic and Competitive Edge* (New York: Free Press, 1988).

[56]P. J. Robertson, D. R. Roberts, and J. I. Porras, "Dynamics of Planned Organizational Change: Assessing Empirical Support for a Theoretical Model," *Academy of Management Journal* 36 (1993): 619–34.

[57]J. M. Nicholas, "The Comparative Impact of Organizational Development Interventions on Hard Criteria Measures," *Academy of Management Review* 7 (1982): 531–42; J. I. Porras, "The Comparative Impact of Different OD Techniques and Intervention Intensities," *Journal of Applied Behavioral Science* 15 (1975): 156–78; J. I. Porras and P. O. Berg, "The Impact of Organizational Development," *Academy of Management Review* 3 (1978): 249–66.

[58]R. A. Guzzo, R. D. Jette, and R. A. Katzell, "The Effects of Psychologically Based Intervention Programs on Worker Productivity: A Meta-Analysis," *Personnel Psychology* 38 (1985): 275–91.

[59]G. A. Neuman, J. E. Edwards, and N. S. Raju, "Organizational Development Interventions: A Meta-Analysis of Their Effects on Satisfaction and Other Attitudes," *Personnel Psychology* 42 (1989): 461–83.

[60]C. Faucheux, G. Amado, and A. Laurent, "Organizational Development and Change," in M. R. Rosenzweig and L. W. Porter, eds., *Annual Review of Psychology*, vol. 33 (Palo Alto, Calif.: Annual Reviews, 1982), pp. 343–70; French and Bell, *Organizational Development*.

[61]L. J. Bourgeois III and M. Boltvinik, "OD in Cross-cultural Settings: Latin America," *California Management Review* 23 (1981): 75–81.

[62]Faucheux, Amado, and Laurent, "Organizational Development."

[63]G. Hofstede, *Culture's Consequences: International Differences in Work-Related Values* (Beverly Hills, Calif.: Sage Publications, 1984); G. Hofstede, *Cultures and Organizations: Software of the Mind* (New York: McGraw-Hill, 1991).

[64]A. M. Jaeger, "The Appropriateness of Organizational Development outside North America," *International Studies of Management & Organization* 14 (1984): 23–35.

[65]F. Steele, "Is the Culture Hostile to Organizational Development?" in P. H. Mirvis and D. N Berg, eds., *Failures in Organizational Development and Change: Cases and Essays for Learning* (New York: John Wiley & Sons, 1977), pp. 23–31.

[66]Bourgeois and Boltvinik, "OD in Cross-Cultural Settings."

[67]W. J. Holstein, "The Stateless Corporation: Forget Multinationals—Today's Giants Are Really Leaping Boundaries," *Business Week*, May 14, 1990, pp. 98–105.

[68]Bourgeois and Boltvinik, "OD in Cross-Cultural Settings," p. 79.

[69]Ibid.

[70]P. E. Connor and L. K. Lake, *Managing Organizational Change* (New York: Praeger Publishers, 1988; G. A. Walter, "Organizational Development and Individual Rights," *Journal of Applied Behavioral Science* 20 (1984): 423–39; L. P. White and K. C. Wooten, "Ethical Dilemmas in Various Stages of Organizational Development," *Academy of Management Review* 13 (1983): 690–97.

[71]Beer and Walton, "Organizational Change."

20

Future Directions of Organizations and Management

· *As we move into the next century, extensive communications networks will form audio and video links with all parts of the world.*

After reading this chapter, you should be able to . . .

· Summarize the domestic and international future for work, organizations, and management.
· Discuss the role a global orientation will play as organizations strive to be competitive in the future.
· Describe the types of technological changes that will affect organizations and their management in the future.
· Explain the direction that organizational design is expected to take in the future.
· Understand the changes in management behavior that will be necessary both to compete in a global environment and to manage within new organization structures.
· Describe the ethical issues that will emerge in the future.

Chapter Overview

. . . .

OPENING EPISODE

- *The Lone Star brewery in San Antonio, Texas. Lone Star, a well-known Texas brand, has entered international markets.*

Lone Star Beer Overseas

Lone Star Beer, once the choice of urban cowboys, will become a chic, imported brew in London pubs and the Australian outback if Heileman Brewing Co. has its way.

However, some experts say "The National Beer of Texas" is sticking out its long neck.

"There is a great mystique for people in other countries about America and that relates to Texas," said Barry McAlister, an Australian who is the vice president of sales for Lone Star, brewed in San Antonio.

"All our reports show that if you've got that Texas flavor that you're going to succeed if you do it correctly and Lone Star Beer is just one of the things that is going to succeed in niche markets around the world," he said.

The beer is moderately priced in Texas, but in Australia, Japan, Britain and Mexico, the beer will be sold as a premium import with a higher price tag.

"It has been tried before and failed," said Jerry Steinman, publisher of an industry newsletter. "But with a different approach it might work, but it will surprise a lot of people if it does."

"Many companies are trying to make their brand appear international, but the amount of Lone Star they are going to sell internationally, two people could drink together in a short time," Steinman said. . . .

Lone Star . . . increased its world-wide push, sending 100,000 cases into Canada, 26,000 to Britain and Australia and then another 100,000 to Tokyo and San Antonio's sister city, Kumamoto City, Japan.

Source: Excerpted from D. Sedeno, "Plans Brewing at Lone Star to Introduce Beer Overseas," Associated Press, 1989. (As the story appeared in the *Albuquerque Journal*, July 30, 1989, p. D4. Reprinted with the permission of the Associated Press.

. . . .

Lone Star Beer is common in Texas, but people in other countries view it as a premium import. It is one example of how organizations of the future must look for market opportunities around the globe, not just domestically. This chapter takes you on a journey into the future. It emphasizes the need for managers to develop a worldwide view to compete successfully into the twenty-first century.

This chapter differs in many ways from preceding chapters. Instead of describing and discussing the well-grounded knowledge of organizational behavior, it looks into the future. Although predicting the future carries the risk of being wrong, many published observations about the future direction of organizations and management suggest exciting times ahead for many people.

The basis of this chapter differs from the basis of earlier chapters because most source material came from the press. Although proportionally less material came from academic writers than was used for earlier chapters, the press reports often relied on information from academics or on respected sources of statistical information such as the Bureau of Labor Statistics. You will find the citations in this chapter readable sources for more detailed information about any topic that interests you.

The chapter covers four topics involving different changes in separate sections. Each topic unfolds in a sequence that shows the effects of those changes on organizations and management. The first topic focuses on what is likely to happen in the United States, including demographic changes, economic changes, and changes in the workforce. The next topic is the major international economic developments predicted for the future. This section roams the planet and discusses what it might look like in the future. The third topic involves technological changes that are happening now and will increase in the future. This section does not discuss all possible technological change; instead it describes the changes that will directly affect management of organizations in an increasingly global economy.

The fourth topic brings this book to a close. This section discusses the organizational and management changes implied by the three preceding topics. As their worldwide external environment undergoes sweeping changes, organizations will have to change both their design and management. Many changes discussed in this section are already underway. Others are necessary if managers are to adapt to the environmental changes surrounding organizations in the future.

This chapter uses economic data for many countries. These data were reported as either gross national product (GNP) or gross domestic product (GDP). GDP refers only to the output of the residents and nonresidents of a specific country, whether native born or foreign. GNP is the total output of a country's residents, whether from domestic or foreign sources.[1]

Before examining the major issues that are expected to affect managers and organizations in the future, let's study a snapshot of our future world. This snapshot will give you a quick glimpse of the future and some of its major implications.

. . . .

◢ *Snapshot of Our Future World*

Figure 20-1 is a snapshot of the world by the year 2010. The figure includes 1994 statistics and predictions for 2010 to give you a sense of how much change forecasters predict. Socioeconomic statistics appear in the upper half of the figure; communication and travel statistics appear in the lower half.

Forecasters predict huge growth in the world economy, likely fueled by the growth in per capita income in emerging market nations. These countries are in Asia, Africa, Latin America, and the territory of the former Soviet Union. The increases in population and income in these areas will offer major market opportunities to those organizations prepared to enter new international markets.

The predicted changes in communication, personal computers, and travel will support the increases in world trade. Forecasters expect the needed communication infrastructure to be in place. Communications satellites will support communication by telephone and personal computers. The air travel estimates emphasize the likely increased movement of people around the world, at least in part to support and manage increases in trade.

With this snapshot as background, let's now examine the four topics mentioned earlier. Each section is a tour through the predicted changes leading to the management and organization issues you can expect to face in the future.

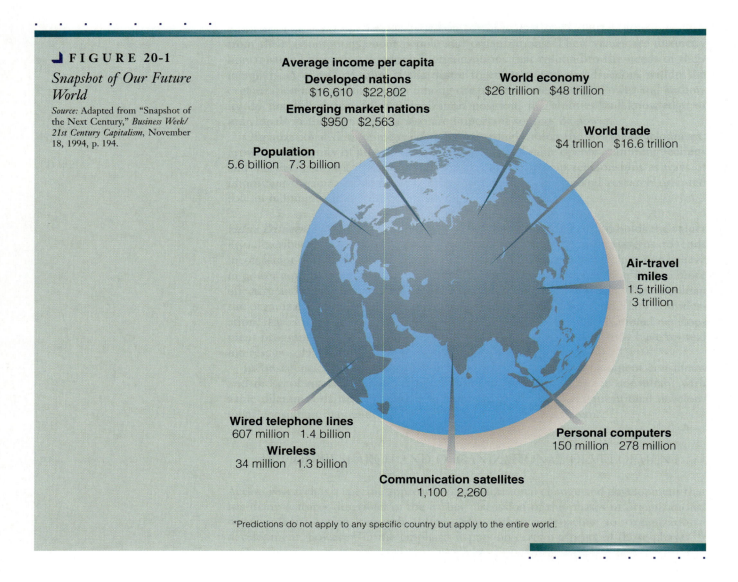

*Snapshot of Our Future
World*

Source: Adapted from "Snapshot of
the Next Century," *Business Week/
21st Century Capitalism,* November
18, 1994, p. 194.

Average income per capita
Developed nations
$16,610 $22,802
Emerging market nations
$950 $2,563

World economy
$26 trillion $48 trillion

Population
5.6 billion   7.3 billion

World trade
$4 trillion $16.6 trillion

**Air-travel
miles**
1.5 trillion
3 trillion

Wired telephone lines
607 million   1.4 billion
Wireless
34 million   1.3 billion

Personal computers
150 million   278 million

Communication satellites
1,100   2,260

Predictions do not apply to any specific country but apply to the entire world.

◢ *Domestic Changes*

The major **domestic changes** predicted for the United States include changes in population demographics, skill requirements of jobs, workforce composition and expectations, and the economy. The U.S. population is expected to have the following demographic profile by the year 2010:[2]

- The total population will reach 282 million people, 41 million more than in 1989.
- Fourteen percent of the annual growth in population will come from immigration. A new law effective October 1991 increased the number of legal immigrants to 700,000 per year.[3] That same law increased the number of skilled worker immigrants by 50,000.
- The population will become older with the number of people age 65 or older increasing by 25 percent.

The U.S. population of the future will be older and more ethnically diverse than it is now. The ethnic diversity will be international in scope, bringing major differences in values, attitudes, and languages among people in the workforce.

The skill requirements of new jobs added to the economy will undergo a major shift.[4] Forty-one percent of the new jobs are predicted to be high-skill jobs compared to 24 percent of existing jobs. This increase in job skill requirements may present a crisis for many organizations. As education quality in the United States declines and the number of school dropouts increases, many people in the workforce will lack the basic skills to do those jobs.

The workforce of the future will bear little resemblance to today's workforce.[5] Growth in the workforce has already slowed to 1% in the 1990s from 2.9% in the 1970s. African Americans, immigrants, Hispanics, and women will be a growing number of the new members of the workforce. Almost two-thirds of the people joining the workforce will be women, including white, nonwhite, and immigrant women. Because of the slow growth in new workers, organizations will turn to older, retired, or disabled people to fill their skill requirements.[6] Many workers of all types will prefer, or only be offered, part-time jobs, especially in the service sector.[7] And the number of dual-earner couples and female heads of households will increase in the future.[8]

Economic forecasts for the U.S. economy in the late 1990s range from "blah" and "mediocre" to prosperous.[9] By the year 2000, forecasters predict investment in technology will increase to offset slow growth in the workforce. They view such investment as a key source of increased productivity. Defense spending will drop as a percentage of the total federal budget, freeing some resources for other programs. The economy will be more stable in the future with few of the major boom and bust cycles of the past.

The global economy will play a major role as more countries adopt market-oriented policies and open their markets to goods from other nations. The United States will not dominate the international economy. Instead it will cooperate with European and East Asian nations in managing the global economy. American organizations will continue to face high competition from rivals in other countries. U.S. multinationals, however, have been strong performers, a trend that should continue into the future.

Although the service sector will be the fastest growing part of the U.S. economy, manufacturing organizations will produce several key innovations in manufacturing processes, organizational design, and management.[10] Competition from other countries has put pressure on managers in these organizations to innovate to increase productivity.[11] The changes in these organizations will provide good lessons for managers of nonmanufacturing firms.

The keynotes of modern manufacturing will be flexibility, speed, and response to customer requirements. Through automation, redesign of processes, and close connections with customers and suppliers, agile manufacturing organizations can make products designed to an individual customer's specifications.[12] Baldor Electric's flexible manufacturing systems, for example, have helped it cut the time needed to fill an order from four weeks to five days.[13] Ross Operating Valve in Troy, Michigan, can deliver custom-designed valves in 72 hours.[14]

Inventory management will change in the future as more organizations adopt just-in-time methods. Inventory levels will be lower, with only enough on hand to manufacture a product for a short time. With lower inventories, manufacturers will become highly dependent on their vendors to supply raw materials and subassemblies as needed. Just-in-time methods force more interdependence within the manufacturing process and require high levels of cooperation among people in separate parts of the process. Management must also decentralize decisions to the shop floor so nonmanagement workers can make the fast decisions required by the redesigned process.

Concurrent engineering, a team-based approach to product design, will spread in manufacturing organizations.[15] Concurrent engineering teams include manufacturing engineers, design engineers, marketing specialists, and customer representatives. Earlier approaches to product design separated such people. Managers in the manufacturing organizations of the future will need to have a good understanding of the concepts about groups and conflict management described in earlier chapters of this book.

The goods-producing sector of the economy, which includes manufacturing, agriculture, mining, and construction is smaller than the service sector. The service sector includes health care, financial services, retailing, and hospitality[16] and accounted for 74% of GDP and 79% of all jobs in 1994. Although employment in the service sector is expected to grow in the future, it will not have the stability of the past. Organizations will consolidate through mergers, acquisitions, and efforts by managers to be cost competitive. The latter will be achieved by laying off workers and moving some operations to other countries.[17] For example, Massachusetts Mutual Life Insurance Co. processes claims in Ireland. The company flies claims to Dublin each day for processing. Modern technology will let many service organizations move unskilled office jobs out of the domestic economy.

Worker productivity in the service sector has been poor, but forecasters expect it will improve because of slow growth in the workforce and increased international competition. Financial organizations in particular will face competition from Japan, the United Kingdom, and Europe.[18] Managers of service organizations will turn to new technologies for help. They are also beginning to borrow innovations from the manufacturing sector, such as managing for quality.[19]

Both domestically and internationally, the consumer will play an increasingly demanding role. The following profile of the American consumer is expected to continue into the future:

> Meet the paradigm of today's tougher U.S. consumers—demanding, inquisitive, discriminating. No longer content with planned obsolescence, no longer willing to tolerate products that break down, they are insisting on high-quality goods that save time, energy, and calories; preserve the environment; and come from a manufacturer they believe is socially responsible.[20]

U.S. consumers may be more discerning than ever. Customers in Japan and Germany are even more demanding. Meeting consumer desires worldwide will be an important challenge for businesses.

· *A diverse international environment will present opportunities in the future to many organizations, large or small.*

International Changes

The **international changes** that observers expect in the future suggest that managers should view the external environment of their organizations as extending beyond the boundaries of their countries.[21] Global markets exist for goods ranging from soybeans to jet aircraft. Even if a company is not competing internationally, its competitors often come from other countries. It is a myopic to think of other countries only as competitors. Managers of successful organizations of the future must view the entire world as potential markets, sources of supply, and places of production. Both large and small organizations will need to think internationally. In a recent year, for example, Avon Products, Inc., had $1.3 billion in sales from international markets, almost equal to its domestic sales in the same year.[22] On a smaller scale, a group of Georgia soybean farmers have found rich market opportunities in Japan for their high-quality soybeans.[23]

In many industries, the successful organization of the future will not be a company with a strong domestic presence and just a few operations around the planet.[24] Managers of the transnational organization of the future will see no national boundaries.[25] Corporate headquarters may be in any country. Managers will choose the locations around the world they consider best for manufacturing, research activities, supply, and capital.

Not all industries require such a transnational view. Managers of organizations making luxury automobiles and some packaged foods can succeed by viewing the world as presenting different markets. The list of industries requiring a transnational strategy is long. It includes pharmaceuticals, appliances, travel services, banking, publishing, consumer electronics, and automobiles.

Some features of the future world that will be important to organizations and management include the following:[26]

- Education levels worldwide will continue to climb, creating an international workforce able to deal with modern technology.
- Computer and communications technology will shrink the size of the world.
- The developing economies of Latin America, Eastern Europe, and Asia will grow at a faster rate than the mature economies of western Europe, Japan, and North America.
- Economic interdependence among countries will continue to expand, bringing impressive opportunities and competition.
- Trade wars, import quotas, and other forms of protectionism will also rise.
- In the Western world, immigration will be an important and divisive domestic issue.

With these features as background, let's now look at the changes predicted for each major market.

 ## NORTH AMERICA

International trade experts see the world as three dominant market areas: the United States, the European Community, and Japan.[27] Several developments since 1988 point to an even stronger position in world trade for the North American part of this triad.

The 1988 United States–Canada Free Trade Agreement (FTA) opened the borders of both countries to the easy movement of capital, goods, and services. This agreement phases out all tariffs over 10 years and formed Canadian-U.S. panels to hear trade grievances.[28] The goal of the agreement for the Canadians was easy access to a massive and dynamic market with expected economic benefits for Canada. The goal for the United States was tariff-free trade with a country that heavily imports U.S. goods. The collective goal was to position the two countries together as a significant market force against Europe and Japan. Both countries have already experienced economic gains, but noncompetitive companies in both countries have suffered.[29]

The North American Free Trade Agreement (NAFTA) became effective January 1, 1994, opening the borders of Mexico, Canada, and the United States to easy movement of goods, capital, and services.[30] The combined GNP of the bloc was $6 trillion in 1990, more than the $4.8 trillion of the European Community. Total trade among the three nations in 1990 was $219 billion.[31] Ten months after NAFTA became effective, trade among the three nations had increased by about 24 percent.[32]

 ## LATIN AMERICA

Economic changes are also occurring in Latin America from Mexico to the southern tip of South America.[33] The new governments of many Latin American countries have moved away from the economically crippling policies of the 1980s. Governments have worked to reduce tariffs, encourage outside investment, and sell state-owned companies.[34] Many view the market potential of this part of the world as colossal. Brazil's GDP alone is double Eastern Europe's. U.S. companies are especially well positioned to benefit from the future development of this area.

Mexico is a huge market seeking expansion after years of restricted demand. Chile is the largest producer of copper in the world and is experiencing a boom in exports and imports. Brazil commands a market double that of Mexico. Although the country has been hard hit by inflation and a recession, the government is persisting with reductions in tariffs and other import restrictions. Venezuela is a major oil producer, drawing exploration investment from around the globe.

Many countries have formed free trade areas throughout Central and Latin America. Argentina, Brazil, Paraguay, and Uruguay have formed the Mercosur trade zone. Venezuela, Colombia, Bolivia, Peru, and Ecuador have formed the Andean group. Other trade zones include the Caribbean Community and the Central American Common Market.[35] A trading area encompassing the entire western hemisphere could soon dwarf these trade zones. Plans to create a Free Trade Area of the Americas by 2005 are already underway. Western hemisphere leaders agreed in December 1994 to begin negotiations for a free trade zone extending from the northern tip of North America to the southern tip of South America. The proposed trade zone would be the largest in the world with total purchasing power of $13 trillion.[36]

The creation of a western hemisphere bloc will not happen quickly. Serious discussions about such an arrangement will not occur until the late 1990s. Whatever the result, if Latin America continues to experience political and economic stability, the potential for success for properly positioned organizations is almost unbounded.

 THE UNITED KINGDOM, EUROPE, SCANDINAVIA, AND THE FORMER SOVIET UNION

The United Kingdom and much of Western Europe have had close economic ties since the formation of the European Economic Community. The European Union (EU) has forged strong trading relationships between the United Kingdom, Ireland, much of Western Europe, and Denmark. Sweden and Finland moved toward more open trade by accepting membership in the EU in 1994, although Norway rejected membership for the second time since 1972.[37] Several Eastern and Central European countries are moving to market-oriented economies, and Western European countries are trying to build economic relations with them. Poland, the Czech Republic, the Slovak Republic, and Hungary have associate status in the EU possibly followed by Bulgaria and Romania.[38] The economic future of the countries of the former Soviet Union is harder to predict. These countries are trying to develop market-oriented economies and forge economic ties with Europe.[39] If they succeed, the result could be an economy of 520 million people with a $5 trillion GNP.

The United Kingdom and the European countries are building an extensive transportation network to support their integrated markets.[40] This network includes high-speed railroads, tunnels, and bridges. High-speed rail is the centerpiece of the transportation strategy. Trains will travel between 120 and 200 miles per hour across the European continent. Existing lines and lines proposed for completion by 2005 will link major trade and financial areas of the continent. The Eurotunnel linking Great Britain and the Continent will increase commerce in both directions. A new bridge will link critical parts of Denmark that were separated for centuries. Proposed new tunnels and bridges will further connect the Scandinavian countries.

This part of the world may present unprecedented opportunities in the future. Proposed agreements will make it easier for manufacturers to meet standards for products such as automobiles. Instead of different standards for headlight widths in each country, there will be one standard for the entire market. Distribution of products and services will also become easier because approval to sell in one country will automatically apply to other countries.[41]

The Eastern and Central European countries have much pent-up consumer demand. Long without the modern conveniences of the West, the 100 million households will be a massive new consumer market. These countries will also present investment opportunities and a source of inexpensive skilled labor. Between 1989 and 1991, 9,700 foreign joint ventures were built in Hungary, the former Czechoslovakia, and Poland. Companies poured into Eastern and Central Europe from the United States, Sweden, India, the United Kingdom, Japan, Switzerland, and Germany. Many Western European companies have moved part of their manufacturing to Eastern and Central European countries with lower labor costs.[42]

Continuing farther to the east, we find the Russian Federation and the other countries that were part of the former Soviet Union, including the three Baltic republics.[43] The Baltic countries quickly moved for associate membership in the EU, underscoring their break from the former Soviet Union. The rest of the countries of the former Soviet Union are in the process of dismantling their centralized economies and building market-oriented ones. Moving to a decentralized market system will not be easy because state-owned monopolies produce huge amounts of investment and consumer goods.[44] Depending on the success of proposed economic reforms, the hidden consumer demand of the 285 million people in this area is a significant market opportunity.[45]

Reform plans include cutting government spending, removing price controls, and legalizing private property. These economic reforms are part of an effort to make the ruble respectable and convertible. Other reforms include developing an integrated system of commercial law, a single monetary and trade policy, and a banking system similar to the U.S. Federal Reserve.[46]

Russia's relationships with the other countries of the former Soviet Union are uneasy. Nationalistic feelings are growing within the other nations following many years of dominance by Russia. Kazakhstan, for example, was under Russian rule for two centuries. Kazakh efforts to restore their culture and language have led to disputes with the large ethnic Russian population in Kazakhstan.[47]

Although chaos will reign in the early stages of political, economic, and cultural redevelopment in the area, opportunities abound for quick-moving organizations. The countries of the former Soviet Union have rich oil and gas reserves, timber, gold, and unsatisfied consumer desires. Major opportunities exist in communication, roads, petrochemical, medical equipment, and pipelines. Many managers want to wait to see what the future holds. The opportunities will go to the companies that move forward quickly.[48]

PACIFIC RIM

The phrase "Pacific Rim" refers to the burgeoning economies ringing the Pacific Ocean from the northwest to the southwest. Japan's economic development following its rebuilding after World War II led this part of the world. Not far behind came Singapore, Hong Kong, Taiwan, and South Korea. Observers now say a third group of countries will join in regional and international trade: Thailand, Malaysia, Indonesia, and the Philippines. By the year 2000, the economies in the Pacific Rim together are expected to be about as large as the EU or North America.[49] Although these countries are all in the same part of the world, they are highly diverse markets with more differences than similarities among them.[50]

The projected changes in the area present both opportunities and problems. Overall the countries of the area are reducing trade barriers and forming economic alliances, but, as explained later, these developments vary from country to country. The economic alliances could forge a Pacific Rim trading bloc, much like those described earlier for North America and Europe. The formation of those trading areas has encouraged the Pacific Rim countries to do the same as a form of defense.[51]

Japan will continue to be a dominant economic force throughout the region.[52] Sentiment in other countries is not always positive about Japan, however, especially if it becomes a major political force. Japan will undergo major internal changes. The younger Japanese desire Western products, have more money, and value their leisure time more than their elders. Japanese markets are already opening, although Westerners doing business there will find it more difficult than elsewhere in the region.[53] Patience and a long-term view are recommended for anyone who wants to do business in Japan. Opportunities abound in Japan for companies offering consumer products, semiconductors, communications equipment, financial services, and travel services. American Express offered the latter and had about one million cardholders by the end of 1990 with annual growth between 20 and 30 percent.[54]

Singapore, Hong Kong, Taiwan, and South Korea are investing heavily in Pacific Rim countries with low-cost labor and abundant natural resources. Their collective investment is second only to Japan's and is lessening that country's influence in the region.[55]

Singapore will play an increasing role because it has a skilled labor force and is located near countries where labor is cheap. Thus, companies can set up manufacturing operations in nearby Malaysia and Indonesia, which have abundant low-cost labor for labor-intensive subassemblies. Then the subassemblies are shipped to Singapore where its more skilled workers do the technical assembly. Western Digital of the United States is one of many companies using this strategy.[56]

Hong Kong has long been a center of entrepreneurial activity, but its future is uncertain. Few government controls, low taxes, and no tariffs let this 410-square-mile territory produce a GDP of $45.7 billion in 1989 with a population of 5.6 million. In 1997, though, China will take over the administration of Hong Kong. It is unclear whether the Chinese leadership will let this freewheeling business continue.[57]

Taiwan will surge forward as a serious international competitor in the late 1990s. It no longer views itself as a cheap assembler of other people's products and will play an increasing role worldwide in electronics, semiconductors, and personal computers. The country has dropped import barriers and is planning to reduce foreign exchange controls. Some observers predict Taiwan will overtake Hong Kong as a Pacific Rim financial center before the year 2000. Its consumers vie for luxury goods ranging from Jaguar cars to satellite dishes. U.S. investment companies such as Merrill Lynch find Taiwan's large cash assets attractive enough to open brokerage offices in Taipei. All predictions point to Taiwan's playing a major economic role in the development of the Pacific Rim.[58]

South Korea is slowly opening its markets to outside businesses. Both manufacturers and retailers will be allowed to have their own operations within the country. South Korea's financial sector, long closed to outsiders, will become increasingly more open. Citibank finally won approval to enter retail banking and promptly introduced South Koreans to a new idea—24-hour banking. South Korea's growing middle class wants quality goods from other countries. Opening South Korean markets to outsiders not only lets goods enter the country but poses serious competition to the giant conglomerates that have dominated its markets. The result will be more choices for South Korean consumers and more competition for everyone who enters this market.[59]

South Korea's giant conglomerates (*chaebol*) are fierce growth-oriented competitors. Samsung is the 24th-largest industrial organization in the world. These conglomerates reach well beyond the Pacific Rim. They are aggressively pursuing markets others perceive as too risky, such as China, Africa, parts of Latin America, the Caribbean, and the countries of the former Soviet Union.[60] Joint ventures with U.S. companies present significant opportunities for both countries. Daewoo, for example, makes forklifts for Caterpillar and aerospace parts for General Dynamics.[61]

The third group of countries in the Pacific Rim (Thailand, Malaysia, Indonesia, and the Philippines) are emerging as the next generation of low-cost and efficient manufacturing economies in Asia. They are also more open to buying Western products and forming joint ventures with outsiders than is Japan. Singapore, as noted earlier, is taking a leadership role in coordinating low-cost and high-cost manufacturing in the same area. It perceives itself at the head of a "growth triangle" that also includes Malaysia and Indonesia.[62] The four countries in this group will be more open to outside investment in the future. South Korea, Taiwan, and Japan have already made major investments in these nations to offset their higher domestic manufacturing costs. Western firms are well advised to look to this region as a significant source of low-cost manufacturing and a base for export to other Asian countries. American Standard, for example, manufactures sinks and toilets in Thailand and sells them throughout Asia.[63]

OTHER COUNTRIES

Other countries, both in Asia and elsewhere, present some uncertain economic opportunities. With a population of 1.2 billion, China is potentially a massive market, and economic reforms in the 1980s started to open it to outside investment. Although China's leadership recentralized the economy in 1989 by imposing import and credit restrictions, economic reforms moved forward again in the 1990s with the hope of increasing private enterprise, entrepreneurial activity, and foreign investment. Although the political and economic future of China is uncertain, companies from all over the world see it as a burgeoning market.[64]

North Korea is slowly opening its borders to the outside world, a move spurred by its need for hard currency. The collapse of the Soviet Union ended its long-standing barter relationships with those countries. North Korea recognizes that it must now interact with market-based economies while trying to keep its version of a closed, collective society. The United States relaxed its trade embargo with North Korea on January 20, 1995, allowing Americans to travel to North Korea and engage in trade with it for the first time in 45 years. Coca-Cola eagerly awaits access to the country's 23 million people. Carlson Wagonlit Travel of Minneapolis believes significant tourism opportunities exist in a country almost completely closed to the West since 1950.[65]

The Middle East presents an odd mixture of opportunities, threats, and uncertainties. Continuing hostility between the United States and Iran and Iraq has slowed trade to a trickle. Saudi Arabia has a mixture of wealth and poverty with the wealthy desiring Western imports. Israel is prosperous and has strong ties to the United States. Jordan's 1994 peace agreement with Israel might allow these two countries to forge a true economic alliance. Preliminary talks have focused, for example, on a joint $1 billion port on the Red Sea that will help link their economies.[66]

Many African countries offer rich economic opportunities to outside investors. Zimbabwe has a growing manufacturing sector, and Angola has desirable minerals and oil. Namibia has rich fisheries and ample deposits of diamonds and industrial minerals.[67] AT&T has proposed building a fiber-optic telephone network around the continent by 2000. H. J. Heinz sees Africa as a potential rich consumer market for its products.[68] Political stability will play a major role in the economic success of these countries.

EXERCISE — *Scenarios of the Global Economy in the Year 2000*

*T*he following are four scenarios of the future of the global economy. An international business development consultant who specializes in global strategy wrote these scenarios.

Read each scenario and estimate its probability of happening. Use three levels of likelihood: low, moderate,

and high. Summarize your reasons on a separate piece of paper so you can compare them to the consultant's views described later.

SCENARIO I: TOWARD A GLOBAL ECONOMY

The international financial system has achieved fragile stability. World GDP growth has averaged 3.5 percent to 4.5 percent over the past two to three years. Intercontinental trade has reflected a similar growth pattern and is

Source: Adapted from Jan V. Dauman, "The Global Economy in the Year 2000" from THE GLOBAL ECONOMY: America's Role in the Decade Ahead, edited by William Brock and Robert Hormats, with the permission of W. W. Norton & Company, Inc. Copyright © 1990 by The American Assembly.

fluctuating between 5.5 percent and 6.5 percent a year; trade in manufactures is stable at between 7 percent and 8 percent, and there has been a marked improvement in trade in services, now reaching 4 percent on a world basis and as high as 6.5 percent in the Organization for Economic Cooperation and Development (OECD) countries. Oil prices are stable but remain comparatively high at $20 per barrel (1989 U.S. dollars).

Capital flows are good and encouraging development in Latin America, especially Brazil. The U.S., having overcome the problems of the twin deficits by the mid-1990s, is showing every indication of a more balanced growth. The European Single Market, with Austria and Norway as new members and Switzerland and Sweden enjoying a special trade relationship, is experiencing a period of high growth at 4.5 percent; there is renewed talk of closer political federation. Japan has become a high value postindustrial economy, with only marginally slower growth rates than in the early years of the decade. . . .

This period of economic health, with the virtual disappearance of trade wars . . . has been helped by a new stability in currencies. The yen, the U.S. dollar, and the European ECU are strong and show only minor variations in exchange rates.

Communications and information access continue the breakdown of national borders begun in the late 1980s. Global radio and television broadcasting via satellites becomes commonplace. . . . As modern culture becomes more homogeneous, local differences matter less. Products are standardized, manufactured globally, and advertised and marketed. The regional trading blocs, having begun to form in the late 1980s and 1990s to help members build up competitive advantage, start to give way to interregional alliances.

Political regionalism begins to dissolve in response to extraordinary external forces: a debt crisis, an environmental disaster. International organizations such as the International Monetary Fund (IMF) and the United Nations Environment Program (UNEP) gain in power and become de facto "governments," in many cases superseding national authority. The greater similarity in world culture and the strength of the international authorities act as spurs to arms reductions, leading eventually to multilateral disarmament. . . .

SCENARIO II: COMPETITIVE ACCOMMODATION

International debt crises still occur, but the world financial system is able to cope. There have been effective compromises on debt reschedulings and capital is now flowing into the Latin American debtor nations. Africa still presents severe problems. World inflation rates have exhibited a slight downward trend for the past three years after peaking at dangerously high levels in the mid-1990s.

The U.S. is faced with deficits, but the administration has managed to reduce them to a manageable amount; the country is by no means the world's biggest debtor nation.

World trade growth has been at 5 percent for the past two years, though intraregional trade shows somewhat higher growth rates. Nonetheless, protectionist pressures have generally reduced. Both the U.S. administration and European Commission have successfully vetoed protectionist legislation. . . . Oil prices have remained within a 10 percent price band over the past two years.

The European Community (EC) is now an effective global competitor in information technology and telecommunications, due to the success of strategic alliances engineered by leading globalized multinational corporations. Despite this, the Community is only just completing the last steps to turn the dream of 1992 into a solid reality. . . . Exchange rates are stable though the U.S. dollar continues to show signs of uncertainty faced with the continuing strength of the yen.

The trend toward global cooperation is tempered by the need of the developing world to become globally competitive. Regional blocs, such as Europe post-1992 and North America (U.S./Canada/Mexico), view their role as allowing members to work out their competitive strategies in a controlled setting. With growing internationalization, the blocs also form interregional alliances: Europe with Japan, North America with developing Asia. . . .

SCENARIO III: REGIONAL SELF-INTEREST

World GNP growth rates have been disappointing, averaging 2.5 percent to 3 percent a year since the mid-1990s. Growth on a regional basis has, however, been stronger. Intraregional trade grew by as much as 5 percent in the last two years of the decade. The main increase has been in manufacturers, with trade in services being slow to catch up. . . .

Oil prices remain weak and fluctuating; since 1998, they have ranged between $17.50 and $21 per barrel (1989 U.S. dollars). Capital flows have been sluggish, with the industrialized countries having shown a marked reluctance to invest in Latin America and other major debtor nations, the one exception . . . being Japan. The situation is now beginning to improve.

The world financial system is still subject to periodic crises—though these are decreasing—and the decade has seen a series of major moratoriums. The U.S., still faced with major deficits, has been focusing increasingly on the North American market. Europe continues to show marked protectionist tendencies; in many ways, fortress Europe has become a reality to many Asian and U.S. companies. Japan dominates Asia; the relationships with the PRC, Taiwan, and Korea are strained, though the dependence of the latter group on Japan is reluctantly recognized. The PRC is once again experiencing over-heating, not helped by the inability to integrate Hong Kong into the mainland economy; politically there has been a swing back to increased state power.

The Eastern bloc has failed to achieve the growth rates outlined as part of the goals of *perestroika* in the early years of the 1990s. The Western powers' economic summits have only proved marginally effective. After a decade of volatility, interest rates are at long last becoming more stable, as are exchange rates. Governments continue to implement economic programs characterized by short termism, with scant regard for longer-term impacts.

Economic issues predominate as competition intensified the trend toward regionalism. Trading blocs take on a more political character; protectionism increases, as does the likelihood of trade wars. Regional defense organizations such as NATO find renewed purpose even in an environment of reduced nuclear weapons. Distrust persists between blocs; super-power relations, while not worsening, do not improve much. International leadership fails to stimulate cooperation even on critical issues; leading nations attempt unilateral solutions to problems such as Third World debt, with only mixed results. . . .

SCENARIO IV: NATIONAL SELF-INTEREST

The international financial system hovers on the edge of collapse. World GDP growth has been at best minimal at 1.5 percent to 2.5 percent a year; though Japan and East Asia continue to perform well ahead of the world average. Intraregional trade has not realized the promise of the early years of the decade, and intercontinental trade has been static. The [General Agreement on Tariffs and Trade] (GATT) accords are regularly breached and GATT has failed to reach agreement in trade in services. There are trade wars on agriculture, textiles, and many manufactured goods between the U.S., Japan, and Europe. Oil prices are now at an all-time high.

There are no or very little international capital flows; as a result the economies of the major debtor nations (Latin America) remain in a highly perilous state. Currencies fluctuate wildly, though the yen has maintained its strength vis-à-vis the U.S. dollar and the German DM fairly consistently over the past three years.

Not surprisingly, governments continue to introduce ever more restricting protectionist legislation. The economies of Eastern Europe are still suffering the shocks of the failure of *perestroika*. The PRC is retreating into a new period of isolationism, despite moves by Japan and the recovery of Hong Kong.

The maneuvering en route to the creation of regional groupings has degenerated into full-scale global trade war. "Europe 1992" has been exposed as a scheme to benefit the strong countries and exploit the weak; the strong (France, Germany, and the U.K.) disagree over sovereignty and reciprocity issues and decide to take their chances on their own. Meanwhile, Japan's yen-driven economic aggressiveness provokes trade sanctions by the U.S. Military distrust increases, prompting calls for a halt to disarmament and even a new arms build-up.

Developed countries find monetary reserves sapped by the pressures of military build-up, maintaining social services, and virtually solo global competition; social services are the loser. Developing countries are subjected to stringent conditions by their creditors. International organizations are effectively powerless.

A CONSULTANT'S VIEW

The international consultant who wrote these scenarios saw a low probability of Scenario I, A Global Economy. He believes the natural tendency of nations toward self-determination will instead produce a regional view. He estimates the probability of Scenario II, Competitive Accommodation, as moderate. Countries will recognize some pragmatic needs to join with others for a competitive advantage in global markets. The consultant saw a high probability for Scenario III, Regional Self-Interest. Existing and predicted trade agreements will create regional blocs. He gave Scenario IV, National Self-Interest, a low probability of happening. Twenty years of building alliances are not likely to crumble into economic isolation.

Clearly, these are the views of a single consultant. You and others may disagree with them. They are offered here as one possible set of views of an international future.

Technological Changes

The major **technological changes** that are underway now and expected to grow in the future will help further the economic changes described above and will let managers respond to these global challenges. This section does not discuss all technological change expected for the future. The changes described are those expected to most directly affect organizations and their management in the four areas of information, materials, manufacturing, and transportation.[69]

INFORMATION

Advances in technologies for creating, collecting, sending, and processing information will continue well beyond present capabilities. These advances will change the way business is done in many parts of the world and help managers respond more quickly and more flexibly to change.

Computers of all types have simplified the task of creating written words or collecting numerical information for later analysis. Innovative contributions of modern computing to information creating and management will continue well into the future.

Electronically based measurement systems will monitor manufacturing processes in modern factories and collect sales information at stores' checkout stands. Future computer technologies will digitize information directly from voice interaction and handwriting on a digital tablet. Hand-held computers will allow retailers to track their inventories and send their orders electronically. Navigation satellites will let trucking and shipping firms track their entire fleet. Communication satellites will allow managers to talk to drivers and ship captains anywhere in the world.

Modems and facsimile machines will be commonplace in organizations of the future. The communication network connecting these devices will use satellites and fiber-optic cables. The latter will cross land and go under the oceans.

Modems allow direct connection between any pair of computers. Such connections will allow direct computer conferencing, for example, among individual researchers working on a common problem, whatever their location on the planet. Facsimile machines will speed signing of contracts and sending orders from buyers on any continent.

Electronic mail (E-mail), voice mail, videoconferencing, and teleconferencing will also increase in use as costs of these forms of communication drop. Videoconferencing adds a two-way video connection to the now common teleconference. According to one prediction, the cost of home teleconferencing will drop in the future, allowing as much as 22% of the workforce to work from their homes.[70] Many organizations will eventually replace or supplement their E-mail systems with voice mail systems. Oral messages, not written ones, will appear in a person's electronic mailbox.

E-mail will take on a new complexion as it reaches well beyond the systems within an organization to public E-mail services.[71] Some public carriers offer E-mail service such as AT&T, Western Union, and MCI. As communication protocols for electronic messages are established, any subscriber to an E-mail service will be able to communicate with a subscriber to any other service. And with future global communication systems, such messaging can happen anywhere in the world.

The essence of what the expected advances in information technology will do for future organizations and management is captured in the following observation by Wayne Calloway, chief executive of PepsiCo:

> In 1980 I could have told you how Doritos were selling west of the Mississippi. Today I can tell you how they're selling not only in California, but also in Orange County, in the town of Irvine, in the local Von's, in the special promotion at the end of aisle four, on Thursday.[72]

MATERIALS

A true revolution in materials technology and engineering will unfold in the future. Materials with names more exotic than wood, steel, and copper will see common use in the years ahead. Some materials already in use are carbon fiber composites and optical fibers, the basis of tennis rackets and communication cable, respectively. Others, such as superpolymers, amorphous metal alloys, and superconductors, will add to a growing list of human-created materials. Innovations in product ideas and technological solutions no longer will depend on naturally existing materials.[73] As two materials scientists put it in the late 1980s, "advances . . . have made it possible to start with a need and then develop a material to meet it, atom by atom."[74]

Advances in materials and methods of bonding them will bring new opportunities for businesses and ways of solving information, manufacturing, and transportation problems. Fiber-optic cables will continue to make near-revolutionary contributions to information handling. Fiber-optic cables are much lighter than copper cables, reducing the costs of laying transoceanic lines. New materials will replace steel and aluminum, allowing lighter cars and trucks that will carry heavier loads. New ceramics technology allows designing jet engines with more thrust. The new engines weigh less than aluminum engines, letting larger planes go longer distances with more people and cargo.

Advances in materials technology will not be positive for all people. New materials may replace many naturally existing materials such as cobalt, manganese, chromium, nickel, and copper. These materials are major exports for some African and Latin American countries, so declines in their use will have adverse effects on the economies of these countries.

New materials also lead to new manufacturing processes. The process called powder-metallurgy forging, for example, requires less direct labor than conventional forging processes. Less direct labor means fewer jobs within the manufacturing process, an adverse future effect for some labor markets.

MANUFACTURING

Manufacturing in the future will feature agile manufacturing processes that keep almost no inventory and use computer-based technology to maintain direct links with customers or end-users. These processes will be cost-effective and competitive in producing both single custom-made items and large production runs, all within the same manufacturing plant. The products moving through these processes will never need to be the same from one product to another.[75]

Innovations in manufacturing will happen because of new advances in computer-assisted manufacturing (CAM), computer-integrated manufacturing (CIM), modern materials, robotics, laser methods of cutting and bonding, and the like. The list is almost endless, and no one can predict all the new technologies of the future that will help manufacturing processes.

The advances in manufacturing suggest opportunities for manufacturing organizations and implications for some international observations made earlier. Modern manufacturing methods will let organizations more closely tailor their products to individual customer needs. Such tailoring should increase the competitiveness of organizations that are willing to recognize worldwide differences in customer needs. The combined effects of future advances in information, materials, and manufacturing technology will create a stronger tie between builder and buyer— much as it was in the days of craftsmen.

Another effect of the changes in manufacturing will come from the reduced role of direct labor costs in the manufacturing process. Automated processes use fewer people directly in the manufacturing process. Of course, many people, such as engineers and computer programmers, support the processes. Such changes in labor costs could affect the decisions of managers to locate manufacturing in countries with low-cost labor. Future location decisions will also consider proximity to customers for closer ties, or to transportation points for moving goods to market.

TRANSPORTATION

The major advances in transportation technology will be in air and space travel. A confluence of forces in information, materials, and manufacturing technologies will

· *A Eurostar high-speed train in Waterloo Station, London. Such trains move passengers through the Eurotunnel between Great Britain and the European continent.*

produce important innovations in aircraft design. Those same forces will also affect ground and sea travel.

New materials and bonding methods allow lighter, faster aircraft that can travel farther and carry more people. They also allow more flexibility in airport location because planes will make less noise and will be able to use shorter runways for takeoff and landing. Major U.S. and European aircraft makers already have preliminary designs for 800-seat aircraft, complete with children's playroom, duty-free stores, and business centers. Other designs focus on supersonic aircraft that could fly from Los Angeles to Tokyo in about 4 hours, not the 10 hours it now takes.[76]

Communication and navigation will be affected by advances in information technology. Satellites will allow communication, navigation, and tracking anywhere on the globe, day or night. Laser-based methods of tracking rail cars and trucks allow real-time knowledge of the location of shipments en route. Knowing the location of something already shipped could let a customer-oriented company divert products to meet urgent customer needs, whether the products are aboard a truck, train, ship, or plane.

. . . .

 Organization and Management Changes

The challenges of the future will press many changes on organizations and their management. This section first describes the key points of new strategies for the future. It then examines the **organization and management changes** such strategies will require.

NEW STRATEGIES

The hallmarks of new strategies for future success will be a long-term view (about ten years) coupled with extraordinary patience. The latter will help when a firm is entering new markets where it has not competed before. Negotiations with government agencies in many countries take much time and an understanding of convoluted processes. It often will be necessary for managers to spend several years building relationships with government officials and local business people before introducing a product or service.[77]

Flexibility will also be a key feature of new strategies. Such flexibility will permeate the design and response of manufacturing and service operations. It will include a thorough understanding of customer needs and variations among markets. The latter will be especially true for companies that compete globally. Markets in different countries feature high diversity even between countries that are not far apart. Management must respond to those differences by treating the customers of the different countries in the way they expect. For example, the giant insurance company, AIG, has local agents collect monthly premiums at each insured's home in Taiwan but uses electronic bank transfers in Hong Kong.[78]

A variety of alliances will be created by many companies trying to compete in the future. Managers will find it easier and mistakes less costly to team with local business people. The local people know their markets better than outsiders do. Such alliances will often be joint ventures but may also involve many local people as managers of local operations.[79]

ORGANIZATIONAL DESIGN

The strategies of the future will require some basic changes in the design of many organizations.[80] Recall the discussion and analyses of organizational design in the earlier chapters. Changes in an organization's strategy often require changes in its design. The latter is a major management tool to achieve the goals of the strategy.

A decentralized organizational design is needed to attain the goals of a strategy that emphasizes flexibility and customer needs. This organizational design moves decisions down to the lowest level in the organization where quick responses are needed to shifting markets and customer needs. The close ties to both suppliers and customers will require cross-functional teams that tightly integrate many parts of the total business process. Local teams with broad decision-making and problem-solving authority help even large organizations decentralize. The modern information technologies described earlier will let the most globally dispersed organization reach decentralization on a scale previously not possible. As a result, organizations in the future will be flatter with fewer layers of management.

MANAGEMENT BEHAVIOR CHANGES

The organizational design changes just described imply some changes in management behavior that are needed to compete effectively in the future.[81] The first, and most obvious, is for management to let go of many decisions and move them to lower levels in their organizations. This change is especially true for organizations competing in global markets. Often only those working in certain markets and with certain consumers will have intimate knowledge of those markets and consumers. The diversity of markets worldwide will not let an organization be competitive with centralized decision making.

Organization-wide self-managing work teams will be an important management change into the next century. An organization forms such teams around a specific base of customers or focused on a product. In the first example, such teams are authorized to make all decisions in response to customer needs. In the second example, cross-functional teams conceive, design, build, and market a product. In both instances, the self-managing teams are involved in all aspects of the business process affecting a product or customer. Such teams will also become involved in the hiring process by doing much of the selection and early socialization of new employees completely within the team.

Motivation and reward systems of the future will be designed to focus people on performing the part of the process for which they are responsible. Skill-based pay systems and various forms of profit sharing, gain sharing, and stock ownership, will see increasing presence in organizations of the future. Skill-based pay systems tie a person's pay to the number of skills the person has learned. The result will be a flexible workforce where people can easily move from job to job. Gain sharing plans let those who contribute to the success of the organization share in that success.

New information technologies will help managers meet the challenge of the future.[82] Computer networks, satellite video and audio links, international E-mail systems, and the like will help managers decentralize decision making to self-managing teams, no matter where they are on the planet. Such information links will also integrate cross-functional teams and give them fast market and customer feedback.

Managers of the future will have different roles than their predecessors. Instead of perceiving themselves as controllers of processes and people, they will be leaders, facilitators, coaches, resources, and helpers. The decentralized organizations of the future, built upon self-managing work teams, will still need direction. The direction will be ingrained into the culture of the organization and come from the leadership of those in management roles.

The following case illustrates some observations made in this section about organizations and management in the future. Use the following questions as a guide for your analysis:

1. How did this company use its organizational design to reach its goals?
2. What effects did the design have on people's behavior?

CASE DESCRIPTION

The archaic name is entirely appropriate: The sun never sets on ICI's far-flung nerve centers, and the company has probably moved as near as any to being truly global. The world's 38th-largest industrial corporation, ICI sells $21 billion a year of pharmaceuticals, film, polymers, agricultural chemicals, explosives, and other products.

In 1983, ICI began to abandon its traditional country-by-country organization and establish world-wide business units. The company concentrated its resources on its strongest ones. Within each, it focused activity where the most strength lay. Four of the nine new business units are headquartered outside Britain. Two are in Wilmington, Delaware—ICI is growing 20% a year in the U.S. but only 2% to 3% at home. A factory in Britain or Brazil producing advanced materials or specialty chemicals answers to a boss in Wilmington.

To avoid overlapping research around the world, labs were given lead roles near the most important markets. Advanced materials research went to Phoenix to be near clients in defense industries, while leather dye research went to the south of France, the heart of the market.

The strategic shift created wrenching changes. ICI reduced its manufacturing jobs in Britain by 10,000 to 55,000; other people were transferred or taken off pet projects. "It's hard on people who have built national empires and now don't have such freedom. We are asking people to be less nationalistic and more concerned with what happens outside their country." The upheaval has been especially worrisome to British employees, since ICI's stronger growth rate elsewhere attracts more resources.

The payoff, says Miller, is better decision-making. "Before, each territory would work up projects and you'd have warring factions competing in London for the same

money. Now with one man responsible for a global product line, it becomes immaterial where a project is located. His profits will be the same. When you start operating in this manner, it takes a lot of steam out of the defense of fiefdoms." In pharmaceuticals, for example, better—and quicker—decision-making has helped ICI reduce the time lag in introducing new drugs to different markets from half a dozen years to one or two. ICI hopes eventually to make the introductions simultaneous.

A global company needs a world view at the top. Until 1982, ICI's 16-person board was all British. Now it includes two Americans, a Canadian, a Japanese, and a German. Among the 180 top people in the company, 35% are non-British.

British or non-British, they may go anywhere. Ben Lochtenberg, the new chairman of ICI Americas Inc., is an Australian who also has worked for ICI in Britain and Canada. He quickly learned that a common language is no insurance against cultural shocks. When he went to England, he couldn't get any respect with his direct Australian manner, so he learned the oblique ways of the English. For example, he says, if an English boss reacts to a pet project by saying, "Perhaps you ought to think about this a little more," what he really means is "You must be mad. Forget it." In the U.S., Lochtenberg had to unlearn the lesson. He told a manager, "Perhaps you ought to think about this a little more." The manager took him literally. Asked why he had gone ahead, the man replied, "Well, I thought about it, like you said, and the idea got better."

CASE ANALYSIS

The distant operations of ICI required its managers to have an unwavering worldview. The company partly achieved a worldview by designing its organization around worldwide business units. Such an organizational design almost forces managers to think and act globally, not locally or nationalistically. The culturally diverse board and group of senior managers increased the probability of culturally based differences in perceptions. Such differences in perceptions could create conflict during decision-making processes.

The experiences of Ben Lochtenberg at the end of the case illustrate other possibilities. Successful movements from country to country require a sensitivity to cultural differences among countries. The international sections of the previous chapters in this book tried to show you the size of those differences and their implications.

*S*everal ethical issues could arouse increasing interest in the future. Some issues follow from increased awareness about such matters. Others follow from the worldwide changes expected for the future as described earlier in this chapter.

The public reaction to the Wall Street scandals of the 1980s and the increased action against white-collar crime both point to increased sensitivity about ethical issues in the future.[83] The results of a survey done by the business school at Columbia University also point to some shift in the future. Eighty-five percent of the 1,500 senior managers surveyed said an emphasis on ethics will be a dominant quality of a successful year 2000 executive. Seventy-four percent of those executives said ethics was an important quality in 1989.[84] Lastly, American organizations have increasingly developed codes of ethics and are now using training to reshape the ethics of their cultures.[85]

Another major area of ethical issues are employee rights to privacy about their nonwork activities.[86] Activities such as smoking, sky diving, auto racing, alcohol consumption, cholesterol level, obesity, and the like are increasingly becoming of interest to employers. They argue that such activities create an unhealthy lifestyle that adds to the high cost of group health insurance and reduces employee productivity. Some employers, for example, already charge smokers more per month for health insurance than nonsmokers. Questions of employee privacy will surely stir much debate and litigation well into the next century.

The increasing global activity of many firms will raise many questions in the future. Those questions will center on the differences in ethical systems between the home country and other countries. A common ethical conflict arises for U.S. firms when a government official in another country wants a payoff to quickly process routine requests. Such payoffs do not violate the Foreign Corrupt Practices Act of 1977 but often violate an individual firm's code of ethics.[87] Bribes to get business are illegal under the act. Payments to hasten routine actions, such as processing license applications, are not. The dilemma for many business people in the future is squaring what is legal in global business with their traditional standards of doing business.

Personal and Management Implications

*M*any personal and management implications follow from the observations about the future made in this chapter. This section discusses those implications for you as an individual or as a manager, now or in the future.

The projected diversity of the domestic workforce implies much variety in attitudes, background, ethnicity, and language. Such diversity offers major opportunities for those organizations that manage the diversity well.[88] The opportunities arise from the variety of viewpoints people can bring to problems. Such variety, if managed poorly, can cause dysfunctional levels of conflict in the organization. The implications for you as an individual come from your level of personal comfort with participating in the diverse workforce of the future and from working in situations with high conflict potential.

The changes predicted for the future in both the level and use of computer and communication technology implies the need to be ready to use that technology. If you are not ready, the technology will be a stressor. Look at your college curriculum to see whether it is preparing you for the technologies of the future. If it is not, you may need to do some preparation separately from what you learn in college.

The increasing global orientation required of competitive future organizations implies a need for sensitivity to cultural differences. There is a large chance you will either work in another country or have managers and coworkers from other countries. Cultural differences affect people's perceptions of events in their work lives. You will need to understand such differences to interact comfortably and effectively. The international aspects sections of the previous chapters gave you many observations on cultural differences that should help you.

The predicted changes needed in the design of organizations and their management imply some differences in your future roles in organizations. The need to flatten organizations through decentralization of decisions implies more areas of decision making for you in the future. Such moves can broaden the scope of your job and possibly increase your job satisfaction and intrinsic motivation. You must also be ready and willing to accept that authority. These changes in job requirements can increase decision latitude but can also increase stress. You will find it helpful to review the discussions about decentralization in Appendix A and the organizational design discussions in Chapters 17 and 18.

The management implications follow from the international aspects of managing in the future, workforce diversity, increases in customer focus, changes in organizational design, and using new technologies. Managing effectively in the future global environment requires deep understanding of cultural and market differences among countries. The international implications sections of the earlier chapters should help you. You may also want to read some business press citations in this chapter to get more detail about specific parts of the world.

Workforce diversity will be a major management challenge in the future. It implies a need for you as a manager to understand the composition of your workforce, the opportunities it offers, and the difficulties it presents to management.[89] Chapters 4 and 11 may also help you understand differences in perceptions and the management of conflict.

The organizational design predictions for the future point to decentralized organizations and using self-managing work teams. These moves will require you to let go of some decision authority and move it to people below your organizational level. Although you can move authority to lower levels, you do not lose the responsibility for the actions of those people. Because of that responsibility, many managers find it difficult to decentralize and trust others to make decisions.

The technologies of the future will help you manage more efficiently but can have some latent dangers. Computer and communication technologies will help managers in the future communicate farther, faster, and with more people. Such far-flung communication will let you manage a decentralized organization. The latent dysfunction lies in the impersonality of some forms of communication. Instead of face-to-face meetings, you will talk to your subordinates by facsimile or direct computer interaction. There is even the chance you will rarely meet the people who work for you. Two-way videoconferencing, though, can let people see and talk to each other concurrently. The management implication is clear. Use future technologies wisely to help you manage effectively. Do not use technology as a substitute for personal interaction among those who work for you.

↵ Summary

The future holds many domestic changes, including demographic changes, skill requirements of new jobs, and workforce diversity. The future population of the United States will be older and more ethnically diverse than it is now. The ethnic diversity will introduce different languages, values, and attitudes into the workforce. Future jobs will have higher skill requirements than now, increasing the pressure on the educational system to prepare young people for them. Older, disabled, and retired people will enter the workforce in greater numbers because of slow growth from more traditional sources.

There will also be an increase in female heads of households and two-earner couples.

The expected international changes emphasize the need for a global view by managers of the future. Successful organizations in international markets will be transnational with their managers behaving as if no national boundaries exist. The scope of their decisions for location of operations and capital investment will be global.

Advances in information, materials, and manufacturing technologies will have major effects on transportation technologies. Lighter and stronger airplanes, trucks, and ships will carry larger loads for longer distances. Navigation satellites and automated tracking systems will let vehicles and vessels move around the clock. Centralized computer systems will track their movements. Changes in information technology include communication satellites, navigation satellites, electronic mail, voice mail, interconnection of computers, teleconferencing, and videoconferencing.

Managers will need to build new strategies based on long-term views, flexibility, customer needs, and business alliances. Global participation will require much patience if managers are to deal successfully with the diverse ways of doing business. Future organizations will have more decentralization than they do now. The decentralization will use self-managing work teams and modern information technology to do the work of the organization worldwide. The roles of managers in the future will shift from controlling to helping, leading, and coaching.

The ethical issues of the twenty-first century will feature increased sensitivity to white-collar crime, questions of employee rights of privacy, and comparative ethical questions from global operations. Employee rights of privacy should be especially controversial as more organizations ask questions about employees' non-work behavior.

. . . .

⮕ Key Terms

domestic changes 592

international changes 594

management changes 604

organization changes 604

technological changes 601

. . . .

⮕ Review and Discussion Questions

1. This chapter emphasized the global orientation that will be a major feature of managing in the future. Discuss how you see that orientation affecting you and others in your class in your future career.

2. Communication and computer technology will play leading roles in letting managers span the globe. How do you feel about such technology? Do you feel comfortable with it? How much have you learned about it in your education to date?

3. The U.S. workforce of the future will be highly diverse in gender and ethnic composition. Discuss the implications of such diversity for you as a manager or nonmanager in the future.

4. The chapter described several large trading blocs proposed for North America (Canada, United States, and Mexico) as well as Europe. The latter includes Eastern Europe, Central Europe, and special relations with the Baltic nations and the countries of the former Soviet

Union. Discuss the long-range implications of such arrangements.

5. The chapter described the emerging transnational organizations that will be common in the future. The Imperial Chemical Industries case described how it manages its worldwide operations. What career opportunities do such organizations present for you and others in your class? Has your education prepared you to participate effectively in such organizations?

6. Review the discussion questions at the end of Chapter 3 and the earlier discussion about ethical issues in the future. Discuss those questions and issues with special emphasis on what the world of organizations will look like over the next 20 years.

7. The chapter presented several scenarios of the global economy. Those scenarios were prepared by an experienced international consultant. Discuss each scenario. Which scenario is most likely to emerge in the future?

. . . .

⮕ Exercise

DRIVING FORCES

Stop now and ponder what you have learned about the future of organizations and management from reading this

Source: Adapted from Jan V. Dauman, "The Global Economy in the Year 2000" from THE GLOBAL ECONOMY: America's Role in the Decade Ahead, edited by William Brock and Robert Hormats, with the permission of W. W. Norton & Company, Inc. Copyright © 1990 by The American Assembly.

chapter. The chapter emphasized the need for global view by managers as they move into the twenty-first century. Many different forces will bear on organizations and their managers, compelling that global view. The following lists driving forces viewed by many observers as compelling a global economy in the next century. On a separate sheet of paper, rate the likelihood of each force to produce a global economy using the following scale:

Highly unlikely to be a driving force in the future	1 2 3 4 5 6 7	Highly likely to be a driving force in the future

Pulls to inter-dependence	The vast investments needed for high-technology research and development (R&D); the growth in mass communications; the convergence of consumer taste; the demands of economies of scale.
Monetary flows/exchange rates	Capital investment and consumer savings; balance of payment and trade credits and deficits.
Technology/information	Effects on the maintenance of political boundaries and the cycle of global events.
Energy	The price of oil as a determinant of the nature and pace of economic development. Stability of supply as an influence on world peace.
Regionalism	Economic nationalism versus economic regionalism.
Debt	Third World indebtedness effects on the world financial system and the markets and stability of the indebted countries.
Population/demographics	Birth rates, aging trends, and the size and prosperity of the workforce.
Leadership	Leadership effects on the progress of international initiatives such as the fight against trade protectionism and debt.
Growth	Economic growth and political maturity.
Ideology	The effect of ideologies of all types.
Military-industrial complex	The effects of conventional versus nuclear weapons debates.
Environment	Concern for the environment effects on economic development.
Weather	Climate and natural disaster effects on economic development.

. . . .

 Case

MANAGEMENT FOR THE 1990S: TO COMPETE, U.S. FIRMS WILL HAVE TO BE COST-WISE, CREATIVE—AND CARING

Read the following press account about how management will look through the 1990s. Consider the following questions both for your own review and for class discussion:

1. Making quality the focal point of an organization's strategy is repeatedly described in the case. Do you believe a quality emphasis will be needed for U.S. organizations to be competitive in the future?
2. Note the observation that high-morale organizations will be more innovative in the future. Is that observation consistent with what you have learned from this book about human motivation in organizations?
3. A customer focus is also a major theme of this case. What implications do you see for a customer focus in U.S. organizations of the future? How can managers harness customer feedback to build improvements into their products or service?
4. Hewlett-Packard Co. did not cut research and development spending. Assess the wisdom of this action for that company. Is it an orientation typical or atypical of U.S. managers?
5. Notice how bonuses were used in one company. Were those plans designed properly? You may want to review

the summaries of earlier chapters on motivation to discuss this question.

Ultimately, stress-management programs, after-work aerobics and late-night back rubs can do only so much to alleviate the morale problems dogging so many U.S. companies. Perhaps the biggest cause of the stress epidemic is the wave of restructuring and cost-cutting that has swept corporate America in the past decade. Since 1977, the Fortune 500 companies alone have slashed 2.8 million employees from their payrolls; millions more have surrendered jobs or taken pay cuts in the name of corporate streamlining. The downsizing has boosted share values and helped save several huge companies—including USX Corp., Caterpillar Inc. and Ford Motor Co. But the cuts have taken a huge toll—one that's not easily quantified but that can, over time, cripple organizations just as surely as high labor or spiraling energy costs.

To be competitive in the next decade, companies will have to find ways of staying lean while becoming considerably less mean to their employees. The bunker mentality in corporate America is already beginning to fade as the weak dollar creates stronger demand for exports and strengthens balance sheets. As managers poke their heads up into the light for the first time in years, they are realizing that surviving in the 1990s will require a new, more imaginative set of tactics. Budget cutting "is only a reaction," argues Professor Mitroff of USC. "It isn't a vision. It isn't even a strategy. A manager had better have more meaningful plans now than slashing budgets."

The most common plan is deceptively simple: ease up on retrenchment and go for growth. The next phase for American industry will not be dominated by bloodless executives

Source: J. McCormick, and B. Powell, "Management for the 1990s: To Compete, U.S. Firms Will Have to be Cost-wise, Creative—and Caring," *Newsweek*, April 25, 1988, pp. 47–48. From *NEWSWEEK*, April 25, 1988. © 1988, Newsweek, Inc. All rights reserved. Reprinted by permission.

with green eyeshades and iron fists. The game, in industry after industry, has changed. If a company has achieved "cost parity" with competitors, new ways to increase profitability are necessary. "Cutting price is usually insanity if the competition can go as low as you can." says Harvard Business School professor Michael Porter. "You have to find a different competitive tack. Quality becomes central—and so do service and innovation."

But finding that "different tack" isn't easy. Companies will have to encourage employees to communicate and work together more effectively. "The more you want people to have creative ideas and solve difficult problems, the less you can afford to manage them with terror," says Daniel Greenberg, chairman of Electro Rent Corp., a leading leaser of electronic equipment to the aerospace industry among others.... The ideal manager of the future will combine cost-consciousness with creativity and a new ingredient, caring. McKinsey & Co. director Richard N. Foster stresses that the last two of the three c's are linked: firms with high morale will usually be the most innovative. The '90s, Foster says, will pit "attackers—those who try to make money by changing the order of things—[against] defenders, those who protect the status quo." And morale, he adds, is important to the attacker—the innovator. He is "often more powerful than he appears, because he is more motivated."

The shift will force a change in leadership at many top companies, bringing the bloodletting full circle. Few executives, after whacking costs by closing divisions and laying people off, have the energy or the ideas to preside over an era of fertile innovation. Even if they did, the remaining employees may not be in the mood to follow the men who wielded the ax. "I have never seen a situation in which the guy who cuts a company down is the one who brings it back," says Richard Lindenmuth, a former ITT executive, now the chief executive at Robinson Nugent Inc., a supplier to the computer industry.

↵ WRENCHING CHANGE

A recent shuffle at Westinghouse Electric Corp., the giant conglomerate, illustrates the point. Former CEO Douglas Danforth presided over a wrenching but successful restructuring. Now he has been succeeded by a tough company veteran, John Marous Jr. His challenge, says one analyst, is to "rev up growth" by stressing basics: better quality and enhanced productivity.

A few executives have managed the difficult trick of downsizing while maintaining reasonably good morale. According to management consultant Robert H. Waterman Jr., they have done so by recognizing the urgent need for change and communicating it quickly and honestly to every employee. Most important, they have linked cost cutting to a broader goal that everyone can work toward. In Waterman's view, Henry Schacht, the chairman and chief executive at Cummins Engine, has accomplished nearly all of that recently. Faced with a ferocious Japanese assault in Cummins' main market—diesel engines—Schacht pushed quality improvement, not cost cutting, as the company's primary goal.

When work-force reductions *were* necessary, Schacht avoided a mistake that's standard operating procedure at most companies: cutting largely from the bottom. Says Chriss Street, who studies failed companies for a Los Angeles brokerage house: "The guys at the upper levels are the boss's friends. The remarkable contributions of the employee three rungs lower isn't as visible." At Cummins, Schacht took a "a slice off the pyramid" as he puts it—that is, he lopped off people at every level, from top to bottom. That sense of equity was important to those who remained, creating a "we're all in this together" attitude that was crucial in improving quality.

Quality, of course, is an overused slogan in corporate America. Few companies actually succeed in differentiating products by establishing a reputation for being better. Those that do reap clear rewards: they can avoid brutal head-to-head price competition that can produce nothing but losses, layoffs, and bruised feelings.

Since the publication of books like "In Search of Excellence" in the early '80s, some of the principles of smart decision making have become cliches. Companies with a knack for targeting a market niche and developing the right technology for it, management gurus say, are those with loose hierarchies that facilitate free exchanges of ideas. The best firms encourage contact with customers and allow employees to run with good ideas. Yet it is remarkable how few companies fit the description—and how much those that don't pay for it. A former executive at a big steel producer recalls his shock when a Toyota manager from the Fremont, Calif. joint venture with General Motors arrived to inspect the quality of the company's sheet steel. The Toyota rep rejected sample after sample. " 'No good,' he kept saying, 'no good.' Our guys were furious. Instead of wanting to make the changes the Toyota guy wanted, they wanted to tell him to go f— himself. So we lost the business."

↵ CUSTOMER-CONSCIOUS

That kind of attitude can keep firms from tapping into a prime source of ideas—the customer. Many companies allow little room for responding to customer feedback. A few, like Western Digital Corp., are exceptions. Kathy Braun works for Western, a specialized electronics company in Irvine, Calif. Five years ago she oversaw production of a new disc-drive controller board that cost $150 to produce. A major customer insisted on paying only $100 for each board. Braun expected her boss, CEO Roger Johnson, to sympathize with her. He didn't.

His order: attack. "Roger told me that if $100 was all the customer could pay, I'd have to redesign the board," she says. The result was a less expensive design that not only satisfied the original customer but opened a flood of new markets for the product. Johnson, who keeps elephant figurines in his office to remind him of the lumbering style of managers at so many big companies, insists that his whole organization pay attention to customers. "A company has to be more customer-oriented now. Do workers think they're manufacturers, sellers or distributors? Or do they think they're all part of a broader, all-inclusive group trying to satisfy the marketplace?"

Cynics at big companies that don't have fast-growing markets all to themselves usually ridicule such rhetoric. But a handful of corporate giants have displayed the attributes needed to compete in the postretrenchment age. The constantly innovating 3M Corp is one. Hewlett-Packard Co. is another. Three years ago HP went through a traumatic period. Competition, particularly from the Far East, intensified. Earnings growth stalled, and HP's return on investment fell below its historic norm. Fabled for a loose, campuslike atmosphere (it borders Stanford University), the company buckled down. Weekly beer blasts were dropped, and some employees were offered early retirement (despite emotional pleas from them that that wasn't "the HP way"). The entire company—from CEO John Young on down—went on a shortened workweek with less pay.

Many companies would have panicked and done anything to maintain quarterly earnings. HP remained calm and stuck to an ambitious research and development budget. Never, says chief operating officer Dean Morton, did management think about cutting R&D, despite screams from analysts to keep earnings up. At the same time, HP centralized purchasing for all manufacturing—a controversial move in a very decentralized firm. Young made the decision, in part, because the R&D effort was aimed at standardizing the design of HP's new Spectrum computer line. That standardization has allowed HP to churn out a series of high-powered products at dramatically lower cost.

◻ SAFE HAVEN

For many companies, adopting that kind of long-term view hasn't seemed possible lately. Bill Roberts can explain why. At 39, the corporate communications expert may be the ultimate victim of the 1980s. In 1982 Roberts left his job at Signode Corp., a manufacturer of packaging machines, when it was under attack by raider Victor Posner. He went to Stauffer Chemical, but quit when the company was on the verge of a leveraged buyout. Then he got fired from Chicago conglomerate Borg-Warner when *it* was taken over. Today Roberts is a vice president at Philips Corp., a small Dayton, Ohio–based building-materials producer. Philips is the kind of firm that wouldn't attract a corporate raider. It's solid, unspectacular and, Roberts says proudly, "We're cheap."

But the company does treat its "stakeholders"—employees and shareholders—very well. It has a generous bonus and profit-sharing plan. And there's wealth to share: Philips has posted 11 straight annual-earnings increases. The company runs a Japanese-style, how-can-we-save-some-money program, in which nearly everyone can participate. It has saved Philips $62 million in six years. The program allows groups of five employees, from various departments, to work together for five days to improve Philips products. Last year 150 teams went at it. Roberts says that no team effort has ever failed to yield some savings. Even better (especially given his travails), not once has the group decided to save money by laying people off. For Roberts, most of the 1980s meant "going to work every day wondering if you'd have a job after lunch." In Philips, he says, he's found a safe haven. A lot of other American workers wish they could say the same.

. . . .

◣ *References and Notes*

[1]"Alphabet Soup," *The Economist*, September 21, 1991, p. 33.

[2]T. R. King, "A Centennial View: Changing Markets—Catering to the Maturing Baby-boom Generation," *Wall Street Journal*, June 23, 1989, p. A7; J. Carey, "The Changing Face of a Restless Nation: Population Shifts, Notably the Baby Boom, Are Still Remolding America," *Business Week*, September 25, 1989, pp. 92–95, 98, 99, 102, 106.

[3]"More Skilled Workers Coming to the U.S.," *Fortune*, September 9, 1991, p. 14.

[4]A. Bennett, "The Second Century—Company School: As Pool of Skilled Help Tightens, Firms Move to Broaden Their Role," *Wall Street Journal*, May 8, 1989, pp. A1, A4.

[5]R. R. Thomas, Sr., *Beyond Race and Gender* (New York: American Management Association, 1991).

[6]A. Bennett, "A Centennial View: Issues to Watch. The Work Force: Firms Become a Crucial Agent of Social Change," *Wall Street Journal*, June 23, 1989, p. A22.

[7]S. Nasar, "Preparing for a New Economy," *Fortune*, September 26, 1988, pp. 86–87, 90, 92, 96.

[8]C. Knowlton, "Consumers: A Tougher Sell," *Fortune*, September 26, 1988, pp. 63, 66–70, 74; A. Kupfer, "Managing Now for the 1990s," *Fortune*, September 26, 1988, pp. 44–47.

[9]K. Pennar, "Economic Prospects for the Year 2000," *Business Week*, September 25, 1989, pp. 158, 159, 162, 166, 170; Nasar, "Preparing for a New Economy," p. 87.

[10]G. Bylinsky, "The Digital Factory," *Fortune*, November 14, 1994, pp. 92–94, 96, 100, 104, 106, 110; O. Port, "Custom-Made, Direct from the Plant," *Business Week/21st Century Capitalism*, November 18, 1994, pp. 158–59; T. D. Schellhardt and C. Hymowitz, "Economy—The Second Century: U.S. Manufacturers Gird for Competition," *Wall Street Journal*, May 2, 1989, pp. A2, A8.

[11]Pennar, "Economic Prospects," p. 159.

[12]Bylinsky, "The Digital Factory"; Port, "Custom-Made."

[13]A. Farnham, "Baldor's Success: Made in the U.S.A.," *Fortune*, July 17, 1989, pp. 101–2, 104, 106.

[14]Port, "Custom-Made," pp. 158–59.

[15]O. Port, "A Smarter Way to Manufacture: How 'Concurrent Engineering' Can Reinvigorate American Industry," *Business Week*, April 30, 1990, pp. 110–13, 116–17.

[16]R. Henkoff, "Service Is Everybody's Business," *Fortune*, June 27, 1994, pp. 48–50, 52, 56, 60; R. E. Kutscher and J. A. Mark, "The Service-producing sector: Some Common Perceptions Reviewed," *Monthly Labor Review* 106 (1983): 21–24; C. Stein, "Boom Is Over for Nation's Service Industries," *Boston Globe*, August 27, 1991, p. 37. You will find a good summary of the service sector's economic performance in J. B. Quinn, *Intelligent Enterprise: A Knowledge and Service Based Paradigm for Industry* (New York: Free Press, 1992), Ch. 1.

[17]Stein, "Boom Is Over."

[18]Stein, "Boom Is Over."

[19]"Quality in Services," *Business Week*, October 25, 1991, pp. 99–128.

[20]F. Rice, "How to Deal with Tougher Customers," *Fortune*, December 3, 1990, p. 39.

[21]R. I. Kirkland, Jr., "Entering a New Age of Boundless Competition," *Fortune*, March 14, 1988, pp. 40–42, 46, 48.

[22]V. Byrd, "The Avon Lady of the Amazon," *Business Week*, October 24, 1994, pp. 93, 94, 96.

[23]J. Martin, "Georgia Farmers Go Global," *Fortune*, May 16, 1994, pp. 16–17.

[24]J. Main, "How to Go Global—and Why," *Fortune*, August 28, 1989, pp. 70–73, 76.

[25]C. A. Bartlett and S. Ghoshal, *Managing across Borders: The Transnational Solution* (Boston: Harvard Business School Press, 1989).

[26]P. Nulty, "How the World WILL CHANGE," *Fortune*, January 15, 1990, pp. 44–46, 50–54; L. S. Richman, "Global Growth Is on a Tear," *Fortune*, March 20, 1995, pp. 108–11, 112, 114.

[27]C. M. Aho and S. Ostry, "Regional Trading Blocs: Pragmatic or Problematic Policy?" in W. E. Brock and R. D. Hormats, eds., *The Global Economy: America's Role in the Decade Ahead* (New York: Norton, 1990), pp. 147–73; S. Ostry, "Governments & Corporations in a Shrinking World: Trade & Innovation Policies in the United States, Europe & Japan," *Columbia Journal of World Business* 25 (1990): 10–16.

[28]M. W. Walsh, " 'Yukon to Yucatan' " Accord within Sight," *Los Angeles Times*, March 19, 1991, World Report Section, p. 4.

[29]L. Kraar, "North America's New Trade Punch," *Fortune*, May 22, 1989, pp. 123–25, 127.

[30]B. Davis and J. Calmes, "The House Passes Nafta—Trade Win: House Approves Nafta, Providing President with Crucial Victory," *Wall Street Journal*, November 18, 1993, p. A1.

[31]W. J. Holstein and A. Borrus, "Inching Toward a North American Market," *Business Week*, June 25, 1990, pp. 40–41.

[32]D. Harbrecht, W. C. Symonds, E. Malkin, and G. Smith. "What Has NAFTA Wrought? Plenty of Trade," *Business Week*, November 21, 1994, pp. 48–49.

[33]J. Main, "How Latin America Is Opening Up," *Fortune*, April 8, 1991, pp. 84–87, 89.

[34]S. Baker, "As Argentina Strides Ahead, Will Its Neighbors Follow?" *Business Week*, October 7, 1991, p. 56.

[35]H. Cooper and J. De Cordoba, "Chile Is Invited to Join NAFTA as U.S. Pledges Free-Trade Zone for Americas," *Wall Street Journal*, December 12, 1994, pp. A1, A3.

[36]Cooper and De Cordoba, "Chile Is Invited to Join NAFTA," p. A1.

[37]"Norway Rejects EU Again," *Albuquerque Journal*, November 29, 1994, p. A3.

[38]G. E. Schares, "Why Eastern Europe Is Getting a Warm Embrace from the EC," *Business Week*, September 16, 1991, pp. 46–47.

[39]R. Brady, "Baby, It'll be Cold Outside COMECON," *Business Week*, January 22, 1990, pp. 41–42.

[40]S. Tully, "Full Throttle Toward a New Era," *Fortune*, November 20, 1989, pp. 131–32, 134–36.

[41]J. McCormick, "Holding Pep Rallies for 1992: States Coach U.S. Firms on How to Win in Europe," *Newsweek*, November 6, 1989, p. 60; M. Meyer, "Storming 'Fortress Europe:' U.S. Companies Brace for the Fallout of '1992,' " *Newsweek*, November 7, 1988, p. 82.

[42]K. L. Miller, "Europe: The Push East," *Business Week*, November 7, 1994, pp. 48–49; J. Templeman, "Eastward, Ho! The Pioneers Plunge in," *Business Week*, April 15, 1991, pp. 51–53; S. Tully, "What Eastern Europe Offers," *Fortune*, March 12, 1990, pp. 52–55.

[43]A. Borrus and B. Javetski, "The West Is Asking: Who's in Charge Here?" *Business Week*, September 9, 1991, pp. 32–33; Brady, "Baby, It'll be Cold Outside"; L. Trei, "The Balts Are Free—But 'Winter Is Coming,' " *Business Week*, September 9, 1991, p. 31; I. T. Ginsberg, "Leaders of 12 Soviet Republics Agree to Form Economic Union," *Albuquerque Journal*, October 2, 1991, p. B6.

[44]R. Brady and P. Galuszka, "Big Deals Run into Big Trouble in the Soviet Union," *Business Week*, March 19, 1990, pp. 58–59.

[45]P. Hofheinz, "Let's Do Business," *Fortune*, September 23, 1991, pp. 62–65, 68.

[46]Hofheinz, "Let's Do Business"; J. B. Levine, "The Great Soviet Sell-off," *Business Week*, September 30, 1991, pp. 38–39.

[47]J. Rossant and P. Galuszka, "Why the West May Come Up Empty in a Monster Oil Patch," *Business Week*, May 30, 1994, p. 57.

[48]L. Kraar, "Top U.S. Companies Move into Russia," *Fortune*, July 31, 1989, pp. 165–66, 168, 170, 171; Hofheinz, "Let's Do Business"; M. Maremont and M. Ivey, "Why Soviet Oil Wells Won't Be Gushing Soon," *Business Week*, September 9, 1991, pp. 36, 38; R. A. Melcher, "For Investors, 'After One Step Backward, It's Two Steps Forward,' " *Business Week*, September 9, 1991, pp. 28–29; Rossant and Galuszka, "Why the West May Come Up Empty."

[49]"A Strategic Guide to the Rim," *Fortune*, Pacific Rim 1989, pp. 72–74, 76, 78; L. Kraar, "Asia's Rising Export Powers," *Fortune*, Pacific Rim 1989, pp. 43, 46, 50; L. Kraar, "The Rising Power of the Pacific," *Fortune*, Pacific Rim 1990, pp. 8–9, 12.

[50]B. Javetski and S. Hutcheon, "Is a Grand Alliance in the Making on the Pacific Rim?" *Business Week*, November 6, 1989, p. 70; L. Kraar, "The Growing Power of Asia," *Fortune*, October 7, 1991, p. 118; Kraar, "The Rising Power."

[51]K. E. House, "The '90s and Beyond: Though Rich, Japan Is Poor in Many Elements of Global Leadership," *Wall Street Journal*, January 30, 1989, pp. A1, A8.

[52]B. Powell and P. McKillop, "Sayonara, America," *Newsweek*, August 19, 1991, pp. 32–33.

[53]Kraar, "The Rising Power"; C. Rapoport, "How the Japanese Are Changing," *Fortune*, Pacific Rim 1990, pp. 15–17, 20, 22.

[54]C. Rapoport, "You Can Make Money in Japan," *Fortune*, February 12, 1990, pp. 85, 88, 90, 92.

[55]F. S. Worthy, "Japan's Spreading Regional Power," *Fortune*, Pacific Rim 1990, pp. 95–98; Kraar, "The Rising Power."

[56]Kraar, "The Rising Power."

[57]"A Strategic Guide to the Rim," pp. 77–78.

[58]D. J. Yang, "The Other China Is Starting to Soar," *Business Week*, November 6, 1989, pp. 60–62.

[59]S. Glain, "Shackled 'Tiger': South Korean Leader Struggles to Free Up a Regulated Economy," *Wall Street Journal*, March 30, 1994, pp. A1, A6; L. Nakarmi, "Korea Throws Open Its Doors," *Business Week*, July 29, 1991, p. 46.

[60]L. Kraar, "Korea's Automakers Take on the World (Again)," *Fortune*, March 6, 1995, pp. 152–54, 158, 162, 164; L. Nakarmi and R. Neff, "Can This Tiger Burn Bright Again?" *Business Week*, December 3, 1990, pp. 56–57.

[61]L. Kraar, "The Tigers Behind Korea's Prowess," *Fortune*, Fall 1989, pp. 36–37, 40.

[62]Kraar, "The Rising Power."

[63]Kraar, "The Tigers."

[64]J. Barnathan, "Behind the Great Wall: The U.S. and China Are Privately Deepening Ties," *Business Week*, October 25, 1993, pp. 42–43; J. Barnathan, "China: Birth of a New Economy," *Business Week*, January 31, 1994, pp. 42–45, 48; A. Borrus and J. Barnathan, "China's Gates Swing Open: U.S. Companies May Well Become Key Partners," *Business Week*, June 13, 1994, pp. 52–53; F. S. Worthy, "Doing Business in China Now," *Fortune*, Fall 1989, pp. 21, 24, 28, 32.

[65]L. Nakarmi, "A Coke with that Kimchi?" *Business Week*, February 6, 1995, p. 4; L. M. Simons, "The Hermit Kingdom," *Albuquerque Journal*, April 2, 1995, pp. B1, B4; L. M. Simons, "Cash Shortage Fuels Push for Tourism," *Albuquerque Journal*, April 2, 1995, pp. B1, B4.

[66]D. Beveridge, "U.S. Not Essential to Iran; Embargo in Vain, Experts Say," Associated Press, May 2, 1995 (As the story appeared in the *Albuquerque Journal*, May 2, 1995, p. D5.); J. Rossant, "The Race to Come Up with a Peace Dividend," *Business Week*, October 31, 1994, p. 68; J. Rossant, "Are the Sands About to Shift under Saudi Arabia?" *Business Week*, February 15, 1993, pp. 50–52.

[67]T. Wells, "Tiny Namibia Settles into Its Democracy Just Fine, Thank You," *Wall Street Journal*, December 6, 1994, pp. A1, A8.

[68]E. Schoonfeld, "Into Africa," *Business Week*, September 19, 1994, pp. 16, 18.

[69]Developed from H. B. Malmgren, "Technology and the Economy," in W. E. Brock and R. D. Hormats, eds., *The Global Economy: America's Role in the Decade Ahead* (New York: Norton, 1990), pp. 92–119 and other cited sources.

[70]Kupfer, "Managing Now for the 1990s."

[71]L. Simone, "E-Mail, the Global Handshake," *PC Magazine*, August 1989, pp. 175–78, 181–182, 185–93, 196, 198–202.

[72]P. Sellers, "Pepsi Keeps on Going After No. 1," *Fortune*, March 11, 1991, pp. 62–63, 68, 70.

[73]J. P. Clark, and M. C. Fleming, "Advanced Materials and the Economy," *Scientific American* 255 (1986): 51–57.

[74]Clark and Fleming, "Advanced Materials," p. 51.

[75]Bylinsky, "The Digital Factory"; Port, "Custom- Made."

[76]J. Cole, "Jet Makers, Once Keen for a Giant Aircraft, Are Drawn to Fast One," *Wall Street Journal*, June 12, 1995, p. A1; C. Rapoport, "Ready for Jumbo Jumbos?" *Fortune*, May 16, 1994, p. 17; B. Sweetman and S. F. Brown, "Megaplanes," *Popular Science*, April 1995, pp. 54–57, 93.

[77]Suggested by House, "The '90s and Beyond"; L. Kraar, "How Americans Win in Asia," *Fortune*, October 7, 1991, pp. 133–34, 136, 140; F. S. Worthy, "Getting in on the Ground Floor," *Fortune*, Pacific Rim 1990, pp. 61, 64, 66, 67; F. S. Worthy, "Keys to Japanese Success in Asia," *Fortune*, October 7, 1991, pp. 157, 158, 160.

[78]Kraar, "How Americans Win."

[79]Schares, "Why Eastern Europe."

[80]Developed from M. S. Gerstein and R. B. Shaw, "Organizational Architectures for the Twenty-First Century," in D. A. Nadler, M. S. Gerstein, Robert B. Shaw, and Associates, eds., *Organizational Architecture: Designs for Changing Organizations* (San Francisco: Jossey-Bass Publishers, 1992), pp. 263–73; E. E. Lawler III, "The New Plant Revolution Revisited," *Organizational Dynamics*, Autumn 1990, pp. 5–14; E. E. Lawler III, "The New Plant Approach: A Second Generation Approach," *Organizational Dynamics*, Summer 1991, pp. 5–14; M. S. Scott Morton, ed., *The Corporation of the 1990s: Information Technology and Organizational Transformation* (New York: Oxford University Press, 1991).

[81]Gerstein and Shaw, *Organizational Architecture*.

[82]Scott Morton, *The Corporation of the 1990s*.

[83]T. Smart, "The Crackdown on Crime in the Suites," *Business Week*, April 22, 1991, pp. 102–4.

[84]L. B. Korn, "How the Next CEO Will Be Different," *Fortune*, May 22, 1989, pp. 157–58.

[85]S. J. Harrington, "What Corporate America Is Teaching About Ethics," *Academy of Management Executive* 5 (1991): 21–30.

[86]C. Kleiman, "Privacy: A Growing Issue among Workers, Bosses," *Chicago Tribune*, August 25, 1991, Section 8, p. 1; Z. Schiller and W. Konrad, "If You Light up on Sunday, Don't Come in on Monday," *Business Week*, August 26, 1991, pp. 68–70, 72.

[87]F. S. Worthy, "When Somebody Wants a Payoff," *Fortune*, Pacific Rim 1989, pp. 117–118, 120, 122.

[88]Thomas, *Beyond Race*.

[89]Thomas, *Beyond Race*.

VI *Organizational Change and the Future*

*T*he two chapters in this section discussed organizational change, organizational development, and the future directions of organization and management. The following case concludes Section VI by integrating those observations.

◁ TIMES ARE GOOD? CREATE A CRISIS

Craig Weatherup faced a dilemma. The numbers at Pepsi-Cola looked great—earnings were up 10%, and the business was more profitable in the U.S. than Coca-Cola's. But looking out a few years, Weatherup, president of a PepsiCo division with sales of over $7 billion, feared that the soda market would turn flat and the competition only get tougher. How, then, to convince his 30,000 highly successful, hardworking people that they needed to tear apart this money machine and rebuild it?

Weatherup's answer: He created a crisis. During a three-day meeting with his top 11 managers, Weatherup bluntly explained that while most executives would be satisfied with 10% annual growth in earnings, he was not. From now on it was 15% or bust. "There's a freight train out there," he said to the startled group, "and it's called 15% earnings. We're standing on the track, and we'd better figure out something or it will run us right over." To emphasize his point he handed each manager a model train featuring an engine with 15% painted on its side. On the accompanying toy tracks, facing the oncoming train, were 11 tiny, frightened figures.

It didn't take long for Weatherup's managers to catch his drift. Over the next two years he and his team, working from headquarters in Somers, New York, restructured the organization, redesigned how it did its work, and redefined jobs. The change included breaking the division into 107 customer-focused units and dramatically revising processes like beverage delivery and special sale promotions, moves that ended up saving Pepsi-Cola tens of millions. The division, says Weatherup, will make its 15% earnings growth target by the end of this year, three years after he declared the crisis.

If all stays on track, Weatherup will have pulled off one of the hardest acts in corporate life. Call it doomsday management. Simply defined, doomsday management is a strategy leaders can use to radically transform a successful and profitable company before its success—and overconfidence and complacency and bloat—catches up with it.

The idea is based on a familiar phenomenon: Most organizations, like most people, won't change fundamentally until they absolutely have to. Any doctor will tell you how folks often refuse to give up the Camels or the Häagen-Dazs Chocolate Chocolate Chip until after a heart attack or stroke. Similarly, in a study of 40 companies, Gibb Dyer, a management professor at Brigham Young University, found that before any could change, each first had to hit bad times and, in many cases, call in a new CEO to bail itself out.

Smart managers don't wait for the crisis to overtake them. They see it coming far off and tell other employees about it so persuasively that everybody gets scared. Then, advises Dan Ciampa, CEO of Rath & Strong, a consulting firm in Lexington, Massachusetts, the leader must give people an idea or vision or picture that allows them to do something about the crisis. In most cases this means offering people a plan, plus the resources, time, and trust, to address the crisis and devise solutions.

And what might the crisis be? The rich history of human calamity suggests any number of possibilities, but in practice three categories seem to cover the worst that most companies will face. . . .

At Pepsi-Cola, Weatherup divined that if he was going to change the company, he would have to make everyone in the organization feel a sense of urgency. Saying that he wanted 15% earnings growth was not enough. To send a strong message, from 1990 to 1992 he held a number of backbreaking, three-day meetings that ultimately included each of his 30,000 employees. Weatherup used the meetings for two purposes: to keep hammering away at his message that a crisis was at hand, and to fill every employee with his vision of a new, customer-driven organization and the tools they would together use to build it.

At the start of each meeting Weatherup would tell what he called the burning-platform story. It seems that a few years ago a North Sea oil rig caught fire. One worker, trained not to jump from the 150-foot-high rig into the icy sea but to wait for help no matter how bad things got, leaped anyway. He survived. Asked afterward why he stepped off the edge, the worker said he looked behind him and saw an approaching wall of fire and looked down and saw the sea: "I chose probable death over certain death."

For Pepsi-Cola, business as usual was the equivalent of certain death, Weatherup argued. To make sure everyone in the audience understood this, he spent the next few hours of each meeting talking about what he calls customer pain. He would tell about a run-in he'd had a few years back with David Glass, CEO of Wal-Mart, an important Pepsi customer. The first time Weatherup met Glass, the retailer told him, "There is nothing about the way your company does business with us that I like." Weatherup related the story as a way to open discussion on such customer complaints as missed or inaccurate deliveries, poor merchandising, and bad communications. All this criticism, remember, was coming from an executive of one of America's most successful companies.

After thoroughly shaking up his people, Weatherup used the meetings to show employees how they could respond to the crisis. He explained his new vision: Pepsi-Cola would become an organization focused on customer needs and filled with employees who know how to reengineer the processes by which they do their work. That may sound like managerial babble, but he backed it up with specific proposals.

Weatherup designed the meetings as a mechanism to get one layer of the organization to train the next, which in turn would train the next. Attending the first meeting in 1990—with the trains—were Weatherup's top 11 managers, who had three months to learn such disciplines as reengineering, continuous inprovement, and mapping of work flows. In most cases, this learning required the managers to actually go out and find a function, system, or service that needed improving. After the 90 days, the 11 spearheaded another three-day meeting, where they used their real-world experiences to train the next 70 managers at Pepsi, who then got three months to prepare themselves to train the next 400. By the fall of 1992, at a series of meetings around the country, Weatherup had reached out to all 30,000 of his people. Says he: "To enroll the next group of people, the managers had to understand the changes going on and the vision."

An example of the resultant change: The meetings encouraged one team, made up of Pepsi-Cola managers and hourly workers, to analyze the way the company delivered soft drinks to supermarkets, stores, and restaurants. Before long, the team realized that the company was wasting lots of time and money by having an employee check soft drink stock on delivery trucks at the gates of the bottling factory each morning. Now the people loading the trucks make sure the soda orders are correct, thus speeding the trucks off directly from the loading dock. Weatherup estimates the new system gives each of his 10,000 trucks a precious 45 minutes of extra delivery time each day, which lets them make more stops and sell more soda.

Once all of Pepsi-Cola's people had been through the meetings, Weatherup, in September 1992, announced a massive reorganization, breaking his traditional hierarchical organization into 107 fairly autonomous units. Each is defined by how Pepsi's customers—supermarkets, restaurants, theaters—see their market, not by some arbitrary territory. Now instead of, say, a Southeast region, there's an Orlando, Florida, market unit that focuses all its energy on customers there. Besides giving customers more attention, the reorganization sent a strong message that the crisis Weatherup declared was real, not just the latest flavor-of-the-month management fad.

It's still too early to tell for certain, but Pepsi-Cola's transformation seems to be working. Profits for the first quarter of 1993 rose 22%, and employees are changing the organization with gusto.

Case Analysis

Craig Weatherup at Pepsi-Cola faced an unusual problem. His company was highly successful, but his view of the future said it had to change.

Weatherup's approach was planned organizational change. His first major step was to develop a need for change in all employees. Weatherup started with his 11 top managers by laying down a nonnegotiable goal— 15% annual growth in earnings. To get their attention, he used a form of cultural symbolism. The model train was a symbol of part of his vision of a new Pepsi-Cola. The train also likely helped reduce resistance to change among those 11 managers.

Weatherup had a clear vision for the company. He wanted it to be customer driven, process focused, and dedicated to continuous improvement. The basic transformation that Weatherup was after is an example of the revolutionary model of planned change described in Chapter 19.

All employees of the company learned about the new vision in a series of meetings. Those meetings played the important role of moving Pepsi-Cola closer to Weatherup's vision. The meetings also gave employees common information about the change, reducing their resistance to it. In 1992, the company formed the 107 customer-based divisions. The new organizational design marked a key point in the tranformation of the company.

A

Foundation Ideas about Organizations and Management

· Telephone relay assemblers at Western Electric Company's Hawthorne Plant in 1920. Workers such as these were the subjects of the now famous Hawthorne Studies.

After reading this appendix, you should be able to . . .

- Understand some foundation ideas about organizations and management.
- Know the cornerstone role the concept "division of labor" plays among the foundation ideas.
- Describe Scientific Management and the way it develops the division of labor of an organization.
- Have insights about the distinction between bureaucratic, bureaupathic, and bureautic behavior.
- Explain group dynamics, power, conflict, and leadership in organizations.

Appendix Overview

◢ FIGURE A-1

Adam Smith's
Observations on the
Functions and
Dysfunctions of the
Division of Labor

Manifest functions	Latent dysfunctions
Greater productivity	Intellectual degradation
Increased dexterity	Low political and social involvement
Save time by not moving from one task location to another	Low physical activity
Innovations	
Greater expertise	

Smith also felt the division of labor could have some latent dysfunctional consequences. Doing the same task repeatedly could lead to mental degradation. The workers would no longer perceive the task as stimulating, and their mental processes would slow. In a related effect, the workers might lose interest in their political and social environment outside the work setting. Smith felt that lack of involvement in work led to decreased political and social involvement. Workers also would become physically inactive because their work did not require them to move about.[4]

Smith described a high degree of task specialization in the 18 operations of making a pin. Division of labor, however, does not always lead to high specialization and routine work. Figure A-2 shows the relationships between the division of labor and task specialization. Division of labor spans the entire continuum from low to high task specialization. Smith's description of making a straight pin is on the far right of the task specialization continuum. The job of a heart surgeon is on the far left. As described in Chapter 9, the degree of routine in jobs with high task specialization is an important consideration in designing jobs.

◢ *Scientific Management: Frederick W. Taylor (1911)*

"The principal object of management should be to secure the maximum prosperity for the employer, coupled with the maximum prosperity for each employee."[5] Those words are from the opening paragraph of Frederick W. Taylor's book, *The Principles*

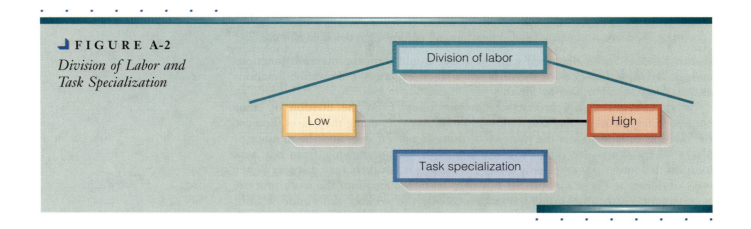

◢ FIGURE A-2

Division of Labor and
Task Specialization

of Scientific Management. Taylor felt he had developed a new approach to management that produced positive results for both employer and employee.[6]

The usual approach to management in Taylor's day was based on antagonistic relationships between management and labor. Management wanted to get as much output from labor at the lowest possible cost. Workers tried to protect their interests by not working too hard. They believed they would put themselves or their coworkers out of work if they worked at a faster pace. Neither side felt cooperation could lead to maximum prosperity for both.

Management wanted to maximize profits, and workers wanted the highest possible wages. Disputes between management and labor centered on what each viewed as mutually exclusive goals. Taylor felt his system of Scientific Management could maximize both goals. Both sides had to undergo a "mental revolution." Each side had to rid itself of antagonistic views of the other. Taylor felt they should view the profits of the organization as coming from cooperation between management and workers. In short, management needed the workers and workers needed management to get what they both wanted.

Scientific Management is based on the following four principles.[7]

- Develop a science for each element of work. Carefully study the jobs to develop standard work practices. Standardize the tools used by workers.
- Scientifically select each worker. Carefully train and continually develop each worker to produce at maximum potential.
- Management and workers must cooperate to ensure that work is done according to standard procedures. Management's behavior toward the workers should include "better treatment, more kindly treatment, more consideration for their wishes, and an opportunity for them to express their wants freely."[8]
- Change the division of labor between management and workers. Management plans and makes task assignments. Workers carry out tasks assigned by managers.

· *Frederick W. Taylor, author of the* Principles of Scientific Management.

The four principles of **Scientific Management** describe a division of work between management and workers. Managers planned and designed the work. They made task assignments, set performance goals, and made time schedules. Managers also selected and trained the workers to do the tasks according to standard procedures and gave the workers quick feedback about how they were doing. Under Taylor's system, increased individual productivity was rewarded with economic incentives. Taylor urged paying piece rates and daily bonuses for improved and sustained worker productivity.

Taylor's Scientific Management sharply contrasted with the management practices of his day. Under his system, jobs were designed after careful study. Workers were selected carefully and assigned to the tasks after the jobs were designed. No longer would jobs be done by "trial-and-error" methods handed down from one worker to another. Lastly, cooperation was substituted for the antagonistic worker-management relationship that existed at the time.

. . . .

↵ *Toward a Theory of Administration: Henri Fayol (1919)*

Henri Fayol began his work career in 1860 at age 19 as a mining engineer for the Commentry-Fourchambault Company. He eventually became the managing director of the company, a position he held until he retired in 1918. When he was the chief executive, Fayol brought the company from the brink of bankruptcy to a high level of success.[9]

Fayol believed that an organization's success depended on both technical and administrative skills. The farther one moved up the management hierarchy of the organization, the more administrative skills were needed, and the less technical skills were needed.

Schools in Fayol's time taught technical skills such as accounting, finance, and engineering, but did not teach administration. Believing that administration was neglected due to the absence of any theory of administration, Fayol set out from 1918 until his death in 1925 to contribute to and encourage the development of a theory of administration.

Fayol took a broad view of administration. He felt his theory of administration applied to all types of organizations, public or private. He made these comments about "administration" in a speech two years before he died:

> The meaning which I have given to the word *administration* and which has been generally adopted, broadens considerably the field of administrative science. It embraces not only the public service but enterprises of every size and description, of every form and every purpose. All undertakings require planning, organization, command, co-ordination and control, and in order to function properly, all must observe the same general principles. We are no longer confronted with several administrative sciences, but with one alone, which can be applied equally well to public and to private affairs.[10]

Note two aspects of this quotation: First, Fayol felt all organizations required planning, organizing, command, coordination, and control. Fayol felt these were the five major functions and activities of a manager.

Fayol's five management functions have endured the test of time. A review of research that focused on managerial activities showed that an impressive number of activities fell into Fayol's five functions. Managers not only did these classical functions, but they *should* do them. The time spent on these areas and the skills required to do them were associated with higher performance of the manager's unit or organization.[11]

Second, note Fayol's comment that managers "all must observe the same general principles." Fayol described some principles of management along with the functions of management. The principles were central to his theory of administration. They are a set of tools a manager needs to perform the functions of management.

A dictionary defines a "principle" as "a fundamental truth, law, doctrine . . . the law of nature by which a thing operates . . . the method of a thing's operation."[12] Fayol's principles, then, should be useful in almost any situation. Possibly recognizing the literal meaning of "principle," Fayol said the following early in his chapter entitled "General Principles of Management":

> For preference I shall adopt the term principles whilst disassociating it from any suggestion of rigidity, for there is nothing rigid or absolute about management affairs, it is all a question of proportion. Seldom do we have to apply the same principle twice in identical conditions; allowance must be made for different changing circumstances, for men just as different and changing and for many other variable elements.
>
> Therefore principles are flexible and capable of adaptation to every need; it is a matter of knowing how to make use of them, which is a difficult art requiring intelligence, experience, decision and proportion. Compounded of tact and experience, proportion is one of the foremost attributes of the manager.[13]

Note Fayol's use of the term "proportion." He was warning managers that they cannot apply his principles rigidly and absolutely in all circumstances. They must tailor the application of the principles to the specific circumstances they face, using a clear **sense of proportion**.

Fayol's first principle was the division of labor. The importance of this principle to his scheme can be seen in his remark: "Specialization belongs to the natural order."[14] The division of labor applied not only to tasks done by individuals, but to the total organization as well. Like Adam Smith, Fayol described the manifest functional consequences of the division of labor. Fayol warned, though, that the "division of work has its limits which experience and a sense of proportion teach us may not be exceeded."[15]

Fayol described the principle of **authority and responsibility** as follows:

> Authority is the right to give orders and the power to exact obedience. Distinction must be made between a manger's official authority deriving from office and personal authority

compounded of intelligence, experience, moral worth, ability to lead, past services, etc. In the makeup of a good head personal authority is the indispensable complement of official authority. . . . Responsibility is a corollary of authority, it is its natural consequence and essential counterpart, and wheresoever authority is exercised responsibility arises.

[G]enerally speaking, responsibility is feared as much as authority is sought after, and fear of responsibility paralyzes much initiative and destroys many good qualities. A good leader should possess and infuse into those around him courage to accept responsibility.[16]

Official authority is in the function the individual performs. Personal authority arises from the characteristics of the manager. The organization gives official authority to the manager; the manager brings personal authority to the organization. Fayol felt both types of authority must be present to have a good executive.

You can see Fayol's idea of a sense of proportion most clearly in his description of the principle of centralization:

Like division of work, centralization belongs to the natural order; this turns on the fact that in every organism, animal or social, sensations converge toward the brain or directive part, and from the brain or directive part orders are sent out which set all parts of the organism in movement. Centralization is not a system of management good or bad of itself, capable or being adopted or discarded at the whim of managers or of circumstances; it is always present to a greater or lesser extent. The question of centralization or decentralization, is a simple question of proportion, it is a matter of finding the optimum degree for the particular concern.[17]

As noted earlier, delegation of authority is the management tool used to get the desired degree of centralization or decentralization. Although Fayol did not use the phrase "delegation of authority," he clearly implied its use.[18]

Another of his principles was **unity of command**, which he described as follows:[19]

For any action whatsoever, an employee should receive orders from one superior only. . . . Should [this principle] be violated, authority is undermined, discipline is in jeopardy, order disturbed and stability threatened. This rule seems fundamental to me, so I have given it the rank of principle. As soon as two superiors wield their authority over the same person or department, uneasiness makes itself felt, and should the cause persist, the disorder increases, the malady takes on the appearance of an animal organism troubled by a foreign body, and the following consequences are to be observed: either the dual command ends in disappearance or elimination of one of the superiors and organic well-being is restored, or else the organism continues to wither away. In no case is there adaptation of the social organism to dual command.[20]

A principle related to unity of command was **unity of direction**: "One head and one plan for a group of activities having the same objective."[21] Fayol was describing a principle for determining the division of labor of the organization. Set up a department or unit and have a single goal for that particular unit. He closed his description of the principles of management with the following observation:

Without principles, one is in darkness and chaos; interest, experience and proportion are still very handicapped, even with the best principles. The principle is the lighthouse, fixing the bearings but it can only serve those who already know the way into port.[22]

We are all capable of reading his principles, but Fayol was not certain we would all make good managers. There is much more to management than a set of principles. For some people, the principles of management will be of no help in making them good managers. Others may have little book knowledge about management, but are good intuitive managers.

Fayol began his description of management principles by saying their application often is hampered by various factors. Unfortunately, Fayol offered no guidelines for applying his principles, nor did he identify the factors. You will find in other parts of this book that his principles continue to be applied today. We are now guided systematically, however, by many considerations unknown to Fayol in the early 1920s.

Figure A-3 summarizes this discussion of Fayol's concepts and shows some relationships among them. Delegation of authority gets the desired degree of centralization or decentralization. Delegation also leads to a division of labor in the

"A sense of proportion"

"A sense of proportion"

Delegation of authority

↓

Centralization—decentralization

↓

Division of labor

↓

| Unity of command | Unity of direction |

". . . generally speaking, responsibility is feared as much as authority is sought after, and fear of responsibility paralyzes much initiative and destroys many good qualities. A good leader should possess and infuse into those around him courage to accept responsibility.

organization. Unity of command and unity of direction are guides for the design of the organization. Think of these concepts as Fayol's tools for designing and managing organizations.

Bureaucracy: Max Weber (1922)

Max Weber was a prominent German political scientist, economist, and sociologist. A major contribution was his analysis of bureaucracy as a form of organization and management. He believed bureaucracy was an efficient and successful form of administration.[23] Before discussing Weber's description of bureaucracy, let's find out what the word *bureaucracy* means to you.

WHAT "BUREAUCRACY" MEANS TO ME

Note on a separate sheet of paper the words or phrases you associate with *bureaucracy*.

Table A-1 shows words and phrases students often associate with the word *bureaucracy*. Check your list to see if you associated some of those words or phrases with bureaucracy. If you perceive bureaucracy in only negative terms, you will find Weber's analysis unusual. He clearly felt bureaucracy was an efficient and effective form of organization and management.

It is useful to distinguish between bureaucratic behavior as defined by Weber and other behavioral responses often found in bureaucracies. Although Weber expected bureaucracies to have good features (manifest functions), many words and phrases in Table A-1 describe the latent dysfunctions. This section first describes the manifest functions of bureaucracy and then turns to some latent dysfunctions of this form of organization and management.

· *Max Weber, German sociologist and political scientist, framed a theory of bureaucracy.*

BUREAUCRACY

Bureaucracy is an administrative structure with well-defined offices or functions and hierarchical relationships among the functions. The offices or functions have clearly defined duties, rights, and responsibilities. Each office or function is designed without regard for who will hold the office. Relationships within a bureaucracy are impersonal. Decisions are made according to existing rules, procedures, and policies. Bureaucracies attain goals with precision, reliability, and efficiency.[24]

Bureaucracies use a form of authority Weber called legal or rational authority. **Legal or rational authority** is in a position and exists before a person takes the position or function in a bureaucracy. The authority is defined by the bureaucracy when it develops its division of labor. The person who takes a position then assumes the authority of that position. Although authority is initially in the function, the person holding the function can change that authority.

Weber identified two other types of authority that he felt were not characteristic of a bureaucracy. **Charismatic authority** is based on the personal qualities of the individual. A person has **traditional authority** because of family relationships. With traditional authority, people assume organizational positions because of their ancestry, a common situation in medieval Europe. You already have seen these types of authority in the discussion of Fayol's theory of administration. Recall Fayol's distinction between official and personal authority.

It is possible to find the three types of authority in modern organizations. Weber felt rational authority brought stability to a bureaucracy because the authority stayed in the function after the person left. Charismatic and traditional authority are unstable because the authority goes with the person when the person leaves the organization. Weber felt legal or rational authority was a basic feature of bureaucratic organization and was a reason bureaucracy was more successful than earlier organizational forms.

Weber believed the following features account for the efficiency of bureaucracies. Bureaucracies in their ideal form have all these qualities.

- Clearly defined and specialized functions—the division of labor of a bureaucracy
- Use of legal authority
- Hierarchical form
- Written rules and procedures
- Technically trained bureaucrats
- Appointment to positions based on technical expertise
- Promotions based on technical competence
- Clearly defined career path

Weber felt bureaucracies were rational and predictable systems. The rationality followed from the objectivity and impersonality of decisions. Decisions were based on fact and made according to existing written rules and procedures so that the decisions would be consistent. The unusual features of any specific case were not to be considered. Predictability followed from the fixed formal relationships among clearly defined hierarchically organized functions.

The following excerpt from Weber summarizes his view of bureaucracy. Compare his view to commonly held views of bureaucracy, including your own.

> The fully developed bureaucratic mechanism compares with other organizations exactly as does the machine with the non-mechanical modes of production. Precision, speed, unambiguity, knowledge of files, continuity, discretion, unity, strict subordination, reduction of friction and of material and personnel costs, these are raised to the optimum point in the strictly bureaucratic administration.
>
> Its specific nature ... develops the more perfectly the more the bureaucracy is "dehumanized," the more completely it succeeds in eliminating from official business, love, hatred, and all purely personal, irrational, and emotional elements which escape calculation.[25]

TABLE A-1

Words and Phrases Students Often Associate with Bureaucracy

Communication difficulties
Cumbersome
Doesn't do anything
Government
Hierarchy
Inefficient
Inflexible
Large
Maze of departments
Paper work
Red tape
Regulations
Slow
Uncooperative

From this point on, the word *bureaucracy* is used in the strictly Weberian sense. All behavior Weber saw in the bureaucracy such as impersonality and reference to written rules and procedures will be called "bureaucratic behavior." Individuals who hold administrative positions in a bureaucracy are "bureaucrats." The latter term also is used in the Weberian sense and does not connote anything negative.

BUREAUPATHOLOGY

The words you associated earlier with bureaucracy reflect your experiences with such organizations. If those words were negative, you probably experienced the latent dysfunctions of bureaucracy, not the speed, precision, and efficiency Weber expected. We now need to find out why bureaucracies often do not display the manifest functions described by Weber.

The term bureaupathic behavior refers to the latent dysfunctions of bureaucracy. **Bureaupathology** is an exaggeration of bureaucratic behavior; the following is a good description:[26]

> excessive aloofness, ritualistic attachment to routines and procedures, and resistance to change; . . . associated with these behavior patterns is a petty insistence upon rights of authority and status.[27]

Bureaucracies often exhibit two major types of bureaupathic behavior. **Trained incapacity**[28] occurs when a bureaucrat's training and experience make him unable to respond to new and unpredictable events. Bureaucracy works well when events are predictable. A bureaucrat is trained and has experience in handling situations A, B, C, and D. When suddenly faced with situation F, the bureaucrat finds it difficult to adapt to the new demand. Trained incapacity refers to training that prepares a bureaucrat to handle events A, B, C, and D, but leaves the individual almost incapable of dealing with F.

The second type of bureaupathic behavior is the means-ends inversion.[29] Recall that bureaucracies have written rules, procedures, and policies to deal with usual and routine events. These are usually designed to help reach the goals of the bureaucracy. The inversion of policies (means) with service to clients (ends) occurs when a bureaucrat focuses on the policy as if it had a life of its own. Instead of believing policies further the goals of the bureaucracy, the bureaucrat believes the policies are ends in themselves. Describing bureaucracies as "red tape" is a common reaction to a means-end inversion.

The reasons for bureaupathic behavior are found both in the characteristics of bureaucracies and in the individual characteristics of some bureaucrats. Bureaucracies pressure bureaucrats to apply the rules and policies uniformly. In the desire to provide impersonal service and avoid appearing to favor any individual client, bureaucrats try not to consider the individual qualities of any specific case. Bureaucrats are expected to deal competently with repeated and routine events and are rewarded for having done so.[30]

Bureaucrats vary in their degree of personal insecurity and desire to control others.[31] Insecure bureaucrats may emphasize existing rules, policies, and procedures for fear of making a mistake. Bureaucrats who wish to control the behavior of others can do so by ignoring the unique qualities of a client's case. They may simply say "We don't handle that in this department" or "You will have to see Ms. Wright for authorization."

Figure A-4 summarizes the relationships between bureaucratic and bureaupathic behavior. Weber described the manifest functions of a bureaucracy; bureaupathology describes some latent dysfunctions. These latent dysfunctions of bureaucracy are the negative experiences we all remember.

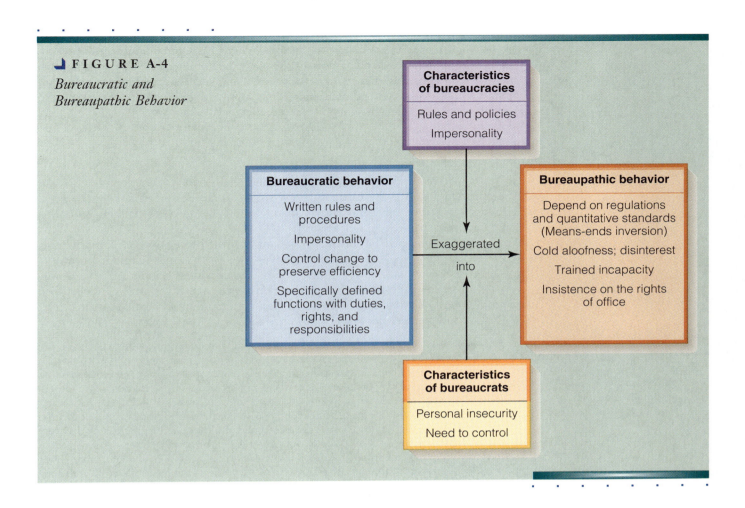

FIGURE A-4
Bureaucratic and Bureaupathic Behavior

Characteristics of bureaucracies

Rules and policies

Impersonality

Bureaucratic behavior

Written rules and procedures

Impersonality

Control change to preserve efficiency

Specifically defined functions with duties, rights, and responsibilities

Exaggerated

into

Bureaupathic behavior

Depend on regulations and quantitative standards (Means-ends inversion)

Cold aloofness; disinterest

Trained incapacity

Insistence on the rights of office

Characteristics of bureaucrats

Personal insecurity

Need to control

BUREAUSIS

A third dysfunction is sometimes seen in people who are clients or members of a bureaucracy. It is called bureausis; its victims are bureautics. **Bureausis** is a condition where the client or member is intolerant of bureaucratic behavior. The person does not like the application of written rules, procedures, and policies or the routine character of bureaucracies. He views bureaucracies as manifestations of "red tape." Bureautics want their individual case attended to in a personal way. They do not understand why exceptions cannot be made to existing policies. Bureautics will either have negative reactions to bureaupathic behavior or view all bureaucratic behavior as bureaupathic.[32]

Mary Parker Follett's Observations on Organizations and Management (1925)

Mary Parker Follett worked mainly as a social worker among the poor in the Roxbury section of Boston. Although her work career did not involve management, she made several basic and enduring observations about organizations and management.[33]

Follett was born in Boston in 1868. She graduated from Radcliffe College in 1898 and established herself as an important contributor to political science. She made her observations on organizations and management from the mid-1920s to the early 1930s. She lectured to many business groups in both the United States and England.

To fully appreciate the contributions she made, try to remember how long ago she made her observations. Check them for yourself and see whether you agree they are basic and elegant in their substance and logic. Here are three of her observations on organizations and management—power, conflict, and leadership.

· *Mary Parker Follett, an early observer of organizations and management, offered many basic ideas that have lasted to this day.*

 POWER

Follett conceived of power as capacity. Although her point was not completely clear, she apparently meant the capacity to get things done. Power cannot be delegated although authority can. She clearly distinguished between power and authority, treating each separately in her analysis.[34]

Follett distinguished power-over from power-with. **Power-over** is dominance or coercion; it is control based on force. **Power-with** is "a jointly developed power, a co-active, not a coercive power."[35] She offered power-with as an alternative to power-over, because she believed human organizations were cooperative systems. Follett had a positive view of power and saw it as basic to organizations and management.

Follett summarized her view of power as follows:

> [I]f we have any power, any genuine power, let us hold on to it, let us not give it away. We could not anyway if we wanted to. We can confer authority; but power or capacity, no man can give or take. The manager cannot share *his* power with division superintendent or foreman or workmen, but he can give them opportunities for developing *their* power. Functions may have to be redistributed; something the manager does now had better perhaps be left to a division superintendent, to a foreman, even to a workman; but that is a different matter; let us not confuse the two things. Indeed, one of the aims of that very redistribution of function should be how it can serve to evolve more power—more power to turn the wheels. More power, not division of power, should always be our aim; more power for the best possible furtherance of that activity, whatever it may be, to which we are giving our life.[36]

 CONFLICT

Follett's analysis of conflict appeared in a paper entitled "Constructive Conflict."[37] The title of the paper gives you a clue about her views on conflict in organizations. Follett felt conflict was neither good nor bad. Conflict is difference, not warfare. The differences may be in opinions or interests. She felt conflict cannot be avoided. Instead of running from conflict, managers should put conflict to use in their organizations.

Follett felt there were three main ways of dealing with conflict: dominance, compromise, and integration of desires. The first two are ways of reducing conflict. **Dominance** means one side to a conflict wins over the others. **Compromise** means each side gives up something to settle the issue. In each of these instances, the basic conflict issue is not settled. Although one party may win, or both parties agree on a basis for settling the dispute, the reason for the conflict remains. Conflict could occur about the same matter or issue at a later time.

Integration of desires was Follett's creative suggestion about how to manage conflict. This approach finds a solution that fully meets the goals of each party in a dispute. Both parties get what they truly want. Neither party gives up anything.

Follett's concept of integration probably seems strange to you. Here is her example of how integration of desires worked to settle a dispute among some dairymen:

> A Dairymen's Co-operative League almost went to pieces last year on the question of precedence in unloading cans at a creamery platform. The men who came down the hill (the creamery was on a down grade) thought they should have precedence; the men who came up the hill thought they should unload first. The thinking of both sides in the

controversy was thus confined within the walls of these two possibilities, and this prevented their even trying to find a way of settling the dispute which would avoid these alternatives. The solution was obviously to change the position of the platform so that both up-hillers and down-hillers could unload at the same time. But this solution was not found until they had asked the advice of a more or less professional integrator. When, however, it was pointed out to them, they were quite ready to accept it.[38]

Integration of desires unshackles us from existing alternatives and lets us creatively discover alternatives that are not mutually exclusive. Integration discovers something; compromise uses only what exists. With integration, conflict is put to work to help discover new, creative solutions to problems and issues in organizations.

Follett's integration approach to conflict involved two steps. First, the differences of the parties in conflict must be laid out without hiding or suppressing any information. Complete facts about what the parties to the conflict want is a necessary first step. Second, the information must be carefully broken into its various parts. It may also be necessary to understand the symbolic meaning of elements of the dispute.

Follett recognized that integration would not always be possible. Some conflict situations are limited by the physical resources available. Assume, for example, there is only one copying machine in an office. Two employees both need the machine simultaneously to meet their individual deadlines. Integration usually is not possible in this situation.

LEADERSHIP

Follett felt the prevailing view of leadership was based on qualities such as aggressiveness and domination. The leader tried to impose his will upon others. Leadership meant giving orders and getting compliance to those orders.[39]

Follett's alternative view of leadership was filled with positive qualities. A leader has a vision of the future and can describe the purpose toward which the organization is striving. He focuses the energies of people toward that purpose. A leader not only knows the technical aspects of his job, but also understands the total situation and the relationships among its many parts. Problems are not just solved. Events are structured and decisions made to head off problems before they happen.

Decisions are made with an understanding of their long-term effect. Leaders do not make decisions that focus only on the present. They know that any situation constantly evolves and that a decision made now affects future states of the situation.

Leaders train and develop their subordinates to become leaders. By developing leaders below them, Follett believed, managers increase the total power in the situation they are managing.

Good leaders do not want passive followers. Follett regarded blind obedience to orders and directives as undesirable. Instead, followers should try to influence their leaders by suggesting alternative courses of action. They also should question directives that are either wrong or cannot be carried out.

Follett's view of the personal qualities of a leader gives a vivid picture of the characteristics of a good leader: "tenacity, steadfastness of purpose, tactfulness, steadiness in stormy periods."[40]

Extended discussions about power, conflict, and leadership appeared in earlier chapters; see Chapters 15, 11, and 12. Follett's observations appeared many years before the publication of much of the research described in those chapters.

. . . .

The Functions of the Executive: Chester I. Barnard (1938)

Chester Barnard was an engineer by training who became the president of the New Jersey Bell Telephone Company and later the first executive head of the United

Services Organization. His book, *The Functions of the Executive*, is rich in basic contributions to our thinking about organizations and management.[41]

Barnard defined an organization as "a system of consciously coordinated activities or forces of two or more persons."[42] Barnard's definition implies that any system of two or more people with consciously coordinated activities is an organization. Organizations are based on cooperation and have a conscious, deliberate purpose.[43]

Barnard believed organizations formed because individuals had a purpose or purposes, but also had limitations. The limitations could be knowledge, financial resources, or physical resources. The person with the purpose needed the cooperation of one or more other people to achieve that purpose. **Purpose plus limitations** leads to a system of cooperative action.

How does an organization get people to join this system of cooperative action? Organizations offer inducements in exchange for contributions. Inducements include salary and fringe benefits. Contributions are things such as the job to be done. Barnard felt a person joined an organization when the inducements slightly exceeded the contributions.[44] Today this relationship between inducements and contributions is called the "**inducements-contributions balance**."[45] Maintaining the balance such that people join and stay with the organization is an important executive function.[46]

Barnard distinguished between two types of motivation in organizations— motivation to participate and motivation to perform. **Motivation to participate**[47] is the motivation of an individual to join and stay with the organization and perform at a minimally acceptable level. The minimally acceptable level varies from one organization to another, and from one part of the same organization to another. When you first join an organization, you learn the minimum performance standards. If you fall below this performance level, you could experience sanctions, particularly during a period of probationary employment. The inducements-contributions balance is closely related to the motivation to participate. Maintenance of the inducements-contributions balance lets managers affect the motivation to participate.

Barnard's definition of an organization asserted that membership of people is a basic building block of organizations. Motivation to participate must be influenced by the executive. The inducements-contributions balance is the major tool available to the executive to affect this type of motivation.

Barnard felt managers must first attend to the motivation to participate. Once they have solved the problem of membership, they can attend to the second type of motivation, the **motivation to perform**.[48] This type of motivation focuses on performance levels higher than the minimum. Managers use both monetary and nonmonetary incentives to get higher performance levels. Earlier Chapter 8 examined the role of incentives in motivation.

Notice the relationships among Barnard's observations. First, the simple definition emphasizes consciously coordinated activities of two or more people. Second, purpose plus limitations cause people to engage in cooperative behavior with one or more others. People need to be attracted to this system of coordinated activity and induced to participate. The need to attract people to the system and keep them there leads to a concern about motivation to participate and the inducements-contributions balance. With these five concepts, you can analyze the birth and growth of any organization.

Barnard used the concept of the **zone of indifference** to describe how people could respond to orders and directives from others.[49] Figure A-5 shows the zone of indifference. People execute orders falling within their zone of indifference without any particular thought or question. A person questions, and possibly does not act on, orders that fall outside the zone. These orders might be demeaning, such as being told to sweep the office floor, or they might be orders that could be interpreted as illegal or immoral. In both cases, the order falls outside the zone of indifference and will not be accepted by the person.

The zone of indifference is closely related to the inducements-contributions balance. Managers affect the width of the zone of indifference by changing inducements offered for contributions requested from a person.

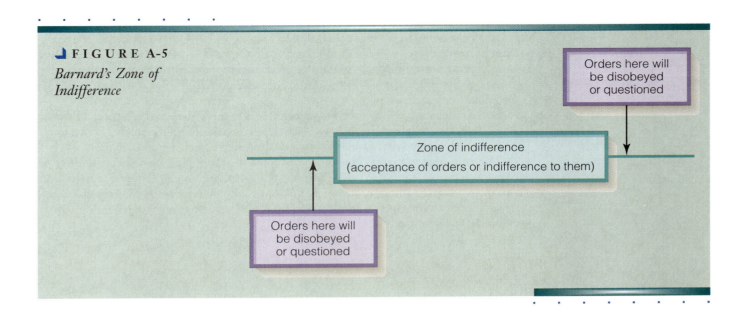

FIGURE A-5

Barnard's Zone of Indifference

Orders here will
be disobeyed
or questioned

Zone of indifference
(acceptance of orders or indifference to them)

Orders here will
be disobeyed
or questioned

The Hawthorne Studies (1939)

The Hawthorne Studies were a large research program done at the Hawthorne Plant of the Western Electric Company from the late 1920s to the mid-1930s. The plant produced various parts for telephone switching systems. This research was a landmark work in the social sciences in the United States.[50]

The Hawthorne Studies were preceded and stimulated by a set of illumination experiments done in the Hawthorne plant in the early 1920s. These studies were designed to determine whether various lighting levels affected human productivity. The experimental design used a control group where lighting was not varied. An experimental group experienced changes in light levels.

The results of the experiments baffled the investigators. Lighting was increased and productivity went up. Then it was decreased and productivity went up. The lighting was severely reduced and productivity went up! The lighting for the control group was not changed, but the group's productivity also increased! Eventually, the researchers concluded that simply being part of the experiment, which focused new and greater attention on the workers, increased productivity.[51] Previously, interaction between supervisors and coworkers was limited. Attention had focused mainly on the work, not on the workers themselves.

Following the illumination experiments, several researchers from Harvard University began studying some groups of workers in the plant. Their goal was to understand the factors that contributed to differences in human productivity. The researchers concluded that a more empathetic or people-oriented form of management led to more productivity than a directive, authoritarian, and money-oriented form of management. People wanted more than monetary incentives for working.

The Hawthorne Studies also made original contributions to understanding the dynamics of informal groups in organizations. The groups studied had norms of behavior—rules that governed the behavior of group members. The groups differed in types of norms. Some groups were cooperative and agreed with the aims of management. Other groups had norms that were antagonistic. The groups put immense social pressure on members to conform to their norms.

Two broad conclusions usually are attributed to the Hawthorne Studies: (1) a people-oriented approach to management is superior to a more oppressive form of management, and (2) the social dynamics within a work group can affect worker productivity.

Some researchers doing secondary analyses of data published in the original reports have come to varying conclusions. One researcher found support for a driving form of management and use of monetary incentives.[52] He felt the researchers moved from presenting descriptive results to promoting a new form of management. By doing so, the original Hawthorne researchers went well beyond the results of their research.[53]

A lively debate has also focused on whether group dynamics affect productivity.[54] Some researchers felt their analyses showed no association between group dynamics and worker productivity. Others felt social dynamics affected productivity.

The importance of the Hawthorne Studies in developing our understanding of organizations should not be diminished by disputes about research design and research results. Although strong conclusions cannot be drawn directly from the research, the studies were an impetus to further developing our understanding about behavior in organizations.

Summary

Figure A-6 graphically summarizes the foundation ideas about organizations and management described in this appendix. The three tiers represent different levels of analysis and different orientations of the concepts within a tier.

The tier at the bottom of the figure shows the basic building blocks for the design and management of organizations. Several concepts in the first tier have deep historical roots. Henri Fayol brought many together when he first developed a theory of administration. These

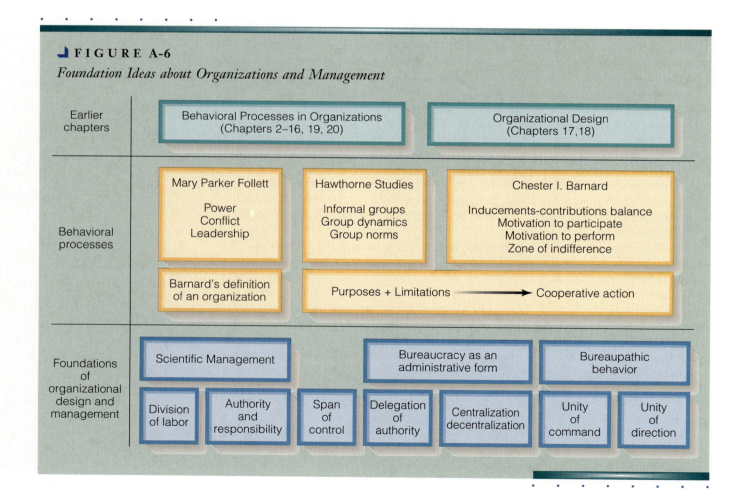

FIGURE A-6

Foundation Ideas about Organizations and Management

concepts are useful today and have played an important role throughout this book.

Weber's analysis of bureaucracy showed the manifest functions of bureaucracy and the conditions under which it works best. Bureaupathic behavior, the dysfunctions of bureaucracy, can also occur. The emergence of that behavior has strong implications for managing bureaucracies.

The second tier in the figure shows concepts that deal more with the behavioral processes of an organization than with organizational design. Mary Parker Follett and Chester I. Barnard each gave us some basic insights into those organizational processes. The contributions of Follett, Barnard, and the Hawthorne Studies are the groundwork upon which this book was built.

The tier at the top of the figure shows the earlier parts of this book that described behavioral processes and organizational design. Our understanding of those processes now is deeper than the ideas of the early writers; nevertheless, the basic ideas in this appendix continue to have utility.

. . . .

➥ Key Terms

authority and responsibility 622	dominance 628	purpose plus limitations 630
bureaucracy 625	inducements-contributions	Scientific Management 621
bureaupathology 626	balance 630	sense of proportion 622
bureausis 627	integration of desires 628	span of control 618
centralization-decentralization 618	legal or rational authority 625	traditional authority 625
charismatic authority 625	motivation to participate 630	unity of command 623
compromise 628	motivation to perform 630	unity of direction 623
delegation of authority 618	power-over 628	zone of indifference 630
division of labor 618	power-with 628	

. . . .

➥ Review and Discussion Questions

1. Review the basic organizational and management concepts illustrated by the biblical passage describing Jethro's advice to Moses. How are those concepts related to each other? What is the value of those concepts to managers today?

2. Review the four principles of Scientific Management and the way in which Scientific Management was supposed to be implemented. Can you see these principles in modern organization life?

3. Discuss the cautions that must be observed when applying Scientific Management to the design of jobs.

4. Henri Fayol developed the beginning of a theory of administration. Review the major concepts of his theory discussed in this appendix. What are the relationships among the concepts?

5. Discuss the differences between bureaucracy, bureaupathology, and bureausis.

6. Review each of Chester Barnard's concepts. Discuss the relationships among them. Have you seen any of these concepts in your own experiences with organizations?

7. Discuss the differences between dominance, compromise, and integration as approaches to reducing conflict. Mary Parker Follett described these approaches to conflict reduction. Does integration of desires impress you as a feasible approach to conflict reduction?

8. What important contributions did the Hawthorne Studies make to our understanding of organizations?

9. Review the characteristics of leadership described by Follett. Have you ever worked for an individual with those qualities? Discuss why those qualities contribute to effective leadership. What is the relationship between Follett's concept of power-over and leadership?

. . . .

➥ References and Notes

[1] W. G. Scott, "Organizational Theory: An Overview and an Appraisal," *Journal of the Academy of Management* 4 (1961): 9. Emphasis removed.

[2] Developed from A. Smith, *An Inquiry into the Nature and Causes of the Wealth of Nations* (London: George Routledge & Sons, 1893), originally published in 1776, Ch. 1.

[3] Adam Smith, *An Inquiry into the Nature and Causes of the Wealth of Nations*, 1776.

[4] Smith, *An Inquiry*.

[5] F. W. Taylor, *The Principles of Scientific Management* (New York: W. W. Norton, 1967, originally published in 1911), p. 9.

[6] Ibid.

7Ibid., pp. 36–37, 85.

[7]Ibid., pp. 36–37, 85.

[8]F. W. Taylor, "The Principles of Scientific Management," *Bulletin of the Taylor Society* (December 1916): 13–23.

[9]H. Fayol, *General and Industrial Management*, trans. by C. Storrs. (London: Sir Isaac Pitman & Sons, 1949).

[10]H. Fayol, "The Administrative Theory in the State," in L. Gulick and L. Urwick, eds., *Papers in the Science of Administration* (New York: Institute of Public Administration, 1937), p. 101. Emphasis in original.

[11]S. J. Carroll and D. J. Gillen, "Are the Classical Management Functions Useful in Describing Managerial Work?" *Academy of Management Review* 12 (1987): 38–51.

[12]*Webseter's New World Dictionary of the American Language* (New York: World Publishing Company, 1960), pp. 1158–59.

[13]Fayol, *General and Industrial Management*, p. 19. Copyright © 1949 by Lake Publishing Company.

[14]Ibid., p. 20.

[15]Ibid.

[16]Ibid., pp. 21–22. Copyright © 1949 by Lake Publishing Company.

[17]Ibid., p. 33. Copyright © 1949 by Lake Publishing Company.

[18]For example: A supervisor can "extend or confine . . . his subordinates' initiative." "Everything which goes to increase the importance of the subordinate's role is decentralization, everything which goes to reduce it is centralization." Fayol, *General and Industrial Management*, p. 34.

[19]Ibid., p. 24.

[20]Copyright © 1949 by Lake Publishing Company. Matrix and project organizations violate this principle, and conflict does occur. When the conflict is properly managed, it does not become dysfunctional. People seem to be able to live with a violation of the principle of unity of command more successfully than Fayol felt. See Chapter 18 for a discussion of matrix organizations.

[21]Fayol, *General and Industrial Management*, p. 25.

[22]Ibid., p. 42. Copyright © 1949 by Lake Publishing Company.

[23]Developed from M. Weber, *The Theory of Social and Economic Organization*, trans. by A. M. Henderson and T. Parsons (New York: Free Press, 1964; originally published by Oxford University Press, 1947).

[24]R. K. Merton, *Social Theory and Social Structure* (New York: Free Press, 1968), p. 252.

[25]M. Weber, *From Max Weber: Essays in Sociology*, trans. by H. H. Gerth and C. W. Mills (New York: Oxford University Press, 1946), pp. 214, 215–216.

[26]V. A. Thompson, *Modern Organization*, 2d ed. (University, Alabama: University of Alabama Press, 1977), Ch. 8.

[27]Ibid., pp. 152–53.

[28]"Trained incapacity" was originally coined by Thorstein Veblen. See Merton, *Social Theory*, Ch. 8 or R. K. Merton, "Bureaucratic Structure and Personality," *Social Forces* 18 (1940): 560–68 for a discussion of this and related concepts.

[29]Also called "displacement of goals." See Merton, *Social Theory*, p. 253.

[30]Ibid., pp. 251–54; Thompson, *Modern Organization*, pp. 166–68.

[31]Thompson, *Modern Organization*, pp. 154–57.

[32]Ibid., pp. 170–77.

[33]Developed from E. M. Fox and L. Urwick, eds., *Dyanamic Administration: The Collected Papers of Mary Parker Follett* (London: Pitman Publishing, 1973).

[34]Developed from ibid., Ch. 4.

[35]Ibid., p. 72. Used with permission.

[36]Ibid., pp. 83–84. Emphasis in original. Used with permission.

[37]Developed from ibid., Ch. 1.

[38]Ibid., pp. 3–4. Used with permission.

[39]Developed from ibid., Ch. 12–13.

[40]Ibid., pp. 224–5. Used with the permission.

[41]C. I. Barnard, *The Functions of the Executive* (Cambridge, Mass.: Harvard University press, 1938).

[42]Ibid., p. 73. Emphasis removed.

[43]Ibid., p. 4.

[44]Ibid., pp. 58, 82.

[45]Name of the concept taken from J. G. March and H. A. Simon, *Organizations* (New York: John Wiley & Sons, 1958), Ch. 4.

[46]Barnard, *Functions of the Executive*, pp. 227, 231.

[47]Name of the concept taken from March and Simon *Organizations*, Ch. 4.

[48]Name of the concept taken from March and Simon *Organizations*, pp. 52–81.

[49]Barnard, *Functions of the Executive*, pp. 168–69.

[50]E. Mayo, *The Human Problems of an Industrial Civilization* (New York: Macmillan, 1933); F. J. Roethlisberger and W. J. Dickson, *Management and the Worker* (Cambridge, Mass.: Harvard University Press, 1939).

[51]The effect on people's behavior because they are part of an experiment has come to be known as the "Hawthorne Effect."

[52]A. Cary, "The Hawthorne Studies: A Radical Criticism," *American Sociological Review* 12 (1967): 27–38; R. H. Franke and J. D. Kaul, "The Hawthorne Experiments: First Statistical Interpretation," *American Sociological Review* 43 (1978): 623–43.

[53]L. Yorks and D. A. Whitsett, "Hawthorne, Topeka, and the Issue of Science versus Advocacy in Organizational Behavior," *Academy of Management Review* 10 (1985): 21–30.

[54]S. R. G. Jones, "Worker Independence and Output: The Hawthorne Studies Reevaluated," *American Sociological Review* 55 (1990): 176–90. Jones summarizes the debate and presents his results that support the group dynamics arguments.

B

Research Methods: The Ways We Learn about Behavior in Organizations

· B. F. Skinner did laboratory experiments with pigeons to form parts of his theory of operant conditioning.

After reading this appendix, you should be able to . . .

· Describe the advantages and disadvantages of different research strategies.
· Understand the types of variables used in organizational research.
· Distinguish between the major sampling methods used by organizational researchers.
· Explain the limitations of methods of measurement used in organizational research.
· Discuss some ways researchers collect data.

Appendix Overview

The Nature of Organizational Research

The material that forms the basis of this book came from the extensive research literature about organizations. Many researchers in the social and behavioral sciences developed the ideas and concepts described. The research process they used involves many steps that produce information adding to our understanding of organizations. The purpose of this appendix is to provide a broad outline describing how such research gets done.[1] Some understanding of the process of organizational research should help you grasp its complexity.

The social or behavioral scientist uses several research methods to do organizational research. The scientist often begins with a theoretical model and derives one or more hypotheses or research questions from the model. Hypotheses are tentative explanations of the phenomena the scientist wants to understand. The purpose of the research is to discover whether the hypothesis is or is not correct.

The scientist collects data using one or more methods. In choosing a method, the scientist weighs the advantages and disadvantages of different methods and selects the one best suited to the requirements of the research problem. She may do the research in an organization or in a more controlled setting such as a laboratory. She chooses a research site based on her understanding of the phenomena of interest and the specific goals of the research.

You likely have done research yourself. Anytime you asked questions and sought answers, you have done what an organizational researcher has done. Your question is similar to the researcher's hypothesis. Your method may have been to go to the library or to collect information (data) from any other source you considered helpful. You then formulated some knowledge about your question that you did not know before you started your investigation. Students commonly use the procedure just described when developing a term paper, a process often called "library research." The research process is really not foreign to you at all!

Research Strategies

A researcher chooses a research strategy from four groups of strategies: field research, experimental research, longitudinal research, and qualitative research.[2] Each set of strategies varies along the following dimensions:

- Cost.
- Realism. The setting in which the research is done will vary in how closely it resembles a real organization.
- Generalizeability of the research results. The strategies vary in how much they let the researcher make statements beyond the group that was the object of study.
- Control over the variables used in the research. The strategies vary in how much control the researcher has over extraneous factors affecting the results of the study.
- Strength of the relationships that can be found among the variables being studied.
- Causal statements. Cause and effect statements are not equally possible from each of the research strategies.

Each group of strategies includes several different design possibilities. The following sections describe the purpose of each strategy and its advantages and disadvantages.

FIELD RESEARCH

Field research uses existing groups of people in a real organization. Researchers often use questionnaires and interviews to collect their data. This research strategy is used to understand relationships among variables. The expected relationships are derived from existing theory. Although the relationships can be discovered and understood, the researcher cannot state causal effects because they require the use of an experimental design.

As an example of field research, assume a researcher wants to understand the effects of job design on people's attitudes and motivation. The researcher could collect data from people in an organization about the degree of routine they perceive in their jobs. She could collect separate information about their level of satisfaction and motivation. Then she can examine the two sets of variables to learn whether people in routine jobs are less satisfied and motivated than those in nonroutine jobs. If the researcher's data show that pattern, she could conclude that people doing routine jobs are less satisfied and motivated than people doing nonroutine jobs. The researcher cannot conclude that the design of a person's job caused the observed level of satisfaction and motivation. That question must be addressed by laboratory or field experiments.

Field research has a high degree of realism because the research setting is real. Control over variables is not high, so many unknown factors may affect results. The researcher cannot always generalize the findings beyond the group studied. Cost is moderate to high depending on the scope of the research and the size of the sample used.

EXPERIMENTAL RESEARCH

Experimental research has two major forms: a laboratory experiment or a field experiment. A researcher does a laboratory experiment in a highly controlled setting, which gives the researcher control over various factors that may affect the results of the research. At least two groups are used in experimental research—an experimental group and a control group. The experimental group is exposed to the conditions of the experiment that are expected to affect the result. The control group is not exposed to those conditions and is not expected to change. Experimental research lets a researcher infer causal relationships among the variables studied.

Here is an example. Assume our researcher wants to understand the relationship between money and individual performance. The research question says that if monetary rewards closely follow individual performance, people will produce more than when they do not get the reward. The researcher chooses a laboratory setting so she can control many factors that might affect performance, such as the design of the task, its physical environment, and the timing of the rewards for performance.

The experimental group would receive the monetary reward for what they did; the control group would not. If the researcher's theory is right, the experimental group will perform better than the control group. The researcher can then conclude that monetary rewards caused increased performance.

A laboratory experiment's lack of realism affects the extent to which the results can be generalized beyond the laboratory. Although control over variables is high, the strength of relationships among variables often is not as high as in more realistic settings. Cost is low to moderate compared to the other strategies.

Researchers also do experimental research in organizations. The setting is more realistic, and the researcher can have moderately high control over the variables of interest. This research design is called a field experiment to convey the greater realism of the setting. The controls in a field experiment, however, are not as tight as in a laboratory experiment. The same research question about rewards and performance that was studied in the laboratory could also be studied in the field.

Field experiments usually are more costly but more realistic than laboratory experiments. The strength of the relationships among variables often is higher than in a laboratory experiment. The researcher can also make causal statements about the relationships among the variables of interest. The lack of control reduces the ability to generalize the findings beyond the research site.

Researchers use **longitudinal research** designs when they want to observe attitudes and performance over time. The length of time of the study depends on the research purpose. Such studies usually are done in real organizations and are less frequently used in laboratory experiments.

Here is an example from a real longitudinal study. The researcher wanted to understand the effects of introducing a centralized word processing facility in an organization.[3] Two separate groups were studied. The operators in the centralized facility were the experimental group. Others outside the facility were the control group. Data were collected over a five-month period from both groups. A questionnaire was used to measure perceptions of the characteristics of the employees' jobs and their levels of satisfaction and motivation. Employees completed questionnaires one week before the change to a central facility and one week, one month, and five months after the change. Collecting data over time is a central feature of longitudinal research.

Figure B-1 shows part of the results.[4] Perceptions of the job characteristics increased sharply after the introduction of the new word processing facility. They also dropped one month after the change and then rose again after five months. Notice that satisfaction and motivation followed about the same pattern.

The control group was level in both perceptions of job characteristics and satisfaction and motivation. The latter result was expected, because no changes had been made in the work setting of those employees.

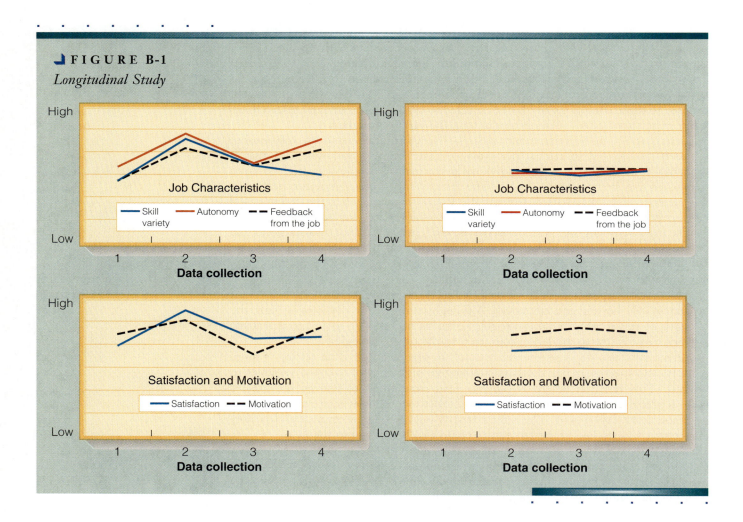

FIGURE B-1
Longitudinal Study

The word processing facility clearly affected employees in the facility. Because perceptions and attitudes varied, more time would have been needed to see whether the pattern continued.

 QUALITATIVE RESEARCH

The research strategies just described are broadly classed as a quantitative approach to organizational research. Such research often results in data that are then analyzed using many different statistical techniques. Research based on quantitative approaches may explain only a small amount of what was observed. Such research also may use variables that are so abstract they lose touch with the underlying phenomena of interest.

Qualitative research methods are an alternative to quantitative methods.[5] In **qualitative research,** the researcher is highly involved in observing the phenomena of interest. Observations are made in the natural setting within which the phenomena of interest occur. The researcher may participate in an organization to understand firsthand the work experiences of the people under study. She may not always use prior models and theories. The underlying explanations for observations are derived from the setting and the observations themselves.

Methods of collecting data in qualitative research include participant observation, interviews, videotaping, still photography, graphic portrayal of people's feelings,[6] tape recordings, and direct monitoring of interactions in an electronic mail system. The ways in which data are collected are limited only by the imagination and resources of the researcher and what the target organization will allow.

Qualitative research usually does not generate data that can be submitted to sophisticated statistical techniques. The data generated are rich in detail and may cover many volumes of paper, tape cassettes, or individual photographs. By analyzing the data, a skilled researcher can develop a greater understanding of the real work of organizations.

 Variables

Researchers move from the conceptual level of theory and general propositions to specific hypotheses and empirical research. The process includes specifying a set of variables. Variables are terms or symbols representing concepts the researcher wants to study. As the name implies, variables can have different values. Organizational researchers typically want to know the relationship among variables they designate in their studies. The three major groups of variables are independent variables, dependent variables, and moderator variables. The specification of which variables fall within those groups comes from the theory underlying the research.[7]

Independent variables are those the researcher believes occur earlier in time than the dependent variables. They also are the variables the researcher believes will explain or predict levels of the dependent variables. Under an assumption of causality, the levels of the independent variables in a study cause different levels of the **dependent variables.** Typical examples of independent variables in organizational research on employee attitudes are a person's gender, age, supervisor, and work unit. A researcher analyzes her data for variations in attitudes attributed to different categories of the independent variables. The dependent variables in such a study are employee attitudes such as job satisfaction, pay satisfaction, supervisory satisfaction, and so on.

Moderator variables affect the relationship between independent and dependent variables. That effect can be on both the level of the dependent variable and the rate of change in the dependent variable per unit change in the independent variable. The

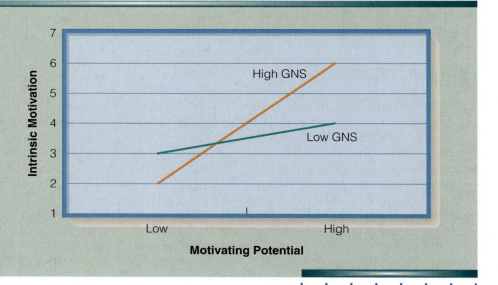

■ FIGURE B-2

*The Expected Effect of
GNS as a Moderator
Variable in the Job
Characteristics Theory*

theory guiding the researcher will describe any expected moderator effects. For example, the Job Characteristics Theory of Work Motivation described in Chapter 9 says a person's level of Growth Need Strength (GNS) affects the relationship between the motivating potential of a job and the person's level of intrinsic motivation. People high in GNS will have a higher level of intrinsic motivation for a given level of motivating potential than people low in GNS. The rate of change in motivation will also be faster for high-GNS people than for low-GNS people.

Figure B-2 shows the expected moderating effect of GNS. The figure also shows the three types of variables just discussed. The independent variable, motivating potential, is on the *x*-axis. The dependent variable, intrinsic motivation, is on the *y*-axis. The two lines in the body of the graph show the moderating effect of GNS. The line for high-GNS people has a steeper slope than the line for low-GNS people. The steeper slope shows a faster rate of change in motivation for high-GNS people than for people with low GNS.

■ Sample Designs

Most research done in organizations uses samples of people from a defined population. A population is the total group of people, or total number of organizations, of interest to the researcher. Each member of the population is a population element. The population could be all organizations that have well-developed quality management programs. An element of the population would be one such organization. If the population is defined as people with specific characteristics, then its elements are individual members of an organization.

A sample is a subset of a population. Properly designed samples offer a less expensive approach to a research problem than a census of the population. Because a sample often has fewer people than an entire population, the researcher can spend more time with each member of the sample. For example, an interview-based study of a 5,000-person organization would likely be prohibitively costly and time-consuming. A properly designed random sample of the same organization would yield trustworthy results at far less cost and in far less time.[8]

The major issues in sample design center on how well the sample represents the characteristics of the population. Researchers also concern themselves with whether they can generalize their sample results to the population. The two major groups of sample designs are nonprobability samples and probability samples. Probability sample designs are the only designs that let researchers assess error in projections from sample results to a population.

The next two sections describe the major nonprobability and probability sample designs. Many variations exist within each group. You can consult advanced treatments of sampling theory for more detailed descriptions.[9]

NONPROBABILITY SAMPLE DESIGNS

Nonprobability sample designs do not try to assure that each population element has the same chance of being in the sample. It also is not possible for a researcher to estimate the accuracy of sample estimates of population characteristics. The major reasons for using nonprobability designs are convenience, economy, and ease of building a sample. In organizational research, nonprobability samples are sometimes the only choices available to a researcher. For example, a researcher's ability to use probability designs is restricted if an organization's managers do not allow access to personnel records.

The three major nonprobability sample designs are convenience samples, purposive samples, and quota samples. A **convenience sample design** takes advantage of the handy presence of the population elements to be studied. This sample design is also called an "accidental sample." As the name emphasizes, the people in the sample just happened to be available to the researcher. For example, a professor interested in business students' attitudes about ethics uses students in her classes as the sample. That professor cannot generalize her results beyond the characteristics of that sample of students.

A **purposive sample** uses judgment to select people considered typical of the population of interest to the researcher or to get a range of opinion about an issue. Either the researcher or knowledgeable people inside a target organization select the people for the sample. The researcher does not try to estimate population values from such sample values as the average opinion about the issue. Researchers can use purposive sampling in the early stages of research when the parameters of the research problem are ambiguous or when the research is still in an exploratory stage.

A **quota sample** design sets targets for various classes of population characteristics to ensure that enough population elements with those characteristics are in the sample to allow reliable analysis and represent the proportions of the characteristics found in the population. For example, if Native Americans are 1 percent of an organization's workforce, simple random sampling would not ensure their proper representation in a sample. The researcher could deliberately draw enough Native Americans from the population to ensure they are 1 percent of the final sample. The targets for the quotas can be anything the researcher considers important to the goal of the research. Organizational research typically targets job groups, types of workers, or work units. Although a researcher can use random methods to draw elements from a population, forcing representation in the final sample does not guarantee the same chance of everyone in the population getting into the sample.

PROBABILITY SAMPLE DESIGNS

The four basic probability sample designs are a simple random sample, systematic random sample, stratified sample, and cluster sample. A simple random sample is the most basic probability design and is used within the other designs described in this section. **Simple random sampling** uses an unbiased method of ensuring that each population element has a known and equal chance of appearing in the sample. A typical method starts with a list of all elements of the population of interest. Each

• *Random sampling is the preferred method of estimating the percentage of different-colored gum balls in this bowl.*

element is sequence numbered starting with 1 from the beginning to the end of the list. The researcher then uses a table of random numbers, or a computer-based random number generator, to select elements based on the sequence numbers. If a random number matches an element number in the list, it is included in the sample. Each element is thus selected independently of any element before or after it.

Systematic random sampling works from a list of population elements. Common lists in organizational research where people are the elements include personnel listings, payroll listings, and the like. The researcher enters the list at a random point selected from a random number table. The researcher then takes every *K*th element in the list with the spacing decided by the number of the elements the researcher wants in the sample. For example, from a list of 1,000 employees, the researcher selects every tenth element to get a target sample of 100. Any bias in the list disturbs the randomness of the final sample. If older or younger people are grouped at one end of the list, their position affects their probability of appearing in the sample. Unless they are exactly equal in number, each of those groups has a different chance of appearing in the sample.

Stratified sampling is a multiple-step process that helps a sample be more representative of different groups in the population. The groups usually are of central interest to a researcher. A stratified sample design lets the researcher get the right representation of important target groups. For example, a researcher assessing the attitudes of a diverse workforce would want the sample to properly represent different racial and ethnic groups. A stratified design does a better job of getting people from each group than simple random sampling. This feature is especially important when some groups have only a small representation in the population.

The researcher first identifies the strata of interest to the research problem. Organizational research uses strata such as job title, sex, ethnicity, and the like. The researcher randomly samples from the strata assuring the randomness of the final sample. This step distinguishes stratified sampling from the quota sample design described earlier.

Studies of large organizations often use a **cluster sample design** to build a probability sample that well represents the natural clumps of elements in the target population. Organizations have many such clumps such as specific work groups, locations, or departments. Cluster sampling uses a well-controlled multiple-step process that efficiently builds a probability sample. The researcher first randomly selects the clusters. She then randomly samples within each cluster using either simple random sampling or stratified random sampling.

Measurement in Organizational Research

Measurement in organizational research assesses degrees or levels of each variable. The measurement process yields either a numeric value or an alphabetic code for variables. Researchers use four basic types of measurement scales: nominal scales, ordinal scales, interval scales, and ratio scales. Each generates a different type of information for the research.[10]

TYPES OF MEASUREMENT SCALES

Nominal scales let a researcher separate objects or individuals into mutually exclusive groups. The objects or individuals are assigned to one and only one group. Nominal scales allow only counting of people or objects in the groups. Statistics such as the average or standard deviation cannot be used with nominal scales.[11]

Examples common to organizational research are a person's sex and job title. The following question might be used in a questionnaire about employee attitudes:

Are you?

     ____Female
     ____Male

The researcher codes the answer to the question with either a numeric value or an alphabetic character. If a person checked "Female," a code "1" or "F" is assigned to the answer. If a person checked "Male," a code "2" or "M" is assigned.

Item 1 in Table B-1 is a nominal scale used to measure job satisfaction. A nominal scale measure of job satisfaction only tells a researcher whether the person is, or is not, satisfied with the job. It cannot tell her the degree of satisfaction.

Ordinal scales let a researcher assess the relative position of an object or individual on a variable. Items 2 through 5 in Table B-1 are examples of ordinal scales measuring job satisfaction. Such scales tell a researcher whether a person is high or low in job satisfaction but do not show the amount of difference in job satisfaction. Such scales can only show the relative position of the person on the scale.

Statistics based on counting such as the median or percentages can be used with ordinal scales. Other statistics that use the relative position of an item in a series are also allowed.

Interval scales have the same properties as ordinal scales but have the additional quality of equal distance between scale intervals. A thermometer is a common example of an interval scale. The distance between points 2 and 3 on an interval scale is the same as the distance between points 8 and 9. Interval scales can measure the relative size of differences between objects and individuals on a variable. A shift of 4 points on an interval scale is twice as large as a shift of 2 points.[12]

Measurements of individual productivity in units produced or the number of accidents in a plant are both done with interval scales. Properly constructed attitude scales approach interval levels of measurement. Calculating averages and standard

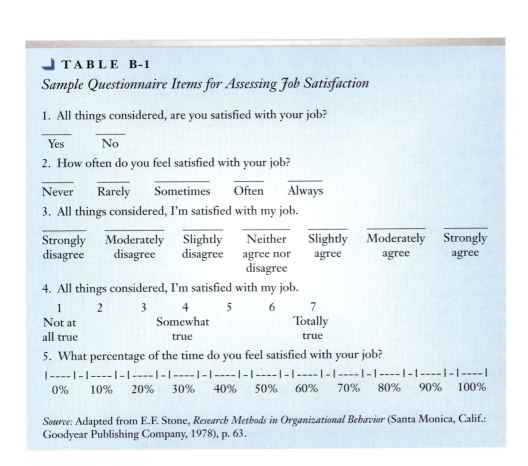

◢ TABLE B-1

Sample Questionnaire Items for Assessing Job Satisfaction

1. All things considered, are you satisfied with your job?

  ____   ____
Yes   No

2. How often do you feel satisfied with your job?

____   ____   ____   ____   ____
Never Rarely Sometimes Often Always

3. All things considered, I'm satisfied with my job.

Strongly disagree	Moderately disagree	Slightly disagree	Neither agree nor disagree	Slightly agree	Moderately agree	Strongly agree
____	____	____	____	____	____	____

4. All things considered, I'm satisfied with my job.

  1   2   3   4   5   6   7
Not at   Somewhat   Totally
all true   true   true

5. What percentage of the time do you feel satisfied with your job?

|----|-|----|-|----|-|----|-|----|-|----|-|----|-|----|-|----|-|----|-|----|
0%   10%   20%   30%   40%   50%   60%   70%   80%   90%   100%

Source: Adapted from E.F. Stone, *Research Methods in Organizational Behavior* (Santa Monica, Calif.: Goodyear Publishing Company, 1978), p. 63.

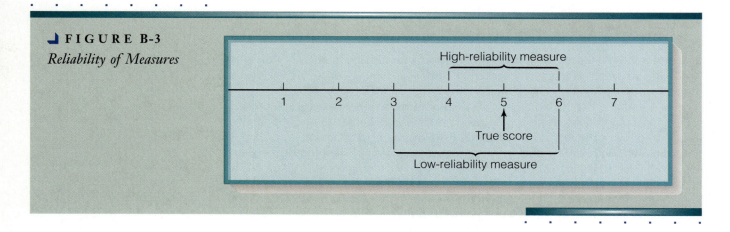

deviations is allowed. Many attitude scales used in organizational research are assumed to be interval in nature. This is the major reason researchers use statistics such as the average in their work.[13]

Ratio scales are the strongest form of measurement available and the one least commonly found in organizational research. Those scales have an absolute zero point that expresses the absence of the quality being measured. Ratio scales are the only scales that allow comparisons, such as "twice as much" or "half as many." Such scales are common in the physical sciences, but not in the social and behavioral sciences. Weight and time are measured with ratio scales. Individual productivity and accident information are ratio scales as well as interval scales. There are no restrictions on statistical or mathematical operations with ratio scales.

RELIABILITY AND VALIDITY

Reliability is a concept used in organizational research to describe measurement error.[14] Measures with high reliability are more error-free and accurate then measures with low reliability.

Figure B-3 graphically portrays reliability. Assume one can assess the "true score" of an item with a perfect measuring device. Because measurement methods used in organizational behavior research do not have perfect reliability, we cannot expect a measure to fall exactly on the "true score." A measure with high reliability gets closer to the "true score" than does a measure with low reliability. The latter misses the "true score" by a wider margin than does a more reliable measure. Measures with low reliability introduce error into data collected with such a measure.

Validity refers to whether the measurement device measures what it claims to measure. A questionnaire may be designed to measure job satisfaction, but does it really measure job satisfaction? It could appear to us to be measuring job satisfaction, but it may really be measuring satisfaction with life in general. High reliability of a measurement device is a necessary but not a sufficient condition for its validity. Low-reliability measures have so much error of measurement that the researcher finds it hard to gather repeatable evidence of the measurement's validity.

Data Collection

Several data collection methods are available to the researcher. The following sections describe four commonly used methods: questionnaires, interviews, observation, and archival records. Each has its advantages and disadvantages that must be assessed before selecting a method of data collection.

QUESTIONNAIRES

Questionnaires are paper-and-pencil devices used to collect data about people's opinions or attitudes. The questionnaire may also be used to collect demographic data such as a person's age, sex, and job title.

Questionnaires present an individual with one or more statements about which the person expresses an opinion. The format of the response categories varies. Table B-1 shows several possibilities. Item 1 allows the simplest and most restricted response, a "yes" or "no." The other four formats allow more choice with Item 5 being an almost continuous response scale.

The advantages of questionnaires include low cost compared to other forms of data collection. They can be mailed to people, or people can be assembled into groups to complete the questionnaire. Less skill is required of the questionnaire administrator than for other forms of data collection. Questionnaires are a uniform method of data collection because each person in a study reads the same items. Lastly, the questionnaires can be completed without names, allowing more honest answers.

The disadvantages of questionnaires include their lack of flexibility. They have a structured format that is not easily altered to fit the unique circumstances of each person in a sample. People may skip questions they do not understand causing incomplete data. Questionnaires require a certain level of reading ability, making them difficult to use with target groups that have reading problems. If questionnaires are mailed, probably not all will be returned. In that case, the final data collected may not strongly represent the target group.

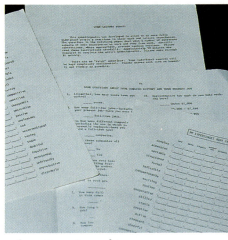

· *A questionnaire used to assess people's perceptions of their work and nonwork experiences.*

INTERVIEWS

Interviews require a person (the interviewer) to ask questions of another person (the interviewee) and record the response to the questions. The interview often is done in a face-to-face meeting. It can also be done without such a meeting, as with telephone interviews. An important distinction between questionnaires and interviews is the degree of interaction between two people required by the interview process. . . .

Interviews vary in the degree of structure brought to the interview process. A structured interview presents questions and a predefined set of responses to the interviewee. An unstructured interview has neither predetermined questions nor predetermined responses. The interviewer focuses the interviewee on the general topic of the interview and records the responses. Table B-2 shows a semistructured interview schedule. The interviewer asks the questions, but the interviewee can answer them in any way desired.

The advantages of interviews are a high degree of flexibility and the ability to get information from people who have reading difficulties. An interviewer can get more information about a question by probing with additional questions that are not always on the interview schedule. The interviewer can also record other information such as nervousness, lack of eye contact, or delays in responding.

The disadvantages include potential reaction to the interviewer. The social interaction required by the interview process can produce reactions from the person interviewed. Such reactions can affect the honesty of the interviewee's answers. Personal characteristics of the interviewer, such as age, ethnic background, and manner of speech, can all trigger positive or negative reactions. The reactions of the interviewer may cause the interviewee to distrust the interviewer. Such distrust may lead the interviewee to change her answers to what she feels the interviewer wants to hear. If an interview is trying to measure a person's attitudes, reaction to the interviewer could change the expressed attitude. Such reactions are less possible in the more impersonal questionnaire data collection technique.

Interviews usually are more expensive than questionnaires. They take more time than questionnaires to get information. Training of interviewers can add to cost depending on the degree of skill the specific interview requires.

TABLE B-2

The Management Accounting System: Sample Interview Form

1. In your opinion, what does the company consider to be the major purposes of the management accounting system? Rank them in order of their importance to the company.

   _____
   _____
   _____

2. Do you personally agree with these purposes (and their ranking) or do you believe some other purpose should be considered more important? Explain.

   _____
   _____
   _____

3. What accounting reports do you receive regularly? What do you do as a result of receiving them?

   _____
   _____
   _____

4. Please list any negative consequences (in terms of the goals of your organization) that result from the operation of the management accounting system.

   _____
   _____
   _____

5. Do you believe that the performance measures in use sometimes encourage managers to take actions that are inconsistent with accomplishing the major goals of the company? If so, how often? What kind? Why?

   _____
   _____
   _____

6. How frequently do you feel users provide inaccurate input to the management accounting system?

	Intended	Unintended
Very often	_____	_____
Often	_____	_____
Occasionally	_____	_____
Never	_____	_____

   Why do you think users do this?

   _____
   _____
   _____

Source: E. H. Caplan and J. E. Champoux, *Cases in Management Accounting: Context and Behavior* (New York: National Association of Accountants, 1978), Page 62, Part B, questions 1, 2, 3, and 6; page 72, question 19; page 63, question 7. Copyright by the Institute of Management Accountants, Montvale, N. J.

If interviewers do many interviews in a day, they can become fatigued and lose interest in the task. They may not ask questions the same way as in earlier interviews or record responses as accurately.

OBSERVATION

Observation methods of data collection record behavior as it happens in its natural setting with or without the knowledge of the people observed.[15] Researchers can gather data about a population independently of people's willingness to participate in a study. Trained observers collect data with audio and video recording devices. The ethics of organizational research require the informed consent of those observed.[16] While the observation is underway, there often is no direct interaction between the researcher and members of the population.

Organizational researchers use an observational approach when the target population has people unwilling or unable to complete questionnaires or participate in interviews. The latter may happen increasingly in the future as researchers begin to do empirical studies in organizations with diverse workforces. As described in Chapter 2, an increasing proportion of new entrants to the workforce will not have English as their first language. Exploratory workforce diversity research will benefit from using observational methods.

Researchers also use observation instead of questionnaires or interviews to avoid dependence on people's self-reports of behavior and the associated error caused by dependence on memory of past events. Observation also avoids distortions of data such as occur in interviews when people give answers they believe the interviewer wants to hear.

An unstructured observation method freely and flexibly records the behavior under observation. Researchers use an unstructured method when they cannot predict the events that will happen or when the important variables for the researcher are still unclear. Structured observation has a well-defined data collection plan. It includes what will be observed, when the observations will happen, and a structured method of recording data in predefined groups. The latter method could be used in workforce diversity research where a researcher wants to understand the quality of social interaction within work groups among people of diverse backgrounds. Past small group research would give the researcher clear theoretical guidance about the important variables.[17]

Researchers can also choose to participate directly with the people they are studying by observational methods. This version of observation has strong anthropological roots and is called participant observation. The research can either be known to the surrounding people or be a disguised observer. The latter approach is selected when the researcher believes people would behave less naturally if they knew she was a researcher.

 ## ARCHIVAL RECORDS

Organizations have naturally occurring data that let researchers collect it without requiring the cooperation of the population they want to study. The researcher collects data from ongoing processes of the organization or routine **archival records** maintained by the organization. For example, manufacturing organizations, typically maintain databases of data about their processes. Those data track costs such as direct labor, direct materials, scrap, rework, and the like. The researcher goes to the database for her data and does not use people as the source as with questionnaires and interviews. Other data available from organization records include turnover rates, absenteeism, use of sick leave, and so on.[18]

There are both advantages and disadvantages to using archival records in organizational research. This method of data collection lets a researcher get data without directly interacting with members of the organization. The lack of direct contact makes the study less obtrusive by not revealing the researcher's purpose or presence to the people who are the target of the study. Collecting data from archives is often less expensive than directly collecting data with questionnaires or interviews. A final and major advantage of archival information is the time-series quality of many organization databases. If an organization collects data regularly about its people and processes, then researchers can do low-cost longitudinal studies. Such research is especially important for discovering and understanding trends in processes and people's behavior.

A major disadvantage follows from the researcher not directing the data collection. Organizations usually collect archival data for reasons different from those of the researcher. The data may not be as complete as the researcher desires, leading to changes in a study's goals. The researcher also needs to know how the data were collected and know the accuracy of the data collection and data recording. Such information lets a researcher know the limitations of the database she wants to use for her research.

⌐ Internal and External Validity of Research Designs

Researchers have two major concerns when designing their research. Will the results of the research be real for reasons the researcher believes they are real? Can the researcher reliably attribute the results to the factors she believes are responsible for them? Both questions address the **internal validity** of a research design. The second concern focuses on the **external validity** of a design. This concern asks whether the researcher can generalize from results of her research to a larger group such as an entire organization.[19]

There are many threats to the internal validity of research designs. Changes in people who participated in the study could account for results, not the variables controlled by the researcher. The method of measurement could affect people's attitudes, not the variables of interest to the researcher. For example, people vary in whether they enjoy completing questionnaires or being interviewed. Because of those factors, the method of measurement could produce positive or negative attitudes, not the variables suggested by the researcher. Still a third threat to internal validity comes from sample mortality. People drop out of samples because they transfer, quit, get promoted, retire, die, are arrested, and so on. A high mortality rate reduces the internal validity of a study design.

The threats to external validity come from some of the same sources but also have unique contributors. Nonprobability sample designs do not let researchers generalize beyond the sample. Uncontrollable events surrounding the study can affect external validity. A major earthquake or hurricane during the data collection phase could affect people's attitudes about their jobs. The uncontrollable event accounts for the level of attitudes, not the variables of interest to the researcher. People can also react either positively or negatively to the setting within which the researcher collects her data. Data collection in a conference room with coffee and donuts provided by the organization could affect people's attitudes, not the work-related variables of interest to the researcher.

⌐ International Aspects of Research Methods

Many well-designed questionnaires and surveys were originally created in English-speaking countries to use with people from the country of origin. Researchers can easily get such instruments and then adapt them for use in other countries and cultures. Several guidelines are now available for the cross-cultural use of questionnaires, surveys, and other measurement devices.

A minimal requirement is the translation of the questionnaire or survey into the language of the target country. A widely accepted procedure in organizational research is translation forward to the target language and then back to English. Separate translators who are not familiar with the research goals do the translations in both directions. The researcher compares the back-translated English version to the original and continues the process until she gets equivalency. Knowledgeable people from the target culture review the translated questionnaire or survey for consistency in grammar and language usage.[20]

Cross-cultural researchers also must attend to potential problems beyond language and translation. Cultures can differ strongly in underlying values that shape people's perceptions and behavior.[21] People can view the content of questionnaires and surveys from differing frames of reference. The following is an example from a survey created in the United States to assess satisfaction with supervision.

The survey asks employees to rate their satisfaction with several items. One item reads: "The way my supervisor gives me credit for my ideas."[22] People from countries with individualistic values such as the United States could easily understand the individual-based orientation of such an item. People from countries with more collectivistic and group-based values such as Korea would likely find such a personal orientation strange.[23]

Some research evidence points to differences in scores from questionnaires and surveys that were traced to different frames of reference. Questionnaires and surveys with a frame of reference bias should not be used in cross-cultural research. Researchers should redesign such questionnaires with wording that is culturally neutral for all groups they intend to study.[24]

People from different cultures may also interpret measurement scales differently. For example, sample questionnaire Item 3 in Table B-1 has a midpoint defined as "neither agree nor disagree." Does this mean the same to Korean and U.S. employees? Perhaps Korean employees interpret it as "mild agreement" and U.S. employees interpret it as "no opinion."[25] Possibly people from individualistic cultures such as Canada and the United States avoid the midpoint more often than people from collectivistic cultures such as Taiwan and Japan.[26] Fortunately for cross cultural researchers, statistical procedures exist to find and account for such differences in their analysis.[27]

. . . .

Summary

This appendix described four organizational research strategies: field research, experimental research, longitudinal research, and qualitative research. A researcher uses a field research strategy to understand relationships among variables in a real organization setting. Experimental research strategies include laboratory and field experiments. An experiment uses at least two groups: an experimental group and a control group. A researcher compares the results for the two groups to see if the experimental conditions had the expected effects. Longitudinal research designs let researchers observe trends in attitudes and performance over time. With qualitative research strategies, the researcher is highly involved in observing the phenomena of interest.

Researchers use three major classes of variables to do their research. Dependent variables are variables a researcher wants to explain. Independent variables are variables a researcher believes will explain levels of the dependent variables. Moderator variables are variables expected to alter the relationship between an independent and dependent variable.

Nonprobability sample designs do not let the researcher say anything beyond the sample. Probability designs are more difficult to do right but let the researcher generalize to a target population.

Organizational researchers choose from four types of measurement scales: nominal, ordinal, interval, and ratio. Each gives a researcher different types of information and produces data that she can use with different types of statistics. In choosing a scale, the researcher also considers the scale's accuracy of measurement (reliability) and whether it really measures what it claims to measure (validity).

The data collection methods available to researchers include questionnaires, interviews, observation, and archival records. Questionnaires typically cost less than the other methods but lack flexibility in people's answers. Interviews have flexibility in people's answers, and can get more information than questionnaires, but they are costly and time-consuming. Observation methods record behavior as it happens in a natural setting. Archival data collection lets a researcher collect information from regularly maintained records of the organization.

Key Terms

archival records 647
cluster sample design 642
convenience sample design 641
dependent variables 639
experimental research 637
external validity 648
field research 636
independent variables 639
internal validity 648

interval scales 643
interviews 645
longitudinal research 638
moderator variables 639
nominal scales 642
observation methods 646
ordinal scales 643
purposive sample 641
qualitative research 639

questionnaires 645
quota sample 641
ratio scales 644
reliability 644
simple random sampling 641
stratified sampling 642
systematic random sampling 642
validity 644

Review and Discussion Questions

1. Discuss the major research strategies used by organizational researchers. What are the major advantages and disadvantages of each?
2. Review the section describing sample designs. Discuss the difference between nonprobability and probability designs. What major features distinguish those two approaches to sampling?
3. Discuss the different types of measurement scales, giving examples of each type. What are reliability and validity? How are they related?
4. Many different methods of data collection are available to organizational researchers. Review the four basic methods described in this appendix. What are the major issues an organizational researcher faces in selecting a method?
5. Internal and external validity are key concerns facing those who design organizational research. Discuss the major threats to each form of validity of research design.

References and Notes

[1]Developed from C. Selltiz, M. Jahoda, M. Deutsch, and S. W. Cook, *Research Methods in Social Relations* (New York: Holt, Rinehart & Winston, 1959); E. F. Stone, *Research Methods in Organizational Behavior* (Santa Monica, Calif.: Goodyear Publishing Company, 1978).

[2]This section gives only an overview of research designs. Detailed descriptions are available in D. T. Campbell and J. C. Stanley, *Experimental and Quasi-Experimental Designs for Research* (Chicago: Rand McNally, 1966); T. D. Cook and D. T. Campbell, "The Design and Conduct of Quasi-Experiments and True Experiments in Field Settings," in M. D. Dunnette, ed., *Handbook of Industrial and Organizational Psychology* (Chicago: Rand McNally, 1976), pp. 223–326.

[3]J. E. Champoux, "A Serendipitous Field Experiment in Job Design," *Journal of Vocational Behavior* 12 (1978): 364–70.

[4]Circumstances beyond the researcher's control prevented collecting data from the control group one week before the change.

[5]Based on H. B. Schwartzman, *Ethnography in Organizations* (Newbury Park, Calif.: Sage Publications, 1992); J. Van Maanen, J. M. Dabbs, Jr., and R. R. Faulkner, *Varieties of Qualitative Research* (Beverly Hills, Calif.: Sage Publications, 1982); J. Van Maanen, "Reclaiming Qualitative Methods for Organizational Research: A Preface," *Administrative Science Quarterly"* 24 (1979): 520–26.

[6]A. D. Meyer, "Visual Data in Organizational Research," *Organization Science* 2 (1991): 218–36; J. P. Spradley, *The Ethnographic Interview* (New York: Holt, Rinehart & Winston, 1979).

[7]C. Frankfort-Nachmias and D. Nachmias *Research Methods in the Social Sciences* (New York: St. Martin's Press, 1992), pp. 54–55.

[8]Developed from I. Chein, "An Introduction to Sampling," in C. Selltiz, M. Jahoda, M. Deutsch, and S. W. Cook, *Research Methods in Social Relations* (New York: Holt, Rinehart & Winston, 1959), Appendix B; Frankfort-Nachmias and Nachmias, *Research Methods*, Ch. 8.

[9]See A. Stuart, *The Ideas of Sampling* (New York: Oxford University Press, 1987).

[10]Developed from C. H. Coombs, "Theory and Methods of Social Measurement," in L. Festinger and D. Katz, eds., *Research Methods in the Behavioral Sciences* (New York: Dryden Press, 1953), pp. 471–535; S. S. Stevens, "On the Theory of Scales of Measurement," *Science* 103 (1946): 677–80.

[11]This text can give only a cursory treatment of scale types and related statistics. See Selltiz, et al., *Research Methods*, and Stone, *Research Methods*, for a more extended treatment.

[12]Selltiz, et al., *Research Methods*, p. 194.

[13]Ibid., pp. 193–94.

[14]Developed from W. L. Neuman, *Social Research Methods* (Boston: Allyn & Bacon, 1991), Ch. 6.

[15]Selltiz, et al., *Research Methods*, Ch. 6; Frankfort-Nachmias and Nachmias, *Research Methods*, Ch. 9.

[16]Frankfort-Nachmias and Nachmias, *Research Methods*, Ch. 4.

[17]Chapter 10 earlier in this book discusses much of that research.

[18]Selltiz, et al., *Research Methods*, Ch. 9; Frankfort-Nachmias and Nachmias, *Research Methods*, Ch. 13. Using archival data also is called "secondary analysis" because the researcher is not the primary source of the data.

[19]Campbell and Stanley, *Experimental and Quasi-Experimental Designs.*

[20]R. W. Brislin, "Translation and Content Analysis of Oral and Written Material," in H. C. Triandis and J. W. Berry, eds., *Handbook of Cross-Cultural Psychology* (Boston: Allyn & Bacon, 1980), pp. 398–444.

[21]G. Hofstede, *Culture's Consequences: International Differences in Work-Related Values* (Beverly Hills, Calif: Sage Publications, 1984); G. Hofstede, *Cultures and Organizations: Software of the Mind* (New York: McGraw-Hill, 1991).

[22]C. M. Riordan and R. J. Vandenberg, "A Central Question in Cross-Cultural Research: Do Employees of Different Cultures Interpret Work-Related Measures in an Equivalent Manner?" *Journal of Management* 20 (1994): 643–71. The item appears on p. 648.

[23]Ibid., p. 667.

[24]Ibid.

[25]Ibid., p. 644.

[26]C. Chen, S. Lee and H. W. Stevenson, "Response Style and Cross-cultural Comparisons of Rating Scales Among East Asian and North American Students," *Psychological Science* 6 (1995): 170–75.

[27]Ibid. This citation describes a statistical procedure for finding and accounting for differences in scale interpretation.

Glossary

achievement-oriented leader behavior In path-goal theory, behavior that emphasizes excellence in subordinate performance and improvements in performance.

action research An approach to organizational change and development that emphasizes strong collaboration between consultant and client and is both action oriented and research based.

active listening A form of listening in which the listener is responsible for hearing the speaker's message correctly; requires accurately hearing the facts in the message and making a deliberate effort to understand the speaker's viewpoint.

activities An organization's formal requirements for group members, e.g., job duties and responsibilities; the same as required behavior.

actual power The presence and use of power, whether that use is successful or not.

act utilitarianism Form of utilitarianism that asks a person to assess the effects of all actions according to their greatest net benefit to all affected.

affective Part of an attitude; refers to a person's feeling of like or dislike for the object of the attitude.

affective outcomes In Job Characteristics Theory, the individual's internal reactions to a job's design; e.g., job satisfaction and motivation.

Alarm The first stage in the stress response in the General Adjustment Syndrome model; heart rate, respiration, muscle tension, and blood sugar increase as the body prepares to fight, adjust to, or flee from the stressor.

analytical perspective The ability to examine and explain organizational behavior by using concepts and theories.

Analyzer A type of organization that both emphasizes efficiency in producing stable products or services and scans the environment for new products that it can adapt to produce its own version; combines centralized, formal elements in part of the organization with decentralized, less formal elements in other parts.

anchoring and adjustment The tendency of decision makers to select a starting point for a decision and then adjust beyond that point.

archival records Naturally occurring data generated or maintained by an organization; e.g., absenteeism rates or costs of an industrial process.

artifacts The most visible level of organizational culture; e.g., architecture, layout of interior space, and formality of working relationships.

assets of group decision making The benefits of group decision making; include increased information and knowledge, increased acceptance of the decision, greater job satisfaction, and personal development of the participants.

attitude A learned predisposition to respond in a consistently favorable or unfavorable manner with respect to a given object.

attitude change A shift in an attitude; can be due to persuasion, to the norms of a social group important to the person holding the attitude, or to the person becoming uncomfortable with some aspects of the attitude.

attitude formation The shaping of attitudes based on a person's beliefs, both positive and negative, about an object and on the amount and type of information available about the object.

attribution of leadership A view of leadership perception that holds that to determine whether someone is a leader, people compare observed and inferred behavior to an implicit leadership theory.

attribution of power The process of ascribing power to another person based on his characteristics and work context; may not be the same as the person's actual power.

attribution process The process by which people explain the behavior they see in others. Attributions can be personal (based on the observed person's personal qualities) or situational (based on the context of the behavior).

authority and responsibility In Fayol's theory, authority is the right to give orders and the power to exact obedience; responsibility or accountability is a corollary of authority.

availability heuristic The tendency for decision makers to recall and use easily retrievable information, e.g., vivid and recent events.

bases of attraction Factors that explain why people who can potentially interact are sufficiently attracted to each other to form a cohesive group; e.g., similarities in age, attitudes, or ethnic background.

bases of power Sources of power for a leader; can come from both the person's formal management position and her personal characteristics.

basic assumptions The least visible level of organizational culture; e.g., beliefs about behavior that develop over time and guide decision making without being consciously articulated.

basic communication process Involves a sender, receiver, and message flowing over a communication channel; also includes feedback to the sender via the receiver's response to the message; surrounded by noise that helps to distort the message.

behavioral intentions Part of an attitude; how the person holding the attitude wants to behave and what he says about his behavior toward the object of the attitude; may differ from actual observed behavior.

behavioral outcomes In Job Characteristics Theory, observed employee behavior in response to a job design; e.g., individual productivity and quality of work.

behavioral response The action a person takes in the presence of a stressor; can lead to distress or eustress.

Behavior Modification An approach to motivation that relies on various techniques of controlling the consequences of behavior to direct and shape behavior; assumes people engage in behavior that has positive outcomes and avoid behavior that has unpleasant outcomes.

belongingness and love needs In Maslow's theory, the desire to give and receive affection and to be in the company of others.

Big-Five **personality dimensions** Dimensions that many personality psychologists use to describe human personality: agreeableness, conscientiousness, emotional stability, extroversion, and openness to experiences.

biological approach An approach to job design that focuses on the job's physical demands.

biological theory Holds that at least some personality characteristics are inherited; includes ethological theory, which holds that behaviors that have helped humans survive become inborn characteristics, and behavior genetics, which sees personality development as a series of interactions between genetically based predispositions and environmental influences.

boundary transition A person's movement into and within an organization; e.g., joining an organization; has three dimensions: functional, hierarchical, and inclusionary.

Bounded Rationality Model A decision-making model that assumes decision makers face limitations that constrain rationality; limitations include incomplete information and time constraints.

brainstorming The spontaneous generation of ideas while deferring critical evaluation of those ideas; used to create decision alternatives, not to select the final alternative.

buffering Stockpiling raw materials or warehousing finished products as a means of uncoupling the technical process from the organization's external environment.

building power The process of creating a power base; involves doing a diagnosis and then amassing power based on one more of the sources of power. *See also* sources of power.

bureaucracy An administrative structure with well-defined offices or functions and hierarchical impersonal relationships; duties and responsibilities are clearly defined without regard for who will hold the office.

bureaupathology The latent dysfunctions of bureaucracy; involves exaggerated forms of bureaucratic behavior; e.g., resistance to change and excessive attachment to rules, policies, and procedures.

bureausis The condition when clients or members of a bureaucracy are intolerant of bureaucratic behavior and want their own case to be handled in a personal way rather than by existing policies.

burnout A special type of work-related distress characterized by a chronic state of emotional exhaustion.

centralization-decentralization Refers to whether an organization's decision authority is concentrated at the upper levels or extends down to the lower levels.

centralized communication networks Networks in which a single person is a key figure in sending and receiving messages; only one or a few parts of the network have the potential to get information.

change: metamorphosis The final stage of the socialization process in which the new employee begins to feel comfortable in his new role.

changing organizational culture Involves breaking from some features of the old culture and creating new features.

charismatic authority In Weber's theory, authority that is based on the personal qualities of the individual; not characteristic of bureaucracy.

choice: anticipatory socialization The first stage of the socialization process; occurs before the person joins an organization or takes a new position in it; builds expectations and prepares the person for the new situation.

cluster sample design A probability design that uses a multiple-step process to ensure that the sample represents natural clusters of elements in the target population.

coalition An alliance of individuals who share a common goal.

cognitive Part of an attitude; a person's perceptions and beliefs about the object of the attitude.

cognitive dissonance Discrepancies among a person's cognitions or beliefs about the object of an attitude; leads to tension, which may motivate the person to change one or more cognitions to reduce the dissonance.

cognitive theory Holds that people develop their thinking patterns over time through a series of cognitive development stages; as people have varied experiences and interact with their environment, each person develops a unique personality.

cohesive group formation, factors affecting Include factors in the physical work area, the work processes, or the organizational design that encourage or restrict social interaction; e.g., proximity of people and the noise level.

cohesiveness The condition when a group's members are attracted to its task, to its norms, and to other members of the group.

communication effectiveness, improving Methods include training, asking for feedback from a receiver, understanding cultural differences, avoiding complexity and jargon, and reducing noise.

communication roles Five roles played by individuals in organizations: initiators, relayers, liaisons, terminators, and isolates.

compliance conformity Occurs when a person goes along with the group's norms without accepting those norms.

compromise In Follett's view of conflict, one of the three ways of dealing with conflict; each side gives up something to settle the issue, but the reason for the conflict remains; a lose-lose method of conflict reduction.

concepts Explanations of parts of the phenomena to which a theory applies; useful tools for understanding behavioral phenomena in organizations.

confirmation bias The tendency to accept information that confirms an initial impression and to hold to that impression despite contradictory evidence; can take the form of belief perseverance and self-fulfilling prophecy.

conflict In organizations, includes interactions in which (1) one party opposes another or (2) one party tries to prevent or block another from reaching his goals; involves opposition, incompatible behaviors, or antagonistic interaction.

conflict aftermath The conclusion of a conflict episode; often linked to the latent conflict of a later episode.

conflict episode A model that views a conflict process as beginning with antecedents that lead to conflict behavior and ending with an aftermath that links it to other conflict episodes; also includes perceived, felt, and manifest conflict.

conflict management Focuses on maintaining conflict at functional levels; does not mean the elimination of all conflict; includes increasing and decreasing conflict.

Consideration The people-oriented dimension of leader behavior (in Ohio State Leadership Studies).

content innovation A response in the metamorphosis stage of the socialization process; the new employee changes or improves the knowledge base and process characteristics of the role.

context satisfaction The degree of satisfaction with the work context; a moderator variable in the Job Characteristics Theory can affect a person's response to the motivating potential of the job.

continuous process A technical process characterized by high capital investment in plant and equipment; usually involves fast-moving automated processes.

continuous reinforcement schedule A system of timing reinforcement in which a consequence is applied after each behavior.

contracting The second phase of organizational development; the consultant and the client organization draw up a contract describing their expectations and outlining their duties.

convenience sample design A nonprobability design that uses people who happen to be available to the researcher, e.g., the students in the researcher's classes; also called an accidental sample.

core job characteristics Five characteristics identified by the Job Characteris-

tics Theory as inducing the critical psychological states; include skill variety, task identity, task significance, autonomy, and feedback from the job.

coupling the technical process Connecting the organization's technical process with the external environment; e.g., through just-in-time production methods.

creating organizational culture Involves a deliberate effort to build up a specific type of organizational culture.

critical psychological states In Job Characteristics Theory, the states that must be present to produce the highest level of positive affective and behavioral outcomes; include experienced meaningfulness of work, responsibility for work outcomes, and knowledge of actual results of work.

cultural relativism An approach to international ethics that considers differences in ethical values among cultures and takes a normative ethical view based on the premise that right and wrong should be decided by each society's predominant ethical values.

cultural symbolism A system of symbols that have meaning only to an organization's members and reflect its culture; can include action, verbal, and material symbols.

custodial response A possible result in the metamorphosis stage of the socialization process; the new employee accepts the new role and conforms to its requirements.

decentralized communication networks Networks in which communication flows freely with no one person playing a central or controlling role; all parts of the network have equal information status.

deception Behavior that tricks another party into arriving at incorrect conclusions or selecting the wrong alternative in a decision process; aimed at building and holding power.

decision support systems Dynamic computer-based systems that support an organization's decision-making processes; are interactive and can be used to retrieve data and test alternatives.

deep structures In the revolutionary model of organizational change, the enduring features of an organization's design, processes, and relationships with its

external environment that enable the organization to succeed.

Defender A type of organization with well-designed functions, centralization, and formal procedures; has a committed customer based that lets it provide a predictable flow of products or services; suited to stable environments.

deficiency cycle In E.R.G. Theory, the condition when an individual cannot satisfy existence needs and comes to desire them ever more strongly.

delegation of authority Moving decision authority to positions below a manager in an organization.

Delphi Method A structured technique for making decisions surrounded by uncertainty; members interact through questionnaires or computer, but not face-to-face.

dependent variables Variables that the researcher believes are explained or predicted by the independent variables.

descriptive theory Explains behavioral phenomena as they actually exist.

detection threshold The point in the perceptual process at which a person notices that something has changed in her environment.

devil's advocate technique A decision-making technique in which one or more persons play the role of critic, finding fault with a proposed alternative and arguing for its rejection; helps ensure the alternative can withstand criticism.

diagnosing organizational culture Studying an organization's culture in order to understand it; can be done as an outsider before joining an organization or as an insider.

diagnosis The third phase of organizational development; the consultant gets information about the client system and diagnoses its condition.

dialectical inquiry A structured, analytical method of examining multiple decision alternatives; involves a structured debate about an alternative and a counter alternative, including the assumptions underlying the alternatives.

differentiation A concept in the Information Perspective; refers to the variations in the formal structure and behavior of members of different units of an organization that develop in response to environmental uncertainty.

differentiation perspective Focuses on the various subcultures dispersed throughout an organization's culture.

dimensions of organizational culture Ways of examining and understanding an organization's culture; include the levels, pervasiveness, implicitness, imprinting, political, plurality, and interdependence dimensions.

dimensions of social responsibility Include economic and legal responsibilities (required of organizations and managers), ethical responsibilities (expected), and discretionary responsibilities (desired but not required or expected).

dimensions of workforce diversity Factors that lead to variations in the composition of the workforce; include age, gender, ethnicity, race, education, religion, union status, sexual orientation, family status, physical ability, and part-time or full-time work.

directive leader behavior In path-goal theory, behavior that focuses on the task to be done, when it must be done, and how it must be done.

dissatisfiers *See* hygiene factors.

distress The dysfunctional result of stress that occurs when the person does not adapt successfully to the stressor or remove it from his environment.

divisional organizational design A configuration featuring decentralized divisions; typically, the organization produces several different products or services and emphasizes customer satisfaction.

division of labor Partitioning the total tasks, duties, and responsibilities of an organization among its members.

domestic changes Anticipated developments within the United States; include changes in population demographics, skill requirements of jobs, and workforce composition.

dominance In Follett's view of conflict, one of the three ways of dealing with conflict; the conflict is resolved with one party winning over the other, but the basic reason for the conflict remains; a win-lose method of conflict reduction.

dysfunctional conflict Conflict that blocks an organization or group from reaching its goals.

dysfunctional consequences The results of behavior that are negative for an organization and restrict its adjustment and adaptation.

dysfunctional consequences of groups Negative aspects of groups; include taking more time to accomplish tasks, loss of individual identity for members, free-rider effects, groupthink, and pressure for conformity to group norms.

dysfunctions of organizational communication Errors and problems that can occur in organizational communication; include selective perception, semantic problems, distortion of messages, information overload, and poorly timed messages.

dysfunctions of organizational culture Potential negative consequences of an organization's culture; include communication failures, conflict from differing views, resistance to change, and difficulties of merging incompatible cultures.

effective socialization process A process that succeeds in helping a new employee become an efficient member of the organization; provides realistic descriptions, focuses on day-to-day activities the employee needs to know, and offers ample feedback at early stages.

Effort-Performance Expectancy ($E{\to}P$) A concept of Expectancy Theory; refers to a person's belief that effort leads to a desired or required level of performance.

egoism Ethical system that has two forms: individual (individuals judge their actions only by the effects on their own interests) and universal (individuals include others' interests when assessing the effects of their own actions).

electronic and video communication Communication via modern technological devices such as electronic mail, computer networks, and videoconferencing.

emergent behavior Behavior that grows from interactions among group members; can focus on work tasks or be purely social.

employee-centered behavior Leadership behavior that focuses on the people in the work units, their personal success, and the quality of the social system that forms in the work units (in University of Michigan Studies).

enhancers Processes or persons that strengthen the connection between leader behavior and subordinate satisfaction and performance.

enrichment cycle In E.R.G. Theory, the condition when a person satisfies

growth needs and comes to desire ever more growth.

entry The first phase of organizational development; the consultant and manager have their first direct contact and establish a working relationship.

entry/encounter stage The second stage of socialization; the new employee joins the organization and begins to learn its culture, acquires a new self-image, learns the norms of his immediate work group, and learns his duties and responsibilities.

equilibrium periods In the revolutionary model of organizational change, the periods of stability when the organization moves steadily toward its mission and goals.

equity The condition that exists when a person perceives the ratio of the outcomes she receives from an employment exchange and the inputs she brings to it as being roughly equal to her coworkers' ratio of outcomes and inputs.

equity sensitivity The degree of response to a state of inequity; can be one of three types: equity sensitive, benevolent, or entitled.

Equity Theory A theory of motivation that focuses on exchange relationships and holds that people try to balance the ratios of outputs to inputs in such relationships.

E.R.G. Theory An extension of Maslow's theory that focuses on three groups of needs that form a hierarchy: Existence, Relatedness, and Growth. A need does not have to be fully satisfied for upward movement to occur; downward movement can occur when a need is dissatisfied.

escalation of commitment The process of committing more resources to a losing course of action in the hope of recovering past losses.

"espoused values" The values that an organization claims to follow.

esteem needs In Maslow's theory, a person's desire to be valued by others and the desire to have a feeling of self-worth.

ethical absolutism Holds that an ethical system applies to all people, everywhere, and always; based on an authority such as religion, custom, or written code.

ethical behavior Behavior judged to be good, just, right, and honorable based on principles, rules, or guides from a specific ethical theory, character traits, or social values; may vary from person to person or country to country.

ethical realism Holds that morality does not apply to international activities, behavior, and transactions.

ethical relativism Holds that ethical behavior is based on personal feelings or opinions and is whatever a person or society says is ethical; rejects the view that moral judgments have objective validity.

eustress The positive result of stress; occurs when a person has successfully adapted to the stressor or when the degree of stress does not exceed the person's ability to adapt.

evaluation The seventh phase of organizational development; the activities focus on whether the development effort has had the effect the client wanted.

evolutionary model A model of organizational change that views change as happening in small steps or increments.

Exhaustion The final stage in the stress response in the General Adjustment Syndrome model; the body begins to wear down after long exposure to a stressor.

existence needs In E.R.G. Theory, a person's physical and material wants.

Expectancy Theory A theory of motivation that focuses on the internal processes and holds that people try to maximize the outcomes of behavior and choose among outcomes based on this maximization.

experimental research A research strategy that uses either a laboratory experiment or a field experiment; allows the researcher to infer causal relationships.

expert systems Interactive computer-based systems that support decision making by simulating the knowledge and decision process of an expert.

external environment Persons and institutions outside an organization that nevertheless affect it; e.g., the organization's competitors, customers, suppliers, government regulators, and labor unions; one of the contingency factors affecting organizational design.

external validity A quality of a research design; refers to whether the researcher can generalize from the results to a larger group.

extinction A means of Behavior Modification in which a positive event is withdrawn to decrease the frequency of undesirable behavior.

extrinsic outcomes Outcomes for a performance that people receive from someone else.

factors affecting cohesive group formation. *See* cohesive group formation

factors affecting group effectiveness. *See* group effectiveness.

false consensus An attribution error; the tendency to overestimate the degree to which other people agree with one's perceptions of another's behavior.

feedback The fourth phase of organizational development; the consultant has a series of meetings with the client where the original diagnosis is discussed and modified.

felt conflict The emotional part of a conflict episode; also includes the values and attitudes the parties to the conflict hold about each other.

field research A research strategy that uses existing groups of people in a real organization; expected relationships are derived from existing theory, but causal effects cannot be stated.

Foreign Corrupt Practices Act (FCPA) A U.S. statute enacted in 1977 that prohibits a company from using bribes to get business in another country or prevent the restriction of its business; allows small payments that are part of the ordinary course of doing business in another country.

formal groups Functional or task groups within an organization. Functional groups are formed by the organization's design, e.g., departments; task groups are formed temporarily to perform a specific duty, e.g., committees.

fragmentation perspective The perspective an organizational culture that focuses on the ambiguity present in organizations.

framing effect The tendency for the presentation of a problem to affect the decision that is made; e.g., whether an alternative is presented as a gain or a loss can affect the decision.

frustration-regression A form of movement in E.R.G. Theory in which behavior focuses on a lower level of needs when a person is frustrated in achieving a higher level.

functional analysis An analytical tool borrowed from anthropology; focuses on whether the consequences of behavior are manifest or latent and whether they are functional or dysfunctional for society.

functional conflict Conflict that works toward the goals of an organization or group.

functional consequences The results of behavior that are good for an organization and help its adjustment and adaptation.

functional organizational design A configuration that groups an organization's tasks into separate units or departments; typically, the organization produces a few standardized products or services in a stable external environment.

functions of organizational communication Include information sharing, feedback, integration, persuasion, emotion, and innovation.

functions of organizational culture Positive roles of an organization's culture; e.g., defining rewards and sanctions, defining group boundaries, and developing a consensus about the organization's mission, goals, and means of achieving those goals.

fundamental attribution error The tendency to underestimate the situation and overestimate personal qualities as the cause of observed behavior; also, the tendency to overestimate the situation and underestimate personal qualities as the cause of one's own behavior.

Garbage Can Model A decision model for high ambiguity situations; sees decision making as a time-sensitive process involving problem, solutions, participant, and choice opportunity streams. The streams' confluence results in a decision.

General Adjustment Syndrome An early stress model that emphasized the physiological aspects of the stress response; viewed the response as involving three stages: Alarm, Resistance, and Exhaustion.

global environment The international environment of modern organizations; will become increasingly important in the future.

Goal Setting Theory Holds that specific, challenging, reachable, and accepted goals lead to higher performance than goals without those characteristics.

goals of organizational design Consist of getting information to the right people for effective decision making and coordinating the interdependent parts of the organization.

group-based job design A job design for a task to be done by a team; must design both the task and some aspects of the group.

group effectiveness, factors affecting Factors that enhance the group members' satisfaction and increase the group's ability to meet goals; include the physical environment, social environment, and the group's size and task.

groupthink Excessive conformity to a group norm that supports agreement among group members in decision making. Afflicted groups lose the ability to critically assess alternatives and lack ethical concern for the effects of their decisions.

growth needs In E.R.G. Theory, the desires to be creative and productive, to use one's skills, and to develop additional capabilities.

growth need strength (GNS) A concept that describes the variability in growth needs among different people; a moderator variable in Job Characteristics Theory.

Herzberg's Motivator-Hygiene Theory Distinguishes factors in the job (motivators) from those in the work context (hygiene factors). The motivators contribute directly to motivation; the hygiene factors can lead to dissatisfaction but not to motivation.

horizontal integration The acquisition of a company in the same line of business as the acquiring organization.

human process interventions Organizational development interventions that focus on interpersonal, intragroup, and intergroup processes; goals include reducing dysfunctional conflict and enhancing fulfillment of human values.

human resource management intervention Organizational development interventions that use goal setting and rewards to shape individuals' behavior in the direction desired by the organization.

humble decision making Adaptive, dynamic decision-making processes that recognize humans' inability to absorb and process all available information; involves a series of trial-and-error decisions.

hybrid organizational design A configuration that combines elements of functional and divisional designs; the organization typically is characterized by many different products or services, a complex external environment, and both routine and nonroutine technical processes.

hygiene factors (dissatisfiers) In Herzberg's theory, factors in the work context that can lead to high levels of dissatisfaction; improving them leads only to less dissatisfaction, not to higher satisfaction.

improving communication effectiveness. *See* communication effectiveness

increasing conflict Methods of raising the level of conflict when it becomes dysfunctionally low; include forming heterogeneous groups, using a devil's advocate, and increasing interdependence.

independent variables Variables the researcher believes occur earlier in time than the dependent variables and explain or predict levels of the dependent variables.

individual blockages Obstacles deriving from a person's skills and abilities, both real and perceived, his experience with the task, and the difficulty of the task that cause the person to perceive a low effort-performance expectancy.

individual differences and socialization People's reactions to socialization vary depending on their skills, abilities, and self-efficacy beliefs.

individual stress management The process of maintaining stress at an optimal level for a particular person by using strategies for stress reduction, stress resilience, and stress recuperation.

inducements-contributions balance In Barnard's theory, the relationship between salary and fringe benefits (inducements) and the job performed (contributions); people join organizations when the inducements slightly exceed the contributions.

informal groups Groups formed within and across formal groups in organizations; not formally established; may be based on shared interests or friendship.

Information Perspective A way of describing the relationship between organizational design and the external environment; emphasizes the management information requirements of that environment. Managers assess uncertainty in their environment and use information to reduce risk.

initiating structure The task-oriented dimension of leader behavior (in Ohio State Leadership Studies).

inputs In Equity Theory, the personal characteristics and behaviors a person brings to the employment exchange.

Integrated Model of Stress A detailed model that combines elements of earlier models. Its elements include a description of stressors as occurring during work, nonwork activities, and life transitions; the role of perception in filtering stressors; moderators of the stress response; and the results of both distress and eustress.

integration A concept in the Information Perspective; refers to the collaboration and cooperation among various units of an organization that must achieve a unified effort to meet the demands of the external environment.

integration of desires In Follett's view of conflict, one of the three ways of dealing with conflict; the parties find a solution that fully meets each party's goals so that neither has to give up anything.

integration perspective The perspective on organizational culture that emphasizes the consensus on values and basic assumptions among an organization's members and consistency in its artifacts and in the actions of its members.

intensive technology A technical process that draws different elements from the organization's available technology and applies them to a single object; as the object responds, the technology applied is varied; e.g., a hospital applying technology to a patient.

interaction Social interaction between two or more people; can be face-to-face or can be conducted through written materials or telecommunication devices.

intergroup conflict Conflict between two or more groups in an organization.

intermittent reinforcement schedule A system of timing reinforcement in which a consequence is applied based on the time between behaviors or the number of behaviors.

internal validity A quality of research design; refers to whether the results are real for the reasons the researcher believes and whether the results can be reliably attributed to the factors the researcher believes are responsible.

internal work motivation A feeling of self-reward from doing a job; in Job Characteristics Theory, the affective outcome most closely associated with work effectiveness.

international changes Anticipated developments worldwide; include faster growth in developing economies than in mature economies, rising education levels, increasing connections through computer and communication technology, and increased emphasis on global markets.

international rights An approach to international ethics that holds that certain fundamental rights can be identified that organizations have a minimal duty to uphold.

interorganizational linkages Connections between organizations; can be achieved by negotiating long-term buying contracts, adding vendors to the board of directors, and engaging in joint ventures.

interorganization conflict Conflict between two or more organizations that results from relationships between them.

interpersonal conflict Conflict between two or more people.

interval scales Measurement scales with equal distance between scale intervals, e.g., a thermometer; allow the use of averages and standard deviations.

intervention The sixth phase of organizational development; the consultant and client collaboratively intervene in the client system to move it to the desired future state.

interviews Data collection method in which an interviewer asks questions of another person and records the responses; can be face-to-face or over the telephone.

intimidation The act of frightening or inducing a sense of inferiority in others as part of the process of building power.

intragroup conflict Conflict among members of a group.

intraorganization conflict Conflict that occurs at the interface of organization functions, e.g., between manager and

subordinate or between departments; includes all types of conflict occurring within an organization.

intrapersonal conflict Conflict that occurs within an individual.

intrinsic outcomes Rewards for a performance that people give to themselves, e.g., satisfaction for completing a challenging task.

"in-use values" The values that actually guide the behavior of organization members as opposed to the "espoused values" that the organization claims to follow.

"It's Good Business" The assumption that doing business ethically is beneficial for organizations, especially in the long term.

Job Characteristics Theory of Work Motivation Describes how job design affects motivation, performance, and satisfaction; specifies core job characteristics that can lead to critical psychological states and induce high levels of motivation and performance; also includes individual and work context factors that can moderate those effects.

Job Demands–Job Decision Latitude Model A model of the stress response that describes the stress effects of jobs in terms of job demands and job decision latitude. High stress occurs in jobs with high demands but low decision latitude.

Job Diagnostic Survey (JDS) A questionnaire that can be used to collect data about jobs in an organization to determine whether they should be redesigned: allows the calculation of the Motivating Potential Score and gives information about levels of context satisfaction.

Johari Window A graphical model of communication that considers two dimensions: information that is known or unknown to one person and information that is known or unknown to the other. Suggests aspects that can affect openness, accuracy, and trust during communication.

judgment biases Tendencies that can lead to errors in decision making: e.g., the tendency to recall recent, dramatic events more than older, less dramatic events.

justice An approach to ethics that uses a comparative process that looks at the balance of benefits and burdens that are distributed among group members or that result from the application of laws, rules, and policies.

knowledge and skill In Job Characteristics Theory, a moderator variable that can affect the motivating potential of a job.

latent conflict Factors in a person, group, or organization that might lead to conflict behavior; the antecedents to conflict.

latent consequences The unintended results of an individual's actions.

leader-member relations In Fiedler's contingency theory, the dimension of leader-subordinate situations that describes the quality of the relationship between subordinates and leader; include trust and whether the leader is respected.

Leadership Categorization A view of leadership perception that holds that people observe behavior and then compare it to a cognitive category describing leaders to determine whether the observed person is a leader.

leadership mystique In Jennings's theory, a set of ideas, values, and beliefs that are the essence of leadership, includes a sense of mission, a capacity for power, and a will to survive and persevere.

leadership traits Qualities characteristic of successful leaders or that distinguish leaders from followers; include self-confidence, cognitive ability, and knowledge of the business.

learning theory Holds that people learn behavior from social interaction and that each person develops a unique personality as a result of the variability of their social experiences.

legal or rational authority In Weber's theory, the form of authority that is inherent in a bureaucratic office or function.

levels of organizational culture Consist of three aspects that vary in their visibility to an outsider: artifacts, values, and basic assumptions.

levels of social responsibility Consist of the institutional level (an organization's broad obligations to society), the organizational level (a given organization's specific function in society), and the individual level (the behavior of people in an organization).

liabilities of group decision making The drawbacks of group decision making; include pressure for conformity, more time required to reach a decision, a tendency for one person to dominate, and the development of strong preferences for certain alternatives.

listening The mental process of assigning meaning to the sounds that are heard.

listening process An active combination of intrapersonal and interpersonal activities in which one person receives a message from another (interpersonal), tries to interpret it (intrapersonal), and responds to show meaning imputed to the message (interpersonal).

longitudinal research A research strategy that enables researchers to observe attitudes and performance over time; usually done in real organizations rather than as laboratory experiments.

lying The intentional misstatement of the truth in order to mislead another party; helps to build power by distorting information in favor of the liar.

maintaining organizational culture Involves holding on to the good part of an organization's culture while helping the organization adapt to new challenges.

management changes Anticipated developments in management behavior; include greater use of self-managing teams, skill-based pay systems and gain sharing plans, and information technologies.

management information systems Information processing systems used by organizations to support their daily operating activities and decision-making functions; can be manual or computer based.

managing diversity The process of creating an environment that harnesses the potential of all sources of difference within an organization's workforce.

managing for ethical behavior Involves three steps: understanding the present culture of the organization, acting to improve that culture, and sustaining ethical behavior so it becomes embedded in the organization.

manifest conflict The actual conflict behavior of the parties to a conflict episode; can be oral, written, or physical.

manifest consequences The intended results of an individual's actions.

Maslow's Hierarchy of Needs Theory A motivation theory that condenses all needs into five basic groups that form a hierarchy according to their prepotency.

mass production A technical process that uses a series of interconnected steps to produce a product; commonly features long production runs of a single product.

matrix organizational design A grid-like configuration in which many people report to at least two supervisors (e.g., one in a functional area, one in a project); used where two separate sectors of the external environment demand management attention.

McClelland's Achievement Motivation Theory Focuses on the Need for Achievement, the Need for Power, and the Need for Affiliation; each need is associated with different behaviors.

mechanistic approach An approach to job design based on industrial engineering; uses task simplification and specialization to get higher output, less mental overload, and decreased training time.

mechanistic organization An organizational design characterized by clearly specified tasks, precise definition of members' rights and obligations, a hierarchical structure, and a tendency toward vertical interaction and communication.

mediating technology A technical process that links interdependent individuals or organizations in order to complete a transaction; e.g., a bank linking borrowers and depositors.

moderators of stress Personal characteristics that can cause a person to experience varying degrees of stress; e.g., physical fitness, personality characteristics, and family health history.

moderator variables (1) Variables that affect the relationship between the independent and dependent variables; the theory guiding the researcher describes any expected moderator effects. (2) In Job Characteristics Theory, factors in the person or the work context that affect the response to a job's motivating potential.

motivating potential In Job Characteristics Theory, the concept that summarizes the effect of the five core job characteristics on the critical psychological states.

motivational approach An approach to job design centered on task variety, worker autonomy, and performance feedback; associated with high job satisfaction and motivation but also high training time and costs.

motivation to participate In Barnard's theory, an individual's motivation to join and stay with an organization and perform at a minimally acceptable level.

motivation to perform In Barnard's theory, the individual's motivation to achieve performance levels higher than the minimum.

motivators (satisfiers) In Herzberg's theory, factors in the job or an individual's personal response to job and work experiences that can lead to satisfaction.

move toward the change state The second phase of the evolutionary model of organizational change; the change agent tries to move the organization or part of it to a new state.

multiple sequence model Describes group development in terms of four phases: orientation, conflict, development, and integration.

Murray's Theory of Human Personality A motivation theory that holds that human behavior is governed by both internal factors (physical or psychological needs) and factors in the external environment; allows for a complex collection of needs that often serve as multiple bases of behavior.

need Latent internal characteristic activated by stimuli or objects a person experiences. The person tries to behave in a way that satisfies an activated need.

Need for Achievement In McClelland's theory, the desire to solve problems, achieve goals, and overcome obstacles.

Need for Affiliation In McClelland's theory, the desire to establish, maintain, and restore positive affective relations with others.

Need for Change The first phase of the evolutionary model of evolutionary change; the manager of other change agent develops a need for change among those affected.

need for power In McClelland's theory, the desire to control the means of influencing the behavior of another person.

need hierarchy In Maslow's theory, the order in which people must satisfy needs; once lower-level needs are satisfied, the needs on the next level become the focus of behavior. From the bottom, the needs are physiological needs, safety needs, belongingness and love needs, esteem needs, and self-actualization needs.

negative inequity The condition that exists when people feel underpaid for what they give the organization.

negative reinforcement A means of Behavior Modification in which a negative event is withdrawn or withheld to increase the frequency of desirable behavior.

neutralizers Processes or persons who break the connection between leader behavior and subordinate response, preventing leaders from having an effect.

new self-image One of the goals of the entry/encounter stage of socialization; achieved by unfreezing a new employee's old self-image, changing to a new self-image that incorporates values and behaviors desired by the organization, and refreezing the new self-image in place.

Nominal Group Technique (NGT) A structured approach to decision making in which members first generate and record ideas without discussing them; then the ideas are discussed and members vote privately to arrive at a decision.

nominal scales Measurement scales that allow objects or individuals to be separated into mutually exclusive groups, e.g., male or female; allows counting but not the use of averages or standard deviations.

nonverbal communication One of two main types of communication in organizations; includes eye movements, gestures, facial expressions, tone of voice, and the like.

normative theory Describes alternatives to existing phenomena; describes the way the theorist thinks the world should be, not the way it actually is.

norms Unwritten rules of behavior for members of a cohesive group; define acceptable behavior and roles of group members.

observation methods Methods of data collection in which researchers record behavior as it happens in its natural setting with or without the knowledge of the people observed.

open system A concept describing the relationship between an organization and its external environment in which the organization can act on, be affected by, and have transactions and exchanges with that environment.

oral communication All forms of speech between a sender and receiver; can be face-to-face or by telephone, radio, television, voice mail, or other devices.

ordinal scales Measurement scales that allow the relative position of an object or individual on a variable to be assessed; e.g., whether something is done never, sometimes, or always; allow the use of medians and percentages.

organic organization An organizational design characterized by roles that are not highly defined, the continual redefinition of tasks as members interact, little reliance on authority, decentralized control and decision making, and communication that is both lateral and vertical; fits an uncertain external environment.

organization A system of two or more persons, engaged in cooperative action, trying to reach some purpose.

organizational architecture An approach to organizational design that asks managers to consider the informal organization, political processes, reward system, and culture as well as functions, divisions, and reporting relationships; focuses on achieving balance among the various parts.

organizational behavior The actions, attitudes, and performance of people in organizations.

organizational blockages Obstacles inherent in an organization, such as a lack of resources or high levels of conflict, that cause people to perceive a low effort-performance expectancy.

organizational culture The shared values, standards, customs, rituals, and norms in an organization; what a new employee needs to learn to be accepted as a member of the organization.

organizational development A long-term, systematic, prescriptive approach to planned organizational change.

organizational development consultants Persons from inside or outside the organization who have the training and experience to assist managers in bringing about organizational development.

organizational socialization The process by which people learn the content of an organization's culture.

organizational stress management The process of achieving the optimal level of stress required by the goals of the organization by using strategies of stress reduction, stress resilience, and stress recuperation.

organizational theory Focuses on the design and structure of organizations.

organization changes Anticipated developments in organizations; include new, more flexible strategies and flatter organization structures with fewer layers of management.

orientations to conflict Predispositions toward conflict; include dominance, collaborative, compromise, avoidance, and accommodative.

pair-wise communication Any form of oral or written communication between two people.

participative leader behavior In path-goal theory, behavior that emphasizes consultation with subordinates and serious consideration of their ideas before making decisions.

perceived conflict Conflict that the parties are aware of.

perceived conflict requirements The level of conflict desired. Organizations facing a fast-changing environment or producing innovative products require higher levels of conflict as do organizations with cultures that value debate and questioning.

perceived stress The concept that describes the importance of perception and attribution in determining whether a stressor leads to distress or eustress.

perceptual defense A means by which people shield themselves from negatively valued stimuli; e.g., blocking out disturbing feedback.

perceptual errors Consist of two major types: perceptual set (beliefs about a target based on previous experience with that target) and stereotyping (holding beliefs about a target based on the group to which the target belongs).

perceptual/motor approach An approach to job design that focuses on the mental demands of the job; associated with fewer errors and accidents and less stress but also low job satisfaction and motivation.

Performance-Outcome Expectancy ($P \rightarrow O$) A concept of Expectancy Theory that describes the perceived connection between a person's performance and any outcomes she may get for that performance.

peripheral role behaviors Behaviors that are neither necessary nor desirable for membership in an organization.

personal acceptance conformity Occurs when a group member goes along with the group's norms because his beliefs and attitudes are congruent with those norms.

personal factors In path-goal theory, one of two sets of contingency factors that are important in the choice of leader behavior; include subordinates' perception of their ability and of the source of control over them.

personality types Various characteristics and dispositions that can be helpful in understanding behavior: include extroversion and introversion, Type A and B personalities, Machiavellian personality, and external and internal control types.

Person-Environment Fit Model A model of the stress response that holds that the congruence between a person and his work environment affects the amount of stress he experiences.

philosophies of conflict management (1) Traditionalist: holds that all conflict is bad for an organization. (2) Behavioral: holds that conflict is inevitable and may play a positive role, but does not advocate deliberately increasing conflict. (3) Interactionist: sees conflict as essential and holds that managers should sometimes increase it.

physiological needs In Maslow's theory, the basic requirements of the human body; e.g., food, water, sleep, and sex.

pivotal role behaviors Behaviors an individual must accept to join and remain a member of an organization.

planning the change The fifth phase of organizational development; the consultant and client identify alternative courses of action and select change alternatives.

political diagnosis An examination of an organization to determine the location of power and the type of political behavior that is likely to occur.

political models Decision-making models that see decision making as a power- and conflict-based process involving bargaining and compromise; assume participants pursue their self-interest.

political network A set of alliances and affiliations within an organization that provides support and a common ideological view.

political strategy A plan to reach a goal using specific political tactics; specifies the goal and the political means to reach it.

political tactics Ways of building power or using it unobtrusively; include selectively emphasizing decision criteria, using outside experts, controlling the agenda, and building coalitions.

position power In Fiedler's contingency theory, the dimension that describes the formal organization power of the leader.

positive inequity The condition that exists when people feel they are paid more than their work is worth.

positive reinforcement A means of Behavior Modification in which a positive event is applied to increase the frequency or strength of desirable behavior.

potential for power The chance that individuals or groups have to build a power base with resources they control.

potential power The condition that exists when one party perceives another party as having power and the ability to use it.

power-over In Follett's view of leadership, dominance or coercion; control based on force.

power relationship Involves three dimensions: dependence (reliance on another party), relational (social interactions between parties), and sanctioning (the use of rewards and/or penalties).

power styles Various approaches to using power; include the Impression Management, Directive, Consensus, Charismatic, and Transactional styles.

power-with In Follett's view of leadership, a jointly developed power that is co-active rather than coercive.

prepotency In Maslow's theory, the idea that lower-level needs, e.g., physiological and safety needs, dominate human behavior when all needs are unsatisfied.

pressures on conflict episodes Pressures on the parties to a conflict episode that may prevent the conflict from ending with the most satisfactory result.

process view of organizational design Views the organization as a series of interconnected processes that weave across functions; people use multiple skills to perform all or part of a process rather than doing repetitive tasks focused on only a small part of the process.

production-centered behavior Leader behavior that focuses on the tasks to be done with little concern for the people involved (in University of Michigan Studies).

Prospector A type of organization that focuses on developing new products or services and watching for new markets; typically has little centralization or task specialization and is suited to dynamic, fast-changing environments.

punctuated equilibrium model Describes group development as being interrupted by major change events, conflict, and upheaval, rather than proceeding through an orderly series of stages.

punishment A means of Behavior Modification in which a negative event is applied to decrease the frequency or strength of undesirable behavior.

purpose plus limitations In Barnard's theory, the reason organizations form; an individual has a purpose but also has limitations and must therefore cooperate with others to achieve that purpose.

purposive sample A nonprobability sample design in which the researcher uses judgment to select people of interest or to get a range of opinion about an issue.

qualitative research A research strategy in which the researcher is highly involved in observing phenomena in their natural setting and may participate in an organization to gain firsthand experience; underlying explanations of the phenomena are derived from the setting and the observations themselves.

questionnaires Paper-and-pencil devices used to collect data about people's opinions or attitudes or to collect demographic data.

quota sample A nonprobability sample design that sets targets for various classes of population characteristics to ensure that enough persons with those characteristics are in the sample to allow reliable analysis and represent the proportion of those characteristics in the population.

Rational Model A decision-making model that holds that the decision maker has a clear goal, knows all alternatives and their results, and applies a preference ordering function to the alternatives; sees decision making as proceeding sequentially from beginning to end.

ratio scales Measurement scales that have an absolute zero point that expresses the absence of the quality being measured; not common in organizational research.

Reactor A type of organization that has an unbalanced configuration of external environment, organizational design, strategy, and technical process.

realistic expectations A balanced view of what to expect from an organization based on both its positive and its negative qualities; can be created through Realistic Job Previews for new employees.

Realistic Job Preview A balanced description of the characteristics of a job and organization that includes sources of both satisfaction and dissatisfaction; given to potential employees.

rebellious response A possible response to socialization in which the process fails; the new employee rejects all aspects of the role and leaves the organization or is terminated.

recognition threshold The point in the perceptual process at which a person can identify the target or changes in some attribute of the target.

reducing conflict Methods of lessening conflict; include lose-lose methods, win-lose methods, and win-win methods.

relatedness needs In E.R.G. Theory, the desires to have interpersonal relationships and to develop intimate relationships.

relationship-oriented leaders In Fiedler's contingency theory, leaders who focus on people, are considerate, and are not strongly directive.

relevant role behaviors Behaviors that an organization considers desirable and good, but that are not essential for membership.

reliability In organizational research, refers to the amount of measurement error; high reliability has fewer errors and is more accurate than low reliability.

representativeness heuristic The tendency for decision makers to compare a current event to past events about which they have knowledge; can lead to stereotypes.

required behavior Things that a person must do because of membership in the organization and as part of the person's role in a formal group.

Resistance The second stage in the stress response in the General Adjustment Syndrome model; the body tries to return to normal by adapting to the stressor.

resistance to change Antagonism toward change among people in an organization; reasons for resistance include misunderstanding the goal of the change, having a low tolerance for change, and perceiving that something of value will be lost.

Resource Perspective A way of describing the relationship between an organizational design and the external environment that emphasizes the degree to which the organization is dependent on other organizations. Managers assess the interdependence and develop strategies for dealing with it.

responses to inequity Include changing inputs or outcomes, cognitively distorting one's inputs and outcomes, withdrawing, taking action against or changing the comparison person, and cognitively distorting the inputs and outcomes of the comparison person.

results of distress Behavioral, psychological, and medical consequences that occur when a person does not choose the right behavior to manage a stress response, is predisposed to stress, or has not built resilience to common stressors; e.g., appetite disorders, disturbed sleep, and anxiety.

results of eustress The positive consequences that occur when a person successfully adapts to a stressor; e.g., exhilaration and excitement.

revolutionary model A model of organizational change that sees change coming in bursts that punctuate long periods of stability; after the changes, the organization settles into another stable period.

revolutionary periods In the revolutionary model of organizational change, the times of change activities aimed at changing the strategic direction of the organization.

rights A person's just claims or entitlements; can be legal (defined by the legal system) or moral (universal rights that exist because of ethical standards).

role episode A means of communicating pivotal and relevant role behaviors. A role sender communicates information about a role behavior to a focal person, who then enacts the role behavior as he perceives it; the role sender perceives the behavior and responds with reinforcement or sanctions.

role innovation A response to socialization in which the new employee rejects most aspects of the role and redefines it; the organization accepts the innovation.

rule utilitarianism Form of utilitarianism in which a person assesses actions according to a set of rules designed to yield the greatest net benefit to all affected.

safety needs In Maslow's theory, a person's desire to be protected from physical or economic harm.

satisfaction-progression In E.R.G. Theory, a form of movement in which a person's behavior focuses on the next higher level of needs as one level is satisfied.

satisficing behavior Selecting a satisfactory but not optimal alternative when making decisions.

satisfiers. *See* motivators.

Scientific Management Taylor's approach based on carefully designed jobs, carefully trained workers, cooperation between managers and workers to ensure the use of standard procedures, and a division of labor between management and workers.

self-actualization needs In Maslow's theory, the desire for self-fulfillment.

self-awareness Knowledge of oneself; can take two forms: private self-consciousness (focusing on inner feelings and personal standards) or public self-consciousness (focusing on external standards or norms).

self-concept The set of beliefs people have about themselves.

self-esteem The positive and negative judgments people have about themselves; the emotional dimension of self-perception.

self-managing teams Work units that have the authority to make decisions about product design, process design, and customer service.

self-managing work group An interdependent group that produces a defined product, service, or decision and whose members control the group's task and interpersonal processes.

self-perception The process by which people develop a view of themselves; includes self-concept, self-esteem, and self-presentation.

self-presentation The behavioral strategies people use to affect how others see them and how they think about themselves.

self-schema A set of beliefs that help a person filter and interpret information she gets about herself.

sense-making process An important part of the entry/encounter stage of socialization; consists of change, contrast, and surprise.

sense of proportion In Fayol's theory, a combination of tact and experience that enables managers to tailor the application of management principles to specific circumstances.

sentiments Attitudes, beliefs, and feelings about those with whom one interacts.

shaping A Behavior Modification technique designed to make gradual changes in a person's behavior while aiming for a target behavior.

side effects of punishment Can include emotional reactions such as anger, inflexible behavior, failure to learn new desirable behavior, and the development of negative feelings toward the source of the punishment.

simple random sampling A probability sample design that uses an unbiased method, e.g., a random numbers table, to ensure that each population element has a known and equal chance of appearing in the sample.

size The magnitude of an organization; one of the contingency factors affecting organizational design. Larger organizations have more formal rules and procedures, more management levels, and more structured work activities than smaller organizations.

small group communication Communication that involves three or more people interacting directly; can be face-to-face or conducted through an audio, video, or computer-based medium.

Social Information Processing Theory Holds that interactions with other people affect a person's perception of job characteristics and that supervisors, coworkers, and the job redesign process can affect perceptions even when the job is not changed.

socialization processes The methods organizations use to shape the values and behaviors they want their members to have.

socialization versus individualization The interplay between the organization's efforts to induce members to conform to its values and the members' efforts to preserve their individuality.

social perception The process by which people come to know and understand each other.

social structure of groups The social arrangement of a group; includes several dimensions such as group member roles, relationships among roles, the group's communication network, and influence patterns within the group.

sources of organizational socialization Include the organization, the person's immediate supervisor, the person's coworkers, and the job itself.

sources of power In organizations consist of six major areas that can be used to build a power base: political network, the creation of a perception of dependence, department and work unit power, work activities, charisma, and the individual's knowledge, reputation, and professional credibility.

span of control The number of people reporting directly to a supervisor or manager.

stabilize the change The last phase of the evolutionary model of organizational change; the change agent makes the change an ongoing part of the organization.

stages of group development Include group formation, intragroup conflict, group cohesion, task orientation, and termination; mark plateaus in group evolution rather than discrete and clearly identifiable states.

stages of moral development Stages in which people shift from an individual understanding of morality to a societal one and then to a universal view. Some persons do not progress through all

three stages, and the stages may differ for men and women.

strategy An organization's long-term goals and the way its managers plan to reach those goals; one of the contingency factors affecting organizational design.

strategy interventions Organizational development interventions that focus on an organization's response to shifts in its external environment.

stratified sampling A probability sample design that uses a multiple-step process to ensure that a sample is representative of different groups in the population.

stressors Objects or events in a person's physical and social environment that can induce a stress response.

stress recuperation The process of recovering from exposure to stressors. Strategies include relaxation training, exercise, and meditation.

stress reduction A decrease in the number of stressors a person experiences. Strategies include avoiding situations that cause distress and planning ahead; organizational strategies include training programs and job redesign.

stress resilience An increase in a person's ability to endure stressors without experiencing dysfunctional results. Strategies include exercise, diet, and weight control.

stress response The physical and psychological changes that a person undergoes when experiencing stress; the changes prepare the person to either fight the stressor or run from it.

structural and technological interventions Organizational development interventions that focus on the design of the organization, the jobs within it, and the addition of new technology; goal is to improve individual productivity and organizational effectiveness.

subcultures Smaller, specialized cultures within a larger culture.

substitutes Persons or processes that can act in place of leaders, making the leaders unnecessary.

supportive leader behavior In path-goal theory, behavior that emphasizes concern for subordinates and their needs.

systematic random sampling A probability sample design that uses a list of population elements that is entered at a point selected from a random number table; then evey *K*th element is taken.

target The object of a person's perceptual process.

task-oriented leaders In Fiedler's contingency theory, leaders who focus on the work to be done, are directive, structure situations, set deadlines, and make task assignments.

task structure In Fiedler's contingency theory, the dimension of leader-subordinate situations that describes the extent to which the work is well defined and standardized.

technical process The system an organization uses to produce its products or services; one of the contingency factors affecting organizational design.

technological changes Anticipated developments in technology; important areas include the creating, sending, and processing of information, the development of new materials, advances in transportation, and the development of new manufacturing processes.

technology and communication Rapid changes will occur in communication due to developments in computers, satellites, video displays, fiber optics, optical data storage, distributed computing, and the like.

terminates The final stage of organizational development; the consultant's involvement with a specific intervention ends.

theories and concepts as lenses The use of theories and concepts to examine organizational phenomena from different perspectives, focusing on the broad view or on a small part of it.

theory A plausible explantion of some phenomenon; also describes relationships among its concepts.

theory of distributive justice Theory proposed by John Rawls that is based on three principles: Equal Liberty for all persons, Difference (society should care for its most needy while using its resources as efficiently as possible), and Fair Equality and Opportunity for all.

time and job reactions The concept describing how people's perceptions of job characteristics vary depending on the stage of their employment.

tolerance for conflict A manager's ability to accept conflict.

tools and techniques of TQM Tools and techniques that help organizations manage for quality in services, products,

and processes; include checksheets, flowcharts, control charts, benchmarking, and quality function deployment.

Total Quality Management (TQM) A philosophy and system of management that embraces all programs of quality management and continuous quality improvement.

TQM view of an organization A perspective that emphasizes processes, customers, interdependence with suppliers, and the role of feedback in getting continuous quality improvement.

traditional authority In Weber's theory, authority that exists because of family relationships, e.g., inherited positions; not characteristic of bureaucracy.

transactional leadership A type of leadership that focuses on exchange relationships between leader and followers; involves contingent reinforcement and management by exception.

Transactional Model of Stress Focuses on the psychological aspects of the stress response, such as perceptual processes and learned responses; sees the response as a dynamic transaction that depends in part on the person's earlier experience with the stressor.

transformational leadership A type of leadership that emphasizes charisma, individualized consideration, and intellectual stimulation.

types of listening In organizational communication include two basic types (discriminative and comprehensive) of listening and two alternate forms (empathic and critical) that serve different functions for the listener and the speaker.

uncoupling the technical process Disconnecting an organization's technical process from the external environment to protect the process from environmental disturbances.

unit production A technical process in which an entire product is made to an individual customer's specifications.

unity of command In Fayol's theory, the principle that an employee should receive orders from one superior only.

unity of direction In Fayol's theory, the principle that a department or unit should have a single head and a single goal.

unstructured decision-making models Models in which the decision-making process does not follow an orderly pro-

gression; appropriate for conditions of uncertainty and for complex, unprecedented, and ambiguous problems.

utilitarianism Approach to ethics that asks people to examine the effects of an action to decide whether its total net benefits exceed the total net benefits of any other action.

Valence (V) A concept in Expectancy Theory that refers to the preference people have among outcomes.

validity In organizational research refers to whether a measurement device measures what it claims to measure.

values The level of organizational culture that has medium visibility; e.g.,rules that guide behavior in an organization.

verbal communication One of two types of communication in organizations; includes oral, written, and electronic communication.

vertical integration The acquisition of a company that is a supplier to or distributor of the acquiring organization.

virtual organization A temporary network of companies or individuals that focus on reaching a specific target or responding to new opportunities; all members of the network are linked by information technology.

Vroom-Yetton Model A decision-making model that uses a set of rules to select the approach that is best for a given problem; assesses problem attributes through diagnostic questions in decision tree form.

work environment factors In path-goal theory, one of two sets of contingency factors that are important in the choice of leader behavior; include tasks, the nature of the authority system, and the primary work group.

workforce diversity Variations in the composition of the workforce based on personal and background factors of employees or potential employees.

written communication Any form of handwriting, printed memo or report, or message sent over an electronic medium such as a computer network.

zone of indifference In Barnard's theory, a concept that describes how people respond to orders and directives from others; people execute orders falling within the zone without much thought, but question and may not act on orders outside it.

Name Index

Dobbins, G. H., 352n
Dobrzynski, J. H., 320n
Dollard, J., 99n
Donaldson, T., 63, 70n, 71n
Dorfman, Dan, 434
Dorfman, P. W., 352n, 353n
Dorrance, John T., 512
Dorsett, Tony, 192–93
Doty, D. H., 550n
Dougherty, T. W., 489n
Doughterty, T. W., 489n
Dowling, W. F., 219n
Dröge, C., 550n
Drucker, Peter, 357
Druckman, D., 489n
Dubin, R., 17n, 71n, 166n, 290n, 550n
Dugas, C., 511n, 524n
Dumaine, B., 3, 238, 348, 394n, 568n, 586n, 615
Dunbar, E., 167n
Duncan, K. D., 219n
Duncan, R., 524n, 550n
Duncan, S., 394n
Dunkle, Kim, 141
Dunn, T., 99n
Dunnette, M. D., 219n, 320n, 394n, 650n
Dusky, L., 128
Dutton, J. M., 316, 318, 320n
Dwyer, D. J., 249n
Dyer, Gibb, 615
Dykema, K. W., 392n

E
Earley, P. C., 220n, 291n
Ebbesen, E. B., 70n, 99n, 394n
Ebbitt, W. R., 392n
Echanique, Katherine, 128
Edwards, C., 98n
Edwards, J. E., 588n
Edwards, J. R., 488n
Edwards, W., 431n
Eichenfield, Samuel L., 381
Eisenberg, E. M., 395n
Eisenhart, K. M., 550n
Ekman, P., 98n
Elashmawi, Farid, 258
Elias, M., 222
Ellis, A., 489n
Ellsworth, P., 98n
Entwisle, D. R., 189n
Epstein, Y. M., 98n
Erdley, C. A., 98n
Erez, M., 220n
Erikson, E. H., 70n
Ettlie, J. E., 550n
Ettling, J. T., 430n
Etzioni, A., 430n
Eulberg, J. R., 488n
Evans, M. G., 189n
Evans, W. A., 71n
Ewing, D. W., 70n, 71n, 131n

F
Falbe, C. M., 550n
Fang, Y., 248n
Faris, R. E. L., 17n
Farnham, A., 517n, 550n, 612n

Farrell, C., 320n
Farson, R. E., 394n
Faucheux, C., 588n
Faulkner, R. R., 650n
Fayol, H., 621–24, 634n
Fazio, R. H., 99n
Feigenbaum, A. V., 26, 27, 40n
Feinberg, J., 70n
Feldman, D. C., 166n, 167n
Feldman, J. M., 100n
Feren, D. B., 219n
Ferguson, James L., 551n, 552–54
Fernandez, J. P., 39n
Ferris, G. R., 166n, 248n, 456n
Ferris, Richard, 350
Ferster, C. B., 219n
Festinger, L., 70n, 98n, 99n, 290n, 650n
Fiedler, F. E., 248n, 329–30, 342, 352n
Field, R. H. G., 430n
Filley, A. C., 320n
Fishbein, M., 70n, 99n
Fisher, A. B., 19
Fisher, C., 166n, 167n, 394n
Fisher, R. J., 291n
Fiske, S. T., 98n
Fitch, Dennis, 397
Fitzgerald, M. P., 248n
Fitzgibbons, D. E., 456n
Flanagan, O., 70n
Fleming, M. C., 614n
Folkman, S., 488n
Follett, Mary Parker, 297, 627–29
Fombrun, C. J., 456n
Fonda, Peter, 17
Ford, R. C., 550n
Forgas, J. P., 98n
Fossum, J. A., 218n
Foster, Richard N., 611
Foti, R. J., 352n
Fotie, R. J., 352n
Fox, E. M., 634n
Fox, M. L., 249n
Fox, N. E., 99n
Franke, R. H., 634n
Frankena, W. K., 70n
Frankfort-Nachmias, C., 650n
Franklin, J. C., 39n
Frederick, W. C., 70n
Frederiksen, L., 220n
Freedman, S., 219n
Freeman, A., 71n
Freeman, R. E., 70n
French, J., 351n, 488n
French, W. L., 489n, 588n
Fried, Y., 248n
Friedlander, F., 588n
Friedman, A., 219n
Friedman, H. S., 100n, 489n
Friedman, M., 100n
Friesen, W. V., 98n
Fritzsche, D. J., 431n
Froggatt, K. L., 489n
Frohman, A. L., 588n
Frohman, M. A., 588n
Frost, P., 130n
Frost, P. J., 352n
Fry, F. L., 219n
Fry, L. W., 248n, 550n

Fuchsberg, G., 31, 40n
Fullerton, H. N., Jr., 39n
Funder, D. C., 351n, 352n
Futrell, D., 249n, 291n

G
Gabarro, J. J., 456n
Gagliardi, P., 130n
Galbraith, J. R., 550n
Gallagher, J. M., 99n
Gallo, H., 38, 39n
Gallupe, R. B., 431n
Galuszka, P., 613n
Gambert, S. R., 489n
Gamboa, V., 219n
Gandz, J., 353n
Ganellen, R. J., 488n
Ganster, D. C., 249n, 488n, 489n
Gardell, R., 248n, 488n
Garland, H., 218n
Garrett, D. E., 395n
Garvin, D. A., 40n, 291n, 588n
Gatewood, R. D., 70n, 71n
Gehani, R. R., 40n
Geis, F. L., 100n
Gelman, D., 486n
Geneen, Harold, 350
Gerber, Scot, 164–65
Gergen, K. J., 98n
Gergen, M. M., 98n
Gersick, C. J. G., 290n
Gerst, John, 166
Gerstein, M. S., 550n, 614n
Gerstner, Louis V., Jr., 564
Gerth, H. H., 634n
Ghagat, R. S., 488n
Ghoshal, S., 613n
Giacolone, R. A., 100n
Gibbons, Barry, 586–87
Gibson, A. M., 100n
Gibson, R., 323n
Giges, N., 551n
Gilbert, D. T., 98n
Gillen, D. J., 634n
Gilligan, C., 70n
Gilmore, D. C., 248n
Ginsberg, I. T., 613n
Ginzberg, E., 39n
Gist, M. E., 291n, 430n
Gittler, J. B., 320n
Glain, S., 613n
Glass, David, 616
Glick, W. H., 248n, 249n, 550n
Gobeli, D. H., 550n
Goeddel, David, 261
Goethals, G. R., 98n
Goldberg, L. R., 99n
Goldhaber, G. M., 394n, 395n
Goldman, L. D., 40n, 121, 130n
Goldsmith, Randy, 518
Golembiewski, R. T., 489n
Gooding, R. Z., 291n
Goodman, P. S., 71n, 130n, 219n
Goodpaster, K. E., 70n
Goodstein, L. D., 131n
Gordon, J. R., 320n
Gottfredson, L. S., 39n
Gouldner, A., 252

McCormick, Richard D., 38
McCrae, R. R., 99n
McDade, Jim, 497
McDermott, James J., 586
McDonald, Marsh, 128
McFarland, John, 518
McGoldrick, A. E., 488n
McGoun, E. G., 353n
McGovern, R. Gordon, 512
McGrath, J. E., 488n
McGregor, D., 190n
McGue, M., 99n
McGuigan, F. J., 481–82
McGuire, J. W., 352n
McGuire, W. J., 99n
McKie, J. W., 70n
McKillop, P., 613n
McKinley, W., 550n
McKinzie, Gordon A., 289–90
McLean, A. A., 489n
McLennan, R., 572n
McLeod, P. L., 291n
McLeod, R., Jr., 431n
McMichael, A. J., 488n
McNealy, Scott, 114, 115
McQuilken, George, 156
Mechanic, D., 456n
Meehan, K. A., 100n
Meglino, B. M., 167n
Mehrabian, A., 394n
Melcher, R. A., 613n
Mendenhall, M., 167n
Merrit, N. J., 248n
Merton, P. K., 17n
Merton, R. K., 99n, 166n, 634n
Messick, D. M., 219n, 291n
Metcalf, H. C., 320n
Metz, Frank A., Jr., 247
Meyer, A. D., 550n, 650n
Meyer, J. P., 167n
Meyer, M., 613n
Meyers, R. A., 395n
Miceli, M. P., 71n, 320n
Michaelsen, L. K., 291n
Mikami, C., 188
Miles, E. W., 219n
Miles, R. E., 524n, 550n
Miles, R. F., 550n
Miller, A., 550n
Miller, D., 550n
Miller, D. T., 99n
Miller, Herman, 16
Miller, K. I., 219n
Miller, K. L., 613n
Miller, N. E., 99n
Miller, V. D., 167n
Milliken, Roger, 455
Mills, C. W., 634n
Mintzberg, H., 430n, 550n
Mirvis, P. H., 588n
Mitchell, T. R., 189n, 218n, 352n
Mitchell, V. F., 189n
Mitz, L. F., 488n
Moberg, D. J., 456n
Moeller, N. L., 248n
Monge, P. R., 219n, 395n
Montano, D. E., 99n
Montello, D. R., 99n

Montello, Kenrick, 99n
Moore, L., 130n
Moore, T., 91
Moorhead, G., 249n
Moran, Edward, 522
Moran, R., 37, 131n
Morgenstern, O., 430n
Morian, J., 478
Morrow, D. J., 447n
Morton, Dean, 612
Morton, M. S. Scott, 614n
Moss, L., 489n
Mougdil, P. M., 189n
Mount, M. K., 100n
Mouton, J. S., 588n
Mowday, R. T., 99n, 219n, 291n
Mullen, B., 98n, 290n
Mundel, M. E., 17n
Murninghan, J. K., 431n
Murphy, P. E., 70n
Murray, H. A., 172, 173, 174, 189n,
    193, 290n
Myers, Craig, 524
Myers, Isabel Briggs, 91

N

Nachmias, D., 650n
Nadler, D. A., 218n, 550n
Nahavandi, A., 130n
Nakarmi, L., 40n, 613n
Nanus, B., 353n
Nasar, S., 612n
Nash, L. L., 431n
Nathan, R. G., 489n
Naumann, E., 167n
Naver, M., 164
Naylor, J. C., 219n
Near, J. P., 320n
Neff, R., 613n
Neilsen, E. H., 291n, 320n
Nelson, David, 113
Nemetz, P. L., 248n
Netherton, Tom, 518
Neuijen, B., 131n, 526n
Neuman, G. A., 588n
Newcomb, T., 70n, 99n
Newell, A., 430n
Newman, J. E., 489n
Newman, W. L., 650n
Nicholas, J. M., 588n
Nichols, Gaylord, 250
Nicholson, N., 167n
Niehoff, B. P., 352n
Nielsen, R. P., 70n
Nisbett, R. E., 430n
Noe, R. A., 248n
Nord, W. R., 219n
Norwood, M., 99n
Nougaim, K. E., 189n
Nozick, R., 54, 70n
Nulty, P., 40n, 613n
Nunamaker, J. F., Jr., 382, 431n
Nurius, P., 98n

O

Oberg, K., 167n
Obert, S. L., 290n
O'Connell, S. E., 395n

O'Day, R., 456n
Oddou, G., 167n
O'Hara, K., 219n
Ohayv, D. D., 131n, 526n
Oklewiczs, Ron, 545
Oldham, G. R., 84, 99n, 218n, 229,
    244, 248n, 290n
O'Leary, Hazel, 343
Olian-Gottlieb, J. D., 218n
Oliver, J. A., 354
Olsen, Gary, 293
Olsen, J. P., 430n
Olson, James E., 559
Olson, M. H., 431n
O'Mara, J., 39n
Omura, Haruki, 188
Omura, Mayu, 188
O'Reilly, C. A., 249n, 394n
Ornish, D., 489n
Osborn, A. F., 431n
Osler, J. F., 488n
Ostry, S., 40n, 613n
O'Sullivan, M., 98n
Ott, J. S., 166n
Ouchi, W. G., 130n
Overstreet, P., 87, 99n
Overton, W. F., 99n
Ozan, Terrence R., 31

P

Pace, R. W., 394n, 395n
Paine, L. S., 71n
Pancake, V. R., 99n
Parsons, T., 634n
Pasewark, W. R., 430n
Paulsen, Pat, 115
Payne, R., 488n, 489n
Payne, S. L., 100n
Penar, K., 612n
Penman, R., 395n
Pennar, K., 612n
Perlin, L. I., 489n
Perlman, B., 489n
Perrin, P. G., 392n
Perrow, C., 550n
Peters, Barbara, 355
Peters, C., 320n
Peters, T. J., 130n
Petersen, Donald E., 350
Petrauskas, Helen, 448
Petrock, F., 219n
Pettigrew, A. M., 130n
Pfeffer, J., 249n, 430n, 456n, 550n
Phelan, John J., 350
Pheysey, D. C., 550n
Phillips, Carolyn, 524
Phillips, J. S., 352n
Phillips, N., 70n
Piaget, J., 70n, 99n
Pichler, J., 71n
Pike, Gary, 479
Pilibosian, Elizabeth, 449
Pilnick, S., 290n
Pincus, A. L., 100n
Pitassi, David, 349
Pitcairn, T., 98n
Pitts, Thomas, 497
Platz, S. J., 352n

Company Index

A

Aid Association for Lutherans (AAL), 548–49
Air Force Academy, 165–66
Alger, Fred, Management, 2
Allied Chemical, 354
Allied-Signal, 92, 354–58
Ancilla Systems Inc., 381
Anheuser-Busch, 351
Apex Manufacturing Corporation, 580–81
Apollo Computer Inc., 113–16
Apple Computer, Inc., 3, 84, 92, 114, 351
AT&T, 92, 126, 559–60, 562
Avon Products, Inc., 594

B

Baggies, B. D., 522
Baldor Electric, 517–19, 593
Blue Sky Natural Beverage Co., 33
Boeing, 221, 288–90
Borg-Warner, 612
Broad Street Books, 522
Brookstone, 486
Burger Chef, 551
Burger King, 299, 323, 586
Burpee, W. Atlee, 551

C

Campbell Soup Co., 502, 511–13, 560
Catalyst, 448
Caterpillar Inc., 610
Chaparral Steel, 238
Chrysler Corporation, 188, 447–48, 449
Citicorp, 92
Clorox, 349
Coca-Cola, 615
Cognetics, Inc., 522
Colgate-Palmolive Co., 532–34
Commentry-Fourchambault Company, 621
Communispond, 363
Compass Computer Services, 91
CompuServe, 164–65
Conrail, 351
Consulting Psychologists Press, 91
Corning, 351
Coty Cosmetics, 356, 490
Cray Research, 350
CSC Index, 349
Cummins Engine Company, 497, 611
Cypress Semiconductor, 3, 15–16

D

Datapoint, 391
Decker Communications, 363
Digital Equipment Corp., 114, 116, 289, 429
Douglas Aircraft, 30
Dow Chemical, 429
Drypers, 349

E

Electronic Data Systems Corp., 149
Electro Rent Corp., 611
Emerson Electric, 517
Endymion, 448
Executive Technique, 363
Exxon, 92

F

FCB/Leber Katz Partners, 16
Federal Express Corp., 168, 350, 453, 454
First Fidelity Bancorporation, 585–86
Florida Power & Light Co., 30, 128–29
Ford Motor Co., 289, 311–13, 449, 549–50, 610
Frito-Lay, 429
Fuji, 289

G

Gemini Consulting, 31
Genentech, 250–52
General Electric (GE), 92, 354, 517
General Foods, 551–54
General Motors (GM), 43, 351, 447–49, 502, 611
Grace, W. R., & Co., 432, 454–55
Greyhound Dial Corp., 381

H

Hallmark Cards, 235–37
Harley-Davidson, 16, 17
Harvard Design & Mapping Co., 522
Hasbro, Inc., 490–92
Hertz, 350
Hewlett-Packard Co., 60, 116, 258, 558, 610, 612
Hewlett-Packard Inc., 114
Hilton International Hotels, 350
Honeywell, 92
Hovey and Beard Company, 11–14
Huffy Corporation, 523–24

I

Imperial Chemical Industries, 606
International Business Machines (IBM) Corp., 114, 121, 155–58, 246–47, 382, 528, 529, 545, 564
International Data Corp., 116

ITT, 350, 354

J

Johnson & Johnson, 350, 351

K

Kansai Electric, 128
Kawasaki Heavy Industries, 289
KDD, 188
Kohner Bros., 551
Krogers, 171

L

Levi Strauss, 3, 16, 17
Loews Corp., 73
Lone Star Beer, 590
Love Cosmetics, 356, 490–92

M

Mack Trucks, 354
Maryland National Bank, 23
Mattel. Inc., 355, 356, 490–92
Mazda Motor Corp., 311–13
McDonald's, 299, 323, 350
McDonnell Douglas Corp., 289
McKinsey & Co., 31, 350, 611
Merck, 16
Microsoft Corporation, 563
Mitsubishi, 289
Morton Thiokol, 57–58
Motorola, 289, 354
Muggs, J. J., 323
Mushroom Cooperative Canning, 518

N

National Aeronautics and Space Administration, 540
Naval Service Weapons Center, 91
NCR Corp., 148
Nestlé, 357–58
Nippon Airways Co., 289–90
Northrop Corp., 60, 289
Northwestern Bell, 38

P

Paramount Pictures, 490
PepsiCo., 351, 370, 615–16
Phelps Dodge Mining Co., 382
Pillsbury Co., 323–24
Procter & Gamble Co., 382, 429

R

Raytheon Corp., 60
RCA, 349
Reliance Electric, 517
Rix, 551
Rubbermaid, 16, 17

Subject Index

Internal control, 332
Internal validity for research design, 648
Internal work motivation, 225
International aspects
  of behavioral theories of motivation, 213–14
  of cognitive theories of motivation, 213–14
  of communications, 387
  of conflict, 313–14
  of decision making, 425
  of groups in, 284–85
  of job design, 241–42
  of job stress, 458
  of leadership, 345
  of need theories of motivation, 183
  of organizational change and development, 581–82
  of organizational culture, 122–23
  of organizational design, 519, 546
  of political behavior, 449–50
  of research methods, 648–49
  of stress, 482–83
International changes, 594–95
International rights, 63–64
Interorganization conflict, 299
Interpersonal conflict, 298
Interpersonal skills of organizational development consultant, 574
Interval scales, 643–44
Intervention
  effects of, 578, 580
  human process, 577
  in human resource management, 577
  in organizational development, 571
  strategy of, 577–80
  structural, 577
  technological, 577
Interview in organizational research, 645–46
Intimidation, 447
  in organizational politics, 446–47
Intragroup conflict, 272–73, 298
Intraorganization conflict, 298
Intrapersonal conflict, 299
Intrapersonal skills of organizational development consultant, 574
Intrinsic outcomes, 195–96
Intrinsic rewards and job design, 223–24
Introversion, 91
Inventory management, 593
Invulnerability, 420

J
Japan, international changes in, 597–98
Job characteristics
  factors affecting perceptions of objective, 239
  perceived and objective, 226–27
Job characteristics theory of work motivation, 224–25, 640
Job decision latitude, 462
Job demands, 462
Job demands–job decision latitude model, 462
Job design, 480, 579

contextual factors in, 231–32
group-based, 235–37
international aspects of, 241–42
and intrinsic rewards, 223–24
and management behavior, 234–36
and organizational design, 232–33
personal and management implications, 243
and stress, 240–41
and technical process, 233
Job diagnostic survey (JDS), 234, 244–46
Job enrichment, 183
Job reactions, and time, 239–40
Jobs, diagnosing and redesigning, 234–35
Job stress. *See also* Stress
  international aspects of, 458
Johari window, 374
Joint ventures, 506
Judgment biases, 414, 418–19
  framing effects, 417–18
  heuristics, 414
  thirteen possible biases, 414–17
Justice, 53–54
  distributive, 53
Just-in-time inventory management, 233–34
Just-in-time production, 509

K
Knowledge and skill, 228

L
Labor, division of, 619–20
Laboratory experiment, 637
Labor force
  definition of, 20–21
  number of women in, 21
  projected growth of, 21
Laptop computers, 378
Latent conflict, 299, 304–6
Latent consequences, 8
Latin America, international changes in, 595
Leader
  achievement-oriented, 331
  directive, 331
  participative, 331
  relationship-oriented, 329
  role of group, 407–8
  supportive, 331
Leader-member relations, 329
Leadership, 629
  attribution of, 340–41
  behavioral theories of, 327–28
  categorization of, 339–40
  charismatic, 337, 439
  contingency theories of, 329–33
  ethical issues in, 345–46
  and gender, 342–43
  international aspects of, 345
  and management, 344–45
  path-goal theory of, 330–33
  personal and management implications of, 346–47
  and power, 438
  and self-managing teams, 343–44

trait approaches to, 326–27, 342
  transactional, 335
  transformational, 336
Leadership mystique, 333–35, 342
Leadership prototype, 339
Leadership through quality market driven quality, 26
Leadership traits, 326–27
Learning theories of personality, 87
Legal authority, 625
Legitimate power, 324–25
Levels dimension of organizational culture, 104
Liaison role, 383
Life transition stressor, 466
Line and staff organizations, 500
Listening, 373
  active, 373, 377
  comprehensive, 374
  critical, 374
  definition of, 373
  discriminative, 373
  empathic, 374
  types of, 373–74
Litigation, 506
Lobbying, 506
Locus of control, 90, 332
Longitudinal research, 638–39
Long-term buying contracts, 506
Lose-lose methods of reducing conflict, 308–9
Lying, 447
  in organizational politics, 446–47

M
Machiavellian personalities, 90, 92
Majority rule, 309
Malaysia, international changes in, 598
Management, and leadership, 344–45
Management behavior
  and ethical, 56–57
  in future, 605
  and job design, 234–36
Management by exception, 335
Management information systems, 424
Management perspective on groups, 261–62
Manifest conflict, 301
Manifest consequences, 8
Manifest needs questionnaire (MNQ), 262–64, 285–86
Manufacturing, technological changes in, 603
Maslow's hierarchy of needs theory, 172, 183–84
Mass-production technologies, 508, 510
Materials, technological changes in, 602–3
Material symbols, 108
Matrix organization, behavioral demands of a, 541
Matrix organizational design, 537–40
McClelland's achievement motivation theory, 172, 180–82, 184
Measurement in organizational research, 642–44
Measurement scales, types of, 642–44
Mechanistic approach to job design, 223

Mechanistic organization, 513
Mediating technologies, 508, 510
Meditation and stress recuperation, 476–77
Medium in communication, 377
Mentoring program, 141
Merger, 506
Message in communication, 377
Metamorphosis stage in organizational socialization, 154–55
Michigan, University of, leadership studies, 328
Middle East, international changes in, 599
Mindguards, 421
Minnesota Multiphasic Personality Inventory (MMPI), 96–97
Misconceptions of chance, 415
Moderator variables, 227, 639–70
Money, role of, in motivation, 181
Montreal Protocol Treaty, 63
Morality, 421
Moral philosophy, 46
Motivation
    behavior modification in, 205–6, 211
        criticisms of, 211
        method of, 206–9
    definition of, 171
    equity theory, 200–202, 204
        choosing among the responses, 203
        equity sensitivity, 204
        responses to inequity, 202
    ethical issues
        and behavioral theories, 214
        and cognitive theories, 214
        and need theories of, 184–85
    expectancy theory in, 193, 204
        basic concepts of, 194–97
        equity sensitivity, 204
    goal setting theory in, 211–13
    international aspects of cognitive and behavioral theories, 213–14
    international aspects of need theories of, 183
    job characteristics theory of work in, 224–25
    in job design, 223–24
    to participate, 630
    to perform, 630
    potential of, 227
Motivators, 182–83
Multimedia, 380
Multiple sequence model, 274
Murray's theory of human personality, 172, 173, 175
Myers-Briggs type indicator (MBTI), 91

N

Needs
    for achievement, 262
    for affiliation, 262
    for autonomy, 262
    for belongingness, 176
    characteristics of, 173–75
    definition of, 173
    for dominance, 262
    esteem, 176
    existence, 177
    growth, 178
    hierarchy of, 176–77
    for love, 176
    physical, 173
    physiological, 176
    psychological, 173
    relatedness, 177–78
    safety, 176
    self-actualization, 176
Need theories of motivation use, 172
Negative reinforcement, 207–8
Neutralizers, 338, 342
Nominal group technique (NGT), 422
Nominal scales, 642–43
Nonprobability sample designs, 641
Nonverbal communication, 366, 367–69
Nonwork stressor, 466
Noradrenaline, role of, in stress response, 467
Normative theory, 6
Norms, group, 259
North America, international changes in, 595
North American Free Trade Agreement (NAFTA), 33, 595
North Korea, international changes in, 599
Notepad computers, 378
Nurturance, need for, 173, 174

O

Observation in organizational research, 646–47
Occupational Safety and Health Administration, in setting standards for stressor, 483
Official authority, 523
Ohio State University, leadership studies, 328
Old Boy network, challenging of, 141
Openness in communication, 374–76
Openness to experience, 89
Open systems, 500
Open-systems planning, 579
Operant-learning theory, 87
Oral communication, 366
Order, need for, 174
Ordinal scales, 643
Organic organization, 514
Organization
    adaptive, 3
    communication in, 377–78, 383
    definition of, 4
    ethics and behavior in, 34–36
    global environment of, 32–34
    intergroup processes in, 283–84
    performance of, and culture, 118–19
    political maneuvering in, 442–44
    size of, 511
    social responsibility of, 43–45
    strategy of, 500
    TQM view of, 27
    understanding groups in, 259–60
Organizational architecture, 545
Organizational bases of power, 324–25
Organizational behavior, 4
    ethical issues in, 46

implications of Murray's theory for, 175
Organizational blockages, 196–97, 215
Organizational change, 560, 604
    ethical issues in, 582–83
    evolutionary model of, 562–63
    forces for and against, 560–61
    international aspects of, 581–82
    management behavior in, 605
    new strategies in, 604
    organizational design in, 604–5
    planned, 562
    resistance to, 565
        managers' orientation, 566
        managing the change process to reduce resistance, 566–67
        reasons for, 565–66
    revolutionary model of organizational change, 563–65
    targets of planned, 562
    unplanned and planned, 561–62
Organizational commitment, 83
Organizational culture, 80, 103–4, 311, 579
    changing, 121–22
    creating, 120
    cultural symbolism in, 107–8
    definition of, 103, 142
    diagnosing, 111–13
    dimensions of, 104–5
        implicitness dimension, 104
        imprinting dimension, 104
        interdependency dimension, 105
        levels dimension, 104
        pervasiveness dimension, 104
        plurality dimension, 105
        political dimension, 105
    dysfunction of, 110–11, 113
    effects on, 116–18
    ethical issues in, 123–24
    functions of, 108–10
    international aspects of, 122–23
    levels of, 105–6
    maintaining, 120–21
    and organizational socialization, 119
    and organization performance, 118–19
    personal and management implications of, 124–25
    perspectives on, 106–7
Organizational design, 498–99, 579
    background concepts, 499–500
    configuration view of, 513
        analyzer organizations, 515
        defender organizations, 514
        mechanistic organization, 513
        organic organization, 514
        prospector organizations, 514–15
        reactor organizations, 515
    contingency view of, 500–502
        external environment in, 503–6
        strategy in, 502–3
        technical process, 507–11
    definition of, 498
    by division, 532–33
        behavioral demand, 534–35
        strengths and weaknesses, 534
    ethical issues in, 519–20, 582–83